be a part of Slow Food's diverse, international community

be a part of a convivium and organize dinners, tastings, visits and other events and projects to get to know the foods and producers in your area and educate others about them

help save biodiversity and support the Slow Food Foundation for Biodiversity and its projects all over the world

support the world's first and only University of Gastronomic Sciences, created to teach the Slow Food philosophy to a new generation

receive the latest news and stories about important food issues written by some of the foremost writers in the food world today

find out about Slow Food's international Presidia and Terra Madre projects and save endangered animal breeds, vegetable varieties and traditional foods

take part in Slow Food's grand international events, where you can get a taste of the remarkable foods we are working to save and meet the producers we support

OSTERIE & LOCANDE D'ITALIA

A guide to traditional places
to eat and stay in Italy

Slow Food Editore

OSTERIE & LOCANDE
D'ITALIA

Osterie e Locande d'Italia. Why an Italian title for a book in English? The fact is that the two terms, 'osteria' (an old-fashioned eating place, part restaurant, part tavern) and 'locanda' (a sort of inn cum hostelry), if not impossible to translate, are at least hard to render concisely. The subtitle 'A guide to traditional places to eat and stay in Italy' sums everything up. The cover sidebar '2,100 addresses recommended by Slow Food' clarifies the concept further. Which raises another question: what is Slow Food? Let's start at the very beginning...

Slow Food was founded in Bra, in the Italian region of Piedmont, in July 1986, to counter the standardization of taste and the manipulation of consumers around the world. The fundamental importance of conviviality and the right to pleasure are still the basic principles upon which all Slow Food events and activities are built. The movement believes that any traditional product encapsulates the flavours of its region of origin, not to mention local customs and ancient production techniques. With this in mind, Slow Food works not only to protect the historic, artistic and environmental heritage of places of gastronomic pleasure (cafés, inns, bistros), but also to safeguard the food and agricultural heritage (crop biodiversity, artisan techniques, sustainable agriculture, rural development, food traditions) in Italy and abroad.

The Italian writer and gastronome Mario Soldati wrote that, 'It's my firm opinion that one should , as far as possible, eat and drink produce from the area in which one finds oneself or at least from the surrounds'. This is the principle that, in 1990, inspired Slow Food to publish *Osterie d'Italia*, a guide of old-fashioned restaurants, osterias, trattorias, holiday farms and wine shops selected according to the criteria of faithfulness to tradition, quality, atmosphere and value for money. The 17 editions published to date have contributed to the revival of the tradition of regional gastronomy in Italy and the proliferation of eating places that particularly reflect local flavor and character. Two separate symbols are awarded for the best stocked cellars and the finest cheese selections, while the most prestigious symbol of all, the distinctive Slow Food snail, is assigned to addresses that best represent the philosophy of the movement.

In 2004 Slow Food came up with a new idea: a guide to B&Bs, small hotels, holiday farms, guest houses and hostels that recapture a sense of good old-fashioned hospitality. Hence *Locande d'Italia*, a list of places to stay in Italy, complete with address, telephone number, number of rooms, facilities and so on.

This new publication, *Osterie e Locande d'Italia*, brings together the two Italian guides in English as an all-round companion for tourists. Compiled by hundreds of Slow Food collaborators throughout the Italian peninsula and islands, the book seeks to capture the incredible variety of the country's cultural and culinary traditions. Language is a problem of course; here you'll find the most weird and wonderful names for dishes and lots of apparently impenetrable dialect terms. We hope that the clear, concise definitions in the gastronomic glossary at the end of book, which we've done our best to make as comprehensive and exhaustive as possible, will help the reader find her or his way around. Having said that, we'd be delighted to answer any queries or consider any comments, suggestions or recommendations from readers who do decide to use our guide on their travels round Italy.

At this point, all that remains for us to say is *Buon viaggio!,* and, of course, *Buon appetito!*

Carlo Petrini
Slow Food International President

CONTENTS

Edited by
Daniela Battaglio, Paola Gho,
Grazia Novellini

Project Coordination
Maria Vittoria Negro

Editorial Desk
Silvia Ceriani, Elisabetta Dutto,
Kathy Gilsinan, Bianca Minerdo,
Alessandro Monchiero, Grazia Novellini,
Carlo Petrini, Gigi Piumatti,
Carla Ranicki, Giovanni Ruffa,
Angelo Surrusca, Winnie Yang

Regional Coordination
Antonio Attorre, Annabella Bassani,
Paolo Battimelli, Carlo Casti,
Giulio Colomba, Massimo Di Cintio,
Antonello Del Vecchio,
Alberto Adolfo Fabbri,
Giampiero Giordani, Carmelo Maiorca,
Marino Marini, Nereo Pederzolli,
Nicola Perullo, Diego Soracco, Maria-
grazia Tomaello, Gabriele Varalda

Translations
Dialogue International, Turin

Layout
Maurizio Burdese

Art Director
Dante Albieri

Front cover: Jonathan Blair/Corbis
Back cover: Owen Franken/Corbis

Printed in October 2006 by Rotolito
Lombarda, Pioltello (Mi)

Slow Food® Editore srl
Via della Mendicità Istruita, 14-45
12042 Bra (Cn)
Tel. 0172 419611-419670
Fax 0172 411218
E-mail: ost.info@slowfood.it

For advertising
Slow Food Promozione srl
Enrico Bonura, Gabriele Cena,
Erika Margiaria, Ivan Piasentin
Tel. 0172 419611-419606
Fax 0172 413640
E-mail: promozione@slowfood.it

Internet website:
www.slowfood.com
www.slowfood.it

ISBN 88-8499-114-5

Contributors

Val d'Aosta Davide Ghirardi, Silvia Manfredi, Flavio Martino, Letizia Palesi, Daniela Vesan.

Piedmont Loredana Aprato, Silvio Arena, Cristiano Baldi, Stefano Barolo, Maria Edi Bevilacqua, Maura Biancotto, Paola Blanch, Carlo Bogliotti, Dino Borri, Bruno Boveri, Dario Bragaglia, Fulvio Brizio, Luigino Bruni, Corrado Calvo, Luigi Carbonero, Davide Cavagnero, Bruno Chionetti, Marco Cicerone, Enzo Codogno, Lorenzo Conterno, Pier Antonio Cucchietti, Marco Del Brocco, Paolo D'Abramo, Bruno Darò, Fabrizio Dellapiana, Maurizio Fava, Gianni Ferrero, Nicola Ferrero, Tiziano Gaia, Armando Gambera, Giancarlo Gariglio, Enrico Giordano, Giovanni Iacolino, John Irving, Augusto Lana, Marcello Marengo, Serena Milano, Tullio Mussa, Giovanni Norese, Valter Oleastro, Tiziana Percivati, Nicola Piccinini, Franco Pippione, Armando Povigna, Leopoldo Rieser, Piero Sardo, Lorena Sivieri, Franco Turaglio, Gabriele Varalda, Eric Vassallo, Marco Villa.

Lombardy Alberto Alfano, Luca Amodeo, Francesco Amonti, Annamaria Barbi, Elena Barusco, Annabella Bassani, Cristina Bertazzoni, Giandomenico Bomba, Marcello Calendi, Luciano Carrara, Sabina Carta, Carlo Casti, Pietro Cavenaghi, Giovanni Ciceri, Marcella Cigognetti, Giorgio Ferrazzi, Marino Marini, Ezio Marossi, Alessandra Mastrangelo, Giacomo Mojoli, Francesca Molteni, Silvano Nember, Maddalena Onofri, Marisa Radaelli, Enrico Radicchi, Daniela Rubino, Alberto Segalini, Maria Pia Sparla, Silvia Tropea, Massimo Truzzi, Patrizia Ucci, Gilberto Venturini, Carla Verzeletti.

Trentino Elisabetta Alberti, Alda Baglioni, Andrea Bassetti, Mario Demattè, Roberto Degasperi, Giancarlo Lotti, Enzo Merz, Nereo Pederzolli.

Alto Adige Alda Baglioni, Angelo Carrillo, Peter Dipoli, Karin Huber, Gianni Mantoanello, Christine Mayr, Enzo Merz, Nereo Pederzolli, Helmut Riebschlaeger.

Veneto Enrico Azzolin, Giuseppe Bedin, Luisa Bellina, Valerio Belotti, Gino Bortoletto, Luigi Boscolo, Mariano Braggion, Marco Brogiotti, Gianni Breda, Nicoletta Destro, Maria Lucia Filippi, Sanzio Folli, Danilo Gasparini, Barbara Grando, Renato Grando, Stefania Guiotto, Sandra Longo, Valeria Pavan, Renato Peron, Angelo Peretti, Fabio Pogacini, Evaristo Pretti, Patrizia Pretti, Giancarlo Riganelli, Sara Ronzini, Morena Sacchetto, Attilio Saggiorato, Cristiano Saletti, Renzo Scarso, Michela Scibilia, Silvano Sguoto, Mariagrazia Tomaello, Giuseppe Toppan, Galdino Zara.

Friuli Venezia Giulia Lorenzo Amat, Giuliano Bardi, Luisella Bellinaso, Piero Bertossi, Gianna Buongiorno, Cristina Burcheri, Eleonora Carletti, Giulio Colomba, Giorgio Dri, Alberto Fiascaris, Mariagrazia Gerardi, Renzo Marinig, Michele Mellano, Karen Miniutti, Sergio Nesich, Fabio Pogacini, Renato Tedesco, Massimo Toffolo, Luca Tomaia, Luca Vidoni, Giles Watson, Pier Paolo Zanchetta.

Liguria: Piero Arnaudo, Luciano Barbieri, Sandro Biavaschi, Walter Bordo, Livio Caprile, Ettore Casagrande, Michele Castaldi, Maurizio Cozzani, Bruna Eusebio, Paolo Fardin, Lucia Fosella, Pietro Garibbo, Franco Lanata, Cristina Maddaluno, Monica Maroglio, Linda Nano, Gianfranco Palmero, Vincenzo Ricotta, Manuel Rossini, Enrico Sala, Luca Scatena, Barbara Schiffini, Diego Soracco, Maurizio Stagnitto, Enrico Tournier, Attilio Venerucci.

Emilia Romagna Lamberto Albonetti, Barbara Ansaloni, Artemio Assiri, Alessandro Barzaghi, Paolo Berardi, Antonio Cherchi, Marco Epifani, Alberto Adolfo Fabbri, Roberto Ferranti, Piero Fiorentini, Romualdo Ghigi, Giampiero Giordani, Fabio Giavedoni, Albano Gozzi, Mirco Marconi, Giancarlo Melandri, Stefania Pampolini, Giovanni Pendenti, Alberto Perari, Massimo Pezzani, Gianni Sacchetti, Armanda Sacchetto, Maurizio Tassinari, Luisella Verderi, Massimo Volpari, Mauro Zanarini.

Tuscany Piera Alberta, Giordano Andreucci, Bruno Bacci, Mauro Bagni, Ermanno Baldassarri, Alberto Baraldi, Arianna Bartoli, Marco Bechi, Mario Benvenuti, Sabino Berardino, Carlo Bernardini, Luciano Bertini, Paolo Bracci, Simone Brogi, Andrea Brogiotti, Fabrizio Calastri, Michele Castaldi, Roberta Cellai, Luciano Ciarini, Fausto Costagli, Fabio D'Avino, Leonardo Dell'Aiuto, Alessandro Draghi, Carlo Eugeni, Stefano Ferrante, Stefano Ferrari, Fausto Ferroni, Daniela Filippi, Laurana Fornelli, Alessandro Frassica, Francesco Funaioli, Carlo Gazzarrini, Marco Ghelfi, Gaetano Guacci, John Irving, Giovanna Licheri, Cristiano Maestrini, Fabrizio Marcacci, Piero Morelli, Marco Mucci, Marco Nardi, Roberto Neri, Renato Nesi, Nicola Perullo, Luigi Pittalis, Leonardo Romanelli, Paolo Saturnini, Barbara Schiffini, Sandra Soldani, Roberto Tonini, Franco Utili, Pasquale Varriale, Alessandro Venturi.

Umbria Luisa Borgna, Fabio Canneori, Sonia Chellini, Gianpaolo Ciancabilla, Sergio Consigli, Salvatore De Iaco, Antonio Metastasio, Pier Giorgio Oliveti, Carlo Rossi, Gabriele Violini, Laura Zoia.

Marche Antonio Attorre, Emidio Bachetti, Pier Antonio Bonvicini, Silvio Broccani, Maurizio Capponi, Renzo Ceccacci, Valerio Chiarini, Alessia Consorti, Roberto Coppi, Franco Frezzotti, Fabio Giavedoni, Tiziano Luzi, Alessandro Morichetti, Alfredo Palazzetti, Fosca Pallai, Francesco Quercetti, Pierpaolo Rastelli, Gloria Rotolossi.

Lazio Enrico Amatori, Stefano Asaro, Paolo Battimelli, Ugo Bonomolo, Roberto Bianchi, Edoardo Bondatti, Gabriella Brogi, Antonio Chichierchia, Beatrice Capoferri, Claudia Caprarola, Roberto Cardella, Dionisio Castello, Alberico Ciccarelli, Tommaso De Massimi, Patrizia Eliso, Paola Fattibene, Mirella Filigno, Mario Fiorillo, Fabio Fusina, Rita La Rocca, Paolo Luxardo, Daniele Maestri, Raffaele Marchetti, Antonio Marcianò, Domenico Mariani, Patrizio Mastrocola, Roberto Perrone, Matteo Rugghia, Fabrizio Russo, Massimiliano

Sbarra, Maria Rosaria Specchio, Dosolina Tonti, Fabio Turchetti.

Abruzzo-Molise Davide Acerra, Francesco Agostini, Antonio Attorre, Anna Berghella, Francesco Biasi, Paolo Castignani, Raffaele Cavallo, Ugo Cittadini, Roberto De Viti, Massimo Di Cintio, Eliodoro D'Orazio, Severino Forcone, Erminia Gatti, Raffaele Grilli, Francesco Martino, Lello Mattoscio, Loredana Pietroniro, Fabio Riccio, Fabio Turchetti.

Puglia Antonio Attorre, Paolo Benegiamo, Francesco Biasi, Michele Bruno, Paolo Costantini, Antonio Del Vecchio, Andrea De Palma, Maria Antonietta Epifani, Angelo Iaia, Giuseppe Incampo, Marcello Longo, Vincenzo Mazzei, Francesco Muci, Guido Pensato, Pasquale Porcelli, Sergio Pugliese, Gregorio Sergi, Salvatore Taronno, Francesco Zompì.

Campania Rita Abagnale, Michele Amoruso, Giancarlo Capacchione, Giustino Catalano, Michele Cinque, Francesco Colonnesi, Antonino Corcione, Enzo Crivella, Gesualdo Della Corte, Patrizia Della Monica, Mirella Di Giorgio, Lorena Falato, Sergio Galzigna, Pino Mandarano, Gaetano Marrone, Alessio Massimo Masone, Gabriele Matarazzo, Nicola Matarazzo, Peppe Nota, Antonio Pasqua, Giuseppe Paladino, Gaetano Pascale, Italo Picciau, Fernando Poppiti, Vito Puglia, Sabatino Santacroce, Mario Stingone, Vito Trotta.

Basilicata Michele Calabrese, Gabriella Cenci, Donata Larotonda, Francesco Linzalone, Francesco Martino.

Calabria Giuseppe Antonini, Michele Bisceglie, Gregorio Carratelli, Elvira Chiefali, Valeria Cinisi, Marisa Gigliotti, Vincenzo Nava, Raffaele Riga.

Sicily Nino Aiello, Aldo Bacciulli, Nino Bentivegna, Alfredo Bordone, Nanni Cucchiara, Anna Fava, Salvatore Giunta, Claudio Grosso, Rosario Gugliotta, Massimo Lanza, Giancarlo Lo Sicco, Carmelo Maiorca, Pippo Privitera, Franco Saccà, Pasquale Tornatore, Sabina Zuccaro.

Sardinia Fabio Atzeni, Massimiliano Cao, Corrado Casula, Luca Galassi, Nicola Migheli, Anna Paola Murtas, Stefano Olla, Nino Scampuddu, Anna Sulis, Eric Vassallo.

How to use this Guide

Order

The guide is arranged by Italian regions, and every establishment is listed alphabetically under the municipality in which it is situated. Where possible, area, district and/or neighborhood names are also specified.

Typologies

The typology of each establishment osteria, trattoria, restaurant, holiday farm (agriturismo), wine shop/bar, hotel, bed & breakfast etc – is specified.

Information

Opening hours, holiday periods and so on have been supplied by the proprietors of the establishments listed.

Prices

Prices are approximate and, unless otherwise stated ('wine excluded'). are inclusive of beverages. Where applicable, set menu prices are also stated.

Symbols

    ⌣   Indicates a place to eat (osteria, restaurant, trattoria…).

    🗝   Indicates a place to stay (bed & breakfast, hotel, holiday farm, locanda, residence…).

    @   An address that, in terms of cooking and atmosphere, reflects the philosophy of Slow Food.

    Ⓒ   An address that stocks a particularly interesting selection of cheeses.

    🍾   An address that boasts a particularly comprehensive and distinguished wine cellar.

    🎁   A shop, an artisan or a company that sells high quality gastronomic specialties and produce.

    🪑   A particularly commendable bar, café, wine shop, ice-cream parlor or cake shop.

Unless otherwise indicated, it is always advisable to book meals
or stays at the addresses listed in advance.

Unless otherwise indicated, it is always advisable to book meals or stays at the addresses listed in advance.

To phone from abroad, add the code '+ 39' to the number stated.

In the credit card indications, CartaSi refers to the Italian card in the MasterCard/Visa circuits, while Bancomat is the Italian term for cards utilizable in Automated Teller Machines (ATM).

Road directions: A = autostrada (motorway, freeway), SS = strada statale (A-road, state route), SP = strada provinciale (secondary provincial road).

A Slow Food Presidium is a tailor-made local initiative (involving the creation of micro-markets, marketing and production activities etc) to raise funds to save threatened vegetable species, animal breeds, quality beverages, culinary preparations and so on.

The guide, the joint effort of hundreds of contributors and translators, is aimed at the entire English speaking-world. While the spelling adopted is American, the choice of terminology used deliberately varies between American and English.

Printed on October 2006, the guide obviously fails to take into account any alterations that may have been made to prices, telephone numbers, addresses and so on since that date.

VALLE D'AOSTA

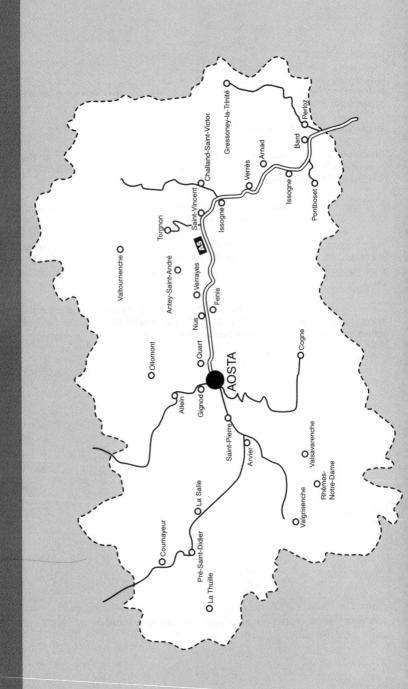

ALLEIN
Ville

ANTEY-SAINT-ANDRÉ
Poutaz

15 KM NORTH OF AOSTA

32 KM NORTHEAST OF AOSTA SR 406

LO RATELÉ

🗝 Holiday farm
Località Ville 2
Tel. & fax 0165 78265
Closed end October to Christmas
and from Epiphany to Easter

HOTEL DES ROSES

🗝 2-Star Hotel
Place Poutaz 5
Tel. 0166 548527
Fax 0166 548248
E-mail: info@hoteldesroses.com
Internet: www.hoteldesroses.com
Closed in May and October-November

On five hectares of fields and pasture-land on the slopes of Mount Chénaille, between the Great St. Bernard and Valpelline valleys, the Conchâtre family rears cows, goats, chickens and rabbits and produces butter, eggs, cheese, jam and marmalade. An old farmhouse has been restructured into seven comfortable rooms (four with terrace) and a dining room. The traditional breakfast at table includes mountain milk and butter, fruit, preserves and cakes baked by Signora Paola, as well as home-made cured meats and cheeses. These and other specialties are also served as snacks (10 euros). Half board 40-45 euros for complete relaxation in a delightful setting.

• 5 double and 2 triple rooms, with bathroom • Prices: double used as single 50 euros, double 54, triple 81, breakfast included • Credit cards: none • Parking in front of the premises. No pets allowed. Owners always available • Restaurant. Breakfast room. Reading room. TV room. Terraces. Solarium

Along the road to Valtournanche, the Via del Cervino, lies the tiny village of Antey-Saint-André. Less than one kilometer from the center of the village, the hamlet of Poutaz consists of a handful of houses. The bedrooms in the small, family-owned hotel are plain but the wide-spread use of wood gives them a friendly feel. The hotel is totally independent to ensure a quiet, relaxing stay. The Valtournenche ski lifts are easy to get to and Breuil itself is only half an hour away by car. The lovely garden has tables for snacks and a solarium. The restaurant, open to non-residents if they book ahead, serves traditional Val d'Aosta and Italian dishes prepared by the owner (18-20 euros, wine included). Half board 38-56, full board 45-63 euros per person.

• 21 double and 2 single rooms, with bathroom, satellite television • Prices: single 34-39 euros, double 51-60; breakfast 7 euros • Credit cards: all, Bancomat • Parking, garage. Small pets allowed. Owners always available • Bar, restaurant. Breakfast room, reading room and lounge, TV room. Garden, solarium, children's playground

🍲 Excellent local cuisine is served at this holiday farm, also open to non-guests for Sunday lunch (set menu about 25 euros, wines included).

VAL D'AOSTA

2 KM FROM CITY CENTER

LE CHARABAN

3-Star Hotel
Località Saraillon 38
Tel. 0165 238289
Fax 0165 361230
E-mail: info@lecharaban.it
Internet: www.lecharaban.it
Closed from early November to December 8

TRATTORIA DEGLI ARTISTI

Restaurant-trattoria
Via Maillet 5-7
Tel. 0165 40960
Closed Sunday and Monday, open in
August for Sunday lunch
Open: lunch and dinner
Holidays: 2 weeks in June, 2 weeks in November
Seating: 50 + 24 outdoors
Prices: 26-30 euros
All credit cards, Bancomat

Charaban, in French-Provençal patois, means a wagon with hatches as once used by traveling salesmen and companies of actors who, during the Carnival period, used to travel up and down the valleys entertaining audiences. This is still the name of the hotel run by the family of Ernesto Margueret, nicknamed Etto, a restaurateur and painter. The hotel was built north of the city in 1965 on the road up to the Great St Bernard. The bedrooms and common rooms are furnished in a simple but attractive style with a great use of wood. Breakfast is served with coffee, fresh bread, fruit and sweets, and savories are available on request. Half board in a single room costs 66-71 euros, or 49-55.5 euros per person in a double room.

• 22 double rooms, with bathroom, minibar, television • Prices: double used as single 44-80 euros, double 68-90 (supplement for additional bed 12-22 euros), breakfast included • Credit cards: all, Bancomat • 2 rooms furnished for the mobility challenged. Outdoor parking. Small pets allowed. Janitor service 7.30 - 24 • Restaurant (for individuals June-September only, for groups all year round). Lounge. Park. Solarium

Older habitués still call the place the 'Pam Pam', from the time when, from the 60s to the 80s, it was frequented by gourmets and lovers of jazz and the figurative arts. Inside, pictures and sculptures hark back to that time, giving a touch of originality to the Alpine decor. It is hidden away in a small alleyway in the old town center, but can find it easily from Via Aubert, where the owners display a menu board at the street entrance.
Apart from a few dishes from other regions of Italy, prepared on request for local patrons who come with their families at lunchtime or dinner, the cuisine is that of the Aosta Valley, hearty and substantial throughout the year. The classic starter, nicknamed the 'fireplace antipasto', is a selection of typical cured meats (**mocetta**, lardo, ham, sausage). If you prefer to start with something hot, go for **cotechino with fondue**. Then come **polenta grassa**, **seupa vapellenentse**, crespelle, gnocchi or tagliatelle or tortelli alle erbette, **rice with** lardo, **Savoy cabbage and Fontina cheese**. The main courses include **carbonade**, **brasato al Blanc de Morgex**, roe deer venison, casseroled or al civet, polpettone al ginepro, **boiled kid** and rabbit with mushrooms. To finish, the Pam Pam ice-cream cup, fruit tart or zabaglione tart.
Alongside some good wines by the carafe, Corrado also serves top Piedmontese and Aosta Valley wines.

ARNAD
Champagnolaz

ARVIER

42 KM SOUTHEAST OF AOSTA SS 26 OR 5 VERRÈS EXIT

14 KM SOUTHWEST OF AOSTA SS 26 OR SAINT-PIERRE EXIT 5

L'ARCADEN

🍲 Osteria opened recently
Località Champagnolaz 1
Tel. 0125 966928
Closed Monday and Thursday, only on Thursday in summer
Open: midday -9pm
Holidays: 2 weeks in June, 2 weeks in November
Seating: 45
Prices: 15-18 euros, wine excluded
All credit cards, Bancomat

CAFÉ DU BOURG

🍲 Restaurant
Via Lostan 12
Tel. 0165 99094-333 3486273
Closed Monday
Open: dinner, lunch Sunday and in summer
Holidays: first half of June, first half of October
Seating: 25
Prices: 25-33 euros, wine excluded
All credit cards accepted

The 'glass and plate' symbol means 'not a complete menu but cold meals or snacks'. In the case of the Arcaden, the symbol is relevant in that the hot dishes are limited to a few **zuppe**, or soups (of cabbage and Fontina cheese, barley and chestnuts), but if you combine these with the great selection of cured meats, cheeses and other delicious foods, you're sure to satisfy your appetite after a day's skiing or walking.

Hikers, skiers and free climbing enthusiasts (we are near a famous rock face here) are the main patrons of this hostelry, which was set up five years ago by the Bertolins, a family that is famous for the production of excellent typical cured meats. Here, you can sample them all: **lardo di Arnad**, **mocetta**, teteun (cow's udder), boc (cooked goat's salami), cacciatorini di asino, coppa al ginepro, bon bocon and **cotechino with potatoes**. The selection of fresh and matured local cheeses is also excellent: Fontina, Toma, Fromadzo and **Salignon**, the traditional peppery Walser ricotta. Plus pickled or preserved vegetables, lingua al verde and peppers with bagna caoda. The custom here is to finish with a hot soup, but for those who can't do without a pudding, tarts and other pastries abound.

To drink, there are good wines by the carafe and excellent bottled Val d'Aosta and Piedmontese wines.

🏺 In the Glair district of Arnad, typical cheeses can be purchased at the Evançon cooperative cheese-factory outlet. At Arnad-le-Vieux, the Cargnino bakery sells bread with chestnuts and sultanas and walnut grissini.

Situated in the beautifully restored hamlet of Arvier (famous for its production of Enfer wine), this charming restaurant – rustic stonework with a dash of modernity – has been around for years. Chef Daniele Martinotti and his wife and maîtresse d'h, Silena Vuillermoz, offer a warm, happy welcome… not to mention a huge choice of mainly regional dishes. The bread, fresh pasta and puddings are home made, and the menu changes with the season. Starters could include flan of spring greens with melted Camembert, **boiled veal musetto with vegetables and bagnet verd**, pear and mocetta salad with warm goat's cheese, **Jerusalem artichoke timbale with sweet Toma cheese fondue** or mountain goat's cheese mousse with warm sweet pepper cream. For the first course: **rye flour stracci with sausage, Savoy cabbage and cheese fondue** or **chestnut flour tagliatelle** with mushrooms and ham. Excellent **cheese fondue** is also available all year round. Of the main courses, we particularly liked the **venison in civet** and the beef fillet with brown bread croutons, bacon and blackcurrant sauce. Of the puddings, we recommend the toasted brown bread semifreddo with pear cream, Saint-Pierre apple cake and **Martine pears stewed in Enfer d'Arvier wine**.

The excellent wine list features around 400 wines from the Aosta Valley and the rest of Italy, plus hundreds of grappas and other liqueurs.

47 KM SOUTHEAST OF AOSTA SS 26

43 KM SOUTHEAST OF AOSTA SS 45 EXIT 5 VERRÈS

LE BON REVEIL

Bed and breakfast
Via Vittorio Emanuele II 85
Tel. 0125 803986-340 5116725
E-mail: bonreveil@libero.it
Internet: www.bonreveil.valleaosta.it
Closed in November

LOCANDA AI PONTI ROMANI

Restaurant
Frazione Vervaz 10-11
Tel. 0125 967608
Closed Tuesday and Thursday evening
Open: lunch and dinner
Holidays: 3 weeks in January, 2 weeks in June, 1 week in October
Seating: 40
Prices: 25-30 euros, wine excluded
All credit cards except AE, Bancomat

At this ancient hamlet, which nestles beneath the spectacular fort of Bard, a bright-colored wooden cockerel welcomes guests to the delightful b&b of Anita Treves and Cesare Bottan: it's as if it wanted to wish you a good sleep before it wakes you up! The sign is the handiwork of the owner, a skilled craftsman who works with wood and oil stone and has his studio in the building (on request, he gives lessons on sculpture, bas-relief and engraving). The bedrooms are comfortable and pleasant (freshly baked cakes and, on request, savories) are served next to the fireplace in an attractive room, where at other times of day it is possible to play cards or checkers and dip into the hosts' library of books and CDs.

• 2 double rooms and 1 triple, with bathroom • Prices: double used as single 40-45 euros, double 50-55, triple 62-65, breakfast included • Credit cards: none • Free public parking 30 meters away. Small pets allowed. Owners always present • Lounge, reading room and TV. Terrace

Challand-Saint-Victor, a small village of just over 500 inhabitants, lies at the entrance to the Val d'Ayas, an important valley for the history of the region. The Viscounts of Aosta took the name of Challant from the castle, acquired from the Savoys in the 13th century, the ruins of which can be seen in Villa, the main village.

The restaurant, named after two fine Roman bridges over the Evançon river, is housed in an intelligently restored mountain hut. Owner Corrado and his staff offer three types of menu, traditional with the odd innovative touch. First, sample the **lardo di Arnad**, **mocetta** and other local cured meats, then choose between a **zuppa** of vegetables, pulses or cereals, a risotto (with Gamay wine, Fontina cheese or mushrooms) and **polenta**, often served with **Salignon**, the peppery ricotta typical of the valleys in the Monterosa area. For main course, you'll find roast or casseroled beef, **cotechino with potatoes**, game in season (wild boar or **venison cutlets with polenta**), snails and **mushrooms**. The puddings are home-made and the bread is baked in an old wood oven, the centerpiece of the dining room.

The wine list includes the finest wines from the Val d'Aosta and a good selection from other Italian regions. Expect a hearty welcome and efficient service.

27 KM SOUTH OF AOSTA SS 47

27 KM SOUTH OF AOSTA SR 47

LA BRASSERIE DU BON BEC

Osteria recently opened
Rue Bourgeois 72
Tel. 0165 749288
Closed Monday, never in May-
August and Christmas
Open: lunch and dinner
Holidays: variable, in autumn
Seating: 47
Prices: 24-28 euros, wine excluded
All credit cards, Bancomat

LA MADONNINA DEL GRAN PARADISO

3-Star Hotel
Rue Laydetré 7
Tel. 0165 74078
Fax 0165 749392
E-mail: hotel@lamadonnina.com
Internet: www.lamadonnina.com
Open from Christmas to Easter
and from end-May to early-October

After a day on the ski slopes or hiking through the Gran Paradiso National Park, this lovely osteria in the center of Cogne is the ideal place to eat. Run by the Jeantet-Roullet family, owners of the historic Bellevue Hotel, it has a typical mountain atmosphere, without being folksy or kitsch and the different menus —including a children's, an unusual feature for an Italian restaurant – have been carefully devised to satisfy all tastes.

Large groups will struggle to resist the temptation to try the **braserade** (cured meats, Reblochon cheese, potatoes and crèpes) or the **pierrade** (mixed meats cooked on a lòsa, or stone slab) hotplate). Equally 'convivial' are the fondue chinoise, the bourguignonne and the Piedmontese bagna caoda. If you wish, you can order a single dish, choosing from a zuppa (the onion is excellent), crespelle, **favò** (pasta with broad beans), **venison in red wine with polenta**, breaded lamb cutlets, or **trout baked in the oven with cheese and herbs**. For a snack or an antipasto, choose from the excellent **cured meats** and **cheeses**, salads - both large and small - and in winter, **frecacha**, a delicious hot beef and potato pie. As a pudding, a slice of cake, delicious **chocolate fondue** or **crema di Cogne** with tegole biscuits.

Wines and liqueurs are mainly from the Aosta Valley and Piedmont.

Opposite the Sant'Orso meadows, along the road to Valnontey and the Paradisia Alpine Park, one of the many attractions of the Gran Paradiso National Park, stands this locanda, managed by the Chillod family since 1975. The center of Cogne, with its attractive piazza, is barely 300 meters away, while the ski pistes are literally outside the door. This establishment is housed in a refurbished cottage, in which wood has been used lavishly in every room; the rooms (two double rooms are in the superior category) are large, bright and comfortable. Breakfast includes home-made jam and marmalade as well as fruit, milk and coffee. The small restaurant (also open to non-residents) offers prevalently creative cuisine. The à la carte menu costs around 20-40 euros, wine excluded.

• 3 single rooms, 16 double rooms and 3 mini-suites, with bathroom, balcony, television • Prices: single 53-83 euros, double 53-85, mini-suite 70-110, breakfast included • Credit cards: all except DC, Bancomat • Mini-suite equipped for the mobility challenged. Parking, garage (19 places). Small pets allowed. Porter service 8am-midnight • Bar, restaurant. Breakfast room, reading room, games room for children, tavern. Outside seating, garden

LES PERTZES

🍲Brasserie-wine bar with kitchen
Via Grappein 93
Tel. 0165 749227
Closed Tuesday and Wednesday, never in the high season
Open: lunch and dinner
Holidays: November and May-June
Seating: 50 + 20 outdoors
Prices: 25-30 euros, wine excluded
All credit cards except DC, Bancomat

LOU RESSIGNON

🍲Restaurant
Rue des Mines 22
Tel. 0165 74034
Closed Monday evenings and Tuesday,
never in October-May and August
Open: lunch and dinner
Holidays: November and first 10 days in June
Seating: 75
Prices: 25-28 euros, wine excluded
All major credit cards, Bancomat

On the right, as you climbing towards the market square and the church, stands a chalet , not unlike the many others in the village, that houses a warm, welcoming restaurant. You can go in the afternoon or late in the evening for a snack of cheeses and cured meats, or at meal-times to sample the mainly traditional cuisine in the refined ambience of a top-class wine bar (stocking 800 different types of wine from all over the world, some of which available by the glass).
A virtual must for starters is the assiette cogneintze, sliced **cured meats** with **chestnuts**; other options are vegetable flan, potato and leek pie with fondue and **marinated Lillaz trout**. Then come **polenta concia** and ravioli in game sauce, **gnocchi al seirass** or **gnocchi alla toma di Gressoney**, **carbonade with polenta**, and braised veal. Depending on the season, there are also maize or buckwheat **maltagliati with cabbage and bacon** or game sauce, tagliolini with cep mushrooms, jellied quail breast in Chambave Moscato wine, baked shin of pork, and **lamb cutlets** alla provenzale. The excellent **cheese board** features products from the Val d'Aosta and beyond. Desserts include **crema di Cogne,** crêpe suzette, cakes and bavarois.
The charming owners, Emanuele Comiotto and Luisella Biolcati, will happily take you to see their wonderful wine cellar. It's also pleasant to sit by the fireside after dinner and sip a dessert wine, a beer or a liqueur.

In the patois of the Gran Paradiso valleys, a lou ressignon is a night-time snack that friends eat together: a few tasty dishes and a bottle of wine or two. This is the name Arturo Allera, a ski instructor and a leading light in the social life of the Val d'Aosta, gave the restaurant he opened with his sister Elda in 1966. After Arturo's death, his children Elisabetta and Davide continued to run the business in the same spirit and they are now restoring part of the chalet as a four-bedroom guesthouse.
Davide is responsible for the cuisine, which reflects traditions influenced by neighboring Piedmont. First courses: **se-upetta cogneintze** (not a zuppa at all, but a risotto), rye-flour crespelle, **spinach gnocchetti with fondue** and **polenta concia** (an absolute must!), homemade **tajarin** with cep mushrooms when in season, **seupa vapellenentse** (winter) and penne alla Ressignon, with raw ham, courgettes and peppers (summer). Main courses: **carbonade** with polenta or potatoes, **casseroled chamois venison**, **roast saddle of lamb** with mustard seeds, goose breast with pears, **grilled** meats or Lillaz **trout**, and boeuf bourguignonne. The fondue chinoise and the selection of cured meats and cheeses listed in the antipasti menu could all be eaten as main courses. To finish, tarte tatin, **crema di Cogne** with tegole (biscuits) and other puddings eaten with a spoon.
The choice of wines and liqueurs is extensive. On Saturdays and Sundays, the wine bar, with its stone fireplace, is open until late at night.

COGNE
Lillaz

LOU TCHAPPÉ

Restaurant
Frazione Lillaz 126
Tel. 0165 74379
Closed Monday, never in July and August
Open: lunch and dinner
Holidays: 15/5-15/6 and 15/10-30/11
Seating: 50 + 25 outdoors
Prices: 25-28 euros, wine excluded
All credit cards except DC, Bancomat

Here you'll find pleasant waiters in period costumes, a well-lit, bright atmosphere inside, and an outside seating area shaded by a gazebo that looks out onto the northeastern peaks of the Gran Paradiso National Park. If you add to this good traditional food, with a wide choice of dishes and large helpings, efficient service and reasonable costs, you will understand why the Artini family restaurant is always crowded. Skiers are among the patrons in winter (the place is near one of the finest cross-country pistes in the region) and hikers stop by in summer (there are some strenuous walks in the vicinity, as well as short 'family-size' excursions to the Valeille river waterfall).
The typical Val d'Aosta cured meats (**mocetta**, lardo di Arnad, and Bosses ham) are the most popular antipasti: alternatively you can have cheese (the **caprini al ginepro**, goat's cheese aged in juniper berries, are not to be missed) and various patés. As a first course, there are **orzotto**, crespelle, bread or **chestnut gnocchi**, malfatti du Tchappé (with smoked bacon and a little tomato) and at least one **zuppa**. Main courses include the specialty of the chef, Giuseppe Artini: **soça**, an old Cogne recipe, a pie made of meat, cabbage, potatoes and Fontina cheese. In addition, depending on the season, fondue, **carbonade with polenta**, **roast lamb**, **scaloppina alla valdostana**, grilled Lillaz **trout** or trout served with almonds, baked breast of duck with apples, and **game**. To finish your meal, crema di Cogne with tegole (biscuits), panna cotta, fruit cake, bavarois and exquisite home-made **cinnamon ice-cream**. The best wines from the valley are served alongside wines from other regions of Italy.

COGNE
Cretaz

NOTRE MAISON

3-Star Hotel
Frazione Cretaz 8
Tel. 0165 74104
Fax 0165 749186
E-mail: hotel@notremaison.it
Internet: www.notremaison.it
Closed from May to mid-June
and from October to Christmas

The center of Cogne is just over a kilometer away from this characteristic chalet, managed by Angelo, Irma, Stefania and Andrea Celesia, and surrounded by spacious grounds (8,000 square meters). Inside, some of the bathrooms are shared, others are inside the rooms: standard (16 sq m), superior (30 sq m), suites (60 sq m). The general impression is one of warm, kindly hospitality, and the generous breakfasts include local ingredients and produce. The restaurant, also open to non-residents, serves local cuisine at a price of around 25-30 euros per head, wine excluded. In summer, it is also possible to dine in a mountain hut in the park.

• 21 double rooms with bathroom, television (some also with balcony, safe, hi-fi) and 2 suites with bedroom, bathroom, lounge, mini-bar, television, fireplace • Prices: double used as single 60-100 euros, standard double 80-120, superior double 120-160, suite 180-220, breakfast included • Credit cards: all except AE, Bancomat • 2 rooms equipped for the mobility challenged. Inside parking, garage. Small pets allowed. The owners are always available • Bar, restaurant. Breakfast room. Lounge, reading room, tavern. Park, solarium. Fitness Center with swimming pool, Turkish bath, sauna

COURMAYEUR
Ermitage

40 KM NORTHWEST OF AOSTA SS 26 D

BAITA ERMITAGE

🍲 Restaurant
Località Ermitage
Tel. 0165 844351
Closed Wednesday, never in July and August
Open: lunch and dinner
Holidays: June and November
Seating: 50 + 40 outdoors
Prices: 20-30 euros, wine excluded
All credit cards except AE, Bancomat

It's summer and it's lunchtime and you find yourself near Courmayeur. You haven't booked anywhere and a few hurried phone calls serve to no avail. But you can count on Ermitage, because even when it's full of inside, there's always room in the garden. And if there are no seats at the tables, you can fill up a tray at the counter (provided there's food left!) and sit on the grass. Self-service but in a very charming atmosphere (with a spectacular view of Mont Blanc) that adds to the friendly welcome and the quality of the cuisine. Piero Savoye, the owner, takes care of diners, while his mother, Valentina Pellissier, takes great pains to create traditional dishes in the kitchen. The mainstays of the menu at lunchtime are sausages, **rabbit** or mushrooms, **polenta concia** with **carbonade**, and in the evening any variations are announced by the waiter. You can start with mixed **cured meats**, apple salad (an Aosta Valley specialty, with celery, turnip and walnuts), tomini al verde, and **warm ham involtini filled with fonduta**. Then the **zuppa dell'Eremita**, made with **brown bread, spinach and Fontina cheese**. Alternatively, you can opt for baked pasta with a cheese topping, tagliatelle, or the classic cheese-filled **crêpe**. Meat dishes include **scaloppina alla valdostana**, paillard, or **snails** alla parigina and, in the hunting season, **roe-deer or chamois venison casserole** accompanied by polenta. You can end with a slice of cake or tart with honey-glazed chestnuts or, in summer, woodland berries and ice-cream.
To drink, honest Val d'Aosta and Piedmontese wines.

COURMAYEUR
La Palud

35 KM NORTHWEST OF AOSTA SS 26 AND 26 D

DENTE DEL GIGANTE

🔑 3-Star Hotel
Strada La Palud 42
Tel. 0165 89145
Fax 0165 89639
E-mail: info@dentedelgigante.com
Internet: www.dentedelgigante.com
Open December-April
and end June-end September

Little more than three kilometers from the center of Courmayeur and 200 meters from the cable car to Chamonix, a warm welcome awaits you at this hotel-restaurant, built in 1947 and managed since the 1960s by the Angelini family and refurbished on several occasions. Wood and stone are the characteristic elements of the mountain style of the simple yet comfortable rooms and common areas. Breakfast is served in the restaurant (which serves essentially local cuisine from set menu: 30-39 euros, wine excluded). A lounge with a fireplace provides the backdrop for moments of relaxation, and wines can be served from the impressive cellars and the equally well-stocked bar, with its comprehensive selection of spirits, infusions and herbal teas). Mont Blanc itself looms large over the hotel.

• 3 single rooms, 8 double rooms and 2 mini-suites with bathroom (mini-suites with jacuzzi), television • Prices: single 35-55 euros, double 60-96, mini-suite 104-140 (supplement for additional bed: 21-34 euros), breakfast included • Credit cards: all except AE, Bancomat • Outside parking. Small pets allowed. Porter service 7am-1am • Bar, restaurant. Lounge

Courmayeur
Val Veny-Peindeint

41 km northwest of Aosta SS 26 d

La Grolla

Restaurant with rooms
Località Peindeint
Tel. 0165 869095-869783
Always open
Open: lunch and dinner
Open 1/12-15/4 and 15/6-10/9
Seating: 85 + 75 outdoors
Prices: 30-35 euros, wine excluded
All major credit cards, Bancomat

This is an archetypical mountain chalet: stone walls, sloping roofs made with slates (called lòse), wooden doors, window frames and shutters, and wood paneling everywhere inside. The landscape is dominated by the steep, looming mountains, their wooded slopes overshadowed by the glaciers of Mont Blanc. The place has been a refreshment post since 1973 and is run by the Truchet family, who also rent out five apartments. The cooking is traditional, home-made, based on high-quality prime ingredients, while the service is charming and attentive.
Since the head of the household is a keen mushroom picker, in season you'll find **porcini** mushrooms, fried, stewed or grilled. On good days, you may even be treated to the very rare 'Caesar's mushrooms', served raw as an antipasto. Other starters include mocetta, lardo and other Val d'Aosta **cured meats**, carpaccio and warm Tomino cheese salad. For your first course, there are several varieties of **polenta** – alla valdostana, with mushrooms, or with milk - crêpes, **risotto** with herbs or mushrooms, ravioli, **seupa vapellenentse** and other soups, including varieties cooked with cereals. Main courses include **carbonade**, **polenta and roe deer venison**, bistecca alla valdostana and, if you book, you can also have fondue and sorça (pork cooked with cabbage, potatoes and sausage). To finish, a delicious apple compote.
The wine list comprises mainly Val d'Aosta labels and, though not comprehensive, does provide a good selection of what the area has to offer.

Courmayeur

38 km north-west of Aosta SS 26 d

Le vieux pommier

Restaurant with rooms
Piazzale Monte Bianco 25
Tel. 0165 842281-846825
Closed Monday, never in July, August and Christmas
Open: lunch and dinner
Holidays: two weeks in May, October
Seating: 180 + 40 outdoors
Prices: 30-35 euros, wine excluded
All credit cards except AE, Bancomat

Although the tables are set out over three rooms and separated by partitions, this is no place for intimacy. But the authentic, mountain atmosphere, the efficient service and the cooking (always carefully prepared despite the large number of diners who flock to the place) make it a place to be recommended.
The most attractive feature of the restaurant, which also has five bedrooms is its convivial atmosphere; ever since the 1960s it has been managed by the Casale Brunet family. The building itself has a welcoming atmosphere, especially the large dining room at the center of which stands a real, old apple tree around which the antipasti and desserts are displayed. A lot of the food is cooked for groups of people, rather than couples. The dishes that particularly stand out on the menu are the 'communal' ones such as bourguignonne, fondue savoiarde, pierrade, raclette, reblochonnade), while other conmvivial mountain dishes such as **polenta concia** are ever present on the menu. After mixed **cured meats** or insalata degli alpeggi, you can order **onion soup**, **seupa vapellenentse**, **seupetta courmayeurentse** (with vegetables, Fontina cheese and brown bread), gnocchi, or **risotto**, either alla valdostana or with cep mushrooms. Then come **carbonade**, scaloppa alla valdostana, chicken breast alla Vieux Pommier, with apple fritters, or **game** in season. The choice of desserts is very wide, too, with cakes, tarts, pastries, mousses and chocolate fondue, crema di Cogne, and cold zabaglione.
The wine list offers several Piedmontese and Tuscan wines alongside those from the Val d'Aosta itself.

GIGNOD
La Clusaz

LA CLUSAZ ◎ ⃔ 🍾

🍲 Trattoria – 3-Star Hotel
Frazione La Clusaz 1
Tel. 0165 56075-56426
Fax 0165 56426
E-mail: info@laclusaz.it
Internet: www.laclusaz.it
Closed Tuesday, never in August and Christmas-Epiphany
Open: lunch and dinner, in winter only for dinner
Holidays: 3 weeks between May and June, November
Seating: 40
Prices: 27-35 euros, wine excluded
All credit cards, Bancomat

The hospice, built in the 12th century, is now an enchanting locanda and one of the best restaurants in the region. The walls of two of the rooms are decorated with prints and in the dining room suffused lighting and stone vaulting create a friendly, elegant environment. The cuisine of Maurizio and Sevi Grange is local, and the menu kicks off with **mocetta**, **teteun** (cow's udder, to which Gignod dedicates a festival round about 20 August) and other excellent Val d'Aosta cured meats, or **chestnut pie with pancetta**, lardo and rye bread. Not to be missed among the first courses, **seupa vapellenentse**, **polenta with fondue**, **straccetti of rye flour with Savoy cabbage and Toma**: among the main courses, **carbonade** with polenta or potatoes and **loin of lamb**. A good selection of **cheeses** is followed by delightful desserts such as **chestnut tart** and sorbet al vin brulé. The wine list offers a lavish array of the best in the Val d'Aosta and the rest of Italy, as well as important international labels.
Half board in a double room costs from 58 to 85 euros per person.

🛏🍽● 14 double rooms with bathroom, television, several with sauna and minibar ● Prices: double room single use 48-78 euros, double 62-115 euros; breakfast 6 euros per person ● Parking, garage (6 places). Small pets allowed (5 euros per day). Owners always present ● Restaurant. Breakfast room, reading room. Terrace

GRESSONEY-LA-TRINITÉ

CAPANNA CARLA

🍲 Restaurant
Località Tschaval 33
Tel. 0125 366130
Closed Monday, never during summer
Open: lunch and dinner; winter dinner also (Sat. and Sun. also at lunch), Spring and Autumn Sat. and Sun.
Seating: 50
Prices: 25-27 euros, wine excluded
All credit cards except AE, Bancomat

This characteristic chalet is located at an altitude of over 1800 meters in the upper Lys valley. A short passageway leads to three small rooms with a few tables, a lot of wood and low ceilings, with framed embroidery and old kitchen utensils adorning the walls. As you come into Gressoney-la-Trinité, you reach the restaurant along the road that leads to the Staffal cable cars; just before the ski-lifts, turn off into the little road that climbs to the restaurant car-park. Susanna Tarello (the cook) and her husband Gigi Barozzi run this perfect place to taste the typical food of the Walser valleys, home to descendants of the Germanic populations who came to the Monte Rosa area in the Middle Ages.
The menu offers a range of traditional dishes, which often derive from exchanges of information between the cook and the old housewives of the village. It's virtually compulsory to start with chestnuts with honey or the classic plate of Aosta Valley cured meats, including lardo di Arnad, though another excellent antipasto is **tomino in chicory sauce**. As a first course, **zuppa valdostana** or **ueca**, cooked on a wood stove, crespelle alla fonduta, **polenta concia**, ravioli filled with wild boar meat or chamois with fondue. Main courses include **carbonade**, **roast beef with blackcurrants**, baked shin of pork or shin of veal with mushrooms, **venison with herbs**, wild boar and **camoscio in salmì**, stewed chamois venison, and simple but tasty **sausages in sauce.** You can finish by sampling **Gressoney Toma cheese** and **Salignon**, the traditional Walser peppery ricotta, and round things off with a slice of homemade tart. The wine-list includes about fifty labels.

ISSOGNE

AL MANIERO

Restaurant – Rooms
Frazione Pied de Ville 58
Tel. and fax 0125 929219
E-mail: almaniero@tiscalinet.it
Internet: www.ristorantealmaniero.it
Closed Monday, never in summer
Open: lunch and dinner
Holidays: 15-30 June
Seating: 50 + 30 outdoors
Prices: 25-30 euros, wine excluded
All credit cards exceptAE, Bancomat

Emanuela and Giovanni started up the restaurant in 1984 and added six rooms with large bathrooms twenty years later. The place is well furnished and in summer you can eat out on the terrace. Although the menu is mostly traditional there is no lack of dishes with fewer local ties but prepared with vegetables grown by the owners.

Whatever the season you can start with the classic Val d'Aosta cured meats – lardo di Arnad, **mocetta**, **boudin**, jambon de Bosses – or with raw meat roulades, flans, **vegetable strudel with fondue**. If you don't want to continue with the **polenta concia**, you can try first courses of home-made pasta, such as **tagliatelle** or **ravioli** topped in season with cep mushrooms, **gnocchi with fondue**, **crespelle** alla valdostana. Seconds include **carbonade with polenta**, **lamb with herbs**, roasts and tagliate. For dessert, fruit pies and creams, including reinvigorating zabaglione.

The wine list includes a hundred or so labels, a third of them from the Val d'Aosta, the rest from other regions of Italy.

The locanda has no closing day and does not accept credit cards.

• 6 double rooms with bathroom, mini-bar, television, safe • Prices: double room single use 40 euros, double 60-90 (15 euro supplement for extra bed), breakfast included • Off-road parking. No pets allowed. Owners always reachable • Restaurant. Breakfast room. Terrace. Garden

LA SALLE
Cheverel

LES COMBES

3-Star Hotel
Località Le Combe
Tel. 0165 863982-335 7464218
Fax 0165 861932
E-mail: lescombes@libero.it
Holidays variable

Le Combe is an ancient hamlet in an enchanting position in the Mont Blanc chain. Abandoned and derelict since the late-1800s, this building has been salvaged and converted, with full respect for its original features, into a family-run hotel. The many common areas – garden, terrace, bar and reading room – are all meticulously kept. Bedrooms are in the local style with the extensive use of wood and stone creating a warm and friendly atmosphere. A baby sitting service is available on request. The restaurant serves traditional cuisine at around 35 euros, wine excluded. Half board 40-76 euros, full board 55-86 euros per person. The hotel is close to Courmayeur and La Thuile.

• 3 double rooms and 5 triple rooms, with bathroom, mezzanine or small balcony, television • Prices: double used as single and double 60-94 euros, triple 80-122, breakfast included • Credit cards: Visa, Bancomat • 2 rooms equipped for the mobility challenged. Inside parking, garage. Small pets allowed. 24-hour porter service • Bar, restaurant. Breakfast room. Reading room, TV room. Tavern. Terrace, garden, playgrounds

La Salle

Lo Peillo de Mamagran

🍲 Restaurant-brasserie
Via Chanoux 4
Tel. 0165 862574
Closed Wednesday, never in the high season
Open: lunch and dinner, Nov. and Apr-May dinner only
Holidays: second half of October
Seating: 50
Prices: 25-28 euros, wine excluded
Credit cards: CartaSi, Visa, Bancomat

La Salle is a small village on the Aosta-Courmayeur road, well known for its Morgex and La Salle white wines and for the Derby and Chatelard castles. In this tastefully renovated restaurant, on a street in the old village center, just a few yards from the parish church, Simone does the cooking and Alessandra welcomes guests. The wood of the tables and the wall paneling, decorated with kitchen utensils, creates a warm, cozy atmosphere.

The assiette on which the local **cured meats** – the classic Aosta Valley antipasto – are served, is also made of wood. All the first courses are traditional; worth trying are the delicious **asulette** (a sort of rye flour polenta with butter and Fontina cheese) and the **polenta grassa**, the **seupetta cogneintze**, the **favò**, the **seupetta di Cogne-Peilà**, the **seupa vapellenentse**, and the **ueca** (a light, savory pudding made with barley). Moving onto main courses, we find **carbonade**, **soça** and **frecacha** (a meat and potato pudding). If you book, you can also have **pierrade** (mixed meats cooked on a hotplate) and bourguignonne. Note that the choice of dishes may be greatly reduced in the low season, in November and at the end of winter. The desserts are all delicious: from crema di Cogne with corn biscuits and chestnuts to wild black cherry crème brulée. The restaurant also serves a vegetarian menu and a children's menu.

There is a full wine list with the top Val d'Aosta labels and a good selection of other Italian wines too (some available by the glass).

La Thuile
Thovex

Le Thovex

🗝 Bed and breakfast
Località Thovex 188
Tel. 0165 884806-347 4211233
Fax 0165 804806
E-mail: info@lethovex.it
Internet: www.lethovex.it
Closed from mid-May to mid-June, October and November

At an altitude of over 1,500 meters, opposite the bus stop for the ski slopes (skiing is possible around the Piccolo San Bernardo November thru April), the Bovio family live in a typical mountain home, with warm friendly interiors. The b&b has two double rooms and a spacious attic with simple but carefully chosen furnishings and walls that are either plastered or wood-faced. Breakfast is continental buffet style. The Bovio family also opened a restaurant a few months ago serving traditional and international cuisine (average price per head 25 euros, wine excluded).

• 1 double room, with bathroom and television, and 2 mini-suites, with bathroom and lounge • Prices: double used as single 43-59, double and mini-suite 61-84, breakfast included • Credit cards: Visa, Bancomat • Outdoor parking on the premises. No pets allowed. Owners always contactable • Breakfast room, lounge

Nus
Saint-Barthélemy

28 KM EAST OF AOSTA

CUNEY

🔑 2-Star Hotel
Località Lignan 36
Tel. & fax 0165 770023
E-mail: marisagrun@libero.it
Closed in October

PERLOZ
Marine

58 KM SOUTHEAST OF AOSTA - SR 505

A MASOUN DOU CARO

🔑 Bed and breakfast
Frazione Marine 56
Tel. 0125 807491-347 4101583
Fax 0125 801447
E-mail: willymarine@libero.it
Internet: www.masoundoucaro.it
Open all year round

Just a few steps from the Church of Lignan (fewer than 30 inhabitants, at an altitude of 1630 meters) and close to the Saint-Barthélemy observatory, this mountain home was refurbished in 1986 by the Grun family of keen organic farmers. The bedrooms are simply furnished but offer everything needed for a comfortable stay. Breakfast includes fresh bread, butter, jam and marmalade, fruit juices and pastries made by Marisa, the mother of the family. The restaurant (also open to non-residents, 18-23 euros, wine excluded) also serves organic and vegetarian menus. Half board 43 euros, full board 50 euros.

• 3 single rooms and 5 double or triple rooms, with bathroom (except for one of the single rooms) • Prices: single 29 euros, double 48, triple 77, breakfast included • Credit cards: all, Bancomat • Outdoor parking on the premises. Small pets allowed. The owners are always available • Bar, restaurant. Lounge. Massage room. Garden, children's playground

Two roads, the local road to Perloz and the regional road to Gressoney, lead to the home of the Vuillermoz family, a baita (mountain refuge) with wooden balconies and staircases in a sunny spot 850 meters above sea level on the right bank of the Lys. Albeit very close to the valley floor and not far from the Monte Rosa skiing resort, this is a peaceful, secluded place. Alfredo and his family ensure a warm welcome; here you can relax in the lounge (wood ceiling and flooring, a stove and a fine view over the surrounding mountains), where a generous breakfast is served in the morning. The comfortable rooms, decorated in Alpine style with a lavish use of wood, are ideal for resting after an excursion to the Mont Mars Reserve (6 km) or the rock gym at Arnad (12 km).

• 3 double rooms, with bathroom • Prices: double used as single 25-30 euros, double 45-65, breakfast included • Credit cards: none • Outside parking on the premises, garage. Small pets allowed. Owners always present • Breakfast and reading room. Terrace. Garden

PRÉ-SAINT-DIDIER

EDELWEISS

⚷**2**-Star hotel
Via Monte Bianco 1-3
Tel. 0165 87024
Fax 0165 87025
E-mail: info@albergo-edelweiss.it
Internet: www.albergo-edelweiss.it
Closed May, October and November

The Pré-Saint-Didier tourist resort has been famous for more than two centuries: here, skiing has never been the only tourist attraction, the locality being renowned also for its spa waters. The Edelweiss is located midway between La Thuile and Courmayeur, an ideal starting point for excursions in and around the valley. The bedrooms are welcoming and peaceful. There's just about everything you need to relax and entertain yourself close to the hotel: from an indoor swimming pool, five-a-side football pitch and tennis court to fishing, canoeing, riding and pony trekking. The restaurant (also open to non-residents) offers meals at around 18-23 euros, wine excluded. Half board costs 46-59 euros and full board 53-72 euros per person.

• 4 single rooms and 34 double rooms, with bathroom, satellite television • Prices: single 28-43 euros, double 56-80, breakfast included • Credit cards: all except DC, Bancomat • Outdoor parking on the premises. Owners always available • Bar, restaurant. Breakfast room. Lounge and reading room. Sauna. Garden

QUART
Villair

VILLAGE BOURICCOT FLEURI

⚷**3**-Star hotel
Frazione Villair 1
Tel. 0165 774911
Fax 0165 774999
E-mail: info@bourricotfleuri.it
Internet: www.bourricotfleuri.it
Open all year round

Situated in a secluded position outside Villefranche, near Quart, just a few kilometers from Aosta, this hotel, built about twenty years ago, is a place of peace and quiet, The relaxing atmosphere is enhanced by the friendly service that still characterizes the hotel even under its new management. The village consists of a number of delightful wooden chalets and several rooms of various kinds. Breakfast is served in a special room and is included in the price. Guests may also use a quiet lounge and a reading/relaxation room.

• 1 single room, 3 double rooms and 1 mini-suite, with bathroom, air conditioning, mini-bar, television; 10 chalets (rooms with toilets and lounge) for 2, 3 or 4 guests • Prices: single 50-60 euros, double 80-105, mini-suite 100-128, chalet used as single 75-97, chalet 100-178, breakfast included • Credit cards: all, Bancomat • Outdoor parking on the premises. Small pets accepted. Porter service 7.30-23.30 • Bar. Breakfast room. Reading and television room, small lounge. Park, terrace

RHÊMES-NOTRE-DAME
Chanavey

GRANDE ROUSSE

2-Star hotel
Località Chanavey 22
Tel. 0165 936105
Fax 0165 936191
E-mail: info@granderousse.com
Internet: www.granderousse.com
Closed May, October and November

The Berard family manages this large hotel, which boasts spacious, comfortable rooms. The overall setting is delightful: Chanavey is on the Rhêmes-Notre-Dame road one kilometer from Bruil, the chief town in the area. It is an ideal starting point for skiing treks, walks and climbs. The hotel also has a hire service for all winter sports equipment. The restaurant is open to non-residents and serves traditional dishes at a very reasonable price (12-18 euros - wine excluded). Half board in a double room 36-46 euros, full board 45 euros per person.

• 37 double rooms (13 in the annex), with bathroom, television • Prices: double used as single 48-56 euros, double 60-70 (supplement for additional bed 30-35 euros); breakfast 5 euros per person • Credit cards: all except DC, Bancomat • Parking outside. Small pets allowed. Porter service 7am-midnight • Bar, restaurant. Breakfast room. Lounge, children's play room. Terrace, solarium

RHÊMES-NOTRE-DAME
Chanavey

29 KM SOUTHWEST OF AOSTA

GRANTA PAREY

3-Star Hotel
Località Chanavey 23
Tel. 0165 936104
Fax 0165 936144
E-mail: info@rhemesgrantaparey.com
Internet: www.rhemesgrantaparey.com
Closed in October and November

The tiny village of Rhêmes-Notre-Dame (90 residents) closes the valley of the same name southeast of Aosta, in the direction of the Gran Paradiso National Park. Climbing a further 1.5 km amidst unspoilt fields and pastures, you come to this locanda, managed by the Bertò family. Built in the 1920s, it offers every comfort, service and facility in a truly relaxing environment. The facilities for sport and children's entertainment are particularly impressive. Breakfast is based on fresh local produce, while restaurant cuisine is mostly typical and fairly priced (20-25 35 - wine excluded).

• 4 single rooms, 26 double rooms and 3 suites, with bathroom, mini-bar, satellite television • Prices: single 52-60 euros, double 74-80, suite 110-120, breakfast included • Credit cards: Visa, Bancomat • 1 room equipped for the mobility challenged. Outside parking. Small pets allowed. Owners always available • Bar, restaurant. Breakfast room. Lounge, reading and television room, children's play room. Meeting/film room. Five-a-side soccer/volleyball court, sauna, gym

SAINT-PIERRE

10 KM WEST OF AOSTA - SS 26 OR A 5

LA MERIDIANA

☎🗝3-Star Hotel
Place Château Feuillet 17
Tel. 0165 903626
E-mail: info@albergomeridiana.it
Internet: www.albergomeridiana.it
Open all year round

Set in a large independent house, surrounded by a beautiful lawn, La Meridiana offers impressively modern services. The simply but elegantly furnished bedrooms are very welcoming, large and comfortable. Common facilities – from the lounge to the restaurant hall (managed separately since summer 2005) – create a warm, spacious environment. Wood is used extensively in the interiors to create a pleasing rustic effect. The hotel is an excellent starting point for excursions to the nearby Valsavarenche and Cogne valleys. The Pila ski slopes are also close by.

• 14 double rooms, 2 triple rooms, 1 with 4 beds and 1 suite, with bathroom, balcony or terrace, satellite television • Prices: double used as single 45-70 euros, double 80-120, triple 108-162, with 4 beds 132-198, suite 100-160, breakfast included • Credit cards: main, Bancomat • 2 rooms equipped for the mobility challenged. Adjacent parking area, inside parking (5 euros /day). Small pets allowed. Porter service 7am-midnight • Restaurant. Breakfast room. Reading room and lounge. Tavern. Garden, solarium

SAINT-PIERRE
Homené Dessus

15 KM WEST OF AOSTA

LES ECUREUILS

☎🗝Holiday farm
Frazione Homené Dessus 8
Tel. 0165 903831
Fax 0165 909849
E-mail: lesecureuils@libero.it
Internet: www.lesecureuils.it
Closed December and January

A refuge at an altitude of 1,500 meters in an enchanting position with a superb view, excellent facilities, a warm, friendly atmosphere and courteous management (though arguably a tad inflexible: breakfast is served strictly at the times indicated). In this particular case, the agriturismo label is more than just a name: cured meats and cheeses are all home-made, ands even wool is still spun with traditional methods. The bedrooms are comfortable. The generous breakfasts, snacks and dinner (only for guests, half board 35-43 euros) feature truly home-made flavors. Guests can dine outside in summer and enjoy the superb view. It doesn't take long to reach the valley bottom by car, and Aosta, skiing facilities and Alpine trails are all easily reachable.

• 5 double rooms, with adjacent bathroom • Prices: double used as single 22-30 euros, double 44-60, breakfast included • Credit cards: none • Parking. No pets allowed. Owners always present • Restaurant (only for guests at dinner). Library. Garden

Saint-Pierre

21 KM WEST OF AOSTA

Vetan

🍲 Bar-restaurant
Frazione Vetan Dessous 77
Tel. 0165 908830
Closed Tuesday; January-March open Saturday and Sunday
Open: lunch and dinner
Holidays: November
Seating: 50
Prices: 23 euros, wine excluded
Credit cards: none, Bancomat

Setting out from the Saint-Pierre town center, from the motorway exit or from SS 26, to reach this restaurant, located at an altitude of 1,700 meters, go through Saint-Nicolas, then double back into the area of Saint-Pierre,. First-time visitors feel they are really high up, just below the peaks of the surrounding mountains. Elida, who has been a fixture here ever since she was a little girl, and who manages the restaurant with her husband Battista, proudly says that the Vetan has the oldest public commercial license in Saint-Pierre (it dates from 1940). In a building nearby their daughter Antonella runs an agriturismo: L'Abri (French for 'shelter').

The restaurant is open at weekends only during the winter, but seven days a week in summer. It is recommended for anyone who wants to sample simple, traditional mountain cuisine. Antipasti include **beetroot and potato salad** made with locally produced vegetables, **lardo with chestnuts** and **cured meats**. The **polenta concia** and the **seupa vapellenentse** are a must, and another substantial first course is riso della nonna, a local dish in which rice and vegetables are supplemented by a good helping of Fontina cheese. For your main course, you can have **carbonade** or, if you book ahead, chamois venison. Alternatively, there's **braised** or **casseroled beef**. For dessert: Saint-Pierre **apple cake** with zabaglione and **panna cotta** made with dairy cream from the Alpine pastures.

Antonella is in charge of the wine department, which features a fairly good choice of Val d'Aosta wines and a few Piedmontese varieties as well.

Saint-Vincent

27 KM EAST OF AOSTA

Le Rosier

🔑 Bed and breakfast
Frazione Romillod Crotache 1
Tel. 0166 537726-333 2384401
Fax 0166 537726
E-mail: ada@lerosier.it
Internet: www.lerosier.it
Open all year round

Driving along the road towards the Colle di Joux, three bends after the spa at Saint-Vincent, you come to the b&b of Ada Vesan, a typical stone house built in 1755. The two rooms and the small apartment (ideal for families) are comfortable and friendly. The breakfast room is very characteristic, with stone vaulting and local antique furniture. For breakfast, brown, white and raisin bread, cakes, jam and marmalade, honey, cornflakes, muesli, yoghurt, and fruit juices. A pedestrian track takes you to the center of town and the Casino in just five minutes. Monte Rosa and the Matterhorn, the most important castles in Valle d'Aosta and the Mont Avic nature park are all close by.

• 2 double rooms, with bathroom, minibar, television; 1 small apartment with 2-4 beds, lounge, kitchen range, bathroom, television • Prices: double used as single 40 euros, double 65, apartment 75-105, breakfast included • Credit cards: none • Parking in front of the premises. Small pets allowed. Owners always present • Breakfast room. Garden, solarium

SAINT-VINCENT

27 KM EAST OF AOSTA SS 26 OR EXIT A 5

TRATTORIA DEGLI AMICI

🍲 Trattoria
Via Biavaz 11
Tel. 0166 513472
Closed Wednesday, never in summer
Open: lunch and dinner
Holidays: 10 days in March, 15 in October
Seating: 35 + 40 outdoors
Prices: 20-24 euros, wine excluded
All credit cards except AE, Bancomat

Famous for its social life and casino Saint-Vincent also opportunities to find out more about the history and traditions of the area. The old Roman bridge provides the history, this trattoria the tradition, at least within the context of food. Strolling down Via Chanoux, turning into a side street you'll immediately see the old-fashioned neon sign above the entrance. It's a very simple but tidy and welcoming: the tables on the veranda have paper tablecloths, while, inside, you'll find the décor basic but cozy ... plus, tables laid with fabric tablecloths. Pina Baudin's home cooking mainly consists of traditional regional dishes which are delightfully served by her daughter, Barbara Ternavasio. You start with **mocetta**, **lardo di Arnad** and various kinds of ham accompanied by butter and chestnuts. Moving on to first courses, there are homemade **tagliatelle** with cep mushrooms, when in season, cheese fondue, crespelle, wholewheat flour **polenta concia**, and **rice with fondue**. Main courses include **carbonade**, **tripe with beans**, bistecca alla valdostana, **wild boar with polenta** and fondue bourguignonne. For dessert: apple pie, crème caramel, panna cotta and, in summer, stuffed peaches. Wine is served by the carafe, but a small selection of Val d'Aosta and other Italian labels is available on request.

🍮 Pasticceria Morandin, Via Chanoux 105: excellent tegole biscuits and Chantilly cream. Les Saveurs d'Antan, Via Roma 103: cured meats, cheese and other Aosta Valley specialties. At **Bosses di Châtillon** (15 km), Douce Vallée produces vinegar made from raspberries and other woodland fruits.

VALGRISENCHE
Bonne

32 KM SOUTHWEST OF AOSTA

PERRET

🔑 2-Star Hotel
Località Bonne 2
Tel. 0165 97107
Fax 0165 97220
E-mail: info@hotelperret.it
Internet: www.hotelperret.it
Closed 1 October - December 26 and May 10- July 1

At an altitude of 1,800 meters, on a ridge overlooking the entire Valgrisenche, this small hotel is run by the Gerbelle family. The position is secluded, the silence total (the village of Bonne has just 25 inhabitants). The bedrooms are cozy and friendly, with telephone and, on request, a modem socket. The garden is large and well-groomed. The restaurant serves typical dishes prepared by the owners (set menu 25 euros, booking required for specialties). Half board costs 58 euros and full board 64 euros per person. The only concession to modernity, albeit very useful, is the small meeting room. Skiing facilities, trekking and excursion trails and climbing centers are all easy to get to.

• 2 single rooms and 16 double rooms, with bathroom, • Prices: single 34, double 64 euros, breakfast 10 euros per person • Credit cards: all except AE • 2 rooms equipped for the mobility challenged. Adjacent parking area. No pets allowed • The owners are always available • Restaurant. Meeting room. Sauna (in winter). Garden

VALSAVARENCHE
Eau-Rousse

VALTOURNENCHE
Crépin

30 KM SOUTHWEST OF AOSTA

43 KM NORTHEAST OF AOSTA SR 406

A L'HOSTELLERIE DU PARADIS

🗝️🔾3-Star Hotel
Frazione Eau-Rousse
Tel. 0165 905972
Fax 0165 905971
E-mail: info@hostellerieduparadis.it
Internet: www.hostellerieduparadis.it
Closed November and December

PANKEO

🗝️🔾Bed and breakfast
Frazione Crépin
Tel. 0166 92956-338 9025305
Fax 0166 92049
E-mail: rosset.adelaide@pankeo.com
Internet: www.pankeo.com
Variable holidays

Marisa Dayné and Alberto Gianni have managed this typical locanda, three kilometers from Dégioz, the chief town of Valsavarenche, for the last 15 years. The surrounding mountain peaks, especially the towering Gran Paradiso, unspoilt nature and delightful views create a magical environment. The Hostellerie is characterized by simple yet attractive wood-lined bedrooms, some under the roof itself but no less warm and welcoming. The restaurant serves traditional dishes 'revisited' (15-20 euros, wine excluded, half board 55-75 euros per person). The garden and solarium outside offer magnificent views of the valley.

• 7 single rooms and 23 double, triple or 4-bed rooms, with bathroom, telephone, television • Prices: single 55 euros, double 85, triple 129, 4 bed 172; breakfast 8 euros per person • Credit cards: all, Bancomat • 3 rooms furnished for the mobility challenged. Parking in the square outside. Small pets accepted. Owners always contactable • Bar, restaurant. Breakfast room. Reading room, lounge. Garden. Solarium. Sauna, indoor swimming pool with whirlpool

Pankeo is the shortened Franco-Provençal name for Pancherot, the mountain west of Pâquier, the chief town in the Valtournenche area. At the foot of this mountain, nine kilometers from Breuil-Cervinia, the Maquignaz family lives in a recently-refurbished 18th-century stone building (three storeys with a built-in wooden granary). One unusual feature of this b&b is that breakfast is served not in a common room but in small rooms adjacent to two of the bedrooms and the daytime corner of the third room (also rented as a single room). Guests can naturally use these facilities all day, so that Pankeo is ideal for both a mountain vacation as well as for study or pure relaxation. The price includes entrance to the municipal swimming pool and there are also discounts for university students and cyclists, as well as for longer stays.

• 3 double rooms, with bathroom, refrigerator, television • Prices: double used as single 30-37 euros, double 60-74, breakfast included • Credit cards: none • Adjacent parking area, garage for motorcycles and bicycles. Small pets allowed. Owners always present • Breakfast and reading rooms. Seating facilities outside

VERRAYES

LA VRILLE

🛏️🔑Holiday farm
Place Grangeon
Tel. 0166 543018
E-mail: lavrille@tiscali.it
Internet: www.lavrille-agritourisme.com
Open all year round

It's not easy to find this agriturismo among the steep vineyards that dot the mountain above Chambave, at the heart of the Val d'Aosta a few kilometers from Nus. Owned by Hervé Deguillame and his wife Luciana, and built solely with traditional materials, it boasts bio-architecture and solar panels to heat water. The bedrooms are jewels of wood and stone, large and comfortably furnished with period furniture. Breakfast offers the fragrant cakes and pastries of Signora Luciana, as well as typical Aosta cheese and cured meats. More recently, staying guests have also been able to enjoy dinner (half board 47-56 euros per person). A wine cellar will be opened soon for tastings.

• 4 double rooms, 1 triple and 1 with 4 beds, with bathroom • Prices: double used as single 45-55 euros, double 64-82, with 3 beds 90-120, with 4 beds 110-160, breakfast included • Credit cards: none • One room equipped for the mobility challenged. Parking in front of the premises. Pets are accepted in one room. Owners always present • Restaurant. Lounge

VERRÈS
Omens

OMENS

🍲Bar-trattoria
Località Omens 1
Tel. 0125 929410-347 4775334
Closed Monday; June-October open Saturday and Sunday
Open: lunch and dinner
Holidays: January 6-February 15
Seating: 80
Prices: 19 euros, wine excluded
No credit cards accepted

The name 'Omens' is said to derive from the word 'uomini' or, to be more precise, the 'uomini' (men) who lived in and defended the underlying castle, one of the most visited in the Val d'Aosta. It's no coincidence that 'medieval dinners' are staged frequently here in the course of the year. To reach Omens, take the road that leads from the center of Verres to the castle, then continue along the road through the woods that comes to an end at the hamlet.

When talking about the Omens trattoria, two people are definitely worth a mention: Elvia, the owner, who manages the business started up by her family in 1974, and Anna, who moved to Verrès and Omens from Chivasso. Continuous opening hours and weekend opening in the winter months show how the place is a favorite haunt for lovers of Sunday jaunts and merende sinòire, substantial late-afternoon snacks.

This is a simple restaurant, very much in the rustic style that was fashionable in the Sixties. The specialties are all from the tpical Val d'Aosta repertoire. You can sample a very special **polenta concia**, **seupa vapellenentse**, and **zuppa di Omens**, made with bread, Toma and Fontina cheeses and courgettes. There are also home-made cured meats, locally picked, glazed chestnuts served with butter, and **potatoes with cotechino and salignon** (peppery ricotta cheese typical of the Gressoney valley). The meat is mainly casseroled: wild boar, **rabbit** and the classic **carbonade**. The desserts on offer include an excellent **crema di Cogne**.

To drink, you can choose from a selection of Val d'Aosta and Piedmontese wines.

PIEMONTE

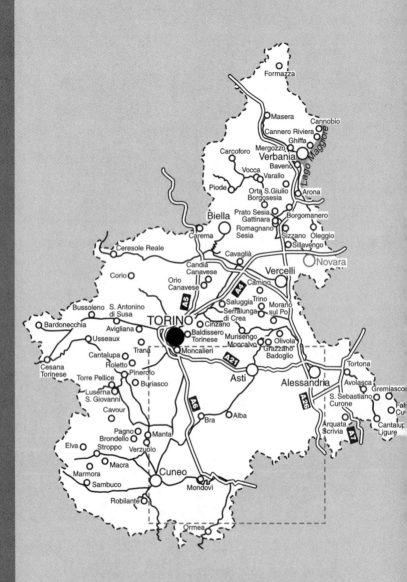

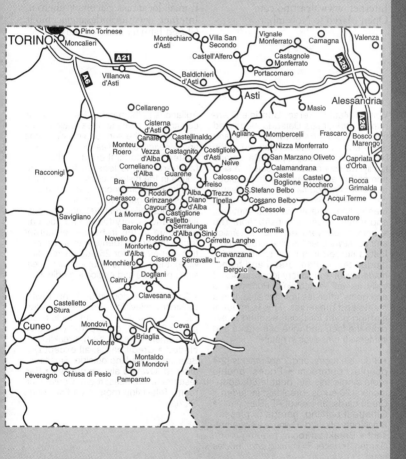

IL CARTINO

LOCANDA SAN GIACOMO

Bed & Breakfast
Passeggiata Bellavista 36
Tel. and fax 0144 323483
E-mail: baccalario@ilcartino.com
Internet: www.ilcartino.com
Open March to November

Rooms for rent
Via Arullani 4
Tel. 0141 954831
Fax 0141 964563
E-mail: locanda.s.giacomo@libero.it
Internet: www.locandasangiacomo.it
Closed January and February

Writers Matilde Serao, Gabriele D'Annunzio and Grazia Deledda all passed through Il Cartino's drawing rooms, and this literary heritage is reflected in the huge library built up by the Baccalario family. It's now possible to stay in a section of this ancient winery, in spacious rooms with period furniture and valuable carpets. An extension houses two apartments, one suitable for small families, and a third is under construction. The spacious courtyard leads to the terrace and its views over the vineyards. Breakfast is served in a cozy room and includes tea, coffee, bread and homemade sweet and savory focaccia baked daily, as well as Robiola di Roccaverano and goats' cheeses from the area, cured meats and preserves. This is an ideal starting point for those wanting to explore the food and wine of the area and immerse themselves in nature.

Agliano is in the heart of Barbera d'Asti country, and offers an ideal base for explorations of the surrounding vineyards and wineries, as well as the recently renovated traditional thermal baths. This family-run inn is located in a period house in the historic center of the town, and its spacious rooms and communal areas are elegantly furnished.
The buffet-style breakfast includes both sweet and savory foods and you can also dine in the in-house restaurant (open to non-residents with a reservation, set menus for 25 euros excluding wine): the cuisine is local and uses seasonal produce and choice ingredients.

• 3 double rooms and 2 apartments (2-4 people), bathroom • Prices: double room single use 60, double 80, apartments 120 euros, breakfast included • Credit cards: all except AE, Bancomat • Off-street parking, garage (5 places). Small pets allowed. Owners always present • Breakfast room, reading room. Garden, terrace. Swimming pool, boules court

• 5 rooms with double bed and 1 twin, bathroom, television, 2 rooms with a terrace • Prices: double room single occupancy 80 euros, double 104 (25 euros supplement for extra bed), breakfast included • Credit cards: all except DC, Bancomat • Parking outside. Small pets allowed. Owners always present • Bar, restaurant. Breakfast room. Conference room. Television room. Reading room. Garden

ALBA

LALIBERA

� Osteria
Via Pertinace 24 A
Tel. 0173 293155
Closed Sunday and Monday lunch
Open: lunch and dinner
Holidays: 20 days in February, last 15 days of August
Seating: 40
Prices: 32-35 euros, wine excluded
All major credit cards

This modern osteria with its tasteful, welcoming atmosphere in the old center of Alba is a pleasant place to stop and eat. The food is always top quality and oncludes a blend of classic Langhe and lesser known Piedmontese dishes. From the Langhe there's **coscia di fassone battuta al coltello**, **vitello tonnato** (very good), pepper roulade with tuna and capers, **tajarin al ragù di coniglio**, maltagliati with various sauces, **agnolotti dal plin with butter and sage**, while the Piedmontese dishes include **insalata di testina di vitello** or **eel**. Forays are also made into other regional cuisines, with Gragnano pasta accompanied by Mediterranean sauces (paccheri with tomato, capers and tuna) or scamone flavored with Pantelleria capers. As for main courses, pride of place goes to local dishes such as grilled veal chops, Cesare Giaccone's **galletto all'aceto**, **roast lamb** and, in the fall, Borgo San Dalmazzo snails. There are also some exquisite new treats such as tripe baked with Bronte pistachio nuts and angler fish served with ratatouille.
And what a repertoire of desserts! When in season try the vineyard peaches with vanilla and pistachio ice-cream, or damsons with lavender ice-cream, or chocolate cake, or coffee-flavored bonet... enough said! There's always a carefully chosen selection of various cheeses, and a well-stocked wine cellar offers wide range of (above all) Langhe and other Piedmontese wines.

🍷 Fine selections of local Langhe and other Italian wines are available from Enoteca Fracchia, Via Vernazza, 29 and from Grandi Vini, Via Vittorio Emanuele, 1a.

ALBA
Altavilla

LA MERIDIANA CA' REINÉ

🛏Holiday farm
Località Altavilla 9
Tel. and fax 0173 440112
E-mail: cascinareine@libero.it
Open all year round

Just a kilometer from the center of Alba, nestling in the hills on the road to Neive and Treiso, is this lovely farm run by the Giacosa family. Current owner Andrea is assisted by father Giuseppe and mother Giuliana, who prepares hearty breakfasts of home-made jams and sweets, local cheeses and cured meats and eggs cooked in special ceramic dishes from Scotland. The tastefully furnished bedrooms are filled with light, located in converted barns next to the 18th-century villa which has been renovated in Art Nouveau style. The surrounding vineyards, fields and woods can be explored on foot or by bicycle (bicycle can be hired).

• 4 double rooms with bathroom, television; 4 apartments (2-4 people) with kitchen, 2 rooms with terrace • Prices: double room single occupancy 70 euros, double 80, apartment 85-100, breakfast included • Credit cards: none • 1 room designed for the mobility challenged. Off-street parking. Small pets allowed. (5 euros per day). Owners always contactable • Breakfast, reading and television rooms, billiard room, library. Garden. Swimming pool, gym

OSTERIA DELL'ARCO

Osteria
Piazza Savona 5
Tel. 0173 363974
Closed Sunday and Monday
Open: lunch and dinner
Holidays: variable
Seating: 50
Prices: 28-32 euros, wine excluded
All major credit cards, Bancomat

SAN LORENZO

2-Star Hotel
Piazza Rossetti 6
Tel. 0173 362406
Fax 0173 366995
E-mail: info@albergo-sanlorenzo.it
Internet: www.albergo-sanlorenzo.it
Closed one week in January and one in August

The history and inspiration of this modern osteria are closely associated with Slow Food and in 2006 it celebrates its 20th anniversary. Even though the original patron, Daniele Sandri, has gone his own way (today he's chef at the Agenzia di Pollenzo hotel), this milestone means a lot to his successor Maurizio Dellapiana. The osteria owes its name to the place where it first welcomed customers in Vicolo dell'Arco before moving over ten years ago to its current home in a charming courtyard in Piazza Savona. Elegantly furnished but with no frills, though one stand-out feature is the series of climatized showcases containing top-label Langhe wines and a wide selection of the best of Italian and international production.
Now down to business. For antipasti, depending on the season, you'll find **vitello tonnato**, cardoon gratiné with fondue, **carne cruda battuta al coltello**, leek pie, Jerusalem artichokes with cream of bagna caoda, cod with potatoes and shallot cream sauce, poached eggs with white truffle dressing. After this, some classical Piedmontese first courses: **gnocchi al raschera**, risotto al Barolo, **tajarin** and **agnolotti dal plin** with butter and sage dressing, **sausage sauce**, cepe mushroom sauce, or with courgettes and cherry tomatoes. Tasty main courses usually include **rabbit Arneis**, **tench** or trout **in carpione**, **beef braised in Barolo**, guinea-fowl spiced with rosemary, Fassone steak, trippa in umido, **Sambucano lamb**.
To end, a fine **cheese** board and a wide choice of puddings: our favorites are the **panna cotta**, and the hazelnut and chocolate cake with vanilla sauce.

Just a few steps from the cathedral, this hotel is located in a recently restored 18th-century building in the center of historic Alba. The bright, attractive rooms are furnished in a modern, minimalist style, and some are decorated with the works of local artists. The substantial buffet breakfast is served in a lounge which doubles as a reading room and offers the customary cold and hot beverages as well as cakes, pastries, cereals, sweet rolls, jams, butter, cured meats and cheeses. Apart from the comfortable rooms and friendly staff, the hotel's strong point is its location, which is both central and peaceful.

• 9 double and 2 triple rooms with bathroom, satellite television, modem connection; several rooms with air conditioning, terrace • Prices: double room single use 60-70 euros, double 83-90, triple 108-115, breakfast included • Credit cards: all, Bancomat • Facility accessible for the mobility challenged. Off-street parking. Small pets allowed. Reception open from 7am to 9pm • Breakfast room with reading area

ALESSANDRIA

ARONA
Campagna

CAPPELVERDE

🍲 Trattoria
Via San Pio V 26
Tel. 0131 251265
Closed Tuesday
Open: lunch and dinner
Holidays: variable
Seating: 50
Prices: 22-26 euros, wine excluded
All major credit cards, Bancomat

CAMPAGNA

🍲 Trattoria
Via Vergante 12
Tel. 0322 57294
Closed Monday evening, never in summer, and Tuesday
Open: lunch and dinner
Holidays: 15-30 June, 15 days in November
Seating: 50 + 30 outdoors
Prices: 30-35 euros, wine excluded
All major credit cards except DC, Bancomat

Cappelverde is one of those places everybody would like to have next door: the welcome's cordial, the food is home-cooking without frills, and the bill is reasonable. In a word, an ideal place when you don't feel like messing around with pots and pans, and you don't want to spend a fortune. You can have a full meal – antipasto, first and main courses – for just 18 euros if you take the day's set menu, but it won't cost you that much more even if you decide to eat à la carte.

What you'll find here are simple, local, well-prepared dishes like **anchovies in green sauce**, stuffed vegetables or carne cruda battuta a coltello. The choice of first courses is dominated by homemade pasta, including stuffed varieties: **trenette al pesto**, with green beans and potato, spaghetti alla chitarra with Taggia olives and capers, gnocchetti di ricotta or **agnolotti al brasato**, a classic Alessandrian dish. The influence of nearby Liguria and the chef's origins are reflected in the cuisine, and the same can be said for the main courses too. **Coniglio alla ligure**, tasty dried cod and stuffed squid, but there are traditional Piedmontese dishes too, like the **fritto misto** and **carne in carpione**. To finish, a sampling of little known cheeses bought from local producers or the home-made puddings, such as apple pie, panna cotta, semifreddo and **bonet**.

The wines are mainly from the province of Alessandria with occasional forays into other regions.

Campagna is run by the capable Zanetta brothers whose energy has never betrayed them. The trattoria is located in a peaceful, picturesque setting in an early 1900s house just a few kilometers from Arona. Rustic, well-kept furnishings inside, while in summer the cool atmosphere of the garden will help you work up an appetite. The formula is always the same and years of appreciation have discouraged modification: the menu changes often and traditional dishes are offered along with one or two attractive innovations.

The antipasti include really fresh vegetables (in frittatas, flans, terrines, aspic or **warm strudel**) and **cured meats** (lard, coppa, culatello, raw ham, fidighin). Then come handmade pasta dishes – tagliatelle with leeks, **tagliolini with rabbit sauce** or with duck sauce or with chard and ricotta, and tortellini with eggplant and courgette filling. Always recommended – and almost always available – **pasta and beans** and various **risottos**. Lightly spiced cuts and fillets of fassone beef, the typical **tapulone d'asino**, donkey stew, **rabbit dous e brusch** (with chocolate, vinegar and amaretti) or cooked with potatoes and peppers, and fish like trout, lake whitefish or **baccalà** are excellent ideas for your main course. Local and national cheeses and puddings created by the inventive cook: semifreddi, crème brûlée, cassata, cakes, are a fitting end to proceedings.

The wine cellar offers a good selection of Piedmontese labels, with just regard for wines from the Novara hills and Gattinara.

Arquata Scrivia

34 km southeast of Alessandria, 15 km from Novi Ligure

Lo Casale

Holiday farm
Strada Pratolungo 59
Tel. 0143 635654
Open Friday evenings, Saturday and Sunday at lunch and dinner
Holidays: January and February
Seating: 30
Prices: 25 euros, wine excluded
No credit cards accepted

To reach this agriturismo, surrounded by woods and nature paths, make for Arquata Scrivia's sports field and then take a right turn and follow the narrow, winding road. A friendly welcome awaits you in two cozy, decidedly informal (paper napkins, tiny wine glasses) dining rooms.
Most dishes are prepared using home vegetables, fruit and cheeses, with meat and wines purchased from small local producers. The seasons clearly play a fundamental role in the menu. So at the right time of year you'll find **wild mushrooms** served raw with a condiment of oil and lemon as an antipasto or impeccably **breaded and fried**. Among the other antipasti we can recommend the sliced meats such as **testa in cassetta**, 'di risulta' cured meat typical of the winter months, good home-cured bacon and **vegetables in carpione**. For first course there are several kinds of homemade pasta and sauces: from tagliatelle **ai rabatòn** to **agnolotti with stew** or **gravy from the roast meat**. You'll find them on the menu in both winter and summer. Main courses are mostly white meat (try the **coniglio grigio di Carmagnola alla ligure** or with herbs), but you'll also find roast veal or **Sambucano lamb with capers**, prepared according to an old Cuneo recipe. To round things off, homemade puddings such as fruit tarts or peaches and whipped cream.
There isn't a wine list, so the few local labels available are announced by Anna Maria, your hostess, who has worked hard to set up this holiday farm and now runs it with flair.

Asti
Quarto Inferiore

3 km from city center SS 10

Antica Dogana

3-Star Hotel
Frazione Quarto Inferiore 5
Tel. 0141 293755
Fax 0141 293803
E-mail: info@albergoanticadogana.it
Internet: www. albergoanticadogana.it
Closed two weeks in August and December 24-31

A few kilometers outside of Asti on the road to Alessandria, this hotel in the village of Quarto is named after its former incarnation as the customs house for goods on their way into Asti. In 1996 the Amalberto family, building on many years of hotel experience, completely renovated the original 19th-century building and fitted it with all mod cons. The hotel is still in the family, now run by Carla and Luisa. All the rooms have views of the grounds away from the busy state road, and eight are furnished with antiques. All are en-suite and air-conditioned, and some have computer access points. Breakfast is served buffet-style and features delicious homemade cakes.

• 1 single, 21 double and 3 triple rooms, bathroom, air conditioning, mini-bar, satellite television • Prices: single or double room single use 52-60 euros, double 78-88, triple 95-105, breakfast included • Credit cards: all, Bancomat • 1 room designed for the mobility challenged. Off-street parking. Small pets allowed. Reception open 24 hours • Bar. Breakfast room. Garden

6 KM FROM TOWN CENTER SS TO CHIVASSO

DA ALDO DI CASTIGLIONE

⌒ Restaurant
Via Giobert 8
Tel. 0141 354905
Closed Thursday
Open: lunch and dinner
Holidays: different periods in summer
Seating: 70
Prices: 30-35 euros, wine excluded
All credit cards, Bancomat

OSTERIA AI BINARI

⌒ Osteria
Frazione Mombarone 145-SS Asti-Chivasso
Tel. 0141 294228
Closed Monday
Open: dinner, on holidays for lunch also
Holidays: 2 weeks between January and February
Seating: 70
Prices: 25-30 euros, wine excluded
No credit cards acceptped

This little restaurant, located in a refurbished palazzo in the old town center, is a reliable place to taste quality Piedmontese cuisine. It's run by the Cavagnero family who moved here from the village of Castiglione: Aldo, with his daughter, has a wealth of experience in the kitchen, while his wife Franca welcomes guests with her obliging, efficient style. There are no menus on the tables (you can get a rough idea of prices from the list in the showcase outside), but Franca will tell you all about the day's dishes and advise you on wines (mostly Asti and Langa labels), which you can also inspect for yourself on the shelves.
To start with, classic Piedmontese antipasti: Insalata russa, **raw meat salad**, Robiola cheese mousse, liver pâté, vitello tonnato, cod and potatoes, **peppers with bagna caoda** (in summer with tuna, basil and egg), **vegetable flan with fondue**. Go for Aldo's excellent **risottos**, or choose the **agnolotti with cheese** or meat filling, tortelli di magro, **bean minestrone**, tagliatelle and gnocchi with various sauces. The main courses are the real highlight in terms of the quality and variety of meat, especially in winter: roast veal, pork shank, **oven-baked duck**, **kid**, pigeon and **finanziera** all show up on a rotation basis. Wild mushrooms also appear, when in season. Home-made desserts (bonet, chocolate and **nougat mousse**, freshly whipped **zabaglione**) or fruit preserved in liqueur bring the meal to an end.

Just outside town, you come to one or two houses on the side of the main road and an ex-railwayman's house. Ex- yes, but not abandoned. On the contrary, It's now more lively than ever since Mara and Claudio Bione turned it into the osteria. You'll enjoy your evening meal (it's only open at lunchtime on Sundays) in a setting that, it almost goes without saying, evokes railway life: sturdy wooden tables set tastefully in the original living room and the closed veranda – whose attraction owes a lot to the choice of materials – which was added later.
Go for the 'Littorina' menu or the 'Littorina allegra' menu (for 24 or 30 euros), or order à la carte from the list of simple but beautifully prepared seasonal Piedmontese dishes. A few examples of the antipasti: raw Fassone beef, **vitello tonnato alla maniera antica**, anchovies in green sauce, **insalata di galletto**, pies and flans made with vegetables in season. Other pleasant memories are the **maltagliati with beans**, **agnolotti with three roast meat sauces**, tajarin (with nettles, for example), risottos, gnocchi with sausage and tomatoes. For second course, you can order **shank of pork**, roulade of rabbut, and **fricandò** (an old Asti beef stew), all with roast potatoes.
Always available, the cured meat and cheese boards, various wines served by the glass, home-made desserts (try the **semifreddo** made with Barbero **torrone** or the warm chocolate cake) and, of course, a well structured wine list of Piedmontese and other Italian labels.

AVIGLIANA
Drubriaglio

29 KM WEST OF TURIN

OSTERIA DEL DIAVOLO 🕲

Osteria
Piazza San Martino 6
Tel. 0141 30221-339 4286857
Closed Monday and Tuesday
Open: dinner only
Holidays: in August
Seating: 40 + 25 outdoors
Prices: 22-28 euros, wine excluded
All credit cards, Bancomat

LA BURNIA

Traditional osteria
Via Drubriaglio 18
Tel. 011 9342045
Closed Monday
Open: lunch and dinner, in August dinner only
Holidays: 2 weeks after the Epiphany
Seating: 80 + 50 outdoors
Prices: 24-28 euros, wine excluded
All major credit cards except AE, Bancomat

The musical and cultural events organized by the Diavolo Rosso Association, which has its headquarters in the deconsecrated church of San Michele, make Piazza San Martino one of the liveliest places in town. The osteria has tables in this little square on summer evenings, while inside the former church you can enjoy a combination of Piedmontese and Ligurian culinary specialties in one of three air-conditioned dining rooms. It's only taken a few years for Fabrizio Barberis and Paola Passuello (with chef Cristina) to come up with some interesting blends of local dishes, as well as seafood and vegetables from the western Ligurian coast. Hence – usually at weekends – **cappon magro**, **brandacujun**, minestrone alla genovese, pasta with pesto, tripe or **steamed dried cod**, fried anchovies, rabbit alla ligure and tuna fillet. As for the Piedmontese component, we can recommend the **vitello tonnato**, warm cooked salami with red onions, summer carpionata, tajarin served with seasonal mushroom sauces, vegetables or sausage, agnolotti dal plin, **shank of veal** or the locally reared **galletto tonchese**. There are also many Slow Food Presidium products, such as lardo di Colonnata served with warm fugassette, bottarga di Orbetello, filetto baciato di Ponzone and a very well assorted **cheese board**. The home-made desserts are good: white bonet with hazelnuts, bavarese alle fragole, semifreddi and apple pie.
Apart from Piedmontese labels, the wine list also carries a personal selection of other Italian and international wines.

Two years ago, Pierpaolo Aschieri and Consuelo Lupo left the Osteria di Vaie and moved to this building in Drubiaglio, just outside Avigliana, which houses the local cooperative store stands. The osteria is on two floors, the downstairs room being warmer and cozier. The larger upstairs room gives on to a terrace which is used in summer. Everything has the look and feel of an old-style osteria with straw-seated chairs, heavy wooden-topped tables, paper 'tablecloths' and prints on the walls depicting scenes from the cooperative's past.
A basket full of **crescentine** accompanied by lardo and cream of tomini leads into the antipasti which, in summer, include vegetable ratatouille, Robiola cheese en papillote spiced with herbs, loin of pork, **carpione of meatballs and zucchini** with brusca sauce and, in winter, **stuffed onions** and polenta crostino with honey-soaked chestnuts. The first courses (you can always ask for a taste of three dishes) use fresh homemade pasta (tagliatelle or **tajarin**) with vegetables, game or **sausage ragù** and gnocchi with local Toma cheeses. After this you can try the **ham cooked in hay**, mixed barbecued meat or **braised donkey meat** with roast potatoes and, in the cold season, **tofeja** and **pork shank**. To finish, there's a good choice of desserts: bonet, panna cotta, two-chocolate mousse and baked apple with amaretto. Finish it all off with a local grappa or arquebuse, a digestive drink produced from mountain herbs.
The wine list is expanding and now includes about 70 labels, mostly Piedmontese reds (some from the Val Susa) with a few whites from other regions. Excellent value for money.

AVOLASCA

LA VECCHIA POSTA

Holiday farm restaurant
Via Montebello 2
Tel. 0131 876254
Open Friday and Saturday for dinner, Sunday for lunch
Holidays: variable
Seating: 50
Prices: 30 euros
No credit cards accepted

Roberto Semino and his wife Annemie run this small farm and its nine hectares of land dedicated to biological agriculture. The location is Val di Grue, an area famous for white truffles and farm tourism – there are also a few rooms for guests – and the view over the surrounding hills is breathtaking.
The restaurant serves well-prepared seasonal dishes. For antipasti, assorted **cured meats** (lardo and pancetta) produced on the farm, rabbit pâté presented on the lightest of fritters, aubergine roulade with goat cheese and a salad freshly gathered from the garden, with radishes, beans and small chunks of meat. The first courses were good too: **nettle tagliolini with courgette flowers** or with basil and nettle pesto or **risotto with broad beans** and nettles. In the cold season, herbs are replaced by wild mushrooms and truffles in excellent sauces for gnocchi or other homemade pasta. There follow dishes made from meat of animals raised on the farm or bought from small local breeders. We tried a tasty **roast beef** with mashed potatoes and broccoli and were treated to second helpings. The desserts are nothing short of superb and confirm our impressions from visits in previous years: try the **semifreddo al Moscato** with strawberry cream or the lemon and strawberry-flavored tiramisu.
As one would expect in an agritursimo, the wine list includes mainly local wines from the Tortona hills, among which Timorasso produced from a local grape of the same name. Given the small number of seats available, it's always wise to book.

BALDICHIERI D'ASTI

CASCINA LANÉ

Holiday farm
Via Nazionale 120 - SS 10 km 49/IX
Tel. and fax 0141 66512
E-mail: cascina@cascinalane.it
Internet: www.cascinalane.it
Open all year round

Though it's easy to reach from the main Asti-Turin road, this pleasant farm is situated in the countryside in a peaceful setting. The main farmhouse and small annex have been well-restored, maintaining original features like wooden beams running the length of the corridor. The comfortable rooms and bathrooms show attention to detail, and in summer breakfast is served outside next to the botanical garden full of rare species of herbs and medicinal plants. Fresh pastries, bread, butter and jams are available and toast, eggs and cured meats can be prepared on request. The agriturismo is run by the Mottura family, who also rear animals and produce organic vegetables and grains. The restaurant is open to non-residents. Average prices are around 20 euros including wine; half board 55 euros per person.

• 1 single room, 9 doubles and 1 quadruple, bathroom, television, modem connection, some rooms with private living room, • Prices: single 40 euros, double 80, quadruple 160, breakfast included • Credit cards: all, Bancomat • 2 rooms designed for the mobility challenged. Covered and open-air off-street parking. Small pets allowed. Owners always present • Restaurant. Breakfast room, reading room, library. Meeting room. Garden

BALDISSERO TORINESE
Superga

BARDONECCHIA

14 KM EAST OF TURIN

90 KM NORTHWEST OF TURIN SS 24 AND SS 335, A 32

BEL DEUIT

VILLA MYOSOTIS

Trattoria
Via Superga 58
Tel. 011 9431719
Closed Wednesday
Open: dinner, Saturday and Sunday also lunch
Holidays: in September
Seating: 60 + 40 outdoors
Prices: 30-33 euros, wine excluded
All major credit cards

2-Star Hotel
Via General Cantore 2
Tel. 0122 999883
Fax 0122 99429
E-mail: info@biovey.it
Internet: www.villamyosotis.it
Closed 3 weeks in May and 2 in October

This trattoria in the hills outside Turin, not far from the landmark Superga Basilica, is named after the dialect for 'warm welcome'.
To start there's always as much salami as you can eat. Then for antipasti **vegetable flan with fondue**, or crêpes with Castelmagno cheese, vitello tonnato or ham roulade in aspic. Moving on to the first courses, take your pick from the excellent **tajarin** with either **rabbit,** asparagus, mushrooms or braised meat sauces, the **agnolotti dal plin gravy** or ravioli with leek sauce. For seconds, alongside popular dishes such as roast or **braised beef** or rabbit cooked in herbs, there are seasonal specialties: **busecca** (tripe) and **tofeja** (pork and beans) in winter and **fried mushrooms** in summer and fall. When available, the trout with butter or in carpione is well worth trying. If, despite the generous portions, you can't resist dessert, treat yourself to **zabaglione**, bonet, stuffed peaches or fruit tart.
The admirable wine list contains a wealth of information and a good selection of Piedmontese labels, plus a small, carefully chosen collection of bottles from other Italian regions. In the warmer months it's also possible to eat outside. Occasionally the service leaves a bit to be desired.

In the upper Susa Valley, Villa Myosotis is run by Paolo Romano with his wife Iole and offers comfortable and tastefully decorated rooms, six with jacuzzis. Triples and quadruples are effectively small apartments with interconnecting rooms. The lavish buffet breakfast of sweets and savories provides a good start to the day. Half board is available for 50-65 euros per person.
Bardonecchia is a historic ski resort, site of the first-ever ski lift, built in 1934. A shuttle service to the slopes departs a few steps from the hotel.

• 2 single rooms, 4 double, 1 triple and 1 quadruple, bathroom (power shower), television, modem connection • Prices: single 40-55 euros, double 60-80, triple 90-100, quadruple 100-115, breakfast included • Credit cards: Visa, Bancomat • Off-street parking. Small pets allowed. Reception open from 8 am to midnight • Restaurant. Breakfast room, Reading room. Garden

In **Turin** (14 km), to enjoy a glass of wine and assorted nibbles: Caffè Elena, Piazza Vittorio Veneto 5, or Vinicola al Sorij, Via M. Pescatore 10. For torcetti biscuits baked according to the old Agliè recipe, Mautino, Via Vittone 20.

The Biovey restaurant seats 35 and is open to non-residents and offers good, creative cuisine. Price 35-40 euros, wine excluded.

BAROLO
Vergne

BAROLO

CÀ SAN PONZIO

IL GIOCO DELL'OCA

🔑Rooms
Via Rittane 7
Tel. 0173 560510-339 7834506
Fax 0173 560510
E-mail: sanponzio@areacom.it
Internet: www.casanponzio.com
Closed last two weeks in January

🔑Agriturismo
Via Crosia 46
Tel. 0173 56206-338 5999426
Fax 0173 56206
E-mail: gioco-delloca@piemonte.com
Internet: www.gioco-delloca.it
Closed from mid-December to March 1

A typical Piedmontese farmhouse with a wooden balcony and green-shuttered windows, in the shade of a huge mulberry, Cà San Ponzio is 100 meters from the road that leads from Fondovalle Tanaro up to Vergne, on the edge of the Barolo zone. The old barn has been converted into rooms and the wine cellar also restored, making it the ideal location for whiling away a long night with a good bottle of wine. The spacious rooms are fitted with antiques and pieces from local craftsmen and include a mezzanine floor for extra beds. There's even a camping area for trailers or tents, with 30 spaces in a hazelnut grove round the back. Breakfast is served buffet-style, with sweet and savory items made with local produce. Hosts Luciano and Maurizio can help recommend places to visit for culture enthusiasts, food and wine lovers or keen cyclists.

• 6 double rooms, triple or quadruple, bathroom • Prices: double room single use 47-52 euros, double 62-68, triple 78-84, quadruple 88-101; breakfast 5-8 euros per person; camping space 6 euros plus 5 euros per person a day • Credit cards: all, Bancomat • Off-street parking. Small pets allowed. Owners always contactable • Breakfast room, living room. Wine-tasting room. Garden, solarium.

A mid-19th-century Langa farmhouse was completely restored seven years ago, creating this charming agriturismo run by Raffaella Pittatore. The original structure has been carefully maintained, and the rustic decor of the welcoming rooms includes furnishings from the local arte povera movement. The pleasant communal areas include a reading room with plenty of information on surrounding monuments, castles and historical sites; a porch with a barbecue that guests can use; and a garden with children's play area, deckchairs and tables. Here you can have breakfast in the summer with bread, butter, jams, homemade cakes, yogurt, cured meats and cheeses, fruit juices and hot beverages.

• 5 double rooms and 1 triple, with bathroom; 1 apartment (2-3 people) with living room and kitchenette • Prices: double single use 45 euros, double 60-65, triple 70, apartment 60-70, breakfast included • Credit cards: Visa, Bancomat • Facility accessible to the mobility challenged. Off-street covered parking. Small pets allowed. Owners always contactable • Breakfast room, reading room, kitchen. Garden

BAROLO

LA CANTINELLA

Trattoria
Via Acquagelata 4 A
Tel. 0173 56267
Closed Monday evening and Tuesday
Open: lunch and dinner
Holidays: in August and in January
Seating: 35 + 25 outdoors
Prices: 26-31 euros, wine excluded
All major credit cards, Bancomat

The drive down to Barolo from La Morra is a magnificent experience, the Langa opening up in a sea of rolling hills covered in vineyards. A few bends in the road and you catch a glimpse of the Marquis Faletti family castle, home to the regional enoteca. Ten years Nella Cravero opened this little trattoria in the square in front of the castle and it provides an excellent taste of the classic Langa cuisine. The two dining rooms are cozy in the winter, while in warmer weather you can eat outside on the square. Either way Nella's husband Andrea will seat you and bring you a menu, from which you can choose the prix fixe of 23, 30 or 38 euros or make a selection à la carte.
Nella's cooking is based on Piedmont's rich culinary heritage: antipasti like raw meat battuta al coltello, warm cotechino sausages, vegetable timbale with cheese fondue, **anchovies in green sauce**, Russian salad, **bagna caoda**; homemade pastas, such as **tajarin** with meat sauce, **ravioli dal plin** with butter and sage sauce, maltagliati with vegetables or sausage and superb **gnocchi**; **sausage in wine**, **braised beef**, excellent rabbit and – not to be missed in winter – **bollito misto**. To finish, a small selection of Piedmontese cheeses and desserts: bonet, panna cotta or hazelnut cake with zabaglione.
Inevitably the wine list focuses on Barolo, though there are wines from the rest of Piedmont. The page of half-bottles is much appreciated.

BAVENO

VILLA AZALEA

3-Star Hotel
Via Domo 6
Tel. 0323 924300
Fax 0323 922065
E-mail: info@villaazalea.com
Internet: www.villaazalea.com
Open all year round

This recently refurbished hotel is located in a very peaceful area in the historical center of Baveno, some of which dates back to the 10th century. It's also close to the banks of Lake Maggiore and a church with the Romanesque bell tower. The rooms are very comfortable, many with terraces and views of the lake. In addition to the rooms, a one-bedroom apartment and four studios are also available, each with kitchenettes and large enough for two to four people. Breakfast is served in the dining room, and there is also a generous continental buffet, offering hot and cold beverages, sweet items (jams, butter, croissants) and savories (cheeses, cured meats). The communal areas are pleasant and so is the terrace with its sundeck and swimming pool.

• 4 single rooms, 19 double and 9 triple rooms, bathroom, air conditioning, mini-bar, safe, television • Prices: single 52-58 euros, double 72-90, triple 103-109, breakfast included • Credit cards: all, Bancomat • 2 rooms designed for the mobility challenged. Off-street parking, garage (15 places, 5 euros per day). Small pets allowed. Owners always present • Bar. Breakfast room, lounge with TV and corner bar. Garden, terrace. Swimming pool with hydro-massage

BERGOLO

BIELLA

'L BUNET

🍲 Restaurant and hotel
Via Roma 24
Tel. 0173 87013
Closed Tuesday, never from April to November
Open: lunch and dinner
Holidays: January
Seating: 50
Prices: 33-35 euros, wine excluded
All credit cards except DC, Bancomat

BARACCA

🍲 Restaurant
Via Sant'Eusebio 12
Tel. 015 21941
Closed Saturday and Sunday
Open: lunch and dinner
Holidays: June 15-July 15
Seating: 35 + 15 outdoors
Prices: 18-22 euros, wine excluded
No credit cards

It's about 40 minutes from Alba and there are many twists and turns before you get there, but you won't be sorry when you finally reach Bergolo and its view over the whole upper Langa area. Emilio Banchero has created a truly hospitable haven here: his restaurant, a single room with rose-colored curtains, is pleasant enough, but it's the food and wine you're here for. The kitchen is run with a light, steady hand, the ingredients used are truly top quality and the Piedmontese dishes are well-prepared and often original.

The set menu (35 euros) starts with three antipasti, **rotondino in salsa antica**, a puff pastry caramella of asparagus with fonduta and cocotte of porcini mushrooms, followed by the famous **macaron del fret** (pasta made with seven different stone-ground flours, wound around a knitting needle) with sausage ragù, a tasty **oven-roasted kid** and desserts, including the ever-popular **bonet**, hazelnut and chocolate mousse, and semifreddo with nougat and Barolo Chinato. Other dishes worth a try are **caponet with zucchini flowers** with creamed peas and basil, vegetable flans, **agnolotti dal plin** with butter and sage and the figure of green pasta filled with Sarass del Fen and, among the main courses, **wild boar al civet**, rolled rabbit with thyme or chicken cacciatora. Don't skip Emilio's carefully chosen **cheeses,** with a selection of around 20 of the best Piedmontese specialties.

The wine list focuses heavily on regional wines (bottles are also on sale to take away). There are some other choices but it's moving towards being exclusively local, which is fitting given the location.

A visit to Patrizia and Paolo Mancastroppa's restaurant will give you a chance to get to know the old part of Biella, with its elegant palazzos and solid culinary traditions. The restaurant is located in a renovated building dating from the early 1800s, furnished with refined elegance and today one of Biella's 'in' places for its good food at reasonable prices.

In the kitchen Massimiliano Rasi prepares authentic, no-frills Piedmontese dishes that are unapologetically old-fashioned The meal opens with mixed antipasti that can include savory vegetable and cheese pies, frittatas, **peppers in bagna caoda**, Biella lardo and prosciutto crudo or **cotechino with potatoes**. For firsts you can't go wrong if you order either the **risotto in cagnone** made extra-creamy with Biella toma cheese and melted butter or the **paniscia** with sausage and beans. Other good risottos come with asparagus or artichokes depending on the season, or try the **agnolotti with roast meat sauce** and the ravioli di magro. Then it's time for beef braised in red wine, trout cooked in butter or the **bollito misto** (tongue, cotechino, head and other meats, all boiled). And finally, the selection of cheeses and homemade desserts: bonet, panna cotta, apple pie and **peaches stuffed with amaretti and chocolate**.

There's been a vast improvement in the wines available, thanks to Paolo's intelligent work. Due attention is paid to local wines, and the list of grappas has become even better and more extensive.

32 KM NORTH OF NOVARA SS 229

32 KM NORTHEAST OF NOVARA SS 229

TRATTORIA ⊘🍾
DEI COMMERCIANTI

🍲 Trattoria
Via Cornice 35-37
Tel. 0322 841392
Closed Tuesday
Open: lunch and dinner
Holidays: 3 weeks in August
Seating: 40
Prices: 28-30 euros, wine excluded
All major credit cards, Bancomat

TRATTORIA 🍾
DEL CICLISTA

🍲 Trattoria
Via Rosmini 34
Tel. 0322 81649
Closed Wednesday
Open: lunch and dinner
Holidays: 3 weeks in September-October
Seating: 60 + 30 outdoors
Prices: 25-30 euros, wine excluded
No credit cards

A recently renovated building dating back to the 16th century houses this well-run trattoria in the old part of Borgomanero. Managed by Mauro Agazzone with wife Lucia, the four dining rooms with exposed wooden beams are welcoming, warmly lit and characterful.

Mauro prepares dishes influenced by the seasons and local traditions, as can be seen from his frequent use of horsemeat. Alongside more typical dishes from the Novara area, such as **paniscia** and **donkey tapulone**, often served with polenta, there are many other specialties, of which recommend antipasti like peppers in bagna caoda, vegetable pies, rabbit terrine and guinea-fowl salad, horsemeat carpaccio and an interesting selection of local **cured meats**. Apart from paniscia, the first courses always include **risotto** (with Arneis wine and courgette flowers, pigeon, with Ghemme wine and saffron), but also tagliolini with various sauces, gnocchetti with Castelmagno or vegetable soups. Then horse fillet with rosemary, donkey stew or alternatively boned **stuffed quail** and braised beef cooked in nebbiolo. Or try the great selection of **cheeses** ranging from Valsesia and Ossola toma to Novara Gorgonzola, goat's cheeses, Bettelmat, Bitto and Castelmagno. Puddings include bonet, crème caramel, meringue pie, pear and chocolate cake.

For accompaniment choose one of the 120 bottles from the wine cellar, which highlights producers from around Novara and Vercelli.

This trattoria in the historic center of Borgomanero exudes the informal air of a village tavern. The cycling theme is carried over from the name to the pictures, prints and photos covering the walls of the dining room and bar, while outside in the courtyard a wide, covered area offers al fresco seating during warmer months. The menu is firmly grounded in the local gastronomy, with a few appearances from dishes from the rest of Piedmont.

Among the antipasti you might try the vitello tonnato, **insalata russa**, a mousse of fresh cheese and, above all, the assortment of **cured meats**, especially the salam 'd la doja and other interesting horsemeat salumi, such as bresaola and salami. Then there are the bread gnocchetti with gorgonzola, risotto with herbs and the ever-present Novara-style **paniscia**, a typical risotto with salami and vegetables. **Tapulone** (chopped donkey meat cooked in wine) is the outstanding dish among the main courses although there are other equine specialties too, like **picula** (horsemeat steak) or a roast.

The extensive wine list includes many nebbiolos from northern Piedmont, wines from locally grown grapes and other regional and national labels. Lunchtime sees a reduced menu for regulars who drop in for a quick bite. The full evening menu, from antipasti through to dessert, will set you back around 25-30 euros.

BORGOSESIA

Agnona

51 KM NORTHWEST OF VERCELLI

TRATTORIA BELVEDERE ▮

◇ Trattoria
Via Solferino 31
Tel. 0163 24095
Closed Tuesday
Open: lunch and dinner
Holidays: 15 days in February
Seating: 40 + 12 outdoors
Prices: 30-35 euros, wine excluded
All major credit cards, Bancomat

Good raw materials allow excellent results to be achieved with minimal manipulation: This is the lesson that Belvedere exemplifies. A simple trattoria, it's run by Francesco and Marinella Mussini, who are constantly searching for the best seasonal ingredients, whether mountain herbs and river fish or carefully selected bread, eggs, vegetables and olive oil.

Antipasti include cured meats, **tongue** in green parsley sauce or **al bagnet ross**, raw meat from Piedmontese breed cattle battuta al coltello, zucchini in carpione, vitello tonnato, Russian salad and **caponet** wrapped in cabbage in winter and in lavassa (Alpine rhubarb) leaves in summer. Then there are mountain **potato gnocchi** (or made with pumpkin or nettles) and handmade pasta dishes such as tagliatelle with zucchini and mint or **agnolotti al sugo d'arrosto**, risottos and, in winter, **creamed cod** and pasta e fagioli. For your main course we'd recommend the Val Vogna **trout** cooked in butter and sage or fried small river fish, which is not to deny the quality of the meat: **braised** lamb and kid, boiled meat salad and beef tagliata, all served with large portions of vegetables. To finish, cheeses from the area and the rest of Italy and excellent desserts, including the blueberry pie and peaches cooked with amaretto.

Francesco has organized the wine list that includes over 100 excellent labels.

🍷 In **Borgosesia**, at Via San Grato 9, Antonio De Giorgi produces fine salam 'd la doja, mortadella made from pig's liver in fat, cotechino, lardo and other cured meats.

BOSCO MARENGO

13 KM SOUTHEAST OF ALESSANDRIA, 8 KM FROM NOVI LIGURE

LOCANDA DELL'OLMO

◇ Ristorante
Piazza Mercato 7
Tel. 0131 299186
Closed Monday and Tuesday evening
Open: lunch and evening
Holidays: August, 26/12-6/1
Seating: 40 + 10 outside
Prices: 30-34 euros, wine excluded
All credit cards except AE, Bancomat

Situated on the main piazza of the pretty village of Bosco Marengo, the restaurant has been famous for years for its good local cooking and hospitable atmosphere. The whole Bondi family work together to ensure its success: father Domenico produces wonderful wines, including Dolcetto di Ovada and Barbera, while his son Gianni cooks the traditional dishes of the plains round Alessandria in the kitchen. For antipasto, hand-chopped **raw beef**, seared peppers with anchovy sauce and vegetable flan with fondue. Be sure to taste **agnolotti di stufato** (filled with stewed meat and served with the gravy), **rabatòn** (baked giant gnocchi filled with ricotta), served in spring with wild herbs, **corsetti novesi** (pasta disks) and tagliolini, all home-made. The main courses also reflect the old-fashioned cooking of southern Piedmont: stews, **rabbit in Gavi wine** or with peppers, **cod** and stockfish. The comprehensive **cheese selection** ranges from the Alps to the Apennines and embraces numerous Slow Food Presidia. Apart from bonet, on the menu all year, desserts are seasonal: **timbales** and stewed Martin pears in winter, peaches and amaretti in summer. There's no written menu with prices but we recommend the value-for-money tasting menu. At any rate, the cook's brother Andrea is always on hand to explain things.

The magnificent wine list features not only the big names in Piedmont but also worthy local producers. The house wines are good too.

BATTAGLINO

🍲Restaurant
Piazza Roma 18
Tel. 0172 412509
Closed Sunday evening and Monday
Open: lunch and dinner
Holidays: 2 weeks in January, 3 in August
Seating: 80 + 30 outdoors
Prices: 30 euros, wine excluded
All major credit cards, Bancomat

BOCCONDIVINO

🍲Osteria
Via Mendicità Istruita 14
Tel. 0172 425674
Closed Sunday and Monday
Open: lunch and dinner
Holidays: variable
Seating: 60
Prices: 26-31 euros, wine excluded
All major credit cards, Bancomat

Owner, chef and host Beppe is the grandson of Sebastiano Battaglino, who back in 1919 founded this restaurant which looks out onto the park in front of the train station. Through the decades it has remained true to the canon of classic Piedmontese cuisine, accumulating many fond memories. Photos recall the times when the town's theater hosted top national performers and after the show everyone would end up da Batajin. Today Beppe's wife Maria Teresa and daughter Alessia – together with regular incursions from Beppe himself – welcome diners.
In the summer many prefer to be seated in the cool courtyard, while the rest of the year the long, narrow dining room becomes a kind of track along which the trolley of **bollito misto** has traveled many, many miles over the past eighty-plus years. As soon as you're seated you'll be served **Bra sausage**, made mainly with veal, heavily spiced and traditionally eaten raw. To follow, egg and zucchini carpione, **vitello tonnato**, raw meat or, in the cold months, Jerusalem artichoke tortino with a cheese cream and baked crêpes with mushrooms. First courses are all based on fresh homemade pasta and include **gnocchi with Castelmagno**, tagliatelle with ragù and the highly recommended **agnolotti dal plin with roast meat sauce**. Then there's the famous boiled meats plus a dish that is becoming a bit of a rarity – **finanziera** – plus brasato al Barolo, **tripe** and stewed and **fried mushrooms**. To finish, homemade puddings: bonet, panna cotta, topolino (pastry cream, chocolate and amaretti soaked in coffee) and brutti e buoni.
A short list of Piedmontese wines.

This osteria is located in Casa Casalis, a building in the old town center used over the centuries for a wide variety of purposes and today the headquarters of the Slow Food movement. The Boccone ('Mouthful' in Italian – the name by which it's affectionately known in Bra) is much more than an osteria. It was in facty one of the very first pieces (it opened in December 1984) in the multi-colored mosaic that forms the movement founded by Carlin Petrini. Today, as in the past, the menu is founded on the region's gastronomic heritage and use of carefully selected ingredients, among which a number of Slow Food Presidia. 'Beppe Gepis' Barbero has run the kitchen for some time now, supervising the work of his team of cooks.
You can either eat à la carte or choose from one of the four set meals. To start with there's **boiled meat salad**, **vegetable flan with Raschera cheese fondue**, stuffed peppers, Bra sausage, **carne cruda al coltello**, **anchovies with red sauce**, **tripe salad** with beans and cream of shallot. First courses always include the excellent **agnolotti dal plin** and **tajarin** with butter and sage sauce or **sausage sauce**, as well as gnocchi, **risottos**, spelt and vegetable soup. **Coniglio grigio all'Arneis**, Sambucano lamb, roast goose leg and **veal braised in Barolo** are some of the best of the main courses. The interesting **cheese** board includes some excellent Roccaverano goat cheeses from various crus and at various degrees of aging, and you can end the meal with bonet, **panna cotta**, or torrone and honey pudding.
About 1,000 bottles of Piedmontese and other Italian wines and some carefully selected foreign wines fill the showcases.

BRA

L'OMBRA DELLA COLLINA

Rooms
Via della Mendicità Istruita 47
Tel. 0172 44884-328 9644436
Fax 0172 44884
E-mail: lombradellacollina@libero.it
Internet: www.lombradellacollina.it
Open all year round

The name of this locanda comes from the title of a famous novel by Giovanni Arpino, whose mother came from Bra. Opened a few years ago, it's located in a beautiful old house in the historic center of town and run by the family of antique dealers. Not coincidentally all the rooms are furnished with antiques, and the building also contains a Toy Museum. John welcomes guests on arrival and provides a wealth of information and useful tips about the town and the surrounding villages in the Langhe and Roero countryside. Rooms are spacious and comfortable, and for breakfast guests can enjoy coffee, milk, tea and croissants from the pasticceria as well as jams, fruit, yogurt and savory items on request.

• 4 doubles and 1 triple room with bathroom, satellite television • Prices: double room single occupancy 62 euros, double 78, triple 78, breakfast included • Credit cards: AE, CartaSi, Visa, Bancomat • Off-street parking. Small pets allowed. Owners always contactable • Breakfast room. Garden. Modem connection in the lounge

BRIAGLIA

MARSUPINO

Restaurant/3-Star Hotel
Via Roma 20
Tel. 0174 563888
Fax 0174 563035
E-mail: info@trattoriamarsupino.it
Internet: www.trattoriamarsupino.it
Closed for lunch on Wednesday and Thursday
Open: lunch and dinner
Holidays: 15 days between January and February
Seating: 80
Prices: 28-32 euros, wine excluded
All major credit cards, Bancomat

Nestling in a small village in the Monregalesi hills, Marsupino offers seven spacious rooms with all mod cons and late-19th-century furniture plus a restaurant specializing in traditional cuisine. Service is obliging and the delicious breakfasts feature home-made pastries and jams and local cured meats and cheeses. The hotel is open all week.
At the restaurant we recommend starting off with hand-chopped **ciapulà raw meat**, prosciutto all'inglese with tartare sauce and seasonal vegetables. First courses include **maltagliati with duck ragù** or chestnuts, potato gnocchi with Castelmagno, **agnolotti dal plin** with **chicken** filling in a sweetbread and toasted-hazelnut sauce, and marvelous **chicken ravioli** with vegetable sauce. To follow, you can choose **snails with Cervere leeks**, rabbit with freisa, pork shank with Barolo and an exceptional **glazed oxtail**, or mushrooms and truffles when in season. To finish off, there is a selection of Piedmontese **cheeses**, or desserts like mousse or **chestnut pudding**, semifreddo with zabaglione and homemade sorbets and ice cream.
The wine cellar offers a vast range of labels, focusing mainly on Piedmontese wines, at very reasonable prices.

• 5 double rooms and 2 suites, with bathroom, air conditioning, minibar, safe, TV, modem connection • Prices: double room at single occupancy rate 55, double room 105, suite 135-225 euros, breakfast included • Access and 1 room with facilities for the mobility challenged. On-site uncovered parking and free external public parking. Small pets accepted. Owners always present • Bar, restaurant. Reading room. Terrace

BRONDELLO

LA TORRE ⊘▮

Ristorante
Via Villa 35
Tel. 0175 76198
Closed Monday evening and Tuesday
Open: lunch and dinner
Holidays: January 7-31
Seating: 70 + 30 outside
Prices: 25-28 euros, wine excluded
All major credit cards, Bancomat

An excellent restaurant in an interesting out-of-the way area that raises the profile of local produce: cep mushrooms, Pagno ramassin (luscious damsons), Toumin dal Mel, chestnuts and Pelaverga wine. Very good value for money.
The place is housed in a villa opposite the village's medieval tower and its walls are covered with certificates of merit and photographs that reveal the great passion for **cheese** of owner Ivano Maero. In the kitchen, his wife Vanna cooks local produce traditionally but imaginatively. To start, frittata of herbs with mousse of toumin dal Mel, old-style **vitèl toné** (without mayo in the sauce), courgette flowers stuffed with herbs and vegetables. To follow, **coujette with mountain cheeses**, ravioli dal plin with butter and cheese, tajarin and **buckwheat maltagliati** with various sauces. For mains, rabbit with juniper berries or **peppers**, **baked Sambucano lamb**, fillet of char with spring herbs or **mountain salmon trout**. As for cheeses, two well-assembled selections are served at the end of the meal accompanied by specially chosen wines. When in season, **cep mushrooms** appear in pies and risottos or by themselves, sautéed and fried. To finish, splendid homemade desserts.
The wine list is comprehensive, ranging from local Pelaverga to the rest of Italy and abroad.

BURIASCO

TENUTA LA CASCINETTA

Farm holiday
Via Pinerolo 9
Tel. 0121 368040
Fax 0121 368039
E-mail: info@tenutalacascinetta.it
Internet: www.tenutalacascinetta.it
Open all year round

This estate dates back to the 16th century, when the monks of the Verano Abbey abandoned their sheltered life and founded the farm. It's been the home of the Carretto family for more than a century, and now Paola has turned it into a charming place to stay. The stylish rooms are are all furnished differently and named after women in history. In the summer, breakfast is served on the porch in the form of cakes, biscuits, focaccia, homemade jams, fruit and cured meats. Laundry service, babysitting, horse-riding, relaxing massages and beauty treatments are available on request. Nearby you can visit the Stupinigi hunting lodge, the fortress of Fenestrelle, the talcum mines of the Val Germanesca, the Rocca di Cavour Park, and the Pinerolo Cavalry Museum.

• 10 double rooms and 3 suites, bathroom, air conditioning, mini-bar, satellite television, modem connection • Prices: double room single occupancy 80 euros, double 100, suite 150, breakfast included • Credit cards: all except DC, Bancomat • 1 room designed for the mobility challenged. Off-street parking. Small pets allowed. Owners always present • Breakfast room, reading room. Garden

CALAMANDRANA
San Vito

BIANCA LANCIA DAL BARÒN

⌒ Restaurant/3-Star Hotel
Regione San Vito 14
Tel. 0141 718400
Fax 0141 718800
E-mail: ristorantehotelbiancalancia@virgilio.it
Closed Tuesday
Open: lunch and dinner
Holidays: in February
Seating: 60 + 50 outdoors
Prices: 25-30 euros, wine excluded
All credit cards, Bancomat

The Bianca Lancia was originally just a hotel until it was bought by Beppe Gallese, aka the Baron, who opened a restaurant also. The rooms are well-equipped for a comfortable stay, and as the mustachioed Beppe will tell you, 'If something is Piedmontese, you can sample it here'. Indeed, apart from a few creations of Signora Giovanni (who works with Beppe in the kitchen), the menu revolves around regional classics. Pancetta, **chopped raw meat**, vegetable frittatas, veal in tuna sauce, **cold tripe** and **roast peppers** (with anchovy sauce or rolled and stuffed in the summer) for antipasti, then **pasta and beans**, tajarin or **agnolotti dal plin**, not just with meat but also with pumpkin or artichokes. The best main course is **roast scaramella** (a cut of beef) but other well-made dishes include rabbit with herbs and **guinea fowl with Moscato**. When in season you will find mushrooms, truffles and **game**, including jugged wild boar and hare. The desserts are home-made (bonet, panna cotta, pear cake, **nougat spumone**, and **home-baked petits fours** with delicious baci di dama biscuits) and wines are mostly from the Langhe and Monferrato.
The service is friendly and the hotel is open all week.

⌐ • 7 double rooms, with bathroom, air conditioning, mini-bar, TV, modem connection • Prices: double room at single occupancy rate 55 euros, double room 70 euros, breakfast included • Garage (for 8 cars). Small pets accepted. Owners always present • Bar, restaurant. Reading room. Garden.

CALAMANDRANA

LA CORTE

⌐ Holiday farm
Regione Quartino 6
Tel. 0141 769109
Fax 0141 769991
E-mail: lacorte@agrilacorte.com
Internet: www.agrilacorte.com
Closed in January

Just 200 meters from the road between Nizza Monferrato and Canelli which runs along the River Belbo lies this grand farmhouse, built around a courtyard and dedicated since the 19th century to wine production. It's now run by the Cusmano family, with part of the recently restored main building converted into an agriturismo. The old barn has also been converted and houses a lovely lounge and restaurant (set menu 30 euros, including home-produced wines; half board supplement 18 euros per person). Rooms and suites are elegantly furnished with all mod cons, and soon there will be 24 more. Breakfast, made using local produce, is served in the lounge. Also available are cooking classes, wine tasting and truffle-hunting expeditions with a trifolao.

• 9 double rooms and 3 suites (4-5 people), bathroom, mini-bar, safe, satellite television • Prices: double room single occupancy 60-75 euros, double 75-108, suite 105-160, breakfast included • Credit cards: all except DC, Bancomat • 1 room designed for the mobility challenged. Off-street parking. Small pets allowed (5 euros per day). Owners always contactable • Bar, restaurant, wine-tasting room. Breakfast room. Meeting room. Terrace. Playground, swimming pool

CALAMANDRANA
Valle San Giovanni

VIOLETTA

🍲 Restaurant
Via Valle San Giovanni 1
Tel. 0141 769011
Closed Wednesday, Tuesday and Sunday dinner only
Open: lunch and dinner
Holidays: in January and August
Seating: 80
Prices: 28-35 euros, wine excluded
All major credit cards, Bancomat

The picturesque upper part of Calamandrana, a small community in the heart of Asti's Monferrato area, is dominated by the castle, which is well worth a visit. To get to Violetta turn off into Valle San Giovanni on the road from San Marzano Oliveto to Nizza Monferrato, in the midst of fruit trees and vineyards. The restaurant is pleasantly unpretentious, and you'll receive a sincere welcome from Carlo and his wife, who will tell you about the day's menu and advise you on the right local wine to combine with your food.

The antipasti include meats and vegetables, like the **aspic** that we'd recommend in summer. Otherwise, try the **vegetable timbales** (perhaps with artichokes or asparagus) with or without cheese fondue, vitello tonnato, delicate stuffed peppers and raw meat all'albese. Chef Maria Lovisolo's skill becomes evident when you taste her fine golden egg pasta: **tajarin** with mushrooms or other seasonal sauces or the classic **Monferrato-style agnolotti** with butter and sage or gravy from the roast. Gnocchi with sausage ragù is a good alternative. The excellent meats then steal the show, from **stuffed guinea fowl** to **veal stracotto** in Barbera. Not always available but absolutely recommended are the Piedmontese fritto misto and the superb **finanziera**. Lastly, bonet, semifreddo with nougat, yogurt or chocolate mousse and parfait with gianduia.

🛍️ On the Nizza-Canelli provincial road, in the hamlet of **Quartino**, at Via Roma, 13, the Saracco bakery sells excellent grissini (breadsticks).

CALOSSO

CROTA 'D CALOS ☙

🍲 Trattoria-enoteca
Via Cairoli 7
Tel. 0141 853232
Closed Wednesday, Nov.-Mar. also Tuesday
Open: lunch and dinnerHolidays: variable
Seating: 60 + 60 outdoors
Prices: 24-27 euros, wine excluded
All major credit cards, Bancomat

The road from Asti to Calosso winds through the hills, offering spectacular views over the vineyards. Once you arrive, you'll find this restaurant in the town hall. The dining room is all exposed brick walls and vaulted ceilings, with the corner of an ancient wall on display, while the balcony overlooking the rolling green countryside offers al fresco dining.

This is the municipal wine cellar, and as one would expect there's an excellent selection, with many interesting Piedmontese labels and some from the rest of Italy, all offering good value. You could just stop by for a glass of wine, helping yourself from the board of cured meats and cheeses, or let Patrizia (assisted by Sebastiano in the dining room) prepare you a full meal. The set menus change frequently and feature traditional dishes, and the check is always reasonable.

To start there's a choice of cured meats, **vegetable flans** (the one with peppers and bagna caoda is particularly good), **vitello tonnato**, anchovies in hazelnut sauce and Russian salad. Among the first courses, the **agnolotti dal plin**, gnocchi and **tajarin** with seasonal sauces or **porcini mushrooms** are all outstanding. For main course, there are traditional roasts and stews and pork and rabbit prepared in various ways. Taste some of the many well-chosen **cheeses** (the goat formaggette is particularly recommended) and then make an assault on the formidable list of dessert: **bonet**, pear timbale, hazelnut cake with zabaglione and semifreddos.

CALOSSO
Piana del Salto

CAMAGNA
MONFERRATO

OSTERIA DELLA GALLINA SVERSA

▽ Trattoria
Via Battibò 9
Tel. 0141 853483
Closed Monday
Open: lunch and dinner
Holidays: 1 week in January and 1 in August
Seating: 40 + 20 outdoors
Prices: 24-28 euros, wine excluded
No credit cards accepted

TAVERNA ⊗🍾
DI CAMPAGNA DAL 1997

▽ Restaurant
Vicolo Gallina 20
Tel. 0142 925645
Closed Monday
Open: dinner, weekends also for lunch
Holidays: last 2 weeks of February, first 2 weeks of September
Seating: 30
Prices: 28-32 euros, wine excluded
All major credit cards, Bancomat

A tipsy hen eyes you whimsically from the sign; a sheltered outside area leads to the bar and a pleasant little dining room with brightly colored tablecloths and photos on the walls. This fairly new osteria is located in an old bakery, on the road linking the hamlet of Piana del Salto to the center of Calosso. It's simple but comfortable, with a well-organized kitchen turning out traditional Piedmontese dishes prepared with quality ingredients cooked to perfection. The Boursier family are responsible for the pleasant atmosphere and good food, with Ediliano and Rosaria in the kitchen and Elena, Emanuela and Eva ruling over the dining room.

There's a wide choose on the menu; we tried the hand-chopped raw meat and the **vitello tonnato** and a tasty **egg and Robiola cheese tortino** (pies and frittatas change with the seasons). This was followed by gnocchi with ragù and exquisite **agnolotti gobbi filled awith three roast meats**, and there's a monthly rotation of agnolotti dal plin, baked pasta, tajarin and **maltagliati with beans.** Roast pork is cooked with honey, outstandingly flavorful and tender. The **roast rabbit** is also good, as are the mixed carpionata (in summer), **chicken alla cacciatora**, **brasato al Barolo** and tripe. The traditional puddings – home-made and beautifully prepared – include panna cotta, semifreddos (with zabaglione, for instance), and stuffed peaches in summer. You can choose from an adequate list of regional wines, including some good local producers. Prices are reasonable.

Roberto Miglietta's place in this pretty little village in the Monferrato hills, with its old brick houses and domed parish church, is a bit off the beaten track. You may be able to find the narrow alley that opens up into a generous parking area, but a few more road signs would still be useful. Don't let this put you off, however, because once you make it to the dining room, Paola's smiling welcome will make you feel at home.

The chef defines the cuisine as 'creative Monferrato', classic dishes discreetly revisited. On our own visit we had **raw ground beef** with Castelmagno cheese, rabbit terrine with vegetable caponatina, courgettes with Toma cheese fondue, **agnolotti monferrini al fondo bruno**, **tajarin** with beetroot, beef cooked with herbs, finely sliced potatoes and a surprise dessert (customers take what comes). And if you can manage it, for just under 3 euros you can sample the board of Piedmontese and French **cheeses**. There's just one set menu but it changes every day. So you might find excellent **risottos**, polenta (in winter), **aspic di bolliti** and many other meat specialties and seasonal vegetables.

All of this accompanied by a long list of recommended wines, excellent and rather unusual labels priced very reasonably. A number of dessert wines are also available by the glass.

🍯 Excellent honey from Elio Debernardi, in the hamlet of Bonina: lime, acacia, chestnut and rhododendron.

CAMINO
Castel San Pietro

CANALE

CA' SAN SEBASTIANO

VILLA CORNAREA

🗝️🗝️ Holiday farm
Via Ombra 52
Tel. 0142 945900-339 5030545
Fax 0142 945900
E-mail: info@casansebastiano.it
Internet: www.casansebastiano.it
Open all year round

🗝️🗝️ Holiday farm
Via Valentino 150
Tel. 0173 979091-440415
Fax 0173 979091
E-mail: info@villacornarea.com
Internet: www.villacornarea.it
Closed in January

The two connected farmhouses that make up Ca' San Sebastiano have been recently restored, maintaining the original character: outside the walls alternate brick with tuff and some rooms have frescoed ceilings. Eight apartments all have a kitchenette a mod cons such as DVD players. Breakfast can be requested and includes cereal, croissants, savory items and various beverages. The restaurant (25-30 euros, excluding wine) is also open to non-residents with reservations. Wine tastings and musical soirees are often organized in the spacious communal areas, and guests can also enjoy wine therapy and aromatherapy treatments. Bicycles can be rented and there's also a swimming pool and barbecue.

On top of a hill in the middle of the Cornarea vineyards stands a splendid 1908 villa built in the Piedmontese Art-Nouveau style. The views from the terrace and towers stretches across the Roero hills all the way to the Alps. Inside, the original décor has been maintained and rooms are furnished with antiques and other pieces of good craftsmanship. Rooms are exquisite and comfortable (those on the third floor with sloping roofs have air conditioning). The buffet breakfast offers various sweet and savory items like ham, salami and local Toma cheeses.

•8 apartments (2-5 people), bathroom, mini-bar, satellite television, kitchen; several rooms with modem connection • Prices: double room single use 60 euros, double 80-150, with 4 beds 120-200 (10 euro supplement for extra bed); breakfast included • Credit cards: major ones, Bancomat • Some apartments designed for the mobility challenged. Off-street parking. Small pets allowed. Owners always contactable • Restaurant. Breakfast room, Conference room. Garden, terrace, veranda. Swimming pool, fitness center with Turkish bath, gym

• 7 double rooms and 2 suites with bathroom, mini-bar, (4 with terrace, 2 with air conditioning) • Prices: double room single use 65-75 euros, double 75-90, suite 110-120 (20 euro supplement for extra bed), breakfast included • Credit cards: all, Bancomat • 1 room designed for the mobility challenged. Off-street parking. No pets allowed. Owners always contactable • Breakfast room. Terrace. Garden, park. Swimming pool

CANDIA CANAVESE

CANNERO RIVIERA

35 KM NORTHEAST OF TURIN SS 26 OR A 5

13 KM NORTHEAST OF VERBANIA-INTRA, 7 KM FROM CANNOBIO SS 34

RESIDENZA DEL LAGO

🔑 3-Star Hotel
Via Roma 48
Tel. 011 9834885-9834886
Fax 011 9834885
E-mail: info@residenzadelago.it
Internet: www.residenzadelago.it
Open all year round

LA RONDINELLA

🔑 2-Star Hotel
Via Sacchetti 50
Tel. 0323 788098
Fax 0323 788365
E-mail: hrondine@tin.it
Internet: www.hotel-la-rondinella.it
Closed 20 days in January and 15 in November

Erbaluce, a classic Piedmontese white wine, is produced in the hills that run down towards Lake Candia, a nature reserve, and it's here, on the edge of the village, that you'll find the Residenza,. Owned by Elena Ferrari, who's helped by son Federico Nuccio and Nella Mancini, the original atmosphere of the old Canavese home has been preserved, with brick walls and barrel vaulting. Rooms are spacious and fitted with period furniture. Some rooms have a fireplace, others a terrace, some a mezzanine-level sleeping area. A buffet breakfast is available in the airy restaurant lounge and includes hot beverages, fruit juices, fresh and dried fruit, jams, honey, muesli, pastries, cured meats and cheeses. The restaurant (25-34 euros, excluding wine) offers genuine traditional cuisine and wine from local producers. Half board in a double room is 78 euros per person.

• 11 double rooms with bathroom, minibar, satellite television, modem connection • Prices: double room single occupancy 70-75 euros, double 80-85 (30 euro supplement for extra bed), breakfast included • Credit cards: all, Bancomat • 2 rooms designed for the mobility challenged. Outside free parking 50 meters away. Small pets allowed (15 euros per day). Owners always present • Restaurant. Reading and television room. Garden

A characteristic 1930s villa with original Art Deco decor now houses this small, comfortable hotel just outside Cànnero, a holiday destination on the northwest shore of Lake Maggiore. The well-furnished rooms have lake views, and about half have balconies too. There's a path from the hotel grounds leading down to the water. The often mild weather means breakfasts are usually served on the picturesque terrace. Sweet and savory items are available. Dinner is also served (set menu 17 euros, à la carte menu from 25 euros, excluding wine). La Rondinella makes a good base for those who enjoy water sports or who want to hike in the surrounding mountains and valleys, either in Italy or nearby Switzerland.

• 13 double rooms with bathroom, safe, satellite television; 3 apartments (2-4 people) with kitchenette • Prices: double room single occupancy 47-54 euros, double 78-90, apartments (4 people) 95-113, breakfast included • Credit cards: all, Bancomat • Off-street parking, garage (8 places). Small pets allowed. Reception open from 7 am to midnight • Bar, restaurant (residents only). Garden, terrace. Public beach 100 meters away

20 KM NORTHEAST OF VERBANIA-INTRA SS 34

33 KM SOUTHWEST OF TURIN

ANTICA STALLERA

☎ 3-Star Hotel
Via Zaccheo 3
Tel. 0323 71595
Fax 0323 72201
E-mail: info@anticastallera.com
Internet: www.anticastallera.com
Closed from mid-January to mid-February

LA LOCANDA DELLA MAISON VERTE

☎ 3-Star Hotel
Via Rossi 34
Tel. 0121 354610
Fax 0121 354614
E-mail: information@maisonvertehotel.it
Internet: www.maisonvertehotel.it
Open all year round

Once a coaching station where travelers could change horses and rest, the Antica Stallera is now a cozy hotel, refurbished in 2000 by siblings Fabrizia and Paolo Soncini and equipped with everything a modern traveler might need. The stunning summer garden contains ancient plants, including two yews that date back almost three centuries and a camellia imported by the English in the 18th century. The hearty breakfast is varied and reflects the tastes of the regular northern European guests. Patrons have a choice of three different types of bread, cured meats, a selection of local cheeses and fresh ricotta, cereal, yogurt, milk and regular and low-sugar jams. In the roomy restaurant, also open to non-residents, meals average at about 26 euros, excluding wine; the half board supplement is 16 euros per person.

• 2 single and 16 double rooms with bathroom, television; several rooms with balcony • Prices: single 55-60 euros, double 84-94 (15-25 euro supplement for extra bed), breakfast included • Credit cards: all, Bancomat • 2 rooms designed for the handicapped. Off-street parking. Small pets allowed (5 euros per day). Owners always contactable • Bar, restaurant. Breakfast room, Reading and television room. Conference room. Garden, terrace

The Maison Verte started out as a health center, run by the Ferrero family drawing on their 40 years of experience producing herbal remedies. In 2001 they converted the 19th-century farmhouse next to the herbalist's shop, creating about 30 rooms, each unique and furnished with great attention to detail with classic furniture and modern comforts. The buffet breakfast offers a wide selection of homemade cakes, jams, cured meats and cheeses. The restaurant (half board 61-94 euros) and the well-equipped fitness center and spa offering natural remedies are additional draws.

• 3 single rooms, 21 doubles, 3 junior suites and 1 suite, bathroom, air conditioning, mini-bar, safe, satellite television, modem connection • Prices: single 73-80 euros, double 90-108, junior suite 120, suite 160, breakfast included • Credit cards: all, Bancomat • Communal spaces and 3 rooms designed for the mobility challenged. Off-street parking. Small pets allowed. Reception open from 7am to half-past midnight • Bar, restaurant. Lounges. Conference room. Park, terrace. Well-being center with swimming pool, sauna, Turkish bath, gym

CANTALUPO LIGURE
Pessinate

CAPRIATA D'ORBA

25 KM SOUTHEAST OF ALESSANDRIA SS 35 BIS

25 KM SOUTH OF ALESSANDRIA, 10 KM FROM NOVI LIGURE

BELVEDERE

IL MORO

Restaurant
Località Pessinate 53
Tel. 0143 93138
Closed Monday
Open: lunch and dinner
Holidays: January
Seating: 45
Prices: 32-35 euros, wine excluded
Credit cards: Visa, Bancomat

Restaurant
Piazza Garibaldi 6
Tel. 0143 46157
Closed Monday, Sunday dinner by reservation only
Open: lunch and dinner
Holidays: variable between February and March
Seating: 35 + 30 outdoors
Prices: 35 euros, wine excluded
All major credit cards, Bancomat

It's a tortuously winding road to get to Pessinate, but the beautiful view over Val Borbera makes it worth the drive, as does this restaurant housed in a building reminiscent of a 1960s pension. The Pagano family has been running it since 1919, and when the latest generation took over things have changed dramatically, particularly with Fabrizio in the kitchen. Typical products and the traditional dishes of this border area remained on the menu, but the chef has introduced some innovations.

Try the vol-au-vent filled with asparagus, porcini and fonduta of Montébore cheese (a Slow Food Presidium), the squash flowers stuffed with **stockfish alla brandacujon** with zucchini, anchovies and garlic or the **snails** with herb butter. The balanced yet complex flavor of the **risotto al Timorasso** with Montébore makes it a winner, and other memorable dishes include **ravioli al tocco di manzo** and the potato tortelli with speck and peppers. Among the main courses, try the saddle of rabbit in a pistachio crust with polenta and Taggia olives, or the **beef cheek** in tuna sauce accompanied by asparagus flan. There's also a very good selection of cheeses produced by the Vallenostra cooperative. Another highlight of this restaurant is the choice of desserts, among which the strawberry sorbet with elderflower croquembouche with a white-chocolate and hazelnut filling, the bonet with orange biscuits and Carla's apple and muscat sorbet.

The wine list contains mostly local wines with a few labels from the rest of Piedmont.

Close to the Ligurian border, this old restaurant on the main square reflects the local cuisine of both Piedmont and its neighbor. Simona and Claudio Rebora have done much to boost its reputation, creating an unpretentious and pleasant atmosphere, warm in the winter and cool under the rustic portico in the summer. The seasonal menu draws on the traditions of Monferrato, Genoa and the Langhe.

Antipasti include two renowned salamis, Acqui filetto baciato and Gavi' testa in cassetta (a Slow Food Presidium), **sweet-pepper sformato** with anchovies or tonno di coniglio, Castelnuovo **onions with fonduta** and flan with Piedmontese cheese. For first courses there are always **agnolotti al tocco** and fresh homemade pastas: lasagne, taglierini or green tagliatelle. Other appealing dishes include the gnocchi alla robiola, **corzetti with marjoram and pine-nut pesto** or sausage and mushroom sauce, not to mention the risotto with nettles and freshwater shrimp. Main courses: top quality horsemeat and Fassone beef cuts are grilled in summer, Mandrogne beef sausage and **suckling pig**, bollito misto in winter, **freshwater fish** and **stockfish with olives**. There's a rich, carefully chosen selection of Piedmontese cheeses: from the local Presidia (Roccaverano and Montebore) to Bettelmatt, from natural Gorgonzola to famous Langa varieties. You can round off the meal with Simona's desserts: pear and bitter-chocolate tortino, a chocolate sampler, milk pudding, jam tarts and ice cream made from seasonal fruits.

A very extensive wine list with an appropriate emphasis on the best Gavi wines and Dolcetto di Ovada.

CARCOFORO

SCOIATTOLO ⊘▮

◁Restaurant
Casa del Ponte 3 B
Tel. 0163 95612
Closed Monday and Tuesday, never in summer
Open: lunch and dinner
Holidays: February, 1 week in June and 1 in September
Seating: 30 + 6 outdoors
Prices: 33-35 euros, wine excluded
All credit cards, Bancomat

Scoiattolo is situated In one of the small-est communes in Italy, up in the moun-tains of the Valsesisa where menories of the Waldensian communities are every-where to be seen. As in the building in which the restaurant is situated (an old wood and stone hay loft with a gneiss slate roof) and its cooking. Over the years, Pier Aldo and Mariangela Manet-ta have gradually added touches of re-finement to the menu, but this is one of the few addresses in the area where you can still taste the Waldensian dishes of yesteryear. New shapes and forms for old flavors: that could be the slogan to sum up the cooking of Mariangela.
Antipasti include a **fantasia of freshwa-ter fish** (steamed trout on a bed of chick-pea purée, trout 'in carpione' with Mosca-to and home-smoked fillet of trout), a 'tavolozza', or palette, of sheep ricotta, bresaola, lardo, white meats in aspic, vitello tonnato and mousse alla car-bonara. First courses are all made with local produce: **gnocchetti filled with fresh ricotta**, **agnolotti** filled with roast meats (or **wild spinach**) and barley soup with dried mushrooms, ham and Toma cheese, plus the very typical **polenta concia carcoforese** with potatoes and celery, **gnucheit** (polenta with butter and Toma cheese). Main courses: cockerel stuffed with vegetables, **baked fillet steak** in Gattinara sauce, rabbit in coffee sauce and, when in season, caffè, **game**. Be sure to taste the wheel of cow's and goat's **cheeses**, including Bruss, Salig-nun and local Toma. The desserts are home-made and creative and the coffee is flavored with a variety of aromas.
The wine list offers excellent labels from all over Italy, but obviously places the onus on local production.

CAREMA

RAMO VERDE

◁Trattoria
Via Torino 42
Tel. 0125 811327
Closed Monday, Saturday lunch and Sunday dinner
Open: lunch and dinner
Holidays: 2 weeks in June, 1 in September
Seating: 35
Prices: 28-30 euros, wine excluded
All major credit cards except AE, Bancomat

On the road to the Valle d'Aosta is Care-ma, known for the nebbiolo-based wine of the same name. The village in the hills is worth visiting for the wine and also to eat at this trattoria, in business since 1924 and run by the Vairettos since 1989. Fabrizio cooks and Graziella serves, in a cozy, informal setting typical of a country trattoria.
There's no written menu or wine list; in-stead you'll be told what your choices are. We recommend the cured meats and mocetta, as well as **vitello tonnato**; the raw meat tartare with capers, onions and anchovies; the **caponet**, the as-paragus tortino with Parmesan fonduta and the eggplant strudel. There are nu-merous first courses, including paccheri with rabbit ragù, artichokes, dried toma-toes and Taggia olives; long fusilli pasta with lardo di Arnad and asparagus and **agnolotti with gravy and thyme**. When in season the **Canavesana soup** made with Savoy cabbage is well worth trying. As for main courses, these are generally the traditional meats of Piedmont and the Valle d'Aosta: veal roll, **beef stew**, rabbit with herbs, **roast Donnaz kid**, lamb chops with almonds, tripe. There's a good selection of cheeses and desserts, including various types of mousse, chocolate and pear cake, apple pie and cherries with fiordilatte.
There's decent selection of wines, but with this food you're best off with a local Carema.

🍷 In **Pont-Saint-Martin** (5 km into the Valle d'Aosta), at Via Chanoux 73, Gauden-zio Porté butchers certified Piedmontese meat and produces salamis, mocetta and lardo.

CARRÙ
Sant'Anna

IL BRICCO

🔑 Bed and breakfast
Strada Sant'Anna 5
Tel. 0173 75558-333 3464485
Fax 0173 75558
E-mail: pri@interfree.it
Internet: www.val-bb.it/ilbricco.asp
Open from April to mid-November

The 'bricco' itself, a small rise in the land, is not that high, but it's enough to offer magnificent views over the countryside of the Tanaro Valley out to the Alps. The Calleri family's 18th-century country house is still where Wilman spends the summer with her husband, author Pier Luigi Berbotto. Rooms and common areas are comfortable and well-furnished. Breakfast is served under the portico with views of the flower garden, an experience made even more enjoyable by Wilma's homemade cakes. In summer yoga courses are also available. Nearby are the Langhe hills and other attractions of southern Piedmont.

• 2 double rooms with bathroom, and 1 suite with living room, kitchen, terrace • Prices: double room single occupancy 44-54 euros, double 70-82, suite 80-92, breakfast included • Credit cards: none • Parking outside. Small pets allowed. Owners always present • Breakfast room, lounge, reading room. Garden, solarium

CARRÙ

MODERNO 🍾

🍲 Restaurant
Via Misericordia 12
Tel. 0173 75493
Closed Tuesday, Monday and Wednesday dinner
Open: lunch and dinner
Holidays: August, 1 week at end of December
Seating: 80
Prices: 31-33 euros, wine excluded
All major credit cards, Bancomat

Some towns boast monuments to kings, knights, saints or poets. Carrù's monument, in a piazza at the entrance to the town, is an enormous bronze sculpture of a Piedmontese ox. Each December a festival dedicated to the cattle brings thousands of visitors to the town, and the meat features on the menus of all the local restaurants.
Il Moderno, run by Carluccio and Domizia, is an institution for beef from the "bue grasso," or fat ox, and in general for traditional Piedmontese cuisine. This is the place to come on the day of the festival for a robust breakfast of beef broth washed down with a glass of Dolcetto wine, but it's worth a visit all year round, particularly for the **bollito misto alla piemontese,** seven traditional cuts accompanied by the prescribed sauces. Start with raw Alba-style meat, **vitello tonnato**, Russian salad or salt-cured ox meat. For a first there's always **tajarin** (also made with wholemeal flour) and **agnolotti dal plin** with ragù, butter and sage or, in winter, cream of leek sauce. Also recommended are the gnocchi with Raschera cheese, **tripe soup**, agnolotti filled with fondue and, in summer, maltagliati with sausage and eggplant. Apart from boiled meat, for a main course you'll often find the **fritto misto**, oven-baked shoulder of pork and **roast shank of beef**. The dessert trolley offers something sweet to round out the meal.
A generous selection of Piedmontese red wines is available to accompany the dishes.

🍷 Pasticceria Artigiana, at Corso Einaudi, 28, run by 'confectioner/photographer' Roberto Reineri: splendid photos, cakes, semifreddos and chocolates.

CARRÙ

OSTERIA DEL BORGO

◯ Osteria
Via Garibaldi 19
Tel. 0173 759184
Closed Tuesday dinner and Wednesday
Open: lunch and dinner
Holidays: 2-3 weeks between June and July
Seating: 45
Prices: 18-28 euros, wine excluded
All major credit cards, Bancomat

Every time you eat in a traditional restaurant with someone who's not from Piedmont it's quite likely you'll be amazed at how lyrical they can get about boiled meat. They pile on the superlatives whereas we – perhaps a bit maliciously – think, 'but what could be easier than boiling a piece of beef?' If, instead of being so supercilious, we ponder the quality of this simply sublime offering, we might have to admit it's not that easy to cook a good helping of boiled meat. It requires a big hunk of excellent meat to make a superb dish, and, of course, the right dose of condiments (salt, vegetables, herbs) and real sauces, but without going overboard. It's not all that easy to find a truly harmonious blend of these ingredients, but at the Borgo you'll find it every day of the year.
Carrù is the homeland of fat oxen: noblesse oblige. But nothing can be taken for granted. Pina and Daniele, chefs and owners of this squeaky-clean osteria have managed to make the seven traditional cuts of **Piedmontese boiled beef** a magnet that attracts customers! Having said all this, the rest of the menu is good too: **raw meat**, stuffed zucchini flowers, vitello tonnato, **oven-baked peppers**; then the ever-present **tajarin** and **agnolotti dal plin**. Good, when in season, the gnocchi with cep mushroom sauce and tripe soup. As for main courses, if you want to give the boiled meat a miss, then opt for either the excellent **punta di petto** cooked in a wood-fired oven or the **rabbit stew**.
Classic home-made puddings (bonet, panna cotta and stuffed peaches), with the occasional fruit pie and a well-balanced, reasonably priced choice of wines.

CASTAGNITO

OSTU DI DJUN

◯ Osteria-trattoria
Via San Giuseppe 1
Tel. 0173 213600
Closed Sunday
Open: dinner only
Holidays: 1 week in August, between Christmas and January 6
Seating: 40 + 100 outdoors
Prices: 30-33 euros
No credit cards

While they are some customers at the Marsaglia brothers' osteria who leave vowing never to return, the majority become firm aficionados. The food is never the problem, instead some people find the service a little too laid back, the lack of a written menu frustrating, and the absence of choice in wine irritating. But others fall in love with the friendly, informal atmosphere, the recital of the day's menu and the constant stimulation of many food-and-wine pairings as magnums are whisked from table to table (an unusual solution which is appreciated by both palate and wallet), and come back again and again. The interior decor is basic but cozy, with some old-fashioned touches, red-brick arches and a big wooden counter. The large courtyard in front provides lots of space for al fresco dining when the weather's good.
Prior to the antipasti (raw meat, rabbit salad, Jerusalem artichoke flan with fonduta) you always get **bagasce**, flat bread warm from the oven and served with lard. Then classic first courses: **tajarin** with melted butter or meat sauce, **ravioli dal plin**, risotto with red wine and, in winter, vegetable, bean and lentil soups. For seconds, **roast rabbit**, **quail** cooked **al babi** (flattened in the pan), **braised beef**, ox shank or roast **Sambucano lamb**. In summer you may even find some nice fish dishes as an alternative to traditional Piedmontese cuisine.
Desserts are not bad: cream budino, zabaglione with peaches, hazelnut cake, bonet and ice-cream gnugnu (with an addition of dried fruit). As a finishing touch, coffee with a glass of grappa.

CASTAGNOLE MONFERRATO

LOCANDA DEI MUSICI

🗝—0 Rooms
Via al Castello 40
Tel. 0141 292283-335 8327450
Fax 0141 292283
E-mail: locandamusici@hotmail.com
Internet: www.locandadeimusici.com
Open February 1-July 20 and
August 20-December 31

Castagnole Monferrato is home to Ruché, a palatable wine of mysterious origins, and this locanda, in a 17th-century house, sits on the Muraja, a bastion offering panoramic views. The pastel rooms have antiques and terraces with views of the Monferrato hills and the Alps. Access to the locanda is through a secluded courtyard and garden which guarantee absolute peace and quiet. Breakfast is varied and plentiful (biscuits and homemade cakes and savory items like cured meats and cheeses) and guests can use the kitchen to make their stay even more comfortable. Wine tastings are organized in the common lounge where guests can sample the unique local wines and Barolo chinatos. Bicycles are available for excursions in the hills and around the nearby vineyards of Monferrato.

• 5 double rooms with bathroom, terrace or balcony, television on request • Prices: double room single use 55-65 euros, double 65-75 (20 euro supplement for extra bed), breakfast included • Credit cards: Visa, Bancomat • Off-street parking. Small pets allowed. Owners always contactable • Reading room, kitchen. Conference room. Garden, terrace

CASTEL BOGLIONE
Gianola

LA CARLOTTA

🗝—0 Holiday farm
Frazione Gianola 28
Tel. 0141 762496-347 1627005
Fax 0141 762496
E-mail: cascinalacarlotta@interfree.it
Internet: www.agriturismocascinalacarlotta.com
Closed from January 7 to the end of
February

A noble house built around a courtyard, sheltered but easy to see from the road between Nizza Monferrato and Acqui Terme, provides a pleasant home for this agriturismo. The winery, which produces DOC and DOCG wines, the reception area, guestrooms and breakfast room all open onto the courtyard which in summer is full of flowers, tables and comfortable chairs. Restored conservatively and with refined taste by Carla Bellotti, every detail has its place. The rooms are large and feature wrought-iron beds in classic or modern styles, some period furniture and designer lamps. The buffet breakfast offers a choice of sweet and savory items: homemade cakes, jams, grape mostarda, cured meats and local cheeses; yogurt and fresh fruit are available on request. Amaretto biscuits from Mombaruzzo and a glass of sparkling Brachetto make for a warm welcome.

• 2 double and 2 triple rooms with bathroom, safe, TV (in 2 rooms satellite); 1 apartment (4 people) with kitchen range • Prices: double room single use 50 euros, double 70, triple and apartment 85, breakfast included • Credit cards: all, Bancomat • Off-street parking, some covered. Small pets allowed. Owners always present • Breakfast room. Furnished courtyard. Swimming pool

12 KM NORTH OF ASTI

11 KM NORTH OF CUNEO, 12 KM FROM FOSSANO

L'OSTERIA DEL CASTELLO 🐌

◻️ Restaurant
Via Castello 1
Tel. 0141 204115
Closed Monday and Tuesday
Open: lunch and dinner
Holidays: January
Seating: 70 + 50 outdoors
Prices: 33-35 euros, wine excluded
All major credit cards except AE, Bancomat

TRATTORIA ROMA

◻️ Trattoria
Via Roma 3
Tel. 0171 791109
Closed Monday dinner and Tuesday
Open: lunch and dinner
Holidays: variable
Seating: 40 + 30 outdoors
Prices: 28-30 euros, wine excluded
All major credit cards

It's said that Piedmontese cuisine reaches its peak in the fall and winter, but we think Osteria del Castello really shines in the summer. That's when you can eat the traditional dishes prepared by Marisa Torta and her mother on the splendid breezy terrace overlooking the Monferrato hills and valleys dotted with villages and castles. The restaurant itself is in an 18th-century castle.

The antipasti are served on large trays, and popular favorites include **raw meat** salad, vitello tonnato and **insalata russa**, always very fresh and delicious. You might be offered a just-made frittata, carpionata or a potato and mushroom flan or one with artichokes. There's a variety of first courses: **agnolotti dal plin with roast meat sauce**, **gnocchi** with sausage or fresh tomato sauce and the always suberb **pasta and beans**. Quality ingredients also underpin the main courses, among which you'll always find **stracotto al Barbera**, **roast rabbit**, **roast kid**, tripe, chicken in aspic in summer, and the rare **finanziera** in winter. The top dessert is definitely the **chocolate mousse**, but there's also panna cotta and bonet, caramelized fruit compote, cherries cooked in wine, pears soaked in Moscato and peaches with amaretto.

There are some really good bottles in the cellar, above all wines from around Asti and Alba: let young Giacomo, whose tasks include preparing wine lists and menus, help you out.

This part of the province of Cuneo is a far cry from the Langhe and Monferrato vineyards, dominated by fields of cows and maize, with intensive agriculture and light manufacturing the main industries. But five years ago Davide Rabbia and Annalisa Brizio decided to take over the well-known trattoria in Castelletto Stura, at the end of the Stura Valley, which had been in business since 1931.

With Annalisa in the kitchen and Davide in the dining room, slowly but surely they improved the standard of cooking and the sources of their ingredients, and now the Trattoria Roma is an appealing destination. The veal and beef come from the La Granda association of producers, the rabbit is the Carmagnola Gray variety, a Slow Food Presidium, as is the Saluzzo white chicken. The cured meats come from Beppe Dho in Centallo, while the trout and char – both highly recommended – are supplied by what Davide calls an extremist breeder who has banned oxygenation, industrial waste, hormones and integrators from his pools. Annalisa showcases these jewels in dishes like **carne battuta al coltello**, tonno di coniglio, superb **salt-cured meat with honey vinaigrette** and vegetable pies. The **ravioli with herbs** is good as is the **bean soup**; while the **beef** from Piedmontese-breed cows is the very best the region has to offer.

The wine list offers a good selection, particularly the whites (something of a rarity in Piedmont) and lesser-known labels. The assortment of cheeses is well-balanced, the homemade ice cream has a delicate flavor and prices are very reasonable. Castelletto might not be on your itinerary but this trattoria makes it a must-visit destination.

CASTELLINALDO

CASTEL ROCCHERO

IL BORGO

ANTICA OSTERIA

🍲 Holiday farm
Via Trento 2
Tel. and fax 0173 214017
E-mail: agriturismoilborgo@tiscali.it
Internet: www.ilborgoagriturismo.it
Open all year round

🍲 Trattoria
Via Roma 1
Tel. 0141 760257
Closed Wednesday
Open: lunch and dinner
Holidays: always open
Seating: 60
Prices: 25-30 euros, wine excluded
All major credit cards, Bancomat

Castellinaldo is a lovely village in the Roero hills north of Alba, surrounded by vineyards which produce Nebbiolo, Arneis, Barbera and other wines. The agriturismo run by Patrizia Ferrero is located right in the old center of the village beneath the walls of the medieval castle. Rooms are basic but clean and quiet, fitted with rustic furniture and boldly colored bedspreads and curtains. Every room is named for a local wine and all have a small terrace with a panoramic view. The lounge used to be the cellar, which was dug out of tufa, and it's where you'll enjoy the hearty buffet breakfast of sweet and savory items; in addition tasting sessions of local wines are arranged here. When the weather is mild, guests can relax in the shade of one of the courtyard gazebos.

• 5 double rooms with bathroom, terrace, mini-bar, TV; 1 apartment (2-5 people) with living room, kitchen range • Prices: double room single use 50 euros, double 66, apartment 82-125, breakfast included • Credit cards: all except AE, Bancomat • Off-street parking. No pets allowed. Owners always present • Breakfast room, wine tasting room

This quiet, old-fashioned village in the Monferrato, in the heart of Barbera and Brachetto wine country, is home to the Antica Osteria, which has recently been greatly improved thanks to the efforts of Massimiliano Morandi, a businessman from Lombardy. The old building has been renovated, maintaining vestiges of the past and designed to look like a country home, with pots and pans hanging on the walls. The two dining rooms have air conditioning and one has a veranda; both are pleasant.
Morandi has put Deborah Vacca and Pietro Amato in charge of the service and the kitchen, and the three of them have put together a wide choice of dishes, including Morandi's personal gastronomic passion, fish, at the weekends. In the "antipasti dell'oste" (four tastes for 9 euros) you might find Russian salad, garlic and onion crostini, marinated anchovies, frittata, pickled vegetables and peperonata. Or you can order **raw meat**, vitello tonnato, **stuffed anchovies** and pinzimonio. Traditional **agnolotti**, **pasta and beans**, tagliolini with porcini mushrooms, gnocchi (some made with Toma cheese) and **lasagnette al ragù** are common first courses, followed by **chicken alla cacciatora** (sublime), meatballs, tagliata (splendid), roast rabbit, **frittura all'italiana** (highly recommended) tripe and **polenta with wild boar** in winter. And that's just a sampling of the extensive menu. The desserts are simple but well-made, and there are also excellent home-baked breads and **cured meats** from Maragliana, an estate also owned by Morandi.
Prices are reasonable and the wine list contains some carefully selected local wines.

CASTIGLIONE FALLETTO

LE TORRI

🗝️❶3-Star Hotel
Via Roma 29
Tel. 0173 62961-339 7822241-328 3772631
Fax 0173 62961
E-mail: info@hotelletorri.it
Internet: www.hotelletorri.it
Closed from January 7 to end of
February

Just down from the medieval castle is this hotel, run by Renata and Silvana Ferrero. Rooms and apartments are comfortable and tastefully decorated and most of them enjoy splendid views of the Langhe hills and the distant Alps. All have a small balcony and one of them – the most expensive – has a sun-deck. The buffet breakfast is lavish, with cured meats, six types of local cheese, five choices of cereal, fruit salad and fresh fruit, croissants, homemade cakes, butter, jams, honey and yogurt. A choice of beverages – milk, coffee, fruit juices and a selection of 15 different types of tea – are served at the table. Bicycles are available for guests.

• 7 double rooms and 2 triples with bathroom, mini-bar, safe, television; 8 apartments (2-4 people) with living room; 4 with kitchen • Prices: double room single use 60-99 euros, breakfast included; double 84-96, triple 108-115, apartment 102-157 euros; breakfast 10-13 euros per person • Credit cards: all, Bancomat • 1 room designed for the mobility challenged. External public parking, free garage (7 places). Small pets allowed (5 euros per day). Owners always contactable • Restaurant in same building with different management, wine shop. Breakfast room with bar service. Furnished courtyard, garden

CAVAGLIÀ

OSTERIA DELL'OCA BIANCA

🍲 Recently opened osteria
Via Umberto I 2
Tel. 0161 966833
Closed Monday, Tuesday, Wednesday
Open: lunch and dinner
Holidays: second half of June
Seating: 45
Prices: 35 euros, wine excluded
All major credit cards, Bancomat

Cavaglià is an agricultural village near Lake Viverone and the Serra d'Ivrea ridge, and for some years it has been home to this osteria run by Paolo Mazzia and his wife Monica. It's a pleasant place with three lovingly furnished rooms, a welcoming atmosphere and a strictly Piedmontese menu. Not just in terms of the food but also the extensive selection of wines – about 300 on the list – focusing on Barbera, the host's passion.

The seasonally changing menu will be recited to you, starting with a long list of traditional antipasti, from **insalata russa** to **carne cruda**, frittatas, Chiaverano cheeses with vinegar and hot chili peppers and the selection of cured meats, of which the highlight is coppa served with lingue di suocera (mother-in-law's tongues), actually crunchy slices of bread, or giardiniera. Most of the first courses are based on fresh pasta (**agnolotti dal plin** and **tagliolini** with meat, fresh tomatoes or mushrooms), but in winter also include **pasta and bean soup** and vegetable minestrone. Also in winter visitors can enjoy an authentic treat from times gone by, **goose with cabbage**; when in season, **snails** and **game**, and throughout the year, pork chops and fillet cooked in Barbera accompanied by vegetables. The **cheese board** includes Slow Food Presidia like Roccaverano Robiola and Macagn, but you'll also find goat cheeses, Toma, Pecorino and Gorgonzola. For dessert, try the Novecento cake or crème brûlée and, for a digestif, one of the many grappas.

CAVATORE

DA FAUSTO 🍶

🍲 Restaurant
Località Valle Prati 1
Tel. 0144 325387
Closed Monday and Tuesday at lunch
Open: lunch and dinner
Holidays: January 1-February 10
Seating: 55 + 40 outdoors
Prices: 28-32 euros, wine excluded
All major credit cards, Bancomat

Cavatore is a small village in Valle Erro, just a few minutes from Acqui. Carved out of a stone-built farmhouse, the restaurant lies near the center of the village, its rooms decorated with a mix of old and new. Sitting in the spacious outdoor area you can see Monviso and Monte Rosa. Rossella's cuisine is a halfway house between Piedmont and Liguria and she proposes two set menus. Fausto's job is to let clients know what they're going to get – and he does so at inordinate length.

You can start with sliced raw meat, **peppers in anchovy, caper and tuna sauce**, vegetable pies, swordfish marinated with cherry tomatoes and Tropea onions or **filetto baciato di Ponzone** (Slow Food Presidium). In the fall you'll often be offered royal agaric and cep mushroom salad and **tripe with bean purée**. Among the first courses, **potato gnocchi with pesto** made from Prà basil and fettuccine with eggplant and Pecorino, while in the colder months there are soups, **meat-filled ravioli in gravy** and **tagliatelle with wild boar** or hare sauce. Depending on the season, main courses include a good selection of game (hare, wild boar and roe deer venison) and **mushroom** dishes, and you'll almost always find lamb chops, **tonno di coniglio with balsamic vinegar**, roast duck and rabbit cooked with olives and pine kernels. To round things off, the cheese board and desserts such as chocolate soufflé and nougat semifreddo with a chocolate fondue.

The well-stocked cellar boasts numerous Italian and foreign wines and, understandably, the best labels from the Acqui area.

CAVOUR

LA POSTA

🔑 3-Star Hotel
Via dei Fossi 4
Tel. 0121 69989
Fax 0121 69790
E-mail: posta@locandalaposta.it
Internet: www.locandalaposta.it
Open all year round

Just a short distance from the Rocca di Cavour regional park in the historic center of town is this 17th-century building, home to the Genovesio family who've been hoteliers for four centuries. Common areas are furnished with antiques, as are the large and bright rooms. A buffet breakfast is served in a lovely little lounge with a fireplace and includes hot beverages, fruit juices, cereal and home-made jams, biscuits and cakes. An English-style breakfast is available on request. Guests can also purchase home-made products: wines, grappa, cured meats, sweets and preserves. The restaurant offers mainly traditional Piedmontese dishes (25-30 euros, wine excluded; half board 60 euros per person).

• 17 double rooms, 2 triples and 1 quadruple, bathroom, air conditioning, mini-bar, satellite television, modem connection • Prices: double room single use 55 euros, double 80, triple 150, with 4 beds 180, breakfast included • Credit cards: all, Bancomat • 1 room designed for the mobility challenged. Off-street parking (2 places) and reserved external parking. Small pets allowed. Reception open 24 hours a day • Bar, restaurant. Breakfast room. Meeting room, smoking room. Hanging garden

CELLARENGO

29 KM NORTHWEST OF ASTI, 35 KM FROM TURIN

CASCINA PAPA MORA

Holiday farm
Via Ferrere 16
Tel. 0141 935126
Fax 0141 935444
E-mail: papamora@tin.it
Internet: www.cascinapapamora.it
Closed in January and February

The extensive grounds of this country farm produce fruit for preserves and wines. The Bucco sisters run the farm organically and believe strongly in a natural lifestyle (guests can take advantage of the special well-being weeks described on the website).

A tempting buffet is usually served out on the veranda and offers cakes, biscuits, pastries, home-baked breads, cereal and jams, with savory items available on request. Second-floor and mezzanine rooms are pretty, painted in different bright colors like yellow, pink, ivy-green and grape-purple, and fitted with retro furniture; bathrooms are roomy and have windows; the restaurant is open to non-residents if they book (20-27 euros, excluding wine) and offers enjoyable meals. Guests can also play table tennis, rent a mountain bike or go horse riding.

• 5 double rooms, triple or quadruple and bathroom • Prices: double room single use 35-40 euros, double 60-70, triple 70-85, quadruple 80-95, breakfast included • Credit cards: all, Bancomat • Off-street parking. No pets allowed. Owners always contactable • Restaurant. Veranda for breakfasts, television and reading room. Garden, solarium. Swimming pool, horse-riding

CERRETTO LANGHE
Cavallotti

57 KM NORTHEAST OF CUNEO, 22 KM FROM ALBA

TRATTORIA DEL BIVIO

Rooms
Località Cavallotti 9
Tel. 0173 520383-339 2299474
Fax 0173 520383
E-mail: info@trattoriadelbivio.it
Internet: www.trattoriadelbivio.it
Closed in January and 10 days in July

This trattoria takes its name from the crossroads between the road from Alba to Albaretto Torre and Sinio in one direction and Cerretto in the other, which if you continued for some time would eventually take you to the coast. Cerretto is a small village in the hills of the upper Langhe and you're guaranteed a relaxing stay and wonderful views of the surrounding countryside. Massimo Torrengo finished restoring this large farmhouse in 2003, and it boasts a three-room restaurant offering traditional dishes with a modern twist (28 euros, excluding wine) on the first floor and guest rooms on the second, basic but tastefully decorated. Breakfast offers traditional croissants, juices, yogurt, hot beverages, homemade bread, butter and jam. Savory items are available on request.

• 5 double rooms and 1 suite with bathroom, satellite television, modem connection; 2 with balcony • Prices: double room single use 55 euros, double 60 (9 euro supplement for extra bed), suite 70, breakfast included • Credit cards: all except AE, Bancomat • Communal spaces and 1 room designed for the mobility challenged. Off-street parking. Small pets allowed. Owners always contactable • Bar, restaurant. Garden

CESSOLE
Madonna della Neve

CEVA

MADONNA DELLA NEVE

Trattoria/1-Star Hotel
Località Madonna della Neve 2
Tel. 0144 850402
Fax 0144 80265
E-mail: info@ristorantemadonnadellaneve.it
Internet: www.ristorantemadonnadellaneve.it
Closed Friday
Open: lunch and dinner
Holidays: December 23-January 31
Seating: 100
Prices: 28-32 euros, wine excluded
All credit cards, Bancomat

ITALIA

Restaurant
Via Moretti 19
Tel. 0174 701340
Closed Sunday dinner and Monday
Open: lunch and dinner
Holidays: 2 weeks in July, 2 in January
Seating: 70
Prices: 15-25 euros, wine excluded
All major credit cards, Bancomat

The atmosphere is homely and the staff attentive but not overbearing, and the hotel offers a few comfortable rooms, each painted a different color. In the restaurant, the Piedmontese menu starts off with farmhouse **cured meats**, **rice and artichoke pie** and vitello tonnato. There are some wonderful **agnolotti dal plin sul tovagliolo** (served without sauce so you can really taste the filling and appreciate the fineness of the pasta), with butter and sage or ragù. Main courses include **roast kid from the Langhe**, **roast rabbit**, **game**, **griva** with pork offal, and when in season, **porcini mushrooms** and Gobbo cardoons. There are some outstanding **Robiola** di Roccaverano cheeses at varying stages of aging. Puddings include an exquisite **tiramisù with Moscato** and hazelnut cake with zabaglione. The wine list includes some bottles from outside the region as well as a good Piemontese selection.

Half board (for a minimum of three days) in a double room costs 47 euros per person, in a single room 50; full board in a double room is 54 euros, in a single room 56. The hotel is open all week.

🛏🔌• 9 double rooms, with bathroom, air-conditioning, mini-bar, satellite TV • Prices: double room at single use rate 38, double room 65 euros (15 euro supplement for extra bed), breakfast included • 1 room with disabled facilities. On-site uncovered parking. Small pets accepted. Owners present 8am-midnight • Restaurant. Reading room. Garden. Boules court

Once a hotel and coaching station, we found Italia living up to its legacy of hospitality, receiving a warm welcome from Vicenzo Bella even when we dropped in without a reservation at an unusual hour. We were impressed from the start as we took our seats in the peach-pink dining room with its vaulted ceiling.

As for the food, there's a huge choice: apart from the à la carte options, there's a tourist menu for 15 euros or a prix fixe at 23 euros. We opted for a not-too-ambitious lunch – **tajarin al sugo langarolo** (the fresh tomatoes were a nice touch) followed by guinea fowl supreme with raisins and wild blueberries. Paolo Pavarino's skill was evident in each dish, which combined tradition, creativity and simplicity. The menu ranges widely, with classical antipasti like stuffed zucchini flowers, rabbit galantine, herb flan with Raschera cheese fondue and **vitello tonnato con salsa all'antica**. Then various risottos, **agnolotti dal plin** and **ola** (minestrone cooked in the oven), a local specialty. Depending on the season, main courses might include game, horsemeat entrecôte, **tripe** and **ox shank cooked in dolcetto**. A high point is the generous use of local ingredients, from Bagnasco beans to Caprauna turnips (a Slow Food presidium).

Then there are the usual popular desserts – bonet, panna cotta, stuffed peaches, gianduia parfait – and while the wine list logically focuses on Piedmont, it also takes in almost all other regions of Italy and a few wines from abroad too.

LA TORRE

🍲 Osteria
Via Garibaldi 13
Tel. 0172 488458
Closed Mondays
Open: lunch and dinner
Holidays: variable
Seating: 40
Prices: 25-30 euros, wine excluded
All major credit cards, Bancomat

OSTERIA DELLA ROSA ROSSA

🍲 Trattoria
Via San Pietro 31
Tel. 0172 488133
Closed Wednesday and Thursday
Open: lunch and dinner
Holidays: 10 days in January and 2
weeks in summer
Seating: 45
Prices: 28-32 euros, wine excluded
All major credit cards except AE, Bancomat

This osteria that Marco Falco opened a few years ago, is in the center of Cherasco, a short distance from the 15th-century municipal tower. It is welcoming and peaceful and furnished in a tastefully elegant, functional manner. Marco's brother, Gabriele, is in charge of the courteous and pleasantly laid-back service. The menu varies a lot from day to day depending on the season, what's available on the market and the chef's inspirations.
For antipasti, you might find insalata russa, **anchovies in salsa verde**, **giardiniera casalinga**, egg drowned in Raschera fondue and **peppers with bagna caoda** in winter and with tuna pâté in summer. After this, there might be **gnocchi al Castelmagno**, tajarin al ragù bianco, **steamed ravioli** served wrapped in a napkin, various risottos and, in winter, chickpea or bean soup. Marco has a real passion for offal and less prized cuts of meat in general, which, particularly in colder months, he uses to prepare memorable dishes like **tajarin with chicken livers**, **tripe soup**, rabbit liver and onions, sweetbreads with lemon or mushrooms, **testina fritta** or al Barolo and **batsoà**. Snails are emblematic of Cherasco, and a dish is always available here, whether **fried**, Parisian style or steamed. Other main courses include roasts, boiled meats and **ox cheek braised in red wine**. At the right time of year there are also game dishes and truffle garnishes. For dessert, there's bonet, panna cotta and, in summer, stuffed peaches and semifreddo zabaione and amaretti.
While the wine list isn't particularly extensive it does include some reliable, mostly local labels, all reasonably priced too.

The Rosa Rossa is one of the very few remaining examples of a genuine Savoy trattoria. The kitchen opens onto the dining room, the walls are covered with rose prints and the tables nestle together with no regard to privacy. And then there is the timeless art of Piedmontese cuisine offered by Laura Dotta and Amelia Chiarla.
This is a place where you come to savor **snails**, the pride and joy of Cherasco, cooked in the pan with onions and rosemary, stewed with tomato, al verde or in a risotto. Then there's a host of fresh, simply prepared antipasti: **girello al sale** with salad, roast peppers on toasted bread, courgettes stuffed with amaretti and onions stuffed with Bra sausage. Try a classic like **insalata russa**, carne cruda al coltello, **vitello tonnato**, insalata di galletto or vegetable timbale. Choose from a range of first courses: there's **agnolotti dal plin**, gnocchi al Castelmagno or with tomato and basil sauce, **tajarin with chicken livers**, or alla salsiccia di Bra or with snails, tagliatelle with tomato sauce and risotto ai funghi. For main courses, you might find **roast rabbit**, roast veal, stewed tripe, **Sambucano lamb** (a Slow Food Presidium) and beef braised in Barolo, all cooked with an unusually light touch. The Rosa Rossa offers a good choice of Piedmontese **cheeses**, but be sure to save room for dessert, whether it be the **panna cotta**, semifreddo or berries in raspberry sauce.
On the wine list you'll find the best of the region's production with particular attention to Langhe wines.

CHERASCO
Moglia

47 KM NORTHEAST OF CUNEO, 17 KM FROM ALBA

CHIUSA DI PESIO
San Bartolomeo

22 KM SOUTHEAST OF CUNEO

PANE E VINO

Trattoria with rooms
Via Moglia 12
Tel. 0172 489108
Closed Monday and Tuesday
Open: lunch and dinner
Holidays: 2 weeks in August, 2 weeks in winter
Seating: 50
Prices: 22-30 euros, wine excluded
All major credit cards

LA LOCANDA ALPINA

Restaurant with rooms
Via Provinciale 71
Tel. 0171 738287
Closed Tuesday and Wednesday lunch, never during summer
Open: lunch and dinner
Holidays: February
Seating: 45
Price: 23 euros, wine excluded
All major credit cards except AE, Bancomat

It may not be in the more picturesque parts of tiny Cherasco, but then isn't it nice to get away from the busy main road, park in the large courtyard and find yourself seated inside the trattoria in no time at all? It's because of its strategic position that this trattoria has managed to survive so long, but Emiliana, Rosanna and Flavio also make it well worth a visit. Without outside distractions, you can turn your attention to the bottle-filled shelves and the trolley load of cheeses (if the weather's not too hot) and the food on your table.

You'll be welcomed with a basket of homemade bread and the wine list, which is comprehensive and well presented. Many of the wines are available by the glass and with recommended accompanying menus.

Antipasti include **peppers** stuffed with tuna mousse, **vitello tonnato**, faggot of sausage and mushrooms and rolled rabbit with quail eggs. For your first course, you can't go wrong with the **tajarin with sausage** or **ravioli dal plin** with butter and sage sauce. The freshly made maccheroncini with tomato, basil and burrata sauce is particularly interesting. Main courses are fine but not quite as attractive as the previous ones. Neverthless, you might try either the leg of rabbit alla langarola, roast veal with mushrooms or **lamb chops** in Chardonnay. Or skip ahead to classic bonet, semifreddo with torrone and moscato or warm chocolate cake. Cherasco is one of the capitals of the snail business and there's a special menu here dedicated to **snails** most of the year. This trattoria also has four rooms for guests wishing to stay overnight – this is the gateway to the Langa area, after all.

Dinner at this osteria makes the perfect conclusion to a hike in the Parco della Valle Pesio. From Cuneo, follow the signs for Peveragno and once you've passed Chiusa di Pesio, take the road for the monastery as far as San Bartolomeo. The Lebra family (Gianfranco and his wife waiting tables, their children in the kitchen) also lets rooms. As soon as you enter there's a bar and some tables where regulars often sit and play cards, while the two dining rooms have a warm atmosphere.

The menu, which is recited, includes classics from the valley with some innovations. The well-presented antipasti include **vitello tonnato**, **tuna-stuffed peppers**, raw meat carpaccio, trout mousse, zucchini flan, **tongue in salsa verde** and Robiola cheese with walnut sauce. The generous firsts include tajarin with zucchini, butter and saffron or other sauces depending on the season; **gnocchi with Raschera** and **agnolotti with ragù** or butter and sage. In the fall and winter there's risotto with mushrooms or fonduta. For a main course choose from **duck with chestnuts**, wild boar in a thyme-flavored bread crust, **game with polenta**, roast lamb, roast rabbit and **trout cooked in butter**. To conclude: coffee panna cotta, peach cake, mint and coffee semifreddo and, in winter, **martin sec pears in cinnamon sauce** and chestnut montebianco. The wine list includes just a few labels, mainly Piedmontese, at reasonable prices.

A In **Boves** (17 km), at Via Roma 7, Martini's butcher's shop sells mountain-reared veal, Morozzo capon, Bisalta kid, Carrù bue grasso and its own cured meats.

CISSONE

LOCANDA DELL'ARCO

Restaurant/rooms
Piazza dell'Olmo 1
Tel. 0173 748200
E-mail: giuseppe.giordano@locandadellarco.com
Internet: www.locandadellarco.com
Closed: Tuesday and Wednesday lunch
Open: dinner, lunch by reservation
Holidays: January 10-February 15
Seating: 30
Prices: 26-35 euros, wine excluded
Credit cards: CartaSi, Visa, Bancomat

A restored 19th-century farmhouse in a tranquil setting offers seven rooms, some with antique furniture. The hotel is open all week and includes a lounge for guests to relax with a book or read up on the surrounding alta Langa area.
Owner Maria Piera Querio prepares her dishes with ingredients of the best quality: stone-ground flours, wild boar and Piedmontese beef, traditional Toma cheeses, tonda hazelnuts, truffles and mushrooms. Recommended antipasti include **cold rabbit with Toma di Murazzano** cheese, marinated trout, **hand-chopped raw meat**, and in the winter months, cauliflower flan with mushroom cream and truffles. As for the first courses, there are potato gnocchi with toma, **tajarin with chicken livers**, risotto with Barolo and **ravioli with mutton and borage**. The most interesting main courses include **wild boar with chestnuts**, **braised beef with Barolo**, rabbit with raspberries and roast beef with hazelnuts. The many desserts include peach and apricot sfogliatina, **semifreddo with nougat**, bonet and panna cotta. There is also a good cheese board.
The extensive wine list offers a good selection of wines from the best producers of the Langhe and Piedmont, and first-rate grappas and liqueurs. Guided tours of the wine cellars are available.

• 7 double rooms, with bathroom • Prices: double room single use 40-50, double room 62-75 euros, breakfast included • External free parking. Small pets accepted. Owners always present • Restaurant. Breakfast room, lounge. Terrace

CISTERNA D'ASTI

GARIBALDI

Restaurant/3-Star Hotel
Via Italia 1-3
Tel. and fax 0141 979118
E-mail: ilgaribaldi.vaudano@libero.it
Closed Wednesday
Open: lunch and dinner
Holidays: 2 weeks in January and 2 after Aug. 15
Seating: 100
Prices: 20-30 euros, wine excluded
All credit cards, Bancomat

This hotel was founded in 1885 by a former soldier who fought under Garibaldi. The Vaudano family took over the attractive frescoed building in the 1940s, keeping the original decor. The rooms are plain but comfortable, and the hotel offers information on local history and the medieval castle's Museum of Historic Arts and Crafts.
There is one main dining room and three attractive little ones. Start with chicken salad, zucchini pie, peppers and an excellent **home-smoked salmon trout**. As for the first courses, house specialties include **tagliolini with 22 herbs** served with a mushroom sauce, but there are also tajarin with rabbit ragù, agnolotti with robiola and walnuts and **square agnolotti**. The **spiced roast rabbit** is also a specialty, as is **fritto misto** (during the week only when booked in advance), quail in white wine and roast duck. To finish off, **apple pie** with chocolate, amaretti biscuits and spices, a time-honored local classic, or **ice cream with grape mostarda**, zabaglione mousse or dark-chocolate bonet. The wine list gives due regard to Cisterna DOC and offers a careful selection of wines from the Monferrato, Roero and Langa.
The hotel is open all week.

• 3 single and 4 double rooms, with bathroom, television • Prices: single 35, double 60 euros, breakfast included • External free public parking. Small pets accepted. Owners present from 7 to 23 • Bar, restaurant. Breakfast room. Conference room. Terrace

CLAVESANA
Palazzetto

CORIO

37 KM NORTHEAST OF CUNEO SS 22

32 KM NORTHWEST OF TORINO

IL PALAZZETTO

Holiday farm
Borgata Palazzetto 18
Tel. 0173 790381-333 4285896
Fax 0173 732992
E-mail: info@agriturismoilpalazzetto.it
Internet: www.agriturismoilpalazzetto.it
Closed 15 days in January

TRATTORIA DELLA SOCIETÀ AGRICOLA

Trattoria
Via Regina Margherita 21
Tel. 011 928887
Closed Tuesday dinner and Wednesday,
in summer open Thursday to Sunday
Open: lunch and dinner
Holidays: 1 week in January, 1 in June
Seating: 30 + 15 outdoors
Prices: 30 euros, wine excluded
All major credit cards, Bancomat

Il Palazzetto lies on a small hill surrounded by dolcetto vineyards. From the summit there's a scenic view of the surrounding hills, the Tanaro valley and the distant Alps. A former convent, the farm has now been restored to offer rooms and apartments fitted with 19th-century furniture made by local craftsmen, plus all mod cons. Breakfast is served in the restaurant (meals cost 22 to 30 euros, excluding wine) and offers cakes, hot beverages and a good selection of cured meats and cheeses. Guests can join in a truffle hunt or see how bread and grissini are prepared and baked in the wood-fired oven.

• 5 double rooms and 1 suite with bathroom, balcony, mini-bar, safe, TV, modem connection; 1 apartment with kitchen • Prices: double room single use 40-45 euros, double 60-70, suite 60-70, breakfast included; apartment 250-350 euros a week • Credit cards: Visa, MC, Bancomat • Communal areas and 1 room designed for the mobility challenged. Off-street parking. Small pets accepted. Owners always contactable • Restaurant. Tavern. Garden, terrace

Corio lies on the border between the Lanzo valleys and the upper Canavese, and is surrounded by tiny hamlets full of slate-roofed mountain houses with dry-stone walls. The trattoria, run for several years by Roberto Aimone and his wife Patrizia, is in the center of the old town. The cuisine is based on traditional local dishes, with a set menu that changes seasonally. We've tried antipasti like the warm spelt salad with turkey, **tongue in parsley sauce**, asparagus with a sorrel sauce, ricotta flan and endive and a vol-au-vent with fonduta. Among the sampling of first courses you'll find various types of **risotto – with porcini mushrooms**, with zucchini and Taleggio cheese, **al salam 'd torgia** (made with beef and pork) – tagliolini with eggplant and dried tomatoes or home-made **agnolotti**. We also recommend the superb **sacòcia** with asparagus filling, **stewed tripe** with beans and the sautéed **Piemontese fassone fillet**, all made using meat from a farm in nearby Nole. There's an interesting selection of goat's and cow's milk cheeses served with fruit jellies; among the desserts, the choice ranges from fruit cake with amaretti caramel cream to ghiacciata al gianduia.
An extremely competent selection of wines is reasonably priced and is full of labels by lesser-known producers.

At Giovanna Alice's bakery (Via Regina Margherita 6), you'll find excellent meliga, pampavia and gallette biscuits.

CORNELIANO D'ALBA

LOCANDA DEI VAGABONDI

🗝🗝Rooms
Via Ruata 6
Tel. 0173 610590
Fax 0173 614731
E-mail: locandadeivagabondi@tiscali.it
Closed August 16-September 1

A few years ago Stefano and Chiara Giraudo, managers of the Podio trattoria in Santo Stefano Roero, relocated the restaurant business to their home in Corneliano, renovating the second floor to accommodate four guest rooms. The building is simple and attractive, located on a side street which opens onto the main square of the village, and has typical 'gallery' balconies, a peaceful cobbled courtyard and a veranda where guests can dine in good weather. Breakfast includes hot and cold beverages, butter, jams, pastries and biscotti. The restaurant serves a set menu of four antipasti, two first courses, two main courses and desserts for 22 euros, excluding wine.

• 3 double rooms and 1 triple with bathroom, balcony, television • Prices: double room single 45 euros, double 52-60, triple 75, breakfast included • All major credit cards, Bancomat • Public parking 30 meters away. Small pets allowed. Owners always present • Restaurant. Outside seating when weather permits

CORTEMILIA

VILLA SAN CARLO

🗝🗝3-Star Hotel
Corso Divisioni Alpine 41
Tel. 0173 81546
Fax 0173 81235
E-mail: info@hotelsancarlo.it
Internet: www.hotelsancarlo.it
Closed December 22 to February 26

The hotel is situated in a modern building on the outskirts of Cortemilia (a small village in the Bormida valley, near Alba, high up in the Langhe hills) and is managed by wine enthusiast Carlo Zarri. Rooms are well furnished and comfortable and common areas are spacious. Pets have the run of a special area set aside just for them on the grounds. For breakfast there is a buffet of savory items like cheeses, eggs and cured meats, as well as yogurt, cereal, bread, butter, jams, pastries, homemade cakes and various beverages. Bicycles are available for guests who wish to explore the countryside, and cooking courses and tastings offered as well. In the family-run restaurant, also open to nonguests, meals cost between 30 and 40 euros, excluding wine. There is a special pet shelter.

• 7 single, 14 double rooms and 2 mini-suites (2-4 people) with bathroom, minibar, satellite TV; several rooms with air conditioning and terrace • Prices: single 50-60 euros, double room single occupancy 65-75, double 92-102, mini-suite 120-160, breakfast included • All major credit cards, Bancomat • External parking, garage (5 euros per day). Small pets allowed (not in the rooms). Reception open from 7 am to midnight • Bar, restaurant. Breakfast room. Television room. Garden, park. Terrace. Swimming pool

Cossano Belbo

Universo

🍲 Trattoria
Via Caduti 6
Tel. 0141 88167
Closed Monday, Tuesday and Wednesday
Open: lunch and dinner
Holidays: June 15-July 15
Seating: 50
Prices: 25-30 euros, wine excluded
Credit cards: Visa, Bancomat

Universo retains the feel of those trattoria of yesteryear, where families went on Sunday outings in the Langa to indulge in a substantial meal with a glut of antipasti, sizable first and main courses and numerous desserts. Things are still pretty much the same today at Universo, so if you happen to drop in during the week you won't find the same choice of dishes you would during the weekend. The menu offered by the Cortese family is pretty much a set one, with a repertoire anchored in Piedmontese tradition: waiters pass by with trays from which they'll serve you generous portions. And they don't mind if you ask for more.
So you can enjoy **insalata di carne cruda**, Russian salad, savory flans with **fonduta**, roasted peppers with tuna sauce and cotechino with mashed potatoes. High point of the meal – though everything is really top quality – are the first courses, especially the very thin, fragrant **tajarin**, but the **agnolotti dal plin** with either a butter and sage, mushroom or ragù sauce are a real treat too. For main courses, there's a series of classic dishes, from roast to **braised beef**, from game (available from fall through winter, like the wild mushrooms) to **rabbit**, from **guinea-fowl** to maiale **al Furmentin** (a lively white wine found only here).
Desserts deserve a special mention: bacio with torrone, panna cotta, **bonet** with amaretti, hazelnut cake, peach pudding and pies. Service in the squeaky-clean, well-lit dining room is friendly and no-frills and the bill is quite reasonable. Wines are mainly from the Belbo valley with a few others from Piedmontese producers.

Costigliole d'Asti

Caffè Roma

🍲 Wine cellar with kitchen
Piazza Umberto I 14
Tel. 0141 966544
Closed Monday and Sunday dinner
Open: lunch and dinner
Holidays: variable
Seating: 50
Prices: 18-25 euros, wine excluded
All major credit cards, Bancomat

Now that the outside area has been set up and the rooms inside reorganized, Caffè Roma has become more functional and welcoming. They seem to have grown in confidence in the kitchen too, as there's been an increase in the number of dishes offered and the quality and presentation have improved a great deal. Anna and Gino seem much more at home in their role as hosts, and they still keep an eye on the wine cellar. You can have a glass of wine or an aperitif at the counter, a snack or simply a cup of coffee at any time of the day.
The cuisine largely features well-known dishes like **insalata russa**, vitello tonnato, insalata di galletto, **carne cruda with Robiola cheese and Bra sausage**, **tajarin** and agnolotti dal plin al ragù and **maltagliati con beans**. There are also some typical local offerings too, like the mousse di Gorgonzola, Robiolina cheese with celery and black truffle, the unusual **cod cooked in moscato**, duck breast with grapes and rabbit with Taggia olives. In season you'll always find carpionata, eggplant with pepper sauce, raw vegetables with oil, salt and pepper, Nizza Monferrato **cardoons with bagna caoda**. And there's always a good selection of **cured meats** and **cheeses**.
Cold zabaione with peaches and amaretto, **bonet**, tiramisu, vanilla ice cream with grape must and Anna's fruit pies are some possibilities for dessert. As for wine, there's an extremely wide choice, including many quality local and other Piedmontese bottles and carefully chosen selections from other Italian regions. Attentive service, honest prices and an obliging host make this informal, relaxing place an all-around excellent destination.

COSTIGLIOLE D'ASTI
Traniera

CRAVANZANA

CASCINA COLLAVINI

DA MAURIZIO

Bed and breakfast
Strada Traniera 24
Tel. and fax 0141 966440
E-mail: info@ristorantecollavini.it
Internet: www.ristorantecollavini.it
Closed for two weeks in August

Trattoria/2-Star hotel
Via San Rocco 16
Tel. 0173 855019
Fax 0173 855016
E-mail: ristorantedamaurizio@libero.it
Internet: www.ristorantedamaurizio.it
Closed Wednesday, Thursday for lunch
Open: lunch and dinner
Holidays: 08/01-10/02 and 25/06-06/07
Seating: 50 + 20 outdoors
Prices: 32-35 euros, wine excluded
Credit cards: Visa, Bancomat

A restaurant business professional, Bruno Collavini is now applying his skills in the country. Together with his wife, his daughter Cristina and son Gianpietro, he has refurbished a 19th-century farmhouse and converted it into a friendly, peaceful oasis of hospitality. On the ground floor are two rooms used for catering purposes: breakfast, which can be eaten outside during the summer, is served in the smaller of the two and this one also has a fireplace. Cristina serves savory fare (cured meats, cheeses and eggs) and cakes (croissants and bread fresh from the bakery, jam and butter). The guest rooms are on the top floor and are sizeable and tastefully furnished. The restaurant (meals range from 30-35 euros, excluding wine, closed Tuesday nights and Wednesdays) serves well-prepared Piedmontese cuisine, plus some dishes from other regions.

Surrounded by hazelnut groves, this hotel has been run by the Robaldo family since 1902 and has just over 10 rooms (open all week) and a spacious courtyard with wonderful views over the hills between the Belbo and Bormida rivers. The mini-suites, with mezzanine levels, offer the last word in comfort. Breakfast, whether sweet or savory, also includes homemade cakes. The food – hearty, local, seasonal fare – is among the best you will find in these hills. Antipasti include **carne cruda all'albese** with shavings of Macra cheese, **vitello tonnato, murazzano cheese pie**, baccalà with potatoes and taggiasca olives, turkey galantine with ratatuja and polenta crostone with mushrooms. Continue with **agnolotti dal plin**, **tajarin with ragù** or mushrooms depending on the season or chestnut lasagne with potatoes, hazelnuts and broccoli. Main courses to try include **roast Langa lamb**, **chicken alla cacciatora**, roast breast of veal, roast guinea fowl and medallions of wild boar in Barolo. For dessert there is the trio with hazelnuts: bonet, hazelnut cake and sweet salami.
The Piedmontese **cheese board** and an exhaustive wine list (around 250 labels) complement everything that's on offer.

• 5 double rooms, with bathroom, some with balcony • Prices: double room single use 55-65 euros, double 80 (20 euros supplement for extra bed), breakfast included • Credit cards: major ones, Bancomat • Off-street parking. No pets allowed. Owners always present. • Breakfast room. Restaurant. Garden, terrace

• 9 double rooms and 3 suites with bathroom; suites with TV, mini-bar, safe • Prices: double room at single occupancy rate 45, double room 60, suite 85 euros, breakfast included • Accessible to the mobility challenged, 1 room furnished for their use. On-site uncovered parking. No pets allowed. Reception open from 8am to midnight • Bar, restaurant. Garden, sun deck. Playground

70 KM FROM CUNEO, 8 KM SOUTH OF ALBA

OSTERIA DELLA CHIOCCIOLA

Enoteca-restaurant
Via Fossano 1
Tel. 0171 66277
Closed Sunday
Open: lunch and dinner
Holidays: first 15 days in January and August 15
Seating: 60
Prices: 28-33 euros, wine excluded
All major credit cards

TRATTORIA NELLE VIGNE

Trattoria
Via Santa Croce 17
Tel. 0173 468503
Closed Monday, also Wednesday in low season
Open: dinner, also for lunch on Saturdays and Sundays
Holidays: January
Seating: 80 + 40 outdoors
Prices: 18-22 euros, wine excluded
All credit cards, Bancomat

In Cuneo's aristocratic and orderly center you'll find this enoteca-cum-restaurant that has been in our guide for some years now. The reason for this is simple: it offers a welcoming, pleasant setting, courteous, professional staff in the dining room and excellent food. On the first floor, you'll find the wine cellar with counter and tables; on the second, the dining area with wooden caisson ceiling and pastel colored walls. The wine list is monumental – not only Piedmontese labels but a wealth of other Italian regional bottles and selections from France too. Bottles are priced competitively, with reasonable mark-ups.

You can eat à la carte or take the set menu. For the latter, lunch runs 17 and 22 euros, and there's a more varied set menu for 28 or 33 euros. In the fall and winter it's worth heading to the Chiocciola to taste their famous **snails** cooked in all manners and sauces: Bordeaux-style, skewered, with polenta or with aioli. From October to December you can also enjoy a wide selection of truffles, in addition to an excellent **Sambucano lamb** and **gnocchi al castelmagno**. In spring and summer, there are a few fish dishes, mushroom and potato pie, tomato and eggplant timbale and fried courgette flowers. Among the main courses we recommend the **rabbit with Taggiasca olives** and pork with mustard. Desserts include the ubiquitous panna cotta, chocolate mousse, **hazelnut cake with zabaione** and bonet.

This trattoria boasts two really pleasant panoramas so that summer and winter visitors will be equally happy. In nice weather you can eat your dinner on the veranda looking out over the Langa countryside and enjoy the view of those vineyards indicated on the sign. Inside, on the other hand, Franco Fausone's wistful ladies give you the eye from the walls. The pictures express a softened eroticism, one of the two forms of expression this Piedmontese artist is famous for (the other is more intense, but would probably seem a bit out of place in the osteria).

Head of the small kitchen staff is Sabrina Farioli, the artist's wife, who offers traditional dishes at an absolutely retro fixed price: you'll pay 21 euros for five antipasti, two samplings of first course dishes, a main course and dessert. So off you go with fried bread and herb-infused lardo, tasty **anchovies in hazelnut sauce** and **tongue in giardino**, peppers and tuna in a sweet and sour sauce, **insalata russa** and vegetable pies. In colder months you'll find **potato subrich** with lardo, **batsoà**, vegetable flans with bagna caoda and **vitello tonnato**. To follow, maltagliati or **tajarin al sugo di salsiccia**, **ravioli dal plin** with melted butter and rosemary, potato gnocchi with cheese sauce and **cisrà** (chickpea soup). Seconds range from **roasted beef shank, rabbit with peppers** or al civet and pork lonza cooked in milk and onions. Conclude your meal with **bonet, panna cotta**, stuffed peaches, apple pie or torrone semifreddo.

The wine list includes some 200 labels, nearly all local. Service is friendly and informal.

DOGLIANI
Madonna delle Grazie

ENOLOCANDA DEL TUFO

🔑 Holiday farm
Borgata Gombe 33
Tel. and fax 0173 70692
E-mail: deltufo@deltufo.it
Internet: www.deltufo.it
Open all year round

Bruno Del Tufo's agriturismo lies on a gentle hill with views over the celebrated Langa vineyards dotted with villages and castles, and also over a long stretch of the Maritime Alps. The panorama can be viewed from all the tastefully furnished rooms, each of which is different. The buffet breakfast consists of honey, jams, cookies, coffee, milk, fruit, cured meats and cheeses. On request you can visit the vineyards, learn grape-growing techniques, participate in farming activities and buy the farm's wines. Apart from the Langhe and Roero, Dogliani, Cherasco, Alba and Saluzzo are nearby and well worth a visit, while the major skiing resorts in the Cuneo area are within easy reach. There's a swimming pool one kilometer away, while it's only two km to the nearest tennis courts and 12 to a golf course.

• 6 double rooms and 2 suites, with bathroom (2 rooms with bathroom in common), terrace or balcony, fridge, TV, modem connection • Prices: double room single use 44-55 euros, double 55-70, suite 80-100, breakfast included • Credit cards: all, Bancomat • 2 rooms accessible to the mobility challenged. Off-street parking. No pets allowed. Owners always present • Use of kitchen on request. Breakfast room Garden, grounds, terrace

DOGLIANI
Sant'Eleuterio

FORESTERIA DEI PODERI LUIGI EINAUDI

🔑 Bed and breakfast
Borgata Gombe 31
Tel. 0173 70414
Fax 0173 742017
E-mail: foresteria@poderieinaudi.com
Internet: www.poderieinaudi.com
Open all year round

Created from an old family home on the estate of the descendants of the first president of the Italian Republic, this facility offers guests a magnificent view of the vineyards of the Langa district. Rooms are pleasant, elegant and extremely comfortable, and furnished with antiques. The buffet breakfast consists of honey, jam, cookies, coffee, milk, fruit, cured meats and cheeses. During your stay, you absolutely must visit the estate's vineyards and the cellars where they age extremely prestigious wines, among which Barolo Costa Grimaldi and Barolo nei Cannubi, awarded the prestigious three-glass symbol in the 2005 Slow Food-Gambero Rosso guide. Places well worth a visit in the neighborhood are Dogliani, Alba and Cherasco, with its pretty old town center where antique and rare book markets are often held.

• 8 double rooms and 2 suites, with bathroom, terrace or balcony, fridge, TV, modem connection; several rooms with air-conditioning • Prices: double room single use 93 euros, double 114, suite 135, breakfast included • Credit cards: all, Bancomat • Facility accessible to the mobility challenged, 1 room designed for their use. Covered off-street parking. Small pets allowed. Owners contactable until 9 pm. • Lounge, reading room, TV room. Garden, grounds, terrace. Pool

ELVA
Serre

54 KM NORTHWEST OF CUNEO ON SS 22

LOCANDA SAN PANCRAZIO DI HANS CLEMER

Bed and breakfast
Borgata Serre 10
Tel. 0171 997986
Fax 0171 997989
E-mail: locandasanpancrazio@tiscalinet.it
Internet: www.ghironda.com
Closed in November

To reach Elva, follow the directions from Stroppo and take a road that climbs uphill through the greenery; alternatively you can drive past Stroppo but then you have to tackle the dauntingly steep valley road. The village itself is a little gem, mainly thanks to its parish church, built in the 13th century, later altered, where you can admire frescoes by Hans Clemer, known as the 'Master of d'Elva'. This charming place, run by Edoardo Laria and Caterina Rostagno, offers hospitality for singles, couples and even larger groups. The rooms are simple, common areas are spacious and all around the facility are fields against the backdrop of Mount Pelvo. Breakfast is very generous and includes bread, butter, jams, local cakes and various beverages. Half board ranges from 35-50 euros per person; packed lunches are available for guests embarking on mountain excursions.

• 8 double, 1 triple and 1 four-bed rooms, with bathroom and terrace, some with fridge, TV; 4 dormitories for 5-7 persons • Prices: double room single use 28 euros, double 52, triple 75, four-bed 96, bed in dormitory 18 euros, breakfast included • Credit cards: all except AE, Bancomat • Restaurant accessible to the mobility challenged. Free public parking. Small pets allowed. Owners always reachable. • Bar, restaurant. Reading room. Terrace

FABBRICA CURONE
Selvapiana

62 KM SOUTHEAST OF ALESSANDRIA, 32 KM FROM TORTONA

LA GENZIANELLA

Hotel-Restaurant
Via Forotondo 7
Tel. 0131 780135
Closed Monday and Tuesday
Open: lunch and dinner
Holidays: September
Seating: 60
Prices: 28-30 euros, wine excluded
All credit cards, Bancomat

When we go to a restaurant we look for many things: courtesy, attention to detail, cleanliness and, obviously, great food. You'll find all of this at Genzianella, in addition to dishes representative of the local area, a factor that is entirely in line with our philosophy.

To start with, there are **cured meats** prepared by artisan and family patriarch Angelo accompanied by crostini, **turta in tra biela** (dry bread and milk flan), an example of reviving a dish from peasant tradition, montèbore budinetti with acacia honey and vegetable flans that vary with the seasons. First courses are this restaurant's forte and they change frequently – sometimes even daily. Don't miss autumn's **wild mushrooms** and **truffles** served with freshly made pasta and in risottos and delicious soups. In spring you'll find lasagna with fresh tomatoes and basil, **cannelloni di patata quarantina** and **ravioli di magro**. Among main courses the star is meat – in the hunting season go for the **game**. Vegetarians can always opt for a selection of cheeses served with preserves and Italian honeys. Three homemade desserts complete the meal. We recommend Tortona strawberries (Slow Food Presidium), only available for twenty days a year, served with Moscato d'Amburgo.

There's a respectable wine list based primarily on local wines, although there are labels from the rest of Piedmont and a few other Italian regions as well.

In **Fabbrica Curone** Andrea Fittabile, via Roma, 47, sells excellent cured meats and tasty cacciatorino salami.

FORMAZZA
Riale

FRASCARO

WALSER SCHTUBA

Bed and breakfast
Località Riale
Tel. 0324 634351-339 3663330
E-mail: sormanimatteo@locandawalser.com
Internet: www.locandawalser.com
Closed in May and October

HOSTERIA
DE' FERRARI

Restaurant
Via Cavour 3
Tel. 0131 278556
Closed Monday
Open: dinner, Sunday and festivities lunch too
Holidays: June 6-16
Seating: 40
Prices: 25-28 euros, wine excluded
All credit cards, Bancomat

Located in the very north of Piedmont on the border with Switzerland is Matteo and Francesca Sormani's B&B, which boasts six rooms with mansard ceilings. Rooms are paneled with pine and are simply furnished in a rustic manner, in keeping with the setting. The generous buffet breakfast offers a wide variety of typical local products, such as cured meats and cheeses as well as yogurt and home-baked cakes. There are many alternative activities for mountain lovers – whether experts or first-timers – with organized excursions accompanied by nature guides and, in winter, excursions with snowshoes. The restaurant offers home cooking (typical recipes from the Waldensian tradition, a Germanic minority that settled in the Rosa Valleys in the Middle Ages) at 25 euros, excluding wine. Half board costs 53 euros per person.

• 6 double rooms, with bathroom (jacuzzi), satellite TV • Prices: double room single use 46 euros, double 72 (32 euros supplement for extra bed), breakfast included • Credit cards: none • Common areas accessible for the disabled. External parking. No pets allowed. Owners always reachable. • Bar, restaurant. Breakfast room. Garden

Located midway between Alessandria and Acqui, Frascaro is a village of fewer than 500 inhabitants. The restaurant is near the town hall and comprises a single room with brightly colored walls and tables set well apart from one another. Lucio Ferrari, your very experienced host, in addition to his tried and tested seasonal menus, often proposes theme evenings at which the highlights are the most popular dishes voted for in surveys carried out among his regular customers.
Among the antipasti you can try the tris Hosteria of **paniccia** (fried chickpea polenta), coppa, courgette flan and a tasty **stuffed tomato**. There are also flans made with seasonal vegetables, veal tartar and oven-baked Roccaverano cheese with toasted bacon, hazelnuts and honey. The first courses include pulse soups, fresh pasta and risottos. We tried pasta with olive, pepper, tomato and caper sauce and a Ligurian dish of **ravioli di magro with light pesto**. Among the main courses you'll often find oven-baked trout with cherry tomatoes and basil and **steamed cod** with Taggia olives or hazelnut cream. The meat dishes include steak with aromatic herbs, roast turkey and **rabbit** in various versions. Cheeses, often used as ingredients in the dishes on the menu, are Lucio's passion. He chooses them himself and proposes a set selection, often accompanied by honey and fig compote or dried apricots. There's a wide selection of desserts: coffee-flavored bonet, panna cotta with Barbera sauce, crème caramel...
The wine list offers an adequate if not particularly original choice, and rightly includes a number of local wines.

FRASCARO
Tacconotti

GATTINARA

TRATTORIA ⊘ DEI TACCONOTTI

◇Trattoria
Frazione Tacconotti 17
Tel. 0131 278488
Closed Wednesday
Open: dinner, lunch also on Saturdays, Sundays and holidays
Holidays: January 1-20
Seating: 40 + 30 outdoors
Prices: 28-30 euros, wine excluded
All major credit cards

ANZIVINO

🔑Holiday farm
Corso Valsesia 162
Tel. 0163 827172
Fax 0163 820910
E-mail: info@anzivino.net
Internet: www.anzivino.net
Closed for two weeks in August

The Ricci family's trattoria is located in a farmhouse on the square in Frascaro, not far from Alessandria. We're in lower Piedmont here and the Liguria-influenced cuisine is well interpreted by Anna Ricci, including her use of both wild and cultivated herbs.

Warm **focaccia** is always on the table, accompanied by mixed antipasti that change regularly. There's goat cheese with Tropea onion, rice and Albenga zucchini pie, eggplant medallions, frittatas and cured meats. In winter you'll also find warm antipasti. First courses include pasta made from flours produced at the highly regarded Marino di Cossano Belbo mill: **corzetti novesi** with marjoram pesto, **panigacci** with Prà basil and Vessalico garlic pesto, herbed tagliolini and **agnolotti ovadesi**. Alternatively there's a good minestrone made with the season's vegetables. Stuffed and fried anchovies and vegetables stuffed with meat are among the main courses, as well as **vitello tonnato all'antica**, beef carpaccio with mustard sauce, **braised beef** and chops sold by weight. In season there are excellent porcini mushrooms, bagna caoda and – advanced notice required – **fritto misto piemontese**. It's also possible to have an all-fish menu. There's an extensive selection of both local and other Piedmontese **cheeses**, while desserts change depending on where Anna takes her inspiration from. There might be pear cake, mint- or rose-flavored whipped cream, peach or herb spumone.

Carlo oversees a wine list that, in addition to a good selection of half-bottles, includes a wide selection of Barbera and Dolcetto wines from little-known though high quality producers.

Famous winemakers, the Anzivino family produce prestigious varieties, such as Bramaterra, Gattinara, Faticato and Tarlo Rosso. In 2001, Emanuele and his wife Sabrina completed the refurbishment of their old farmhouse to take in guests. As a result, double rooms are now available (all of them can be converted into triples), as well as one apartment, all made particularly snug and comfortable by antique furnishings. All common areas are spacious, as is the restaurant, which is open to non-residents but only at weekends (meals are 25 euros per person, including wine), the garden, the terraces and the patio, shaded by umbrellas for quiet moments of relaxation. The Italian/German-style breakfast offers sweet fare (cakes, croissants, honey and jams) and savories (eggs, cured meats and a variety of local cheeses).

• 5 double rooms, with bathroom, air-conditioning, satellite TV; 1 apartment (2-4 persons) with kitchen • Prices: double room single use 55 euros, double 75 (15 euro supplement for extra bed), apartment 75-120, breakfast included • Credit cards: all, Bancomat • Restaurant accessible for the disabled. Off-street parking, open and covered. Small pets allowed. Owners always reachable. • Bar, restaurant. Breakfast room. Patio, garden, 2 terraces

GHIFFA

CASTELLO DI FRINO

🗝 2-Star Hotel
Via Colombo 8
Tel. 0323 59181
Fax 0323 59783
E-mail: laforet@tiscalinet.it
Internet: www.castellodifrino.com
Open from March until October

The building looks more like a Tuscan villa than a house beside an Alpine lake, but there used to be a medieval castle here before it was destroyed by wars at the end of the 17th century. It was rebuilt in this imposing manner and many of the architectural features remain intact, as do many of the original furnishings. The rooms are austere yet elegant and nearly all of them have a view of the lake, while 650 square-meter grounds with age-old trees contribute to the charm of this hotel. Breakfast includes both sweet and savory fare and is served in a special room or in the garden. In the restaurant, which is also open to non-residents, they serve homemade pasta and grilled meat (25 euros, excluding wine). Full board is 95 euros per person. While you're here, be sure to visit the Sacro Monte della Trinità Nature Reserve in the shadow of Mount Carciago: 200 hectares crisscrossed by paths, flanked by low dry-stone walls and with many characteristic votive chapels.

• 11 double, triple or four-bed rooms, with bathroom • Prices: double room single use 60 euros, double 120, triple or four-bed 180-240, breakfast included • Credit cards: all, Bancomat • 3 rooms designed for use by the mobility challenged. Off-street parking. Small pets allowed. Reception open 24 hours a day. • Bar, restaurant. Breakfast room. Garden, grounds. Pool, tennis court

GRAZZANO BADOGLIO
Madonna dei Monti

L'ALBERGOTTO

🗝 3-Star Hotel
Viale Pininfarina 43
Tel. 0141 925185
Fax 0141 925252
E-mail: albergotto@libero.it
Internet: www.albergotto-natalina.com
Open all year round

This hotel, which lies in the hills in the lower Monferrato area, offers hospitality with something of an old-world flavor, but it in no way lacks comfort or services (there are a small swimming pool in the grounds and jacuzzis in all suites). The house, where the owner Francesco Redoglia was born, has been converted into a hotel, though it retains the features of an old farmhouse: the facade of the building is made of tufa blocks, and it has a traditional old kitchen. Breakfast is classic with bread, butter, homemade jams and croissants. Piedmontese tradition is also evident in the comfortable rooms, furnished with antiques but the five apartments 300 meters from the hotel are brand-new. In the Natalina restaurant you'll taste the typical cuisine of this area in a warm, family atmosphere (meals cost from 30-35 euros, excluding wine).

• 6 double rooms and 3 suites, with bathroom, air-conditioning, fridge, safe, TV; 5 apartments (2-4 persons) with kitchen • Prices: double room single use 60 euros, double 75, suite 105, apartments 75 (30 euro supplement for extra bed), breakfast included • Credit cards: all, Bancomat • Some rooms designed for use by the mobility challenged. Off-street parking. No pets allowed. Staff always reachable • Bar, restaurant. Breakfast room. Conference room. Grounds. Pool

GREMIASCO

BELVEDERE

⌖Restaurant
Via Dusio 5
Tel. 0131 787159
Closed Tuesday
Open: lunch and dinner
Holidays: 20 days between February and March
Seating: 100 + 30 outdoors
Prices: 28-30 euros, wine excluded
All major credit cards, Bancomat

Gremiasco is a hillside village between San Sebastiano and Fabbrica Curone, villages that are only slightly larger. The entire area is famous for its fruit, which is often used here to prepare excellent desserts, and for its woods, which provide both wild mushrooms and game. The Delucchi family uses all this to great advantage in a menu in which the seasons and territory remain decidedly in the foreground.

The wide choice of antipasti includes Val Curone salami, homemade **insalata russa** and the season's **vegetable flan** (for instance, in summer eggplant, in winter leek) **with fonduta di Montébore**. If you like this kind of dish, between April and May don't miss the **rice timbale with spugnole** and prugnoli mushrooms (the same used to liven up the roast veal). First courses offer a thorough taste of local traditions, from **agnolotti al brasato** or with mushroom sauce to gnocchi di ortica or winter polenta, which is often served as a complete meal with stew. For the main course, pork, veal and, when in season, wild boar and game are on the menu. Remember that Val Curone is well known for its **white and black truffles** which can be used to perfume any number of dishes from June to December.

The wine list grows year by year and is very reasonably priced. It also includes a good house wine.

🍶 Just a few meters from the restaurant is the Arsura delicatessen, which sells one of the best raw salamis in the entire valley.

GUARENE
Lora

CASALORA

⌐O Rooms
Località Lora 3
Tel. 0173 611013
E-mail: info@casalora.it
Internet: www.casalora.it
Open all year round

Managed by Maurizio Perucca, Casalora is a B&B in an old farmhouse, recently renovated but maintaining the distinctive features of the original building. What stands out in this bright, cozy place are the beautiful wooden floors, ceilings with wooden beams and the well-chosen combination of antique and modern furniture. The suite is particularly attractive with its large arched windows that let in plenty of light. All the rooms are personalized by works of contemporary artists. During summer the buffet-style breakfast is served in the portico adjacent to the old barn, and consists of cakes, cheeses, cured meats, yoghurt, fruit and various types of jam. The position is ideal for people wishing to combine the pleasure of a relaxing stay with the possibility of visiting sites of cultural interest, as well as pursuing food and wine-tasting trails.

• 5 double rooms and 1 suite, with bathroom, terrace, TV, modem connection • Prices: double room single use 60 euros, double 85, suite 100, breakfast included • Credit cards: all, Bancomat • 1 room designed for use by the mobility challenged. Off-street parking. Small pets allowed. Owners reachable 8am-7pm. • Breakfast room. TV room. Garden, terrace

GUARENE
Coscia

LA MORRA
Rivalta

62 KM NORTHEAST OF CUNEO, 52 KM SOUTHEAST OF TURIN

54 KM NORTHEAST OF CUNEO, 12 KM FROM ALBA

SOLESTELLE

🗝Holiday farm
Località Coscia 1
Tel. 0173 611718
Fax 0173 611947
E-mail: info@solestelleonline.it
Internet: www.solestelleonline.it
Open all year round

BRICCO DEI COGNI

🗝Bed and breakfast
Località Bricco Cogni 39
Tel. 0173 509832–335 6497532
Fax 0173 500014
E-mail: info@briccodeicogni.it
Internet: www.briccodeicogni.it
Open all year round

Marinella Delpiano and Claudio Fissore will give you a friendly welcome to this renovated farmhouse, which belongs to their aunt and uncle. It lies in a beautiful position between vineyards and hazelnut trees in the Roero area, bordering on the lower Langa hills. The bright rooms and common spaces are decorated with paintings and sculptures and are named for flowers: 'Primrose' and 'Sunflower' are apartments with kitchens and can comfortably accommodate up to four people. The cost of the sweet and savory buffet-style breakfast is calculated apart according to items consumed. Common areas are pleasant, like the terrace solarium where aperitifs are served in summer. You can rent bicycles and there are guided tours to the surrounding area. That's not all: to make your stay completely relaxing, anti-stress massages are also available. A shuttle service to Alba station and Turin airport is available on request.

• 2 double and 2 triple rooms, with bathroom, fridge, satellite TV, modem connection; 2 mini-apartments (4 persons) with kitchen • Prices: double room single use 45-50 euros, double 65-70, triple 85-90, breakfast included; mini-apartment 90-100 euros • Credit cards: all except AE, Bancomat • 1 room designed for use by the mobility challenged. Off-street parking. Small pets allowed. Owners always reachable • Corner bar. Reading room. Terrace, garden with children's playground

Not too far from the square in Rivalta, a village between Verduno and Pollenzo, is the Bollano family's beautiful country house, now a dream home thanks to excellent renovation work and the addition of exquisite antique furnishings. The original floors, ceilings and fixtures have been conserved and antique furniture, carpets and other precious items create a warm, elegant atmosphere in all areas of the house, especially the spacious bedrooms. Breakfast (jams, homemade cakes, but also cheeses and cured meats) is served in a room with a fireplace and view over the Langa hills. Livio, his wife Claudia and mamma Vittorina, are always ready to cater for the needs of their guests.

• 6 double rooms, with bathroom • Prices: double room single use 60-90 euros, double 70-100 (14-18 euro supplement for extra bed); breakfast 7.50 euros per person • Credit cards: major ones, Bancomat • Off-street parking. Small pets allowed. Owners always present. • Breakfast room, lounge. Garden. Pool, solarium

La Morra

Corte Gondina

🛏️ 3-Star Hotel
Via Roma 100
Tel. 0173 509781
Fax 0173 509782
E-mail: info@cortegondina.it
Internet: www.cortegondina.it
Closed from beginning of January until mid-February

A few years ago Elena Oberto and Bruno Viberti finished restoring what had been the home of Radegonda Oberto, nicknamed 'Gondina', a teacher who was an institution in La Morra. As a result, there are now 14 elegant rooms (standard and superior) decorated and furnished with painstaking attention to detail. Common areas are pleasant and relaxing too, with many secluded corners where guests can sit and read. The buffet breakfast offers an extraordinary selection of foods to satisfy all palates: jams, honey, croissants, pastries, home-made sweet and savory cakes, yogurt, cereals, fresh fruit, ham and local cheeses such as Raschera, Bra and Testun. Plus, milk, coffee, tea and fruit juices. In warmer months guests can use the swimming pool. A pleasant place to stay while visiting the famous Langa vineyards and wine cellars.

• 12 double and 2 triple rooms, with bathroom, terrace, air-conditioning, fridge, satellite TV, modem connection • Prices: double room single use 75-90 euros, standard double 90-110, superior double 115-125, triple 135-155, breakfast included • Credit cards: all, Bancomat • 1 room designed for use by the mobility challenged. Off-street parking. Small pets allowed. Owners present until midnight • Coffee-shop. Breakfast room. Reading room. Internet point. Cellar with conference room. Garden. Swimming pool

La Morra
Santa Maria

L'Osteria del Vignaiolo

🍲 Osteria
Regione Santa Maria 12
Tel. 0173 50335
Closed Wednesday and Thursday
Open: lunch and dinner
Holidays: January, 15 days in July
Seating: 40 + 20 outdoors
Prices: 28-32 euros, wine excluded
All credit cards, Bancomat

It's a young but already expert, tried-and-tested team that, led by Luciano Marengo, caters to guests in a carefully furnished space with a menu that moves nimbly among the many traditional Langa specialties. The seasonal, 28-euro menu offers two antipasti, a first and a main course and dessert.
After nibbles of peppery coppa you can start with warm **rabbit salad**, Parma culatello served with rosemary-flavored focaccia, **carne cruda** spiced with black truffle or the Parma-style eggplant pie. First courses are well-executed: choose from **agnolotti dal plin** (firm pasta and a tasty filling) with butter and sage, **tagliatelle with gallinacci mushrooms** and risotto with Raschera fonduta. For your main course go for the meat dishes: **veal stew**, lamb chops (the breading might be a bit too much), quail and **roast leg of goose**. There's almost always a fish dish too. Don't skip out on dessert – among your options there may be panna cotta with berries, peach cake with fior di latte ice cream, **chocolate cake** and semifreddo al torrone.
The extensive wine list includes some very nice local labels as well as some foreign ones, most notably French. Top-notch service lets you fully enjoy your meal without overlong pauses or any feeling of being hurried.

🛒 At La Morra, via Roma 110, you'll find stone-ground flour at Molino Sobrino. To taste and purchase wines, visit the Cantina Comunale, Via Carlo Alberto 2, and Vin Bar, Via Roma 56.

LA MORRA
Annunziata

LUSERNA
SAN GIOVANNI

VILLA AGNESE

Bed and breakfast
Frazione Annunziata
Borgata Plucotti, 76 a
Tel. and fax 0173 50255
E-mail: villa.agnese@libero.it
Internet: www.villaagnese.it
Open from Easter to end of December

LOU CHARDOUN

Holiday farm
Via Vecchia di San Giovanni 99
Tel. 0121 90761
Open dinner, lunch also on Saturday, Sunday and holidays
Holidays: 1 week in January, 1 in August
Seating: 45
Prices: 25 euros, wine excluded
No credit cards accepted

From Piazetta dell'Annunziata you take a narrow road that skirts the vineyards of the Cordero di Montezemolo estate until you come to the gate of the Agnese family's house, a beautifully refurbished late 19th-century building. The guest rooms on the ground floor are comfortable and elegant, furnished with an extensive use of warm-colored fabrics. In an equally charming room adjacent to the lounge you'll enjoy a generous breakfast, partially organized as a buffet and including beverages, yogurt, jams, fruit salad, cooked fruit, cookies and hazelnut cakes, bonet and other sweet treats from the Langhe, as well as cured meats, cheeses and omelets. The owner organizes cooking courses while her husband will accompany you for excursions by bicycle or on foot.

• 3 double rooms, with bathroom (1 with a jacuzzi), small garden, fridge • Prices: double room single use 80-90 euros, double 100-120, breakfast included • Credit cards: major ones, Bancomat • Reserved parking alongside. Small pets allowed. Owners always present. • Breakfast room, lounge. Garden

In the rather unpredictable world of agriturismos, here's a place that's really worth trying. Why? Because it's a real farm, where your hosts tend to your needs only when not carrying out their chores to run the farm. After crossing the Bibiana bridge, follow the indications on the right to reach the hamlet where you'll find the refurbished farmhouse. It's a clean, unpretentious environment with Provençal accessories and table settings.
Enjoy a set menu of three antipasti, a first and main course with side dish, cheeses, two desserts, coffee and house wine, all excellent dishes at an attractive price. Portions are generous and no one minds if you ask for second helpings. We had onion pie with an aperitif, salami and lardo, **rotolo di cappone** and sarass del fen (a Slow Food Presidium cheese), nettle flan with Toma cheese fonduta, **basil-spiced gnocchi** with asparagus and zucchini flowers, **rabbit filet** with green peppercorns, local cheeses, strawberry semifreddo and chocolate cake. Typical dishes in cold months are **cardoon and Jerusalem artichoke flan with bagna caoda** and walnut oil, chicken terrine, pumpkin gnocchi with vegetable sauce, **boned rabbit cooked with herbs**, chestnut mousse and caramel apple fritters. The menu takes shape around what the seasons bring.
The wine list could be better, as could the quality of the glasses in which wine is served. However, there are a few good Piedmontese selections.

MACRA
Camoglieres

MANTA

LOCANDA DEL SILENZIO

🔑 Rooms
Borgo Camoglieres 1
Tel. and fax 0171 999305
E-mail: info@locandadelsilenzio.com
Internet: www.locandadelsilenzio.com
Variable holidays

IL GIARDINO DEI SEMPLICI

🔑 Bed and breakfast
Via San Giacomo 12
Tel. 0175 85744-347 7617987
E-mail: demafam.bb@libero.it
Variable holidays

The name of this locanda couldn't be more appropriate. Silence, peace, tranquility: you'll find them all here. Coming from Dronero, you leave Saint Damiano behind you; shortly before reaching Macra, a red sign on your right will guide you and for about a kilometer you follow the narrow road that climbs up to Camoglieres. Surrounded by majestic mountains is a beautiful renovated stone house that's well maintained both inside and out. Nanni, who also does the cooking with help from Paola and Rossana, will be there to welcome you. The refuge for groups and the rooms are basic: no TV – a prerequisite for silence. Breakfast is very generous and consists of yogurt, muesli, homemade jams and cakes, cookies, bread, locally made butter, beverages and juices. A meal at the restaurant (also open for non-residents) costs 25 euros, excluding drinks; half board, which is preferable during the winter season, costs 60 euros per person based on double room occupancy.

• 3 double rooms, with bathroom, modem connection; 1 dormitory for 10 persons • Prices: double room single use 60 euros, double 80 (27 euro supplement for extra bed), bed in dormitory 24 euros, breakfast included • Credit cards: Visa, MC, Bancomat • Free external public parking. Small pets allowed. Owners always reachable. • Bar, restaurant. Breakfast room, reading room. Garden

Il Giardino dei Semplici covers a small part of the hill above Saluzzo: large grounds surrounding an old house in an atmosphere that's so quiet it seems unreal. To think it's practically in the center of Manta, just a minute away from the main road and a stone's throw from the famous castle (open for visits). Here the Dematteis husband-and-wife team live with their 'semplici' (simple ones), their six children who inspired the name of the place. Passing through a pretty little garden, you come to the part of the house dedicated to guests: a large lounge and three bedrooms, two doubles (with a comfortable additional bed) and a single room, all very pleasant. You'll be able to wake up slowly with some help from Maria's cakes and a tasty selection of savory fare, including the ever-present Toumin dal Mel cheese or the exquisite goat cheeses of the Maira valley.

• 1 single and 2 double or triple rooms, with adjacent bathroom • Prices: single 25-35 euros, double 50-60, triple 60-75, breakfast included • Credit cards: none • Off-street parking. Small pets allowed. Owners always present. • Breakfast room, lounge. Garden, grounds

MARMORA
Finello

MASERA
Cresta

51 KM NORTHWEST OF CUNEO ON SS 22

44 KM NORTHWEST OF VERBANIA ON SS 34 AND 33

LOU PITAVIN

🔑 Rooms
Borgata Finello 2
Tel. and fax 0171 998188
E-mail: info@luopitavin.it
Internet: www.loupitavin.it
Holidays: beginning of November until Christmas

OSTERIA ⌇🍴
DEL DIVIN PORCELLO

🍲 Osteria
Borgata Cresta 11
Tel. 0324 35035
Closed Monday
Open: lunch and dinner
Holidays: January 15-30
Seating: 60 + 20 outdoors
Prices: 30 euros, wine excluded
All credit cards, Bancomat

After leaving Stroppo in Val Maira behind you, continue towards Acceglio and then, once you reach Ponte Marmora, take a left, following the directions for Marmora. 500 meters from the main village you'll find this B&B run by Valeria and Marco Andreis. The guest rooms are located in a 19th-century house carefully renovated in 2000 while retaining its original features. The rooms have mezzanines and are simply yet tastefully furnished. Communal areas are particularly appealing, as is the restaurant, also open to non-residents (meals cost 23 euros, excluding beverages), which was previously an old stable. There are tables and wooden benches outside.
More adventurous hikers should visit Rocca la Meja. Let Marco advise you on the routes.

• 4 double rooms with bathroom, terrace, modem connection; 1 dormitory for 8 persons • Prices: double room single use 60-68 euros (22 euro supplement for extra bed), place in dormitory 19 euros, breakfast included • Credit cards: all except AE, Bancomat • Restaurant accessible to the mobility challenged. Free external public parking. Small pets welcome. Owners always reachable. • Bar, restaurant. Breakfast room. Garden, terrace

True to its name, Divin Porcello is notable for the **cured meats** produced by the Sartoretti family in Masera, a town in the Ossola area close to the Swiss and Lombardy borders. This tradition, begun in the 1950s by grandfather Pierino, has been handed down to the present generation. Here, they continue to seek absolute quality by selecting only the best meats, processing them with natural methods and aging them in the cellars of the osteria.
Once seated, you absolutely must taste the **Val d'Ossola mortadella** (a Slow Food Presidium), goat and lamb violini and cotechini accompanied in winter by polenta, lardo, coppa, pancetta, culatello and bresaola, not to mention salami and fresh salamini. These antipasti are followed by **gnocchi all'ossolana,** made with potatoes, pumpkin and chestnuts, tagliolini and **risotto ai funghi**, soups of all kinds and **tripe**. And if you enjoy convivial rituals, ask for lausciera: a dish of potatoes and various fine cuts of meat that diners themselves cook on the hot shale stone and enjoy with various sauces. Otherwise, go for the classic grilled meats, steaks and **porcini**. The **cheeses** are also an excellent choice, with Bettelmatt, Tome d'alpeggio and local fresh goat and other cheeses. Be sure to try the **bread and milk cake** for dessert.
We recommend the local red Prünent to help you on your way, but the cellar, with more than 300 labels, is impressive and Massimo, the owner and a wine connoisseur, is always on hand to advise you.

20 KM SOUTH OF ALESSANDRIA

12 KM NORTHWEST OF VERBANIA-PALLANZA ON SS 33

ANTICA TRATTORIA LOSANNA

Trattoria
Via San Rocco 36
Tel. 0131 799525
Closed Sunday evening and Monday
Open: lunch and dinner
Holidays: August, 15 days after Christmas
Seating: 60
Prices: 25-27 euros, wine excluded
All major credit cards, Bancomat

LA QUARTINA

3-Star hotel
Via Pallanza 20
Tel. 0323 80118-80328
Fax 0323 80743
E-mail: laquartina@libero.it
Internet: www.laquartina.com
Holidays: January and December

This trattoria once served the wagoners of Val Tiglione carrying wine to Switzerland. Today, it attracts gourmets and admirers of the cuisine of Franco Barberis, who goes by the nickname 'Scarpetta'. Diners always enjoy the superb quality of his dishes, simple and closely linked to local traditions.

Guests are welcomed to the restaurant by a display of bottles, including the best Piedmontese labels but wines also from elsewhere in Italy and a fine selection of French ones as well. Franco Strabella is a delightful host; he'll start things off perhaps with lingue di suocera from the Rocchetta Tanaro bakery to go with his excellent salami.

Antipasti are served quickly and in generous portions on trays left for diners to enjoy as they please. Dishes always include **insalata russa**, frittatas with mixed herbs and onion, **stuffed peppers** and savory flans with seasonal vegetables. Special mention must be made of the marinated pork with slivers of black truffle that we tasted on our last visit. First courses include **agnolotti with gravy**, potato gnocchi with tomato and basil or seasonal sauces, **tagliatelle with porcini mushrooms** or vegetables and various soups. Main courses: stewed rabbit, roast or braised beef as well as traditional dishes like **tripe** or **stockfish**, both **stewed**. For dessert, there are traditional preparations like panna cotta, bonet, hazelnut cake and, in summer, ice-cream. Meals can be finished off with superb Piedmontese grappas.

This hotel-restaurant overlooks the small but lovely Lake Mergozzo, one of the cleanest lakes in Europe. The village of the same name is surrounded by woodland and makes an ideal base for excursions into Val d' Ossola and the splendid natural parks in the neighboring area. Suitable for those who are looking for a quiet, totally relaxing vacation, the hotel offers well-furnished rooms with every modern comfort. Breakfast, lunch and dinner are all served in the airy restaurant dining room located right by the lake and, when the weather permits, on the beautiful panoramic terrace (meals range from 30-45 euros, excluding wine; half board is 82 euros per person based on double room occupancy). Laura Profumo and her staff are professional and attentive.

• 2 single and 8 double rooms with bathroom, fridge, safe, satellite TV • Prices: single 40-78 euros, double 92-112 (20-28 euro supplement for extra bed), breakfast included • Credit cards: all, Bancomat • Off-street parking. Small pets welcome. Owners always present. • Bar, restaurant. Reading room, TV room. Terrace, solarium. Public beach

MOMBERCELLI

MONCALIERI
Revigliasco

20 KM SOUTHEAST OF ASTI

10 KM SOUTHEAST OF TURIN

LOCANDA FONTANABUONA

Restaurant
Via Nizza 595
Tel. 0141 955477
Closed Tuesday and Monday
Open: dinner, lunch also on Saturday and Sunday
Holidays: 2 weeks in January and 1 week between June and July
Seating: 80 + 40 outdoors
Prices: 28-33 euros, wine excluded
All major credit cards, Bancomat

LA TAVERNA DI FRA FIUSCH

Restaurant
Via Beria 32
Tel. 011 8608224
Closed Monday
Open: for dinner, lunch also on Saturday and holidays
Holidays: 2 weeks in August
Seating: 50
Prices: 28-33 euros, wine excluded
All major credit cards except DC, Bancomat

In this green valley near Asti, on the road to Nizza Monferrato-Canelli halfway up the hillside, you'll find this renovated farmhouse with outside tables. Here, you can enjoy a bottle of wine with a platter of cured meat, some **cheeses** and tasty **focaccine with lardo**.
Moving on to the menu (the set 'Locanda' menu is 26 euros, drinks excluded, for three antipasti, first and main courses and dessert, but you can also order à la carte), there are antipasti like **vitello tonnato**, salad of raw Piedmontese fassone beef, peppers with tuna sauce, insalata di galletto, **terrine** made with three kinds of meat, vegetable tarts and flans. The fresh pasta dishes (made with organic flour from the Marino di Cossano Belbo mill) are well prepared: try the classic **agnolotti dal plin with gravy**, Monferrato-style ravioli (but also with asparagus, artichoke, chicken sauces) with meat and sausage ragù, gnocchetti al Castelmagno and, in the spring, **nettle tagliolini with melted butter and mint**. For your main course, we recommend the **duck al Moscato**, **veal al Barbera** and local rabbit with olives. Desserts are also traditional Piedmontese specialties, and our favorites are **bavarese al Moscato** and semifreddo di torrone.
The extensive, original wine list ranges from Piedmont to selections from all over the world.

Up in Revigliasco, a small village in the hills outside Turin strewn with luxurious villas and residences, you'll find this warm, unpretentious restaurant that immediately gives you a sense of the passion and taste of the person who runs it. Here, the menu offers the entire classic repertoire of Piedmontese cuisine, surprising in terms of its comprehensive variety and reasonable prices. The set menu runs just 28 euros for three antipasti, a first and main course and dessert. We chose the **vitello tonnato**, always good, the savarin di sarass del fen and the basil pie. For firsts, there's **agnolotti stuffed with fonduta**, gnocchi al Castelmagno – which could have been a bit more tender – and an interesting rice dish with finferli mushrooms and burrata. You might also find a rarity like **agnolotti filled with donkey meat** in Barbera sauce or **tajarin with porcini mushrooms**. Boned quail, **brasato al Nebbiolo** and fried mushrooms are just some of the main courses, but how can one not be tempted by the succulent **finanziera**? And on Fridays you may also find a fritto misto and, if ordered in advance, bagna caoda. The desserts are all well prepared and the **cheeses** are superb. Two pages of the menu are dedicated to a detailed description of types of Piedmontese cheese; get a full tasting for 14 euros. As for wine, selections run to more than 200 labels, all very carefully selected and with fair mark-ups. In short, Fra Fiusch continues to be one of the best restaurants in the Turin area.

On the Mombercelli plain, the Barbero Astigiana Distillery, via Alessandria 154, produces excellent single-varietal grappas and other exceptionally elegant spirits.

MONCALVO

LA BELLA ROSIN ⊘

🍲 Restaurant-enoteca
Piazza Vittorio Emanuele II 3
Tel. 0141 916098
Closed Wednesday
Open: for dinner, lunch also on Saturday and Sunday
Holidays: two weeks in February
Seating: 50
Prices: 28-33 euros, wine excluded
All major credit cards except DC, Bancomat

Bella Rosin is in cozy Piazza Vittorio Emanuele, a little frequented corner far from the steep streets of Moncalvo's pretty town center. In one of the last towns in the province of Asti, bordering on the Cavalese Monferrato hills, you'll find this establishment, which is named after the wife of a Savoy king. It's a quiet place where you can savor quality food and enjoy one of the enticing labels from the cellar overseen by your host, Guarino. His selections include Piedmontese and other Italian and world wines that are not too pricey.

The kitchen turns out Monferrato specialties that spring from Mamma Rosa's lifetime of experience cooking traditional dishes. She in turn has recently passed on the baton to the younger generation. Among the antipasti you'll find cruda al coltello, **vitello tonnato** (the old lesser-known recipe without mayonnaise), Tonchese chicken in aspic, pepper flan with cream of Montèbore cheese (a Slow Food presidium), anchovies in red sauce and baccalà carpaccio. Some plates reveal a desire to innovate, but always in a modest manner. In winter there's **cardoons** and, on request, white truffles. Good first courses: **agnolotti dal plin** (also with **donkey meat** filling as is customary in the nearby village of Calliano), **tajarin with chicken livers**, gnocchi al Castelmagno and pleasant soups. For main courses there are lamb scottadito and duck breast, but the really outstanding dishes are beef cuts – brasato al Barbera and **bollito misto**.

To finish there's an excellent selection of **cheeses** and classic desserts, like **bonet**, panna cotta, stuffed peaches, hazelnut cake and sorbets made with fruit in season.

MONCHIERO
Monchiero Alto-Santuario

TRA ARTE E QUERCE

🛏️ Rooms
Via Monchiero Alto 11
Tel. 0173 792156-335 5750385
E-mail: ezioetclelia@tiscali.it
Internet: www.traarteequerce.com
Holidays: January and February

This establishment is situated in an ancient village that for half a century was the 'buen retiro' for artist Eso Peluzzi. It is located close to the 18th-century church of the Rosario with its adjacent lodgings for pilgrims. Clelia Vivalda's place is a delightful farmhouse restructured with full respect for the architectural style of the Langa region. Rooms are spacious and elegant and offer every comfort, and the communal areas are pleasant and furnished with great attention to detail. The buffet breakfast consists of honey, jams, cookies, coffee, milk, fruit and local produce (cured meats, cheeses and the local specialty, eggs flavored with truffles). There are bicycles for rent and the owners organize truffle-hunting excursions, a passion they inherited from their uncle Copa, a famous truffle hunter. You can eat lunch and dinner in the small restaurant (seating only 25) provided you book in advance. There's a menu of traditional Piedmontese dishes, with a set menu for 25 euros per person, excluding wine. You can go for long walks in the forest below, and ski resorts and spas are less than an hour's drive away.

• 6 double rooms with bathroom, fridge, satellite TV, modem connection; some with balcony • Prices: double room single use 50-60 euros, double 90-110, breakfast included • Credit cards: all, Bancomat • Facility accessible to the mobility challenged, 1 room designed for their use. Free external public parking. Small pets welcome. Owners always reachable. • Restaurant. Reading room

MONDOVÌ
Piazza

MONFORTE D'ALBA

27 KM EAST OF CUNEO ON SS 564

48 KM NORTHEAST OF CUNEO, 74 KM SOUTHEAST OF TURIN

SOCIETÀ OPERAIA DI MUTUO SOCCORSO

☞**⚷** Guest rooms
Via Vasco 8
Tel. 0174 42931-3SS80 5221763-338 8011616
E-mail: societao@socalnuovosoccorso.191.it
Open all year round

GIARDINO DA FELICIN

☞**⚷** 3-Star Hotel
Via Vallada 18
Tel. 0173 78225
Fax 0173 787377
E-mail: albrist@felicin.it
Internet: www.felicin.it
Closed in July and from end of December to beginning of February

The Società Operaia is located in the old center of Mondovì Piazza in an 18th-century building with a bar, a restaurant open for dinner if booked in advance (20-25 euros), a conference room, billiard and bridge rooms and two apartments with contemporary furnishings, completely refurbished in 2003. For an additional 2 euros you can have breakfast – a hot drink, a pastry and fruit juice – in one of the three bars on Piazza Maggiore. A pub is currently being built in the basement of the building and will also be open to non-residents. It's worth noting that there's a 10% discount for guests arriving by train or bicycle and for those who stay more than a week.

• 2 quadruples, with bathroom, fridge, kitchenette • Prices: quadruple for 1-4 persons 50-60 euros; breakfast 2 euros per person • Credit cards: none • Free external public parking. Small pets allowed. Management always contactable. • Bar, restaurant. TV room, billiard room, bridge room, lounge

This renowned Piedmontese restaurant, run by Giorgio Rocca with his wife Rosina, son Nino and daughter-in-law Silvia, has always had a few rooms on offer and recently three apartments have been added. The rooms feature old family furniture, large bathrooms and a splendid view over the Langhe hills and vineyards. Basic breakfast is included in the room price, but for a 12 euros per person supplement you can have something more substantial – really almost a lunch. At the time of booking guests may choose the half board option, which includes dinner with a great gourmet menu. A building in the historic center of Monforte with 15 new apartments has recently been added.

• 11 rooms and 18 apartments, with bathroom, fridge, safe, satellite TV • Prices: double room single occupancy 75 euros, double 80-110, apartment 90-160; breakfast included • Credit cards: all except DC, Bancomat • Off-street parking, garage (18 spaces). Small pets allowed. Reception open from 8am to midnight. • Restaurant. Outdoor area, garden

🍲 Restaurant with classic local cuisine, full meal from 28 to 49 euros, excluding wine.

MONFORTE D'ALBA

48 KM FROM CUNEO, 12 KM SOUTH OF ALBA

LA SALITA

🍲 Osteria
Via Marconi 2 A
Tel. 0173 787196
Closed Monday and Tuesday
Open: dinner; also for lunch on Sunday, but not in summer
Holidays: January through February; 1 week, end of June and end of August
Seating: 40
Prices: 26-30 euros, wine excluded
Credit cards: MC, Visa, Bancomat

La Salita is one of those places loved by Langhe winemakers. They stop off here to drink a glass, have a chat or get together with customers and friends. The merit for these visits belongs to Emilio, who, after years of following the wine trails, decided to put down roots here.

The owner has organized a wide-ranging wine list in terms of both choice and price and he never says no to pouring a glass. He's always ready to suggest just the right food to accompany your wine and also to accompany you while you enjoy it. The atmosphere is relaxed and pleasant – just like the furnishings and cuisine, which includes just a few solid dishes written up on a blackboard.

Mariangela and Ornella Scarzello put their inventiveness and respect for local customs into each dish and make particularly notable use of herbs, many of which are grown in their own garden. You'll find delicately flavored frittatas, carne cruda all'albese, **insalata di gallina**, stuffed courgette flowers, excellent vegetable flans and summer dishes like a beautifully balanced **carpione**. Try **maltagliati** and choose from a wide variety of sauces (especially those **with Roccaverano cheese and sausage**). There's also gnocchi, **tajarin** and at least one soup as well. The **rabbit** is not to be missed, but you might also try the cartoccio di salsiccia, porcini and potatoes with rosemary and the unusual **stuffed veal roulade**. Desserts like peaches with chocolate, bonet, panna cotta and the lovely **peach tart** are the perfect way to finish off your meal here.

MONTALDO DI MONDOVÌ
Corsaglia

38 KM SOUTHEAST OF CUNEO, 18 KM FROM MONDOVÌ

CORSAGLIA

🍲 Hotel-restaurant
Località Corsaglia 27
Tel. 0174 349109
Closed Tuesday
Open: lunch and dinner
Holidays: always open
Seating: 60
Prices: 22-27 euros, wine excluded
All major credit cards, Bancomat

At least two roads lead to this hamlet of just 20 or so houses. From the center of Mondovì itself you make for Torre di Mondovì and then follow the Corsaglia valley; alternatively follow the signs for the Frabosa Soprana ski slopes and then head for Bossea. The building housing the hotel-restaurant is just a short way from the center, with a stream and provincial road running on either side. Both outside and inside the building looks vaguely démodé, with the entrance through a bar where old folks play cards leads to a dining room with matchboarded walls and tables set with only the bare essentials.

Margherita, Sebastiano and Mauro serve hearty traditional dishes. You begin with **insalata russa**, **vitello tonnato**, game medallions, donkey or wild boar cured meats and carpione di trota. The first courses change often and you may well find **lasagnasse** (like whole meal wheat pizzoccheri) **al raschera**, polenta of nettles with Gorgonzola cheese and mushrooms (also served as a main course), **ravioli di magro or with meat** and potato gnocchi with meat or vegetable sauces. After this there's a roast with mushrooms, **lamb stew**, **fried frogs**, fried trout, **rabbit cooked with herbs** and substantial game dishes in winter. Desserts include bonet, stuffed peaches in summer and chestnut tarts in the fall.

There's a small but noteworthy list of bottles from the local area. Always remember to book, even during the week; that way you'll be sure the restaurant is open and that the more interesting dishes are available.

Monteu Roero
Villa Superiore

Cantina ⊘🍾
dei Cacciatori

🍲 Restaurant
Località Villa Superiore 59
Tel. 0173 90815
Closed on Monday and for lunch on Tuesday
Open: lunch and dinner
Holidays: 10 days in January, 10 in July
Seating: 45 + 25 outdoors
Prices: 23-30 euros, wine excluded
All credit cards except DC, Bancomat

Here, on the right-hand bank of the River Tanaro, the steep hills form the buttresses that are typical of the Roero area. To reach the restaurant run by the Forno family, go through the small village of Monteu Roero and continue towards Ceresole d'Alba. Bruno and his daughter-in-law Flavia run the dining room in a friendly and respectful manner, while his wife Paola and son Fabrizio coordinate the kitchen.

In the dining room or outside in the courtyard in summer you can enjoy traditional dishes from two set menus or eat à la carte. In summer we recommend the **carpionata** and **l'albese di fassone** with a delicate anchovy sauce. Always available: vegetable **flans** accompanied by fonduta or, in summer, diced tomatoes. First course dishes include **tajarin with Bra sausage** or mushrooms, **ravioli**, potato gnocchi and risottos, either classic or al brut with egg yolk, endive and Gruyère cheese or pumpkin flowers and stracchino cheese. Among the main courses there's rabbit cooked in white wine, but also accompanied by garitole or olives, **shank of veal** cooked in wine or with hazelnuts and tripe all'Arneis. In spring or summer try the **fried Ceresole tench**. On the long list of desserts you'll certainly find something you like: maybe stuffed peaches or hazelnut cake with an excellent **zabaione al Marsala**, white chocolate semifreddo or even an unusual apricot-flavored bonet or darmassin (a local variety of plum) compote with lingue di gatto. In the fall the sumptuous cheeses reappear and include about twenty carefully selected cheeses.There's a good wine list offering the best of the Langhe and Roero area production and various labels from outside the region.

Morano sul Po
Due Sture

Tre Merli

🍲 Trattoria
Via Dante 18
Tel. 0142 85275
Always open
Open: lunch and dinner
Holidays: between Christmas and Epiphany
Seating: 40 + 15 outdoors
Prices: 24-26 euros, wine excluded
No credit cards accepted

You can reach Morano sul Po from Casale Monferrato along the main road to Turin. On reaching the town, the turn for Due Sture is on the right. Here, you'll find a village surrounded by paddy fields. Massimo Bobba and his wife Elena offer a simple yet warm welcome to this classic country inn. Local history is proudly displayed on the walls in period photographs of village inhabitants.

Tre Merli is a small place off the beaten track where booking is not only recommended but absolutely essential, especially if you want to try dishes featuring frogs and snails – ingredients that are not easy to procure. The small paddy-field **frogs** are eaten whole and are served with zingy salsa verde, breaded or fried in frittatas. The traditional Vercelli risotto, **panissa,** is always available and served **with beans and salam d' la doja** (a salami stuffed in cow intestines covered with melted lard). The menu combines dishes typical of Monferrato and Vercelli and follows the seasons. In spring and summer, you can order freshwater fish and vegetables **in carpione**, vegetable pies, asparagus cooked in various ways, **ravioli di magro, roast rabbit** or duck. In winter be sure to get the classic agnolotti, **cotechino with polenta,** verze in bagna caoda and pork shank. You and six or seven of your friends can dig into the inimitable fritto misto piemontese – as long as you reserve it ahead of time. Elena makes all the desserts herself. There's apple crostata, **chocolate salame,** bonet, bavarese alla frutta or al caffè.

The wine list is fairly good, with bottles from Casale Monferrato and the Langhe.

LA CANTINA DEL RONDÒ

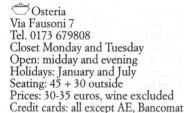Osteria
Via Fausoni 7
Tel. 0173 679808
Closet Monday and Tuesday
Open: midday and evening
Holidays: January and July
Seating: 45 + 30 outside
Prices: 30-35 euros, wine excluded
Credit cards: all except AE, Bancomat

HOTEL VILLA LAURI

3-Star Hotel
Via Fausoni 7
Tel. 0173 679874
Fax 0173 678141
E-mail: info@hotelvillalauri.com
Internet: www.hotelvillalauri.com
Closed for two weeks in the winter

In their pretty osteria at Rondò di Neive, accomplished hosts Emanuela e Francarlo serve truly authentic Langa cooking. All ingredients are sourced from trusted producers (apart from the vegetables, which they grow themselves, and the wines, which they make themselves), and all are organic. Emanuela and Francarlo's approach is not simply to 'reproduce' classics (though, when they do, they invariably add an extra touch, as in the case of the **tajarin with farmyard chicken livers and sausage** in mountain butter, and **raviole del plin**), but seek constantly to highlight unusual, stimulating aspects. Witness their most recent passion offal and innards – which gives rise to dishes such as **pig's snout in carpione**, tripe with fava beans and peas, **frisse** and **minestrone of tripe**. The menu, which changes with the seasons, reads like an anthology of peasant civilization (which Francarlo sees as a sort of golden age of cooking). In the 35 euro set menu (two antipasti, first, second, dessert) or à la carte, you'll find cured meats, **anchovies**, insalata russa, vegetable flans and **vitel tuné**. Pastas, including gnocchi and lasagnette, are followed by a varied array of mains, such as **roast bullock**, loin of pork with hazelnuts, **free-range cockerel in red wine,** or alla cacciatora, stewed shin of beef, rabbits and guinea fowl, **lamb cutlets** and kid. In season, of course, strictly local mushrooms and truffles also come into play.

To accompany your meal, a special 'house wine' formula: Arneis, Tocai del Collio, Barbera and Barbaresco selected and aged on the premises and aged in carafes.

You'll find this charming hotel in a recently restored late-19th-century villa just outside the medieval hill town of Neive. The spacious rooms are fitted with classic furniture and fine fabrics; the suites also have a private balcony with view of the vineyards. Breakfast is served in an elegant room next to the scenic terrace, where they will soon be creating a winter garden. There's a vast choice of sweet and savory fare, from cakes and jams to cured meats and several types of local cheese.

• 9 double rooms and 2 junior suites, with bathroom, fridge, satellite TV, modem connection; some rooms with air-conditioning • Prices: double room single use 80-100 euros, double 100-120, junior suite 120-140, breakfast included • Credit cards: all except AE, Bancomat • 7 rooms accessible for the mobility challenged. Off-street parking. Small pets allowed. Reception open from 7.30am to midnight. • Bar. Breakfast room. Terrace

LA CONTEA

🔑1-Star Hotel
Piazza Cocito 8
Tel. 0173 67126
Fax 0173 677558
E-mail: lacontea@la-contea.it
Internet: www.la-contea.it
Closed in February and 1 week at Christmas

PALAZZO DEMARIA

🔑Bed and breakfast
Via Demaria 19-21
Tel. 0173 677724-338 3894110
Fax 0173 677991
E-mail: info@palazzodemaria.it
Internet: www.palazzodemaria.it
Open between Easter and New Year's Eve

La Contea is located in a fine 15th-century palazzo with a charming annex, located in a small square close by the castle. It only has one star because of the size of the reception, but the quiet, well-furnished rooms are of a higher standard, as are the common areas like the dining rooms with decorated ceilings and romantic fireplaces. Upon arrival you'll be greeted by members of the Verro family – Tonino, who takes care of the restaurant and the Cinciallegra wine cellar, and his wife Claudia Francalanci who manages their farm – with a welcome aperitivo and snacks. The sweet and savory breakfast includes a wide range of choices. The restaurant can also be used as a conference room. Half board ranges from 80-90 euros per person, excluding wine.

• 22 double rooms, with bathroom, fridge, TV • Prices: double room single occupancy 55-70 euros, double 72-90, breakfast included • Credit cards: all, Bancomat • 2 rooms designed for use by the mobility challenged. Free external public parking, garage (1 space). Small pets allowed. Reception open from 7.30am to midnight • Bar, restaurant, wine cellar. Breakfast room. Garden

Palazzo Demaria stands in front of the castle, next to the arch of San Rocco, which marks the entrance to the historic center of Neive. The 16th-century building has its own park within the ancient town walls: 1,600 square meters of grounds, with centuries-old trees. It's as elegant as the palazzo's interior, furnished with antiques, paintings, beautiful carpets and other treasures. Maria Giunipero serves a breakfast with sweet and savory foods, prepared from family recipes. Guests stay in luxurious suites, and have access to a swimming pool and a Finnish sauna. The hosts also organize various activities in which guests can participate, like bridge, cooking and stretching.

• 3 suites, with bathroom, walk-in wardrobe, fridge • Prices: suite 120 euros, breakfast included • Credit cards: none • Parking very close by, garage (5 euros per day). No pets allowed. Owners always present • Breakfast room. Games room. TV room. Library. Grounds. Pool, sauna

🍲 Thanks to its careful reinterpretations of local cuisine, the restaurant (28-63 euros, excluding wine) is considered a classic in the Langa area.

NIZZA MONFERRATO

27 KM SOUTHEAST OF ASTI

LE DUE LANTERNE 🍶

🍲 Restaurant
Piazza Garibaldi 52
Tel. 0141 702480
Closed Monday evening and Tuesday
Open: lunch and dinner
Holidays: July 20-August 10
Seating: 80
Prices: 28-35 euros, wine excluded
All major credit cards, Bancomat

This restaurant in Piazza Garibaldi is a landmark for people seeking traditional Piedmontese cuisine served with a touch of sophistication and prices in keeping with the quality (the set menu at 28 euros brings you four antipasti, two first courses, two main courses and dessert). The rooms are maybe a bit too standardized as far as furnishings go, but service is highly professional under the guidance of owner Luca Ivaldi, who pays the same attention to the wine list. The emphasis here with regard to the latter is on Barbera and Monferrato labels, but other Italian wines are also available as well as a selection of international varieties.
Be sure to check out the specials, since these reflect seasonal produce. The spring menu opens with **vitello tonnato**, stuffed peppers, **insalata russa**, **carne cruda**, insalata di galletto, courgette flan and asparagus crepes with melted cheese, while winter dishes include **cardo gobbo** flan or **with bagna caoda**. The **agnolotti dal plin with gravy**, butter and sage or al ragù are excellent. Green gnocchetti with sausage, tajarin with asparagus, risottos or pasta e fagioli are equally fine alternatives. Main courses include **stracotto alla Barbera**, roasted veal shank, guinea fowl, rabbit cooked in white wine and duck with sweet and sour sauce. **Bollito**, **fritto misto** and **finanziera** are available if you order ahead.
Classic desserts to end the meal include semifreddo al torrone, bonet with chocolate or chestnuts, stuffed peaches and rum pastries.

NIZZA MONFERRATO
San Nicolao

28 KM SOUTHEAST OF ASTI ON SR 456

CASCINA MONSIGNOROTTI

🔑 Holiday farm
Regione San Nicolao
Tel. e fax 0141 721100
E-mail: info@monsignorotti.it
Internet: www.monsignorotti.it
Open all year round

This farmhouse surrounded by vineyards has been renovated by owners Marisa and Carlo Lacqua, creating a holiday farm that's a great destination for anyone who loves the outdoors. The theme is wine, from the views of rows of vines to the names of the rooms: Barbera, Moscato, Cortese, Chardonnay. The hearty farmhouse-style breakfast includes bread, cured meats, cheeses, seasonal fruits and wine. From the center of Nizza follow the signs for Acqui Terme, then make a right turn straight after the railway station and drive up San Nicolao hill. It's possible to rent the apartment by the week for 500 euros.

• 1 single and 7 double rooms, with bathroom, TV; 1 apartment (4-6 persons) with kitchenette • Prices: single 40-50 euros, double 60-70, apartment 35 euros per person, breakfast included • All major credit cards, Bancomat • 1 room designed for the mobility challenged. Off-street parking. Small pets allowed. Owners always present. • Wine-tasting room. Breakfast room. Garden, terrace

NIZZA MONFERRATO   NOVELLO

VINERIA DELLA SIGNORA IN ROSSO

Osteria
Via Crova 2
Tel. 0141 793350
Closed Monday and Tuesday
Open: dinner, lunch also on Saturday and Sunday
Holidays: July
Seating: 40 + 50 outdoors
Prices: 20-25 euros, wine excluded
All credit cards, Bancomat

ABBAZIA IL ROSETO

Bed and breakfast
Via Roma 38
Tel. 0173 744016-328 7654370
Fax 0173 744016
E-mail: info@abbaziailroseto.com
Internet: www.abbaziailroseto.com
Closed in January

Originally a wine bar, the Signora in Rosso has come a long way, thanks to the hard work of owner Tullio Mussa, in promoting the wine production of Nizza and the surrounding hills. This is one of the best viniculture areas in Piedmont, with long wine producing traditions and a hallmark product, the excellent Barbera, now complete with Nizza's denomination of origin recognition. What's more, the rediscovery of the **cardo gobbo**, a local variety of cardoon, owes a great deal to this osteria, which offers it with the classic **bagna caoda** and in many other ways when it is in season.
Cristiano runs the osteria with great skill and enthusiasm, while his father works in the kitchen. His expert hands produce superb local dishes like **carne cruda** with anchovies and green and red bagnèt, **agnolotti,** gnocchi, tajarin, pasta e fagioli, and **chickpea and spare rib soup**. Among the main courses, **pork chops alla Barbera** is one of the osteria's classics, along with **roast kid**, **rabbit** and chicken alla cacciatora. There are also carefully selected cured meats from all over Italy. The **cheeses** live up to the high standard here as well, with selections of typical Piedmontese and other cheeses. Excellent traditional desserts to finish.
Remember that on November 4, the day honoring San Carlo, Nizza Monferrato holds a bagna caoda marathon dedicated to the town's symbolic dish.

This B&B run by Anna Demichelis is in a well renovated 16th-century abbey surrounded by vineyards. The bright, basic rooms line a corridor with high plaster ceilings: each room has a bathroom en suite, a fireplace and personalized antique Piedmontese-style furnishings. The buffet breakfast consists of various types of beverage and sweet and savory fare served in the room that was once the abbey's kitchen. From the garden equipped with tables and chairs for relaxation you can enjoy a beautiful view of Monviso. Common areas include a reading room and a billiard room, which are currently being renovated and are not open to the public.

• 4 double and 2 triple rooms, with bathroom • Prices: double room single use 60 euros, double 75, triple 95, breakfast included • Credit cards: none • Facility partially accessible for the mobility challenged. Off-street parking with video surveillance. No pets allowed. Owners always reachable. • Breakfast room. Garden with solarium. Small gym

At Via Maestra 45, you'll find Marabotti, where delicious amaretti, baci di dama and soft torrone are made.

NOVELLO

AL CASTELLO DA DIEGO

3-Star Hotel
Piazza Marconi 4
Tel. 0173 744502
Fax 0173 731250
E-mail: info@castellodinovello.com
Internet: www.castellodinovello.com
Closed from December 20 to March 15 and 1 week in summer

The hotel occupies a singular neo-Gothic style castle surrounded by greenery and situated in a panoramic spot on the hill of Novello. From here the view takes in the surrounding hills and in the distance, the Alps. Rooms and suites all have antique furnishings, are comfortable and have direct access to the large terrace, which can also be used as a solarium. Buffet breakfast includes coffee and light refreshments, fruit juices, sweet fare such as jams and excellent hazelnut cakes, and savories such as cured meats and cheeses. Novello is a good base for excursions in the hills as well as for gastronomic and wine-tasting itineraries: Barolo is just 4 kilometers away, Alba.

• 7 double rooms and 3 suites (1-4 persons), with bathroom, fridge, safe, satellite TV • Prices: double room single use 80 euros, double 93, suite 135-180, breakfast included • Credit cards: all, Bancomat • Communal areas accessible to the mobility challenged. Off-street parking. Small pets allowed. Owners always reachable. • Restaurant under separate management. Breakfast room. small lounge with corner bar, fridge for beverages, wine, ice cream and a coffee machine. Garden, terrace

OLEGGIO

IL GATTO E LA VOLPE

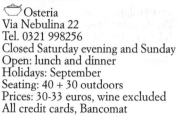

Osteria
Via Nebulina 22
Tel. 0321 998256
Closed Saturday evening and Sunday
Open: lunch and dinner
Holidays: September
Seating: 40 + 30 outdoors
Prices: 30-33 euros, wine excluded
All credit cards, Bancomat

In the center of Oleggio, just a short walk from the car park and from a breathtaking view over the Novara plain, Daniele Bonini's inn is known for its traditional dishes. In the attractive dining hall with its open fire or out on the terrace in summer, you will be served by the patron and his daughter Arianna, while wife Mercede and son Alessandro work in the kitchens.

The menu changes often depending on seasons and what's available, with special attention paid to methodically prepared local produce. There's a buffet of antipasti to start, with vegetables cooked in numerous ways, **carne cruda** in pastry or chopped, **nervetti salad,** stuffed peppers, **tongue in parsley sauce,** cotechino, cheese mousse, pumpkin flowers and insalata russa. First courses include **agnolotti** with butter and sage or **with gravy from the roast,** tagliatelle al Gorgonzola and pumpkin flowers, lasagne and the typical Novara **paniscia** with salami and vegetables. Meat reigns supreme for main courses. Particularly excellent: **roast veal shoulder** and a tender ossobuco with peas. A wide selection of Piedmontese cheeses are served with locally produced honey. For dessert, try the pear tart, **bonet,** panna cotta or gelato with wild berries.

The osteria's wine cellar is well worth a visit: you'll find open brickwork and an abundant selection of labels from northern Piedmont, Italy and France. The mark-up is minimal and, although an official wine list is not printed, wines will be recommended to go with the dishes you have chosen.

Olivola

La Presidenta

🍴 Holiday farm
Via Vittorio Veneto 23
Tel. 0142 928294
Fax 0142 928086
Closed in January and for two weeks in August

La Presidenta was once the 18th-century country seat of the Callori Counts: a large recently replastered villa at the bottom of a private tree-lined road. The rooms are spacious and fitted with period furniture, all essential comforts and brand-new bathrooms. Outside there is a large garden and a terrace that offers a magnificent panorama over the surrounding hills. Breakfast is traditional, with bread, butter and jam, hot drinks and fruit juices. Your two young hosts, Luca Bevilacqua and Emanuele Monzeglio, prepare the meals personally, drawing on their previous experience in restaurants in the Monferrato and Asti areas (a meal costsfrom 35-40 euros, excluding wine). Interesting visits to historic wine cellars.

• 1 single and 3 double rooms, with bathroom, air-conditioning, TV • Prices: single 50 euros, double 80-100, breakfast included • Credit cards: all, Bancomat • 1 room designed for use by the mobility challenged. Off-street parking. Small pets allowed. Owners always reachable. • Restaurant. Conference room. Garden, terrace

Orio Canavese

Barba Toni

🍲 Restaurant
Via Torino 9
Tel. 011 9898085
Closed Sunday evening and Monday
Open: lunch and dinner
Holidays: 3 weeks in August, 1 week in January
Seating: 30 + 30 outdoors
Prices: 25-30 euros, wine excluded
All major credit cards, Bancomat

On the Turin-Aosta road, exit at San Giorgio and continue towards Caluso until you reach the turn-off for Orio on the left. The restaurant is located in the center of the village, in a courtyard with parking where, in summer, you can sit outside in the shade. It is a very tastefully furnished, discreet and quiet place to stop and there is no doubting the passion Alain and his wife Sara put into their work, starting with the warm welcome they offer all their guests and the joyful manner with which they describe the dishes. Just take the amazing variety of **cheeses** from Valchiusella, which are very carefully selected and varied throughout the year, or the extensive wine list, with its excellent labels and very reasonable mark-ups.
The same care and passion goes into the genuine manner they prepare dishes using only local produce. The guiding theme in the menu remains constant but changes with the season. For example there is a menu dedicated entirely to **mushrooms** with the odd freshwater fish popping up. For antipasti, there's marinated filet of Piedmontese veal, river prawn and walnut salad, **polenta with stewed porcini mushrooms, stuffed courgette flowers**. Follow this with **risotto** all'**Erbaluce with eel**, **agnolotti di brasato al Nebbiolo** with butter and thyme, tagliolini al radicchio, mocetta and walnuts. Among the main courses, there is excellent **salmon trout** from Valchiusella served with sage, breadcrumbed and fried porcini mushrooms, **veal sirloin al Carema**. Get the exquisite zabaglione with Caluso raisins and wild berries for dessert – but there might also be bonet and excellent fresh figs and fig ice cream and a lot more besides.

IL BORGO

Restaurant
Via Roma 120
Tel. 0174 391049
Closed Monday and Tuesday, never in August
Open: lunch and dinner
Holidays: vary
Seating: 35
Prices: 22-25 euros, wine excluded
No credit cards accepted

VILLA PINUS

Bed and breakfast
Viale Piaggio 33
Tel. 0174 392248-348 6701878
Fax 0174 392248
E-mail: marco.costalla@libero.it
Open from May to October

This time-honored restaurant in the historic center of Ormea is highly appreciated for its loyalty to the cuisine of the upper Tanaro valley, that corner of Piedmont that borders on Liguria. It offers unusual cuisine, based on mountain produce – potatoes, buckwheat, pulses – which all go to create some very original, tasty dishes.

To begin, there are numerous antipasti, served in a sequence of small portions: **tultea** (ravioli stuffed with herbs), **bruss**, **fozza** (flat bread with lardo), **panizza** (chickpea polenta), buckwheat polenta with bagna caoda, leek flan with creamed peas (or with fonduta), various frittatas. You can then choose from first courses, such as the **Ormea agnolotti** stuffed with potatoes and seasoned with rosemary and pine nuts, **tajarin** with nettle sauce, **buckwheat polenta** served in various ways and cornmeal pappardelle with mushrooms. The main courses are all worth a try: there's stewed venison and **bocconcini di vitello with Taggiasca olives, rabbit with thyme**, beef in aspic and stewed lamb. Conclude your meal with some of the local cheeses or perhaps **potato cassata** (a sort of gelato cake), blackcurrant mousse, cooked cream with wild berry sauce, jam tarts or fresh fruit cooked in grappa.

The wine list is short but excellent, with Piedmont and Liguria labels.

In the small capital of the upper Val Tanaro (at an altitude of 750 meters, on one of the roads linking the Cuneo area to the Ligurian coast), Marco Costalla runs this B&B which, on request, now also offers half board and full board options. It's a prestigious place, an early 20th-century villa (arriving from Ceva you'll find it on your right, just before entering Ormea) that has retained its Art Nouveau architecture and furnishings, and has secular pine trees in the grounds. The rooms are comfortable and very well furnished. The traditional breakfast comprising sweet and savory fare is served in one of the rooms on the ground floor or, on request, in your own room. Imperia, Albenga and the seaside resorts on the Riviera are less than three quarters of an hour away by car, though the Maritime Alps are much closer and there you can enjoy winter sports or go on nature hikes in all seasons.

• 4 double rooms, with bathroom, TV • Prices: double room single use 35 euros, double 50, breakfast included • Credit cards: none • Facility accessible to the mobility challenged. Off-street parking. Small pets allowed. Owners always reachable. • Corner bar. Breakfast room, lounge. Grounds

45 KM NORTHWEST OF NOVARA   39 KM NORTHWEST OF CUNEO, 7 KM SOUTHWEST OF SALUZZO

SANTA CATERINA   LA CANONICA

3-Star Hotel
Via Marconi 10
Tel. 0322 915865
Fax 0322 90377
E-mail: orta@email.it
Internet: www.orta.net/s.caterina
Open from April to October

Bed and breakfast
Via Provinciale 20
Tel. 0175 76333-338 1393145
Fax 0175 76333
E-mail: info@lacanonicadipagno.it
Internet: www.lacanonicadipagno.it
Open all year

Lake Orta been called the most romantic of the Alpine lakes and this, a place that has inspired superb pages of literature, certainly does have a magic all its own. Located in a street crossing the main road at the entrance to the village arriving from Gozzano, this recently refurbished building has various types of rooms, suites and common areas furnished with taste. In addition there's a lakeside villa 400 meters from the main facility, with different sized apartments that have balconies or gardens. The same management has other apartments in the old center of town and one more located on the hill of the Sacro Monte. The buffet-style breakfast is served in one of the rooms in the hotel, while main meals are served in the Olina restaurant (Via Olina 40, in the historic center). Moreover, every afternoon guests are offered coffee, tea and homemade cakes in the snack area.

• 28 double or triple rooms and 2 suites, with bathroom (the suites have jacuzzis), satellite TV; 7 apartments (for 2, 4 or 6 persons) with kitchen • Prices: double room single use 45-50 euros, double 58-75, triple 70-85, suite 85-100, apartments 145-220; breakfast 7 euros per person • Credit cards: all, Bancomat • 2 rooms designed for use by the mobility challenged. Free garage parking. Small pets allowed. Reception open from 7 am to midnight. • Breakfast room, lounge, snack corner. Garden

This vicarage dating from the 18th-century is a little gem of history and good taste. Part of it is used by the new owners, Daniela Gerbino and her husband Robert, and the other part has been organized as a B&B. There are spacious rooms furnished in a way that reflects the style of the original building. Before you enter the property there are two splendid gardens, one with a gazebo in the center and a unique 'reading house' built in a very old tree. Breakfast is served in the main room among antiques and a beautiful table on which you'll find exquisite sweet and savory fare. A swimming pool and sauna are under construction.

• 3 double rooms and 1 suite, with bathroom, satellite TV • Prices: double room single use 42 euros, double 55 (25 euro supplement for extra bed), suite 65, breakfast included • Credit cards: major ones, Bancomat • Off-street parking and free external public parking. Small pets allowed. Owners always present • Breakfast room, reading room with Internet access. Courtyard, gardens

PAGNO

LOCANDA DEL CENTRO 🍷

☞ Restaurant
Via Caduti della Liberazione 2
Tel. 0175 76140
Closed Wednesday, Thursday at lunchtime
Open: lunch and dinner
Holidays: 15 days in January, 1 week from August 15
Seating: 60 + 60 outdoors
Prices: 23-25 euros, wine excluded
All credit cards

The diminutive village of Pagno is just a few miles from Saluzzo and is built around the Abbey of Saints Peter and Colombano, which contains a series of important frescoes. When you are here you might also take time off to enjoy a pleasant walk through the woods in Val Bronda or relax at Gemma Lamberti and Marco Negri's restaurant. The Locanda is lovely and offers efficient, courteous service. There's a large patio for dining al fresco in summer.

For antipasto, try the classic **girello di vitello** with toumin del Mel. In the summer the focus is on freshness, with vegetable rolls in puff pastry, chicken salad with valerian, balsamic vinegar and hard-boiled eggs. The first and main courses are the real highlights, pointing up the quality of the fresh ingredients used to make them. We liked the **agnolotti dal plin** stuffed with meat and vegetables and the maltagliati made from chestnut flour with trout and cherry tomato sauce. There are also **tajarin** and a variety of risottos with **mushrooms,** when they are in season. Choose from **roast rabbit,** roast beef, **roast shoulder of veal** and pork with passito to follow. To conclude your meal, local cheeses or desserts such as stuffed peaches, grappa cream and hazelnut gelato cake with chocolate.

The extensive wine list offers labels from all over Italy.

🍯 At Marco Soleri's farm, via Romani 7, you can buy honey and ramassin (damsons) from the Val Bronda.

PAMPARATO
Serra

RESIDENZA PIETRABRUNA

🔑 Bed and breakfast
Via Chiesa 36 A
Tel. 0174 351268-45041 or 338 5609905
E-mail: pietrabruna3@virgilio.it
Open all year round

Pamparato is a mountain village in the Mondovì area, famous for its Raschera cheese and for the Festival of the Saracens, dedicated to early music. Here, just a few hundred meters from the San Giacomo di Roburent skiing facilities. This is where Giovanna Ferrua restructured the small building that was once the family hotel's dining room, closed in the 80s, to create this small B&B located. Rooms are pleasant and furnished with local antiques, but it's breakfast that deserves a special mention. Giovanna makes you focaccia, tarts, chocolate and almond cakes, ramassìn (damsons), peach, apple and cherry jams, and she'll not let you go without tasting the paste di meliga, or corn pastries (a Slow Food Presidia), milk, tea and coffee, and acacia, chestnut and millefiori honey.

• 1 single and 2 double rooms, with bathroom, TV; terrace • Prices: single 30-35 euros, double 52-60, breakfast included • Credit cards: none • 1 room designed for use by the mobility challenged. Off-street parking, some covered. Small pets allowed. Owners always reachable • Breakfast room. Garden, terrace

PEVERAGNO
Santa Margherita

PINEROLO

11 KM SOUTHEAST OF CUNEO

37 KM SOUTHEAST OF TURIN ON SS 23 OR SS 589

CASCINA LA COMMENDA

REGINA

🗝️🔑Holiday farm
Frazione Santa Margherita 16
Tel. e fax 0171 385351
E-mail: cpeano@tiscalinet.it
Internet: www.paginegialle.it/cascinalacommenda
Open all year round

🗝️🔑3-Star Hotel
Piazza Barbieri 22
Tel. 0121 322157
Fax 0121 393133
E-mail: info@albergoregina.net
Internet: www.albergoregina.net
Closed first 15 days of August

Just a few kilometers from Cuneo, near the imposing Mount Bisalta, Mariangela and Claudia Peano have recently opened this agriturismo and have thus made their father's dream come true. He, Michele, had rented the surrounding land for a long time before managing to buy the most important farmhouse in the entire hamlet. The building has recently been refurbished and divided into nine rooms located on two levels, a lounge with a small library, and a fitness area equipped with sauna, jacuzzi and a small gym. The rooms are simple but offer every comfort; the buffet breakfasts consist of home-made cakes and jams, fruit preserves, cured meats and local cheeses. Let your hosts advise on possible itineraries in the upper Pesio Valley.

• 5 single and 4 double rooms, with bathroom, fridge, TV, modem connection, 4 rooms with air-conditioning, 3 with kitchenette • Prices: single 35 euros, double 50-60 (10-20 euro supplement for extra bed); breakfast 3-5 euros per person • Credit cards: major ones, Bancomat • Common area and 1 room designed for use by the mobility challenged. Off-street covered parking. Small pets allowed. Owners always reachable. • Breakfast room. Reading room. Sauna, gym

In the 19th-century, what is now Hotel Regina was a staging post where people changed carriages on their way to France. Today the building fits in perfectly with the architecture of Piazza Barbieri. It was purchased from the Rissolo family in 1927 and Michele, who has been managing it since the 80s, represents the third generation of his family to do so. There are only a few rooms, furnished classically and with every comfort, including a free ADSL Internet connection. On the ground floor there's the restaurant where the buffet breakfast is laid out. This consists of hot and cold beverages, home-made cakes, jams, cereals, cured meats and cheeses. The cuisine draws inspiration from Piedmontese tradition and guests may also opt for half board (ranging from 62-73 euros per person) or full board.

• 8 single and 7 double rooms, with bathroom, mini-bar, satellite TV, modem connection, some rooms with safe • Prices: single 54 euros, double 80, double single use 65, double 80; breakfast 7.70 euros per person • Credit cards: all, Bancomat • Communal areas accessible for the mobility challenged. Off-street parking and paid external parking. Small pets allowed. Reception open from 6.30 am to midnight. • Bar, restaurant. Small lounge. Small conference room

PINO TORINESE

PIODE

PINO TORINESE

GIARDINI

3-Star Hotel
Via Roma 34
Tel. 011 843404
Fax 011 842655
E-mail: info@hotelpinotorinese.it
Internet: www.hotelpinotorinese.it
Closed for 3 weeks in August

Restaurant/3-Star Hotel
Via Umberto I 9
Tel. 0163 71157-71135
Fax 0163 71135
E-mail: ristorantegiardini@virgilio.it
Internet: www.ristorantegiardini.it
Closed Monday, never in summer
Open: lunch and dinner
Holidays: first 2 weeks of September
Seating: 40 + 15 outdoors
Prices: 25-30 euros, wine excluded
All major credit cards, Bancomat

The hotel is housed in a beautiful, completely refurbished 19th-century building on the main street in Pino Torinese. There is a second entrance in Via Molina, right in front of the park. Originally it was called Albergo Nazionale con Stallaggio, a name that evokes carriages and change of horses (Pino Torinese was a popular vacation spot). Now the stables have become a parking facility for the hotel's patrons. Even though the rooms were modernized by owner Renato Ferrauto in 1994, they still evoke an atmosphere of days gone by. They have rustic furniture and all possible comforts, some have air-conditioning and two rooms are reserved for non-smokers. The buffet breakfast is prepared using quality products.

This 19th-century former post office now offers self-catering accommodation (open all week). The rooms, with country-style furniture and all modern conveniences as well as cooking facilities, are studio apartments that sleep two or four. Food at the restaurant is prepared using local produce. Start off with cured meats like lamb prosciutto with herbs, lardo and **mocetta**, **caponet from Valsesia** with fonduta, gratin of zucchini flowers and smoked trout. Besides the **risottos**, including one with **Gattinara wine**, there are fresh pastas like **ravioli with roast beef** and borage and baci di Piode (spinach and ricotta gnocchi). If you see it on the menu, you should definitely order the **river trout with butter and sage**, but there are also meat options, including veal with Toma and porcini mushrooms, herbed rabbit saddle and, when in season, **venison** with polenta. Cheeses include Alpine Toma from local dairies but save room for the wild strawberry cake or millefeuille with Moscato cream sauce.
Owner Mauro Alberti's wine cellar contains 250 labels featuring wines from Gattinara and Novara producers.

• 7 double rooms, with bathroom, terrace, mini-bar, safe, TV • Prices: double room single use 60 euros, double 70; breakfast 5 euros per person (included in the room price for Saturday and Sunday overnight stays) • Credit cards: all except DC, Bancomat • Off-street covered parking (8 spaces, 5 euros a day). No pets allowed. Reception open from 7.30 am to 8.30 pm. • Bar. Breakfast room. Garden, terrace

• 9 double rooms and 2 quadruples with bath, mini-bar, satellite TV, modem connection, cooking facilities; some with balcony • Prices: double room single use 48, double 60, quadruple 70 euros, breakfast included • Common areas and 5 rooms accessible to mobility challenged. Free external public parking. Small pets welcome. Owners always present • Bar, restaurant. Terrace

PORTACOMARO
Cornapò

BANDINI

⌒Restaurant
Via Cornapò 135
Tel. 0141 299252
Closed Monday
Open: lunch and dinner
Holidays: in January
Seating: 40 + 25 outdoors
Prices: 25-30 euros, wine excluded
All major credit cards, Bancomat

At Bandini (the name comes from the hero in John Fante's novels) in the countryside just outside Asti, regular customers always find something new and passing visitors can count on tasty traditional dishes from the area and exceptional value. In the dining room Antonella Bera offers courteous service and dispenses a fine assortment of regional and national wines (some also served by the glass), while in the kitchen Massimo Rivetti, without deviating from the high road of tradition, successfully experiments with ideas like smoking and marinating salmon. In addition to ordering à la carte you can choose one of two set menus: one presents personal recipes that include some fish dishes (**brandade di baccalà**, octopus carpaccio, risotto with squid, sea bream filet) and the other focuses on typical Piedmontese dishes. In both cases the price is reasonable: 25 and 29 euros, excluding wine, for a full meal.

For antipasti, we recommend carne cruda, the rosy and tender **vitello tonnato**, pilchard or **eel in carpione**, rabbit tonno, warm tripe and pepper salad and tasty **marinated testina**. Pastas include agnolotti alla piemontese, **tajarin with mushrooms** and maltagliati and beans. There's a very light merluzzo al verde, **rabbit in white wine**, fried porcini mushrooms, **tripe** and bollito misto (in winter), all of which bow to tradition, as well as beef chops or donkey cheek with polenta. Last but not least, choose from the worthwhile selection of local cheeses and desserts, including **vanilla gelato with spiced oranges** (our favorite), bonet, warm chocolate cake and hazelnut cake with zabaglione.

PRATO SESIA

CASTELLO

⌒Trattoria
Piazza Marconi 3
Tel. 0163 852149
Closed Wednesday
Open: lunch and dinner
Holidays: 2-3 weeks in August, first week of November
Seating: 60
Prices: 20-25 euros
All major credit cards, Bancomat

Situated under the shade of a ruined castle that used to guard the entrance to Valsesia, this trattoria has been in business for over 40 years. The grandfather of the present owners opened what resembles a tavern of bygone days. A glass panel separates the entrance from the trattoria proper, which is divided into two rooms. The walls are lined with racks stacked with bottles – a good selection of Gattinara, Ghemme and Coste della Sesia wines, in addition to other good Piedmontese labels. The wine list also includes wines by the glass and Biella's Menabrea beer.

Elena takes care of service while Massimo runs the kitchen with Paolo, the other young partner. Dishes change weekly depending on what they're selling in the market: the Gorgonzola is from Prato and the other cheeses and meats are from Valsesia. On our last visit we tasted a **mocetta** lightly spiced with **frachet**, a fresh cheese dressed with walnut oil, and a version of **tongue in salsa verde** with grilled peppers. Not to be missed: Val Vigezzo raw ham, zucchini pie and Venere rice salad. Among the first courses try the excellent **risotto with porcini mushrooms**, **gnocchetti di castagne**, pear and ricotta ravioloni with Gorgonzola fonduta, **tagliatelle al ragù and finferli mushrooms**. To follow there's **trout**, rabbit, scottata di puledro (sautéed foal meat) and an original dish, maialino rosolato al tabacco toscano, suckling pig sautéed in Tuscan tobacco. The cheese selection is serviceable; desserts range from lavender-scented crème brûlée to semifreddo di croccante and ratafià. The set menu costs 20 euros (10 euros for lunch, including wine).

RACCONIGI

CASALE

⚓ Bed and breakfast
Corso Regina Elena 1
Tel. 0172 86479-348 8823238
Fax 0172 86479
E-mail: serena.casale@libero.it
Closed in August

Racconigi is in the extreme north of the province of Cuneo on the main Turin-Cuneo road and is famous for its Savoy castle with its magnificent grounds, now State property (both can be visited). Just a short distance away from the entrance to the castle, on the first floor of a large building that was once a royal hunting lodge, this splendid b&b is run by Giuliana Casale and her daughter Serena, an architect. It boasts a large courtyard, a lovely lounge and rooms furnished in a subdued and elegant manner: one of them has Louis-Phillippe furniture, another is Art Nouveau in style and the third has been eclectically furnished and painted by Serena. The breakfast, served in silverware, is sumptuous and includes jams and crêpes made by Serena and Giuliana, as well as savories on request.

• 3 double rooms with adjacent bathrooms, terrace, TV • Prices: double room single use 35 euros, double 50-60, breakfast included • Credit cards: none • Off-street parking, with surveillance. Small pets allowed. Owners always present. • Breakfast room, lounge. Garden

ROBILANTE

LEON D'ORO   ⊛

🍲 Restaurant
Piazza Olivero 10
Tel. 0171 78679
Closed Wednesday
Open: lunch and dinner
Holidays: 1 week at end September, 2 weeks after Carnival
Seating: 50 + 15 outdoors
Prices: 25-28 euros, wine excluded
All credit cards, Bancomat

Robilante is about 20 kilometers from the French border, on the road that leads from Cuneo up to the Colle di Tenda and the popular Limone Piemonte ski slopes. Here, in the Vermenagna Valley, silica quarries alternate with green woods and nature trails that can be explored on foot or by bicycle. Located in the middle of the village, in its two rooms and, whenever mountain weather permits, in a small outdoor area, the Leon d'oro hosts passing visitors and locals with a menu of carefully prepared traditional dishes using choice prime ingredients.
In the kitchen, Marco Fantino prepares a buffet of antipasti that, according to season, includes **vitello tonnato**, **rabbit terrine**, aubergines in olive oil, various vegetable pies with cheese fondues and a good selection of cured meats, among which an excellent venison fillet. For first courses, in summer, **gnocchi alle erbe** or al castelmagno or pastas from the Setaro brothers or Pastificio Gragnanese with vegetable sauces. In winter, you'll find **tagliatelle with sausage** and polenta with beef stew. All the beef and veal comes from the Piedmontese cattle breed, a Slow Food Presidium, and the various cuts are grilled or **braised in red wine** and, in summer, roasted. The excellent selection of Italian **cheeses** is supplemented by varieties from the nearby French Alps too. Marcella, who serves guests in the dining room, is from Sardinia and, as a tribute to her origins, some of the island's fare features in the menu. Lastly, the desserts: bonet, **stuffed peaches**, cream puddings, **blueberry tart**, semifreddi, lemon pie and ice creams. The wine list offers a good, well-balanced selection and mark-ups are very reasonable.

Rocca Grimalda

30 km south of Alessandria on A26, exit Ovada

Alla Rocca

Restaurant
Piazza Borgatta 12
Tel. 0143 873333
Closed Tuesday and Wednesday
Open: lunch and dinner
Holidays: January through February
Seating: 60 + 20 outdoors
Prices: 22-25 euros, wine excluded
All major credit cards except AE, Bancomat

Alessandra Fossa, a Milanese native with roots in Casteferro, a village not far from Rocca Grimalda, has returned to the Orba Valley after running two restaurants in Madagascar. She has reopened an old trattoria that sits under the magnificent Malaspina Castle in this tiny village perched up on a rocky spur overlooking the river and surrounded by the famous Dolcetto d'Ovada vineyards. The proximity to Liguria strongly influences the cuisine, so you'll also find some seafood dishes even though the fresh fish used tend to be the humbler anchovy, rock-fish and octopus.
Ravioli with toccu, a Ligurian dish, is always available at Rocca Grimalda, as is **perbureira**, a bean and lasagna soup flavored with olive oil and raw garlic. There's also **gnocchi** and tagliolini with sauces that vary from season to season. Main courses change every week according to the seasons. You might find **coniglio alla ligure** or rabbit roulade with asparagus, fassone or Angus beef steak, cima alla ligure with a green sauce, **Genoa-style baccalà**, **faraona with cherries** and honey. Vegetables that accompany the meat dishes or come as antipasti are grown locally. Among them there's **carpaccio di fassone** with onions and broad beans, zucchini and goat cheese and Zibello culatello with melon and grapes. In winter, you can choose from risottos, **braised meats** and bagna caoda on cardoon tarts. Desserts are made in-house and there's an honest wine list.
In the kitchen, Andrea oversees the cooking with the help of Alessandra. The two pastel-colored rooms are warm and inviting (especially with the fire going in the hearth).

Rocca Grimalda
San Giacomo

30 km south of Alessandria on A26 exit Ovada

Locanda Montebello

Trattoria
Località Montebello 249
Tel. 0143 876365
Closed Monday, Tuesday and Wednesday
Open: lunch and dinner
Holidays: August 1-15
Seating: 36
Prices: 30 euros, wine excluded
No credit cards accepted

This trattoria, run by Roberto Bisio and Charlotte Beck, lies inside the Tenuta Montebello, a grape and wine producing farm surrounded by 20 hectares of slopes famous for their production of Dolcetto d'Ovada. Wine is a common thread in the lives of this couple, who, prior to coming to this village in the Monferrato, ran a wine-bar in Milan's Navigli area. The place is cozy and welcoming, with large windows looking out onto the garden and bottles laid out just about everywhere.
Vegetables, meat and bread are all purchased in Ovada, Novi or Carpenato. The delicious grissini and focaccia come from this last town. Among the antipasti you'll find **rabbit liver pâté** with orange marmalade, savoiarda (a meat and vegetable salad), sausage in carpione and a rather unusual **fritto misto** that includes elder and acacia flowers, fruit, snails and sausage, with seasonal variations. First courses include **ravioli al sugo di stufato** (a real Alessandria specialty), fresh **tagliatelle**, broad bean soup and **rabatòn** flavored with poppy and kale. To follow, try oven-cooked lonza di maiale, **chicken cacciatora**, vitello tonnato or rabbit with chocolate and ginger. The winter menu also includes **cotechini with fonduta**, pork shank and braised beef or donkey. For cheese there's Montébore and Roccaverano, whereas the desserts show evidence of the cook's German origin.
Wines are dominated by Dolcetto d'Ovada (from the vineyards surrounding the trattoria) although there are wines from all over Italy too. The quinquina-flavored wines produced in the Asti area as digestive drinks are worth trying. Given the limited seating you must book in advance.

RODDI
Toetto

RODDINO

CASCINA BARIN

🔑 Holiday farm
Località Toetto 21
Tel. e fax 0173 615159
E-mail: cascinabarin_roddi@libero.it
Open all year

OSTERIA DA GEMMA

🍲 Osteria-trattoria
Via Marconi 6
Tel. 0173 794252
Closed Monday
Open: lunch and dinner
Holidays: end of March through April
Seating: 80 + 20 outdoors
Prices: 20-22 euros, wine excluded
No credit cards accepted

Giuseppina Nervo and Giulio Baracco's farm is specialized in growing fruit, especially grapes and hazelnuts. Renovation of the beautiful two-story farmhouse was completed in 1999, and the guest rooms are simple and are furnished with carefully restored antiques. All the rooms have large windows that give on to the garden, with tables and sun umbrellas for moments of relaxation. Giuseppina prepares superb breakfasts consisting of omelets made with seasonal vegetables, focaccia, savory pies, tarts and fresh and preserved fruit from the farm. Being an expert, during the right season Giulio will be happy to guide you in a hunt for Alba white truffles.

• 1 single, 5 double and 1 triple rooms, with bathroom, some with balcony • Prices: single 42 euros, double 65, triple 83, breakfast included • Credit cards: major ones, Bancomat • 1 room designed for use by the mobility challenged. Off-street parking. Small pets allowed. Owners always present • Lounge. Garden, veranda

Gemma's new digs are clean and tidy, but the place still lacks that lived-in feel reminiscent of an osteria of yesteryear, despite the fact that the area near the bar is reserved for habitual customers who drop in for a game of cards and a glass of wine. The main dining room does, however, have a big picture window overlooking the Langhe, and you're here less for the surroundings than for the convivial meal you'll find here – definitely one of the best values in the area. Gemma Boeri has finally realized her dream: to work in a larger kitchen where she has plenty of room (which is not to say that there's much room for anyone besides her and her helpers in there) to prepare really traditional dishes served family-style. Once you're seated the **cured meats** arrive: raw and cooked (excellent) to slice up as you like. Then, in rapid succession, insalata di carne cruda, **insalata russa** and **vitello tonnato**. You may sometimes find seasonal variations, like peppers with bagna caoda and cotechino with mashed potato or fonduta. You'll need the short break afterwards to prepare for the two first courses of **tajarin** and **agnolotti dal plin** with a classic ragù or butter and sage. Roast or stewed rabbit, **shank of veal**, braised or diced veal cooked in Barolo and **chicken alla cacciatora** are the main courses that alternate throughout the year. It goes without saying that the set menu will be served complete with house wine and, of course, desserts as well: a magnificent **bonet**, meringata and a terrific **strudel**. As an alternative to the house wine you'll find a a few Langa options as well. In the dining room Daniele and Silvana provide pleasantly straightforward, no-frills service.

ROLETTO

IL CIABÒT

� Restaurant
Via Costa 7
Tel. 0121 542132
Closed Sunday evening and Monday
Open: lunch and dinner
Holidays: 1 week in January, 3
between June and July
Seating: 50 + 15 outdoors
Prices: 25-30 euros, wine excluded
All major credit cards, Bancomat

Mauro Agù (in the kitchen) and his wife Lorena Fenu (in the dining room) run this delightful restaurant in the center of Roletto, at the foot of Mount Muretto, just a few kilometers from Pinerolo. The inviting dining room has been reorganized and the table layout improved to seat a good number of customers. The cuisine focuses on local products with a few well-considered forays beyond these There's also a 26-euro menu that includes freshwater and ocean fish. Traditional dishes can be ordered à la carte from a choice of four antipasti, four first courses, four main courses and six desserts.

You start with **Fassone beef tartar** with quail egg yolk, char terrine with porcini mushrooms, **fagottini alla mostardela** or three warm vegetable antipasti and flans. Among the first courses, we recommend **agnolotti alla piemontese**, pasta millefoglie with seirass, asparagus and luvertin or the nest of **tagliolini with rabbit** and hazelnut **ragù**. To follow, there's **rack of lamb with Alpine herbs**, sottofiletto di fassone alla provenzale or filet of pork with porcinis. Finish off with a selection or local cheeses or one of the delicious desserts – among them, bavarese allo zabaglione and mousse al gianduia with cinnamon and chili pepper.

The wine list focuses on important Piedmontese reds (the number of Barolos and Barbarescos is growing), but there is also a choice of more economically-priced bottles. The selection from other regions is limited. You can round out the meal with excellent digestive drinks from the Pinerolo area.

ROMAGNANO SESIA

ALLA TORRE

⌀

⌀ Restaurant
Via I Maggio 75
Tel. 0163 826411
Closed Monday
Open: lunch and dinner
Holidays: December 27 to January 7
Seating: 60 + 20 outdoors
Prices: 30 euros, wine excluded
All major credit cards, Bancomat

Lucia and Andrea expertly manage this restaurant in the town's old watchtower. In these lovely interiors you can choose from a very interesting menu that is constantly being changed, a sign of the owners' assiduous search for top quality produce that goes beyond local boundaries.

We particularly like the **Val Vigezzo prosciutto crudo** served with a wild asparagus flan, **mocetta** from Val d'Ayas with zucchini flan, **carpione of River Sesia trout**, Jerusalem artichoke flan with bagna caoda and the savory pie with **furmagina** di Romagnano. There is a wide choice of first courses, ranging from the **skilà** (soup eaten by Val Sesia shepherds with toma cheese and croutons) to gnocchi with bettelmatt cheese fonduta, **tajarin al ragù marinato al Gattinara**. In summer, order maltagliati with eggplant, classic **paniscia from Novara** or one of the various fresh vegetable soups. Among the main courses, in the winter we highly recommend **tapulone d'asino**, donkey meat stew, with cabbage or polenta and **glazed stewing steak** al ginepro and al Gattinara; alternatively you can go for grilled beef, river prawns with ginger or stuffed zucchini blossoms. The cheeses – the Val Sesia Toma cheese and Bettelmatt being the most typical of the area – are served with pickled fruits and honey. There is also a wide range of excellent desserts, like gelato cakes, fresh fruit tarts, bonet and raspado di caffè.

There is an excellent wine list, with northern Nebbiolos, the classic reds and whites wines of Piedmont, and also a great beer list with brews from three local makers (Beba, Baladin and Città Vecchia).

SALUGGIA

LA PIAZZETTA

🍲 Restaurant
Via Faldella 2
Tel. 0161 480470
Closed Monday
Open: lunch and dinner
Holidays: August, 1 week in January
Seating: 30
Prices: 30-35 euros, wine excluded
All major credit cards, Bancomat

Giovanni Faldella wrote: 'Saluggia is the last town in the Vercelli district in geographical terms only, because it is located where the province of Vercelli meets the Canavese hills, the environs of Turin and the Monferrato'. La Piazzetta is right opposite the writer's home, a reliable stopping place in this part of the province. The dining room is managed by Alessandro Zanella, who will guide you through the dishes prepared by Paolo Ugazio and the wine list.
The dishes are based primarily on ingredients from the area – where there are numerous Slow Food Presidia – and some of them come together in inventive combinations. Start with the **cured meats**, such as culatello di Zibello, **mortadella from Val d'Ossola**, filetto baciato from Ponzone, onion flan with mountain raschera fonduta, **carne cruda piemontese** or stuffed peppers from Carmagnola. In the summer, there are **tinche gobbe dorate** from Poirino in carpione and, sometimes, fried or stewed frogs. Follow with an excellent **panissa**, **potato ravioli** with goat cheese, **rabbit with thyme** and Piedmontese fassone steak. Over the past year, the choice of excellent **cheeses** has increased considerably. To finish, order the dark chocolate tegole with rum, bonet, panna cotta and **timbala** (a typical cake from Cigliano), all made here.
In addition to the extensive wine list, there is a broad selection of liqueurs and Italian and Belgian artisan beers.

🍶 In **Livorno Ferraris** (7.7 km), the Colombara di Rondolino farm produces organic carnaroli rice that is stone polished and matured at cold temperatures.

SAMBUCO

PACE

🍲 Restaurant/3-Star Hotel
Via Umberto I 32 and 38
Tel. 0171 96628 or 0171 96550
Fax 0171 96628
E-mail: info@albergodellapace.com
Internet: www.albergodellapace.com
Closed Monday, never in summer
Open: lunch and dinner
Holidays: 1 week in June, 20 days in October
Seating: 48
Prices: 25-27 euros, wine excluded
All credit cards except DC, Bancomat

The ideal place to stop off on trips to the mountains, this hotel is situated in the village square and is always open. The rooms are simply appointed with plain wooden furniture. There is a breakfast buffet. Half board costs 46 euros per person, full board 56.
Owner Bartolo Bruna promotes the culinary traditions and products of the valley. He will take you through the menu, which might include **lamb liver paté**, rabbit roulade, ricotta with basil sauce and **potato with leeks and baccalà**. From the first courses, try ravioli, gnocchi al nostrale, **tripe minestrone** and the signature traditional dish, **cruset** (which are like orecchiette) **with leeks** or meat ragù. **Sambucano lamb** (a Slow Food Presidium), **roast** or **braised**, is the highlight of the main courses, but there are roast venison and veal as well. Desserts include montebianco, fruit crostatas, apple soup and Bavarian cream.
The wine list merits a mention for its variety and selection of wines offering great value, and for your digestif, try one of the Alpine herb liqueurs, which are the house specialty.

• 1 single, 8 double and 2 triple rooms with bath, terrace and TV • Prices: single 35, double 65, triple 79 euros, breakfast included • 1 room accessible to the mobility challenged. Free external public parking. Small pets welcome. Reception open from 6:30am to 11pm • Bar, restaurant. Reading and TV lounge. Conference room. Terrace

SAN MARZANO OLIVETO
Mariano

25 KM SOUTH OF ASTI

LE DUE CASCINE

🚜 Holiday farm
Regione Mariano 22
Tel. 0141 824525
Fax 0141 829028
E-mail: info@leduecascine.com
Internet: www.leduecascine.com
Open all year round

This very well managed, recently built yet tasteful agriturismo is situated in a small, secluded valley planted with vineyards (mostly producing Barbera). The location is perfect, almost equidistant between Nizza and Canelli, the two small wine capitals of this part of the Monferrato area. Wine is one of the main attractions of the place and you'll be able to taste it with the traditional cuisine in the restaurant (meals range from 15-22 euros, wine excluded). Besides sampling the production of Le Due Cascine, you'll also be able to visit other producers in what is considered one of the most important wine producing areas in the province of Asti. Breakfast includes sweet and savory foods prepared using products from the farm's own organically cultivated orchard and vegetable garden.

• 10 double rooms, with bathroom, TV, modem connection, several rooms with balcony • Prices: double room single use 50 euros, double 75 (20 euro supplement for extra bed), breakfast included • Credit cards: all, Bancomat • Off-street parking. Small pets allowed. Owners always present. • Bar, restaurant. Breakfast room. Conference room. Garden. Pool, children's playground

SAN MARZANO OLIVETO
Valle Asinari

25 KM SOUTHEAST OF ASTI, 5 KM FROM CANELLI

DEL BELBO DA BARDON

🍲 Trattoria
Via Valle Asinari 25
Tel. 0141 831340
Closed Wednesday and Thursday
Open: lunch and dinner
Holidays: between December and January, 1 week following August 15
Seating: 50 + 60 outdoors
Prices: 30-35 euros, wine excluded
All major credit cards

The close-knit teams in the kitchen (Anna and Giuseppino) and the dining-room (Gino and Andrea) direct the true passion they have for what they do into ensuring you a welcoming environment in an enjoyably rustic atmosphere. The food here is all substance, firmly rooted in tradition and made with excellent ingredients. There's a superb wine cellar with thousands of labels for every taste and every pocket. Bardon has been open for over a century on the banks of the river Belbo, halfway between Canelli and Nizza Monferrato, surrounded by vineyards, orchards and fields of the famous **cardoons** (which are prepared in a variety of ways when in season).

Sitting down at one of these tables means running through the whole catalogue of the cuisine of the Monferrato and Langhe, starting with **carne cruda** battuta a coltello and vegetable flans, seasonal salads of **wild mushrooms** (which can also be **fried**) and vitello tonnato. The first courses are all worth trying: try **agnolotti** dal plin or **quadrati monferrini** with ragù, gnocchi with a sausage or tomato sauce, tajarin with seasonal sauces (from wild mushrooms to leeks) or the incomparable **pasta and beans**. Then comes a truly exemplary array of meats: **Langhe kid**, roast rabbit, **shin of veal**, chicken alla cacciatora, bollito misto, chicken with lemon and **tripe stew**. When Gino finds the right animals, he also prepares hare, duck, and goose, as well as **stewed cod**.

The **cheese** board is extensive and changes every day but always includes some good Robiola di Roccaverano. Desserts are simple and include the traditional mattone with cream made with butter.

SAN SEBASTIANO CURONE

45 KM SOUTHEAST OF ALESSANDRIA, 25 KM FROM TORTONA

SANT'ANTONINO DI SUSA
Cresto

35 KM NORTH OF TURIN ON SS 25 OR A32

CORONA

🍷Restaurant
Via Vittorio Emanuele 14
Tel. 0131 786203
Closed Monday and Thursday
Open: lunch only
Holidays: between June and July
Seating: 60
Prices: 30-35 euros, wine excluded
All credit cards, Bancomat

IL SENTIERO DEI FRANCHI

🍷Restaurant
Borgata Cresto 16
Tel. 011 9631747
Closed Tuesday
Open: lunch and dinner
Holidays: vary
Seating: 25
Prices: 32-35 euros, wine excluded
All major credit cards, Bancomat

Located at the entrance to the historical part of the town, the Corona conveys the atmosphere of a small mountain hotel from the moment you enter. It has been run by the Fontana family for over 100 years and is now in the hands of Matilde, who has made the search for top quality ingredients the starting point and the star feature of her simple, traditional food. After you take your seats in the welcoming dining-room, you will be served a long list of antipasti, including **Brignano salami**, lardo and pancetta with acacia honey, sausage with peppers, various quiches and delicate ham and tuna mousses. First courses include **potato gnocchi with cream**, **meat-stuffed ravioli** with porcini sauce, **pasta and beans** and artichokes al Montébore. And because we are on the borders of Liguria, you will often find stuffed cima alla genovese as well as wild mushrooms and game prepared in various ways when in season. Try the **kid with rosemary** or the **tripe stew** prepared in the best country tradition. Where desserts are concerned, Matilde herself prepares the excellent gelato and bonet and selects the **chocolates**.

The wine list is very interesting and includes about 200 labels, focusing in particular on Piedmontese and local wines, and there are often several vintages of a single label.

Borgata Cresto, located right below the Sacra di San Michele, is an important starting point for excursions and is easily reached from the center of Sant'Antonino. Here you will find a small restaurant named after the road along which Charlemagne's army marched when he descended the Susa Valley before the battle of Le Chiuse. At Sentiero, you wil be offered cuisine inspired by traditional Alpine dishes, which are often served accompanied by Celtic music.

The menu offered by owner Renzo Andolfatto, assisted by his wife Maria Pia, features antipasti such as lardo from Arnad, mountain toma cheese, cured meats made by the local butcher, **insalata russa**, **lingua salmistrata** and crostini with fonduta and mushrooms. You can choose between **agnolotti** with wild boar or venison sauce, malfatti of potatoes and peas with gorgonzola and cream and classic **polenta** made with Storo cornmeal. The main courses are substantial and include brasato al vino bianco, caponet, **carbonade** alla valdostana and **wild boar in red wine**, all accompanied by fried polenta and mountain potatoes. Cheeses include those in the 'Shopping Basket' prepared by the Turin Provincial Authority. Finally, for dessert, you might choose from pan del conte, semifreddo and a simple cake made with cornmeal, raisins and chestnut sauce from Villar Focchiardo. The wine list is on the short side and focuses on Piedmont and Val d'Aosta producers (with a good number of wines from the Susa Valley). The water comes from a local spring.

🦪 Dino Medicina's butcher shop, at Via Anselmi 7, sells raw and cooked salamis, pancetta and Piedmontese beef.

Santo Stefano Belbo
Valdivilla

81 KM FROM CUNEO, 25 KM FROM ASTI ON SS 292

Santo Stefano Belbo

81 KM FROM CUNEO, 25 FROM ASTI ON SS 592

Ca' d' Gal

🍲 Farm restaurant
Strada vecchia di Valdivilla 1
Tel. 0141 847103
Always open for bookings
Open: lunch and dinner
Holidays: in January and during grape harvest
Seating: 40 + 15 ourdoors
Prices: 35 euros
All major credit cards, Bancomat

Osteria dal Gal Vestì

🍲 Tavern-cantina
Via Cesare Pavese 18
Tel. 0141 843379
Closed Mondays and Tuesday, never in July or August
Open: lunch and dinner
Holidays: between January and February
Seating: 45 + 40 outdoors
Prices: 25-30 euros
All major credit cards, Bancomat

Ca' d' Gal is a simple farm restaurant where you can enjoy well prepared dishes that offer great value. The place can be reached from Neive, following the signs for Coazzolo and Villalta, or from Santo Stefano Belbo, up splendid hills planted with moscato vines. The farm is run by Alessandro and Laura Boido, who have been working as both wine producers and restaurateurs for several years. The dining room is welcoming, illuminated by large panoramic windows, and the food is based on local tradition and whatever is in season.

Start with **cured meats** made by pork butcher Silvio Brarda of Cavour: lardo, cooked and raw, salamis and excellent corned beef. There are also **frittatas of courgettes** or other seasonal vegetables, as well as **carpioni** and cotechino. Among the first courses, we recommend the **agnolotti dal plin** or **tajarin paglia e fieno** dressed with butter and sage or with a meat sauce and gnocchi served with mushrooms and truffles when in season. The flour used to make the fresh pasta is stone ground. Chickens and rabbits raised on the farm feature in the main courses: try the **rabbit** cooked with wine or **al civet**. Cheeses are served with homemade **cognà al Moscato**, and this same wine lends its perfume and flavor to the desserts too. It is added to peaches or used to make moscatella, a semifreddo made with sponge and covered with chocolate.

If you decide on the house wine, the price of a complete meal will be about 35 euros, otherwise you can choose from a small selection of Piedmontese labels.

This area was the setting for Cesare Pavese's books Paesi tuoi, La luna e i falò and I mari del Sud, in which the poet's cousin complains, 'This year I am going to write it on the poster: Santo Stefano has always been the first of the feast days in the Belbo valley'. We are in Pavese country, his town and the osteria that occupies a part of the house he was born in, an old lobster-pink farmhouse not far from the center. If there were still any doubt about whose legacy still reigns supreme here, the bust of the writer is in the garden in front of the patio under the wisteria.

There is a choice of two set meals or you can choose à la carte from an array of dishes that changes with the seasons. The antipasti include soft, hot **friciole** with lardo, **carne cruda battuta al coltello**, rabbit tonno, fagottini stuffed with eggplant, various vegetable flans and, in the winter, a **cardoon flan**. Go on to the **potato gnocchi with seirass** with a sauce of fresh tomatoes and basil or cheese, **tagliatelle with rabbit liver**, tajarin alla monferrina, **agnolotti dal plin**, vegetable lasagne and pasta e fagioli. Then veal rump cooked in salt, grilled lamb chops, **rabbit liver with potatoes and peppers** and, in the right season, **boar in red wine**, **brasato di bue grasso al mosto** and wild mushrooms baked in foil. Themed meals are organized on Friday evenings and if you book in time you will be able to try mushrooms, bollito misto or **fritto misto**. The meal ends with **stuffed peaches**, bonet and various types of semifreddo. The rich wine list, primarily Piedmontese, dedicates the right amount of space to small local producers.

Santa Vittoria d'Alba
Villa

53 KM NORTHEAST OF CUNEO, 11 KM FROM ALBA ON SS 231

Savigliano

33 KM NORTH-EAST OF CUNEO SS 20

Cascina Valdispinso

Holiday farm
Via Rolfi 5
Tel. 0172 478308
Fax 0172 478465
E-mail: info@valdispinso.com
Internet: www.santavittoria.org
Open all year

Antica Osteria dell'Orsa

Osteria recently opened
Piazza Battisti 5
Tel. 0172 717606
Closed Wednesdays and Thursday
Open: lunch and dinner
Holidays: 3 weeks in January, 1 week
between August and September
Seating: 35 + 18 outdoors
Prices: 25-28 euros, wine excluded
Credit cards: MC, Visa, Bancomat

The headquarters of Antonella Chiarlone's vineyards and winery is a historic farmhouse, part of the Santa Vittoria Castle estate. The two buildings shared a common destiny before and after 1838, the year when Carlo Alberto of Savoy purchased the feudal properties of the Romagnano family (Pollenzo, Verduno and Santa Vittoria). Today Valdispinso, which is only 800 meters from the castle, is an annex of the 4-Star Hotel Castello (39 rooms, double room with breakfast costs 140 euros). An apartment and a studio flat have been added to the old farmhouse. The common spaces consist of a lounge with fireplace and a kitchen; outside, in addition to the oven and barbecue grill, there is also a small swimming pool. For breakfast – a rich buffet with sweet and savory fare – you have to go to the Hotel Castello.

• 2 double and 1 triple rooms, with bathroom, air-conditioning, safe, TV; 3 apartments with 1-2 bedrooms, bathroom, living room, kitchen • Prices: double room single use 70 euros, double 100, triple 115, breakfast included; four-bed apartment 130 euros, five-bed 140, breakfast included • Credit cards: all, Bancomat • Parking right outside. Small pets allowed. Reception at the Castello Hotel (800 m) • Lounge. Kitchen. Garden, pool

This delightful inn, where ancient and modern flavors go hand in hand, is in an old-fashioned little square that has recently been restored, just a short walk from the town's more famous Piazza Santarosa. Go through the small entrance hall and two rooms with austere walls, tall windows, and very simple furnishings open up on either side. The food reflects the same straightforward approach. It's a joy to find such simple, basic, even poor cuisine in a gastronomic world that seems to want to amaze all the time.
The antipasti include carpaccio of Piedmontese veal served with Robiola di Roccaverano cheese in salsa verde, a flan of peppers or other vegetables with **zucchini in carpione**; in the colder months, vitello tonnato with mushroom pâté and **chicken with old-fashioned salsa tonnata**. The first courses are homemade: **tagliatelle al ragù**, ravioli with butter and thyme, **gnocchi al raschera**, cavatelli with meat sauce and panzerotti with butter and herbs. And various types of soup in the winter. The main courses include classic **stracotto al Nebbiolo**, rabbit all'Arneis and **kidneys**; or try the grilled fillet of veal with a sauce from an ancient recipe and baccalà alla ligure with potatoes and parsley. The menu always includes a classic **Piedmontese beef steak (**as you can see, the Osteria tends to favor the excellent local meat). On cold days, you'll find stewed ox-tail and tripe.
To finish, cheese and desserts, including sorbet of raisins, crema catalana and semifreddo with nougat. The wine list is adequate and the prices are reasonable.

PIEDMONT

SAVIGLIANO
Santa Rosalia

SERRALUNGA D'ALBA

33 KM NORTH-EAST OF CUNEO

58 KM NORTHEAST OF CUNEO, 14 KM FROM ALBA ON SP 125

SANTA ROSALIA

CASCINA SCHIAVENZA

⚷ Bed and breakfast
Strada Santa Rosalia 1
Tel. 0172 726386
E-mail: santarosaliacamere@libero.it
Internet: www.santarosaliacamere.it
Open all year round

🍲 Restaurant
Via Mazzini 4
Tel. 0173 613115
Closed Tuesday and evenings on festivities
Open: lunch and dinner
Holidays: in January, July 15-August 15
Seating: 40 + 20 outdoors
Prices: 28 euros, wine excluded
All major credit cards, Bancomat

Turn off the busy main road linking Savigliano and Turin to Santa Rosalia and you'll notice the entrance to this very well restructured farmhouse, surrounded by a garden with a small lake and fruit trees.

The interiors are characterized by brick vaults, terracotta floors and wooden beams across the ceilings. The small, pleasant lounge that leads to the restaurant is rendered even more attractive by a 100-year-old cast-iron stove. The rooms are all spacious and give access to the small grounds. Pastel colors on the walls, wrought-iron bedsteads and period wardrobes contribute to creating an old-style Piedmontese atmosphere. Breakfast includes caffelatte or tea, fresh brioches, cakes and jams made by Loredana. For dinner, home cooking, cured meats and a splendid Castelmagno (meals cost from 25-30 euros per person, excluding wine).

• 1 single and 5 double rooms, with bathroom, mini-bar, TV, modem connection• Prices: single 48 euros, double 72 (12 euro supplement for extra bed), breakfast included • Credit cards: major ones, Bancomat • Facility accessible to the mobility challenged. Off-street parking (covered for motorcycles). No pets allowed. Owners always present. • Restaurant (for residents only). TV room in the reception area. Garden, grounds

Above the small medieval village of Serralunga d'Alba rise three towers, each one different, known as the cิòche, which are part of a fortress built in the mid 14th century for Pietrino and Goffredo Falletti; below, a lovely church looks out onto the vineyards that surround the hill. Between these two symbols of the power of the past is a small house which still respects age-old 'Langarola' cooking traditions. Service is prompt and courteous, the dining room is simply but well furnished, and in the summer guests can dine al fresco on the terrace, from which they can admire the gentle slopes of the hills covered with their intricate network of vines.

The set meal starts with a classic array of antipasti, including **carne cruda**, cooked and raw salamis, excellent fried **stuffed zucchini flowers**, vitello tonnato, insalata russa, and **peppers with bagna cauda** and spinach flan with fondue in the winter. The first courses include excellent crisp homemade **tajarin** made with plenty of egg yolk, rolled by hand and cut with a knife, **agnolotti dal plin**, and crespelle with bechamel and mushrooms, or artichokes when in season. The main courses always include **brasato al Barolo**, guinea fowl with herbs, chicken alla cacciatora and **rabbit al civet**, accompanied by fried polenta and plenty of whatever vegetables are in season.

The wine list is not very long but with the right mark-ups, and favors the labels from the Schiavenza cellar and winemakers from the Serralunga area, meaning Barolo, Barbera and Dolcetto. To end, local cheeses served with honey or cognà, and a number of tasty desserts such as panna cotta, bonet and **hazelnut cake with zabaione**.

SERRALUNGA D'ALBA
Fontanafredda

SERRALUNGA D'ALBA

56 KM NORTHEAST OF CUNEO, 12 KM FROM ALBA ON SP 125

58 KM NORTHEAST OF CUNEO, 14 KM FROM ALBA ON SP 125

FORESTERIA DELLE VIGNE

☛—⚷3-Star Hotel
Via Alba 15
Tel. 0173 626191-626184
Fax 0173 626194
E-mail: villacontessarosa@fontanafredda.it
Internet: www. villacontessarosa.com
Closed the first 15 days of August
and during the Christmas period

L'ANTICO ASILO

☛—⚷Rooms
Via Mazzini 13
Tel. 0173 613016
Fax 0173 613956
E-mail: elena@anticoasilo.com
Internet: www.anticoasilo.com
Closed 20 days between January and February

Great wines have been produced on the estate that Vittorio Emanuele II donated to the children he had from his morganatic wife Rosa Vercellana, Countess of Mirafiori and Fontanafredda since 1878. Secular parkland surrounds the buildings of the complex that have now been renovated to include not only wine cellars and offices, but also conference and hospitality facilities. The guestrooms are located in a building adjacent to the villa of the Countess popularly known as 'Bela Rosin' (she was not of noble birth) that is now a comfortable hotel with 11 very well furnished rooms, each of which is named for a vineyard. The continental-style buffet breakfast is served in a room on the first floor. The Contessa Rosa restaurant is located in the royal villa (closed on Wednesdays and Sunday nights) and offers traditional dishes from Piedmontese cuisine at a price starting from 30 euros per person, excluding wine.

• 11 double rooms, with bathroom, minibar, TV • Prices: double room single use 80 euros, double 100, breakfast included • Credit cards: all, Bancomat • Facility accessible to the mobility challenged. Off-street parking. No pets allowed. Reception open from 8am to 9pm • Breakfast room. Restaurant. Congress center. Grounds

Originally a kindergarten (1901-1963), the Picedi family home is a beautiful building in Art Nouveau style near the medieval castle of Serralunga among the Barolo hills. The part of the house dedicated to guests is the ground floor. The elegant, spacious rooms lead off the luminous entrance hall-corridor and its inlaid floors: three rooms have a mezzanine floor, the fourth faces directly onto the garden, as does the breakfast room. Here, every morning, Elena prepares a sumptuous buffet with beverages, sweet and savory homemade cakes, cured meats, cheeses and other Langa specialties. The top price charged for a double room for single occupancy is in September and October, the peak tourist period in an area famous for truffles and wines.

• 4 double or triple rooms, with bathroom • Prices: double room single use 65-95 euros, double 95, triple 126, breakfast included • Credit cards: all, Bancomat • Facility accessible to the mobility challenged. Parking right outside. Small pets allowed. Owners always present. • Breakfast room. Garden

SERRALUNGA D'ALBA
Parafada

50 KM FROM CUNEO, 12 KM SOUTHWEST OF ALBA

LA ROSA DEI VINI

Restaurant with rooms
Località Parafada 4
Tel. 0173 613219
Closed Wednesday
Open: lunch and dinner
Holidays: 2 weeks in January
Seating: 45 + 70 outdoors
Prices: 24-28 euros, wine excluded
All major credit cards except AE, Bancomat

This family-run osteria just outside Serralunga d'Alba is surrounded by vineyards and has a breathtaking view over Castiglione Falletto with La Morra in the distance. Eat outside in the summer to appreciate the beautiful scenery. The restaurant has six rooms for those who wish to stop and get to know the area better. As you would expect, the cooking is pure Piedmontese, and every dish is made just as it should be.
You can choose à la carte or opt for one of the two set meals: the first (**vitello tonnato**, a pie of cep mushrooms, **tajarin with Bra sausage**, **veal stew al Barbaresco**, a combination of three puddings with panna cotta, bonet, and strawberry mousse) costs 24 euros, the second 35 euros is richer at. Both offer excellent value for money. The antipasti include peppers with bagna caoda, **tongue with salsa verde**, caponet with Castelmagno puré, and small frittatas. First courses: ravioli di magro gravy, tajarin with a choice of sauces, **agnolotti dal plin** and risotto with seasonal ingredients. For the main course: cod with leeks from Cervere, **rabbit with peppers** and **galletto alla babi** (in Piedmontese dialect, 'babi' means a toad, and the name refers to the shape of the bird, when it is slit down the front and squashed flat), but also – a real treat! – fritto misto, boiled meats and bagna caoda (book ahead). The desserts include those mentioned above but also **Madernassa pears** al Barolo, stuffed peaches, sorbets and bavarois.
The wine list is impeccable, particularly as far as wines from the Langhe are concerned. Service is prompt and pleasantly informal, like the ambience.

SERRALUNGA DI CREA
Guazzaura

40 KM NORTH-WEST OF ALESSANDRIA, 28 KM FROM ASTI

TENUTA GUAZZAURA

Holiday farm
Via Guazzaura 9
Tel. 0142 940289-335 8039509
Fax 0142 940289
E-mail: info@guazzaura.it
Internet: www.guazzaura.it
Closed from 20 December to end of January

Luca and Marie-Helen Brondelli opened their very singular agriturismo in 1998 in this beautiful family farm lying at the foot of the Sacred Mount of Crea. There are five very attractive apartments – one two-bedroom and four studios, all with cooking facilities – where you'll be completely independent. The apartments are very comfortable and airy, and are furnished with antiques. An avenue of age-old plane trees leads up to the farmhouse, which is in an ideal position for enjoying the 'Walking in the Monferrato' trails and for playing golf (there's a golf course close by). In the season your host organizes trips to go truffle hunting or you can visit other Monferrato wine producers and savor the very best Grignolino and Barbera wines. You can either make your own breakfast or, on request, the owners will prepare it for you and serve it in your room. A swimming pool is under construction.

• 4 double rooms and 1 suite, with bathroom, kitchenette; 2 with a balcony • Prices: double room single use 40 euros, double 60 (23 euro supplement for extra bed); breakfast 5 euros per person • Credit cards: none • 1 room designed for use by the mobility challenged. Covered off-street parking. Small pets allowed (6 euros per day). Owners always present. • Grounds

SERRAVALLE LANGHE

SILLAVENGO

54 KM NORTHEAST OF CUNEO, 22 KM FROM ALBA

19 KM A NO DI NOVARA SS 299

LA COCCINELLA

Restaurant
Via Provinciale 5
Tel. 0173 748220
Closed Tuesday and Wednesday for lunch
Open: lunch and dinner
Holidays: 1 month after the Epiphany, 1 week mid-July
Seating: 45
Prices: 33-35 euros, wine excluded
All major credit cards, Bancomat

TENIMENTO AL CASTELLO CANTINETTA

Osteria
Via San Giuseppe 15
Tel. 0321 824221
Closed Monday, Tuesday and Wednesday
Open: dinner, Saturday and Sunday lunch also
Holidays: always open
Seating: 70
Prices: 30-35 euros, wine excluded
All major credit cards, Bancomat

La Coccinella is unusual, first of all because it is run entirely by men. The three Dellaferrera brothers do everything: from cooking to serving at table, carefully selecting the wines on the list (which also includes interesting varieties by the glass), and choosing the cheeses for the very attractive board, and the single-grape grappa. Secondly, you don't often find a restaurant off the beaten track which proposes a cuisine that shows such strong links with local tradition, but also experiments with creative ideas which, luckily for us, are well worth trying.

The menu varies with the seasons and how the chef is feeling. So be prepared for new surprises on every visit. We tried several antipasti, including excellent smoked trout with polenta and Gorgonzola, salted veal rump with quail's eggs, **soufflé of asparagus and ricotta** and millefoglie of suckling pig with onion preserve. For the first course, we can certainly recommend the classic **tajarin** with various sauces, hazelnut gnocchi with Castelmagno and herb puré. Freshwater fish play an important part among the main courses: we tried char and crayfish in an unusual combination with saddle of rabbit. People who prefer more traditional dishes can choose veal tagliata and **rolled leg of lamb**. To conclude, fantastic desserts, such as **hazelnut cake** with Moscato sorbet, **bonet**, strawberry meringues and panna cotta with honey.

Tenimento al Castello is a large accommodating structure, suitable for parties and celebrations which can be held in the large banqueting rooms, or for small groups for small lunches and dinners based on local produce. It also boasts a large garden where guests who wish to do so can enjoy a drink as they wait for their meal, weather permitting. Sabrina and Antonio Pappalardo manage the restaurant competently, no easy task, proposing a menu that varies with the seasons.

The interesting range of antipasti includes **cured meats** purchased from small producers, from salam 'd la doja to fidighina, from salame d'oca to cured horsemeat. But you will also find roast peppers with anchovies, pies and vegetables in season prepared in various ways. Follow this with the typical **paniscia**, or ravioli with herbs or pumpkin, **pasta and beans**, and various types of soup. The beef and veal are supplied by the La Granda cooperative, a Piedmontese breed Presidium, and is always recommended: tagliata di fassone, **carne cruda battuta al coltello**, and stracotto with cep mushrooms when in season, and **mixed boiled meats**. Book in advance to enjoy **friteura**, meatballs of a combination of capocollo, liver and kidney. The cheese board includes Toma from Valsesia and Macugnaga, goats' cheese, and different types of Gorgonzola. Finish with fruit in syrup served with whipped cream or vanilla sauce, carrot, apple or chocolate cake, and crostata with raspberry or bilberry preserves.

There are more than 180 labels in the cellar, and a choice of home-made liqueurs at the end of the meal.

PIEDMONT

SINIO

OSTERIA DEL MAIALE PEZZATO

☞◦Bed and breakfast
Via Carlo Coccio 2
Tel. e fax 0173 263845
E-mail: osteria@maialepezzato.com
Internet: www.maialepezzato.com
Open all year round

Sinio, at the beginning of the Val Talloria, is a tiny village that goes back to medieval times and here you'll find this cozy restaurant with rooms. The rooms themselves and common areas have been furnished with great attention to detail and guests will certainly feel comfortable. The owners have a beautiful orchard and so breakfast never lacks fresh seasonal fruit, in addition to other sweet fare. On request you can also have savory dishes made for you. Among the sites to visit nearby are the 15th-century castle built for Marquis Franceschino del Carretto, the parish church dedicated to San Frontiniano and the 17th-century Oratory of the Disciplinati, which has been restructured to become a theater, which Oscar Barile's local drama company uses for performances. The restaurant, which is also open to non-residents, serves typical Langa cuisine with a personal touch (meals range from 20-25 euros per person, excluding wine).

• 3 double and 3 triple rooms, with bathroom, TV • Prices: double room single use 75 euros, double 90, triple 110, breakfast included • Credit cards: all except AE, Bancomat • Public parking close by. No pets allowed. Owners always present. • Bar, restaurant. Garden. Pool

SIZZANO

CAFFÈ RISTORANTE IMPERO

🍲Restaurant
Via Roma 13
Tel. 0321 820290-820576
Closed Sunday evening and Monday
Open: lunch and dinner
Holidays: August, 12/26-01/07
Seating: 50
Prices: 30-35 euros, wine excluded
All major credit cards, Bancomat

Sizzano lies on the left bank of the Sesia, in the Novarese part of the Nebbiolo district in the north of Piedmont. The Caffè Ristorante Impero is a historical restaurant at the center of town, which has been run by the same family for over 70 years, and is now in the hands of Paola and her mother Vittoria in the kitchen and Manuela and Federico in the dining-room. The cooking has its roots in the local territory, which also provides the raw ingredients for the dishes that vary every day according to the cook's imagination.

At lunchtime, the set meal is lighter (22-25 euros including a quarter liter of house wine), while in the evening there is a choice of classic dishes such as **tapulone**, **mixed boiled meats** (every Wednesday) and stewed pork with **frittura dolce** (book in advance at midday). Among the antipasti we recommend the lentil salad (cold in summer and warm in winter), the vegetable aspic, the terrine of Gorgonzola with balsamic vinegar and the **local cured meats** such as fidighin (liver mortadella from Novara) and salam 'd la duja. Follow this with **paniscia** (also served reheated in a frying pan), straccetti with courgettes and saffron, stuffed tortelloni with various sauces and gnocchetti with spring onions and tomato. For the main course, in addition to the dishes mentioned above, the menu often includes **boiled stuffed chicken** with mostarda, bagnetto verde and figs. The puddings include bavarois, mousses and crostata with fruit.

The wines on the wine list tend to be local – Sizzano, Ghemme, Boca and Gattinara – but there are also some other excellent Piedmontese and Italian labels.

STROPPO
Bassura

ALLA NAPOLEONICA

🔑 Rooms
Frazione Bassura 43
Tel. 0171 999277
Fax 0171 999814
E-mail: locandanapoleonica@libero.it
Internet: www.locandanapoleonica.it
Closed in October

The Maira Valley is possibly the wildest and most uncontaminated part of the mountainous area around Cuneo and many villages there have lost nothing of the typical local architecture. On the road that continues towards Acceglio, just after passing through the main square of Bassura, a sign will direct you to the Napoleonica. For years Elena Fino and her husband Roberto Ravasio have been running this locanda in a house dating from the 1800s that was carefully restored a few years ago. Five basic, airy rooms with beautiful wooden false-ceilings. The common areas are pleasant and cozy: there's a restaurant, a gym and a room where they serve breakfast, consisting of yogurt, home-made jams and cakes, cereals and fresh fruit. A set menu in the restaurant, also open to non-residents, costs 26 euros, excluding wine; half board ranges from 50-60 euros per person.

• 5 double rooms, with bathroom, balcony, satellite TV, modem connection • Prices: double room single use 40-45 euros, double 70-80 (25 euro supplement for extra bed), breakfast included • Credit cards: major ones, Bancomat • Free external public parking. Small pets allowed. Owners reachable from 9 am to 9 pm. • Restaurant. Breakfast room, reading room. Terrace. Small gym

STROPPO
Ruata Valle

CODIROSSO

🍲 Trattoria annexed to locanda
Frazione Ruata Valle 8
Tel. 0171 999101
Closed Wednesday, Apr-Jun open festivities only
Open: dinner, festivities at lunch only
Holidays: mid-October-March
Seating: 20
Prices: 22 euros, wine excluded
All major credit cards, Bancomat

This locanda is situated in Ruata Valle, halfway between the church of San Peyre and the sanctuary of Santa Maria. This delightful hamlet can be reached on foot, taking a short walk from the church or a longer path from Paschero through the woods.
The cooking is based on local produce and offers good value for money. The set menu includes three antipasti, one first course, one main course with vegetables, cheese and a dessert, all for 22 euros, but you can go à la carte if you prefer. The antipasti might include **anchovies al verde** or **with raisins and pine-nuts**, pepper flan with saffron, salads of wheat and spelt with vegetables, lentils and roast peppers, or tomato and mozzarella (to appeal to tourists, particularly Germans). The first courses include hand-made **tagliatelle with gravy**, maltagliati of spelt and borage with butter and sage, in the fall **chestnut flour fettuccine with potatoes and Elva Toma** cheese, or maccheroncini of rye or buckwheat. Then come a delicate turkey breast with potatoes, various **roasts** flavored with wild thyme or savory, chicken or **Sambucano lamb**. To finish, an assorted cheese board, home-made puddings, sorbet and sweet salami.
The wine list offers a choice of bottles from various regions of Italy, with a bias for labels from the Langhe and Roero, all proposed with a reasonable mark-up. If you don't finish your bottle, you'll be asked if you wish to take it with you.

🍲 In **Prazzo** (12 km), at Maslerio de Mountanho, Via Nazionale 46, Nicola Cesano sells good meat and excellent raw salami.

STROPPO
Bassura

TURIN

LOU SARVANOT

AI SAVOIA

🍲Restaurant
Frazione Bassura 64
Tel. 0171 999159
Closed Monday through Thursday,
never August 15 and Christmas
Open: dinner, festivities also at lunch
Holidays: March 10-25 and November 1-15
Seating: 28
Prices: 23-29 euros, wine excluded
All major credit cards, Bancomat

🛏Bed and breakfast
Via del Carmine 1 B
Tel. 339 1257711
Fax 011 5212848
E-mail: aisavoia@libero.it
Internet: www.aisavoia.it
Open all year

Paolo, with his quiet, courteous manner, is the host in this small restaurant, at the top of a winding road in the Maira valley. Silvia rarely appears as she juggles her jobs as cook and mother, but the skill with which she handles the raw materials, dosing out herbs and giving the right touch of lightness to her Provençal cuisine, but also carefully combining new flavors, speaks for itself.

There are two set menus, for 19 and 25 euros, and they change nearly every day. You begin with a salad of baccalà and potatoes, **sage flan** with fondue of local blue cheese and **pepper pie**. In winter you could try artichokes with anchovy sauce, **caponet**, or **liver pâté** with chestnuts. The pasta is home-made: **strangolapreti** with collard greens or spinach dressed with **butter and sage**, or buckwheat pasta served with vegetable sauces (try the courgette flower sauce in the summer). You'll often find classic local specialties such as **comaut**, **ravioles**, pasta and potatoes with leeks and baccalà. Follow this with **River Maira trout** in a variety of sauces (alla provenzale, with fresh tomato and capers, with orange or Cognac), or meats such as veal with raisins, culatta alle erbe, **Sambucano lamb with spices**, or rabbit with white wine and mustard. Then cheese from local dairies and desserts: strawberry sorbet, apricot, apple and plum cakes, aspic of raspberries, and torta dei Tetti with pears and chocolate (we advise a taste of all three).

The wine list offers an interesting selection of Piedmontese bottles and some outstanding labels from further afield.

The B&B is located in a wing of Palazzo Saluzzo di Paesana, one of the most beautiful buildings in the city, complete with a splendid courtyard. The stairway giving access to the palazzo is shared with an insurance office, but once you cross the threshold there are caisson ceilings, antique furniture and paintings, glasses and cups, all from the turn of the century. The buffet breakfast is laid out in a luminous hall and includes hot and fresh drinks, seasonal fruit, jams, honey, brioches from the bakery, cakes, butter and yogurt. If you pay a bit extra you' can enjoy a 'court breakfast', with three slices of the cakes once served at the Racconigi royal castle, where a relative of the current owners used to work. The rooms are furnished in imitation antique style and are in no way inferior to those you might find in a higher class hotel. 100 meters from the main facility, in a palazzo with an elevator in Via della Consolata, are five additional rooms of the same caliber.

• 3 double rooms, with bathroom, air-conditioning, safe, TV • Prices: double room single use 90 euros, double 95, breakfast included • Credit cards: Visa, Bancomat • Public parking (payment up to 7.30pm) and garage at a special rate nearby (18 euros for 24 hours). Small pets allowed. Owners always reachable.
• Breakfast room

CITY CENTER

AMADEUS

🔑 3-Star Hotel
Via Principe Amedeo 41 bis
Tel. 011 8174951
Fax 011 8174953
E-mail: info@hotelamadeustorino.it
Internet: www.hotelamadeustorino.it
Closed for 3 weeks in August

ANTICHE SERE

🍲 Traditional osteria-trattoria
Via Cenischia 9
Tel. 011 3854347
Closed Sunday
Open: dinner only
Holidays: two weeks in August and
two at Christmas
Seating: 50 + 50 outdoors
Prices: 30-35 euros, wine excluded
Credit cards: none, Bancomat

In the lively area behind Piazza Vittorio and Via Po, with its many cafes, restaurants and places where young people meet, you'll find the Amadeus Hotel managed by Luisa Balbo, a peaceful oasis in the heart of the city. The River Po is only a few hundred meters away, and on summer evenings the Murazzi riverside embankment attracts large crowds. The rooms are functional and nicely furnished, and some have a kitchenette for guests who prefer residence-style accommodation. The five mansard rooms on the fifth floor are not particularly large, though they have been furnished with great attention to detail. The buffet breakfast offers sweet and savory fare and hot and cold drinks. In the surrounding area you can visit the Accorsi Foundation and the Mole Antonellina, which houses the not-to-be-missed Cinema Museum.

• 10 single and 16 double rooms and 2 suites (2-4 persons), with bathroom (with showers or jacuzzis), air-conditioning, mini-bar, safe, satellite TV; some rooms with kitchenette • Prices: single 60-109 euros, double 98-120, suite 119-152, breakfast included • Credit cards: all, Bancomat • Off-street parking (2 spaces), garage at a special rate (15 euros a day). Small pets allowed. Reception open 24 hours a day. • Breakfast room. Lounge with TV.

We have always included this address in our guide, because it embodies just what we expect from an osteria today. First, it is located in a historical working-class part of the city, Borgo San Paolo, and it was founded about 15 years ago on a spot where they used to play 'bocce' (boules), retaining some of its original features, like the wood facing halfway up the walls, and the pergola in the courtyard, which provides comfortable al fresco dining in the hot summer months. Guests are looked after by the vivacious Antonella Rota in the dining-room and her skilled brother Daniele in the kitchen.

The cuisine is all Piedmontese, with a few dishes from Ghemme, the town in the province of Novara where the Rota family comes from. The wine list, carefully compiled and priced, is also based on this area. Together with good local and Italian labels, it features some of the best Nebbiolos in North Piedmont. The meal starts with excellent cured meats, vegetable pies and frittata, **stuffed vegetables**, including sweet onions, a real delicacy. Then, pasta and beans, tagliolini with asparagus, **gnocchi al ragù di salsiccia**, traditional **agnolotti** and an unmissable **paniscia**. The same must be said of the **tapulone** (a dish from Borgomanero, made with chopped donkey meat and herbs, cooked in red wine and served with polenta), or the **leg of pork**, cooked to perfection, or the delicate but tasty rabbit in white wine. At the end of the meal, a good selection of traditional desserts, from bonet to panna cotta, zabaione with corn biscuits and delicately perfumed Moscato soufflé. It is impossible to recommend one particular dish: better to try them all!.

ARTUÀ & SOLFERINO

🗝️● 3-Star Hotel
Via Brofferio 1-3
Tel. 011 5175301
Fax 011 5175141
E-mail: info@artua.it
Internet: www.artua.it
Open all year round

CON CALMA

🍲 Restaurant
Strada Comunale del Cartman 59
Tel. 011 8980229
Closed Monday
Open: dinner, Sunday and, on festivities, lunch too
Holidays: always open
Seating: 80 + 60 outdoors
Prices: 30-32 euros, wine excluded
All credit cards, Bancomat

The Artuà & Solferino Hotel is housed in a beautiful late 19th-century building on the corner of elegant Piazza Solferino, a really convenient address for anyone wishing to stay in the city center and find the main theaters and museums within easy reach. Strictly speaking, there are two hotels here: one at number 1 and the other at number 3, ten rooms each with standard, full comfort and two economy rooms at a lower price than the minimum, but not including breakfast. You'll feel as if you're staying in a family home, where the period details (thick wooden doors, brass handles, wooden floors) combine top create an informal, friendly atmosphere. Breakfast is buffet style, with hot drinks and sweet and savory fare. 10% discount on room prices at weekends.

• 3 single, 13 double, 2 triple and 2 four-bed rooms, with bathroom, air-conditioning, safe, satellite TV, modem connection • Prices: single 72-90 euros, double 96-120, triple 120-150, four-bed 128-160, breakfast included • Credit cards: all, Bancomat • Public parking (5 euros per day), garage (15 euros per day). Small pets allowed (in some rooms). Reception open 24 hours a day • Breakfast room. Reading room

You will find this refurbished restaurant in the hills above Corso Casale. It is particularly inviting in summer, when you are looking for respite from the heat. An elegant terrace and two carefully decorated rooms make up the restaurant, where you will be welcomed by Renata, her mother and the members of her young, professional staff. In the kitchen, chef Sandro Tonnera prepares traditional and 'reinvented' dishes, making good use of seasonal and local produce.
Choosing from the ample menu, you can order cured meats (such as potato salami from the Canavese and Biella areas), Piedmontese fassone veal marinated with Lanzo toma cheese, **carpionata mista**, **cold Piedmontese antipasti**, and salad of scaramella, as well as a number of dishes with wild herbs (friar's beard, costmary). Classic first courses such as **agnolotti alla monferrina** and **tagliolini** alternate with more imaginative dishes, from Venere rice with smoked trout to risotto with Barbera and smoked carp. Tradition then takes the upper hand, with roasts, **brasato** and **finanziera**, but many of the recipes are reinterpreted: roulade of rabbit filled with Lanzo Toma and Savoy cabbage from Montalto Dora, or tonno di coniglio with string beans and bilberry sauce. There is always a choice of cheeses from the board, to be enjoyed with a glass of Moscato Passito, a wine that is also be perfect with the desserts: bavarois, millefeuilles with chocolate, lugli (small hand-made biscuits) with zabaione, and others, depending on the chef's imagination. The cellar offers Piedmontese labels at reasonable prices, and guests who enjoy liqueurs can choose from a good selection of whiskies.

CONTE DI BIANCAMANO

3-Star Hotel
Corso Vittorio Emanuele II 73
Tel. 011 5623281
Fax 011 5623789
E-mail: info@hotelcontebiancamano.it
Internet: www.hotelcontebiancamano.it
Closed in August and 15 days at Christmas

A few minutes away from the city center, a hotel that's really worth discovering. Under the wide porticos of Corso Vittorio Emanuele II (almost on the corner with Corso Re Umberto), you climb the stairs to the 'piano nobile' of an elegant 19th-century palazzo originally built by the Counts of Barbaroux. Inside, the space is divided into a small reception area and a magnificent lounge with stuccoes and frescoes, while the rooms are spread over three floors. The bathrooms are sometimes a bit small, but there was no alternative when renovating an old building like this. Breakfast is buffet style, with sweet and savory fare. Prices are lower at weekends, but when there are fairs or soccer games and bank holidays, prices are approximately 10 euros above the maximum. The bus terminal to go to Caselle airport is within easy reach, as are Turin's famous coffee bars and restaurants and, for art lovers, the Gallery of Modern Art.

• 10 single and 10 double rooms and 4 suites (2-3 persons), with bathroom, mini-bar, satellite TV, modem connection • Prices: single 75-95 euros, double 95-120, single suite 95-110, double suite 120-145 (34-50 euro supplement for extra bed), breakfast included • Credit cards: all, Bancomat • Reserved parking (2 spaces), garage at special rates. Small pets allowed. Reception open 24 hours a day • Bar. Breakfast room, lounges. Conference room

DAI SALETTA

Trattoria
Via Belfiore 37
Tel. 011 6687867
Closed Sunday
Open: lunch and dinner
Holidays: August
Seating: 50
Prices: 33 euros, wine excluded
All credit cards

This is one of the few, real trattorias left in Turin, where Sonia and William Saletta keep both the original environment and the food unaltered. The two small dining-rooms, the checked tablecloths, and the friendly, affable manner of the proprietors create a familiar, down-to-earth atmosphere that isn't easy to find these days.
The dishes served are the typical fare of the Piedmontese capital, but there are also others borrowed from the Langhe and the mountain valleys. Local produce is transformed into succulent dishes, some of which are on the menu all year round, others, obviously, only when in season. Start with the cured meats, **tripe from Moncalieri** or, in true Piedmontese fashion, with the rustico della casa, a tray of seven typical antipasti. Of the first courses, it is a pleasure to recall the **tagliolini alla langarola** and the **agnolotti dal plin** but the gnocchi al Castelmagno, trifulin (ravioli di magro flavored with truffle), rustiche alla montanara (with potatoes and Toma from Lanzo) are equally inviting, or vegetable soup with tripe in winter. For a main course, we recommend the **brasato al Barolo**, rabbit with plums and fesotto alla senape. You will have to wait for the colder weather to enjoy the really classical dishes like **bagna caoda** and **stewed tripe**, and it may be necessary to order before you go. To conclude, traditional puddings like panna cotta, **bonet**, and cold zabaione.
The wine list is mainly Piedmontese, and is quite extensive, but in the summer the reds are not always served at the correct temperature.

10 KM FROM CITY CENTER

FORESTERIA DELLA BASILICA DI SUPERGA

Guestrooms
Strada della Basilica di Superga
Tel. 011 8980083
Fax 011 8987024
Open all year round

L'OCA FOLA

Trattoria
Via Drovetti 6 G
Tel. 011 4337422
Closed Sunday
Open: dinner only
Holidays: 10 days in August
Seating: 50
Prices: 30-32 euros, wine excluded
All credit cards except AE

The Basilica of Superga towers at an altitude of 670 meters on one of the highest points in the hills to the east of Turin. For some time now it's been possible to stay in one of the key baroque buildings in Piedmont, completed by architect Filippo Juvarra in 1726. The guestroom facility in the basilica's foresteria is managed by the monks – the Padri Servi di Maria – who for centuries have looked after the monument. Everybody is welcome to stay here, but while there are no religious obligations guests are expected to behave appropriately given the nature of the place. Located only 10 minutes by car from Turin, it is perfect for those seeking peace and quiet and who enjoy art and nature. The prices are very competitive indeed. The large rooms with period furniture have thick wooden floors and caisson ceilings. Breakfast is very simple and offers coffee, tea, milk, bread, jam and fruit. In the evening you can come back at any time, provided you pick up your room key before 8.30 pm.

• 22 double rooms, with bathroom • Prices: double room single use 25-30 euros, double 50-60, breakfast included • Credit cards: none • 2 rooms designed for use by the mobility challenged. Off-street parking and free public parking 30 meters away. No pets allowed. Monks always present. • Breakfast room. Conversation room with TV

Located in the Piazza Statuto area, easy to reach from Corso Francia or from Corso Inghilterra, the Oca Fola is a typical Piedmontese osteria. The interior is simply and carefully decorated with arte povera furniture, white curtains, and shelves with bottle. The restaurant's logo, a goose, pops up on the tablecloths and plates, and even decorates the walls. The restaurant is run by three men, Claudio, Massimo and Dario, who do everything between them, from shopping to coordinating service in the dining-room and cooking.

The menu varies almost every day, to reflect what is in season or available on the market. You will find five antipasti in small trays on the table when you sit down. So while you savor the raw and cooked salamis, **vitello tonnato**, veal cutlets in carpione, tomini al verde and **peppers with bagna caoda**, you can concentrate on choosing one of the three first courses on the menu: for example **agnolotti with gravy**, pasta e riso all'ortolana, **cabbage soup alla canavesana** in winter, rice and bean soup or cream of vegetable soup alla contadina. One of the two main courses on offer may be tagliata of fassone or **fillet of pork** alla boscaiola, and in winter we recommend the **tripe** (on Fridays), which is replaced in summer by a fairly varied cheese board. The puddings range from **bonet** to torta langarola with peaches and amaretti, panna cotta, and pandorino with chocolate.

The wine list is well stocked: about 100 labels of Piedmontese reds and whites, all reasonably priced.

PIEMONTESE

☎🍴 3-Star Hotel
Via Berthollet 21
Tel. 011 6698101
Fax 011 6690571
E-mail: info@hotelpiemontese.it
Internet: www.hotelpiemontese.it
Open all year

The hotel is in a 19th-century building in the multiethnic San Salvario quarter. To the right of the reception desk, there's a comfortable hall where newspapers are available for guests. At the back there's another pleasant lounge-cum-library and two other rooms where a buffet breakfast is served (with hot drinks, fruit juices, seasonal fresh and dried fruits, jams, honey, brioches, cakes, cured meats, cheeses and a few organic products). The four rooms on the fifth floor have mansard ceilings, with warm and cozy furnishings, wooden beams and a view over the city's rooftops, the fourth floor rooms are a little smaller. During the recent refurbishment various bathrooms were fitted with jacuzzis or sauna showers; the minimalist-style rooms are very pleasant. Prices are increased during the months of April-May and September-October.

• 32 double rooms and 5 suites, with bathroom, air-conditioning, mini-bar, TV, modem connection, some rooms with terrace • Prices: double room single occupancy 69-93 euros, double 89-119, suite 119-159, breakfast included • Credit cards: all • 2 rooms designed for use by the mobility challenged. Covered parking at special rates next door. Small pets allowed. Reception open 24 hours a day. • Breakfast rooms, reading and conference room, TV room. Garden

SOTTO LA MOLE   ⊗

🍲 Restaurant
Via Montebello 9
Tel. 011 8179398
Closed Wednesday, Sunday in summer
Open: dinner, October-May, Sunday at lunch too
Holidays: 3 weeks in June, 10 days in winter
Seating: 40
Prices: 33-35 euros, wine excluded
All major credit cards

The restaurant is located in a quiet pedestrian precinct in the town center in front of the entrance to the Mole Antonelliana, now the home of the popular Cinema Museum. The renown and excellent visibility of this monument are a perfect magnet, and people can enjoy a pleasant encounter with Piedmontese traditional cooking before or after they visit the museum. Professional skill and a careful selection of raw materials are evident in the dishes prepared by chef Simone Ferrero, and served in the dining-room with efficiency and courtesy by his wife Anna Rosa and her assistants.

The menu changes with the seasons, but among the antipasti you will nearly always find an excellent **timballo di carne cruda** with horseradish sauce. In the summer: **caponet di seirass** with pureed tomato, home-made **insalata russa**, chicken liver pate with compote or an excellent lardo with hot focaccia. In winter, you can choose between terrine of tongue and **testina with green or red sauce**, flan of cardoons and Jerusalem artichokes with bagna caoda, and insalata di galletto alla moda rustica. For your first course, you will be offered **agnolotti** alla piemontese, risotto with sausage and Barbera and **tajarin**: with courgettes and peppers in summer, or with chicken liver sauce in winter. For a main course: **finanziera**, boned rabbit alla canavesana, steamed cod with Taggiasca olives, fassone stew, **tapulone** from Borgomanero, stewed Bra sausage with polenta. There is a good selection of Piedmontese cheeses. End your meal with a **gianduiotto** on melted chocolate, bilberries au gratin or panna cotta.

The wine list concentrates on Piedmont and contains some interesting labels.

TORINO

TORRE PELLICE

50 km southwest of Turin, 13 km southwest of Pinerolo

TRATTORIA VALENZA

Trattoria
Via Borgodora 39
Tel. 011 5213914
Closed Sunday and Monday at lunch
Open: lunch and dinner
Holidays: August
Seating: 40 + 20 outdoors
Prices: 26-28 euros, wine excluded
No credit cards accepted

FLIPOT

3-Star Hotel
Corso Gramsci 17
Tel. 0121 91236
Fax 0121 953465
E-mail: flipot@flipot.com
Internet: www.flipot.com
Holidays vary

This authentic Piedmontese pìola lies in the historical heart of Turin, near to the multiethnic Balòn market and its stalls of second-hand goods and foods. While you eat, or after you've finished, you'll often be entertained by guitarists or by the proprietor himself, Walter Braga, a great exponent of bel canto and of the cuisine of yesteryear. When you enter the restaurant you get the impression that time has stood still: old clocks hanging on the walls, paintings of every description and here and there a variety of ciapa póver (dust collectors, a humorous term for ornaments) witnesses to times gone by.

Tomini cheese, anchovies, **peppers with bagna caoda** and insalata russa to start with. Followed by classical **agnolotti, tajarin** and gnocchi with all the usual sauces. For seconds, as a sign of continuity, try the **boiled meats** with the traditional Piedmontese bagnet, cotechino with sauerkraut, tripe and **brasato** and, in the summer, veal cutlets in carpione or tasca ripiena. And to finish, panna cotta, torta della nonna, and fresh or stewed seasonal fruit.

The cellar offers an honest Barbera by the carafe, and some labels of Dolcetto, Grignolino and Bonarda. At the end of the meal, don't miss the house coffee made from a secret recipe. The dishes may not all fill you with enthusiasm, but if you want to relive emotions of the past, this is a trattoria where you will discover a city that you thought had vanished.

At the Ceni grocer's shop, at Piazza della Repubblica 5 h, you'll find 20 types of rice, beans, lentils, seeds and cereals, plus a vast range of ethnic foods.

Flipot is a name more famous as a restaurant than a hotel. Yet this establishment began life as a locanda in the same building, an 18th-century farmhouse. In 1903 it was called Locanda del Persico, but soon the personality of the first owner, Filippo Gay, gained the upper hand and the place took his name. Since then much has changed and Walter and Gisella Eynard, who have owned the place since 1981, have made it more comfortable without modifying the old Piedmontese locanda atmosphere. Here guests can take time out for a vacation with a yesteryear feel to it. For breakfast there are two options: Italian style, with homemade pastries, jellies and jams, or American style, with a variety of cured meats and local cheeses from the valley.

• 8 double rooms, with bathroom (and jacuzzis), satellite TV, modem connection • Prices: double room single occupancy 80 euros, double 100, breakfast included • Credit cards: all, Bancomat • Restaurant accessible for the mobility challenged. Off-street parking. No pets allowed. Reception open 9am-midnight (except Mondays and Tuesdays) • Restaurant. Breakfast room, reading and TV room. Garden

The restaurant (set menu 80 euros, excluding wine) serves a perfect blend of traditional cuisine and contemporary reinterpretation.

TORTONA

VINERIA DERTHONA

🍲 Osteria-wine bar
Via Perosi 15
Tel. 0131 812468
Closed Monday, Saturday and Sunday lunch
Open: lunch and dinner
Holidays: August, 1 week after Christmas
Seating: 50
Prices: 28-30 euros, wine excluded
All major credit cards, Bancomat

Since this wine bar, now run by Gianni Respighi, first opened, it has owed its success on its wide choice of wines – bottles or by the glass – and a well balanced menu with a limited number of dishes (never more than twelve), mainly designed to show off the local cuisine, with interesting incursions into the surrounding regions.
Start with Piedmontese classics: insalata russa, tongue with salsa verde, **anchovies**, vitello tonnato and a good warm tripe salad accompanied by cannellini beans. For first course, we tried the **cream of asparagus soup**, but on other days you will find **ravioli tortonesi**, **pasta and beans**, soups, polenta or excellent pisarei e fasò (pasta and beans Piacenza-style). Follow this with meat – we tried the roast beff al sale, served with a sauce of mayonnaise and Dijon mustard – or fish, **stoccafisso** or **baccalà**, poached and served with good mashed potato. Worth a special mention is the board of Piedmontese **cheese**, which includes Montébore (a Slow Food Presidia), back in production again since 1999 after all but disappearing in the 1980s. Last but by no means least in terms of quality, the **Tortona strawberries** with Barbera and sugar, otherwise you can't go wrong with crostata, aspic, meringue or tiramisù.
The wine list is extensive with a preference for bottles from Tortona, but there are also several labels from the rest of Italy and abroad.

TRANA
San Bernardino

LA BETULLA

🍲 Restaurant
Strada Giaveno 29
Tel. 011 933106
Closed Monday
Open: lunch and dinner
Holidays: January 7-21
Seating: 60
Prices: 26 euros, wine excluded
All credit cards except AE, Bancomat

La Betulla was once one of the brightest stars in the firmament of restaurants in the Turin area. It is now enjoying a revival, thanks to today's chef and owner Franco Giacomino who, after gaining the necessary experience in Italy and abroad, decided to return to raise the profile of his home town. The ambience is elegant with large, light-filled dining-rooms, beautiful curtains and lovely fittings, and the welcome from the dining-room staff is professional. Choose à la carte as you enjoy a glass of bubbly and you'll find dishes that exploit raw ingredients from the Sangone and Susa valleys, Slow Food Presidia products, such as Sambucano lamb and Cevrin from Coazze, as well as a number of imaginative fish dishes.
To start with, raw Piedmontese fassone meat salad with black truffles or Santena asparagus and poached eggs, fried fillet of perch with artichokes and a fantastic **vitello tonnato in salsa antica**. This is followed by **rabatòn** from Alessandria flavored with sage and tomato, gnocchi with sarass del fen and courgette flowers with crayfish sauce, **agnolottini dal plin** in gravy or nettle gnocchi au gratin with Gorgonzola fondue. For main course, we recommend **Sambucano lamb flavored with hay**, finanziera, stewed rabbit with olives and artichokes or a **kebab of frog's legs** in herb bread. To conclude, **cheese** from the rich cheese board or desserts such as zabaglione al Moscato or chocolate drop and cinnamon pie. From Tuesdays to Fridays it is possible to order **fritto misto piemontese**, with 21 pieces of meat and vegetables. The wine list is very extensive, with almost 1,000 labels, mainly Piedmontese and Italian.

OSTERIA DELL'UNIONE

RISORGIMENTO

Restaurant
Via Alba 1
Tel. 0173 638303
Closed Sunday dinner and Monday
Open: lunch and dinner
Holidays: 2 weeks between December and January
Seating: 25
Prices: 30-35 euros, wine excluded
No credit cards accepted

Trattoria
Viale Rimembranza, 14
Tel. 0173 638195
Closed Mondays
Open: lunch, Fridays, Saturdays, also Sunday dinner
Holidays: 15 days in January and July
Seating: 60
Prices: 18-28 euros, wine excluded
Credit cards: Visa, Bancomat

25 years have passed since that first of May when this classic eating place re-opened to the public with the help of the Libera e Benemerita Associazione degli Amici del Barolo (the original nucleus of the future Slow Food organization). It is run by the Marcarino family: Beppe, his wife Pina Bongiovanni, an excellent cook and daughter of the former owner Cesarin, and their daughter Patrizia, who has been playing a more important role in the kitchen in recent years. This small inn is easy to reach along a beautiful, scenic road from Alba. The simple, tastefully decorated restaurant exudes charm: brick-vaulted ceilings, bottles displayed on good-looking wooden shelves, and fresh flowers. The service is efficient and somewhat reserved.

You usually start with a selection of local cured meats, followed, when in season, by small **herb frittatas**, insalata di carne cruda, **tongue in sauce**, Toma from the Langhe with **bagnet verde**, carpione of chicken with zucchini, **stuffed zucchini flowers** or quail's eggs, **vitello tonnato**. Patrizia makes the home-made pasta, which is served with meat sauce or butter and sage; the **tajarin** are excellent (they take their intense yellow color from the quantity and quality of the eggs used), as are the **agnolotti dal plin**. Possible main courses are **rabbit with Barbaresco** (or with peppers or herbs) and **brasato al Barolo**. To complete the meal, cheese served with cognà, **bonet**, panna cotta or **hazelnut cake with zabaglione**.

The carefully chosen wine list includes all the best labels from the Langhe. This is Beppe's department and he'll be able to recommend the best wines to go with your meal.

The building is not particularly attractive, but the dining-room – next to the bar where the locals meet for a coffee or a glass of wine – is carefully furnished and the décor combines tables and chairs from the new premises with a number of 'antiques' transferred from the former premises (which incorporated a food store) a short distance away. But the pride of the restaurant remains its cuisine, which is strictly Langa-style, prepared with care by the owner Maria Settima Vola, assisted by her daughter Elisa. Husband Ilario, the other daughter Cinzia and a waitress serve at table. Age-old customs are preserved here: the menu is presented vocally, and only the antipasti and desserts are served on plates – everything else arrives on generously filled trays.

You can start with **carne cruda all'albese**, **vitello tonnato**, excellent **insalata russa**, or vegetable pie or flan with fondue. For a first course, all year round you'll find the icons of tradition, such as **tajarin** and **agnolotti dal plin** with meat sauce or with butter and sage, **gnocchi** with sausage, and **risotto**, and, in summer, maltagliati with whatever vegetables are in season. The main courses include excellent boned and **sautéed rabbit**, **brasato al Barbaresco**, **roast lamb shank**, and, in the fall, wild boar stew. If you book, you can enjoy a huge **fritto misto**. To conclude, bonet, panna cotta, apple cake, and peaches with Moscato or, in summer, stuffed.

Enjoy your meal with a good bottle of wine from the Langhe from the selection displayed on a long counter in the dining-room.

ANTICO BORGO DEL RIONDINO

Holiday farm
Via dei Fiori 13
Tel. e fax 0173 630313
Open from beginning of March to
end of December

Irene Poncellini's friendliness is exemplary. This agriturismo is just outside Trezzo Tinella, in a farmhouse that probably dates back to the 17th century. Guest rooms are all painted in different colors and furnished with antiques. As for the common areas: the 'black room' looks out onto the inside garden through big windows and has comfortable divans where you can read and engage in conversation; the breakfast room, where a different type of cake is served up every day along with brioches, bread, butter and jams (for a small supplement you can also have a variety of cured meats and local cheeses); the restaurant, only open to residents who must also make a reservation (dinner ranges from 35-37 euros per person, wine excluded). Recently a small pond has been added to the garden where you can swim. As for pets, only dogs are allowed.

• 8 double rooms, with bathroom • Prices: double room single use and double 105 euros, breakfast included • Credit cards: major ones, Bancomat • Public parking. Small pets allowed. Owners always reachable. • Restaurant (for residents only). Breakfast rooms, reading room. Garden

MASSIMO

Restaurant with hotel
Via Ferrari 7
Tel. 0161 801325
Closed Saturday at noon and Sunday evening
Open: lunch and dinner
Holidays: end-July to end-August
Seating: 70
Prices: 28-30 euros, wine excluded
All major credit cards, Bancomat

Trino lies where the southern part of the province of Vercelli meets the River Po, where rice-growing was introduced by the Cistercians and where the Partecipanza wood conserves the last remains of the province's primeval forest. A few years ago, Giorgio Bonato, his wife Sandra and their children, took over the Massimo hotel and restaurant, making it one of the most reliable addresses in the area.
In addition to the Piedmontese dishes that vary almost every day according to the market and the season, on Fridays there's also a fish menu. Keeping to the most traditional dishes, the meal begins with cured meats – **salam 'd la doja**, cooked salami from nearby Monferrato, lardo and mortadella di fegato – and other antipasti which include fresh Robiola cheese with spicy pear, peppers with bagna caoda, carne cruda battuta al coltello, **giardiniera with tuna**, **vitello tonnato** cooked in salt and salad of baccalà. The first courses always include **panissa** and **agnolotti in gravy**, the emblems of local cuisine, but the tajarin with cep mushroom or frog-meat sauce and panzerotti with ricotta and eggplant with pesto are also good. For main course, **roasts**, guinea-fowl, fillet steak, an array of boiled meats, **stewed donkey**, tripe or snails. But if you are around between July and November, and if the ranatè, or frog catcher, provides the raw ingredients, order the **fried frog's legs**. To conclude, panna cotta, pancakes with chocolate or peaches with Brachetto.
The cellar is well supplied, with over 300 labels, the majority of which Piedmontese.

USSEAUX
Laux

VARALLO
Sebrey

LAGO LAUX

☎—🔑3-Star Hotel-Residence
Via al Lago 7
Tel. and fax 0121 83944
E-mail: info@hotellaux.it
Internet: www.hotellaux.it
Closed for a few days after Easter and
from end of September to mid-October

MONTE ROSA

☎—🔑2-Star Hotel
Via Regaldi 4
Tel. and fax 0163 51100
E-mail: albergo.monterosa@laproxima.it
Internet: www.albergomonterosa.com
Open all year round

Originally the hotel was a vacation home, enlarged by the Salesians in 1943 and then destroyed during the war. Currently managed by Marinella Canton and Gianfranco Aimo, it has comfortable, simply furnished double rooms (during summer and Christmas the price goes up to 126 euros), all with a view of the lake and the surrounding park, whence paths lead to the forests and the nearby mountains. In summer the area surrounding the hotel is equipped for mobile homes. In the immediate vicinity there are a hang-gliding field, a mountain bike track and, in winter, ski-lift facilities. Breakfast offers classic fare, honey, jams, bread, cookies and homemade cakes. The restaurant, which is also open to non-residents, specializes in Piedmontese and Provençal cuisine (ranging from 20-30 euros per person, excluding wine). For a stay of at least three days there's a half board option ranging from 74-84 euros, and full board ranging from 95-105 euros per person.

• 7 double rooms, with bathroom, mini-bar, TV; 5 with kitchenette • Prices: double room single use 105 euros, double 105 (15 euro supplement for extra bed), breakfast included • Credit cards: all, Bancomat • Free external public parking. Small pets allowed (in some rooms only). Reception open from 8 am to midnight. • Restaurant. Breakfast room, TV room. Grounds

In the capital of the Valsesia district, right in view of Mount Rosa and close to one of the oldest of Piedmont's sacred mounts (a nature reserve), the Del Boca family has been running this small hotel, which is also their home, for nearly a century. Built by great-grandfather Annibale in 1908, it's a typical building surrounded by trees on a road that crosses Via Brigate Garibaldi as you leave the city traveling towards Civiasco-Lago d'Orta. The interiors, common areas and rooms retain the original furnishings, with parquet floors, fabrics and furniture dating from the early 1900s. The simplicity of the whole setting is made even more attractive by the kindness shown by Maria Paola and her family. There is table service for breakfast and savory dishes are served on request. The restaurant is only open in July and August and offers homely cooking with prices ranging from 15-20 euros per person, wine excluded (half board is 45 euros, full board is 55 euros).

• 5 single and 10 double rooms, with bathroom, TV • Prices: single 25-35 euros, double 50-60 (10-15 euro supplement for extra bed), breakfast included • Credit cards: none • Communal areas accessible to the mobility challenged. Off-street parking, garage on request. Small pets allowed. Owners always present. • Bar, restaurant (closed in winter). Breakfast room, living room. Outside space, garden, grounds

VERCELLI

VERDUNO

VECCHIA BRENTA

CA' DEL RE

� Restaurant
Via Morosone 6
Tel. 0161 251230
Closed Thursday
Open: lunch and dinner
Holidays: July
Seating: 100
Prices: 20-30 euros, wine excluded
All major credit cards, Bancomat

� Holiday farm restaurant
Via Umberto 14
Tel. 0172 470281
Closed Thursday
Open: lunch and dinner
Holidays: December 15- February 31
Seating: 40 + 40 outdoors
Prices: 25 euros, wine excluded
All major credit cards, Bancomat

This historical restaurant is a short walk from the central Piazza Cavour in the heart of Vercelli old town, near the former ghetto, and used to be a hotel too. People would come here specially for the agnolotti, but the restaurant then suffered a decline. Today things are on the up again, and the clients are back, young people included. The credit goes above all to the hard work of Massimo Magagnato and his family: his mother helps in the kitchen, his fiancée, Michela, is in the dining-room and his father works the bar. The restaurant, with its wonderful old sign, has a large entrance with a counter and two cozy rooms with soft lighting. The menu varies three times a year and is strictly 'alla piemontese' with some diversions, fish dishes included. Select the specialties that reflect local customs. For antipasto: **salam d'la duja**, lardo, tomini, **acquadelle in carpione**, pinzimonio of vegetables, and **bagna caoda** in season. We can recommend the first courses: **agnolotti al sugo d'arrosto** or with a vegetable filling, potato gnocchi, and **risotto** with artichokes and lardo, or with courgettes and fondue, or with truffles, as well as the traditional **panissa**. Then try the grilled vegetables, **mixed boiled meats** with various sauces, roasts, **fritto misto**, or **fried frogs** and snails, when in season. The cheese selection is fair, with plenty of Toma and Gorgonzola. Desserts include home-made soft puddings and panna cotta, and **tartufata** from a local pastry shop.
The wine list is limited but includes some good Piedmontese labels.

The very name of Verduno conjures up hillsides in bloom. And that is exactly what you see as you approach this lovely village, overlooking the rolling hills of the Langhe. The holiday farm restaurant run by the Burlotto family is in the old part of the village. Here guests eat in a spacious dining-room that is rustic but tastefully decorated, or al fresco in the inner courtyard in the summer.
Gabriella Burlotto lists the day's dishes, prepared in a kitchen that is the epitome of simplicity. In the summer try the tray of cured meats (good raw and cooked salamis), **tomatoes stuffed with bagnetto verde**, salad of calf's head and occasionally meatballs in carpione. In winter – but increasingly rarely – try **oriot** (head of pork boiled and diced, and served with a sauce of vegetables and peppers), or vitello tonnato, tongue or a frittata of onions. The pasta is all home-made: **tagliatelle** (the ones made with corn flour are particularly good) served with ragù, **butter and mint**, or fresh tomato, and **minestrone** prepared with vegetables from the garden or with chickpeas. Then come excellent **roast rabbit**, **veal stewed in Barolo**, roast pork and chicken alla cacciatora. Simple, traditional puddings such as bonet or, in the summer, stuffed vineyard peaches, semifreddo al torrone and apple cake.
The family farm produces one of the best Verduno Pelavergas, the wine that is the symbol of the town. The wine list includes not only the Burlotto family's own wines, but also a good selection of labels from the Langhe with a reasonable mark-up. Book in advance.

REAL CASTELLO

2-Star Hotel
Via Umberto I 9
Tel. 0172 470125
Fax 0172 470298
E-mail: info@castellodiverduno.com
Internet: www.castellodiverduno.com
Open from March to November

SAN BERNARDO

Trattoria
Via San Bernardo 63
Tel. 0175 85822
Closed Tuesday and Wednesday
Open: lunch and dinner
Holidays: 3-4 weeks after the Epiphany
Seating: 50 + 60 outdoors
Prices: 25-28 euros, wine excluded
All major credit cards, Bancomat

The rooms of this interesting hotel are situated in a part of Verduno Castle and in its annexes (the 'castalderia' overlooking the garden, the 'foresteria' in a 17th-century farmhouse and the Ca' del Re vacation farm – 0172 470281 – not far from the castle itself). The rooms are all spacious and beautifully appointed with antique furniture. Great care has also been taken over the choice of colors. The hotel garden is surrounded by a wonderful garden. In the morning guests are welcomed by a generous buffet breakfast with sweet and savory fare.

• 14 double rooms, 4 junior suites and 2 senior suites, with bathroom (next door in three rooms); in the Ca' del Re vacation farm, 5 double rooms, with bathroom • Prices: double room single use 105 euros, double 100-115, suites 135-180 (40 euro supplement for extra bed), breakfast included. At Ca' del Re, double room single use 50 euros, double 60, breakfast included • Credit cards: all, Bancomat • 2 rooms designed for use by the mobility challenged. Off-street parking, in part covered. Small pets allowed (in 2 rooms). Owners always present. • Restaurant, wine cellar, wine-tasting room. Garden, grounds.

The local cuisine in the hotel and holiday farm restaurants is excellent (40-45 euros, excluding wine, at the castle).

Who's to blame the monks and hermits who chose the hills around Saluzzo as a refuge from the world? Traveling up to San Bernardo, through the woods, small vegetable gardens and farmhouses, you have a sense of peace and fresh air, not to mention the opportunity for a relaxing stop. Paolo is the host in this scenic osteria – with beautiful views from both the summer and the winter dining areas – and he is certainly not lacking in good humor and courtesy.

The creations that come out of the kitchen, most of which devised and prepared by Paolo's partner, Alberto, all start from quality raw ingredients: **cured meats** from Beppe Dho of Centallo, meat from Silvio Brarda of Cavour, cheese from small local dairies and producers, vegetables from the garden and **mushrooms** picked in the surrounding hills (ceps and garitole used to flavor pasta and risotto, or fried and served as a main course). Start with **vitello tonnato**, **carne cruda**, flans and soufflés of vegetables with various sauces, summer **carpionata**, and a variety of other first courses. Tagliolini with zucchini and zucchini flowers, risotto with herbs, **agnolotti** with butter and sage, and **ravioles**. Plus, to warm you up in winter, tripe soup and **pasta and beans**. The meat courses include roast beef cooked to a turn, **stracotto di bue**, boiled meats, coppa of pork and **boar in white wine**. You can also order fritto alla piemontese. Many of the summer desserts are made with fruit (apricot cake, semifreddo with berries, stuffed peaches), but bonet, panna cotta and other goodies are also on the menu.

The cellar contains approximately 200 labels, from Piedmont.

VERZUOLO
Villanovetta

VEZZA D'ALBA

27 KM FROM CUNEO, 6 KM SOUTH OF SALUZZO SS 589

47 KM FROM CUNEO, 17 KM SOUTHWEST OF ALBA

TRATTORIA SOCIETÀ ⊘❚

DI VIN ROERO

⌒Trattoria
Via Griselda, 29
Tel. 0175 88743-85495
Closed Wednesday
Open: lunch and dinner
Holidays: 1 week in February, 2 in June
Seating: 30
Prices: 23-25 euros, wine excluded
All major credit cards, Bancomat

⌒Osteria with rooms
Piazza San Martino, 5
Tel. 0173 65114
Closed Monday
Open: dinner, Saturday and at lunch on festivities
Holidays: 1 week in January, 1 in July
Seating: 50 + 50 outdoors
Prices: 20-23 euros, wine excluded
All major credit cards, Bancomat

It is restaurants like this that keep alive the production of foods that would otherwise disappear. We refer only to Slow Food Presidia, though they are widespread in this area, but also to the fact that the proprietors never cease to encourage local farmers to cultivate their land with care and to avoid abandoning tradition. Verzuolo is a sleepy village in the foothills of the Alps near Cuneo, where you really have to work hard to survive. Which is why chef Charlie Zuchuat, Swiss in origin but now a naturalized Provençal, and his wife Marcella in the dining-room never deviate a single millimeter from their determination to serve guests the best the land can offer. Our enjoyable investigation of local fare began with an antipasto of ramassin with Grigio di Becetto, an almost unknown marbled cheese, followed by bruschetta of tapenade and anchoyade, typical flavors of Provence, salad of babi beans with Tomin dal Mel and a delicious **salad of Saluzzo white chicken** with tarragon and hazelnuts. As a first course, **tagliatelle made with chestnut flour**, spätzle (small Swiss gnocchi) with ratatouille, and **finanziera of chicken giblets**. As a main course, **roast veal shank** and a fine selection of local cheese. To conclude, home-made desserts: wild bilberry pie and mint flan. The dishes express a true passion for local traditions and are all well made. In other words, not only a lesson in Provençal biodiversity but also in good cooking.

The wine list consists mainly of labels from this area of minor production, with the addition of a few Swiss and French gems. Prices are extremely reasonable.

Nestling in the heart of the Roero district, Vezza is like so many other small towns on either side of the Tanaro, with a perfectly maintained, discreet old center perched on top of a hill, and a lower part that has been plundered by the building mania of the nouveau riche, with all the accompanying concrete monstrosities. But when you are up in the airy square, with the two churches on the right and the wooden door to the inn on the left, you can forget all the rest: the air is better and the warm welcome from the Grasso family prepares you for the pleasures of the restaurant's simple home cooking, which has never changed over the years. It is difficult to find more traditional recipes, carefully chosen raw ingredients, unbeatable prices, great skill and courtesy to help you choose. So just relax and enjoy yourself.

The antipasti always include tagliata of veal with Provençal herbs, **peppers with bagna caoda** (or with tuna sauce in the summer), **trout in carpione**, vitello tonnato and various pies prepared with seasonable vegetables. This is followed by good fresh pasta: **gnocchi al raschera**, tajarin, and **ravioli dal plin** with melted butter, meat sauce or mushrooms. The main courses don't stray far from the typical fare of the Tanaro area: rabbit all'Arneis, **stracotto al Nebbiolo, boned turkey** or **boar al civet** in winter. End the meal with a traditional dessert: bonet, salame del papa, panna cotta or stuffed peaches.

The short wine list consists mainly of wines from the Langhe and Roero, which deserves a special mention for their honest mark-ups.

VICOFORTE
Santuario di Vicoforte

32 KM EAST OF CUNEO ON SS 564 AND 28

PORTICI

🗝️3-Star Hotel
Piazza Carlo Emanuele 47
Tel. 0174 563980
Fax 0174 569027
E-mail: info@hotelportici.com
Internet: www.hotelportici.com
Open all year round

VIGNALE MONFERRATO

24 KM NORTHWEST OF ALESSANDRIA, 17 KM FROM CASALE

DRÉ CASTÉ MONGETTO

🍲Holiday farm-Restaurant
Via Piave 2
Tel. 0142 933442
Open Friday and Saturday dinner, Sunday at lunch, other days for groups (if booked)
Holidays: August and January
Seating: 40 + 16 outdoors
Prices: 26-28 euros, wine excluded
Credit cards: CartaSi, MC, Visa

In the 17th century the Bishop of Mondovì and the Savoy family decided to build a place to accommodate pilgrims arriving in the area. The result was an extraordinary architectural complex comprising several sacred buildings, delimited by the Palazzata. In the wing of this building constructed in 1751 is the Portici hotel, with its 29 elegant and comfortable rooms. This facility, managed by the Bezaleel company, is the ideal place to stay to explore the beauties of the area round Mondovì. Common areas are spacious and refined and a relaxing stay is guaranteed. The highly professional staff will be pleased to suggest itineraries to meet your requirements. The continental-style breakfast focuses particularly on sweet fare from the adjacent pastry shop: besides the classic brioches, also risole, paste di meliga, pan polenta, and santuariesi with rum or nuts.

• 2 single, 18 double, 4 triple, 1 four-bed rooms and 4 suites (2-4 persons), with bathroom, mini-bar, safe, satellite TV, modem connection • Prices: single 44 euros, double room single use 49, double 70, triple 78-87, four-bed 95-103, suite 93-105, breakfast included • Credit cards: all, Bancomat • Entire facility accessible to the mobility challenged. Free external public parking. Small pets allowed (3.50 euros per day). Reception open 24 hours a day • Bar. Breakfast room, TV room. Conference room next to the facility. Garden

The Santopietro brothers, Roberto and Carlo, share out tasks between them: the former produces jams, sauces and preserves in the cooperative in nearby Mongetto, the latter manages the farm and the farm restaurant. But the two activities are closely linked because the restaurant serves many products from the cooperative, including grape mostarda, the sauces to accompany the boiled meats, martin sec pears al Grignolino and vineyard peaches al Moscato. Housed in an elegant farmhouse, the restaurant has a large courtyard, a portico that is ideal for an al fresco aperitif or a merenda sinoira, or afternoon snack, and a terrace with a wonderful view over the lower Monferrato. There are two well furnished dining-rooms with fireplaces; upstairs there are four comfortable bedrooms for people who wish to stay longer.

The menu is recited aloud; it offers little choice, but is all traditional Monferrato fare, from the antipasti that might include **peppers with bagna caoda**, **giardiniera**, stuffed vegetables, frittata and fried garden vegetables. The first courses include excellent **tagliolini** with mushrooms, **al sugo di stufato** or with truffles, and among the main courses we recommend the **mixed boiled meats**, the **brasato**, the chicken alla cacciatora and the tasty **roast rabbit**. The vegetables are those in season and the fruit in the crostata may be bottled or fresh, produced by the Mongetto cooperative. Other desserts worth trying are the bonet, panna cotta and various types of bavarois.
All the wines are produced on the farm and are all very good.

VIGNALE MONFERRATO

UNIVERSO

⌒ Restaurant
Via Bergamaschino 19
Tel. 0142 933052
Closed Monday and Tuesday
Open: dinner only
Holidays: 2 weeks of August
Seating 70
Prices: 30 euros, wine excluded
Credit cards: CartaSi, Visa, Bancomat

The restaurant, situated in a street beside Palazzo Callori, the home of the Regional Wine Cellar, is close to the square where the International Dance Festival is held every year. During the festival, a path round the stage permits access to the restaurant, where the atmosphere created by the furnishings, frescoes and fireplaces takes you back in time. The tables are well laid and the service is professional. Maria welcomes the guests courteously and describes the day's specials. Following a habit adopted in the Seventies, the courses come in such a way that all guests are served at the same time.

You can start with the excellent **carne cruda**, peppers in sauce and tuna mousse. The menu often includes a tasty, delicate risotto with white wine and rosemary, **home-made agnolottini** and, in season, **tagliolini with truffle** or **game sauce**. Although the main courses follow gastronomic tradition, they are often 're-visited' and enhanced with unusual flavors (hazelnuts, citrus fruit, balsamic vinegar and so on): breast of duck, chicken, rabbit and, in the fall, wild birds and game, including excellent **wild boar**. The puddings are traditional: bonet, panna cotta and the house specialty, **apple cake**, well worth trying.

There is no wine list and the labels proposed are all local (Barbera, Grignolino del Casalese and Cortese). You'll have to insist to find out if there are any other labels available, even if you do see a number of outstanding bottles of Langhe wine at the end of the room.

VIGNALE MONFERRATO
Ca' Cima

ACCORNERO

⚷ Holiday farm
Località Ca' Cima
Tel. 0142 933317
Fax 0142 933512
E-mail: info@accornerovini.it
Internet: www.accornerovini.it
Open all year (possibly holidays in January)

The Accornero family's restored farmhouse is halfway along the road from Vignale to Altavilla. It offers rooms for overnight stays and serves a generous breakfast of everything from home-baked krumiri cookies to local cured meats. A perfectly equipped kitchen is available for guests staying in the double rooms, while the apartment in what used to be the barn has its own kitchen. The family vineyards and those of other prestigious producers surround the farmhouse, a great base for pleasant walks in the hills. Wine tastings are organized in the owners' cellar and those of other winemakers in the area. There are many restaurants within easy reach of the farm.

• 3 double rooms, with bathroom; 1 apartment (3-6 persons) with small lounge, kitchen • Prices: double room single use 55-60 euros, double 84, apartment 42 euros per person, breakfast included • Credit cards: major ones, Bancomat • Off-street parking, garage. Small pets allowed. Owners always present • Breakfast room, reading and TV room. Conference room. Garden

VIGNALE MONFERRATO

San Lorenzo

CASCINA INTERSENGA

☛—○Holiday farm
Cascina Intersenga 1
Tel. 0142 933415
Fax 0142 930942
E-mail: czarnetta@vignale.de
Open all year round

This farmhouse, restored by Rena Czarnetta and Uwe-Jenz Burchard, natives of Bremen, has an apartment consisting of two bedrooms, a bathroom, lounge and kitchen, and also a four-bedroom vacation house. Each room has an en-suite bathroom, and all are furnished with country-style furniture. There's also a shared, fully equipped kitchen. For breakfast they serve home-made products, while in the tasting room you can taste the wine the Burchard family has been producing since 2000, as well as other wines from the surrounding area. What was previously the barn has been converted into a relaxing common area complete with musical instruments. The swimming pool offers a view of the surrounding vineyards. Trips can be organized to visit the historic towns of Casale and Asti, the Parco di Crea, or excursions in the Monferrato area, following recommended itineraries.

• 3 double rooms, with bathroom, terrace, mini-bar, 3 apartments, (2-4 persons) with lounge, kitchen • Prices: double room single use 40 euros, double 60, breakfast included; for the apartment, double 60 euros, triple 75, four-bed 90, breakfast included • Credit cards: none • Facility accessible to the mobility challenged, 2 apartments designed for their use. Off-street parking. Small pets allowed. Owners always present. • Wine-tasting room. Breakfast room, kitchen, reading and music room. Garden, terrace. Swimming pool

VIGNALE MONFERRATO

San Lorenzo

COLONNA

☛—○Holiday farm
Frazione San Lorenzo, Cuccaro road
Tel. & fax 0142 933239
E-mail: info@vinicolonna.it
Internet: www.vinicolonna.it
Closed in January

In an 18-century farmhouse built over cellars where important wines are made, Alessandra Colonna has opened this agriturismo, which boasts beautiful rooms, a well-stocked library and a meeting and conference room in what used to be a barn. In the morning, the generous breakfast comes with home-made cakes, jams, cheese, fruit and cereals. The farm also offers a signposted trekking trail that winds through the vineyards. The in-house Osteria dei Sapori serves a set menu (typical local cured meats and cheeses, first course and dessert) for 25 euros per person, excluding wine.

• 4 double rooms and 5 suites (2-4 persons), with bathroom; several rooms with terrace • Prices: double room single use 60 euros, double 85 (15-30 euro supplement for extra bed), suite 115-175, breakfast included • Credit cards: all, Bancomat • Off-street parking. Small pets allowed. Owners always reachable • Restaurant. Breakfast room, reading and TV room, library. Conference room. Garden, terrace

VILLANOVA D'ASTI

ALBERGO DEL MULETTO

🗝3-Star Hotel
Via Roma 86
Tel. 0141 946595
Fax 0141 946634
E-mail: albergodelmuletto@virgilio.it
Internet: www.albergodelmuletto.com
Open all year round

In the early twentieth century, this hotel operated as a staging post for changing horses. Giuseppe Vergnano reopened it a few years ago after meticulous refurbishment work that maintained the pink color and original structure of the facade. More modern solutions were adopted for the common areas and rooms, however, with the comfortable, functional furnishings that today's guests have come to expect. Traditional breakfasts include coffee, cappuccino, tea, brioches, bread, jam and butter. Easy to reach, this hotel is halfway between Asti and Turin. Excellent value for money.

• 12 double rooms, with bathroom, air-conditioning, mini-bar, satellite TV, modem connection • Prices: double room single occupancy 60-66 euros, double 80-88, breakfast included • Credit cards: all, Bancomat • 1 room designed for use by the mobility challenged. Off-street parking. Small pets allowed. Reception open from 6am to midnight. • Bar. Breakfast room

VILLA SAN SECONDO
San Carlo

PERBACCO

🍲Trattoria
Via Montechiaro 26
Tel. 0141 905525-905333
Open Friday, Saturday and Sunday
Open: dinner, lunch by reservation only
Holidays: variable
Seating: 40
Prices: 30-35 euros, wine excluded
All major credit cards, Bancomat

The inhabitants of Asti return to dine at the Perbacco with the pride of parents who have watched their children growing up (it was one of the first 'modern' osterias to open in the area). Visitors return to enjoy the refined but sound local cuisine again. Leave the city behind you and travel up this quiet, green valley, interspersed with small groups of houses, to enter the osteria's small dining-room, which is simply but tastefully furnished.
The menu, prepared by Fausto Rocchi and served by his wife Sara, varies daily. You may be offered tripe salad with mustard or a delicate pie of Jerusalem artichokes with fondue of Castelmagno or the ever-present but always enjoyable **carne cruda** or vitello in salsa tonnata. In cold weather, try the **mushrooms** (crisp fried porcini), or the rustic cod and potato pie. The first courses of home-made pasta are all exquisite: **tajarin with giblets** or vegetables, **agnolotti** (especially with duck filling) and ravioli di magro. The main courses are equally enjoyable: leg of duck, **rabbit casserole**, fillet steak cooked in salt and, in colder weather, **fritto misto alla Piemontese**, stracotto al Barbera and stewed boar. To conclude, you can always count on good cheeses, and sweets served with a glass of dessert wine: panna cotta, aspic of berries, and in winter, **gianduia pudding**, **persimmon jelly**, nougat semifreddo and chocolate bavarois.
The comprehensive wine list offers a balanced choice of local, Italian and foreign wines: the mark-up is modest and it is also possible to buy bottles over the counter.

LOMBARDIA

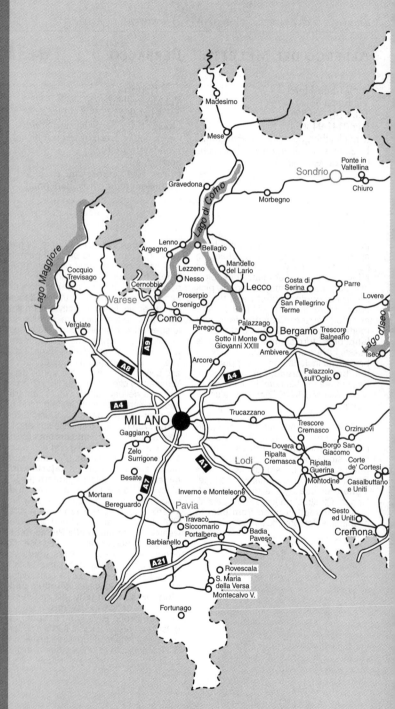

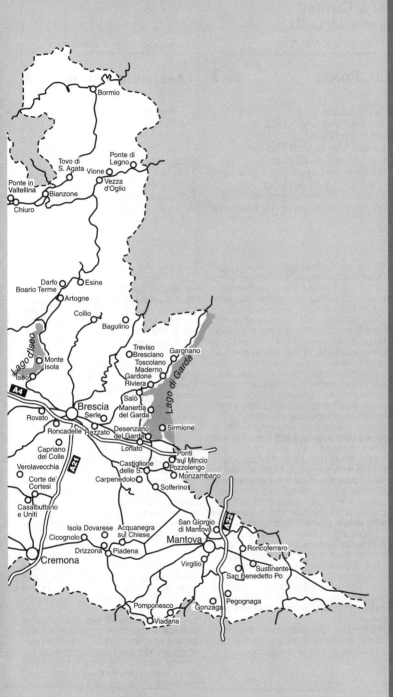

ACQUANEGRA SUL CHIESE
Ponte sull'Oglio

33 KM WEST OF MANTUA

AL PONTE

Trattoria
Via del Ponte Oglio 1312
Tel. 0376 727182
Closed Monday and Tuesday
Open: lunch and dinner
Holidays: one week in January, two weeks in August
Seating: 40 + 20 outdoors
Prices: 27-30 euros, wine excluded
All credit cards except AE, Bancomat

Off the main road between Mantua and Cremona, through the town of Calvatone and along the River Oglio, you'll find this trattoria by an old iron bridge, surrounded by the marshes, poplars and corn fields of the Le Bine nature reserve. Run by the same family for three generations, current young chef-owner Vania offers traditional dishes, some given an original twist, prepared with local, seasonal ingredients. Front of house, Dario welcomes guests in a courteous professional manner. The menu includes handmade pasta and freshwater fish, all flavored with a wide range of herbs.

Lunch could start with a selection of local **cured meats**, **fried zucchini and river prawns**, sturgeon pâté and carpaccio of river bass. Pastas include **tortelli with pumpkin**, **bigoli al torchio with sardines**, stuffed caramelle pasta filled with pike, ravioli with costmary, and in the winter season, tortelli with prunes and guanciale and **maccheroni with salami pesto**. The fish-based main courses are excellent – river bass fillets with herbs or **pike** alla Vania e Dario – and for meat-lovers, roast rabbit, **goose stew**, **margiuola** (a sausage made with pork tongue) with mashed potato, and pigs' trotter soup. Leave a little room for Vania's delicious desserts, like peach cake, chocolate budino and pumpkin pie,

The wine list specializes in the best local labels, as well as offering a number from Italy's best-known wine regions.

AMBIVERE

12 KM NORTH-WEST OF BERGAMO

TRATTORIA VISCONTI

Restaurant
Via De Gasperi 12
Tel. 035 908153
Closed Tuesday and Wednesday
Open: lunch and dinner
Holidays: two weeks in June
Seating: 60 + 40 outdoors
Prices: 35 euros, wine excluded
All credit cards, Bancomat

This has been recognized by the Lombardy Regional Authority as a historic establishment of local importance. In 1932 it was a bar and wine shop, serving meals on special occasions, where the locals came to play bowls and cards. Since 1960 it has been more of a trattoria. It occupies an ancient manor house with a veranda and arches, and has been elegantly renovated, respecting the original layout. The Visconti family have always been at the helm. You will be welcomed in by Fiorella and Giorgio, who will explain the menus on offer and you will be able to sample appetizing dishes prepared using local produce, according to time-honored family recipes.

The antipasti include cured meats, vegetable pies and warm **sweet and sour vegetables**; as well as roe deer paté, timballe of zucchini with a mousse of fresh goats' cheese and cured lonzino sausage with vegetables. Worth a mention are nonna Ida's **casoncelli**, and the **green tortelli with goosebreast filling** and malga butter, spelt fettuccine with garden vegetables, and risotto with nettles or taleggio or cardoons from the Bergamo hills. To follow, a tender **beef guanciale** in white Valcalepio wine with polenta, vegetable puff pastry parcels with formai de mut, braised venison with dark chocolate and prunes, and an unforgettable **manzo all'olio** with Bergamo **polenta**, and to finish up a cheese board served with homemade jams. The puddings are excellent: parcels of pear, almonds and raisins with creamy wild berry sauce, **jam tart**, semifreddo with nut brittle or nougat, and peaches with Moscato in aspic.

The wine list offers good quality Italian wines and a fine selection of local wines.

ARCORE

L'ARCO DEL RE

Recently opened osteria
Via Papina 4
Tel. 039 6013644
Closed Monday, Saturday lunch and Sunday dinner
Open: lunch and dinner
Holidays: vary
Seating: 45 + 8 outdoors
Prices: 35 euros, wine excluded
All credit cards, Bancomat

Just beyond the Milanese suburbs, this osteria is a destination for both locals and diners from further afield, who come to sample excellent cuisine in a spacious, convivial dining room, accompanied by a glass or a bottle of good wine recommended by owner Gino Santoro. There's a good choice of set dishes if you don't want a full meal, and often culinary educational events like tasting sessions, courses and workshops.

Start off with the extraordinary selection of **cured meats**, which includes truly outstanding cured meats made by artisanal producers and some Slow Food presidia, or with vegetable tortini, fish depending on availabilty and foie gras – a must if it's on the menu. The first courses of homemade pasta paired with seasonal sauces are all of a high standard. In the winter there are good soups, minestrone and **risotto**, as well as **polenta** served **with stews**, Gorgonzola, Taleggio and lardo. In warmer weather the meat and fish dishes are light but satisfying, and there are also tempting vegetarian options. When it's in season order the local **pink Mezzago asparagus**, prepared in a variety of ways but always excellent. The homemade desserts deserve a mention, especially the **chocolate salami**, or if you prefer to finish off with the **cheese board** a good selection is guaranteed, accompanied by mostarda, jams and honey.

The extensive wine list (over 400 Italian and international labels) features a number of small producers sourced by Gino, and several are available by the glass. Don't forget to dip into the great selection of excellent spirits.

ARGEGNO

SANT'ANNA

3-Star Hotel
Via per Schignano 1
Tel. 031 821738
Fax 031 822046
E-mail: locandasantanna@libero.it
Internet: www.locandasantanna.it
Closed last two weeks of November

This hotel on Lake Como, in a late-19th-century building once used by the church as a spiritual retreat for priests, has been owned for decades by the Peroni family, and was renovated by the second generation. The rustically furnished, comfortable rooms are named after the typical flowers of the Intelvi Valley, and at least half have splendid views. The nearby valley is ideal for pleasant walks. Home-baked cakes make the typical buffet breakfast even more delicious. The restaurant offers traditional cuisine, which guests can enjoy with a good bottle of local wine (a meal costs 25-35 euros, wine excluded). Service is professional and polite. A number of maps and leaflets giving information on the area are available for consultation by guests.

• 8 double rooms and 1 suite (4 persons), with bathroom, TV; safe in the office • Prices: double room single occupancy 65-75 euros, double 84-94, suite 110-130; breakfast included • Credit cards: all except DC, Bancomat • Off-street parking and also outside in front of hotel. Small pets allowed. Reception open from 7.30am to 0.30am • Bar, restaurant. Garden, terrace.

Artogne

Le Frise ◎◁

Farm-restaurant
Località Rive dei Balti 12
Tel. 0364 598298-598285
Open Saturday dinner and Sunday lunch,
groups only Thursday and Friday evenings
Holidays: in January
Seating: 60 + 50 outdoors
Prices: 30 euros, wine excluded
No credit cards accepted

A little paved road takes you from Artogne through a chestnut wood to the farm run by the Martini family for over 25 years. The father, Gualberto, works in the dairy, Luigi breeds sheep and Camosciata goats, and mamma Emma's job is keeping everyone happy. The simply decorated dining rooms offer an inviting ambience. All the produce from the farm ends up on the dinner tables, along with wild vegetables, Alpine herbs and berries from the forest.

To start with, a selection of **cured meats** – culatello, lardo, pancetta and salami made with pork, sheep, goat and donkey meat; flavored and plain **fresh goats' cheese**; terrines; pigeon pâté; fried, battered squash flowers, elderflowers, acacia flowers and borage. Then nettle gnocchetti, crêpes with ricotta, stuffed **casoncelli camuni**, a spicy, aromatic **zuppa del pastore** and cream of mushroom, asparagus or wild herb soup. Main courses use meat from animals raised on the farm (goat, chicken, hen, turkey, pigeon, pork, donkey and mutton): **roast kid**, **lamb, roasted** or cooked whole **on a spit**, and **braised donkey meat**, while wild boar with mountain herbs is also available in season. To finish off, there is an amazing range of **unpasteurized goat's milk cheeses**, matured for varying lengths of time, and flavored with over 30 different ingredients. Desserts change seasonally, with tarts, mousses or millefeuilles with blueberries, currants, rhubarb, sour black cherries or pears. There are some good fruit sorbets, including an interesting mulberry sorbet.

The wine list is based on the region, dominated by wines from the Valle Camonica, Valtellina and Franciacorta.

Badia Pavese

Ai Due Taxodi

Farm-restaurant
Cascina Pezzanchera 2
Tel. 0382 728126-78094
Closed Tuesday and Sunday dinner
Open: dinner and Sunday lunch
Holidays: last two weeks of July, first week of August, first two weeks of January
Seating: 40 + 70 outdoors
Prices: 23 euros, wine excluded
Credit cards: CartaSi, Bancomat

Keen botanists will recognize the two incredibly tall conifers at the entrance to the attractive 18th-century farmhouse as taxodium cypresses, close relatives of the sequoia. In addition to running this restaurant and offering four welcoming rooms, the Capelli family also grows rice and farms cattle. These are exclusively of the Chianina breed, an unusual choice in these lowlands between the provinces of Pavia, Piacenza and Lodi.

The restaurant is well-appointed and the food simple and delicious. The set menu changes with the season, generally kicking off with a selection of **cured meats**, followed by fragrant filled focaccine and frittata made with garden herbs. Then **risotto** and filled pastas: we sampled a good nettle risotto and meat-filled **ravioli**.

The main courses were satisfying: a tender, succulent **roast with mushrooms** and an excellent English-style roast beef, which really brings out the quality of the meat, plus unusual bread bocconcini with Chianina beef sausages. If you order in advance, you can have chops and steak char-grilled in the huge fireplace, and depending on the time of year, poultry like chicken, goose and guinea fowl. To round off, delicious homemade desserts: tarts, cakes and creamy gelato, served with wild berries when in season.

The modest wine list is notable for its low mark-ups, and offers some good labels from the Oltrepò Pavese, San Colombano and Colli Piacentini.

BAGOLINO

AL TEMPO PERDUTO

🔑 3-Star Hotel
Via San Rocco 46
Tel. 0365 99145
Fax 0365 99665
E-mail: info@altempoperduto.it
Internet: www.altempoperduto.it
Open all year

The sign outside – 'to time gone by' – says it all. Restored in 1990 and 2004, this used to be an old inn providing food and lodging. It is located on the main street of a charming mountain village of narrow alleys and little flights of steps. The rooms have rustic furniture and some offer the wooden balconies typical of this area. Nearby are ski resorts (there's a shuttle to Gaver and Maniva) and the Caffaro and Chiese Valleys and Lake Idro are also easy trips. Two kilometers away is a beautiful pine forest and a brook where trout are farmed. Carnival period is considered high season, with some really original entertainment on offer: dancers in local costume and masks perform the traditional dances and music of the area. The restaurant offers typical cuisine (a meal costs 15-25 euros, excluding wine) and for breakfast guests can enjoy cappuccino, pastries with butter and jams.

• 10 single and 3 double rooms, with bathroom, safe, TV, modem connection • Prices: single 30-40 euros, double 60-80, breakfast included • Credit cards: all, Bancomat • Facility accessible for the mobility challenged. Public parking next to the hotel, 700 meters away (20 spaces). No pets allowed. Reception open 24 hours a day • Bar (open from 8am to midnight), restaurant. Lounge.

BARBIANELLO

DA ROBERTO

🍲 Trattoria
Via Barbiano 21
Tel. 0385 57396
Closed Sunday dinner and Monday
Open: lunch, Friday and Saturday dinner
Holidays: July and one week in January
Seating: 50
Prices: 15-25 euros, wine excluded
All major credit cards, Bancomat

This inviting trattoria is located in the center of a small farming village in an uncharacteristically flat part of the Oltrepò, and bears the distinction of being the headquarters of the Brotherhood of Cotechino Caldo. Roberto Scovenna and Maria Rosa, owners since 1986, offer more than just cotechino, but this **cooked salami** is a classic winter favorite, and you might find it on the menu until spring, perhaps served as an antipasto and accompanied by polenta or fonduta. During our last visit it was followed by some excellent salami and pancetta, sweet-and-sour red onions, bresaola and fresh goat's cheese, a flavorful rustic frittata with wild chicory and a delicate fresh herbed cow's milk cheese. Then came a memorable **risotto with asparagus and Castelmagno** cheese and an excellent traditional **ravioli with braised meat**. In the right season borage or vartis (the tips of wild hops) might be used in the ravioli. Razza Piemontese beef is succulent and presented on a hot stone slab, so you can have it cooked as you please. Depending on the season and availability there might also be chicken, duck, **rabbit** with herbs from the salt roads and braised pork, and game, mushrooms and truffles always appear in the fall. The **cheese board** offers, among many others, Robiola di Roccaverano, a rare sheep's milk Taleggio, Montébore, Saras del Fen, and Don Verri goat's milk tomini, all accompanied by honey and mostarda. Round off everything with melon and Madeira ice cream and classic San Contardo cake. The reasonably priced wine list revolves mainly around the Oltrepò Pavese, with some interesting labels from Piedmont, Liguria and Tuscany.

BELLAGIO
Loppia

BEREGUARDO

30 KM NORTHEAST OF COMO, 21 KM FROM LECCO ON SS 583

13 KM NORTHWEST OF PAVIA

SILVIO

HOTEL DE LA VILLE

🔑2-Star Hotel
Via Carcano 12
Tel. 031 950322
Fax 031 950912
E-mail: info@bellagiosilvio.com
Internet: www.bellagiosilvio.com
Closed November 20-December 20
and January 10–February 20

🔑3-Star Hotel
Via Ticino 44
Tel. and fax 0382 928097
E-mail: info@hotel-delaville.com
Internet: www.hotel-delaville.com
Closed two days at Christmas and 15 days in August

This hotel was originally a inn opened by Silvio Ponzino just after World War I. Four generations later, it's managed by his great grandson Silvio with his wife Giuliana and children Christian and Elena. Located in Loppia, just a short walk from the center of Bellagio, it offers beautiful views of the Villa Melzi gardens and the lake. Rooms are spacious and tastefully furnished. The buffet breakfast includes homemade cakes, croissants, bread, butter and jam, cured meats, cheeses, fruit juices, tea, coffee and milk. Weather permitting guests can enjoy an aperitivo on the veranda and lunch on the terrace. A fishing service for tourists (the first in the area) has recently been organized so guests can go out on the lake with fishermen. Silvio also rents comfortable apartments for longer stays.

• 17 double rooms, 3 triple and 1 quadruple, with bathroom, satellite TV, safe • Prices: double room single occupancy 50-77 euros, double 70-100, triple 90-105, quadruple 95-115, breakfast included • Credit cards: CartaSi, Bancomat • Garage parking. Small pets allowed. Reception open from 7.30 am to 11 pm. • Bar (for guests only), restaurant. Reading room. Conference room. Garden, solarium, terrace.

🍴 The restaurant serves both local cuisine and more creative dishes, including homemade pasta (average cost 22 euros, excluding wine).

This family-run hotel is located in Bereguardo (from beau regard, or pleasant view) in the Ticino Park and is an ideal stop for guests traveling to or from Milan or Pavia. The comfortable rooms are fitted with modern furnishings and the suites have jacuzzis. The buffet breakfast offers bread, butter and jam, cakes, coffee, tea, milk and fruit juices. Cured meats and local cheeses are available on request. Worth visiting is the nearby castle and, a few kilometers away, the famous barge bridge, one of the few remaining in Italy. The hotel is a good base for cyclists wanting to explore the park: the Zelata wood are worth a visit and don't miss the heron breeding grounds.

• 1 single, 16 double rooms and 2 suites, with bathroom, air-conditioning, fridge, safe, TV, modem connection • Prices: single 50 euros, double room single occupancy 64, double 78, suite 100, breakfast included • Credit cards: all, Bancomat • Some rooms designed for use by the mobility challenged. Off-street parking. Small pets allowed by prior agreement. Reception open 24 hours a day • Bar. Billiard room. Conference room. Garden with children's playground. Pool, tennis court, five-a-side soccer pitch.

BERGAMO

AGNELLO D'ORO

🔑☎ 2-Star Hotel
Via Gombito 22
Tel. 035 249883
Fax 035 235612
E-mail: hotel@agnellodoro.it
Open all year

This comfortable, well appointed hotel is located in a 17th-century building in the historic center of Bergamo, overlooking the small medieval Piazza San Pancrazio, the Gombito tower (the tallest in Bergamo), the parish church and a distinctive fountain dating from 1549. Only a few minutes away are Piazza Vecchia, considered one of the most beautiful squares in Europe, and the Remembrance Park with its views over the entire city. The comfortable and welcoming rooms are simply furnished, and for breakfast guests can enjoy coffee, tea, milk, fruit juices, jams, cakes, bread, cured meats and cheeses. Owner Pino Capozzi is a risotto maestro, and the hotel restaurant offers other typical local dishes (set menu 32 euros).

• 4 single and 16 double rooms, with bathroom, satellite TV, some with a small balcony • Prices: single 52 euros, double 92; breakfast 6 euros per person • Credit cards: all except DC, Bancomat • Facility partially accessible for the mobility challenged. Paid parking nearby. Small pets allowed. Reception open from 6 am to 1 am • Bar (for guests only), restaurant.

BESATE

CASCINA CAREMMA

🍲 Farm-restaurant with rooms
Strada per il Ticino
Tel. and fax 02 9050020
E-mail info@caremma.com
Internet: www.caremma.com
Closed Monday, Tuesday and Wednesday
Open: dinner, Sunday and holidays also lunch
Holidays: August
Seating: 80
Prices: 26-28 euros, wine excluded
All major credit cards, Bancomat

Rooms in this agriturismo, a converted 19th-century mill, can be rented by the week, giving guest a chance to make the most of all the hiking, mountain biking and canoeing opportunities in the surrounding countryside. The restaurant uses produce from the farm (also on sale in the shop), and the seasonally changing menu starts with a dozen antipasti like homemade **cured meats**, barley salad with fresh vegetables and **liver mortadella** cooked in mulled wine, all served with home-baked bread. These are followed by two first course tastings, a **risotto** that varies almost every day (including one **with six herbs from the nearby Parco del Ticino**) and a homemade pasta – the **papardelle with duck ragù** is excellent. Then two main courses, poultry and beef or pork, maybe **stracotto cooked in Barolo** and **roasted shank of pork**. In season there's **polenta** made with the farm's Maranello corn. To finish, two desserts: choices include millefeuille with wild berries and **pan mein**. The wine list is interesting.

🔑☎ • 8 double, 3 triple, 2 quadruple rooms, 1 with 6 beds, en-suite, air conditioning, TV • Prices: double room single occupancy 45-52, double 65, triple 147-156, quadruple 208, with 6 beds 312 euros, breakfast included • Entire building is accessible to the mobility challenged, and one bedroom is specifically designed for such guests. External open parking area. Pets welcome. Owners available from 6.30am to midnight • Restaurant. Conference room. Fitness center, indoor swimming pool, sauna, Turkish bath, exercise trail, five-a-side football, tennis

BIANZONE

21 KM EAST OF SONDRIO SS 38

ALTAVILLA

⌒Trattoria–1-star Hotel
Via ai Monti 46
Tel. 0342 720355
Fax 0342 721626
E-mail: benvenuti@altavilla.info
Internet: www.altavilla.info
Closed Monday dinner and Tuesday
Open lunch and dinner
Holidays: variable
Seating: 30 + 30 outdoors
Prices: 30 euros, wine excluded
All credit cards, Bancomat

This excellent trattoria and cozy hotel make a good base from which to visit the local wineries and mountains of the Valtellina. Run by Anna Bertola, the hotel has just one star only because the comfortable rooms lack telephones.
A meal will begin with bresaola or other **cured meats** from the valley, **sciatt** (cheese-filled buckwheat fritters) with chicory, similar but flatter **chisciöi** and **manfrigole** (buckwheat pancakes filled with casera and butter). To follow, **pizzoccheri** with onion, soups, broths and polenta made from wheat or buckwheat. In the summer seasonal vegetables accompany mains like lamb or **trout fillet in aromatic herbs**, mixed grills, grilled sausage and venison. The **cheese board** offers a selection of local Bitto and fresh goat's cheese, plus other top cheeses from around Italy. End with chocolate sciatt or a thirst-quenching **sorbet made with Braulio**, a historic Bormio liqueur.
The cellar offers a choice selection of wines from Valtellina and the rest of Italy, plus many by the glass.
The hotel is open every day and also sells local produce. Half board is 37-48 euros, full board 42-52.

🚂🌙• 4 single rooms and 10 doubles, en-suite; 9 rooms with TV, 4 with fridge-bar • Prices: single 22-45, double 40-68 euros; breakfast 8 euro per person. External parking in front of the trattoria, garage. Pets welcome • Restaurant. Terrace.

BORGO SAN GIACOMO
Padernello

33 KM SOUTHWEST OF BRESCIA

LOCANDA DEL VEGNÒT

⌒Trattoria with rooms
Via Fornello 10
Tel. 030 9408045
Closed Tuesday to Thursday
Open: dinner, Sunday lunch
Holidays: last week in July, first two weeks in August
Seating: 160 + 60 outdoors
Prices: 25-26 euros, wine excluded
All credit cards except AE, Bancomat

This pretty locanda was renovated in 2000 by Omar Pansera and Natale Gallia, and the name refers to the local wine production. Fronted by an attractive veranda, inside there are two floors offering four air-conditioned dining rooms with exposed wooden beams and five inviting bedrooms. Omar's courteous welcome will get you in the mood for their excellent food.
Start with the house antipasti: a selection of prosciutto, coppa, pancetta, lardo, salamella and Gorgonzola with polenta, **snails**, and porcini mushrooms when in season. Then move on to good homemade pasta – tortelli with herbs, **bigoli with jugged duck**, tagliatelle with mushrooms, maltagliati with smoked provola cheese and speck – and in season, a superlative **pumpkin risotto**. Main courses all revolve around meat: beef or horsemeat tagliata, lamb chops, grilled venison fillets, wild boar stew and various braised meats. **Spiedo bresciano with polenta** is available on request from September to June. To finish off, a good selection of Lombardy and Piedmont cheeses with jams and honey, and many desserts: chocolate cake and apple pie, semifreddo with nougat served with hot chocolate, homemade ice cream, pear tarte tatin. The 25 euro set menu, including house wine, is interesting: during the grape and spelt fair at the end of September it includes risotto and braised meat with white grapes, splet tortelloni and biscotti, red grape cake and homemade grape gelato.
The wine list features over 150 labels, with a good price-to-quality ratio. About ten wines can be ordered by the glass, plus around 40 Italian and international spirits.

BORMIO

BRESCIA

VECCHIO BORGO

Inn with rooms
Via Monte Braulio 1
Tel. 0342 904447
Fax 0342 911522
Open all year

LA GROTTA

Trattoria
Vicolo del Prezzemolo 10
Tel. 030 44068
Closed Wednesday
Open: lunch and dinner
Holidays: in August
Seating: 80 + 40 outdoors
Prices: 18-35 euros, wine excluded
All credit cards except AE, Bancomat

Just minutes away from the spa, this family-run locanda and osteria in a restored 18th-century building is a charming place to stay in Bormio, a well-known vacation destination in the summer and winter. Simply furnished rooms are comfortable and clean. The osteria's wooden counter and card-playing guests make for an old-fashioned atmosphere. Breakfast can be customized and includes bread, butter and jam, cured meats, cheeses and hot and cold beverages. The restaurant offers typical dishes from the Valtellina (average cost of a meal is 15-20 euros, wine excluded). The locanda is the perfect base for excursions to surrounding areas, including demanding hikes in the Ortles-Cevedale mountains and the Stelvio Park.

• 1 single, 14 double and 1 triple rooms, with bathroom, TV; 3 with balcony • Prices: single 30-35 euros, double 60-70, triple 90-105, breakfast included • All major credit cards, Bancomat • Off-street parking. No pets allowed. Owners always reachable. • Bar, restaurant. Garden.

A little alley off Corso Cavour in the historic center of Brescia leads to this ancient trattoria, where past generations of locals used to come to enjoy a glass of fine wine accompanied by simply, authentic fare. A skilful renovation has brough La grotta back to life while retaining its original charm: the two air-conditioned dining rooms are decorated with local dialect phrases and old photographs of the former wine shop, and chef Luciana turns out delicious traditional dishes. When the weather's nice you can lunch in the pretty internal courtyard or on the street, and the cool cellar, hollowed out of a cave, has a long table for wine tastings.
Danilo and Luigi will welcome you, bringing antipasti based on Brescia **cured meats**: lardo con la vena, coppa and outstanding hand-cut prosciutto (crudo and cotto); then it's on to **casoncelli** with meat or herbs, tagliatelle with jugged hare and **tripe in stock** (in the fall). Don't miss the fabulous **zuppa paesana** with beans or pumpkin. Main courses include a few great classics: **rabbit, roasted** or alla cacciatora, **salt cod alla bresciana**, beef tagliata, veal cutlets, young horse fiandre and **kid with polenta di Storo**. To finish off, a great selection of cheeses from the local valleys, homemade apple or pineapple pie, **sbrisolona cake** or chocolate pudding.
Danilo has put together an interesting wine list, including some by the glass.

Claudio Fantoni's butcher's shop at Corso Cavour 52 is a historic establishment of superb quality and variety.

OSTERIA AL BIANCHI

🍲 Traditional osteria
Via Gasparo da Salò 32
Tel. 030 292328
Closed Tuesday and Wednesday
Open: lunch and dinner
Holidays: August
Seating: 60 + 20 outdoors
Prices: 22-28 euros, wine excluded
All credit cards , Bancomat

OSTERIA DEL QUARTINO

🍲 Recently opened osteria
Via Fabio Filzi 92
Tel. 030 383574
Closed Saturday lunch and Sunday
Open: lunch and dinner
Holidays: August
Seating: 70 + 30 outdoors
Prices: 25-32 euros, wine excluded
All major credit cards, Bancomat

Owner Franco Masserdotti is justly proud of the old-fashioned atmosphere of his osteria, which can be found 100 meters from piazza della Loggia. Locals come to sit and play cards all day, for a glass of good wine, to sip a pirlo (a Brescia specialty which can vary but generally includes white wine, Campari and lemon rind) or on Saturday, market day, to sample a plate of bertagnin (cod). As in any self-respecting authentic osteria the kitchen shuts at 10pm and idle chit-chat and card games once again dominate the tables.
Wine is sold from a bar counter at the entrance, and there are two simple dining rooms where you can try Domenico's cooking, based on traditional Brescia dishes: antipasti of cured meats, then **malfatti with herbs**, pappardelle with porcini mushrooms, **gnocchi** made with potatoes or chestnut flour, **pasta e fagioli** or **tripe**. Tempting main courses include **salt cod** served hot or cold, **donkey stew with Barolo wine**, sautéed kidneys, snails with Swiss chard, **braised donkey meat**, stuffed roast pork, beef stew and **bolliti**. Fruit or jam tarts, **sbrisolona** cake or zabaglione mousse are an excellent way to finish off.
There is a good wine list overseen by Michele Masserdotti, mainly featuring Brescia wines but with a few good labels from Trentino, Sicily and Friuli.

🍯 On the Valpersane farm near the ex-Polveriera, husband and wife team Cristina and Alberto Guidi have a herd of 100 Camosciata goats, producing around ten kilos a day of excellent cheese. It can be bought from the farm shop or tasted in Brescia's top restaurants.

Osteria del Quartino's peaceful, inviting setting and excellent Brescia cooking make it one of the few establishments still worthy of the name osteria. Formerly a monastery, it's been carefully restored and furnished with antiques and is now run by siblings Ivonne, Mario and Pietro with dedication and skill. The kitchen is open until midnight and you can choose from set menus of 25, 30 and 35 euros, which include some good house wines.
Antipasti include Pozzolengo salami, bresaola di punta d'anca with fresh Valcamonica goat's cheese, lardo and prosciutto, paired with hot focaccia, redolent of extra-virgin olive oil and rosemary. The excellent first courses (Ivonne makes the pasta fresh every day) include **tortelloni del Quartino, tripe**, **malfatti al bagòss,** cream of zucchini soup, multigrain zuppa di cereali, tagliolini with garden vegetables and gnocchi with Gorgonzola. Then choose between a good **beef all'olio**, **roast rabbit with polenta** di Storo, horse tagliata, breaded cutlets and fillet steak. The cheese board is a must: unfortunately bagòss is not always available, but there is Robiola bresciana, Pasubio from the Ledro Valley and cheeses from Tremosine. To finish, homemade tarts, pear cake, homemade tiramisù, rice cake della nonna and homemade ice cream.
The list of over 350 Italian wines stands out for its good value.

🍯 200 meters from the osteria, at Via San Donino 25, is a pasticceria called Le paste di Luca, where you can buy cakes, mini-fruit pastries, cream puffs and traditional local sweets, all without spending a fortune.

Busto Garolfo

A Casa di Alice

🗝️ Bed and breakfast
Via Espinasse 12
Tel. 0331 536165-3475273261
Fax 0331 536165
E-mail: acasadialice@hotmail.com
Internet: www.acasadialice.it
Closed in November and December

Maria Giovanna Savaris's B&B is close by Milan and Malpensa airport, but in a quiet, leafy residential area. Rooms, in a detached house built in the 1970s, are spacious, simple and tastefully furnished. In the summer guests can enjoy breakfast in the beautiful garden, with fruit juices, coffee, tea, milk, butter and jam, cookies, croissants, yogurt and fresh fruit, with savory items available on request. Nearby Parco del Roccolo, woodlands full of birds and animals, is best explored by bicycle. The name derives from a structure formerly used for bird-catching, an activity now prohibited. If you're interested in history, don't miss the town of Magenta.

• 3 double rooms with bathroom, TV •
Prices: double room single occupancy 45 euros, double 60, breakfast included
• Credit cards: none • Off-street parking (1 space). Small pets allowed. Owners always reachable • Garden.

Capriano del Colle
Fenili Belasi

Antica Trattoria 🍾
la Pergolina

🍲 Trattoria
Via Trento 86
Tel. 030 9748002
Closed Sunday dinner and Monday
Open: lunch and dinner
Holidays: August, one week in January
Seating: 80
Prices: 32-35 euros, wine excluded
All credit cards, Bancomat

The small hamlet of Fenili Belasi is after Capriano, on the road between Brescia and Quinzano d'Oglio, and is home to this historic trattoria in an old country house. The spacious courtyard in front serves as a car park when necessary. Teresa Bianchetti in hte dining room and Omar Bertocchi in the kitchen offer a wide range of traditional local dishes.
To start there's a tempting range of cured meats, including a good homemade lardo; frittata and seasonal vegetable pie, then simple, seasonal first courses: **tortelli al bagòss** (a Slow Food presidium), pappardelle with hare and wild-duck ragù, **pumpkin gnocchi** and pheasant ravioli with thyme butter. All the mains are local specialties well worth trying, with **stews (beef stew with red wine** is superb), roasts, hare, kid, **stewed salt cod** alla bresciana, calf kidneys with chanterelle mushrooms, sautéed porcini with polenta and gorgonzola, cotechino sausage and salami from Bassa. You can sample **vineyard snails**, large snails with a nut-brown shell which are gathered from June onwards and served in consommé or sauce. The excellent **spiedo bresciano** is available in season when ordered in advance. Then there's some good cheeses, served with homemade mostarda, followed by homemade desserts – chocolate cake with ice cream, apple pie with zabaglione, citrus mousse and semifreddo with wild berries.
Bruno Bianchetti, an experienced sommelier, knowledgeably handles the wine list, which features a vast range of Brescia, Italian and international wines, plus many by the glass.

CARPENEDOLO

LA FARMACIA DEI SANI 🍷

⌣ Enoteca with kitchen
Via Santa Croce 9
Tel. 030 969015
Closed Sunday and Monday
Open: lunch, Friday dinner,
Saturday dinner only
Holidays: two weeks in August
Seating: 50 + 10 outdoors
Prices: 25-28 euros, wine excluded
All credit cards, Bancomat

This enoteca boasts well-stocked cellars, with a vast range of Italian and international wines, and the adjacent wine shop guarantees a constant supply of new labels. Over the years Giuliana's cooking and her son Riccardo's wine expertise have built up a reputation for good food and a convivial atmosphere. The opening hours – from 10am to 8pm Tuesday to Thursday, from 10 am to 12 am on Fridays and from 7pm to 12 midday on Saturdays, were dictated by the habits of the regulars, who pop into the 'pharmacy' for a simple snack – ham, salami and cheese – and a glass of good wine.
Lunch is à la carte, and the menu changes seasonally, often kicking off with **polenta and porcini mushrooms**, prosciutto crudo di Parma, buffalo mozzarella from Campania, grilled formaggella or a **salad of raw mushrooms**. Then **tagliatelle with jugged game**, crêpes with mushrooms, **malfatti with herbs** and delicate **pumpkin gnocchi**. Main courses include grilled donkey and horse chops, beef tagliata, fiorentina steak and to finish off there is a tempting cheese board and a great platter of **vegetable crudités**. The homemade ice cream served with seasonal fruit salad and cookies is also good.
The prices are reasonable and the wine mark-ups are fair. A regularly changing roster of wines is also sold by the glass. Reservations are advised.

🍷 At Via Deretti 1, the Da Umberto deli offers wonderful cheeses from the valleys around Brescia.

CASTIGLIONE DELLE STIVIERE
Fontane

HOSTARIA VIOLA 🍷

⌣ Restaurant
Via Verdi 32
Tel. 0376 670000-638277
Closed Sunday dinner and Monday
Open: lunch and dinner
Holidays: variable
Seating: 60
Prices: 25-30 euros, wine excluded
All credit cards, Bancomat

The family that runs Hostaria Viola, just outside Castiglione delle Siviere, has almost a century's experience in the restaurant business. For over three years Alessandra has been in charge, sourcing fresh, high-quality ingredients from local products and introducing innovations like biodynamic wines, organic and unpasteurized cheeses and vegetarian options. Look out for extra virgin olive oils from Garda, Tuscany and Puglia.
The meal starts with the unmissable **sorbir d'agnoli** –perfect washed down with Lambrusco – a sampling of local cured meats, a generous helping of **pike in salsa** served with slices of grilled polenta, and a polenta sformato with bitter herbs. Then it's on to some traditional Mantuan first courses: **risotto alla pilota**, traditionally prepared for the workers who husked the rice; the typical **capunsei** of bread and cheese tossed in melted butter; an excellent **onion soup**; **tortelli with pumpkin** or other seasonal fillings; agnoli with sauce or in broth; and **tortelli amari** from Castelgoffredo, the Viola family's hometown, prepared with costmary. Main courses include **stracotto alla mantovana**, braised donkey and horse, roast pork stinco, beef tagliata and **capon alla Stefani**, invented by the famous chef of the Gonzaga family. Side orders include homemade mashed potato and raw or cooked seasonal vegetables. Finish off with the cheese board and desserts: pies with pears, amaretti and chocolate or Rennet apples and traditional **sbrisolona** cake.
The well thought out wine list offers over a hundred Italian labels and a selection of all-natural, double-fermented beers.

CERNOBBIO

GIARDINO

2-Star Hotel
Via Regina 73
Tel. 031 511154
Fax 031 341870
E-mail: albergogiardino@tin.it
Internet: www.giardinocernobbio.com
Open all year

Cernobbio is a charming village on the western shore of Lake Como, a summer destination for visitors from all over the world and an excellent base for exploring the lake and Como itself. Located in a completely restored house from the last century with a beautiful courtyard garden, the comfortable hotel and pizzeria/restaurant (meals cost 15-45 euros, wine excluded) are managed by Cristino De Cillis. The restaurant offers classic, well-presented cuisine, and a traditional Italian-style breakfast is served.
Nearby is Villa Erba, an exhibition center which often hosts interesting events.

• 3 single and 9 double rooms in the main building, 1 single, 1 triple and 4 quadruple rooms (2 with balcony) in the annex, with bathroom, fridge, TV • Prices: single 70-90 euros, double 85-120, triple 100-130, four-bed 110-140, breakfast included • Credit cards: all, Bancomat • External paid parking, paid garage parking 20 meters away. No pets allowed. Owners always reachable • Bar, restaurant. Conference room. Garden.

CHIURO
Castionetto

DA SILVIO FANCOLI

Restaurant
Via Madonnina 2-4
Tel. 0342 563006
No closing days
Open: lunch and dinner
Holidays: none
Seating: 120
Prices: 18-22 euros, wine excluded
All credit cards, Bancomat

After a visit to the picturesque village of Chiuro to admire its aristocratic palazzi and narrow cobbled streets, take the road which winds up through the vineyards to Castionetto. A couple of kilometers further is this 15-year-old restaurant run by Silvio, on two floors with a terrace for eating al fresco in the summer. A favorite with locals for its old-fashioned cooking, it manages to strike the perfect balance between modernity and tradition, using local produce in seasonally changing menus. On arrival you'll find a good rye bread and a carafe of local red wine, or if you prefer you can choose from a decent selection of Valtellina reds from established Chiuro producers.
Silvio gets his high quality **cured meats** from local suppliers, and you can start your meal with luganega, bresaola, salami and pancetta. Then continue with **pizzoccheri**, slightly more rounded than the normal, served with Savoy cabbage or other seasonal vegetables, or traditional **sciàtt** ('toads' in the local dialect), lumpy, odd-shaped buckwheat fritters filled with cheese. The game ravioli are equally good, as are **pappardelle with porcini mushrooms**. Depending on the season main courses could include a beautifully prepared **jugged game** with buckwheat **polenta**, venison either grilled or in a mushroom sauce, as well as spare-ribs or pork chops and hearty mixed grills.

CICOGNOLO

COCQUIO TREVISAGO

14 KM EAST OF CREMONA SS 10

12 KM WEST OF VARESE

OSTERIA DE L'UMBRELEÈR

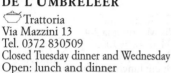

🍲 Trattoria
Via Mazzini 13
Tel. 0372 830509
Closed Tuesday dinner and Wednesday
Open: lunch and dinner
Holidays: in August or September
Seating: 80 + 30 outdoors
Prices: 28-33 euros, wine excluded
All credit cards, Bancomat

ANTICA OSTERIA ITALIA

🍲 Osteria Via Roma 74
Tel. 0332 700150
Closed Sunday evening and Monday
Open for lunch and dinner
Holidays: August
Seating: 50 + 25 outside
Prices: 30 euros, wine excluded
All major credit cards, Bancomat
bottiglia

The Luccini family has been running this place for as long as anyone can remember, with mamma in the kitchen preparing her own brand of traditional rustic cuisine and Diego, Paolo and Pier in the dining room and taking care of the wine cellar. They know this is an area where some very good food is produced, and they do their best to make the most of. An excellent homemade mostarda accompanies the mainly Italian selection of **cheeses** at the end of the meal, and you can buy some of their other products in the trattoria. The aim is to appeal to those who appreciate the simplicity of local dishes prepared attentively, served with care and priced fairly.

The menu reads like a tour of the local area: **cured meats** from around Cremona, ravioli with Provolone, the more classic **marubini in stock** (actually three kinds of broth) or **pumpkin tortelli** from neighboring Mantua. The **donkey stracotto**, beef stews and **roast goose** are all good. On the subject of goose, at the beginning of the winter it is delicious with Savoy cabbage, and you can also try foie gras or stuffed goose neck in sauce. If you happen to arrive at the right time don't miss the maialata – a rural celebration where you can taste an endless variety of **pork** dishes. Just make sure you're ready to eat and eat and eat: a fast beforehand is probably a good idea. The meal ends with **sbrisolosa** cake or some tempting tarts and sponge cakes. As for the wine, Pier will insist on giving you the complete low-down, so let him be your guide to his well-stocked cellar.

Massimiliano Condello and his brother Christian, the cook, recently took over this osteria, first opened in 1918: three small dining rooms with vaulted ceilings, plain brickwork and beautiful floors.

The meal starts with cured **Cinta Senese pork,** venison and wild boar. First courses range from home-made pasta (pappardelle to ravioli) to **risottos (with ossobuco,** cep mushrooms, Castelmagno cheese and wild fennel, sausage, radicchio and pine kernels, Cabrales cheese) and soups, which change from week to week. The meat dishes are delicious and also varied: bistecca fiorentina, Piedmontese Fassone veal and beef, **stracotti,** stuffed rabbit ... Plus local favorites such as tripe, **casoeula, polenta** with various matchings and much, much more. The meal comes to an end with a good assortment of local cheeses with mostarda and preserves, followed by plain chocolate cake with caramelized oranges, jam crostata or seasonal desserts accompanied by sweet wines suggested by Massimiliano.

A small point of sale sells extra virgin olive oil, mostarda, jams and other local delicacies.

🍯 In **Varese** (12 km), at Viale dei Mille 51, Il laboratorio di Chiara sells pastries, cookies, fruit jellies, cream cakes and seasonal fruits.

COMO
Lora

CORTE DE' CORTESI

CROTTO DEL SERGENTE

IL GABBIANO

🍲Restaurant
Via Crotto del Sergente 13
Tel. 031 283911
Closed Wednesday
Open: dinner, Sunday and holidays also for lunch
Holidays: in September
Seating: 70 + 20 outdoors
Prices: 25-30 euros, wine excluded
All credit cards

🍲Trattoria
Piazza Vittorio Veneto 10
Tel. 0372 95108
Closed Thursday
Open: lunch and dinner
Holidays: in July
Seating: 60 + 40 outdoors
Prices: 25-35 euros, wine excluded
All major credit cards except DC, Bancomat

Over the years this restaurant has established itself as one of the few serving authentically traditional cuisine in Como, and it's appeared in our guide for the last five years. Current owners, brother and sister Anna and Gianni Castiglioni, have restored the interior with great dedication and good taste. Out of the two dining rooms, the one with great old wooden tables and a vaulted brick ceiling is very attractive, and there's also a pleasant terrace for when the weather is fine.

In the winter Massimo recommends you start with **missoltini** (dried shad) **and polenta** or a selection of local cured meats, or a gorgonzola parcel in spinach sauce. Then wild boar agnolotti with butter and sage or the classic **saffron risotto with sausage**. You can continue with beef and lardo kebabs, **beef cheek in red wine** or **guinea fowl stuffed with Savoy cabbage and honey mushrooms**. From spring onwards you can sample a radicchio roulade of with a salt cod and potato mousse, potato and beetroot gnocchi with mascarpone and broccoli, and wholemeal straccetti with asparagus and bresaola. If available, try the **onion soup** and the zander in a horseradish crust. Every Thursday, from September to April, Massimo offers **bollito misto**. There's always a cheese board, which includes fresh goat's milk cheese and flavorsome mature cheeses in oil, and to finally zabaglione foam with strawberries and torta saracena with berries.

The good wine list is reasonably priced.

The main piazza of the village is home to this trattoria, which has an attractive interior with wooden beams and simple decor, plus two verandas, one in the front and the other in the courtyard, for summer al fresco dining. Inside the walls are lined with glass-fronted cabinets of tasting glasses and bottles of wine, which are on sale at reasonable prices. Giusy and Gianni Fontana, together with their children Stefania and Andrea in the dining room, are responsible for the classic regional cuisine, sometimes reworked slightly to bring it into line with modern tastes. The set menus are interesting: a traditional Cremona menu for 25 euros and a seasonal menu for 27, with no cover charge.

The traditional **cured meats** served at the start of the meal are outstanding – be sure to try the culatello di Zibello. The goose specialties are also delicious, as are the seasonal vegetable antipasti. The first courses are so good, you'll wish you could try them all: classic Cremona **marubini in stock**, **casoncelli with herbs**, pink gnocchi with duck and honey-mushroom ragù, **pumpkin tortelli**, risottos, and tagliatelle with porcini mushrooms. The very traditional **Nonna Bigina's guinea fowl** with homemade mostarda is a must; then there is **roast foal meat** marinated in red wine, tagliata of duck breast, escalopes, medallions of wild boar and freshwater fish, with some excellent sturgeon. At the end of the meal there is a fine **cheese board** and sweets accompanied with dessert wines served by the glass.

The wine list features around 350 quality labels, with at least 30 which can be ordered by the half-bottle, plus Italian and international liqueurs.

COSTA DI SERINA
Gazzo

CREMONA

30 KM NORTHEAST OF BERGAMO

LA PETA   ⓒ

🍲 Farm-restaurant with rooms
Via Peta, 3
Tel. 0345 97955
Open from Friday dinner to
Sunday lunch, always in the summer
Holidays: One week in June, two in August
Seating: 75 + 20 outside
Prices: 24 euros, wine excluded
All credit cards, Bancomat

HOSTERIA 700

🍲 Restaurant
Piazza Gallina 1
Tel. 0372 36175
Closed Monday dinner and Tuesday
Open: lunch and dinner
Holidays: one week mid-August
Seating: 80
Prices: 25-30 euros, wine excluded
All credit cards except DC, Bancomat

The attractively restored 15th-century building that houses this farm is in a picturesque clearing in the woods of the shady Val Serina, along the ancient Via Mercatorum. There's all kinds of amenities: six rooms for guests wishing to stay the night, a conference room, two spacious dining rooms and a little farm shop where you can buy fresh goat's cheeses, honey and other local specialties. There's some pleasant walks around the area, or you can wander around the open areas where barnyard animals and goats are raised, and see the gardens which produce the vegetables for the restaurant. The traditional dishes of the set menu are made from organic ingredients from the farm or others in the area.

The restaurant's own bread, made from organic flour and baked in a wood-fired oven, accompanies rich antipasti like fresh and matured goat's cheeses, frittata with herbs, goat salami, **smoked leg of kid**, pancetta, **giardiniera** (pickled vegetables) and apple compôte. There's two first courses, with a choice between dishes like tagliatelle with zucchini and tomato ragù, homemade **vegetable lasagne** (with porcini in season) and goat's cheese ravioli. Then meat-lovers can choose the **rabbit roulade**, **roast kid** or roast pork with walnuts, accompanied with **polenta** bergamasca and roast potatoes.

The simple desserts are well worth sampling: walnut, peach or amaretti cakes or chocolate bavarese. Don't miss the coffee, made in a moka coffeepot.

The wine list has room for improvement, currently offering around ten local organic labels.

This osteria is housed in a historic 1837 palazzo in the center of Cremona, once the residence of the Barbò family. You can dine in one of the three rooms: the yellow, white or red room, adorned with frescoes by local painters, antique furniture and mirrors. The red room in particular has a beautifully preserved caisson ceiling.

Since being taken over by new management in 1994, it has offered high-quality cuisine at reasonable prices, with careful service and simple presentations. The osteria has become a destination for foodies and risotto fans, and every second Thursday in the month there's a special menu of of around 20 dishes.

Start with the Cremona **cured meats** and other seasonally changing antipasti. The first courses include some noteworthy **risottos** – a winter risotto with Savoy cabbage and salami pesto, or "risotto 700," the restaurant's signature dish, made with scamorza and speck. There are also **pumpkin tortelli**, **marubini** with sauce or in the traditional stock, and handmade **tagliolini with salami pesto**. Main courses include **duck breast in red wine**, tagliata with scamorza, **bollito misto with Cremona mostarda, beef cheek in Barolo** and medallions of fillet steak alla Stradivari. The good cheese board served with the ubiquitous mostarda, and there are desserts like as dolceluca, semifreddo with nougat or a cream of yogurt, lemon and ginger, to finish off in style.

The wine list of over 150 Italian labels also deserves a mention.

LA SOSTA

Recently opened osteria
Via Sicardo 9
Tel. 0372 456656
Closed Sunday dinner and Monday
Open: lunch and dinner
Holidays: two weeks in August
Seating: 60
Prices: 32-35 euros, wine excluded
All major credit cards except AE, Bancomat

Around the corner from the piazza with the Torazzo is La Sosta, an attractive osteria about to celebrate its 20th birthday. As of this year the sole proprietor is Claudio Nevi, who attends to guests in one of two inviting and tastefully decorated dining rooms. His cuisine is anchored in tradition, interpreted with innovative flair and using the best ingredients. The restaurant takes part in various culinary events dedicated in the fall to local traditions and in the spring to freshwater fish. During these events there are interesting set menus which also include drinks.
Start with warm chicken salad with radicchio and walnuts, local **cured meats** with sweet-and-sour vegetables, culatello di Zibello and melon, or warm cuttlefish with spelt and grilled zucchini. Then green ravioli with taleggio and asparagus served with butter and sage, paccheri di Gragnano with black pepper and pecorino, **fettuccine with ragù of rabbit and vegetables** or **gnocchi vecchia Cremona** filled with salami pesto. In winter there are the classic **marubini with three stocks**, followed by **bollito misto** and **cotechino sausage with lentils**. Or there's beef tartare, grilled beef tagliata, **roast suckling pig with potatoes** or caramelized duck breast with balsamic vinegar. It is hard to resist the tempting **cheese board** with mostarda and jams. To finish off, fruit, sorbet, ice cream, wild mint panna cotta with bitter chocolate or semifreddo, together with a good selection of sweet passito wines served by the glass.
There is a good range of Italian wines, mainly from Piedmont and Tuscany.

CREMONA

PORTA MOSA

Recently opened osteria
Via Santa Maria in Betlem 11
Tel. 0372 411803
Closed Sunday
Open: lunch and dinner
Holidays: in August and around Christmas
Seating: 36
Prices: 33-35 euros, wine excluded
All credit cards, Bancomat

Diners are well taken care of in this small, cozy osteria, from the warm friendly welcome from Roberto Bona (a chemist who quit his day job to work, with great success, in the restaurant business) to the simple and unique food. Bona is assisted by his mother, Annamaria Lupi, whose decades of experience show in the range of dishes which approach perfection.
Start with traditional **garlic salami** and **fiocco di culatello**, lardo and pancetta or rustic cured meats made with game; there's also **foie gras** on toast, a tempting **aged goose salami**, smoked goose speck and turkey fillet. Then try Annamaria's **tagliatelle** with **porcini mushroom sauce** or vegetables, pumpkin-stuffed caramelle drenched in melted butter, and a memorable **shallot soup** with black pepper. In the winter you can sample the classic **marubini ai tre brodi**, mixed mushroom soup, **cotechino** and cooked salumi. We tried a delicate duck breast tagliata with juniper berries and perfectly cooked pré salé lamb chops in an orange sauce. Other main courses include **roast suckling pig** in beer sauce, fillet steak with pink peppercorns and freshwater fish. There is a tempting **cheese board** and a high quality plateau fromage fermier. To finish off, try the creamy zabaglione ice cream, **sbrisolona cake** and a tiramisù worthy of the name.
The wine list is impressive thanks to the family-run wine shop: let Roberto advise you on the right choice.

DARFO BOARIO TERME
Angone

DESENZANO DEL GARDA

GABOSSI

PIROSCAFO

Osteria-trattoria
Via Fratelli Bandiera 9
Tel. 0364 534148
Closed Tuesday and Wednesday
Open: dinner only
Holidays: August
Seating: 50
Prices: 26-28 euros, wine excluded
All credit cards, Bancomat

3-Star Hotel
Via Porto Vecchio 11
Tel. 030 9141128
Fax 030 9912586
E-mail: piroscaf@tin.it
Internet: www.hotelpiroscafo.it
Open from March to December

The interior of this rustic restaurant boasts wide arches set on columns, a wood-burning grill and oven, and a lower dining area in what was once the old wine cellar, with stone walls, a wooden-beamed ceiling and an open fire which is lit almost year round. Run by Oliviero and Eugenia Gabossi and their daughter, they've managed to create a homely and inviting ambience in an already attractive setting.

To whet your appetite you'll be served a little slice of pizza to nibble on while trying to decide from the large menu. The antipasti include a good selection of **cured meats** accompanied by polenta, salads and grilled vegetables. The menu always includes **casoncelli camuni**, or choose from **potato gnocchetti** with local scorzone truffles, pasta alla pastora, **tripe** and **pasta and beans**. Then it's on to **duck with Savoy cabbage, baby wild boar** (reared by Oliviero's father) roasted in the wood-fired oven and served with deeply savory potatoes with rosemary or char-grilled Brescia meats – the beef is excellent. To finish off, a selection of Alpine cheeses and fresh caprini accompanied by **polenta taragna** and **sweet-and-sour pickled vegetables**, served with passito muffato wine. Homemade fruit tarts and seasonal fruit round off the meal.

The cellar offers around 40 prized regional wines, particularly from Franciacorta and Garda and the increasingly popular wines of the Valcamonica area (Merlot, Baldamì etc.). There's also a wide range of spirits, including a good genepy.

This renovated 1920s guesthouse overlooks the old fishing port right in the center of town, with its busy market, characteristic arcades and Palazzo del Tourismo, which often hosts art exhibitions. From Desenzano you can take any of a number of boats to the sights around Lake Como. The Villa Romana, the Sirmione baths and the Garda hills with their beautiful vineyard views. Just 500 meters from the hotel is a pleasant beach with a sailing school. Rooms have modern furnishings, and some have lake views. Breakfast is buffet-style.

• 2 single and 30 double rooms, with bathroom, air-conditioning, safe, satellite TV • Prices: single 52-70 euros, double 70-91; breakfast 9 euros per person • Credit cards: major ones, Bancomat • Special conditions for municipal paid parking. Small pets allowed. Reception open 24 hours a day • Bar. Reading and TV room. Terrace.

DESENZANO DEL GARDA

28 KM SOUTHEAST OF BRESCIA

LA CONTRADA

Restaurant
Via Bagatta 12
Tel. 030 9142514
Closed Wednesday and Thursday lunch
Open: lunch and dinner
Holidays: variable
Seating: 40 + 12 outdoors
Prices: 30 euros, wine excluded
All credit cards, Bancomat

Via Bagatta is a quiet little street which leads from the porticos to the upper part of Desenzano and is home to this tastefully decorated restaurant with just a few tables, owned by Marta Zancarli. She is committed to promoting the local area and its produce, and her menu revolves around specialties from the lake.

The antipasti, for example, include fish like **pike in salsa** and marinated **trout and char terrine**. There are also **cured meats** from local artisanal producers. On our visit we then sampled the lake-fish-filled **ravioli al pescato di lago** and garganelli with trout ragù; as well as some tasty **bigoli** made the traditional way, then tossed in **salami pesto**, and the excellent tagliolini with Valle Sabbia Bagòss (a Slow Food Presidium). The main courses included a light **mixed fry of lake fish** and river prawns with zucchini tempura. Highly recommended are the **pike alla pescatora** and the roast whitefish. For those who prefer meat, there's **roast quail**, in season stuffed with porcini, or rack of lamb with aromatic herbs. A good Italian cheese board and a millefeuille with fresh fruit or chocolate cake provide the perfect finish.

The meal is accompanied with good wines from the area or various regions of Italy.

🐟 Just around the corner in Via Castello, Cavallaio sells fresh fish from the lake, plus wonderful sardines perfect for grilling.

DOVERA
Barbuzzera

52 KM NORTH OF CREMONA, 7 KM NORTH OF LODI

LA CUCCAGNA 🍾

Restaurant
Via Milano 14
Tel. 0373 978447
Closed Wednesday and Thursday lunch
Open: lunch and dinner
Holidays: December 27- January 2
and two weeks in August
Seating: 50
Prices: 30-35 euros, wine excluded
All credit cards except DC, Bancomat

The tiny village of Barbuzzera, in the countryside between Dovera and the Paullese highway, may not be the most likely location for this interesting restaurant run by the Magnani family, but it's a pleasure to find it here. Roberto and Marco are in charge of the kitchen and dining room, and their parents behind the bar. There've been several stages of restoration, and there are now three tastefully decorated, air-conditioned dining rooms.

The seasonally changing menu reflects the chef's creative flair, as well as the rich resources of nearby Milan's markets – though there's plenty of room for local produce like **Mezzago asparagus**, and **cured meats** from Cremona and Parma are always on the menu. The first courses should not be skipped: **tortelli cremaschi** or **with pumpkin filling** or in many other variations, well-made asparagus or mushroom **risottos**, seasonal soups, and in the winter **busecca** (tripe) or **cotechino**. None of the dishes is heavy-handed: everything is beautifully presented with a creative touch.

The beef, served raw, grilled or roasted, is supplied by Franco Cazzamali, who has a farm just a few kilometers away where he rears some of the best Italian breeds. In the winter the menu features superb local **bolliti** accompanied by the classic **mostarda**, as well as pork, duck and rabbit cooked in a variety of different ways, and in the summer there's fish. The extensive wine list has over 400 labels, with wines from indigenous Italian varietals featuring strongly. The spirits and liqueurs have been carefully selected.

DRIZZONA
Castelfranco d'Oglio

ESINE

28 KM EAST OF CREMONA ON SS 10

62 KM NORTHEAST OF BRESCIA, 8 KM FROM DARFO AND BRENO SS 42

L'AIRONE

LA CANTINA

━●Holiday farm
Strada Comunale per Isola Dovarese 2
Tel. 0375 389902
Fax 0375 389887
E-mail: info@laironeagriturismo.com
Internet: www.laironeagriturismo.com
Open all year

▽Trattoria
Via IV Novembre 7
Tel. 0364 466411-46317
Closed Wednesdays
Open: dinner, Saturday and Sunday lunch
Holidays: from June 20-July 20
Seating: 50 + 30 outdoors
Prices: 23-25 euros, wine excluded
No credit cards, Bancomat

A beautifully restored farmhouse surrounded by the tranquil countryside of the Oglio Sud nature reserve provides the lovely setting for L'Airone. Rooms are named after flowers and are all airy, clean and furnished in a rustic style. Breakfast includes sweet and savory foods, produced on the farm or typical of the area. The restaurant serves traditional Cremona cuisine and an average meal costs 28 euros, excluding wine. The farm also houses an interesting museum of country life and has a special children's area in a shady walnut grove. Guests can enjoy cycling, horse riding and canoeing and the cities of Mantua, Parma and Cremona are all within easy reach.

• 1 single, 9 double and 2 triple rooms, 1 junior suite and 1 suite (6 persons), with bathroom, fridge, TV, modem connection • Prices: single 45 euros, double room single occupancy 54, double 60, triple 70-75, junior suite 100, suite 150, breakfast included • Credit cards: all, Bancomat • Facility accessible for the mobility challenged. Off-street parking. Small pets allowed. Reception open from 8 am to 8 pm • Restaurant with bar. Breakfast room. Conference rooms. Garden, playground. Pool, gym.

When Oriana Belotti and Giacomo Bontempi took over this osteria in the historic center of Esine a few years ago, they completely remodeled it, bringing out original architectural features and creating some lovely, welcoming dining areas. Oriana's menu is based on Valcamonica specialties, and every day she sources local ingredients in the valley before arriving in the kitchen to make the day's fresh pasta.
Antipasti include lardo, Italian beef sausage, spalla salmistrata di Angolo, carne salada with onion, salmon trout in carpione in summer and **polenta** – made with stone-ground corn, buckwheat or wholemeal flour – with anchovies in winter. First courses include **barley with loertis** (wild hops), porcini mushrooms or onions and wild herbs; **taedèi** (rustic chestnut-flour tagliatelle) with butter and sage; polenta gnocchetti with duck ragù or porcini or strachitund cheese; **gnocc de la cùa**; **foiade pasta with potatoes and wild cabbage**; **bigoi** with truffles in season and porcini soup. As for the main courses, try the **game**, roast pork stinco or **donkey stracotto**. In the winter there's hearty **boiled cotechino** and **soppressa** and **baccalà in milk** with leeks and parsley; in spring **lamb sausage** with boiled potatoes and frogs' legs tortino with spinach and wild herbs; and in summer **grilled sardines** from the nearby Lago d'Iseo. The desserts are homemade: apple pie, jam tarts, and in season, a fluffy chestnut cake.
There is a good selection of regional wines, all IGT labels from Valcamonica.

FORTUNAGO
Casareggio

GAGGIANO
Vigano Certosino

38 KM SOUTH OF PAVIA, 10 KM SOUTHEAST OF VOGHERA

15 KM SOUTHWEST OF MILAN

CASCINA CASAREGGIO

Holiday farm
Località Casareggio 1
Tel. 0383 875228
Fax 0383 875637
E-mail: segreteria@cascinacasareggio.it
Internet: www.cascinacasareggio.it
Open all year

ANTICA TRATTORIA DEL GALLO

Trattoria
Via Kennedy 1-3
Tel. 02 9085276
Closed Monday and Tuesday
Open: lunch and dinner
Holidays: 3 weeks in August, 2 weeks at Christmas
Seating: 100 + 120 outdoors
Prices: 33 euros, wine excluded
All credit cards, Bancomat

It's not far from the muggy heat and crowds of the lowlands, but the 500-meter altitude of the Casareggio farm makes all the difference. In the midst of peaceful woods and meadows, close by many historical fortresses and castles, it's an ideal base for walks, cycling and horse riding. Rooms are tastefully furnished, with great attention to detail. The farm boasts a large open-air area used for events, where guests can enjoy an alfresco breakfast. The owner, Lucia Rossotti, offers her guests genuine local cuisine (average price 35 euros) with a modern twist. Farm ingredients are used in the restaurant and for the buffet breakfast of cereals, jams, home-baked cakes and fruit.

• 14 double and 1 triple rooms, with bathroom, fridge, TV • Prices: double room single occupancy 50-60 euros, double 75-85 (20 euro supplement for additional bed), triple 110, breakfast included • Credit cards: major ones, Bancomat • Facility accessible for the mobility challenged. Off-street parking. Small pets allowed. Reception open from 7.30 am to 1 am • Bar, restaurant. Meeting and conference rooms. Pool.

This trattoria is a classic destination for Milanese who want to escape the city. Here they can dine alfresco under the lovely arbor, or inside the pleasant, rustically furnished dining rooms. Dishes from the restaurant's history are balanced by a number of interesting additions, all prepared with carefully selected, seasonal ingredients. The set menu for 30 euros is worth a try, and there's also a children's menu. The fresh pasta and excellent bread are both made in-house.

You can start with an antipasto of **cotechino** and **cured meats** produced under the watchful eye of owner Paolo Reina; then whipped salt cod, **smoked goose breast** and **tonno di campagna**, a local dish which has all but disappeared. The **veal ravioli** tossed in melted butter are part of the restaurant's gastronomic legacy, but you can also sample cream of fava beans with chicory, minestrone (served cold in summer), potato gnocchetti, and crêpes with eggplant and scamorza. The trattoria's signature dish, **pollo alla diavola**, is made using chicken from a trusted local farmer; or try the classic **breaded veal cutlet**, **snails in sauce**, saddle of rabbit, and in summer fresh steak tartare. The side dishes are beautifully prepared, from crunchy fried potatoes to delicious mixed salads. If you still have room, try the good **cheese board** selected by Paolo. The desserts – chocolate mousse is excellent – are homemade and accompanied by sweet wines served by the glass.

The extensive wine list of 800 wines, with half bottles available too, from the various regions of Italy, will satisfy the most demanding customer.

GARDONE RIVIERA
Gardone Sopra

34 KM NORTH EAST OF BRESCIA SS 45 BIS

TRATTORIA AGLI ANGELI

🍲 Trattoria – 2-Star Hotel
Piazzetta Garibaldi 2
Tel. 0365 20832-20746
Fax 0365 20746
E-mail: info@agliangeli.com
Internet: www.agliangeli.com
Closed Tuesday
Open: lunch and dinner
Holidays: November 10 – February 10
Seating: 50 +30 outdoors
Prices: 32-35 euros, wine excluded
All credit cards except AE, Bancomat

This charming establishment has been owned by the Pellegrini family since the 1970s, and recently the new generation has transformed it into a delightful destination, in an ancient village that offers glimpses of the lake. There is a small swimming pool and 14 rooms with original furnishings; the buffet breakfast is rich and varied.
The historic trattoria's cuisine is seasonal and traditional, using lots of **freshwater fish** – tench, trout and sardines – steamed, stewed, baked, grilled; as well as home-smoked round steak, leek and cauliflower flan with walnut sauce and **fresh goat's cheese tortino** with pears and onions. To continue, **tagliatelle with smoked eel**, pasta caramelle with formaggella and herbs, soup with local spelt, maccheroncini al **Bagòss** (a Slow Food Presidium). The main courses offers more fish, or loin of suckling pig glazed with honey and thyme and grilled lamb kebabs. To finish, a choice selection of cheeses and eight different desserts. The wine list offers abundant choice.
Don't miss the nearby Vittoriale villa of Gabriele D'Annunzio and André Heller's botanic garden.

🛏• 1 single room, 7 doubles, 1 triple, en-suite, air conditioning, TV, safe deposit box • Prices: single 45-65, double 75-95, triple 117 euros, breakfast included • Parking: 6 parking spaces reserved on payment at the Vittoriale; public parking at 100 meters. Pets welcome. Owners always available • Restaurant. Reading room. Garden

GARGNANO
Bogliaco

45 KM NORTHEAST OF BRESCIA SS 45 BIS

ALLO SCOGLIO

🍲 Restaurant
Via Barbacane 3
Tel. 0365 71030
Closed Monday
Open: lunch and dinner
Holidays: January-February
Seating: 60 + 30 outdoors
Prices: 25-35 euros, wine excluded
All credit cards, Bancomat

Bogliaco is a small tourist town not far from Gargnano del Garda, and Allo Scoglio has an enviable location on the northeast corner of a tranquil piazza. Keen sailors can watch the start of the well-known Centomiglia del Garda boat race from here. Enter through the charming lakeside garden, where you can dine alfresco in summer. The restaurant is run by Mariska Piantoni with the expert help of husband and chef Mauro. Ingredients are carefully selected and skillfully cooked with a light touch, resulting in flavors and aromas that capture the best of the area's produce.
Fish from the lake feature abundantly, from the antipasti on: **pike in sauce**, **lake whitefish alla gardesana** and **warm salad of char**, as well as artichoke salad and prosciutto crudo. As for first courses, we recommend the delicious **tortelli filled with chub**; **strigoli with perch**; homemade buckwheat tagliatelle with zucchini, whitefish and saffron: and an excellent **tench risotto**. Then try the grilled lake fish or opt for grilled eel, roast perch, or **char in salsa** served with some delicious **polenta di Storo**. If you prefer meat, roast breast of guinea fowl and **veal with porcini mushrooms**. The desserts, from nougat or amaretto semifreddo to a yogurt mousse with hot raspberry sauce to pear and chocolate cake, are very good.
The quality wine list offers ideal pairings for the dishes on offer.

GARGNANO
Bogliaco

GONZAGA

45 KM NORTHEAST OF BRESCIA ON SS 45 BIS

27 KM SOUTH OF MANTUA

BOGLIACO

3-Star Hotel
Via Battisti 3
Tel. 0365 71404
Fax 0365 72780
E-mail: info@hotelbogliaco.it
Internet: www.hotelbogliaco.it
Open from March to December

NEGRI

Restaurant
Largo Martiri della Libertà 14
Tel. 0376 528182
Closed Sunday evenings and Monday
Open: lunch and dinner
Holidays: August
Seating: 40
Prices: 25-30 euros, wine excluded
Credit cards: Visa

In a 19th-century mansion known as Villa Teodora, the hotel is decorated with allegorical frescoes and boasts a beautiful garden which opens onto the lake and nearby Piazza Bogliaco. Once the residence of the Mussolini family, until the 1970s it housed the youth center Casa del Fanciullo. In 1975 it was converted into a charming hotel managed by Noemi Zanini. The restaurant lounge with its paneled ceiling, lovely fireplace and numerous frescoes is a particularly pleasant area, while the suite with its four-poster bed, antique furniture and original flooring is spectacular. A supplement of 5 euros per person is payable for rooms with lake views. The restaurant offers authentic local cuisine and an average meal costs 30 euros. Guests can enjoy a buffet breakfast of homemade cakes and tarts, fresh fruit, milk, yogurt, cereals and savory items. Worth visiting are the nearby Riva del Garda and the castles. For those who love sailing, Bogliaco hosts the Centomiglia del Garda race.

• 3 single, 22 double, 3 triple, 3 quadruple rooms and 1 suite, with bathroom, air-conditioning, satellite TV, safe, (the suite and one double have jacuzzis) • Prices: single 50-60 euros, double 80-110, triple 100-120, four-bed 120-140, suite 150-200, breakfast included • Credit cards: major ones, Bancomat • Facility accessible for the mobility challenged, 2 rooms designed for their use. Off-street parking (30 spaces). Small pets allowed (not in communal areas). Reception open from 7.30 am to midnight • Bar, restaurant. Reading room. Terrace, gazebo. Private beach.

Gonzaga is an important farming town in the lower Po River plains, famous for its time-honored September fair and for being the birthplace of the Corradi family, who, as they rose to power in the city of Mantua, took on the name of their home town. Negri lies just off the porticoed main square, with its two beautiful 15th-century towers, once part of an ancient castle. Three generations of the Negri family have run the restaurant; before Alberto there was his father, and before that his grandfather, and traditions have been impressively maintained.
Start off with **Mantua salami**, vegetable terrine, or a range of different carpaccios, then continue with the excellent traditional Mantuan **nidi di rondine** (swallows' nests), **sorbir di cappelletti** in a rich meat stock with a generous sprinkling of Parmigiano and **pumpkin tortelli**. Some innovations appear in the mains: alongside the traditional dishes there are a few creative touches. They include beef tagliata, rabbit in Prosecco vinegar, **duck breast with Mantua mostarda** or rocket and oranges, goose breast escalopes in Marsala and **vitello tonnato**, served without the traditional mayonnaise dressing. In winter there is the classic **cotechino with beans** or creamed potatoes. The puddings always include **sbrisolona cake**; there is also a curious Gorgonzola pudding with honey and fig jam, along with semifreddo with rum or amaretti and a creamy liquorice and chocolate sauce.
Alberto is a connoisseur when it comes to oils, wines and spirits. The wine list offers some top labels from northern Italy, and particularly around Mantua.

GRAVEDONA

52 KM NORTHEAST OF COMO ON SS 36

LA VILLA

3-Star Hotel
Via Regina Ponente 21
Tel. 0344 89017
Fax 0344 89027
E-mail: Hotellavilla@tiscalinet.it
Internet: www.hotel-la-villa.com
Closed from December 10 to January 20

Gravedona is a charming village full of history and art, on the western bank of Lake Como. It's home to this hotel, managed by the Mallone family. Rooms furnished in a modern style and have all mod cons, and some have lovely views of the lake. The restaurant offers both traditional cuisine from the region and around Italy at an average cost of 22 euros, excluding wine. The buffet breakfast comprises a variety of sweet and savory items and a wide choice of beverages, which in summer guests can enjoy alfresco by the pool. The lakeside can be explored on foot, by bicycle or boat. Don't miss the picturesque church of Santa Maria del Tiglio in the center of the village.

• 15 double rooms, with bathroom, fridge, satellite TV; some have a terrace • Prices: double room single occupancy 70-75 euros, double 85-90, breakfast included • Credit cards: all, Bancomat • Entire facility accessible for the mobility challenged, 1 room designed for their use. External parking out front. No pets allowed. Reception open from 7 am to 11 pm • Bar, restaurant. Garden. Pool.

INVERNO E MONTELEONE
Monteleone

22 KM EAST OF PAVIA SS 235

RIGHINI

Trattoria
Via Miradolo 108
Tel. 0382 73032
Closed Monday and Tuesday
Open: for dinner, Saturday also lunch, Wednesday and Sunday lunch only
Holidays: 1 July-15 September, 7-31 January
Seating: 90
Prices: 25-35 euros
No credit cards accepted

There's only one seating here, and come prepared to eat, as course after course a seemingly endless array of tempting dishes will be brought out. Guests are spoiled and fussed over, treated like grandchildren pushed to have second helpings of their favorite dishes. It's all like it was in the 1950s, when Sundays were the occasion for an outing to the country in search of authentic traditional cooking. From Milan it's a bit off the beaten track, but easily reached from both San Colombano and Miradolo Terme. Chef Ines has a lot of experience and, helped by the rest of her family, serves the best that a lunch in Lombardy can offer. The meal starts as you enter with a glass of the sparkling house wine which, like the other wines, is made in the San Colombano hills. It's paired with lardo and **raspadura** from Lodi. Once seated you'll be offered a selection of cured meats, vegetables preserved in oil or vinegar, hot **mondeghili**, frittata with wild herbs or vegetables, guinea fowl in carpione and other specialties according to the season. Then it's on to homemade fresh pasta, including meat and vegetable ravioli served in a variety of different sauces, and excellent **risottos**.
Watch out for the generous portions of the first courses and leave room for the mains: free-range meats and chicken and amazing **rabbit**, all served with a variety of side dishes. At this point it's time for a sorbet, then how about a hearty plateful of steaming **polenta** with **chestnut soup**, gorgonzola, **snails in sauce** or **sautéed porcini mushrooms**? And before coffee, what about a rich dessert or a fruit salad? You'll leave the table full but happy in the knowledge that you've had a real old-fashioned Sunday lunch.

Iseo
Clusane

Isola Dovarese

28 KM NORTHWEST OF BRESCIA SS 510

24 KM EAST OF CREMONA

Al Porto

Caffè la Crepa 🌀 ⊗ ▮

🍲 Trattoria
Via Porto dei Pescatori 12
Tel. 030 989014
Closed Wednesday
Open: lunch and dinner
Holidays: none
Seating: 200
Prices: 30-33 euros, wine excluded
All credit cards, Bancomat

🍲 Traditional osteria
Piazza Matteotti 14
Tel. 0375 396161
Closed Monday dinner and Tuesday
Open: only for dinner
Holidays: second week of September, one week in January
Seating: 40 + 20 outdoors
Prices: 30-32 euros, wine excluded
All major credit cards, Bancomat

The ancient fishing village of Clusane has been a tourist destination for over two centuries, with visitors coming for both the picturesque charm and the lake-based cuisine. This 200-year-old trattoria is in an old house which has undergone several extensions. On the western side of the first floor a little loggia has mullioned windows and stone columns carved with flowers, dating back to the 17th century. The many dining rooms spread out over the two floors have country-style furniture, and you'll be taken care of by Gabriella Bosio and her family.

Every dish on the simple, seasonal menu is bursting with flavor. The antipasti include a **whitefish terrine** with chives, **char with herbs** and the classic **lake sardines with polenta**. First courses are particularly good, with **tagliatelle with lake prawns** or perch, lake risotto, **casonsei** and char ravioli. The main courses are also fish-based – **roast tench with polenta**, whitefish fillets with lemon, whitefish with capers and **fried lake prawns** – though there are a few meat dishes and a good selection of cheeses. To round off the meal, a variety of desserts: nonna Giuditta's cake, pear pastries, nougat sformato, amaretti budino.

The well-stocked cellars offer over 100 labels, mainly the great wines of Franciacorta, along with a wide range of spirits.

🍯🍴 The Bottega del Porto (in the piazza beside the trattoria), sells lake produce and oil; at Via Mirolte 16, the shop run by the Bonari sisters continues the family tradition, offering a wide selection of cheeses, honey, jams and other specialties.

We're sad to have to report that Signora Elda, who ran this osteria for half a century, has passed away. A guardian of the culinary experience of generations of women, she was a presence in this piazza since 1951, originally on the corner of Contrada de le Gere, and then in 1962 moving her restaurant into the 15th-century Palazzo della Guardia. She used to make a truly suberb frittata, and would never reveal any of her secrets. Now efficiently run by her talented children, the Caffè is the definitive authentic Italian trattoria, with cuisine reflecting the variety of local produce and a commitment to finding the best ingredients.

This is the place to sample classic dishes such as **black-eyed peas with pork rind**, prepared on the Day of the Dead; **baccalà** on Good Friday; meatballs; **rice savarin** with tongue; a selection of **cured meats** – culatello, pancetta, coppa and salami – and a good **cheese board** with cow's and goat's milk cheeses. First courses include traditional Castelgoffredo **tortelli amari** made with costmary, vegetable soups; **tripe** cooked the old-fashioned way, marinated eel, **pike in sauce**, and frogs' legs. You can finish off by sampling the products of the restaurant's own gelateria, or opt for one of the homemade fruit tarts. There's a good range of excellent wines from which you can choose the perfect pairing for your meal. Many of the wines are served by the glass, which can help keep the final check low.

Don't leave without visiting the cellars, where you can admire thousands of bottles, cured meats hanging up to mature and family antiques.

LECCO
Acquate

LENNO

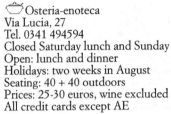

2 KM FROM THE CITY CENTER

27 KM NORTHEAST OF COMO SS 340

ANTICA OSTERIA CASA DI LUCIA

Osteria-enoteca
Via Lucia, 27
Tel. 0341 494594
Closed Saturday lunch and Sunday
Open: lunch and dinner
Holidays: two weeks in August
Seating: 40 + 40 outdoors
Prices: 25-30 euros, wine excluded
All credit cards except AE

SANTO STEFANO

Trattoria
Piazza XI Febbraio 3
Tel. 0344 55434
Closed Monday
Open: lunch and dinner
Holidays: mid-January to mid-February
Seating: 25 + 20 outdoors
Prices: 25 euros, wine excluded
All credit cards

Casa di Lucia has been serving classic local food and wine to the people of Lecco for over twenty years. Located in the historic center of Acquate, the osteria is the creation of owner Carletto Piras, who's passionate about saving local traditions from extinction. In the summer ask to be seated in the garden under the arbor. The rest of the year there's three attractive dining rooms; the favorite with regulars and Carletto's friends is the one with the huge fireplace and antique stone sink.

But the real draw is the food. Antipasti include **brisaola** from Chiavenna, cured meats accompanied with vegetables preserved in oil, and tasty grilled **missoltini with polenta**. You can continue with **pappardelle with hare sauce**, vegetable ravioli tossed in butter and sage or elderflowers, and when in season, garganelli with artichokes, sheep's milk ricotta and bottarga and paccheri with broccoli sauce. Main courses include the classic liver piccatina with creamy onions and, thanks to a local fisherman who supplies Carletto with a daily catch, a some good, traditionally prepared **lake fish**. There is a good **cheese board** – with fresh and mature goat's cheeses, Bitto and Taleggio from Valsassina – as well as some excellent homemade desserts (puddings, cakes and semifreddo).

The historic wine cellar offers fine wines from Italy and abroad.

With the breathtaking setting of Lake Como, the village of Lenno attracts tourists from all over the world. This inviting trattoria in the lakeside square has been run for decades by Claudio Zani and his wife Gloria. The menu features lake fish, supplied daily by the fishermen of Menaggio, and seasonal local produce cooked in simply and according to tradition.

The gracious, ever-patient Gloria will offer you the house antipasti, which includes whitefish in piquant green sauce, fish in carpione and **trout** carpaccio or **terrine**. You can continue with **ravioli** or opt for **tagliolini with smoked trout**. If it's on the menu, we recommend the golden perch, whitefish and **shad served with butter and sage** or grilled and the classic **chub fishcakes**. In winter the chef offers game-based dishes when hunter friends oblige, served with **polenta**. To finish, ask to sample the cheeses or go for one of the delicious desserts.

The wine list deserves a mention: a great deal of work is being done to extend it year by year.

LEZZENO

HOTEL AURORA

2-Star Hotel
Via Sossana, 2
Tel. and fax 031 914645
E-mail: info@hotelauroralezzeno.com
Internet: www.hotelauroralezzeno.com
Open from Easter to November 10

This hotel, managed by the Gregorio family, is located in a recently restored early 20th-century building a few kilometers from Bellagio. Rooms are spacious and comfortable, some with views of the lake and some overlooking the mountains. For breakfast, guests can enjoy a generous buffet of both sweet and savory items. In summer on the veranda overlooking the lake guests can taste delicious fish dishes at an average cost of 30 euros, excluding wine. The surrounding mountains can be explored on foot or by bicycle and the hotel also rents canoes, motor boats, water skis and tennis equipment. Not to be missed: the village of Varenna, built on a rocky promontory, and the island of Comacina.

• 2 single and 10 double rooms, with bathroom, TV; some with balcony • Prices: single 40-45 euros, double 75-90 (20 euro supplement for additional bed), breakfast included • Credit cards: all, Bancomat • Off-street parking, garage (15 spaces). Small pets allowed. Reception open from 8 am to 11 pm • Bar, restaurant. Breakfast room. Jetty with solarium. Beach.

LONATO

OSTERIA SAN CIPRIANO

Recently opened osteria
Via San Cipriano 25
Tel. 030 9131638
Closed Monday
Open: lunch and dinner
Holidays: 15 June-31 July, 30 December-6 January
Seating: 30 + 20 outdoors
Prices: 20-23 euros, wine excluded
No credit cards, Bancomat

On the outskirts of Lonato, the osteria is easy to reach from town and industrial area of Desenzano. Its fetching terrace and ivy-covered pergola offer charming outdoor dining in the summer, while the simply appointed interior offers the down-to-earth atmosphere characteristic of the traditional osteria. Carla Torazzini, who runs the place with her husband Egidio, a well-known gastronome, and their son Gian Mario, a promising chef, will recommend the day's specials, as dictated by market and seasonal availability.
The antipasti, however, do not vary: excellent **cured meats** (pancetta, coppa, local salami), warm beef carpaccio and **pike alla barcaiola**. Then it's on to **spaghetti with freshwater shrimp, risotto with salami pesto**, Brescia **pumpkin tortelli** with walnuts and ricotta, and fresh **tagliatelle with horsemeat sfilaccino**. We recommend following up with the combination of horse meat, beef, local chicken and pork grilled over aromatic oak and beechwood. There's also **lake fish**, depending on the day's catch, **boiled stuffed hen** served with pearà sauce, a Verona specialty, and homemade mostarda, roast duck or **guinea fowl with stuffing**, or an excellent peppered goats' cheese served with a wonderful olive oil. Contorni include sautéed wild chicory and vegetables prepared in a variety of ways. Finish your meal with almond cake and a glass of passito or one of the desserts. The wine list offers some good Garda wines served by the carafe as well as quality local and regional labels. There is a good range of grappas and liqueurs.

LOVERE

41 KM NORTHEAST OF BERGAMO ON SS 42

SANT'ANTONIO

🗝️●3 Star Hotel
Piazza Tredici Martiri 2
Tel. and fax 035 961523
E-mail: info@albergosantantonio.it
Internet: www.albergosantantonio.it
Open all year

Located on the main square of pretty Lovere, this elegant hotel welcomes tourists attracted by the beautiful lakefront, historical buildings (Palazzo Tadini, now an art gallery, Palazzo Marinoni, Villa Milesi) and interesting examples of medieval architecture such as the Arghisi and Torricella towers. All rooms are spacious and comfortable and have views of the lake. The buffet breakfast offers various sweet items but savories are available on request. The restaurant is well known for its cuisine and features freshwater fish in addition to local, regional and national dishes. During the summer, guests can enjoy lunch or dinner on the panoramic terrace on the top floor (average cost of a meal 15-20 euros).

• 20 double or triple rooms and 2 suites, with bathroom, fridge, satellite TV • Prices: double room single occupancy 55-60 euros, double 70-80, triple 81-95, suite 95-105; breakfast 4 euros per person • Credit cards: all except DC, Bancomat • Facility accessible for the mobility challenged, 5 rooms designed for their use with external bathroom. Public parking (paid during the day). Small pets allowed. Reception open 24 hours a day • Bar, restaurant. Breakfast room, reading, TV and conference rooms. Terrace.

MADESIMO
Montespluga

78 KM NORTHWEST OF SONDRIO ON SS 36

POSTA

🗝️●2-Star Hotel
Via Dogana 8
Tel. and fax 0343 54234
E-mail: salafaustoenoteca@tiscalinet.it
Closed January and February

This friendly hotel near the Swiss border was once used as a stopover for horse-drawn carriages. Now refurbished, it offers well furnished, comfortable rooms, some with TV. After a peaceful night's sleep guests can feast on an inviting breakfast of coffee, milk, tea, fruit juices, bread, butter and jam, pastries and savory items on request. Between Madesimo and the Val di Lei there are ski slopes that both experienced skiers and beginners can enjoy, along with the magnificent scenery. Half board is also available (59 euros per person per day) for those wishing to stay a few days, for a minimum of three days. The restaurant offers local dishes with a twist and an extensive wine list (average cost of a meal is 25-30 euros, excluding wine).

• 10 double rooms, with bathroom • Prices: double room single occupancy 45 euros, double 72; breakfast 6 euros per person • Credit cards: all, Bancomat • Off-street parking. No pets allowed. Owners always reachable • Bar, restaurant, wine cellar.

MANDELLO DEL LARIO
Maggiana

MANERBA DEL GARDA

9 KM NORTHWEST OF LECCO, 35 KM NORTHEAST OF COMO

32 KM EAST OF BRESCIA ON SP 572

SALI E TABACCHI

Traditional osteria
Piazza San Rocco 3
Tel. 0341 733715
Closed Monday and Tuesday
Open: lunch and dinner
Holidays: January 10-February 5
and August 18-September 8
Seating: 35 + 10 outdoors
Prices: 25-30 euros, wine excluded
All credit cards

VILLA SCHINDLER

2-Star Hotel
Via Bresciani 68
Tel. 0365 651046
Fax 0365 554877
E-mail: info@villaschindler.it
Internet: www.villaschindler.it
Closed from mid-October to the end of March

Ten minutes out on the winding road from Mondello to Maggiana you'll find a village where time seems to pass more slowly. And there you will find Sali e Tabacchi, the old village bakery, which is now divided into a bar/tobacconist and an osteria. Chef Gabriele, or Lele, as he is known, left a steady job as a cartographer and now ably runs the kitchen, while his wife Giuliana keeps watch over the front of the house. Lele always takes the trouble to find out how everything he serves is grown or produced and his dishes reveal an in-depth knowledge of local traditions.

In winter Giuliana usually recommends starting off with cream of baccalà served with Lario oil, **hot cotechino with Savoy cabbage** or a **quiche of Bitto and porcini mushrooms** with fonduta. Then **gnocchi with duck ragù** and sautéed mushrooms or the classic **tagliolini with missoltini**. For main courses, try the **ossobuco with polenta**, braised venison with Salsella and **polenta concia**. In summer Lele has fresh fish brought in daily by fishermen friends, and he often selects shad, whitefish and danube roach which he serves in carpione or in other dishes. Do try the rice with golden perch and the **whitefish with butter and sage**.

If you are not fond of fish, you can go for the classic cured meats, then ravioli with herbs and mascherpa tossed in a light pesto or lasagne with zucchini and Quartirolo cheese and lamb cutlets with thyme. For dessert: semifreddo with chestnut honey served with raspberry sauce and elderberry meini with zabaglione made using Moscato d'Asti.

Villa Schindler, just outside the village and on the San Felice del Benaco border, is an old mansion in the middle of the countryside offering beautiful views of the lake. Restored by talented local artist Anna Brotto, the building retains the original ceilings, floors and frescoes which make it all the more attractive. The villa is not only a hotel but also an art gallery: paintings and sculptures adorn both guest rooms and communal areas. Once a farm, Villa Schindler still boasts many beautiful, age-old olive trees. Rooms are spacious and welcoming, tastefully decorated and outfitted with fine furniture. The buffet breakfast offers an extensive selection, including coffee, milk, tea, fruit juices, cakes, croissants, bread, butter, eggs, cured meats and cheeses. For art lovers, Anna also organizes art and restoration courses.

• 5 single and 5 double rooms, with bathroom • Prices: single 51-83 euros, double 71-98 (15-20 euro supplement for extra bed), breakfast included • Credit cards: none • Off-street parking. Small pets allowed. Reception open from 8 am to 8 pm. • Breakfast room, small lounge bar. Garden, terrace. Pool. Small beach.

CASA MARGHERITA

Bed and breakfast
Via Portici Broletto 44
Tel. 349 7506117
E-mail: fregna.barbara@tiscali.it
Internet: www.lacasadimargherita.it
Open all year

DUE CAVALLINI

Trattoria
Via Salnitro 5
Tel. 0376 322084
Closed Tuesday
Open: lunch and dinner
Holidays: July 21–August 23, one week in January/February
Seating: 100 + 60 outdoors
Prices: 22-30 euros
All major credit cards, Bancomat

This typical Mantua-style house located under the arcades and among the shops in the town center is managed by Barbara Fregna, who has done an admirable job restoring it. The inner courtyard has been covered with a skylight and the rooms are simple, elegant and outfitted with modern furniture and antiques. All have balconies overlooking Piazza delle Erbe and Palazzo del Podestà. For breakfast guests can enjoy coffee, tea, milk, fruit juices, yogurt, homemade cakes and croissants, while savory items are available on request. Just a stone's throw away from Barbara's house are the Castle of San Giorgio, a Gonzaga family residence, with its celebrated Camera degli Sposi (Wedding Chamber) and many other buildings of historic and architectural interest. During the literary festival week the cost of a double room can reach 125 euros.

• 1 double, 1 suite (double bedroom and lounge with a sofa bed) and 1 apartment (2 rooms, 5 beds), with bathroom, air-conditioning, TV • Prices: double room single occupancy 55-68 euros, double 80-100 (25 euro supplement for extra bed), breakfast included • Credit cards: none • Public parking 500 meters away. Small pets allowed. Owners always reachable • Breakfast room.

Due Cavallini was established 1939 in La Fiera, the poorest district in the city, situated behind the Catena river port among the chimneys of the Ceramica factory and beside the municipal slaughterhouse. For decades the osteria was where factory workers, boatmen and porters enjoyed a quick break for a chat, a jug of red wine, fried cod, hard boiled eggs and tripe.

Now Porto Catena is deserted, the Ceramica factory is derelict and the slaughterhouse hosts the municipal library. The trattoria has not changed its classic dark wood furniture and white tablecloths, strictly traditional food and brisk, down-to-earth service, but they do offer a more varied menu. In summer you can eat in the shade of the pergola outside, but year round the dishes are all authentic Mantua specialties.

Start off with **cured meats** and olives, artichokes, baby onions and peppers preserved in oil. Then have a good helping of **sorbir d'agnoli** – a bowl of agnolini in broth with a shot of red Lambrusco – or **Mantua tripe** in broth with a **ciopa** of bread. Choose between a hearty serving of agnolini (without wine), **pumpkin tortelli** and **maccheroncini al torchio with braised horse meat**, also served as a main course with **toasted polenta**. Main courses include **boiled** hen, beef, cotechino and tongue, or **roast** rabbit, guinea fowl, duck and pork shank. For dessert: **sbrisolona** dunked in white wine or grappa.

Libations run from Lambruscos of the Basso Mantovano area to the reds and whites of the Alto Mantovano.

MESE

MILAN
Città Studi

CROTASC

🍲 Trattoria
Via Don Lucchinetti 63
Tel. 0343 41003
Closed Monday and Tuesday
Open: lunch and dinner
Holidays: last two weeks of June
Seating: 70 + 40 outdoors
Prices: 25-35 euros, wine excluded
All credit cards, Bancomat

ACQUABELLA

🍲 Recently opened osteria
Via San Rocco 11
Tel. 02 58309653
Closed Sundays and Saturday lunch
Open: lunch and dinner
Holidays: three weeks in August
Seating: 80
Prices: 30-33 euros, wine excluded
All major credit cards, Bancomat

This trattoria continues to exert a certain charm, thanks to its two attractive dining rooms and the outdoor area, where you can eat al fresco in summer. It is run by the Prevostini siblings, following in the footsteps of their parents and their grandparents before them. The capable Michela welcomes guests, while Paolo takes care of the vineyards and Mamete handles the cellar and the wine production, which is of a consistently high standard.

For 30 euros the traditional menu will get you **brisaola** from Chiavenna, lardo and salamini bastardell, **pizzoccheri** from Valtellina, white gnocchi from Valchiavenna, **round of roast suckling pig with polenta** and the cheese board, or a cornmeal cake with pears and chocolate. There is an even heartier **game** menu (available at an additional charge), which is composed of roe deer, wild boar ravioli with butter from Alpine pastures, medallions of venison in white wine, and if you still have room, the cheese board and puddings. Other local dishes on the menu include jugged and braised meats with polenta and **barbecued** lamb or venison in the summer. The cheese board offers local classics: bitto from Val Gerola, casera, scimudin and fresh goats' cheeses.

Dessert offerings include meascia, sorbets and semifreddo.

Mamete will be able to recommend a few good labels from the well constructed wine list.

The old Acquabella osteria, which welcomed diners in this area for over a century, was run for almost thirty years by the Artuso family. It was sold in 2003, and reopened by a family in another area, fully retaining its original spirit, atmosphere and, most importantly, food. Acquabella has an authentic trattoria feel, especially in the inner room, with its dark wooden floors and warm tones on the walls. The wine list boasts over 200 Italian wines, with a few additions from France and Spain, and you can order by the glass and also buy wines to take home. The food is traditionally prepared with a light enough touch to make winter specialties enticing in warmer weather too.

Pasta e fagioli (hot or cold), and **risotto** are always on the menu. The sautéed saffron rice is excellent. House specialties include **casoeula**, with all the ingredients cooked separately then assembled when served. Main courses include a succulent **veal ossobuco with vegetable gremolada** served with saffron rice, **mundeghili** and **breaded veal cutlets** on the bone. Another traditional dish, though not from these parts, is baccalà alla vicentina with polenta. Summer brings meat and fish carpaccios, veal with tuna and roast beef. The cheese board offers local selections, including aged bagòss and asiago, along with mozzarella di bufala, brought in twice a week from the Cilento area. The Campania region offers up its pastiera cake, as well as tiramisù and the excellent **brutta ma buona**.

Evenings are organized to feature particular wine-growing areas with bottlings to accompany suitable dishes.

MILAN
Monforte-Cinque Giornate

MILAN
Buenos Aires-Loreto

ALLA CUCINA ECONOMICA

🍲 Trattoria
Via Guicciardini 8 at the junction with via Melloni
Tel. 02 783256
Closed Wednesday
Open: dinner only
Holidays: in August
Seating: 40
Prices: 30-32 euros, wine excluded
All credit cards except AE, Bancomat

AL LESS

🍲 Recently opened osteria
Via Redi at the junction with via Jan
Tel. 02 36533440
Closed Tuesday
Open: lunch and dinner
Holidays: three weeks in August
Seating: 35
Prices: 35 euros, wine excluded
All major credit cards, Bancomat

The menu proudly declares that "Home-cooked Italian food" is served here, and nothing could be more fitting to describe the trattoria run by Adriano Benedetti, with its two simply appointed dining rooms. White tablecloths cover the tables and antique ornaments add a special touch.

The meal starts with a selection of **cured meats** – coppa piacentina, coppa di testa, finocchiona, pancetta from Val Trebbia and salami from Cremona – or with a generous serving of lardo con la vena, accompanied by **beans and cooked guanciale**. The dishes vary according to the seasonal produce available, and many of them belie the Trentino origins of the owner. The menu always features one kind of soup and a vegetarian dish. Alternative first courses include pappardelle with apple, zucchini or leeks and penne with sun-dried tomatoes, basil and oregano. Then there are four different versions of **parmigiana**, lamb with cardoons or artichokes, **rabbit al Teroldego**, **tonco del pontesel** (a Trentino goulash made with four kinds of meat) served with **polenta**, and carne salada. In the summer a few seafood dishes are on offer, such as baby octopus in sauce and fish soup. Choose from their commendable selection of cheeses, which includes vezzena, pecorino lucano, pecorino di Pienza and mascherpa. For dessert: chocolate mousse, tarte tatin, strudel and a **chocolate cake** made without flour.

The house wine is good and served in carafes, or if you prefer you can choose wines to accompany the dishes of the day from the short wine list.

This osteria is near Corso Buenos Aires, Milan's main shopping street. It was opened in June 2003 by the Scaglioni family. Cozy and well-lit with the kitchens on view, Al Less has an authentic feel, with its big wooden tables and smaller marble-topped sewing machine tables, some pieces of arte povera and modern design. And though the decor is somewhat eclectic, the food most definitely isn't. The set lunch menu for 13 euros includes a buffet of antipasti, a first course and a main course of your choice and coffee.

Starting with the antipasti, there is a wide choice from the buffet with grilled and fried vegetables and platters of cured meats. First courses in winter include spelt or bean **soups**, **braised meat ravioli**, and vegetable tortelli; while in the summer there are testaroli with pesto, pici senesi served with vegetables and mozzarella and chilled soups. The signature dish, as the name of the osteria would suggest, is **lesso**, or boiled cuts of meat, including short ribs, chuck steak, veal shanks, calf's head and guanciale. These are accompanied by a variety of sauces, from piquant green sauce to Piacenza pickled vegetables and given a special twist with three unusual gelatos flavored with horseradish, green sauce and mustard. The summer version of lesso is served cold with a side salad. The summer menu also offers **breaded veal cutlets**, **veal cartilage**, pickled tongue and burrata with cherry tomatoes, while in winter there is **tripe**, coppa and **roast pork shank**. Desserts include apple pie and tarts, panna cotta and gelato – the chocolate, ginger and cinnamon flavors are the best. There is a remarkable wine list with over 500 labels.

AL PONT DE FERR

Traditional osteria
Ripa di Porta Ticinese 55
Tel. 02 89406277
No closing day
Open: lunch and dinner
Holidays: two weeks over Christmas and New Year
Seating: 50 + 80 outdoors
Prices: 35 euros, wine excluded
All major credit cards

BED AND BREAD

Bed and breakfast
Via Vetta d'Italia 14
Tel. 02 468267-333 8396441
E-mail: info@bedandbread.it
Internet: www.bedandbread.it
Closed July and August

With its 120 years of history, the last 18 in the hands of Maida Mercuri – this establishment has remained authentic and kept its simple feel with its brick walls and wooden tables. This osteria boasts a highly respectable **cheese board** – with fresh goats' cheeses, pecorino, taleggio, gorgonzola and castelmagno – and an outstanding wine list, with around 400 labels. Highly regarded bottles sit alongside others of excellent value, and wine can always be ordered by the glass.
The seasonal menu changes every three weeks. At lunch the choice is more limited, with hot and cold antipasti, four first courses, some served with vegetables, and three main courses. For a first course and a main course without wine you can spend under 15 euros, a rarity in Milan. In the evening, alongside a good selection of **cured meats** there are some of the more creative offerings from Uruguayan chef Juan Lema Pena: pumpkin soufflé with cheese fonduta, **bean soup** with pumpkin, fish ravioli, whole wheat ribbon pasta with sun-dried tomatoes and black olives, a salad of Sardinian fregola with bottarga and fresh fava beans and gazpacho. The main courses always include a fish option, sometimes carpaccio, and Piedmontese beef, which might be seared **rump steak** with creamed potatoes, timballe of beef with potatoes, olives and provola, or veal stew with beer, served with polenta. Desserts include fresh ices, **hot chocolate cake** and a pleasingly bitter chocolate praline.

This lovely B&B run by Donata Giovannetti in an early 20th-century detached house is situated in a quiet city center neighborhood not far from the Exhibition Center. The name of the B&B offers a hint of the good night's sleep you'll find here, as well as the morning's generous breakfast of homemade bread, puddings and jams, yogurt, fruit juices, tea, milk and coffee, with cheeses and cured meats on request. Rooms are comfortable, colorful and outfitted with modern furniture. In the communal lounge with its vaulted ceiling, guests can relax, read books from the well-stocked library, watch TV or surf the Internet.

• 3 double rooms, with bathroom •
Prices: double room single occupancy 70 euros, double 110, breakfast included • Credit cards: major ones, Bancomat • Small pets allowed. Owners always present • Breakfast room, lounge with TV, DVD, library and Internet point.

BOTTIGLIERIA DA PINO

Trattoria
Via Cerva 14
Tel. 02 76000532
Closed Sunday
Open: lunch, dinner on reservation
Holidays: August, 10 days around Christmas
Seating: 58
Prices: 20 euros, wine excluded
No credit cards accepted

BUON SOGGIORNO

Bed and breakfast
Via Carlo Forlanini 1
Tel. 02 717951-340 5076109
E-mail: info@buonsoggiorno.it
Internet: www.buonsoggiorno.it
Closed June to August and 20 days in December

If you can't be bothered with a quarter of an hour's wait during rush hour, go elsewhere. You will make another customer very happy, and you won't know what you've missed out on. This is a haven for those who appreciate food and offers a truly convivial atmosphere and great prices. Situated right in the heart of the city, just around the corner from San Babila and the Duomo, the Bottiglieria is a well-known haunt for construction workers and blue-collar workers who head here at midday on the dot, along with professionals, managers and clerical workers. Mauro has followed in his father's footsteps and works in the kitchen, while his brother Marco works the front of the house and deals with the wine, most of which is from northeast Italy, with a few additions from Tuscany.

Beautifully prepared soups, **risottos** and pasta are on offer, along with seasonal vegetables, tomato, ragù or ricotta. The celery and almond pesto is excellent. You definitely can't go wrong with any of the day's specials. Mauro changes the menu daily, depending on what he can find at the market or as the mood strikes him. Much care goes into the main courses, which include liver alla veneziana, **roast pork coppa**, **rump steak stew**, and **boiled beef** and **hen**. There is always **raspatura**, seasonal vegetable pies, a wonderfully fresh burrata from Andria and a good Italian cheese board. Desserts include cakes, tarts and panna cotta, all simple but irresistible.

In the last few years the Ferri brothers have had the right idea when it comes to wine, which is poured into big balloon glasses and offers a good value.

This B&B run by Giulia Garbi is located in an elegant 1930s house that can be easily reached by public transport (bus stops and two taxi ranks are just a few minutes walk away). Rooms are friendly and comfortable. The one called 'The Den' was once the house's air-raid shelter and is very spacious – it can accomodate three guests – and has its own entrance and small kitchen. Breakfast is tailor-made to the needs of guests and tables are set with period linens and china. Those not wishing to have breakfast will receive a discount of 5 euros.

• 1 single and 2 double rooms, with bathroom, TV; 1 with small balcony • Prices: single 70 euros, double 80-100, breakfast included • Credit cards: Visa, Bancomat • Paid parking 100 meters away. No pets allowed. Owners always present • Breakfast room, Lounge with library, TV, Internet point. Garden.

IN THE SOUTHERN SUBURBS AT THE ENTRANCE OF THE MAIN ROAD TO PAVIA

CASCINA GAGGIOLI

Holiday farm
Via Selvanesco 25
Tel. 02 57408479-57408357
Fax 02 5391151
E-mail: cascina.gaggioli@virgilio.it
Internet: www.cascinagaggioli.it
Open all year

DONGIÒ

Trattoria
Via Corio 3
Tel. 02 5511372
Closed Saturday for lunch and Sunday
Open: lunch and dinner
Holidays: three weeks in August
Seating: 50
Prices: 30 euros, wine excluded
All credit cards, Bancomat

The interesting thing about this agriturismo is its location on the outskirts of Milan. Located on the road parallel to the Naviglio di Pavia, the farm offers a peaceful respite from city traffic. The building is a typical Lombard farm estate with 45 hectares of land where Francesco and Paolo Bossi raise cattle and grow grain, all certified organic. On the farm, which dates back to 1640, you can purchase rice, polenta, cheeses, sausages, meat, eggs, honey and jams. Francesco and Paolo's sister Giuditta and their mother look after the accommodation. There aren't many rooms but they are very comfortable. For breakfast, which is served in the room, guests can enjoy delicious homemade cakes, cookies, yogurt and various beverages.

• 2 single and 2 double rooms with shared bathroom, TV; 1 mini-apartment (3 beds) with use of kitchen • Prices: single 35 euros, double 68, mini-apartment 95, breakfast included • Credit cards: all except AE, Bancomat • Facility designed for the mobility challenged and mini-apartment equipped for their use. Off-street parking. Small pets allowed. Owners always present.

Just around the corner from Porta Romana is this lively trattoria where you'll find good food at reasonable prices. The Criscuolo family has been running the place since 1989, and their Calabrian origins come through in the flavorful dishes. Friendly, courteous Antonio and the excellent food he offers more than compensate for the not exactly rapid service and the level of noise in the restaurant.

The menu features a rich selection of specialties from Calabria. Among the antipasti are **cured meats**, including spicy sausage and capocollo, chilli peppers stuffed with tuna or crushed olives preserved in oil and grilled vegetables. First courses, all with fresh pasta made in-house, include the classic **fusilli alla 'nduja**, a very spicy pork sausage flavored with chilli pepper (much loved by chef Pietro), pasta all'etrusca with Tropea onions, pecorino and pancetta, tagliatelle alla re Ferdinando, and **gnocchi with sausage**. For main courses, choose from **grilled Caciocavallo silano**, which can be served with a filling of spicy sausage or grilled meats – especially good are the **fillet steak** flavored **with rosemary** or fennel or garlic, parsley and Pecorino. There are excellent crostatas for dessert; try the apple, chocolate, pear or walnut.

The wine list offers around a hundred bottles with a good range from southern Italy and much attention to value.

Solci's, via Morosini 19: a wine bar belonging to the well known distributors Solci, with 40 wines served by the glass (out of a total of over 800) to accompany hot and cold dishes.

MAGENTA AREA, 3 KM FROM PIAZZA DEL DUOMO

LA DOLCE VITE

🔑 Bed and breakfast
Via Cola di Rienzo 39
Tel. 02 48952808
E-mail: info@ladolcevite.net
Internet: www.ladolcevite.net
Closed in August

LA MADONNINA

🍲 Trattoria
Via Gentilino 6
Tel. 02 89409089
Closed Sunday
Open: lunch Thurs, Fri and Sat, Sat also for dinner
Holidays: August
Seating: 60 + 30 outdoors
Prices: 30 euros, wine excluded
Credit cards: MC, Visa, Bancomat

This friendly B&B, run by the gracious and helpful Enrica, is located in a lovely 1920s house just a minutes away from the Duomo and the Exhibition Center. The three-story building has a beautiful garden where, in the summer, guests can enjoy a continental breakfast of bread, butter and jam, honey, cakes, pastries, coffee, milk, cocoa and fruit juices. The guest rooms, located on the third floor, are comfortable and tastefully furnished. Antique pieces lend a bit of character to an atmosphere already made cheerful by the presence of a dog and two cats. The property does not have parking facilities, though it is easily reached by public transport.

• 3 double rooms with bathroom, air-conditioning, TV; safe and modem connection in the office • Prices: double room single occupancy 75 euros, double 110-120, breakfast included • Credit cards: major ones, Bancomat • No pets allowed. Owners always present • Breakfast room, TV room. Garden, terrace.

This trattoria, located in a traditional Milan courtyard surrounded by craft workshops and little boutiques, offers a little corner of authentic simplicity.
It is not always easy to find a place to park, but once you are here the infectious enthusiasm of Fabio, who has been running the place with a group of friends for the last few years, and the wonderful food on offer will work their magic. The tables, covered with white and red checked tablecloths, are amply spaced apart. In summer you can eat outside under the pergola in the courtyard.
Risotto is always featured on the menu, whether **with ossobuco**, al salto, with mushrooms, alla mantovana, or with seasonal produce, depending on how the chef is feeling, but strictly according to tradition. Or you could indulge in minestra, gnocchi, tagliatelle, **soups** – we recommend the **bean** and onion soups in particular. There is, of course, the classic **cotoletta alla milanese**, served with cherry tomatoes in the summer, **casoeula**, cotechino and lentils, **bollito misto**, and polenta and baccalà on Fridays. There is also a good selection of vegetarian dishes which vary according to what is available at the market. For dessert, the exquisite fruit tarts and crostatas are not to be missed.
The wine on offer is all local, with a few exceptions from outside of Lombardy and Piedmont, and the mark-up is very reasonable.

🍴 L'Osteria, at number 46 on Naviglio Grande, offers over 300 wines from large and small producers, with excellent cured meats and cheeses served by Francesco and Marco.

MILAN
Porta Venezia

MILAN
Brera

LA PIOLA

🍲 Trattoria
Viale Abruzzi 23
Tel. 02 29531271
Closed Sunday and public holidays
Open: lunch and dinner
Holidays: 2 weeks in August
Seating: 40
Prices: 35 euros, wine excluded
All credit cards, Bancomat

LATTERIA SAN MARCO

🍲 Trattoria
Via San Marco 24
Tel. 02 6597653
Closed Saturday and Sunday
Open: lunch and dinner
Holidays: August and Christmas
Seating: 25
Prices: 30-32 euros, wine excluded
No credit cards accepted

La Piola maintains an old-fashioned trattoria ambience and offers solid knowledge of traditions and good food, with an emphasis on excellent ingredients. Alberto and Lucia's menu covers all of Lombardy. Lucia, a native of Cape Verde, will astound you with her knowledge of local culinary traditions and her skill in the kitchen. There is a real family welcome and guests are well cared for and given expert help while choosing their courses.

Start with the **nervetti**, which come with the traditional accompaniment of sweet and sour baby onions, or opt for the Valtellina specialties of bresaola and **sciatt** (little buckwheat fritters filled with Valtellina cheese). You can choose from all the most classic Milanese dishes, everything from risotto to **cotoletta** to **ossobuco and risotto**. In the winter they do a succulent **casoeula with yellow polenta**. If you are looking for something a little less traditional, you will be surprised by the range of first courses on the menu, all freshly made pasta dishes. Main courses include roasts, **pork shank**, and **bollito**, which in summer makes way for tagliata with zesty parsley sauce. The short list of desserts includes chocolate and pear cake, tart and tiramisù.

The modest wine list ranges over an interesting selection of labels and regions. Wines are also served by the glass.

This trattoria, situated in one of Milan's most exclusive districts, recalls the days when, at lunch time, dairies stopped selling milk and cheese and offered the dishes they happened to have in the house at the time. There are not many establishments like this left in Milan now, and they generally don't sell dairy products any more as they have been converted into inviting trattorias.

Arturo and Maria Maggi have been running this place for forty years now with complete dedication and a clear vision. Dishes vary daily depending on what Arturo finds at the market. There is always spaghetti with seasonal sauces, **soups**, good **risottos**, **bollito**, **cotoletta alla milanese** and **bruscitt**. The **meat balls** and Arturo's rice salad, tossed in a blend of ripe fresh tomato and basil, are very popular. One new dish served to help you keep fresh in summer is the crudaiola: lettuce, carrot, fennel, tomatoes and basil blended and served with bulghur wheat. From beyond the confines of Lombardy come testaroli and cod alla livornese with potatoes. For dessert, try the bavarese with bitter orange and apple purée. The wines (Ortrugo, Riesling and Gutturnio) are served by the carafe and come from a producer in the Piacenza area.

They don't take reservations, so get there early (there are not many tables). You may also be sharing your table with other diners.

🍯 At Sugartree (Via Bellotti 11), Venezuelan Jenny Sugar sells some excellent preserves and certified organic savory products.

🍷 At the Ostarie Vecjo Friùl, Via Rosmini 5, there are over 800 wines from all over the world, delicious cheeses, cured meats and a few hot dishes too.

LE VIGNE ▣

🍲 Recently opened osteria
Ripa di Porta Ticinese 61
Tel. 02 8375617
Closed Sundays
Open: lunch and dinner
Holidays: none
Seating: 65
Prices: 35 euros, wine excluded
All credit cards, Bancomat

L'OSTERIA DEL TRENO ▣

🍲 Trattoria-Railway workers' cooperative
Via San Gregorio 46-48
Tel. 02 6700479
No closing days
Open: lunch and dinner
Holidays: over Christmas and New Year, and 10 days in August
Seating: 70 + 40 outdoors
Prices: 31-35 euros, wine excluded
Credit cards: Visa, Bancomat

The Navigli is one of Milan's most popular neighborhoods and has a high turnover of new restaurants often serving up some outlandish offerings. Le Vigne is not one of those.
Start with a selection of **cured meats** and **cheeses**. The cheeses – both Italian and foreign – are served with homemade preserves and mostarda. Other tempting antipasti include bruschetta and the delectable **soups**. Be sure to try the **fava bean and asparagus endive soup**, if it's on the menu. Pastas include ravioli with a potato filling, timballe of spelt and artichokes and spaghetti alla chitarra with Navelli saffron. The main courses vary according to season: try the boned guinea fowl or **roast suckling pig**, or choose more traditional dishes like **braised donkey meat** or **cotoletta alla milanese**. Summer brings a host of interesting fish and vegetable dishes as well as some excellent gelati.
The wine list offers good value bottles from little-known Italian producers.
Remember that the trattoria is open on the last Sunday of every month to coincide with the big antiques market held along the Naviglio Grande.

Angelo Bissolotti's historic osteria is a little oasis for foodies in a city that can often prove disappointing, as far as dining goes anyway. The atmosphere is warm and inviting, with a stunning art nouveau dining room for special occasions. The wait staff are attentive and courteous.
Here, they do their utmost to source unusual products, including several Slow Food Presidia. We were pleased to sample mortandela from the val di Non, tasty lucanica from Trentino and petuccia della Carnia, made from mutton and goat meat. The menu also features **goose** specialties, cured meats from val d'Orcia, anchovies from Amalfi and much more. Try also **tagliatelle with leeks and salami**, wonderful **tortelli with Alpine cheese, pears and cinnamon**, lasagne with goose speck and chives and the unusual chocolate gnocchi with creamy gorgonzola sauce. As for main courses, we enjoyed **goose with juniper and white corn polenta**, duck breast in Moscato and an inviting platter of zucchini flan with ginger, Savoy cabbage rolls and broccoli flan with cheese fonduta. There are som twenty cheeses, including Bitto, Pannerone, Vezzena and Provola dei Nebrodi. You might finish your meal with a Malvasia sorbet and the millefeuille with goat ricotta and orange sauce.
The balanced wine list offers some good drinking with a few wines served by the glass.

MARTIN PESCATORE

🍲 Trattoria
Via Friuli 46
Tel. 02 5462843
Closed Sunday and Saturday for lunch
Open: lunch and dinner
Holidays: three weeks in August
Seating: 25 + 10 outdoors
Prices: 35 euros
All credit cards except DC, Bancomat

OSTERIA GRAND HOTEL

🍲 Recently opened osteria
Via Ascanio Sforza 75
Tel. 02 89511586-89516153
Closed Monday
Open: dinner, Sundays also for lunch
Holidays: August
Seating: 60 + 60 outdoors
Prices: 35 euros, wine excluded
All major credit cards, Bancomat

Small and cozy, but the tables are generously spaced apart. The sea-themed tablecloths and nets hanging on the walls leave no doubt about the focus of this trattoria (whose name means 'kingfisher'). Bruno Corbatto and his wife offer classic seafood preparations that don't indulge in any flights of fantasy and provide especially attentive service. Bruno assembles his menu every morning with the ingredients his wife has procured at the market. Guests are welcomed to the table with hot, freshly-baked bread. The signature antipasto platter features a wide range of hot and cold dishes, including fried whitebait, squash blossoms with anchovies and mozzarella, gratinéed scallops and salmon en croute, as well as a selection of raw scampi, shrimp, canoce and anchovies with lemon that offer up the breezy salt tang of the sea. Try the penne with tuna or swordfish with eggplant, tagliolini with pesto and shrimp and other dishes which vary daily. **Fritto misto** is the yardstick to measure a chef by, and Bruno passes with flying colors. There's also sea bass or gilthead carpaccio and **turbot in a potato crust**. Desserts include zabaglione and wild berries, meringue with strawberries, cherry crostata with gelato, tarte tatin or a chocolate basket with chestnuts. The wine cellar boasts some thirty labels, including half bottles, and offers excellent value.

Fabrizio Paganini, a native of Ostiglia, runs this little gem in a courtyard just around the corner from Naviglio Pavese, which is fortunately well separated from the hectic pace of the chic Milan night life. Walls hung with mirrors and old theater posters, a bar counter, an attractive garden with a pergola and two bocce courts give this place that definitive old-fashioned osteria ambience. At the end of May the scent of jasmine blossom and roses mingles with aromas from the kitchen. The meal starts off with local **cured meats**, a tatin of caramelized shallots and, when in season, an **asparagus sformato** with taleggio fonduta. First courses include the tasty **ziti with duck ragù**, trenette with fresh tuna and wild dill, and some memorable whole wheat **pappardelle with smoked goose breast and herbs**. As for the main courses, you could opt for a simple timballe of artichokes and potatoes, rabbit saddle stuffed with asparagus or **lamb** prepared in various ways. In winter, they do meats in sauce or **braised**. The meal ends with a good **cheese board** – pecorino di fossa, blu del Moncenisio, robiola di Roccaverano – and simple, well-made desserts like zabaglione and coffee-flavored bavarois, almond brittle, nougat semifreddo with chocolate sauce and apple tarte tatin. The wine list is worth a mention as it boasts a few hundred labels, many of which are served by the glass. Keep an eye out for those with the prices marked in red, which denotes a particularly good value.

🍾 Spazio Sicilia, Corso di Porta Vittoria 47 (at the intersection of Via Dandolo), offers a range of Sicilian specialities such as legendary cannoli, wine, jams and honey.

NEAR PIAZZA SICILIA, SOUTH OF THE EXHIBITION CENTER

PIEMONTE

🗝🔑 2-Star Hotel
Via Ruggiero Settimo 1
Tel. 02 463173
Fax 02 48193316
E-mail: info@hotelpiemonte.it
Internet: www.hotelpiemonte.it
Closed August and a few days at Christmas

PONTE ROSSO

🍲 Trattoria
Ripa di Porta Ticinese 23
Tel. 02 8373132
Closed Sunday and Monday lunch
Open: lunch and dinner
Holidays: one week at Christmas and one week in mid-August
Seating: 40 + 25 outdoors
Prices: 32-35 euros, wine excluded
All credit cards except DC, Bancomat

The recently restored Piemonte, easily reached by public transport, is in an ideal central location for both tourists and business people. Rooms are comfortable and quiet. Two of the doubles are large enough to accommodate extra beds. Continental breakfast is served in a beautiful lounge and offers cakes, croissants, bread, butter and jam, fruit, yogurt, milk, tea, coffee and fruit juices. Eggs and cured meats are available on request. The bar also offers 24-hour room service, something that's rarely available these days even in higher category hotels.

• 3 single rooms, 13 double and 1 triple and 1 suite (3 persons), with bathroom, safe, TV, modem connection • Prices: single 70-80 euros, double 90-120, triple 135-160, suite 150-175, breakfast included • Credit cards: all, Bancomat • Off-street parking (costs 13-16 euros per day). Reception open 24 hours a day • Bar. Breakfast room.

This is a rare find in the chaotic Navigli: no happy hours, thumping music or inedible food. A few years ago Stefania Giannotti – architect, well-known feminist, talented chef and cookbook author – decided to turn a long-held dream into reality. She took over an old osteria, spruced up the wonderful bar and updated the place with warm, welcoming colors and a few family heirloom sideboards, creating a wonderful place to spend an evening with friends. Stefania's time in Rome and Carloforte lend the menu Mediterranean flavor and mingle with Claudio Vanin's Lombard and Trieste influences, resulting in a menu with regional focus and innovative highlights. Antipasti include **creamed baccalà,** Carloforte bottarga, cured tuna with grapes or figs, eggplant and scamorza quiche and **liver paté**. Particularly notable are the **soups**, like the one of favas, peas, artichokes and asparagus offered in the summer, and pasta dishes, **risotto** and gnocchi. The Neapolitan rice timballes are superb; choose from sartù, cerino, or gattò, made according to an ancient Cavalcanti recipe. Main courses range from Lombardy specialties – meatballs with savoy cabbage, **cotoletta** or **ossobuco** – to Roman lamb chops scottadito or braised oxtail to dishes from the south – baccalà and escarole, tuna alla ghiotta, baby anchovies and onions, stuffed lettuce leaves, arancini and onion calzone. Leave some room for the tarte tatin, rum babà, hot chocolate soufflé and strawberry or orange gelati.
The respectable wine list offers pretty good values. The trattoria is open for lunch too on the last Sunday of the month to coincide with the antiques market.

TAGIURA ⊘

☺ Trattoria
Via Tagiura 5
Tel. 02 48950613
Closed Sunday
Open: lunch, Thursday and Friday dinner bookings only
Holidays: August, Christmas and Easter
Seating: 150
Prices: 18-30 euros, wine excluded
All major credit cards, Bancomat

When you find a charming eatery like this out in the charmless periphery of Milan, you absolutely have to tell everyone about it. Here, you can get a really solid lunch without spending a fortune. Consider yourself doubly lucky if you manage to get a table for dinner (reservations only). The restaurant, located between Baggio and Piazza Napoli, offers a number of dining rooms with frescoes on the walls, wood paneling, beautifully laid tables and a pleasant atmosphere. Signora Tullia is the heart and soul of the place – and not only in terms of food.

Begin with **cured meats** like strolghino, coppa di Pianello and the exquisite culatello di Zibello, a Slow Food Presidium. There is also a wide range of vegetable dishes. Among the fresh pastas, try ricotta ravioli with leeks or asparagus and the wonderful **marubini**, or choose one of the seasonal soups or minestrone instead. For main courses, there are braised and roasted **rabbit**, **donkey** and **goat meat**. End your meal with **sbrisolona** or slice of one of the tarts, or sample some of the extensive cheese selection, which are served with jams and honey.

As for wines, there is an adequate range on offer, but the list requires a little attention.

TRATTORIA DEGLI ORTI

☺ Trattoria
Via Monviso 13
Tel. 02 33101800
Closed Sunday
Open: lunch and dinner
Holidays: three weeks in August, one at Christmas
Seating: 50
Prices: 25-30 euros, wine excluded
No credit cards accepted

This quiet street is lined with old houses and offers a snapshot of a Milan from years past. The historic trattoria was taken over by the Bedeschi family in 1999. Rosi helms the kitchen, while her husband Giorgio and son Camillo take care of the guests. The tables are so close together that even the owner can hardly get around them, but you could say it helps to make dining here a friendlier affair. Rosi's cooking is simple but full of flavor, changing with the seasons and making the most of what the market has to offer. In addition to traditional Lombardy specialties there are dishes from Emilia, from Giorgio's home town, and Veneto recipes from Rosi's.

While you peruse the menu you will be given a taste of **mondeghili**. Antipasti worth sampling: **fried gnocchi** with cured meats, onion frittata and cold sliced **nervetti**. The ravioli alla mantovana is wonderful, but there are also tagliatelle with ragù, gnocchi, and **pumpkin ravioli** to be had as well as **risotto alla milanese** or with sausage, soup with leeks or spelt or simple minestrone. Main courses include **cotoletta alla milanese** and depending on the day, **bollito misto**, game with polenta, **tripe**, **ossobuco**, creamed baccalà, **casoeula**, stuffed squash blossoms and **snails in sauce**. For dessert, there are pear cake, tiramisù and panna cotta, all made in-house,
There are a hundred reputable labels on the wine list, all of which pair well with the food here.

TRATTORIA DEL PESCATORE

☜Trattoria
Via Vannucci 3
Tel. 02 58320452
Closed Sunday
Open: lunch and dinner
Holidays: August, 10 days around both Christmas and Easter
Seating: 90
Prices: 30-35 euros, wine excluded
All credit cards except AE, Bancomat

TRATTORIA MILANESE

☜Trattoria
Via Santa Marta 11
Tel. 02 86451991
Closed Tuesday
Open: lunch and dinner
Holidays: August and from Christmas to Epiphany
Seating: 100
Prices: 31-35 euros, wine excluded
All credit cards, Bancomat

If you want to a taste of Sardinia in Milan, this is the place to go. Giuliano Ardu and Franco Marceddu offer charming service, while tireless chefs Agnese and Renzo turn out excellent fish dishes. Tables are placed quite close together and fill up quickly every meal: reservations are a must here, especially for dinner.

The antipasti we were served featured sautéed clams, mussels alla marinara, whelks in sauce and sea food gratin. The first courses included **spaghetti with clams, baby squid and bottarga**, tagliolini with a crab sauce or scampi, **fish soup** and **seafood risotto**. The fish on display on the counter are a testament to the freshness of the day's catch, selected every day by Giuliano. Customers can choose between **gilthead**, sea bass, crab and lobster, which are then cooked in a variety of simple, traditional ways – **roasted in a salt crust**, grilled or baked in foil. The most expensive dish is, without a doubt, lobster alla catalana, with tomato and onion. To finish off the meal, a tasty young Sardinian Pecorino and some fresh sorbets.

The wines come from Sardinia, as well as other parts of Italy and beyond, and, in keeping with Sardinian tradition, you will also be offered the typical myrtle liqueur, mirto.

Located in the heart of the historic city center right behind piazza Affari, Trattoria Milanese has offered quintessential Milanese food to locals and tourists since 1933. The atmosphere is a throwback, with spacious areas furnished with antique furniture and white tablecloths that can only be found in historic buildings of this kind. When the restaurant is full you have to take a seat wherever you can get one, so you share your meal with an English tourist, a couple of Germans or a group of locals with a passion for Milanese specialties. The menu is the same all year round and features the cornerstones of traditional Milanese food, along with a few other northern Italian dishes.

For antipasti, choose from **cured meats**, **nervetti** or tuna paté. Then some excellent **tagliolini** (called tagliatelle) with **roast beef sauce**, meat ravioli, **risotto alla milanese** with ossobuco or without and riso al salto. Main courses include roast breast of veal, **ossobuco in sauce**, **mondeghili**, **foiolo** (tripe) **alla milanese** and the peerless **cotoletta alla milanese**. Choose between crème caramel, a bowl of hot zabaglione and superb **panettone** to finish off your meal.

The wine list is limited but carefully edited, and the selection of half bottles is worth a mention. The prices, plus cover charge, are in line with the rest of Milan.

Ⓦ There are two excellent confectioners near Porta Romana: Paradiso, in corso di Porta Vigentina, offers chocolate and pear cake, Sachertorte and artisanal ice-creams; Panarello, at Piazza San Nazario in Brolo 15, features Genoa specialties, cannoncini with custard cream, jam tarts and much more.

Ⓦ At Viale Brianza 11, the butcher shop run by Ercole Villa offers the finest Piedmontese meat, cheese and other high quality products, such as rice, pasta and cured meats.

MONTECALVO VERSIGGIA
Versa

34 KM SOUTHEAST OF PAVIA, 35 KM FROM VOGHERA

PRATO GAIO

⌂ Hotel restaurant
Località Versa 16 - at the junction for Volpara
Tel. 0385 99726
Closed Monday and Tuesday
Open: lunch and dinner
Holidays: 7 January-6 February
Seating: 60
Prices: 30-35 euros, wine excluded
No credit cards accepted

With the painstaking attention it pays to rediscovering local traditions and sourcing ingredients, Prato Gaio is probably the establishment which best corresponds to our idea of an authentic osteria in the Pavia area. It lies among the vineyards of the Oltrepò Pavese in the Versa valley, and though not that easy to get to, it is definitely worth the trip. It has been run by the Liberti family for four generations, going back to 1890. Current owner Giorgio presides over the front of the house, while Daniela Calvi runs the kitchen. The original menu gives a description of each dish, its origins and the source of the produce, all seasonal.

Antipasti include **cured meats** from the upper Versa valley, **dus in brüsc** (chicken in a sweet and sour sauce, an old country recipe), **cotechino** and cupa (salami made from the head) with salad, grana, pear and balsamic vinegar. Daniela makes the pasta for **braised meat ravioli** and **tagliolini in gravy**. There are also **risotto with wild herbs**, onion and baccalà soup and potato gnocchi with cherry tomatoes and leeks. Of the many main courses we recommend **goose neck** stuffed with Mortara foie gras, veal guanciale in white wine, stuffed **duck** and, in summer, **tempura**, carpaccio of baccalà and herring rolls with freshly picked tomatoes. Desserts include pear cake served with chocolate sauce or vanilla gelato, baked reinette apples with raisins in Moscato grappa or lemon sorbet.

The best of the Oltrepò area is represented on the wine list. Caveat emptor: the establishment's sole downside is its exorbitant cover charge.

MONTE ISOLA
Peschiera Maraglio

23 KM NORTHWEST OF BRESCIA

LA FORESTA

⚷ 1-star hotel
Via Peschiera Maraglio 174
Tel. 030 9886210
Fax 030 9886455
E-mail: laforesta@monteisola.com
Open from beginning of March to 20 December

After years working on cruise ships, Silvano Novali moved to the island in Lake Iseo in 1974 and started a new life as a hotelier. Silvano offers his guests delicious dishes made from freshwater fish – provided by his fisherman brother – and excellent wines which he selects himself from the best labels (average cost of a meal is 40-50 euros, excluding wine). You can catch a boat to Peschiera Maraglio from Sultano or any of the other ports on the mainland. There are no cars on this little gem of an island and fishermen still employ traditional techniques to make their nets and to dry freshwater sardines and shad. Tourists can spend their holiday sunbathing on the dock or beaches, visiting the castles and the sanctuary of the Madonna della Ceriola or using the Sassabanek sports center. Guests here can also taste traditional products like the Monte Isola salami, which is sliced by hand.

• 10 double rooms with bathroom, terrace • Prices: double room single occupancy 70 euros, double 80, breakfast included • Credit cards: all, Bancomat • Discount available for paid parking. No pets allowed. Owners always reachable • Bar, restaurant. TV room. Veranda.

MONTODINE

IL POSTIGLIONE

🍲 Trattoria
Via Roma 10
Tel. 0373 66114
Closed Monday
Open: lunch and dinner
Holidays: August 20 – September 15, January 7-14
Seating: 45 + 35 outdoors
Prices: 28-33 euros
All credit cards except AE, Bancomat

We have been faithfully following Jury and Nadir for many years. Here, they continue to offer their own simple, special cuisine, alternating between the kitchen and front of house with the same level of care and attention. The big country house by the Serio was undoubtedly once a mail depot, hence the restaurant's name, in view of its position at the crossroads leading to the fortified town of Castelleone. The dining room has a big fireplace, a lounge at the back and a roomy veranda which is particularly welcome in the summer months.
The menu begins with good **cured meats** from Crema and Cremona, **Salva** cheese at varying degrees of maturity or in **a potato crust**, country frittatas – the onion one is delicious – creamed cod fritters, focaccine filled with cooked shoulder and finferli mushrooms and potato. In summer you can choose between a warm bean soup with raw scallions, eggplant ravioli, **risotto** with squash blossoms or mushrooms and boned quail. In winter they do a superlative **Savoy cabbage and sausage soup** and tagliatelle with a **ragù of veal kidney and sweetbreads** or the potato raviolo with beans, a tribute to the hearty appetites of local farmers. Main courses include cockerel stuffed with potatoes and lardo and **roast suckling pig** with caramelized onions. For dessert, try the semifreddo with meringue served with a strawberry sauce or the classic torta margherita with custard cream and fresh fruit in liqueur.
Jury and Nadir's passion for fine wines can be seen in the remarkable cellar – ask for a tour – with its numerous vintages of Bartolo Mascarello's Barolo, as well as hundreds of other labels.

MONZAMBANO
Castellaro Laguselle

ANTICO BORGO

🔑 2-star hotel
Via Castello 1
Tel. and fax 0376 88978
E-mail: info@anticoborgosas.it
Internet: www.anticoborgosas.it
Closed 15 days in January

The building housing the Antico Borgo dates back to the 15th century and is located in the historic center of Castellano Laguselle, close to Mantua and Verona. The hotel has a pleasant, relaxing atmosphere, while the rooms are furnished in keeping with the style of the building and evoke times gone by. The buffet breakfast is traditional, and savory items are available on request. The restaurant offers classic Mantuan cuisine and the wine list boasts 250 types of Italian wines (an average meal costs 29 euros, excluding wines). If you're a nature lover, you can't miss Parco Natura Viva, a nature reserve that protects endangered animals. The amusement parks of Gardaland and Caneva World are also nearby.

• 7 double rooms with bathroom, air-conditioning, satellite TV • Prices: double room single occupancy 55 euros, double 65, breakfast included • Credit cards: all except DC, Bancomat • External parking in blue zone reserved for guests. No pets allowed. Owners always reachable • Bar, restaurant. Breakfast room. Garden.

MONZAMBANO
Castellaro Lagusello

IL FILOS

🔑 Agriturismo
Località Perini-Strada Nuvolino 19
Tel. e fax 0376 800197
E-mail: info@ilfilos.it
Internet: www.ilfilos.it
Closed from Epiphany until the end of February

Located in the center of the Mantuan countryside, Il Filos (filos means 'friend' in Greek) has welcomed guests since 1996. The former stables now house two dining rooms and the old barn has been converted into three bedrooms. This family-run agriturismo is peaceful and friendly. Many animals (turkeys, peacocks, lambs, donkeys, chickens and geese) can be found on the grounds, which are also scattered with fruit trees. Guests can purchase the peaches, prunes, kiwi, apples and pears that are grown here. Rooms are spacious and comfortable and breakfast here is varied and generous. The restaurant offers typical Mantuan cuisine prepared with the farm's own produce (average price 18 euros, excluding wine). Guests can enjoy a pleasant bicycle or horse ride in the countryside or visit the beautiful cities of Desenzano, Peschiera and Sirmione.

• 3 double rooms with bathroom, air conditioning, TV; 2 mini-apartments (2-3 persons) with kitchenette • Prices: double room single occupancy 45 euros, double 52-62, mini-apartment 31 euros per person, breakfast included • No credit cards • 1 apartment accessible for the mobility challenged. Off-street parking. Small pets allowed (not in rooms or the restaurant). Owners always reachable • Restaurant. Garden, children's playground, portico.

MONZAMBANO
Olfino

LUPO BIANCO

🔑 Agriturismo
Strada dei Colli 94
Tel. e fax 0376 800128
E-mail: agritur.lupobianco@libero.it
Open from March to October

This farm, managed by Daniele Ramponi, is nestled in the hills overlooking Lake Garda. Grapes are grown here for wine production and for eating. A lovely courtyard leads into the recently refurbished building where rooms are elegantly appointed with wooden furniture. Some of the farm's own produce is used for breakfast and in the restaurant (open Thursday to Sunday) where the host offers his guests local specialities (average cost of a meal is 25 euros, excluding wine). The Romponi family is very hospitable, ensuring that guests will have a pleasant stay. The farm is a good base for those wanting to enjoy Lake Garda or explore cities in Lombardy and the Veneto.

• 3 double and 1 triple rooms with bathroom, 2 apartments with bathroom and small kitchen • Double room single occupancy 32 euros, double 56, triple 66, breakfast included, apartment 70-85 euros • No credit cards, Bancomat accepted • 1 room designed for use by the mobility challenged. External parking in private area. No pets allowed • Restaurant (open from Thursday to Sunday, subject to reservation). Breakfast. Garden.

MORBEGNO

25 KM WEST OF SONDRIO SS 36

OSTERIA DEL CROTTO

☞Restaurant
Via Pedemontana 22
Tel. 0342 614800
Closed Sunday
Open: lunch and dinner
Holidays: 3 weeks in August and September
Seating: 80 + 50 outdoors
Prices: 28-32 euros, wine excluded
All credit cards

L'Osteria del Crotto takes its name from the old, naturally cooled larder that the osteria has developed over the years. This restaurant boasts traditions that owner Maurizio Vaninetti continues to maintain and offers a selection of well-made local specialties.
Maurizio, together with a number of local restaurant owners, recently set up the Slow cooking association to promote local crops and encourage sales to support the producers. It seems to be going well, as you will see when you sample the set menus featuring **lake fish** from Como (caught by Marco Vanoli from Gera Lario), locally sourced goat meat and delicious **tortelli with goat ricotta and nettles** tossed in butter and wild thyme. You must try the **Bitto** cheese and the delicate fior di latte gelato, made from the milk of cows reared by Mosé Manni from Cosio Valtellino. Restaurant classics include **violino di capra**, local salami, lardo and pancetta, made by a butcher friend. In summer they offer **ravioli** filled with braised meat and **bigoli** al torchio served with a superb **missoltini sauce**. When it gets cold, there are **crêpes made with Teglio buckwheat** (a Presidium) with Savoy cabbage and Bitto fondue. In spring, order the garganelli in Taleggio and asparagus sauce. Meat dishes include breaded lamb cutlets flavored with aromatic herbs and sirloin steak cooked in red wine. Top it all off with some of the excellent cheeses on offer and one of Maurizio's desserts: parfait with grappa, white chocolate mousse or hazelnut semifreddo with honey zabaglione and chocolate sauce.
The extensive wine list has over three hundred labels, with bottlings primarily from local producers.

MORTARA
Guallina

37 KM NORTHWEST OF PAVIA SS 35 AND 596

GUALLINA

☞Restaurant
Via Molino Faenza 19
Tel. 0384 91962
Closed Tuesdays
Open: lunch and dinner
Holidays: 3 weeks in June and July
Seating: 40
Prices: 30-35 euros
All credit cards, Bancomat

In the heart of the Po valley, where the province of Milan meets that of Pavia, a few kilometers out of Mortara lies the village of Guallina and the restaurant of the same name. The sign here depicts a goose, one of the gastronomic specialties of the area. Rita Resente will welcome you into this traditional country house, where the atmosphere is inviting, the tables well-appointed with high quality linen and tableware. Talented chef Edoardo Fantasma offers seasonal local food.
From October to April you can sample a menu based entirely on goose, beginning with goose livers or a sumptuous **foie gras terrine** then continuing with **ravioli with goose meat filling** tossed in melted butter and **roast goose**, which should be reserved in advance. Of course, there are many other equally tempting local specialties, from the **risottos**, with classics such as risotto with goose salami and black eyed peas or with **frogs' legs**, now somewhat of a rare find. The onion soup and classic **pasta e fagioli** are also good. Excellent main courses include roast pigeon with pancetta, sautéed kidneys, **snails alla borgognona**, duck breast in orange sauce or lamb cutlets. For cheese, you can try Seirass, Castelmagno and many others. The homemade desserts always include apple strudel and classic chocolate mousse.
The wine list reads like an encyclopedia, with labels from all over Italy and some international names too. Mark-ups are fair.

NESSO

ORSENIGO

16 KM NORTHEAST OF COMO ON SS 583

10 KM SOUTHEAST OF COMO ON SS 342

TRE ROSE

LA CASSINAZZA

3-Star hotel
Via Borgonuovo 4
Tel. 031 910137
Fax 031 910678
E-mail: info@trerosehotel.com
Internet: www.trerosehotel.com
Closed in December

Agriturismo
Cascina Cassinazza 2
Tel. 031 631468
Internet: www.cassinazza.it
Closed from Epiphany until mid-February

Nesso is an old village located on the banks of Lake Como, halfway between Como and Bellagio. The Tre Rose Hotel, restored twelve years ago, was traditionally a trattoria where travelers would stop over, and it now offers eight rooms, four of which have balconies overlooking the lake. Lying beyond the village, just a few kilometers away, are the plains of Nesso and Tivano. From here you can take trips to the area's most attractive mountain locations and enjoy an unusual and enchanting view of Lake Como. In winter there are some good ski slopes nearby – some of which are specially designed for children – or the long cross-country ski runs. The restaurant offers both local and international cuisine (a meal averages 30-35 euros) while breakfast varies according to the needs of guests.

• 8 double rooms with bathroom, TV • Prices: double room single occupancy 40 euros, double 55; breakfast 8 euros per person • Credit cards: all except DC, Bancomat • Free external public parking. Small pets allowed. Reception open 24 hours a day • Bar, restaurant. Reading room, TV room. Garden.

The farmhouse was completely restored seven years ago and is located in the heart of Brianza, in the green countryside surrounding Orsenigo, about ten kilometers from Lake Como. Rooms are simply but comfortably furnished and the restaurant offers local specialties, including cured meats, cheeses and vegetables grown organically on the farm (average cost per meal is 20-25 euros). The traditional breakfast also offers delicious tarts made with fruit grown here and cheeses made with milk from the farm's own cows.

• 2 single and 9 double rooms and 3 suites with bathroom, fridge, satellite TV • Prices: single 42 euros, double 70, suite 80, breakfast included • Credit cards: all, Bancomat • Some rooms designed for use by the mobility challenged. Off-street parking. Small pets allowed (10 euros per day) • Bar, restaurant. Breakfast room. Conference room.

ORZINUOVI
Barco

30 KM SOUTH OF BRESCIA SS 235

EL PURTÙ

🍲 Trattoria
Via Filippo Turati 8
Tel. 030 9940513
Closed Monday and Tuesday
Open: dinner, weekends and
holidays also for lunch
Holidays: one week in January, one in August
Seating: 130 + 30 outdoors
Prices: 20-30 euros, wine excluded
All credit cards, Bancomat

El Purtù is just outside Orzinuovi in an ancient village which once belonged to the counts Martinengo da Barco. It is a stone's throw from the Oglio river and the menu often features the now under-appreciated fish that were once staples in the Bassa area of Brescia and Cremona, including frogs, bose (gobies) and eels. Along with frittatas and meatballs, these were often the only things on offer in osterias.

This is an attractive trattoria, featuring two air-conditioned dining rooms with vaulted brick ceilings. On the upper floor there is a big room with an open fireplace for large groups and a veranda. Manuela and Mauro, gracious and professional hosts, recommend traditional local dishes and wines, while talented young chef Michela helms the kitchen. The dishes on offer are all local specialties, from the **casoncelli** of the Bassa area, taken from an ancient local recipe, or those of Longhena, with a meat filling. The cured meats are all made here and served with homemade pickles and vegetables. There are also some tempting vegetarian dishes. When in season, there is **spiedo bresciano** or spit-roasted suckling pig, **manzo all'olio** and braised donkey meat with **polenta** made from Castegnato cornmeal. They regularly offer an excellent **bollito misto** served with sauces. You should also try the travagliatina, a **horse meat steak** and so-called in honor of the village of Travagliato, which hosts a horse fair. Then you can finish off with a good gelato alla crema, citrus sorbet, nougat semifreddo, **sbrisolona** or a tart with custard cream and peaches.
There is a good variety of Italian wines from key production regions.

PALAZZAGO
Burligo

18 KM NORTHWEST OF BERGAMO

OSTERIA BURLIGO

🍲 Trattoria
Via Burligo, 12
Tel. 035 550456
Closed Monday and Tuesday
Open: dinner, holidays lunch also
Holidays: vary
Seating: 35 + 20 outdoors
Prices: 30 euros, wine excluded
All major credit cards, Bancomat

It is a great pleasure to visit Norma and Felice Sozzi in Burligo, safe in the knowledge that you will find simple, well-prepared food, variety (though with a few time-honored classics) and attention to the quality of ingredients, the seasonal availability of produce and authentic local specialties. The trattoria has a simple feel, with plain decor that reflects the surrounding countryside – a hilly landscape which may appear rather forbidding at first. But on the terrace in front of the entrance you will feel that welcome evening breeze that makes it worth the trip out here on a summer evening. There is a homey atmosphere of disarming simplicity, and the service is most attentive. Felice will help you choose your wine from an ever-increasing wine list, which offers both local labels and wines from the rest of Italy.

You can sample antipasti like **polenta and salami**, roasted peppers with tuna sauce, a salad of fresh goats' cheese with herbs in a raspberry vinegar dressing, some wonderful fava bean croquettes with sesame sauce and spinach frittata. Then it's on to basil gnocchetti with tomato, **barley risotto**, **nettle soup**, roasted black rice with vegetables, **casoncelli**, or tagliatelle with zucchini and sun-dried tomatoes. As for the main courses, you can choose between baccalà with monk's beard, goat goulash, chicken served with fresh peas or in carpione, a good **rabbit roulade** or the traditional **wild asparagus with egg**. You can finish off with a cheeses from small local dairies or try a slice of the delicious hazelnut or chocolate cake, crema al caramello, gelato with strawberry sauce, pineapple semifreddo or crême catalane.

PALAZZOLO SULL'OGLIO
Calci

28 KM NORTHWEST OF BRESCIA, EXIT AT 4

PEGOGNAGA

28 KM SOUTH OF MANTUA

OSTERIA DELLA VILLETTA

Osteria – Rooms for rent
Via Marconi 104 and 116
Tel. 030 732316-7401899-348 0407816
Fax 030 7401899
Closed Sunday and Monday
Open: lunch and dinner
Holidays: 1 week in January, the first of July, 3rd August
Seating: 60 + 40 outdoors
Prices: 27-35 euros, wine excluded
All major credit cards, Bancomat

To the right of the station you will find a cozy osteria managed by the Rossi family, who have been in the restaurant business since 1870. The accomodations offered here are furnished in a rustic style and savory foods are available for breakfast on request.
They've got a small menu, but dishes are particularly well prepared. The meal starts with local **cured meats** – pancetta and coppa di Val Nure, ham aged for over thirty months – **large freshwater carp** and golden perch. Among the first courses, we recommend the vialone rice sautéed with vegetables and sausage, **orzotto** with vegetables**, bread and onion soup** and **tripe**. Main courses include a few great classics: **beef guanciale in green sauce** with homemade **pickled vegetables** and fried veal brains. On Fridays, **baccalà**, **frittelle di bertagnino** and freshwater fish. Cheeses include mature grana padano and Vigolo taleggio. For dessert, try one of the fruit crostatas and, in season, peaches filled with amaretto.
Great selection of wines, including the most celebrated Franciacorta labels.

• 1 single room and 4 doubles, ensuite, TV • Prices: single 45 euro, double 65 euro (10 euro supplement for extra bed), breakfast included • Accessible in part to the mobility challenged with 1 bedroom specifically designed for their use. Internal open parking area. Pets welcome (check first) • Owners always available • Restaurant. Breakfast and reading room. Garden

CA' ROSSA

Agritourism farm
Strada Provinciale Est 6
Tel. 0376 559072-348 6929358
E-mail: agriturcarossa@libero.it
Internet: www.agriturcarossa.it
Open all year

This professionally run agritourism farm in the Mantuan countryside is easily accessible from the motorway and is organized in an old farmhouse renovated with great attention to detail. Rooms are basic but tastefully furnished. Traditional breakfast offers coffee, milk, tea, yoghurt, homemade cakes and seasonal fresh fruit. A short walk or bicycle ride away from the farm is Parco San Lorenzo with its three lakes and the Falconiera Oasis, with a wealth of vegetation and bird species. About twenty kilometers away is San Benedetto Po and the famous Polirone Abbey founded by Tebaldo di Canossa.

• 4 double rooms, with bathroom, air conditioning, TV; 1 apartment with 2 bedrooms and kitchenette • Prices: double room single occupancy 39 euros, double 60 (20 euro supplement for extra bed), breakfast included; apartment 61 euros, breakfast 3 euros per person • Credit cards: none • 1 room designed for use by the mobility challenged. Off-street parking. No pets allowed. Reception open from 8 am to 9.30 pm. • Breakfast room.

PEREGO

17 KM SOUTH OF LECCO, 27 KM FROM COMO ON SS 342

LA COSTA

🚜 Holiday farm
Via Curone 15
Tel. 039 5312218
Fax 039 5312251
E-mail: info@la-costa.it
Internet: www.la-costa.it
Open all year

The La Costa farm, nestling between Parco Montevecchia and the Curone Valley, is managed by the Crippa sisters. It comprises vineyards, pastureland, woods and the old Costa, Scarpata and Galbusera Nera farmhouses, restored with due respect for the original architecture. Rooms in the Costa farmhouse are spacious and cozy and guests can enjoy breakfast in the comfort of their own rooms. The restaurant in the Scarpata farmhouse is only open on Sundays and the average cost of a meal is 35 euros, excluding wine. The Galbusera Nera farmhouse boasts all the necessary equipment for winemaking (this year its wines are featured in the Slow Food/Gambero Rosso Italian Wines guide) and it also houses a small agricultural museum. Not to be missed, inside Parco Montevecchia, are noble mansions and archeological finds dating back to Celtic and Roman times.

• 8 mini-apartments, with double bedroom, small lounge, kitchenette, fridge, TV, modem connection • Prices: double room single occupancy 40-50 euros, double 90, breakfast included • All major credit cards, Bancomat • 1 mini-apartment designed for use by the mobility challenged. Off-street parking. Small pets allowed (if very small in the rooms, otherwise in a special outdoor area). Owners always available • Restaurant (only open for Sunday lunch) in an adjacent farmhouse. Reading room, TV room.

PIADENA
Vho

31 KM EAST OF CREMONA, 35 KM WEST OF MANTUA SS 10

TRATTORIA DELL'ALBA

🍲 Trattoria
Via del Popolo 31
Tel. 0375 98539
Closed Sunday dinner and Monday
Open: lunch and dinner
Holidays: August and Christmas vacation
Seating: 40
Prices: 28-32 euros, wine excluded
All major credit cards, Bancomat

If you get the chance to stay on after dinner to chat with the owner you'll find that little here has changed since the war. The trattoria has been carefully remodeled, with the addition of air-conditioning and better bathrooms, but Angela still uses her mother's saucepans, the same methods in the kitchen and the same recipes for her wonderful mostarda, made with apples, pears, white watermelon and mandarin oranges.
The food of the Casalasco area is simple country fare, but on feast days special meat dishes are prepared: roast stuffed breast of veal, **stuffed guinea fowl** with potatoes, and boiled tongue. Then come **pumpkin tortelli,** here served in a tomato sauce and, from the River Oglio, **minnows in vinegar**, or **carp in sauce**. Taken from the famous recipe book by Platina (Bartolomeo Sacchi, a librarian in the Vatican in the 15th century) the **pollo in agresto'** is a delight of a summer's evening. Chef Ubaldo cooks up some wonderful **soups** with vegetables, spelt, tuna belly and tomato, beans and mixed legumes, and others still according to season. Omar, on the other hand, is an expert with **mostarda** and cures a fantastic **shoulder of pork**, served raw after hanging for 28 months. Omar also manages the extensive wine list, which is constantly being enhanced. Be sure not to miss the desserts, the raw milk goats' cheeses from a small nearby dairy, and the Brozzi culatello, which D'Annunzio used to be wild about.

POMPONESCO

PONTE DI LEGNO
Pezzo

SALTINI

DA GIUSY

🍲 Trattoria
Piazza XXIII Aprile 10
Tel. 0375 86017-86710
Closed Monday
Open: lunch and dinner
Holidays: 15 July-14 August
Seating: 100
Prices: 28-30 euros, wine excluded
All major credit cards, Bancomat

🍲 Restaurant
Via Ercavallo 39
Tel. 0364 92153
Closed Tuesday, no closing day in summer,
closed in winter Monday to Thursday
Open: lunch and dinner
Holidays: none
Seating: 70
Prices: 24-27 euros, wine excluded
No credit cards, Bancomat

After a visit to the Gonzaga town of Sabbioneta, it's worth heading on to Viadana, then following the signs for this village on the border with Emilia. Under the arcades of the lovely main square, this trattoria was opened in 1970 and is now run by the children of the founder, Cavalier Saltini: Maria Stella in the kitchen and her two brothers front of house. It is a spacious establishment (seating up to 120 people) with an informal, country feel, and serves local food prepared with excellent quality ingredients.

The antipasti feature a rich assortment of **cured meats** (culatello, pancetta, salami, spalla cotta and prosciutto crudo), served with luadel, farmhouse bread, brought to the table still warm and deliciously fragrant. The first courses are traditionally Mantuan: **pumpkin tortelli**, **tagliatelle with duck sauce**, **bigoli al torchio** and **agnoli in brodo**. Then come the house specials: **braised donkey meat with polenta** and, when in season, **game**; excellent roe deer venison with mushrooms and roast wild boar. The menu also offers roast duck and shin of pork accompanied by quince mostarda, a Viadana specialty, and **snails in sauce**. Finish off a great meal with simple but delicious puddings: ice-cream, tiramisù, **chocolate salami**, meringata and **sbrisolona**.

The wine list is well thought out, comprising Lambruscos, rustico or amabile, around 80 Italian labels and a few good Champagnes.

Da Giusy is located in Pezzo, the highest village in the Valcamonica. With the exception of a few minor improvements to the houses, time seems to have stood still here. It's wonderful to explore the narrow lanes on foot, taking in lungfuls of its fresh mountain air. You'll be welcomed into this plain but comfortable restaurant by the children of signora Giusy, who runs the place.

Start off with a mixed antipasto of **cured meats** from the valley, then try the excellent local **gnocc de la cùa**, made with wheat flour, local potatoes and herbs and tossed in a mixture of Alpine cheese, butter and more potatoes. Other first courses include **orzotto** – barley risotto with cep mushrooms – and **scandela**, a soup made with barley and vegetables. The main courses reveal the influence of the nearby Trentino region, with **boiled speck** served with **braised red sauerkraut** and braised venison with **polenta**, which also served with a range of sauces or butter and grated Parmigiano-Reggiano, **cotechino** with spinach, horse meat or beef grilled or cooked in a variety of ways and melted or grilled mountain cheese. To finish off, seasonal fruit or housedesserts: from **pumpkin pie** and chestnut pudding to woodland fruit tart and a variety of cream puddings.

The wine list offers bottles from Franciacorta, Valtellina and Trentino, and, as a digestif, classic genepy and other herb-based liqueurs.

PONTE IN VALTELLINA

PONTI SUL MINCIO

OSTERIA DEL SOLE

CORTE SALANDINI

Trattoria
Via Sant'Ignazio 31
Tel. 0342 565298
Closed Monday evenings and Tuesday
Open: lunch and dinner
Holidays: one week in March, one in July
Seating: 70
Prices: 15-20 euros, wine excluded
All credit cards, Bancomat

Holiday farm
Strada della Colombara 7
Tel. 0376 88184
Fax 0376 813147
E-mail: info@agriturismosalandini.com
Internet: www.agriturismosalandini.com
Closed in February and November

Signora Olimpia is still in charge of the kitchen at the Osteria del Sole, but her daughter Monica has now taken over the running of the restaurant. This trattoria, which dates back to before the Second World War, when it was run by Olimpia's grandparents, has remained true to its original style: one of simplicity, authenticity and quality, especially when it comes to the food itself.

The meal starts with local **cured meats** from tried-and-tested suppliers, after which the abundant first courses range from the definitive classic handmade **pizzoccheri**, made using only local produce, to **sciàtt**, irregularly shaped buckwheat fritters filled with tasty Casera cheese and accompanied by fine-chopped chicory from Olimpia's own fields. Try also the **polenta taragna**, made with buckwheat, but remember to book it in advance. Sample it by itself or with cured meats, sausage and pork ribs. The winter menu offers **jugged game** and succulent roasts. If it happens to be on the menu, don't miss **taròzz**, a side dish of potatoes and green beans tossed in butter and cheese. To finish off, cheeses from local producers and homemade desserts.

The wine list features a good selection of labels from the Valtellina, though the house wine made by Olimpia's husband Menico also holds its own. All in all, a real old fashioned trattoria, especially in terms of value for money. Which is why it may be a good idea to book ahead.

The Corte Salandini farm is located in the Parco del Mincio, a few kilometers from Lake Garda. The building was once a courtyard farmhouse and some parts of the structure date back to the 16th century. The Fontana family has carefully restored the building, partly to enhance the views over both the courtyard and the countryside, with its orchards, vineyards, corn fields and pastures. Rooms are basic but comfortable and and breakfast is simple but tasty. A saltwater swimming pool, jacuzzi and barbecue area are also at the disposal of guests. An ideal base for lovers of hiking, cycling (bicycles are available to guests), horse riding and sailing.

• 4 double rooms, with bathroom, air-conditioning, fridge, safe, satellite TV; 10 apartments with separate kitchen • Prices: double room single occupancy 30-45 euros, double 60-90, breakfast included; apartment 30-45 euros per person, breakfast 5 euros per person • Credit cards: all, Bancomat • Facility accessible for the mobility challenged, 1 apartment designed for their use. Off-street parking. Small pets allowed. Owners always reachable • Breakfast room. Conference room. Garden, playground. Pool, jacuzzi, table tennis.

In **Sondrio** (9 km), Tommaso Tognolina, in Via Beccaria, sells traditionally produced butter, Casera cheese and dairy products.

PORTALBERA
San Pietro

OSTERIA DEI PESCATORI

Trattoria
Località San Pietro 13
Tel. 0385 266085 320 3713052
Closed Wednesday
Open: lunch and dinner
Holidays: first two weeks in January, last three in July
Seating: 60
Prices: 30 euros, wine excluded
All credit cards, Bancomat

It is always a pleasure to return to this old Po Valley osteria, a stone's throw from the river itself. Lorena Schiappelli will be glad to welcome you into the simply decorated but comfortable dining room, where only the pendulum of the grandfather clock marks the passing of time. Her husband Massimo Borgognoni, an accomplished chef, serves a menu mainly based on freshwater fish, with a few typical Lomellina antipasti and Piacenza-inspired first courses.

Start with a mixed antipasto: fish (trout, tench and superb salmon), smoked, in carpione and marinated, plus **goose salami**. For first course, don't pass up on the delicious **tagliolini with freshwater shrimp**, though the traditional **pisarei e fasò**, local pasta with beans, the filled pastas and the aromatic vegetable minestrone are tempting too. As for the main courses, the choice is yours: grilled sturgeon, classic fillets of **perch in butter**, or pike, tench and catfish prepared in various ways. Phone in advance, though, if you fancy fried **frogs' legs** or, in winter, **eel in sauce** with peas. If you aren't a fish person, Massimo also prepares roast or braised meat (pork, goose and duck), **casoeula** and **tripe** with white beans, depending on the season. Desserts are simple and homemade. One such is **Torta Paradiso** (which here also comes in a version with a chocolate filling), which is traditionally dunked in wine – or maybe it's just an excuse for an extra glass!

All the wines on the short list are from the Oltrepò area and the mark-up is fair.

POZZOLENGO
Martelosio di Sopra

ANTICA LOCANDA DEL CONTRABBANDIERE

Bed and breakfast
Località Martelosio di Sopra 1
Tel. 030 918151-333 7958069
Fax 030 918151
E-mail: info@locandadelcontrabbandiere.com
Internet: www.locandadelcontrabbandiere.com
Closed for a fortnight in January

This lovely 15th-century building in the hills between Brescia, Mantua and Verona is owned by Imerio and Lorenzo Bonato. The inn's original name has been retained and, in the converted first-floor rooms, guests can enjoy local cuisine at very reasonable prices (30 euros, excluding wine). Breakfast is traditional, consisting of homemade jams, tarts and cakes, as well as local cured meats. Rooms on the second floor have antique furniture and views over the countryside and swimming pool. The B&B is close to many tourist attractions in the area (the battlefields of San Martino and Solferino, Sirmione and Lake Garda, the cities of Brescia and Verona) but, given its surprisingly peaceful surroundings, is enchanting in its own right.

• 3 double rooms, with bathroom, air-conditioning, fridge, satellite TV • Prices: double-room single occupancy 80 euros, double 100 euros, breakfast included • Credit cards: none • Off-street parking. Small pets allowed. Owners always reachable. • Restaurant. Terrace. Pool.

PROSERPIO

INARCA

☞Trattoria
Via Inarca 16
Tel. 031 620424
Closed from Monday to Wednesday
in winter, no closing day in summer
Open: lunch and dinner
Holidays: two weeks in October
Seating: 35 + 40 outdoors
Prices: 35 euros, wine excluded
All credit cards, Bancomat

Arriving at owner Pierdinarca's chalet is a bit like returning to a rural idyll. At the end of a path through the woods, you will hear the braying of the 'mad donkey' and see the slouching brindled dog, the mascots of the Inarca farmyard.

In this part of Brianza, where agricultural traditions are dying out, the quest for local produce continues and the specialties of the Lario area are being rediscovered. Meanwhile Pierdinarca's first son Manuel, 'il cuochino', works in fresh new culinary creations.

In the dining room, the other son Jonathan and mamma Ade offer classic dishes in winter – **casoeula**, **intragli** (offal), **rustisciada** – cooked salami with creamed potatoes – buckwheat pasta with **missoltini** and calf's head. In summer under the pergola, you can sample boned rabbit salad, carpaccio of Chianina beef with cannellini beans, **Valtellina bresaola**, and cured meats and lardo from Brianza. Thanks to Claudio, a young fisherman from Lezzeno, the menu also features risotto with lake angler-fish or whitefish, butter and sage, and **common sunfish, bleak and perch in carpione**.

Otherwise, you can opt for veal kidneys or **braised donkey meat with polenta**. To finish off, a regional and local **cheese board** – the fresh goats' cheeses from Caslino d'Erba are excellent – and the now legendary battle between 'il cuochino' and Pierdinarca over who makes the best **laciada**, otherwise known as cotizza (a batter of flour and water fried and sprinkled with sugar).

REZZATO
Virle

ALPINO DA ROSA

☞Trattoria
Via Trieste 27
Tel. 030 2591968
Closed Wednesday
Open: lunch and dinner
Holidays: three weeks in August
Seating: 70 + 20 outdoors
Prices: 25-32 euros, wine excluded
All credit cards except AE, Bancomat

This classic trattoria has been running for years and has recently been given a smart new look, with two small dining rooms carved out in the old wine cellars. Here you'll be welcomed by chef Rosa Goini and her daughter Simona, who will recommend the best wines to accompany their authentic Brescia-style cooking.

The menu starts off with a simple antipasto of local salami, frittata, stuffed tomatoes and hot seasonal vegetables, then continues with a very popular specialty, a trio of **casoncelli** filled with vegetables, meat and pumpkin. Alternatively, try the **ravioli al bagòss**, tagliolini with venison ragù or **pappardelle with jugged hare**, or the various seasonal **risottos**, all delicious. Second courses include **bollito misto**, **stuffed chicken** alla bresciana, **beef in oil**, lamb cutlets, horsemeat T-bone steak (for two people), a Fiorentina steak and, if you book in advance, **spiedo bresciano,** with larks roasted on the spit and served with **polenta** made with flour from Storo. To finish off, a cheese board with exceptional local Bagòss and desserts: tarts, crème brûlée, tiramisù, bavarois with chocolate and pears, and the wonderful homemade traditional **biscuits** stored in the glass jars on display as you enter the restaurant.

An interesting set menu for 26 euros (wine excluded) includes an antipasto, a trio of first courses, two main courses – bollito and beef in oil – and dessert.

The wine list, beautifully compiled by Simona, boasts over 150 important Italian labels plus a good range of the finest Italian and foreign spirits.

REZZATO

LA PINA

🔑🗝️ 3-star Hotel
Via Garibaldi 98
Tel. 030 2591443
Fax 030 2591937
E-mail: info@lapina.it
Internet: www.lapina.it
Open all year

This hotel-restaurant, renowned for its cuisine and professional service takes its name from Giuseppina (Pina) Merlo, who built and opened it in 1949. Renovated in 1995, it is now managed by the Abruzzese and Franzoni families. Located near Brescia only half an hour from Lake Garda, the hotel is perfect for vacations or business trips. Rooms are comfortable and fitted with modern furniture; some have balconies. The buffet breakfast offers yogurt, cereals, homemade cakes and fruit juices, while savory items are available on request. The restaurant offers both local and Mediterranean cuisine at an average price of 25-30 euros, excluding wine. At Rezzato guests can play tennis and bowls or swim in the pool. Those wishing to travel a little further afield can visit Carzago di Calvagese or play on the lovely Palazzo Arzaga golf course.

• 6 single, 11 double and 4 triple rooms, with bathroom, air-conditioning, fridge, satellite TV, modern connection; some rooms with terrace • Prices: single 55-70 euros, double 75-90, triple 85-95, breakfast included • Credit cards: all, Bancomat • Facility accessible for the mobility challenged, 1 room designed for their use. Off-street parking. No pets allowed. Reception open from 6.45am to midnight. • Bar, restaurant. Reading and TV room. Conference room. Garden, terrace.

RIPALTA CREMASCA
Bolzone

VIA VAI

🍲 Trattoria
Via Libertà 18
Tel. 0373 268232
Closed Tuesday and Wednesday
Open: dinner, Saturday and Sunday also for lunch
Holidays: variable
Seating: 40 + 20 outdoors
Prices: 28-35 euros, wine excluded
No credit cards

Green is the color of choice in the dining room, green for hope. And hopeful is how we feel when we meet the Via vai team: brothers Marco and Stefano Fagioli, Stefano's wife Monica, and promising young chef Ivan Gorlani. The brothers never forget the influence of their mentor, in life and in the kitchen, Clementina Tacchini, a leading light in the dine dining business in this part of the Crema area. Here, among the raised flood embankments along the River Serio, rural culture reigns supreme and the plains are full of cattle and pig farms. Farmyard animals such as geese are also reared.

This is the setting for this inviting trattoria, where you can sample excellent **foie gras pâté** and, in winter, a whole range of **goose**-based dishes, such as stuffed **goose neck with Savoy cabbage**, a reminder of the days when no part of the animal went to waste. Then comes a fine spread of local **cured meats**, including salami with a hint of garlic and excellent Cremonese **cotechino**. This is the homeland of **tortelli cremaschi** and the local trattorias do battle to offer the most authentic recipes. As a second course, apart from goose, you can enjoy stuffed rabbit legs or **jugged guinea fowl** and, in winter, a range of pork dishes.

Marco, the wine waiter, and will recommend the right accompaniments from a prevalently Italian list (which also includes a few high quality, reasonably priced French labels). A good cheese board and a selection of homemade desserts round off a pleasurable dining experience. Good value for money.

Ripalta Guerina

36 km north of Cremona

Toscanini

Trattoria
Via XXV Aprile 3
Tel. 0373 66171
Closed Monday
Open: lunch and dinner
Holidays: one week in July
Seating: 50
Prices: 28-33 euros, wine excluded
All credit cards, Bancomat

The great Arturo Toscanini lived in Ripalta Guerina before his exile to the United States. The trattoria which now bears his name was opened in 1919, and the musician himself often came here for a glass of good wine. In thoswe days it had a small room which served as an osteria, kitchens which were also used by the family, and a wine shop. A few years ago it was renovated by Francesco Foppa Vicenzini, who converted the arcade into another dining room and left the back room with a small number of tables. The walls are adorned with musical instruments, mementos and a portrait of the maestro, and there is a piano in the corner of the main room for the regular classical music evenings.
Keen chef Vanna Galvani excels herself in first courses: **casoncelli** filled with prosciutto and served with pancetta, a real treat, **tortelli cremaschi,** an old traditional dish made with wafer-thin pasta and excellent **risottos** all year round. One local specialty which always features on the menu is **Salva**, a cheese which was at risk of dying out altogether, here served as an antipasto either 'al naturale', young after a month of maturing, seasoned with an aromatic bouquet of wild berries, or fried. Popular main courses include **roast shin of veal**, local duck or goose prepared in a variety of ways, and a delicate beef tartare with poached egg. The homemade desserts are also good: they range from the classic pears and chocolate to **apple pie**, **chocolate salami**, and tiramisù, both in the usual version or in a summer version with fresh fruit.
The well thought out Italian wine list satisfies regulars and occasional visitors alike.

Roncadelle

6 km southwest of Brescia SS 235

Trattoria Conti

Trattoria
Via San Bernardino 23
Tel. 030 2780147
Closed Monday; June-August closed Sunday
Open: lunch and dinner
Holidays: first week of January, two weeks in August
Seating: 70 + 20 outdoors
Prices: 30-35 euros, wine excluded
All credit cards, Bancomat

In the center of the village, just past the parish church, lies this trattoria, a safe haven for lovers of good food. Recent renovation work has given the place a warm, homey feel: three little dining rooms, a courtyard dominated by an ancient olive tree, where you can dine al fresco in summer, and an upstairs room for groups (of 24-30 people) on special occasions. The walls are lined with previous photographs showing the building in its previous life as a workshop for repairing carts and a barn for keeping livestock.
The menu changes with the seasons. To start off, try the classic Conti antipasto – a combination of cured meats, vegetables, frittata – or lardo d'Arnad with honey, baked figs, Gorgonzola and candied orange, and a selection of high quality **cured meats**, such as culatello di Zibello and pata negra. The first courses feature homemade pasta, including **casoncelli** with a filling of herbs, pumpkin or meat, tagliatelle with cep mushrooms, maccheroni with cherry tomatoes and ricotta, and the authentic signature dish of Franco Foti, assisted by Francesco Lanotte: **risotto all'onda** made with vialone nano rice, either with **Bagòss** cheese and saffron pistils or with Groppello and smoked Scamorza. Then come the meat dishes; **tagliata al bagòss** and lamb cutlets with extra virgin olive oil. A comprehensive cheese board is accompanied by wine jellies, pears and honey. Excellent grilled vegetables are also available. To finish off, crème brûlée, tiramisù and pear tart. The wine list offers an extensive choice with a number of good labels at the right prices. Pinuccia, who works front of house and is also an expert wine waiter, will help you choose.

RONCOFERRARO
Garolda

ROVESCALA
Luzzano

DAL GAIA

CASTELLO DI LUZZANO

▱ Trattoria
Via Garolda 10
Tel. 0376 663815
Closed Monday and Tuesday evenings
Open: lunch and dinner
Holidays: mid-July to mid-August
Seating: 40
Prices: 25-30 euros, wine excluded
Credit cards: AE, Visa

🛏 Holiday farm
Frazione Luzzano 5
Tel. 0523 863277
Fax 0523 865909
E-mail: info@castelloluzzano.it
Internet: www.castelloluzzano.it
Open all year round

Dal Gaia in Garolda, near Roncoferraro, is one of the few remaining authentic trattorias in the countryside near Mantua. It's a place with a timeless feel: the entrance, originally used as a bar and wine shop, is packed with furniture and mementos which recall the old osterias which used to offer shelter and refreshment to carters and hired hands. The two adjoining dining rooms, with country-style decor and well-appointed tables, have a pleasant, homely, farmhouse atmosphere. Two generations work in the trattoria, the men front of house and the women in the kitchen. The food takes its inspiration from traditional recipes reworked to satisfy the modern demand for a lighter touch.
All the dishes on the menu are simple and carefully prepared.
The antipasti include good prosciutto and culatello; while the first courses we recommend are ravioli with ricotta and egg plant, **pumpkin tortelli**, **agnoli in stock**, tortelloni with asparagus and artichokes and, in season, **tagliolini with pigeon** and morel mushrooms. Then come fillet of veal with green peppercorns accompanied by excellent roast potatoes, tagliata, **duck legs** with balsamic vinegar and **pike in sauce with polenta**. For dessert, **pumpkin budino** with caramel, nougat mousse, bavarois with peaches and raspberries...
The wine list features almost 150 Italian labels, mostly from Piedmont, Tuscany, Friuli and Trentino. Desserts may be accompanied by passito wines served by the glass and, to round off, there are excellent spirits (the bottles are attractively displayed on the antique dressers which add to the quaint charm of the trattoria).

The Castello di Luzzano holiday farm is located in the hills of Pavia and Piacenza. The lovely locanda and excellent restaurant have been carved out of the restored manor house and adjacent farm cottages and are surrounded by 120 hectares of land, 90 of which are vineyards. The farm utilizes modern winemaking techniques and produces an excellent red wine which, together with the cuisine, reflects the cultures of both Pavia and Piacenza. The farm's own produce is also available for purchase. Rooms are well designed and tastefully furnished. The buffet breakfast offers cereals, jams and homemade cakes and the restaurant excels in local cuisine at an average cost of 30 euros, excluding wine.

• 2 double rooms and 2 mini-apartments (2 people), with bathroom, TV • Prices: double room single occupancy 85 euros, double 95 (30 euros supplement for extra bed), breakfast included; mini-apartment 90-105 euros, breakfast 10 euros per person • All major credit cards: Bancomat • Off-street parking. Small pets allowed (in mini-apartments, 5 euros per day) • Restaurant. Veranda.

Salò

Osteria di Mezzo

Recently opened osteria
Via di Mezzo 10
Tel. 0365 290966
Closed Tuesday
Open: 12pm-11pm
Holidays: January 10-February 8
Seating: 30 + 8 outdoors
Prices: 28-33 euros, wine excluded
All major credit cards, Bancomat

This off-the-beaten-track osteria takes its name from the little street where it is situated, one of the oldest in town. From Via San Carlo, which runs parallel to the lakeside, a gentle climb takes you up to the building. Simple, well-appointed decor and a cordial welcome complement the food, based on lake produce and accompanied by excellent wines, also served by the glass. The osteria is run by the Vanni family – Dory in the kitchen, Gino and Mauro front of house – and serves meals and simple snacks non-stop from midday to 11pm.

You can opt for a set dish or a selection of **cheeses** or **cured meats**, all outstanding, or choose from the menu. On our last visit we tried a mixed 'lake antipasto' with delicately aromatic **pike** accompanied by polenta, marinated char with carrots, and trout and **sardines in saor**. Then **tagliolini with perch**, kamut flour pappardelle with tomato and almonds, and excellent **char en papillote** and grilled sardines. Main courses include fillets of perch with leeks, **marinated lake fish**, and meat dishes such as lamb or rabbit with herbs. To finish off, an interesting **almond tart**, made without butter or flour, and a chocolate zuccotto.

The extensive wine list comprises the best Garda and an interesting range of spirits, including excellent whiskies and cognacs.

At Via San Carlo 86, Pasticceria Vassalli, which specializes in chocolate, sells an array of goodies.

Salò

Trattoria alle Rose

Restaurant
Via Gasparo da Salò 33
Tel. 0365 43220
Closed Wednesday
Open: lunch and dinner
Holidays: vary
Seating: 65 + 65 outdoors
Prices: 35 euros, wine excluded
All credit cards, Bancomat

This restaurant in the historic center of Salò is as inviting and reliable as ever. It boasts a large car park and an attractive terrace which takes over from the inside dining room in summer. It interprets local identity with style and its good old-fashioned food is prepared with painstaking care, starting with the selection of the raw materials. Particular attention is devoted to the olive oil, the various dishes being matched with different labels.

Owner Gianni Briarava is a genial host, and it's a pleasure to hear him talking about 'his' lake, which provides the fish his mother-in-law Rosanna Faé and brother-in-law Marco Giacomini cook with such skill.

The menu is wide-ranging and linked to the seasons. Antipasti: tartare of pike or whitefish, marinated eel, **pike in consa with wholemeal polenta**, carpaccio of sardines, cream of zucchini soup with fresh water shrimp. Pasta dishes: wafer-thin **ravioli** stuffed with **whitefish** or **Bagòss** cheese, tortelli with chub, bigoli with sardines. Second courses: **steamed carp**, **fillets of perch in butter**, grilled sardines and whitefish; excellent meat dishes, especially the **kid** and the typical Brescia-style spit-roasts, with pork, rabbit, chicken and songbirds (when available), potatoes and sage, and **spatchcock with a stuffing of chanterelle mushrooms**. There is a wide choice of desserts, all homemade.

The wines, featuring labels from Garda and Franciacorta sourced from little-known but reliable wineries, have a fair mark-up and are served by the glass.

San Benedetto Po

22 km south of Mantua

L'Impronta

Restaurant
Via Gramsci 10
Tel. 0376 615843
Closed Monday
Open: lunch and dinner
Holidays: last two weeks of January and June
Seating: 40
Prices: 25-30 euros, wine excluded
All credit cards, Bancomat

L'Impronta is a small restaurant run by Matteo Alfonsi, a young chef who trained in the best local establishments. His food is inspired by a great respect for local traditions and high quality Mantua produce, sourced from small producers and treated with an original touch.
For antipasto, the finest San Benedetto **cured meats**, including excellent salame casalino and culatello, followed by the best from the day's market: **pike in sauce**, **frittata with frogs' legs** and peas or **with snails** and courgettes, or fried pumpkin flowers filled with cheese and served with tomato sauce. In winter, first courses are likely to include **sorbir d'agnoli**, **pumpkin tortelli**, **risotto** with apple, gorgonzola and lardo, with red onions and provola or with **braised horse meat**, and excellent **maccheroncini al torchio**, either with **pumpkin**, rosemary and sausage or with wild honey mushrooms. Freshwater fish also feature in pasta dishes such as **bigoli with pike and sardine sauce**, and in main courses such as fillet of perch with sun-dried tomatoes, capers and oregano. Other main courses include soused salt cod with fried polenta and sweet and sour carrots, **pork loin with aromatic herbs**, duck legs with pork and chestnut stuffing, and **casserole of spatchcock** with seasonal vegetables. To finish off, some elaborate desserts: bitter chocolate mousse, vanilla panna cotta with strawberry sauce, caramelized pears with saffron in chocolate sauce, and fior di latte and chilli-pepper ice-cream. **Sbrisolona** and **tagliatelle cake** with the coffee.
The wine list is well thought out, with numerous fairly priced bottles from local wineries and the rest of Italy.

San Giorgio di Mantova

3 km northeast of Mantua

Locanda dell'Opera

Locanda with rooms
Via Bachelet 12
Tel. e fax 0376 371414
E-mail: info@operaghiotta.com
Internet: www.operaghiotta.com
Open all year

The Locanda dell'Opera is located in a new building surrounded by a delicately scented, shady garden, just minutes from the historic center of Mantua, easily accessible by bicycle or bus. Rooms are spacious and tastefully furnished, all with wooden floors. Traditional breakfast offers coffee, tea, milk, local cakes and homemade tarts, while savory items are available on request. In summer, breakfast can be taken on the terrace. The place is in a perfect location for visitors keen to visit Verona and Lake Garda.

• 6 double rooms, with bathroom, air-conditioning, TV • Prices: double room single occupancy 50 euros, double 80 (20 euros supplement for extra bed), breakfast included • Credit cards: all, Bancomat • 2 rooms designed for use by the mobility challenged. Off-street parking and also in front of the locanda. Small pets allowed. Management contactable at all times • Breakfast room. Garden. Terrace.

Santa Maria della Versa
Ruinello

29 KM SOUTHEAST OF PAVIA, 8 KM NORTH OF STRADELLA

Serle
Castello

21 KM EAST OF BRESCIA SS 45 BIS

AL RUINELLO

CASTELLO

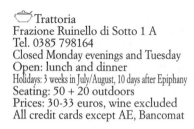

Trattoria
Frazione Ruinello di Sotto 1 A
Tel. 0385 798164
Closed Monday evenings and Tuesday
Open: lunch and dinner
Holidays: 3 weeks in July/August, 10 days after Epiphany
Seating: 50 + 20 outdoors
Prices: 30-33 euros, wine excluded
All credit cards except AE, Bancomat

Trattoria
Via Castello 38
Tel. 030 6910001
Closed Tuesday
Open: lunch and dinner
Holidays: in July
Seating: 90 + 60 outdoors
Prices: 28-30 euros, wine excluded
All major credit cards, Bancomat

In the heart of the Oltrepò area, among the vineyards on the hills around Santa Maria della Versa, a historic production area for spumante, this trattoria in the tiny hamlet of Ruinello has been run by the Bersani family since 1988. The dining room is well appointed and a spacious veranda overlooks an attractive garden that guests are free to visit.

Front of house owner Pietro and his son Cristiano will help you choose from the wide range of local wines, while Donatella and daughter Raffaella run the kitchen. Things get off to a good start with a taste of the local **cured meats** – the culatello di Castell'Arquato with mostarda is outstanding – followed by Russian salad with homemade mayonnaise and grilled peppers. From our last visit we have fond memories of **ravioli with braised meat** and the classic **pisarei e fasò**, local pasta and beans. As an alternative, seasonal **risottos** made with ceps and chanterelles, spumante, asparagus or strawberries, and in summer, crespelle with ricotta and herbs or spinach, and **lasagne with pesto and vegetables**. The main courses are mostly meat-based: the winter menu features **braised beef with** wholemeal **polenta**, roast beef with walnuts, **quail with Pinot Grigio** or grapes, guinea fowl stuffed with vegetables and duck with grappa. In summer, the same meats appear in lighter dishes: hence **guinea fowl with lemon**, roast beef with orange and rabbit in beer. Phone ahead if you want fish (and there's not much in the way of cheese, by the way). To finish off, coffee semifreddo, panna cotta, cherry cake and homemade jam tarts.

The interesting wine list focuses on the wide range of locally produced labels.

The Castello-Brescia road through the Botticino area, where the wine of the same name is produced, is winding but picturesque, and it's enjoyable to explore the thickly wooded countryside on foot or by mountain bike. The trattoria has been renovated and three new little dining rooms and a wine cellar have been added to the old osteria dining room. It is run by Emilio, a professional wine waiter, his wife Lorena, who runs the kitchen, and mamma Rosy, who makes sure that everything runs smoothly and takes care of the guests, mostly regulars.

This is a land of **mushrooms** and **spiedo bresciano** (spit-roasted pork, chicken, rabbit and birds), which are also the hallmark dishes of the trattoria. On our last visit we sampled **chanterelles with polenta** and local truffle, **polenta taragna** (with cheese) and a delicate tarte tatin. The menu varies with the seasons and the availability of ingredients. You can start off with a classic antipasto of **cured meats** and continue with **tagliatelle ai finferli**, **soup of cep mushrooms, casoncelli**, tagliolini al sugo di spugnole and, among the main courses, kid Brescia-style, **cheek of beef,** and rabbit with herbs. If you are not a meat lover, choose from the rich **cheese board**, served with mostarda. To finish off, Lorena's excellent desserts: chestnut flour and chocolate cake, **sweet salami** with Marsala cream and pears and chocolate.

The professional skill of Emilio, a Brunello expert, shines through in the wine list: hundreds of labels – mainly Tuscan and Piedmontese and the best from Franciacorta and Botticino. This year a few beers and a separate list for dessert wines and spirits have also been added.

SIRMIONE

40 KM EAST OF BRESCIA

MARCONI

🗝3-star Hotel
Via Vittorio Emanuele 51
Tel. 030 916007
Fax 030 916587
E-mail: hmarconi@tiscalinet.it
Internet: www.hotelmarconi.net
Open from March to November

The Marconi hotel in the historic center of Sirmione (the town center is closed to traffic but hotel guests are given a special pass) is an ideal base for shopping, motorboat rides and sightseeing. The building dates back to the 1970s but was restored in 2001 and refurbished with modern furniture. The Visani family offer their guests a relaxing holiday enhanced by the mouthwatering creations of pastry chef Giampaolo. The buffet breakfast offers a vast array of homemade pastries and other meals are simple but tasty (average cost 16 euros, excluding wine). Guests can go to the lake or visit the baths of Sirmione, Catullus's villa and the Sigurtà di Valeggio Park near Verona, a unique garden that can be visited on foot, by bicycle or by electric train.

• 3 single and 14 double rooms, with bathroom, air-conditioning, balcony, safe, satellite TV, modem connection; in the annex, 2 single and 4 double rooms, with bathroom • Prices: single 36-58 euros, double 62-95 (20-30 euros supplement for extra bed), breakfast included • Credit cards: all, Bancomat • Off-street parking. Small pets allowed. Reception open 24 hours a day • Bar, restaurant (for hotel guests only). Garden, solarium, terrace. Private jetty for mooring boats.

SOLFERINO
Sorgive

35 KM NORTHWEST OF MANTUA, 30 KM SOUTHEAST OF BRESCIA

LE SORGIVE-LE VOLPI

🗝Holiday farm
Via Piridello 6
Tel. 0376 854252
Fax 0376 855256
E-mail: info@lesorgive.it
Internet: www.lesorgive.it
Open all year

This facility is located in the Mantuan hills amidst vineyards and woods, about ten kilometers from Lake Garda, and comprises two farmhouses dating back to the 19th century: Le Sorgive, the lodging unit managed by Vittorio Serenella, and Le Volpi, the bar and restaurant managed by his sister Anna. The two buildings are located on a vast agricultural estate specializing in organic fruit, vegetables and medicinal plants and the Serenellas also breed geese, ducks, chickens, rabbits, pigs, cattle and bees. Guests also have access to the estate's stables, where horses are bred and trained. Rooms are spacious, quiet and welcoming and buffet breakfast offers hot beverages and home-produced fruit juices, honey, jams and cakes (savory items are available on request). The restaurant serves local cuisine at an average cost of 20-30 euros, excluding wine.

• 8 double, triple or four-bed rooms, with bathroom, TV; communal fridge in the breakfast room • Prices: double room single occupancy 55-65 euros, double 80-105 (13-23 euros), breakfast included • Credit cards: all, Bancomat • Facility accessible for the mobility challenged, 2 rooms designed for their use. Off-street parking. Small pets allowed. Owners always reachable. • Breakfast room. Garden. Pool, gym, mountain bike tracks, grass 5-a-side soccer field, table tennis, archery.

Sotto Il Monte Giovanni XXIII

16 KM WEST OF BERGAMO

Casa Clelia

🗝Holiday farm
Via Corna 1-3
Tel. 035 799133
Fax 035 791788
E-mail: info@casaclelia.com
Internet: www.casaclelia.com
Open all year

Casa Clelia is located in a 17th-century manor house surrounded by vegetable gardens, orchards, barns and stables. The structure has been refurbished using environmentally friendly materials and respecting the original architecture. Rooms are all named after a flower and are spacious, simply furnished, colorful and very welcoming. Breakfast is generous and offers a variety of sweet and savory items. In summer, guests can enjoy wholesome dishes prepared using the farm's own produce (set menu 29 euros, excluding wine) and relax in the shade of the wisteria and jasmine-scented arbor. The farm's seasonal fruit and vegetables, jams and cured meats are also available for purchase. Guests can enjoy beautiful walks or explore the countryside on horseback and there's also a lovely golf course nearby.

• 8 double and 2 triple rooms, with bathroom, TV, modem connection • Prices: double room single occupancy 55-65 euros, double 85-120, triple 130-150, breakfast included • Credit cards: Visa, MC, Bancomat • Facility accessible for the mobility challenged. Off-street parking. Small pets allowed. Reception open from 8 am to 11 pm. • Restaurant. Breakfast room. Conference room. Gazebo, children's playground.

Sustinente

22 KM SOUTHEAST OF MANTUA ON SS 482

Ca' Guerriera

🗝Holiday farm
Vai Martini 91
Tel. 0386 437343
Fax 0386 437342
E-mail: infocaguerriera@corterestara.com
Internet: www.caguerriera.com
Open all year

Located on the banks of the River Po within the grounds of the Corte Restara farm, this holiday farm is managed by the Marquis Odoardo Guerrieri Gonzaga, his wife and two daughters. The original structure was an 18th-century farmhouse, now restored with the aid of one of the marquis's architect daughters. Rooms are spacious (some double and triple rooms are large enough to accommodate an extra bed), comfortable and have antique furniture. Traditional breakfast also offers seasonal fresh fruit grow on the farm and homemade jams. Guests can enjoy the outdoor swimming pool, children's playground and, just a few kilometers away, the riding center for those wanting to explore the countryside on horseback. The restaurant offers local cuisine featuring the farm's own produce, at an average cost of 23 euros, excluding wine.

• 1 single, 8 double and 2 triple rooms, with bathroom, air-conditioning, TV, modem connection • Prices: single 46 euros, double 86, triple 120 (20 euros supplement for extra bed), breakfast included • Credit cards: all, Bancomat • Facility accessible for the mobility challenged, 1 room designed for their use. Off-street parking. Small pets allowed (not in the rooms). Reception open 24 hours a day • Restaurant. Lounge, conference room, exhibition room. Garden, children's playground. Pool.

5 KM SOUTH OF PAVIA

14 KM EAST OF BERGAMO SS 42

L'Ustaria di Giugaton

Conca Verde

Trattoria
Via Battella 65
Tel. 0382 571040
Closed Monday lunch and Thursday
Open: lunch and dinner
Holidays: two weeks in July/August, two in January
Seating: 50 + 10 outdoors
Prices: 25 euros, wine excluded
No credit cards, Bancomat

Trattoria
Via Croce 31
Tel. 035 940290
Closed Monday, Tuesday evenings and Saturday lunch
Open: lunch and dinner
Holidays: two weeks in June and August
Seating: 40 + 30 outdoors
Prices: 35 euros, wine excluded
All major credit cards, Bancomat

The trattoria lies inside the Ticino Park, on the outskirts of Pavia, just past the Ponte Vecchio. Here, ten years ago, Domenico Pietra (Nico) and Aurora Annamaria took over a time-honored establishment, well known to university students as a wine shop and snack bar. With the assistance of Daniela Vallata in the kitchen, they have created a pleasing, attractive eatery. Once through the door, we were taken by the room with the brick ceiling and wood beams, a pretty wood-burning stove, quaint checked tablecloths and cups instead of glasses (though you can ask for wine glasses, if you prefer). Nico recites the menu and helps customers choose between local wines or a few labels from Piedmont. We started off with a selection of **cured meats** from a local producer, **nervetti** (veal cartilage), Russian salad, a roll of salami in bread crust and **cotechino**. First courses include homemade pasta dishes: **ravioli with braised meat**, sumptuous yellow tagliolini with cherry tomatoes and river shrimp, and pisarei e fasò (pasta and beans Piacenza-style, revealing Nico's origins). There's also a delicious-smelling herb soup with river shrimp and a rice patty with salami past and Bonarda wine. The main courses include roast beef in a salt crust or alla giugatun (with spices) served with baked potatoes, braised meats and sautéed kidneys. In summer, the menu also features freshwater fish – **sturgeon** cooked in various ways, **fried fillets of perch** – as well as **sautéed snails** and frogs' legs. The puddings are the pride of the chef: **sabbiosa**, the Pavia version of Torta Paradiso, chocolate cake, pear cake, meringues with hot chocolate sauce or strawberries and cream.

Slightly isolated among the green hills of Trescore Balneario, this big white building opens to reveal a trattoria with a family atmosphere. The summer outdoor area and the fireplace that heats the dining room in winter help to create the warm feel typical of a country house. The food on offer – organic vegetables, farmyard animals and the produce of the nearby lakes – is the fruit of the seasons and the work of Antonio Mutti, who runs the trattoria with his family: wine.
The menu starts with all kinds of homemade **cured meats**, made from pigs reared by Alessandro and served with toasted polenta. Then come excellent **grilled snails**, a beautifully prepared timbale of rice and numerous hot and cold seasonal delicacies. Continue with the homemade pasta dishes, from tortelli with potatoes and light pesto or with taleggio di malga to **pappardelle with duck ragù** to the traditional **casoncelli with pumpkin and amaretti biscuits**.
There is a wide range of main courses: pike in anchovy sauce, snails in piquant parsley sauce, and **braised donkey meat**, all served with **polenta**, or lamb cutlets and roast potatoes. At the right time of year, do sample the **barbecued spatchcock**, a simple but tasty dish which they do particularly well here. To finish off, you can choose between the cheese board with honeys and jams, and the house puddings (the fruit tarts and pies are good).
The small but interesting wine list focuses on labels from the Bergamo area.

TRESCORE CREMASCO

TREVISO BRESCIANO
Vico

48 KM NORTHWEST OF CREMONA

46 KM NORTHEAST OF BRESCIA

BISTEK

LAMARTA

Restaurant
Viale De Gasperi 31
Tel. 0373 273046
Closed Tuesday evenings and Wednesday
Open: lunch and dinner
Holidays: January 1-10, 3 weeks from the last week in July
Seating: 50
Prices: 25-33 euros, wine excluded
All major credit cards, Bancomat

Trattoria
Via Tito Speri 36
Tel. 0365 83390
Closed Thursday, no closing day in summer
Open: lunch, dinner book first
Holidays: variable
Seating: 50 + 24 outdoors
Prices: 26-30 euros, wine excluded
All credit cards, Bancomat

The restaurant is on the left side of the road to Pandino. In the three comfortable dining rooms on the upper floor, you can sample the best specialties in the Crema area.

Antonio Bonetti, helped in the kitchen by Paolo Bombelli, puts all his enthusiasm into his seasonal theme menus, which range from freshwater fish to frogs, goose, pork and mushrooms. The set menus, wine included, are reasonably priced at 27 euros for lunch and 38 for dinner. Front of house he is capably welcomed by Ornella and Lucia.

They serve a vast range of dishes. To start, **frittata with cress** and Salva cheese, homemade focaccia with herbs, and minced Piedmontese fassone beef. And don't miss the Crema **cured meats** (muleta, culatello di Zibello, giro dell'oca). Then, depending on the season, risotto with wild asparagus, **pipeto of savoy cabbage**, **bean and pork rind soup**, goose tortelli, tagliatelle with porcini mushrooms and gnocchi with buffalo ricotta, and handmade **tortelli cremaschi**. To continue, **soused eel**, fried frogs' legs, tender **escalope of catfish**, sautéed kidneys, tagliata of Piedmontese fassone beef, roast stuffed quail, **spiced goose legs**, and lamb loin chops. At the end of the meal, a rich **cheese board** and local desserts, such as **spungarda** and treccia d'oro, with dessert wines served by the glass. Try Ornella's rosolio, too.

The wine list features over 150 labels at reasonable prices. On the ground floor, brother Angelo and his wife Agnese run a pub, popular with young people, which serves many of the dishes from the restaurant.

The trip to out of the way Vico is certainly worth it. The mountain atmosphere stimulates the appetite, and Lamarta – the name is a tribute to grandmother Marta – offers a pleasant welcome. The whole family is involved in continuing the place's tradition for hospitality, paying great attention to the quality of the ingredients used and to guests, who they treat like friends. Leave your address and they'll invite you for special occasions: when they're cooking up **mushrooms** from the surrounding mountains, for example, or when they're preparing the local spit-roast specialty, **spiedo valsabbino**, with the meat of farmyard animals and birds.

Behind all this is Graziella Massari, who works front of house and in the kitchen, and her husband Dario Piccinelli, who picks mushrooms and wild herbs in the woods for aromatic dishes and delicious frittata, and also rears chickens, hens, goats and pigs. Hence the excellent quality of the **cured and other meats** (if available, try the wonderful **roast kid**).

The atmosphere is that of a village osteria, with a bar and fireplace warming up chilly guests in the one dining room. You will be waited on by the polite, cheerful daughter Rubina, just out of school, who helped design the delightful decor and would love to see the little hamlet come back to life. Try Graziella's authentic creations: **tortelli in stock** and **casoncelli**, the pasta for which includes pumpkin, when in season, the roast served with frittata and roast potatoes, and the local cheese expertly matured by Dario.

The wine list, worthy of a great enoteca, is compiled by Alessio, who offers a truly outstanding range of labels. Reservation essential.

TRUCAZZANO
Albignano

23 KM EAST OF MILAN

LE DUE COLONNE

📟 Trattoria
Largo Conte Anguissola 3
Tel. 02 9583025
Closed Monday
Open: lunch and dinner
Holidays: August 16-31
Seating: 60 + 40 outdoors
Prices: 30-35 euros, wine excluded
All credit cards, Bancomat

Albignano is near Trucazzano, about 20 kilometers from Milan in the direction of Rivolta d'Adda. The trattoria, which occupies the ground floor of an 18th-century palazzo looks onto an attractive courtyard. The current owners (Corrado Invernizzi, his wife Bianca and his sister-in-law Piera) are the latest members of the family which has been running the restaurant since 1956. In recent years they have focused on local produce, sourcing high quality raw materials, and greatly improving the wine list with the help of Alessandro Ridolfi, a knowledgeable wine waiter: they now offer 500 labels, and guests can order half bottles and wine served by the glass. In the kitchen, Piercarlo Testa and Eros Modolo create heartier fare during the winter and fresher, lighter offerings in the heat. The quality of the meat deserves a mention: fiorentina or succulent fillet steaks, roast shoulder or breast of veal, **braised donkey meat** or wild boar, served with some good **polenta**. Thursday is the day for a very popular **bollito misto**. For antipasto, an excellent selection of **cured meats** or, alternatively, parmigiana di carciofi , baked artichoke with cheese) and **stewed snails**. Then the ever-present **risotto** (**alla milanese**, with salami, with chestnuts or with creamy **Bagòss**), tagliatelle with wild boar, tagliolini with pesto and fava beans, and linguine with cabbage and sausage. At the end of the meal, a fine cheese board features Castelmagno, Caciocavallo podolico delle Murge, mature Söra and naturally-fermented Gorgonzola) and Bianca's homemade puddings: **chocolate salami**, **mattonella di Albignano** (with chocolate, walnuts and Barolo chinato), and pear and chocolate tart.

VERGIATE
Corgeno

18 KM SOUTHWEST OF VARESE

LA CINZIANELLA

🔑 3-Star Hotel
Via Lago 26
Tel. 0331 946337
Fax 0331 948890
E-mail: info@lacinzianella.it
Internet: www.lacinzianella.it
Closed in January

This quiet, relaxing hotel on the banks of Lake Comabbio is managed by the Gnocchi family. Rooms are spacious, comfortable and tastefully furnished, and all have terraces overlooking the lake. The more than ample breakfast comprises coffee, tea, milk, orange juice, cakes, bread, butter, jam, cured meats, eggs and cheese. The restaurant serves a set menu for 35 euros, excluding wine. Guests can windsurf and row on the lake, go horse riding in the nearby equestrian center or play on the Laghi golf course just ten kilometers away. Worth visiting is the parish church of San Giacomo in Comabbio or, in the Lake Maggiore direction, the monastery of Santa Caterina, Stresa, the Borromeo Islands and Cannero castles.

• 2 single, 6 double and 2 triple rooms, with bathroom, air conditioning, terrace, fridge, satellite TV; modem connection in the office • Prices: single 75 euros, double 100, triple 130, breakfast included • Credit cards: all, Bancomat • Facility accessible for the mobility challenged. Off-street parking. Very small pets allowed (10 euros per day). Owners always reachable. • Bar (for residents only), restaurant. TV room. Rooftop solarium.

VERGIATE
Cuirone

VEROLAVECCHIA
Monticelli d'Oglio

18 KM SOUTHWEST OF VARESE

30 KM SOUTHEAST OF BRESCIA

LA VITTORIOSA

LA ROSA ROSSA ⊘

☞Trattoria
Via Matteotti 1
Tel. 0331 946102
Closed Monday
Open: lunch, Friday and Saturday also for dinner
Holidays: August
Seating: 80
Prices: 20-25 euros, wine excluded
No credit cards

☞Trattoria
Frazione Monticelli d'Oglio 95
Tel. 030 931280
No closing day
Open: dinner, Friday and Saturday lunch
Holidays: a week in February
Seating: 100 + 100 outdoors
Prices: 20-30 euros, wine excluded
All credit cards except AE, Bancomat

The tiny hamlet of Cuirone, near Vergiate at the foot of Monte San Giacomo, is surrounded by woods, lakes and the rolling hills of the Ticino Park.
La Vittoriosa, simple but comfortable, is run by a cooperative and also operates a food store that sells cakes, fruit preserves, jams, dessert wines, cured meats and cheeses. The trattoria proper consists of a bar and a spacious dining room, where you will be welcomed by Maria Rosa and Pia Gerosa. The menu features both local specialties and a number of the chef's own creations, all carefully prepared using high quality ingredients.
To start off, superb **cured meats**, followed by seasonal vegetable flans and pies. First courses always include a **risotto**, with sausage, asparagus or mushrooms, **tortellini in stock** or ravioli with meat ragù. The chef's talent really shines through in the meat department with excellent **bollito misto**, **casoeula**, **bruscitt** served **with polenta**, **rustisciada**, when in season, and, in summer, veal in tuna sauce, at once delicate and full-flavored. Plus, roast or stuffed rabbit, with olives or asparagus, **roast shin of veal**, braised meat and, every Wednesday, cod, stewed or fried. To finish off, sample Maria Rosa's fragrant fruit or jam tarts.
To accompany the food the choice is between the very respectable house red or a quality bottle (the list contains around 80 labels, mostly from the north of Italy).
All in all, excellent value for money.

From Verolavecchia, follow the signs for Monticelli d'Oglio: about five kilometers further on, inside the Parco dell'Oglio, you'll find the old trattoria that partners Beppe Bonetti, Amedeo Guarneri and Pierluigi Permon have renovated. There are two spacious dining rooms, one of which is air-conditioned, with country-style furniture and straw-covered seats, and a large outdoor area that makes for pleasurable summer dining.
The meal starts with classic antipasti: salami, culatello di Zibello, lardo, seasonal vegetable frittata, and polentina with mushrooms and Gorgonzola. This traditional trattoria stands out for its handmade pasta dishes, prepared by mamma Maria and Sergio: **tortelli with herbs**, **casoncelli** with a meat filling, tagliatelle with pheasant, duck or rabbit sauce, **chestnut flour tagliolini al Bagòss** and mountain butter, and aubergine gnocchi. For main course, we sampled good **roast duck** and **baked rabbit** with polenta; alternatively, you can choose from beef tagliata or fillet steak, flash-fried lamb cutlet scottadito and, in winter, red and roe deer venison and wild boar served in a variety of ways. If you reserve it in advance, they'll also prepare you the **classic spiedo alla bresciana**, a spit of mixed meats, with **polenta di Castegnato** and in summer, **fried frogs' legs** or river minnows. To finish off, noteworthy among the homemade desserts are the nougat semifreddo, tarts, **chocolate salami**, hot zabaglione with biscuits and various bavaroises made with seasonal fruit. The wine list does justice to the food, as do the grappas, all from distinguished distilleries.

Vezza d'Oglio
Fontanacce

Viadana

LE FONTANACCE

DA BORTOLINO

🍲 Trattoria
Via Valeriana 49
Tel. 0364 76171
Closed Wednesday, no closing day in summer
Open: lunch and dinner
Holidays: two weeks in June
Seating: 100 + 20 outdoors
Prices: 22-27 euros, wine excluded
All credit cards, Bancomat

🍲 Recently-opened osteria
Via al Ponte 8
Tel. 0375 82640
Closed Thursday
Open: lunch and dinner
Holidays: December 27-January 4
Seating: 40 + 60 outdoors
Prices: 28-30 euros, wine excluded
All credit cards, Bancomat

This recently renovated trattoria is situated in the little valley down from Vezza d'Oglio, opposite a trout farm on the River Oglio. It is easy to get to, whether you are coming down from the center of Vezza or heading up from Edolo, and has a large car park, a children's play area and a paddock for horses – pony trekking is an attraction in summer. The trattoria is family-run: owner Umberto Rizzi receives customers and helps them choose from the menu, while his mother Beatrice and wife Cristina run the kitchen.

The food is simple but tasty and fragrant, without frills.

The antipasti include classic **cured** pork and game, served with excellent **rye bread** and **quiches** made with seasonal vegetables. First courses invariably include meat-filled **casoncelli** and **tortelli al bagòss** (a Slow Food Presidium cheese from the neighboring Caffaro Valley), plus **chestnut flour tagliatelle** with hazelnut or wine sauce, ricotta and nettle gnocchi, and risotto with sausage or mushrooms. For main course, char-grilled **trout**, jugged roe deer venison, char-grilled venison steak, a variety of poultry dishes, excellent **porcini mushrooms**, char-grilled or **with polenta**, and grilled mountain cheeses. Seasonal crudités or grilled vegetables are anointed with superb Lake Garda extra-virgin olive oil. **Wild berry tart** and almond or yoghurt cake round off the meal.

The wine cellar offers over 30 labels, mostly from Franciacorta or the PGI Valcamonica area. For digestif, locally made grappas and genepy.

Situated on the lower flood plain of the Po, which runs alongside the village of Viadana, near the bridgehead where the Stradivari motorboat is now moored, Da Bortolino has been open since 1891.

The old photographs and mementos on the walls show the history of the establishment, back in the days when there was no electricity, when the Po regularly broke its banks and when fishermen would stop off here for a frugal lunch. Since 1996 the place has been run by two young restaurateurs who have created a friendly country-style atmosphere inside and serve al fresco dinners in the shady garden in summer. The food revolves around the produce from this area on the border between Mantua and the Emilia region. Along with wines selected from a list of over 500 labels (the place also functions as an enoteca and serves snacks), you can sample a whole range of local produce and specialties.

To start with, traditional **cured meats**: culatello, spalla cotta, salami, gola, bondiola, and **donkey bresaola**. The first courses are excellent: **cappelletti** served in stock, both in winter and summer , according to local custom, **pumpkin tortelli**, **bigoli with duck**, delicious **tripe** – plus, in summer, maccheroni with cherry tomatoes and capers or mange-touts and pancetta. Main courses are hearty: **pork guancialino**, round of beef with piquant green sauce, roast shin of pork and **braised donkey meat**. The **cheese board** is good and features Parmigiano-Reggiano, served with **mostarda di Viadana**, and many other Italian cheeses.

From the assortment of homemade desserts, try the traditional **sbrisolona**, zuppa inglese, **sweet salami**, ricotta cake or the seasonal fruit tarts.

VIONE
Canè

CAVALLINO

Hotel restaurant
Via Trieste 57
Tel. 0364 94188
Closed Tuesday, but not at
Christmas, Easter and in summer
Open: lunch and dinner
Holidays: none
Seating: 80
Prices: 25-27 euros, wine excluded
All major credit cards, Bancomat

To get to the restaurant in Canè, a hamlet near the village of Vione, turn off the main highway to Ponte di Legno at Stadolina, just opposite the white peaks of the Adamello. This recently renovated restaurant features warm wooden interiors, the work of skilled local craftsmen, and exudes a warm welcome. Like many other typical Alpine village establishments, it doubles as an inn, bar and wine shop. It is family-run and the food reflects the traditions of the valley. Ernesta and Marilena are experts on the wild fruit and herbs which grow in the area and use them to prepare aromatic dishes.

For antipasto, you will be brought a wooden tray of traditional **cured meats**, roe deer paté, **formai parat** (melted cheese) and **smoked ricotta** with onion compôte and homemade mushrooms preserved in oil. Then come excellent **meat-filled calsù** (curious half-moon casoncelli), ravioli flavored with wild herbs, **bread gnocchi** with local cheese fondue and **barley soup**. Try the braised beef and, in season, the game – classic **jugged roe deer venison**, red deer venison chops flavored with juniper, served with chestnut and redcurrant jam – and the **mushrooms**, preserved in oil, sautéed, breaded or grilled. Also on the menu **polenta** made from stone-ground flour, and a cheese board with good goats' cheeses served with homemade mostarda. The cakes and **fruit tarts** are all casaline ('homemade', in the local dialect) and when, in season, wild berries are alo served.

The wine list is basic but with some good regional labels and some from neighboring Trentino. To round off your meal. spirits and liqueurs made from Alpine herbs.

VIONE
Stadolina

LISSIDINI

Recently opened osteria
Via Nazionale 13-15
Tel. 0364 906127
Closed Wednesday, but not at Christmas and in summer
Open: lunch and dinner
Holidays: June 10-24
Seating: 25 + 30 outdoors
Prices: 18-20 euros, wine excluded
All credit cards, Bancomat

Nothing flash from the outside, the osteria is still exactly how it looked when it first opened at the beginning of the last century. The dining room preserves the same decor and original carved wooden frames, and from October to May it is heated by a big ceramic stove which dates back to 1924. Coming here (leave the highway from Edolo to Ponte di Legno and turn right at the hamlet of Stadolina). is like going back in time. Fabio Ferrari has been running the place for around ten years now, with the precious help of companion Ramona. The food is traditional: there are few dishes on the menu but almost all of them are local specialties prepared using top quality ingredients.

The meal starts with an antipasto of **cured meats**, featuring traditionally-made salami, soppressa cruda with **guanciale** cut by hand as it used to be, and smoked beef with straw mushrooms and shavings of Grana. Then it's gnocchi with a mushroom filling, classic **calsù** (casoncelli), **gnocc de la cùa**, and risotto with truffle and Taleggio. The main courses are **braised donkey meat**, which was so delicious we asked for second helpings, fillet of veal al Teroldego, and, in fall and winter, venison chops with juniper, and braised **game**. To finish there is an excellent local cheese served grilled with **polenta taragna**. Chestnut crêpes with ice-cream or caramel and homemade biscuits round off the meal.

The wine list is not extensive but suitable for the cooking of the osteria. For a digestif, good traditional grappas and genepy.

VIRGILIO
Pietole

ZELO SURRIGONE

4 KM SOUTH OF MANTUA ON SP 413

21 KM SOUTHWEST OF MILAN SS 494

CORTE VIRGILIANA

Holiday farm
Via Virgiliana 13
Tel. 0376 448009 –328 4269237
Fax 0376 282483
E-mail: info@cortevirgiliana.it
Internet: www.cortevirgiliana.it
Open all year

ANTICA TRATTORIA DI SAN GALDINO

Trattoria
Via Vittorio Emanuele 18
Tel. 02 9440434
Closed Sunday evenings and Thursday
Open: lunch and dinner
Holidays: in August and one week at Christmas
Seating: 80
Prices: 25-30 euros, wine excluded
All credit cards except AE, Bancomat

This noble old farmhouse is located inside the Parco del Mincio, specifically in an area called Pietole, where the Roman poet Virgil was born. It is part of a vast agricultural estate which grows grain and breeds animals. Rooms are elegant, spacious with antique furniture. Guests can enjoy breakfast in the comfort of their own room: the fridge is stocked with jams, butter and yogurt produced on the farm, while freshly baked bread and milk from the farm's catttle is delivered every morning. Not to be missed, inside the Parco del Mincio, is the Vallazza Nature Reserve, which can also be reached by boat from Mantua. Otherwise, guests can explore the Mantuan countryside on foot, by bicycle or on horseback.

1 studio and 5 two-room apartments, with bathroom, use of kitchen, fridge • Prices: double room single occupancy 50 euros, double 80, triple 100, 4-bed 110, breakfast included • Credit cards: none • Entire facility accessible for the mobility challenged, 1 room designed for their use. Off-street parking. Small pets allowed. Owners always reachable. • Garden, playground, 5-a-side soccer pitch.

The little village of Zelo Surrigone lies between Milan and Abbiategrasso in an area typical of the Bassa Milanese, where the Naviglio Grande irrigates the rice fields. This traditional, family-run trattoria has been open since the beginning of the 1920s.

The grandmother of current owner Giovanni Marmondi started up the establishment, which used to be a bar, trattoria and butcher's shop. The latter was subsequently closed, though Giovanni keeps the tradition going, buying pigs from a farm in the nearby village of Ozzero and producing excellent cotechino and blood sausages. In the style of the old trattorias of the area, the place is plain but inviting, with a large garden that is used in spring. The owner and his wife Gianna work front of house, while in the kitchen their son Paolo prepares the local specialties.

The meal starts off with excellent, traditional **cured meats**, accompanied by **nervetti** (veal cartilage), pickled vegetables and Russian salad, plus, in winter, Giovanni's **cotechino** and **blood sausage**. Then come tempting **risottos**, meat-filled **ravioli** tossed **in melted butter**, excellent lasagne and, in winter, **polenta with casoeula**, a typical Milanese dish made of pork and cabbage. Main courses feature more polenta, served with braised meats, **breaded veal cutlets**, **tripe** and, in summer, char-grilled meat. Worth a taste too is the sumptuous Gorgonzola, especially the natural version available in winter. You can finish off with homemade fruit tarts, apple pie or tiramisù with coffee, or in summer, with fruit. The wine list – 20 or so carefully selected labels from the nearby Oltrepò area – is simple with reasonable mark-ups.

TRENTINO

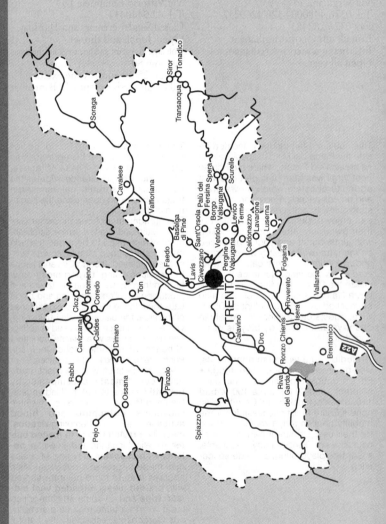

BASELGA DI PINÉ

18 KM NORTHEAST OF TRENTO

DUE CAMINI

Restaurant/3-Star hotel
Via XXVI Maggio 65
Tel. 0461 557200
Fax 0461 558833
E-mail: info@albergo2camini.com
Internet: www.albergo2camini.com
Closed Sunday evening and Monday, never during high season
Open: lunch and dinner
Holidays: 2 weeks in November, 1 week before Easter
Seating: 70
Prices: 28-30 euros
All credit cards, Bancomat

This place has all the charm of a typical mountain dwelling, including an impressive fireplace in the hall. Everything about the Due Camini is homey, comfortable and simple. The rooms, open all week, are mansard-roofed and fitted entirely with wood furnishings.
The menu here is seasonal and offers traditional Trentino dishes. Begin with **cured meats**, vegetables preserved in oil and **mushrooms** – fresh or preserved in vinegar or oil or cooked in a variety of ways. The most representative dish from the area, **rufioi** – ravioloni with savoy cabbage and cheese – is prepared according to an old traditional recipe. There are also three fresh pastas available: taglierini, tagliatelle, pappardelle with mushrooms, vegetables and sometimes even local truffles. You can then choose from **rabbit roulade**, venison filet, goulash, **ossobuco**, and **carne salada**, not to mention **polenta**, vegetable soup and mushrooms. There's a host of local **cheeses** to finish off your meal and excellent puddings like chocolate cake, **strudel**, semifreddo and different variations of bonet, a Piedmontese specialty that Mamma Lucia has brought here from her home town. The wine list is plentiful and offers great variety, and the wines can also be tasted by the glass.

• 10 double rooms with bath, TV • Prices: double room single use 45-56, double 80-90 euros, breakfast included • Restaurant dining room accessible to the mobility challenged. Uncovered internal and external parking reserved for guests. Small pets welcome. Owners present until midnight • Restaurant. TV room. Garden

BORGO VALSUGANA
Sella

40 KM SOUTHEAST OF TRENTO ON SS 47

LEGNO

Osteria
Località Valle di Sella 16
Tel. 0461 761084
Closed Monday and Tuesday, never in high season
Open: lunch and dinner, winter dinner only
Holidays: January
Seating: 40 + 20 outdoors
Prices: 25 euros, wine excluded
All major credit cards

Valle Sella, the valley of art. Arte Sella is an association that transforms the territory's natural features into artistic events, promoting new cultural happenings every year: performances by artists, shows, guided tours among the numerous works on display in the woods, the now famous 'vegetable cathedral' and many other structures made out of branches, trunks and bark. While this tiny high mountain valley above Borgo Valsugana exhibits its art, Michele Pasquazzo continues to serve traditional mountain cuisine in his rustic osteria, thus adding to the fascination of the place. You won't find any elaborate dishes here: everything is kept simple, tasty, made with prime raw ingredients and reasonably priced. The aim is to capture a young public curious to discover both local art and local cuisine.
To start with, a wide variety of cured meats and cheeses from local producers and then the dish that's the emblem of the area: hand-made wholemeal pasta with mountain potatoes, cabbage and malga cheese. To follow, traditional **strangolapreti**, tagliatelle with sausage and chicory, vegetable minestrone and ravioloni alle erbe with a melted butter sauce. For the main course, **carne salada**, but also **puntine di maiale with sauerkraut**, lamb and pork fillet and, when in season, **cep mushrooms** gathered in the surrounding woods in which politician Alcide De Gasperi used to walk. To finish, home-made desserts: chocolate or woodland fruit cake, panna cotta with blueberries, **apple strudel** and home-baked biscuits.
The decent wine list also includes a good selection of liqueurs.

BRENTONICO

San Giacomo

BRENTONICO

BRENTONICO

45 KM SOUTH OF TRENTO, 23 KM FROM ROVERETO

45 KM SOUTH OF TRENTO, 20 KM FROM ROVERETO

MAS DEI GIRARDEI

MASO PALÙ

🗝️ Bed and breakfast
Via Peneze 4
Tel. 0464 391541-347 2208315
Fax 0464 391541
E-mail: eliogirardelli@virgilio.it
Closed for two weeks in November

🍲 Trattoria
Località Palù
Tel. 0464 395014
Closed Tuesday, except in August
Open: dinner, Friday, Saturday, Sunday also lunch
Holidays: June
Seating: 90 + 20 outdoors
Prices: 30 euros, wine excluded
Credit cards: Visa, Bancomat

Elio Girardelli had been in the restaurant business for years before deciding to retire to the old family farmhouse, lovingly refurbished over many years of hard work. Now he's pleased to welcome you to his beautiful, secluded house in the woods overlooking Vallagarina. This mountain retreat made of wood and stone is meticulously equipped to guarantee peace and quiet and make you feel in touch with nature. It's a strategic base for people keen to exercise – cycling and on or off-slope skiing are available – but it's also ideal for those who just want to 'pull the plug' on their jobs for a few days and enjoy the relaxing atmosphere of Brentonico and the botanical gardens of Mount Baldo. There is no charge for children up to the age of 3 and those aged between 4 and 10 pay half the already reasonable price, which includes breakfast, (sweet or savory, it consists of top quality local products). For their other meals guests can eat at either the Maso Palù di Brentonico trattoria run by Eliana Amadori Girardelli (30 euros per person, excluding wine) or the San Giacomo Hotel (25 euros per person, excluding wine).

• 2 double or triple and 1 four-bed rooms, with bathroom • Prices: double room single use 25 euros, double 50, triple 70, four-bed 90, breakfast included • Credit cards: none • Internal open parking area. Small pets allowed. Owners always present • Restaurant. Breakfast room, lounge. Garden

A fixed menu and huge portions for everyone, a well-organized sequence and rhythms tried and tested over the years ... always the same, some might say, but always inviting. Only come up here when you've got a really big appetite!. Maso Palù was – and still is – one of the prime movers in the revival of Brentonico's typical plateau gastronomy, now fueled by typical eateries, holiday farms, bed & breakfasts, dairies and wine bars. Emiliana Amadori, an indefatigable cook who prepares a consolidated menu of gastronomic delights, is assisted by her two children, Camilla and Tobia.

There's always the same succulent, long succession of dishes, at least a dozen of them served on rustic tables in a cordial Alpine atmosphere, accompanied by as much of the house wine as you can drink (in our opinion, a more meditated selection wouldn't be amiss...). For starters, cornmeal **polenta** prepared in many ways, fresh hand-made pasta, bread gnocchi with mountain cheese, various vegetable soups, **orzotto** and tagliatelle. Main courses, **shin of veal with sauerkraut** and, in the right period, **game** (the venison is a must). There are always **wild mushrooms** and herbs – Monte Baldo is an immense botanical garden with unique, rare species – in combination with cheeses from nearby farms or vegetables and **trout** from the valleys. Home-made desserts: freshly made ice cream every day, served when in season with warm woodland fruit, and **apple strudel**.

To finish, very reasonably priced liqueurs and spirits. Given the location and periods, when open you must book in advance.

CALAVINO
Lagolo

FLORIANI

▯ Restaurant/3-Star hotel
Via al Lago 2
Tel. and fax 0461 564241
E-mail: albergo.floriani@tin.it
Internet: www.albergofloriani.it
Closed Tuesday, never during high season
Open: lunch and dinner
Holidays: November
Seating: 60
Prices: 25-30 euros, wine excluded
All credit cards, Bancomat

You'll find this tiny hotel-restaurant, run by Domenica and Stefano, on the shores of Lake Toblino. The rooms, partly mansarded, are available all week. Each is furnished in wood and named for an Alpine plant. In the restaurant, the tables are tended to with the greatest attention to detail.
Suggested dishes: terrine of goat's cheese or vegetable flan with smoked ricotta, savory herb pie with Vezzena, **trout marinated** in juniper with butter and wild herbs, and veal meatballs with mushrooms in wine sauce. Home-made pastas include **tagliatelle** with seasonal sauces and ravioloni with cheese or **lake fish**. Plus **game with polenta**, venison with cherry grappa and rabbit prepared any number of ways. Particularly notable are dishes featuring **mushrooms** in season, gathered just under the beech trees in front of the house. Puddings include **strudel**, mousse, white chocolate with mango and crostatas made with fresh fruit accompanied by artisan ice-cream. Wines here are excellent with reasonable mark-ups; most of the options are from Trentino.

• 18 double rooms with bath, safe and TV • Prices: double room single use 38-56, double 56-92 euros, breakfast included • Accessible to mobility challenged, 1 room furnished for their use. External parking reserved for guests. Small animals welcome (not permitted in communal spaces). Owners always present • Bar, restaurant. TV room. Terrace. Beach

CALDES
San Giacomo

SOLASNA

Holiday farm
Località San Giacomo 4
Tel. 0463 902073-338 5964846
Fax 0463 902124
E-mail: info@agritursolasna.it
Internet: www.agritursolasna.it
Open all year round

Managed by the Andreis family, this was one of the first agriturismos to open in the Trentino region. The farm has a stable and also raises poultry; its apple trees yield the prized Val di Non golden variety, and other fruit and vegetables are also produced, not to mention honey. The farm is outside the village in a quiet area, well exposed to the sunshine. The restaurant on the ground floor offers dishes from the local cuisine: canederli, strangolapreti and local cured meats. Half board ranges from 30-45 euros per person. The top floor is divided into comfortable rooms, all with en-suite bathrooms. Breakfast is all home-made: yogurt, jams, fresh fruit, cakes and sometimes home-baked. There are many things to do in the surrounding area, including mountain bike outings, excursions in the Stelvio Park, and summer and winter skiing on the Passo del Tonale slopes.

• 4 double rooms, with bathroom, fridge, TV; 2 apartments (4-6 persons) with kitchenette • Prices: double room single use 30 euros, double 60, apartment 30 euros per person, breakfast included • Credit cards: all, Bancomat • Facility accessible for the mobility challenged, 1 room designed for their use. Small pets allowed. Owners always reachable • Restaurant. Garden

CALDONAZZO

AQUILA D'ORO

🛏️2-Star Hotel
Via Roma 13
Tel. 0461 723116
Tel. 0461 723162
E-mail: info@albergoaquiladoro.it
Internet: www.albergoaquiladoro.it
Open all year round

This hotel is located in a small alley in the old town center and has a large private courtyard. It was founded 150 years ago and still has an early 1900s feel to it, though today it is managed with a pleasantly deft touch by a young couple, Ida and Carlo Pondero. She is from the Abruzzo region and takes care of service in the restaurant, while Carlo from Friuli runs the kitchen. Guests will find a series of soberly furnished, vaguely retrò but comfortable and quiet rooms, the real charm of which is their unpretentiousness. Breakfast, which on request can also include savory fare, consists of bread, croissants and small homemade pastries. Restaurant cuisine is dominated by seafood. This is precisely why people come here: to enjoy well-prepared, tasty fish dishes served in a friendly atmosphere. There's also a short, but carefully chosen wine list.

• 6 single and 8 double rooms, with bathroom, TV • Prices: single 30 euros, double 50-60, breakfast included • Credit cards: all, Bancomat • Facility accessible for the mobility challenged. Internal parking and, nearby, external parking. Small pets allowed. Owners always present. • Bar, restaurant. TV room, reading room. Outdoor area

CARANO

MASO EL GIATA

🛏️Holiday farm
Località Aguai 3
Tel. 0462 231456-339 1202691
E-mail: info@masoelgiata.it
Internet: www.masoelgiata.it
Closed in November

Secluded, attractive, relaxing and perfectly refurbished. A characteristic farmhouse dating from 1842, built entirely in stone and wood, located on the border between Trentino and Alto Adige, close to the San Lugano Pass and just below the road between Carano and Cavalese in the Dolomites. While this is classified as a holiday farm, for an additional charge it also has a small but modern spa offering a sauna, and cold fog and special showers. The soundproofed rooms are furnished mountain-style. There are fields and woods round about for walks or cycle tours. Andreina Degiampietro manages operations and prepares breakfast that consists of yoghurt, cakes, small homemade pastries, cured meats and local cheeses – a must – but also organic products, herbal teas and body-cleansing beverages.

• 5 double rooms, with bathroom • Prices: double room single use 80 euros, double 120, breakfast included • Credit cards: none • Facility accessible for the disabled, 1 room designed for their use. Off-street parking. No pets allowed. Owners always present • Breakfast room. TV room, lounge. Garden, solarium. Gym, spa

CAVALESE

CAVALESE

53 KM NORTHEAST OF TRENTO SS 48

53 KM NORTHEAST OF TRENTO

COSTA SALICI

Restaurant
Via Costa dei Salici 10
Tel. 0462 340140
Closed Monday and Tuesday at lunch
Open: lunch and dinner
Holidays: October
Seating: 35 + 25 outdoors
Prices: 28-35 euros, wine excluded
All credit cards

LAURINO

3-Star Hotel
Via Antoniazzi 14
Tel. e fax 0462 340151
E-mail: info@hotelgarnilaurino.it
Internet: www.hotelgarnilaurino.it
Closed for ten days in May

Traditional Val di Fiemme cuisine at very affordable prices, with a good variety of dishes and even some titillating surprises. Maurizio Tait, his wife Rosalba and young son Stefano are persisting with the osteria formula, changing the sequence of dishes to follow the seasons in this all-wood restaurant among the trees on the outskirts of Cavalese.
A few examples: delicious **cep mushroom flan** with Lake Garda extra-virgin olive oil, an appetizing antipasto, **tortelli di formaggio di malga** with finferli mushroom cream, and **tonco de pontesél**, a typical Trentino dish similar to goulash, with sausage, polenta and tomato sauce. Round this off with cheese ice-cream with pears and cooked must, plus a shot of the elderberry liqueur Maurizio prepares following the very old recipes of high-altitude farmsteads. Then come **frittelle di formaggio puzzone** with cabbage salad and speck or **smoked suckling pig** with shavings of Trentino Grana cheese. If you wish to choose more elaborate dishes from the menu, there's venison tartar with toasted pine nuts, mint and apple praline or diced venison cooked in an infusion of hay. You can eat in the cozy wooden stuben or in the garden where your food is cooked right in front of the table on a large porphyry stone barbecue. To round off the meal, a large selection of local **cheeses**, not only from Val di Fiemme, and desserts: chocolate terrine, **pear strudel** and ice cream with cinnamon.
The good selection of wines and spirits contains many well chosen labels.

The Chelodi family's hotel is in a 17th-century building in the old part of Cavalese. The paintwork is immaculate and the place is surrounded by courtyards and shady green spaces. There is also a playground for children. The rooms, on three floors of the central part of the palazzo and corner tower, have either modern or traditional Tyrolean furnishings. The attic suites are particularly well designed and include a small living room. Breakfast mainly focuses on organic products, cakes and homemade breads. The reading room is a typical stube, with wood-lined floor, walls and ceiling, and comfortable sofas where guests can relax. The apartment, located in another building, has a fully equipped kitchen.

• 12 double rooms and 2 suites, with bathroom, fridge, safe, TV; some rooms with balcony; 1 apartment (2-5 persons) with kitchen • Prices: double room single occupancy 45-60 euros, double 76-90, suite 96, breakfast included; apartment 48 euros per person • Credit cards: all except DC, Bancomat • Common areas accessible to the mobility challenged, 2 rooms designed for their use. Off-street parking. Small pets allowed. Owners always present • Breakfast room, reading and TV room. Garden with children's playground

CAVIZZANA

LOCANDA SAN MARTINO

🍲Trattoria with rooms
Località Cavizzana 30 and 31
Tel. 0463 900222
Closed Monday
Open: dinner, also for lunch on Sunday
Holidays: none
Seating: 50 + 20 outdoors
Prices: 22-23 euros
All major credit cards, Bancomat

You'll find the building, all stone and wood, on the right bank of the Noce, in an isolated location well exposed to the sunshine. On the second floor, there are six sizable rooms (available all week long by reservation), four of which can hold additional beds for children. Breakfast is generous and brings you sweet items and cured meats, all home-made. This place, in fact, is also a farm that produces goat's and cow's milk cheeses, smoked meats and vegetables. The menu they offer is a set one, but varies widely and according to season. You'll be able to try a host of different **cured meats** and excellent freshly made pasta, such as **gnocchi**, lasagne with chicory and ravioli with spicy cheese. Follow this up with delectable meat dishes made from animals raised on the farm, including **rabbit with polenta**, pork lombatina, **beef braised in wine** and sometimes even just-made **cotechini**. Don't miss out on the freshwater fish: fried trout, for instance, or **trout marinated in raspberry vinegar**. For puddings, try anything made with fruit, although the semifreddo, chocolate cake and **apple strudel** (made from either golden delicious or reinette apples) are highly recommended as well.
There is a serviceable selection of wines and spirits here.

🗝• 2 double and 2 triple rooms with bath • Prices: double room single use 30, double 44-50, triple 66-75 euros; breakfast 3 euros per person• Accessible to mobility challenged, 1 room furnished for their use. External parking reserved for guests. Small pets welcome. Owners always present. • Restaurant. Garden, terrace

CIVEZZANO

LOREDANA

🗝Bed and breakfast
Frazione Bosco 57
Tel. 0461 851019-339 5737505
Fax 0461 851019
E-mail: 3394406707@tin.it
Closed from Epiphany until beginning of February

Once you leave the main Valsugana highway, traveling from Trento in the direction of Venice, take the road leading up towards the hills of Divezzano. Here Loredana Coser has restored her attractive 18th-century house to make it one of the most pleasant B&Bs in the Trentino region. The hilly location in Bosco di Civezzano provides a lovely view of the Valsugana and the temperature in summer is ideal, far-removed from the oppressively clammy heat in the valley below. The comfortable, airy rooms are furnished with family furniture dating from the early 1900s. The common kitchen may be used 'within reason'. Breakfast is very filling: bread, cakes, jams made with small fruits and herbal teas, but also good cured meats and cheeses. In addition to other common rooms, there is a small library.

• 1 single room with separate bathroom, 2 double rooms with bathroom en suite • Prices: single 30 euros, double room single use 30, double 60, breakfast included • Credit cards: none • Off-street parking. Small pets allowed. Owners always present. • Breakfast, reading and music room. Garden, terrace, solarium

CIVEZZANO
Forte

COREDO
Tavon

7 KM NORTHEAST OF TRENTO ON SS 47

39 KM NORTH OF TRENTO

MASO CANTANGHEL

🍲 Trattoria
Via della Madonnina 33
Tel. 0461 858714
Closed Saturday and Sunday
Open: lunch and dinner
Holidays: in August and Christmas
Seating: 30
Prices: 33 euros, wine excluded
All credit cards, Bancomat

PINETA

🍲 Restaurant/3-Star hotel
Via al Santuario 17
Tel. 0463 536866
Fax 0463 536115
E-mail: info@pinetahotels.it
Internet: www.pinetahotels.it
Closed Wednesday, never in summer
Open: lunch and dinner
Holidays: November
Seating: 50
Prices: 28 euros, wine excluded
All credit cards, Bancomat

A splendid farmstead just a few kilometers from Trento, managed since 1981 by Lucia Gius whose mother taught her traditional Trentino recipes from childhood and those she continues to offer with her own personal touch. Two small, cozy rooms and a kitchen where guests can see exactly how everything is prepared. As the place is so small, you clearly have to book in advance. The unpretentious local dishes possess that added something thanks to Lucia's extraordinary skill and are served in an ambience where care has been taken over every last detail, from the furnishings to linen tablecloths. The menu is fixed, although it changes daily, depending on what's available in the vegetable garden or the market and on local farms.
We had **carne salada**, a warm antipasto with **trout** and a delicate flan baked leeks and zucchini from the vegetable patch. Then homemade **gnocchi** with chard and hand-rolled **tagliatelle** with **vegetable sauce**: the shape of the homemade pasta is always changing and is very fresh indeed. For our main course we had **roast pork** and braised beef, with a mixed salad and braised vegetables. In other periods there are stuffed zucchini flowers, Savoy or regular cabbage flan, tasty Trentino sausages, **risottos** with asparagus or finferli mushrooms, **rabbit with polenta**, **roast guinea-fowl** with potatoes and cabbage. The cheese board always offers a wide selection of **local cheeses**, some of which homemade, then there's **hazelnut ice-cream** and, with coffee, a small selection of pastries prepared fresh every day.
The wine list offers an intelligent choice of Trentino labels – the region's best – plus other Italian and international varieties.

This hotel, hidden away in the woods, offers a wellness center, with saunas, as well as an open-air amphitheater and three wooden cottages. Room rates reach 132 euros at the peak of high season in mid-August.
The old osteria serves up traditional dishes of the region, prepared according to recipes passed down through generations of the Sicher family. The menu is seasonal and the one featuring beef (from cattle raised by the family) includes antipasti of steamed beef with onions and apple cider vinegar, **canederli with goulash** and sirloin with onions. The menu almost always features **potato pie**, barley soup, **orzotto al Teroldego**, **carne salada**, various roasts, **baccalà alla trentina** (in the cold months) and a selection of cheeses from the Val di Non area. The delicious home-made desserts include **apple strudel** and cakes of wild berries. The cellar is open for a visit and is well stocked.
The hotel is open all week and offers half board for a double room for 59-82 euros per person.

🛏️ • 9 single and 20 double rooms with bath, TV • Prices: single 43-66, double 85-78 euros, breakfast included • Accessible to the mobility challenged, 3 rooms furnished for their use. External parking reserved for guests, garage (3 euros per day). Small animals welcome. Reception open from 7:30 am to 10 pm • Bar, restaurant. Reading and TV rooms. Garden. Multi-purpose gym, wellness center with sauna, Turkish bath and indoor pool

DIMARO

KAISERKRONE

🔑🗝3-Star Hotel
Piazza Serra 3
Tel. 0463 973326
Fax 0463 973016
E-mail: info@kaiserkrone.it
Internet: www.kaiserkrone.it
Closed for ten days in May

The crown referred to in the name of this hotel is that of Emperor Franz Joseph, undoubtedly the establishment's most distinguished guest. The hotel is a characteristic three-floor building located in the center of the village: the windows on the facade are arranged in a geometric pattern and capped by a sloping roof. The rooms are all spacious, with a generous use of light-colored wood, and occupy the attic and part of the third floor. On the first floor is the elegant coffee room embellished by marble floors, inlays and a majolica fireplace. This is where the very generous buffet breakfast is served. The hotel has an agreement with a few restaurants in the area guests who wish to opt for the half board option. On request, gastronomic tours can be organized in the environs.

• 7 suites, with bathroom, fridge, satellite TV • Prices: suite with single use 40-65 euros, suite 60-110, breakfast included • Credit cards: all except DC, Bancomat • Facility accessible to the mobility challenged, 1 room designed for their use. Free garage parking. Small pets allowed. Reception open from 7 am to 2 am • Coffee room

DRO

MASO LIZZONE

🔑🗝Holiday farm
Località Maso Lizzone
Tel. 0464 504793-333 5232846
Fax 0464 504793
E-mail: info@masolizzone.com
Internet: www.masolizzone.com
Closed from 10/11 until 01/03

This attractive farmhouse in Basso Sarca, just a few kilometers from Arco and Lake Garda, is one of the nicest agriturismos in the Trentino. It's a place with a magical air about it: quiet and breezy, surrounded by olive trees and herbs. The building retains all its original rural charm. Weather permitting, breakfast is served outside in the fresh air. Worth mentioning among the common facilities are the fully equipped kitchen, though every room also has its own kitchenette, including cooker and fridge (the dishwasher is shared). A small, fully furnished apartment s also available for let. The farm lies in grounds with secular trees, surrounded by vines and olive trees (the farm's oil and wine are on sale). People with campers or tents can also make short stays in one of the seven small spaces marked out along walls around this farmhouse.

• 5 double rooms and 1 apartment, with bathroom • Prices: double room single use 45-55 euros, double 68-88, breakfast included; apartment 72-90 euros (minimum 3 nights) • Credit cards: all except DC, Bancomat • Facility accessible for the mobility challenged, 2 rooms designed for their use. Off-street parking. Small pets allowed (only in the apartment). Owners always reachable • Fully equipped kitchen. Breakfast room, reading room. Grounds, pool

FAEDO

AI MOLINI

🍲 Holiday farm
Località Molini 6 and 8
Tel. 0461 650817, 0461 651088 or 347 2371577
Internet: www.comune-faedo.it/agriturmolini
Closed Monday and Tuesday
Open: lunch and dinner
Holidays: during grape harvest
Seating: 35
Prices: 18-20 euros, wine excluded
Credit cards: CartaSi, Bancomat

This agriturismo offers traditional comforts and breakfasts of Rabelaisian proportions: you'll be offered apple pies and homemade cookies, fresh fruit or preserves, yogurt, honey and eggs from the nearby coop. Lunch brings a somewhat lighter menu, with **carne salada**, **orzotto** with chicory, hand-rolled pasta with vegetables (asparagus in spring), **polenta and rabbit** and roasts, followed by **apple strudel** and **crostatas** made with fruit preserves. In the evening, the must-try dish is **tortèl de patate** – chips of the tubers roasted in lardo – with carne salada, beans and vegetables from the garden. Choose from first courses like **strangolapreti**, gnocchi made with potatoes or herbs, **pork with sauerkraut** or mushrooms and roasted cabbage. You'll often find **game** here, particularly in winter. Many of the cheeses as well as the cured meats are made by shepherds in the mountains. Conclude your meal with berries and one of the tempting desserts: fresh fruit tarts, tiramisù and panna cotta.
Often the owner will treat you to a drink of his own wine, made from the grapes that surround the place, at the beginning of the meal. Choose also from all the wines made in Faedo and others from the nearby Piana Rotaliana. The locanda does not accept credit cards.

🛏🔌 • 5 double rooms with bath, TV • Prices: double room single use 22, double 44 euros, breakfast included • Accessible to the mobility challenged, 1 room furnished for their use. Uncovered internal parking, garage (for motorcycles). No pets allowed. Owners always reachable • Restaurant. Breakfast room. Garden

ISERA

LOCANDA DELLE TRE CHIAVI   🍲🚫📱

🍲 Trattoria
Via Vannetti 8
Tel. 0464 423721
Closed Sunday evening and Monday
Open: lunch and dinner
Holidays: 2nd week in January, first two in July
Seating: 80 + 80 outside
Prices: 33-35 euros, wine excluded
All credit cards

Sergio Valentini has turned this trattoria into a sort of taste workshop, choosing local farmers' produce, encouraging initiatives to promote biodiversity, proposing Slow Food Presidia, not only from Trentino but also from outside Italy. He's enlarged the place, making it more attractive and placing greater emphasis on the cuisine and wine and **cheese** selections. Every dish highlights the uniqueness of Trentino's farming and food production. From **tortèl de patate** con Puzzone di Moena to a platter with lucanica, **mortandela**, smoked horsemeat, speck, carne salada and lardo from a butcher in Trambileno, a village in the nearby Vallarsa. Alternatively, **marinated trout** or melted cheese with **polenta di Storo**. Then **strangolapreti** with Asiago cheese fondue, **potato gnocchi and fresh lucanica**, ravioloni with saffron-flavored farmhouse butter or **spelt-flour pappardelle with pike sauce**. Main courses, **braised beef al Marzemino with polenta**, pork filet with speck in chamomile-flavored pastry and vegetable millefeuille, **carne salada with beans**. To finish, **apple or cherry strudel**, cinnamon ice-cream, buckwheat cake with redcurrants, strawberry tiramisu, pear and walnut zuccotto with Trentino Vino Santo. Tasty dishes carefully prepared by Annarita, Emanuele and Nora, who are bent on relaunching this trattoria, which is always ready to host meetings, wine tastings – the wine list is well thought out with numerous labels available by the glass – and other pleasant opportunities to get together. Recommended by the Italian Celiac Disease Association, on request the trattoria serves gluten-free dishes.

LAVARONE
Azzolini

RUZ

🍲 Osteria-wine cellar
Località Azzolini 1
Tel. 0464 783821
Closed Thursday, never in high season
Open: lunch and dinner
Holidays: 2 weeks in October
Seating: 35
Prices: 18-20 euros, wine excluded
No credit cards, Bancomat

Don't expect a wide selection or elaborate dishes. This is a village osteria where people drop in for a chat and to sip a glass of wine poured by host, Franco Bertoldi, sommelier and ski instructor. It's in front of the tiny honey museum near the road that links a number of hamlets in the area, in a field where in winter you can learn to ski – with Franco to teach you, of course!
Wife Laura and daughter Raffaella take care of the flavorsome, unpretentious cooking. After a taste of the local cheeses and cured meats – lucanica, speck, coppa – onion soup, **canederli with cheese**, tagliatelle with rabbit sauce, pork with mushrooms. Then come **brasato al Teroldego**, roast pork, game, **polenta** (made with **potato**, Lavarone-style, only in certain periods during winter, and only on request). Various types of cheese from the plateau of Vezzene, mainly from the nearby Cappella dairy, are accompanied by a wonderful selection of honeys. The meals ends with omelets with home-made jam and delicious apricot tarts.
The wines and liqueurs are ideal for quaffing after summer outings on mountain bikes or at the end of a day's skiing (the annual Millegrobbe, a classic cross-country race, is run in legs over a mountain circuit). All are priced reasonably.

🍯 A few meters from the osteria, Casa del Miele sells mountain honey and other beehive products. At **Cappella**, a hamlet near Lavarone, the Cheesemakers Cooperative is the only place you can buy authentic Vezzena cheese.

LAVIS
Sorni

VECCHIA SORNI

🍲 Trattoria
Piazza Assunta 40
Tel. 0461 870541
Closed Sunday evening and Monday
Open: lunch and dinner
Holidays: 3 weeks in January-February
Seating: 20 + 20 outdoors
Prices: 30 euros, wine excluded
All credit cards except AE, Bancomat

Sorni white or Sorni red? The question refers to the Trentino DOC wine, the smallest label in all the entire Dolomites. Because the grapes (nosiola, chardonnay and pinot bianco for the white, schiava, teroldego and lagrein for the red) mature on the Lavis hills, in Sorni, founded by the Schorns, a noble Tyrolean family, on steep rows of vines cultivated garden-style. In the old village, among the courtyards, you'll find this tiny, squeaky-clean trattoria run by Maria Teresa. Although her son Lorenzo Callegari learned to cook abroad, here he serves impeccably cooked traditional dishes.
The rich menu varies with the seasons. In spring, asparagus grown along the banks of the River Adige and wild herbs; in the fall, mushrooms, chestnuts and grapes. First courses include incomparable **canederli** with ricotta cheese and potato **gnocchi served with speck** or local cured meats. Then come a tasty **cep mushroom strudel** with cheese and potatoes, eggplant roulade stuffed with vegetables, creamed potatoes cooked in the oven. Normally the boned, dressed rabbit is served wrapped in herbs; there are also calf's cheek in wine, char and the traditional **groestl,** roast potatoes with beef and onions. For dessert, raspberry cake, a bowl of seasonal fruit with homemade yogurt or ice-cream, **fruit pie** and terrines.
To accompany the dishes, white Sorni or one of the many other reasonably priced wines on the list. On warm days you can eat on the terrace, a magnificent balcony overlooking the Adige valley and the vineyards that yield the Trentino region's best wines.

LEVICO TERME

BOIVIN – ROMANDA 🍷

◁▷ Traditional osteria-wine shop/3-Star hotel
Via Garibaldi 7-9
Tel. 0461 701670 or 0461 707122
Fax 0431 701710
E-mail: info@hotelromanda.it
Internet: www.hotelromanda.it
Closed Monday, never in summer
Open: dinner, also for lunch on Sunday
Holidays: vary
Seating: 50
Prices: 26-28 euros
All major credit cards, Bancomat

Rooms in the Romanda hotel are decorated with colorful tapestries and fabrics and look as if they're straight out of the 1500s. The Boivin restaurant is housed in the same building and overseen by the same management (the Bosco family). The food here varies with the seasons, with wild herbs at the beginning of spring (potato ravioloni con silene, **bread gnocchi with nettle sauce**), followed by cherries and other small fruit (cold black cherry soup with **ricotta canederlotti**), then **mushrooms** and products made by mountain shepherds, and apples and chestnuts in dishes like tortelli with golden apples and **chestnut soup** feature at the end of the year. The kitchen highlights the Ischian origins of both the resident signora and nonna in dishes like **strangolapreti** flavored with onions and cinnamon and mortandela from the Valsugana, filled with lardo and offal and markedly different from the Val di Non version. These are served alongside dishes of Gragnano pasta and puddings of southern Italian origin. There are also carrot cake, **apple strudel** and seasonal desserts.
Wines from here are quite good, but labels from outside the region are also available.

⚷ ● 3 single, 37 double rooms with bath, satellite TV ● Prices: single 42-55, double 66-90 euros, breakfast included● Uncovered internal parking. Small pets welcome. Reception open from 6am to 1am ● Bar, restaurant. TV room. Garden

LUSERNA

LUSERNARHOF

⚷● 2-Star Hotel
Via Tezze 43
Tel. 0464 788010
Fax 0464 788235
E-mail: info@lusernarhof.it
Internet: www.lusernarhof.it
Always open during high season, by reservation for rest of the year

You'll be surprised by the peculiar dialect the locals speak. Their ancestors were ancient Cimbri people who originally came to the Lavarone and Luserna highlands to cut wood. The hotel managed by the Zotti family is the result of renovating three stone mountain houses, an operation that was completed in 2001. The interiors are simple, the dominant feature being an extensive use of light-colored woods. Breakfast consists of a generous buffet with sweet and savory fare to suit the tastes of the mainly Italian and German customers laid out daily in a spacious room in the attic. In winter, cross-country skiing fans can enjoy this sport on well-signposted pistes, which can be followed in summer by bicycles or on horseback.

● 3 single, 7 double and 2 triple rooms, with bathroom ● Prices: single 30-35 euros, double 60, triple 90, breakfast included ● Credit cards: Bancomat ● Facility accessible for the disabled, 2 rooms designed for their use. External parking reserved for customers and public parking. Small pets allowed. Owners present from 7 am to midnight ● Bar, restaurant. Hall with TV. Solarium

OSSANA

71 KM NORTH OF TRENTO TAKING SS 43 AND 42

ANTICA OSTERIA

🍲 Trattoria
Via Venezia 11
Tel. 0463 751713
Closed Wednesday, never in high season
Open: lunch and dinner
Holidays: 2 weeks end of June
Seating: 38
Prices: 28-30 euros, wine excluded
All credit cards except AE

Don't be distracted by the appearance of this old place – it looks like the archetype of the mountain refuge – or by its cozy furnishings, comfortable seating and friendly service. Instead you should focus on the food prepared by Mariano Dell'Eva, the latest in a dynasty of hosts. Seasonal dishes, the majority prepared using homemade ingredients, from speck to goats' milk ricotta cheese with dandelion honey. Start with wild chicory with roasted lardo and **mortandela** from the Val di Non, herb flan with cured meats and vegetables, then go on to **potato ravioli** with pears and braised red cabbage or fritters with grappa and fresh cheeses from the Pejo dairy. In spring we had **gnocchi with nettles**, risotto with calendula and hops, while during our fall visit the star dish was **risotto with chestnuts** and the year's new wine. All pasta – and the bread too – is home-made, while meats are cured and local cheeses aged on the premises, and **game** is selected from what is bagged by local hunters (venison and wild boar, but also **pheasant**, which is cooked **with juniper berries** accompanied by roast cabbage. In season, **wild mushrooms** galore; don't miss the malfatti with mint and cep mushrooms. For dessert, fruit and chocolate cakes, cornmeal cake flavored with walnuts and raisins, semifreddi, **strudel**, and home-made ice cream.
There's a really well-selected wine list, something rare to find at these altitudes. Recently a grotto has been prepared to store the rarer vintages and to taste them, along with Alpine grappas and liqueurs.

PALÙ DEL FERSINA

30 KM NORTHEAST OF TRENTO

SCALZERHOF

🛏️ Holiday farm
Località Frotten 108
Tel. 0461 550074-338 9591987
Fax 0461 550074
E-mail: scalzerhof@virgilio.it
Internet: www.agriturscalzerhof.it
Open all year round

The Mocheni Valley between Pergine Valsugana and Lagorai is an ethno-linguistic enclave populated by the descendants of immigrants from northern Europe who jealously retain their own traditions, language and way of life: indeed, the valley enjoys special administrative autonomy within the province of Trento. Finding a pleasant place to stay with adequate rooms and filling mountain-style breakfasts is no easy task in this area. That is, unless you choose this agriturismo, where your every whim is taken care of. It also includes a restaurant that is open at weekends and serves dishes such as cuccalar and krapfen. The valley is a paradise for amateur photographers, ethnographers and hikers: among places to visit we recommend the Grua va Hardoembl mine-museum, the fascinating Filferhof farmhouse and Lake Erdemolo at an altitude of 2,400 meters.

• 1 single and 4 double rooms, with bathroom, 3 rooms with balcony • Prices: single 19-23 euros, double 38-46; breakfast 3 euros per person • Credit cards: none • Facility accessible for the mobility challenged, 1 room designed for their use. Off-street parking. No pets allowed. Owners always present. • Restaurant. Garden

PEJO
Cogolo

PEJO
Comasine

CHALET ALPENROSE

1-Star Hotel
Via Malgamare
Località Masi Guilnova
Tel. 0463 754088
Fax 0463 746535
E-mail: alpenrose@tin.it
Internet: www.chaletalpenrose.it
Closed in November

IL MULINO

Restaurant
Località Comasine 2
Tel. 0463 754244
Always open from June 15 till end of September
and from early December to Easter
Open: dinner, summer also for lunch
Seating: 100
Prices: 28-30 euros, wine excluded
Credit cards: Visa, Bancomat

The building, which is considered part of the museum complex within the Stelvio National Park (at an altitude of 1,300 meters) was renovated a few years ago, though the external structure with its old 18th-century frame and original plank floors were left intact – a job that took four years to complete. Tiziano and Martina Rossi manage the place with dedication and passion. All rooms have bathrooms with massage showers and some have four-poster beds. The cuisine, based on traditional local dishes, is of high standard. The buffet breakfast includes home-made bread and cakes, milk and cheeses – among which casolèt, exclusive to the Pejo area – that are produced locally. Three kilometers away, at the famous Pejo Spa, guests may take advantage of the curative powers of the local waters.

• 8 double, 1 triple and 1 four-bed rooms, with bathroom (massage shower), safe, satellite TV • Prices: double room single use 40-50 euros, double 80-100, triple 120-150, four-bed 160-200, breakfast included • Credit cards: all except AE, Bancomat • Facility accessible to the mobility challenged, 1 room designed for their use. External parking reserved for guests. Small pets allowed. Owners always reachable • Bar, restaurant. Reading room. Garden, solarium

Surrounded by snow and ice, this mill has a daunting look, almost like a mountain stronghold, but when the snow melts it becomes one of the most interesting buildings not only in the Valle di Pejo but also in the whole of Trentino. A structure dating back centuries, magnificently restored and converted into a welcoming restaurant where the food is a blend of tradition and innovation. All thanks to Agnese Pegolotti, who has decided to preserve the original charm of the old mill.

The service has improved of late and the menu has been expanded. Taste the **fagotto di Bernardo Clesio**, a roulade of beef, venison and pork, spiced with apple and plums that was made by cooks at the bishop-prince's court at Cles, not far from the Mulino. For antipasto, a classic **apple salad with walnuts and Casolèt**, a fresh cheese made only in Pejo. From the choice of first courses, which also included **mushroom risotto** with barley and spelt, cappellacci filled with venison and poppy seeds and polenta gnocchi with melted butter, we chose an open raviolone with really fresh goats' milk ricotta and braised vegetables. To finish, bitter chocolate cake and spumone allo yogurt with woodland fruit. Other desserts included **wholegrain krapfen** with blueberry jam, warm vanilla strudel, **torta de fregolòti** with apple, fruit bavarois and semifreddo with honey.

The selection of wines, mainly from Trentino, is impressive as is the assortment of grappas and liqueurs. Given the seasonal nature of the menu, reservation, booking is compulsory.

PERGINE VALSUGANA

PINZOLO

CASTELLO

MASO MISTRIN

🗝 1-Star Hotel
Via al Castello 10
Tel. 0461 531158
Fax 0461 531329
E-mail: verena@castelpergine.it
Internet: www.castelpergine.it
Open from April to November

🗝 1-Star Hotel
Località Sant'Antonio di Mavignola
Tel. e fax 0465 507293
E-mail: info@masomistrin.com
Internet: www.masomistrin.com
Open all year round

Pergine Castle, which dominates the entire valley from the Colle del Tegazzo has stylistic features from many different periods in the past. Originally built by the Dukes of Austria, it was reconstructed in the 15th century, though its present appearance is the result of alterations by prince-bishops in the 16th and 17th centuries. Since 1900 it has been privately owned, most recently by a Swiss family. Though the rooms have a distinct medieval feel to them, the meticulous, obliging and friendly style of the management ensures efficiency and dynamism. The generous breakfasts, prepared with the fresh, fragrant ingredients typical of the Trentino region, are served in the inner courtyards or in rooms lined with suits of amour. The restaurant is ideal for candlelight dinners (meals cost about 28 euros per person, excluding wine) and serves local dishes and a fine selection of wines. Every year the castle displays a collection of sculptures or installations by outstanding modern artists.

• 4 single and 17 double rooms, with bathroom (7 rooms have shared bathroom facilities) • Prices: single 31-49 euros, double 62-98 (30 euro supplement for extra bed), breakfast included • Credit cards: all major ones, Bancomat • Off-street parking. Small pets allowed (not in communal areas). Owners reachable up to midnight • Bar, restaurant. Breakfast room. TV room, reading room. Internal and external grounds

This fascinating and relaxing hideaway has been created by Alice Bugna Collini's family in a location very near Madonna di Campiglio that is untouched by mass tourism. Nothing here is left to chance. The building is new and in a beautiful position; the furnishings are charming, with extensive use of old pine, fine fabrics and lace (which is why the owner says that, unfortunately, pets are not allowed). Apart from the rooms – each of which is personalized and different – there are also a couple of apartments. Guests are welcomed as if they were friends and the hospitality is impeccable, elegant and courteous. The buffet breakfast includes at least three types of home-baked cake, a variety of yogurts, desserts, preserved fruit, honey, and home-made elderberry juice, but also a good selection of local cheese, cured meats, warm crêpes and eggs galore.

• 1 single and 7 double or triple rooms, with bathroom, TV; 2 apartments (4 persons), with kitchenette • Prices: single 30-62 euros, double 60-110, triple 80-120, apartment 30-60 euros per person, breakfast included • Credit cards: all, Bancomat • Facility accessible for the mobility challenged, 2 rooms designed for their use. Off-street parking, garage (6 spaces). No pets allowed. Owners always reachable. • Breakfast room. 2 gardens

RIVA DEL GARDA

RESTEL DE FER

🗝 1-Star Hotel
Via Restel de fer 10
Tel. 0464 553481
Fax 0464 552798
E-mail: info@resteldefer.com
Internet: www.resteldefer.com
Closed from mid-February to mid-March

The iron gate is still the outstanding feature of the facade of this otherwise unpretentious building that has always belonged to the Meneghelli family. Now this country house has become a small hotel managed by Ennio with help from his wife Ida. It's just outside the town center and only a short distance from the lake. There are only a few rooms and each one is unique, furnished with wrought-iron beds, bedspreads and curtains in subdued, elegant colors, and furniture sourced from local antique dealers. Breakfast is mainly based on local products such as cheeses, cured meats and homemade plum, fig and persimmon jams. For your meals you will be seated at the tables in the winter garden (meals cost around 35 euros per person, excluding wine). Recently a space entirely dedicated to smokers has been added.

• 7 double rooms, with bathroom, TV, 3 apartments (4-5 persons) with use of kitchen • Prices: double room single use 70 euros, double 80, apartment 110 (10-20 euro supplement for extra bed), breakfast included • Credit cards: all, Bancomat • External parking reserved for guests, garage (for motorcycles and bicycles). Small pets allowed. Reception open from 7 am to midnight. • Restaurant, wine cellar. Lounge. Winter garden, lawn. Chalet for smokers

ROMENO
Malgolo

NERINA

🍲 Trattoria/2-Star hotel
Via De Gasperi 31
Tel. 0463 510111
Fax 0463 510001
E-mail: info@albergonerina.it
Internet: www.albergonerina.it
Closed Tuesday, never in summer
Open: lunch and dinner
Holidays: October 15-30
Seating: 45
Prices: 23-25 euros, wine excluded
All major credit cards, Bancomat

You'll find this simple establishment hidden away in the apple orchards. Its rooms are distributed on two floors and there's also a spartanly appointed restaurant strewn with bottles. For breakfast, bread, jam, home-made pastries and cookies, artisan butter and fruit from the orchard. The hotel is open all week and offers half board (with a three-night minimum) for 40 euros per person. At table, the Di Nuzzo family turns the spotlight o to Val di Non **cured meats** and **goat cheeses**, the most notable of which is the Montesòn. Of the antipasti, we recommend **carne salada** and vegetables. Follow this with potato ravioloni with fresh cheese, thyme and poppy seeds, **canederli with speck**, **strangolapreti** or **stracci with smoked trout**. There's more trout in the main courses, then **lamb**, **venison with polenta**, pork and grilled beef and **quail with rosemary**. Desserts: try **strudel** made from apples or figs and raspberries, schwarzwalderkirschtorte (made with buckwheat flour and cherry preserves) or maybe even a babà or pastiera, if Signor Di Nuzzo, the Neapolitan pastry chef, is feeling so inclined. There are abundant wines and cheeses to choose from.

🗝 • 12 double rooms with bath, TV; 9 with balcony • Prices: double room single use 35-37, double 56-60 euros, breakfast included• Uncovered internal parking. Small pets welcome. (not in communal spaces). Owners present from 7:30am to midnight • Restaurant. TV room. Terrace

RONZO CHIENIS
Valle di Gresta

ROVERETO

50 KM SOUTH OF TRENTO, 25 KM TO 22 ROVERETO SUD

25 KM SOUTH OF TRENTO ON SS 12

MARTINELLI

⌒ Hotel-Restaurant
Via del Car 4
Tel. 0464 802908
Closed Monday, never in high season
Open: lunch and dinner
Holidays: 2 weeks, end of January
Seating: 70 + 30 outdoors
Prices: 28-30 euros, wine excluded
All credit cards, Bancomat

PETTIROSSO

⌒ Recently opened osteria
Corso Bettini 24
Tel. 0464 422463
Closed Sunday
Open: lunch and dinner
Holidays: July
Seating: 70
Prices: 30 euros, wine excluded
All credit cards

On the road sign it says 'Gresta', though people from Trento know it as the 'cabbage village' after the local specialty. Here, any vegetable that can survive the altitude is grown biologically: cabbage, parsnips, carrots, potatoes, beans, pumpkins, zucchini, Savoy cabbage. Each season the local trattorias, agriturismos and farms offer what is grown in the surrounding fields. They include the family-run place Martinelli hotel-restaurant in the village center, furnished simply in mountain style. Here you'll be welcomed by young Mirko Martinelli.

Some extremely tasty dishes are served up. The menu changes every month, depending on the harvest. After the grilled vegetable crostini, **leek soup**, zucchini, chicory and tomato flan, cheese and parsnip medaglione, cream of carrot, and **parmigiana di zucchini**. In other periods, mixed grain focaccia with raw cabbage salad, **chicory, mushroom and cheese strudel**, spelt and parsnip. Then, **canederli with Savoy cabbage**, **potato gnocchi with onion**, elderberry flower and potato frittata. Among the main courses, sirloin steak with onions and potatoes, venison with polenta and mushrooms, **shin of pork with cabbage** and white meats with vegetables. There are usually vegetarian dishes too, as well as **Vezzena cheese** with pear mostarda and farmhouse cheeses with jam. For dessert, apple sorbet, vanilla ice-cream with Gresta jams, raspberry tart and skewers of caramelized fruit.

Dishes can be accompanied by some good wines, mainly from the Trentino.

Rovereto is not only famous for feasts and festivals dedicated to Marzemino wine, but also for its numerous cultural events: art exhibitions, the Mozart festival and the international dance and theater festival. On the strength of experience gained working for years in Trentino and beyond, Paolo Torboli has created this pleasant two-story meeting place in the street leading to the Mart. On the ground floor you can drop in for a snack and a glass of wine, while traditional dishes are served on the basement floor below.

A typical menu starts with **tortèl de patate** flavored with **mortandela** from Val di Non and cabbage salad. Then you can choose from **canederli** with various fillings, potato gnocchi or handmade tagliatelle. Another local specialty, **tonco de pontesèl**, is served with corn or buckwheat **polenta**. Always in demand are the **orzotto al Marzemino**, freshwater fish from the lake, Alpine **trout** and, in winter, **baccalà with potatoes and milk**. In the warmer months, **gnocchi d'ortica**, dandelion and lardo and canederli with beet, savoy cabbage and cheese, all prepared by chef Antonio Pederzolli. Among the puddings, chocolate cakes and a new one, red wine cake, of course, made with Marzemino. There are also apple cake, strudel, pies and homemade ice cream. Nor is there a lack of selection on the cheese board – courtesy of Remo Scozzini, goat farmer and cheese maker at Boccaldo di Vallarsa – or of cured meats and wines (the list comprises over 700 labels).

SIROR
San Martino di Castrozza

BEL SITO DA ANITA

Trattoria
Via Dolomiti 6
Tel. 0439 768893
Always open, October to Christmas weekends only
Open: lunch and dinner
Seating: 70 + 15 outdoors
Prices: 28-30 euros, wine excluded
All credit cards, Bancomat

SORAGA

ARNICA

3-Star Hotel
Via Barbide 30
Tel. 0462 768415
Fax 0462 768220
E-mail: info@hotelarnica.net
Internet: www.hotelarnica.net
Open from Easter to mid-June, and
from September 20 to December 1

Anita Corona and her children Elisabeth and Michele continue to improve their gastronomic offering in this splendid corner of the Trentino, a paradise for climbers keen to tackle really testing peaks. The trattoria is tucked away between buildings facing onto the main square in San Martino di Castrozza, pearl of the Dolomites. Eat here on a summer's day at the tables outdoors and you'll feel at peace with the world. Add to this the excellent quality of the food served and the very reasonable tab at the end, and your day is complete.

If you go for the local menu, there's carpaccio di **carne fumada** from Siror with fine **Tosèla cheese** made from the fresh milk of the day and produced only in Primiero. Then comes **leek and finferli mushroom soup** and a first course of home-made pasta with cheese and bilberries. The meats – **game** and beef – are grilled and accompanied by **mushrooms** or seasonal vegetables. A Sachertort-style cake and a ricotta mousse with woodland fruit round out the meal. The owners also offer alternatives to the previous menu: Tosèla with mushrooms, **roast sausage with corn polenta**, the ever-present **canederli**, followed by **shin of pork** and a small cheese board offering only Primiero cheeses. Compared with previous visits the wine list has improved, with bottles from a number of Italian regions.

A stone's throw from the trattoria and run by the same family is Eder, a store that sells specialty foods, jams (without pectin or thickeners) and their own homemade biscuits, local honey and cured meats, the same you eat at the Bel Sito.

A small mountain-style hotel on the sunny slopes of the valley diligently managed by Marco Pederiva, a good cook and expert hotelier. In accordance with local custom, wood is much in evidence both externally and in the rooms: the hall has inlaid ceilings, while the stube is Tyrolean in style. The comfortable rooms can be reached by elevator and have superb views over the Dolomites. A fitness center with a sauna and jacuzzis is available for guests. The cuisine is excellent, while breakfast consists of cereals, bread, croissants, yogurt, local jams, cakes and seasonal fruit. All of the Val di Fassa's ski-lift and mountaineering facilities are within easy reach of the hotel.

• 4 single, 11 double and 1 triple rooms, plus 2 apartments, with bathroom, TV • Prices: single 40-60 euros, double 60-120, triple 90-180, breakfast included • Credit cards: major ones, Bancomat • Facility accessible to the mobility challenged. Off-street parking. No pets allowed. Owners present up to midnight. • Bar, restaurant. TV room, reading room. Garden, solarium. Fitness center

SORAGA
Fuchiade

SPERA
Val Campelle

96 KM NORTHEAST OF TRENTO ON SS 48 AND SS 346   42 KM EAST OF TRENTO ON SS 47

FUCHIADE

CRUCOLO – SPERA

🝙 Restaurant/Mountain refuge
Località Fuchiade
Tel. 0462 574281 or 0462 768194
Internet: www.fuciade.it
Always open from mid-June to mid-October
and from December to Easter
Open: lunch and dinner
Seating: 80 + 60 outdoors
Prices: 35 euros
All major credit cards except AE, Bancomat

🝙 Trattoria/3-Star hotel
Località Val Campelle – Via Carzano 7
Tel. 0461 766093, 0461 762042 or 0461 763710
Fax 0461 782781
E-mail: info@crucolo.it e hotelspera@crucolo.it
Internet: www.crucolo.it e www.hotelspera.it
Closed Tuesday evening and Wednesday, never in summer
Open: lunch and dinner
Holidays: January 10–March 15
Seating: 180 + 70 outdoors
Prices: 20-25 euros
All major credit cards except AE, Bancomat

This is a magic refuge, reachable on foot or by skiå, by shuttle service, snowmobile or SUV. The Rossi family loves to spoil their guests. They have even created a play area for children here. For breakfast, they serve local produce, like fresh milk and home-churned butter. The menu, which has a Ladino stamp to it, changes often but you will always find **game** and local cheeses, such as **Puzzone**, Spetz tsaorì or Nostran de Fàsa – also used to make **panzerotti di patate**. Choose also from **beef guanciale**, cured meats made in-house, polenta gnocchi with beef, pork or **venison stew**, **braised veal cheek**, lamb, roasts and Val di Fassa cheeses. Cakes are the specialty of the house and are made with buckwheat flour or blueberries, carrots or chocolate. Don't forget that there's also **rosada**, crème brûlée with grappa and wild berries. The wine cellar is well stocked and organizes convivial tastings that might last well into the wee hours.
Half board is 70 euros per person.

🚪•❶ 2 double, 2 triple e 2 quadruple rooms with bath • Prices: double room single use 40, double 80, triple 120, quadruple 160 euros, breakfast included • Public parking 3.5 km away. Small animals welcome (not in rooms). Owners always present • Restaurant. Garden

This place is comfortable and spartan, like all the best rifugi. The hotel, open all week, is ideal as a base for excursions up to mountain pastures or biking trips. The Purin family, managers of the establishment, are friendly and informal, and apart from making their own cured meats and cheeses, also raise and butcher pigs. In the hotel (half board 45 euros per person), specialty food items from the Valsugana area are available for purchase.
On the menu, you'll find **cured meats** and fresh and aged cheeses that may also be served hot. First courses include **canederli**, vegetable soup and fresh pasta. Then there are roasts, a variety of pork preparations – **shank with sauerkraut**, ribs, **polenta with sausages** or **cotechini** – sometimes game and, in the summer, **mushrooms** as well. Don't miss the great cheese selection, with the classic fuso just melted on the grill. For puddings: cakes made in-house from buckwheat, carrots or berries, **strudel** and artisan ice-cream.
There's a small selection of Trentino wines, and the Parampampolo served hot is not to be missed.

🚪•❶ 34 double rooms with bath, TV • Prices: double room single use 39, double 66 euros, breakfast included• Accessible to the mobility challenged. Uncovered external parking. Small pets welcome (not in common spaces). Owners present from 7:30 am till midnight • Bar, restaurant. Terrace

SPIAZZO
Mortaso

TESERO

MEZZOSOLDO

DARIAL

Restaurant/3-Star hotel
Via Nazionale 196
Tel. 0465 801067
Fax 0465 801078
E-mail: info@mezzosoldo.it
Internet: www.mezzosoldo.it
Closed Thursday, never in summer
Open: lunch and dinner
Holidays: September 20 – December 1, after Easter until June 15
Seating: 50
Prices: 30-35 euros, wine excluded
All major credit cards except AE, Bancomat

Holiday farm
Via Cavada 61
Tel. 0462 814705a
Fax 0462 812647
E-mail: info@agriturdarial.it
Internet: www.agriturdarial.it
Open summer and winter

Each room is furnished differently with a mixture of neoclassical, rustic and oriental elements. Meals are served in two different rooms: one with wooden tables and antique craft items, the other more elegantly with an earthenware stove.
Begin your meal with a taste of **radic de l'ors**, followed by a salad of finferli mushrooms and Spressa (a local cheese), **capuc** in cabbage or grape leaves, vegetable strudel with mountain cheeses and **sfoiade**, large buckwheat tagliatelle with garlic. Main courses are particularly good; try **lamb shanks with patugol**, braised meat with herbs and lichen with **tortèl di patate**, larded **venison**, and, moving on to fish, **roasted char** or baccalà mousse. For dessert, pears in moscato, **cake of mountain herbs** with grappa and artisan ice-cream. Plus a great choice of wines and spirits, the best of which made with gentian and imperial herb.
The hotel is open all week and half board costs 48-70 euros per person.

• 2 single, 21 double and 3 triple rooms with bath, TV • Prices: single 50, double 82, triple 100 euros, breakfast included • Accessible to the mobility challenged. Uncovered internal parking. Small pets welcome (not in communal spaces). Owners present from 8 am to midnight • Bar, restaurant. TV and reading rooms. Garden

This newly built Fiemme-style three-story farmhouse is located outside the village at an altitude of 1,100 meters, in a sunny position close to the Volcan family's farm, which raises Saanen goats, the milk from which is ideal for making local cheeses. The Volcan family supplies milk to the local cheese factory in Cavalese rather than producing cheese themselves, and they dedicate their own time to running their comfortable agriturismo. The splendid rooms are all airy. Breakfast consists of home-made products such as cakes, jams and honey, as well as local cheeses, cured meats and vegetables. Guests have to book to use the restaurant (the supplement for half board ranges from 5-8 euros per person). There is also a fitness center with a Finnish sauna, Turkish bath, cold fog treatment and jacuzzi. Guided visits are organized to mountain homes and high-altitude farms managed by the same family.

• 6 double, 2 triple and 2 four-bed rooms, with bathroom, TV; 8 rooms with balcony • Prices: double room single use 35-37 euros, double 58-62, triple 87-93, four-bed 106-124, breakfast included • Credit cards: major ones, Bancomat • Facility accessible to the mobility challenged, 2 rooms designed for their use. Off-street parking, garage (2 spaces). Small pets allowed. Owners always present • Restaurant. TV room. Garden. Fitness center

TON
Toss

TONADICO
Val Canali

GOLDEN PAUSE

CANT DEL GAL

Holiday farm
Via Verdi 16
Tel. 0461 657688-335 5430624
Fax 0461 657177
E-mail: scrivi@goldenpause.it
Internet: www.goldenpause.it
Open all year round

Trattoria/2-Star Hotel
Località Sabbionade 1
Tel. 0439 62997
Closed: Tuesday, never in high season
Open: lunch and dinner
Holidays: November
Seating: 60 + 20 outdoors
Prices: 27-29 euros, wine excluded
All credit cards

This is one of the least known localities in the lower Val di Non, where apples and honey reign supreme. Claudio Fedrizzi, expert fruitgrower and pork butcher (his mortadella is exquisite) and friendly host, and his family are waiting to welcome you. Rooms are rustic, albeit furnished with taste and equipped with every comfort, while common areas are very roomy. Snacks and dinners – available only for guests by reservation – are served in the ground-floor dining room. Breakfasts are really huge and include, among other things, strudel, apple juices, wholewheat bread and jams, all of which home-made. The Golden Pause is the ideal place to be in every season: in springtime, the apple trees in blossom are a sight not to be missed; during winter it's a good base for skiing on the Raganella or on the famous Valle di Sole slopes.

• 4 double rooms, with bathroom, TV; 1 apartment (2-4 persons) with kitchen • Prices: double room single use 33 euros, double 56-60, breakfast included • Credit cards: none • Facility accessible to the mobility challenged, 1 room and the apartment designed for their use. Off-street parking. No pets allowed. Owners always present • Breakfast room. Garden

This trattoria in Val Canali, a mountain paradise, is named for the mating call of the wood grouse, a rare bird that fortunately continues to nest in these woods. With the help of his wife Marzia, Nicola Cemin has restructured the place – adding ten rooms in the process – so that it blends in perfectly with the Alpine surroundings. The menu consists of traditional Trentino and Primiero area specialties. To start, **carne fumada** with a Lake Garda olive oil condiment, ricotta cheese gnocchi, **strangolapreti**, **canederli** with cheese and mushrooms, venison chops, and **apple strudel**. Or you can tackle the huge helpings of **tosèla with mushrooms**, **polenta** and **sausage**, the melted cheese dish called **patugol**, with grilled lucanica, red cabbage and pork ribs. In cold months, game, from **stewed roe deer venison** to roast red deer venison; then there's tagliate di manzo, **roast pork** and about ten different Trentino cheeses, including Tosèla. For dessert, tarts, puddings and mousses with berries.
The wine list boasts about 100 labels: bottles are chosen and uncorked by your host, and prices are fair.

• 12 double rooms, with bathroom. satellite TV • Prices: double room single use 40 euros, double 64, breakfast included • Credit cards: all, Bancomat • Facility accessible to the mobility challenged, 1 room designed for their use. Off-street parking. Small pets allowed (not in communal areas). Owners always present • Bar, restaurant. Garden with children's playground, solarium

TRANSACQUA

BAITA ZENI

🔑 Bed and breakfast
Località Pezze Alte
Tel. 0439 64813-333 4749382
Fax 0439 64813
E-mail: iassi@libero.it
Open all year round

This tastefully furnished, renovated farmhouse is located in the middle of a forest at an altitude of 1,100 meters, three kilometers from the center of Fiera di Primiero. As the place can only be reached by a rough road, unless you have a jeep or a similar vehicle, the managers will be pleased to pick you up. This apparent inconvenience is more than offset by the location of this B&B: a place with a view stretching from the Primiero Valley to the surrounding mountains that makes it an ideal base for excursions on foot or by bicycle, immersed in nature, far from the chaos and noise of city life. Alba Salvatori and her family run things and she also makes tasty breakfasts, consisting of cakes, fruit salads, yogurt, honey and homemade jams, plus local cheeses and cured meats.

• 3 double rooms. with bathroom, satellite TV • Prices: double room single use 25-35 euros, double 50-70 (20-30 euro supplement for extra bed), breakfast included • Credit cards: none • Public parking 1 km away. Small pets allowed. Owners always reachable • Fully equipped kitchen. Breakfast room, reading room. Garden

TRENTO
Cognola

ALLE COSTE

🔑 Bed and breakfast
Via alle Coste 24
Tel. 0461 983783-346 2309185
E-mail: a_dallape@yahoo.com
Internet: www.bedandbreakfastallecoste.it
Holidays variable

The Dallapè family's B&B is perhaps the most comfortable of the places located near the city. This country house has two cozy double rooms (you can add a third bed) and is close to the science university complex, but also to wine cellars and sun-baked vineyards. This is an area where you can wander around on foot or by bicycle, but also attempt easy climbs on the surrounding mountains or take off to the hills to enjoy moments of genuine Trento-style relaxation, only minutes away from the old town center. The building has quiet, airy rooms, and guests are treated almost like old friends of the family. Apart from the breakfast room, there's a TV lounge room furnished in an unpretentious rustic manner.

• 2 double rooms, with bathroom; 1 with TV • Prices: double room single use 35 euros, double 65 (15 euro supplement for extra bed), breakfast included • Credit cards: none • Covered off-street parking. No pets allowed. Owners always reachable • Breakfast room, TV and relaxation room. Garden, terrace

ASTRA

⌣ Osteria
Corso Buonarroti 16
Tel. 0461 829002
Closed: never
Open: only for dinner
Holidays: August
Seating: 25
Prices: 20 euros, wine excluded
Credit cards: none, Bancomat

IL LIBERTINO

⌣ Osteria
Piazza Piedicastello 4
Tel. 0461 260085
Closed Tuesday
Open: lunch and dinner
Holidays: two weeks end-July
Seating: 50
Prices: 25-30 euros, wine excluded
All credit cards

Fool and food: it's a combination that works in this pleasant osteria opened by the Artuso family, famous in Trento as cinema managers, – in a multi-screen complex where they only shows films of a certain level. As you enter, there's a sign prohibiting consumption of popcorn, crisps and canned drinks. There are just a few seats on the mezzanine floor beside the projection room, exactly above the area next to the ticket office with a counter where you can drink a glass of locally produced wine accompanied by snacks. The timing of showings is organized so people can have a bite to eat or a full dinner before or after the film.

The food is based on clear ideas and precise aims. The cook is the enthusiastic Anna Artuso, self-taught but highly competent. She proposes a series of soups: **cream of pumpkin**, lentil with sturgeon or **potato and baccalà**. Plus **lasagne** with trout and broccoli, served with local cheeses or **rabbit ragù**. To follow, **breast of duck**, veal roulade and **smoked char**. There are always vegetarian dishes too. Desserts are homemade: from torta tenerina – with eggs, bitter chocolate, sugar, butter and flour – to apple strudel and various terrines. Every Thursday there's a theme evening, for get-togethers with other osterias or for menus based entirely on baccalà, mushrooms, asparagus, seasonal vegetables, or tripe cooked in various ways. Many wines are up for tasting, some by the glass, accompanied by local cheeses and cured meats. An original idea is to offer guests dishes that appear on screen with appropriate wines.

This curiously named osteria has become a place not to be missed for connoisseurs of good food in Trento. Launched by Fabrizio Pedrolli, a well-known wine importer-exporter, it's professionally managed by the husband-and-wife team of Luca and Maria Assunta Maurina, who have many years' experience in preparing typical Trentino food. The osteria is located in one of the old palazzos in the ancient quarter of Piedicastello on the river bank, an area now traversed by the highway and ring road. The environment is vaguely Art Nouveau, with dark wood on the walls: there are two small inside rooms and, as you enter, a tiny wine bar.

Now for the cuisine. The focus is on local **cured meats** and cheeses – including Slow Food Presidia produce – while the menu, which changes weekly, always includes certain dishes: **tortèl de patate** and the traditional homemade **tajadèle** with a sauce made from the season's vegetables. In colder months, tasty **canederli** in stock or with a saucet, **carne salada** and various roasts. Almost always available, **brasato al Teroldego**, cut of beef cooked in balsamic vinegar, beef and pork cooked in various ways. Alternatively, freshwater fish and the usual **baccalà alla trentina**, cooked with milk and served with **polenta**. The service is good and there's a wide selection of desserts: fruit cakes, **torta de fregolòti**, a Trento specialty, creams and tiramisu.

There's also a very wide range of wines, almost all available by the glass and your host will always be ready to advise you on the right one for the occasion.

5 KM SOUTHWEST OF TRENTO CITY CENTER

PRÀ-SEC

🔑 Holiday farm
Via di Malebis 1 a
Tel. 0461 349204-328 5775635
Fax 0461 349204
E-mail: danilo.baldo@tin.it
Internet: www.agriturpra-sec.it
Open all year round

SCRIGNO DEL DUOMO ⊗ 🍾

🍲 Osteria
Piazza del Duomo 29
Tel. 0461 220030
Closed: never
Open: lunch and dinner
Holidays: none
Seating: 50 + 30 outdoors
Prices: 25-30 euros, wine excluded
All credit cards

Prà-Sec is in a farmhouse surrounded by apple orchards on the southern outskirts of the city in the direction of Aldeno. It's hard to find a more comfortable agriturismo anywhere: the building is new and welcoming, the rooms splendid and the service extremely courteous. The apartments, equipped with kitchenettes and washing machines, are ideal for small families. Breakfasts are very tasty and mainly prepared with home-made ingredients. On request you'll be able to taste and purchase typical local farm produce, such as wine and fruit. There's plenty of room to relax in the spacious, green outdoor area and you can go for excursions on foot or by mountain bike (numerous paths wind up the slopes of Mount Bondone). Not too far away there's also an area organized for rock-climbing with routes of various levels of difficulty.

• 3 double, 4 triple and 1 four-bed rooms, with bathroom, TV; 4 apartments (2-4 persons) with kitchen, balcony • Prices: double room single use 45 euros, double 65-74, triple 80-85, four-bed 95-100, breakfast included • Credit cards: major ones, Bancomat • Facility accessible to the mobility challenged, 2 rooms designed for their use. Off-street parking. Small pets allowed. Owners always reachable • Breakfast room. Garden

Alessandro Bettucchi is the manager of this splendid establishment, which occupies the ground floor and picturesque courtyard of the building. It is at once an osteria, wine bar and meeting place for young people and wine-lovers. In the basement room, among sculptures and pictures by well-known artists, the Scrigno is an exclusive restaurant with seating for only a few guests, impeccable service and a kitchen directed by Alfredo Chiocchetti, for years a top chef in the field of mountain cuisine. Two places in one or, if you wish, one place that offers two different, quality, alternatives. The osteria is always crowded and an enormous blackboard behind the bar counter offers a wide selection of wines served by the glass at extremely reasonable prices.
You'll be served traditional Trento dishes – in good weather outside in the courtyard that leads directly into the piazza. Local **cured meats** are followed by potato gnocchi, **strangolapreti**, home-made pasta and bread, or vegetable, mushroom or cheese **soups**. The osteria's most famous dish is **roast rabbit** with collard greens or other seasonal vegetables, served with **corn polenta**. The rabbits are reared in a semi-wild state and are fed according to the criteria of organic agriculture, which makes their meat particularly tasty. Other dishes are **carne salada**, trout and char cooked in various ways. To end the meal, woodland fruits and various types of **strudel**, mousse and cake.
There are wines to suit all tastes and pockets: about 1,000 labels, from the traditional to grands crus from France and even further afield.

TRENTO
Cognola

VALFLORIANA

VILLA MADRUZZO

🔑 3-Star Hotel
Località Ponte 26
Tel. 0461 986220
Fax 0461 986361
E-mail: info@villamadruzzo.it
Internet: www.villamadruzzo.it
Open all year round

FIOR DI BOSCO

🔑 Holiday farm
Località Comuni
Tel. 0462 910002-329 0125349
Fax 0462 910002
E-mail: Glozzer@libero.it
Closed for 15 days in May and November

Leave the city center and follow the road to Padua until you reach the Ponte Alto waterfall. A few hundred meters away you'll find this hotel surrounded by extensive grounds with old trees, bamboo, roses and magnolias. The rooms are equally divided between two communicating buildings: the villa, which in the 16th century was home to one of the main participants at the Council of Trento, and the modern wing, added in the Fifties. The rooms are big and tastefully furnished; the ones on the top floor have ceilings with wooden beams and all of them are very comfortable. The continental breakfast includes sweet and savory fare and is served in one of the rooms of the restaurant, which is also open to non-residents. The cost of a meal is approximately 38 euros per person, excluding wine; the supplement for half board is 22 euros per person.

• 50 double rooms, with bathroom, air-conditioning, fridge, safe, TV • Prices: double room single occupancy 62-72 euros, double 95-105, breakfast included • Credit cards: all, Bancomat • Facility accessible to the mobility challenged, 2 rooms designed for their use. Off-street parking. Small pets allowed. Reception open 24 hours a day. • Bar, restaurant. Conference room. Grounds, outdoor spaces

A model agriturismo at an altitude of 1,000 meters on the mountain that separates Val di Fiemme from the Val di Cembra. Getting there isn't exactly a cake-walk, but the winding road leading up to the farm has a charm all of its own. The facility is run by Graziano Lozzer, a likeable, theatrical character, together with his wife Isabella and the rest of the family. The Lozzers own a herd of Grigia breed cows, produce cheese and offer the possibility of a stay in this fully renovated farmhouse setting. All the rooms have wide balconies and, though they maintain the rustic charm of a mountain farmhouse, they are equipped with all modern comforts. The cuisine is country style: local dishes, home-made bread and cakes, butter and cured meats and really fresh milk. They also have a malga – an Alpine farmhouse – nearby that's open in the summer.

• 1 single and 9 double rooms, with bathroom, some with a balcony • Prices: single 30 euros, double 60, breakfast included • Credit cards: Visa, CartaSi, Bancomat • Facility accessible to the mobility challenged, 2 rooms designed for their use. Off-street parking. Small pets allowed. Owners always present. • Restaurant. Reading room. Garden

ALTO ADIGE
SÜDTIROL

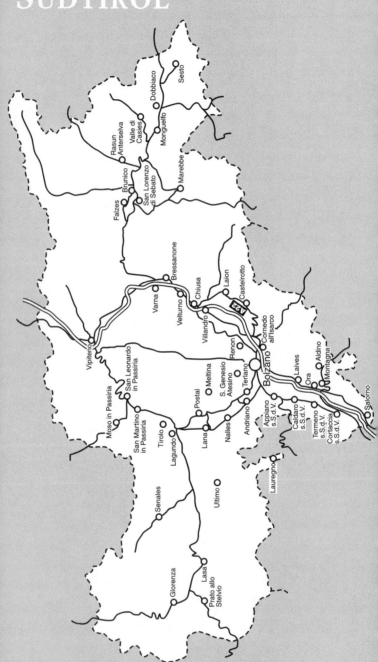

ANDRIANO-ANDRIAN

13 KM WEST OF BOLZANO

APPIANO SULLA STRADA DEL VINO
EPPAN AN DER WEINSTRASSE
Monte-Berg

12 KM SOUTHWEST OF BOLZANO SS 38

WEINSTUBE SICHELBURG SCHWARZER ADLER

Trattoria-inn
Piazza Sant'Urbano 2
Tel. 0471 510288
Closed Monday and Tuesday lunch
Open: lunch and dinner
Holidays: January 15-March 15
Seating: 70 + 50 outdoors
Prices: 25 euros, wine excluded
All major credit cards accepted

TURMBACH

3-Star Hotel
Via Rio della Torre 4
Tel. 0471 662339
Fax 0471 664754
E-mail: gasthof@turmbach.com
Internet: www.turmbach.com
Closed from Christmas to Easter

This settlement, surrounded by vineyards and fruit orchards, on the Rio Gaida, between the fairy tale castles of Wolfsturm and Festenstein, dates back over 1,000 years, The roads that run through the estates are perfect for a bike ride or to stretch your legs after a good lunch in one of the trattorias in the valley. Among these, the Aquila Nera (its Italian name) is the most characteristic. Situated behind a pleasant hotel, looking onto the mountains, it has its own entrance in a garden surrounded by old vines. It's pleasant to eat in their shade during the summer, or when there's no room left in the two main dining rooms, one large and modern, the other smaller with attractive old-fashioned wood decor.

To start, home-cured meats and speck, seasonal dishes like **asparagus and eggs, boiled ham and horseradish**, **vegetable soups**, orzotto, hand-made pasta with fresh herbs and dandelion gnocchi (with mushrooms in the summer). Plus uperb **schlutzer**, ravioli stuffed with ricotta and spinach, followed by toothhsome pork, **roast** potatoes, beef and onions, loin of lamb and spicy **goulash**. To close, **apple strudel**, buckwheat cake, soft apple fritters and, in the autumn, chestnuts with grape must freshly drawn from the bottle. The selection of local cheeses is also excellent, In the summer tasty snacks are served outside with white Pinot and Terlaner or red Lagrein from the oldest winemakers' cooperative in the region.

Not many people know this but the spa in Monte di Appiano has been operating for centuries, exploiting the crystal clear waters of the area for herbal infusions with pine resin and other conifer flavors. The Turmbach, a typical gasthof, is located in one of the few residences that have stood the test of time and has been managed by the Worndle family for as long as anyone can remember. This friendly, well kept place has balconies with flowers and adequate space for dining: in short, it is fully equipped for anyone wishing to enjoy a relaxing break. In summer you can eat outside under the apple trees, close to the river where the trout can be seen darting through the water. Rooms are comfortable and, though they vary from one room to the next, furnishings are all typical. A buffet breakfast is available with a selection of home-made sweet and savory food. The restaurant serves 'revisited' local dishes at a price of 40-45 euros, excluding wine.

• 15 double rooms with bathroom and balcony • Prices: double room single use 38-45 euros, double 64-80, breakfast included • Credit cards: all except DC, Bancomat • Off-street parking. Small pets are allowed. Reception open from 8 am to 12 am • Bar, restaurant. Garden. Swimming pool

CAVALLINO BIANCO

Traditional Osteria
Via Bottai 6
Tel. 0471 973267
Closed Saturday evening and Sunday
Open: lunch and dinner
Holidays: 3 weeks at the end of June, Christmas–New Year
Seating: 100
Prices: 25 euros, wine excluded
No credit cards accepted

HOPFEN & CO.

Osteria-pub
Piazza delle Erbe 17
Tel. 0471 300788
Closed Sunday, never in winter
Open: lunch and dinner
Holidays: never
Seating: 150
Prices: 15-25 euros, wine excluded
All credit cards accepted

To find an authentic Alto Adige gasthaus just take a walk along the charming streets the in old part of town. The Cavallino Bianco is an old inn that has been open for centuries. Behind the large green and white entrance door on Via Bottai, just a short walk from Piazza Walter, a daily ritual takes place that has changed very little over the years. From early in the morning you are likely to bump into people in traditional costume or, more simply, in their blue work overalls who come down into town and stop off at the osteria for a delicious snack of **sauersuppe** or **canederli with liver** before going home. Towards midday the three large dining rooms (as of this year there's also an inside garden) start filling up with craftsmen, factory workers, white collars, bankers and shop owners. Sharing the large dark tables, they enjoy **canederli in stock**, **goulash** with sauté potatoes or large breaded **wiener schnitzel** with potato salad or sauerkraut. In the fall, try the **homemade sausage** (auswurst), **sanguinaccio** and the 'farmers' dish': generous portions of sausages, wurstel and corn beef with canederli on the side. The boiled meat and tongue, served with green parsley sauce and boiled potatoes, is also very tempting,. The menu includes 'Mediterranean' first courses that are very popular with the German visitors.
The all-South Tyrol wine list has been much improved and, a note of merit this, the osteria only charges for bread that is actually eaten. We recommend eating here in the evening, when the place is less hectic than at lunchtime.

Hopfen is the German name for hops, to which, not by chance, the owners have dedicated their inn. The latter occupies three floors in the historic palazzo in Piazza Erba where Bozner Bier, the first beer to be produced in Bolzano, is made, served and drunk with great gusto. It is made in the cellars, which can be seen through a number of round windows. The ground floor, still complete with original furnishings, is divided into two halls. The first is occupied by the bar, which takes up two thirds of the room, with two copper boilers where the must boils. The second contains the large tables and benches where dishes – recently not as good as they used to be – can be tasted. Perhaps success has undermined part of the original charm of the place, which has been an inn for centuries. In the menu, you often find Mediterranean first courses and vaguely exotic dishes.
We enjoyed the **canederli**, **rosticciata** of potatoes and boiled meat and we always recommend the **weisswurst**, which can be enjoyed from 10am served with sweet mustard and bretzel, a type of soft bread. As a snack, the Nuremberg roast sausages are very good and, for heartier appetites, **shin of pork** or veal, served with sauté potatoes, canederli or **sauerkraut**. The menu contains lots of specialties using beer, steak in beer being one. Climbing up a narrow spiral stairway you reach the other two floors, where the furniture is more modern and the atmosphere cozier and generally more relaxed.
There's a great selection of wine, mainly regional labels. Generally Hopfen is more suitable for the young and food is served well into the night.

BOLZANO-BOZEN
Colle di Villa-Bauernkohlern

BRUNICO-BRUNECK
Ameto-Amaten

8 KM FROM THE CENTER OF TOWN

75 KM NE OF BOLZANO SS 49

KOHLERN

OBERRAUT

Trattoria with rooms
Località Colle 11
Tel. 0471 329978
Closed Monday
Open: lunch and dinner
Holidays: January to Easter, Christmas
Seating: 50 + 30 outdoors
Prices: 28 euros, wine excluded
All credit cards accepted

Trattoria – 1-Star Hotel
Località Ameto 1
Tel. 0474 559977
Fax 0474 559997
E-mail: gasthof.oberraut@dnet.it
Closed Thursday, always open in summer
Open: lunch and dinner
Holidays: end of January, end of September and Christmas
Seating: 40 + 25 outdoors
Prices: 32-35 euros, wine excluded
All major credit cards, Bancomat

This smart locanda in the refined jugendstiel style was built to cater for the first tourism at the end of the 19th century in what was considered the garden of the Tyrol. This is where the Bolzano merchant class used to come to eat. To avoid the long winding road up into the hills, in 1908 the first owner had a passenger cable car built at his own expense. Externally very little has changed since then, and the menu tends to follow tradition, with scrupulously prepared dishes and only local produce whenever possible.

We recommend the **calf's head all'agro** with canederli carpaccio, smoked beef and fresh goats' cheese. A good selection of **speck** and other home smoked meats prepare the palate for the delicious dishes that follow: the variation on **canederli**, potato tortelloni with white cabbage and speck, and **schlutzer**, typical half-moon pasta stuffed with ricotta and spinach. Tagliatelle al Gewürztraminer with **rabbit ragù** are a new entry on the menu. Among the main courses, we recommend the excellent **gröstel**, roast veal and boiled potatoes, **liver and onions** and breaded calf's head with potatoes. In season, the special dishes with **mushrooms** picked fresh in the fields and cooked in all imaginable ways. The home-made desserts are very good: canederli with apricots or ricotta, **strudel**, and kaiserschmarrn or **apfelschmarrn**, rich whipped omelet with raisins or apples.

The cellar offers a good selection of wines, many available by the glass, and the service is attentive and rapid.

Atop the so-called 'balcony of Brunico', seductive for the beauty of the natural surroundings and panorama, Teresa and Christof Feichter run their trattoria with typical South-Tyrolean grace and professionalism. They are also in charge of the small adjacent farm. The rooms (available all week) are comfortable and basic, while the copious breakfast is regional in style. Meals are served in two stuben or on the veranda in summer.

The Feichters produce cured meats and Graukäse, and uselocal game for some of their antipasti and main courses, such as the remarkable **venison goulasch**. Among the soups, cream of fresh Alpine cheese and traditional **tirtlan with barley soup**. Other local specialties: **groestel, canederli with nettles**, schlutzer stuffed with ricotta and spinach, **tagliatelle with game ragù**. In season, mushrooms abound. A couple of pleasant novelties are **open** potato **ravioli** with mushrooms and crispy speck and lamb in croute. The dessert menu offers browned blueberries, apricot-**filled canederli** and caramelized fritters.

The South Tyrolean **cheese** selection (one produced and matured on the farm) is respectable, and the wines are mainly regional.

● 6 doubles en-suite (2 of which with shared facilities) ● Prices: double single use 26-32, double 52-64 euros, breakfast included ● Private outdoor parking. Pets welcome. Owners always on premises ● Restaurant. Breakfast room

BRUNICO-BRUNECK

GOLDENE ROSE

☛➊ 3-Star Hotel
Via Bastioni 37
Tel. 0474 413000
Fax 0474 413099
E-mail: info@hotelgoldenerose.com
Internet: www.hotelgoldenerose.com
Closed 2 weeks in June and 2 weeks in September

75 KM NORTHEAST OF BOLZANO

This hotel, housed in an old building next to a medieval tower, has been owned by the Hinterhuber family since 1879 and was entirely refurbished in 1999. Two types of rooms available – 8 standard and 13 superior – and all feature large windows giving on to the old town. All rooms are spacious and well furnished, with pale wood furniture and beds with continental quilts as opposed to sheets. Breakfast is served on the first floor and consists of a wide variety of foods to suit the tastes of an equally varied clientele: stewed fruit, muesli and cereals, different types of honey and jam, cheeses and cured meats. The building is situated in an ideal location for those who wish to visit the lively town center with its typical Nordic-style houses.

• 21 double rooms with bathroom, minibar, satellite television; many rooms with balcony • Prices: double room single use 57-103 euros, standard double room 94-124, superior 124-156 (31-41 euro supplement for extra bed), breakfast included • Credit cards: all except DC, Bancomat • Accessible for the mobility challenged, 1 specially equipped room. Garage (7 euros per day), free underground parking 150 meters away. Small pets allowed (10 euros per day). Reception open 7am-11pm • Coffee. Breakfast room. Conference room.

CALDARO SULLA STRADA DEL VINO
KALTERN AN DER WEINSTRASSE

MARLEN

☛➊ Pension
Via Barleit 13
Tel. and fax 0471 963355
E-mail: pension.marlen@rolmail.net
Internet: www.kalterersee.com/marlen
Open all year round

15 KM SOUTHWEST OF BOLZANO

This hotel, efficiently managed by the friendly Tulzer family, is housed in a pristine mountain building just 10 minutes on foot from the center of Caldaro. Most of the simply furnished rooms have terraces which, in the summer, are decorated with pots of flowers. The buffet breakfast, served in the common area, seeks to satisfy Italian and German guests alike: home-made strudels, jams, bread, muesli, fruit, yogurt and a selection of cheeses, cured meats and eggs. Summer and winter gardens complete the facilities. All guests are given a free entry pass to an exclusive club located on the nearby lake, where they can practise sports activities such as windsurfing.

• 10 double rooms and 2 triples with bathroom, safe, television; many rooms with balcony • Prices: double room single use 38-40 euros, double 64-76, triple 99-111, breakfast included • Credit cards: none • Outdoor parking reserved for customers and covered parking (2 places). Pets not allowed. Reception open from 8 am to 10 pm, owners always present • Breakfast room. Garden, terrace

CASTELROTTO
KASTELRUTH

BINTERHOF

🔑 Holiday farm
Via Panider 49 A
Tel. and fax 0471 700071
E-mail: info@binterhof.com
Internet: www.binterhof.com
Open all year round

This white house, with its wide roof and balconies with flowers in the summer, rises from the middle of the field like some giant mushroom. A splendid location and an ideal departure point for excursions, it is situated on the sunniest plateau in Alto Adige, halfway to the Siusi Alps or the Gardena. Here Albin Plunger's family opens his hof to guests as a stopover to relax during an excursion or to rest before setting out on a hike or bike trip to the mountains. The delicious food served for breakfast is true farmhouse-style: fresh home-baked bread every day, excellent butter, local jams and many other mountain specialties, served with informal kindness. If you really want, they'll even let you help clean the stable or mow the fields. Comfortable apartments are available for longer stays and two of them are equipped with washing machines.

• 2 double rooms with bathroom, and 3 apartments (2-5 beds) with kitchen • Prices: double room single use 28-34 euros, double 48-60, breakfast included; apartments 39-95 euros • Credit cards: none • Covered off-road parking, garage (2 euros per day). Small pets allowed. Owners always present • Breakfast room. Reading and television rooms. Garden

CASTELROTTO
KASTELRUTH
Sant'Osvaldo-Sankt Oswald

TSCHOETSCHERHOF

🔑 2-Star Hotel
Località Sant'Osvaldo-Sankt Oswald 19
Tel. 0471 706013
Fax 0471 704801
E-mail: info@tschoetscherhof.com
Internet: www.tschoetscherhof.com
Open from March to November

The Sciliar plateau is one of the loveliest places in the Dolomites. This airy, wide-open, relaxing area allows you to discover all that a holiday in Alto Adige has to offer. The village maintains its medieval character and the farmhouses their original appearance, given that agriculture is still important here and manages to coexist in harmony with tourism.

Among the Sciliar farmhouses in this isolated location you'll find this little gem. It shouldn't come as a surprise that the place also boasts a rural museum and produces a few specialties, speck first and foremost. Rooms are furnished in spartan fashion and are located above the common areas. Good country meals and snacks are available (a meal costs around 19 euros, wine excluded). This is a quiet location near the woods, a good departure point for excursions, ideally after a substantial breakfast of typical cakes and farmhouse produce.

• 1 single room and 7 doubles, with bathroom • Prices: single 27-30 euros, double room single use 34-39, double 54-62, breakfast included • Credit cards: MC, Visa, Bancomat • Parking right outside. Small pets allowed. Owners always contactable • Restaurant. Breakfast room. Garden

Chiusa-Klausen
Gudon-Gufidaun

Cortaccia sulla Strada del Vino
Kurtatsch an der Weinstrasse

30 KM NORTHEAST OF BOLZANO SS 12 OR A 22

28 KM SOUTHWEST OF BOLZANO SS42

Unterwirt

3-Star Hotel
Località Gudon-Gufidaun 45
Tel. 0472 844000
Fax 0472 844065
E-mail: info@unterwirt-gufidaun.com
Internet: www.unterwirt-gufidaun.com
Closed 3 weeks in January and 2 end-June

Santlhof

Trattoria
Hofstatt 7
Tel. 0471 880700
Closed Monday, Tuesday and Wednesday
Open: dinner, lunch on weekend
Holiday: Christmas-February, 3 weeks in June-July
Seating: 40 + 12 outdoors
Prices: 20-25 euros, wine excluded
No credit cards accepted

The Haselwanter family has been running this enchanting gasthof for generations. Young Thomas – 'jeune restaurateur d'Europe' – has recently changed the style of the restaurant, three centuries-old stuben (one dates back to 1300), and the hotel, which communicates with the old building. The apartments are spacious and luxurious, while rooms include every comfort and offer a splendid view over the nearby mountains: an ideal place for a completely relaxing holiday. Breakfast is simply delicious: ams, yogurt, bread and cakes are all home-made and eggs, cured meats, local cheeses, muesli and fruit are also available. The Unterwirt is very well known and much appreciated by gourmets for its cuisine: for many years it was a simple, charming osteria, but now it's a top quality restaurant (price 40-50 euros, wine excluded).

• 3 double rooms and 4 apartments (2-6 beds) with bathroom, balcony, living room with cooking facilities • Prices: double room single use 34-37 euros, double 48-54, apartment 54-120; breakfast 10 euros per person • Credit cards: major ones, Bancomat • Outdoor private parking. Small pets allowed. Owners always contactable • Restaurant. Garden. Swimming pool

More than a hill, this place resembles a garden! So tidy that you can count the vines as you climb the steep road from Cortaccia to the hilly hamlets of Penone, Corona and Favogna, The grapes that grow in this strangely Mediterranean climate (here the wind arrives from far off Lake Garda) at 1,000 meters above sea level, produce a rare Müller Thurgau. Georg Mayr's farmstead is the most characteristic and original on the slopes. Nothing has ever changed here, apart from the house itself, recently renovated Everything is in tune with tradition, including the branch on display at the entrance, compulsory under Austro-Hungaric law for peasants who sold homemade wine. An expert winemaker and friendly host, Georg also servesw up typical rustic dishes, with the help of his aunt and his sister: potato gnocchi, cheese **canederli** or **knödel in stock**, the ever present **schlutz**, homemade raviolioni di magro, barley soup and fresh vegetable soup made of produce from the gardens of the buschenschank. Plus **rosticciata with potatoes** with or without onion, depending on personal taste, served with **strips of boiled beef, lean sausage of loin of pork**, sauerkraut, potatoes and often, when the weather's cold, delicious **black pudding.** The meal ends with **apple strudel**, omelets with homemade jam and buckwheat fritters.
In the summer, thirst-quenching homemade juniper or apple juice is served at the tables under the bower; in the fall, chestnuts and new wine.

DOBBIACO-TOBLACH
Gandelle-Kandellen

FALZES-PFALZEN

100 KM NORTHEAST OF BOLZANO

85 KM NORTHEAST OF BOLZANO SS49 PUSTERIA

SEITERHOF ⊘▮

KOFLER AM KOFL

▱Holiday farm
Località Kandellen-Gandelle 7
Tel. 0474 979114
Fax 0474 979049
Closed Tuesday, always open in high season
Open: lunch and dinner
Holidays: January 10-31
Seating: 30
Prices: 28 euros, wine excluded
All major credit cards, Bancomat

▱Farmhouse osteria
Via Kofler 41
Tel. 0474 528161
Closed Monday, but not in the high season
Open: lunch, dinner by reservation only
Holidays: never
Seating: 50 + 20 outdoors
Prices: 20-22 euros, wine excluded
All major credit cards are accepted

Sieglinde and Herbert Kamelger's farm, a mountain refuge and an osteria, is a place of rural magic, a place to relax. The comfortable, warm, wood-lined rooms, comlplete with new facilities and televisions are available all week. Almost all the food, both sweet and savory is home-produced.

Lunch starts off with tasty **cured meats**, smoked meat, **calf's head** and tartare. To follow, **canederli** (including a beetroot vgersion) and other types of fresh home-made pasta or, alternatively, **soups**: with seasonal vegetables, al vino or 'povera', with onion, black bread and speck. To follow, **hash browns** with boiled beef, home-butchered grilled meats, **goulasch** and other dishes prepared on request. To close off the meal, the choices are fruit **strudel**, raspberry ice-cream, strawberry and lemon or elderflower sorbet.

The **cheese board** offers variety as does the well thought out wine selection. The prices, though not always exactly low, are appropriate in relation to the quality of the food served.

🛏🍽• 6 doubles, en-suite, balcony, television • Prices: double single use 26, double 52 euros, breakfast included • Public outdoor parking. Pets welcome. Owners always on premises • Restaurant. Breakfast room. Garden. Patio

🍮 In **Dobbiaco**, buy delicious fruit preserves at Alpe Pragas, via Maximilian 6.
In **Villabassa** (8 km from Dobbiaco), Franz Weissteiner's butcher's shop, in Via Frau Emma, sells traditional speck pusterese, more smoked than other South Tyrolean versions.

You would never come here by chance or if you were lazy. In this ancient mountain farmstead with 700 years' history behind it, culinary dissertations or discussions about the ingredients or the recipes are not allowed. Here the strictest country traditions rule supreme: tasty dishes without frills with no room for fleeting trends or stereotypes. Here the mountains, farming, cattle breeding and food become an indivisible unicum. For antipasto tasty **Graukäse,** 'gray cheese', made by the farmers of the area with fresh cow's milk. It is followed by a series of first courses of **canederli**, including the ones typical of this area that are 'pressed' and look like thick fritters. Then come eggs with potatoes and speck, **beef goulash with polenta** and excellent **pork** (mainly chops, grilled or roast). If you want to be certain to find a special dish it's best to book, and if you want to have dinner here you must always phone first. To finish the meal, typical **schmarrn**, omelets made with fresh eggs and jam covered with a sprinkling of sugar, homemade buckwheat cakes and krapfen.

The osteria serves a few good wines from Alto Adige cellars. In the fall, it's nice to come to the Kofler for the törggelen feast or rest here after walks at altitudes in excess of 2,000 meters.

🍮 In the village of Vallarga near **Vandoies** (10 km), an assortment of typical breads is on sale at Kersbaumer. At Easter, animal-shaped cakes, a tradition of Val Pusteria

GLORENZA-GLURNS

POSTA

🔑 3-Star Hotel
Strada Flora 15
Tel. 0473 831208
Fax 0473 830432
E-mail: hotel.post.kg@rolmail.net
Internet: www.hotel-post-glurns.com
Closed from Epiphany to Easter

Glorenza a medieval village in the upper Val Venosta, close to the borders with Switzerland, still surrounded by the original walls, where life is taken at a very slow pace, is a magical place. Fewer than 1,000 people live here in houses in alleyways, among arcades and irrigation canals, proud to be part of a civitas recognized as early as 1291. It's as if time has stood still here, While the exterior of this historical gasthof, built in the 15th century isn't particularly striking, the spacious, stone-walled rooms with wood décor create an atmosphere of times gone by. Essentially, they are airy stuben, furnished in traditional Venostana style, with comfortable beds, spotless duvets and 'well-trodden' wooden floors. The traditional cuisine is excellent (menu at 17 euros, wine excluded): farmhouse cheeses, freshwater fish, local fruit. This is the ideal spot for a vacation with zero stress.

• 22 double rooms with bathroom, television • Prices: double room single use 50-62 euros, double 80-84, breakfast included • Credit cards: all except DC • Facilities accessible for the mobility challenged. Adjacent parking. Small pets allowed. Owners always contactable • Bar, restaurant. Breakfast room

LAGUNDO–ALGUND
Plars di Sopra-Oberplars

33 KM NORTHWEST OF BOLZANO, 8 KM FROM MERANO

KÖESTENWALDELE

🍲 Trattoria with rooms
Plars di Sopra 36
Tel. 0473 448374
Closed Thursday
Open: lunch and dinner
Holidays: winter months
Seating: 80 + 40 outdoors
Prices: 30 euros, wine excluded
Credit cards: Visa, Bancomat

Chestnuts are typical of the Merano valley and are grown where vines are unable to sustain the jumps in temperature and where the mountain slopes are particularly steep. Leaving Merano behind, in the direction of the Val Venosta, urbanization has eliminated all borders and divisions and territorial diversity is marked by the chestnut groves.
The Köestenwaldele or 'Chestnut Wood' is a lovely Tyrolean trattoria, with a few rooms for guests and a wonderful view of the valley. The Gamper family, for years leading players on the local catering scene, run the inn.
To start, delicious dishes with river asparagus, wood mushrooms and, of course, **chestnuts**, ingredients that are mixed and matched according to the season. Plus home-made cured meats and **speck**, **schlutzer**, ravioli stuffed with spinach and ricotta, and **tagliatelle**, lasagnette, **potato gnocchi** and other types of home-made pasta (not to mention the home-baked **bread**, made with walnuts or chestnut flour). An unusual and tasty dish is the home-farmed **trout** cooked in vine leaves, served with chestnuts and white wine sauce. Other second courses include beef, local **lamb** and roast pork with potatoes and speck.
For dessert, **apple strudel** with almond liqueur and cold cappuccino cream, fruit tarts and, in the fall, a delicious tiramisu made with chestnuts. The wine list offers the best regional labels, also available by the glass.

LAGUNDO-ALGUND
Plars di Mezzo-Mitterplars

LAGUNDO-ALGUND
Velloi-Vellau

30 KM NORTHWEST OF BOLZANO, 5 KM FROM MERANO

39 KM NORTHWEST OF BOLZANO

LEITER AM WAAL

🍲 Trattoria
Plars di Mezzo 26
Tel. 0473 448716
Closed Monday evening and Tuesday
Open: lunch and dinner
Holidays: Christmas to February 15
Seating: 50 + 70 outdoors
Prices: 30-35 euros, wine excluded
All major credit cards accepted

OBERLECHNER

🗝 2-Star Hotel
Frazione Velloi 7
Tel. 0473 448350
Fax 0473 222557
E-mail: oberlechner@rolmail.net
Closed from mid-January to mid-March

The name refers to the waal, an ingenious irrigation system devised in medieval times to reclaim the Merano valley floor; the canals are still functioning and play an important farming and environmental role. Philip Hafner is the owner of this lovely trattoria amid vines, canals and apple orchards on the road to the Val Venosta. A well kept, you might almost say pretentious, inn, in true South Tyrolean style. The menu changes with the seasons: it opens with **river asparagus** – the Adige flows nearby – and wild herbs (nettles in the gnocchi mixture and the ravioli stuffing, dandelions in the salad), and continues with mushrooms, apples, chestnuts and grapes.
You'll always find **sliced roast canederli**, then a trio of canederli, **ricotta gnocchi** and **schlutzer** (ravioli with spinach), all served with melted butter. The traditional dish is **roast pork with onions**, a tasty sauce and potatoes. Among the puddings, we must mention the **krapfen filled with poppy seeds and blackcurrants**. Then, in season, come asparagus, eggs and boiled ham with horseradish cream, a typical spring dish along the banks of the Adige, and risottos, meat and puddings with apples. You'll also find game and sometimes **trout**, raised in the running waters of the waal canals. In the fall, the ritual of törggelen is celebrated, with sauerkraut, sausage and chestnuts being washed down with jugs of new wine under the large bower.
The meal is rounded off with a fair selection of local cheeses and a good wine list, with labels mainly from local cellars.

Velloi is a charming village at an altitude of over 900 meters above in the Burgraviato mountains, the district of which Merano is the main town. The road leading up from the valley floor ends here (alternatively you can use the chair-lift), which means there's little traffic. The hotel is an ideal base for climbs and excursions in the Gruppo di Tessa nature park. In Velloi the Gamper family provide courteous hospitality in their gasthof, which consists of a few rooms and additional apartments suitable for longer stays. The rooms are simply furnished in classic Tyrolean style. Breakfast is served in one of the restaurant's stuben and will make you want to try the Oberlechner's cuisine for lunch and dinner too (25-30 euros, wine excluded).

• 5 double rooms with bathroom (TV on request), and 5 mini-apartments for 2 people, living room, kitchen • Prices: double room single use 30 euros, double 52, breakfast included; mini-apartment (minimum 3 days) 45 euros (10 euro supplement for extra bed) • Credit cards: major ones, Bancomat • Parking right outside. Pets not allowed. Owners always contactable • Bar, restaurant. Living room. Outside area

LANA
Foiana-Völlan

LAUREGNO-LAUREIN
Gosseri-Gassern

NIEDERHOF

🚜 Holiday farm
Via San Giorgio 16
Tel. and fax 0473 557008
E-mail: info@niederhof.it
Internet: www.niederhof.it
Open all year round

SONNE

🍲 Trattoria
Gosseri-Gassern 11
Tel. 0463 530280
Closed Wednesday, never in the summer
Open: lunch and dinner
Holidays: never
Seating: 30 + 20 outdoors
Prices: 20 euros, wine excluded
Credit cards: none, Bancomat only

When the apples are on the trees, you can either help pick the crop or give the Frei Family a hand with their overall agricultural workload (Herbert and Annelise Frei are skilled fruit growers, beekeepers and winemakers). The farmhouse is surrounded by greenery and lies in a scenic position (you can admire Merano in all its central European beauty) near woods and mountain paths. The apartments are all beautiful, fully equipped to cater to the needs of children, while the staff at the small health center specialize in plantar reflexology, Ayurvedic massage and lymph-draining. Local produce, from bread to fresh milk, is served for breakfast. Collective barbecues are organized complete with house wine, and in the fall you can taste the famous törggelen, a dish prepared with chestnuts and grape must, along with other typical specialties of the grape-harvesting season.

• 4 apartments with bathroom, balcony, safe, TV, kitchen • Prices: apartment for 2 people 32-52 euros, for 4-6 people 42-82; breakfast 6.50 euros per person • Credit cards: major ones • Off-street covered parking. Small pets allowed (on request). Owners always contactable • Bar. Garden with playground. Solarium, swimming pool. Fitness center

The boundary between Trentino and Alto Adige is fine but almost palpable, The two regions have always disputed this area under the Maddalene, a mountain chain in the upper part of the Valley di Non that links typically Italian country life to that of the South Tyrol. Political and administrative questions have co-opted the municipalities of Lauregno and Proves into the autonomous province of Bolzano. Lauregno is a mixture of houses, farmsteads, hay barns, stables and small agricultural sheds. The greenery explodes in spring in a triumph of meadow flowers, with dandelions everywhere (this wild medicinal plant is widely used in the typical dishes of Lauregno). Indeed, local restaurateurs almost compete to see who can come up with the best **dandelion** dishes.

In her isolated Sonne gasthof in the meadows, Anna Ungerer uses the flowers when they are in season, from the end of April to the beginning of June. Then the normal mountain dishes return. Hers is a clean and tidy rustic inn with a terrace for eating outdoors in the summer. Here the cuisine is simple and peasant–style; we recommend the various **soups**, pasta, roast meat and tasty salads, served with hard-boiled eggs and speck, and garnished with melted lardo. Home-made **cured meats**, very good **vegetable soups** and **canederli**, pork chops, **grilled and braised meats**, **apple strudel**, fruit tarts and **omelets with jam** complete the repertoire.

The few wines available come from the Caldano cellars. Given the location and limited seating capacity, it's essential to book.

MAREBBE-ENNENBERG
San Vigilio-Sankt Vigil

MAREBBE-ENNEBERG
Mantena-Welschmontal

84 KM NORTHEAST OF BOLZANO SS12 AND SS 49

84 KM NORTHEAST OF BOLZANO SS12 AND SS49

FANA LADINA

GARSUN

🍲 Restaurant
Via Plan de Corones 10
Tel. 0474 501175
Closed Wednesday, never in the high season
Open: lunch and dinner, only dinner in the winter
Holidays: 20-09/30-11, Easter-June 15
Seating: 35 + 15 outdoors
Prices: 33 euros, wine excluded
All credit cards, Bancomat

🍲 Traditional osteria
Località Mantena, 9
Tel. 0474 501282
Closed Monday
Open: lunch and dinner
Holidays: June and November
Seating: 30
Prices: 20 euros, wine excluded
All major credit cards, Bancomat

Alma Kastlunger welcomes you wearing traditional Ladino costume, lace and a dark apron covered with mountain flowers. You thus feel the atmosphere of the valley rightaway. The inn is dedicated to that humble, essential kitchen tool: the pan. The stuben, dating back to the 17th century, is all wood, soft warm lighting and typical furnishings. The cooking is inspired by Ladino traditions and holds pleasant surprises in store.
The antipasti of cured meats, speck and smoked salamis has to be tried, but the strong points of the restaurant are the traditional dishes (which used to be meals in one) with their complicated names: **crafun** (savory fried doughnuts) served with butter and cheese; ancj, **ravioli** seasoned with poppy seeds and cheese, and potatoes and ricotta, **feies da sonj**, green potato leaves served with blackcurrants or sweet krauten. All fully respect the customs of the Ladino people, fewer than 30,000 of whom live in the three provinces of Trento, Bolzano and Belluno. Returning to the food, noteworthy is the game – **venison medallions** and **goulash**, chops, including lamb – and other meat dishes, including pork and **roast shin** with vegetables and beef stew. The desserts include other delicious specialties, such as **omelet soufflé**, cooked in the oven with berry jam, and gnoc de fiara, large semolina gnocchi, sprinkled with sugar and garnished with jam. Plus few good cheeses rediscovered in recent years and a wine list with local labels. Booking is essential.

At the end of a really memorable meal, the Kastlungher family tells you that the price will shortly be going up by one euro, the meal will cost 20 euros, but only during the winter. You couldn't find a better, more honest place! Mamma Maria Luisa and her daughters Maddalena, Cecilia and Francesca have refurbished the old building, which is in the heart of Ladinia, home of the ancient Dolomite people, keepers of a whole heritage of mountain knowledge. The osteria, a sort of farmstead with a stall for the cows, is formed of two recently modernized stuben on the ground floor, and is hard to notice as you enter San Vigilio di Marebbe. There is no written menu and the ladies are proud to suggest you try Ladino cuisine in the simplest manner possible, always with the same dishes.
No antipasti. You start with **panicia**, hot barley soup served with **turtla**, large round ravioli stuffed, depending on availability, with spinach and ricotta, krauten or potatoes, and then fried. You'll always find **cancj**, homemade ravioli served with melted butter and poppy seeds, typical of the country dwellings in this Alpine area. Main courses: **pork shin with potatoes** or, in season, roast **game** served with various preparations of mushrooms freshly picked in the surrounding woods. You finish with Ladino desserts, all homemade, including **jam krapfen**, **puncerle**, fritters filled with blackcurrant jam or small wild berries, **apple strudel** with fresh cream from the milk of the cows. Simple wines from the Caldano cellars. Booking is recommended.

ALTO ADIGE

MELTINA-MOELTEN
Salonetto

REIDER

Rooms to rent
Località Salonetto 1
Tel. 0471 668007
Fax 0471 668407
E-mail: info@gasthof-reider.com
Internet: www.gasthof-reider.com
Open all year round

MONGUELFO-WELSBERG
Tesido-Taisten

SEPPILA

Farm restaurant
Via Haspaberg 30
Tel. 0474 950204
Closed Wednesday, low season open Thursday-Sunday
Open: lunch and dinner
Holidays: one week at Christmas
Seating: 30 + 15 outdoors
Prices: 25-28 euros, wine excluded
All major credit cards, Bancomat

Meltina is a tiny village on the Tschoegglberg plateau at an altitude of 1,000 meters, between Bolzano and Merano, just above Terlano, which can be reached by cable car. Any stay here is particularly pleasant as the location gets a lot of sunshine and is ideal for long walks or mountain biking. This is also where Europe's highest wine cellar, the Arunda, is located. The Reider— an unpretentious place but at once very functional, with wide outdoor spaces and a playground for children – has always been run by the same family. The rooms are simply furnished with a lot of wood everywhere and duvets on the beds; many have a balcony, where you can relax or soak up the sun. The buffet breakfast includes both sweet and savory foods and locally made organic produce.

• 2 single rooms and 6 doubles with bathroom, 5 with balcony • Prices: single 25-29 euros, double 50-68, breakfast included • Credit cards: all, Bancomat • Facility accessible for the mobility challenged. Off-street parking. Small pets allowed. Owners always contactable • Bar, games room. Garden, playground

A secluded farmstead that is hard to find, at the entrance to Val Casies, between Monguelfo and Dobbiaco, where Sepp Hofer (Seppila is the local nickname for Joseph) and his family breed cows, ostriches, boar, **lambs and kid.** They started out as a holiday farm, but given their success they have gradually changed the organization without upsetting the environment. They make their own beer and put an increasing amount of emphasis on their food. Hence they have recently renovated the dining rooms.

The meal, served in the attractive stube or outside in the summer, is presented by Gabrielle Bucher, the farmer's wife. It starts with **home-cured meats** and speck, as well as various types of cheeses. The first courses feature various types of **canederli** from traditional to ones **with wild herbs**, **mushrooms,** beetroot and liver. The delicious **vegetable strudel** is made with freshly picked vegetables. Meat comes from the animals which the family breed and butcher themselves. The **wild boar** is cooked in various manners, as are the beef and, sometimes, the ostrich. The bread is home-baked using cereals grown in the high mountain fields.

The wines are selected from around ten South Tyrolean wine makers, who do not bottle their wine but sell it exclusively to friends. A few labels from other famous cellars are also available.

In **Monguelfo**, the Hell butcher's shop in the center of the town sells game salami, speck and kaminwürstel, smoked sausages.

Montagna-Montan
Casignano-Gschnon

29 km south of Bolzano SS12 or A22

Moso in Passiria
Moos in Passeier

55 km from Bolzano SS44-b towards the Rombo Pass

Dorfnerhof

🍲 Traditional osteria
Località Casignano, 5
Tel. 0471 819798
Closed Monday
Open: lunch and dinner
Holidays: 2 weeks between January and February
Seating: 55 + 40 outdoors
Prices: 24 euros, wine excluded
No credit cards accepted, only Bancomat

Tannenhof

🍲 Hotel trattoria
Località Plata 34
Tel. 0473 649088
Closed Monday
Open: lunch, dinner booking only
Holidays: 3 weeks in November and February
Seating: 60 + 20 outdoors
Prices: 25 euros, wine excluded
No credit cards accepted

The Dorfnerhof is an isolated farmstead on the sunny slopes of the Montagna mountain (it's not a play on words, this really is the name of the place!), a vine-growing hamlet between Egna and the narrow inner road – the old road for the Val di Fiemme – that leads to Trodena and the Mount Corno Park. It's not easy to find the Vescoli family's spartan farm, with its few outside tables outside, a skittle alley and two scenic verandahs, but it's well worth the effort.

Reinhilde with her daughter Anita serve the dishes her young son Anton prepares in the kitchen: **home-cured meats**, courtesy of father Hubert, and appetizers of smoked trout, mousse of baccalà in milk, toasties with seasonal herbs and **ox snout** served hot. First courses: **ravioli with ricotta and spinach** or mushrooms, potato gnocchi (in the spring with river asparagus) and four types of **canederli**, liver, spinach, cheese and speck. The **tagliatelle with game sauce** or fresh vegetables are hand-made. Main courses include **gröstl**, with potatoes and boiled meat, or pork chops with lucaniche, krauten and polenta. You'll often find beef or venison and sometimes rabbit **goulash** too. The **strudel** is always fresh (excellent with **ricotta**) and the jam omelets are delicious. In the fall, for the törggelen, you'll find buckwheat cakes, krapfen and chestnuts.

The cheeses are excellent as is the wine list, including all the best labels from Montagna, the Pinot Nero area par excellence.

A toll must be paid to drive along the Rombo Pass from Austria. The same annoying tax probably has to be paid at the Italian customs point as well. Road maintenance is very costly on this border crossing, and the respective customs offices are still operational, despite the fact that the euro is the common currency. Complaints have come from travelers and also several hotel operators in the area, since the tax discourages travelers and perhaps discourages them from stopping off at the local restaurants. The doubt is confirmed by Prinoth family, who have been running this trattoria and bar for generations. It sleeps ten and guests are mainly people traveling to and from Rombo, a few kilometers away, half an hour's journey in one of the most isolated and loveliest spots in Italy. They stop at Moso for a hot drink or a snack, but less and less to appreciate the traditional food the place has to offer. It's a shame, because the dishes are delicious, the service excellent and the prices very reasonable.

The menu is seasonal: **mushrooms** in summer (excellent soup), game in winter (when the snow hasn't closed the Pass) and, throughout the year, hot **barley soup,** pasta with game sauce, **ravioli with spinach and ricotta**, potato gnocchi and **canederli**. Plus **game with polenta** and typical **groestl** with slices of boiled beef, onions and potatoes. Homemade desserts include typical krapfen and strudel. Some young dairy farmers in the area – there are several goat and sheep farms in the mountains – supply locally matured cheeses. The wine list is short but honestly priced.

Alto Adige

ORA-AUER

PRATO ALLO STELVIO
PRAD AM STILFSER JOCH

20 KM SOUTH OF BOLZANO A22 OR SS12   85 KM NORTHWEST OF BOLZANO, 50 KM FROM MERANO

TSCHÜRTSCH

ZUM DÜRREN AST   ⊗

🍲 Traditional osteria
Piazza della Chiesa 3
Tel. 0471 810648
Closed Wednesday
Open: dinner
Holidays: July
Seating: 90 + 30 outdoors
Prices: 20-25 euros, wine excluded
All credit cards

🍲 Traditional osteria
Località Valnera 6 A
Tel. 0473 616638
Closed Friday, never in high season
Open: lunch and dinner
Holidays: December to Easter
Seating: 30 + 60 outdoors
Prices: 25-27 euros, wine excluded
No credit cards accepted

A hamlet near Bolzano, on the cross-roads leading to Caldaro and the high valleys of Fiemme and Fassa: elegant mansions, courtyards, high walls, orchards, vineyards in the homesteads, here called hof and an integral part of the town. In one of these country dwellings, Edy Pichler has housed the Tschürtch (which means pinecone). In the basement the wine used to be made from the grapes harvested from the vines on the hills. The osteria has a lovely garden with a few tables for summer evenings. Throughout the rest of the year, you eat inside. The dishes are traditional, cooked with seasonal ingredients.

River asparagus – served with cooked ham, eggs and horseradish – features in the spring, **mushrooms** later in the year and, in the fall, the törggelen ritual is accompanied by new wine, chestnuts and homemade **speck.** On the menu you can normally find **polenta with local cheeses, canederli with beef goulash**, calf's head, **barley soup** or vegetable soup, filling **rosticciate** with beef, potatoes and onions, roasts and lots of good cheeses. Home-made puddings range from **apple strudel** to wild berry tarts. The vegetables are all home-grown, and the Lagrein, Schiava and Pinot Bianco wines come from a nearby cellar where they are made from the family's own grapes.

It is advisable to book, especially during the fruit and grape harvest periods, when the host has to divide his time between the fields and the kitchen.

The sign of this simple osteria, popping up out of the meadows on the way to the Stelvio Pass, shows a dry branch: hence the German name for the farmstead. A dry name but warm and friendly welcome. Petra and Klaus Theiner, who run the inn, have improved the interior decorations – rather spartan but in line with Venosta style – and created an attractive garden, with comfortable tables for eating outside during the summer and a good play park for the children. The menu is recited as opposed to written, offering food from the family orchard or bought from local farmers: from the flour to the fruit, from the free-range eggs to the various Venosta Valley cheeses.

Each dish that is served speaks of tradition, starting with the **cured meats** and the **Alpine cheeses**. You start with classic smoked meats, spicy salami, slices of **speck**, **calf's head** or boiled meat with onions and 'gray cheese' (**Graukase**). Then come **vegetable soups**, home-made pasta, gnocchi, followed by **game** – venison, above all, from deer hunted locally and butchered at home – or superb **trout** farmed in the local stream and served with asparagus, home-grown vegetables and **polenta**. In season, you'll find **canederli** with plums or apricots, as well as **gröestl** and eggs, potatoes and speck served straight from the iron pan. Desserts feature **apple strudel**, ricotta or cocoa cake and nevelatte, a sort of mousse with cream and milk. If you want to try the **ribi**, the house specialty made from black polenta and blackcurrants, you must book beforehand.

A small but careful selection of local wines.

RASUN ANTERSELVA
RASEN ANTHOLZ
Anterselva di Mezzo-Antholz Mittertal

98 KM NORTHEAST OF BOLZANO ON THE A22 AND SS49

RENON-RITTEN
Signato-Signat

8 KM NORTHEAST OF BOLZANO

EGGERHOEFE

🍲 Trattoria-farm
Località Masi Egger 42
Tel. 0474 493030
No closing days
Open: lunch and dinner
Holidays: Christmas-Easter
Seating: 30 + 20 outdoors
Prices: 20-25 euros, wine excluded
No credit cards accepted

PATSCHEIDERHOF

🍲 Trattoria-farm
Località Signato 178
Tel. 0471 365267
Closed Tuesday
Open: lunch and dinner
Holidays: two weeks in February, July
Seating: 35 + 70 outdoors
Prices: 30 euros
All credit cards

Anterselva is a closed valley leading off the Val Pusteria, a wedge of land that leads to the Austrian border: luxuriant in the summer, cold and frozen in winter, an area of woods, lakes and winter sports, such as the biathlon. Any time is right to relax, but the summer is best. And the place to do it is at a farmstead like this one, which belonging to Marlies and Christian Leitgeb and is at least 200 years old. Beautifully renovated, it is situated on the mountainside, a little way from the village in an area where the simple language of local tradition reigns supreme. Here guests can try their hand at mowing the grass, shearing the sheep and milking the cows reared in the nearby barns, gentle animals of the local Pinzauner or Pustertaler Sprinze breeds, ideal for these mountain pastures and great milk producers (though their meat is also excellent).

The farm comprises two lovely stuben, where the food is served, and four holiday apartments. During the summer, tables are set outside and guests can savor all the home-made produce – '**gray cheese'**, plus cured meats and **speck**. Menus are simple but excellent. You are sure to find **canederli with goulash**, potato or barley **soup**, roast meat with maize polenta, **grilled or braised beef, and** lots of home-made desserts, such as **apple fritters,** krapfen, buckwheat cake and blackcurrant tart. The bread too is home-baked using wholemeal or rye flour. In autumn you'll find the **tirtlan**, pasta stuffed with vegetables, cheese or poppy seeds (for the sweet version), and fried in lard,

Three different South Tyrol wines are up for tasting, and you'll always find a selection of home-made cheeses.

This old farm is one of the many scattered among the chestnut groves and forests on the steep sunny side of the Renon plateau. The beautiful panorama and wide choice of tracks make this a favorite area for trekkers. Gourmets love to come here too, especially in the fall when they can take part in an unforgettable törggelen.

Following the hairpin bends that lead from the famous wine hills of Santa Maddalena (whose red wine was one of the first in Italy to be protected), the signpost points to the farm. The place has been partly renovated but the original stuben, more than three centuries old, have been conserved and a scenic terrace gives a breathtaking view of the Bolzano valley and the Rosengarten Mountains. Alois Rottensteiner, the owner, does the cooking himself, faithfully reproducing the traditional recipes and the delicious flavors that have never changed over the years.

To start, a rich choice of **cured meats**, all home-smoked, delicious seasoned **speck** and traditional **spleen croutons in stock**. Then come **canederli**, which vary according to the chef's fancy and the season's produce (fillings range from beetroot and spinach to various types of cheese and, very occasionally, with ricotta). When it's on the don't miss the **weinsuppe** (wine soup). The main courses include the very popular baked **pork ribs**, served with sauerkraut when the season is right and potato **gröstel** with roast beef, rabbit or **lamb**. To finish, buckwheat tart and **apple strudel**.

Besides the local Santa Maddalena, other wines from Bolzano are available, as well as excellent labels from other regions of Italy and abroad.

RENON-RITTEN
Soprabolzano

15 KM NORTHWEST OF BOLZANO

SCHLUFF

2-Star Hotel
Località Maria Assunta 2
Tel. and fax 0471 345139
E-mail: info@schluff.it
Internet: www.schluff.it
Holidays variable

To find this hotel, follow the signs to the old shooting range, where it's said Emperor Franz Joseph himself loved to keep his eye in. The hotel is located in an old farmhouse on the edge of the woods, where the road from Bolzano to Renon ends. Don't expect an ultra-modern environment and – be warned! – everything at this gasthof happens at a relaxing pace. Your hosts offer restful rooms, all furnished in traditional Tyrolean style (lots of wood and eider down), balconies with pots of geraniums, gardens and maximum privacy. This pleasantest of settings also includes a children's play area. The food, featuring local traditional, dishes is exquisite too (à la carte meals around 20 euros, excluding wine; half-board 42 euros per person). This romantic, vaguely retro hotel is an ideal base for walks in the woods and mushroom hunting, or for ice-skating when the temperature is low enough.

• 2 single rooms, 4 doubles and 2 triples with bathroom, satellite television; several rooms with a terrace • Prices: single 31 euros, double 62, triple 93, breakfast included • Credit cards: Visa, Bancomat • Off-street parking. Small pets allowed. Owners always contactable • Bar, restaurant. Breakfast room. Garden

RENON-RITTEN
Signato-Signat

6 KM NE OF BOLZANO

SIGNATERHOF

Trattoria – 3-Star Hotel
Località Signato, 166
Tel. 0471 365353
Fax 0471 365480
Closed Sunday dinner and Monday
Open: lunch and dinner
Holidays: January 6-February 1, June15-30
Seating: 50 + 20 outdoors
Prices: 28-30 euros wine excluded
All major credit cards except AE, Bancomat

Two beautiful, wooden old stuben, rooms in traditional Tyrolean style, a gorgeous patio and verandah for the warmer season: this place is family-run and offers a superb breakfast – sweet and savory buffet – and simple but gratifying cuisine.
Meals star with platters of sweet and sour gherkins, local cured meats, speck and smoked sausages. The pasta is homemade daily and features **tagliolini with lamb ragù** and **schlutzkrapfen** stuffed with ricotta and spinach or field herbs, but often available is amore rustic version with sauerkraut filling. Meat choices range from **pork** or lamb **shank** to **gulasch** and ox cheek, of which Erika and Gunther Lobiser offer generous portions. The home specialties are **poppyseed cake with buttermilk**, apple strudel and omelets. The gasthof is well-equipped to welcome tourists on their autumn trips, serving wine must, cheeses, roast meat, sauerkraut and pork. The **cheese**, all local, is carefully chosen and the variety of wines is great, including the area's own Santa Maddalena.
The hotel is open all week long, but if you want to enjoy all the peace and quiet it can offer, October weekends are best avoided.

• 7 doubles, en-suite, television; 3 with balcony • Prices: double single use 40, double 68 euros (extra bed 34 euros), breakfast included • Adjacent public parking. Pets welcome (3-4 euros per day). Owners always on premises • Bar, restaurant. Breakfast room. Patio. Garden

RENON-RITTEN
Collalbo

WEIDACHERHOF

⌒ Holiday farm
Via Viehweider 1
Tel. 0471 356691
Fax 0471 358955
E-mail: info@weidacherhof.com
Internet: www.weidacherhof.com
Open all year round

This vacation farm located at an altitude of 1,000 meters is similar to many others in the area: a rural building that has been continuously maintained and refurbished without altering its original function of dwelling place with cow shed. Markus and Margit Rottensteiner have exploited this combination in a very pleasant way by converting their rural home into beautiful apartments (one of which is suitable for up to eight people), with a fitness center with a relaxing sauna. That's not all. You can also bathe in the mineral waters that spout from the springs, or even in the milk produced by the cows in their shed. Various activities are also possible, although the main emphasis is on body care (you pay for services separately, but prices are affordable), and typical South Tyrolean specialties are also available: homemade speck, local cheeses and a variety of jams.

🍴—0• 4 apartments (2-8 people), with 1-3 bedrooms, bathroom, living room with kitchenette or living room and separate kitchen, satellite television • Prices: for 2 people 42-55 euros, for 2-4 people 55-90, for 6-8 people 85-160; breakfast 8.50 euros per person • Credit cards: none • Parking nearby. Small pets allowed. Owners always contactable • Breakfast room. Terrace. Garden. Fitness center

SALORNO-SALURN
Cauria-Gfrill

FICHTENHOF

⌒ Trattoria – 1-Star Hotel
Località Cauria 23
Tel. and fax 0471 889028
E-mail: uli.pardatscaer@rolmail.net
Internet: www.fichtenhof.it
Closed Monday
Open: lunch and dinner
Holidays: November 7- December 25
Seating: 50
Prices: 22-25 euros, wine excluded
All major credit cards, Bancomat

On the border with Monte Corno nature park stands an old farmstead where the food is good (35-38 euros half board) and the rooms (available all week) are simple but stylishly Tyrolean. From the veranda of the Fichtenhof, which has belonged to the Pardatschers for almost 50 years, the view over the valley is breathtaking: on a clear day you can admire the silhouette of the Brenta and the white peaks of the Adamello and Presanella. The neighboring Trento province influences a few of the recipes and the way the slightly-smoked homemade salamis are prepared; the fine Teroldego wine served at the bar is also from there.
You can't turn down the home-made **speck** to start, but the first courses top the list: potato **gnocchi** with **nettle and finferli mushrooms** and wild **herb risotto** (the herbs are picked in the park) are two late spring specialties. In the fall, **game** rules: **leg of chamois** and **carpaccio of venison** are recommended. Also worth a mention are the typical **canederli**, **polenta nera**, and spinach and ricotta cheese parcels. Twice a week **dark bread** is baked in the house oven and the puddings are home-made too: we suggest you try the **strudel** and the strawberry mousse.
A small selection of wines with a few renowned labels. Accommodation unavailable from January 10 to February 10.

🍴—0• 1 single and 8 doubles, en-suite • Prices: single 25-28 euros, double 50-56, including breakfast • Private outdoor parking, garage (4-5 spaces). Pets welcome. Owners always on premises • Restaurant. Breakfast room, TV room. Patio. Sauna

San Genesio Atesino
Jenesien
Avigna-Afing

San Genesio Atesino
Jenesien

UNTERWEG

🍲 Trattoria-hotel
Avigna 128
Tel. 0471 354273
Closed Wednesday
Open: lunch and dinner
Holidays: 3 weeks in February and 2 weeks in June
Seating: 50 + 60 outdoors
Prices: 23-25 euros, wine excluded
All credit cards, Bancomat

SCHOENBLICK-BELVEDERE

🔑 3-Star Hotel
Località Pichl 15
Tel. 0471 354127
Fax 0471 354277
E-mail: info@schoenblick-belvedere.com
Internet: www.schoenblick-belvedere.com
Closed from 15 January to 10 March

A maze of tracks, country roads and flights of steps run through the farms that line or cut across the road between San Genesio and Bolzano below.
It's not always easy to find this traditional gasthof, which is situated right beneath the main road, between the green woods and the vineyards. The Furggler family, thoroughbred South-Tyroleans, people of few words, are always ready to offer their local specialties. Besides cured meats, speck and **smoked meat,** all strictly home-made, they breed their own farmyard animals and use fresh eggs to make appetizing omelets for you to enjoy during a break in your walks and summer trek.
In the dining hall, beneath a few bedrooms for around ten people – they serve delicious **canederli**, in stock, tomato sauce or country style, tossed in butter. Other first courses are **potato gnocchi**, ravioli with spinach, **barley soup** and vegetable soup made from homegrown produce. Goulash and **roast beef** with potatoes and onions – served with white cabbage salad seasoned with speck tossed in the pan – are just a two of the alternatives to boiled beef or **calf's head in parsley sauce**. In the summer, normally on Thursdays, you can sit under the bower and enjoy a great barbecue with spare ribs, loin, sausages, pork chops, beef and veal. Fried krapfen, apple strudel and fruit tarts are served as desserts.
The hous wine comes from a local cellar, where the must is also used for the postgrape harvest törggelen, and excellent labels are also available from other Bolzano wineries.

The name says it all: this hotel, in fact, offers a breathtaking scenic view over the mountains surrounding Bolzano. San Genesio is a quiet little village above the city, which you can just see in the valley below. Over the centuries it has been frequented by Bolzano's better off and visitors to the Alto Adige. In this renovated gasthof the rooms all have superb views, and some have been converted into suites with small mezzanines for families. Every last detail has been studied meticulously to ensure you have a memorable stay. The cuisine is equally good, combining refined and typically local dishes prepared with organic ingredients selected or produced in mountain farmhouses on the Bolzano plain (meals range from 23 to 30 euros, excluding wines; the convenient half board option is about 8 euros more expensive than B&B). Longer stay packages are available and include various recreational activities such as excursions and cultural and gastronomic tours. The price for a double room in August is 134 euros.

• 2 single rooms and 18 doubles with bathroom, 4 junior suites and 2 suites • Prices: single 51-69 euros, double 84-100, junior suite 102-138, suite 114-156, breakfast included • Credit cards: all, Bancomat • Facility accessible for the mobility challenged. Off-street parking. Small pets allowed. Owners always contactable • Bar, restaurant. Breakfast room. Terrace. Garden. Fitness center

SAN LEONARDO IN PASSIRIA
SANKT LEONARD IN PASSEIER
Vàltina-Walten

58 KM FROM BOLZANO, 29 KM NORTH OF MERANO

SAN LORENZO DI SEBATO
SANKT LORENZEN
Sares-Saalen

75 KM NORTHEAST OF BOLZANO, 7 KM FROM BRUNICO

JÄGERHOF

Restaurant – 3-Star Hotel
Via Passo del Giovo 80
Tel. 0473 656250
Fax 0473 656822
E-mail: info@jagerhof.net
Internet: www.jagerhof.net
Closed Monday
Open: lunch and dinner
Holidays: November 1-December 10
Seating: 80
Prices: 30 euros wine excluded
Credit cards: Visa, Bancomat

About 10 kilometers from San Leonardo, the Augscheller family runs a homely gasthof, ideal for either quick snacks or full meals. The rooms, available all week, are well furnished. There is also a spa with numerous wellness facilities, including hay and steam baths. The excellent breakfast is prepared with local produce.

In the kitchen, tradition and modernity combine: witness the fresh goat's cheese terrine with tomato sauce and the steamed **char** with fresh herbs. Pasta, and often the bread too, are made fresh daily: **canederli,** traditional large-size ravioli (schlutzer), **potato gnocchi** and durum wheat tagliatelle with garlic pesto are ever present on the menu. Main courses: **savory strudel** filled with wild herbs, '**padella del cacciatore**' (venison and lamb cutlets and pork chops), **braised chamois venison Lagrein wine sauce**, game and local lamb. At the end of the meal, buttermilk with blueberries, elderflower sorbet and hay flower semifreddo. Cheeses and vegetables come from surrounding farms. Well-stocked cellar.

• 2 singles, 1 double, 8 triples and 2 with 4 beds, en-suite, safe, television; balcony for most rooms • Prices: single 30-60, double 60-120, triple 87-174, 4 beds 96-192 euros, breakfast included • Private outdoor parking. Small pets welcome (5 euros per day). Porter available from 8 am to midnight • Bar, restaurant. Breakfast included. Spa

MARIA SAALEN

3-Star Hotel
Località Sares-Saalen 4
Tel. 0474 403147
Fax 0474 403021
Closed from November 5 to mid-December and 2 weeks in Spring

Situated under Plan de Corones, one of the most renowned sky resorts in the Dolomites, on the old road between the Pusteria and Badia valleys (nowadays only used by cyclists and pedestrians), this very old gasthof was originally built to accommodate pilgrims traveling to the nearby sanctuary, one of the most famous in the South Tyrol region. The Tauber family has renovated the buildings while keeping the osteria's monumental stuben intact. The equally charming rooms are spacious and equipped with every comfort. In the adjacent fitness center you can have a sauna and, on warmer days, take a dip in the water that gushes from the mountain. The breakfasts are delicious and filling, and much of the food is homemade. The restaurant offers traditional Pusteria-style dishes (18-25 euros, wine excluded). Half board costs around 45-65 euros per person.

• 2 single rooms, 20 doubles with bathroom, television, safe, modem connection, several with balcony • Prices: single 38-58 euros, double 60-100, breakfast included • Credit cards: all, Bancomat • 2 rooms with facilities for the mobility challenged. Parking right in front. Small pets allowed. Owners always contactable • Bar, restaurant. Reading room, relaxation room. Fitness center with sauna and bathing pool

San Martino in Passiria
Sankt Martin in Passeier

45 km northwest of Bolzano SS38

All'Agnello-Lamm ⊗

🍲 Trattoria
Via Paese, 36
Tel. 0473 641240
Closed Wednesday
Open: lunch and dinner
Holidays: November and one week in February
Seating: 80 + 20 outdoors
Prices: 25 euros, wine excluded
All credit cards, Bancomat

Val Passiria is the most characteristic yet least known of the valleys near Merano. In the Merano valley, where the Passirio flows into the Adige, tourists tend to be German, well-off and rather sedentary. Go to Val Passiria for mountain walks, trips on mountain bikes, riverside excursions and tours of the abandoned mines. In this unspoilt valley, goats and sheep are still reared and, hough there are several hotels and other types of accommodation, mass tourism is still unknown.

Arnold Fontana, the cook and owner, buys most of his ingredients from local farmers, one of whom is a goat breeder who uses organic farming methods to guarantee totally genuine meat. A traditional menu offers cured meats and **speck**, lots of different types of **canederli**, home-made pasta, potato gnocchi, cheese **or cep mushroom ravioloni**, risotto with wild herbs and **orzotto with smoked meat**, the house specialty. For second course, lamb and **roast kid**, mainly in the spring, then roasts and **game**, and, only on Fridays, trout or **char** cooked in **wine** or served with various sauces.

The home-made desserts include fruit tarts and **apple strudel,** while an excellent **cheese board** offers at least twelve different varieties, mainly from Alto Adige. Three different types of white and red wine are served also by the glass, and are supplemented by a valid selection of important labels, not all of them from the South Tyrol.

Sarentino-Sarntal

20 km northwest of Bolzano

Auenerhof

🛏️ 3-Star Hotel
Via Auen, 21
Tel. and fax 0471 623055
E-mail: info@auenerhof.it
Internet: www.auenerhof.it
Open all year round

The Val Sarentino road takes you from Bolzano to what is still an isolated area of the Alto Adige. This valley community firmly believes in keeping the landscape, as well as traditions, intact and rethinking development in order to preserve its identity. The villages are indeed very beautiful, as are the mountain resorts. Berghotel is one of the best preserved farmhouses, ideal for a pleasant stay. The Schneider family has long experience in the culinary and wine fields and has decided to add accommodation facilities to its restaurant. The apartments are equipped with every comfort, and there's also a fitness area with sauna and solarium. Breakfast is varied and filling and the half board option is quite economical (48-57 euros per person). Avelignese breed horses are available for treks and snowshoes may be rented for high-altitude excursions. Don't fail to visit the local farmhouses and small museums that conserve precious traditional Sarentino costumes.

• 7 apartments (2-6 people), bathroom, living room, balcony or terrace, television • Prices: apartment for 1-2 people 64-70 euros, for each additional person 25 euros, breakfast included • Credit cards: all, Bancomat • Off-street parking. Small pets allowed (3 euros per day). Reception open from 7 am to 10 pm • Bar, restaurant. Breakfast room. Terrace. Garden. Fitness center

🍲 The Ausner is one of the most famous eateries in the South Tyrol (around 40 euros, wine excluded).

SENALES-SCHNALS
Madonna-Unser Frau in Schnals

OBERRAINDLHOF

Restaurant with accommodation
Località Madonna 49
Tel. 0473 679131
Closed Wednesday
Open: lunch and dinner
Holidays: three weeks in November
Seating: 80 + 20 outdoors
Prices: 30 euros
All major credit cards

This beautiful valley is a place for skiing (possible on the glacier even in August) or for a really relaxing holiday. For some time now South Tyrolean tourism has focused on the rediscovery of local cooking. If you come to this gasthof, given the beautiful furnishings and scrupulous care paid to the smallest details, you have the impression you are staying in a 5-star hotel. There are twelve comfortable rooms all wood-furnished, the genuine local food is served at more than fair prices.

Here you can sample typical **rye flour spaghetti**, not boiled in water but fried in butter or lard and served with ricotta. Another classic is **schlutzkrapfen**, ravioli stuffed with mushrooms or nettles, depending on the season, and **knödl**, canederli usually made from bread dough with different fillings, from liver to spleen or simply cheese, and served in stock. Plus a variety of soups and minestrone. Meats include **game** – medallions of venison in herb crust with cep mushrooms – lamb and pork. Some of the local dairies make ricotta or fresh cheese from fresh milk and serve them directly at the table, or as whipped cream on chocolate cake and vanilla strudel and ib nevelatte, dessert with raisins, pine nuts, honey, cinnamon and lots of buttery cream. Fruit tarts (with apricots from the nearby Val Venosta), poppy seed and chestnut krapfen and other typical desserts are also available. The wine selection is comprehensive.

Nearby in the Madonna district, home-made speck can be bought at Schnalser Speck, which also offers an excellent choice of other typical cured meats.

SESTO–SEXTEN

HOLZER

3-Star Hotel
Via San Giuseppe 18
Tel. 0474 710340
Fax 0474 710602
E-mail: info@hotelholzer.it
Internet: www.hotelholzer.it
Closed from after Easter to mid-June and in November

The name Holzer is very common in Sesto Pusteria, but this is the only family to boast real expertise in hotel management. Young Stefan keeps up the tradition impeccably by constantly improving the hotel, with its beautiful rear garden, located near the road leading to the Dolomites. Everything is geared to the comfort of guests, even those who stop off for just a few hours. The rooms are very comfortable and the kitchen bakes fragrant breads and cakes. The Holzer family provides guests with a variety of local and international food specialties from their nearby store, Feinkost (one of the brothers, Georg, is a wine connoisseur). The Holzers will also be glad to suggest itineraries, pointing out curiosities and places where you'll find genuine Pusteria products. In short, a stay here is sure to be enjoyable. Booking essential.

• 2 single rooms, 13 doubles and 5 triples with bathroom, safe, satellite television • Prices: single 35-50 euros, double 80-120, triple 120-180, breakfast included • Credit cards: all, Bancomat • Off-street parking. Small pets allowed. Owners always contactable • Bar, restaurant. Breakfast room, games room. Garden. Fitness center

TERLANO-TERLAN
Vilpiano

TIROLO-DORF TIROL

SPARERHOF

🗝️ 3-Star Hotel
Via Nalles 2
Tel. 0471 678671
Fax 0471 678342
E-mail: info@hotelsparerhof.it
Internet: www.hotelsparerhof.it
Open all year round

MAIR AM TURM

🗝️ 3-Star Hotel
Via Principale 3
Tel. 0473 923307
Fax 0473 923432
E-mail: info@mairamturm.com
Internet: www.mairamturm.com
Open from March to November

In the Terlano area, the old road that runs from Bolzano to Merano is dotted with tiny village communities, set among vineyards, apple orchards and fields of white asparagus, which grows in spring. The place is full of wineries, holiday farms, boarding houses and typical gasthofen. The Sparerhof is one of the most charming. Unpretentious and modern, but with authentic local touches, it boasts a few well designed rooms, some small suites, lots of wood decor, large beds with duvets and carefully chosen furnishings. Plus a good restaurant, a sauna and an outdoor swimming pool. This gasthof offers a series of theme-based vacation packages, focusing on biking, wine and asparagus tasting, and it's particularly convenient as a base for short stays to enjoy gastronomic itineraries or excursions in the mountains. Breakfast offers a selection of traditional local sweet, or if you prefer, savory fare.

• 15 double rooms with bathroom, safe, satellite television; several with mini-bar • Prices: double room single use 46-57 euros, double 80-92 (29 euro supplement for extra bed), breakfast included • All major credit cards, Bancomat • Off-street parking. Small pets allowed (5 euros per day). Reception open 7am-1am • Bar, restaurant. Breakfast room. Garden. Swimming pool, solarium, sauna

Tirolo is a small town above Merano which, in the early years of the eleventh century saw the beginning of the saga of the noble Counts of Tyrol, a decisive chapter for the Brenner Pass area. The magnificent castle bears witness to the legend. Given the beauty of its houses and hotels that cater for mainly German and Swiss tourists, Tirolo has an exclusive air about it. But there are also some typical gasthofen that are constantly being renovated. The one owned by the Prantl family dates from 1420 and has always offered a pleasant stay in Tyrol. The rooms are completely modern, fully equipped for a relaxing stay and with a splendid view over Merano, the Tessa mountains and the River Adige valley. The cuisine is wholesome, with vegetarian and gluten-free menus (15-20 euros, wine excluded, half board 49.50-56.50 euros per person). There are many things to do in the area: long walks along the ancient irrigation canals and visits to museums, the castle and the unique bird recovery center, where birds of prey in difficulty are first treated and then released. You can see demonstrations of falconry there too.

• 3 single rooms and 8 doubles with bathroom, safe, satellite television • Prices: single 40-44 euros, double 72-87, breakfast included • Credit cards: major ones, Bancomat • Off-street parking. Small pets allowed. Owners always contactable • Bar, restaurant. Breakfast room. Garden. Terrace

Ultimo-Ulte
Santa Gertrude-Sankt Gertraud

57 km west of Bolzano SS38

Falschauerhof

Trattoria
Santa Gertrude 14
Tel. 0473 790191
No fixed closing days
Open: lunch and dinner
Holidays: in January
Seating: 15
Prices: 20-25 euros, wine excluded
Credit cards not accepted

The panorama is amazing. A farmstead surrounded by green meadows and larches, high mountains in the background and the tinkling of goat bells as you climb you to the top from Lana through one of the most uncontaminated valleys in the Alps, the Val D'Ultimo.
On this picturesque farm, the Gruber family grow their own vegetables and berries and breed sheep, goats and cattle. Everything in this magical place is rigorously home-made using mountain farming methods and it really is worth your while to stop off here, if only to enjoy a drink, taste an apple fritter or **knodel with cheese** or **barley soup**, or buy the produce. The Gruber family butcher their own animals, make their own dairy products and serve all the area's typical dishes. Elisabeth will welcome you to the wooden stube and describe the various dishes on the menu, which changes with the season. Not to be missed are the **speck**, **smoked beef**, cured meats, desserts such as the **apple strudel**, and, above, all the freshly made **cheeses**, soups – **muas**, roasted flour with milk – and a special broth with goats' milk. Other classics are **schluter**, large ravioli stuffed with herbs and cheese, roast pork, beef, veal, goat and kid, served with freshly picked vegetables (delicious prepared in sweet and sour sauce).
Desserts include cider, raspberries, juniper syrup and other local specialities, while the wine list features the best labels from the South Tyrol.

Valle di Casies-Gsies
San Martino-Sankt Martin

99 km northeast of Bolzano

Kahnwirt

2-Star Hotel
Frazione San Martino 19
Tel. 0474 978409
Fax 0474 978013
E-mail: info@kahnwirt.com
Internet: www.kahnwirt.com
Closed June and 9-25 December

The hotel rooms are all furnished in traditional Pusteria style with snug corners and lots of wood everywhere to conserve memories of the past. The rooms fascinate by their sheer simplicity. In the building next door, a residence with 14 apartments was inaugurated not long ago. Guests are treated like friends to traditional food, breakfast with the morning's fresh milk, yogurt, jams and other Pusteria treats. This gasthof has been in operation for fully five centuries, a veritable monument to Valle di Casies hospitality. Many of the ingredients used in the kitchen (menu 14-17 euros, wine excluded, half board 32-45 euros) are produced on the nearby farmhouse, which has its own stable, cattle and other animals. Booking is essential, but a stay here is well worth the trip.

• 3 double rooms, 2 triples and 1 with 4 beds, bathroom, balcony, 14 apartments (2-4 people) with kitchen • Prices: double room single use 18-35 euros, double 32-64, triple 48-96, 4 beds 64-128, breakfast included; apartment 35-80 euros • Credit cards: none • 1 apartment with facilities for the mobility challenged. Off-street parking. Small pets allowed. Owners always contactable• Restaurant (evenings only, for residents only). Terrace

VALLE DI CASIES-GSIES
Planca di Sotto-Unterplanken

VARNA-VAHRN
Novacella-Neustift

99 KM NORTHEAST OF BOLZANO SS49 TURN OFF AT MONGUELFO

45 KM NORTHEAST OF BOLZANO

DURNWALD

PACHERHOF

🍲 Trattoria
Planca di Sotto, 33
Tel. 0474 746920
Closed Monday
Open: lunch and dinner
Holidays: second half of June
Seating: 80
Prices: 28 euros, wine excluded
Credit cards: CartaSi, Bancomat

🔑 3-Star Hotel
Località Novacella-Neustift
Tel. 0472 835717
Fax 0472 801165
E-mail: info@pacherhof.com
Internet: www.pacherhof.com
Closed mid-January and end-February

Erich Mayr is a refined cook, having gained experience in kitchens all round the world. He decided to come home though to continue in the family business and give the trattoria's authentic, simple, tasty cooking a more modern touch, at once reviving the gastronomic specialties of Pusteria, the Val Casies in particular.
Instead of turnips he uses Graukäse to make his **canederli**, or mushrooms and potatoes to make the **spelt flour soup** after browning them in butter. Not to be missed are his hand-made pappardelle with Graukäse, **schwoassnudeln mit gaukas**. In this comfortable restaurant with its wooden stube, veranda overlooking the meadows and excellent basement wine bar, the rest of dishes follow the seasons and local eating habits: **home-cured meats**, cheeses such as Zieger and **Graukäse** served with onions and vinegar, wholemeal pasta, different types of **schlutzer**, large ravioli stuffed with cheese or herbs, lots of different varieties of canederli, as well as 'revisited', lighter dishes, using **game** – mainly venison – lamb, veal from animals bred in the nearby stables, pork, and all sorts of roasts. Plus home-made cheeses, several aged on the family farmstead.
To conclude, home-made desserts: strudel, fritters, fruit canederli, **krapfen**, buckwheat cake, served with herb drinks, homemade fruit juice and an amazing selection of wines, which can be personally chosen in the wine bar and tasted at the bar.

Novacella Abbey, a bulwark of religious culture and witness to centuries of experience in wine growing, is just a stone's throw away, This characteristic gasthof used to be a farmhouse with a vineyard – wine-grower Josef Huber produces excellent Sylvaner and other Valle d'Isarco whites – but has now been converted into a modern holiday home. Everything is original, from the entrance to the rooms, pleasantly furnished in perfect South Tyrolean style, with the focus on attention to detail and wine. Rooms are designed to offer a view of the vineyards or valleys, and a small annex is available for families. The wholesome home-made breakfast includes fresh baked bread, jams and eggs in true northern European style. The farmhouse also has a swimming pool, a small fitness center, a trattoria (around 20 euros, excluding wine; half board 46-78 euros per person) and a good wine cellar. In August the price of a double room can go up to 140 euros.

• 18 double rooms and 4 suites with bathroom, safe, television, modem connection, several rooms with balcony • Prices: double room single use 55 euros, double 84-120, suite 120-160, breakfast included • Credit cards: all, Bancomat • Facility accessible for the mobility challenged, 1 specifically designed room. Off-street parking. Small pets allowed (8 euros per day). Reception open 24 hours a day • Restaurant. Breakfast room. Swimming pool, fitness center

VILLANDRO
VILLANDERS
San Valentino-Sankt Valentin

VIPITENO-STERZING
Tulve-Tulfer

ROCKHOF

Holiday farm
Località San Valentino 9
Tel. and fax 0472 847130
Closed from January to end-March

PRETZHOF

Restaurant
In Tulve
Tel. 0472 764455
Closed Monday and Tuesday, always open in August
Open: lunch and dinner
Holidays: 10 days during the Carnival period
Seating: 50 + 20 outdoors
Prices: 32-35 euros, wine excluded
All major credit cards, Bancomat

This agriturismo is not too far away from the Chiusa highway exit, on the sunny slopes of the Villandro, where vineyards are still to be found even at an altitude of almost 700 meters. It will come as no surprise to learn that the Augschoell family are winegrowers who make excellent wines, from fruity whites to a robust red made from Lagrein and local grapes. A few rooms are available for guests, all of whom are welcomed like friends. In this wonderful stube, the farm also serves hot meals, including new wine with chestnuts for the fall törggelen feast. The farmhouse cures pork and age Alpine cheeses. You'll be treated to these products and others in filling breakfasts, served in a pleasant, informal way in this relaxing rustic setting. For longer stays there are also two comfortable apartments.

• 4 double rooms with bathroom, and 2 apartments (2-4 people) with kitchenette • Prices: double room single use 25 euros, double 40 (10 euro supplement for extra bed), breakfast included; apartment 20 euros per person• Credit cards: none • Off-street parking, garage. Pets not allowed. Owners always contactable • Restaurant (from October to March for residents only). Breakfast room. Terrace.

The first member of the family that now owns the restaurant bought the farmstead in 1695 from Christian Prez of Stilves, hence, presumably, the current name. Val di Vizze is situated off the usual tourist track in a natural, wild area surrounded by green meadows and luxuriant woods. Cattle breeding, cheese and speck production and hunting were routine activities for all the local families, and they now guide the philosophy of the present owners of the restaurant. Farmsteads dot this extreme region of Italy, which extends into Austria along the Brenner Pass, and the last before the border is Pretzhof, which enjoys an extremely attracrive position and which we highly recommend.

Here the smoked **speck**, home-made according to the traditional maturing techniques, is exceptionally sweet and the **cured meats** are very good too, especially those made from game. Seated in the warm stube, it's a delight to taste the various types of cheeses (the Graukäse is excellent) made in the family's mountain cottage at over 2,000 meters above sea level. Besides snacks and cold dishes, always available, the kitchen also serves **canederli with speck** or with Graukäse, or gray cheese. We suggest trying the variation of canederli with fresh seasonal fillings. The traditional soups are very tasty, in particular the barley soup and **weinzuppe** made with wine. Then come **game** and beef dishes, made with meat from the cattles raised in the valley. To close the meal, a good selection of home-made typical or creative desserts, the latest invention being white poppy cake.
The wine list offers a very good selection of labels from the Alto-Adige region.

VENETO

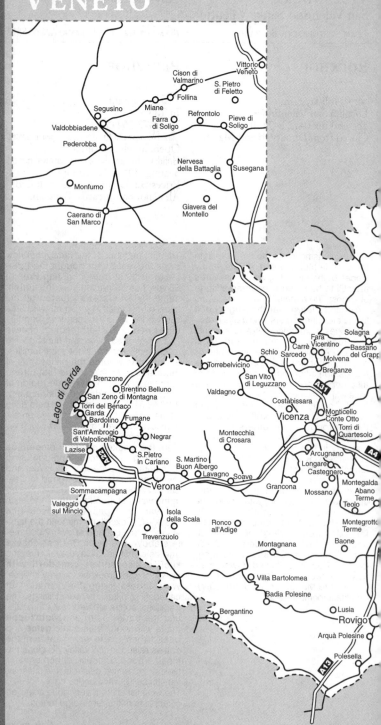

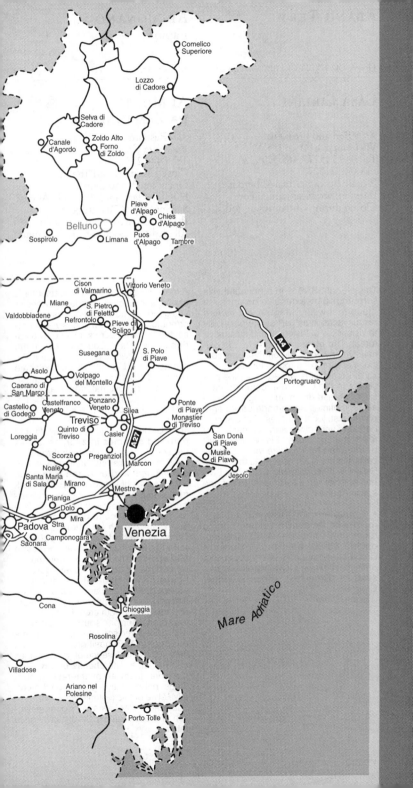

ABANO TERME

11 KM SOUTHWEST OF PADUA ON SS 250

CASA CIRIANI

Bed and breakfast
Via Guazzi 1
Tel. 049 715272-368 3779226
Fax 049 715272
E-mail: bb.casaciriani@libero.it
Internet: www.casaciriani.com
Closed during Christmas period

This elegant B&B is in a beautiful villa surrounded by extensive grounds – a place that will guarantee you have a restful vacation as well as the possibility to visits sites of historical and cultural interest. The pleasant house is approximately thirty years old and features spacious and relaxing rooms furnished with style. Breakfast is served under the portico or in the breakfast room and consists of bread, fresh fruit, yoghurt, cereals, sometimes homemade cakes and, on request, local cheeses. The center of Padua is very close and you can easily reach the Euganean Hills (your host will be pleased to organize visits to wine cellars in the area) as well as the Brenta Riviera with its splendid villas. The B&B has special rates for guests to use the spa in Abano.

• 3 double rooms, with bathroom; 1 room with balcony • Prices: double room single occupancy 40-50 euros, double 65-80, breakfast included • Credit cards: none • Off-street parking. Small pets allowed. Owners always present. • Breakfast room. Lounge. Grounds

ARCUGNANO
Lapio

12 KM SOUTH OF VICENZA

AI MONTI DA ZAMBONI

Restaurant
Via Santa Croce 14
Tel. 0444 273079
Closed Monday and Tuesday
Open: lunch and dinner
Holidays: January 1-10 and in August
Seating: 120 + 70 outdoors
Prices: 35 euros, wine excluded
All credit cards except AE, Bancomat

A meal at Severino Trentin's restaurant is always a rewarding experience, whether you go for the traditional à la carte menu or opt for innovation which is well-represented in the 40-euro set menu (two antipasti, two first courses, two main courses and two puddings). What these two aspects of Zamboni's cuisine share is careful selection of seasonal ingredients and professional presentation; the difference lies in the continuity of the former and the continual evolution of the latter.
The classic menu includes **brasolara** of pork and **sardines in saor**, as well as seasonal dishes such as salads with ovoli mushrooms and garlic bread with ciccioli; followed by **bigoli with arna**, **risotti** ai bisi of Lumignano, Berici black truffles or Bassano del Grappa white asparagus and fettuccine with finferli mushrooms. Second courses include fish dishes such as **pike** from Lake Fimon and **baccalà** alongside **polastrelo in tecia** and, in fall-winter, **torresano allo spiedo**. The creative menu, on the other hand, is changed every day: antipasti may include girello di manzo steeped in spices and salt and then smoked, burrata with cherry ice cream and calf's head with cren; then come fig and black pepper soup, pappardelle with spiced venison sauce, chicken in a peppermint and basil crust, duck in a herb crust with a sauce of green apples and red wine. The **cheese board** is impressive, followed by interesting puddings that once again focus on the creative style of this restaurant.
The wine cellar has a very good selection and offers an excellent quality-price ratio.

ARIANO NEL POLESINE

36 KM SOUTHEAST OF ROVIGO ON SS 495

DUE LEONI

☛●3 Star Hotel
Corso del Popolo 21
Tel. 0426 372129
Fax. 0426 372130
E-mail: italiaservisi@tin.it
Closed in the first half of July

ARQUÀ POLESINE
Granze

8 KM SOUTHWEST OF ROVIGO

TRATTORIA DEGLI AMICI

🍲Trattoria
Via Quirina 4
Tel. 0425 91045-91187
Closed Wednesday
Open: lunch and dinner
Holidays: in fall/winter and the week of Aug. 15
Seating: 80 + 35 outdoors
Prices: 30-35 euros, wine excluded
All credit cards, Bancomat

Between the Po delta and lower Polesine is this small village that mainly lives off agriculture and raising cattle; only recently has the development of aquaculture been increased. In past times the hotel was a staging post where carriages changed horses and on the façade of the building you can still see two bronze lions. Today it's modern, elegant and friendly, furnished with great attention to detail. The very generous breakfast made using top quality products can either be eaten in the breakfast room or bar. In the restaurant a meal costs an average of 35 euros per person, excluding wine. A stone's throw away when you cross the Po di Goro you're in Emilia Romagna, and not far away towards the Adriatic coast we can recommend a visit to the island of the Donzella with its interesting vegetation, which includes water buttercups, bulrushes, water-lilies, cane, and bird life.

• 5 single and 8 double rooms, with bathroom, TV, modem connection • Prices: single 50 euros, double 70 (10 euro supplement for extra bed), breakfast included • Credit cards: all except DC, Bancomat • Communal areas accessible to the mobility challenged. Off-street parking, some covered (there is a charge) and free parking right outside. Small pets allowed. Owners always reachable. • Bar, restaurant. Breakfast room, reading and TV room

Granze, a small village with the atmosphere of times gone by, is nestled in the verdant Venetian countryside south of Rovigo. Here you'll find this trattoria, managed since 1996 by Valerio and Nicola with their mother Edda in the kitchen. Dishes reflect the cuisine of the Polesine region with a personal touch: in the summer Valerio uses lots of fresh fish, herbs and mushrooms, while in the winter the emphasis shifts to game and pork. The trattoria has several rooms, with a simple main dining room and a smaller room for a more intimate experience; in summer, meals are served on the veranda.
Antipasti always include excellent cured meats (Montagnana cured ham, homemade salami), joined in spring and summer by raw langoustines, zucchini carpaccio with Grana Padano cheese and grilled asparagus with balsamic vinegar. First courses include homemade pasta in dishes like **pasta e fagioli** with maltagliati, **bigoi in salsa**, **tortellini in capon broth**, tagliatelle with mixed meat sauce and peas and green gnocchi with porcini mushrooms. The most characteristic main course is **eel in coccio** baked in the wood-burning oven; also try the **baccalà** with polenta, marinated beef carpaccio with mixed greens, the excellent **bondola** with creamed potatoes, wild duck, breast of guinea fowl with stuffed vegetables and grilled lamb chops with mostarda; sides include delicious patate della nonna. Homemade desserts such as tiramisù or warm apple pudding are worth trying.
The local osteria-enoteca is an enjoyable place, with cheeses and cured meats accompanied by a wide selection of excellent wines.

CA' DERTON

LA TRAVE

Restaurant-wine cellar
Piazza D'Annunzio 11
Tel. 0423 529648
Closed Sunday and Monday for dinner
Open: lunch and dinner
Holidays: 20 days in winter, 20 in summer
Seating: 35
Prices: 35 euros, wine excluded
All credit cards, Bancomat

Traditional osteria-trattoria
Via Bernardi 15
Tel. 0423 952292
Closed Monday
Open: lunch and dinner
Holidays: 20 days in winter, 20 in summer
Seating: 70
Prices: 27-30 euros, wine excluded
All major credit cards

The historic town centre sees Nino and Antonietta Baggio welcome guests to their delightful restaurant. The windows in the elegant dining room (35 seats) offer a splendid view of the streets close to the castle; there is also an snug little dining room on the first floor and a small enoteca (wine store), with tables outside. Antonietta, helped by her children, discreetly welcomes guests and suggests the best dishes. Traditional Venetian fare includes several elegant variants prepared by Nino.
To start - depending on the season - try pumpkin flowers stuffed with finferli mushrooms and Ricotta del Grappa, the rabbit terrine or moscardini with vegetables. First courses include the superb **pasta e fagioli** with Levada beans and home-made **bigoi al torchio** (the pasta-making press is also home-made) topped **with duck sauce** or tuna roe, green onion and mint. Other excellent dishes include **risotto al morlacco**, **risi e bisi** from Borso del Grappa, and **sopa coada** in winter. The fall is the ideal period to taste traditional Venetian meats: **goose in onto**, pork, guinea fowl with **peverada**, and a large selection of game. **Alpagotto lamb** and **quails** are served all year round. Alternatives include guanciale di vitello all'Amarone or fillet of sea bream with zucchini purea and cream of egg plant. Close with a fig strudel, Asolana cream, tortino della nonna with hot chocolate and green apple sauce, or blancmange with Maser cherries. For those preferring a savory finish, a selection of local **cheeses** is served with home-made conserves.
The carefully selected wine list meets every preference.

Pietro Bembo made a wise decision when he decided to spend a few years at the court of Queen Cornaro. He must have passed through Pagnano, past the 15th-century forge (recently restored) and almost certainly enjoyed a glass of wine or two - ombra - in the local osterias, which were then more common. Today the Contrada Bernardi is home to this osteria which dates back more than a century, and still serves as a meeting place where people of the village stop by to drink a glass or enjoy the excellent local cuisine served with style. The evocative setting is dominated by the knotty beam that gives the place its name. The delightful hosts Franca and Veronica have been serving dishes prepared by Guido since 1994.
First courses focus on local traditions, particularly dishes like **sopa coada**, **pasta e fagioli**, **pumpkin gnocchi with smoked ricotta**, **bigoli (thick spaghetti) with chicken-liver sauce and pungitopo**. Main courses include meat and fish dishes: **guinea fowl with peverada** sauce, **polenta and sc'ios** (snails), lamb chops, duck tagliata with porcini mushrooms, game with mushrooms (in the fall), **polenta and baccalà**, cuttlefish al nero, a tasty zuppa di pesce, spaghetti with langoustines and mussels and **stuffed doves**. A must among the homemade desserts is the D'Annunzio cake.
The wine list is quite good, with labels from various Italian regions, particularly the Veneto and Friuli.

BADIA POLESINE

BAONE

LE CLEMENTINE

☛—◐ Holiday farm
Via Colombano 1239 b
Tel. e fax 0425 597029
E-mail: agriturismo@leclementine.it
Internet: www.leclementine.it
Open all year

BROLO DI CA' OROLOGIO

☛—◐ Holiday farm
Via Ca' Orologio 7 a
Tel. 0429 50099-336 376100
Fax 0429 610875
E-mail: caorologio@tin.it
Internet: www.caorologio.com
Open from end of March to mid-November

Le Clementine is a vacation farm managed by Luciana Vallese with help from her husband, the ideal place to stay for those who want to explore the Polesine area. It's located approximately 50 meters from the River Adige in a setting you can get to know using mountain bikes provided by the farm or simply on foot. The land is cultivated with vines, cereals and vegetables and the farm also raises pigs and poultry. Produce from the farm is used in the restaurant, which is open to non-residents from Friday to Sunday and every evening for residents. For non-residents a meal costs from 20-25 euros per person, whereas guests will pay less. Breakfast is homemade, generous and inviting. The Art Nouveau-style rooms are frescoed and furnished with antiques, features that will make your stay even more pleasant. Rovigo, Ferrara, Adria, Padua, the Palladian villas, the Averto Valley Oasis, Delta del Po Park and the Mount Baldo Nature Reserve are easily reachable from the farm.

• 5 double, 2 triple and 1 four-bed rooms, with bathroom, air-conditioning, TV • Prices: double room single occupancy and double 52 euros, triple 68, four-bed 78, breakfast included • Credit cards: major ones, Bancomat • Communal areas accessible to the mobility challenged. Off-street parking. No pets allowed. Owners always present. • Restaurant. Breakfast room, lounge. Garden

This vacation farm is in the Euganean hills, inside an estate mostly given over to vineyards and with a few olive trees. The facility run by Maria Gioia Rosellini is in a very old villa, part of which dates back as far as the late 15th century. The rooms have wooden floors and beamed ceilings, and are furnished with antiques. Those who book for a whole week will only pay for six nights instead of seven. The buffet-style breakfast includes produce from the farm: eggs, yoghurt, jams, bread and inviting homemade cakes. Inside the Euganean Hills Regional Park there are many interesting trails with picnic areas equipped with tables and benches. Here you'll be able to admire the very varied flora and also animal species that are no longer found in the surrounding areas.

• 2 double rooms, with bathroom, fridge, TV, modem connection; 2 studios (2-3 persons) and 2 two-room apartments (2-4 persons) with kitchenette • Prices: double room single occupancy 59-90 euros, studio 72-90, two-room apartment 87-110; breakfast 7 euros per person • Credit cards: MC, Visa, Bancomat • Off-street parking. No pets allowed. Owners always reachable. • Breakfast room, lounge. Garden, solarium

28 KM NORTH-WEST OF VERONA

28 KM NORTHWEST OF VERONA SS 249

COSTADORO

IL GIARDINO DELLE ESPERIDI ⊗ 🍾

🔑 Holiday farm
Via Costabella 29 a
Tel. 045 6210493-7211668
Fax 045 6227330
E-mail: info@agriturismocostadoro.com
Internet: www.agriturismocostadoro.com
Open all year

🍲 Restaurant
Via Mameli 1
Tel. 045 6210477
Closed Tuesday and Wednesday lunch
Open: lunch and dinner
Holidays: variable
Seating: 35 + 35 outdoors
Prices: 32-35 euros, wine excluded
All major credit cards, Bancomat

Valentino Lonardi's farm, left for him to manage after the recent retirement of his father, Gianni, can boast a small record: it's the only one to produce all the listed types of Bardolino wine. 200 meters away from the wine cellar, on a road offering a beautiful view, the Lonardi family has opened a pleasant vacation farm, which is managed by Valentino's wife Mariangela. The rooms are furnished with taste and bedsteads are in wrought iron. Apart from the rooms there are two apartments that can be rented on a weekly basis (price ranging from 500-700 euros). In front of the house there's a garden where you will be able to chill out and soak up the sun. The buffet breakfast is served in the basement and includes homemade cakes, fruit juices, yoghurt and cured meats. For those who want to have lunch they have an agreement with the Costadoro restaurant (which doesn't belong to the Lonardi family, although it's again a family business where you'll be able to enjoy the local cuisine). In the surrounding area, visits to the grounds of Villa Cedri and the Olive Oil Museum are a must.

• 10 double rooms, with bathroom, air-conditioning, mini-bar, satellite TV, almost all rooms have balconies; 2 mini-apartments (2 persons) with kitchenette • Prices: double room single occupancy 50 euros, double 75-85, breakfast included • Credit cards: all except AE, Bancomat • 1 room designed for the mobility challenged. Off-street parking. No pets allowed. Owners always present. • Breakfast room, tea room. Conference room. Garden, solarium. Pool

In the summer the Giardino delle Esperidi on Lake Garda is like a sip of fresh water on a hot day. The few tables here in the historic centre of Bardolino aren't crowded with holiday-makers but filled instead by local people enjoying aperitivi and snacks in typical Veneto osteria style, or well-informed tourists looking for fine cuisine and excellent wine. The thirty-five seats inside are set amidst antique furniture, bottles and knick-knacks, and there are the same number outside in the pedestrian area. The restaurant - as the almost obsessive care over details suggests - is managed entirely by women: Susy Tezzon and Annamaria Vedovelli look after the dining room, while shy and reserved Mari Vedovelli in the kitchen has been continually improving her culinary skills year after year. The wine list boasts around 700 labels, with around 30 wines available by the glass.
The cooking strictly follows the seasons and the market: **lake fish fritters**, salt cod fritters, aged bull meat, lavender **fettuccine** with **whitefish**, barley soup, **cappellini with rabbit**, lemon and olives, fillets of lake fish with a balsamic sauce and green beans, whitefish rosette with zucchini and stuffed squash flowers, **parmigiana with black truffles**. Alternatively, try the platter of cured meats or the cheese board. Desserts include soft chocolate cake and crème brûlée with rosemary or lavender. The tiny inside courtyard has a cigar room.

💧 Valentino Lonardi is one of the best producers of DOP Garda extra-virgin olive oil: the Costadoro farm, which he manages with his father Gianni, is on the panoramic Bardolino road.

MELOGRANO

Restaurant
Via Chiesa 35
Tel. 0424 502593
Closed Monday
Open: lunch and dinner
Holidays: Jan. 15-30/June 15-25
Seating: 80 + 80 outdoors
Prices: 30-35 euros, wine excluded
Credit cards: Visa, Bancomat

TRATTORIA DEL BORGO

Trattoria
Via Margnan 7
Tel. 0424 522155
Closed Wednesday and Saturday at lunch, in
summer Sunday and Saturday for lunch
Holidays: variable
Seating: 40 + 40 outdoors
Prices: 28-32 euros, wine excluded
All credit cards except AE, Bancomat

Starting out from Bassano del Grappa in the direction of the Asiago plateau you have an easy drive to Valrovina through delightful hills planted with olive trees. The restaurant is close to the church and has two fine dining rooms, a garden and a veranda. The atmosphere is friendly and the attentive and courteous staff ensure efficient service even when the restaurant is full. Owner Gigi suggests wines and describes the dishes that his wife Carla prepares using typical, seasonal produce.
The star of the spring menu is unquestionably the **Bassano white asparagus**, which also features in themed set menus. There is a consistent focus on local produce, including seasonal wild herbs, in the first courses: **risotto** with creamed spring vegetables **with Vezzena cheese**, nettle gnocchetti with cherry tomatoes and smoked ricotta, tagliolini with squash blossoms, asparagus and scallops. We also recommend the tasty **guinea-fowl ravioli** with pancetta, asparagus and shavings of pecorino cheese. Autumn flavors include **radiccio and ravioli gnocchetti with Morlacco del Grappa cheese and walnuts**, as well as chestnut ravioli with sweet potato and guinea fowl. Roasts include **fillet of beef cooked with teroldego wine**, wild-asparagus-like **bruscandoli and pine nuts**; **guinea fowl** stuffed with chestnuts and pomegranate; and **duck breast with radicchio** and juniper. The summer menu concentrates on fish dishes and, occasionally, special themed menus. Desserts are homemade, well-presented and delicious: parfait with almonds and amaretto, crunchy semifreddo with chocolate, **caramel pears** with spumone allo zabaione and chocolate. The wine list consists of Triveneto labels, with wines from other Italian regions and abroad.

Just 400 meters from the historic centre of Bassano, this delightfully welcoming trattoria has a fine interior and a quiet garden with a superb arbor of vines, wisteria and roses. On our last visit, we missed the friendly, informal style that had struck us in the past, but even the new restaurant atmosphere still offers attentive service and presentation.
The menu is largely based on seasonal ingredients, especially the antipasti (**smoked beef** with asparagus or mushrooms, lardo with fioroni figs, and the classic **soppressa with yellow polenta** and a generous sea-food salad) and first courses (**ravioli** stuffed with cep mushrooms, asparagus or other vegetables, smoked ricotta or crustaceans, the classic **risotti**, fettuccine with asparagus or mushrooms). The main courses in spring focus on **Bassano white asparagus** (try them **with eggs**), while other seasons offer **snails with polenta**, **mutton kebabs**, speck cooked with artichokes (winter) and the very traditional **baccalà alla Vicentina.** Puddings include biscuits served with a glass of dessert wine, panna cotta, mousse with strawberries or other fruit.
The wine list is reasonable; a white and a red are also served by the glass.

Near Ponte degli Alpini are two historic grappa distilleries: Nardini - a typical old shop with bar on the old bridge itself; Salita Ferracina: the sales outlet of the Jacopo Poli distillery, with an interesting Grappa Museum. In viale Asiago 84, at the Azienda Due Santi, Stefano has excellent extra virgin olive oils - frantoio and leccino varieties.

BELLUNO
Castion

BERGANTINO

3 KM SOUTHEAST OF BELLUNO

52 KM WEST OF ROVIGO SS 16

TENUTA DI NOGHERAZZA

🛏️🔑 Bed and breakfast
Via Gresane 78
Tel. 0437 927461
Fax 0437 925882
E-mail: amiarif@tin.it
Internet: www.nogherazza.it
Closed 3 weeks in February

DA LUCIANO

🍲 Restaurant with hotel
Via Cavallotti 81-86
Tel. 0425 805120
Closed Monday
Open: lunch and dinner
Holidays: July 27-August 25
Seating: 120 + 20 outdoors
Prices: 30 euros, wine excluded
All credit cards, Bancomat

This estate in the hamlet of Castion is the ideal place to stay, even for the most demanding guests. The rooms have been very well refurbished and are furnished with great attention to detail: mountain-style floors and furniture made of hand-planed wood, beautiful curtains and linen sheets. Every room has cable TV and a video recorder, and you will be able to borrow cassettes from the well-stocked video collection. Andrea Miari Fulcis has converted what were once the homes and workplaces of share-croppers on the estate of his father, Count Giacomo, so that today it looks like an old rural hamlet. During summer you can have lunch on the beautiful terrace with view of the Dolomites (meals cost about 25 euros per person, excluding wine) and explore the surrounding area. On Lake Santa Croce you can sail and windsurf; in winter, skiing enthusiasts can use the Nevegal facilities.

• 6 double rooms, with bathroom, mini-bar, satellite TV • Prices: double room single occupancy and double 80 euros (20 euro supplement for extra bed), breakfast included • Credit cards: major ones, Bancomat • Communal areas accessible to the mobility challenged. Off-street parking. Small pets allowed. Owners always reachable. • Bar, restaurant. Breakfast room. Conference room. Terrace

Bergantino is renowned worldwide for the skill of its craftsmen in building fair-ground attractions; their creativity means they can build machines capable of meeting even the most unusual of requirements. The town has even dedicated a museum in Palazzo Strozzi to these craftsmen, chronicling the evolution of theme parks from their origins to the current use of modern technology. The town enjoys a position at the crossroads of three regions - Veneto, Lombardy and Emilia: this could cause some confusion, especially in terms of cuisine, but Da Luciano avoids this quandary. Instead the family management takes a balanced approach that makes the most of the different surrounding culinary traditions.
Start with the excellent cured meats – the influence of Emilia is evident here, with Parma ham, Valtellina bresaola, superb homemade salami, coppa and pancetta. The first courses blend the traditions of the Veneto and Emilia: **pumpkin tortelli with butter and sage** (at the end of August, Bergantino holds a festival dedicated to pumpkins), cappelletti in broth, **pasta e fagioli**, **bigoi in salsa** (pasta al torchio with anchovies), strozzapreti with various sauces. The main courses are also good and include **donkey stew with polenta**, cotechino, **luganega with white wine** and excellent **baccalà with polenta**. There is also a wide selection of grilled meats served with seasonal vegetables. Homemade desserts include **zaleti**, cornmeal biscuits served with vanilla or chocolate cream, and **sfregolota**, a dry cake rather like the Mantuan sbrisolona.
Good selection of wines, with very fair mark-ups.

LA CIACOLA ⊗❚

Enoteca with bar and kitchen
Via Marconi 9
Tel. 0445 300001
Closed Monday
Open: 6pm - 0.30am
Holidays: variable
Seating: 40
Prices: 20-25 euros, wine excluded
No credit cards

LA CUSINETA

Trattoria
Via Pieve 19
Tel. 0445 873658
Closed Sunday evenings and Monday
Open: lunch and dinner
Holidays: Juy 15-30
Seating: 50
Prices: 30 euros, wine excluded
All credit cards, Bancomat

Interesting things to see in Breganze include the bell tower, a historic forge and traces of the story of Pietro Laverda - a pioneer of agricultural mechanization. It is also home to "La Ciacola", once a popular Arcigola center and now a friendly osteria skillfully run by Lorella and Enrico. Menus follow the seasons and, as Lorella says, "whatever is available."

Antipasti include superb, traditional Vicenza cured meats, such as **soppressa**, local pancetta, **brasolara** (pork fillet wrapped in salami meat), **bocconata** (pancetta mixed with salami meat), as well as a selection of cheeses from the Asiago, Grappa and Colli Berici regions. Worth a mention are **stravecchio di malga**, **Morlacco** (a Slow Food Presidium along with the Burlina cow) and various goat's milk cheeses - all perfectly matched with honey, fruit conserves and vegetables preserved in olive oil.

Warm dishes in autumn and winter include **bigoli mori with sardines, gargati with fiolaro broccoli** or **consiero** (a tomato-less meat ragù), **spelt and lentil soup** or **pasta with pumpkin and smoked Burlina ricotta**. In the spring and summer try **ziti with tomato and Morlacco cheese, snow peas with silene** or **spaghettini with bruscandoli** which showcase the restaurant's superb use of wild herbs. There are no main courses as such, so move straight onto the homemade desserts: semifreddo with Torcolato wine, **zaleti** and **tarts**.

The excellent wine list reflects an impressive cellar with about 300 labels, with Breganze DOC and other fine Italian wines.

This is a small, family-owned trattoria in Breganze, not far from the main square and dominated by the bell tower. The dishes served up by Marzia and Terenzio, helped in the dining room by daughter Chetti, are admirable. The cuisine faithfully reflects the traditions of the province of Vicenza and especially the typical dishes of Breganze.

First and foremost, the **torresani** (young tower doves that have never flown) **cooked on spits**, a dish whose invention is disputed between the towns of Breganze and Torreglia; then bigoli alla breganzese, with pigeon sauce and homemade **soppressa** served **with hot polentina**. The menu contains many other specialties, such as pony bresaola with chicory in batter with venison ham; first courses include potato and pumpkin gnocchetti with butter and sage or, in season, fettuccine with cep mushrooms and ravioli with local black truffles; grilled meat and meats cooked in other ways follow, served with mushrooms, melted mezzano cheese and polenta, as well as **baccalà alla vicentina**. These dishes can always be joined by fish (prawns in pasta sauces, filets of sea-bass with rosemary) but, excepting the baccalà, we recommend the products of dry land. Lastly, fruit tarts and almond biscuits dipped in Breganze torcolato.

The wine cellar has labels from the Veneto and several other regions. An excellent choice of grappas and spirits.

Todesco wine shop, in via Marconi 1: an extensive selection of Breganze wines, grappas by Jacopo Poli, Dalla Vecchia, Capovilla spirits, extra virgin olive oils and other food specialties.

BRENTINO BELLUNO
Belluno Veronese

BRENZONE
Castelletto

AL PONTE

🍲 Trattoria
Piazza Vittoria 12
Tel. 045 7230109
Closed Wednesday
Open: lunch and dinner
Holidays: end of July to Aug. 15
Seating: 50
Prices: 25 euros, wine excluded
All major credit cards, Bancomat

ALLA FASSA

🍲 Restaurant
Via Monsignor Nascimbeni 13
Tel. 045 7430319
Closed Tuesday, never during summertime
Open: lunch and dinner
Holidays: between January and February
Seating: 80 + 80 outdoors
Prices: 32 euros, wine excluded
All major credit cards, Bancomat

The many military fortresses built by the Austrians and Italians have given this area the name of Terra dei Forti, also used to designate the wines of Valdadige, between Verona and Trento. These days many people, instead of simply following the main highway through the valley, turn off at Affi or Avio for a peaceful drive along the roads flanking the River Adige, between the vineyards at the foot of Monte Baldo and the Lessini mountains. The Trattoria Al Ponte, at Belluno Veronese, is an ideal stopoff for such travelers: Stefano Bridi and his mother Annamaria prepare dishes that reflect the valley's gastronomic Veneto and Trentino influences.

On the second floor (there is a bar downstairs) Monica and Grazia - Stefano's wife and sister - helpfully explain the menu. Start with the classic **polenta and soppressa**; excellent **raw carne salàda** made by the local butcher, Renato Segabinazzi; polentina with cheese and black truffles or **trout in carpione** from the local trout farm. Then come the pasta dishes: **tagliatelle with duck and guinea fowl**, rabbit or truffles, **bìgoli with sardines**, and - in spring - risotto with Rivoli asparagus. The main courses include grilled carne salàda, **baccalà**, polenta and chanterelle mushrooms, **stewed bogóni** (snails), roast rabbit and **donkey stew**, typical of Valdadige. As one might expect, wines come from Verona and Trentino; there is a good selection.

🫒 Grissinificio Zorzi, Via XXIV Maggio 10, in **Brentino**, produces thick, crunchy homemade breadsticks, sold in 250-gram bags.

Unfortunately, not many restaurants on Lake Garda focus their cuisine on lake fish: tourism has too often pushed interest elsewhere. Yet one of the best places to enjoy lake fish is undoubtedly the Alla Fassa, at Castelletto di Brenzone, not far from the Convent of Piccole Suore della Sacra Famiglia. It overlooks the beach and the gentle waves can be heard from the veranda. Children can play in the small park beneath the olive trees.

Roberto Brighenti confines his interest almost exclusively to local produce. Fish are caught at night by the last remaining professional fishermen; alborelle in salamoia are prepared by his mother; his father makes oil from the olives that grow around the trattoria. The same passion for the territory is shared by Mario Zanolli, front of house: he explains the dishes and will serve wine by the glass if you do not wish to choose a bottle from the hundred or so labels in the list.

Start with **pike in sauce**, **sarde in saor**, **cavedano with peas**, stewed tench, **carp salad** or trout carpaccio. Classic first courses include **bìgoi co le àgole in salamoia**, tagliolini with perch and pumpkin flowers, tagliatelle with finferli mushrooms and smoked trout. Main courses include the not-to-be-missed and fragrant **fried chub, sardines and eels** cooked in slices. Then try **perch in melted butter**, **grilled eel**, fillet of lavarello with truffles. Desserts include peach mousse with marasca cherry conserve.

🫒 Castelletto - the gastronomy shop of Tonino Veronesi, Via Don Angeleri 41, has Garda extra virgin olive oil, Monte Baldo honey and the very rare filets of lake sardine preserved in olive oil.

BRENZONE
Porto di Brenzone

52 KM NORTH-WEST OF VERONA

TAVERNA DEL CAPITANO

🍲 Trattoria
Via Lungolago 8
Tel. 045 7420101
Closed Tuesday, never in summertime
Open: lunch and dinner
Holidays: from November to Easter
Seating: 40 + 40 outdoors
Prices: 20-30 euros, wine excluded
Credit cards: CartaSi, Visa, Bancomat

CAERANO
DI SAN MARCO

25 KM NORTHWEST OF TREVISO ON SS 248 OR 667

COL DELLE RANE

🔑 Holiday farm
Via Mercato Vecchio 18
Tel. 0423 650085
Fax 0423 650652
E-mail: info@coldellerane.it
Internet: www.coldellerane.it
Open all year

The road at Brenzone was only opened in the 1920s: before then, the only approach was from the lake or along the winding tracks of Monte Baldo. Perhaps it was this long isolation that ensured that the customs of Garda are still strong here and have managed to withstand the impact of tourism.

The fishing tradition survives in a small, plain trattoria near the quay at Porto di Brenzone: it is closed in winter because there are no inside rooms and the veranda is open only in milder seasons. You approach a meal at the Taverna del Capitano in much the same way as you would tackle an ethnographic museum: dishes are marked by their use of vinegar, garlic, onion and salt - essential ingredients of a cuisine that in the past had to ensure food conservation. Leaving aside the rustic impact, enjoy the huge lake antipasto, prepared by Gianlucia Brighenti and explained by her husband Bortolo. Large, tasty helpings often include rare recipes, such as **sisàm** (dried alborelle filled with onion and vinegar), **pike in salsa**, **polpettine di cavedano** , marinaded lake sardines, **salted fillets of sardines**, fried sardine eggs, cavedano with a sweet and sour sauce, **lavaret with an alborella sauce** or smoked, and many other delights. First courses include the typical **bìgoi co le àgole salàe** (salted alborelle), while the **fish zuppetta** is also interesting. For those who prefer main courses, try **fried** or grilled **lake fish** and other lake cooking. Home-made puddings. The wine list is small - mostly easy-drinking wines appropriate for this kind of place.

The Gallina family has recently restructured the old country house where the vacation farm facility is located, retaining all its original architectural features. Since 2000 the farm has gone over to organic agriculture. All rooms are pleasant and spacious; some have a mezzanine floor to enable them to accommodate larger families. Four of the apartments can be rented at a very attractive rate, if you intend to stay longer than one night. Breakfast is prepared using natural, quality products: jams, fruit juices and cakes, everything is homemade. You are welcome to bring your pets and there are two shelters equipped to accommodate them. There are wonderful Palladian villas in the immediate vicinity and a few kilometers away there is Asolo, with its famous fortress.

• 4 single and 10 double rooms, with bathroom, air-conditioning, fridge, TV, modem connection, some rooms with balcony; 4 apartments (1-2 persons) with kitchen • Prices: single 37 euros, double room single occupancy 45, double 63, breakfast included. • Credit cards: all, Bancomat • 1 room and 1 apartment designed for use by the mobility challenged. Off-street parking, some covered. Small pets allowed (not in rooms). Owners always reachable. • Breakfast room, reading room. Garden

CAMPONOGARA

CANALE D'AGORDO

HOSTERIA
AI MITRAGLIERI

Recently opened osteria
Piazza Marconi 28
Tel. 041 5150872
Closed Sunday
Open: lunch and dinner
Holidays: first three weeks of August
Seating: 40 + 25 outdoors
Prices: 35 euros, wine excluded
All major credit cards, Bancomat

ALLE CODOLE

Restaurant/3-star hotel
Via XX Agosto 27
Tel. 0437 590396
Fax 0437 503112
E-mail: direzione@allecodole.it
Internet: www.allecodole.it
Closed Monday, except from July to August and at Christmas
Open: lunch and dinner
Holidays: 15 days in October or November
Coperti: 60
Prezzi: 25-30 euro, wine excluded
All major credit cards, Bancomat

Don't be put off by the name of this osteria: it is simply the old name of the nearby square. You will be welcomed by Cristina who, together with Signora Graziella and Monica, in the kitchen, has put this old osteria - formerly a pizzeria and later closed for years - back on track. In summer, a garden with 25 seats is used as well as the two inside rooms.
The cuisine is naturally local and often based on the organic produce of the area and the fish market in Chioggia. The menu changes on average every month and follows the seasons. On our last visit in summer, we tasted antipasti such as crudo serrano with fresh fruit, a basket of zucchini and fresh goats' cheese with smoked lamb, pumpkin flowers au gratin filled with speck. First courses include **spaghetti ai moscardini** and gnocchetti with scampi and cherry tomatoes. Main courses include **leg of duck cooked in red wine with cherries**, beef tagliata in balsamic vinegar and Cervia salt and fillet tartar. Other seasons offer **sardines in saor**, **bigoli in salsa**, **cuttlefish in tecia**, **stewed bisato** (eel). The excellent cheese board is accompanied by honey and conserves. Home-made puddings: chocolate mousse, cocoa cream with rum and ice-cream, ice-cream with wild strawberries, bavarese.
The excellent wine list contains local and national wines - and the two wines of the day are also served by the glass. The cellar is climate-controlled at 14°C for both red and white wines.

This hotel is one of the oldest in the Biois Valley on the Veneto side of the Dolomites. Established as a stopping point for pioneering mountain climbers, today Alle Codole offers inviting quarters for visitors to the area. The rooms, available all week, are furnished simply and comfortably. Help yourself to the buffet breakfast, which offers sweet items (as well as savory items on request). Siblings Livia and Diego capably tend to guests' needs front of house, while their brother Oscar and mother see to the kitchen.
The menu changes every two months, with traditional dishes always featured. Parties of two or more can order one of the prix fixe menus (18, 24 or 29 euros a person). There is a wide selection available à la carte as well. Start with speck (homemade) and cucumber, Trento-style **carne salada**, quail and foie gras with an olive and celery sauce and potato and truffle crema cotta with sautéed artichokes. Interesting first courses include **farro mantecato** with spinach, goat cheese and filacci, while traditional main courses are the way to go, like the roasted **Alpago lamb shanks** (made from a Slow Food Presidia) or the veal guanciale. The wine cellar, overseen by Diego, a professional sommelier since 1989, holds more than 600 labels.

• 3 single rooms, 6 doubles with 1 to 4 beds, all with bath, safe, TV; some with balcony • Prices: single 25-40, double 50-80, with 4 beds 100-160 euros, breakfast included • Uncovered parking in front. No pets allowed. Front desk open from 8am to 10pm • Bar, restaurant. Lounge.

CARRÈ

DA RICCARDO

☞Restaurant
Via Val d'Assa 31
Tel. 0445 314694
Closed Sunday for dinner and Monday
Open: lunch and dinner
Holidays: August and one week at Christmas
Seating: 100
Prices: 30-33 euros, wine excluded
All credit cards, Bancomat

Along the State Road from Thiene to Pi-
ovene, near the A31 underpass, Riccardo and Annalisa have managed this
restaurant with skill and passion for
many years. Riccardo – a gentle giant -
explains the menu, that changes frequently in relation to seasonal produce.
Annalisa in the kitchen prepares traditional dishes, with a dash of "Mediterranean" style.
Antipasti include **schie** (grey prawns)
with Marano polenta, flan of bruscandoli with cheese fondue, local **soppressa** with home-made preserves in vinegar
and oil. First courses include **tagliatelle
with rabbit sauce**, **bigoli with duck** (in
winter) and the typical **gargati col consiero**. The weekend especially offers
pasta dishes with sea-food sauces, such
as scialatelli with mussels, cherry tomatoes and pecorino cheese or fusilli with
swordfish, capers and bottarga. The
most traditional second course is **baccalà alla vicentina**; otherwise, springtime offers chicken fillets with asparagus:
grilled steaks all year round, tenderized
fillet with aromatic herbs or salmon in
carpione. At lunchtime, in keeping with
tradition, the trolley with **boiled** and
roast meats makes its appearance, accompanied by the vegetable trolley.
The good wine list has local labels and
wines from various Italian regions.

CASIER
Dosson

OSTERIA ALLA PASINA ⓖ▮

☞Restaurant with rooms
Via Marie 3
Tel. 0422 382112
Closed Sunday for dinner and Monday
Open: lunch and dinner
Holidays: December 28-January 2 and August 15
Seating: 120 + 50 outdoors
Prices: 30-35 euros, wine excluded
Credit cards: MC, Visa, Bancomat

Elegant furnishing, high quality table
settings and professional service: one
wonders what remains of an osteria in
this restaurant set up in a renovated
1800s farmhouse. Yet the osteria atmosphere is all there in the warm welcome,
the passion with which the Pasin family
(Giancarlo and daughter Nicoletta in the
kitchen, Teresa and son Simone front of
house) do their work and a cuisine inspired by tradition even in the more unusual proposals. Meals are served in
three small rooms with a fireplace and
20 seats each, a large hall for receptions and another room with a view over
the garden, for tasting sessions and buf-
fets; the former granary now contains
six very comfortable bedrooms.
Casier is in the area of **Treviso red
chicory**, a product which the Pasin family use with great skill (they promote it
abroad too) and which they prepare in
various ways, from the most traditional
to the most unusual: breast of guinea
fowl with chicory, involtini with chicory
and salmon. Another extensively used
local product is **mais biancoperla** (Slow
Food Presidia) used to make **polenta**
served, when available, **with schie**
(prawns). All the pasta, like the bread, is
homemade: **ravioli**, **tortelli** and **gnocchi**, often topped **with rabbit sauce** or,
in season, with mushrooms. The main
courses include free range animals
(**guinea fowl**, **rabbit**), **snails** and straccetti alla Pasina (two types of meat, two
cheeses and black truffles); in summer,
several fish dishes are also served. An
excellent **cheese board** and homemade puddings.
A large and varied wine list, with regional, national and international labels.

Castelfranco Veneto

Treville

28 KM WEST OF TREVISO SS 52

PIRONETOMOSCA

Recently opened osteria
Via Priuli 17 C
Tel. 0423 472751
Closed Monday for dinner and Tuesday
Open: lunch and dinner
Holidays: variable
Seating: 50 + 20 outdoors
Prices: 25-30 euros, wine excluded
All major credit cards, Bancomat

Just a couple of kilometers outside Castelfranco – hometown of the renowned painter Giorgione – you will find this small osteria managed by two friends, Giulio and Moreno, in an old farmhouse at Treville. It is an intimate, charming place and in good weather guests can also enjoy the views of the surrounding countryside. The seasonal dishes, for the most part prepared using organic ingredients, offer one delight after another.

Antipasti – explained personally – include salami and **pancetta de casada**, squash blossoms filled with ricotta and basil, various kinds of savory pies and, in season, **marinated Treviso radicchio**. In the fall calf's **nervetti with onions** or various dishes prepared with fresh **porcini mushrooms** (served with fresh polentina, in small pies, as a pasta sauce or as topping for pork fillet). First courses always include **gnocchi** and **risottos**: the former are made with eggplant and ricotta, potatoes or pumpkin; the later are served **alla sbiraglia**, with wild herbs and asparagus. The broad, hand-sliced tagliatelle with meat sauce is also recommended. Then come slow-cooked meats, such as baked breast of Garronese beef. In summer, try the **tris dei marinati** (marinated beef medallion, duck breast and pork loin) served with sweet-and-sour eggplant and zucchini. There is also an excellent **rabbit alla veneta** or chicken prepared in various ways. Close with a crostata with walnuts, ricotta, lemon or fruit preserves; chocolate puddings with red-wine caramel or the typical **zaeti**.

The small wine list has an interesting selection of local labels. There is also a fair selection of grappas.

Castello di Godego

31 KM NORTHWEST OF TREVISO ON SP 245

LOCANDA AL SOLE

2-Star Hotel
Via San Pietro 1
Tel. 0423 760450
Fax 0423 768399
E-mail: info@locandaalsole.it
Internet: www.locandaalsole.it
Closed for 15 days in August

Luigi Baggio and Gianni Martinello's hotel building, which dates back to the period of Austrian domination and was previously used as an army barracks, is located on an important crossroads in the countryside outside Treviso. Careful renovation has updated the place to offer all modern conveniences while maintaining the warm atmosphere typical of Veneto-style hospitality. The rooms – recently 12 more have been added in a new building – are different from one another, although in common they have wooden beams and have been furnished with great attention to detail. Breakfast served on the tables in a communal room is traditional and includes orange juice, croissants and homemade cakes. In the adjacent restaurant (also open to non-residents every evening except Monday and for lunch only on public holidays) they serve a creative-style cuisine with traditional roots for 30 euros per person, excluding wine.

• 5 singles and 15 doubles, with bathroom, air-conditioning, mini-bar, satellite TV, modem connection • Prices: single 42 euros, double 62, included • Credit cards: all, Bancomat • Communal rooms and some bedrooms accessible to the mobility challenged. Free parking 50 meters away; internal garage. Small pets allowed.. Owners always reachable. • Corner bar, restaurant. Small TV lounge, reading room

CHIES D'ALPAGO
San Martino d'Alpago

CHIOGGIA
Sottomarina

CHIOGGIA

23 KM NORTH-EAST OF BELLUNO

53 KM SOUTH OF VENICE SS 309 OR FERRY

SAN MARTINO

ALL'ARENA

☞Trattoria
Via Don Barattin Montanes 23
Tel. 0437 40111-470191
Closed Monday, Tuesday for dinner and Wednesday
Open: lunch and dinner
Holidays: none
Seating: 60
Prices: 25-27 euros, wine excluded
All credit cards

☞Restaurant
Via Vespucci 4
Tel. 041 5544265
Closed Tuesday
Open: lunch and dinner
Holidays: 1 week in January and 1 in September
Seating: 30
Prices: 30-35 euros, wine excluded
No credit cards, Bancomat

In a splendid but somewhat isolated position (booking advisable), 865 meters above sea level, this welcoming, age-old trattoria, whose second room was recently renovated, sees the Barattin family ply its trade with growing passion. Aldo breeds animals including Alpagote sheep (Slow Food Presidia), Norina ensures superb service and Gabriella, at times helped by Enrica, looks after the kitchen. Here, almost everything is homemade, beginning with the warm bread (baked in the wood oven just like the potato bread, focacce and (if you book), Aldo's suckling pig) served at table together with **salami alpagoto**, coppa and preserves in olive oil (the latest innovation is dandelion flowers). Depending on the season, you can try fried cep mushrooms, **vegetable flans**, frittatine with herbs, and pork carpaccio marinaded with orange. First courses include **potato or pumpkin gnocchi** and tagliatelle with a **roe-deer** or mushroom sauce, crespelle with herbs, fine **soups** with beans or barley and vegetables, cream of pumpkin and cep mushrooms. The specialities among main courses are **Alpagoto lamb** (Slow Food Presidia) and **roast kid**, as well as other meats such as **rabbit** - all highly recommended for the traditional way they are cooked and the very best quality. In July and August, you can order **s'cios** (snails) **all'alpagota** - occasionally also available at other times of year. Puddings include torta di ricotta all'alchermes, home-made jam tarts and semifreddi.
The wine list is improving, and there are some excellent mountain grappas.

This restaurant, just one hundred meters from the beach at Sottomarina opposite the entertainment arena, has been managed since 2004 by the Scuttari brothers, with Alessio in the kitchen and Diego front of house. Almost all fish-based, the preparations are refreshingly simple. Even when the chef decides to unleash his creativity, the authentic flavor of the ingredients always shines through.
We tried the well-balanced **baked lasagne with a seafood ragù**, spaghetti with little squid and cherry tomatoes, the excellent **sadines in saor** and a series of delicious cicheti: razor clams, mantis shrimp, garusoli (murex). The menu changes daily depending on what's available at the Chioggia fish market: **roast scallops**, **canestrelli** (little scallops) and **fasolari** (cockles) raw or **au gratin**, various crudités, risotto alla marinara, tagliolini with langoustines and zucchini, **cuttlefish** cooked in various ways - even **baked** (a typical dish in the cuisine of Chioggia) – **sautéed giant shrimp**, raw or grilled langoustines, fried moeche (soft-shell lagoon crabs) in season, not to mention sea bass, gilthead bream, sole and other seasonal fish. The restaurant began by specializing in pesce azzurro (fish like anchovies and sardines) but unfortunately has had to expand its menu to meet the preferences of clients (not always a good idea). Luckily, however, the focus on genuine local cuisine has not been lost. The wine list, primarily whites, is limited but sufficient, with a few good bottles at fair prices.

VENETO

LA TAVERNA DAL 1887

OSTERIA DA PENZO

🍲 Restaurant
Calle Cavallotti 348
Tel. 041 400265
Closed Monday
Open: lunch and dinner
Holidays: first 2 weeks in October,
December 25-January 15
Seating: 42 + 20 outdoors
Prices: 35 euros, wine excluded
All credit cards except DC

🍲 Traditional osteria-trattoria
Calle Larga Bersaglio 526
Tel. 041 400992
Closed Monday dinner and Tuesday,
summer Tuesday only
Holidays: 1 week in September,
December 25-January 6
Seating: 40 + 20 outdoors
Prices: 33-35 euros, wine excluded
Credit cards: Visa, Bancomat

Calle Cavallotti faces Chioggia Town Hall and n° 348 is home to this Taverna. The most important fish market of the upper Adriatic plus the passion of the three brothers who manage the restaurant, add up to this landmark for sea fish cuisine.

Tradional Venetian dishes are also to the fore: **sarde in saor, luserna incovercià** (grilled gallinella di mare marinated with vinegar), risotto al nero di seppia, **peoci and bibarasse in cassiopipa**, canestrelli bianchi (excellent baked, truly superb raw). Excellent first courses include **spaghetti ai garusoli** (murici), penne with calamaretti, **mezzemaniche with moscardini and pine nuts** and (if you book) fish soup. There is also an extensive choice of raw sea food from the nearby market, from scampi to tuna by way of cicale, various mollusks and sea bass, gilthead or swordfish. Two seasonal dishes must be tasted: moleche (crab with soft shells) in spring and fall and sepoline de burcelo in August, served fried with a fresh salad. Main courses include **mixed fried fish** or **eel**, sea-bass, and turbot cooked in various ways depending on size.

The wine list has a good selection, essentially whites, in harmony with the menu.

This small osteria is near the Colonna del Vigo in a side street off Corso del Popolo. A simple, welcoming place, the interior is decorated with delightful historic photos of Chioggia, interspersed with some of Ascoli, since chef Fabrizio comes from the Marches region. Roberta describes the day's specialties, and Anna suggests appropriate wines.

The hand-written menu changes every day, following the seasonal offerings available at the always well-supplied Chioggia market. First courses might include gnocchetti with local clams, white onion and Chioggia radicchio, spaghetti with prawns and zucchini or tagliolini with asparagus and scallops. Typical local and regional specialties feature heavily: **sardines in saor**, mixed cicheti (a selection of local delights: **boboli da vida, garusoli, sepa rosta, whipped baccalà, folpeti** and other seasonal delicacies, accompanied by a glass of wine), **luserna incovercià**, cuttlefish de burcelo, fried moleche (soft-shell crabs), scallops and canestrelli (small white scallops) au gratin. Excellent baked fish are also served: bass, gilthead bream, corvina, star-gazer and other large fish served with potatoes and vegetables. In winter, you could choose an interesting cheese board, served with conserves. Dishes can also be prepared for diners with food allergies.

The good, reasonably priced wine list has a selection of Italian whites plus a few international labels.

🍷 Behind Palazzo Granaio: every morning except Monday - the fish market. Pasticcerie Artigiane Ciosote (Pac) has ciosota - a dessert made with chicory and carrots; all traditional bakers have bossolà, the typical biscuit-bread.

39 KM NORTHWEST OF TREVISO, 15 KM FROM VITTORIO VENETO

41 KM NORTH-WEST OF TREVISO, 17 KM FROM VITTORIO VENETO

AL MONASTERO DI ROLLE

Trattoria
Via Enotria 21
Tel. 0438 975423
Closed Monday and Tuesday
Open: dinner, Saturday and Sunday lunch
Holidays: two weeks in January
Seating: 50 + 40 outdoors
Prices: 27-33 euros, wine excluded
All credit cards

CA' DEI LOFF

Osteria-trattoria
Via Vittorio Veneto 15
Tel. 0438 85962
Closed Wednesday
Open: dinner, Sunday for lunch also
Holidays: Feb. 20-March 10
Seating: 50 + 40 outdoors
Prices: 20-25 euros, wine excluded
All credit cards, Bancomat

After twenty years' experience in famous restaurants, Roberto Martin has returned to his roots with this trattoria, housed in the outbuildings of a Benedictine monastery at Rolle, an ancient, well-preserved village in the hillly Valemarena vineyards. Roberto manages the trattoria with Marinella Businaro (front of house) and - helped in the kitchen by Milan Cernic – takes great care over the quality of ingredients and their preparation. The charming dining room, with an open-beam ceiling and a small fireplace, is decorated with old kitchen equipment.

The set menu, hand-written on a blackboard at the door, includes three antipasti, two first courses, one main and a dessert. Seasonally changing antipasti focus on cured meats and fried vegetables, while first courses include home-made pasta (**bigoli**, tagliatelle, lasagne, **gnocchi**) or a risotto. The main courses are rotated during the week: Wednesday is grilled meats, Thursday fish from the Adriatic (the bill goes up to 33 euros), Friday and Saturday evenings has **spiedo** with whole **pork neck** and **belly** respectively, Saturday and Sunday lunches see tagliata and **roast veal** while Sunday dinner is a platter of hot foods (the only dish served, 15 euros with a bottle of wine and coffee). Desserts are homemade.

All the wines are from the Marca Trevigiana. If at least twenty bookings are made, Roberto will also open on Tuesday evening.

Don't be put off by the name - Ca' dei loff (Wolf House): this friendly, welcoming and comfortable osteria-trattoria is tastefully furnished to reflect tradition. Annamaria ensures a professional welcome while Beatrice in the kitchen prepares local, seasonal dishes. The menu is in dialect but is fairly comprehensible to outsiders: if necessary Annamaria is happy to translate.

Start with the antipastin: lardo conzà, porchetta trevisana with peveroni, schenal de' porzel or aciughete agre or formai tendr or tastes of all these cichetìn - as well as an impressive selection of fortàje **(frittate).** Then come the minestre and pastasut: **tagliolini** (home-made); in spring, tortei con sambuc (as well as rust, with sciopet or sparasi). Main courses include classic dishes such as **poenta and s-cioss** (snails), **sopa coada, tripe,** as well as typical local dishes including **guinea fowl with peverada sauce** alla **panada.** The cheese board focuses especially on local produce: cacio cheese from Pedemontana (morlac) and Belluno (renaz), cheese from the plains (piave vecio) and an excellent selection of imbriaghi. There is a fine selection of Veneto wines and sgnape. Home-made dolzet: crostata coa marmeata, **buzolà col Marzemin de Refrontol**, strudel coi pon, chocolate salami.

At **Bagnolo di San Pietro di Feletto** (10 km), Via Cervano 2: Latteria Perenzin uses milk from the Felettano hills to make excellent cheeses.

CISON DI VALMARINO
Rolle

39 KM NORTHWEST OF TREVISO, 15 KM FROM VITTORIO VENETO

DA ANDREETTA

🍽 Restaurant
Via Enotria 5-7
Tel. 0438 85761
Closed Wednesday and Thursday for lunch
Open: lunch and dinner
Holidays: three weeks in January
Seating: 120 + 80 outdoors
Prices: 30-33 euros, wine excluded
All credit cards, Bancomat

Anna Maria and Alberto have managed this delightful restaurant, set amidst the prosecco vineyards around Rolle, for many years, and it's earned the nickname "Terrazza Martini" from clients who enjoy the cool summer terrace and its splendid view.

The menu is seasonal: try the winter salad (Treviso radicchio, brillo cheese and pomegranate), Mondragon goose prosciutto with celeriac, **soppressa** costea with homemade pickles, prosciutto di Montagnana with marinated rosa di Castelfranco radicchio or marinated asparagus, carne salata, baccalà di nonna Santina (boiled salt cod, rice, potatoes and onions), **lumache alla veneta** (snails) with **polenta made from Biancoperla corn**, a Slow Food Presidium. First courses include soups with nettles and potatoes, pumpkin, chestnuts and chicory; sopa coada with stewed chicken; **bigoi col conzier rustego** (in a sauce with radicchio and chicken livers); tortelli with elderflowers; wild herb flan with silene and nettles; and **tagliolini with castel de Conajan** cheese. Main courses include maiale in agro (a whole pork coppa cooked with vinegar and onions), Vicenza-style **baccalà**, **guinea fowl in peverada** sauce, **rabbit leg with rosemary**, mixed skewers and **leg of lamb with herbs**. The excellent **cheese board** focuses on the Veneto. To close, try **torta rustica with peaches** or pears and chocolate, **buzolà with Refrontolo Passito**, apple strudel and torta della nonna with almonds and walnuts.

Alberto's wine cellar is impressive: about 400 Italian and international wines with a particularly interesting selection of local varieties, joined by around 50 spirits.

COMELICO SUPERIORE
Padola

73 KM NORTHEAST OF BELLUNO SS 52

MOIÈ

🍽 Holiday farm
Via Valgrande 54
Tel. 0435 470002
Open from Friday to Sunday, always July-September and for Christmas, Easter
Holidays: June 15-30, October 15-30
Seating: 50
Prices: 19 euros, wine excluded
All credit cards, Bancomat

This farm holiday center in Valgrande - as its name suggests - is an ideal place to take a breather. Recently renovated, it offers relaxation in a rural, family setting with wooden beams and an imposing bar counter. The farm is run by Germano and his wife Loretta, helped by young Tiziana in the dining room. The typical local menu is largely based on the farm's own produce.

Cured meats are served as an antipasto – with excellent speck – together with wild mountain chicory preserved in olive oil and a barley and home-grown vegetable salad. Barley is also served in a tasty soup; then come the typical **casiunzei**, **canederli** with melted butter or in broth, **gnocchi made with ricotta**, **spetzli with roe-deer sauce** and, in season, a perfumed **soup of cep mushrooms and spelt**; not to mention creamed zucchini, leek soup, pasta and beans, rolled Savoy cabbage, melted cheese with polenta. Main courses include beef and pork dishes (the animals are reared on the farm), grilled or braised; in winter, try the **gröstl** (roast pork with onion and potatoes), **roe-deer with polenta**, **goulasch** with beef or roe-deer. Finish with an excellent Comelico cheese variously seasoned and homemade puddings, such as wild fruit tarts, ricotta and chocolate cake, apple and amaretti cake, strudel, or ice cream with a hot wild fruit topping.

Try the Cabernet Franc and Merlot house or bottled wines. There are six comfortable rooms for overnight stays.

CONA
Conetta

AL PORTICO

🍲 Trattoria
Via Leonardo da Vinci 14
Tel. 0426 509178
Closed Wednesday
Open: lunch and dinner
Holidays: 20 days in August
Seating: 60 + 25 outdoors
Prices 30-35 euros, wine excluded
Credit cards: Visa, Bancomat

The Vegro family trattoria tells its story through its architecture: the old, well-restored portico - the most ancient shop in town - is topped by the family home and flanked by new premises. Hoping that his children, who are attending Hotel School, will join the business, Tiziano Vegro runs the trattoria with great passion and impressive scrupulousness as regards sourcing and using new ingredients. He also makes a point of meeting and learning from experts and chefs to keep up to date. He personally greets guests and describes the menu (not written).
Signora Maruzzella manages the kitchen, creating delicate, tasty dishes. The menu follows Veneto traditions and also uses Slow Food Presidia products such as mais biancoperla. Typical cured meats are served as antipasti: prosciutto crudo, **soppressa**, lardo accompanied by homemade preserves in vinegar. The other ingredients are also local, including the meat that Tiziano personally supervises. We tried a **risotto with vegetables, gnocchi with duck** and tomato, **shin** and **cheek of veal**; other kinds of grilled meat were also available, as well as a risotto served in a Parmesan cheese mold. From May through September an entire menu is dedicated to **frogs' legs**: we tried the fried dish but there is also an antipasto with pumpkin flowers stuffed with frogs' legs, cannellini with a frog sauce, and a risotto. Pasta and gnocchi are home-made, like the puddings: the selection includes sfogliatine with creamed strawberries, baked cream, mousses, semifreddi.
There is a fine **cheese board**, while the cellar (a new area below ground is being built) is being continually expanded with new labels; there are also good house wines from the nearby Colli Euganei.

COSTABISSARA
Motta

IL GRANDE PORTICO

🔑 Holiday farm
Via San Cristoforo 44
Tel. 0444 970718
E-mail: ilgrandeportico@libero.it
Internet: www.ilgrandeportico.it
Open all year

This facility in a farmhouse dating from the 1700's is in an area of great environmental and archaeological interest. During the restructuring phase the owner, Renato Forte, intentionally retained features recalling the building's peasant-farming past. The garden is full of plants that makes it inviting on hot summer days. The rooms all have beautiful views and are tastefully furnished. Silvia, Renato's daughter, manages the facility in a friendly, professional, homely manner. Breakfast is traditional, with homemade jams and cured meats produced in the farm. On Friday and Saturday for dinner and Sunday at lunchtime there's restaurant service, also available to non-residents, offering dishes made using products from the farm and local producers (the price of a meal ranges from 20-25 euros per person). Cured meats produced on the farm are for sale. They often organize recreational activities and there are tennis courts and a beautiful swimming pool a few kilometers away,.

• 3 single and 3 double rooms, with bathroom, air-conditioning, TV • Prices: single 36-55 euros, double 60-85 (15 euro supplement for extra bed), breakfast included • Credit cards: none • Communal areas accessible to the mobility challenged. Off-street and external parking reserved for guests. No pets allowed. Owners always present. • Restaurant (closed in August). TV room. Conference room. Garden

COSTABISSARA

LOVISE

🗝️2-Star Hotel
Via Marconi 22
Tel. 0444 971026
Fax 0444 971402
E-mail: trattorialovise@yahoo.it
Internet: www.ilbaccalaallavicentina.it
Closed for 10 days in January and 20 days in August

The Lovise family has been in the restaurant business since 1893, testifying to an industrious continuity that has kept Vicenza's gastronomic tradition alive (including baccalà). From generation to generation the business has grown to become a restaurant with rooms – a 2 star hotel that could easily aspire to a higher category. Sandra has furnished the rooms with taste and there's also a quiet little lounge on the first floor. The large, romantic garden with gazebo provides the right setting to relax in the shade of the trees or in the recently built swimming pool. The buffet-style breakfast is prepared with their own products. A meal in the restaurant (seating 200) ranges from 28-30 euros per person, excluding wine.

• 6 single, 11 double and 1 four-bed rooms, with bathroom, air-conditioning, mini-bar, TV, modem connection • Prices: single 40 euros, double 60, four-bed 120, breakfast included • Credit cards: all, Bancomat • 1 room designed for use by the mobility challenged. Off-street parking. Small pets allowed. Reception open from 6 am to midnight (Monday, from 7 am to 7.30 pm). • Bar, restaurant. Lounge. Garden, grounds. Pool

DOLO

VILLA ALBERTI

🗝️3-Star Hotel
Via Ettore Tito 90
Tel. 041 4266512
Fax 041 5608898
E-mail: info@villalberti.it
Internet: www.villalberti.it
Open all year

On the banks of the River Brenta, Venetian families used to build sumptuous holiday homes to reflect their wealth and power. In the municipality of Dolo, one kilometer from the center of Mira, on the quieter side of the river, you'll find this 18th-century Venetian villa surrounded by grounds with very old trees, completely refurbished by the Malerba family in 2003. Five of the rooms have been created in the outhouse next to the villa. Each is different but all contain a piece of period furniture and other furnishings are coordinated with the fabrics. Rooms in the villa itself cost slightly more. Thanks to the owner's sons who are architects, all the original floors have been retained (Venetian terrazzo or wood) as well as the original glass windows. Breakfast is traditional buffet style offering sweet and savory fare. A meal in the restaurant costs around 20 euros, excluding wine.

• 18 double and 2 triple rooms, with bathroom, air-conditioning, mini-bar, satellite TV, modem connection; some with balcony • Prices: single 65-85 euros, double 90-120, triple 100-130, breakfast included • Credit cards: all, Bancomat • Facility accessible for the mobility challenged, 2 rooms designed for their use. Off-street parking. Small pets allowed. Reception open 5 am-1 am • Bar, restaurant (for residents only). Conference room. Grounds.

FARA VICENTINO

25 KM NORTHWEST OF VICENZA SS 248

COSTALUNGA

Holiday farm
Via Costalunga 10
Tel. 0445 897542
Open Friday, Saturday for dinner and Sunday
During the week, book
Holidays: 20 days in August
Seating: 45 + 20 outdoors
Prices: 20-22 euros
All major credit cards, Bancomat

FARRA DI SOLIGO
Col San Martino

32 KM NORTHWEST OF TREVISO SS 13

LOCANDA DA CONDO

Restaurant
Via Fontana 134
Tel. 0438 898106
Closed Tuesday dinner and Wednesday
Open: lunch and dinner
Holidays: July
Seating: 80 + 30 outdoors
Prices: 25 euros, wine excluded
All credit cards, Bancomat

We are in the foothills to the Asiago plateau, well off the beaten track, in the relaxing countryside. Costalunga means authentic farm vacations, and nobody here has any intention of becoming holiday apartments or a restaurant or even a riding school. After fifteen years of hard work, Rosalina always manages to satisfy us and even to surprise us, with her products, her dishes and her constant desire to make almost everything at home (from the flour to all types of bread, pickles and cured meats), and she even finds the time to entertain visiting school groups. It is necessary to book, and when you call, by all means order some of the dishes we suggest.

For antipasti, you could try an excellent **soppressa**, pancetta, vegetables in oil or vinegar, and **pies** with seasonal vegetables. Among the first courses, try the homemade **gnocchi**, **tagliatelle** and **bigoli** with various sauces, including an excellent **meat sauce made with duck**; but the vegetable sauce in the summer and the wild asparagus sauce in the spring are equally good. The **miserie de le femene** (soft gnocchi made with flour and eggs) are also inviting and more unusual, and Rosalina will tell you the story behind them. The meat for the main courses is all produced on the farm, and we recommend the **rabbit all'oseleta**, the **stuffed guinea-fowl**, **duck with shallots** and, in winter, the **cotechino en croute** which are all excellent. End the meal with **macafame** or another traditional pudding (do not miss those at Christmas and Carnival).

The house wines and liqueurs are all reasonable.

Included in Osterie d'Italia since the first edition, this is the perfect "slow" eating place: a comfortable, pleasant environment, furnished with care; a courteous welcome and food that always meets your expectations. Owner Enrico is devoted to the land, a devotion which is reflected in the traditional, local cuisine, and friendly, attentive Beatrice, known as Bea, looks after the wine and the dining room.

Many antipasti change seasonally, and they include several based on historic recipes from old cookbooks, such as **fresh salami with vinegar and onions** or asparagus and cheese crostatina. The first courses include traditional **pasta e fagioli** and tagliatelle with seven herbs. **Speo** (meat cooked on the spit) has always been the Locanda's strong point, particularly in the winter, but the **guinea fowl with peverada** and **roast lamb with rosemary** also hold their own. In the summer there are some lighter dishes. Try the menu prepared for "Biso e Verdiso," an event promoting the local production of peas and wine. The array of desserts is very appealing: mulberry mousse, biscuits with passito wine, wild berry pies, crostatina with apples and plenty more. When in season chestnuts from the many surrounding trees are used in a variety of ways.

Different wines, often local, are proposed each day, including a house wine by the carafe, and the wine list includes a good selection of Italian wines.

Just down the road, the Damuzzo butcher's shop and salumeria offers traditional homemade musetto, soppressa and salami.

A LA BECASSE

🍲Trattoria
Via Brumal 19
Tel. 0438 970218
Closed Tuesday for dinner and Wednesday
Open: lunch and dinner
Holidays: Jan. 15-31 and August 15-31
Seating: 45 + 25 outdoors
Prices: 25-27 euros, wine excluded
All credit cards

OSTERIA DAI MAZZERI

🍲Restaurant
Via Pallade 18
Tel. 0438 971255
Closed Monday and Tuesday lunch
Open: lunch and dinner
Holidays: Feb. 20-March 10, Christmas
Seating: 80 + 30 outdoors
Prices: 33-35 euros, wine excluded
All credit cards, Bancomat

Otello Zaia opened this typical trattoria with his family 18 years ago, after experience in a number of excellent restaurants in Veneto and farther afield. His son Michele is a great support in the kitchen, so that during our visit, Otello was able to leave it to show off his kitchen garden, his collection of oils (about a hundred) and the salamis hanging in the cellar, all with great pride.
You will be greeted with appealing nibbles and an aperitif under the pergola or in one of the two dining-rooms, and Otello's wife Rosanna, assisted by her daughter Monica, will present the day's menu. Otello occasionally offers dishes from his beloved Tuscany (the ribollita is excellent) and ostrich meat, but most of the cuisine is strictly Veneto. The antipasti include a classic **salami with vinegar**, **soppressa with polenta**, various flans (with mushrooms, chicory, artichokes, etc.), vegetable tartlets, and **Treviso chicory au gratin with pancetta**. Tagliolini with bilberries, walnuts and speck, crêpes with seasonal fillings, eggplant rolls, pasta shells au gratin, zucchini and basil soup, **risotto with herbs** and **pasta e fagioli** are just some of the first courses. Some days you can enjoy barbecued tagliata di chianina or **lamb chops**; in the winter there is always **baccalà alla vicentina** and **tripe stew**, at other times of the year, veal stew with mushrooms, fillet of pork with finferli mushrooms or chicory, and **guinea-fowl with peverada sauce**. On Thursday evenings, for 13 euro you can enjoy a monumental fritto misto. And do not miss the puddings: **pansopà**, cinnamon ice cream with a warm wine sauce, coffee soufflé with toffee cream, and panna cotta with strawberry sauce. The wine list is extensive, with more than 100 labels.

Good food, courteous service and a familiar ambience: this is what we like about Al caminetto, run for 19 years by the Mazzero brothers. The fireplace that gives the restaurant its name helps create the warm atmosphere.
Mauro welcomes the guests, presenting a menu built around the flavors of regional traditions and the seasons. His brother Vito, the cook, explains that it takes time and passion to create a dish, or to make homemade pasta, preserve vegetables in oil, raise chickens or check the origins of the processed meats. His great attachment to the local territory is underlined by the fact that many Slow Food Presidia products from the Veneto region are used in the kitchen, for example Biancoperla sweet corn, morlacco cheese, lamb from Alpago, and rice from Grumolo delle Abbadesse.
Start your meal with **soppressa and Treviso radicchio in saor**, duck and chanterelle mushroom salad, crostini, snails à la bourguignonne. Ravioli of duck and porcini mushrooms, **tagliolini with radicchio**, pappardelle with kid and artichokes, filled pastas or pasta served with a sauce of wild herbs, bruscandoli or asparagus, and mushrooms when they are in season, are just some of the first courses that you may find during the year, together with the ever-present **pasta e fagioli** and the traditional **tripe**. Meats are grilled, or cooked on the spit on Saturday evenings and Sunday lunchtime. Vito also prepares an excellent **cock in red wine**, **duck with peverada and polenta**, and **liver alla veneziana**. Mauro is responsible for the desserts: cakes with homemade preserves, semifreddo and sorbets. There is an extensive wine list with honest mark-ups.

Forno di Zoldo
Mezzocanale

Fumane

Mezzo Canale da Ninetta

⌒ Trattoria-osteria
Via Canale 22
Tel. 0437 78240
Closed Tuesday for dinner and
Wednesday, never in the high season
Holidays: September
Seating: 80
Prices: 25 euros, wine excluded
All credit cards

Enoteca della Valpolicella ⊘🍾

⌒ Trattoria
Via Osan 45
Tel. 045 6839146
Closed Sunday dinner and Monday
Open: lunch and dinner
Holidays: variable in summertime
Seating: 90 + 45 outdoors
Prices: 35 euros, wine excluded
All major credit cards, Bancomat

There is no better introduction to the beautiful landscape of the Dolomites than a stop in this trattoria which is over 160 years old, and was once a staging post where horses were changed and riders stopped for refreshment. Since 1966 it has been managed by the Col and Pancera families, now in the fifth generation: Umbertina and her daughter Manuela are in the kitchen, another daughter, Tiziana, front of house with Angelo, Manuela's husband, while father Gino keeps an eye on everything else. The restaurant is right on a busy main road (particularly bad at peak tourist season, in mid summer and mid winter), but when you cross the threshold you are in another world. Wood everywhere, tables laid with care, numerous pictures, a small fire at one end of the room and a large fireplace in the first reception room, on the right as you go in.

The menu is recited by Angelo and Tiziana, and as it is rather long, there is always the risk that you will miss some delicacy. The first courses include extraordinary **cappelletti of potato filled with spinach** and served with melted butter, but the **gnocchi** and the **bean soup alla zoldana** are also worth trying. **Game** is always present in the right season, as is **lamb** from the surrounding pastures. The **pastin with peperonata** and **rabbit with white wine** are both excellent. Schiz cooked on the griddle is served with corn polenta. The desserts are traditional and homemade.

The wine sold by the carafe and in bottles is not yet up to the standard of this excellent cuisine.

As a result of the improvement in the quality of Valpolicella wines over the last decade, its global image has likewise improved, and wineries are often full of tourists seeking out a bottle of Amarone or other local red wine. These same wine tourists will often be found at the tables of Enoteca della Valpolicella, a must for anyone visiting the area. The restaurant's two rooms are on the upper floor of an old farmhouse. As you might expect the wine list is spectacular: 800 choices, with the best local and Italian producers represented. Bottles can be bought to take away, or if you just want to try one glass, ask Ada Riolfi and Carlotta Marchesini, as there's always some bottles already open.

The cuisine reflects the seasons and showcases local produce. To start with, **soppressa with homemade vegetable giardiniera**, wild radicchio with Monte Veronese cheese and pancetta, and stuffed zucchini flowers. To follow, **tagliatelle with a rustic ragù**, the ever-present **risotto with Recioto** wine, risotto with duck and various types of ravioli: with nettles and Monte Veronese cheese, with asparagus, and with truffles and ricotta from Lessinia. For a main course, lamb chops, **roast rabbit, beef stracotto with Amarone** or grilled meats. And to close, sbrisolona cake or a plate of cheeses from Lessinia with homemade mostarda and preserves.

🍦 In **Valgatara di Marano di Valpolicella** (5 km from Fumane), in Via Cadiloi 55, Marco Scamperle's Il Gelato serves excellent homemade fruit ice creams.

FUMANE

LA MERIDIANA

🔑 Bed and breakfast
Via Osan 48
Tel. 045 6839146-6839228
Fax 045 6839228
E-mail: lameridiana@valpolicella.it
Internet: www.lameridiana-valpolicella.it
Open all year

Built in the seventeenth century, this small rural complex in Fumane in the heart of Valpolicella country has six spacious rooms furnished with wrought-iron bedsteads and period wardrobes; one of the rooms also has an ancient fireplace that can be lit on winter evenings. The meridiana – a sundial – that figures on the sign is painted on the facade of the house and is dated 1879. The facility is run by Carlotta Marchesini, with help from her husband Fosco Frapporti and the staff of the nearby Valpolicella Wine Shop where breakfast is served: homemade cakes, jams, various types of local honey, cheeses from the Lessinia area, eggs, cured meats and juices. And at the wine shop you'll also be able to check your e-mail free of charge. Guided tours are organized to nearby wine cellars and to Molina Park and Waterfalls.

• 6 double rooms, with bathroom (2 rooms with shared bathroom), TV • Prices: double room single occupancy 70 euros, double 90 (30 euro supplement for extra bed), breakfast included • Credit cards: all, Bancomat • 2 rooms accessible for the mobility challenged. External car park reserved for guests. Small pets allowed. Owners always reachable. •Reading room. Internal courtyard, garden

GARDA

SILVESTRO

🔑 3 Star Hotel
Via San Giovanni 19
Tel. 045 7255522
Fax 045 6278442
E-mail: albergoristorantesilvestro@simail.it
Internet: www.hotelsilvestro.com
Closed in November

Angelo Castelletti's hotel in Garda is not far from the picturesque little Piazza Calderini. The rooms are comfortable and simply furnished: nothing memorable, although decent rooms at a fair price are something of a rarity in this area. Breakfast is traditional, while the restaurant offers a complete meal at an average price of 25 euros per person, excluding wine. Places to visit in the town are Piazza del Porto with Palazzo dei Capitani, Palazzo Fregoso over the west gate of the historic center, the parish church. Moreover, from Garda you can go to Punta San Vigilio to reach the famous Baia delle Sirene, the site of the 16th-century Brenzoni-Guarienti villa. Alternatively, before reaching San Vigilio you can take the path dotted with rock inscriptions that climbs up the slopes of Mount Luppia, and from there go on to Torri del Benaco. Or simply just take a walk in the peaceful greenery of Rocca del Garda.

• 2 single and 9 double rooms, with bathroom, air-conditioning, mini-bar, safe, TV; 1 room with balcony • Prices: single 50-68 euros, double 70-83 (28-33 euro supplement for extra bed), breakfast included • Credit cards: all, Bancomat • Facility accessible for the mobility challenged, 1 room designed for their use. External parking, free garage 50 meters away. Small pets allowed (7 euros per day). Owners always reachable. • Bar, restaurant.

GIAVERA DEL MONTELLO

ANTICA TRATTORIA AGNOLETTI

🍲 Trattoria
Via delle Vittorie 190
Tel. 0422 776009
Closed Tuesday
Open: lunch and dinner
Holidays: none
Seating: 120 + 120 outdoors
Prices: 25-28 euros, wine excluded
All credit cards

The most pleasant route to this restaurant is the road along the Montello, which runs past restored villas and farmhouses. The trattoria itself is housed in a mid-17th-century nobleman's house. It's been a restaurant since the end of the following century, initially called Agnolotti and then, from 1780, Agnoletti. Held in high repute, it was known particularly for its excellent mushroom dishes. However it was in a decline until four siblings took it over in May 2000, Maria Lucia and Massimo as chefs and Fabio and Andrea running the front of house. The dining rooms are carefully decorated in Old Veneto style, including a small one on the upper floor that's charmingly intimate, and there's also a summer veranda with views over the grounds surrounding the restaurant.
The menu continues the tradition of serving **mushrooms**, which are particularly abundant in the spring. A growing number of products pass themselves off as being made with "Montello mushrooms," and it's a pleasure to enjoy here an extraordinary **soppressa** with chiodini (honey mushrooms) that really have been picked locally. Pasta is homemade with flour from the artisanal mill at Cusignana, and traditional utensils like a special press for **bigoi.**
Don't miss the **porcini mushroom soup** if it's on the menu. Then move on to **roast kid**, **kebabs** of pork and chicken, or quail and marzorini when in season, and other main courses of **game**. Most of the side dishes also feature mushrooms.
There is a ample selection of good-quality wines from the area, plus interesting labels from the rest of the country.

GRANCONA
Pederiva

ISETTA

🍲 Trattoria/2-star hotel
Via Pederiva
Tel. 0444 889521-889992
Fax 0444 889992
E-mail: info@trattoriaalbergoisetta.it
Internet: www.trattoriaalbergoisetta.it
Closed Tuesday evening and Wednesday
Open: lunch and dinner
Holidays: none
Seating: 70 + 30 outdoors
Prices: 35 euros, wine excluded
All credit cards, Bancomat

This trattoria is really typical of this area, the Colli Berici, and is managed with profound respect for tradition by the Gianesin family. The small hotel (no weekly closing day) it is attached to offers a base for excursions to the Veneto region's renowned cities of art. The rooms here are simple and practical, the breakfasts generous and homely.
The food here is a blast from the past, with antipasti like their home-cured meats, including the local specialty **soppressa**, an excellent **baccalà mantecato**, cuttlefish with peas and mashed potatoes and, in season, soffiotto with cep mushrooms, fonduta and black truffles. Follow this with the very traditional **gargati con i durelli**, homemade tagliatelle served with morels and squash blossoms, **bigoli with ragù** and a soup of **risi, bisi and tagliatelle**. You can watch the delicious meats cook in the hearth after they've been shown to you for your approval. Also recommended: **pheasant with plums**, **roast pigeon**, rabbit with olives, **baccalà alla vicentina** and **snails**. Save room for the cherry strudel and the delightful orange gelato.
Vintages from all over Italy as well as abroad can be found on the interesting wine list.

🛏🔌 • 4 single and 5 double rooms with bathroom, air conditioning, satellite TV, modem connection; some with balcony • Prices: single 36, double 46 euros (additional bed surcharge 13 euros); breakfast 8 euros per person• Communal spaces accessible to mobility challenged. Uncovered parking within. Small pets welcome. Owners always reachable • Bar, restaurant. Breakfast room. Veranda

Isola della Scala

Risotteria Melotti

🍲 Recently opened osteria
Piazza Martiri della Libertà 3
Tel. 045 7300236
Closed Tuesday
Open: lunch and dinner
Holidays: August
Seating: 50
Prices: 20 euros, wine excluded
All major credit cards, Bancomat

Isola della Scala is the gateway to the vast plain usually called the Bassa Veronese. Here the landscape is given over to rice fields: it is the area where vialone nano veronese rice is grown, protected by the IGP designation. The Melotti family are among the oldest producers, and they recently opened a small but welcoming osteria in the main square of the town, close to the place where a Sagra del Riso is held every September, attracting tens of thousands of visitors.
The menu is based entirely on vialone nano rice and avails itself of the diversified range of products created by the Melottis, which include polenta, biscuits, cakes, ice cream, grappa and beer. Start your meal by tasting the **rice polenta**, proposed in various ways: with smoked breast of duck, with vegetables, with Verona cured meats, with Gorgonzola, and with mushrooms. But let it be clear that you really come here for the risotto. You will always find **risotto all'isolana**, with hand-chopped meat. The other risottos follow the seasons: with duck, **with Amarone**, with **red chicory and monte veronese** cheese, with pumpkin, or with pheasant and spugnole mushrooms. Try the unusual **risotto with melon**, typical of nearby Erbè. And as pudding, **rice biscuits with zabaione**, rice ice cream with a caramel and rosemary sauce, semifreddo of rice with amaretto, crostata of rice with fruit and cream of rice with a kiwi or berry sauce. The limited wine list concentrates on bottles of wine from the Verona area.

Jesolo
Lido di Jesolo

Alla Grigliata

🍲 Traditional osteria-trattoria
Via Buonarroti 17
Tel. 0421 372025
Closed Wednesday, never in summer
Open: dinner, summer festivities also for lunch
Holidays: end of December to mid-February
Seating: 80 + 30 outdoors
Prices: 25-28 euros, wine excluded
Credit cards: Visa

It may seem odd to come to this well-known seaside town and visit an all-meat restaurant. But the Lorenzon family wanted it this way when they opened Alla Grigliata in 1976, offering an alternative to meat-loving diners and to avoid problems with fish supplies. It's not hard to find the welcoming trattoria – just head for the Acqualandia park and take Strada del Cavallino. Luigi is in the kitchen, while Moreno and Luigi's sister Manola are in the dining room.
As the name indicates, grilled meats are the specialty. You might have to wait for your food because it is cooked to order at the last minute, first directly on the flame to melt the fat, then over glowing coals. It's well worth the wait, as the cooking style and quality of the raw ingredients makes for an excellent result. While you wait for main attraction, try an appetizer of soppressa, coppa, and **grilled fresh salami, sausage in crosta**, and, as a first course, spaghetti or **gnocchi with ragù** or tomato, **pasta e fagioli, radici e fasioi** (pasta and beans served warm with red radicchio from Chioggia). Then enjoy the **grilled meats**: pork spare ribs and sausages with polenta, pork or veal chops, kebabs, fillets and giant steaks grilled to perfection. Luigi occasionally experiments with ostrich, particularly the fillet, and he also grills vegetables like eggplant and bell peppers. And to finish, tiramisù and homemade sweet salami. There is a generous wine list, but the wine by the carafe is also good.

JESOLO
Cortellazzo

LAVAGNO
Vago

44 KM FROM VENICE SS 14, JUNCTION FOR PORTEGRANDI

12 KM EAST OF VERONA SS 11

LA TAVERNA ▮

LA CANTINA

🍲 Trattoria-pizzeria
Via Amba Alagi 11
Tel. 0421 980113
Closed Monday dinner and Tuesday, June-July Monday lunch
Open: lunch and dinner
Holidays: Dec. 20-Jan. 20
Seating: 50 + 40 outdoors
Prices: 22-26 euros, wine excluded
All major credit cards, Bancomat

🍲 Trattoria-wine shop
Via Provinciale 18
Tel. 045 982381
Closed Tuesday for dinner and Wednesday
Open: lunch and dinner
Holidays: Jan. 1-10, three weeks in August
Seating: 65 + 30 outdoors
Prices: 28-30 euros, wine excluded
All major credit cards, Bancomat

The old fishing port of Cortellazzo is overrun with campers in the summer, but relatively tranquil the rest of the year. Gianni Bettio's trattoria was once just a pizzeria, but now serves simple seafood made with good ingredients supplied by the local fishermen and the Caorle market. The set menu at 22 euros varies depending on the day's catch and includes two antipasti, a first course, a main and dessert, and there's also a longer à la carte menu.

You can start with grilled pilgrim scallops, **lagoon shrimp** with polenta, **sardines in saor**, a plate of mixed steamed fish, smoked swordfish, or the special Taverna antipasto that might include crustaceans, clams, mussels, octopus, **scallops**, crab, and **fried schie with polenta**. The list of first courses starts with minestra del porto, followed perhaps by spaghetti with clams, **gnocchi with langoustines** or crab, black tagliolini and **risotto alla marinara**. There is a vast choice of main courses, from grilled or **stewed baby cuttlefish** to **baccalà alla veneziana**, sole, turbot, jumbo shrimps, grilled giant shrimp and langoustines, **fritto** misto and fried **moeche** crabs, langoustines or small calamari. There is also a meat menu, with local soppressa, spaghetti or gnocchi with ragù, fillet with mushrooms or pepper, and veal scaloppine. The puddings include crostatina, tiramisù and panna cotta.

The wine list presents about 120 labels from well-chosen wineries from all over Italy and a small international selection; there are also six wines sold by the glass.

A glass door opens from the large car park right onto the bar/wine shop area, where it is worth stopping just for a good glass of wine chosen from the 50 local and other labels listed on the blackboard at the entrance, the same wines that you will enjoy with your meal – unless, of course, you prefer to choose one of the 700 bottles on the wine list. The restaurant extends to the right, with two delightful, clean rooms where, in spite of the vicinity of the main road, the atmosphere is relaxing. The women of the Veronesi family are your hosts, and Giuseppina is in charge of the dining-room with her daughter Alessandra (let her guide you in the choice of wines), while Luciana and Federica are in the kitchen.

The appetizers include classic but excellent **sardines in saor**, a pie of carrots and zucchini and a good selection of cured meats from Verona, accompanied by fried grana padano cheese. Going on to the first course, you must try the **pasta e fagioli**, made from an old family recipe, the delicate **ravioli di monte veronese**, **taglierini with chicken livers**, and maltagliati with white asparagus when they are in season, an excellent **risotto al Durello** or risotto all'Amarone in a wafer of grana padano. For a main course, we recommend a traditional **baccalà with polenta**, **liver alla veneziana**, also with polenta, and an excellent fillet with Amarone; but we must also mention the lamb chops with mint sauce, tagliata of beef with zucchini and slivers of mezzano, roast breast of duck and orata ubriaca with cherry tomatoes. And to finish, an excellent choice of local and other **cheeses**, accompanied by jellies, jams and honey. For pudding, try the **sweet ravioli filled with rum and figs**, served with honey and amaretti.

AL VAJO

IL PORTICCIOLO

Holiday farm
Via Rocchetti 11
Tel. e fax 045 7581248
E-mail: agriturismo@alvajo.com
Internet: www.alvajo.com
Holidays vary, in winter

Restaurant
Lungolago Marconi 22
Tel. 045 7580254
Closed Tuesday
Open: lunch and dinner
Holidays: January
Seating: 70 + 50 outdoors
Prices: 30-35 euros, wine excluded
All major credit cards, Bancomat

It seems impossible, but even on the hottest days there's always a light breeze here: all thanks to the tiny Vajo stream that runs close to the house, forming a small waterfall where hens flutter about. The location is Lazise, on the eastern bank of Lake Garda. Esterina Gregori's vacation farm is not too far from the town surrounded by the Scaligere walls, and just one kilometer from the lake, on the side of the road that climbs inland. The rooms built only a couple of years ago are spacious while the furniture once belonged to Esterina's grandmother: beds, wardrobes and bedside cabinets dating from the middle of last century. Breakfast is served in a room on the ground floor. The garden is available for those who want to get a good suntan. Apart from the season when he needs to tend the vineyards, head of household and wine-making expert Emilio Fasoletti is happy to take guests for a fishing trip on the lake.

• 4 double rooms, with bathroom; fridge available in a communal room • Prices: double room single occupancy 40-50 euros, double 50-60; breakfast 5 euros per person • Credit cards: none • Facility accessible to the mobility challenged. Off-street parking, some covered. (3 spaces). No pets allowed. Owners always present. • Breakfast room. Garden, solarium

The breeze from Lake Garda wafts through the restaurant's large windows overlooking the lakeshore. Because of its position, it is easy to understand why Il Porticciolo is often packed with tourists of various nationalities, and the service may be a little hurried on really busy days. But Renato Azzi will provide a good interpretation of lakeside cuisine. For antipasti, you can serve yourselves from the buffet: **trout in agrodolce**, lavarello with a sauce, **sardines in saor**, **pike alla Gonzaga** or alla gardesana and plenty of other dishes (note that the price is fixed regardless of quantity). If you prefer to be served at table, Renato's wife Loredana, or their son Alessandro, will be pleased to help. The traditional first course is **risotto with tench** (or alternatively, with lavarello or eel), but one of your companions will have to join you, as these dishes are only prepared for a minimum of 2 people. Otherwise, **tagliolini with fish and truffles** or spaghettini with lake crawfish or smoked trout. The fireplace turns out large portions of **eel**, **whitefish**, and **lake sardines**: the dish takes time to make and must be enjoyed. The wine list is essential, but includes some good local bottles.

However, if the lake air induces you to stay out late to enjoy the cool of the evening and the reflections of the sunset, you must remember that the kitchen will not wait for you: it closes at 10 pm, but then no one will stop you from lingering in the garden to meditate under the stars with a glass of grappa.

LIMANA
Valmorel

LONGARE

AL PEDEN

Restaurant
Via Peden 6
Tel. 0437 918000
Closed Monday and Tuesday
Open: lunch and dinner
Holidays: January 15-February 28
Seating: 50 + 20 indoors
Prices: 30 euros, wine excluded
All credit cards, Bancomat

LE VESCOVANE

Holiday farm
Via San Rocco 19
Tel. 0444 273570
Fax 0444 273265
E-mail: info@levescovane.com
Internet: www.levescovane.com
Open all year

The Al Peden restaurant is a rustic, warm environment, all in wood, with copper saucepans hanging on the walls. And if it is warm enough, you can eat outside and enjoy the view.
The menu is rich and varies with the seasons. Ledi prepares tasty, wholesome dishes, which are presented with passion and enthusiasm by her son Massimo, a sommelier, who will help you choose from the 200 labels on the wine list. The **cured meats** that start the meal are prepared by the family with raw materials they select themselves, and there is an interesting fact: they only use salt from the Himalayas because it is particularly wholesome. We can recommend a number of first courses: **rolls of pasta with a sauce of chicken livers and smoked ricotta**, pasta with asparagus and béchamel, and **mose** (a mousse of polenta with herbs); in the fall and winter there is an excellent **bean soup**, risotto with mushrooms (the rice used is Grumolo delle Abbadesse, a Slow Food Presidia) and cream of cep mushrooms, in the Summer pasta with herbs and **gnocchi of pumpkin** or potatoes. For a main course, the **game** is unbeatable, like the stew (if it is on the menu, try the **Alpago lamb**, another Slow Food Presidia); the **fried cheese** and the cheese filled with onion are both delicious. And towards the end of August, try the mushrooms stuffed with mushrooms. There are about a dozen **cheeses**, almost exclusively from the Veneto region, including some raw-milk varieties. Ledi's husband, Roberto, has a talent for puddings: trifle with strawberries, pastries with herbs, confectioner's custard with elderberry or chocolate and amaretto. End the meal with huehue coffee from Guatemala (a Slow Food Presidia).

Just one kilometer from the border between Longare and Vicenza, this vacation farm has been created in a building that was erected around the 1400-1500s as a hunting tower, and then expanded many times until, in the 1800s, it became the home of a noble Venetian family, with farmhouses and cattle sheds attached. The elegant guest rooms are located in the more refined part of the building, and those in the apartment (with mezzanine) have windows that face onto the park. The farm produces wines, extra-virgin olive oils, cereals, vegetables and fruit, and raises 500 head of cattle. Farm products can be tasted at breakfast (jams, cakes) and during main meals (homemade local dishes, à la carte prices range from 20-30 euros, the menu for residents 8-20 euros per person).

• 8 double rooms, with bathroom, air-conditioning, TV, mini-bar; 1 apartment with 2 bedrooms, living room with kitchenette, lounge • Prices: double room single occupancy 45-60 euros, double 60-99 (18-22 euro supplement for extra bed), breakfast included; apartment 700-1000 euros per week • Credit cards: all, Bancomat • Off-street parking. No pets allowed. Owners always present. • Restaurant. Lounge, reading room, living room. Garden, grounds.

LOREGGIA

LOCANDA AURILIA

◻Trattoria-wine shop with hotel
Via Aurelia 27
Tel. 049 5790395
Closed Tuesday
Open: lunch and dinner
Holidays: August 1-15
Seating: 60
Prices: 25-30 euros, wine excluded
All major credit cards

The word locanda conjures up images of carriages and men on horseback, wayfarers and carters; those were the days, one hundred and fifty years ago, when the Locanda Aurelia first opened, a stable for horses and an inn with beds. Recent history says that the De Marchi family took it over in 1952: now Dino and Antonietta have handed control over to their children Osorio, Ferdinando and Lucia, who are in charge of the kitchen, the dining-room and the hospitality respectively. One of Osorio's best dishes is **capon in canavera**, a way of preparing it that prevents the juices from being lost in the cooking water because the capon is cooked inside a pork bladder together with various herbs. This dish has a very short season, from December to January. But you will find numerous other local specialties: polenta pasticciata with mushrooms and soppressa (here they call it sopressa, with one p), **baccalà** mantecato, **alla barcariola** or even alla vicentina, **sardines in saor**, **carne salada**. The first courses include homemade **bigoli** and tagliatelle, gnocchi of potatoes or pumpkin, **pasta e fagioli**, risotto with seasonal vegetables or, at certain times of the year, with **rovinassi** (chicken giblets). As a main course, **rabbit in agrodolce**, **mixed boiled meats**, **snails alla veneta**, kid or **roast lamb** and various cuts of beef on the grill. The puddings are also homemade: bavarese, fruit crostata, mousses, and local specialties like **zaleti** and **pinza**. Ferdinando waits at table but is also in charge of the **cheese board**: to ensure that it is always varied.
The Locanda includes a wine cellar, where you can choose from the wines on the monumental wine list, which are on sale, reasonably priced.

LOZZO DI CADORE

LA FAVORITA ◻

◻Trattoria with rooms
Via Giouda 226
Tel. 0435 76142
Closed Sunday, never in July and August
Open: lunch and dinner
Holidays: January
Seating: 40 + 16 outdoors
Prices: 25 euros, wine excluded
Credit cards: MC, Visa

In one of the small lanes that lead off from the main square, an old vine growing up the wall of a typical Cadore house tells you that you have arrived. The interior is simple and austere, and although it has improved, it still does not have the mountain atmosphere that is expressed perfectly in the kitchen. This is run by Andrea Forni who, after working in important restaurants, has for some years now been running the family restaurant with his father Antonio, front of house, and his brother Alessandro.
The menu is rich and varied. If you wish to try something typical and appetizing, but all served on a single generous plate, order one of the 'one-plate traditional Cadore meals', named for the poacher, the woodcutter, the farmer and the landowner. If you prefer a conventional menu, order the inexpensive set meal. Or choose from the hand-written menu. You can start with **local salami with marinated dandelion**, excellent Sauris ham, **pastin with polentina** or carpaccio of pork fillet with herbs. The first courses are particularly inviting, and most of the pasta is homemade: tagliolini with a sauce of sausage and shallots, **bigoli with game sauce**, small vegetable strudels with nettle sauce, the typical **casunziei of red turnips**; in the right season, excellent local **mushrooms** flavor the pasta and orzotto. Mushrooms reappear in the main courses, in the fillet alla cadorina or the sausages. Then try the **smoked loin of pork** with apples, honey and thyme, delicious **lamb** or venison chops, a superb **pigeon with herbs** and the interesting board (tajer) of mainly local **cheeses**, served with honey and raspberry preserve. And to close, fruit pies and homemade crostata.

LUSIA
Bornio

9 KM NORTHWEST OF ROVIGO SS 499

MIANE
Combai

38 KM NORTH-WEST OF TREVISO, 19 KM FROM VITTORIO VENETO

AL PONTE

🍲 Trattoria
Via Bornio 13
Tel. 0425 669177
Closed Monday
Open: lunch and dinner
Holidays: August
Seating: 80
Prices: 30-35 euros, wine excluded
All credit cards, Bancomat

AL CONTADIN

🍲 Traditional osteria
Via Capovilla 17
Tel. 0438 960064
Closed Monday
Open: lunch and dinner
Holidays: none
Seating: 80
Prices: 20-22 euros, wine excluded
No credit cards, Bancomat

Leaving the autostrada at Rovigo and following the road for Lendinara you'll soon come to Bornio di Lusia, a town renowned for its vegetable cultivation and flourishing local market.

Trattoria Al Ponte has always been run by the Rizzato family, first Luciano's parents and now Luciano himself, a sommelier by trade. His wife Giuliana is in the kitchen, where she skilfully prepares traditional local dishes.

There are always plenty of **vegetables**, **battered and fried** or transformed into pies and strudels; **pinza onta**, made with pork rind and once considered a food for the poor, now provides an excellent accompaniment to the **home-cured meats** which are cut by hand at the table. The first courses include seasonally varying **risottos** (with beans, asparagus, peas or mushrooms); **tagliatelle** with speck, walnuts or mushrooms; potato or **pumpkin gnocchi** with ragù or with butter and sage. The main courses include **stuffed chicken**, duck, **tripe**, **muset** (cotechino sausage), **catfish** and **fried eel**. The menu always includes grilled meat seasoned with rock salt. Desserts include zuppa inglese and tiramisù.

The wine cellar is well-organized, and contains Italian and foreign wines, as well as some rare or forgotten vintages which – as Luciano says – must be enjoyed in the right company.

🍴 In the center of **Lusia** (8 km), the Piccolo bakery, Via Garibaldi 6: special breadsticks made with vegetables, various types of bread and pinza, stuffed focaccia.

The last village in Valmareno, at the foot of Monte Cesen, Combai is a village of stone and wood houses built on various levels, that is famous for its chestnuts. The osteria that the Stefani family has run for over a century is in one of its narrow streets. Carla and Diego do the cooking, while their daughters Laura and Moira welcome guests and serve at table. A new dining-room, where local painters exhibit their work, has now joined the simple, orderly original room, whose walls are covered with photographs, drawings and pictures all related to the theme of women.

Start your meal with the cured meats produced on the family farm: an excellent **soppressa**, prosciutto and ossocollo, or **musetto** (a sort of cotechino) served **with cren**, and vegetables conserved in oil or vinegar, all homegrown. The most popular dish is always the excellent **kebab of pork, chicken and rabbit**, a specialty of the Treviso foothills which is served with exquisite **peperonata**. In the right season, you can book game (**wild boar**, **venison**, **hare**) and free range poultry such as goose and guinea-fowl, or **rabbit stew** with potatoes. The first courses include **tagliatelle**, **risotto** and **pasta e fagioli**, and in winter **sopa coada**, a soup made with pigeon meat. A particular mention must go to the **raw-milk cheese** made on the farm. And the excellent homemade puddings, such as tiramisu, panna cotta, and fruit crostata.

In addition to the Stefanis' house whites, Prosecco and Verdiso, there is a wine list with about thirty labels including some good reds from Friuli, Veneto, Tuscany and Alto Adige.

295

VENETO

MIRA
Marano

MIRA

DA CONTE

ISOLA DI CAPRERA

Traditional osteria
Via Caltana 133
Tel. 041 479571-479569
Closed Sunday and Monday
Open: lunch and dinner
Holidays: 15 days in September
Seating: 35 + 15 outdoors
Prices: 33-35 euros, wine excluded
All major credit cards, Bancomat

3 Star Hotel
Via Silvio Trentin 13
Tel. 041 4265255
Fax 041 4265348
E-mail: info@isoladicaprera.com
Internet: www.isoladicaprera.com
Closed first week in August and last week in December

The restaurants along the Riviera del Brenta traditionally serve fish, and Da Conte's menu (more elaborate for dinner and on Saturday, and simpler during weekday lunches) certainly offers plenty of fish. But you'll also find a good choice of meats and a particularly excellent selection of Italian **cheeses**.

The osteria has two welcoming rooms, plus the cellar, and a recently refurbished terrace which is much appreciated during the summer. Owner Giorgio Zampieri will help you choose your meal and your wine from the 400-strong list. His wife Emanuela is in the kitchen, recently joined by Claudio Viato. His experience in restaurants all over northern Italy has brought in a breath of fresh air, but traditional Veneto dishes are by no means ignored.

You could start with a mixed antipasto of cooked or raw fish, a soup of radicchio and mushrooms, or monkfish with artichokes. For a first course, there is always **zuppa di pesce** and spaghetti with mullet bottarga, and, depending on the season, you might enjoy tagliatelle with octopus, bell peppers and zucchini; **bigoi with goose sauce** and tagliolini with little cuttlefish and a light pesto. The main courses always include **steamed baccalà with parsley sauce**, fried fish and **cuttlefish in ink with polenta**, plus dishes like bream with porcini mushrooms, swordfish with Taggiasca olives and capers, lamb chops with a gorgonzola sauce or breast of duck with figs. And to finish, zabaione of Moscato passito with cookies, dark chocolate flan, chestnut mousse, fragola grape sorbet, apricot cream and other delicacies. Several dishes are prepared with products from Slow Food presidia when available.

Water and boats, sandbanks and lagoons have always been protagonists in the history of Mira, apart from its close ties with Venice and its people. Comfortable and personalized, Roberto Frezza's hotel opened in 1988 after he had refurbished the outhouse that was part of a nineteenth-century villa on the bank of the River Brenta. It was then restored again in 2001. The rooms are all different, spacious and provided with all comforts. Breakfast is buffet style, with a variety of sweet and savory fare. This is a peaceful place, the ideal base for anyone wanting to visit cities of artistic interest in the Veneto region.

• 1 single and 13 double rooms, with bathroom, air-conditioning, terrace or balcony, mini-bar, satellite TV, modem connection • Prices: single 55-80 euros, double room single occupancy 60-80, double 80–120 (20 euro supplement for extra bed), breakfast included • Credit cards: all, Bancomat • Facility accessible to the mobility challenged, 2 rooms designed for their use. Off-street parking. No pets allowed. Reception open from 6 am to 1 am. • Bar. Breakfast room, reading and TV room. Conference room. Garden. Pool.

MIRANO

ART HOTEL

🔑 2 Star Hotel
Via dei Pensieri 13
Tel. 041 430062
Fax 041 432922
E-mail: info@art-hotel.it
Internet: www.art-hotel.it
Open all year

This hotel located in the center of town is an ideal base for those who are interested in the festivals organized in Mirano or want to visit Venice, which is easily reachable by coach. Originally opened in 1970 and then refurbished at the beginning of 2003, this hotel is now managed by Ernesto Leo. There's a traditional-style buffet breakfast, with the addition of cheese and eggs. In the eighteenth and nineteenth centuries Mirano underwent remarkable expansion, as well as experiencing a period of great artistic ferment. In the historic center there are numerous old villas and very well kept gardens. The Tiepolo family (Giandomenico and Lorenzo) also had a country house in Mirano: a small villa in Zianigo where they came to relax. This is where Giandomenico offered his interpretation of the life and customs of the time in a series of paintings which today are in the Ca' Rezzonico Museum in Venice.

• 2 single and 14 double rooms, with bathroom, air-conditioning, TV, modem connection • Prices: single 42-51 euros, double 54-74 (16-20 euro supplement for extra bed); breakfast 6 euros per person • Credit cards: all except DC, Bancomat • External parking reserved for guests. Small pets allowed. Owners always present • Bar. Reading room. Garden, terrace.

MIRANO

BALLARIN

🍲 Traditional osteria-trattoria
Via Porara 2
Tel. 041 431500
Closed Tuesday for dinner and Wednesday
Open: lunch and dinner
Holidays: August
Seating: 80
Prices: 24-30 euros, wine excluded
Credit cards: MC, Visa

The number of tourists, many of them foreign, that visit the Venetian villas and stop at this historical restaurant, continues to grow. But the locals do not have to worry, because the osteria is always ready to serve its magnificent "cicchetteria" at all hours of the day – crostini, folpeti, fried cuttlefish and baccalà and plenty more – accompanied by a good ombra of Cabernet, Verduzzo or Riesling. Emilio Voltan presides over the beautiful wine bar with his daughter Marina, who also waits at the tables in the two dining-rooms. In the kitchen wife Marina guides her son-in-law Andrea with an experienced eye.

The menu changes with the season and what the market offers, but certain elements are constant: mushrooms, baccalà and tripe, for example. Some examples of appetizers: **soppressa with polenta and pioppini mushrooms, pumpkin and chicory in saor**, salad of baby cuttlefish, bauletto of vegetables with sfilacci. The first courses include spaghettoni with zucchini, shrimp and cuttlefish, tagliatelle with mushrooms, **gnocchi** with various sauces, ravioli of ricotta and cep mushrooms with poppy seeds and melted butter. Then **baccalà** prepared in various ways, **guinea-fowl with peverada sauce**, cuttlefish alla veneziana, **tripe alla parmigiana, stewed horsemeat**, or tagliata of beef. And when they are in season, a menu based on **mushrooms**. Good oils and vinegars dress the side servings of vegetables. The puddings are homemade: semifreddo alla stracciatella, panna cotta, biscuits with passito wine, trifle, crostata of ricotta, and catalan cream.

In addition to the wine by the carafe, Andrea also offers excellent labels from the Triveneto area.

MIRANO
Campocroce

BELVEDERE DA PULLIERO

Trattoria
Via Braguolo 40
Tel. 041 486624
Closed Thursday
Open: lunch and dinner
Holidays: none
Seating: 80
Prices: 30-33 euros, wine excluded
Credit cards: Visa, Bancomat

Mauro and Stefania work hard to maintain tradition, highlighting the pleasures of simple, good food while constantly looking for new ideas. An entrance with a wine bar and other classic osteria features is still open for people to stop in for an ombra, or you can move through to the two main dining rooms, the domain of Mauro.
Stefania's cuisine is rooted in tradition, but reveals a certain added elegance in the preparation and presentation of the dishes. The ingredients are all typical and traceable, particularly the horsemeat, which is always on the menu: **donkey mocetta** with marinated porcini mushrooms, **horse sfilacci**, **strigoli with musso** (donkey), **tagliatelle with a foal sauce**, **foal stew**. We tried a delicious warm tortino of asparagus and bell peppers, local **soppressa** and porcini as antipasti; **tagliolini with bruscandoli and fossa cheese** as a first course; a good selection of Italian and French cheeses; and for dessert, almond crostata with coffee sauce, coffee tortino with grappa sauce and zabaione with cantuccini biscuits, all homemade. During the year, there are themed evenings that focus on typical local products: **mushrooms**, **Treviso radicchio**, **pork**, **goose** or **baccalà**. In the right season, there's an all-mushroom menu for just 25 euros.
Mauro's wine cellar is growing and currently has about 70 labels from Veneto, Trentino, Friuli, Tuscany, Piedmont, Abruzzo and Puglia, plus some wines from Chile and Uruguay. The outstanding spirit selection includes 170 types of grappa, 26 whiskies and 14 rums, displayed on the shelves around the walls.

MIRANO
Scaltenigo

CASA COUNTRY

Bed and breakfast
Via Formigo 22
Tel. 041 488005–338 1537490
Fax 041 488005
E-mail: casacountry@libero.it
Internet: www.bbcasacountry.it
Closed in December and January

Maria Tagliapietra and Paolo Talamini have given over a few rooms in their refurbished late nineteen-century farmhouse to a B&B facility. The rooms for the guests, elegantly furnished and with great attention to detail, are on the first and second floors, the third room is in an annexe. Breakfast offers classic fare – coffee, brioches and jams – served in a spacious, airy room with a large window facing onto the garden, where, from 15 April to 15 October guests can make use of a kitchenette. On request they provide transport to and from the railway station, and a laundry/ironing service. In the surrounding area you can visit Venice and the villas along the Brenta, but don't forget that Scaltenigo has one of Europe's most beautiful skating rinks.

• 3 double rooms with 3 or 4 beds, with bathroom, balcony, 1 room with air-conditioning • Prices: double room single occupancy 35-45 euros, double 65-75, triple 90-95, four-bed 115-125, breakfast included • Credit cards: none • Off-street parking. Small pets allowed. Owners always present. • Breakfast room, lounge. Garden with relax area.

MIRANO
Scaltenigo

MOLVENA
Mure

18 KM NORTH-WEST OF VENICE A 4 EXIT DOLO

28 KM NORTH-WEST OF VICENZA

LA RAGNATELA

AL POZZETTO

Restaurant
Via Caltana 79
Tel. 041 436050
Closed Wednesday
Open: lunch and dinner
Holidays: none
Seating: 80
Prices: 30-33 euros, wine excluded
Credit cards: CartaSi, Visa, Bancomat

Agritourism farm
Via Michelina 1
Tel. e fax 0424 419051
E-mail: info@agriturismoilpozzetto.it
Internet: www.agriturismoalpozzetto.it
Open all year

The story of the Ragnatela restaurant, which is now managed by a cooperative of about ten people, began in August 1984. At first, the kitchen only prepared meals of the type normally eaten at home, for friends and acquaintances; today the clientele is much more diversified, particularly at midday, when the restaurant caters for blue and white-collars on their lunch break. The atmosphere becomes more relaxed in the evening, and diners choose à la carte. There are two menus, traditional and innovative, both of which make extensive use of Slow Food Presidia: padovana hen, biancoperla sweet corn, vialone nano rice from Grumolo delle Abbadesse, morlacco del Grappa, and stravecchio cheese made by Asiago shepherds.

If you choose the traditional menu, you will be served the extraordinary **fried moeche**, **savor of shrimp**, **folpeti** with potatoes, **sardines in saor**, **bìgoi in sauce**, **padovana hen in tocio**, and **baccalà alla veneziana**. If you go for the more daring proposals of the second menu, you might find yourself eating stewed nervetti with borlotti beans and marinated chicory from Treviso, tagliata of duck with marasca cherries or berries, pigeon stuffed with foie gras and plenty more besides. And why not try the specialties of both menus with the very reasonably priced set meal? To end with, a rich board of Italian and local **cheeses**, and the pudding list, with about ten choices, including zabaione with Port and cinnamon mousse with pears in red wine.

The wine list offers the best labels from Veneto, the rest of Italy and abroad (approximately 400) and a good selection of liqueurs.

This vacation farm lies at an altitude of 200 meters on the hill that dominates Molvena in the Mure area, surrounded by cherry trees and with a magnificent view of the plain below. The farm produces asparagus, vegetables, wine, cherries, olive oil, marano corn for making polenta, and other raw materials that are then used for the preparation of dishes. This farm is in a strategic position, approximately an hour away from Venice, Verona and Treviso, only 4 kilometers from Marostica and 10 kilometers from Bassano del Grappa. Breakfast consists of tea, coffee, homemade cakes and jams, fresh fruit, cured meats, eggs and local cheeses such as Morlacco or Asiago stravecchio. At weekends you can dine in the adjoining restaurant at an average price of 25 euros per person. Your host will be Florindo, although everyone calls him Floris, helped by his wife, father and his mother Rosina who takes care of the cooking.

• 4 double rooms, with bathroom, balcony, TV • Prices: double room single occupancy 45 euros, double 60 (15 euro supplement for extra bed), Breakfast included • Credit cards: Visa, Bancomat • Off-street parking. No pets allowed. Owners always present. • Restaurant (only open at weekends). Communal sitting-room with fridge. Garden, solarium.

MONASTIER DI TREVISO
Chiesa Vecchia

15 KM EAST OF TREVISO

MONFUMO
Castelli

38 KM NORTHWEST OF TREVISO

IL TIRANTE

Restaurant
Via San Pietro Novello 48
Tel. 0422 791080
Closed Monday dinner and Tuesday
Open: lunch and dinner
Holidays: variable in summertime
Seating: 16
Prices: 35 euros, wine excluded
No credit cards, Bancomat

OSTERIA DALL'ARMI

Traditional osteria
Via Chiesa 1
Tel. 0423 560010
Closed Wednesday
Open: lunch and dinner
Holidays: August 20-September 15
Seating: 36 + 30 outdoors
Prices: 20 euros
No credit cards, Bancomat

Luigi Dall'Antonia's grandfather opened a salumeria and osteria in this 16th-century house near the Benedictine abbey of Santa Maria del Pero about 80 years ago, and it was recently restored, leaving on display the original metal tie-beam which reinforces the building. Luigi's wife Caterina prepares traditional dishes with a personal touch for the small number of guests. The menu changes monthly, and the dinner menu offers a wider selection; however diners can also enjoy a good lunch at a decent price.

Start with Monastier cured meats, lardo with rosemary or **baccalà mantecato** quenelles. First courses are based on homemade pasta, and **bigoi** made using an old bigolaio. During Lent you can try the classic version served **in salsa**, and at other times of the year a less traditional sauce of zucchini and smoked salmon. The **ravioli with Treviso radicchio and Piave cream** are also good, as are the risotto with black cuttlefish and the eggplant flan. The main courses include **lamb chops** with balsamic vinegar, cooked cheese with grilled vegetables, **rabbit in an aromatic herb crust**, **pork cubes in saor**, and a guinea fowl roulade with radicchio sauce. There is an appealing selection of **cheeses**: aged latteria, bastardo, formajo imbriago, Piave Mezzano, Vezzena and gorgonzola, which can be accompanied by homemade jams and preserves. The desserts are also homemade: a delicious **apple cake** served warm, **zonclada** (a medieval cake), ricotta and chocolate cake, sabbiosa and crostata with orange marmalade.

The wine list of over 100 labels is of interest, with wines mainly from the area and the rest of Italy but also some from outside the country

You won't find a long menu, a wine list or elegant surroundings in this unapologetically unstylish restaurant, and don't come eat here if you're in a hurry. This is one of the last true osterias around Treviso, and simplicity is key, from the unchanging, limited menu to the sometimes exasperatingly basic service. On our last visit we had to wait two and a half hours for two courses, which is too much even for Slow diners. However Dall'Armi is such a classic example of an authentic osteria that it would be remiss to overlook it, especially with all the fake imitations that have sprung up in recent years. The name comes from the family which has run it since 1850, and it's been in its current location for almost 60 years.

The lack of choice is particularly true for the first courses, or rather the first course, as it is always **tagliatelle** with different sauces: **green beans**, asparagus or tomatoes and basil. For antipasti, there are local cured meats, including an excellent **soppressa**, grilled vegetables, **anchovies with butter** and occasionally marinated fish. For a main course, grilled meat, **fried cheese** and **frittata**, which is particularly popular with today's customers: made with soppressa and onion, s'ciopeti or bruscandoli, herbs or seasonal vegetables. Chicken in tecia must be ordered in advance. Don't expect fancy desserts, which weren't served in traditional osterias, instead there's some good biscotti to dip into bianchetta. It's homemade, as are the other wines on tap – Cabernet and Prosecco – all included in the price of the meal.

In summer you can eat al fresco under the inviting arbor. The service may be slow but is always courteous.

MONTAGNANA

47 KM SOUTH-WEST OF PADUA ON SS 10

ALDO MORO

🔑🔸3 Star Hotel
Via Marconi 27
Tel. 0429 81351
Fax 0429 82842
E-mail: info@hotelaldomoro.com
Internet: www.hotelaldomoro.com
Closed from 2-12 January and 8-18 August

This pleasant hotel in Montagnana, one of Europe's most famous walled medieval towns – is managed by Sergio Moro. Breakfast is buffet style, with bread, butter and jam, homemade cakes, seasonal fresh fruit and various types of drink. The restaurant offers regional and international dishes at a price averaging from 30-40 euros per person, wine excluded (half board costs 78 euros per person). Places to visit in town are the tower of San Zeno Castle, with finds from pre-Roman, Roman and medieval times; Piazza del Duomo, the Romanesque church of San Francesco that probably dates from the fourteenth century and, in the outskirts, magnificent villas. For bikers there are some itineraries in the countryside where you can enjoy the panorama and architectural treasures.

• 24 double rooms and 5 suites (4 persons) and 5 suites (4 persons), with bathroom, fridge, TV; 5 mini-apartments (2 persons) with kitchenette • Prices: double room single occupancy 66 euros, double 96, mini-apartment 106, suite 106-125; breakfast 8 euros per person • Credit cards: all, Bancomat • Facility accessible to the mobility challenged, 2 rooms designed for their use. Off-street parking, some covered. No pets allowed. Reception open from 7 am to 1 am. • Bar, restaurant. Reading room, TV room. Conference room. Garden.

MONTECCHIA DI CROSARA
Pergola

28 KM EAST OF VERONA SS 11 OR A 4 EXIT SOAVE

ALPONE   ⊘🍷

🍲 Restaurant
Località Pergola 51
Tel. 045 6175387
Closed Sunday for dinner and Tuesday
Open: lunch and dinner
Holidays: 15 days in January, 15 in August
Seating: 50 + 30 outdoors
Prices: 30-35 euros, wine excluded
All major credit cards, Bancomat

Simone Tessari is a cook and a restaurateur, but more than that, he is an enthusiast about the countryside and produce of the Soave and Lessinia areas: a passion that he manages to convey perfectly in his cooking. He is assisted in the restaurant, which is halfway between Monteforte d'Alpone and Montecchia di Crosara, by his sister Marialuisa, who greets guests in the dining-room.
The menu changes constantly according to what is available. The appetizers might include budino di monte veronese with smoked pancetta and **soppressa from Val d'Alpone with cren and polenta**. The first courses include **bìgoli co la sardèla and breadcrumbs, gnocchi of nettles and potatoes** with mushrooms, tortelli of pumpkin and rosemary. The main courses range from **bogóni** (snails) **alla veronese with Soave and polenta** to **tongue imbrìaga** (cooked in wine), and rolled kid. On Sunday in winter, try the classic **boiled meats with pearà, cren and green sauce**. There is a good selection of **cheeses** from Lessinia (monte veronese, cimbro and other small local varieties) and elsewhere, all served with the jams and jellies that Simona prepares herself. And finally, plain puddings, such as **zaletti** and **nocciolini** served with Recioto di Soave, or creams such as **budino di puìna** (ricotta), Recioto di Soave ice cream and a soft cake with spicy cherries.
The cellar is well stocked with local labels, both well-known and new, and special attention is paid to those from the Soave area; the Tessari family also produce their own excellent wines (which can be ordered by the glass).

MONTEGALDA

DA CULATA

☞ Traditional osteria
Via Roi 47
Tel. 0444 636033
Closed Tuesday
Open: lunch, plus dinner Wed., Sat, Sun.
Holidays: August
Seating: 50
Prices: 22-25 euros, wine excluded
Credit cards: Visa, Bancomat

One of the last traditional old osterias in the Vicenza area, maybe the last to be annexed to a a grocer's store (a combination that used to be common in Veneto but has now virtually disappeared). The place is on the road to Longare and is without a sign (you can spot it because it's virtually next door to the Brunello distillery). It's famous throughout the province and beyond for Signora Carla's baccalà (which here refers to the type of dried cod known as stoccafisso, or stockfish, in other regions). The rest of the fare is, quite frankly, pretty average (book all the same, though) but a dish of **baccalà alla vicentina** is worth the journey on its own.
Besides this, the culinary symbol of the province of Vicenza, made less and less these days on account of the time and care it takes to make it, at Da Culata you'll also be able to savor **boiled** and **creamed baccalà**, **salad** of baccalà and **bigoli** with baccalà. Other dishes on the menu include **tagliatelle** with chicken livers, meat and vegetable stew, roast and grilled meats and, in winter, boiled meats with horseradish sauce. The meal ends with strudel, tiramisù and biscuits. Besides the house wine, a few bottles are also available.

🐐 Enrico Grandis's goat farm at Via Carbonare 45 sells fresh, aged and herb-flavored cheeses. The Brunello distillery at Via Giuseppe Roi 27 produces excellent spirits and fruit preserved in grappa.

MONTEGROTTO TERME

DA MARIO 🍾

☞ Restaurant
Corso Terme 4
Tel. 049 794090
Closed Tuesday and Wednesday lunch
Open: lunch and dinner
Holidays: first 2 weeks of July
Seating: 80
Prices: 30-35 euros, wine excluded
All credit cards

Diego Gomiero handed control of this restaurant over to the Bernardi brothers two years ago, and we are pleased to report there's been no lowering of standards. Marco makes sure the menu continues to respect the culinary traditions of the Veneto, thanks to his skill and experience.
Among the antipasti there are seasonal salads, like porcini or asparagus with Parmesan, and ricotta-filled zucchini flowers, plus meat terrines and fish fritters. Classic first courses include **pasta e fagioli** and **bigoli in salsa**; the homemade pappardelle and **tagliatelle** are served **with peas** or fish and there's also **risotto** and pasta with tomato and basil or with shellfish. Many of the main courses use fish bought by Marco from the nearby Chioggia market: the fritto misto is always good, or you might find de-boned sea bass, grilled amberjack and cod with asparagus and pancetta. Beyond fish there's **fried rabbit**, **roast lamb with thyme** and first-rate grilled meats: beef and **guinea fowl with sage and rosemary**. All the main courses, whether meat or fish, cost the same: The desserts, Marco's pride and joy, are presented in a separate menu and each is offered with a glass of dessert wine.
In the dining room is his brother Francesco, who can help you choose the best pairing for your meal from a list that includes several Colli Euganei wines and a good selection of labels from the rest of Italy and abroad.

MOSSANO

DA SAGRARO

Agritourism farm
Via Olivari 1
Tel. e fax 0444 886217
E-mail: sagraro@inwind.it
Open all year

Sagraro was great-grandfather Pietro, so nicknamed because on Sunday he and his son Mario would sell homemade sweetmeats from a table set up in the village square: meringues, spumiglie (in dialect sagre) and other delicacies. He bought this 20-hectare farm in 1916 and it still belongs to the Rigo family, who today cultivate olive trees, vines, cherries, forage herbs and raise free-range pigs and poultry. The rustically furnished apartments are in a refurbished farmhouse located 300 meters away from the main center, whereas the restaurant (meals cost 20 euros per person, excluding wine) is in what was originally a farmworkers' dwelling. Guests prepare their own breakfast with the products supplied by their hosts (milk, fruit and jams). This vacation farm is a good starting point for excursions in the Berici Mountains.

• 4 mini-apartments (2-4 beds), with bathroom, lounge, kitchen • Prices: mini-apartment single occupancy 30 euros, mini-apartment 50-100, products to make breakfast included. • Credit cards: all, Bancomat • One apartment accessible to the mobility challenged. Partly covered off-street parking. Small pets allowed. Owners always reachable. • Restaurant (open at weekends from March to July and September to December). Conference room.

MUSILE DI PIAVE
Fossetta

ANTICA TRATTORIA ALLA FOSSETTA

Bar-Restaurant
Via Fossetta 31
Tel. 0421 54756-330296
Closed Tuesday
Open: lunch and dinner
Holidays: first 15 days of January
Seating: 120 + 150 outdoors
Prices: 27-29 euros, wine excluded
All credit cards

There's been an osteria here since the 16th century, on the road between Mestre and San Donà, and now its a charming trattoria with several dining rooms, a flower garden and an airy arbor. Often helped by their parents, it's run by Alessandro Doretto, his brother Flavio and Flavio's wife Mariella, with passion and a good sense of humor.
The menu is printed every day, and varies with in accordance with the seasons, with rotating ingredients like radicchio, anchovies and sardines, asparagus and mushrooms. The restaurant actively participates in two annual events that aim to raise the profile of the area's produce and gastronomic traditions: Magnaloca in November and Maialonga in November and December.
The well-made dishes are simple, and start with antipasti like **soppressa with polenta**, brasiola de Piave (a unique sausage invented by Flavio) with marinated vegetables and **sardines in saor**. Follow with **tagliatelle with duck**, ravioli with herbs and crema del Piave or spaghetti with clams or allo scoglio from the nearby sea. In winter the specialty is **bollito misto**, and grilled meats in summer, but we also recommend the **roast pork shank**, **guinea fowl in peverada sauce** and fried fish. Desserts include pineapple upside-down cake and **apple strudel**, and are all homemade. There is a special children's menu for 7 euros.
The "wine diary" offers a good selection of local and national wines, with very reasonable mark-ups; if any wine remains in the bottle, you can take it home in a special "sporta del vin." Every week the wine diary extract proposes a selection available by the glass.

VENETO

NEGRAR
Mazzano

NEGRAR
Torbe

ALLA RUOTA

Restaurant
Via Proale 6
Tel. 045 7525605
Closed Monday dinner and Tuesday
Open: lunch and dinner
Holidays: 1 week in January, 10 days in June
Seating: 60 + 40 outdoors
Prices: 30-35 euros, wine excluded
All major credit cards, Bancomat

CAPRINI

Trattoria
Via Zanotti 9
Tel. 045 7500511
Closed Wednesday
Open: lunch and dinner
Holidays: none
Seating: 100
Prices: 20-25 euros, wine excluded
All major credit cards, Bancomat

La Ruota is up in the hills around Negrar, and from its recently renovated terrace the view to the left sweeps down through the Valpolicella vineyards to Verona and beyond to the Appennines on a clear day, while to the right the fields lead to Lessinia, the rugged mountains. The restaurant, managed by Odilla and Lorenza Peretti, is spacious yet at the same time warm and inviting, and maintains close links to the countryside and the seasons. Almost everything is homemade, including the bread, and Lorenza's husband Stefano will be happy to explain the menu to you.

To start with don't miss the **savory galàni with lardo and pancetta** (galàno is a typical Carnival fritter, here in a savory version). First courses include **wholemeal tortelli with ricotta**, lasagnette with rabbit and mushrooms, **meat tortelli** with black Lessinia truffle, maltagliati with ricotta and pancetta and **pasticcio di Monte Veronese** with zucchini and sausage. Save room for meats like suckling pig with apple, veal shank with mushrooms, **loin of lamb**, **rabbit meatballs** and succulent **guinea fowl**. Alternatively there's a selection of mostly local **cheeses** with mostardas and jams. To round off the meal, strawberry pie with chantilly cream, semifreddo and a cart of chocolate desserts. Or you could choose the traditional **biscotti with recioto from Valpolicella**.

The wine list is extensive, with local varieties and labels from other regions, some available by the glass.

Past the center of Negrar a side road takes you to Torbe, perched on the side of the valley in the countryside that links the vineyards of Valpolicella with Lessinia. Opposite the church is Caprini, with the nondescript entrance between the bakery and cafè. You'll find the dining rooms on the upper floor, opposite the kitchen, and there's also a terrace for summer al fresco dining. The simplicity of the ambience is reflected in the menu, which has no frills but lists good traditional dishes prepared by mamma Pierina Caprini, the fifth of eight daughters. Sons Davide and Nicola help her in the kitchen. Sergio, the other son, runs the dining room, while papà Francesco looks after the kitchen garden and the trattoria's vines. The first thing to try is the excellent **soppressa** with cornéti, the typical bread of Torbe, and the homemade **vegetable giardiniera**. Then, **paparèle in broth with fegadìni** (fettuccine with chicken giblets), tagliatelle with a generous helping of butter from the mountain dairies of Erbezzo, **lasagnette with rabbit sauce** or Lessinia truffles and risotto with pumpkin and Amarone. Main courses include lepre in salmì (jugged hare), **rabbit in teglia**, **brasato all'Amarone** and, in winter, bollito misto co la pearà on Sunday and baccalà on Friday. Round off your meal with fragrant buttery pastries or stewed cherries.

The wine list has some 80 reds from Valpolicella, plus a couple of excellent unlisted whites.

Silvana Caprini's bakery, below the trattoria, produces cornéti, treccia (sugared bread) on Saturday and traditional cakes: always pastafrolla, brasadèle broè at Easter and nadalìn at Christmas.

NEGRAR
Arbizzano

10 KM NORTHWEST OF VERONA

STELLA

Trattoria
Via Valpolicella 42 A
Tel. 045 7513144
Closed Sunday dinner and Wednesday
Open: lunch and dinner
Holidays: variable
Seating: 70 + 40 outdoors
Prices: 25 euros, wine excluded
All major credit cards

The road from Verona to Valpolicella starts climbing into the hills at Arbizzano, and on the right by the first traffic light stands Cristina Righetti's classic trattoria, which she runs with most of her family. At lunchtimes on weekdays you share the dining room with workers who are looking for more than just a quick bite, and the conversation tends to turn to wine and the vines, the major industry around here. The generous portions are served with relaxing pauses in between and the food wil calm even the most heated debate. You can start with **soppressa**, **gnocchi** or **bìgoli** with meat ragù, **tagliatelle with rabbit** and truffle caramelle from Valpolicella. **Stracotto all'Amarone** leads the traditional main courses, which include **pastissàda of horsemeat** and **bollito misto con la pearà**. The **roast rabbit** is recommended, and there's also a wide selection of seasonally changing side dishes. If your visit coincides with the first week of Lent, you can sample a special Lent menu including salted sardines and herring, tied into the popular Ash Wednesday celebrations a few kilometers away in Parona, just outside Verona.
The wine list is good, dominated by local and national reds. Try a glass of Valpolicella recioto with your homemade dessert.

NERVESA DELLA BATTAGLIA

35 KM NORTH OF TREVISO

LA PANORAMICA

Restaurant
Strada Panoramica del Montello 28
Tel. 0422 885170
Closed Monday and Tuesday
Open: lunch and dinner
Holidays: Jan. 15-30, 1 week July or August
Seating: 140 + 40 outdoors
Prices: 27-30 euros, wine excluded
All credit cards, Bancomat

Up at Montello, past the World War I battlefields and around a few bends, you'll come across an estate that produces an excellent prosecco and then a huge late-19th-century villa, carefully renovated and home since 1966 to the Furlan family's restaurant. There are several well-appointed dining rooms and a terrace with a magnificent view over the River Piave valley. The mother, Antonella, is in charge of the kitchen, while service is handled with great skill by Eddy and his children Giuliano and Francesca.
The local cuisine uses seasonal produce; in springtime wild herbs, local **asparagus** and Sant'Erasmo castraure (young artichokes), in the summer and fall local Montello **mushrooms** – porcini, finferli and chiodini – are used with pasta, meat and in salads. In the cold season, pride of place is taken by the famous **Treviso radicchio**.
Among the antipasti special mention goes to **soppressa with artichokes**, salads of porcini or folpi and vegetables. The **risottos** and **tagliolini** with mushrooms or **radicchio**, risotto with bruscandoli and mushroom soups are among the noteworthy first courses, while **fillet of beef al Margottino**, **kid with thyme** and **roast rabbit** are excellent choices from among the mainly meat-based mains. Desserts are all homemade; wild-apple tart, almond parfait with hot chocolate and bavarese.
The generous wine list, compiled with care by Eddy, a wine expert and sommelier, combines the restaurant's own wines with others from Italy and abroad, many available by the glass.

NOALE

PADUA
Camin

26 KM NORTHWEST OF VENICE, 23 KM SOUTHEAST OF TREVISO   5 KM FROM THE CENTER OF TOWN

OSTERIA STALLO

AL CANCELLETTO

Recently opened osteria
Via Tempesta 57
Tel. 041 5801199
Closed Monday and Tuesday
Open: dinner only
Holidays: 15 days in summer
Seating: 50
Prices: 25-28 euros, wine excluded
Credit cards: Visa

Restaurant
Via Corsica 4
Tel. 049 8702805
Closed Saturday, and Sunday lunch during summer
Open: lunch and dinner
Holidays: 1 week around Aug. 15
Seating: 50 + 25 outdoors
Prices: 30 euros, wine excluded
All major credit cards, Bancomat

This osteria was once a stable for horses and then an inn (stallo in Veneto dialect), serving visitors to the livestock and hay market still held in Noale every Thursday. After crossing to moat to the north of the castle keep a close look out for the restaurant because there's no sign outside. Renovated in 1992, the interior is spartan, with visible ceiling beams and tables set with paper tablecloths, just like an old-style osteria. But the service is friendly and efficient, with Antonella and her helpers in the dining room while her husband Alberto runs the kitchen with skill.

The menu follows the seasons, though some products may be defrosted. The cuisine is for the most part fish-based and you can start with **baccalà mantecato with warm crostini** or marinated swordfish fillet. The first courses include the excellent **risotto di gò** with goby from the Venice lagoon or **risotto with pumpkin and shrimp**, spaghetti with local clams and macaroni with carletti (herbs), sausages and smoked ricotta. In addition to a generous serving of **mixed fried fish** the main courses include **canestrelli au gratin**, grilled scallops, **stuffed calamari** and a traditional eel dish called **bisato sull'ara**. For dessert, buttery biscuits, crema catalana and tiramisù in the winter.

In addition to the house wine there are some reasonably priced choices from Veneto and Friuli-Venezia Giulia. The carob grappa makes an excellent finish. Reservations are recommended.

It might be near the industrial zone, on the eastern outskirts of town, but this restaurant is refined and inviting, with careful attention paid to the service and the presentation of the dishes. Angela attends to guests, while Davide cooks, sometimes with creative touches but more often than not turning out well-prepared traditional plates that focus on horse meat, a key element of the local gastronomic culture. **Foal bresaola** is always on the menu as well as **sfilacci**, costata, fillet steak and **straeca** (steak from the horse's belly). There are also 13 different cuts of grilled pork, lamb and beef as well as poultry prepared in a variety of ways. The **bigoli in salsa** with salted sardines or with **duck** are excellent, as are the **pasta e fasoi**, maccheroncini with pesto and datterini tomatoes, ricotta chicche with eggplant and **potato gnocchi with chives and smoked ricotta**. The menu changes approximately every three weeks and is always attentive to seasonal produce. Seasonally changing dishes might include zucchini flowers, served in batter or alla paprica with a delicious caper sauce; wild boar ham with burratina; smoked tuna with celery, cherry tomatoes and thyme oil; **smoked pork chop** or saddle of pork with juniper. For dessert choose from the vast array of biscotti on a table by the entrance or try the bavarese with nougat, tiramisù and ciambella all'amaretto.

There are some 50 wines, mostly red and all very reasonably priced.

One of the entrances to the city in the southeast is Via Facciolati, and at number 12 you'll find the Pasticceria Biasetto, with excellent cakes, small pastries and chocolate specialties.

PADOVA

L'ANFORA

Osteria with bar and enoteca
Via dei Soncin 13
Tel. 049 656629
Closed Sunday
Open: 9am-11pm
Holidays: August
Seating: 40
Prices: 22-28 euros, wine excluded
Credit cards: AE, Visa

Along a narrow porticoed street not far from Piazza delle Erbe, this osteria is a great place for a sponcion (a warm or cold snack) and an ombra (glass of wine). The setting is rustic with beams and dark-wood paneled walls peppered with notice boards that reflect the owner's passions for rugby and jazz. The tables are set with simple paper tablecloths and napkins. In the morning the clientele is mostly elderly, students and office workers come in for lunch, then there's the aperitivo ritual, followed by dinner, all at affordable prices. Owner Alberto Grinzato alternates at the bar with Domenico Cortes, and he'll be happy to advise you on a good wine to taste, drink or buy to take away.
The menu changes daily and the dishes are very simple. Antipasti could be cured meats, **horsemeat sfilacci**, mussel impepata or fillet of smoked mackerel with herbs. For a first course there is the classic **pasta e fagioli** and **bigoli in salsa**, but also fusilli with sausage and eggplant or tagliolini with shrimp and zucchini. Alberto follows the Padua tradition of keeping poultry and rabbits, and they provide the raw materials for traditional dishes of **hen**, guinea fowl, **goose**, duck, **turkey** and rabbit. Or there is roast saddle of beef, stewed cuttlefish with peas or mixed fried fish; vegetarians are also catered for. The puddings range from panna cotta to **sweet polenta**, and from fruit cakes to fruit agli zaeti. The sponcion bar features various fried foods, unshelled hard-boiled eggs, sardines in saor, meatballs and crostini with cured meats.
Naturally there is no shortage of wines to choose from; around 40, mostly from Veneto and Friuli, are sold in the shop.

PEDEROBBA
Onigo

32 KM NORTHWEST OF TREVISO SS 348

LE RIVE

Trattoria
Via Rive 46
Tel. 0423 64267
Closed Tuesday and Wednesday
Open: lunch and dinner
Holidays: 3 weeks in January, 1 in August
Seating: 50 + 50 outdoors
Prices: 25-30 euros, wine excluded
Credit cards: CartaSi, MC, Visa

Channeled through the 15th-century Bretella canal, the waters of the River Piave turned the wheels of scores of flourmills, power hammers, sawmills and fulling mills. For centuries, hydraulic engineers (including fra' Giocondo da Verona, renowned architect and humanist), stone cutters and other workers labored to build the canal and keep it working, and many osterias sprung up along its banks to serve them. One of these is Le Rive, tranquil and off the beaten track. Silvia Rebellato warmly welcomes her guests to two warm rooms or, weather permitting, to the little courtyard.
The menu is dictated by the seasons. In the spring you'll see crespelle with herbs, homemade **risottos** and **tagliatelle**, while in other seasons you can choose between **potato and beet ravioli**, **leek and potato soup** and fresh or marinated **Treviso radicchio**, served as an antipasto with bresaola and marinated endives. Cold-weather main courses include **skewered pork and chicken**, an excellent **turkey roll** stuffed with red Tropea onions, a boneless **roast leg of lamb** and cooked cheese with radicchio, while the warmer days bring **rabbit salad** de casada and fried or grilled cheese. The trolley of homemade desserts features tiramisù, apple and amaretto tart, fruit pies and apple strudel.
There are some good bottles to choose from.

PIANIGA

DA PAETO

🍲 Traditional osteria-trattoria
Via Patriarcato 78
Tel. 041 469380
Closed Monday, Tuesday
Open: lunch and dinner
Holidays: August
Seating: 60
Prices: 24-28 euros
No credit cards

This lively, welcoming osteria is housed in a simple building in the old Roman grid area. Galdino, the owner, is an experienced cook and retaurateur, hence the ideal person to guide you though your meal, describing dishes, filling you in on the ingredients used and suggesting the right wines to drink. Tasting the dishes prepared by Eddy in the kitchen, you'll be sure to appreciate the use of special extra virgin olive oils, the choice of quality pastas such as Gragnano and Campofilone and a penchant for carefully chosen traditional prime ingredients such as smoked codfish and Veneto Slow Food Presidia products as Grumolo delle Abradesse rice.

Antipasti: **baccalà in insalata**, **sardines in saor** and a cast of cured meats starring aged pancetta with peppers. First courses: **risotto di baccalà**, **tripe soup**, **bigoli in salsa** and other pastas with seasonal vegetables. **Baccalà**, reappears, inevitably, among the main courses, **alla vicentina**, **mantecato** or **alla veneziana** with fresh tomatoes (if you wish you can have a taste of each of the three recipes). Other mains include **mixed fried fish** and stewed tripe. All dishes are accompanied by **polenta di mais biancoperla**. The meal is rounded off by cakes and biscuits from the nearby Pasticceria Vianello served with Marsala.

The cellar offers Franciacorta fizzy wines, Prosecco, Marzemino and Raboso. Honest mark-ups.

PIEVE D'ALPAGO

RIFUGIO CAROTA 🍾

🍲 Restaurant with rooms
Località Carota 2
Tel. 0437 478033
Closed Tuesday
Open: lunch and dinner
Holidays: mid-January to the beginning of February
Seating: 70 + 30 outdoors
Prices: 20-22 euros, wine excluded
Credit cards: MC, Visa, Bancomat

The Pellegrinotti family's restaurant is up a thousand meters, above the lake of Santa Croce, but easily accessible from the autostrada. Peaceful and quiet, you'll find Luca in the dining room and Daniele in the kitchen, preparing dishes based on local mountain ingredients.

You can start with cured meats or venison carpaccio with the addition, in summer, of sweet-and-sour veal. Then there is **mouflon** or wild boar **soup**, first courses of homemade pasta (tagliolini and **tortellini with roe deer** or venison **sauce**, **lasagne with lamb and artichokes**, gnocchetti with speck and leeks), pasticcio with wild boar ragù, **risottos** with seasonal ingredients and vegetable rolls and strudels. There is a wide choice of main courses: roe deer or **wild boar with polenta**, pork with morels, fried lamb chops, **rabbit alla bellunese**, **pheasant in a bread crust**, fillet al Carota with a sauce of local bacò grapes if pre-ordered, **pastin** (fresh salami meat) and **s'cios** (snails). There are also **mushrooms** in season. The cheese is homemade as are the bread and desserts mousses, pear tart and berry pie.

The wine list has a good selection, especially of reds from all over Italy. The sparkling and the dessert wines are also good.

🍯 In **Schiucaz di Pieve d'Alpago** (3 km) the De Pizzol mill sells good flour made from locally grown corn. In **Tambre** (10 km), two places for buying cheese: the Centro Caseario del Cansiglio, at Pian Cansiglio (they use organic milk), and Diego Bortoluzzi, località Sant'Anna, Via Cansiglio 23.

PIEVE DI SOLIGO
Solighetto

POLESELLA

35 KM NORTH OF TREVISO

13 KM SOUTH OF ROVIGO SS 16

DA LINO

CORTEVECCHIA

🗝️❶3 Star Hotel
Via Brandolini 31
Tel. 0438 82150
Fax 0438 980577
E-mail: dalino@tmn.it
Internet: www.locandadalino.it
Closed in July, 10 days between January and February

🍲Trattoria
Strada Statale 16 2672
Tel. 0425 444004
Closed Wednesday, Saturday and
festivities also for lunch
Holidays: August 1-15
Seating: 100 + 30 outdoors
Prices: 25-30 euros
All credit cards, Bancomat

The hotel is in a restructured farmhouse. The rooms are embellished by valuable pieces of furniture, as well as antiques, paintings and copper pots. You'll be welcomed by Marco and Chiara Toffolin, who have given each room a different personality by their selection of furnishings and colors dedicated to the famous people who have stayed here in the past. The generous buffet breakfast includes sweet items like tarts and fagottini, and savory fare too. On request you'll be able to visit the vineyards from which Prosecco is made, wine cellars, and follow cultural trails involving Asolo and other towns of artistic interest. Bicycles are available for guests to explore the surrounding area.

• 2 single and 8 double rooms, and 7 suites (2-4 persons), with bathroom, air-conditioning, balcony, fridge, satellite TV, modem connection • Prices: single 70 euros, double 90, suite 115-138, breakfast included • Credit cards: major ones, Bancomat • Facility accessible to the mobility challenged, 1 room designed for their use. Covered off-street parking. Small pets allowed. Reception open from 7.30 am to midnight. • Restaurant. Breakfast room. Conference room. Garden.

This family-run trattoria along the main Rovigo-Ferrara road has been skillfully renovated in keeping with its 17th-century origins. The three dining rooms have a warm, welcoming atmosphere, and at the end of the largest room there's a huge fireplace which is always lit to heat charcoal for the grill, and often there's a suckling pig turning leisurely on the spit.
There's no printed menus, but the choices are simple, with Montagnana prosciutto and mixed cured meats for an antipasto, followed in the colder months by **polenta with tastasal** and **fasoi in potacin**. The pasta for the **bigoli** with beef ragù and the maccheroncini with rabbit are homemade and there are also **gnocchi** and **risottos** with seasonal produce. Main courses include the excellent **suckling pig alla brace**; cuts of grilled pork, beef or lamb; **salt-roasted loin of veal**, **duck**, guinea fowl and **roast turkey**. The dessert cart boasts tiramisù, trifle, panna cotta, tarts and the ever-present zaleti.
The wine on tap could be improved but there's also a wine list with good labels at reasonable prices. The efficient service deserves a special mention. It's recommended you book to ensure that the best dishes are still available.

🍲 Marco manages the restaurant, which offers some quite creative dishes (55-55 euros, excluding wine).

PONTE DI PIAVE
San Nicolò

PONZANO VENETO
Paderno

5 KM NORTH-EAST OF TREVISO ON SS 19

6 KM NORTH OF TREVISO

RECHSTEINER

Agritourism farm
Via Montegrappa 3
Tel. 0422 807128-752074
Fax 0422 808084
E-mail: rechsteiner@rechsteiner.it
Internet: www.rechsteiner.it
Open all year

DA SERGIO

Trattoria
Vi dei Fanti 14
Tel. 0422 967000
Closed Sunday and Saturday lunch
Open: lunch and dinner
Holidays: Aug. 1–21, Dec. 24–Jan. 2
Seating: 90 + 60 outdoors
Prices: 26-28 euros, wine excluded
All credit cards

This vacation farm is in the plain of Treviso on the border with the province of Venice and the Friuli region. The Rechsteiners, like other important families, settled here in the days of the Venetian Republic and created this farm in 1881. It is managed by Stepski Dolina, a man of German origin who speaks fluent Italian. The facility is in a restructured farmhouse that has retained all its original architectural features. As it's surrounded by fields and vineyards you'll be guaranteed peace and quiet. Rooms and apartments (which have the use of a kitchen), are furnished tastefully. The farm raises chickens, ducks and geese and grows vegetables, and these raw materials are used in the restaurant (open to non-residents from Friday to Sunday, and always open for residents). Just a few minutes away is Oderzo and an important Roman archeological site.

• 10 double rooms, with bathroom, almost all with TV; 4 apartments (2-4 persons) with kitchenette • Prices: double room single occupancy 39-45 euros, double 62-71, breakfast included; apartment 85-120 euros • Credit cards: major ones, Bancomat • Communal areas accessible to the mobility challenged. Off-street parking. Small pets allowed. Owners always present. • Restaurant. Conference room. Garden.

Don't be followed by the sober modernity of the decor; this restaurant run by Sergio and his family sticks closely to local traditions. The open kitchen, looking out over the beautiful dining room, is presided over by his wife Pina. The tables continue out to the veranda, surrounded by a hedge and trees which also shade the handy car park at the rear. Daughters Raffaella and Daniela and their brother Leo are always welcoming and the trattoria has a family, homely atmosphere despite its size. The large tables are generous and well-spaced, making normal conversation possible, and the clientele is primarily regulars.

The menu, based on excellent seasonal ingredients, varies often but always includes dishes which link the restaurant to its history and the local cuisine: **potato gnocchi** with tomatoes or ragù, **risottos** with vegetables or **alla sbiraglia**, classic **pasta e fasoi**, beef carpaccio with Parmesan and arugula (Sergio has had it on the menu every day since 1966), Veneto-style snails, **sardines in saor**, **baccalà alla vicentina**, and cuttlefish in rosso. The first courses include the freshly made **tagliatelle** with mushrooms or zucchini flowers and mascarpone, while main dishes include **tripe alla parmigiana** and flash-fried sirloin steak on a bed of radicchio. Pina's desserts vary with the season. Don't miss Leo's ice cream if it's available.

There is no wine list but bottles with price tags are on display, and Leo is only too happy to guide you through the hundred or so selections on hand, mainly from the Triveneto and Tuscany.

PORTOGRUARO

66 KM NORTHEAST OF VENICE SS 14, A4 OR A28

VENEZIA

Trattoria
Viale Venezia 10-12
Tel. 0421 275940
Closed Sunday
Open: lunch and dinner
Holidays: between August and September
Seating: 40
Prices: 30 euros, wine excluded
All credit cards, Bancomat

A mainland town architecturally inspired by the city of Venice, Portogruaro is home to this restaurant, located in Viale Venezia, the state road to Venice. Renowned for its regional seafood, it's run by Claudio and Maria, with the lively trio of Renzo, Lucia and Rosanna in the kitchen.
Fishing stocks might be low, but here you can stil find a rich selection of the best of the day's catch fresh from the market. Start with a **carpaccio of amberjack with pickled seaweed**, a splendid eggplant and shrimp tart with smoked ricotta, **sardine cartoccio**, crostini with calamaretti and cherry tomatoes. The pasta dishes are excellent: **pasta with sardines**, **spaghetti** with bottarga and cherry tomatoes or **with clams**. Then **brill, sea bass** and **langoustines** served with seasonal vegetables. The desserts, homemade by Maria, include a delicious chocolate tart and nougat semifreddo.
The reasonably priced wine list pairs well with the cuisine and ranges from Veneto to Trentino-Alto Adige.

PORTO TOLLE
Bonelli

70 KM SOUTHEAST OF ROVIGO SS 309 AND SP 38

DA RENATA

Trattoria with rooms
Via del Mare 2
Tel. 0426 89024-389322
Closed Wednesday
Open: lunch and dinner
Holidays: first week of July
Seating: 100
Prices: 30-35 euros, wine excluded
All credit cards, Bancomat

This trattoria is located in one of the most beautiful landscapes of the Po estuary, between the Sacca degli Scardovari bay (source of many lagoon fish) and the open sea. There's a mooring for boats alongside, and nine double rooms for guests who want to stay the night. Make sure you reserve, so as not to be disappointed after a long journey – Rovigo is an hour away – but the food is well worth the trip.
Owner Maurizio will welcome you to a simple but comfortable setting. There is no menu as such as it changes every day based on what's available in the market, so quality and freshness of the fish are guaranteed. The house specialties are **mussels**, **clams** and **oysters** (blanched and served with chopped onion), **fish risotto**, spaghetti with seafood sauces and grilled **shellfish**. The most typical dishes are **grilled eel** and fish from the estuary. Grilling is the principal cooking method and it is done using excellent extra-virgin olive oil. To end the meal try the warm **focaccia** accompanied by a glass of local sweet wine.
There are some good wines, but we hope they will soon expand the selection.

Pasticceria Toffolo, viale Matteotti 46: a broad selection of top-quality products from simple mignon pastries to savories. They also produce exquisite chocolate Easter eggs and panettoni.

PREGANZIOL

EL PATIO

🍲Restaurant
Via Croce 35
Tel. 0422 93292-633240
Closed Tuesday and Wednesday
Open: lunch and dinner
Holidays: none
Seating: 100 + 40 outdoors
Prices: 28-30 euros, wine excluded
All credit cards

Though it's just a few hundred meters from the Terraglio, the tree-lined road that runs from Treviso to Venice, you'll be pleasantly surprised by the quiet of the farm and adjoining garden where Vanda Pistolato has her restaurant. The menu varies frequently with the seasons and features traditional local cooking, with a light touch and the occasional flash of creativity.

Depending on the season, the antipasti might include duck carpaccio with arugula, rabbit on a bed of salad, bresaola with an eggplant involtino, artichoke salad with flakes of Parmesan, a prosciutto sfogliatina with spring herbs, smoked swordfish with crostini, wild boar prosciutto with asparagus gratin and speck and rusticacio cheese salad. The selection of first courses ranges from the traditional **pasta e fasoi** to homemade **maltagliati with duck**; lean ravioli with speck, walnuts and parmigiano; orecchiette with broccoli; **cottage cheese gnocchetti** with speck and vegetables and a crêpe sformato. The spring-herb **risotto** and the tagliatelle with smoked swordfish and artichokes are recommended. Main courses give a better idea of the local specialties: **baccalà alla vicentina**, **cuttlefish** alla veneta **with polenta**, guancette with stuffed peppers, **stewed veal ossobuco** with mashed potato, **lamb cutlets alla scottadito**, turkey involtino, asparagus and provola cheese; there's always a selection of grilled vegetables and cheeses, tagliata with rosemary and beef fillet with balsamic vinegar. For dessert sample the vast array of homemade biscotti.

The wines are limited to around 30 labels, most of which are regional and reasonably priced, making it easy to select a good wine to accompany your meal.

PREGANZIOL
San Trovaso

OMBRE ROSSE

🍲Osteria with kitchen
Via Franchetti 78
Tel. 0422 490037
Closed Sunday
Open: 6pm-2am
Holidays: 2 weeks August or September
Seating: 40 + 30 outdoors
Prices: 30-35 euros, wine excluded
All major credit cards

This attractive enoteca/osteria on the Terraglio has been run for many years by Claudio Borin, together with his wife Tessa Candiani. The atmosphere is rustic, with paper napkins just like in the old bacari, and it's a popular spot to come after a concert or event to listen to Claudio tell stories about the latest wine that he's just discovered.

The menu changes continuously according to what the market has to offer and the imagination of Tessa and her staff. Antipasti include an excellent prosciutto from Montagnana or San Daniele, pork guanciale, **chicken liver paté, vegetable flan with morlacco cheese**; in spring, the small castraure artichokes from Sant'Erasmo (a Slow Food Presidium). First courses contain typical Treviso vegetables (**Lamon bean soup with Treviso radicchio**, tortelli with asparagus) and a local classic, **sopa coada**. Main dishes range from **baccalà alla veneta** to eggs and asparagus, fish couscous and gilthead bream roasted in salt. In addition there is Chianina beef tagliata, guinea hen breast and carne salada from Trentino. The **cheese board** is varied as is the dessert cart. The first-rate cellar has a good selection of wines by the glass.

Puos d'Alpago

Quinto di Treviso

20 KM NORTH-EAST OF BELLUNO

8 KM SOUTHWEST OF TREVISO SS 515

Locanda San Lorenzo

Stella d'Oro

🗝️3 Star Hotel
Via IV Novembre 79
Tel. 0437 454048
Fax 0437 454049
E-mail: info@locandasanlorenzo.it
Internet: www.locandasanlorenzo.it
Closed for 20 days between January and February

🍲Restaurant annexed to hotel
Via Vittorio Emanuele 38
Tel. 0422 379876
Closed Saturday lunch and Sunday
Open: lunch and dinner
Holidays: Aug. 8-28
Seating: 50 + 35 outdoors
Prices: 35 euros
All credit cards, Bancomat

The Locanda San Lorenzo is located in peaceful Puos d' Alpago and welcomes guests to the warm, relaxing atmosphere typical of mountain hotels. At the entrance there's a wrought-iron sign reproducing the martyrdom of San Lorenzo. The hotel is managed by Renzo Dal Farra's family, who runs the attached restaurant that offers the typical local cuisine, with pride of place given to Alpago lamb (half board ranges from 70-80 euros per person). The big rooms on the first floor have been furnished with great attention to detail. Breakfast is continental and prepared with quality home produce. Within easy reach is Lake Santa Croce, famous for its passeggiata, a long, shaded path that skirts the lake for approximately two kilometers.

• 2 single and 8 double rooms, and 2 suites, with bathroom, mini-bar, TV, modem connection; 6 rooms with air-conditioning, 3 with balcony • Prices: single 61 euros, double 88 (15-20 euro supplement for extra bed), suite 95 euros, breakfast included • Credit cards: all except DC, Bancomat • Communal areas accessible for the mobility challenged. Off-street parking. Small pets allowed., Owners always reachable. • Bar, restaurant. Breakfast room, lounge. Terrace.

🍲 Restaurant open for lunch and dinner, offering local cuisine and an extensive wine list (average cost of a meal 50 euros).

Apart from its proximity to the airport the Locanda Stella d'Oro enjoys a quiet, peaceful setting in an 18th-century former post house. The beautiful palazzo, elegant and sober inside and out, stands on the banks of the River Sile just before it flows through Treviso. The current owner is Giuseppe Graziati, and his family's history has always been closely linked to the inn, which in addition to the restaurant and hotel also provides snacks like bruschetta, cure meats and cheeses for those looking for a quick bite.
Apart from some seasonal variations the menu is invariable. Antipasti include the bruschettas mentioned earlieras well as the typical **sardines in saor**. For a first course there is traditional **pasta e fagioli**, **gnocchi della casa** with speck, **tagliatelle with duck sauce**, agnolotti di magro and spaghetti with clams or bottarga. As a second course try schitz with chiodini mushrooms and polenta, **baccalà alla vicentina**, **cuttlefish alla veneziana**, veal stew with porcini, fillet of Angus steak, tagliata with rosemary, beef carpaccio or caprese salad with buffalo mozzarella and tomatoes; we also enjoyed an excellent **eel stew**. The menu lightens in the summer with salads and cold pastas. Desserts are homemade and mostly spoon sweets like tiramisù and semifreddo.
There are 40 or so Italian wines, and Cabernet Franc, Prosecco and Sauvignon from the area of Lison Pramaggiore available on tap.

Refrontolo

34 km northwest of Treviso, 14 km from Conegliano

Trattoria al Forno

Traditional osteria-trattoria
Viale degli Alpini 15
Tel. 0438 894496
Closed Monday and Tuesday
Open: lunch, weekends also dinner
Holidays: second half of January and August
Seating: 40
Prices: 25-30 euros, wine excluded
All credit cards, Bancomat

This beautiful osteria-trattoria is located in a centuries-old house looking out over Refontolo's main piazza. Owners Mario and Rosita Piol live out in the country at the San Boldo pass, where they grow vegetables and gather the wild herbs used in the kitchen. Look out for the grisol (catchfly) and peruch (mountain spinach that grows above 800 meters). The cuisine reflects seasonality, tradition and local produce, and the Piols' corn, potatoes and other vegetables are organically grown.

The pleasant atmosphere of the restaurant is enhanced in the winter by the fireplace, where meats are grilled. If you preorder there's excellent meat kebabs available. Antipasti always include **pastin** (sausage paté) in balsamic vinegar with **polenta and cheese sauce** and eggplant or **pumpkin in saor**. The first courses include such classics as **bigoli with duck ragù**, ravioli with speck and blueberries, **rice with wild herbs**, gnocchi with arugula, tagliolini with porcini and truffles in season, **soup** with chestnuts and honey mushrooms or **beans and grains**. The main courses highlight poultry and rabbit with **chicken stew with fasioi sofegai**, duck with basil sauce, **roast rabbit** and **guinea fowl in peverada sauce**. The homemade desserts include excellent biscuits to accompany the Marzemino Passito di Refrontolo, semifreddo al croccante, Catalan cream with strawberries or cherries, or crostate with seasonal fruit.

The list of 60-plus wines boasts a good price-quality ratio.

Ronco all'Adige

26 km south-east of Verona

Sofia

Trattoria
Via Baldo 10
Tel. 045 6615407
Closed Monday for dinner and Tuesday
Open: lunch and dinner
Holidays: 2 weeks mid-August
Seating: 60 + 50 outdoors
Prices: 20-25 euros, wine excluded
All major credit cards, Bancomat

If you stop to ask for directions you have to be really unlucky to find someone who does not know where the Sofia trattoria is. East of Verona, Sofia Meneghello is an institution – a long-time hostess. There are no signposts pointing to the establishment nor is there one telling you you've arrived. Quite simply, signposts are not needed. She is the one who welcomes you while her daughters Maria Antonella and Angelita run the kitchen in a way deeply rooted in local tradition.

The menu follows the seasons, drawing its products from the countryside, the rice fields, the river Adige and the wetlands. From January to March you must try the tastiest of Verona's traditional dishes, namely **risotto with meat**, lasagnette with meat sauce, **lesso co la pearà**. With springtime comes risotto with white Ronco asparagus which is also the main ingredient in the pasticcio. When the weather gets warmer, it's time for meat from the rice fields with **fried frogs legs**, risotto with frogs legs, **risotto with pessìn de fosso** (the fry which breed when the rice fields are flooded). With the passing of summer, duck becomes the specialty and it is used to make meat sauce for risottos or to serve roasted. Puddings include fritters made with Zevio apples, **apple saccottini**, and **galani**.

A very interesting idea (you need to book however) is the regular theme-based menu on weekdays. Early in the year there are risottos served in various ways while late fall generally features the pumpkin. There are some twenty wines.

ROSOLINA
Volto

ROVIGO

RISTORANTE AL MONTE

⌒Restaurant
Via Venezia 60
Tel. 0426 337132
Closed Monday
Open: lunch and dinner
Holidays: 2 weeks in September, 3 in January
Seating: 50
Prices: 33-35 euros, wine excluded
All credit cards, Bancomat

AL SOLE

⌒Traditional osteria-trattoria
Via Bedendo 6
Tel. 0425 22917
Closed Sunday
Open: lunch and dinner
Holidays: 8 days mid-August
Seating: 25
Prices: 20 euros
All credit cards except AE

This is the place to come for seafood, always bought fresh from the nearby Chioggia market. You'll find the restaurant on the main Romea road, at the junction for Rosolina Mare. Stefano is in the dining room, with wife Melita and mamma Antonietta in the kitchen.

The dishes are simple but well-prepared and highlight the local cuisine, with **calamaretti gentili with soft polenta**, **little cuttlefish in tecia** and **risottos** with local clams, langoustines or bass. The mixed grill, also traditional, focuses on sole, langoustines and eel with variations according to the season, and is always cooked to perfection. The raw seafood we sampled on our last visit was also very good, the fish at the peak of freshness and served with a light dressing that did not mask the flavor. Then there is **granseola**, gratineed **scallops**, langoustines, giant shrimp and bigger fish grilled or roast and, in season, moleche crabs, little cuttlefish, a **mixed fry of lagoon fish** and more, depending on the day's catch. A special mention for the potatoes, which are rough cut and freshly fried like they used to be, a far cry from the omnipresent pre-fried variety which you usually find these days.

The wine list is good with a fair selection of reasonably priced whites to combine with the menu.

Al Sole has been around for over a century and is Rovigo's most traditional restaurant. In a narrow street nearby the Chamber of Commerce, it was originally an osteria where wine on tap would be served directly from the barrel at the bar in sturdy glasses or brought to the tables in carafes. It's still a place for locals to come and play cards, with an ombra and a couple of slices of good salami to nibble on. In classic osteria style, regulars who ask for something to eat outside normal hours (noon-2.30pm, 7.30-9.30pm) are usually accommodated.

Maurizio Astolfi runs the place together with his wife Gabriella and his mother Ippolita, who works in the kitchen. The menu posted outside advertises typical Polesine dishes like **rice and chicken livers**, **pasta e fagioli**, potato **gnocchi** with meat sauce, homemade **tagliatelle**, **muset** sausage, **tripe in broth**, **roast baccalà**, **boiled chicken**, guinea fowl, **liver alla veneziana** and cooked bondola sausage with mashed potato. The desserts, all homemade, include **brazadela**, apple tart and dark salami (made with chocolate).

The wines are mainly local Treviso or Friulian varieties on draught but it's also possible to select from a few good bottles. Booking recommended.

ROVIGO

SAN DONÀ DI PIAVE

TAVERNETTA DANTE

TONETTO

Trattoria
Corso del Popolo 212
Tel. 0425 26386
Closed Sunday
Open: lunch and dinner
Holidays: in August
Seating: 50 + 35 outdoors
Prices: 30 euros
All credit cards, Bancomat

Restaurant
Via Code 1 A
Tel. 0421 40696
Closed Sunday
Open: lunch and dinner
Holidays: one week mid-August
Seating: 150 + 35 outdoors
Prices: 27-32 euros, wine excluded
All credit cards

In the Rovigo's main street, this trattoria is fairly elegant but in its own way, for example the napkins printed with traditional sayings which change weekly. The dedicated Renato Santamaria and Mario Coloschi have owned it for ten years. Renato is a Montello native and a sommelier who looks after the dining room, building on his experience working all over Italy from Rome to Venice. Mario in the kitchen prepares faithful interpretations of Veneto dishes, using the best seasonal produce the market has to offer.

There is a good balance of meat and fish on the menu, starting with soppressa, ossocollo and other typical **cured meats**; the classic **sardines in saor** or a warm antipasto of cuttlefish, shrimp and octopus. Then you can choose from firsts like **bigoli in salsa**, **tortelli with pumpkin and smoked ricotta**, fettuccine with white asparagus when in season, tagliatelle with porcini and **risotto with radicchio and sausage**. Second courses include beef steak and pork chops, **horse costata, cuttlefish al nero**, **baccalà alla vicentina**, fresh tuna or grilled swordfish. The cheese board is good with attention paid to Veneto specialties. Mario also makes the desserts: fruit tarts, almond sweets and chocolate salami.

The wine list has an extensive selection of reasonably priced Italian and foreign wines, some of which are available by the glass.

Hostaria La Zestea, via X Luglio: a good selection of cured meats, cheeses and substantial toasted sandwiches with wines by the glass.

The Tonetto family started this restaurant in 1969, and it soon became known as the place for a good, affordable lunch. While still catering for the busy lunchtime clientele, Carlo has been improving the restaurant's appeal for a couple of years, and some good renovation work has given it its own identity. We recommend visiting for dinner in order to enjoy his hospitality and that of Stefano, who runs the dining room.

To begin with don't miss the cured meats which Bruno, Carlo's father, makes from pigs raised and slaughtered on the family farm (**soppressa, ossocollo**, pancetta, guanciale, salami), accompanied by marinated vegetables. First courses vary seasonally but the pasta is always homemade, from **tagliatelle al tastin** (with fresh soppressa meat) to **gnocchi al ragù**; then there is the classic **risi e bisi**. Main courses center on **grilled meats** cooked in the great open hearth, with fillets, sliced Sorana beef chops and the excellent cube rolle, a sort of tagliata marinated in Raboso wine. There are always a few fish dishes available, made with fresh fish that Carlo gets at the Caorle and Venice markets: gilthead bream carpaccio with orange, marinated swordfish, razor clams (in season) and the specialty orto-mar, or sea garden, a **fritto of fish with vegetables**.

The cellar has a good selection of reasonably priced wines from Veneto and Friuli.

SAN MARTINO BUON ALBERGO

Campalto

8 KM SOUTH OF VERONA

CORTE PELLEGRINI

🗝️Agritourism farm
Via Campalto 18
Tel. 045 8820122
Fax 045 8798172
E-mail: info@cortepellegrini.com
Internet: www.cortepellegrini.com
Open all year

This old eighteenth-century corte surrounded by age-old trees is located in a vast estate where they grow cereals, and raise rabbits, goats and horses. The Pellegrinis are a noble family from Verona; Bernardo and Cristiana welcome their guests to rooms furnished rustically but with a touch of refinement. Breakfast is served in a pleasant room and it's really mouth-watering: freshly baked bread, butter and jams, croissants, yoghurt, cereals, fresh seasonal fruit. The riding school means you'll be able to go on excursions on horseback along the banks of the River Adige and in the surrounding hills. On the estate itself you can visit an exhibition of ancient farm implements. Verona is really close and other cities of great artistic interest – Vicenza, Padua, Treviso, Mantua, Ferrara and Trento – are within easy reach.

• 5 double, 3 triple and 2 four-bed rooms, with bathroom, air-conditioning, mini-bar, TV • Prices: double room single occupancy 50 euros, double 75, triple 90, four-bed 110, breakfast included • Credit cards: all, Bancomat • Facility accessible for the mobility challenged. Off-street parking. Small pets allowed. Owners always reachable. • Breakfast room, reading room. Garden with children's playground. Pool, riding school.

SAN PIETRO DI FELETTO

Borgo Frare

35 KM NORTH OF TREVISO ON SP 635

IL FAÈ

🗝️Bed and breakfast
Via Faè 1
Tel. 0438 787117
Fax 0438 787818
E-mail: mail@ilfae.com
Internet: www.ilfae.com
Closed from December to end of February

This is an old farmhouse arranged in three different height modules, each being painted in a different color. Around the building is a large lawn which in turn is surrounded by a vineyard from whose grapes the owner makes a pleasant Prosecco. Salvatore Valerio and Sabina Brino Bet live here and have been running the B&B for five years. They offer cookery lessons, visits to wine cellars and cheese factories and excursions on horseback. From a ground-floor room, with its monumental fireplace and very long table, a wooden staircase leads you to the rooms on the two other floors: wooden beams and parquet, rough whitewashed walls, wrought-iron bedsteads of various colors and small lacquered wardrobes made just after the end of the war. Breakfast consists of freshly made brioches from the local bakery, honey, jams, and Sabrina's cakes. In a small adjacent building your hosts sell their own homemade ware: gastronomic products, necklaces and clothing accessories, candles, clothes hangers and other household objects.

• 6 double, 1 triple and 1 four-bed rooms, with bathroom • Prices: double room single occupancy 60 euros, double 70-75, triple 95, four-bed 130, breakfast included • Credit cards: major ones, Bancomat • Off-street parking. Small pets allowed. Owners always present. • Breakfast room and lounge, TV room. Garden, pool.

SAN PIETRO IN CARIANO
Bure

14 KM NORTH-WEST OF VERONA ON SS 12

LA CAMINELLA

🔑 Bed and breakfast
Via Don Bertoni 24
Tel. e fax 045 6800563
E-mail: corra.giuliana@libero.it
Internet: www.lacaminella.com
Open all year

Giuliana Corrà has created three pleasant rooms in what was formerly a tobacco-drying room built in the nineteenth century. We are at Bure, a hamlet near San Pietro in Cariano surrounded by vineyards. To get there, leave the autostrada at the Verona nord exit and drive along the main road for Valpolicella right to the end. The building is very light and airy as the numerous original windows of the plant have been retained. The sizeable, elegant rooms have terracotta floors, wooden beams and stone walls. They are furnished with a double bed, a divan (that can be used as a third or fourth bed), and a small table-bureau. Only one of the rooms has a kitchenette. Breakfast is served in the living room during winter and on the terrace in summer. It includes freshly squeezed fruit juices, yoghurt, cakes, focaccia, homemade jams and fruit. You can also book pottery and cookery lessons, and olive oil, wine and cheese-tasting sessions.

• 2 double rooms and 1 suite (2-5 persons), with bathroom; suite with kitchenette • Prices: double room single occupancy 60-65 euros, double 65-70, suite 110-130, breakfast included • Credit cards: none • Off-street parking. Small pets allowed: Owners always reachable. • Breakfast room. Garden with jacuzzi. Terrace. Pool.

SAN POLO DI PIAVE

23 KM NORTH-EAST OF TREVISO

GAMBRINUS 1847

🔑 Rooms
Via Roma 20
Tel. 0422 855043
Fax 0422 855044
E-mail: locanda@gambrinus.it
Internet: www.gambrinus.it
Closed from 1-15 January and 2-20 August

This B&B in the countryside outside Treviso has been created in a period residence that retains all of its original identity. The rooms have been given the names of flowers and are furnished according to the impeccable taste of the owner, Marianna Zanotto, and in fact the furniture used, imitation antique, has always belonged to the family. Breakfast is served in a room on the ground floor and consists of sweet items, such as locally made cookies, and savory fare. Bicycles are available for trips in the countryside. At the locanda you can also buy a drink known as Elisir Gambrinus, which was first produced in 1847.

• 6 double rooms, with bathroom (2 with jacuzzi), air-conditioning, mini-bar, safe, satellite TV, modem connection; 2 with kitchen • Prices: double room single occupancy 55-65 euros, double 80-120 (20 euro supplement for extra bed), breakfast included • Credit cards: all, Bancomat • Facility accessible to the mobility challenged, 2 rooms designed for their use. Off-street parking. Small pets allowed (on request). Staff present from 8 am to midnight. • Bar, restaurant. Breakfast room. Garden, terrace, solarium.

🍲 In the nearby restaurant Adriano Zanotto uses products in season in his traditional and creative dishes – a meal costs 35 to 40 euros.

SANTA MARIA DI SALA
Caltana

SANT'AMBROGIO DI VALPOLICELLA

PAPAVERI E PAPERE

AL CÒVOLO

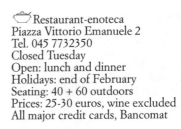

🗝Agritourism farm
Via Caltana 1 b
Tel. 041 5732462
Fax 041 5732155
E-mail: info@papaveri-papere.com
Internet: www.papaveri-papere.com
Open all year

🍲Restaurant-enoteca
Piazza Vittorio Emanuele 2
Tel. 045 7732350
Closed Tuesday
Open: lunch and dinner
Holidays: end of February
Seating: 40 + 60 outdoors
Prices: 25-30 euros, wine excluded
All major credit cards, Bancomat

This facility – recognized as an organic production farm – in the green countryside of Santa Maria di Sala is managed by Raffaella, with help from her children Gigliola, Cinzia, Anna, Maurizio and Nicola. You can tell by the way they go about their work that they have a real passion for cultivating the land and raising animals, such as poultry, pigs and wild boar. But they also manage their vacation farm in an equally professional and efficient manner. The building housing the rooms is clean and well kept. Although the farm is located in the province of Venice it's a member of an association based in Padua called Pro avibus nostris. The aim is to preserve and restock local poultry breeds, among which the Padua hen and Euganei Hills turkey. The small shop at the farm is open at weekends and you can buy the farm's produce, which is also used to prepare dishes served in the restaurant (meals cost about 25 euros per person).

• 5 double rooms, with bathroom, TV •
Prices: double room single occupancy 30 euros, double 48 (13 euro supplement for extra bed), breakfast 3 euros per person • Credit cards: Visa, MC, Bancomat • Communal areas accessible to the mobility challenged. Off-street parking. Small pets allowed. Owners always present. • Restaurant. Garden.

As one might expect from the name wine is made here in Sant'Ambrogio di Valpolicella, but it's also known for marble and stone which are exported all over the world. The town hall is built on a stairway vaguely reminiscent of the Campidoglio in Rome. On one side of the square stands Adelino Molinaroli's enoteca. Laid-back, quiet and attentive, Adelino runs the dining room with the help of his family, catering to many tourists from nearby Lake Garda or on a wine-tasting tour around the surrounding vineyards.

The seasonally changing menu always follows local traditions. Start with **polenta and soppressa, lardo** and **pancetta** in winter when you dine in the small room inside, or prosciutto rolls with Monte Veronese cheese in the summer out in the courtyard. If it's cold we recommend a generous portion of **bìgoli with duck** or **pasta e fagioli** for a first course. Mains include **stracotto all'Amarone**, **rabbit with polenta** and **duck breast on red Verona radicchio**. End your meal with homemade desserts, or if it happens to be the right season don't miss the fresh strawberries with Recioto and fresh mint.

The list of wines is extensive and they can be ordered by the glass – making it possible to follow Adelino's advice and pair a different wine with each dish.

🍯 The 8 Marzo agricultural cooperative in the Cà Verde area produces organic cheese, yogurt, cured meats, fruit, vegetables and wine.

SANT'AMBROGIO DI VALPOLICELLA

San Giorgio

19 KM NORTH-WEST OF VERONA

DALLA ROSA ALDA

☞●1 Star Hotel
Strada Garibaldi 4
Tel. 045 6800411
Fax 045 6801786
E-mail: alda@valpolicella.it
Internet: www.dallarosalda.it
Closed in January and February

In San Giorgio, a tiny hamlet near Sant'
Ambrogio di Valpolicella, you climb up
towards the splendid Romanesque
parish church to enjoy the view and it's
there that you'll find the Dalla Rosa Alda
hotel, considered a temple of traditional
Verona-style cuisine. Thanks to a recent
refurbishment the rooms have been
made more comfortable and now have
beautiful marble floors, and the restaurant area has been improved as well.
Owner Lodovico Testi has further promoted this area's most typical product –
wine – by creating a very well-stocked library with numerous publications on the
subject. More often than not opera
lovers returning from a performance at
the Arena di Verona will find a tray of
Lessinia cheeses and a good glass of
wine ready for them. In front of the trattoria is a wine shop in a small medieval
building where you'll be able to taste a
nice glass of Recioto.

• 1 single and 9 double rooms, with
bathroom, TV • Prices: single 60-75
euros, double 90-105, breakfast included • Credit cards: all, Bancomat • Facility accessible to the mobility challenged,
2 rooms designed for their use. Public
parking 20 meters away. Small pets allowed. Owners always present. •
Restaurant, wine cellar. Terrace.

☞ Restaurant with excellent traditional
cuisine at an average price of 35-45 euros,
excluding wine.

SAN VITO DI LEGUZZANO

21 KM NORTHWEST OF VICENZA SS 46

DUE MORI

☞ Trattoria with rooms
Via Rigobello 41
Tel. 0445 671635
Closed Monday
Open: lunch and dinner
Holidays: Aug. 1-20
Seating: 160 + 40 outdoors
Prices: 28-30 euros, wine excluded
All credit cards, Bancomat

This welcoming trattoria run by Rosalia
Saccardo and her staff always provides
a pleasant experience. The dining room
is run with efficiency and warmth, and in
the summer you can eat outside in the
small, well-tended garden. Rosalia is a
skilled chef whose dishes follow local
tradition using carefully selected, top-
quality ingredients.
The menu varies with the season and features many antipasti. We suggest garden
vegetables and local wild herbs in oil,
grilled or in a frittata, **sardines in saor**
and various mushroom dishes when available. The pumpkin-stuffed tortelli are excellent as are the **homemade tagliatelle
with duck sauce** (also available with fish
and vegetables); the menu always has a
soup – the **onion** is really very good –
and some **risottos**, including an original
one served in a round of Parmesan
cheese. The mains feature lots of meat:
grilled lamb skewers, kid, rabbit and
game in the winter, also served stewed.
The trattoria has an interesting way of
serving **grilled meats** at the table "al pati-
bolo," on the scaffold, hanging from a
steel tube for one last flaming. To end the
meal there is a good selection of local
cheeses and a rich dessert cart including
torta della nonna, wild fruit tart and trifle.
The ice cream is homemade as are the
petits fours offered with your coffee.
The wine list has a selection from all
over Italy at reasonable prices. For
those wishing to stay the night, the trattoria also has a few comfortable and
simply furnished rooms.

🍴 At **Thiene** (8 km) the La Pistoria wood
fired bakery in Via Dante 7 produces rustic
loaves, special breads and rolled focaccia
with raisins and sugar.

SAN ZENO DI MONTAGNA

SAN ZENO DI MONTAGNA

39 KM NORTHWEST OF VERONA SS 12 OR A22

39 KM NORTHWEST OF VERONA SS 12 OR A22

COSTABELLA

3 Star Hotel
Via degli Alpini 1
Tel. 045 7285046
Fax 045 6289921
E-mail: hotelcostabella@hotelcostabella.it
Internet: www.hotelcostabella.it
Open all year

TAVERNA KUS

Restaurant
Via Castello 14
Tel. 045 7285667
Closed Wednesday, never in summer
Open: lunch and dinner
Holidays: Jan. 6 to mid-March
Seating: 80 + 20 outdoors
Prices: 35 euros, wine excluded
All major credit cards, Bancomat

You'll find this hotel in the center of San Zeno, a short distance from Lake Garda and with Mount Baldo as a backdrop. Guests on vacation here will find it relaxing while at the same time it offers them a wealth of opportunities for cultural and naturalistic excursions and sport. It's run by the Perotti family, who will give you a friendly welcome and are always available to cater for your needs. The rooms are spacious, airy and nicely furnished, and many of them have a terrace with a view of the lake or the mountains. Breakfast is rich and generous, with a variety of foods to suit every taste. In the restaurant you'll be able to savor typical dishes of this area at an average price of 35 euros, which includes a bottle of wine for two (half board ranges from 40-50 euros per person). A must to see in San Zeno is Ca' Montagna, a historic building in Gothic-Venetian style that in the past belonged to the Montagna family but today is owned by the municipality.

• 5 single and 29 double rooms, with bathroom, TV; some with balcony • Prices: single 45 euros, double 78; breakfast 6 euros per person • Credit cards: all, Bancomat • 2 rooms designed for the mobility challenged. Off-street parking, in part covered (4 spaces). Small pets allowed. Owners always reachable. • Bar, restaurant, tavern. TV room. Terrace.

Driving up towards Monte Baldo there's a great view down over Lake Garda. Right after San Zeno di Montagna you'll find Taverna Kus, an elegant restaurant which has managed to maintain a warm family atmosphere. Located in a historic farmhouse, the beams, vaults and stone walls have been well-maintained. Ask to visit the old ice-house, where the wines are stored. The staff are young and full of energy, coordinated by Giancarlo Zanolli. Ten years ago he decided to turn this restaurant into the gastronomic focal point of Monte Baldo, and by all accounts he's succeeded.

The cuisine puts local, seasonal ingredients to good use in dishes like **chestnut minestrone**, **canederli with cabbage**, **bigoli with duck ragù**, **ricotta gnocchi with truffles from Monte Baldo** and orzotto with local field herbs. Move on to a roll of potatoes and cherries, **rabbit stew, carne salà**, tender beef cooked on a huge skewer and a selection of local **cheeses**, all paired with excellent wines. The desserts also follow the seasons. We recommend the **chestnut and chocolate roll**.

Seasonally themed set menus change monthly, and in the fall don't miss the San Zeno chestnut menu, based on the renowned Monte Baldo chestnuts.

In Pra Bestemà you can buy Ugo Bonafini's cheeses, which he and his family make in Bait dei Santi using milk from cows pastured high up on Monte Baldo.

SAONARA

ANTICA TRATTORIA ⊚ ▮
AL BOSCO

� Trattoria
Via Valmarana 13
Tel. 049 640021
Closed Tuesday
Open: lunch and dinner
Holidays: two weeks after Christmas, first week of June
Seating: 120 + 100 outdoors
Prices: 28-32 euros, wine excluded
All credit cards, Bancomat

Once an inn, this trattoria still features the original long bar where ombre and cicheti would be available outside regular service hours. There's also three attractive rooms and a beautiful summer arbor. Stefania and her father Luigino welcome diners.

Saonara is a center for nursery gardening, and has long been famed for its horsemeat. At Bosco you can start with **soppressa**, **horsemeat** bresaola and the typical hand-cut **sfilacci** (meat dried over a wood fire). **Tagliatelle** comes with sfilacci, or a horsemeat ragù; but the main courses really showcase the delicacy, with foal **spezzatino** or tagliata **of foal**, grilled steak or **straeca** (a cut from the belly of the horse). Apart from horsemeat dishes, the trattoria also has excellent **goose salad** and **veal tongue with beets** for antipasti, **risottos** with seasonal vegetables, **pasta e fagioli**, **bigoi in salsa**, and mains like **baccalà**, **roast rabbit**, and lamb and kid grilled over an open fire. The meal is rounded off with an excellent selection of cheeses, or one of the homemade desserts such as focacce with pears or apples, tarts or pies. Stefania has personally selected each wine on the extensive list which covers the whole of Italy, and will be happy to advise you on the perfect pairing for your meal.

SARCEDO

VILLA DI BODO ▮

⌣ Enoteca with kitchen
Via San Pietro 1
Tel. 0445 344506
Closed Monday
Open: 11.00 am-3.00 pm/6.30 pm-12.00 am
Holidays: 3 weeks Jan. or Febr., 10 days September
Seating: 50 + 50 outdoors
Prices: 25-32 euros, wine excluded
Credit cards: AE, Visa, Bancomat

You'll find this enoteca in the hills between Sarcedo and Thiene, at the beginning of the road that leads to the small restored church of San Pietro. Renovated from the outbuildings of an old aristocratic mansion, it's run by Gianfranco Zenari and Marilena Cavedon, with Piero Menegante in the kitchen. The local, seasonal cuisine places much emphasis on wild herbs.

They appear in antipasti like a **wild-herb flan with a taleggio fonduta**, which in the springtime might be joined by dishes like plumcake with green asparagus and smoked goose breast with a shallot sauce. There's always a **soup** of the day, or try **cannelloni of Marano corn with Asiago cheese and soppressa** from Vicenza or fagottini with dandelions and ricotta. There is a broad selection of main courses, **baccalà alla vicentina**, **liver alla barcarola**, Sorana beef tagliata with aromatic herbs and **tosella cheese from the Asiago plateau** with seasonal vegetables. There is also a good selection of Italian and French cheeses. The desserts are homemade, with the traditional **macafame** joined by hazelnut cake, blancmange with strawberry sauce and various mousses depending on the season.

The monumental wine list (some 500 labels, both Italian and foreign) shows Gianfranco's passion for wine. He'll be only too pleased to advise you on the choice of a bottle, or just a glass. There is also a good selection of grappas.

◐ In **Thiene** (5 km), Gianni Genovese is dedicated to finding the best wine production in Italy and abroad, and you can appreciate the fruits of his research at Enogamma, Via San Simone 32.

SCHIO
Magré

SCORZÈ

ALL'ANTENNA

PERBACCO

Trattoria
Via Raga Alta 4
Tel. 0445 529812
Closed Tuesday
Open: dinner only
Holidays: in August
Seating: 40 + 15 outdoors
Prices: 25-30 euros, wine excluded
Credit cards: Visa, Bancomat

Osteria-wine bar
Via Moglianese 37
Tel. 041 5840991
Closed Sunday
Open: lunch and dinner
Holidays: one week in August
Seating: 60 + 30 outdoors
Prices: 30-35 euros, wine excluded
All credit cards, Bancomat

Follow the signs for Magré, then Via Raga will take you up to the trattoria. On top of a hill, Antenna offers a broad panorama of the surrounding countryside, also the source of many of the restaurant's ingredients. While it has become more refined over the years the simplicity of its beginnings has never been abandoned. Laura explains the primarily traditional menu while Giovanni uses seasonal produce to prepare the food.

The many antipasti include **baccalà mantecato with fried polenta, soppressa**, lardo from Arnad **with radicchio in oil**; in spring try the cheese fonduta and asparagus sfogliatina and the browned asparagus with egg sauce. First courses include the classic **gargati al consiero, ricotta gnocchi with chives**, fagottino dorato with wild chicory and truffle. For a main course, in addition to the typical **rabbit alla valleogrina** and **baccalà alla vicentina**, try the pork rosettes with artichokes and loin of lamb with herbs. The desserts are delicious: crème brûlée, soft chocolate cake and zabaglione, biscotti with pastry cream and seasonally changing semifreddo.

The wine list contains some good wines from Italy and abroad, divided by origin. There's a particularly large choice of sparkling wines.

Just outside the center of Scorzè, on the road to Mogliano, an 18th-century mill on the banks of the River Desa houses the Perbacco and the Piccolo Hotel, run separately. The atmosphere of the tastefully refurbished interior is pleasant, and a relaxing meal on the outside terrace is accompanied by the sound of running water. The efficent and cordial service is overseen by the likeable Stefano Tosato while Claudio Pigozzo, an enterprising young chef, is painstaking in his selection of produce (Slow Food presidia, local meats and vegetables). The daily changing menu ranges from the traditional to the creative.

Alongside the **schie** (tiny gray shrimp) **with polenta** and the **scallops au gratin** with marinated tomatoes, the antipasti include tomatoes stuffed with burrata and pesto and cod salad with seasonal vegetables. Then, **spaghetti with squid ink,** strozzapreti with zucchini and saffron, tagliolini with little squid, giant shrimp and tomato, and in winter, **bean soup with Treviso radicchio**. Main courses include **guanciale braised in red wine**, roast Sorana beef with roast potatoes and tuna tagliata with olives and cherry tomatoes. The selection of Italian and French **cheeses** is excellent, with 12 varieties always on the board. Marco the pastry chef contributes his homemade white-chocolate and raspberry mousse with pistachio biscuits, fruit torta, banana mousse with strawberry and passion fruit and lemon mousse with melon and peach puree.

The wines on the list (there are some 300 Italian and foreign labels) are stored in a cellar with properly regulated temperature and humidity. The selection of spirits is also excellent.

In Magré there is a wide selection of cheeses in the shop run by Carlo Bernello inside the Vivo supermarket, Viale Roma 30. In **Schio**, Cooperativa Produttori Latte, Via Vicenza 20, for Grana Padano and pressed and extra-mature Asiago d'Allevo.

SEGUSINO
Milies

DA MIRKA E MARCELLO

🍲 Osteria
Via dei Narcisi 5
Tel. 0423 979120
Open June-September from Tuesday to Sunday
and October-May from Friday to Sunday
Open: lunch and dinner
Seating: 50
Prices: 20-25 euros, wine excluded
No credit cards

Segusino is on the left bank of the River
Piave, known here as the sacred river,
the last town in the Province of Treviso
after Valdobbiadene. To get to this osteria, take the road up by Riva Grassa,
with views down to the River Ariù,
through Stramare to Milies, a plateau at
700 meters altitude. Here cattle and
sheep would stop in June on their way
to the high summer pastures, and in
September on their way back down,
with the cowherds and shepherds stopping in the old osteria for an ombra.
Now Mirka and Marcello, together with
their children Isabella, Federica and
Lorenzo, have been running the osteria
for over ten years, Mirka in the dining
room and Marcello in the kitchen
preparing simple, direct dishes.
Don't miss Marcello's own cured meats
for antipasti, like **fresh smoked salami**
or the **soppressa**, to enjoy together with
the **marinated dandelion** if available.
The first courses include homemade
tagliatelle with **duck or donkey ragù**, or
risottos which, depending on the season will be with radici de camp (dandelion) or mushrooms (don't miss the porcini soup when in season) or vegetable
flans. Main courses include the tasty
stracotto di muss (donkey), the **mixed
spiedo** (rabbit, chicken, pork and beef),
game (roe deer, venison) and **grilled
cheese**. The meal ends with homemade
desserts: **strudel**, tiramisù and fruit in
mountain-herb-flavored grappa.
The wine list is starting to include some
excellent choices.

SELVA DI CADORE
Pescul

GARNÌ LADINIA

🗝3 Star Hotel
Località Pescùl 125
Tel. 0437 521249
Fax 0437 520063
E-mail: ladinia@dolomiti.com
Internet: www.garniladinia.com
Closed from 1 May to mid-June and in November

This hotel run by Elena Del Zenero and
Mario Zuliani, an alpine aid volunteer, is
located in a new building in front of the
ski lift facilities of Val Fiorentina, crossed
by Alta Via No. 1. As it's not far away
from the Sella mountains and Cortina
D'Ampezzo it's an excellent starting
point for skiing (downhill, cross-country
and alpine) and scaling Dolomite peaks.
Wood is the dominant feature in the furnishings of the comfortable rooms as
well as the communal areas. The buffet
breakfast includes homemade cakes.
By special arrangement guests may use
the nearby Nigritella Hotel's indoor
swimming pool.

• 2 single and 3 double, triple or four-
bed rooms and 2 suites, with bathroom,
terrace or balcony, TV, modem connection • Prices: single 34-46 euros, double
52-70 (31 euro supplement for extra
bed), suite 100-140 euros, breakfast included • Credit cards: major ones, Bancomat • 2 rooms designed for use by
the mobility challenged. Off-street parking. No pets allowed. Owners always
present. • Bar. Reading room, TV room.
Garden.

SOAVE
Carcera

SOLAGNA

RONCOLATO

Bed and breakfast
Via Carcera 21
Tel. 045 7675104
Fax 045 7675935
E-mail: antonioroncolato@libero.it
Internet: www.cantinaroncolato.com
Open all year

DA DORO

Trattoria
Via Ferracina 38
Tel. 0424 816026-558081
Closed Sunday dinner, Monday,
Thursday for lunch
Holidays: end June, beginning July
Seating: 45
Prices: 25-30 euros, wine excluded
No credit cards, Bancomat

Right in the heart of the countryside three kilometers from Soave, in a renowned winemaking facility run by Antonio Roncolato and Anna Maria Petrin, you'll find this B&B located in an old renovated farmhouse. It opened three years ago and allows you to combine relaxation with wine, gastronomic and culture-related tourism. This vineyard is part of the Soave wine trail and complies with the quality requirements set by the association. The rooms are comfortable and spacious, and one in particular can accommodate a small family. Breakfast is prepared on the spot to each guest's liking, with a choice of honey, jams, bread and cookies (all made with organic ingredients), ham, eggs and cheeses. In the vicinity you can visit the Regional Park of Lessinia, Lake Garda, whereas Verona, Vicenza and Venice are easily reachable by car.

• 2 double and 1 five-bed rooms, with bathroom, air-conditioning • Prices: double room single occupancy 50-60 euros, double 62-72, five-bed 130-150, breakfast included • Credit cards: CartaSi, MC, Visa, Bancomat • Off-street parking. No pets allowed. Owners always present • Shared kitchen. Garden. Pool.

Walking into this old, family-run trattoria is like stepping back in time. Located in a historic building on the main street in Solagna, a small town on the way up to the Valsugana. A brief ascent, with the church to your right, takes you to the warm welcome of Giovanni and Anna Scapin and their simple dishes which help you discover the flavors and history of the area. The short menu changes daily but there's always at least one risotto, two soups and two pasta dishes (one vegetarian) plus one red meat, one white meat and one fish, usually trout. Bread is homemade using organic flour. For antipasti, choose from home-smoked meats, **sardines in saor**, trout paté or snails when in season. Then try the rice tortino with steamed vegetables, **canederli with trout**, onion soup au gratin, **Lamon bean flan** with seasoned lardo, **gargati with ragù bianco** (veal, guinea fowl and pork) and, in summer, cold potato dumpling with gorgonzola. The main courses include veal cheek in Cabernet, **rabbit**, kid in season, and **trout with horseradish**. The **cheese** board is replete with quality produce from local farms: Morlacco, smoked ricotta, Allevo and extra-mature Asiago. The traditional desserts include **pinza**, **ferdinands** (a sweet made with double-leavened bread), apple tart, fruit semifreddos and chocolate mousse.
Next to the regular wine list is a list of everyday wines with nothing over 10 euros a bottle – a brilliant idea.

SOMMACAMPAGNA

SOSPIROLO
Mis

AL PONTE

ALLA CERTOSA

Trattoria
Via Corrobiolo 38
Tel. 045 8960024
Closed Tuesday dinner and Wednesday
Open: lunch and dinner
Holidays: Christmas, Easter and August
Seating: 80 + 40 outdoors
Prices: 20-25 euros, wine excluded
All major credit cards, Bancomat

Traditional osteria
Via Mis 83
Tel. 0437 843143
Closed Monday and Tuesday
Open: dinner, Sunday also for lunch
Holidays: 20 days in June
Seating: 40
Prices: 18 euros, wine excluded
All major credit cards

Al Ponte is great place to stop for lunch or dinner if you happen to be driving along the Serenissima highway. Turn right after the toll plaza and carry on for about a kilometer, and you'll find a simple, country trattoria which has somehow managed to survive as shopping malls and indutrial estates have sprung up around it. Make sure to call ahead for a reservation, because Andrea Pedrazzi's straightforward home cooking attracts a lot of regulars. After parking in the courtyard next to the trattoria, take a peek into the kitchen – under the faded sign reading "vendita vini," wines sold – and you'll see Andrea busy with the pots, pans and the grill.
The unchanging menu includes **tagliatelle**, served with just a knob of butter. You can then help yourself to tomato or meat ragù directly from the sauce dishes brought to the table. There's also delicate **tortellini with melted butter**, pappardelle with mushrooms, **pasta e fagioli** and porcini soup. Among main dishes **vitello tonnato** is a house classic as is the pike in sauce, **baccalà with polenta**, **liver alla veneziana** and grilled meats. The desserts are rustic but delicious, especially the trifle and fruit tarts.
The wines are few but the list has some good local varieties. The tables are set with white tablecloths and small glasses, but if you want proper wine glasses just ask.

This osteria takes its name from the nearby 15th-century Carthusian monastery of Vedana, located in the Lake Mis valley in the middle of the the Belluno Dolomites national park. Inside the focus is on a beautiful sideboard, overflowing with bottles of wine and spirits, through which Casimiro and Nadia can help you browse. While the cooking is excellent and the atmosphere pleasant, there are certain limitations: no main courses (though there is an excellent **cheese** selection), and apart from soups the whole table must order the same first course.
There's no written menu, and generally one starts with various warm and cold antipasti: vegetable **frittata** or flan, **savory pies** and stuffed or gratineed vegetables. **Pastin** (a chopped salami mixture) is served alone or used in fillings and sauces. There is a wide choice of first courses: soups, risottos, pasta al forno and stuffed pasta. **Onion soup** is ever-present, and in season there's porcini mushroom soup and tripe soup with chanterelles or porcini cabbage and beans, traditionally served between the feast days of St. Nicholas (December 6) and St. Giuliana (16 February). In addition, there is always **risotto** with chanterelles or porcini and pastin, with radicchio or pumpkin. The baked pasta could be with zucchini and squash flowers or mushrooms, or you could choose freshly made pasta like **bigoli with duck or rabbit sauce** as well as **pumpkin gnocchetti**. The desserts, all homemade, include walnut, hazelnut and chocolate cake (in the winter months) and amaretto and lemon cake, fruit cakes, mousses and peach ice (in summer).

Near the sports complex in **Bussolengo** (6 km), in Piazza del Grano 6, Zeno Gelato e Cioccolato has chocolates and ice cream made with top ingredients (try the Reciota flavor).

STRA
Paluello

DA CARONTE

Osteria-trattoria
Via Dolo 39
Tel. 041 412091
Closed Tuesday dinner and Wednesday
Open: lunch and dinner
Holidays: beginning of January, 15 days in August
Seating: 45 + 45 outdoors
Prices: 25-30 euros, wine excluded
All major credit cards, Bancomat

The banks of the River Brenta are lined with luxury villas set in a stunning landscape, and are home to this osteria. On the less-visited by equally interesting right bank, its housed in an old renovated villa which has an arbor outside for summer dining. Inspiration for the cuisine comes from the Veneto traditions of the land and the sea, interpreted by Maria Grazia in the kitchen. Roberto takes care of the dining room.

Antipasto includes a wide choice of cured meats (Montagnana prosciutto crudo, homemade **soppressa**, **foal sfilacci**, **horsemeat bresaola**), raw vegetables and savory torte. Then for a first course, **bigoi in salsa**, **tagliolini** with porcini mushrooms in season, tagliatelle with mussels, spaghetti with lobsters, maccheroncini with langoustines and vegetables and ricotta foulard with poppy seeds. In addition to the classic **mixed fried fish,** fish mains include **mixed saor** (sardines, sole, langoustines and fried vegetables, all marinated with onions); there is also the traditional **black Venetian-style cuttlefish**, **schie** (gray shrimps) with polenta, and a trio of **cod** (**mantecato**, **in tocio** and **Vicenza style**). For meat lovers there are **bocconcini of foal** with artichokes, breast of duck with roast potatoes, cold sliced veal with tuna sauce and **ossobuco** with vegetables. For dessert the homemade tarts are excellent.

As for wines, Roberto has now built up an excellent cellar linked to the old building by an underground passageway, in which he holds theme-based wine tastings. The easy-to-read list contains reasonably priced wines, especially from the Triveneto region, plus you can choose from more than 130 grappas.

SUSEGANA
Colfosco

ALL'ANTICA TRATTORIA DA CHECCO

Osteria-trattoria
Via San Daniele 70
Tel. 0438 781386-780027
Closed Monday dinner and Tuesday
Open: lunch and dinner
Holidays: 15 days in January
Seating: 70 + 70 outdoors
Prices: 20-25 euros, wine excluded
All major credit cards

The name comes from the original owner Francesco, known as Checco, and for many years it was a place for families and tourists to stop for cicheti and ombre on their way up to Parco Tombola at the top of the hill. Now run by Matteo Spinato and his parents, this attractive trattoria, while a bit off the beaten track, makes a pleasant destination in its own right. In the warm weather you can sit out on the spacious terrace, enjoying a magnificent view, while inside the dining room is warmed by a fireplace and decorated with a painting of the nearby castle of San Salvatore. Watch Matteo and his friend Loris working over the charcoal grill in the open kitchen while mamma Floriana and young Elisa explain the day's menu to you, then help yourself from the antipasto buffet in the center of the room.

Start with **tagliolini with duck** or **maccheroni al torchio** with a rustic meat ragù; in springtime there are garganelli with asparagus and gorgonzola or **risotto** with fresh wild herbs from the Conegliano hills, while the bauletti alla mediterranea are also very tempting. The main courses feature excellent grilled meats (including **donkey**), but if you want to stay traditional try the **donkey stew with polenta, rabbit stuffed with pork fillet** and quail in a potato crust. The recommended set menu includes with wines and offers good value for money. Round off the meal with something from the dessert cart or a selection of cookies.

Wines and sparklers are available by the glass, drawn from a rich collection of labels from Veneto and the rest of Italy.

TAMBRE

CENTRO CASEARIO E AGRITURISTICO DEL CANSIGLIO

Agritourism farm
Via Marconi 82
Tel. e fax 0437 439722
E-mail: caseifcansiglio@iol.it
Internet: www.cansiglio.com
Open all year

In Tambre, on the plateau of Alpago, the milk production unit founded in 1930 by cattle farmers in the Cansiglio-Alto Alpago area was restructured in 2003. In line with the original project, part of the building is used for cheese production while the rest is now used to host guests in spacious, pleasant rooms. The part of the building under the mansard ceiling, where sturdy wooden beams support the roof, is used as the breakfast room, which of course includes exquisite organic milk and the butter produced below, together with jams prepared with fruit from this area. Currently you'll still be able to hear the bustle of activity in the cheese factory, although the plans are to transfer it to a more remote building. You will find detailed maps indicating itineraries for walks and excursions by bicycle or on horseback. Guests will also be able to participate in guided tours to learn about this territory, its history and traditions, including its gastronomic traditions. There's a golf course not far away.

• 1 single and 11 double rooms, with bathroom, TV • Prices: single 32-35 euros, double 56-60 (14-28 euro supplement for extra bed), breakfast included • Credit cards: Visa, Bancomat • 2 rooms designed for use by the mobility challenged. Off-street parking. No pets allowed. Owners always reachable. • Breakfast room.

TEOLO
Castelnuovo

AL SASSO

Trattoria
Via Ronco 11
Tel. 049 9925073
Closed Wednesday
Open: dinner, Saturday and Sunday also for lunch
Holidays: 15 days in January, 10 in September
Seating: 80 + 60 outdoors
Prices: 31-35 euros, wine excluded
Credit cards: CartaSi, Visa

In spring the Euganei hills are covered with wild herbs, some of which end up in the dishes prepared by Lorenzina, the owner of this lovely trattoria together with husband Lucio Calaon. You might find fried orsino garlic leaves, **salad greens with fried ciccioli**, tani in salad with onion grass, nettle flan or rosole with warm uncured Montagnana ham, and then **risotto** with bruscandoli (wild hop shoots) or carletti (bladder campion). In other seasons the risottos are made with mushrooms and you can try **pasta with santi** (a local variety of bean), **gnocchi with chicken ragù**, ravioli with eggplant and tomato, **agnolotti with Vezzena cheese and walnuts**. Among the main courses, apart from meat (chicken, **guinea hen**, **lamb chops** and various cuts of beef) grilled on an open wood fire, there's breast of guinea hen with finferli mushrooms, snails with spugnole mushrooms, rack of rabbit wrapped in bacon and the excellent **stuffed torresano pigeon**, a dish claimed by both the Colli Euganei and Breganze area near Vicenza as a local creation. The **fried chicken** gets a special mention, as it really is superb. There's a short fixed menu for 18 euros and the service is courteous and competent.
The wine list is very interesting, including many Colli Euganei wines as well as some other good Italian and foreign wines at reasonable prices.

Praglia Abbey, in **Presseo** (11 km), produces a variety of exceptional honeys, liqueurs and herbal teas.

TEOLO

VILLA LUSSANA

3 Star Hotel
Via Chiesa Teolo 1
Tel. e fax 049 9925530
E-mail: info@villalussana.com
Internet: www.villalussana.com
Closed from 7-31 January

This Art Nouveau-style country house is in the center of Teolo, a village of Roman origin in a delightful valley of the Euganei Hills. The rooms (4 of which are in an annexe) are all pleasantly sizeable and enjoy a delightful view. Since July 2003 the hotel-restaurant has been managed by the Crestati children. Barbara takes care of the general hospitality side of things, while Franco prepares traditional Veneto dishes for meals priced from 30 and 40 euros per person, excluding wine (half board costs 67 euros per person). There's an Italian-style part buffet and part served breakfast with orange juice, coffee, milk, tea, bread, butter and jam, croissants and homemade cakes. Only two kilometers away is the Madonna del Monte Sanctuary and from its terrace you can enjoy a magnificent view of the Euganei Hills Park, of which Teolo is part. The Park is the ideal place for walks to keep you in close contact with Nature.

• 11 double rooms, with bathroom, air-conditioning, mini-bar, TV • Prices: double room single occupancy 60 euros, double 90 (20 euro supplement for extra bed), breakfast included • Credit cards: all, Bancomat • Facility accessible to the mobility challenged, 1 room designed for their use. Off-street parking, garage (4 spaces, 10 euros per day). No pets allowed. Owners always reachable. • Restaurant. Lounge with TV corner. Terrace, garden.

TORREBELVICINO
Pievebelvicino

ALLA SORGENTE

Trattoria
Via Tenaglia 4
Tel. 0445 661233
Closed: Monday and Tuesday
Open: dinner, festivities also for lunch
Holidays: variable
Seating: 40
Prices: 18-25 euros, wine excluded
No credit cards, Bancomat

You'll find this trattoria by continuing straight after the old parish church, taking the little road on the right (the corner is marked by a stone) through a narrow valley, passing through a hamlet and going on until you see a wide courtyard on the right. Lorenza provides a warm welcome while her husband Claudio will be busy in the kitchen. He's passionate about cooking and very meticulous, choosing his ingredients with care and following local traditions with just the odd touch of inventiveness.

The menu is heavy on fish, raised by the owners in ponds fed by the sorgente, or spring, which gives the place its name. So start with **smoked trout** with homemade **sauerkraut** or fresh goat's cheese and radicchio, then try **lasagnette with trout** or trout ravioli with tomato sauce, **oven-baked trout** and fillet of trout with vegetables and speck or mustard. Other options include vegetable or **barley soup**, macaroni or other pasta served with seasonal sauces, **polenta with renga** (herring) or **baccalà**, grilled beef or pork and lamb around Eastertime. For dessert we recommend the buckwheat cake, apple puree with cinnamon, or in summer, watermelon with pistachio nuts. There's an extensive and varied wine list, with a some really good value options: Claudio is a real connoisseur and is always on the lookout for little-known and up-and-coming producers.

TORRI DEL BENACO
Albisano

PANORAMA

☎—◑3 Star Hotel
Via San Zeno 9
Tel. 045 7225102
Fax 045 6290162
E-mail: info@panoramahotel.net
Internet: www.panoramahotel.net
Open from March to November

Albisano is a sleepy hillside village near Torri del Benaco, on the eastern shore of Lake Garda. The name 'Panorama' given to the Martinelli family's hotel is very apt as it lies in a position dominating the lake. On summer evenings while dining on the hotel terrace (the restaurant offers many seafood dishes, but also some local cuisine, at a price ranging from 25-30 euros, excluding wine) you'll see the houses on the opposite shore gradually lighting up like a crib. Every winter when they close, Giancarlo, his wife Anna and their children Teresa and Mauro, dedicate the time to modernizing the rooms or improving the services. Breakfast consists of homemade cakes, jams, honey, cured meats and cheeses, and in summer it's served on the terrace overlooking Torri. On request the hotel books excursions and tickets for shows and museums.

• 3 single and 25 double rooms, with bathroom, safe, satellite TV; many have air-conditioning • Prices: single 49-52 euros, double 76-88, breakfast included • Credit cards: all except AE, Bancomat • Facility accessible to the mobility challenged, 1 room designed for their use. External parking reserved for guests. Small pets allowed. Owners always present. • Restaurant. Reading room. Conference room. Terrace. Pool with jacuzzi.

TORRI DI QUARTESOLO
Lerino

LE GUIZZE

☎—◑Bed and breakfast
Via Guizze
Tel. 044 4381977
Fax 044 4381992
E-mail: info@leguizze.it
Internet: www.leguizze.it ⸙
Closed for 3 weeks in August

This ancient farm refurbished in 2001 lies in the midst of the green Vicenza countryside. It features wooden and terracotta ceilings, wooden floors and cherry-wood furniture in keeping with the tradition of the Veneto region. The rooms all have a good view and are pleasant and quiet: you'll find a family atmosphere here and the owners are happy to provide newspapers, transport timetables, maps of the city and informative material on the environs. The restaurant offers local dishes, with some variations, at approximately 30 euros per person, excluding wine. The continental breakfast is buffet style. This B&B is in a strategic position for visiting the province of Vicenza and the entire Veneto region. It's the ideal place to stay to visit the nearby Venetian and Palladian villas, the walled cities of Marostica, Montagnana, Citadel, Este and Monselice, and cities of artistic interest such as Padua, Verona, Venice, Treviso, Asolo and Bassano.

• 6 double rooms, with bathroom, air-conditioning, safe, TV modem connection • Prices: double room single occupancy 55 euros, double 65-110, breakfast included • Credit cards: all, Bancomat • Communal areas accessible for the mobility challenged. Off-street parking. Small pets allowed. Owners always reachable. • Bar, restaurant. Conference room. Garden.

TREVENZUOLO
Fagnano

TREVISO

22 KM SOUTH OF VERONA

ALLA PERGOLA

🍲 Trattoria
Via Nazario Sauro 9
Tel. 045 7350073
Closed: Monday and Tuesday dinner
Open: lunch and dinner
Holidays: January and between July and August
Seating: 50
Prices: 20-25 euros, wine excluded
All major credit cards, Bancomat

IL BASILISCO 🍾

🍲 Restaurant
Via Bison 34
Tel. 0422 541822
Closed: Sunday and Monday lunch
Open: lunch and dinner
Holidays: variable
Seating: 40 + 40 outdoors
Prices: 28-35 euros, wine excluded
All credit cards, Bancomat

If you're not familiar with the area it can be hard to find the tiny village of Fagnano, hidden away in the Verona countryside, surrounded by fields and rice paddies. You leave the A22 del Brennaro at Nogarole Rocca, and drive a few kilometers on to get to Fagnano. Here we're off the beaten tourist track, yet the large area of the Province of Verona known as the Bassa is full of surprises and can reward visitors with some culinary delights.

The menu at Pergola is influenced by the hearty cuisine of both Verona and Mantua. First courses include **tortelli di zucca** or ravioli stuffed with seasonal vegetables. The **meat tortelli** are exceptional, whether with a sauce or in broth, as are the **fettuccine col ragù di musso** (donkey). As the dwarf Verona variety of rice is grown here, don't miss the traditional dish of **rice and meat** served with pieces of beef and pork. Other main courses include classics such as **a platter of roast and boiled meats** (boiled beef, tongue, calf's head and cotechino) with green sauce, horseradish, mostarda and the ever-present **pearà** veronese. For puddings, the **sbrisolona** will remind you that we're quite near Mantua, or try the fresh seasonal fruit. The wine list may be short, but there's some quality choices.

The chef-patron of Il Basilisco is a Trentino native, but before coming to Treviso he worked in restaurants around Europe and the United States. His recently renovated restaurant uses only fresh ingredients (there's no freezer in the kitchen), including some Slow Food presidia, sourced from carefully selected suppliers. The finished dishes reflect Diego's passion and curiosity, including an interest in offal.

The menu changes every day and there's always a choice of six antipasti, six firsts and six main courses. A few examples: home-**cured meats**, tartare of fianchetto (diaphragm), the Trentino specialty carne salada and turkey ham cured with vinegar, then **tagliatelle with guinea-fowl sauce** or with fresh tomato and sheep's milk ricotta and **risotto with gizzards** braised in Raboso del Piave wine or with tuna livers. Mains might include **pigs' trotters**, veal heart, warm **nervetti** with parsnip puree and green sauce, ossocollo with herbs and mashed potatoes, browned **leg of Alpagotto lamb**, monkfish tripe, cuttlefish with fresh tomato and zucchini or grilled tuna steak. For dessert there's **torta di pane** with almonds and raisins or chocolate chips, other unusual sweets and homemade gelato.

The wine list contains about 200 labels organized in an original manner, with special categories of wine referred to as "outsiders." There are also a dozen beers which pair well with the dishes. In addition there are always four or five red and white house wines, some quite well known.

🖤 In **Vigasio** (6 km) there's Riseria Gazzani, in Via Zambonina 40, using old wooden basins to process selected rice varieties from trusted farmers in the Bassa area.

TREVISO

VALDAGNO
Contrà Maso

VINERIA ⊖▮

� Recently opened osteria-enoteca
Via Castellana
Tel. 0422 210460
Closed Sunday
Open: 10.30-2.30 pm - 6.00 pm-12.00 am
Holidays: none
Seating: 40 + 50 outdoors
Prices: 30 euros, wine excluded
All credit cards except DC, Bancomat

HOSTARIA A LE BELE

� Trattoria
Via Maso 11
Tel. 0445 970270
Closed Monday and Tuesday lunch
Open: lunch and dinner
Holidays: August
Seating: 70
Prices: 30-35 euros, wine excluded
All credit cards

This modern osteria on the outskirts of Treviso has become a trendy destination for the younger generation since it was opened by owners Andrea and Omar a few years ago. Reflecting wine's new appeal to young people, here there's a choice of 1,700 labels, paired with first-rate food. The casually presented but well-prepared dishes are based on quality products from around Veneto and beyond, many on sale at the shop next door. The wide selection of Italian cured meats dominates the antipasti: from langhirano a coltello to Val Chiavenna bresaola, lardo di Colonnata and **soppressa** veneta served with **Biancoperla corn**. Mention should also be made of the Piedmontese hand-chopped carne cruda. The carefully selected pastas are sauced with vegetables from the surrounding fields (Treviso red radicchio, Badoere and Cimadolmo asparagus, Lamon beans, pumpkin), whereas the **ravioli** are served with **a fondue of Morlacco**, a cheese made from the milk of cows pastured high up on Monte Grappa; in addition, there's the typical dish known as **sopa coada**. For the main course, **tripe, musetto with mashed potatoes** and excellent grilled meats like steak, fillet and lamb. There's an extensive, carefully selected **cheese board**, with Morlacco and Alpago cheeses like a fresh, lightly smoked Alpago ricotta. Care is taken over the desserts and chocolate tastings. To finish, Guatemalan coffee, a Slow Food Presidia.
Omar and Andrea's friendships with many local chefs, plus their professionalism and dedication to research, mean that the restaurant is constantly developing and improving.

It's been many years since carters and shepherds travelling through the Agno Valley would stop at this post station to eat a plate of pasta e fasoi or tripe prepared by the bele, two attractive sisters called Bice and Giulia. That was at the end of the 19th century, and in 1975 the Pianegonda brothers decided to reopen the restaurant, naming it for the sisters and continuing their tradition of hospitality and good food. Modernizations have left intact the family atmosphere and old-fashioned unpretentiousness.
A fixed menu offers a series of local dishes – three small antipasti, three first course tastings and a main course plus dessert. There's also a well-balanced à la carte menu available. You could start with good **cured meats** or **frittatas** with seasonal additions, tongue timbale with basil sauce or **polentina with fonduta**. The pasta used for first courses (**gargati col consiero, gnocchetti with butter and cinnamon**, chitarrine with black truffles) is homemade, and **risottos** are flavored with seasonal vegetables, like bruscandoli in the spring. Among the main courses there's an excellent **lamb in crosta, rabbit roulade** and **Vicenza-style baccalà with polenta**; alternatively, fillets and steaks. There are also some fish dishes, such as shrimp with olives and tuna carpaccio. For dessert try the famous **putana** vicentina, served with zabaglione. The wine list includes wines on tap and in bottles and includes some interesting labels available by the glass.

VALDOBBIADENE
San Pietro di Barbozza

TRATTORIA ALLA CIMA

🍲Restaurant
Via Cima 13
Tel. 0423 972711
Closed Monday dinner and Tuesday
Open: lunch and dinner
Holidays: Jan. 6-31, first week in July
Seating: 90 + 90 outdoors
Prices: 27 euros, wine excluded
All credit cards

The Rebuli family's beautifully renovated farmhouse stands among prosecco vineyards. Founder Antonio Rebuli has been managing this trattoria since May 1969, first focussing his efforts on the kitchen and later confining himself to grilling meat on the enormous open fireplace in the middle of the room. Diners can also watch chef Davide Capovilla and his team preparing the meals in the open-plan kitchen, while son Isidoro and wife Grazia deal with guests in a courteous, professional manner.
The menu is based on local seasonal produce: in spring you'll find dishes based on asparagus, wild herbs and snails; in summer, mushrooms; in the fall, mushrooms and radicchio; in winter, radicchio. The most typical antipasto is the merenda del mazarol, minced **soppressa** heated **in a pan with fresh ricotta cheese.** In season there's **radicchio rolls** and polenta timballo with mushrooms. From the first courses we would recommend the eggplant and smoked-ricotta gnocchi, **potato gnocchi with hare sauce,** tagliolini with chanterelle mushrooms and crescenza cheese and the very good, ever-present **pasta e fagioli.** Main courses include a wide selection of meats: beef, **horse,** pork, **kid** and **game,** all well-chosen by Antonio and, above all, well-cooked, whether **on skewers** or grilled. Also worth mentioning are the sirloin steaks cooked with juniper berries, boned guinea fowl flavored with mint and the **soppressa with polenta.** Rounding out the menu are homemade desserts such as warm apple tart with vanilla cream, semifreddo with coffee or al croccante and amaretto.
Isidoro is also in charge of the wine list, which offers an excellent selection of labels from the area and the rest of Italy.

VALEGGIO SUL MINCIO
Le Bugne

CORTE MARZAGO

🔑Agritourism farm
Località Le Bugne
Tel. 045 6369821
Fax 045 7945104
E-mail: info@cortemarzago.com
Internet: www.cortemarzago.com
Open from mid-March to mid-November

The Corte Marzago, which takes its name from the family that owned it for many years, is in an old convent dating from the sixteenth century that has always been synonymous with hard-working country folk. The fruit and olive trees, and vineyards cultivated on these 20 hectares of land in the morainic hills to the south-east of Lake Garda, create an attractive backdrop to the farm that is so efficiently and enthusiastically run by the Fabiano family. The rooms are spacious and furnished with antiques, the courtyard and farmhouse are entirely at the guests' disposal. Continental breakfast is served indoors or under the portico. Apart from Lake Garda, in the immediate vicinity you can visit Borghetto sul Mincio, with the Ghibelline ramparts of the Scaligero castle; the bell tower of San Marco and the picturesque Visconti bridge; Salionze with the eighteenth-century Tebaldi villa (according to tradition this is where Pope Leo the Great halted the march of Attila). There's a shuttle service to and from Peschiera railway station.

• 6 double rooms, with bathroom (1 next door), air-conditioning, TV; some with mini-bar, 2 with kitchen • Prices: double room single occupancy 60 euros, double 70, breakfast included • Credit cards: all, Bancomat • Off-street parking. Small pets allowed (not in rooms). Owners always present. • Wine-tasting room. Breakfast room, reading room. Garden.

VALEGGIO SUL MINCIO
Salionze

VENICE
City center

ALLA PASSEGGIATA

🍲 Trattoria
Via del Garda 132
Tel. 045 7945009
Closed: Tuesday dinner and Wednesday
Open: lunch and dinner
Holidays: November
Seating: 150 + 30 outdoors
Prices: 20-25 euros, wine excluded
All major credit cards, Bancomat

ACCADEMIA

🔑 Bed and breakfast
Dorsoduro 1054
Tel. 041 5221113-346 3130083
Fax 041 5221113
E-mail: info@bbaccademia.com
Internet: www.bbaccademia.com
Open all year

Travelling to Salionze from Valeggio or Peschiera del Garda you'll have a chance to enjoy the lush vegetation of the Valle del Mincio. Glacier-formed morainic hills are covered in vineyards, ordered fields and the beautiful wooded Sigurtà Gardens, an attractive alternative to the crowded theme parks around Lake Garda.

The cooking of Vittorio and Claudio Mischi and Vittorio's wife Franca is another attraction, as they offer their interpretations of typical local dishes in an unpretentious trattoria with old-fashioned decor. The menu opens with **pike in sauce with toasted polenta** or **cured meats with pickled vegetables**. Then homemade pasta like **tortellini**, pride of the area, a must to try either with delicate melted butter or in broth. As we are near Mantua you'll also find **tortelli with yellow pumpkin**, as well as more typical dishes from Verona such as **pasta e fasoi** and **paparèle coi fegadini** (tagliolini with chicken giblets). For a main course there's **baccalà**, **tripe** and a good selection of grilled meats. Generous helpings of seasonal vegetables, superb fried potatoes (a world away from fast-food fries) and to finish up, homemade dessert like buttery **torta delle rose**, another local specialty.

The wines are all local, a small selection but of good quality.

🍴 Classic tortellini di Valeggio along with other fresh pastas can be purchased at Luciana and Guido Remelli's artisanal pasta production outlet in Via Sala 24, in front of the parish church.

The Accademia occupies the first and second floor of an eighteenth-century building near the gallery where many famous paintings can be seen (Carpaccio, Mantegna, Giorgione, Titian, Tintoretto, Guardi...), and it is just a few minutes from Piazza San Marco and the Peggy Guggenheim Collection (Picasso, Kandinsky, Severini, Giacometti...). Apart from the friendly welcome you'll get from Barbara Terruzzin and her family, the main attraction of this house is the splendid terrace that guests are free to use, which overlooks the campo in front of Ponte dell'Accademia. The rooms are spacious, bright and furnished with period pieces although it can be a bit noisy in summer (there is a water bus stop nearby); two rooms have a beautiful view of the Grand Canal. Breakfast can either be served in your room, in the breakfast room or on the terrace and there's never a lack of freshly-baked croissants and a well-prepared cappuccino with lots of foam and a sprinkle of cocoa.

• 3 double rooms, with bathroom (2 rooms share a bathroom), safe, TV • Prices: double room single occupancy with bathroom 65-110 euros, without bathroom 50-95, double with bathroom 65-120, without bathroom 50-105, breakfast included • Credit cards: all, Bancomat • No pets allowed. Owners always reachable. • Breakfast room. Terrace.

VENICE
Mestre

VENICE
City center

9 KM FROM TOWN CENTER

AL CALICE

Wine bar and osteria
Piazza Ferretto 70 B
Tel. 041 986100
Closed: Sunday for dinner
Open: lunch and dinner
Holidays: none
Seating: 50 + 40 outdoors
Prices: 28-33 euros, wine excluded
All credit cards, Bancomat

AL CAMPANIEL

Bed and breakfast
San Polo 2889-Calle del Campaniel
Tel. e fax 041 2750749
E-mail: alcampaniel@hotmail.com
Internet: www.alcampaniel.com
Closed from 15 July to 15 August

An ancient courtyard where you can have lunch or dinner in summer, three cozy little rooms, the bar area: this is the place run by Emiliano Rispoli, Marco Cardin and Maurizio Ritrovato in the pedestrian precinct of Piazza Ferretto. To reach it you walk under the porticoes, through a gallery festooned with photos of famous visitors from the past (the osteria has been in existence since 1836). Apart from a full meal you can also drop in here for a quick snack, taking advantage of the splendid cicheti and a fantastic choice in terms of quantity and quality of wines by the glass. And you can sample any type of wine by the glass during your meal too.
The menu changes daily and includes both meat and fish dishes. Among the antipasti, a mix of **fish, boiled, marinated or in saor**, smoked swordfish carpaccio and, when it can be found fresh in the market, raw fish; there are also some nice cured meats, including Parma ham seasoned for 24 months. Among the first courses, **fish risotto**, **linguine all'astice** or with clams, pasta and risotto with vegetables and the ever-present **pasta e fagioli**. To follow, **seppie in nero with polenta**, **baccalà mantecato** with warm crostini, 'premium' grilled fish and, for meat-lovers, grilled Florentine steak, filet steak with balsamic sauce and, on Monday, **mixed boiled meat with cren and green sauce**. To end up, a selection of cheeses or a homemade pudding: crema catalana, chocolate salami, apple pie.
As already mentioned, there's a vast selection of wines: the list carries bottles from the world's most important wine-producing areas, including Champagne.

Close to the Grand Canal, about ten minutes from Piazzale Roma and the railway station, and only one minute from the water bus stop of San Tomà, you'll find this B&B located in a building dating from the late nineteenth century. Managed by Marco De Andreis, this facility offers hospitality in elegant, comfortable rooms with a view over a small courtyard. Now it's possible to have breakfast in a cozy room that has been added recently; in addition all rooms have a kettle with which you can prepare your own tea or coffee. The apartment is on the ground floor: the small kitchen always has a supply of honey, jam, slices of bread, butter, tea, coffee, orange juice and milk. In the vicinity you can visit the church of Santa Maria Gloriosa dei Frari built in the XIVth century, which contains works by Titian, Giovanni Bellini and Donatello.

• 2 double and 1 triple rooms, with bathroom (in the case of 1 room, the bathroom is next door), air-conditioning, safe; 1 apartment (2-4 persons) with kitchenette • Prices: double room single occupancy 40-55 euros, double with bathroom next door 54-78, double with bathroom en suite 68-108, triple and apartment 78-118, breakfast included • Credit cards: Visa, MC • No pets allowed. Owners always reachable. • Breakfast room.

ANICE STELLATO

🍲 Osteria-trattoria
Cannaregio 3272-Fondamenta de la Sensa
Tel. 041 720744
Closed: Monday and Tuesday
Open: 12.30-2.00 pm/7.30-10.00 pm
Holidays: 1 week end-January, last two
weeks of August, 15-September 20
Seating: 45 + 12 outdoors
Prices: 35 euros, wine excluded
Credit cards: MC, Visa, Bancomat

Coming from Piazzale Roma you can reach the osteria on foot. It's tastefully furnished, has two rooms, and in good weather there are four tables outdoors, always much in demand. This is a family-run place: mamma Luciana rules over the kitchen, helped by her son Silvio and daughter-in-law Franca, with another son, Alessandro, front of house with his wife Martina. It's mainly a fish-based menu and changes daily depending on what's available in the Rialto and Caorle markets.

You start with the traditional cicheti, **sardines in saor**, clams and **peoci** heated quickly in the frying pan or pilchards spiced with lemon and ginger then cooked in the oven. The **pasta**, either homemade or bought from a Gragnano pasta-maker, is served in various ways: **alla buranella** with a shellfish sauce, **with cuttlefish and cannellini beans**, with scampi and zucchini flowers. Then there's ravioli stuffed with mozzarella di bufala, **risottos** and, in the cold season, **pasta e fagioli** with added shellfish. There are many excellent main courses, from simple dishes like breaded sardines to a generous portion of mixed fried fish, skate cooked in the season's aromatic herbs, salmon spiced with dill or swordfish cooked with juniper berries and thyme. Exceptional dishes, but unfortunately not always on the menu, are the **zuppetta di gransipori** and cappelunghe dorate. As a side-plate, when in season, the Slow Food Presidia, the Sant'Erasmo purple artichoke and the typical **castraure**. To finish, a nice selection of cheeses, including the excellent Vezzena, and puddings.

To drink there's a pleasant white house wine and a few regional labels.

CASA DEL MIELE

🛏️ Bed and breakfast
Via Palliaghetta 2 a
Tel. 041 5416129-338 8300560
Fax 041 5342718
E-mail: info@casadelmiele.com
Internet: www.casadelmiele.com
Open all year

Enrico Giorgiutti – agronomist and formerly an employee of Venice's fishing and aquaculture authority, nature guide and with a passion for meteorology – has refurbished his villa with garden located just 300 meters from the Casino of Ca' Noghera to create a B&B. The three rooms, furnished with taste by his wife Annalisa, are big and comfortable. The buffet breakfast served in the beautiful lounge with fireplace, includes a large variety of sweet fare, among which twenty or so types of honey (Enrico's father is a bee-keeper). A library with books on subjects of interest to tourists is available for guests. The bus for Venice stops 50 meters from the B&B, or alternatively you can go to Piazza San Marco by taxiboat that, for 10 euros, connects the Marco Polo airport to the city center, with stops on the way at the island of Murano and the Lido.

• 3 double rooms, with bathroom, air-conditioning, satellite TV, mini-bar, safe, modem connection • Price: double room single occupancy 65 euros, double 75 (20 euro supplement for extra bed, breakfast included • Credit cards: MC, Visa, Bancomat • Off-street parking. No pets allowed. Owners always present. • Breakfast room. Garden.

CASA PERON

🗝️ 1 Star Hotel
Santa Croce 84-Salizzada San Pantalon
Tel. 041 710021-711038
Fax 041 711038
E-mail: casaperon@libero.it
Internet: www.casaperon.com
Closed for 15 days in January

DALLA MARISA

🍲 Trattoria
Cannaregio 652 b-Fondamenta San Giobbe
Tel. 041 720211
Closed: Sunday, Monday and Wednesday for dinner
Open: lunch and dinner
Holidays: August and Christmas
Seating: 25 + 35 outdoors
Prices: 30-35 euros
No credit cards

Casa Peron is in the historic center, very close to the Piazzale Roma parking area in a palazzo dating from the sixteenth century. Gianrico Scarpa and family have been running it since 1989 and are always ready to provide guests with maps and informative material about Venice. The rooms are pleasant although furnished in a basic way and some of them have a terrace. Breakfast is traditional and includes bread and freshly made brioches from a local bakery, milk, tea, coffee and fruit juices. You must visit the church of the Frari and the Scuola di San Rocco, the Ca' Rezzonico Museum of 18th-century Venice, the church of San Nicolò dei Mendicoli, one of most popular and ancient churches in the city with a square bell tower standing next to it, and the Accademia art gallery.

• 4 single, 5 double and 2 triple rooms, with bathroom (in 4 rooms, next door); 7 with air-conditioning • Prices: single 25-90 euros, double 40-95, triple 60-120, breakfast included • Credit cards: major ones, Bancomat • No pets allowed. Reception open from 7 am to 1 am. • Breakfast room.

The osteria is near Ponte dei Tre Archi but isn't very easy to spot: you'll only find it easily in the warm months when a number of tables are set outside along the canal. It's always a bit chaotic at lunchtime, what with passing visitors, gondoliers and workmen from the surrounding area. However, service is very fast and efficient and dishes are well-prepared and served up in healthy portions. It's very pleasant in the evenings and you can stay there till late in a very relaxed atmosphere. There's no written menu but the owner's children, Wanda and Stefano, will call off what's available. Marisa generally prefers to cook meat and game, but if you order, she'll turn out some excellent fish dishes, for instance, **folpeti in umido**, **peoci al forno**, fried fish depending on what's available on the day, sea bass and gilthead.

It's advisable to start immediately with your first course as you'll undoubtedly find whatever you choose to be superb. The homemade **pasta** is good with either a wild boar or **masaro** (drake) **sauce** or veal ragù, and the **risottos** are excellent: if available, taste the one **in caroman**, with mutton. Again speaking of first courses, which change with the season, there are sauces based on zucchini, asparagus and mushrooms. A choice of numerous meat dishes for your main course: a superb **stuffed roast pheasant**, cooked very slowly and that we found very tasty indeed, venison in salmì, baked breast of duck and, if you're lucky, **sguazzetto alla becera**, with tripe and giblets.

Unfortunately there's no wine list so the choice is either white or red house wine.

DALLA MORA

🔑1-Star Hotel
Santa Croce 42-Salizzada San Pantalon
Tel. 041 710703
Fax 041 723006
E-mail: hoteldallamora@libero.it
Internet: www.hoteldallamora.it
Closed from 7-30 January

GLI ANGELI

🔑Bed and breakfast
Castello 2161-Campo de la Tana
Tel. 041 5230802-339 2828501
Tel. e fax 041 2415350
E-mail: bedgliangeli@hotmail.com, theangels@email.it
Internet: www.gliangeli.net
Open all year

With help from their family, the two brothers Alexander and Francisco Aidone run this cozy hotel located in a late nineteenth century building and in the nearby annexe. The quiet, comfortable rooms are furnished in a restrained, essential manner and some have a view of the canal. Breakfast is traditional, with milk, tea, coffee, croissants, bread, butter and jam. The location is ideal for visiting the city's monuments, churches and museums, starting from the Frari and the Scuola di San Rocco, Ca' Rezzonico, the Carmini and Accademia art gallery. Piazzale Roma and the Tronchetto are within easy reach by vaporetto, lines 1 and 82.

• 4 single and 8 double rooms, with bathroom (for some, next door) • Prices: single 50-65 euros, double 70-95 (20 euro supplement for extra bed), breakfast included • Credit cards: all except AE, Bancomat • 1 room accessible for the mobility challenged. Small pets allowed. Owners always present. • Breakfast room. Terrace.

On the first floor of a fifteenth-century building, just a few steps from the majestic entrance to the Arsenal, you will find this cozy B&B run by Sonia and Antonio. In his spare time Antonio enjoys making leaded windows, which you'll also find in the rooms furnished in eighteenth-century Venetian style with gold leaf inlays on the mirrors and windows. The apartment with two double bedrooms has a kitchen, bathroom and a winding staircase that will lead you to a private garden. Breakfast is available every day when the rooms are being cleaned and the pantry restocked. Walking down Riva dei Schiavoni you get to Piazza San Marco in about ten minutes. Musts to see are the Corderie dell'Arsenale where the Biennale and other events are held, the Naval History Museum and Via Garibaldi, with the small market, stores, ice-cream parlors, pizzerias and restaurants.

• 1 double room, with bathroom, fridge, safe, TV; 2 apartments (2-4 persons) with kitchenette • Prices: double room single occupancy 60 euros, double and studio 79-95, 2-room apartment 129-159, breakfast included • Credit cards: major ones • Small pets allowed (not in double room). Owners always reachable.

CA' REZZONICO FERRY STOP | 9 KM FROM TOWN CENTER

LA BITTA

⌒Osteria with kitchen
Dorsoduro 2753 A-Calle Lunga San Barnaba
Tel. 041 5230531
Closed: Sunday
Open: 6.30 am-2.00 am
Holidays: variable
Seating: 28 + 12 outdoors
Prices: 32-35 euros, wine excluded
No credit cards

LA PERGOLA

⌒Trattoria
Via Fiume 42
Tel. 041 974932
Closed: Saturday for lunch and Sunday
Open: lunch and dinner
Holidays: 3 weeks in January, 15 days in August
Seating: 45 + 40 outdoors
Prices: 30-32 euros, wine excluded
All credit cards, Bancomat

A small osteria that started out as a bàcaro where you could stop for an ombra and a cicheto, but that is now making a name for itself among Venice's restaurants. It's a pleasant place, both in the bar area, in the dining room with its simply set tables and in the outdoor courtyard used in summer.

Front of house is Debora who presents the dishes cooked by her husband Marcellino. The menu changes every day depending on the season and what's available in the market. The focus is mainly on meat and vegetables from the area, always of excellent quality. Among the antipasti we'd recommend you taste the **porchetta trevisana** served with coarse salt and rosemary, the soppressa de casada, zucchini and **Treviso chicory in saor**, snails in guazzetto. For your first course, **tagliatelle with** mutton or **donkey meat sauce**, linguine with white meat ragù, pumpkin agnolotti with melted butter sauce, gnocchi with chicory or Gorgonzola cheese or pappardelle alla Caruso. To follow, beef braised in Cabernet, **ossobuco in tecia**, diced veal with artichokes, roast kid, **duck in peverada sauce**, steamed goose, chicken straccetti with finferli mushrooms, sliced kidney, **liver Venetian-style**. To close, a selection of cheeses or a homemade pudding.

As for the wine, trust Debora, she's young but very competent. The choice will be from around sixty good labels from the Triveneto area, with a number of them available by the glass.

This place has changed over time, from rustic old osteria in the 1930s, visited mainly by railroad workers, to what is today a very sophisticated environment offering an attentive, friendly service. Outside there was once a little boules court covered by a dense pergola; now it's used for eating in the warm months. Paolo takes care of the wine cellar and tables while Davide manages the kitchen. The menu offers dishes based on local recipes and products in season, and is almost exclusively land-based, with a wide use of meat (beef, pork, lamb and other farmyard animals). Above all in summer there's a 'change of taste' to keep the local regular customers happy, with the inclusion of recipes from other Italian regions. So what do we recommend? The regional cured meats, **calf's head with Lamon beans** and, when in season, **Treviso chicory in saor** with soppressa. And again the famous chicory is used as a condiment for **tagliatelle** (in spring with **Bassano asparagus** and guanciale, in the fall with cep and finferli mushrooms) or as an accompaniment to the pork filet in red wine sauce; other first courses include **tagliatelle** with a **stewed duck sauce**, **risi e bisi**, potato gnocchi with wild-duck sauce. Among the main courses, **roast lamb**, **rabbit stew**, duck livers cooked in port with stewed onions, **tripe in umido with polenta**, savoy cabbage sofegae with sausage. Every day there's a selection of cheeses, which are kept in a climatised glass cabinet. For pudding, strawberry bavarese, cassatina with sheep ricotta, chocolate mousse.

Given the type of cuisine the wines are mainly reds. There are about one hundred labels from various Italian regions.

VENICE
Lido-Malamocco

LE GARZETTE

🍲 Agritourism farm
Lungomare Alberoni 32
Tel. 041 731078
Fax 041 2428798
E-mail: legarzette@libero.it
Internet: www.legarzette.on.to
Closed from Christmas to mid-January

About 50 meters from the sea, in an old farmhouse restructured in the Nineties, you'll find this vacation farm managed by Renza Orazio with help from her husband, who's been living in the Veneto region for about 30 years but retains his typical Neapolitan courtesy and accent. The rooms are all bright and pleasant with a view of either the lagoon, the sea or the garden. The restaurant, which is always open for guests but only at weekends for non-residents, offers local cuisine made with seasonal ingredients produced on the farm (average price of a meal is 45 euros per person). Breakfast is traditional and prepared with homemade products: bread, butter and jams, but also eggs laid by free-range hens. Places to visit in the vicinity: the old center of Malamocco, the island of Pellestrina, Chioggia, the Oasi di Ca' Roman and the Alberoni.

• 1 double, 1 triple and 2 four-bed rooms, and 2 bungalows, with bathroom, air-conditioning, satellite TV • Prices: double room single occupancy 60-70 euros, double 80-90, triple 90-100, four-bed 120-140, bungalow 90-140, breakfast included • Credit cards: none • Communal areas accessible to the mobility challenged, 1 bungalow designed for their use. Off-street parking. Small pets allowed. Owners always present. • Restaurant. Garden, terrace. Beach.

VENICE
Mestre

MORO

🍲 Restaurant
Via Piave 192
Tel. 041 926456-926431
Closed: Sunday
Open: lunch and dinner
Holidays: second week in July
Seating: 28
Prices: 27-32 euros, wine excluded
All credit cards, Bancomat

This small, quiet, pleasant and well-furnished restaurant lies near the station in the center of Mestre. It's been in business for over fifty years, always managed by the Moro family. Originally it only operated as a bar (whose founder, Cesco, still manages it today) with the restaurant service, added later, handled by Cesco's son, Lino. He'll give you a warm welcome and is always ready with good advice. Lino's wife, Luisa, helps out with the tables at lunch while for dinner his daughter Federica takes over. Daniele has been working in the kitchen for more than twelve years and can be considered part of the family. To start, try their mixed cold cuts or other **cured meats** carefully chosen by Lino, like the Lucinico (near Gorizia) ham, lardo di Colonnata, breast of goose with butter and crostini, or the artichoke salad. The more traditional first course dishes are **bigoi with duck ragù**, **tortelli di zucca**, and legume soup, but also good are the garganelli with scampi and zucchini, fresh maccheroncini with eggplant and pecorino cheese, pasticcio of baby tomatoes with a light pesto sauce. Among the main courses we can recommend the vitello tonnato, **baccalà Vicenza-style**, **goose with cren**, **liver Venetian-style**; in addition, fresh tuna steak with herbs and boiled potatoes and steak tartar with crostini (prepared at the table). If you're still hungry you won't be disappointed by the **cheese board** with its choice of about ten cheeses. The homemade puddings are good too: when we last visited we had a very nice chocolate and torrone semifreddo topped with melted chocolate. There's a good wine list (Lino is a sommelier) with around 200 labels, mostly Italian, and reasonably priced.

OSTARIA ◉ ⊘ ▮
DA MARIANO

Traditional osteria with kitchen
Via Spalti 49-corner Via Cecchini
Tel. 041 615765
Closed: Saturday and Sunday
Open: lunch, Wednesday-Friday also for dinner
Holidays: August
Seating: 35
Prices: 20-25 euros, wine excluded
All credit cards, Bancomat

S. MARCO

Bed and breakfast
Castello 3385 l-Fondamenta San Giorgio degli Schiavoni
Tel. 041 5227589-335 7566555
Fax 041 5227589
E-mail: info@realvenice.it
Internet: www.realvenice.it/smarco
Closed in January, 2 weeks and August and 2 at Christmas

This osteria has been in existence for40 years: founder Mariano Badesso trained his son Antonio and daughter-in-law Nadia and has now handed it over to them. However, it retains its original character, starting with the customary Venetian cichetteria, and offers a quiet, discreet family atmosphere in which the owners' friendly welcome is an outstanding feature.

Antonio himself always selects the ingredients and the menu changes daily, even though certain typical dishes are always available: **baccalà** prepared in a number of ways, **cuttlefish** Venetian-style, **pilchards in saor**, **bigoli in salsa**, pasta with pilchards, **pasta e fagioli**, **liver Venetian-style**. The menu changes with the seasons: for instance, vegetables like chicory and savoy cabbage, used in numerous traditional recipes, accompany meat or fish. Running the kitchen is Martino, who has been here for three years now after attending hotel school and working in restaurants in Venice for ten years. With the help of another person he prepares the pasta, including ravioli with a vegetable and **cheese** filling, much in evidence in both the bar and the trattoria. They also use Veneto-produced Slow Food Presidia products, such as biancoperla corn and Grumolo delle Abbadesse rice. The chef prepares baked puddings with marano flour: jam, chocolate or fresh fruit pies.

There are more than 200 labels on show in the various bottlrle cabinets: advised by Antonio, you can order by the glass, but there's also a wine bottled for Mariano by a vineyard in Pramaggiore.

The sign doesn't refer to the city's patron saint but to the name of the owner, Marco Scurati, a likeable, enterprising young man who used to work in Milan's new economy until his Venetian parents decided to move to Ravello and leave this property to their son. The rooms are nice and friendly, furnished with antiques, and all have a view. The atmosphere is youthful and informal. The facility overlooks Rio de la Pieda, facing it there's the Scuola di San Giorgio degli Schiavoni, frescoed by Carpaccio, and it's only a stone's throw from the church of San Giovanni in Bragora, the church of San Zaccaria, one of the most beautiful in the city, and San Marco itself. Breakfast consists of fresh bread, croissants, coffee, tea and milk (not available to guests in the apartment) and is prepared and served in Marco's kitchen, which returns to being a private room again at 11 am. A fine library including guides and books on Venice can be used by guests lodging at this beautiful B&B.

• 3 double rooms, with shared bathroom; 1 apartment (4 persons) with kitchen, lounge • Prices: double room single occupancy 50-80 euros, double 80-110, apartment 100-160, breakfast included • Credit cards: MC, Visa • No pets allowed. Owners always reachable. • Kitchen. Library.

AL BERSAGLIERE

Trattoria
Via dietro Pallone 1
Tel. 045 8004824
Closed: Sunday
Open: lunch and dinner
Holidays: variable
Seating: 80 + 30 outdoors
Prices: 25 euros, wine excluded
All major credit cards, Bancomat

AL PARIGIN

Trattoria
Via Trezzolano 13
Tel. 045 988124
Closed: Wednesday
Open: lunch and dinner
Holidays: September
Seating: 80 + 10 outdoors
Prices: 17-20 euros, wine excluded
No credit cards

Walking the narrow streets in the old Filippini quarter, Leo Ramponi welcomes us to a place where you can still feel the atmosphere of a Verona osteria of times gone by. Don't be surprised if they serve gòti of wine at the bar counter and tables by the entrance while excitedly discussing the issue of the day, it's part of the character of this place. Frequented by locals and visiting gourmets, the three small rooms (in summer an inside courtyard is also used) are full of mainly sport-related relics, including those dedicated to Leo himself, a daredevil rally driver in his time. In any event, whether you're a sports fan or not he'll make you feel at home, describe the dishes, suggest the right wine and, why not, the right oil too, chosen from an extensive menu.

The menu combines traditional dishes and the day's proposals, but always prepared with local, seasonal products. For instance, there's **paparèle coi fegadìni** (tagliolini in broth with giblets) or **gnocchi with sugar and cinnamon**, alternatively an excellent **pasta e fagioli**, or in winter, if Marina Tezza with Giancarlo Grava in the kitchen are feeling nostalgic, **gnocchi sbatùi** as they make them in mountain farmsteads. **Pastisàda de cavàl** or **lesso co la pearà** are offered as main courses, even though the most outstanding dish is the **baccalà**, which even visitors from Vicenza recognize as being one of the best "on the road". Don't miss the number one pudding, the **diplomatico**.

Visit the wine cellar: there's a wide choice with a sharp focus on local labels, and reasonably priced too. If you have time, choose from among the 300 grappas and other liqueurs.

Much praise goes to restaurants in out-of-the-way locations with little passing trade which still managed to provide a quality service and food that does credit to the local traditions. This is the case with the trattoria run by Giorgio and his family, where you can find mushrooms and snails from the nearby hills, classic home-cured meats like salami and pancetta and pasta made daily and cooked to perfection. It's off the beaten track, with no frills, no printed menu and dining rooms that could be described as spartan, but the food makes it worth the trip.

After tasting Giorgio's excellent **cured meats**, accompanied by slices of grilled polenta, you can move on to first courses of fresh pasta, such as **tagliatelle** with tomato sauce, ragù or mushrooms, **bigoi with hare sauce** and **tagliolini in broth with chicken livers**. If they have it, try the **risotto alla salsiccia**, a classic Verona dish prepared using the very best beef broth. For your main course choose from **bogòni** (snails) **in tecia** with herbs, **jugged hare**, excellent cuts of grilled meat and, in the colder season, **bollito con salsa pearà**. When Giorgio can he'll put roe deer or wild boar on the menu, which he cooks very, very slowly to bring out all the flavor. The desserts are simple and almost always limited to either a rustic baked **apple focaccia** and semifreddo all'amaretto with chocolate sauce, both of which are exquisite.

As for wine, all that's available is a good house wine and a few bottles from small local producers.

Verona

Verona
Parona di Valpolicella

AL POMPIERE

🍲Recently opened osteria
Vicolo Regina d'Ungheria 5
Tel. 045 8030537
Closed: Sunday and Monday lunch
Open: lunch and dinner
Holidays: in January and between June and July
Seating: 50
Prices: 35 euros, wine excluded
All credit cards

Verona is famous for its Roman Arena and the house of Juliet, Shakespeare's tragic heroine, located in Via Cappello. The street is always crowded with tourists, but you can escape by taking the first, hard-to-spot side alley where you'll find this restaurant, one of the best places in the city to eat authentic Verona cuisine. Until a few years ago Il Pompiere was a typical ostarìa where people went for a gòto accompanied by bocconcini and meatballs. Then the place changed hands and was transformed into a quality restaurant, while still remaining faithful to traditional cooking, offered here in a more refined form.
Guided by Stefano Ganzerla, you'll be able to savor dishes from a menu that offers classics, like gnocchi with horse pastisàda, **pasta e fagioli**, **bigoli with sardines**, **Vicenza-style baccalà**, **bogóni** (snails) **with herbs**, capèl de prete with embogonàdi beans and **horse pastisàda**. If you like **cured meat** and **cheeses** you'll find an exceptional selection, with meats sliced right in front of you at your table. However they aren't cheap and so should be considered as an alternative to a regular meal. A sweet note is provided at the end by chocolate cake with orange sauce, **sbrisolona** and ricotta cheesecake. There's also a good wine list.

🔔 Locals come to the extremely small, always crowded Caffè Tubino, Corso Portoni Borsari 15 D, for their espresso. The hot chocolate is good too.

BORGHETTI

🍲Restaurant/3-star hotel
Via Valpolicella 47
Tel. 045 942366
Fax 045 942367
E-mail: hb@hotelborghetti.com
Internet: www.hotelborghetti.com
Closed Sunday
Open: lunch and dinner
Holidays: none
Seating: 90
Prices: 28 euros
All major credit cards, Bancomat

Though externally the Borghetti seems to have little to recommend it, the rooms are spacious and kept in the style characteristic of those hotel-osterias of yesteryear. The restaurant offers a reliable point of reference for traditional local cuisine and boasts a wine list of 700 bottles –a sizeable number of which are available by the glass. In summer, the buffet breakfast, with both sweet and savory offerings, is served in the small garden.
You can choose one of the two set menus or order à la carte, beginning with local cured meats, traditional dishes like **luccio in salsa** or **sarde in saor**. Pastas made in-house include **tortellini di carne in brodo**, tortelli made with pumpkin, ricotta and spinach or with ricotta and local truffles, **tagliatelle in brodo with chicken livers**, strangolapreti), **pasta and beans**, soups and **risottos**. For a main course, try the **sfilacci**, **pastisàda de caval** with polenta and **costata di puledro**, a dish which upholds the area's tradition of preparing horsemeat dishes. There is also the classic **liver alla veneziana**, carne salada, grilled lamb chops, filet all'Amarone. Desserts include **sbrisolona** with a special version with grappa.

🛏• 12 single and 30 double rooms with bathroom, satellite TV, modem connection • Prices: single 50-60, doubles 75-90 euros, breakfast included • Accessible to the mobility challenged. Garage (40 spaces). Small pets welcome. Reception open 24 hours • Bar, restaurant. Tasting room, wine shop. Conference room. Garden

PORTICHETTI

⬭ Trattoria
Piazzetta Portichetti 6
Tel. 045 8032364
Closed: Saturday lunch and Sunday
Open: lunch and dinner
Holidays: August
Seating: 50
Prices: 25-28 euros, wine excluded
All major credit cards, Bancomat

TRATTORIA ALL'ISOLO

⬭ Trattoria
Piazza Isolo 5 A
Tel. 045 594291
Closed: Wednesday
Open: lunch and dinner
Holidays: 2 weeks in September
Seating: 50 + 30 outdoors
Prices: 25 euros, wine excluded
All major credit cards, Bancomat

Few tourists find their way to this area of the city, and the ones that do are generally here to visit the historic basilica of San Zeno. "The quarter of the black bishop" (Verona's patron saint) and the nearby Regaste neighborhood are not so far from Castelvecchio and the city center, but still they've maintained a kind of village atmosphere. Portichetti is equally unpretentious and casual, a trattoria with an easy-to-miss entrance, the type of place where you're as likely to hear conversations in dialect as regular Italian. You'll be welcomed by Franco Coltri, but his partner, Alberto Poffili, tends to abandon the kitchen to greet regular customers.

There's a very basic menu chalked up on a blackboard, offering just a few traditional Veneto dishes. Among the antipasti you'll find polenta and cured meats, nervetti salad, **pilchards in saor**. For your first course, **bigoli with donkey ragù** or with sardelle, fettuccine with peas or asparagus or pappardelle with hare sauce. The **gnocchi with tomato** are symbolic of Verona's carnival, ruled over by the Papà del Gnòco, elected every year nearby in Piazza San Zeno. Among the main courses, the classic **pastisàda di cavallo**, Vicenza-style baccalà, **brasato all'Amarone**, **stewed bogòni** (snails). And there's always polenta: toasted at lunch time, piping hot in the evening. For dessert, fruit pies or chestnut mousse.

There's a good choice of wines at reasonable prices, with some available by the glass.

Silvana Beghini, husband Enzo and daughter Sabrina run their simple trattoria with a family style which makes it seem like it's in a little village rather than a touristy city. But the Isola neighborhood is like that, even though the center of Verona is just across the River Adige. The few tables are set with immaculate white tablecloths and frequented by locals, office workers and laborers, here for the food which reminds them of good old-fashioned home cooking. During the summer any tourists who find their way here prefer to sit outside under umbrellas. Here they can admire the recent renovation of the large piazza, laid with Verona marble, recalling its history as an island between two branches of the river.

The kitchen serves up soppressa and lardo for antipasto and then **gnocchi with pastisàda di cavallo**, pumpkin ravioli, **bigoli with sardines**, **pasta e fagioli**, fettuccine with duck sauce and tagliatelle with peas. The main courses are classics: **baccalà**, **pastisàda di cavallo**, **ossobuco with polenta**, roast leg of lamb, vitello tonnato and braised veal cheek. In winter there's **lesso co la pearà**. It's not on the menu, but if you ask Silvana will probably cook you up a plate of sausage and embogonè beans (stewed, with just a little tomato). For dessert, carrot cake, diplomatico and sabbiosa. There's a simple selection of wines with a few decent bottles.

🍲 At Giorgio Avesan's horsemeat butchers in Piazzetta Monte 4 you'll find fresh meat and ready-made traditional Verona dishes.

VILLA BARTOLOMEA
Carpi

ANTICA OSTERIA AL BERSAGLIERE

⌒Traditional osteria-trattoria
Contrà Pescheria 11
Tel. 0444 323507
Closed: Sunday
Open: lunch and dinner
Holidays: 1 week in January and 2 in August
Seating: 35
Prices: 30-35 euros, wine excluded
Credit cards: MC, Visa, Bancomat

This traditional osteria in the historic center of Vicenza is a destination for lovers of good wine and classic snacks like crostini with **baccalà mantecato**, **polenta and cotechino**, homemade soppressa and garlic-flavored salami, all served at the counter or at one of the few tables near the entrance. The dining room is on a mezzanine floor, where you can enjoy outstanding dishes from the Vicenza repertoire, prepared by talented Maria Teresa Trentin. Dishes are based on seasonal ingredients, including many local wild herbs and mushrooms.

The wide choice of antipasti includes the small plates mentioned previously, and flans and frittatas made with whatever vegetables are in season. Then fettuccine with various sauces, like porcini or spugnole mushrooms, zucchini and asparagus (the local wild asparagus is excellent) or **maltagliati with duck sauce**, tortelli with goat's milk ricotta and some good **risottos**. Among the main courses, the top dish is Marano corn polenta with flavorful farmhouse cheese (Slow Food Presidia) or **Vicenza-style baccalà**, fish or meat – we enjoyed the braised guinea fowl and lamb chops al corno – and a nice selection of local cheeses. To end the meal you could try an unusual crema flavored with lemony luisa, a chocolate flan and a few semifreddos, accompanied by dessert wine by the glass.

There's a wide choice of wines from the Triveneto and other well-known areas of Italy; many also available by the glass. If you want a full meal it's best to book in advance.

ANTICA TRATTORIA BELLINAZZO 🍷

⌒Trattoria
Via Borgo Chiesa 20
Tel. 0442 92455
Closed: Monday dinner and Tuesday
Open: lunch and dinner
Holidays: August
Seating: 90
Prices: 22-25 euros, wine excluded
All credit cards, Bancomat

This trattoria has been run by the same family since 1855, and currently in charge is young Daniele, ably assisted by his parents and wife. He's been responsible for some updates, a new focus on tradition and the surrounding land, with a constant search for the best ingredients. The setting is basic and very clean, with large, well-spaced tables, with a friendly atmosphere.

You can start with a tasting of two **hams**, dolce di Montagnana and Sauris, a combination of maranin with lardo, pecorino di fossa and cimbro di fossa cheeses and smoked fillet of duck breast, or the classic **soppressa con polentina** and mushrooms. Moving on to the first courses, a real must is the **pasta e fasoi** and also the delicious tagliatelle with blanched Carpi asparagus and Monte Veronese mezzano; among the fresh pastas there's also **bigoli al somarino** and wholemeal pasta with radicchio, speck and Monte Ubriaco, the Verona-style **risotto**, not always available, is highly recommended. In the colder season there's a good **bollito misto with pearà**, **taiadeline with chicken livers** and **fettuccine with hare** or duck sauce. Among the main courses, **pastizzà de musso** (donkey) with polenta, **baccalà**, and **tripe**, also with polenta. Alternatively try grilled lamb chops, foal tagliata or veal chops. Daniele selects **cheeses** and sends them to trusted affinatori to be aged, and it's possible to put togther some interesting regional tasting plates. Stars among the desserts are the apple tart and the homemade biscuits.

The wine list includes over 300 labels, with a marked focus on regional and local wines, but also an excellent selection from other regions, all reasonably priced.

VILLADOSE
Canale

VITTORIO VENETO
Serravalle

8 KM EAST OF ROVIGO ON SS 443

40 KM NORTHWEST OF TREVISO TAKING SS 13 AND 51 OR A 27

DA NADAE

HOSTARIA VIA CAPRERA

◯ Trattoria
Via Garibaldi 371
Tel. 0425 476082
Closed: Tuesday
Open: lunch and dinner
Holidays: mid-August to the beginning of September
Seating: 80
Prices: 25-27 euros
All credit cards, Bancomat

◯ Traditional osteria-trattoria
Via Caprera 23
Tel. 0438 57520
Closed: Thursday
Open: lunch and dinner
Holidays: June 30- July 30
Seating: 40
Prices: 21-26 euros, wine excluded
All credit cards, Bancomat

A few kilometers out of Rovigo on the main road to the sea, you'll see a sign for Canale di Villadose, a small hamlet whose one claim to fame is this trattoria. Formerly their father's, for many years now it has been run by Mariuccia and Gabriella, with the help of their husbands and children.

Their menu is simple but the dishes are good, with the same dishes available year-round, dependent on the daily catch. For antipasti there are always mussels and clams, **mixed boiled fish**, scallops and **schie** (gray shrimp) **with freshly made polenta**. Alternatively there are some excellent **cured meats**. Among the first courses you'll find a seafood **risotto**, spaghetti with clams or allo scoglio and **bigoli** with various sauces. Among the main courses there will be **eel**, **fried catfish**, **roasted baccalà in bianco** and mixed grills; for those who are not fish lovers there's grilled meat or **stinco al forno**. The most common dessert is zuppa inglese. Dishes are usually accompanied by house wines (a red and an excellent prosecco), but for more demanding palates there are also some good bottles.

This restaurant has been around for almost a century; spread out over two floors, it will soon be extended to give it access to a garden. Gianpaolo runs the ground floor, where you can stop in for a quick ombra and the usual range of cicheti, while upstairs you'll get a warm welcome from Roberto, who deals with the restaurant. The seasonally changing menu is subdivided by week and features traditional dishes prepared by Daniela.

You'll find some dishes which are not so common these days, like **sopa coada**, and seasonal specialties, listed in Veneto dialect. In spring, for instance, you can try ravìoi co'e ortiche (ravioli with nettles) and **macheroni col tocio de anara** (duck) while in winter you'll always find **pasta e fagioli**, onion soup, **baccalà**, nervetti and **s'cios** (snails). The main courses use farmyard animals and in the season, game: so there's **guinea fowl rodolada co'a peveràda** or col tocio, **cunicio in tecia**, gévero a la cacciatora or **cavrèt in tecia**. All the desserts are homemade: fruit pies, chocolate salami, pumpkin cake, poppyseed cake with cream.

The wine selection includes about 150 labels, mainly from the Triveneto. There are also around 100 liqueurs, half of them whiskeys.

🍴 In **Villadose**, in his bakery in Via Umberto 30, Sergio Schiesari bakes typical pagnotta del doge cakes. In **Pezzoli** (9 km from Canale), the Associazione Culturale Cerere, Via dei Cappuccini 1, produces fruit, vegetables, cereals and honey without using pesticides, and sells them from the farm and at the Rovigo market.

🍴 Distilleria De Negri, Via Oberdan 101, is worth a visit for its liqueurs made according to traditional methods (flavors include plum and mugo pine).

Volpago del Montello

22 km northwest of Treviso

Bosco del Falco

Agritourism Farm
X Presa-Via Battisti 25
Tel. 0423 619797
Open Thursday and Friday dinner, Saturday and Sunday, if you book
Holidays: 2 weeks in January, 1 in June and 1 in September
Seating: 80
Prices: 35 euros
No credit cards, Bancomat

We strongly recommend reservations, and also calling ahead for directions through the complex streets of Montello. The farm covers four hectares, and the main building is beautifully furnished, from the elegant sideboards and carpets to the spotlights in the chestnut room.
Husband and wife Paolo Comunello and Elena Bordin are the owners. Elena, having studied at hotel school before working in several restaurants and managing a bar, was the driving force behind the project, and she oversees the food chain, running the kitchen with help from young Matteo and assisting her husband, brother and another helper in the dining room. Paolo has a day job as owner of a sporting goods shop, but in the evening he shifts naturally into the role of host.
Chickens, cockerels, guinea fowl, rabbits, ducks, geese and pigs are raised on the farm, and they also have asparagus fields, 220 olive trees, an orchard, a small area dedicated to growing berries and a prosecco vineyard. The unwritten menu includes basic dishes that highlight the quality of ingredients produced on the farm.
You'll find **soppressa with polenta** (with mushrooms when in season); **risotto** with herbs or asparagus, zucchini or Treviso radicchio; and homemade **tagliatelle with rabbit** or duck **ragù**, ricotta or, in winter, pumpkin gnocchi. The farm's animals feature in main course dishes: the winter dishes like **goose with juniper** and **duck in tecia** are particularly recommended. Finish your meal with a slice of berry pie.
The local wines are acceptable, but Elena has promised to dedicate greater attention to the list in the future.

Zoldo Alto
Pecol

46 km north-west of Belluno on ss 251

La baita

3 Star Hotel
Via del Gonfet 4-5
Tel. 0437 789163
Fax 0437 789163
Closed from mid-April to 1 July and from mid-September to end of November

Rustically furnished, this facility is located near the ski-lifts. Since 2002 it's been managed by the Molin Pradel family, who have modernized the hotel, carefully renovating the breakfast room, bar and relaxation areas. Adelino and his son Emiliano look after guests in a courteous, professional manner, while his wife Rita prepares excellent tarts, homemade jams and traditional focaccia, which along with fresh fruit, yoghurt, mountain butter, cured meats and cheeses are a splendid way to start your day. The rooms are simple and pleasant; for those that can become triples and four-bedders there's a 30% reduction for the third bed and a 50% reduction for the fourth. During the summer season the hotel is an excellent starting point for excursions high up in the mountains: the climb up to the foot of Monte Pelmetto to see the footprints of dinosaurs is a unique experience.

• 5 single and 7 double rooms, with bathroom, 8 with balcony • Prices: single 32-50 euros, double 56-94, breakfast included • Credit cards: all except AE, Bancomat • Communal areas accessible to the mobility challenged. External parking reserved for guests. No pets allowed. Owners always reachable. • Bar. breakfast room. Veranda, solarium. Fitness center with sauna and Turkish bath.

Andreis

35 km north of Pordenone

Al Vecie For

Trattoria with rooms
Via Centrale 63
Tel. 0427 764437
Fax 0427 764707
E-mail: lavila00@locandaalvecjefor.191.it
Closed Monday evening and Tuesday, never in August
Open: lunch and dinner
Holidays: 3 weeks in February, 1 in October
Seating: 45
Prices: 28-30 euros
All major credit cards, Bancomat

This place is among the most peaceful of the Valcellina near the Prealpi Carniche Park. Its few rooms are decorated in a tidily romantic alpine style. Available all week long, are located in an old renovated bakery outfitted with locally made furnishings. For breakfast, you can choose from excellent sweets and savories.
The menu here changes every fortnight according to the season. Start your meal off with a **cabbage and Sauris culatello strudel**, leek and potato dumplings, a crunchy crostino with burrata and Grions asparagus spread, **rabbit and zucchini salad with raspberry vinegar** and ricotta and dill gnocco with cep mushroom sauce. Herbs and vegetables also feature prominently in **lasagne with Treviso chicory**, wild rice and pea velouté with mint, **vegetable soup**, **orzotto** with quail and finferli mushrooms. For your main course, try **beef braised in Cabernet** with onion jam, **stewed wild boar**, **veal cheeks braised in white wine**, **suckling pig shank with red cabbage**, smoked pork chops and **lamb loin with herbs**. Not-to-be-missed: the seasonal fruit **crostatas**, chocolate and cinnamon pastry and **apple strudel**.
House wines are available, or you can choose from among the serviceable regional selections.

• 1 single, 3 double and 1 triple room with bath, TV • Prices: single 30, double 60, triple 90 euros, breakfast included • Restaurant accessible to the mobility challenged. Public parking in the immediate vicinity. No pets allowed. Owners always reachable. • Bar, restaurant

Aquileia
Beligna

38 km southeast of Udine on SS 352

Ca' Ospitale

Holiday farm
Via Beligna 107
Tel. 0431 917423
Fax 0431 917168
E-mail: caospitale@agritur.it
Internet: www.caospitale.com
Open from April to October

This typical Veneto-style farmhouse dating from the beginning of the 1900s is located on the Julia Augusta consular road. In addition to a portico, the building has a large green area, with swimming pool, tennis court and a 5-a-side soccer field. There are also 15 spaces for mobile homes with all necessary toilet. Rooms are fitted with rustic-style period furniture. The continental buffet breakfast offers coffee, milk, tea, cakes from the pastry shop, cheeses, cured meats, and homemade jams. Bicycles are available for guests to to explore the countryside around the lagoon. In addition, you can easily reach the nearby archeological site of Aquileia and the beaches at Grado.

• 3 single and 11 double rooms, with bathroom • Prices: single 35-37 euros, double 67-72 (20-25 euro supplement for extra bed), breakfast included • Credit cards: all except AE, Bancomat • 1 room designed for use by the mobility challenged. Off-street parking. Small pets allowed. Owners always reachable • Breakfast room and lounge. Garden. Pool, tennis court and 5-a-side soccer field

ARBA
Colle

ARTA TERME
Piano d'Arta

GRAPPOLO D'ORO

SALON

Osteria-trattoria with lodgings
Piazza IV Novembre 14
Tel. 0427 93019
Fax 0427 789977
Closed Monday and Saturday at lunch
Open lunch and dinner
Holidays: last weeks of January and June
Seating: 50 + 20 outdoors
Prices: 25-28 euros
All major credit cards, Bancomat

3-Star Hotel
Via Peresson 70
Tel. 0433 92003
Fax 0433 929364
E-mail: albergosalon@tiscali.it
Internet: www.albergosalon.it
Closed from 15 January to 15 February

Not far from the Meduna stream, you'll find this historic osteria with six rooms that are available all week long for overnight stays, with a 15-euro supplement for half-board. In the breakfast room, there's splendid antique flooring, the work of local artisans.

The manager, Guglielmo Di Pol, serves the dishes of chef Virgilio. Antipasti include prosciutto di San Daniele and artichoke hearts, **trout filet smoked** or with the delightful **dolcecuore** and larded pork fillet stuffed with meat and spices. There are numerous soups; try the asparagus velouté, cream of leek and zucchini and **barley and chestnut**. Otherwise, there's **fettuccine with venison sauce**, asparagus risotto, herb tortelli with walnuts and smoked ricotta and **horsemeat pitina**. Follow this with **frico with potatoes**, **veal guanciale with Pinot Nero**, lamb cutlets and other grilled meats and steak flavored with rosemary. You can also order grilled bison filet. Of the desserts, the rice and plum cake is particularly good.

Very good regional wines and a few Tuscan labels are available here. Conclude your meal with one of the fine Friuli liqueurs. The locanda closes for a fortnight between January and February and another fortnight between July and August.

• 6 double rooms with bath • Prices: double room single use 40, double 70 euros (additional bed 35 euros), breakfast included • 1 room accessible to the mobility challenged (36 euros). Uncovered parking inside premises. No pets allowed. Owners always reachable • Bar, restaurant. Garden

For nearly 60 years Bepi Salon has managed this hotel-restaurant in the center of Piano d'Arta, a vacation center in the But Valley, on the road to the pass of Mount Croce Carnico and close by a very well-known spa. The Salon is above all famous for signora Fides's ability in the kitchen (her cooking has local roots and she makes a wide use of herbs and mushrooms; meals 25-30 euros, excluding wine), but it's also pleasant to spend the night in one of the rooms. The bar, arranged around a large fogolâr, faces onto a courtyard with garden; in winter guests gather around the fireplace in the lounge, while in the summer you can soak up the sun on one of the large terraces. The abundant buffet breakfast, with sweet and savory fare, will help you get off to a good start for morning walks in the Coglians Park or treatment sessions at the nearby Arta Terme spa.

• 7 single and 17 double rooms, with bathroom, TV • Prices: single 35-42 euros, double 54-68, breakfast included • Credit cards: major ones, Bancomat • Parking behind the hotel (10 spaces). Small pets allowed. Owners always reachable • Bar. Restaurant (in winter only open at weekends and if you book). Lounge, TV room. Outside space, garden. Terraces, solarium

ARZENE

ROVERE DALLA RIVA

🔑Bed and breakfast
Via Alpi 30
Tel. e fax 0434 899401
Closed from 15 January to 15 February

This B&B is part of a typical Friuli-style farmhouse, refurbished in 2003 and surrounded by a beautiful garden with a wide variety of flowers and plants, some of which quite unusual. Ivano Rovere, a hotel manager for 20 years, has a passion for gardening and green fingers to go with it. The rooms are comfortable and simply furnished with the addition of a few antiques. Breakfast is generous and varied and includes bread, butter and jam, croissants, orange juice, tea, milk, coffee and, on request, fruit, cheese and cured meats. Ivano is always happy to take his guests for a little tour of the garden, illustrating the main attractions. In addition to that he'll provide you with bicycles for interesting excursions in the surrounding area. Among places worth visiting, the medieval castle in Valvasone and in Casarsa Della Delizia, places dear to Pasolini.

• 1 single, 1 double and 1 triple room, with bathroom, TV • Prices: single 30 euros, double 40, triple 50, breakfast included • Credit cards: none • Off-street parking. Small pets allowed. Owners always reachable. • Breakfast room, TV room. Garden, grounds

BAGNARIA ARSA
Sevegliano

MULINO DELLE TOLLE

🍵Holiday farm
Via Julia 1-Statale Palmanova-Grado
Tel. 0432 924723
E-mail: mulinodelletolle@tin.it
Internet: www.mulinodelletolle.it
Open Thursday through Sunday, February 4 to April 30 and October 11 to December 23; Wednesday through Sunday, May 1 to August 31; lunch and dinner
Seating: 80
Prices: 20 euros, excluded wine
Credit cards: Visa, Bancomat

The Mulino delle Tolle is an agriturismo where they raise animals and butcher the meat, grow vegetables and grapes. The rooms are modern but offer all the pleasures of an old locanda. All meals include traditional cuisine.
You begin with cured meats and **ossocollo**. The menu always comprise soups, such as **barley and beans**, asparagus and leek velouté or **cream of potato**, **gnocchi** and savory pie with meat or vegetable ragù. Main courses include the very Friulian **frico with potatoes**. We especially recommend **stewed goose, rabbit roulade with herbs** or another version of pheasant and green apple, **stewed chicken with plums** and pork loin with rocket and braised meats. The **polenta** and the puddings are all made in-house – our favorite is the pear cake. Wines are limited to the best local labels. Try the Sabellius (a blend of refosco, merlot and cabernet).
The farm is particularly 'child-friendly', providing toys and a sizeable games yard.

• 1 single, 5 double, 2 triple and 2 quadruple rooms with bath, air-conditioning, mini-fridge, TV, modem outlet; 1 apartment (3 persons) with kitchen • Prices: single 50, double 72, tripe 88, quadruple 105, apartment 88 euros, breakfast included • External facilities and 1 room accessible to the mobility challenged; apartment furnished. Uncovered internal parking. Small pets welcome only in the apartment. Owners always reachable • Corner bar, restaurant. Breakfast room. Garden, park for children. 5-a-side soccer pitch

BORDANO
Interneppo

BUDOIA

ALLA TERRAZZA

CIASA DE GAHJA

Hotel trattoria
Via Principale 89
Tel. 0432 979139
Closed Saturday
Open: lunch and dinner
Holidays: 15 days in February, 15 days end-September
Seating: 40 + 30 outdoors
Prices: 20 euros, wine excluded
All credit cards

4-Star Hotel
Via Anzolet 13
Tel. 0434 654897
Fax 0434 654815
E-mail: info@ciasadegahja.com
Internet: www.ciasadegahja.com
Open all year round

Driving up from the Tre Comuni lake, you come to the hamlet of Bordano – 'village of butterflies' – and your eye immediately catches this welcoming restaurant, part of a small hotel (14 bedrooms). It's family-run (by Cesare, his wife Adriana and daughter Laura), with simple food based on local produce and homegrown vegetables from the family's kitchen garden. Booking is advisable to enable them to prepare the freshest possible food for you – visitors here aren't very frequent!

Sitting in the dining room or, when the weather's fine, on the terrace, after the typical regional San Daniele or Sauris cured meats, you can choose from a menu that varies with the season. So as a first course, there are the soups, or **barley and bean** in winter, pasta with broccoli, **risotto with sclopit** or tagliolini with asparagus in spring, vegetable soups and mezzemaniche in spicy sauce, or with artichokes or zucchini, in summer. As a main course, mixed roast meats, **salsiccia ubriaca**, or 'drunk sausage' (ie, in wine), rolled chicken breast, **grilled rabbit** and **lamb**, and in the fall and winter, **oven-baked shank of pork** or casserole of cockerel meat. For non-meat-eaters, there are **smoked trout, fried Montasio cheese**, vegetable pastries or **herb frittatas** to choose from. The salted meat served cold with **smoked ricotta** is also well worth a try. To finish, you might choose a slice of homemade tart, lemon cake, wild berries or cherries in liqueur.

The choice of wines goes beyond the regional borders, and Cesare will be able to advise you on the best wine-food combinations.

Gahja is a term that has Lombard origins and means 'the lord of the manor's possessions': the area in which this enchanting hotel is situated must have been a gahagium in the early Middle Ages, that is, a tract of land (forest or pasture) classified as off-limits for normal use. In addition to the grounds, reminders of times when the building was a hunting lodge can be seen in features such as the stone well under the wisteria arbor, the fireplace in the communal room, the wood beams in the bedrooms and other architectural details preserved during the intelligent renovation process. The buffet-style breakfast is very filling, whereas the restaurant offers revisited traditional dishes (a meal costs 30-45 euros per person, wine excluded). You'll be able to visit various places in the environs: the Cansiglio plateau, San Floriano Park (environmental education center), the springs of Livenza and mountain cottages and pastures.

• 8 single, 8 double rooms and 1 suite, with bathroom (some with jacuzzi), air-conditioning, satellite TV, modem connection • Prices: single 65-80 euros, double 85-120, suite 150-200, breakfast included • Credit cards: major ones, Bancomat • 1 room designed for use by the mobility challenged. Off-street parking. Small pets allowed (organized enclosure available for larger pets). Reception open 24 hours a day • Restaurant. Lounge. Conference room. Outside space, garden, grounds with children's playground. Pool

BUTTRIO

13 KM SOUTHEAST OF UDINE ON SS 56 AND SP 14

SCACCIAPENSIERI

☛❶Holiday farm
Via Morpurgo 29
Tel. 0432 674907
Fax 0432 683924
E-mail: brutmus@tin.it
Closed in January, open weekends only in February

CAPRIVA DEL FRIULI
Spessa

8 KM WEST OF GORIZIA, 26 KM SOUTHEAST OF UDINE ON SS 56

TAVERNETTA AL CASTELLO

☛❶3-Star Hotel
Via Spessa 7
Tel. 0481 808228
Fax 0481 880218
E-mail: tavernetta@tin.it
Internet: www.tavernettaalcastello.it
Closed for 2 weeks between January and February

Scacciapensieri (meaning to 'drive away cares') is an entirely appropriate name for Marina Danieli's agriturismo. You can hardly remain indifferent to the view of the surrounding hills (beautiful both by day and at night) that can be enjoyed from the balconies of the rooms or from the common terrace. The rooms are fitted with antique furniture and have a rustic though elegant feel to them, inducing you to relax into a slower pace of living. Both the rooms and restaurant are part of the farm (a meal costs 22 euros, excluding wine), and farm produce is used for approximately 65% of menu (in the form of meat, eggs and vegetables). In addition, only farm-produced wine is served. For breakfast you'll be offered homemade cakes, among which tarts and apple or ricotta pies.

• 1 single and 5 double rooms, with bathroom, balcony • Prices: single 65 euros, double 100, breakfast included • Credit cards: all except DC, Bancomat • 1 room designed for use by the mobility challenged. Off-street parking. Small pets allowed. Owners always present • Restaurant. Terrace

The Castello di Spessa estate (30 hectares of vineyards on the hills surrounding the mansion house that over the centuries has belonged to several noble families) has restructured and extended a building that in the past was an old osteria, transforming it into an elegant vacation farm. The rooms all have a mansard roof and are tastefully furnished to provide a warm atmosphere. From the various balconies and small terraces, you'll enjoy the total serenity of the panorama. You'll receive a very friendly welcome from Lucia, Maurizio and Tonino, and will be able to taste and purchase the estate's wines. Wines mature in 14th-century wine cellars or in a bunker built during the previous century for military purposes. You can also play golf on the new course that surrounds the facility. The buffet-style breakfast, with sweet and savory fare, includes home-made bread and cakes. The restaurant (also open to non-residents) serves local cuisine at an average price of 40 euros per person, excluding wine.

• 8 double and 2 triple rooms, with bathroom (some with jacuzzi bath or shower), air-conditioning, terrace or balcony, mini-bar, satellite TV • Prices: double room single use 77 euros, double 118, triple 153, breakfast included • Credit cards: all except AE, Bancomat • Facility accessible to the mobility challenged, 2 rooms designed for their use. Off-street parking. Small pets allowed. Management always reachable • Restaurant. Garden, golf course

Castelnovo del Friuli
Oltrerugo

46 KM NORTHEAST OF PORDENONE

Dal Cjco ⊘

🍲 Osteria with dining room
Via Oltrerugo 119
Tel. 0427 90032
Closed Tuesday and Wednesday
Open: lunch and dinner
Holidays: from January 7 to 17, last ten days of June
Seating: 50 + 30 outdoors
Prices: 28 euros, wine excluded
All credit cards, Bancomat

This osteria, located in the delightful Castelnovo hills, has come a long way in recent years. Since 1996, when twins Liana and Massimo Corsi started up in the restaurant business – Liana in the kitchen and Massimo as front of the house – they have expanded the selection of food on offer, refining it with an intelligent mix of quality, tradition and innovation. Liana, in fact, who is both highly skilled and modest about her cooking, acquired her skills under the tutelage of Gianni Cosetti, the great master chef, who in the latter years of his life was happy to spend his evenings in the kitchen of this restaurant.

From him, Liana learned, among other things, the clever use of herbs. The **lasagna with sclopìt** we sampled recently was excellent both for flavor and lightness – an example of the sophisticated results that simple herbs can impart. Herbs are also used in the antipasti – most notably, the mixed salad with mountain cheeses, **speck with ridric di mont**, and the **frite di prat**. The risotto with morchele and quail legs, the **bleons** with herb or turnip fillings and the vegetable fagottini are excellent. There are some delicious main courses, for instance, **pig's liver cooked in Verduzzo** or Ucelut (an indigenous sweet white wine of the area) **with fried onion**, while the **rabbit rotolo** and, in season, the **game**, are worth sampling as well. There is a good selection of local **cheeses**, such as formadi frant, asìno and the classic montasio. Desserts include cornmeal biscuits with zabaglione and acacia flower mousse.

The wine list contains about 30 labels, some of them interesting and unusual.

Cavasso Nuovo

32 KM NORTH OF PORDENONE SS 552

Ai Cacciatori

🍲 Trattoria
Via Diaz 4
Tel. 0427 777800
Closed Monday evening and Tuesday
Open: lunch and dinner
Holidays: second week in January, September 15-30
Seating: 35
Prices: 30-35 euros, wine excluded
All credit cards

Just ask for Danêl, and you'll have no trouble finding this restaurant, which the personable owner Daniele Corte manages along with his wife Angelina, a formidable cook. They have brought some recipes from the lower Friuli area here, such as the delightful eel with green plums, available only between mid-July and mid-August. In the local area, Danêl has unearthed a rare red onion that is sweet enough to eat raw and several heirloom apples that serve as an ideal accompaniment for some of his dishes. The kitchen garden is tended by his octogenarian mother-in-law and much of it ends up in the dishes served in the restaurant. The meats, too, often come from a butcher shop that Danêl co-owns. In winter, the restaurant is famous for its wide choice of **game**. In summer, recommended dishes include the homemade, slightly smoked **goose ham**, pasta or rice with porcini mushrooms, **tortellacci with mountain herbs**, or the simple tomato and basil tagliolini with sheep ricotta. Slow Food Presidium **pitina** is available all year, or rather, this restaurant's own variation: **pitin'oca**, made with goose. Main courses include **chestnut flour maltagliati with hare,** orzotto with sclopìt, and **buckwheat blecs** (maltagliati) **with lamb ragù**. Then there are small lamb ribs cooked on a griddle, **roasted kid, veal kidneys with tarragon and parsley,** and mixed boiled meats in winter, herring during Lent, and baccalà at Easter. The cooking here truly reflects the seasons, and the extensive wine selection is further proof of the restaurant's close ties to the surrounding area.

CAVAZZO CARNICO
Borgo Poscolle

CERCIVENTO

BORGO POSCOLLE

IN PLÀIT

🍲 Trattoria
Via Poscolle 21 A
Tel. 0433 935085
Closed Tuesday and Wednesday lunch
Open: lunch and dinner
Holidays: three weeks, varies
Seating: 40 + 30 outdoors
Prices: 27 euros, wine excluded
No credit cards accepted

🍲 Restaurant
Via Di Sot 51
Tel. 0433 778412
Closed Monday and Tuesday
Open: evenings, lunchtime booking necessary
Holidays: varies
Seating: 20
Prices: 25-28 euros, wine excluded
No credit cards accepted

Borgo Poscolle stands at the far edge of Cavazzo Carnico and is also the location of the main church and a couple of beautiful, traditionally styled buildings. This may very well be the most pleasant area in the whole village. Lucio Pillinini and his wife bring to the restaurant memories of their childhood. The interior is tastefully appointed with articles from their own homes, creating the atmosphere of a peaceful country dwelling.

The menu is traditional. We recommend a choice of typical antipasti from the area, with cheeses and **cured meats** from small Carnia producers. The first courses are available seasonally and offer more choices: **barley and bean** soup, Carnia **jota (with beans and brovada**), potato and leek velouté, various kinds of **gnocchi**, **ravioli with beets** or with formadi frant, **cjalsòns** with wild herbs (all the pastas are homemade). Of the main courses, most of the meat is not locally sourced (as not much animal husbandry is practiced in this mountain area) except for the **game** and the free-range poultry and rabbits, chosen by Luca Paschini, a promising youngster who looks after the kitchen. **Oven-roasted veal shank** or lamb saddle, **pork fillet** with herbs or with crispy **speck**, and roasted duck breast with glazed onions are just some of the dishes on offer; in spring, there is also roasted kid. **Salmon trout** from Sutrio is often on the menu. You'll find it difficult to choose between the desserts: dark chocolate pie, apple gnocchetti with Verduzzo sauce and a tart made from mirabelle plums.

There's a good selection of wines in the cellar, both from Friuli and from the rest of Italy.

This cozy eatery with its book-lined walls lets you sample food and drink while you leaf through books about the history and culture of Carnia and the Friuli region. William, the village baker, must have remembered that man does not live by bread alone when, along with Stefania, he decided to combine his enthusiasm for culture with the pleasures of eating and open this very unusual restaurant, which also holds musical events, lectures and meetings. In plait is a Carnia term – now little used – that describes a place in which the village community meets for discussions and decision-making.

Alongside traditional local dishes, there are some with roots in Tuscany-Romagna, Stefania's original homeland. For antipasti, try the excellent **cured meats** and cheeses from local producers. Among the homemade pastas, you can choose from **ravioli filled with radic di mont**, meat, potatoes or herbs, **ricotta gnocchi** with vegetables, tagliatelle, tagliolini or lasagna. Main courses range from pork filet, veal meatballs, **tripe**, snails and **smoked trout**. For dessert: crema pasticceria, fruit tart or ricotta cake.

You'll find the wine if you look on the shelves between the bookcases.

🍴 At **Ovaro** (15 km), the Fior bakery produces fragrant bread made from rye, maize and wheat; in the Clavais district, Luisa Puschiasis makes outstanding preserves. We particularly like the blackcurrant jam.

CIVIDALE DEL FRIULI

IL RONCAL

🔑 Holiday farm
Via Fornalis 148
Tel. 0432 730138
Fax 0432 701984
E-mail: info@ilroncal.it
Internet: www.ilroncal.it
Open all year

This agricultural estate, created in 1986 by Roberto Zorzettig, today covers approximately 20 hectares. The name 'roncal' in Friuli dialect means 'a terraced hill farm', and in fact what makes this landscape so attractive are the rows of terraced vineyards that surround the hill of Montebello. Recently Martina, Roberto's wife, opened an agriturismo in a typical farmhouse with a tower. The rooms are rustic and the furniture is arte povera in style, brightened up by colored curtains. In one of the common rooms you'll be able to admire a typical Friuli fogolâr, or fireplace. Breakfast is generous and prepared with great attention to detail: it includes various types of locally cured meats and cheeses, local jams and honey, yogurt, cereals, fruit juices, tea, milk, coffee, bacon and eggs.

• 5 double and 3 triple rooms, with bathroom (1 double and 1 triple share a bathroom), air-conditioning, mini-bar, satellite TV, modem connection; 2 rooms with terrace • Prices: double room single use 50 euros, double 90, triple 120, five-bed 160, breakfast included • Credit cards: major ones, Bancomat • Facility accessible for the mobility challenged, 1 room designed for their use. Off-street parking. Small pets allowed (not in rooms). Owners always reachable • Breakfast room, lounge, TV room. Garden, grounds with children's playground, terrace

CIVIDALE DEL FRIULI

AI TRE RE

🍲 Traditional osteria
Via Stretta San Valentino 29
Tel. 0432 700416
Closed Tuesday
Open: lunch and dinner
Holidays: 1 week in February, 2 in June, 1 in October
Seating: 60 + 40 outdoors
Prices: 20-25 euros, wine excluded
Credit cards: MC, Visa, Bancomat

This lovely osteria in the center of Cividale, a charming historic city and the starting point for pleasant excursions into the Natisone valleys, is managed by the Morandini family. Elsa and Loretta see to the cooking, under the direction of Anna, mother of the exuberant Paolo who supervises the dining room.
The skillfully prepared dishes are mostly traditional, with some interesting forays into local products and recipes that have been reinvented and simplified. Antipasti may include a typical cheese (Asìno or Frant), herb-flecked lardo with pears or **soppressa**. First courses include superb **pasta e fagioli**, **potato gnocchi** ai Tre Re **with speck and smoked ricotta** and rice seasoned with chopped herbs. As a main course, you can choose from **sausage in white wine**, roast veal, pork filet in a cocoa bean crust, **frico with polenta** and **cheese filled with litùmp**, a mixture of natural herbs picked before sunrise. On Fridays, they cook fish: squid, or taccola with sea bass and cherry tomatoes. Desserts include white chocolate semifreddo with candied walnuts, crêpes with cream and fruit or preserves, and traditional homemade **gubana**. The service is gracious, but the wait can be rather long because dishes are mostly prepared once they have been ordered. The serviceable wine list offers wines from outside Friuli as well.

🏺 Excellent gourmet specialties, both local and from farther afield, can be found at the historic Scubla Alimentari, Corso Mazzini 33, and at the Bottega del Gusto, Via Paolino d'Aquileia 14.

AL MONASTERO

Restaurant with rooms
Via Ristori 9
Tel. 0432 700808
Closed for Sunday dinner and Monday
Open: lunch and dinner
Always open in season
Seating: 150 + 30 outdoors
Prices: 25-28 euros, wine excluded
All credit cards

AI MULINARS

Restaurant
Via della Val Cosa 83
Tel. 0427 80684
Closed Monday
Open: lunch and dinner
Holidays: 10 days in February
Seating: 45 + 45 outdoors
Prices: 32-35 euros, wine excluded
All credit cards except AE

The restaurant is in the center of Cividale, a town rich in history that has undergone periods of great cultural development, still visible today in its architectural heritage. Al Monastero was opened by Bepi Pavan in 1990, and true to its name, once housed a monastery in the eighteenth century before becoming an osteria frequented by hunters and travelers, as we can see in the paintings by Jakob Malar (Jacum Pitor) in the dining rooms.

Cristina, who was born into the business, carries on the family tradition. The dishes she prepares are typical of the area and are enhanced with lots of natural herbs from the surrounding countryside. Particularly good: **raw ham** served **with mountain radicchio**, **agnolotti filled with buonenrico** (a sort of wild spinach) and diced turkey with sweet-tasting herbs. In the fall, there are **mushrooms** – porcini, ovoli, galletti – to be eaten as a salad, grilled on a hotplate or as seasoning for tagliolini. **Game** is available in season in dishes like orecchiette with red deer venison and eggplant sauce or roe deer venison with mushrooms and chestnuts or can be tasted all year round with such offerings as cured venison and wild boar ham, the first combined with a cheese compote and the second with pumpkin and pomegranate. Also try the **montasio strudel**, **cjarsòns**, duck maltagliati and **chestnut gnocchetti with montasio**. Second courses include the Monastero tournedos (beef filet with Sauris ham, smoked ricotta and red wine sauce). Among the desserts, there are tarts made with unusual preserves, such as cane apple jam.

The wine list includes wines from both Friuli and the rest of Italy; the house wine is very good.

The restaurant is located below the Cosa river waterfall, just as you come into Clauzetto. The large area in front of the building has a gazebo and wood flooring where visitors can sit in the warmer season. Inside, the décor is fairly typical, with stone walls, exposed beams on the ceilings and floors in a mosaic of marble chippings (the laying of which was the traditional occupation of local skilled workers). The restaurant managers have an interesting history: Ottavio, who was born in a neighboring valley, came back to the region after many years away in Berlin, while his wife Angela is German and has brought a breath of northern Europe to the cuisine. Their three children bring courtesy and professionalism to their roles front of house.

You can start with the Ai Mulinars antipasto, comprising San Daniele ham aged for 24 months, goose breast with crostini, Angus beef fillet and seasonal produce. Alternatively, there's meat salad or grilled vegetables. First courses include **eggplant rolls with guanciale and Montasio**, ricotta and spinach crêpes and home-made pasta dishes: ricciottelle with fresh cep mushrooms, **cjalzòns with speck and malga cheese** and rigatoni with walnut sauce. To follow, **frico with potatoes, grilled lamb ribs**, and loin of venison with wild blackcurrants, as well as other types of **game**. The cheese board selection is very good. The desserts are homemade: in winter, almond tarts or **strudel** and, in summer, fruit pies and cream of yogurt.

The wine list includes many labels from Friuli, especially reds, and some sound bottles from the other Italian wine-producing regions. The grappas, made with herbs or wild berries, are excellent.

COMEGLIANS
Maranzanis-Povolaro

CORMONS

BORGO MARANZANIS

☛❶Diffuse hotel
Frazione Povolaro 36
Tel. 0433 619002
Fax 0433 619621
E-mail: albergodiffuso@libero.it
Internet: www.albergodiffuso.it
Open all year

ANTICA OSTERIA ALL'UNIONE

🍲Trattoria
Via Zorutti 14
Tel. 0481 60922
Closed Monday
Open: lunch and dinner
Holidays: one week in August
Seating: 45
Prices: 28-32 euros, wine excluded
All credit cards except AE, Bancomat

The idea of Friuli poet Leonardo Zanier, chaired by Piero Pascolo and financed by European funds, the Comeglians co-operative aims to relaunch the charming hamlet of Maranzanis using the innovative formula of a 'diffuse hotel' – effectively a holiday village. The place is charming, and the renovation of the old houses have been carried out tastefully with great attention to detail; it is an on-going process and there is no lack of innovative ideas. Maranzanis is an excellent base for those who want to explore nature in the Carnia area and for ski lovers (the Zoncolan slopes and facilities are only 7 kilometers away, while the Pradibosco cross-country piste in Val Pesarina is about 20 kilometers away). The cooperative has agreements with many local businesses and staff members are always ready to suggest excursions and activities. On request, they'll prepare breakfast for you or you can have it in one of the bars offering special terms.

• 14 mini-apartments (from 2 to 6 beds), with bathroom, TV, kitchen or kitch-enette, some with terrace or balcony • Prices: two-bed mini-apartment 19-53 euros, three-bed 42-73, four-bed 51-73, six-bed 84; breakfast 5-10 euros per person • Credit cards: all, Bancomat • 1 apartment designed for use by the mobility challenged. Small pets allowed. Reception open from 9 am to 1.30 pm, staff reachable by telephone outside these hours.

This restaurant already existed back in the 19th century and, until the 1960s, it was an osteria with a kitchen attached to a blacksmith's workshop. It's now a family-run trattoria. Pino Pecorella su-perintends the kitchen, while his wife Giovanna and daughter Veronica look after the dining room with courtesy and professionalism.
The menu changes with the seasonal nature of the produce and also varies in relation to what takes the cook's fancy. Pino does, however, follow certain fixed rules; he always uses fresh, mainly or-ganic ingredients, makes his own pasta and enhances the basic flavors of his dishes with herbs, spices and truffles). To start, mixed **cured meats**, crostini with liver paté and, in season, aspara-gus with Montasio cheese and Cormons ham or royal agaricand cep mushroom salad. Moving on to first courses, you can sample **tagliolini** or **gnocchi** with seasonal vegetables (asparagus and zucchini) or with mushrooms, a **timbale** (the one made **with cheeses** – ricotta, Parmesan and Montasio – is excellent) or sclopit and sausage flavored with white truffle, which we tried on our last visit. As a main course, **fillet steak with lardo and herbs** (including calendula flowers and mallow), **pork fillet al Cabernet**, veal rump steak with polenta, plus, in winter, **tripe**, **stracotto** and **bac-calà in bianco** (without tomato). If you decide to try the cheeses, you mustn't miss the salted sheep's ricotta. To finish, **chocolate and pear pie**, chocolate mousse or other desserts.
The wine list is not very long but it of-fers a high quality selection.

CORMONS
Borgnano

17 KM WEST OF GORIZIA, 25 KM SOUTHEAST OF UDINE ON SS 305

BORG DA OCJS

🔑 Holiday farm
Via Parini 18
Tel. 0481 67204-340 3619874
E-mail: zoffgiuseppe@virgilio.it
Internet: www.borgdaocjs.it
Open all year

This agriturismo was created in 2001 by restructuring an old cattle shed. After returning to his family activity after working for years as a coachbuilder, Giuseppe Zoff now raises cows and produces cheeses here. His wife Patrizia, assisted by daughters Aurora and Laura, supervises the accommodation. The rooms are painted in non-synthetic colors and are fitted with restored and arte poverastyle furniture. For breakfast you'll be offered farm produce: fresh milk and yogurt in summer and 'milk jam' in winter. Patrizia bakes sachertorte and other cakes, strudels and fruit tarts every day. The savory buffet is also appetizing: fresh or smoked and flavored Caciotta cheeses, fresh dairy and mature cheeses and cured meats, all produced on the farm. Milk, yogurt and cheeses can also be bought at a small store.

• 3 double and 2 triple rooms, with bathroom • Prices: double room single use 36-54 euros, double 52-77 (18 euro supplement for extra bed), breakfast included • Credit cards: all, Bancomat • Facility accessible to the mobility challenged, 1 room designed for their use. Off-street parking. Small pets allowed. Owners always present • Breakfast room. Garden

CORMONS
Zegla

17 KM WEST OF GORIZIA, 25 KM SOUTHEAST OF UDINE ON SS 56

EDI KEBER

🔑 Holiday farm
Località Zegla 17
Tel. e fax 0481 61184
Holidays vary

Edi Keber has always been known in the Friuli winemaking world as a serious producer with a very attentive pricing policy. In 2000 he decided to refurbish this house, immersed in a quiet, peaceful country atmosphere, retaining its original features and adding a tower structure, where the agritursimo is now located. His wife Silvana, who manages the facility, will give you a very friendly welcome. Breakfast consists of sweet and savory fare, and is prepared with genuine, quality products. In the area surrounding Cormons there are a few itineraries – the wine and cherry trails are particularly interesting – you can cover on foot, by bicycle or on horseback. The ancient village of San Floriano is worth a visit and golf lovers will also find a nine-hole course nearby.

• 2 double rooms, with bathroom, terrace, mini-bar; 3 mini-apartments (2-4 persons) with kitchenette • Prices: double room single use 50 euros, double 50-80 (10 euro supplement for extra bed), mini-apartment 70-110; breakfast 5 euros per person • Credit cards: none • 1 room designed for use by the mobility challenged. Off-street parking, some covered. No pets allowed. Owners always reachable • Breakfast and TV room. Garden. Grounds

LA BOATINA

🔑 Holiday farm
Via Corona 62
Tel. e fax 0481 639309
E-mail: info@boatina.com
Internet: www.paliwines.com
Open all year

LA CASA DI ALICE

🔑 Bed and breakfast
Via Ara Pacis 22
Tel. 335 377994
Fax 0481 61743
E-mail: annabrandolin@libero.it
Internet: www.wel.it/alice
Closed from December to February

Owned by businessman Loretto Pali, like Spessa in Capriva del Friuli, the Boatina is a 60-hectare estate of which 36 hectares are vineyards in the far western section of the Collio area. In part of this complex (a group of long, low, whitewashed farmhouses with a vaguely Mediterranean air) stands this elegant agriturismo. Only 100 meters away the Ritrovo della Boatina is a small shop where you can taste the estate's wines, as well as cheeses and cured meats from all over the world. The rooms of the farm were refurbished in 2004 and are furnished with rustic elegance. All enjoy a beautiful view over the vineyards. In the ground floor lounge the outstanding feature is the large fireplace, an inviting place to gather for a chat and a nice bottle of wine or grappa. Breakfast offers sweet and savory fare; bicycles are at your disposal for excursions in the surrounding area.

• 5 double rooms, with bathroom, balcony, mini-bar • Prices: double room single use 50-55 euros, double 75-85, breakfast included • Credit cards: all except DC, Bancomat • Off-street parking. Small pets allowed. • Breakfast room. Lounge. Conference rooms. Garden

Ten minutes by foot from the old center of Cormons stands this late 19th-century house, originally a sulfur factory and later used as a hospital during World War I. It was subsequently bought by the grandfather of the current owners who converted it into a farmhouse. In 2002 it was tastefully restructured with great attention to details such as the original stone walls. The bedrooms have been created in the old cattle sheds and barn with wooden beams and floors and are fitted with modern furniture. On display in one of the common spaces are antique farm tools. Breakfast is traditional, with sweet and savory fare: bread, butter, jams, eggs, local ham and cheeses. On request, the owner, Anna Brandolin, organizes guided tours of the wine cellars she works with.

• 3 double rooms, with bathroom (2 with jacuzzis and terrace), TV • Prices: double room single use 50-60 euros, double 75-95, breakfast included • Credit cards: none • Off-street parking. Small pets allowed. Owners always reachable. • Breakfast room, lounge. Garden

CORMONS
Boatina

14 KM WEST OF GORIZIA, 24 KM SOUTHEAST OF UDINE ON SS 56

MAGNÀS

🔑 Holiday farm
Via Corona 47
Tel. e fax 0481 60991
E-mail: info@agriturismomagnas.com
Internet: www.agriturismomagnas.com
Open all year

CORMONS
Monte Quarin

17 KM WEST OF GORIZIA, 25 KM SOUTHEAST OF UDINE ON SS 56

TANA DEI GHIRI

🔑 Bed and breakfast
Località Monte 4
Tel. 0481 61951-335 6173220
Fax 0481 61951
E-mail: tanadeighiri@email.it
Open all year

Magnàs, which can be translated as 'magnanimous', has been the nickname for generations of the branch of the Visintin family that in the early 70s became owners of this farm between Cormons and Corona di Mariano del Friuli. The 8-hectare farm has vineyards and wine cellars, cattle sheds and pig sties. Luciano Visintin, his wife Sonia and their son Andrea restructured the place in 2001 to create this charming agriturismo. The rooms are elegantly furnished with great attention to detail and all of them enjoy a view of the surrounding countryside. Breakfast is served in a beautiful stone-walled room and offers a large selection of bread and jam and fruit cakes home-made by Sonia, in addition to the farm's own cured meats that can also be purchased along with the wines they produce. You'll be able to explore the surrounding area on the bicycles the agriturismo makes available.

• 1 single and 2 double rooms, with bathroom, air-conditioning, terrace or balcony, mini-bar, TV, modem connection; 2 suites, with bathroom, kitchenette, air-conditioning, terrace or balcony, mini-bar, TV, modem connection • Prices: single 40 euros, double 70, suite 70-80, breakfast included • Credit cards: Visa, MC • Off-street parking. No pets allowed. Owners always present. • Breakfast room. Lounge. Jogging course

Originally the summerhouse of Guglielmo and Martina, the Tana dei Ghiri is now an elegant, refined facility in an ancient rural complex that dates from the second half of the seventeenth century. Two of the rooms have been created in the old farmhouse while the other three are in what was once the barn. The heavy wooden antique furniture goes well with the airy rooms, decorated with paintings by the region's most promising artists. The bed and bathroom linen is very refined. In summer guests can soak up the sun on comfortable sun beds in the beautiful garden or on the large terrace. You'll also be able to enjoy breakfast outside: coffee, tea, milk, hot chocolate, yogurt, muesli, honey, jam, eggs, local cheeses and cured meats. The Tana is a good starting point for visiting historical sites in the vicinity, among which the Ossuary of Oslavia and Museum of the Great War in Gorizia.

• 1 single and 4 double rooms, with bathroom; some with terrace • Prices: single 50 euro, double 70 (20 euro supplement for extra bed), breakfast included • Credit cards: major ones, Bancomat • Off-street parking. Small pets allowed. Owners always reachable • Breakfast room with corner bar, reading and relaxation room. Garden, terrace

CORMONS
Brazzano

15 KM WEST OF GORIZIA, 25 KM SOUTHEAST OF UDINE ON SS 56

TERRA & VINI

☞❶Tourist apartments
Via XXIV Maggio 34
Tel. 0481 60028
Fax 0481 639198
E-mail: info@terraevini.it
Internet: www.terraevini.com
Closed last 15 days of January

The estate of Livio Felluga, considered the father of Friuli winemaking, has added another string to its bow with this re-edition of the old formula of 'osteria with kitchen and rooms'. On the upper floors of a building round a courtyard restructured in 2002, already an osteria in the past, are seven very well furnished apartments with kitchenettes (alternatively, you can have breakfast in an adjacent bar where you pay for what you consume). The counter, tables and chairs are those from the previous old osteria and have all been restored: here you'll be able to taste wines by the glass, a selection of local products and set dishes that change every day (average 20 euros per person, wine excluded). The shop above the wine cellar (which you can visit) sells bottles of all the wines produced on the estate plus a selection of other outstanding Friuli labels.

• 7 mini-apartments (2-4 persons), with bathroom, small lounge, kitchenette, terrace or balcony • Prices: double mini-apartment single use 80 euros, two-three-bed mini-apartment 95-120, four-bed mini-apartment 140; breakfast included • Credit cards: all, Bancomat • Facility accessible to the mobility challenged, 1 apartment designed for their use. Off-street parking. Small pets allowed. Management reachable up to midnight • Bar, restaurant, wine cellar. Lounge. Reading room, TV room. Shop selling the estate's products, wine-tasting room. Garden, veranda

DIGNANO

24 KM WEST OF UDINE ON SS 464

CASA PIRONA

☞❶Bed and breakfast
Via Garibaldi 21
Tel. 0432 951215
Fax 0432 200875
E-mail: studiocojutti@libero.it
Open from March to 30 November

This small place, housed in a 17th-century in the open countryside a few kilometers from Spilimbergo, is managed by Maria Bortolan and Emanuele Cojutti. It was here that in 1789 one of their ancestors – Abbot Pirona, author of the first scientifically compiled dictionary of the Friuli language –was born. The rooms are simple and fitted with period furniture; breakfast is traditional and during the summer is served in the garden. Guests can go for bicycle excursions in the surrounding area. Not far away you'll be able to visit Spilimbergo and its picturesque historic center decorated with mosaics and frescoes, the Gothic-style cathedral and the castle. A little further away San Daniele's famous Guarneriana Library houses one of the oldest manuscripts of Dante's Divine Comedy.

• 3 double rooms, with bathroom • Prices: double room single use 22-27 euros, double 44-54 (11-16 euro supplement for extra bed), breakfast included • Credit cards: none • Nearby external public parking and off-street covered parking for motorbikes. Small pets allowed. Owners always reachable • Breakfast room, lounge. Garden

DOLEGNA DEL COLLIO
Cerò

VENICA & VENICA

Holiday farm
Località Cerò 8
Tel. 0481 61264
Fax 0481 639906
E-mail: venica@venica.it
Internet: www.venica.it
Open from April to October

The Venica family's vacation farm is in a farmhouse, restructured in 1995, on an important Collio wine-growing estate famous for its Tocai Friulano wine. You can sense the owners' professionalism and love for the land in the part of the complex dedicated to accommodation, particularly the hand of Ornella, a pioneer of wine tourism. The rooms have been tastefully furnished in country style with great attention to detail. For breakfast, homemade cakes, Cormons prosciutto and cheeses from Borgnano (a hamlet near Cormons). You'll also be able to buy farm produce and visit the surrounding area by bicycle, supplied by the agriturismo free of charge.

• 4 double rooms and 2 suites, with bathroom, terrace or balcony, mini-bar, TV, modem connection; 2 apartments (4-6 persons), with bathroom, lounge, kitchen • Prices: double room single use 80-90 euros, double 85, suite 95 (20 euro supplement for additional bed), apartment 120-180; breakfast 14 euros per person • Credit cards: all, Bancomat • Off-street parking. No pets allowed. Owners present from 8.30am to 6.30pm. • Lounge. Conference room. Garden, grounds. Terrace, veranda. Pool. tennis court, fitness trail

DUINO-AURISINA
Santa Croce

IL PETTIROSSO

Traditional osteria-trattoria
Località Aurisina Santa Croce 16
Tel. 040 220619
Closed Monday and Thursday lunch, Monday and Thursday in winter
Open: lunch and dinner
Holidays: in November
Seating: 55 + 50 outdoors
Prices: 25-30 euros, wine excluded
All credit cards

This restaurant is located in the Santa Croce district, just beyond the Carso provincial road linking Sistiana to Prosecco. Emiliano, the talented cook, is particularly good at coaxing the best out of fish varieties that are underappreciated – unjustly so, it turns out, as they are exquisite when treated properly.
The place has charm in spades, with two dining rooms (one dominated by an imposing period stove, the other smaller and more intimate) that you reach by crossing a trellis-covered courtyard that offers summertime dining alfresco. There's ample room at the bar for you to linger over a glass of wine or a cup of coffee. The welcome is cordial, the service efficient and the bread and pasta are homemade. What else do you need to know?
Well, you should know that the **pedoci a la scotadeo** (scalded mussels) are especially good, as are the salad of small octopus, sardelle and **sardoni in savor**, gulf seafood au gratin and cold seafood antipasti. First courses include **seafood risottos**, tagliatelle alle vongole and **linguine ai crostacei**; then there's **zuppa di pesce**, oven-baked or grilled fish, calamari and an ethereal **fritto misto**. Emiliano's inventiveness and confidence in traditional cuisine result in dishes that highlight local specialties with a personal touch.
The wine list is focused on small producers of the region, particularly the Italian and Slovenian winemakers of the Carso area.

DUINO-AURISINA
Slivia

FAEDIS
Borgo Canal del Ferro

SARDOC

CASA DEL GRIVÒ

Traditional osteria -trattoria
Località Slivia 5
Tel. 040 200146
Open Thursday to Sunday
Open: lunch and dinner
Holidays: vary during summer
Seating: 80 + 30 outdoors
Prices: 25-28 euros, wine excluded
All credit cards

Holiday farm
Via Canal del Ferro 19
Tel. e fax 0432 728638
E-mail: casadelgrivo@libero.it
Internet: www.grivo.has.it
Closed from mid-December to end of February

This osteria has been here for decades, offering good, local cuisine in a friendly atmosphere and at reasonable prices. You enter the restaurant through a courtyard, passing under a portico where you can sit in the summer. The muted interior is divided into two eating areas, while in the back you'll find the bar and kitchen. The tables are well separated from each other and the settings are simple but done with great attention to detail.

The Sardoc family are all involved in running this osteria: there's Ranko who has now moved from the dining room to work in the kitchen, his sister Roberta in the front line serving the patrons and the other members of the family in the kitchen. The family pays little heed to the fickleness of fashion and are more concerned with life in these parts, not just in terms of food, but also in terms of language and culture. Everything on the menu is made in-house. All this has created a rich, substantial cuisine that partly reflects seasonal changes.

After sampling the local prosciutto crudo, you can order potato **gnocchi**, **spinach roll**, herb crespelle and **barley and bean** or other soups. Then there's **lubjanska** (steak with ham and cheese), **roasted pork** or veal shanks and grilled meat accompanied by **potatoes in tecia**. The **fried chicken** alone makes the trip here worthwhile. For dessert, the **strudel** is definitely not to be missed.

Friuli wines are well represented on the wine list, with several dozen wines from the region, and there is also a good selection of spirits.

A pretty 1920s farmhouse with stone walls and a long wooden balcony houses this no-frills, charming agriturismo. Antonio and Paola Costalunga live here with their three children, dogs, cats and two donkeys. They cultivate their vegetable garden, vineyard and fruit trees organically (they also produce a local variety of apple called Zeuka and make apple juice). They refurbished the building back in 1992, equipping it with solar panels, but also salvaging a great deal of old furniture and old agricultural implements. The overall effect is one of enchanting simplicity: in the common room there's a fogolâr, or open fireplace, while the kitchen has an oven for baking bread that will be served to you for breakfast along with Paola's home-made jams. For dinner, dishes are prepared using vegetables from their garden and other quality products (15-20 euros per person; half board is 45 euros). Bicycles are provided for you to explore the surrounding area.

• 1 double room with bathroom ensuite and 3 rooms (1 double, 1 triple and 1 four-bed) that share 2 bathrooms • Prices: single 27 euros, double 54, triple 81, four-bed 108, breakfast included • Credit cards: none • Parking right in front. Small pets allowed. Owners always reachable • Restaurant (only open for dinner and reserved for residents). Lounge. Reading and meeting room, with library and piano. Garden. Terrace

FAGAGNA
Casali Lini

FARRA D'ISONZO

15 KM NORTHWEST OF UDINE

8 KM SOUTHWEST OF GORIZIA SS 351

CASALE CJANOR

BORGO COLMELLO

🚪 Holiday farm
Località Casali Lini 9
Tel. e fax 0432 801810
E-mail: casalecjanor@hotmail.com
Internet: www.casalecjanor.com
Open all year round

🍲 Restaurant-wine bar with apartment
Strada della Grotta 8
Tel. 0481 889013
Closed Monday, also Saturday lunch in
summer and Sunday evening in winter
Holidays: 10 days in January, 10 in September
Seating: 55 + 60 outdoors
Prices: 25-30 euros
All credit cards, Bancomat

The Missana family offers hospitality in the Fagagna hills in this renovated farmhouse, built before 1700. The comfortable rooms are tastefully furnished in local traditional style, and from the windows you can see the storks that inhabit the nearby nature reserve. The farm raises poultry, in particular geese, and produces wines, grappa, olive oil, and vegetables that guests can also buy if they wish. The buffet breakfast consists of home-made jams and cookies and, on request, cured meats and cheeses. The restaurant (Fridays, Saturdays and Sundays also open to non-residents, 15-25 euros, excluding wine) serves local specialties, among which blecs con pestat and casseroled goose. During winter, everybody sits round the open fire, while in summer you can cool off under the kiwi fruit pergola.

• 2 double and 1 triple rooms, with bathroom (some with jacuzzis) • Prices: double room single use 53 euros, double 70-90, triple 110, breakfast included (5 euro supplement for savory fare) • Credit cards: all, Bancomat • Communal areas accessible to the mobility challenged. Off-street parking. Small pets allowed (not in rooms). Owners always reachable • Restaurant. Lounge, reading room. Garden

Thanks mainly to its perfect combination of good value and inviting atmosphere, this is one of the most popular osterias in the Isonzo area. Reservations are highly recommended for both lunch and dinner. The menu is closely tied to the seasons and varies frequently, sometimes even daily. In the kitchen, Claudio Felati, the young Gorizia chef, expresses his enthusiasm for sourcing impeccable ingredients, such as meats selected by Vinicio Carniel, a local butcher renowned for his meat, ham and sausages, fish that arrives from the market in Gorizia and goose and tuna supplied by Jolanda De Colò. The vegetables come from kitchen gardens in Gorizia and the cured meats are made by small producers. The bread, pasta and desserts are made in-house.

For antipasti, try the prosciutto di San Daniele, Sauris culatello and **goose speck**, as well as the sea bass carpaccio and crab salad. First courses: **blecs with cockerel sauce**, panzerotti with prosciutto crudo, dried tomato and ricotta filling, **potato gnocchi with wild boar sauce** or butter and sage, eggplant timbales with montasio cream, **orzotto** with seasonal vegetables and smoked ricotta and risotto al granciporro. There are some traditional main courses, such as **tripe** and **goulash** in winter, and **baccalà**, **bollito misto**, **cotechino**, **brovada** and grilled offerings in summer. All the desserts need to be sampled: there's the classic **palacinke**, apple strudel, bavarois (yogurt or fruit) and white chocolate mousse.

The wine list contains an exhaustive selection of the best wines of the area.

Forni Avoltri

85 km northwest of Udine, 35 km from Tolmezzo on SS 355

Al Fogolar

Trattoria
Via Ponte Nuovo 1
Tel. 0433 727453
Closed Monday dinner
Open: lunch and dinner
Always open in season
Seating: 80
Prices: 26 euros, wine excluded
All credit cards

Set deep in the countryside of the Carnic Alps, Forni Avoltri is the northernmost point of the Val Degano, connecting Carnia to the Comelico area. Al Fogolar lies by the turn-off for Pierabec near the banks of the Degano river, which provides water for a number of trout farming pools. Chef-owner Fabio Gerin concentrates his efforts on researching and using produce from the area, with quality and freshness as his main objectives. The cuisine draws from Carnia tradition and what the kitchen garden, woods and river provide.
Sample cured meats like smoked Paluzza salami, **Sauris prosciutto**, or cheeses from the Alpine pastures of Casera Tuglia and Casera Vecchia. First courses include chestnut-flour tagliatelle with porcinis or sauce made from duck or hare, **gnocchi alla Carnica**, with sausage and maize, rocket and Val Degano cheese or spring herbs, the not-to-be-missed **cjalsòns**, either sweet or with Carnia herbs, tricolor chicchette with sauce made from roe deer, **tagliolini with radic di mont and sausage** and gnocchetti with nettles and fresh ricotta. To follow, there are tagliatas and steak (all the meat comes from local breeders), roe deer venison in salmì with polenta, **cotechino with sauerkraut** from the hillsides, **frico** and grilled **trout**, which is always fresh because it is caught in the restaurant's own waters. For dessert, there are home-made crostatas and, at the end of summer, apple strudel with wild berries.
The wines on offer are limited to house wine by the carafe and some regional wines.

Gorizia

Alla Luna

Traditional osteria
Via Oberdan 13
Tel. 0481 530374
Closed Sunday for dinner and Monday
Open: 8.30am-3pm/5.30pm-10.30pm
Holidays: in February and July
Seating: 60
Prices: 22-25 euros, wine excluded
Credit cards: Visa, Bancomat

Mention was made of this trattoria way back in 1876; it's the oldest in Gorizia and one of the last osterias to be firmly rooted in the cultural tradition of central Europe, proudly adhered to by the Pintar family in the dishes and in the atmosphere they create. The restaurant's name derives from the history of the merchants who, as they traveled by night, had only the light of the moon to see by. In the past, it was both a hostelry for wayfarers and a refuge for animals. There was a small theater, too, where the well-to-do of Gorizia could spend their evenings. The Pintars have been managing this restaurant for just under 50 years, with Milan working in the kitchen, his wife Celestina at the bar and their daughter Elena front of house, dressed, like the rest of the staff, in traditional costume.
The menu follows the traditions of these border peoples, with **jota**, **bread gnocchi**, **potato gnocchi with plums**, barley and vegetable soups, herb frittatas, and mushroom or vegetable risottos. Main courses include **goulash** and excellent **baccalà**. The puddings are home-made: **palacinke**, tarts made with seasonal fruits, and apple strudel.
Some of these dishes (goulash, fried anchovies, **sardines in saor** with onion, meat balls, fried vegetable marrow flowers, **ham baked in bread** and served with fresh horseradish, sliced cured meats and cheeses) can be sampled as snacks at the bar, accompanied by inviting carafes of Collio.

ROSEN BAR

� Trattoria-bar
Via Duca d'Aosta 96
Tel. 0481 522700
Closed Sunday and Monday
Open: lunch and dinner
Holidays: variable
Seating: 50 + 60 outdoor
Prices: 23-32 euros, wine excluded
All credit cards, Bancomat

VECIA GORIZIA

⌫ Traditional osteria
Via San Giovanni 14
Tel. 0481 32424-329 8770248
Closed Saturday and Sunday
Open: lunch only
Holidays: August 7-20
Seating: 40 + 18 outdoors
Prices: 18 euros, wine excluded
No credit cards accepted

The Rosen Bar was set up 20 years ago by two children of the borderland, Michela Fabbro and Piero Loviscek. The two had left to gain experience in restaurants elsewhere in Europe, but eventually came back to open their own trattoria, in which they carry out continual research into the dishes and products they remember from their childhood. From a macrobiotic experience in Holland, Michela learned the paramount importance of balance, which is now the leitmotiv of her cuisine. Flavors may be new and intriguing, but never extravagant or over the top.
Early produce from the kitchen garden and fish are the cook's favorite raw materials. On the seafood menu you'll find (depending on what the market has to offer) salad of sea bass and citrus fruits, fillet of sole with ricotta and orange sauce, **scallops au gratin**, **zuppa di pesce**, spaghetti with zotoli (typical of the late winter period), fresh tuna tagliata, **poached cuttlefish with polenta**, baked **squid filled with** Treviso chicory and a tasty **mixed fry of fish and vegetables**. With certain dishes, the cost of the meal may come to over 35 euros, but an excellent quality-price ratio is always maintained. On the meat menu, apart from cheese and cured meats, there are often **tagliatelle with sausage**, **goulash with potatoes in tecia** and **meat braised in red wine** with polenta. Desserts worth a mention are the gianduiotto, the vanilla bavarois with wild berries, the apple pie with hazelnuts and crema inglese and the ricotta soufflé with zabaglione and chocolate. There are several Italian wines, a lot of Friuli labels and a few Slovenian ones as well.

The Vecia Gorizia, or rather its forerunner, opened at the end of the 19th century as an inn, with about 20 rooms on three floors and with the rather curious name, possibly coined in self-mockery, of Conte Max. At the beginning of the 20th century, it turned into an osteria, as part of a circuit of stopping and refreshment points for the post coaches. Today it is managed by Emanuela Russian and Nini Buttignon and still maintains its traditional snack bar, serving sliced raw or cooked ham, herb frittatas, breaded sardines and top-quality cheeses. You go to the osteria on foot, through the alleyways that formed the ghetto of Gorizia until World War II, and you'll recognize it from its beautiful wrought iron sign.
The menu offers traditional, local dishes. Bread gnocchi or potato **gnocchi with plums,** with goulash or game sauces, are a fixed item on the winter menu, as are the **spetzl**, little green spinach gnocchi served with butter and smoked ricotta. Then there's **tripe, baccalà with polenta**, and **āevapāiāi** (minced veal and pork with spices, garlic and onion). On Fridays you can also have fish, especially sardines, anchovies and other Mediterranean varieties. In summer, the trattoria limits its opening to lunchtimes, offering lighter, cooler dishes such as mixed vegetable salad, chicken salad and grilled vegetables and cheeses. For dessert, there are fruit tarts and apple strudel.
To drink, there's wine by the glass and good quality beer.

GRADISCA D'ISONZO

MULIN VECIO

⌒ Traditional osteria
Via Gorizia 2
Tel. 0481 99783
Closed Wednesday and Thursday
Open: lunch and dinner
Holidays: variable
Seating: 150 + 100 outdoors
Prices: 15-25 euros, wine excluded
No credit cards accepted

This is more of a snack bar than a real restaurant, though the hot food and service mean that you can eat a complete meal with typical local dishes. What happens is that, at aperitif time, the place fills up with local patrons who greatly appreciate the wine and great cured meats on offer. The restaurant has been managed for the last 40 years by Bruno and Alba Spessot, today assisted by their sons Luca and Cesare and by Lara, Cesare's wife. Over 600 pieces of copperware are on display in the Mulin Vecio – cooking pots and utensils – and as well as the charming rooms inside, it also has a well tended garden.

All the cured meats are supplied by small local producers and sliced by hand; San Daniele ham, salami, pancetta, ossocolli and lots of others. The **ham baked in bread crust** and dusted **with horseradish** is excellent, as is the large **mortadella**. Antipasti worth a mention are calf **nervetti** salad and beans with onion. A delicious **pasta and bean** minestrone can be eaten the whole year round, while **tripe** is the classic dish on Tuesdays, and **goulash** with just the right seasoning of paprika is served on Fridays. **Würstel** accompanied by **sauerkraut** is also frequently on the menu. As you can see, the Austro-Hungarian Empire has left its gastronomic imprint on the area. To finish your meal, there's a good selection of Friuli cheeses. Dessert is a delicious handmade **apple strudel**.

The wine is mainly served by the carafe and is carefully researched by Bruno. If you prefer, you can choose from at least ten labels from the Friuli region.

GRIMACCO
Clodig

ALLA POSTA

⌒ Trattoria
Via Roma 22
Tel. 0432 725000
Closed Monday and Tuesday
Open: evenings, lunch by reservation only
Holidays: variable
Seating: 40 + 12 outdoors
Prices: 20-22 euros, wine excluded
No credit cards accepted

In simple, well-tended surroundings with fresh flowers in the vases and an age-old wisteria on the pergola over the entrance, the trattoria perfectly reflects the spirit of the owners: the courtesy and warm spontaneity of Maria Gilda Primosic and the discretion of her husband Peppino. Decades of working in the kitchen have not dimmed Maria's enthusiasm for cooking and discovering ancient recipes.

The main focus of the Posta restaurant is its first courses, with **gnocchi** and, even more so, **soups**, that vary with the season: classic varieties with potatoes and cep mushrooms (or chestnuts) and with herbs, such as rue flowers, and the sweet-and-sour zuppa del vedovo, made of apples and prunes and maize flour. White potatoes are the main ingredient of **boiled strucchi** with a filling of walnuts from the woods around Clodig. Other specialties are **pinza batuda** (flat polenta cake with sour cream and cucumber sauce), **brisa** (white sugar, sour milk and beans) and **marve** (a frittata with eggs, milk and herbs). Salami and ricotta are home-made. The main course menu is seasonal, too. In winter, **game** and red meats, but also pork fillet, rabbit and breast of guinea fowl. In summer, veal, **shank** and **roasts**. Some of these dishes are served with elderberry and other syrups. Seasonal vegetables abound. Apart from tarts, fruit pies and fragrant **strudels**, you can also find traditional strucchi and puddings inspired by the church calendar. At the end of the meal, Maria offers San Giovanni wine, a red flavored with 25 herbs and flowers that were traditionally picked at the summer solstice.

You can drink Colli Orientali and Collio wines and Merlot and Tocai by the carafe.

MAJANO
Susans

24 KM NORTHWEST OF UDINE

MALBORGHETTO-VALBRUNA
Malborghetto

76 KM NORTHEAST OF UDINE, 12 KM FROM TARVISIO SS 54 OR AT 23

ALL'ANTICA SCUDERIA DEL CASTELLO
🔑 Holiday farm
Via Castello 150
Tel. 0432 959115
Fax 0432 947147
E-mail: info@susans.it
Internet: www.susans.it
Open all year

ANTICA OSTERIA DA GIUSI
🍲 Trattoria
Via Bamberga 19
Tel. 0428 60014
Closed Monday and Tuesday
Open: lunch and dinner
Holidays: variable
Seating: 90
Prices: 30 euros, wine excluded
All credit cards, Bancomat

500 meters from Susans Castle is a building once used as a stable. It has now been restructured and turned into an agriturismo, tastefully fitted with period furniture that varies in style from room to room (the Art Nouveau room on the ground floor can be used by the mobility challenged), which have names like Blueberry, Cherry and Laburnum. Breakfast is very filling and offers a selection of sweet and savory fare served in a room reminiscent of an old Friuli-style kitchen with all its accessories. The farm products on sale comprise a small quantity of extra-virgin olive oil. Maria Luisa Zuliani, who runs this place with her husband Valter and daughter Barbara, will be pleased to provide mountain bikes and suggest excursions in the environs: San Daniele del Friuli, the Lake Cornino nature reserve where the griffon-vulture has been re-introduced, and the white stork oasis at Fagagna.

•2 double or triple and 1 four-bed rooms, with bathroom • Prices: double room single use 37 euros, double 62, triple 99, quadruple 106, breakfast included • Credit cards: all, Bancomat • 1 room designed for use by the mobility challenged. Off-street parking, some covered. Small pets allowed. Owners always reachable. • Breakfast room. Garden

Malborghetto is a small border village set deep in a valley where history has unfolded: Napoleonic, Austrian and, of course, Italian troops have all passed through this village. All these comings and goings have generated a population that feels decidedly central European. The cuisine does too, and it's significant that at the Schönbergs' place there are menus named after the Austrian captain Hensel and the French viceroy Beauharnais, rivals in a battle to conquer the fortress of Malborghetto.
As antipasto, various cured meats: speck, raw ham, soppressa, **cooked ham with horseradish**, and **sasaka** (minced, smoked lardo served with brown bread croutons). There are many traditional first courses: vegetable soups, **bean and barley soup**, potato **gnocchi** with ragù or with mushrooms or smoked ricotta or **Montasio** (this cheese takes its name from the high mountain pastures that overlook the village). The zuppa del capitano, a bowl of cereals and slightly spicy meat is served as a meal on its own. There are some substantial main courses: **goulash with polenta, smoked loin of pork with mustard and sauerkraut**, venison in sauce and melted cheese. To finish, **potato kipfel with preserves**, apple strudel, omelet with redcurrant jam and **buchtin** (fritter dough oven-baked as opposed to fried).
There are regional wines or wines by the carafe, and a full selection of grappas and flavored spirits.

MALBORGHETTO-VALBRUNA
Malborghetto

76 KM NORTHEAST OF UDINE, 12 KM FROM TARVISIO ON SS 54 OR AT 23

CASA OBERRICHTER

🍲 Restaurant
Via Superiore 4
Tel. 0428 41888
Closed Wednesdays, never in August and over Christmas
Open: lunch and dinner
Holidays: 2 weeks in March, 2 in September
Seating: 90
Prices: 25-30 euros, wine excluded
All credit cards, Bancomat

Casa Oberrichter is a beautiful little 15th-century palazzo, in the oldest and most elegant village of the multiethnic Valcanale area. After being abandoned for a long time, it was restored by the artist Marina Gioitti and her family. On the ground floor, there's now a carpentry and painting workshop and on the first floor, the restaurant-cafeteria, where concerts, exhibitions and festivals are often held. The young owner, Alessio Nicolavcich Gioitti, is a tenor who combines his passion for music and singing with his enthusiasm for cooking.

You can sample typical dishes from the area that are seldom found in restaurants, all prepared with care and delicacy. **Rollschinken** (smoked ham) **with apples and horseradish**, **liptauer** (spicy cream cheese) and radicchio with ricotta and chives are appetizing antipasti. Meat and vegetables vary with the seasons: there's **goulash** or nettle **zuppa**, calf's liver gnocchetti, **palatschinken** (a kind of omelet) in broth, and radicchio, mushroom or game pies. Main courses include **kaiserteller** (smoked cutlets served with sauerkraut, potatoes and bread gnocchi), roast pork from organically raised animals, **roe deer venison with Sambuco**, **wild boar with pears and Merlot** and, if you're lucky, chamois goulash. Making desserts is one of Marina's hobbies: there's **reiling** (a yeast dough with raisins, cinnamon and a little sugar), **potiza** (with walnuts, raisins or poppy seeds) accompanied by a small glass of dostler (an apple and pear liqueur) and **cock** (ricotta, apples, walnuts, almonds, chocolate and stale bread).

You can choose from a fairly limited list of Italian wines or opt for the very reasonable house wine.

MALBORGHETTO-VALBRUNA
Valbruna

80 KM NORTHEAST OF UDINE, 9 KM WEST OF TARVISIO ON SS 13

VALBRUNA INN

🔑 3-Star Hotel
Frazione Valbruna
Via Alpi Giulie 2
Tel. 0428 660554
Fax 0428 660559
E mail: info@valbrunainn.com
Internet: www.valbrunainn.com
Closed in May and from mid-October to end of November

The boarding house originally opened in 1951 by Egidio Keil in the family home near Valbruna's church is now a pleasant little hotel with traditional mountain-style furnishings. The fabrics, wall colors and floor tiles differ from room to room, each of which has its own special character thanks to features such as fireplaces, dual bathtubs or shower cabins, panoramic terraces and reading corners with book shelves (during Christmas and in August prices for the more luxurious rooms range from 140-185 euros). The room with the fireplace is furnished with antiques and has a library named after mountaineer and writer Julius Kugy. It contains a collection of hundreds of books on the nature, art, cooking and traditions of the area, a meeting point of Italian, Austrian and Slovenian cultures. Breakfast is abundant and the restaurant serves local specialties at 25-30 euros, excluding wine.

• 13 double rooms, with bathroom, mini-bar, satellite TV • Prices: double room single use 70-90 euros, double 65-120 (30 euro supplement for extra bed), breakfast included • Credit cards: all except DC, Bancomat • Facility accessible to the mobility challenged, 2 rooms designed for their use. Off-street parking. Small pets allowed. Owners always reachable • Bar, restaurant. Stube, library. Fitness area

MANIAGO

VECCHIA MANIAGO

🍲 Osteria-trattoria
Via Castello 10
Tel. 0427 730583
Closed Monday for dinner and Tuesday
Open: lunch and dinner
Holidays: 15 August
Seating: 35 + 100 outdoors
Prices: 30-35 euros, wine excluded
All credit cards

Host Claudio Corba is sometimes excessively self-effacing, but he should be given due credit for creating such beautiful surroundings from virtually nothing. You can have a good tajut at the bar and eat in the restaurant or, in the summer months, outside under the pergola. In addition, a traditionally decorated dining room with a fogolar is available for themed evenings or events.
After a long period of trial and error in the kitchen, the restaurant has found the right path to follow, offering dishes from the area alongside grilled meats that have been sourced locally. Beba, the skilled cook, is of Slovenian origin and came of age under the tutelage of the various cooks who have worked there. To start, there is an excellent steak tartare, the more traditional **pitina** in vinegar, **Treviso radicchio, speck and montasio involtini**, and a substantial **polenta with soppressa**. First courses include **bean soup** and tagliatelle with porcini sauce in season, **ravioli di gialletti with wild boar ragù** and pappardelle with pitina and cabbage. Among the main courses, **frico with potatoes and onion, petuccia al cao** and **tripe in white sauce with polenta** are worth trying. You can also have beef guancetta with porcinis and **braised meat al Refosco with spring onions**. To finish, there's gianduia with biscuits or chocolate salami.
There is a wide range of interesting wines on offer, especially from Friuli and Tuscany, with selections from Franciacorta and elsewhere.

MARIANO DEL FRIULI
Corona

AL PIAVE

🍲 Trattoria
Via Cormons 6
Tel. 0481 69003
Closed Monday and Tuesday
Open: lunch and dinner
Holidays: 1-15 February, 1-15 July
Seating: 30
Prices: 30 euros, wine excluded
Credit cards: Visa, Bancomat

By the time this guide arrives in the bookshops, the refurbishment that was underway when we last visited – to give Patrizio and Claudia Fermanelli's trattoria a larger kitchen, a second dining room, indoor restrooms and four or five bedrooms upstairs for overnight stays – should be finished. These improvements, the owners assured us, will not change the style of the premises, which will continue to welcome patrons to a glass of wine at the bar, and to provide them with traditional Friuli dishes.
Before the restaurant closed for its makeover, we were able to sample a tasty summer version of **jota**, with pickled zucchini instead of sauerkraut. In other seasons, you'll find **barley soup, tagliatelle with duck**, and **gnocchi with hare**, while in spring there's bruscandoli strudel. Don't miss out on antipasti like the **cured meats**, which includes San Daniele prosciutto, wild boar prosciutto and homemade salami, venison carpaccio and smoked goose breast. Main courses include **roasted veal shank**, wild boar casserole and a good selection of grilled meats, like tagliata, **lamb chops** and **pork cutlets**. To finish, there's an excellent **apple strudel** or creamy desserts like crème brûlée.
To combine with the dishes cooked by Patrizio, you can order by the bottle or glass of Isonzo DOC wines, which are well represented on the wine list.

MEDEA

KOGOJ

Holiday farm
Via Zorutti 10
Tel. e fax 0481 67440
E-mail: kogoj@kogoj.it
Internet: www.kogoj.it
Closed for 20 days in September

A brief stretch of rough road will take you to this old but recently refurbished farmhouse, which lies at the heart of the Kogoj estate. Silvio wasn't born in Medea, though little more than 20 years ago he decided to live in the countryside and bought this estate: farmhouse, barn, sheds, fields and all. He planted the first vines, then extended his land to include some of the most beautiful vineyards in Pradis and began selling his own wines directly. Adding rural hospitality was a natural move for him, given his frank and sincere nature. The rooms are all charming and furnished with antique tables and chairs, beautiful carpets, paintings and prints. Mr. Kogoj also prepares breakfast, which comprises a sweet menu – the strudels are excellent – and a savory one of mainly local produce. The facility is a good base for visiting Gorizia, Aquileia and Udine.

• 1 single and 4 double rooms, with bathroom (next door for the single), some rooms with access to a communal terrace • Prices: single 50 euros, double 80, breakfast included •Credit cards: all, Bancomat • Off-street parking. Small pets allowed. Owners always reachable. • Breakfast room, small lounge. Grounds. Pool

MONFALCONE
Panzano

AI CAMPI DI MARCELLO

3-Star Hotel
Via Napoli 7
Tel. 0481 486470
Fax 0481 720192
E-mail: locandaaicampi@tin.it
Internet: www.paginegialle.it/aicampi
Closed from Christmas to New Year

At the end of the 19th century, Anna Bregant's hotel was surrounded by fields. Today there are yards where cruise ships are built, as can be seen in the pictures lining the corridor walls. Even though the hotel's name recalls its pre-industrial past, it was refurbished in 2000 and equipped with all modern comforts. Anna is dedicated to satisfying her guests' requirements and serves excellent breakfasts: juices and seasonal fruit salads, bread, butter and jam, honey, yogurt, plus pastries and cakes baked by her son Denis, as well as tea, milk, coffee and hot chocolate. A restaurant offers a set menu at 15 euros per person, excluding wine. Guests are able to use bicycles provided by the hotel to reach the cycle tracks leading to the lagoon of Grado or the Carso where trenches and gun positions still remain from World War I.

• 10 single and 4 double rooms, with bathroom (1 with a jacuzzi), air-conditioning, mini-bar, satellite TV, modem connection, some rooms with a small balcony • Prices: single 50 euros, double 82; breakfast included • Credit cards: all, Bancomat • Facility accessible to the mobility challenged, 2 rooms designed for their use. External parking out front. Small pets allowed. Management always reachable • Bar corner, restaurant. Relaxation room, TV room. Garden, terrace

MONRUPINO
Zolla

MORUZZO

AL CASTELLIERE POD TABROM

🍲 Trattoria-gostilna
Località Zolla 8
Tel. 040 327120
Closed Thursday and Friday
Open: lunch and dinner
Holidays: variable
Seating: 45 + 60 outdoors
Prices: 25-30 euros, wine excluded
All major credit cards

AL TIGLIO

🍲 Osteria
Via Centa 8
Tel. 0432 672126
Closed Monday for dinner and Tuesday
Open: lunch and dinner
Holidays: variable
Seating: 20 + 20 outdoors
Prices: 30 euros, wine excluded
Credit cards: Visa, Bancomat

Times passes slowly and nothing much happens to upset the tranquility of this corner of Carso, close to the Slovenian border. And fortunately, the fragrant smells from the kitchen of this trattoria have remained just as they always were. The restaurant, run by the Gustin family, consists of an entrance hall and an area with a few tables, mainly used by patrons from the village, who come for coffee, a glance at the newspaper and a chat. Further along, on the right, is a brightly lit room with large windows looking out over the valley and a typical Carso landscape. You can eat outside in good weather. The tables are laid in a simple manner and the service is painstaking and efficient.

The kitchen is only partly affected by the changing seasons: both the local clientele and tourists in search of the typical food of the area want substantial, full flavored dishes in the summer as well as in winter. After sampling a good Carso ham, you can order a traditional soup (there's always **jota** at weekends), **gnocchi** (the most typical prepared **with plums**), roasted vegetable or mushroom pie or **cabbage roll**. As a main course, there's veal or **oven-roasted pork shank with potatoes in tecia**, grilled meats and **game**. Call it a day with some **strudel** and other homemade puddings.

As an alternative to the house wine, served by the carafe, there's a choice of bottles, though the list is a very limited one and not on par with the food.

Given how few seats this restaurant has, booking is absolutely essential. This osteria offers many pleasant surprises, from the inviting atmosphere and the professionalism with which you are welcomed, to the flavors you find there and food that steadfastly upholds local traditions.

The menu changes each month, but some things always remain the same. Among the ingredients, this includes Treviso radicchio, cardoons, artichokes, goose, rabbit, guinea fowl, lamb, tuna, moscardini and octopus. Walter Dri's cooks up dishes like **buckwheat tagliatelle with guinea fowl** or cinta senese pork ragù and formadi frant, **cjarsòns**, **panade** (bread, Alpine cheese and radicchio pie), **toc' in braide** with black truffle or with foie gras, tagliatelle with broccoli and Grado lagoon calamaretti, tortelli di burrata and turnip tops. Then there's rabbit sirloin with cherry tomatoes, veal and artichoke millefeuille, **goose with polenta** and sea bass with vegetables and black rice. Antipasti worth sampling include the **cured meats**, selected according to the strict requirements for aging stipulated by tradition. To finish, there's chocolate cake with soft milky cream, crêpes or cannoli with orange cream, chocolate fondant with pineapple sorbet, and nougat tiramisù.

The wine list is short but offers a well-thought-out choice of wines with good value.

🖊 At **Pagnacco** (3 km), Piazza Matteotti 26, the Olivo bakery produces excellent bread. A few yards away, on the Tricesimo road, the Narduzzi dairy sells Brazzacco cheese.

Mossa

BLANCH

🍲 Trattoria
Via Blanchis 35
Tel. 0481 80020
Closed Tuesday for dinner and Wednesday
Open: lunch and dinner
Holidays: last week of August, first 3 in September
Seating: 120 + 50 outdoors
Prices: 25-30 euros
No credit cards accepted

This centuries-old osteria in the Collio area near the Slovenian border offers a family-style welcome. Outside, a few tables are set up under a delightful trellis, while the interior is casually furnished with wood paneling and simply laid tables and not afraid to show its age. In short, this is a real osteria, where they don't feel the need to kowtow to current fashion and the wine – local, obviously – is still bought in bulk to be patiently bottled in the cellar.

The trattoria is very popular and frequented by locals, particularly during **mushroom** season. Mushrooms can be found all over the menu, in salads, sautéed, fried and grilled. And in general, the food here takes into account what the countryside offers, from seasonal herbs to game. After a fine dish of cured meats, you may choose between **zuppa** (of barley, **beans** or vegetables), potato gnocchi with ragù or mushrooms, the local **gnocchi with plums**, tagliatelle with game or mushroom sauce and the most famous specialty of the house: **blecs cul gjal**, or maltagliati seasoned with cockerel sauce – a traditional Slovenian dish. The main courses are quite substantial any time of the year, with choices like **pork shank**, wild boar, roe deer, partridge, **roast kid**, little grilled or breaded ribs of kid, rolls with mushrooms and sausages, **liver alla veneziana** and barbecued meats. Desserts include **apple strudel**, cherry crostata and a superb puff pastry tart with cream. There are also wild berries in season.

Mossa

VECCHIE PROVINCE

🍲 Traditional osteria-trattoria
Via Zorutti 18
Tel. 0481 808693
Always open in season
Open: 11 am-3 pm and 5 pm-2 am
Holidays: variable
Seating: 60 + 30 outdoors
Prices: 20-22 euros
All credit cards

Although the food it offers fully entitles it to be called a trattoria, this eatery run by the Dilena family still has the look and the attributes of an old frasca, or tavern. People come here not just to eat but also to drink a glass of wine, chat with friends and play card games such as briscola or tressette, sitting on benches around the tables inside or in the courtyard shaded by jasmine and by an old trellis with its uva fragola vine.

One thing should be noted: the osteria is open every day except for the last week of each month, when it closes from Monday to Thursday in order to give the owner, Francesco "Mic" Dilena, the time to visit his suppliers and stock up. The results are excellent, from the cheeses and **cured meats** that Mic and his daughter Martina serve as a starter to the traditional Gorizia preparations that follow. This area's cuisine is a product of the Italian, Germanic and Slav cultures and customs that intermingle here, and the dishes prepared by Mic's son Cristiano are praiseworthy. First courses include **gnocchi with radicchio**, **slikrofi** (a sort of potato and herb tortellini and a specialty from neighboring Slovenia) with roast meat sauce, pasta with wild boar sauce, barley and **risottos** with seasonal vegetables. Among the main courses, you will often find **salami in vinegar, prosciutto cotto in bread with horseradish**, **sausage in white wine, frico** – the crisp version – and asparagus with hardboiled eggs in season. Desserts are simple but good.

In the spirit of frasca tradition, the wine is served by the carafe, and it is satisfactory. Both red and white wines are produced by the owner.

NIMIS
Cergneu

PALMANOVA

CASA NONGRUELLA

🍲 Bed and breakfast
Via Nongruella 7
Tel. 0432 797194-333 2668108
Fax 0432 400950
E-mail: info@nongruella.com
Internet: www.@nongruella.com
Open all year

LA CAMPANA D'ORO

🍲 Trattoria
Borgo Udine 25 B
Tel. 0432 928719
Closed Tuesday, Sunday and Monday for dinner
Open: lunch and dinner
Holidays: 1 week after Christmas, 2
weeks in August
Seating: 50
Prices: 28-32 euros, wine excluded
All credit cards

Ornella Barbei's B&B is in the valley of Cergneu, in an old Friuli-style house with loggia, and with wood and stone construction materials visible both inside and out. It sits on a small hill, which offers a view over secular forests of ash, beech and cherry trees through which you can take relaxing walks. Rooms – complete with well-restored family antique furniture – are accessible directly through an outside portico. Breakfast consists of sweet and savory fare, including home-made jams and cakes, and in summer is served in a private garden, an ideal place to soak up the sun. For wine lovers, the area is famous for its excellent Ramando and Picolit. Sites of historical and cultural interest in the surrounding area are Cividale del Friuli and Udine.

• 2 double rooms, with bathroom, TV; 1 mini-apartment (2 persons) with kitchenette • Prices: double room single use 35 euros, double 50, mini-apartment 50-60, breakfast included • Credit cards: none • Adjacent parking. Small pets allowed. Owners always reachable. • Breakfast room, lounge. Garden

This historic restaurant has been licensed since 1864 and has been entirely family-run since 1960. Margherita Gandin, with son Marco and daughter-in-law Elena, does the cooking, paying careful attention to local, traditional recipes and to the use of fresh, seasonal products, including fish. They prepare finely tuned menus with predominantly simple dishes, but there are a few innovative ones as well.
The antipasti will always include locally sourced salami, smoked goose breast, Friuli lardo alle erbe and bresaola. If you prefer fish, there are steamed mantis shrimp, gratinéed scallops, **anchovies in saor**, marinated salmon with horseradish sauce and mattonella di polpo. Traditional first courses include **potato gnocchi with smoked ricotta and cinnamon**, buckwheat gnocchi with prosciutto and bruscandoli (urtizzons), **uardi e fasui** (barley and bean) soup, and tagliatelle with lamb sauce. Also recommended: tagliatelle with prawns and zucchini or spaghetti with baby clams or al nero di seppie. Among the main courses, we particularly like the **goulash, montasio with polenta,** sole, striped bream or grilled monkfish, sea bass or slices of roasted turbot with potatoes, baccalà with cream, ricciola in boreto (amberjack) and **seppie nere in umido** (stewed cuttlefish) with peas and polenta. Elena makes all the desserts, which might include chocolate mousse with coffee or lemon sauce, apple, pear and cinnamon strudel with vanilla sauce and latte cotto spiced with dried flowers. As well as a fair number of mostly Friuli wines, the wine list also offers some interesting organically produced wines by the carafe.

PALUZZA
Timau

PAVIA DI UDINE
Lauzacco

72 KM NORTHWEST OF UDINE, 23 KM FROM TOLMEZZO ON SS 52 BIS

10 KM SOUTH OF UDINE ON SS 352

DA OTTO

Restaurant with hotel
Via Plozner Mentil 15
Tel. 0433 779002
Closed Tuesday, never in summer
Open: lunch and dinner
Holidays: 6-20 January
Seating: 80 + 12 outdoors
Prices: 20-25 euros, wine excluded
All major credit cards, Bancomat

LA FRASCA

Trattoria
Viale Grado 10
Tel. 0432 675150
Closed Wednesday
Open: lunch and dinner
Holidays: first half of January
Seating: 90 + 40 outdoors
Prices: 25-28 euros, wine excluded
All credit cards, Bancomat

Timau is a little village (pop. 400), at the foot of the Monte Croce Carnico pass leading to Carinthia. Here they speak a Austro-German dialect that is incomprehensible to just about everyone else. Because of the isolation of this area, unusual features of agricultural and food production have been preserved. Da Otto opened in 1850 and the management has been passed down through the Matiz family for generations. There's the friendly, good-natured Diego in the dining room and his wife Antonietta in the kitchen, assisted by chef Stefano, who all make this restaurant a very pleasant place to eat.

For antipasti, you can sample strudel with mountain herbs, speck with artichoke cream, croutons with porcini and montasio, smoked pancetta served with mountain radicchio, **frico**, and wild boar speck. The most outstanding of the first courses is the **cjarsòns**, but the **spätzle** with blackcurrants and venison ragù sauce, the **Carnia pasticcio** with sausage and veal, the asparagus and sclopit crespelle and the tagliatelle with scampi and porcini are all well worth trying. Main courses include veal guanciale with polenta, **frico with potatoes**, **game**, kid, lamb and grilled smoked chops. There's also a small selection of goat and cow cheeses – both fresh, matured and, in summer, straight from Alpine pastures. Desserts include a pear tart with confectioner's cream, semifreddo with pine nuts, the ever-popular apple strudel and chocolate pie with chocolate icing and cream.

The wine list contains some interesting Friuli wines, and the sweet Verduzzo house wine is excellent. Good, attentive service.

In its forty years' existence, this restaurant has gone through three incarnations: osteria (a real frasca, or tavern, conceived as a shop window for Scarbolo's wines), a farm holiday center and a bar with a restaurant license. Increasing the surface area and the seating capacity has not, however, meant a reduction in the warmth of the reception they give to visitors, but a great improvement in the quality of the food. The raw materials are all (apart from the wine, the cured meats and some of the vegetables) produced here, or (in the case of the meat, cheeses, oil, grain and flour) they come from suppliers who are very well known and trusted by owners Mariagrazia and Valter Scarbolo. Mimmo, the very able chef, transforms the produce into dishes divided between two menus, which vary from week to week. The more extensive one offers traditional fare, while the other is themed and closely linked to the changing seasons.

You can start with a rich selection of **cured meats** made by in-house (ossocollo, soppressa, salami or guanciale), with **herb frittata** or vegetables au gratin. First courses include **barley and bean soup**, vegetable minestrone, tagliolini with ham or with asparagus in the springtime. Then there are the classical dishes of the area, such as **frico with polenta** and **cotechino with brovada**, vegetable dishes (with asparagus, leeks, artichokes and chicory), fried turkey breast and excellent **grilled meats** (beef tagliata, pork chop and sausage). There is a good selection of Friuli cheeses: Montasio, Formadi frant and formaggi ubriachi from Carnia.

The Scarbolo wines are very satisfying to drink, but the wine list also offers other good wines, both regional and from the rest of Italy.

POLCENIGO

PALAZZO SCOLARI

🔑 Bed and breakfast
Via Gorgazzo 2
Tel. 0434 74100-3200 726080
E-mail: salice@virgilio.it
Internet: www.palazzoscolari.it
Open all year

Anna and Egle Salice will try to make your stay in this ancient village at the foot of the mountains as pleasurable and interesting as possible. The B&B is in an impressive 16th-century building facing onto the main village square, and has been completely renovated while conserving its original features. The rooms are refined and fitted with antique furniture. Both Anna and Egle are excellent cooks and will surprise you in the morning with a generous buffet breakfast of sweet and savory fare and a wide variety of drinks. The Salice sisters will also provide you with bicycles so that you can explore the area in summer: an interesting sight just a few kilometers away is the reappearance above ground of the Livenza and Gorgazzo rivers.

• 3 double rooms, with bathroom, TV (on request) • Prices: double room single use 50-55 euros, double 65-70 (15-20 euro supplement for extra bed), breakfast included • Credit cards: none • Facility accessible to the mobility challenged. Off-street parking places, some covered. No pets allowed. Owners always reachable • Breakfast room, reading room, TV room. Conference room. Garden, grounds

PORPETTO
Pampaluna

16 KM NORTHWEST OF PORDENONE

33 KM SOUTH OF UDINE

DA TARSILLO

🍲 Osteria
Via Pampaluna 27
Tel. 0431 65058-621629
Closed Monday and Tuesday
Open: lunch and dinner
Holidays: 10 days in January, 20 in July
Seating: 50 + 20 outdoors
Prices: 25-30 euros, wine excluded
All credit cards, Bancomat

Like many other Friuli osterias, this restaurant was originally a grocery store and bar serving snacks and wine. It was transformed into a trattoria in 1978. It has belonged to the Berton family since just after World War II and Flavia and her husband Romeo continue to run it today. Its salient feature is the simple, wholesome home cooking that uses raw materials of excellent quality.
The fixed items on the menu are joined by others that alternate with the seasons, such as mushrooms, **pickled salami**, the classic combination of **brovada and musetto**, and vegetables. The antipasti consist of Italian **cured meats** and crostini with venison or goose ham. You can then sample the potato or eggplant or spinach **gnocchi** with fresh tomatoes, the **bread gnocchi** with melted butter and sage, the pasta with gorgonzola and radicchio. In the colder months, there's always **orzo e fagioli** (barley and beans) and in summer, **risotto alla castellana** with mushrooms and ham. There's **game**, too, in season – venison, wild boar and, to order, hare and duck – cooked in a variety of ways and also used to sauce **tagliatelle**. The meat grill, whether beef or pork, is always very popular, as is the **live alla veneziana**, the **tripe alla parmigiana** and the **baccalà in white wine sauce**. **Mushrooms**, asparagus, wild herbs, grilled vegetables and caponata complete the menu in spring and summer. You can finish your meal with desserts like strudel, panna cotta or crème caramel.
The wine list offers a reasonable selection of Friuli and Tuscan wines.

POVOLETTO
Ravosa

POVOLETTO
Belvedere

13 KM NORTHEAST OF UDINE

10 KM NORTH OF UDINE

LA FAULA

VILLA DOMUS MAGNA

⚷ Holiday farm
Via della Faula 5
Tel. 0432 666394
Fax 0432 647828
Internet: www.faula.com
Open all year

⚷ Bed and breakfast
Via del Tiglio 13
Tel. e fax 0432 679054
E-mail: domusmagna1467@libero.it
Internet: www.domusmagna1467.it
Open all year

A typical early 1900s Friuli farmhouse that still has its original wooden floors and furnishings, including a large stone fireplace. The organic farm managed by this family not only produces wine but also raises Aberdeen Angus cows, the rare Plezzana sheep breed and poultry. For breakfast, you can have fresh eggs from the henhouse, yoghurt, jams and home-baked cakes. The restaurant is only open for residents and a reservation is required: it serves local cuisine at a price of 20-22 euros per person, wine excluded. If you wish, you can take part in excursions on horseback in the peaceful surrounding countryside. Places to visit include the small church of San Pietro in the Magredis area, where you'll be able to admire 12 15th-century frescoes of the months of the year.

• 7 double or triple rooms, with bathroom; 2 mini-apartments (2-4 persons) with kitchenette; 2 small houses with kitchen, 1-2 rooms, veranda • Prices: double room single use 55 euros, double 80, triple 100, breakfast included; mini-apartment 70 euros, small house 60-80; breakfast 7 euros per person • Credit cards: major ones, Bancomat • Communal areas accessible to the mobility challenged, 1 small house designed for their use. Off-street parking. No pets allowed. Owners always reachable. • Restaurant. Lounge, reading and TV room. Conference room. Garden. Pool, jogging track

Belvedere di Povoletto is a peaceful place just minutes from Udine, on the left bank of the River Torre, and with a panorama that lives up to its name. In the center of the small village stands the Domus Magna of the noble Partistagno family, a 15th-century building carefully refurbished by the owner, Chiara Pelizzo. The villa is surrounded by extensive grounds protected by walls and five hectares of fields where there's a swimming pool available for guests. The rooms are elegantly furnished, complementing the style of the house. The continental breakfast includes cakes and fresh bread, and is served in a room with a triform window (a window divided into three parts linked by a single architectural motif, typical of Medieval times) or in the garden. There's a laundry service on request, and bicycles are available for excursions in the surrounding area. In Primulacco (only one kilometer away), there's a flying-field with a grass runway for ultra-light aircraft.

• 3 double, 1 triple rooms and 1 suite, with bathroom, air-conditioning, TV • Prices: double room single use 50 euros, double 75, triple 90, suite 90-120, breakfast included • Credit cards: Visa, Mastercard, Bancomat • Suite designed for use by the mobility challenged. External parking out front, garage (3 spaces). No pets allowed. Owners always reachable • Breakfast room, lounge. Garden, grounds. Pool

PRATA DI PORDENONE
Ghirano

PREPOTTO

ALLO STORIONE

🍲 Restaurant
Piazza Mazzini 10
Tel. 0434 626028-626010
Closed Monday
Open: lunch and dinner
Holidays: 3 weeks in August
Seating: 70 + 20 outdoors
Prices: 25-30 euros, wine excluded
All major credit cards

DA MARIO ENOTECA DELLO SCHIOPPETTINO

🍲 Trattoria
Via XXIV Maggio 16
Tel. 0432 713004-713222
Closed Monday and Tuesday
Open: lunch and dinner
Holidays: in July
Seating: 45
Prices: 30 euros, wine excluded
All major credit cards, Bancomat

Allo storione, an osteria that gets better all the time, is situated at the point in which the province of Pordenone borders with Veneto and the Meduna and Livenza rivers. About 60 years have gone by since Bruno Buzzi, the father of the present owner Giacomo, opened the place after deciding he didn't want to cook sturgeons for friends only any more. Today, assisted by his mother, wife and uncle, Giacomo welcomes guests to the spacious dining room complete with fireplace. In the meantime, he has also converted an old granary in front of the restaurant into a 40-room hotel, the Dall'Ongaro.
Mushrooms, artichokes, radicchio di Treviso, asparagus and meadow herbs are the most used ingredients in the kitchen. The menu is read out as opposed to written mainly because it changes frequently according to market availability. The **tortellacci** filled with vegetables and ricotta, the **strichettoni** with spring herbs or **salsa pevarada** (a typical Venetian sauce made of fowl livers, soppressa, pork and herbs) in autumn and, in general, all the pastas are handmade. For main course, generous portions of **game**, brochettes of mixed roast meats, braised meats and **free-range chicken**. Booking ahead, it's also possible to taste **sturgeon** in guazzetto, in carpaccio or baked in the oven. The desserts are home-made too: we recommend the crostatas and cream puddings.
To drink, a tolerable house wine and a few local wines. It's also possible to taste good wines, cured meats and cheeses at the well-stocked enoteca in the family hotel.

There's a lot of talk today about autochthonous vines, so it seems prophetic that in the 1970s, the inhabitants of Prepotto should decide to protect Schioppettino, a wine made with grapes cultivated only in this tiny area of the Colli Orientali. One of its most enthusiastic supporters was and still is Marco Grassi, who hosts an exhibition of the best Schioppettino wines every year in spring, in this restaurant, which his father Mario opened in 1979. And, unless you would prefer to choose a bottle of the more famous Friuli wines, Schioppettino is mainly what you will drink here, in this delightful trattoria where Marco (front of house) and his wife Gioia (in the kitchen) are now assisted by their son Giacomo and daughter-in-law Anna.
The food reflects the changing seasons and what the market suggests, but the maialata, a sumptuous tray of **pork** (filet, chine and rib) cooked in the oven with wild fennel, garlic and a sprinkling of Sauvignon, is always on offer. Alternatively, as a main course, you can have **pork loin**, **baked smoked veal shank** and cooked ham, chine of pork with pepperoni, **lamb**, **boned and stuffed guinea fowl**, a vegetarian fagottino and a **frittata** flavored with a mixture of about a dozen field herbs. Depending on the time of year, sclopìt, asparagus or mushrooms will be used for sauces for the homemade **gnocchi** or will turn up in **risottos**, orzotti and in a dish that combines three different grains (rice, barley and spelt) that may be prepared in winter with sausage or fresh salami. Among the first courses, we should also mention the **tortello with Montasio and smoked ricotta** and the crespelle with leeks. Gioia's desserts are exquisite.

PULFERO

AL VESCOVO-SKOF

Restaurant/3-Star hotel
Via Capoluogo 67
Tel. and fax 0432 726375
E-mail: info@alvescovo.com
Internet: www.alvescovo.com
Closed Wednesday
Open: lunch and dinner
Holidays: February
Seating: 60 + 50 outdoors
Prices: 25-28 euros, wine excluded
All credit cards , Bancomat

Once a staging post, now a superb trattoria shaded by chestnut trees with view of the River Natisone. The adjacent wellness center also looks onto the river. The hotel, open all week, has rooms outfitted with wood furnishings and serves a buffet breakfast.
Of the more traditional dishes, we remember **brovada** (fermented turnip) **and bean soup**, chestnut and mushroom soups, pumpkin gnocchi, gnocchi with rocket and smoked ricotta and **biechi with duck sauce**. Excellent meat dishes include **rabbit with herbs** or with seuka apples, **braised Savoy cabbage with pork ribs**, wild boar and venison. Try also **polenta obiajena** and **stakanje**, gently fried potatoes and vegetables with vinegar. Tradition extends to the puddings, with offerings such as **struki lessi**, crostatas with homemade preserves and apple strudel.
The wine cellar stocks a host of top regional bottles and a decent house wine. For a minimum stay of 3 days in a double room, half-board is 40 euros per person, full-board 45.

• 4 single, 14 double or triple rooms with bath, TV, 2 with balcony • Prices: single 42, double 60, triple 67 euros; breakfast 5 euros per person • 2 rooms accessible to mobility challenged. Uncovered internal parking. Small pets welcome. Owners always reachable • Bar with TV area, restaurant. Garden with play area for children, terrace. Spa with sauna, jacuzzi and solarium

RAGOGNA
San Giacomo

CASA ROSSA AI COLLI

Holiday farm
Via ai Colli 2
Tel. 338 8895548
E-mail: info@casarossaaicolli.it
Internet: www.casarossaaicolli.it
Open all year

Alessandra Negretto and Renzo Zandegiacomo, recently a champion skier, have created a comfortable agriturismo in a large farmhouse on San Giacomo Hill, built in the early 1900s for the Counts of Porcia. The rooms are simply yet elegantly furnished, with extensive use of wood. A buffet breakfast is served in a large room with a fireplace in the middle and consists of freshly baked bread, jams and excellent cakes made by the owner, locally made honey and, on request, savory fare. The house is surrounded by fields, fruit and olive trees and small shady woods for romantic walks. Visits to the local archeological museum and the nearby Tagliamento Park are not to be missed. You'll also find it hard to resist the temptation to taste the famous San Daniele prosciutto.

• 6 double rooms, with bathroom, TV, modem connection • Prices: double room single use 40 euros, double 70, breakfast included • Credit cards: all, Bancomat • Facility accessible to the mobility challenged. Covered external parking. Small pets allowed. Owners always reachable. • Breakfast room, with corner to relax. Grounds

RAVASCLETTO

BELLAVISTA

☞ Restaurant with hotel
Via Roma 22
Tel. 0433 66089
Closed Thursday
Open: lunch and dinner
Holidays: November
Seating: 130 + 40 outdoors
Prices: 28-35 euros, wine excluded
All major credit cards

The green Conca di Ravascletto lies in the heart of Valcalda, which links the But and Degano valleys. The town is dominated by the Crostis, Arvenis and Zoncolan mountains, and their east-facing slopes are always sunny and make the area one of the most popular skiing resorts in the region. In warmer weather, there are trails of varying difficulty for hikers or mountain bikers. Traditions in Ravascletto are kept up not only between the old stone walls of its dwellings but also in a simple and tasty cuisine characterized by the inventive use of mountain produce that the local women used to enhance with spices and dry fruit bought in winter from the cramars – the traveling salesmen of the time.
Antipasti at Bellavista include smoked goose breast, lardo in balsamic vinegar or bresaola with porcini. Try the **fagottini di crespelle with radic di mont**, ravioli with marjoram, mezzelune with wild herbs and ricotta di malga, canederli with melted butter and speck, **plum gnocchi**, **cjarsons di Monaj** – made using as many as eighteen different ingredients – and, in the fall, tagliatelle with porcini and **barley and beans** based on nonna Graziella's old recipe. Main courses are always served with buckwheat polenta and include venison, **spare ribs**, veal stew, **brovade e muset** and roast pork shank. Don't miss homemade pastries like strudel, strawberry or blueberry tart and **pita**, a traditional dessert made from apples.
The wine list is limited; the local grappas infused with cinnamon, licorice or herbs are more interesting.

REMANZACCO
Cerneglons

AI CACCIATORI

☞ Traditional osteria-trattoria
Via Pradamano 22
Tel. 0432 670132
Closed Monday
Open: lunch and dinner
Holidays: from mid-July to end-August
Seating: 50
Prices: 15 euros, wine excluded
No credit cards accepted

Just a few kilometers from Udine, this traditional osteria is a meeting place for a taglietto (glass of wine) and a plate of cured meats, a friendly chat, a glance at the newspapers or a game of bocce on the adjacent court – once an essential part of all trattorias worthy of the name.
It would be truly difficult to find a more genuine place than this, with its bar counter, main room with fogolar, or hearth, and simple, rustic dishes.
The food prepared by the imposing Marcello focuses on Friuli right from the start: home-made cured meats, thick **frittata** with fresh herbs and a majestic, highly original **frico**. As soon as the crust forms, it is tossed into the fersoria (the traditional frying pan) so that the steam trapped beneath swells into a soft "cushion" filled with melted cheese. The menu always has bean soup, home-made pasta with game sauces, polenta, salami cooked with onion and vinegar, **brovade and muset**, broiled and roast poultry and **lidric cuinciat cun lis fricis** (chicory and pork scratchings). Reserve ahead for superb **game** dishes. Local hunters often turn up with hares, woodcocks, partridges, pheasants and boar to eat here.
Delightful table service always ensures enjoyable meals. Colli Orientali del Friuli wines are offered at honest prices; even the house wine is a superb accompaniment to these rich dishes.

RIVE D'ARCANO
Rodeano Basso

17 KM NORTHWEST OF UDINE

SAN DANIELE DEL FRIULI
Aonedis

27 KM NORTHWEST OF UDINE

ANTICA BETTOLA DA MARISA

▽ Traditional osteria
Via Coseano 1
Tel. 0432 807060
Closed Thursday and Saturday for lunch
Open: lunch and dinner
Holidays: 15 days in January, 20 in September
Seating: 50 + 120 outdoors
Prices: 30 euros, wine excluded
All credit cards, Bancomat

DA CATINE

▽ Trattoria
Località Aonedis 78
Tel. 0432 956585
Closed Monday evening and Tuesday
Open: lunch and dinner
Holidays: January 1-10, 2 weeks in August
Seating: 50
Prices: 25 euros, wine excluded
All credit cards, Bancomat

A cellar boasting 850 wines from all over the world with minimum mark-ups is the main draw of this traditional osteria, but the quality of food and service are equally appealing. Roberto Palmieri, co-owner with his wife Rita, who assists him in the kitchens, has clear ideas: the inside rooms are used from October to April, while guests are served May to September outside.

In winter, there is a set menu that changes every month. Dishes are based on fresh local produce and medicinal herbs. In summer the menu consists exclusively of grilled meat, such as superb local sausages and steak, as well as Angus, chianina and ox cuts. Winter menus all begin with an excellent **San Daniele prosciutto** and you can choose from antipasti, first and main courses with side dishes, including magnificent Carnia recipes like **gnocchi** di Sauris and **cjarsons** di Paluzza and traditional Friuli specialties like barley and beans, sclopìt soup, **lamb with fennel**, **broiled goose**, **shin of pork** and **salami cooked in vinegar**.

No meal here is complete without some dessert, coffee with a dash of liqueur and a busulùt (small glass) of grappa.

The new approach at this traditional trattoria began when Caterina and Luca joined their parents Raffaele and Nella and introduced significant improvements in the service and the wine list. The dining room has recently been modernized but without taking away from the classic feel of the old trattoria. The excellent wine list is changed weekly with various Friuli selections also served by the glass; the house wine is delightful.

Menus here usually begin with a tasting of traditional frico, while antipasti include **trota regina**, a traditionall product of the area, served with butter on warm toasts, San Daniele prosciutto, venison prosciutto and Friuli salami with polenta. First courses include not only the traditional **minestra di orzo e fagioli** (barley and brean soup) but also **risotto with sclopit** (silene), **pumpkin gnocchi with melted butter and ricotta cheese**, quiche or pasticcio with seasonal vegetables (such as asparagus, courgettes, aubergines, spinach, peppers or mushrooms). Main courses include trout in a tart sauce (the filet is cooked with herbs and lemon), soft **frico** (quiche with Montasio cheese, onion and potatoes), **brovada con muset** (sour turnips), **stewed veal guanciale**, game and bollito misto. A selection of interesting cheeses are served with honey and mostarda.

There is a large choice of desserts. Particularly recommended: apple strudel, hazelnut cake and biscuits served with a glass of Ramandolo. Book in advance for weekends.

🏺 Arcano, via del Cristo 8, sells a range of organic products, baked in a wood-fired oven, including wholemeal bread, plum cake with hazelnuts and raisins and torta della nonna.

DA SCARPAN

Restaurant
Via Garibaldi 41
Tel. 0432 943066
Closed Tuesday evening and Wednesday
Open: lunch and dinner
Holidays: 2 weeks in July
Seating: 40
Prices: 32 euros, wine excluded
All credit cards

L'OSTERIA DI TANCREDI

Osteria-cantina
Via Monte Sabotino 10
Tel. 0432 941594
Closed Wednesday
Open: lunch and dinner
Holidays: two weeks in July, 1 in January
Seating: 20
Prices: 20-25 euros, wine excluded
Credit cards: MC, Visa, Bancomat

Beneath the cool porticos of via Garibaldi, near the Sant'Antonio church and its frescoes by Pellegrino da San Daniele, this restaurant – renovated in 2000 – serves a delightful selection of local dishes under the discreetly expert guidance of Luigina and Angelico (the owner).

The menu is seasonal and some dishes are only available at certain times of year: examples are frico in flaky pastry with mushrooms, polentina with melted cheese, crespelle with green asparagus or **allo sclopìt**. Antipasti include – of course – San Daniele prosciutto and the less well-known fil di fumo trout, lightly smoked locally. Alternatively, the speck salad and trout fantasia are excellent. First courses include tagliatelle alla San Daniele, **spaghetti with fil di fumo trout**, crespelle with basil and Montasio, vegetable soup and **risotto with radicchio and sausage**. Main courses include **frico** with potatoes and onion, **lamb chops with mint**, **capretto** and trout filet with vegetable caponata. Other frequent dishes include **baccalà alla vicentina** and **tripe**. Luigina's desserts include pistachio crème brulée and mint-flavored bavarese with chocolate.

The wine list is interesting and is made up primarily of regional labels. The house wine is also excellent.

Inaugurated three years ago, the osteria that Silvia Clocchiati dedicated to the memory of her father Tancredi is in a 16th-century building in the town center. The single room is boldly decorated to contrast with the exposed ancient walls and has a large counter and tables for tasting wines and hams and for meals. Here, Silvia presides over the airy, peaceful atmosphere with skill and professionalism, overseeing the kitchen, the counter and the tables, assisted by the kind Didì.

The menu of local dishes makes the most of top quality ingredients. The most classic antipasto is an excellent, 18-month aged **San Daniele ham**, accompanied by Montasio or goat's cheese and vegetables preserved in olive oil, but there's also Sauris speck, **Friuli lardo**, smoked San Daniele **trota regina**, **sarde in saor** (sardines), pheasant paté and local cheeses, including the rare Asìno. First courses include **tagliolini alla San Daniele**, spelt soup and summer vegetables, **barley and beans**, spaghetti with Tagliamento trout capers and fresh tomatoes, **apple gnocchi** with cinnamon, smoked ricotta cheese and melted butter as well as other pastas with seasonal sauces. Main courses: **free-range** chicken **casserole**, **frico** with potatoes and onion, **goulash with potatoes**, Friuli **sausage with polenta**, **baccalà** in winter and tagliate and carpaccio of beef with vegetables in summer. Cheese is served accompanied by conserves. Portions are generous but be sure to leave some room for Silvia's desserts, perhaps the **apple strudel** or cookies to dip in Verduzzo.

More than 200 wines, mostly from Friuli, are also served by the glass.

SAN DORLIGO DELLA VALLE
Pesek

10 KM EAST OF TRIESTE ON SS 14 OR A 4

NUOVO HOTEL PESEK

🚪2-3-Star Hotel
Località Pesek 69 a
Tel. 040 226294
Fax 040 226889
E-mail: info@hotelpesek.it
Internet: www.hotelpesek.it
Open all year

The Karis family has managed this hotel-restaurant in a beautiful corner of the Carso, right on the border – today virtual – with Slovenia for many years. It is housed in separate blocks, one of which is classified as 2-Star and the other 3-Star. The original building houses a large restaurant (mostly local cuisine, 22-30 euros per person, excluding wine) and seven rooms. Only a few yards away they've added an attractive new building with 13 rooms and a pizzeria. Breakfast includes both sweet and savory fare and is either buffet style or served at the bar counter; the reading and TV room is equipped with a bookcase and fireplace. As you step out of the hotel, you find yourself immediately in a Carso setting against the backdrop of Mount Concusso. The equally attractive inland area of Istria is easily reachable by car or bicycle.

• 2 single and 18 double or triple rooms, with bathroom, some with terrace and satellite TV • Prices: single 45-70 euros, double 70-90 (13-18 euro supplement for extra bed), breakfast included • Credit cards: all, Bancomat • Facility partly accessible to the mobility challenged. Off-street parking. • Small pets allowed. Reception open from 7 am to midnight • Restaurant. Pizzeria. Reading and TV room. Garden

SAN GIORGIO DELLA RICHINVELDA
Rauscedo

18 KM NORTHEAST OF PORDENONE

IL FAVRI

🍲 Osteria
Via Borgo Meduna 12
Tel. 0427 94043
Closed Sunday evening and Wednesday
Open: lunch and dinner
Holidays: 10 days in January and 10 in August
Seating: 40 + 40 outdoors
Prices: 25-30 euros, wine excluded
All credit cards except DC

The cornerstone of the Rauscedo economy is the production of vine cuttings: it seems that at least half the vine strains planted all over the world originated here. Historic nurseries include that of a branch of the D'Andrea family – a common surname in these parts – but Mauro's family preferred the restaurant business and he has run this osteria since 1993. The atmosphere is delightfully informal and he offers traditional cuisine and a fine wine cellar with 300 labels.

The menu changes often but always starts things off with **San Daniele prosciutto**, **soppressa** and other typical cured meats to be enjoyed with wood-fire baked bread. Winter offerings include **boiled prosciutto with cren**, **pitina** (meat balls tossed in cornmeal and smoked) **with vinegar** and **toc' in braide** (polenta with melted cheese). In the summer you can order carpaccio, burrata and sometimes fish antipasti. **Zuppa di fagioli with San Daniele prosciutto** always figures on the menu, as well as grain- or vegetable-based soups. First courses are served with fresh pasta, like **ravioli** with spinach, smoked ricotta and poppy seeds, tagliatelle, **bigoli**, lasagne and **pumpkin gnocchi**. Main courses include **frico**, **salami with vinegar**, sausage, pork or **veal guanciale** and **stew**, as well as frittatas, **baccalà** and cuttlefish. Desserts include almond cake and excellent fruit tarts.

🍴 In **San Giorgio della Richinvelda** (3 km), you'll find the Leon butcher's shop, Via Poligono 1, where they offer traditional cured meats. In **Valvasone** (7 km from Rauscedo), you'll find wonderful bread and cakes at Claudio Di Cocetta, Via Roma 2.

SAN QUIRINO

ALLE NAZIONI

🍲 Traditional osteria
Via San Rocco 47
Tel. 0434 91005
Closed Sunday for dinner and Monday
Open: lunch and dinner
Holidays: in August, 15 days in January
Seating: 50
Prices: 25 euros, wine excluded
All credit cards, Bancomat

This restaurant opened way back in 1873 and was initially attached to a grocery store. Tastefully renovated and decorated with interesting paintings and sculptures, it is managed with great attention to detail by the Canton family. Adjacent to the osteria is the famous La Primula restaurant, and chef Andrea Canton, whose cooking is notable for its balanced, delicate style, works in both these places. This style shines through even in the simpler dishes of the varied menu of the osteria, which draws upon tradition and choice ingredients.
Antipasti include cured meats from local producers, as well as home-cured mackerel and anchovies from the Upper Adriatic. Of the first courses, try the toothsome **tagliatelle with mushrooms**, asparagus, or salami sauce (in winter), **soups** made with onions, beans or vegetables or **gnocchi with smoked ricotta**. Winter main courses are hearty: there's **tripe**, baccalà, steamed cuttlefish and the ever-present **brovada con muset**. The summer menu includes stuffed peppers, pickled cold chicken and marinated beef carpaccio. The cheese board also focuses particularly on local producers; if available, don't miss the salted cheese and **Formadi frant**. The desserts – especially the semifreddi – must not be missed.
The excellent wine cellar has regional and national labels, as well as carefully selected international wines at fair prices.

SAURIS
Sauris di Sotto

ALLA PACE

🍲 Trattoria
Via Roma 38
Tel. 0433 86010
Closed Wednesday, never in summer
Open: lunch and dinner
Holidays: 3 weeks in June and 10 days in November
Seating: 50
Prices: 28 euros, wine excluded
All major credit cards

The first houses in Sauris – many built entirely of wood – surround this palazzetto, home to Trattoria Alla Pace, managed since 1804 by the Schneider family. Franca takes care of guests in the dining room, while her husband Vinicio chooses the finest local produce. Their three children have all divvied up the rest of the work: Andrea helms the kitchen, Mauro is in charge of wines and Elena making desserts.
Begin with excellent **cured meats**: smoked speck, culatello and ham accompanied by olive oil-preserved vegetables such as **radicchio di monte**. Don't miss the montasio **frichetti** and the frittatas flavored with seasonal herbs. First courses feature fresh pastas like pumpkin gnocchi, **cjarsòns with herbs and ricotta**, pasta e fagioli, nettle soup, pasta with speck and leeks, **blecs made with buckwheat** with roe deer sauce or porcini mushrooms in late summer. In winter, try the **mues** (soft polenta) **with ricotta affumicata**. The menu continues with traditional **frico** with potatoes and onions, **musetto con brovada**, scaloppina alla saurana, **goulash** and venison stew. The traditional local cheeses are top notch. Elena's desserts include apple pie with filed mint and a strudel with apples, raisins and pine nuts.
The wine list offers the best labels from Friuli and noted Tuscan producers, but there's also excellent local beer. Go with some of the grappa if you're considering a digestivo.

🍷 Prosciuttificio Wolf, Sauris di Sotto 88, sells hams smoked with beech wood, juniper and aromatic herbs, speck and other cured meats.

PA' KRHAIZAR

Hotel-restaurant
Frazione Lateis 3
Tel. 0433 86165
Closed Wednesday, never in high season
Open: lunch and dinner
Holidays: March and October
Seating: 30
Prices: 25-30 euros
All credit cards except AE, Bancomat

RIGLARHAUS

Trattoria/2-Star hotel
Località Lateis 3
Tel. 0433 86049-86013
Fax 0433 86049
E-mail: riglar@infinito.it
Internet: www.sauris.com
Closed Tuesday, never in summer
Open: lunch and dinner
Holidays: January 10 to February 10
Seating: 40 + 40 outdoors
Prices: 25-30 euros, wine excluded
All major credit cards, Bancomat

After ten years of being shuttered and a series of management changes, Pa' Krhaizar returns with a trattoria next to a delightful hotel. In 2004, Sergio Milanato and his wife Mariangela fell in love with this place and took over its management after working for some time in Tuscany and Veneto. The terrific cuisine that came out of their kitchen soon brought it into the public eye. Pasta and desserts are made in-house and, when possible, ingredients are purchased locally. And so, there are **prosciutto**, pancetta and lardo from Sauris di Sotto and salted cheese and **Formadi frant** from the neighboring hill farms. Summer boasts plentiful **mushrooms** served as antipasti, such as porcini crostoni. You'll also find **toc' in braide**, prepared according to an ancient recipe. First courses include gnocchi with radicchio and speck, **cjarsòns** (tortelli with a slightly sweet stuffing), **peintlan**, rough spaghetti with speck, smoked caciotta, radicchio di montagna (Slow Food Presidia) and beef sfilacci. The grilled braciola di cervo and **frico** are served with truly excellent **polenta**. Mention must also be made of **dunkatle**, a sauce with diced salami and smoked pancetta mixed with cornmeal. Desserts, in particular the **apple strudel** and fruit tarts, are well worth tasting.
The wine list is rather limited but nevertheless ensures successful pairings. There are no great labels but you'll get honest wines at fair prices.

A hundred meters above Pa' Khraizar, Pietro Crivellaro's Malga Alta Carnia shop offers cheese (the fresh kind never before July) and ricotta affumicata from nearby hill farms for tasting and purchase.

You'll find Paola Schneider's hotel at more than 1,200 meters above sea level,. The rooms, available all week long, are simple and comfortable and,in the morning, you'll be served a continental breakfast. Half-board for a double room is 36-46 euros, full-board 40-52. The northern influences emerge at the table in the form of cured meats served as antipasti, often lightly smoked and flavored with mountain herbs. Tempting first courses include **Sauris gnocchi** with speck and melted butter, **triangoloni with formadi frant** (aged cheese) and walnuts, **cjarsòns** with butter and foraged baby greens. Follow with **venison stew** with polenta, ossobuco, **leg of lamb with wild thyme** and scaloppine with green asparagus, available in season. For side dishes, you can choose from salads, various cooked vegetables and **cabbage with crunchy pancetta**. Berries from nearby fields are turned into cakes, ice-creams and panna cotta.
The Friuli wines on offer here are worth a try, and the list includes a few selections from further afield too. The beers are terrific.

• 1 single and 6 double rooms in the main building, 7 double rooms in adjacent building • Prices: single 34-40, double 55-75 euros, breakfast included • 1 room accessible to mobility challenged. Parking in front. Small pets welcome. Owners always reachable • Bar, restaurant. Living room with fireplace. Patio, play area for children

SAURIS
Sauris di Sotto

SAVOGNA D'ISONZO
San Michele del Carso

SCHNEIDER

DEVETAK

2-Star Hotel
Via Roma 92
Tel. 0433 86010-86220
Fax 0433 866310
E-mail: sas.sauris@genie.it
Closed for 3 weeks in June and 2 in November

Trattoria-gostilna
Via Brezici, 22
Tel. 0481 882005-882488
Closed Monday and Tuesday
Open: for dinner, lunch also on Saturday and Sunday
Holidays: vary
Seating: 70 + 25 outdoors
Prices: 28-35 euros, wine excluded
All credit cards, Bancomat

The main town of Sauris at an altitude of 1,200 meters jealously preserves the customs and speech of the Carinthian community that moved to this valley in the Middle Ages. A recent building continues the tradition for hospitality of the Alla Pace locanda, originally opened in 1804. The old name has been inherited by the restaurant (excellent Sauris cuisine at 25-30 euros per person, excluding wine; half-board costs 55 euros) that the Schneider family manages only 200 meters away from this small, cozy hotel. The rooms are tastefully furnished in the traditional local style and every morning guests can look forward to a generous buffet breakfast of sweet and savory fare. The main attractions in the surrounding area are Lake Sauris, a myriad of paths that can be covered by mountain bike, museums and local artisan food producers (this is the home of a famous prosciutto). You can count on a warm welcome from Franca and Vinicio Schneider.

• 7 double rooms with bathroom, TV • Prices: double room single use 44-50 euros, double 65-75, breakfast included • Credit cards: major ones, Bancomat • Public parking 50 meters away, garage (4 spaces). No pets allowed. Owners always reachable • Breakfast room, TV room

The Devetak family has managed to combine Italian and Slovenian culinary culture and traditions here since 1870. Gabriella carefully selects all ingredients: pasta is made fresh every day, bread is baked in the home oven, vegetables and aromatic herbs are picked fresh from the garden looked after by father Renato. Ustili proudly explains dishes to diners.
The menu follows the seasons. Spring brings vegetable pies with leeks and garden herbs and wild asparagus sauce, **tortino di Montasio** with sautéed asparagus and egg gratin, turkey stuffed with creamed apples and ricotta with a mustard cream, **mlinci with supeta** (lightly baked pasta with stewed hen), **asparagus soup** with egg stracciatelli, pork with wild fruit sauce, **goulash** and ox cheek with a sauce of peppers and sweet paprika. Summer menus offer tomato and yogurt cream, **gnocchi made with bread and sheep's milk ricotta** with herb-cheese sauce and turkey and pears with honey. Cold first courses include white onion pie with fonduta and black truffles, pan dolce and cotechino with horseradish sauce and balsamic vinegar, **selinka**, a minestrone made with celery and ham bones, beetroot gnocchetti with yellow pumpkin and smoked ricotta, **potato strudel** with smoked ricotta and red chicory, **baccalà** and a trio of poultry. There's a delicious selection of desserts: **krasko pecivo** with amoli sauce, gelato with bitter cocoa and panna cotta with strawberries and peppermint.
The wine cellars – carved out by hand by father Renato among others – contain more than 14,000 bottles from 200 producers from all over the world.

SGONICO

SGONICO
Devincina

MILIC

Holiday farm
Località Sagrado 2
Tel. 040 229383
Fax 040 229383
E-mail: info@zagrajski.com
Internet: www.zagrski.com
Open Friday through Sunday, 10 am to 10 pm
Holidays: January 10 to February 10, several days in August
Seating: 80 + 30 outdoors
Prices: 12-25 euros, wine excluded
No credit cards accepted, Bancomat

SAVRON

Restaurant
Località Devincina 25
Tel. 040 225592
Closed Tuesday and Wednesday
Open: lunch and dinner
Holidays: last week of February, first week of September
Seating: 100 + 60 outdoors
Prices: 22-28 euros
All credit card, Bancomat

Sagrado is a diminutive village in the Trieste Carso area, set among lovely vineyards, stone walls and views of the sea. The two families here have dedicated their lives to agriculture and to farm hospitality. One of them, the Milics, offer traditional dishes with Carso and Austro-Hungarian influences. The bright rooms outfitted with period furniture have functional bathrooms. Breakfast includes home-made pastries, preserves, fruit juices, cured meats, local cheeses and, on request, hot drinks.

The menu offers a variety of preparations closely tied to the seasons and to what the garden has to offer. Hearty dishes are served up in every season, just as the locals would have it. Start with **prosciutto in bread crust, bean and barley soup**, grilled meat, **cevapcici** with polenta or with **potatoes in tecia** and raw milk cheeses. The bread, baked here, is particularly delicious, and the assortment of desserts remarkable: our advice is to try the boiled **boiled strudel**. The wines, some of the best of the Carso, are also made here, some from native varietals such as vitovska, malvasia and terrano, as well as chardonnay. As a digestif, choose from the many home-distilled aromatic grappas. Service is speedy and efficient.

There are numerous osterias and trattorias in the Carso area around Trieste. Although true wine and food excellence is a rare find, the average eating experience hereabouts ranks pretty high. Savron is located in the green area just outside the village of Prosecco. Michele Labbate manages the establishment with the help of her enthusiastic staff and upholds the area's culinary traditions with the cookbooks of Katarina Prato, a historian of the wine and food of the last century. Dishes are inspired by Austro-Hungarian traditions.

Start with the classic **jota**, or **bread gnocchi** that are served with game sauces during hunting season. These dishes are followed by roast wild boar or **pork shank**, vitello lardato, breadcrumb-crusted **pork loin**, **venison with blueberry preserves** and strudel with leeks and courgettes. The substantial country platter includes **bread gnocchi with pork cooked in beer** as a first or second course. Desserts include various types of **strudel**, including **ricotta and apple**.

Service is courteous and low key. There are two small rooms and tables set outside in summer. The wine list has several local wines and a fair selection of national and international labels.

1 single and 4 double rooms with bath • Prices: single 30, double 60 euros, breakfast included • Building accessible to mobility challenged, 1 camera furnished for their use. Uncovered internal parking. Small pets welcome. Owners always reachable • Restaurant open from Friday through Sunday. Kitchen, living room

AL BACHERO

DA AFRO

Osteria
Via Pilacorte 5
Tel. 0427 2317
Closed Sunday and Monday for dinner
Open: lunch and dinner
Holidays: 3 weeks between June and July
Seating: 80
Prices: 16-18 euros, wine excluded
No credit cards accepted

Osteria-trattoria/3-star hotel
Via Umberto I 14
Tel. and fax 0427 2264
E-mail: osteria.daafro@tin.it
Closed Sunday
Open: lunch and dinner
Holidays: two weeks in January
Seating: 45 + 20 outdoors
Prices: 26-32 euros, wine excluded
All credit cards, Bancomat

Managed by Enrico Zavagno and his wife Graziella, this osteria, though renovated and expanded, retains its original features: a comfortable setting to enjoy in the company of others while chatting, drinking at the bar or eating at your table. It is very busy on Saturday – market day – and still exudes the atmosphere that has distinguished it for more than a century, when it began as a bar serving wines and spirits as well as selling olive oil from Puglia.
Dishes include cured meats accompanied by baby onions in balsamic vinegar or crostoni with anchovy sauce to be eaten together with a good glass of house wine – mostly reds like cabernet franc or merlot delle Grave. If you prefer a complete meal, **baccalà** and **tripe with polenta** are the most popular specialties served year round. The standard antipasto is **mature cured ham** from nearby **San Daniele**. First courses: spaghetti with meat or tomato sauce, potato gnocchi and the traditional **barley and bean** soup. These dishes are joined by main courses such as **beef stew with potatoes** and **salami all'aceto**, and sometimes there's roast chicken too. Meals end with the local **cheese** or desserts accompanied by a glass of Zibibbo or Moscato di Pantelleria. Digestivi are usually served at the historic bar.

Da Afro is open all week. Situated in an 18th-century building, the rooms are airy and tastefully appointed. Breakfast is 'international' with both sweet and savory fare. The osteria here is as traditional as they come and, thanks to Dario Martina's extraordinary passion for local products, the menu faithfully reflects seasons and traditions.
Begin your meal with **prosciutto crudo di San Daniele**, bresaola with herbs and, in the right season, sardine or salmon carpaccio. In the spring, you'll find vegetables in abundance in **soups**, **risottos** and savory tarts, while in the winter, there's **bean soup** and pasticcio, or stew. Main courses: try the excellent **pickled salami**, **tripe**, **brovade e muset** (turnips fermented in marc accompanied by a cotechino-like sausage). Alternatively, there are a few dishes that draw less upon Friuli but are equally interesting, such as **Venetian-style liver**, roast pheasant with prosciutto crudo and, on Thursdays in winter, bollito misto. For dessert, choose from sorbets, crema catalana and fruit crostatas.
The wine list is quite good, with excellent selections from Friuli and beyond.

• 6 double and 2 triple rooms with bath (jacuzzi tub or shower) air conditioning, minibar, safe, satellite TV, modem outlet • Prices: double room single occupancy 60-65, double 100-110, triple 120-130 euros, breakfast included • 1 room furnished for use of mobility challenged. Uncovered internal parking. Small animals welcome. Reception desk open from 7 am to midnight • Bar, restaurant. Living room. Outdoor lounge. Boules court

STREGNA
Zamir

STREGNA

27 KM NORTHEAST OF UDINE

31 KM NORTHEAST OF UDINE, 14 KM FROM CIVIDALE

ANGELINA

SALE E PEPE

🗝️ Bed and breakfast
Località Zamir 3
Tel. 0432 723389
Open from Easter to end of December

🍲 Trattoria
Via Capoluogo 19
Tel. 0432 724118
Closed Tuesday and Wednesday,
winter also Monday and Thursday
Open: dinner, lunch also on Saturday and Sunday
Holidays: end of June and end of September
Seating: 40
Prices: 30 euros, wine excluded
All major credit cards

The farmhouse, situated in the green fields and forests of the Natisone valleys, was carefully renovated in 2000 by Maria and Giorgio Chiabai. It now serves both as their home and as an attractive B&B. The guest rooms are comfortable and are furnished with antiques. Bathrooms are functional. You'll be eased into sleep by the sound of the burbling Erbezzo that runs by the end of the garden. On waking you'll find a generous breakfast, with traditional, mainly sweet fare. In the surrounding area there's no lack of places to visit on foot, by mountain bike or on horseback. In addition to Cividale del Friuli, worth visiting are the sanctuary of Castelmonte (5 kilometers away) and the San Giovanni d' Antro hypogeum complex (7 kilometers away).

• 3 double rooms, with bathroom • Prices: double room single use 25-28 euros, double 50-55, breakfast included • Credit cards: none • Off-street parking. Small pets allowed (only in the garden). Owners always reachable • Breakfast room, lounge with TV corner. Veranda. Garden

Teresa in the kitchen and her husband Franco in the dining room and cellar have brought new life to the village where this osteria is the vital center and meeting place. This cozy, sophisticated place serves traditional recipes brought up-to-date but always made with local produce.

The many dishes on the menu are often written in local dialect, but don't worry, Franco is happy to explain every dish. Ricotta and cheese from the valley is accompanied by polenta or potatoes served in various ways with the antipasti and main courses. The spring menu features wild nettles and asparagus, while in the fall **mushrooms** (porcini, chiodini and finferli) are used to embellish dishes. First courses include **brisa** (soup with grated white pumpkin in sour yogurt with beans), creamed barley with elderflower, **màrvice** (pasta with asparagus), **soups** like **brovade** (sour turnip) and **blinis di grano saraceno** with cabbage. In season, there are also excellent **game** dishes; alternatively, try **boned rabbit stuffed with** wild herbs and **rabbit stew with plums wrapped in speck**. There are many delicious desserts: **struki lessi** served with melted butter, a basket of wild fruit, mint and strawberry cream or chestnuts with persimmon fruit sauce, a crunchy semifreddo or torta settembrina.

The cellar is impressive: the wines come from highly regarded production areas in Friuli and are carefully selected.

SUTRIO

62 KM NORTHWEST OF UDINE, 15 KM FROM TOLMEZZO ON SS 52 BIS

62 KM NORTHWEST OF UDINE, 15 KM FROM TOLMEZZO ON SS 52 BIS

ALLE TROTE

🍲Trattoria
Via Peschiera 5
Tel. 0433 778329
Closed Tuesday, never in July or August
Open: lunch and dinner
Holidays: 2 weeks in March and 3 weeks in October
Seating: 70 + 30 outdoors
Prices: 22 euros, wine excluded
All credit cards

DA ALVISE

🍲Trattoria with rooms
Via I Maggio 5
Tel. 0433 778692
Closed Wednesday
Open: lunch and dinner
Holidays: two weeks in July, 1 in September
Seating: 40 + 25 outdoors
Prices: 20-25 euros, wine excluded
No credit cards accepted

From Tolmezzo, cross the Noiaris Bridge and follow the clear indications to reach Sutrio. This peaceful verdant haven stands on the banks of the But tributary, which supplies the water for the historic trout farm that provides the fish for many of Alle Trote's dishes. The trattoria has a large, tidy and bright dining room and a porch where meals are served outdoors in summer.

Antipasti include fried salmon trout, carpaccio of salmon trout and the more traditional smoked trout with crostoni. And since we are in the Carnia mountains, after all, alternatives focus on mixed local cured meats or sliced smoked beef. First courses: risotto with seasonal herbs, **spaghetti with trout sauce**, fresh-made fusilli with zucchini and eggplant, **onion soup** and ricotta gnocchi with zucchini and squash blossoms. You might also find **cjarsòns** (tortelli with ricotta, cocoa, herbs and pine nuts, topped with smoked ricotta and melted butter) and **goulash soup**. The main courses include **trout** – grilleden papilotte, breaded or even in burgers. Meat dishes include beef either grilled or with green pepper, beef carpaccio with celery and fresh goat cheese and venison with grilled vegetables. Soft **frico** is always available. For dessert, try the pear tart with ricotta or red currant, apple strudel and panna cotta with yogurt and a chocolate sauce.

The wine list has Collio and Colli Orientali labels and a few Tuscan and Trentino wines.

Proceeding from Tolmezzo along the state road towards Austria, you come to Sutrio, a village famed for its woodworking. More recently, the center has been made more welcoming by the renovation of many buildings. Da Alvise is a pleasant stop-off after a walk, and you will be welcomed by Elena Di Ronco and her husband Enzo. Their trattoria is simply furnished and cozy, and there are also five rooms for overnight stays.

A glimpse of the menu or a chat with Elena, assisted in the kitchen by Aurora, is enough to convince diners that home cooking is kept very much alive here. Antipasti include local cured meats and **frichetti** (pies with cheese, potatoes and onions). For first courses, there are freshly made pastas, such as tagliatelle, panzerotti, potato gnocchi, **blecs** (maltagliati) or **cjarsòns** and stuffed Carnia tortelli topped with butter and smoked ricotta. While there are numerous versions of this dish, Elena's recipe particularly stands out because of her shrewd use of herbs and flavorings. Then we have the classic **herb frittata**, **veal stew**, pork filet, sausages and various vegetable "pasticci", all prepared with great care and served with taste. In season, **mushrooms** gathered from nearby take pride of place. For dessert, there are fruit tarts, fritters and – of course – **strudel**.

The wine list has a fair selection of labels primarily from Friuli, Tuscany and Piedmont.

🍲 At Caseificio Sociale Alto But, Viale Martiri 1, you'll find excellent traditional Carnia cheeses.

TARCENTO
Zomeais

DA GASPAR

🍲 Trattoria
Via Gaspar 1
Tel. 0432 785950
Closed Monday and Tuesday
Open: lunch and dinner
Holidays: first week of January, 1 month in summer
Seating: 50 + 10 outdoors
Prices: 25-28 euros, wine excluded
No credit cards accepted

Climbing from Tarcento – a delightful town that sits on a moraine – along the right bank of the Torre river, you pass through dense woods until you get to a renovated old mill, standing above a tributary of the Torre. Here you'll find Da Gaspar, a tastefully furnished trattoria overseen by sisters Valentina (in the dining room) and Gabriella (in the kitchen). Piercarlo Cereda, Valentina's husband and the sommelier, alternates between the kitchen and the dining room. His hand-written wine list has as many as 300 labels from Friuli and elsewhere in Italy. The menu offers impressive seasonal, local specialties.

The homemade **cured meats** (a variety of pork preparations) kicks off a list of antipasti that also includes vegetable pies and soufflès. When in season, asparagus can be found all over the menu – the asparagus rolled in pancetta are superb. Pasta is always freshly made. Try the **cjarsòns**, **pumpkin gnocchi**, **risotto** or pasticcio **with sclopìt** or mushrooms. Traditional main courses include **roast veal shank**, **game** and **goulash**. The frittatas with seasonal herbs are also very good.

Cakes and cookies are both made in-house; the latter are ideal with zabaglione or a good glass of Ramandolo.

TARCENTO
Loneriacco

OSTERIA DI VILLAFREDDA

🍲 Trattoria
Via Liruti 7
Tel. 0432 792153
Closed Sunday dinner and Monday
Open: lunch and dinner
Holidays: 3 weeks in January, 1 in August
Seating: 70 + 30 outdoors
Prices: 30-35 euros, wine excluded
All credit cards, Bancomat

You'll find this lovely farm building in the hills near Tarcento, a few kilometers from the road between Udine and Tarvisio. Inside the rooms are plain but comfortable and the kitchen is ably managed by Luca the cook, who works with prime quality ingredients in compliance with regional traditions.

Let his wife Barbara guide you through the meal. You can start with delicious cep mushroom flan with Montasio fondue, **frico**, **frittata with herbs**, lardo with polenta and salami. Firsts range from vegetable soup with basil and **bean and barley soup** to Villafredda **cjalsòns**, crêpe flan with vegetables and herbs and **orzotto** with asparagus. Mains include porcini mushroom fritters, fried chicken legs, calf's kidneys, **duck with polenta**, fillet of pork with herbs, **shin of pork** and, in winter, tripe. The cheeses deserve a special mention, from the fresh ricotta to the Montasio, from the **Latteria sot la trape** with grape jelly to Formadi frant with chestnut honey. Desserts are all home-made and feature apple strudel, pear tart, strawberry cake with rhubarb and semifreddo of amaretto with chocolate sauce.

Good though the wine list is, it's also worth tasting the house wine, produced using organic methods in the Grave area.

88 KM NORTHEAST OF UDINE ON SS 13 OR A 23

EDELHOF

🛏🛎3-Star Hotel
Via Diaz 13
Tel. 0428 644025
Fax 0428 644735
E-mail: info@hoteledelhof.it
Internet: www.hoteledelhof.it
Holidays vary

TSCHURWALD

🍲Osteria
Via Roma 8
Tel. 0428 2119
Closed Wednesday for dinner and Thursday
Open: lunch and dinner
Always open in season
Seating: 40 + 20 outdoors
Prices: 30-33 euros, wines excluded
All major credit cards except DC, Bancomat

Tarvisio, a crossroads leading to Austria and Slovenia, is the region's most popular vacation and winter sports center. A town of Roman origin, Tarvisio lived through difficult times in the Middle Ages and many times it came under siege or was pillaged by the Turks. This comfortable hotel is rather like a typical country house, and the owners have intentionally given a somewhat Gothic look and feel to it. The furnishings in the common areas, heated by large majolica heaters, are rustic but elegant. The rooms are airy with hand-painted furniture in the Val Canal style. The Italian-style buffet breakfast is excellent, with coffee, tea, milk, yogurt, fruit juices, jam, honey and homemade cakes. Good local dishes are served in the nearby restaurant (average 30 euros per person, excluding wine).

• 10 double, 4 triple or four-bed rooms and 2 suites, with bathroom, terrace, satellite TV • Prices: double room single use 80 euros, double 90, triple or four-bed 120-150, suite 150, breakfast included • Credit cards: all except DC, Bancomat • Facility accessible to the mobility challenged. Off-street parking, garage (5 spaces). Small pets allowed. Reception open 24 hours a day • Bar, restaurant. Lounge. Conference room. Garden, terrace

A passion for fine food, a proven team and a continuing search for quality are the defining characteristics of the Tschurwald family. At their osteria, Fabio and sister Emanuela oversee the dining room while their mother Gabriella helms the kitchen. The bar area serves a variety of snacks with interesting wines (the cellar here has regional and national labels), but it is worthwhile to sit down in one of the two delightful dining rooms for a complete meal.

Antipasti of cured meats (Sauris speck, San Daniele cured ham and salami in balsamic vinegar) are followed by fresh pasta, like tagliatelle, spelt tagliolini and **caserecci** served, depending on the season, with radicchio and sausage, artichokes, leeks and prosciutto crudo or **mushrooms** (especially the gialletti variety) foraged by the Tschurwalds. Other first courses include **potato gnocchi alla carnica**, **barley and beans** and vegetable soup. Among the main courses we recommend **szegediner goulash** (pork, knödel and sauerkraut), as well as veal stew in white wine, **grilled venison chops** with apple sauce, and chicken with rosemary. There is also an interesting cheese board – don't miss the **Asìn**.

Desserts include a fine chocolate cake with walnuts, tiramisù or, during festive periods, cookies and **pinze** (a delicious sweet bread).

🍯 In **Ugovizza** (10 km), Statale Pontebbana 24, you'll find the Cooperativa Allevatori Val Canale, which sells excellent local cheeses such as Montasio, Malga, Stravecchio, Latteria and Ricotta as well as smoked cured meats.

TORREANO
Montina

MARIE-THÉRÈSE

🔑 Bed and breakfast
Via Zorutti 19
Tel. 0432 715106-339 4420813
Fax 0432 715106
E-mail: roiattiwalter@libero.it
Closed November 1-March 31

Teresa and Walter Roiatti run this B&B in their country house and can guarantee you absolute peace and quiet during your stay. The rooms are big and furnished in rustic style, with wooden floors and ceilings and wrought iron bedsteads. Breakfast is traditional and offers seasonal fruit grown by the owners, homemade jams and cakes and a variety of drinks; on request you may also have cheeses and cured meats. Cividale del Friuli is only three kilometers away and can easily be reached by bicycle (available from the hosts). There you'll be able to admire the cathedral and visit the National Archeological Museum, the small Longobard temple and the 'devil's bridge' over the River Natisone.

• 1 single, 1 double and 1 triple room, with bathroom, TV (on request) • Prices: single 26 euros, double 55, triple 78, breakfast included • Credit cards: none • Covered off-street parking. No pets allowed. Owners always present. • Breakfast room, reading room with TV corner. Garden

TREPPO CARNICO

CRISTOFOLI

🍲 Restaurant/2-Star hotel
Via Matteotti 10
Tel. 0433 777018
Fax 0433 777408
E-mail: albergocristofoli@libero.it
Internet: www.albergocristofoli.it
Closed Sunday evening and Monday, never in summer
Open: lunch and dinner
Holidays: none
Seating: 150
Prices: 30 euros, wines excluded
No credit cards accepted, Bancomat

Treppo Carnico is a stronghold of traditional Carnic cuisine. This place, already a locanda in the mid-1800s, has been run by the Craighero family for 40 years. The rooms (available all week) are simple and a fogolâr (open hearth) heats the lounge. You are served a continental breakfast or something more substantial on request. For a stay of at least 3 days, half-board is available for 38 euros, full-board for 42.
A meal here begins with cured meats, speck salad, guanciale and walnuts with balsamic vinegar, and the typical **toç' in braide** (salami and sausage with whole grain polenta). Follow this with gnocchi with herbs, pumpkin or potato gnocchi, buckwheat **blecs**, **cjarsòns**, and bean soup. Then there's **frico** with polenta, rump with Schiopettino, roasts and splendid **game**, always accompanied by polenta. The local cheeses are also worth ordering. In summer, mushrooms show up everywhere on the menu in classic dishes. Puddings include chocolate salami, **strudel**, walnut mousse, apple pie and crostata.
The wine cellar offers a wonderful selection of Friuli wines and several Piedmontese, Tuscan and French labels as well. They also distil their own liqueurs here with locally foraged herbs.

🔑 • 7 single rooms with shared bathroom, 6 double and 2 triples with bathroom, some with balcony or terrace • Prices: single 22, double 42, triple 56 euros; supplement for breakfast according to what is consumed • Uncovered internal parking, garage for motorbikes (5 spaces). No pets allowed. Owners always present • Bar, restaurant. Living room, TV room

TRIESTE

ANTICA TRATTORIA VALERIA

🍲 Trattoria with rooms
Strada per Vienna 52
Tel. 040 211204
Closed Tuesday
Open: lunch and dinner
Always open in season
Seating: 80
Prices: 25-32 euros, wines excluded
All credit cards, Bancomat

ANTIPASTOTECA DI MARE

🍲 Osteria
Via della Fornace 1
Tel. 040 309606
Closed Sunday for dinner and Monday
Open: lunch and dinner
Holidays: vary, in summer
Seating: 40
Prices: 18-28 euros, wines excluded
No credit cards accepted

This delightful establishment has been serving its customers since 1904. The heart and soul of the trattoria is Signora Milli, now joined by her son David and young but skilled kitchen staff. Opicina is the place where the Trieste and the Carso's well-to-do come to retire. There are several small tables outside if you wish to enjoy a coffee or a glass of wine. The large entrance opens onto a bar where wines are served, and there are two dining rooms. The tables are set with serviceable glasses and linen and the waitstaff is scrupulously efficient. If she has time, Signora Milli is happy to talk about local cuisine and the culinary traditions of these borderlands.
Traditional food is always featured here. There is the classic **jota**, stuffed cannelloni, **barley and cabbage**, potato **gnocchi** and **plums**, biechi with rocket and **spinach roulade**. Follow any of these with grilled meat, **fried chicken**, **roast shin**, **kipfel with potatoes** or **potatoes in tecia**. In season, mushrooms and truffles come to the fore in the kitchen. Desserts include strudels that vary with the season, chestnut roulade and **torta rigojanci**.
There is a fine, fairly priced list of wines and spirits.

Roberto and Gianni are a splendid team, always ready to enjoy themselves and faithful interpreters of the Trieste motto: 'Everything is fine as it is.... don't worry about the rest'. Their osteria, close to San Giusto Cathedral, is a landmark for lovers of local cuisine based on underappreciated seafood. Roberto's mother ensures that the antipasti – true to its name, the osteria serves many of these – are excellently prepared.
In a cozy room furnished with wooden tables and chairs and perhaps a few too many nautical trimmings, the osteria serves dishes such as **sardoni** au gratin or **in savor**, a salad of barley and calamaretti, **schile and girai fritti**, spuma di molo (a type of hake), sardelline with toasted bread and polenta, zuppe di mare, mussels prepared in various ways, **folpeti** and cuttlefish. Finish off your meal with the excellent **palacinke**, crêpes filled with jam or hazelnut cream. Since neither Gianni nor Roberto particularly enjoy wine, only one house wine is available. Service is speedy and efficient, but if you are not in a hurry, Roberto will take the time to tell you passionately detailed stories about Istrian and Trieste sailing traditions.

🍯 In nearby **Trebiciano** 237 (3 km from Opicina), the Azienda Settimi e Ziani produces limited quantities of highly-prized single-varietal honeys. The marasca honey is particularly unusual.

🍯 At the Pescheria Al Golfo di Trieste, Strada del Friuli 10, Lorenzo and his family offer the best and freshest fish catches every day.

BUFFET BIRRERIA RUDY

Trattoria-buffet
Via Valdirivo 32
Tel. 040 639428
Closed Sunday
Open: 9am-12am
Holidays: between July and August
Seating: 50
Prices: 15-18 euros
All credit cards, Bancomat

This very popular spot for enthusiasts of beer and local cuisine has for many years served dishes prepared according to tradition. Known to older Trieste inhabitants as Alla Spaten, it is something of a shrine to Bavarian beer. The trattoria is situated in the heart of the Theresian quarter and has a single room with walls partially lined with wood and wood tables and chairs. The tables fill up from early morning with clients who come for the boiled meats. Service by dynamic young waiters is quick and efficient. Rudy is very popular with younger clientele, particularly in the evening, although there are regulars who have been coming here for decades for the Mitteleuropäische atmosphere.
Boiled meats include tongue, cotechino, **porzina**, **Cragno** or Vienna luganighe with plenty of mustard and horseradish, accompanied by **potatoes in tecia** and sauerkraut. Not to mention **jota**, **bread gnocchi with goulash**, soups with bobici or beans, **carré of smoked pork**, **boiled ham baked in bread crust**, polpette and roast meats.
Unsurprisingly, very few wines are to be found here – take advantage instead of the numerous beers on offer. Sometimes there are also musicians that perform live.

Enoteca Bere Bene, Viale Ippodromo 2-3, offers local, national and international wines and spirits. At Pasticceria Bomboniera, Via 30 Ottobre 3, you'll find traditional pastries like presnitz.

BUFFET DA MARIO

Trattoria-buffet
Via Torrebianca 41
Tel. 040 639324
Closed Saturday and Sunday
Open: 8am-10:30pm
Holidays: last week of May
Seating: 25 + 20 outdoors
Prices: 18-30 euros, wines excluded
No credit cards accepted

Buffet Da Mario is a longstanding home of local cuisine in the city. Time seems to have come to a standstill here. There are just two rooms: in one, guests crowd at the bar counter all day long, while the other offers seating for lunch and dinner. It has been managed for some years by a Genoese family who, with local help, uphold the culinary features that have made the place so famous.
Even in the morning, you'll find dishes like boiled ham, **porzina**, **cotechino** and various types of **luganiga** – all served, if you wish, with mustard and horseradish. Other preparations include **jota**, **minestra di bobici** or seasonal vegetables, **baccalà**, whipped or **with potatoes in rosso**, muscoli in Terrano wine and seafood dishes that vary depending on the catch that day.
Service is courteous and polite. In summer, diners can eat outside under a gazebo. The range of bottled wines is rather poor and deserves more attention given the quality of the cuisine.

Granmalabar, Piazza San Giovanni 6, is a small and cozy place with a good choice of coffee and an impressive list of wines served by the glass or to purchase to take home. They also organize interesting and popular tastings with producers.

BUFFET DA SIORA ROSA

Trattoria-buffet
Piazza Hortis 3
Tel. 040 301460
Closed Saturday and Sunday
Open: 8am-8pm
Holidays: between September and October
Seating: 55 + 20 outdoors
Prices: 10-25 euros
All credit cards

DA GIOVANNI

Trattoria-buffet
Via San Lazzaro 14
Tel. 040 639396
Closed Sunday
Open: 8am-3:30pm, 4:30pm-10pm
Holidays: three weeks in August
Seating: 25 + 40 outdoors
Prices: 10-22 euros, wines excluded
No credit cards, Bancomat

Off the beaten track but close to the Rive and now undergoing radical but much appreciated restyling, this place has long been familiar to enthusiasts of the local cuisine. Overseen by the Facco family, this trattoria serves interesting dishes even early in the morning, as per tradition in these parts. In one of the trattoria's two rooms, you'll find a bar counter serving wines by the glass accompanied by food. The other at the rear offers dining in a peaceful, quiet atmosphere. In summer, meals are also served outside among the trees in Piazza Hortis, part of a pleasant pedestrian area. Service is informal but courteous and professional.

Classic boiled cuts of meat are available virtually all year round for people seeking a cheap but substantial snack. These might include **porzina**, tongue and Vienna and Cragno **luganighe** as well as **potatoes in tecia**, grilled and stuffed vegetables, roast chicken, **pork shank** or veal shank and seasonal soups such as **jota**. **Steamed cuttlefish** and **baccalà** are the main dishes, along with other less traditional but equally delicious fare.

The wine selection is limited. Since beer is a good match for the local specialities and there is no lack of enthusiasts, perhaps the beer list could also be extended.

Pastificio Mariabologna, Via Battisti 7, offers a huge selection of dry and stuffed pasta, torte salate and takeaway dishes. At Panificio Jerian, Via Combi 26, they sell all kinds of bread made with different kinds of flour. You can visit Penso, via Diaz 11, for traditional Trieste pastries.

The arrival of Robertina, the young scion of the Vesnaver family, has brought an attractive dose of happiness and serenity to this renowned trattoria. All the action here takes place in a single room with a corner counter where warm boiled ham is always on offer, as well as cured prosciutto and a huge mortadella. Close by, dishes ready to be served are displayed in a window. Small barrels of house wine are kept in the back. The kitchen is run with a firm hand by Signora Vesnaver, assisted by her daughters, brother-in-law and other competent staff at the counter and the tables. Sometimes during lunch brother Bruno turns up. He is a well-known figure in the city and is often involved in the family's other gastronomic activities.

The food here focuses on boiled meats, such as cotechino, **porzina**, tongue and various types of sausage, all complemented perfectly by a bread roll, mustard and horseradish. Other delights include **nervetti**, **tripe**, **goulash with potatoes** either roasted or **in tecia**, **sardoni in savor**, stewed beans, roasts, meatballs, seasonal pasta and **gnocchi with apricots**. The fritto misto is also popular. On Fridays, there's **baccalà**.

Service is quick and courteous. The selection of bottled wines is limited but some labels are also served by the glass. In summer, lunch and dinner are served outside under large market umbrellas so that you can admire the Art Déco features in this attractive part of the city.

L'ALBERO NASCOSTO

ALLE ALPI

3-Star Hotel-Residence
Via Felice Venezian 18
Tel. 040 300188
Fax 178 2230629
E-mail: info@alberonascosto.it
Internet: www.alberonascosto.it
Open all year

Trattoria
Via Veneto 179
Tel. 0432 601122
Closed Sunday for dinner and Monday
Open: lunch and dinner
Holidays: August 15-30
Seating: 55
Prices: 20-24 euros, wines excluded
All credit cards, Bancomat

This large old palazzo has been carefully restructured to create a pleasant hotel of discretion and good taste, in line with the intention of its owner, Aldo Stock. It's located right in the center of the city, though in a rather quiet area, and has two entrances: one door leads directly to the rooms and another to the reception, an area that doubles as a small reading room with a bar where you can sip a coffee or glass of wine and even have breakfast (sweet croissants, fruit juices, etc.). The rooms are far larger than you would normally expect and have wooden beams running across the high, airy ceilings, while the walls are partly bare stone: in short, mini-apartments with sofas, armchairs and kitchenette, (during Easter, on August 15 and during the regatta period, prices can be as high as 135 euros per room). Some of the bathrooms have a window, and all are spacious and well-equipped.

• 1 single and 9 double rooms, with bathroom, air conditioning, kitchenette, mini-bar, TV, modem connection • Prices: single 65-75 euros, double 95-115, breakfast included • Credit cards: all except DC, Bancomat • Facility accessible to the mobility challenged, 1 room designed for their use. Public parking nearby, garage 200 meters away (10 euros per day), public garage 50 meters away (15 euros per day). Small pets allowed. Reception open 8am-8pm. • Bar, wine cellar, breakfast and reading room

Alle Alpi is in the southern suburbs of the city in a not particularly attractive area. But on entering, you'll find an immediate, pleasant sensation of warmth and familiarity. The two rooms are both richly furnished with paintings and unusual sculptures: the first holds the bar, the second is dominated by a large hearth that owner Alberto Zilli uses to grill meat, whatever the season. Milan works in the kitchen, while Patrizia and Mirko serve diners with flair and the utmost courtesy.
The mainstays of the menu – which otherwise changes with the seasons – are **sottoli in agrodolce** served as an antipasto, **fagiolata** and grilled meat. For antipasti, there are local cheeses and cured meats as well as asparagus au gratin with speck, **grillled** with honey and speck and orzotto with bresaola. Customary first courses are minestra or **risotto with sclopit**, **tagliolini** or other freshly made pasta with **San Daniele** or gorgonzola and walnuts, **gnocchi with herbs**, crespelle with asparagus and **barley and beans**. Steak and tagliata and suckling pig roasted whole (must be reserved ahead) and kid are among the main courses. There is also baccalà and some dishes with fresh seafood, including octopus salad, fritto misto and **steamed cuttlefish with peas and polenta**. Desserts can be accompanied by one of the many liqueurs on offer.
As for wine, the good house wine is matched by a reasonable selection of well-known Colli Orientali and Collio labels at fair prices.

AL RISTORANTINO

Trattoria
Via Bertaldia 25
Tel. 0432 504545
Closed Sunday
Open: lunch and dinner
Holidays: variable
Seating: 30
Prices: 30 euros, wines excluded
All major credit cards

AL VECCHIO STALLO

Osteria
Via Viola 7
Tel. 0432 21296
Closed Wednesday, Sunday in July and August
Open: lunch and dinner
Holidays: 20 days in August, Christmas
Seating: 100
Prices: 20-25 euros, wines excluded
No credit cards accepted

This small, well-run trattoria is situated near Viale Ungaria in the city center. Pietro Zanuttig is a well-known local restaurateur who serves dishes cooked by his mother Liliana. Her experience ensures the high quality of the seasonal menus.

One of the dishes most loved by the people of Udine is the exceptional **mixed fried vegetables**, each vegetable coated in delicate, crunchy, perfectly fried batter. Antipasti include **soppressa with sauteed polenta, rabbit salami with olives**, ossocollo di Sauris, local cured ham and a vegetable terrine. First courses highlight family classics such as **onion soup** and **gnocchi with red herbs**, but there are also barley and asparagus soup and fagottini with zucchini flowers and pistachios. Choose from a broad choice of meats, including tagliata with rosemary, **smoked carré with horseradish**, chicken with seasonal vegetables and liver alla veneziana. Alternatively, you can ask for grilled vegetables. The cheese board is serviceable. There's a good choice of desserts to conclude your meal. Try chocolate fonduta with fruit, apple fritters with cinnamon and ice-cream, semifreddo with coffee or chocolate and orange mousse. The wine list offers many good labels.

20 years have gone by since brothers Mario and Maurizio Mancini opened this 1950s-style osteria in what was once a post office. Fair prices and a happy, relaxed atmosphere mean the osteria is crowded at tajut time – when Friuli takes its aperitivo – and the large counter is crammed with delicious snacks such as the classic **nervetti with onions** and **sardelle in saor**.

Once seated at table, a strictly traditional menu will be offered with friendly aplomb. Meals start with quality local cured meats that, in summer, may even be served as a main course. Numerous, very tasty firsts: the most typical are gnocchi di Sauris, **sfregolòz** (gnocchetti prepared with spinach), **mignàculis** (gnocchetti made with potatoes and flour) topped with meat sauce, **cjalsòns** and **barley and beans**. The **roast pork shank** and the classic **frico with potatoes** are two mainstays among main courses, often joined by **baccalà with polenta** and veal alla carnica. In winter, among the side courses, don't miss the **potatoes in tecia**. Finish off with Coppa Stallo (a high-calorie variant of tiramisù) with a slice of **gubana** with grappa or **apple strudel**.

The wine selection could be improved. Service is friendly and easy-going but at times can be a little too slow.

📖 Il Laboratorio del Dolce di Danilo D'Olivo, Vicolo Sottomonte 2, produces traditional confectionery such as Quaresima biscuits, Cresima biscuits, gubana and other cakes with chestnuts, walnuts, almonds, ricotta cheese.

2 KM FROM CITY CENTER

CASA RENATA

🛏️○ Bed and breakfast
Via Tissano 8
Tel. e fax 0432 600232
E-mail: casarenata@libero.it
Internet: www.bbcasarenata.it
Closed 5-20 January and 1 week in March, May, November

GIARDINETTO

🍷 Trattoria-cantina
Via Sarpi 8
Tel. 0432 227764
Closed Sunday for dinner and
Monday in October through March
Open: lunch and dinner
Holidays: July 15-31
Seating: 40
Prices: 32-34 euros, wines excluded
Credit cards: Visa, Bancomat

This B&B, surrounded by greenery and located in an area well served by public transport, has been created by tastefully restoring a wing of an old stable with a barn. The rooms under the mansard roof are in a style that the owners define as rural-romantic, and are named by the color of the furnishings. Renata Adami Beltramini, the hostess, is always courteous and happy to satisfy the needs of her guests. Breakfast is continental style and is served in the bright kitchen: you'll be offered coffee, tea, milk, yoghurt, cereals, fruit juices, jams, honey and cakes. By autumn the restructuring of a room with a stove and the reading and TV area should be completed. On request, bicycles and guided tours can be arranged.

• 2 double rooms and 1 suite, with bathroom, air-conditioning, mini-bar, satellite TV • Prices: double room single use 40 euros, double 60-62, suite 62-66, breakfast included • Credit cards: none • 1 room designed for use by the mobility challenged. Off-street parking. Small pets allowed. Owners always reachable. • Breakfast room, lounge. Grounds

It took years of work for Nicolina Rabassi and her sons Paolo and Giovanni Donadon to restore this trattoria in the very center of Udine. Although small, it is elegantly furnished and very functional. There are two dining rooms; one is just beyond the room used as the wine shop and bar, and the other is located above the entrance. The delightful cellar is also well worth a visit for its great wines and its special emphasis on Friuli (though other fine products from all over the world are not overlooked). A glass of wine is always accompanied by snacks and, at 7pm, a taste of risotto. Start lunch or dinner with cured meats like **San Daniele prosciutto**, local pancetta, Sauris smoked pancetta, **Carnico smoked salami**, lardo with rosemary or **frico with potatoes**. On Fridays in winter, don't miss the baccalà alla vicentina. Alternatively, try the **Formadi frant**, cheese topped with sour cream, or the lukewarm guinea-fowl salad with urtizòns (hops). First courses include spaghetti and maccheroncini with a sauce of zucchini – the squash and flowers – as well as ravioli of sole. Main courses include **lamb chops with rosemary** and beef carpaccio with arugula and shavings of Parmigiano. There is a fine choice of desserts. Be sure to try the mousse with hazelnuts, bavarois with melon and Port wine or chocolate and bitter cherry cake.
Professional and friendly service includes suggestions for wines by the glass or the bottle to accompany each dish on the menu. If you are in a hurry, a set menu offers a pasta dish, vegetables, a glass of wine, mineral water and coffee for just 12.50 euros.

LOCANDA AL MUNICIPIO

🍲 Trattoria with rooms
Via Glizoio di Mels 4
Tel. 0432 985801
Closed Monday
Open: lunch and dinner
Holidays: 3 weeks in January, 1 in November
Seating: 30 + 30 outdoors
Prices: 25-30 euros, wines excluded
All credit cards

VECCHIA OSTERIA CIMENTI 🍷

🍲 Trattoria/3-Star hotel/Residence
Via Battisti 1
Tel. 0433 750491
Fax 0433 750807
E-mail: vecchiaosteria@libero.it
Closed Monday
Open: lunch and dinner
Holidays: 1 week in July, 1 in Dicember
Seating: 40 + 15 outdoors
Prices: 30-32 euros, wines excluded
All major credit cards, Bancomat

We recommend arriving in Venzone from the east and walking through Porta San Genesio, the best-preserved gate in the city walls and an outstanding example of medieval architecture. The main square is dominated by the elegant Town Hall in a Venetian-Gothic style that dates to circa 1390-1410. The locanda stands alongside the Town Hall. You will be welcomed kindly and promptly by Signora Giordana, who will lead you to a simple yet likeable dining room or, in summer, to the inside garden, where she explains the dishes on a menu that focuses on traditional, local cuisine and seasonal produce.
Local salami, soft polenta with mushrooms and pies with asparagus, arugula or chicory open the proceedings and are followed by seasonal first courses. There are **tortelloni** with sclopit, pumpkin, asparagus, artichokes or radicchio trevigiano, **risottos** with zucchini, squash blossoms or wild herbs, the ever-present **barley and beans** and **pumpkin soup** in the fall. Main courses include tasty, full-bodied dishes such as **tripe** with or without tomato, shin of veal, **roast wild boar**, salt cod, **frico with potatoes** and game. Fresh seafood is only available if you ask ahead. Alessia's desserts include a delicate tiramisù and a divine panna cotta with chocolate or mint.
There's a reasonable selection of wines. The house wine is also good.

The pleasant apartments of the Cimenti family's restaurant are situated in a building that calls to mind the staging posts of old. Breakfast here, made with the traditional produce of the area, is eaten at the bar. Other meals will begin with ardièl di cjase (home-cured lardo flavored with chives), **salam tà l'asèt** and **jote di d'avaste**. Try also **cjarsons**, **macarons cui lòps** (gnocchi stuffed with local apples), **fregoloz di sudri** (gnocchi with seasonal herbs, ricotta and melted butter) and **blecs**. Main courses: **muset e brovade** (in winter), **formadi salàt cu' la meste**, kid's offal and **frite** (wild herbs lightly fried in butter). The cheese selection is particularly good. The small local apples are used to make the desserts here and are served with zabaglione.
The 'acqua del sindaco' (from the municipal acqueduct) is remarkably good, and there is an excellent selection of the best Friuli labels.

🛏️ • 8 mini-apartments (3 with 2 beds, 5 that can take 3 or 4 beds) with bathroom, kitchen, mini-bar, TV; some with terrace or balcony • Prices: double room single use 59-65, double 82-92 euros (22-27 euro supplement for extra bed), breakfast included • 2 mini-apartments accessible to mobility challenged. Uncovered internal parking (12 spaces). Small pets welcome. Management present 6.30am-1am • Bar, restaurant. Lounge. Terrace

🛍️ Just 10 km away on the SS 355 at **Baus di Ovaro** 43 a, the Molino Donada has been making and selling cornmeal since 1500.

VITO D'ASIO
Anduins

VILLA MARGHERITA

🔑Bed and breakfast
Via Fonte Solforosa 10
Tel. e fax 0427 807780-328 4639409
E-mail: villa_margherita@tiscali.it
Internet: www.villa-margherita.info
Open all year

In the valley of the Arzino, an affluent of the River Tagliamento, you find the scattered municipal area of Vito d' Asio and its center, Anduins, a hillside village famous for the curative powers of its sulfurous waters. 300 meters from the source stands Villa Margherita, surrounded by a beautiful garden, built a century ago and refurbished in 1978. The warm, comfortable rooms are furnished with antiques and have wrought iron bedsteads. In addition to the outside space, guests can also use two other rooms to talk and read, and a characteristic tavern with a fireplace. Your courteous host Ivano Zannier will lend you bicycles for excursions in the surrounding area. 800 meters away there's a practice area for rock climbing, and canoeing and fishing are possible in the Arzino.

• 5 double rooms, with bathroom, air-conditioning, mini-bar, TV; 1 mini-apartment with kitchenette • Prices: double room single use 45 euros, double and mini-apartment 60-65 euros, breakfast included • Credit cards: none • Mini-apartment designed for use by the mobility challenged. External parking. Small pets allowed. Owners always reachable • Kitchen. Lounge, reading room. Tavern. Garden. Pool, solarium, small gym

VIVARO
Basaldella

VILLA CIGOLOTTI

🔑4-Star Hotel
Via San Marco 4
Tel. 0427 976083
Fax 0434 976085
E-mail: villacigolotti@hiponet.org
Internet: www.villacigolotti.it
Closed the first 2 weeks in January

Villa Cigolotti is an 18th-century patrician estate in the Magredi area, between Pordenone and Spilimbergo. The complex consists of a main house with an adjacent barn, plus a more classic stone-built outhouse, all within fenced grounds. The common areas include a particularly attractive large central hall decorated with flower-motif stuccos, and the so-called Counts' Room, which is frescoed and has a large marble fireplace. Each of the bedrooms is different, though all are fitted with period furniture and fine ornaments. The generous buffet breakfast offers sweet and savory fare, while the restaurant serves revisited traditional dishes (30-35 euros per person). Cycling excursions are possible (bicycles are supplied by the hotel) as are horse rides (the stables are only one kilometer away).

• 3 single, 21 double rooms and 5 suites, with bathroom (some with jacuzzis), mini-bar, safe, satellite TV, modem connection • Prices: single 65 euros, double 100, suite 120-240, breakfast included • Credit cards: all, Bancomat • 4 rooms designed for use by the mobility challenged. Off-street parking. Small pets allowed. Reception open 24 hours a day • Restaurant. Breakfast room. Reading room. Conference room. Billiard room. Gym, sauna, solarium. Grounds

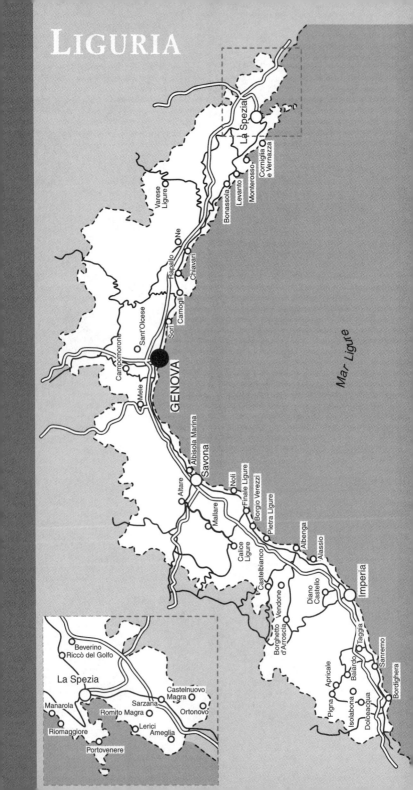

51 KM WEST OF SAVONA, 22 KM EAST OF IMPERIA SS 1 TO 10

4 KM EAST OF SAVONA SS 1 AND EXIT 10

I MATETTI

LA FAMILIARE

Osteria
Viale Hanbury 132
Tel. 0182 646680
Closed Monday, never in July and August
Open: lunch and dinner; August only dinner
Holidays: January
Seating: 40
Prices: 24-28 euros, wine excluded
All credit cards except DC, Bancomat

Trattoria
Piazza del Popolo 8
Tel. 019 489480
Closed Monday
Open: lunch and dinner
Holidays: in November
Seating: 65 + 20 outdoors
Prices: 35 euros, wine excluded
All credit cards, Bancomat

This typical Ligurian trattoria is located on the Via Aurelia east of the center of Alassio. It serves typical regional cuisine and dishes of the day are listed in dialect on a blackboard outside the door. The welcome you receive will be down-to-earth and without frills. On the walls are period photos of classes of children – in Alassio dialect matetti, hence the name of the osteria.

Traditional cuisine is well represented in the menu that changes weekly and follows the rhythm of the seasons. In winter good antipasti are farinata baked in a wood-fired oven or sliced fried **panissa** (made from chickpea flour like farinata). In other seasons you'll find **vegetable pies** and fritters. Soup lovers will enjoy the Ligurian minestrone or the **zemin** (chickpea soup with vegetables and cotiche). Fresh pasta fans can choose from **gasse** (sheets of green lasagna-type pasta) **with pesto**, pansotti with a walnut sauce and **ravioli au tuccu** (meat ragù). The main courses are traditional too: stuffed cuttlefish, **stewed octopus**, **Ligurian-style rabbit**, mixed fried fish platter, **stuffed pilchards**. To end your meal, there's a choice of home-made tarts and delicious **bunetti** (blancmanges). A list of local wines, not many, but all good quality.

The friendship between Giovanni (Stefano) Vassallo and Pina Algerì (of Sicilian origin but brought up in the Ligurian gastronomic tradition) ensures the continuity of this pretty trattoria in a small village famous for its ceramics. The narrow street, the small flower-festooned piazza, the sea just a stone's throw away, the old building and small outdoor eating area make this a very attractive place: the sound cuisine with its blend of meat and seafood dishes does the rest.

The menu features many famous Ligurian specialties, prevalently seafood: **stuffed anchovies**, stewed cuttlefish, anchovy and potato pie, **buridda di stoccafisso** (sometimes also served boiled with potatoes and spices), **trenette al pesto** and traditional **vegetable ravioli**. A meal based on these dishes will certainly keep down the cost (two courses plus dessert about 25 euros), whereas it goes up if you choose **fish ravioli** (excellent) or pasta with seafood sauces (the pappardelle with angler fish are very good), the wonderful **mixed fried fish** or oven-baked fish. Big eaters can start with an antipasto, with a choice of octopus salad, stewed mussels and clams, and marinated tuna or swordfish. As for meat, go for the fillet steak or, even better, **rabbit alla ligure**. To end up, home-made puddings such as blancmanges, tarts, tiramisu.

The wine list covers all the Italian regions with a special focus on Ligurian and Friulian whites. Half-bottles are available.

At Via Neghelli, 43, Pasticceria Briano, excellent confectionery and interesting traditional products, such as baci di Alassio and gobeletti.

ALTARE

QUINTILIO

🍲 Restaurant
Via Gramsci 23
Tel. 019 58000
Closed Sunday for dinner and Monday
Open: lunch and dinner
Holidays: July
Seating: 65
Prices: 33-35 euros, wine excluded
All credit cards

The upper Val Bormida, sadly famous for the ecological disasters that marked its industrial past, is once more becoming an environmental delight (it forms a significant part of Italy's most wooded province, Savona). In the very center of Altare, once famous for its glass production, you'll find the Bazzano family's restaurant, which people living in Savona have long targeted for gastronomical outings. Following recent refurbishment it has somewhat changed its look, though the excellent quality of a cuisine that has always been linked to the local terroir and seasonal produce has been preserved.

The antipasti are partly influenced by nearby Piedmont: so you'll find stuffed peppers, bagna caoda and capon salad. The most representative first courses are also the most traditional ones: **pansotti with walnut sauce**, chickpea zemin, **stuffed lettuce** in stock and oven-baked rice (a traditional Altare dish). It's difficult to choose between the main courses as they're all interesting: among the classics, certainly worth tasting are the **mixed fried platter**, tripe Altare-style and **cappon magro**, difficult to find elsewhere. In season, certain dishes are enhanced by the aroma of local truffles. The rich **cheese board** focuses on Ligurian and Piedmontese products and is truly a delight for the eyes and palate. Among the puddings we advise you to try the ever-present hazelnut cake and delicate blancmange.

There's an extensive wine list featuring mainly Ligurian and Piedmontese labels which you can also purchase to take home in the small wine cellar next to the restaurant.

AMEGLIA
Montemarcello

DAI PIRONCELLI

🍲 Trattoria with rooms
Via delle Mura 45
Tel. 0187 601252
Closed Wednesday
Open: dinner, in winter also Sunday lunch
Holidays: January
Seating: 30 + 10 outdoors
Prices: 30 euros, wine excluded
All credit cards, Bancomat

Montemarcello is one of the prettiest villages in this remote corner of Liguria and from it you can admire both the coastline of Tuscany and the River Magra valley and estuary. The little trattoria is at the entrance to the village, its simple dining room similar to many you would see in local houses, where time seems to stand still. In winter, the rough stone fireplace creates a cozy atmosphere, while in summer you can eat outside by candlelight. The friendly hosts are owner Fabrizio and Lorenzo; Fabrizio's wife, Stefania, rules in the kitchen where she prepares delicate dishes that draw on tradition, but are often enhanced by original touches.

To start, try the vegetable pies, **lardo di Colonnata** with warm focaccia and carpaccio di baccalà with extra virgin olive oil. More traditional first courses comprise **tortelli di ricotta** with basil, borlotti bean soup, lasagna al pesto, spaghetti with mussels, **spaghettoni alla contadina** with red cabbage and potatoes, and an extra virgin olive oil dressing. Main courses feature traditional, inexpensive fish: **stuffed anchovies** either baked or gently fried with spinach instead of the usual potatoes. For meat lovers, breaded rabbit, **roast lamb** or chine of pork with wild fennel.

To end, something off the cheese board or a dessert: **chocolate cake**, stewed cherries with vanilla ice-cream and excellent semifreddi. Good wines and liqueur selection.

🍴 In **Sarzana** (13 km), Pasticceria Gemmi in Via Mazzini sells excellent buccellato and traditional spongata; in the first-floor loggia you can enjoy sweet and savory specialties to the sound of folk music.

APRICALE

APRICUS

☎🔑Locanda
Via IV Novembre 5
Tel. 0184 209020-339 7963193
E-mail: apricuslocanda@libero.it
Internet: www.apricuslocanda.com
Open all year round

The Latin name of Apricale, Apricus, means 'exposed to the sun'. Albanian artisan Artur Kasneci and Dutch manageress Jeanette Van Maiven moved to Apricale where they met in 2003 and decided to renovate a late 19th-century farmhouse to turn it into a locanda. The five comfortable rooms have themed décor, air-conditioning, telephone, mini-bar, satellite TV ... and beautiful views. The suite also boasts a jacuzzi. From the reception area a spiral staircase leads to a lounge with a fireplace where guests can read and relax. The lounge's french windows open onto a large terrace where breakfast is served in summer.

• 4 double rooms and 1 suite, with bathroom, air-conditioning, mini-bar, safe, satellite TV, modem connection • Prices: double room single use 80 euros, double 90, suite 125 (25 euro supplement for extra bed), breakfast included • Credit cards: all except DC, Bancomat • Parking in the immediate vicinity. No pets allowed. Owners always present • Breakfast room, reading room. Garden, terrace

BEVERINO
Casa Villara

CASA VILLARA

☎🔑Holiday farm
Via Castagnarossa 8
Tel. 0187 883356-349 8181269
Fax 0187 884900
E-mail: casavillara@hotmail.com
Internet: www.casavillara.com
Open all year round

Giovanna Simonelli and her husband Vincenzo run this old farmhouse in the wooded hills of Baverino, a small village near La Spezia. From the portico you access the bright, spacious rooms fitted with charming period furniture. From the same portico you also reach the warm, friendly common areas. Guests can relax in front of the fireplace on one of the lounge's many sofas. The dining area with its big rustic tables is the ideal place to savor typical Val di Vara cuisine. The olive oil, honey and homemade pasta are particularly good. When the weather is mild, guests can dine in the lovely garden that overlooks the woods and valley below.

• 2 double and 2 four-bed rooms, with bathroom • Prices: double room single use 40 euros, double 70, triple 95, four-bed 105, breakfast included • Credit cards: none • Off-street parking. Small pets allowed. Owners always present • Restaurant. TV room, reading room. Garden, grounds

BEVERINO
Scortica

LA GIARA

🔑 Holiday farm
Via Federici 15
Tel. 0187 883129-347 9112232
Internet: www.agriturismolagiara.it
Open all year round

In the hills of Beverino, this old farm-house, now tastefully renovated, has stone walls and large windows and rooms that are bright and fitted with solid rustic furniture with views over a wide valley. The owner welcomes her guests in the common area, which comprises two comfortable lounges furnished with wooden tables, all the more attractive thanks to the original stone walls and terracotta floors. Guests can taste typical testaroli with cured meats and cheeses, home-made pasta and barbecued meats. Fruit and vegetables come from the fields and greenhouses behind the main building, and they also produce wine on the farm. For breakfast, guests can enjoy home-baked bread, jams and cakes.

• 2 double and 1 triple rooms, with bath-room, TV • Prices: double room single use 30-40 euros, double 50-60, triple 60-70, breakfast included • Credit cards: none • Facility accessible to the mobility challenged, 1 room designed for their use. Off-street parking. Small pets allowed. Owners always present • Restaurant. TV room. Garden, terrace

BONASSOLA

VILLA BELVEDERE

🔑 3-Star Hotel
Via Ammiraglio Serra 33
Tel. 0187 813622
Fax 0187 813709
E-mail: info@bonassolahotelvillabelvedere.com
Internet: www.bonassolahotelvillabelvedere.com
Open from end of March to early November

Villa Belvedere is an early 20th-century building, once a convent and then a home for underprivileged children, located about 200 meters from the center of the village and the sea front.
Converted into a hotel in the 1960s, it's managed today by Vincenzo Richiello and his wife Barbara Bagnolati. All rooms are en-suite and 16 of them have a sea view. Guests can watch TV in a cozy lounge with veranda, while deckchairs are available in the large garden. The restaurant offers traditional dishes from the Liguria and Campania regions – Vincenzo is originally from Naples. The buffet breakfast is plentiful and offers sweet and savory fare.

• 2 single, 13 double and 4 triple rooms, with bathroom • Prices: single 75 euros, double 98-105, triple 120, breakfast included • Credit cards: all, Bancomat • Off-street parking. Small pets allowed. Reception open 8am-11pm. • Bar, restaurant. TV room. Garden, terrace

AURORA

3-Star Hotel
Via Pelloux 42 b
Tel. 0184 261311
Fax 0184 261312
E-mail: info@hotelaurora.net
Internet: www.hotelaurora.net
Closed from mid-October to Christmas

IL TEMPO RITROVATO

Osteria
Via Vittorio Emanuele 144
Tel. 0184 261207
Closed Sunday and Monday
Open: lunch and dinner, July and
August only dinner
Holidays: first 2 weeks of July, December 9-25
Seating: 30
Prices: 35 euros, wine excluded
Credit cards: MC, Visa, Bancomat

The hotel is located in a quiet area close the town center and the sea (the beach is just 500 meters away). This elegant old building is surrounded by greenery and features spacious, airy lounges with frescoes by Piana. All rooms are fitted with modern furniture and offer all modern comforts. From the terrace you can enjoy stunning views of. The restaurant serves both Ligurian and international dishes. Trips inland and to the Côte d'Azure are organized by the hotel itself. For sports lovers, tennis courts, golf courses and a pleasure harbor are nearby. Rooms are charged at a higher rate during the month of August, at Christmas and Easter, and during the Monte Carlo Grand Prix period.

• 4 single, 24 double rooms and 2 suites, with bathroom, satellite TV; several with air-conditioning • Prices: single 49-74 euros, double 76-128, breakfast included • Credit cards: all, Bancomat • Facility accessible to the mobility challenged, 3 rooms designed for their use. Off-street parking. No pets allowed. Reception open 24 hours a day • Bar, restaurant. Garden, terrace, solarium

'Il tempo ritrovato' (Time Refound) is a literary reference to the two owners' previous lives as booksellers. The book theme can also be found on the table mats, decorated with quotes by famous authors, from Horace to Baudelaire. In the kitchen, Calabria-born cook Franco Cartellà likes to define himself as a perfectionist though rather uptight. His wife Valeria Torchio handles the tables and also organizes the extensive wine list, which includes several distinguished labels.

The menu offers meat and fish dishes that are both equally representative of Ligurian cuisine. Among the antipasti, we can recommend the 'crudo di mare' (three fish carpaccio and sliced tuna), **brandacujon** (creamed stockfish with potatoes), **cappon magro** and **octopus with potatoes**. Then you can move on to tagliatelle with red mullet, tomato and hot spicy breadcrumbs, **straccetti di farro al pesto and pelandrui** (string beans), tagliolini with fish roe and tomatoes, **pastasciutta di trippe**, spaghetti with cuttlefish ink, fish couscous (in winter). Main course dishes vary according to the day's catch: if it's on the menu try the diced fish with zucchini flowers, or grilled swordfish escalope, **spuncia** (baby cuttlefish), rossetti and anchovies. For those who prefer meat, two regional classics: **rabbit alla ligure** and **goat and beans**. Round off the meal with a plate of Alpine pasture cheeses or home-made puddings.

The fresh pasta and bread are made at this osteria with flour from the Marino di Cossano Belbo mill.

BORDIGHERA

BORDIGHERA

MAGIARGÈ

Osteria
Piazza Giacomo Viale
Tel. 0184 262946
Closed: Monday and Tuesday for lunch, never in August
Open: lunch and dinner, summer only for dinner
Holidays: October 15-31, 1 week in February
Seating: 45 + 40 outdoors
Prices: 35 euros, wine excluded
All major credit cards

VILLA SPERANZA

3-Star Hotel
Via Galilei 3
Tel. 0184 261717
Fax 0184 262401
E-mail: hotelvillasperanza@libero.it
Internet: www.hotelvillasperanza.it
Open from mid-April to mid-October and at Christmas

Centuries ago a beautiful slave-girl named Magiargè, the love of a Saracen pirate, died in Bordighera. Not only has this legendary damsel had a statue dedicated to her at the center of an 18th-century fountain near the town hall, but this osteria, managed for ten years now by Mauro Benso, in the ancient fortified quarter is also named for her. The menu offers Mediterranean cuisine with plenty of locally caught fish. In recent months there's been a change in the kitchen (with the arrival of young chef, Aimone Cassini), though the quality of the food has remained unchanged and Paolo and Luisa continue to greet you with their courteous, professional approach front of house. It's a lively, well-designed osteria with a number of brightly colored, pleasantly furnished rooms.

Start with a tasty **marinated fish alla genovese**, octopus cooked in the pan with crunchy vegetables, vellutata di zucchine trombette (in winter, pumpkin) with red mullet sauce, tartare of tuna with broad bean sauce or **brandacujon**. Among the first courses: **fregamai al ragù di moscardini**, lasagne with pesto and chard, rice and baccalà, **ciuppin** (fish soup) and maccheroncini with anchovies. To follow, excellent tuna with Tropea onions, Mediterranean cod on a bed of tomatoes, **stewed bladefish with vegetables** or fillet of white bream with potatoes and olives. Only a few meat dishes: **rabbit alla ligure** or shank of veal allo Sciacchetrà. For dessert, in summer, manbrin (aspic) of watermelon and melon, apple wafers in vanilla sauce and babà with jujube syrup; in winter, chocolate flan with Verduzzo wine sauce.

The wine list is a carefully chosen selection of 500 labels.

This villa, built in the 1920s and originally home to a British ambassador, is surrounded by a large tropical garden and lies only 800 meters from the sea. It has belonged to the Lindinger family for 40 years and is now a hotel. Rooms are bright, tastefully furnished and with all modern comforts. Breakfast offers sweet and savory fare, thus catering for the tastes of both Italian and foreign guests. The German owner speaks Italian, English, French, Spanish, Portuguese and even Indonesian. The in-house restaurant serves typical Ligurian cuisine as well as international dishes. Gluten-free and vegetarian menus are also available.

• 3 single and 9 double rooms, with bathroom, satellite TV • Prices: single 75-90 euros, double 90-110, breakfast included • Credit cards: all, Bancomat • Off-street parking. No pets allowed. Owners always reachable • Bar, restaurant. Garden. Swimming pool

BORGHETTO D'ARROSCIA
Gazzo

34 KM NORTH OF IMPERIA

LA BAITA

Trattoria
Frazione Gazzo 19
Tel. 0183 31083
Open: Friday, Saturday and Sunday,
always in August and Christmas holidays
Open lunch and dinner
Holidays: none
Seating: 80
Prices: 30 euros, wine excluded
All credit cards

Gazzo, a quarter of an hour by car from Pieve di Teco on the main road to Piedmont, is a picturesque village in the Valle Arroscia, which stretches from Vessalico to the plains of Albenga. The Ferrari family have been running this trattoria since 1885 and the latest member of the long line is the current owner, Marco, who is passionately fond of cooking. La Baita is important for the economy of the hamlet, with local farmers supplying the majority of the ingredients. During the summer months, much of the menu focuses on dishes prepared using **wild mushrooms** and **truffles**, all gathered in the woods near the trattoria. Front of house is a young but competent helper, Manuele Donato, who also gives Marco a hand in producing fine olive oil and pleasant Ormeasco wine.

There are many dishes worthy of note: **preve** (stuffed savoy cabbage), tonno di coniglio (shredded rabbit), zucchini flowers with nettle sauce, **ravioli stuffed with borage**, marjoram and other local herbs in Ligurian farmhouse butter, snails gathered in the surrounding countryside and cooked in various manners, panzerotti with Taggia olive paste filling and **rabbit stew**. Several cheeses are produced locally, including the Slow Food Presidium Brigasca sheep's milk variety. Among the puddings, a superb ice-cream made using low-fat yogurt, oil and sugar syrup served with extra virgin Taggia olive oil.

We're happy to say that this year the wine list has been extended considerably, with the addition of good local labels and wines from almost all other Italian regions.

BORGIO VEREZZI

29 KM WEST OF SAVONA SS 1 OR 10

DA CASETTA

Restaurant
Via XX Settembre 12
Tel. 019 610166
Closed: Tuesday
Open: dinner, Saturday and Sunday
never in summer, also for lunch
Holidays: in fall
Seating: 40 + 16 outdoors
Prices: 35 euros, wine excluded
All credit cards, Bancomat

At Da Casetta in Borgio you'll be conscious of a feeling of well-being, and not just because of the pleasant food. First there's the restaurant itself: two tastefully furnished rooms and an outside space on the scenic terraced piazzetta. Plus friendly yet professional service and a very extensive list of wines and spirits. The Morellis, the family who run the place, are experts in making their guests feel at home. So at table Pier, pleasant and with a great sense of humor, his girlfriend Marina and Claudia, the only nonfamily member of staff, are always helpful and courteous, and the service always comes with a smile. The cuisine is Ligurian – dishes are skillfully prepared with great enthusiasm by mamma Elda and her daughter Cinzia – made from produce from the family vegetable garden tended by Giuseppe, head of the family and a farmer. The menu has a marked seasonal bias: we particularly like Da Casetta in spring when it becomes a triumph of artichokes and, from the sea, bianchetti (whitebait).

Start with a mixed antipasto (stuffed vegetables, **vegetable pies**, cheese focaccia, zucchini in carpione…) or with **cappon magro**, a refined dish that combines fish and vegetables (in this case, the meal will cost a bit more). You can continue with **picagge** (or testaroli) al pesto, or with **a walnut** or mushroom sauce, corzetti levantini al ragù, minestrone alla genovese, **ravioli** either with **asparagus** or a peppery hazelnut sauce. For main course, **snails alla verezzina**, **stoccafisso in brandacujun**, cima alla Genovese, stuffed zucchini flowers in tomato sauce or **fish fry alla ligure**. To finish, homemade puddings ranging from sorbets and blancmanges to cakes and pies.

DA VIOLA

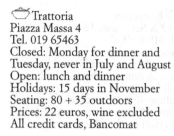

Trattoria
Piazza Massa 4
Tel. 019 65463
Closed: Monday for dinner and
Tuesday, never in July and August
Open: lunch and dinner
Holidays: 15 days in November
Seating: 80 + 35 outdoors
Prices: 22 euros, wine excluded
All credit cards, Bancomat

LA CAMOGLIESE

2-Star Hotel
Via Garibaldi 55
Tel. 0185 771402
Fax 0185 774024
E-mail: info@lacamogliese.it
Internet: www.lacamogliese.it
Open all year round

Secondo Turello, Piedmontese president of one of the first cooperatives inspired by Mazzini, came to Calice Ligure in 1870: he then started a family, obtained a license to serve food and drink and opened this trattoria. The Viola family have now been running it for four generations. In this old building, renovated a few years back, see the medieval well and underground cellar discovered when the work was being done. Roberto and his mother, Gianna, work in the kitchen, while Luca and his wife Michela are front of house. Papà Dino supervises everything and tends the vegetable garden and olive grove that provide many of the ingredients used in the kitchen, among which the oil you'll find on the tables.
There's a fixed-price menu. After a taste of pan fritu, you have a choice of mixed antipasti and the superb and by now rare **cappon magro**. First courses include: **spelinseghi** (typical butterfly-shaped pasta made from buckwheat flour) with **pesto**, ragù, artichokes or mushrooms, pappardelle with octopus and seasonal vegetables, taglierini with cep and finferli mushrooms, ravioli (sometimes filled with fish) and, in winter, **chestnut flour gnocchi** with Brigasca sheep cheese fondue. The wide choice of main course dishes embrace **cima** (stuffed breast of veal), **rabbit alla ligure**, roast or fried fish, **buridda di stoccafisso** and, when in season, wild boar and polenta. If you order in advance, they also do an excellent **Piedmontese mixed fry**. For dessert **gobeletti with zabaglione** and homemade fruit ice-creams; if you go between December and April, don't miss the **giuncata** made from sheep's milk. The reasonably priced wine list has been expanded to include with a number of good labels.

Camogli is an old fishing village on the Golfo di Paradiso. The hotel, managed by the Rocchetti and Laneri families since 1950, is located in a quiet area on the sea front, close to the entrance to Monte Portofino National Park. Rooms are all en-suite and have private telephone, satellite TV and safe; some have a sea view. The nearby La Camogliese restaurant offers special prices for guests staying half-board (extra 18 euros per person) and full-board (extra 30 euros per person).

• 6 single and 15 double rooms, with bathroom, safe, satellite TV • Prices: single 60 euros, double 87 (25 euro supplement for extra bed), breakfast included • Parking 50 meters away (10 euros a day). Small pets allowed (6 euros a day). Reception open 7am-midnight. • Bar. Breakfast room, reading room, lounge

CAMPOMORONE
Isoverde

DA IOLANDA

🍲Trattoria
Piazza Niccolò Bruno 6-7 R
Tel. 010 790118
Closed Tuesday dinner and Wednesday
Open: lunch and dinner
Holidays: August 15- September 10
Seating: 60 + 35 outdoors
Prices: 25-30 euros, wine excluded
All major credit cards, Bancomat

Leaving behind the sea with its salty tang and strong aromas, change to sweeter, more aromatic fragrances by climbing the Val Polcevera and the Val Verde until you come to this village in the Genoa hinterland. Here, on the main square, you'll find this old trattoria which, after falling out of favor for a while, has now got its act together again.
Nothing has changed as far as the cooking's concerned. Dishes are still mainly Ligurian and the place is still run by Silvano with the kitchen in the capable hands of Rosina. What has changed is the atmosphere and it's a real pleasure to see again that genuine passion for food that lately seemed to be lacking.
You can start off with panissa dressed with olive oil and mullet roe, **cuculli di baccalà** (fritters), classic savory flans, **ciulli** (an old Genoa-style recipe based on polenta, red cabbage and beans) or marinated baccalà. Among the first courses, very good **lasagna with pesto** – also used with the trofiette di Recco – green taglierini (with a mix of brain, Parmesan cheese and borage), ravioli with meat sauce, minestrone and **chickpeas in zemin**. Again following tradition, main courses include **lamb with artichokes**, **stoccafisso accomodato** (stewed stockfish), anchovy pie, game (in autumn) and wild mushrooms, when in season. Reasonable selection of cheeses and desserts.
Wines are good and reasonably priced.

CASTELBIANCO

GIN

🍲Restaurant/2-Star Hotel
Via Pennavaire, 99
Tel. 0182 77001
Fax 0182 77104
E-mail: info@dagin.it
Internet: www.dagin.it
Closed Monday, always open in summer
Open: dinner, lunch on Sunday and holidays
Holidays: 2 weeks in-February, 2 weeks in June
Seating: 50
Prices: 28-33 euros wine excluded
All major credit cards, Bancomat

Castelbianco boasts a long gastronomic tradition. The Gin, a restaurant run by the Fenocchios, is very friendly. The rooms (available all week), some overlooking a stream, are en-suite and furnished with antiques. Buffet breakfast.
The antipasti often include the valley's **mushrooms** (fried, sautéed or in a pie), or cream of potato with cep mushrooms (picked in chestnut woods) and zucchini flan with fondue. Tradition lives on in the first courses, mainly consisting of fresh pasta: the **sciancui al pesto** and **pansotti with walnut sauce** are excellent, as are the trofie with zucchini, mint and pecorino cheese, and tagliolini with Caprauna turnips and black truffle (Caprauna turnips and violet asparagus, local Slow Food Presidia, are commonly used). Among the main courses, in addition to **rabbit alla ligure** and **stewed wild boar**, Piedmontese beef undercut and pork with rocket leaves and orange are also worth a mention. The desserts are superb: malted barley blancmange with stewed cherries, Grand Marnier parfait with orange sauce, and bavarois with mint.
The wine list showcases interesting local and national labels.

🛏🔴• 4 doubles, 2 triples and 2 suites, en-suite, satellite tv • Prices: double single use 70, double 95, triple 100-115, suite 115 euros, breakfast included • Outdoor public parking. No pets. Owners always on premises • Restaurant. Reading room

🫒 In **Nasino** (3 km), aty Via Roma 13, the Garello oil mill makes good extra virgin olive oil, pesto, olive paste and sauces.

Castelnuovo Magra

Armanda

🍲 Trattoria
Piazza Garibaldi 6
Tel. 0187 674410
Closed Wednesday
Open: lunch and dinner
Holidays: 1 week in September, during the Christmas season
Seating: 30 + 20 outdoors
Prices: 35 euros, wine excluded
All major credit cards, Bancomat

You'll find this trattoria off the road leading from the plain up to Castelnuovo Magra, just as you enter the old town. It owes its success to its respect for the gastronomical tradition of this area on the border with Tuscany and the special care it takes over the dishes it serves. Front of house is Valerio, in the kitchen, his wife Luciana, who owes everything she has learned to the experience of her mother-in-law, Armanda.
Start with the rosemary-flavored focaccia, **baccalà fritters**, crespelle with asparagus and fondue, **lardo di Colonnata** with chestnut flour bread, vegetable pie and rabbit salad in balsamic vinegar. To follow, **stuffed lettuce in stock**, borage ravioli with pine nut and almond sauce, **pasta and beans Castelnuovo-style**, chestnut flour lasagna with pesto and zucchini, ravioli di baccalà with fresh tomatoes and olives and **panigacci al pesto** or with mushroom sauce. For main course, **stuffed rabbit**, oven-baked baccalà with potatoes and tomatoes, **tripe**, fillet of pork in lardo di Colonnata with red cabbage and apple, lamb in porchetta with herbs and beef tagliata with Alberga artichokes. The best desserts are the typical **rice cake**, semifreddo al torroncino, caramelized pears in red wine, fresh fruit tart with cream and cassatina of dried fruit with hot chocolate sauce.
The wine list is dominated by Ligurian and Tuscan labels, and there's a good selection of spirits.

🛢 Going down towards the plain, Elena and Mirco's Antica Salumeria, at Via Canale 52, sells excellent sausages and home-cured meats, including outstanding prosciutto and mortadella.

Castelnuovo Magra
Colombiera

Cascina dei Peri

🚜 Holiday farm
Via Montefrancio 71
Tel. and fax 0187 674085
E-mail: info@cascinadeiperi.com
Internet: www.cascinadeiperi.it
Closed from January 15-30

This agriturismo, close to the mountains in the green heart of the Lunigiana area and only six kilometers from the Ligurian coast, has been run by Tonino and Mariangiola for 20 years. The farm's eight hectares of land are planted with vines and olive trees and produce extra virgin olive oil and two types of wine. While the place is very comfortable it still has a rustic feel to it. Guests can stay in one of the seven double rooms or in one of the two independent apartments, each with its own two bedrooms, bathroom and kitchen. An area organized for mobile homes is also available. Guests can choose between B&B and half-board. The set dinner menu serves dishes prepared with ingredients from the farm. Breakfast is traditional but also includes home-made cakes and jams.

• 7 double rooms, with bathroom; 2 apartments with kitchen • Prices: double room single use 39 euros, double 70-90, breakfast included; apartment 400-800 euros a week • Credit cards: MC, Visa, Bancomat • Off-street parking. Small pets allowed. Owners always reachable • Restaurant. TV room. Terrace. Swimming pool

CORNIGLIA

A CANTINA DE MANANAN

Traditional osteria
Via Fieschi 117
Tel. 0187 821166
Closed Tuesday
Open: lunch and dinner, summer weekdays only dinner
Holidays: variable
Seating: 25
Prices: 25-33 euros, wine excluded
No credit cards accepted

Mananan is located a narrow alleyway in Corniglia, in the Cinque Terre. Rough stone walls and wooden beams, white marble-topped tables huddled close together, wall shelves lined with home-made jams, liqueurs, mementos from times gone by – all contribute to the warm family atmosphere in ths tiny osteria. The menu is chalked up on a large blackboard and changes daily: interesting comments to dishes are added by owner Agostino Galletti, a Ligurian who can be really amusing when he opens up. You'll be welcomed by his wife Marianne.

Start with the three versions of **Monterosso anchovies**: salt-cured with garlic and oregano, marinated and alla Mananan (marinated with fresh onion). As alternatives, mixed seafood antipasti, mussels alla marinara, cured meats and vegetable pies. There's also a choice between seafood and meat for your first course: spaghetti with seafood – mussels, crab, clams and algae – or tagliolini with ragù or pesto, **pansoti with walnut sauce** or **testaroli with mushroom sauce**. Pan-fried or grilled fish from the day's catch, fried whitebait and excellent **fish soup** appear frequently among the main courses, along with **rabbit alla ligure** with aromatic herbs and local olives. You can round off the meal with the cheese board or one of Marianne's desserts, from delicious semifreddi with seasonal fruit to cantuccini with Sciacchetrà wine.
The wine list is limited and focuses on small local producers.

DIANO CASTELLO

LE RAGANELLE

Holiday farm
Via Case Sparse, Località San Siro
Tel. and fax 0183 401041
E-mail: leraganelle@libero.it
Internet: www.leraganelle.com
Closed from December 12-26

This agriturismo, managed by the Martino family, is located on a green, sunny hill surrounded by old olive trees just 700 meters from the sea. The vegetable garden, orchard and olive grove are all organic and the farm's produce is used in the kitchen. Guests can choose from en-suite rooms, one-bedroom apartments with kitchenette and bathroom or two-bedroom apartments with large kitchen/diner, bedroom and bathroom. Rooms are tastefully furnished with antique furniture, curtains and ornaments. The apartments are independent and bed linen is changed once a week, bathroom linen twice a week. Guests can enjoy trips to San Remo, 29 kilometers away, and Monte Carlo, 80 kilometers away, while many old villages nearby are also worth visiting.

• 2 double rooms with bathroom, TV; 4 apartments with kitchen • Prices: double room single use 50 euros, double 64-90, apartment 20-50 per person; breakfast 7 euros per person • Credit cards: none • Off-street parking. Small pets allowed. Owners always reachable. • Restaurant

DOLCEACQUA
Arcagna

GENOA

LOCANDA DEL BRICCO

AGNELLO D'ORO

☎—◑Holiday farm
Località Arcagna
Tel. 0184 31426
Fax 0184 31230
E-mail: rondelli@terrebianche.com
Internet: www.terrebianche.com
Closed in November

☎—◑3-Star Hotel
Vico delle Monachette 6
Tel. 010 2462084
Fax 010 2462327
E-mail: info@hotelagnellodoro.it
Internet: www.hotelagnellodoro.it
Open all year round

The Locanda del Bricco lies among the vineyards of Arcagna and is part of the Terre Bianche farm, which was founded in 1870 and has produced quality wines and olive oils for the last 20 years.
Rooms are in old farm buildings surrounded by olive groves, vineyards and orchards and can accommodate two to four guests. All rooms are en-suite, with crisp bed and bath linen and arte povera furniture. The restaurant serves dishes from Liguria and Provence, mostly prepared with ingredients from the farm. The Locanda's location between the sea and mountains, close to the Italian and French Rivieras, makes it the ideal base for anyone keen to wishing to explore the area.

• 8 double rooms, with bathroom, TV • Prices: double room single use 50-60 euros, double 100-120 (25 euro supplement for extra bed), breakfast included • Credit cards: all, Bancomat • Off-street parking. Small pets allowed• Restaurant. TV room. Conference room. Boules court, horse-riding

The hotel is located in an old barefoot Carmelite convent dating back to the 1580s, in the heart of the old center of Genoa. The building was restructured by Maddalena Centuriana and, between 1840 and 1849, housed the school 'degli ignorantelli' for underprivileged children. Despite structural changes, some original features are still visible, like the French windows opening onto the courtyard. The Agnello d'Oro was recently renovated and now offers cozy, bright rooms furnished in a restrained modern style. There's a magnificent view from the top-floor guestrooms, which stretches over the rooftops of Genoa down to the harbor. Breakfast is continental.

• 10 single and 10 double rooms, with bathroom, TV; several with air-conditioning • Prices: single 50-100 euros, double 60-120, breakfast included • Credit cards: all, Bancomat • Garage (15 euros per day). Small pets allowed. Reception open 24 hours a day • Breakfast room

GENOA

GENOA
Cremeno

ANTICA OSTERIA DI VICO PALLA

⬭ Osteria with kitchen
Vico Palla 15 R
Tel. 010 2466575
Closed Monday
Open: lunch and dinner
Holidays: 10 days mid-August
Seating: 90
Prices: 25-30 euros, wine excluded
All credit cards, Bancomat

ARVIGO

⬭ Trattoria
Via Cremeno 31
Tel. 010 7170001
Closed Tuesday
Open: lunch, Wednesday, Friday, Saturday also for dinner
Holidays: in August, 15 days in September
Seating: 80
Prices: 27-30 euros, wine excluded
All major credit cards

After years of experience working in shipping and catering, young Maurizio Capurro returned to his native city in April 1999 and, helped by his father, opened this typical seafood osteria. Located near the old port, the historic building and typical Ligurian cuisine give the place distinctive character. It's a pity the service is a bit too laid back at times.

A witty dialect sonnet dedicated to **stoccafisso** (stockfish) decorating the wall and printed on the paper napkins lets you know immediately what fish is the star of the show: boiled with potatoes, accomodato alla genovese (stewed) or in brandacujun (creamed with potatoes Liguria-style), 'dried' cod is cooked here in a variety of ways. The menu continues with **fish fry and vegetables**, stuffed vegetables Genoese-style or vegetable pies. Among the more classic first and main courses, we suggest **minestrone** (cold in summer if you like), mandilli (thin lasagna) or other pasta al pesto, pansoti in walnut and pine nut sauce, **black trofie with fish sauce**, zemino of cuttlefish (or of chickpeas winter), angler fish with artichokes and potatoes and **tripe with broad beans**. The desserts are simple and home-made: apple pie, chocolate blancmange, tiramisu, latte dolce fritto (fried sweet milk), plus a tempting **plum and Sciacchetrà cake**. The wine list, which is already fairly representative, could be further extended.

It's advisable to book for dinner from Thursday to Sunday.

Arvigo is a well-run, functional trattoria, unpretentious with a very pleasant atmosphere, and a menu that includes almost all the classic Genoese recipes. You reach it by taking the Bolzaneto exit from the main Milan-Genoa highway, then driving towards Sant'Olcese as far as the turnoff for Cremeno.

You can start with a delicate Russian salad made with local vegetables or a good selection of cured meats: the traditional **Sant'Olcese salami** (made with equal portions of beef and pork), mocetta d'asino (made of donkey meat) and lardo di Arnad served with toast and honey. The excellent **pesto alla genovese** is used as a condiment for trenette, lasagne and **trofie polceverasche** (made from chestnut flour); alternatively, pansoti with walnut sauce and **meat-filled ravioli al tocco** (meat ragù). In season, you can also find local mushroom-based dishes and, if ordered in advance, **snails**. The choice of main courses is vast (perhaps excessive): delicate **cima alla Genovese** (stuffed breast of veal), vitello tonnato, **liver all'aggiadda**, Italian mixed fry with cep mushrooms, plus numerous meat dishes involving beef, rabbit and lamb. You can close with desserts such as the excellent canestrelli, baci di dama, chocolate, pear or apple cake with zabaglione, and almond-paste dolcetti.

The wine list has improved considerably and is reasonably priced.

🍴 In **Sant'Olcese** (9 km from the Genoa Bolzaneto exit) Salumificio Parodi, at Via Sant'Olcese 63 (there's a sales outlet at number 25 too), sells excellent cured meats.

BARISONE

Trattoria
Via Siracusa 2 R
Tel. 010 6049863
Closed Sunday for dinner and Monday
Open: lunch and dinner
Holidays: August
Seating: 60 + 40 outdoors
Prices: 25-30 euros, wine excluded
No credit cards accepted

CAIROLI

2-Star Hotel
Via Cairoli 14
Tel. 010 2461454-2461524
Fax 010 2467512
E-mail: info@hotelcairoligenova.com
Internet: www.hotelcairoligenova.com
Open all year round

This trattoria is located in the west of town, very close to the famous Sestri shipyards whence in the past some of Italy's largest ocean liners embarked on their maiden voyages. Without paying lip service to modern trends, the Barisone family's trattoria continues to propose classic Genovese recipes in an unpretentious, lively and sometimes noisy environment.

Starting with the mixed antipasti, there are the ever-present **anchovies** (in carpione, fried, **stuffed** and marinated with lemon), scallops au gratin, bianchetti (whitebait) omelet (when in season) and tasty mussels. Seafood predominates in the choice of first course dishes, with **zuppetta di rossetti and artichokes**, linguine with scampi, **fish-filled ravioli** and the hard to find **corzetti** polceveraschi (small eight-shaped pasta) with **octopus sauce**. Obviously some pastas can be accompanied by **pesto** made from fragrant basil gathered on the nearby Pra hills. As for mains, worth trying are the breaded hake, gurnard alla livornese, bianchetti and rossetti cooked in a number of ways, and also the classic **mixed fried platter**.

Among the puddings – almost all homemade – we suggest the fragrant pignolata, ricotta and wild strawberry cheesecake and amaretti and chocolate cake. As for the wine list, it's still rather limited. Book your table in advance.

The hotel is located in the historic center of Genoa, close to the Aquarium, the old harbor, the Palazzo Bianco and Palazzo Rosso Galleries and the Palazzo Reale. The Carlo Felice Theater, Palazzo Ducale and the cathedral of San Lorenzo are also all within walking distance. Rooms offer all modern comforts and are furnished in an up-to-date, simple and functional manner. The hotel has a boat available for guests wishing to swim away from the beach or for trips along the coast.

• 3 single and 9 double rooms, with bathroom, air-conditioning, mini-bar, safe, satellite TV • Prices: single 55-90 euros, double 75-100; breakfast 10 euros per person • Credit cards: all, Bancomat • Garage parking at special rates. Small pets allowed. Reception open 24 hours a day • Bar. TV room, reading room. Gym, solarium

Da Evo, at Via Galata, 46 R, quality jams, pasta, genuine breads and excellent extra virgin olive oils.

GENOA
Fontanegli

16 KM FROM TOWN CENTER

DA PIPPO

Trattoria
Salita Chiesa di Fontanegli 13 R
Tel. 010 809351
Closed Monday, in winter on Tuesday also for dinner
Open: lunch and dinner
Holidays: variable
Seating: 50 + 60 outdoors
Prices: 30 euros, wine excluded
All credit cards

Leave the main highway at Genova Est, take the road that follows the Bisagno stream towards Prato for about ten kilometers and you'll find the sign for Fontanegli. This osteria, which serves classic Genoese cuisine, is managed by the Villa family on premises, opened way back in 1870, where there was once a butcher's shop and a dairy. In a simply furnished dining room with tables set well apart, you'll be greeted by Christian, ready to list the dishes of the day, prepared – after painstaking selection of the best ingredients – by chef Matteo.

To start, you can choose from the seasonal vegetable flans, Pippo's mixed antipasto, **cappon magro** and a delicate rabbit salad dressed with apple vinegar and served with quarantina potatoes. The pasta is fresh and hand-made and it's certainly worth tasting the picagge al pesto, pansoti with walnut sauce and the **ravioli di magro** with Albenga artichoke sauce or meat-filled with **tocco alla Genovese** meat ragù. If it's available, taste the magnificently rich **vegetable minestrone**. Among the main courses, apart from the **mixed fry** (seasonal vegetables, 'sour milk', panissa, cutlet, 'sweet milk'), **cima alla genovese** (stuffed breast of veal) and fricasseed lamb. Plus a recipe dating from the 1950s: **rabbit cooked in milk with thyme**.

Home-made desserts: apple or walnut pie, bacetti di dama and a few sorbets. The wine list is extensive and well-balanced too.

GENOA
Granarolo

4 KM FROM TOWN CENTER

LUIGINA

Trattoria
Via ai Piani de Fregoso 14
Tel 010 2429594
Closed Thursday
Open: only for lunch
Holidays: August 15-September 10
Seating: 30 + 60 outdoors
Prices: 20-26 euros, wine excluded
No credit cards accepted

This is a classic trattoria just outside the city, on a hill about a 20-minute drive from the center. The road leading from Sampierdarena to here offers nice panoramic views over the city and sea below. A wide veranda and arbor provide shade from the hot summer sun, and there are warm rooms inside during the colder winter months: Luigina's really is the ideal place to escape from the chaotic life of the city. The husband-and-wife team of Anna Laura (in the kitchen) and Cesare (front of house) carry on what has been a family passion for more than a century (Luigina's opened way back in 1894).

The menu offers simple antipasti, including salt-cured anchovies in oil, excellent first courses such as **lasagne al pesto**, **meat-filled ravioli with tocco** (meat ragù without tomato), taglierini with artichoke or mushroom sauce (depending on the season). Mushrooms and artichokes also accompany the **veal stew**, or, alternatively, there are quail, roast lamb, **cima alla Genovese** (stuffed breast of veal), vitello tonnato, roasts and, from October to May on Fridays or when ordered in advance, **stoccafisso in umido** or accomodato (stockfish stew). You can finish up with a nice home-made tiramisu, canestrelli or cakes. The wine list includes about 20 labels in addition to a pleasant Val Polcevera white house wine.

GENOA

IMPERIA
Porto Maurizio

SA PESTA

Trattoria
Via dei Giustiniani 16 R
Tel. 010 2468336
Closed Monday for dinner and Sunday
Open: lunch, for dinner on booking
Holidays: end-July, beginning of September
Seating: 60
Prices: 20-25 euros
No credit cards accepted

CA' DEL VESCOVO

Bed and breakfast
Via Carducci 7
Tel. 335 6141677
Fax 0183 91576
E-mail: info@cadelvescovo.it
Internet: www.cadelvescovo.it
Open all year round

This place in the old quarter of the city is easy to reach, whether you come from the Aquarium or from San Lorenzo Cathedral: walking down the old alleyways you'll be able to admire the many, beautifully restored patrician palaces in this area. At Sa Pesta the welcome may seem a bit off hand, but it's the way the Genoese tend to deal with all 'foreigners'. It does have the advantage of cutting out any empty politeness and bonhomie and getting straight down to business.
As you enter, you'll see the wood-fired oven and large copper pans. The dining room is furnished simply in a rustic manner and you sit on stools at tables with paper mats. House wine is pumped directly from the barrel and service is minimal: in short, little has changed since the late 1800s when Felice Paravagna, nicknamed 'il Salpesta', ran this trattoria and was awarded certificates of quality. **Farinate, stuffed vegetables, vegetable pies**, anchovies and **fried baccalà** are the most classical dishes on the menu, together with such as cima (stuffed breast of veal, not produced on the premises), pasta al pesto, octopus salad, **stoccafisso accomodato** (stewed stockfish). In addition, there are also more conventional dishes like gnocchi al ragù, grilled meat and sausages.
The more traditional fried specialties are well in view and are also available (only at lunchtime) for takeaway. This trattoria is only open for dinner by reservation only.

Romeo Viganotti, at Vico dei Castagna 14 R, sells excellent artisan chocolate. At Antica Drogheria Torielli (Via San Bernardo 32 R), you'll find Aleppo pistachio nuts and all types of spices and blends of tea.

This B&B is located in a 160 square-meter apartment renovated in 2003; it comprises two bedrooms, a suite and a lounge where guests can enjoy breakfast. The suite, which can accommodate up to four people (there's also a comfortable sofa-bed), has ceiling frescoes by the famous Porto Maurizio-born, 18th-century artist Carrega, and Venetian mosaic floors. The B&B's location makes it the ideal base for exploring the city on foot or by public transport. A 5-minute walk away is the Parasio neighborhood with its beautiful views over the gulf (on a clear day you can see as far as Corsica). The Marina and Foce neighborhoods – respectively a 15- and 10-minute walk away – boast parks, villas, bathing establishments and sports facilities.

• 2 double rooms and 1 suite, with bathroom, TV • Prices: double room single use 55 euros, double 70 (25 euro supplement for extra bed), suite 110, breakfast included • Credit cards: none • Parking in the immediate vicinity (2 spaces). No pets allowed. Owners always reachable • Breakfast room, reading room.

IMPERIA
Porto Maurizio

ISOLABONA
Molinella

61 KM NORTHWEST OF IMPERIA, 14 KM FROM VENTIMIGLIA

HOSTARIA

� Osteria
Via Sant'Antonio 7
Tel. 0183 667028
Closed Monday, in winter also
Tuesdays for lunch
Open: lunch and dinner, summer dinner only
Holidays: variable
Seating: 45 + 30 outdoors
Prices: 32-35 euros, wine excluded
All credit cards

LA MOLINELLA

� Holiday farm
Via Roma 60
Tel. 0184 208163
Open Saturday for dinner and Sunday for
lunch, June-October always for dinner
Holidays: in November
Seating: 25 + 35 outdoors
Prices: 27 euros, wine excluded
No credit cards accepted

Brothers Giorgio and Loris Campeggio are always ready to give a warm welcome to visitors to their osteria in a characteristic little square in the old fishermen's quarter, Marina di Porto Maurizio, below the medieval Parasio neighborhood. The Hostaria has only one room with a wide barrel-vaulted brick ceiling, though you can also eat outside in the summer. Dishes rotate according to season and daily availability of raw materials (especially anchovies, pilchards and the like).

Among the antipasti, you'll find the typical farinata ligure or a Ligurian mixed platter with a vegetable pie and lovely stuffed vegetables, **fresciöi di giancheti** (whitebait fritters) or baccalà fritters, stoccafisso mantecato (creamed stockfish) and **octopus in zimino** with Pigna beans (Slow Food Presidia). The first course dishes include **linguine al pesto**, risotto with cuttlefish and artichokes, freshly made pasta with zucchini and bottarga or seafood from the day's catch. For main course, tasty **stoccafisso accomodato** (stewed stockfish), pan-fried gilthead with vegetables or mixed grilled fish. Note that the osteria bakes its own bread and breadsticks. Another item worthy of note is the puddings, original creations that are very palatable, if you wish accompanied by one of the passito wines recommended by Loris.

The wine list offers a good variety and mark-ups are low.

🍷🍴 In front of the osteria, you'll find a wine-shop (it belongs to the same owners) where you can have a drink and purchase wines, good beers, olive pâté, anchovies preserved in oil and salted, tuna, honey and jams.

Leaving the sea behind and climbing the Val Nervia, you come to this corner of western Liguria where the landscape is extremely colorful and very varied. Here you'll find the small medieval village of Isolabona and the agriturismo, which is situated nearby. On a hillside among woods and olive groves, the Moro family offersguests a few rooms and cooking that is unpretentious but wholesome and clearly Ligurian, prepared by Gioia with help from her son, Nicola. Her other son, Piermichele, serves in the small, comfortable dining room or, in summer, outside. Gioia's husband Ugo tends the garden that provides all the vegetables they use and he also gathers mushrooms in the woods.

There's a set menu. You can start with an excellent **fugassun** (vegetable flan), herb omelets, **barbagiuai**, cep mushroom flan, **brandacujon**, octopus carpaccio and Pigna beans, tonno di coniglio (shredded rabbit) and marinated eel. Then come fresh pastas: **ravioli di magro with butter and marjoram**, vegetable lasagne with a marjoram pesto, **parpagliui** (butterfly-shaped pasta) **with pesto, string beans and potatoes**, tagliatelle with cep mushroom sauce. For your main course you can have **rabbit alla ponentina** with Taggia olives, lamb with artichokes or **stewed stockfish with potatoes and olives**; typical dishes in winter are goat and bean stew and wild boar with polenta. To end, home-made puddings: apple puff pastry, fruit pies or cubaite (hazelnuts cooked in honey sandwiched between two wafers).

The wine list features a few good Ligurian and other Italian labels. Always book in advance.

ALL'INFERNO

Traditional osteria
Via Costa 3
Tel. 0187 29458
Closed Sunday
Open: lunch and dinner
Holidays: August
Seating: 100
Prices: 15-18 euros
No credit cards accepted

In a corner of the central Piazza del Mercato, a short ramp of steps leads down to a basement room with a low vaulted ceiling: this is All'Inferno, a picturesque osteria that has been here for about 100 years. It was used in the 19th century as a coal warehouse, then run as an osteria for four generations without interruption by the D'Avanzo family. Gianluca, grandson of the founder, will welcome you at the counter and check your booking (strongly recommended, especially for dinner), then he'll show you to your table. Seating in the two rooms is packed close together, a sheet of paper serves as a tablecloth and the menu will be read out to you. In short, It's an atmosphere from times gone by when people cared less about frills and more about substance, But today there is one bonus... air-conditioning.
There's a wide range of dishes, in part reflecting local tradition but also depending on what's available in the nearby market. Among the first courses, certainly worth trying are the **mes-ciua** (a legume and cereal soup), **minestrone**, tagliatelle al pesto or with a vegetable or mushroom sauce. Then you can continue with either **stuffed mussels** or mussel soup, octopus salad, cuttlefish, fried anchovies or red mullet, **baccalà**, stockfish, **tripe** or oven-baked pork. For dessert, there's usually a choice of zuppa inglese, cream with amaretti and panna cotta.
People normally drink house wine, though there are always a few good reasonably priced bottles from other regions (strange though it may seem, there arenone from the Cinque Terre).

ANTICA HOSTARIA SECONDINI

Trattoria
Via Montalbano 84
Tel. 0187 701345
Closed Wednesday
Open: lunch and dinner
Holidays: between September and October
Seating: 50 + 15 outdoors
Prices: 25-28 euros, wine excluded
All credit cards, Bancomat

Perched in the hills above the town, the hamlet of Sarbia overlooks the Gulf of La Spezia, offering a particularly captivating view at night. It's easy to reach from the town center, with two panoramic roads starting either from the east (Piazza Verdi) or west (Via Genova-La Foce) of town. The trattoria's dining room is simply furnished with a display of bottles of wine along the walls. In summer you can also eat on the small patio near the entrance. Endrio takes care of the tables in a professional and courteous manner; the kitchen is the domain of his wife Simona, who cooks the most typical dishes of the La Spezia tradition.
From the menu – the cover decorated with amusing anecdotes about La Spezia – you can start with vegetable flan, vegetables preserved in oil and exquisite cured meats accompanied by **sgabei** (fried bread). Among the first courses, the fresh home-made pasta certainly deserves a mention: plain with seafood or seasonal vegetable sauce, or filled (**ravioli with meat** or vegetable fillings). Gluten-free pasta is available too. You can choose from either fish or meat dishes for your main course: baccalà fritters, **stuffed mussels**, **stoccafisso** (stockfish) or **tripe**, grilled meat or roast **game** (in winter).
In addition to the major local labels, the list has a wide selection of other Italian bottles.

In the town below (7 km) on the continuation of the Via Aurelia, at Via Fiume 186, Gastronomia Ferrini sells a selection of cured meats, cheeses and olive oils. In the same street, at number 108, Forno Rizzoli has one of the best focaccias in town.

LA SPEZIA
Marola

3 KM FROM TOWN CENTER

AÜTEDO

Trattoria-pizzeria
Via Fieschi 138
Tel. 0187 736061
Closed Monday
Open: lunch and dinner
Holidays: end-September, mid-October
Seating: 80 + 80 outdoors
Prices: 18-26 euros, wine excluded
No credit cards accepted

OSTERIA DA GIANNI

Traditional osteria
Corso Cavour 352
Tel. 0187 717980
Closed Sunday
Open: lunch only, wines served at the bar until 8pm
Holidays: last week of August-first week of September
Seating: 35 + 12 outdoors
Prices: 10-15 euros
No credit cards accepted

Despite health problems, owner Giorgio Angelini refuses to give up his work and the pleasure that contact with regular customers brings. Here there's no menu and dishes change day by day: the choice is more restricted at lunchtime, wider choice in the evening. There are two inside rooms, now much more comfortable after recent renovation, but in summer you can also eat under the grapevine arbor (aütedo in dialect). Alessandro, with guidance from Giorgio and his wife Roberta, prepares dishes strictly as prescribed by tradition, plus a number of more creative recipes.
For antipasti, **anchovies** (salt-cured. marinated, fried, in frittatas or topping soia pizzas) and **mussels**, **stewed** with potatoes or stuffed. Other traditional dishes are **stopeta**, strips of baccalà cooked with onions and chili pepper, and **macheto**, prepared in winter with small fresh anchovies in olive oil spiced with chili peppers: in times gone by these specialties were a normal breakfast for the workers who unloaded coal at Porta Marola. First courses: tagliolini with stockfish, **gnocchetti with fresh anchovies** and seafood risotto. Main courses: excellent fried fish platter, **fried mussels** or **baked anchovies** with Vermentino.
In addition to the house wine, a few Ligurian labels. Occasional theme evenings are dedicated to traditional dishes.

In **Portovenere** (6 km) at Bar Lamia in Calata Doria, ice-creams, aperitifs and an excellent selection of wines and liqueurs. Next door La Posàa sells Ligurian food and drink: olive oil, wines, pesto, olives and many other products.

In the heart of the popular old Umbertino quarter, built at the end of the 1800s to house the families of workers who had migrated from the Ligurian hinterland to work at the Military Arsenal, this osteria continues to keep alive the gastronomic tradition of La Spezia. The place, next door to Piazza Brin and near the railway station, is run by Gianni and his wife Rosangela. A small outside area is separated from the footpath by glass panels; inside, next to the small bar in the entrance with three tables, the large, simply furnished dining room.
The menu changes daily and seasonally according to what's available in the market. Among the first courses, traditional hand-made **meat** or vegetable **ravioli** (with thyme to spice the filling) with ragù or pesto, fresh vegetable **minestrone alla genovese**, tagliolini with vegetables or ragù. As a main course you'll often find stuffed vegetables, anchovies marinated with lemon (or stuffed or fried), **stuffed mussels**, savory rice cake or polpettone di patate, and don't miss the **tripe** on Tuesdays or on Fridays and the **stoccafisso** (in winter, accompanied by polenta). You can finish with fresh fruit or one of the few home-made puddings. There's only house wine.
The cost, like the atmosphere, is a pleasant surprise. In the afternoon, you'll always find snacks of baccalà fritters, rice or vegetable flans and focaccia, to be eaten on the spot or for takeaway.

LA SPEZIA
Marola

LA SPEZIA

3 KM FROM TOWN CENTER

OSTERIA PICCIARELLO

🍲 Trattoria
Viale Fieschi 300-302
Tel. 0187 779237
Closed Monday
Open: dinner, Sunday also for lunch
except in July and August
Holidays: in November
Seating: 50
Prices: 25-35 euros, wine excluded
All credit cards, Bancomat

You come to Marola driving along the La Spezia-Portovenere road. The osteria run by Marola-born Stefano Poles and his wife Lara has a warm, welcoming atmosphere with the simple furnishings and brightly colored walls reflecting the popular seaside style of the place. There are two rooms: a large one with a bar counter and a smaller one that's less noisy when the trattoria is full. The marble-topped tables are covered with paper and there are straw mats under the plates.

The food is mostly based on cheap local fish. For antipasto you'll find **mussels** either **fried on a skewer** or **stuffed**, stuffed anchovies, **mixed fried platter** of anchovies, cuttlefish and moscardini, vegetable flans and **seafood salad**. Among the first courses and depending on the season, orecchiette with eggplant, risotto with Treviso chicory, homemade trofie and tagliolini with various seafood sauces; in winter there are also **soups**, often with a Tuscan flavor to them: spelt, ponentina (cannelloni beans, potatoes and pesto) or **piovana**, made with pumpkin and red cabbage with a pinch of corn flour. You can continue with either meat (pork fillet cooked in wine or leg of pork with apple sauce) or fish (**octopus alla diavola** and delicate **stuffed cuttlefish**). The desserts are home-made: crema pasticciera with fruit or hot chocolate and various tarts with cream or jam fillings.

The wine list has grown considerably over the years thanks to Stefano's enthusiasm: you'll find top labels from Colli di Luni producers and a good selection of Tuscan and other Italian wines.

VICOLO INTHERNO

🍲 Osteria
Via della Canonica 21
Tel. 0187 23998
Closed Sunday
Open: lunch, Friday and Saturday
also for dinner, summer dinner only
Holidays: variable
Seating: 30 + 15 outdoors
Prices: 20-25 euros, wine excluded
All credit cards

There's a happy atmosphere in this small osteria just a few steps from the new futuristic market square, all thanks to the simple furnishings, bright colors, pleasant ornaments and Provence-style fabrics. In the entrance there are racks for the bottles and a large display of local cheeses and cured meats, the day's fresh vegetables to eat raw dipped in salted olive oil, vegetable flans and stuffed vegetables. The creator of this pleasant little corner is Barbara, helped front of house by young Dalila.

The menu changes with the seasons and produce available at the market. **Anchovies**, the main 'poor' fish of Ligurian cuisine, are prepared in all the classic manners: stuffed, fried, 'in scabeccio' with onions and vinegar, marinated with lemon, salted with olive oil and oregano. Among the first courses, tagliolini with red mullet, **pennette with mantis shrimps** or with fresh anchovies and tomato, fresh pasta straccetti with Garfagnana ricotta cheese and basil, **lasagne al pesto** with potatoes and string beans, tortelli stuffed with artichokes and thyme. Savory flans, stuffed vegetables, roast veal with potatoes and **rabbit alla spezzina** are some of the regular main courses. You can also order another extraordinary traditional dish, **stoccafisso in umido**, (stewed stockfish) in advance. To finish, cakes: apple, pear and chocolate, ricotta or bitter chocolate.

The wine list includes some bottles of Colli di Luni producers and good Italian wines, also served by the glass. Dishes of the day are available as takeaways.

LA SPEZIA

LOCANDA DEL PRIONE

🔑 Rooms
Via del Prione 152
Tel. 0187 257153
Fax 0187 257222
E-mail: info@locandadelprione.it
Internet: www.locandadelprione.it
Open all year round

The hotel is located in La Spezia's traditional shopping street, close to the railway station and the harbor. The building, completely renovated in 2002, is a 13th-century structure typical of the Liguria region. All rooms have an independent entrance from their own landing and are furnished in a restrained, elegant manner with all modern comforts. Breakfast is available on request, prepared in a nearby café and served in the rooms. Guests can book train, ferry and theater tickets, rent cars, coaches, speed boats or sailing boats at reception, open in the morning until 12 noon. Guided tours of the city's many museums can also be organized.

• 4 double rooms and 2 suites, with bathroom, air-conditioning, mini-bar, safe, TV • Prices: double room single use 40-60 euros, double 40-70, suite 90-120; breakfast 6 euros per person • All major credit cards: Bancomat • Garage parking at special rates nearby (13 euros per day). Small pets allowed. Owners present until noon.

LA SPEZIA
Campiglia

TRAMONTI

🔑 Locanda
Via della Chiesa 56
Tel. and fax 0187 758514
E-mail: campiglia@beta-service.it
Internet: www.locandatramonti.it
Open all year round

Campiglia is located on a hill overlooking the Gulf of La Spezia and the Cinque Terre coast. On a clear day from the windows of the locanda you can see the islands of Corsica, Capraia, Elba and the Côte d'Azure. The facility is located in a 19th-century building and is run by the Bracco family assisted by Giovanna. Rooms have all modern comforts and are fitted with antique furniture. You can purchase good quality saffron grown by the Braccos, jams, lavender perfumes, rosemary condito (a mixture of local aromatic herbs) and wine from the Cinque Terre. Following the paths indicated by Italian Alpine Club signs, you can hike to Portovenere and Riomaggiore.

• 1 single, 3 double rooms and 1 mini-apartment (4 persons), with bathroom, mini-bar, modem connection • Prices: single 70-80 euros, double 90-120, mini-apartment 100-150, breakfast included • Credit cards: Visa, Bancomat • Parking in the immediate vicinity. Small pets allowed. Management always present. • Breakfast room. Terrace

LERICI
Tellaro

MIRANDA

🛏️🔑 3-Star Hotel
Via Fiascherino 92
Tel. 0187 968130-964012
Fax 0187 964032
E-mail: locandamiranda@libero.it
Internet: www.locandamiranda.com
Closed from mid-December to mid-January

Tellaro is a lovely fishing village about four kilometers from Lerici on the Golfo dei Poeti. The Miranda Hotel is located in a beautiful two-storey building dating back to the 1950s and just 100 meters from the beach. Rooms are elegant and attention to detail is visible in the restaurant dining room with its many antiques. Once managed by Miranda herself, the hotel is now in the hands of her son Alessandro. Rooms all have a sea view. The reading room with its fireplace is warm and cozy. The traditional breakfast is varied and filling.

• 5 double rooms and 2 suites, with bathroom, TV • Prices: double room single use 85 euros, double 100, breakfast included • Credit cards: all except DC, Bancomat • Parking in the immediate vicinity. No pets allowed. Reception open 8am-1am • Bar, restaurant. Reading room, TV room

LEVANTO
Legnaro

I PIPETTA

🛏️🔑 Holiday farm
Località Legnaro
Tel. 0187 801342
E-mail: i_pipetta@hotmail.com
Open all year round

This 15th-century farmhouse, renovated in 2001, is in one of the most beautiful medieval villages in the Levanto valley. The farm is family run: Francesco, a graduate in agricultural sciences, manages the olive grove, the vineyard and the orchard; his father, a retired teacher, is responsible for the kitchen and his mother looks after the accommodation. The restaurant is only open in the evening and offers typical local dishes, served on the panoramic terrace when the weather is good. Guests can explore the surrounding areas on foot or visit the beaches just three kilometers away (also reachable by bus). The hosts pick up guests traveling by train and drop them off at the station when they depart.

•1 single and 4 double rooms, with bathroom • Prices: single 40-55 euros, double 55-75, breakfast included • Credit cards: none • Public parking in the immediate vicinity. Small pets allowed. Owners always reachable. • Restaurant. Garden, panoramic terrace.

🍲 The popular restaurant run by Angelo and Giovanna Cabani serves an excellent seafood menu.

Montale

40 KM NORTHWEST OF LA SPEZIA

36 KM WEST OF LA SPEZIA

L'ANTICA PIEVE

L'ANTICO BORGO

Bed and breakfast
Via Piccola 10
Tel. 0187 800755
Fax 0187 807636
E-mail: info@lanticapieve.it
Internet: www.lanticapieve.it
Open all year round

Rooms
Località Dosso
Tel. and fax 0187 802681
E-mail: antico_borgo@hotmail.com
Internet: www.anticoborgo.net
Open all year round

Montale is the oldest village in the hills of Levanto. In 2003, host Cristina decided to give up her job as an accountant and renovate this 16th-century building, which belonged to the family. Rooms are fitted with Genoa-style furniture, wrought-iron bedsteads and crocheted curtains. They offer a generous buffet breakfast of home-made cakes and jams, freshly baked bread, Ligurian focaccia, home-baked cookies, seasonal fruit and honey from Levanto. Cured meats and cheeses are also available and are particularly in demand with foreign guests. Guests can go hiking from Montale to other villages in the Levanto valley, or visit the Cinque Terre and the Val di Vara. The beaches of the gulf of Levanto are only five kilometers away.

• 4 double rooms, with bathroom, air-conditioning • Prices: double room single use 45-60 euros, double 70-100, breakfast included • Credit cards: Bancomat • Free public parking in the immediate vicinity. No pets allowed. Owners always reachable • Breakfast room, lounge with TV corner

Dosso a medieval village just four kilometers from Levanto. This old manor house offers lovely views and spacious, airy rooms, furnished simply but tastefully. All rooms are en-suite: some overlook the the gulf of Levanto, others the valley below. Guests can read or watch TV in the cozy reading room with fireplace. A small stone-walled cellar is used principally for wine-tasting. A varied buffet breakfast to suit all tastes is served in a special room, which also has a fireplace and beautiful views. When the weather's good, it's served on the panoramic terrace.

• 6 double rooms, with bathroom, minibar, satellite TV; 5 with air-conditioning • Prices: double room single use 45-80 euros, double 60-90 (25-30 euro supplement for extra bed), breakfast included • Credit cards: all, Bancomat • Free public parking in the immediate vicinity. Small pets allowed. Owners always reachable • Breakfast room, reading and TV room, tavern, internet point. Garden, terrace

VILLA CATERINA

🗝Rooms
Località Piè di Gallona
Tel. 0187 804013
E-mail: info@villacaterina.com
Internet: www.villacaterina.com
Open all year round

VILLA MARGHERITA

🗝Bed and breakfast
Via Trento e Trieste 31
Tel. and fax 0187 807212
E-mail: villamargheritabythesea@hotmail.com
Internet: www.villamargherita.net
Open all year round

With the aid of his relatives, Vittorio Berlotto, a young graduate in environmental and marine sciences, has renovated this family-owned 19th-century farmhouse and started to grow crops again on the hillside above. Rooms are all decorated with different colors and textiles and are rendered even more attractive by the stunning wrought-iron work, the handiwork of the Berlotto family. Guests can enjoy trips on foot from Piè di Gallona to other villages of the Levanto valley, the Cinque Terre and the Val di Vara. The beaches of the Gulf of Levanto are just two kilometers away. Vittorio is available to drive guests to the beach after breakfast and pick them up at sunset and can, on request, collect you at the train station and drop you off there when you leave.

• 4 double rooms, with bathroom, TV • Prices: double room single use 37-60 euros, double 45-80, breakfast included • Credit cards: major ones, Bancomat • Facility accessible to the mobility challenged. External parking. Small pets allowed. Owners always reachable. • TV room. Grounds, garden

This Art Nouveau villa, built in 1906, now belongs to the Campodonico family, who have renovated it and turned it into a B&B. Rooms are fitted with antique furniture, all have comfortable beds, ensuite bathrooms and telephone, while some have private patios with a sea view. There's also an independent apartment with private entrance on the ground floor, with two bedrooms and a kitchen with fridge, washing machine and dishwasher. The three large gardens have sun-beds, tables and chairs. Breakfast is served in the lounge or out in the garden when the weather is good.

• 2 single and 4 double rooms, with bathroom, mini-bar, satellite TV, modem connection; 1 apartment (4 persons) with kitchen • Prices: double room single use 60-100 euros, double 80-120 (15 euro supplement for extra bed), apartment 90-150 euros, breakfast included • Credit cards: Visa, MC, Bancomat • Off-street parking. Small pets allowed. Owners always reachable • Breakfast room, TV room, reading room, internet point. Garden, solarium

MALLARE

LA LANTERNA

Restaurant
Località Panelli 1
Tel. 019 586300
Closed Thursday
Open: lunch and dinner
Holidays: none
Seating: 35
Prices: 26-30 euros, wine excluded
All major credit cards

Mallare, which you can reach by car from Altare in 15 minutes, may not boast important tourist attractions, but you'll certainly find it a sound benchmark for good food. La Lanterna is capably run by the Minetti family: Elisa and Gianmaria, a close couple in both life and work, take care of the tables and wine cellar, while in the kitchen Daniele is young, down-to-earth and communicative. He's created a menu with seasonal variations based on traditional recipes – you're in Liguria, but there' a strong Piedmontese influence – with a personal touch and a restrained dash of inventiveness.

In a bright, airy, well furnished environment, you'll find dishes with distinct flavours, such as **cockerel breast stuffed with vegetables**, vitello tonnato, **brandacujun** (creamed stockfish with potatoes), steamed shredded guinea-fowl with vegetables (from the garden), flakes of Pecorino cheese and local black truffles. Among the first courses, noteworthy are the **rabbit and olive 'double' ravioli** with butter and thyme, green borage tortelli filled with giuncata (typical local ricotta cheese), **chestnut picagge with pesto, potatoes and string beans**, or **stockfish ravioli with fresh tomatoes**. To continue, roast saddle of suckling pig, boned chicken in crepinette, crispy twice-cooked guinea-fowl or **saddle of rabbit** stuffed with its own liver and pancetta. Finally, there's a good selection of cheeses and the puddings: tartrà of wild berries in a basket of warm chocolate, frozen soufflé with bitter chocolate and coffee, semifreddo with Marsala sauce.

The wine list offers a careful selection of mainly Piedmontese labels and markups are reasonable.

MANAROLA

CA' D'ANDREAN

3-Star Hotel
Via Discovolo 101
Tel. 0187 920040
Fax 0187 920452
E-mail: cadandrean@libero.it
Internet: www.cadandrean.it
Closed November-December

This family-run hotel was created by restructuring the cellars and olive oil press of an old house close to the sea. Rooms are spacious and functional, and some have a terrace. The hall with fireplace and residential bar opens onto the courtyard garden where, in summer, breakfast is served among the lemon trees. A must to see is the Gothic church of San Lorenzo, built with local stone in 1338. The church façade boasts a rosette by Matteo and Pietro Campilio and there's a 15th-century polyptych with a gold background in the apse. One of the most thrilling excursions is the walk through the so-called 'Via dell'Amore', a path cut in the rock on the steep cliff overlooking the sea between Manarolo and Riomaggiore.

• 1 single and 9 double rooms, with bathroom, air-conditioning, satellite TV • Prices: single 60-67 euros, double 60-90; breakfast 6 euros per person • Credit cards: none • Parking before entering the village. No pets allowed. Owners always reachable. • Bar. Garden

MANAROLA

19 KM WEST OF LA SPEZIA

MELE
Acquasanta

21 KM FROM GENOA, 6 KM FROM VOLTRI EXIT A 10, SS 456

MARINA PICCOLA

🔑 3-Star Hotel
Via Birolli 120
Tel. 0187 920103
Fax 0187 920966
E-mail: info@hotelmarinapiccola.com
Internet: www.hotelmarinapiccola.com
Closed in November

OSTERIA DELL'ACQUASANTA @🐌⊘🍶

🍲 Trattoria
Via Acquasanta 281
Tel. 010 638035
Closed Monday
Open: lunch and dinner
Holidays: in January, never during weekends
Seating: 70 + 40 outdoors
Prices: 30 euros, wine excluded
Credit cards: CartaSi, Visa, Bancomat

Located high on a spur of rock, Manarolo is an old village on the Riviera di Levante with typical many-colored houses. This small family-run hotel has well-maintained, functional rooms with all modern comforts. Some rooms have views of the nearby harbor with its typical black rock formations. Guests can enjoy many walks in the luxuriant surroundings with their dry-stone walls and terraced vineyards, moving easily from village to village whilst admiring the scenery.

• 2 single and 11 double rooms, with bathroom, air-conditioning, TV • Prices: single 83 euros, double 105, breakfast included • Credit cards: all, Bancomat • Parking before entering the village. No pets allowed. Reception open 7am-11.30pm. • Bar, restaurant.

This well-managed trattoria, run by the trio of Alessandro, Fabio and Marco, is just a few meters from the sanctuary of the same name, under the shady branches of age-old trees. In a spartan, informal atmosphere, you can enjoy the strictly seasonal menu, which starts with the osteria's well-balanced antipasti: vegetable flans, panissa (a sort of chickpea flour polenta), tasty salt-cured anchovies and delicate creamed baccalà. The hand-made fresh pasta is served with typical Ligurian sauces: **ravioli alla genovese co u toccu** (meat sauce), **lasagnette with Pra pesto**, tagliolini with meat and mushroom sauces, **pansoti di magro** spiced with basil. Ligurian cuisine is also the theme of the main courses: **stoccafisso accomodato** (stewed stockfish), bagnun of anchovies and other 'poor' fish prepared in traditional ways. As the list of old Ligurian recipes doesn't offer much variety in the way of fish, the menu is rounded out with **tomaxelle alla genovese** (roulade of veal), rabbit with vegetables, tripe with broad beans and **liver all'aggiada**. There's a particularly wide selection of Piedmontese cheeses. Among the puddings, you'll find fresh fruit pies, walnut canestrelli, semifreddo al torrone di Visone, chestnut budino with a wine sauce and zabaglione bavarois with chocolate.
The great wine list numbers about 100 carefully chosen labels, all correctly priced.

🍲 The hotel restaurant has a good seafood menu: average 25-30 euros, excluding wine.

LIGURIA   430

MONTEROSSO
Beo

34 KM WEST OF LA SPEZIA

IL CILIEGIO

Restaurant
Località Beo 2
Tel. 0187 817829
Closed Monday
Open: lunch and dinner
Holidays: 1 November-20 December
Seating: 70 + 70 outdoors
Prices: 30-32 euros, wine excluded
All credit cards, Bancomat

The restaurant is in the hills above the old village of Monterosso al Mare. It can be reached from La Spezia by car taking the panoramic coast road along the ridge of the Cinque Terre, or by train: in the latter case, if you telephone ahead, a shuttle service will be provided to take you from the village to the restaurant. In summer you can eat in the shady garden overlooking the sea and a corner of the garden has been organized as a children's playground.
The two owners, Rosanna and Teresa, give their guests a warm welcome and offer traditional Riviera dishes, among which the famous Monterosso **anchovies** (Slow Food Presidium), fried, stuffed or served with extra virgin olive oil and oregano. To complete the antipasti, vegetable flans, marinated fish and warm fish and shellfish antipasti. The best first courses are the typical **trofie al pesto** and **trofie** with scampi and **swordfish**; if you order in advance, you can also enjoy an excellent **fish soup**. The famous Monterosso anchovies reappear in main courses, together with tasty **stuffed mussels**; you can also order Ligurian-style oven-baked fish or cima alla Genovese (stuffed breast of veal). It's a pity the menu also includes occasional 'dishes for tourists'. There's also a vegetarian menu based on local dishes and a good choice of desserts that can be accompanied by a glass of Sciacchetrà.
The wine list includes distinguished Ligurian Cinqueterre and Colli di Luni labels and the house wine is good too .

In the old village center, in Piazza Garibaldi, the Cinque Terre National Park salting workshop sells Slow Food Presidium anchovies.

NE
Conscenti

53 KM EAST OF GENOA OR A 12 EXIT LAVAGNA

ANTICA OSTERIA DEI MOSTO

Trattoria
Piazza dei Mosto, 15/1
Tel. 0185 337502
Closed Wednesday
Open: lunch and dinner, July and August only for dinner
Holidays: second half of October
Seating: 50
Prices: 30-35 euros, wine excluded
All credit cards

It's not difficult to get to this fine trattoria: leave the A 12 highway at the Lavagna exit and follow the signs for Valgraveglia; after passing through Ne you come to Conscenti. In this small village, on the first floor of a palazzo on the main square, you'll find the Osteria dei Mosto. With invaluable assistance from Catia in the kitchen, Franco Solari fills the roles of maître d', sommelier and commis, and for years now has been serving traditional dishes of the valley modeled based on old recipes and made with a wide range of local ingredients.
The warm antipasto is a prime example of the quality and unpretentious nature of the cooking: testaieù (wafer-thin disks made from flour, salt and water) al pesto, mixed vegetable pies, warm focaccia with local cured meats. Among the first courses, all of which use home-made pasta, you'll find the typical chestnut flour trofie al pesto, **mandilli de sea** (thin lasagne) in cream of mushroom sauce, delicate potato ravioli with goat's milk butter and **picagge perse al ragù bianco**. You can follow this with **oven-baked cima alla Genovese** (stuffed breast of veal), fried rabbit spiced with herbs, stuffed vegetables and lettuce and an extremely tender **asado**. There's a wide selection of local and other Italian cheese, plus home-made puddings, including an outstanding **gallanne pinne**, typical cream-filled wraps sweet pastry.
The wine list offers a wide, very carefully chosen, reasonably priced selection.

BARBIN

Locanda
Via San Lorenzo 16
Tel. 0185 337508
E-mail: info@locandabarbin.it
Internet: www.locandabarbin.it
Open all year round

LA BRINCA

Trattoria
Via Campo di Ne 58
Tel. 0185 337480
Closed Monday
Open: dinner and also for lunch
Saturday, Sunday and holidays
Holidays: variable
Seating: 80 + 20 outdoors
Prices: 30-35 euros, wine excluded
All credit cards

Conscenti is a small, very well-preserved medieval village in the Graveglia Valley, inland from the Gulf of Tigullio. This simple, peaceful locanda is located in a building renovated with full respect for its surroundings. Inside it's bright and friendly, fitted with wooden and wrought-iron furniture. Guests without cars can take advantage of the pick-up and drop-off service from the hotel to the railway station in Chiavari. Many trips to the historic and artistic villages nearby are available, as are nature walks in the Ligurian Apennines and visits to the nearby beaches in the Tigullio area.

• 1 single and 4 double rooms, with bathroom, mini-bar, safe, satellite TV • Prices: single 35 euros, double 60 (6 euro supplement for extra bed), breakfast included • All major credit cards, Bancomat • Parking in the immediate vicinity. Small pets allowed. Owners always reachable. • TV room

If you're set on eating fish then spare yourselves the trip – you won't even find an anchovy here! Having said this, you can either go for the very varied fixed-price set menu (together with excellent advice as regards appropriate wines) or a classic à la carte menu offering an interesting itinerary through traditional recipes.

Among the antipasti, the typical **prebugiun** (mixed wild herbs), fried raviolo alla brace and frisciulla al pesto are all worth trying, while the first courses include very good **potato and chestnut gnocchetti with pesto**, ravioli d'erbette, taglierini with mushroom sauce and **lettuce stuffed with meat**, a dish that's almost impossible to find elsewhere. Meat stars in the main courses: **roast rabbit stuffed with herbs**, rump steak with pine nut sauce, breast of veal with juniper berries baked in a wood-fired oven. The cheese board – mostly local – is the result of a long and painstaking selection process. The desserts include a number of classics: semifreddi (the one flavored with rosehip syrup is a must), fluffy sorbets and various creations using seasonal fruit, among which cherries cooked in Brachetto with vanilla ice cream.

The magnificent wine list focuses on organically made products, and the superb selection of liqueurs will suit all tastes.

NOLI

ITALIA

🔑 3-Star Hotel
Corso Italia 23
Tel. 019 748971
Fax 019 7491859
E-mail: info@hotelitalianoli.it
Internet: www.hotelitalianoli.it
Closed between December and January

The Italia Hotel, managed by the Sanna family, is located on the promenade of Noli, between a beautiful bay and green hills. The hotel offers soundproofed rooms, with all modern comforts, direct-dial telephone, TV and mini-bar included. The common areas are spacious, with various lounges and a sun terrace for guests to enjoy. The panoramic terrace is also used as a dining area in summer and boasts stunning views over one of the most beautiful parts of the Ligurian coast. The restaurant uses quality ingredients to produce traditional dishes with a creative twist.

• 1 single, 10 double, 2 triple and 2 four-bed rooms, with bathroom, mini-bar, safe, TV • Prices: single 65 euros, double room single use 65-70, double 98, triple 138, four-bed 196, breakfast included • Credit cards: all except DC, Bancomat • Parking in the immediate vicinity. No pets allowed. Owners always reachable • Bar, restaurant. TV room, reading room. Solarium

ORTONOVO
Nicola

CERVIA

🍲 Traditional osteria
Piazza della Chiesa 19
Tel. 0187 660491
Closed Monday
Open: lunch and dinner
Holidays: first days of November up to Christmas
Seating: 50 + 50 outdoors
Prices: 30-35 euros, wine excluded
All credit cards, Bancomat

Nicola is a fascinating medieval village perched on a hill dominating the Luni plain: to get there, turn off the Via Aurelia at the Roman archeological site. The road is a succession of hairpin bends through vineyards and olive groves directly overlooking the upper Versilia coast. The osteria is in the center of the village in front of the church and occupies all floors of an old house, while in summer there are also tables outside in the old cobblestone square. Sonia and Letizia carefully choose local ingredients and prepare dishes based on traditional recipes, albeit with a interesting personal touches.
You can start with **vegetable flan** and the ever-present **lardo di Colonnata**. Among the first course dishes, delicious lasagne with spinach and Provola cheese, classic, superbly prepared **ravioli with meat ragù** and excellent risottos made with seasonal vegetables and cheese. For main courses, predominantly meat dishes: tagliata of beef or veal, **breaded lamb with herbs**, **filet of pork with hazelnut sauce**, costata di cinta senese, vitello tonnato. To finish, puddings such as almond cake and yogurt or Chantilly cream mousse.
There's a good selection of local wines (Colli di Luni from the top producers) and other Italian labels, some distinguished.

🛍 In **Ortonovo** (4 km), Magnani, at Via Aurelia 168, sells excellent cured meats, Italian cheeses, honey and Colli di Luni wines.

ORTONOVO
Nicola

PIGNA

DA FIORELLA

🍲 Traditional osteria-trattoria
Via per Nicola 46
Tel. 0187 66857
Closed Thursday
Open: lunch and dinner
Holidays: in January and September
Seating: 75
Prices: 25-30 euros, wine excluded
All credit cards except DC, Bancomat

TERME

🍲 Hotel-restaurant
Località Madonna Assunta
Tel. 0184 241046
Closed Wednesday, never in August
Open: lunch and dinner
Holidays: January 10- February 15
Seating: 80
Prices: 26-33 euros, wine excluded
All credit cards

You'll find this place on the road from Dogana di Ortonovo just before entering the ancient medieval village of Nicola. The Osteria Fiorella continues to be a standard-bearer of the Ligurian-Tuscan gastronomical tradition.

The view from the windows of the large, sparsely furnished dining room offers a magnificent panorama over the Luni plains down to the sea at Marina di Carrara and Versilia. You can start with **vegetable pies**, local cured meats (the Castelnuovo raw ham is a must) and rosemary- and walnut-flavored focaccia. You can then choose from typical **testaroli** served with three condiments (olive oil, pesto and mushroom sauce), **quadrucci with chickpeas**, homemade tagliatelle or gnocchi with pesto, ragù or mushroom sauce and, as a tribute to the sea, spaghetti with anchovies or shellfish. Among the main courses, don't miss the **mixed platter** of fried chicken, rabbit and lamb, though there's also a choice of grilled game. Fish dishes include fried or **stuffed anchovies** and a filling mixed fry of seafood. To end your meal, a good choice of home-made desserts: from typical **rice cake** to jam or amaretti tarts.

The wine list boasts the best local labels (Colli di Luni) and a few Tuscan and Piedmontese wines as well.

🍷 In Ortonovo, two bakeries – Paola Ambrosini, Via Isola 13, and Da Cudì, Località Isola, Via Gaggio 48 – produce excellent bread in wood-fired ovens, plus rosemary- or basil-flavored focaccia and several types of cake.

In Roman times, Pigna was a rural district of Albintimilium (Ventimiglia) and was already renowned for the spa waters fed by the springs of Lake Pigo. In the 12th-century medieval village, the church of San Michele with its 16th-century polyptych by Canavesio is worth a visit. The professional and obliging Lanteri family have been running the hotel-restaurant here since 1968. Gloria prepares traditional dishes in the kitchen, while her husband Silvio takes care of the tables with their children, Maura and Claudio (who will advise you on your choice of wine). You can either eat à la carte or choose an 18.50 or 26 euro set menu.

You can start with hard-to-find **gran pistau** (wheat soup), cima (stuffed breast of veal), **barbagiuai**, excellent **zucchini trombetta pie** in summer or cep mushroom pie in winter. First courses include **ravioli di magro**, tagliatelle Verdi al tocco di coniglio (rabbit sauce), **pansotti with walnut sauce**, tortelli di magro with cep mushrooms, **maltagliati and Pigna white bean soup**. Moving on, **rabbit al Rossese and Taggia olives**, unweaned lamb with aromatic herbs, **goat and Pigna white bean stew**, wild boar in salmì, stoccafisso accomodato (stewed stockfish). To finish, home-made pear or apple pie and trifle.

The wine list includes over 300 labels, mostly from Piedmont, Liguria and Tuscany: you'll also find vintage Rossese wines and other rarities. There's a good selection of whisky too.

RAPALLO
San Massimo

RICCÒ DEL GOLFO
Ponzò

31 KM FROM GENOA AT 12 OR SS 1

11 KM NORTHWEST OF LA SPEZIA SS 1

U GIANCU

🍲 Traditional osteria
Via San Massimo 78
Tel. 0185 260505
Closed Wednesdays
Open: dinner, lunch on booking
Holidays: variable
Seating: 90 + 60 outdoors
Prices: 35 euros, wine excluded
All credit cards except AE

ANTICA TRATTORIA CERRETTI

🍲 Trattoria
Via San Cristoforo, 22
Tel. 0187 926277
Closed Wednesday, January and
February open only on weekends
Open: lunch and dinner
Holidays: none
Seating: 50
Prices: 24-33 euros, wine excluded
All credit cards, Bancomat

After passing through the large garden where you can eat when the weather's good, you come to this pleasant, airy, squeaky-clean unusually decorated osteria (the walls are lined with cartoons and drawings collected by Fausto Oneto all over the world). Fausto's obliging son runs the tables. The menu also adopts a cartoon style and describes dishes in a careful, precise manner: it changes with the seasons as most of the fresh ingredients used come from local vegetable gardens, though lots of wild greens and herbs also appear.
The classic antipasti include: fried focaccia with cheese, broad beans and salami, **panissa** and fried borage flowers. Among the first courses, **spelt tagliatelline with pesto, string beans and potatoes** or other vegetable-based sauces, and potato gnocchi with pumpkin sauce. For your main course, you can choose from lamb chops either fried or cooked with aromatic herbs, **rabbit stew with olives**, roast guinea-fowl with chestnuts and onions, shank of roast pork, mixed vegetable pie, **prebuggiun** accompanied by corn meal focaccia and a superb **wild herb salad**. From May to November, you'll always find **wild mushrooms** on the menu: sliced, baked, en papillotte, breaded and fried, in soup, in sauces or simply raw in salads. There's an interesting selection of limited-production cheeses, served with honey or jam.
To finish, home-made ice cream, cakes, pies and biscuits. There's been an admirable increase in the wine list both in terms of quantity and quality.

Ponzò is a peaceful hillside village in Val di Vara that you can reach by taking the Via Aurelia from La Spezia or from the Cinque Terre, passing through the old village of Pignone. Here, with a magnificent view over the surrounding hills, is the Antica Trattoria Cerretti run by the Guastini family: waiting to greet you will be Teano, a sometimes over-enthusiastic host. Paola and her son Matteo run the kitchen. For antipasto you can have **sgabei** (fried bread dough) with lardo di Colonnata and a few vegetable-based dishes. First courses vary according to the season: in winter there's **legume soup**, minestrone alla genovese, polenta di formenton with leek sauce, cornmeal flour gnocchi; throughout the year, meat and vegetable ravioli with spicy meat sauce, **pansoti** di magro **with walnut sauce, tagliolini with cep mushroom sauce** or with baccalà. Cod also plays an important role in main courses: excellent baccalà in agliata, oven-baked or **stewed stockfish**. In summer there are also other fish dishes, such as octopus all'inferno and **cuttlefish in zimino**. Alternatively, roast meats and oven-baked capocollo. To finish, home-made cakes and puddings. Graphically, the wine list is very attractive – Matteo's work – and proposes some good local, Tuscan and Piedmontese labels.
A word of warning, avoid bringing your dog as no animals are allowed in the dining room.

🍴 Following the Via Aurelia (7 km) towards Foce along the road to Beverino, at Via Graveglia 55, you'll see Il Crepuscolo degli Dei, a place for a dinner or a snack with excellent wines, cured meats and cheeses, open until well into the night.

Riomaggiore

Riomaggiore

13 KM WEST OF LA SPEZIA

13 KM WEST OF LA SPEZI

Ripa del Sole

Restaurant
Via De Gasperi 282
Tel. 0187 920143
Closed Monday
Open: lunch and dinner
Holidays: November
Seating: 70 + 50 outdoors
Prices: 30-35 euros, wine excluded
All credit cards, Bancomat

Locanda della Compagnia

1-Star Hotel
Via del Santuario 32
Tel. 0187 760050-920586- 329 3945815
Fax 0187 760700-920586
E-mail: lacomp@libero.it
Open all year round

You'll find the restaurant in the upper part of the village. To get there, take the coast road from La Spezia, go down to Riomaggiore and after you pass the municipal car park, make your way to the little church of San Giovanni Battista. The restaurant nearby is run by the Bertola family, with Daniela in the kitchen whose cuisine closely reflects the local gastronomical tradition with a few small innovations. She runs the place with her brother Matteo, with the advice and help of their parents. The large internal dining room with its huge picture windows is furnished in marine style; when the weather permits, you can also eat on the terrace with its fine view in front of the entrance.

It's worth starting with the antipasti: marinated, salted, stuffed or fried anchovies, soppressata of octopus, **moscardini in guazzetto**, baccalà marinated or in fritters and spuma of hake. For first course, apart from the ever-present **trofie al pesto** and seafood risotto, we can recommend the **fish ravioli** with thyme and marjoram, and the **trenette with fresh anchovies and pine nuts**. For main course, excellent **fried seafood platter**, fillet of bass with fresh vegetables, fish from the day's catch either baked or grilled and, when in season, **stuffed mussels**. For pudding, we suggest **zabaglione allo Sciacchetrà** and chocolate squares in zabaglione sauce.

The wine list includes many Cinque Terre, as well as a few other quality Italian wines.

The hotel is located in the old part of Riomaggiore, surrounded by the tower-houses typical of this area, very close to the sea and the Cinque Terre National Park. The name of the locanda derives from its former use (in the 19th century) as the headquarters of the brotherhood, or compagnia, of the Madonna Assunta, to whom the beautiful church built in 1871 in the piazza is also dedicated. During the 1930s through to the 1950s, the building was used as a cinema and community hall, then converted into a hotel. It's a comfortable, homely, clean place to stay, managed by the courteous, helpful owner, Tommasa Franca Pasini and her son Alessandro.

• 4 double and 1 triple room, with bathroom, air-conditioning, mini-bar, satellite TV • Prices: double room single occupancy and double 90-120 euros, triple 100-150, breakfast included • Credit cards: all, Bancomat • 1 room designed for use by the mobility challenged. Public parking in the immediate vicinity. Small pets allowed. Owners always reachable • Restaurant. Reading room

RIOMAGGIORE
Volastra

13 KM WEST OF LA SPEZIA

LUNA DI MARZO

🗝️3-Star Hotel
Via Montello 387 C
Tel. and fax 0187 920530
E-mail: albergolunadimarzo@libero.it
Internet: www.albergolunadimarzo.com
Closed in January

The hotel is located in an old farmhouse amidst olive groves overlooking the sea, renovated and extended by its young owner Eugenio Rollandi and his mother. Albeit devoid of previous building experience, Eugenio has created a simple, friendly place in keeping with its surroundings. From the panoramic veranda, which presents a sheer drop to the sea below, you access the common area. The rooms are fitted with modern furniture and have been renovated with great attention to detail. Buffet breakfast, served on the veranda in summer, offers organic products and delicious focaccia. Guests can easily walk from the village to the sea by following one of the many paths through the vineyards and olive groves, whilst also enjoying the stunning views.

• 10 double rooms, with bathroom, satellite TV; 2 with terrace overlooking the sea • Prices: double room single use 65 euros, double 95-110 (25 euro supplement for extra bed), breakfast included • Credit cards: all except AE, Bancomat • Facility partly accessible to the mobility challenged, 1 room designed for their use. Private parking 50 meters away. No pets allowed. Reception open 7am-10.30 pm • Breakfast room, reading room. Veranda

SANT'OLCESE
Comago

10 KM NORTH OF GENOA

LOCANDA DEL CIGNO NERO

🗝️3-Star Hotel
Parco di Villa Serra-Via Levi 10
Tel. 010 7262132
Fax 010 7262095
E-mail: info@locandadelcignonero.it
Internet: www.locandadelcignonero.it
Open all year round

Villa Serra is an intriguing 19th-century neo-Gothic building. The property boasts an English garden and a small old palazzo with a crenellated tower where the hotel is located. Managed by the Belforte family, it has simply furnished rooms painted in pastel colors. On the ground floor, a small reception area, bar and elegant restaurant room (traditional Ligurian and Piedmontese cuisine and international dishes are available). The adjoining villa has four large rooms (each seating 80 people) available for meetings, conferences and seminars. Breakfast is basic but the place's peaceful location and closeness to the city center make it a good base. During Euroflora and the Boat Show in Genoa, room rates are higher.

• 2 single, 4 double, 1 triple rooms and 2 junior suites, with bathroom (Jacuzzi, shower), TV, modem connection • Prices: single 80 euros, double 90, triple and junior suite 120, breakfast included • Credit cards: all, Bancomat • Facility accessible to the mobility challenged, 1 room designed for their use. Off-street parking. Small pets allowed. Owners always reachable • Bar, restaurant. Conference rooms. Grounds

SAVONA

SORI
Capreno

16 KM SOUTHEAST OF GENOA SS 1 OR A 12

VINO E FARINATA

🍲 Traditional osteria
Via Pia 15 R
No telephone
Closed Sunday and Monday
Open: lunch and dinner
Holidays: between August and September
Seating: 120
Prices: 18-22 euros, wine excluded
No credit cards accepted

DA DRIN

🍲 Trattoria
Frazione Capreno 66
Tel. 0185 782210
Closed Wednesday
Open: lunch and dinner
Holidays: September 15-October 15 and Christmas
Seating: 70 + 30 outdoors
Prices: 20-25 euros, wine excluded
All major credit cards, Bancomat

This osteria is on Via Pia, Savona's busy central street. Here you can enjoy excellent **farinata**, both the classic version made with chickpea flour and Savona-style, made with wheat flour, and, more generally, unpretentious cuisine with a decidedly Ligurian flavor. As there's no phone, you can't book ahead (you either have to go there to do it in person or write), and given the number of diners, you often have to queue in the entrance in the company of the large oven.

Once you've got a table in one of the two small dining rooms, you can take your pick from a list of the dishes of the day's, mostly fish, though there are alternatives: **minestrone**, stuffed vegetables, tongue in parsley sauce and roast lamb. But the best dishes are seafood, and so you'll find very fresh marinated, fried or stuffed **anchovies**, seafood salad, octopus with potatoes, fillet of hake with olive oil and lemon, and mussels alla marinara. There's a limited choice of first courses, among which fish soup and spaghetti with shellfish. The choice of main courses is broader: **fried pignoletti** and shrimps, moscardini alla diavola, **cuttlefish with peas**, sliced bladefish in a tomato sauce. Plus, when available, baked bass and gilthead.

Low prices and a cordial, welcoming atmosphere compensate for the ready-made desserts they serve and a wine list that leaves room for improvement.

🍴 The covered market in the port area, in Via Giuria, is well worth a visit. Here you'll find a traditional tripe store that, in the morning, not only sells ready-to-cook tripe but also tripe soup. Also look out for the Il Grigio, a fishmonger's stall.

The place now occupied by this trattoria first opened for business almost a century ago, founded by the great grandparents of the current owners as a general food store with osteria attached. The osteria has since been overhauled: in addition to the indoor space there's now a terrace and a veranda with views of the hills and the sea, a convenient car park has been built, and refined tablecloths have made their appearance too. As for the store, today it's no longer commercially viable, though there are still reminders of the early 1900s like the old wood and glass chests of drawers that create an atmosphere of times gone by.

For antipasto, try the fried **cheese-flavored focaccia** or the tasty stuffed vegetables. Moving on to the first course, superb **pansoti in walnut sauce**, gnocchi al pesto, lasagne with meat and mushroom sauce, and ravioli or trofiette al pesto with potatoes and string beans. There's also a classic minestrone but it must be ordered in advance. For the main course, magnificent **cima** (stuffed breast of veal), **stewed rabbit**, mushrooms and a **mixed fried** of meat and vegetables. In winter, you'll also find lamb with artichokes and, ordering in advance, stoccafisso accomodato (stewed stockfish).

There's a wide choice of puddings, all home-made: jam tart, crème caramel, panna cotta, tiramisu, warm apple pie with ice cream, and chocolate budino. While the wine list is reasonable, there's still room for improvement. We'd advise you to book.

TAGGIA

GERMINAL

🍲 Osteria
Via Gastaldi 15 B
Tel. 0184 41153
Closed Monday, Tuesday and Wednesday
Open: dinner, Sunday also for lunch,
in summer Saturday also for lunch
Holidays: variable
Seating: 30
Prices: 30-33 euros, wine excluded
All major credit cards

Located in the middle of town, this osteria was once the workshop of a basket-
weaver. Right from the start the focus
has been on food and music: the two
new owners, Enrica Borelli and Roberta
Ciribilli, have continued this theme,
though they've placed more emphasis
on the gastronomical element. A fundamental change has been the contribution to the kitchen of Danilo Musso, ex-
fisherman turned cook. An informal atmosphere with marble-topped tables,
paper tablecloths and a handwritten
menu. The dishes are simple, made with
good ingredients, reflecting what's available in the fish market and family vegetable garden.
Start with **fried anchovies**, octopus with
string beans and potatoes, **stuffed
pilchards**, tartare of sorallo or palamita
(both vaireities of tuna), stuffed squid,
cima (stuffed breast of veal) al limone,
previ (cabbage leaves stuffed with fish
or meat). The pasta is home-made:
gnocchi or **borage tagliolini with fish
ragù**, maltagliati in ratatuia, parpagliui
(butterfly-shaped pasta) with zucchini
trombette and tuna bottarga. Also for first
course, **fish soup**, cream of broad
beans or zuppa in zemin. To follow,
scabbard fish in parsley sauce, fillet of
palamita with Taggia olives and capers,
stoccafisso accomodato, **fish buridda**,
cuttlefish stew, stuffed rabbit, veal cima
cooked in the oven. To round things off,
an original pumpkin, raisin and pine nut
pie, with apple fritters or vanilla ice-
cream topped with exquisite homemade
marmalade.
The choice of wines is still limited: for
the moment, Vermentino, Pigato and a
few Piedmontese reds.

VARESE LIGURE

GLI AMICI

🍲 Restaurant/3-Star Hotel
Via Garibaldi 80
Tel. 0187 842139
Fax 0187 840891
E-mail: info@albergoamici.com
Internet: www.albergoamici.com
Closed Wednesday, always open in summer
Open lunch and dinner
Holidays: December 15-January 15
Seating: 170
Prices: 25 euros wine excluded
Most credit cards, Bancomat

In one of the best promoted and preserved villages in the Val di Vara sits the
elegant, though at the same time down-
to-earth, Amici hotel and restaurant. Five
of the 30 rooms (available all week) are
in the annex on the opposite side of the
road. The buffet breakfast includes pastries, and, on request, eggs and cold
cuts. The cuisine is typical of La Spezia's
surrounding hilltops with a touch of
Genoa and the region of Emilia.
Local cured meats, vegetables preserved in olive oil, croquettes, vegetable
pies and **baciocca** open the meal. **Meat
and vegetable ravioli**, tagliolini with
mushrooms, trofie al pesto follow. The
crosetti, pasta wheels with the restaurant's name or floral patterns impressed
on them, are good. Among the main
courses you will find organic meats and
cheeses from the local cooperative: try
the **tomaxelle**, stewed stuffed meat
roulades, **stecchi**, **cima** (stuffed breast
of veal) and, in season, roasted or **fricasseed lamb**.
As an alternative to the house wine,
good local, Piedmontese and Tuscan labels,.

• 3 singles and 26 doubles, en-suite, TV
• Prices: single 40, double 50 euros;
breakfast 5 euros per person • Private
indoor and outdoor parking. Small pets
welcome. Porter available 7am-11pm •
Bar, restaurant. Television room. Garden

🛒 In Piazza Vittorio Emanuele, Andrea De
Vincenti sells traditional pastries, fresh
hand-made crosetti and cheeses from the
local cooperative dairy. In **San Pietro Vara**
(6 km), the San Pietro Vara cooperative
sells organic meat.

VENDONE

LA CROSA

Holiday farm
Via Crosa 10
Tel. and fax 0182 76331
E-mail: lacrosa@hotmail.com
Internet: www.lacrosa.it
Open all year round

About 25 years ago Luigi Bodini and his wife Alessandra purchased the property and, after carefully renovating it, turned it into an agriturismo 10 years ago. All apartments have a private entrance and are the ideal location for people in pursuit of a peaceful holiday surrounded by nature. This farm is particularly suitable for children and a special pool has been designed for them. The restaurant serves local cuisine. The owners often organize trips on foot or by bicycle in the countryside. For sports lovers, a golf course, riding stables and tennis courts are available nearby.

• 3 apartments (2-5 persons), with bathroom, kitchen, private garden or terrace • Prices: 35 euros per person, breakfast included; apartment with use of kitchen 60-80 euros • Credit cards: none • Off-street parking. Small pets allowed. Owners always reachable • Restaurant. Reading room. Garden. Swimming pool

VERNAZZA

GIANNI FRANZI

2-Star Hotel
Piazza Marconi 1
Tel. 0187 821003-812228
Fax 0187 812228
E-mail: info@giannifranzi.it
Internet: www.giannifranzi.it
Closed from 6 January to 6 March

This famous hotel-restaurant is located in the main square of the beautiful village of Vernazza. It started out as a simple tavern before World War II before becoming a renowned seafood restaurant with the addition of the hotel in the late 70s. The original set of rooms was extended in 1997 by incorporating an adjacent old building on a sheer cliff. What makes the rooms and the commin areas so unique is the personal touch of theatrical director Aldo Trionfo, responsible for the décor assisted by set designers and sculptors, Luca Crippa and Giorgio Panni. Most rooms have a sea view and the more recent hotel wing also has small gardens overlooking the sea, in the shadow of the Doria castle.

• 7 single and 15 double rooms, with bathroom • Prices: single 42 euros, double 65-80; excluding breakfast (available in the restaurant bar) • Credit cards: all, Bancomat • Parking before entering the village. No pets allowed. Reception open 8am-midnight. • Bar, restaurant. Solarium.

EMILIA ROMAGNA

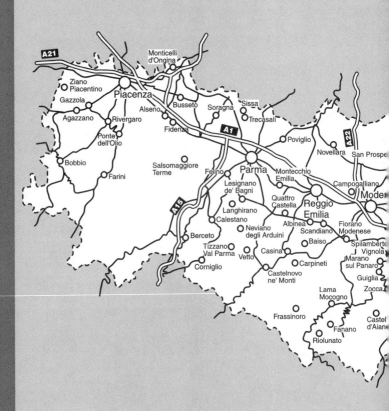

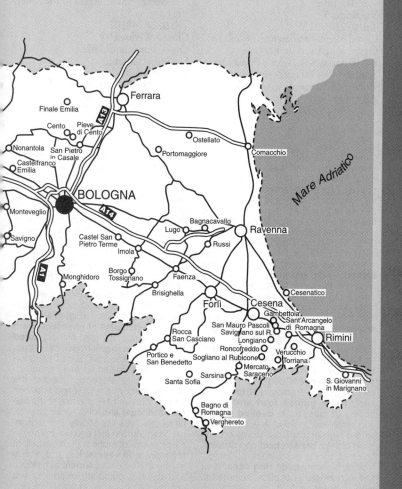

AGAZZANO
Sarturano

ANTICA TRATTORIA GIOVANELLI

📷

Trattoria
Via Roma 5
Tel. 0523 975155
Closed Monday and evening on holidays
Open: lunch and dinner
Holiday: August 16-31, 15 days in February-March
Seating: 60 + 60 outdoors
Prices: 28-30 euros, wine excluded
All major credit cards

Gentle slopes and a relaxing country-side lead you to this typical country trattoria. The Giovanelli family has been running it for three generations now with their warm hospitality and the traditional dishes of Piacenza. If you go there in the summer you can sit and relax in the shade of the gazebo.

Once settled, you start with an Italian antipasto or, rather, Piacenza antipasto, with various selected and home cured **meats:** coppa, salami, bacon, soppressa and in the winter fresh crackling. Piacenza cuisine offers various types of tasty pasta, prepared by the Giovanellis with the excellent **tortelli with ricotta and spinach,** served with separate garnishes: butter and sage and red mushroom sauce. The other pastas: **anolini in hen and capon broth**, **pisarei e fasò**, baked pasta and tagliatelle with seasonal sauces. Good main courses, all true to local traditions: **tripe,** roast veal, **roast guinea fowl and duck,** coppa of roast pork, **cooked salami** and sometimes chicken in aspic. In winter the highlights are two slowly cooked meat dishes: **braised beef** and **donkey**. To close try the homemade puddings: fruit tarts, homemade **ring cake,** pear tart with melted chocolate, semifreddo with yoghurt or fruit, the evergreen sbrisolona.

The cellar offers a good selection of the best local labels, which you can taste in the typical majolica scudlein.

ALSENO
Cortina

BOSCHI

📷

Restaurant attached to the hotel
Via Cortina 59
Tel. 0523 948102
Closed Wednesday
Open: lunch and dinner
Holidays: variable
Seating: 40
Prices: 25-35 euros, wine excluded
Credit cards: MC, Visa

They say that passion, hard work and enthusiasm are needed for any job. For proof of this go to Cortina di Alseno – the first hills of the Arda Valley just a short distance from the lovely medieval village of Castell'Arquato – and have lunch at Giuseppe Boschi's. The dining room is simple but very well looked after, the welcome warm and discreet. Giuseppe's mother Carla works in the kitchen, competently transforming the ingredients which Giuseppe finds or produces with maniacal care.

The result is top quality local dishes interpreted with an individual touch. We can start with the smoked salmon with balsamic vinegar, **pâté of pheasant livers** in apple sauce, the ever present **cured meats** that are excellent: salami, coppa, culatello, raw shoulder (superb) and excellent raw ham served with cep mushrooms in oil. Giuseppe imports the salmon directly from Scotland and then smokes it himself. He also makes the **balsamic vinegar** and, of the cured meats, he follows the entire supply and seasoning chain. Among first courses the home-made pasta triumphs with the excellent **tagliolini with vegetables,** and, above all, the stuffed pasta: **tortelli** with ricotta and spinach, pumpkin, artichokes and cep mushrooms when in season. A very pleasant risotto with pears, cheese and nutmeg. Among the second courses, noteworthy is a Padua dish that is hard to find now, **guinea fowl alla creta** (you have to book), stewed deer and when possible **game**. Among the puddings, bavarese with nougat and doughnut with chocolate chips and macaroons.The cellar offers a personal selection of Italian and foreign labels, together with the wine made by Giuseppe from his own vines.

BAGNACAVALLO

OSTERIA IN PIAZZA NUOVA

☞Restaurant
Piazza Nuova 22
Tel. 0545 63647
Closed Saturday lunch
Open: lunch and dinner
Holidays: variable
Seating: 80 + 80 outdoors
Prices: 35 euros, wine excluded
All credit cards accepted

The beautiful Romagna countryside, its seaside resorts and then Bagnacavallo, with its center rich in history and art, lovely palazzos, roads and squares, and the Trattoria di Piazza Nuova. No matter what the season, these are all good reasons to spend a day visiting the town and trying its specialties. You will be welcomed to the restaurant by Maurizio Bragonzoni. The dishes of fish and meat that Maurizio offers, helped in the kitchen by Matteo Giacomoni, follow the seasons and traditions with a bit of cross-fertilization from other regions as well.

Among the antipasti: **piada and uncooked ham,** basket with fried gnocchi or **squaquerone** with caramelized figs. For first course there are **cappelletti romagnoli al ragù,** strozzapreti cooked according to the season, **tortellacci filled with fossa cheese** or asparagus and, in summer, zucchini. For seconds, a wide choice of **grilled meat,** including mutton. Otherwise: **stuffed rabbit** with Sangiovese sauce or fresh tuna escalopes. Also among the main dishes a delicious **baccalà stew** with polenta. And don't forget the wide choice of cheeses, served with caramelized figs and homemade jam.

For pudding, the ever-present **mascarpone,** also used as filling for the crepes with fondant, chocolate salami, **scroccadenti** with almonds, ricotta blancmange. Only Romagna wine is drunk and the list offers the best labels from the region.

BAGNO DI ROMAGNA
San Piero in Bagno

AL GAMBERO ROSSO 🐌 ▮

☞Trattoria/1-Star Hotel
Via Verdi, 5
Tel. e fax 0543 903405
E-mail: locanda.gamberorosso@libero.it
Closed Sunday dinner and Monday; January-March
also for dinner on Tuesday and Wednesday
Open: lunch and dinner
Holidays: variable
Seating: 60
Prices: 33-35 euros, wine excluded
All major credit cards, Bancomat

The modest rooms and restaurant of the Saragoni family are housed in an 18th century residence. If you breakfast in the locanda, you will appreciate the donuts, sweets and marmalades, all home-made. Half-board (after the third night's stay) is 45 euro per person.

Giuliana uses local and seasonal products in the cuisine. You can choose between a taste of the first courses, of four or six helpings, or the traditional menu: **potato and mushroom pie; passatelli soup,** cannolo with herbs, ricotta and cep mushrooms, potato tortelli with fossa cheese; pork stew with apples or stewed lamb or **trippa in bianco; trifle** or caffè in forchetta. The same dishes are on the menu, but also soups, **farinata di grano con la gota,** passatelli with wild fennel or stridoli, **pigeon with black olives, stewed freshwater prawns** or with green tagliolini (from elsewhere, given that it is forbidden to fish locally)... In fall dishes with pera cocomerina (Slow Food Presidia) are served. Delicious choice of home-made puddings and choice selection of wines, mainly from Romagna and the nearby regions. Other national labels are also available.

🛏🍴• 2 single rooms, 2 doubles and 1 triple, en-suite, TV • Prices: single 40, double 50, triple 65 euros; breakfast 5 euros per person • Building in part accessible to the mobility impaired. Outside public parking available adjacent to the hotel. No pets allowed. Owners available from 11am to 4.30pm and from 6.30pm to 11pm • Restaurant. Relaxation room

BAISO
Lugo

BERCETO
Bergotto

29 KM SOUTH OF REGGIO EMILIA

58 KM SOUTH OF PARMA A15 OR SS62

CA' POGGIOLI

MANUBIOLA

Trattoria
Via Lugo 7
Tel. 0522 844631
Closed Monday evening and Thursday
Open: lunch and dinner
Holidays: between August and September
Seating: 70
Prices: 20-25 euros, wine excluded
All credit cards except AE, Bancomat

Restaurant
Via Fontanelle 78
Tel. 0525 64511
Closed Tuesday
Open: lunch and dinner
Holiday: three weeks in January
Seating: 100
Prices: 23-27 euros, wine excluded
All credit cards are accepted and Bancomat

The trattoria is in a lovely traditional stone building, with the dining room divided in two parts by a lovely open well. Front of house, Gabriele presents the dishes prepared by his mother, Gianna, following typical mountain tradition. On the Reggio Apennines, in the Secchia River Valley where Baiso is situated, the limes Byzantium, used to run, the borderline between Lombard Italy and the land governed by Byzantium. The Lombards used to raise pigs while on the other side of the border they preferred lamb and mutton. These historic roots have left deep marks on this part of the mountains, where cooking traditions are strongly tied to sheep.

The antipasti include cured meats, toasts, chiazze and tigelle with aromatized lardo. Among the first courses **tortelli with herbs**, pumpkin, cabbage and, the mountain classic, with **potatoes and cep mushrooms**. Then **cappelletti in broth, and** potato gnocchi with fried vegetables. Among the main courses we would mention the **barzigole**, a typical local dish, made from marinated wether meat, not sheep's, for a more delicate flavor. Then the **lamb chops** grilled or fried, homemade **cotechino with spinach**, puree and white beans. In winter, boar and **game**. Just a few but very good puddings: cooked cream, **trifle**, semifreddo with chocolate and baked tarts. The wines are mainly local sparking types.

There is no need to go up to Baiso to reach the trattoria, but follow the bottom of the Secchia valley towards Montefiorino, and then the signs for Lugo.

Manubiola is the name of the river that flows through the valley of the same name in the Parma Apennines. The woods supply mushrooms and game which are the basic ingredients for local cooking; a spacious informal restaurant, where the generous portions are one of the main features of the service.

If it is springtime we recommend starting with dishes based on **prugnoli mushrooms**, in summer **cep mushrooms**, prepared fried, sautéed or in salads. As antipasto, we suggest the typical Parma cured meats, including the excellent **culaccia**, or thin slices of lardo that cover the potato pie. Among the first courses, we recommend **taglioline all'ortica** with speck and truffles, **tortelli with herbs** garnished **with mushrooms**, or mushroom soup and croutons. The main courses are nearly all based on meat: we recommend the **pork fillet with truffles, and** the escalopes with cep mushrooms. There is also a wide choice of **game**, including boar chasseur, hare or pheasant chasseur, braised venison or deer. These dishes are all seasonal and should be booked beforehand. To finish a very good strawberry puff pastry, **trifle** or wild berry tarts. The wine list has recently been added to and offers a good selection of regional and national wines.

To reach the restaurant, we suggest taking the Cisa motorway, exit at Borgotaro and then follow the signs for Berceto and then Bergotto.

PIACENTINO

🗝3-Star Hotel
Piazza San Francesco 19 A
Tel. 0523 936266-936563
Fax 0523 936266
E-mail: info@hotelpiacentino.it
Internet: www.hotelpiacentino.it
Holidays vary

A BOLOGNA

🗝Bed and breakfast
Via Cairoli 3
Tel. 051 4210897-348 5939844
Fax 051 4210897
E-mail: takakina@hotmail.com
Internet: www.traveleurope.it/bolognabb
Closed in January

Maria Celestina Bellocchio is the fourth-generation owner of this hotel that faces a peaceful tree-lined public square near the historic center. The hall and bar are located in the older wing of the building, erected over one hundred years ago, while the rooms and restaurant are in the newer part built in the Sixties. The apartments are in a separate building just a few meters from the hotel. The spacious, comfortable rooms are furnished in a classic manner. Buffet breakfast offers a vast choice of sweet and savory fare, along with the usual hot and cold drinks. In the restaurant – open to non-residents – you'll be able to taste traditional dishes (the pasta is homemade) at a price ranging from 20-30 euros per person, excluding wine. There's also a half board option that will cost you from 47 to 68 euros depending on the season.

• 4 single, 14 double rooms and 2 apartments (4-6 persons), with bathroom, air-conditioning, safe, TV; some with balcony • Prices: single 42-52 euros, double 52-73 (16-22 euro supplement for extra bed), apartments 25 euros per person (minimum 4 persons); breakfast 5 euros per person • Credit cards: all except DC, Bancomat • Entire facility accessible to the mobility challenged. Free external public parking, garage (2 spaces). Small pets allowed. Owners always reachable. • Bar, restaurant. Breakfast room, TV room. Garden

This B&B, which opened in 2003, is on the second floor of a modern building in a strategic position in the center of Bologna. The rooms are big, refurbished and freshly painted, with beautiful marble floors; each room is different and they are all tastefully furnished with great attention to detail. The atmosphere is on the whole elegant but at the same time young and happy, like the owner Takako Nagayama who left Japan to marry a man from Bologna. Breakfast is prepared as each customer prefers, with a choice of either sweet or savory fare. It is usually served in your room, although there is also a small communal room equipped with tables, chairs and refrigerator if you prefer. During vacation periods the double room can cost up to 180 euros.

• 2 double and 2 triple rooms, with bathroom (2 with a shared bathroom), satellite TV • Prices: double room single occupancy 50-80 euros, double 65-120, triple 120-200, breakfast included • Credit cards: none • Paid parking and garage in the vicinity. Small pets allowed. Owners always reachable • Breakfast room

ANTICA TRATTORIA DELLA GIGINA

Trattoria
Via Stendhal, 1 B
Tel. 051 322300-322132
No fixed closing day
Open: lunch and dinner
Holiday: first three weeks in August
Seating: 70
Prices: 26-28 euros, wine excluded
All major credit cards and Bancomat

ARCOVEGGIO

2-Star Hotel
Via Spada 27
Tel. 051 355436
Fax 051 363102
E-mail: info@hotelarcoveggio.it
Internet: www.hotelarcoveggio.it
Open all year

On the northern outskirts of Bologna, once the reign of Gigina, and famous for its tagliatelle with beef ragù and tomato concentrate. Gigina is no longer here, but the tagliatelle are made from hand-made dough, like all the other fresh pasta – marked in the menu as "mythical" dishes. For several years now the restaurant has been in the hands of the histrionic Carlo Cortesi and Rosalba who have continued to offer typical cuisine while renovating the restaurant where professional service is given at very honest prices. It was a winning gamble because you will usually find the restaurant full both at lunchtime and dinner with a varied selection of clients.

Cold antipasti, including mortadella mousse and balsamic jelly, loin of pork in tuna sauce and sweet and sour capers; then the Bologna first courses: **tortellini** and **passatelli in broth, tagliatelle with ragù**, lasagna verdi, tortelloni with ricotta, gramignone sporcafaccia with sausage al pasticcio. Among the main courses, dishes that continue in the tradition, such as **roast rabbit** highlight of the trattoria, **muscoletto of boiled beef** with Bologna **friggione, cutlet alla petroniana** or boned roast guinea-fowl cooked in wine, together with a few new dishes like roast shoulder of suckling pig.

Among the puddings, the **fried cream Gigina style** stands out, the homemade **rice cake**, trifle, along with the yoghurt mousse in berry sauce and nougat ice cream cake with balsamic cream. Exceptional wine list, especially the regional labels with very honest mark-ups.

The Arcoveggio Hotel managed by Laura Palazzi is a short distance from the racecourse: a strategic position for reaching the fair and exhibition center and the old city center, which takes only five minutes by bus (number 27) or you can do it on foot in fifteen minutes. The hotel building is in a small green area far away from traffic and other noise. The atmosphere is relaxing: rooms and communal areas are spacious, comfortable and furnished with lively chromatic solutions and great attention to detail. Here, breakfast is a very important moment, it's set out in an elegant room and the generous buffet offers a wide variety of sweet and savory fare, along with hot and cold drinks.

• 1 single, 19 double and 3 triple rooms, with bathroom, TV • Prices: single 60-78 euros, double 70-115, triple 110-150, breakfast included • Credit cards: all, Bancomat • 2 rooms designed for use by the mobility challenged. Garage (7 euros per day). No pets allowed. Reception open from 6am to 1am. • Bar. Breakfast room. Garden

IN THE HISTORIC CENTER

CRISTINA ROSSI

🗝️🔑 Bed and breakfast
Via Porta di Castello 6
Tel. 051 220052-335 6223113
Fax 051 220052
E-mail: info@cristinarossi.it
Internet: www.cristinarossi.it
Open all year round

DA GIANNI
A LA VÈCIA BULÀGNA

🍲 Trattoria
Via Clavature 18
Tel. 051 229434
Closed Sunday evening and Monday
Open: lunch and dinner
Holidays: August and Christmas
Seating: 45
Prices: 32-35 euro, wine excluded
All credit cards accepted, Bancomat

This charming B&B is in a peaceful corner of Bologna's historic center, very close to Piazza Maggiore. A gentle cobblestone hill leads up to the building, with the owner's – the likeable and courteous Cristina – apartment on the first floor, while the four guest rooms are on the second. Access to the rooms is either through the Rossi family's beautiful dining room or, in a more discreet manner, by taking the stairs up to your room directly. The generous, meticulously prepared breakfast is served in a communal room and consists of either homemade sweet fare or that produced by a local quality bakery. The rooms have been tastefully and elegantly furnished, with great attention to detail. The bathrooms are new and comfortable; the shared one has two washbasins. The double room is furnished with antique furniture and has a jacuzzi in the ensuite bathroom. During periods when fairs are going on (this is frequent in Bologna) the price of this room goes up to 160 euros.

• 1 single and 2 double rooms, with bathroom (1 next door), air-conditioning, TV • Prices: single 45-100 euros, double 75-120, breakfast included • Credit cards: all except DC, Bancomat • Ticket for parking in the vicinity. Small pets allowed. Owners always reachable • Breakfast room with satellite TV, reading area, Internet point, fax

For a few years now chef Michele Rode and his wife Barbara Bertozzi have been helping Giorgio Previati run this traditional trattoria, which he took over in 1985 from its historic owner Gianni. It is just a short walk from Piazza Maggiore, in the medieval heart of the town, where there are still several colorful food shops. The restaurant is reached down a narrow alley half way down Via Clavature. The three small rooms, together with the friendliness and warmth of Barbara and Giorgio, make the guests feel at home, Bolognese and tourists alike. Traditional local dishes and homemade pasta using the historic pasta machine Cinzia, reign supreme in the kitchen. After the antipasti (culatello, lardo with croutons, polenta and squacquerone cheese) we have **passatelli** and **tortellini in broth**, onion soup and **pasta and bean soup, tagliatelle ragù**, taglioline with ham, tortelloni with ricotta, butter and sage, **gramigna with sausage**, strozzapreti 'Gianni' style (with asparagus and ham). Among the main courses, meat (but on Friday Michele has some fresh fish proposals): **roast lamb and potatoes**, mixed boiled meat and cotechino with puree, **Bologna cutlet** (with ham and Parmesan), roast pork shank, morsels of chicken with potatoes and artichokes, **stewed tripe au gratin**. Among the traditional puddings, mascarpone with macaroons and coffee, cooked cream with wild berries, crème brûlée and **tiramisù**.
There is also the day's menu, with a dozen different dishes according to what the nearby market has to offer. Barbara pays special attention to the wine list, especially the regional labels. It is advisable to book.

MELONCELLO

🍲 Trattoria
Via Saragozza 240 A
Tel. 051 6143947
Closed Monday evening and Tuesday
Open: lunch and dinner
Holidays: 1 week in January, 3 in August
Seating: 50 + 30 outdoors
Prices: 28-30 euros, wine excluded
All major credit cards, Bancomat

SERGHEI

🍲 Trattoria
Via Piella 12
Tel. 051 233533
Closed Saturday and Sunday
Open: lunch and dinner
Holidays: August, one week at New Year
Seating: 28
Prices: 28-32 euros, wine excluded
Major credit cards, Bancomat

From Porta Saragozza take the road that leads to San Luca; straight after the Teatro delle Celebrazioni you come to the Trattoria Meloncello, which takes its name from the arch. Externally the trattoria has a very friendly air and as you enter you will find a simply furnished room in the best trattoria tradition. On the walls photos of some of the artists who have stopped here to taste a "slice of bologna", and if you want Bolognese cooking this is the right place for you.

There are no menus or wine lists on the tables, but the owner Patrizia will help you by explaining the dishes and suggesting the best. Homemade pasta among the first courses, especially the stuffed variety which is very good. Excellent traditional **tortellini in broth** and **tortelli with ricotta and ragù**. Also the **tagliatelle al ragù**, green lasagna and passatelli in broth. Among the main courses, the highlights are the various stews, including the excellent **rissoles** with peas, **zucchini stuffed with meat**, veal stew. Another classic at the Meloncello is the **rabbit chasseur** or rabbit boned and stuffed (with a summer version as well).

Homemade puddings, including trifle and **rice cake** to close.

Serghei's is in the historic heart of the city in the Palazzo of the Conti Piella, on the road of the same name close by the "torresotto" and the entrance gate to the town when, in medieval times, the town had walls. The trattoria has a small entrance with a bar and a room with just a few tables. The warm atmosphere comes from the wood-panelled walls typical of old osterie. You will be welcomed by Saverio and his sister Diana, who also helps their mother in the kitchen to prepare the typical Bologna dishes, some of which are hard to find elsewhere.

There are no antipasti on the menu; we go straight to the first courses. Homemade fresh pasta: classic **tortellini** or passatelli in broth, **tagliatelle ragù,** tortelloni with ricotta in butter or gorgonzola; not forgetting the classic **lasagna Bolognese** and various soups, such as pasta and beans and pasta and chickpeas. In winter, the **polenta with pork ribs,** or rabbit or **chicken chasseur**. As main courses there is **pork loin in milk,** stuffed zucchini and rissoles in stew, marrowbone with puree, **roast pigeon with junipers, mixed boiled meat** and green sauce. You can close with puddings such as crème caramel, trifle or **semifreddo with mascarpone** and hot chocolate.

A reasonable choice of regional and national labels, mainly red wines. Given the size of the inn, it is best to book.

🍦 The Gelatauro ice cream parlor in via San Vitale 98 B, is one of the best in the city. It offers unusual flavors such as ginger, apple, cinnamon, jasmine. Slow Food Presidia are also used such as Noto almonds, Bronte pistachio and manna delle Madonie.

🍦 You should try the ice cream made by Stefano, an ice cream parlor in the nearby via Galliera at 49 B, made with Sicilian ingredients. Few flavors, excellent quality. Closed on Monday.

Trattoria del Rosso

🍲 Trattoria
Via Augusto Righi 30
Tel. 051 236730
No fixed closing day
Open: lunch and dinner
Holidays: never
Seating: 85 + 40 outdoors
Prices: 20-22 euros, wine excluded
All credit cards, Bancomat

Fita

🍲 Trattoria
Via Roma 3
Tel. 0542 91183
Closed Monday dinner, Tuesday and Saturday lunch
Open: lunch and dinner
Holidays: August and 2 weeks in January
Seating: 50
Prices: 26-28 euros, wine excluded
All major credit cards, Bancomat

What used to be a coffee bar, in the 19th century a meeting place for patriots, artists and men of culture, is today run by Stefano Corvucci who has preserved the original environment with its large mirrors and the period photos on the wood-covered walls. Faithful to Bolognese cooking, he offers good service over long hours (the kitchens are open until midnight) and the prices are very reasonable. The trattoria is in the city center, under the arcade of Piazza August Righi, which links Via dell'Independenza with the University area, just a short walk from the underground car park in Piazza VIII Agosto, where the weekly Piazzola market is held. Three rooms and tables outside on the street in the summer: wooden tables with yellow paper place-mats, always crowded with students and tourists. A very central, lively place (if you are looking for intimacy you won't go there), with a bill, which is very low for Bologna.

The quality of the food is more than satisfying. Starting with the **crescentine** and Pasquini & Brusiani **home cured meats** (with the **classic mortadella** of Bologna, Slow Food Presidia). All the traditional firsts: **tagliatelle** with different sauces, lasagna and **tortellini in broth**, gnocchi with Bolognese ragù, **gramigna with sausage**, pasta and bean soup, vegetable minestrone and **passatelli in broth**. Substantial main courses, with ribs and polenta, roast shank, **stewed tripe**, sausage and **friggione**, stewed meat and peas and classic **Bolognese cutlet**, with a few summer variations to replace the heavier dishes.

Lots of salads and vegetables. For the puddings trust the homemade ones. The wine list is limited to good quality regional wines, sold with a very honest mark up.

Leave Imola following the racing circuit, and take the state road for Florence. You will find this small village as you get to the foothills of the Apennines. The restaurant used to be just a simple osteria: the wine was made in the cellars beneath and travelers could cook their own sausages in the fireplace. The furnishings haven't changed much: in the entrance there are large tables and benches that have darkened with time and the enormous fire is always on. Maria Pia looks after the cooking, preparing typical Romagna dishes, together with her husband Ivo who welcomes guests to the dining room and competently controls the grill in the fireplace.

You can start with antipasti: **chicory with bruciatini** (grilled pancetta) in **balsamic vinegar**, casatella with figs caramelized in wine, platter of local **cured meats**. The pasta is homemade. We recommend the tagliolini alle corniole or al ribes, **tortelli with potatoes or ricotta** with wild asparagus, **garganelli** and **tortellini with butter, rosemary and lemon** (in Romagna it is quite normal to use lemon on the pasta). Among the main courses following the tradition, we recommend the **rabbit with plums, cutlet in onion sauce**, chopped fillet with cep mushrooms and wild berries. If you prefer, Ivo will grill you a **mutton chop**, a T-bone steak, sausage or fillet of beef, and prepare delicious grilled eggplant and tomatoes. A wide choice of puddings, including English cream with hot wild berries, flaky bitter chocolate and mint and an excellent homemade **biscuit assortment** served with passito wine. The wine list contains a good selection of Romagna Sangiovesi and a reasonable choice of other regional labels.

BRISIGHELLA
Monte Romano

BRISIGHELLA

CROCE DANIELE

LA CAVALLINA

Trattoria
Via Monte Romano 43
Tel. 0546 87019
Closed Monday
Open: lunch and dinner
Holidays. Sunday before Christmas – beginning of February
Seating: 120 + 50 outdoors
Prices: 20-22 euros, wine excluded
All major credit cards, Bancomat

Rooms
Via Masironi, 6
Tel. 0546 80520
Fax 0546 81828
Closed for 15 days after Epiphany

It is not easy to reach this corner of the Apennines on the border between Romagna and Tuscany, but it is well worth the trip and you will leave the trattoria fully satisfied. What's more the road that leads up to Croce Daniele is really spectacular: after Brisighella continue towards Marradi and then turn off towards San Martino in Gattara, where you pass through a beautiful wood before reaching Monte Romano. The road continues along a crest with some really breathtaking views, and you can see Brisighella, Faenza, the plains and the Adriatic.
A mountain trattoria, meeting place for the few locals, and an inn competently run by Luciano Gentilini. The surroundings are simple and traditional, like the cooking, which is really something. You can start with the home cured **meats** or the croutons, to continue with the delicious first courses. You should try the **spoia lorda with sausage and chicory,** tortelli with herbs and ricotta, **tortelli with potatoes**, tagliatelle and **cappelletti**. Meat triumphs in the second courses: grilled or roast **guinea fowl**, lamb, **game** and **rabbit,** and if you book **rabbit chasseur**. To finish you can taste the fresh **goat's cheese** made by the local shepherds, and then the homemade puddings: zabaione, **mattonella with coffee,** cream dessert and semifreddo with ricotta and macaroons. The best wine to serve is the house wine, but there are also a few Romagna labels.

This possibly one thousand year-old building was originally a station where horses were changed on the salt road from the Cervia salt-mines to Florence. In addition to its rooms, the B&B has seven miniapartments equipped with two bathrooms and a kitchen, suitable for groups of three to five people, that can be rented for a minimum period of three days. Acquired by the Casadio family, the facility has been restructured with a bio-architectural approach by Vincenzo who also manages it. The surrounding area consists of gardens where squirrels, weasels and hares run about undisturbed, even though the railway station and the center of Brisighella are just a short distance away. The rooms are spacious and comfortable and have been furnished with great attention to detail. Breakfast is served in the restaurant room and offers hot and fresh drinks, and sweet and savory fare; the cost of a meal ranges from 20-30 euros per person. Management supplies bicycles for excursions in the surrounding area.

• 10 double rooms, with bathroom, minibar, satellite TV; some with air-conditioning • Prices: double room single occupancy and double 50 euros, breakfast included • Credit cards: all, Bancomat • 1 apartment designed for use by the mobility challenged. Off-street parking. Small pets allowed. Owners reachable in the restaurant from 7.30am to midnight in the restaurant • Bar (for residents only), restaurant. Reading room. Conference room. Garden, terrace. Pool

BRISIGHELLA

OSTERIA DEL GUERCINORO

Traditional Osteria
Piazza Marconi 7
Tel. 0546 80464
Closed Tuesday
Open: dinner only, from September to May on holidays also at lunch
Holidays: December 20–January 7
Seating: 30 + 15 outdoors
Prices: 30 euros, wine excluded
Credit cards not accepted

Along the road that joins Faenza to Florence you will find the lovely hamlet of Brisighella; enter the historic center and along the Via degli Asini you will find this attractive little inn. The few tables are set in a single room dug out of the chalk walls, chalk being the material that the whole of the village is built on. You will be welcomed by Franco, owner and chef, and by Marco and Alina in the dining room who will help you choose from the day's dishes. The menu is short and dishes change virtually every day because they only cook whatever is found fresh in the market.

Given the vicinity with Tuscany, we recommend starting with the lovely selection of **cinta cured meats** and cheeses from the Apennines, often hand ripened and seasoned. You should also try the fresh goat's cheese, if for no other reason than that it is seasoned with **Brisighella oil**. Among the first courses of homemade pasta, we recommend the **orecchioni** (triangular stuffed pasta similar to ravioli) **with smoked ricotta**, tortelli stuffed with goat's cheese and spinach, tagliatelle with mushrooms. In the winter, you will always find soup in the evenings. Among the main courses we suggest the **combata di cinta**, sliced fillet with vegetables, t-bone steak but, above all, the **lamb dishes:** fried sweetbreads, roast treccia di coratella, or budella with eggs. Sometimes they prepare the Romagna frizzaglio a dish of onions and peppers. To finish the meal excellent apple pie, homemade tarts or fresh ricotta cake with caramelized figs. Attention paid to local produce is confirmed by the excellent Brisighella oil, the Fognano wood cooked bread and lots of good wines from the numerous local producers.

BRISIGHELLA
Strada Casale

TRATTORIA DI STRADA CASALE

Trattoria
Via Statale 22
Tel. 0546 88054
Closed Wednesday
Open: dinner, lunch on Saturday and Sunday
Holiday: January 10-31, September 4-14
Seating: 40 + 30 outdoors
Prices: 25-32 euros, wine excluded
All major credit cards, Bancomat

On winter evenings, the large open fire makes these comfortable surroundings even cozier, and the well-spaced tables create a pleasantly intimate atmosphere, while in the summer you can eat outside on the large veranda.

The service, sometimes rather rushed, is looked after by owners Remo Camorani and his wife Daniela Pompili, helped in the kitchen by Piero Donegaglia. The menu pays special attention to the quality of the raw materials and traditional dishes, and is changed every week. There are not many dishes on the à-la-carte menu (choosing three courses you will spend around 25 euros, drinks excluded) but it is supplemented with a set menu costing 32 euros, with an additional 8 euros, two different wines served by the glass.

Among the antipasti, besides the wild herb fritters, we tasted a very good **loin of pork** which is home seasoned. Among the first courses **ravioli with ricotta**, potato and green bean soup, quadrucci **of pasta in broth with broad beans** and homemade stricchetti with guanciale, peas and sheep's cheese. Among the main courses, besides the roast **musk duck** or guinea fowl, roast pork shank with borlotti beans and herbs, roast veal chops and good raw ham served with rosemary pizza.

A good selection of cheeses from the Apennines or squacquerone with oil and pepper can be a good alternative. Among the puddings, ice creams and homemade cakes, especially the apricot and almond tart. Booking is recommended.

CAMPANINI

Trattoria
Via Roncole Verdi 136
Tel. 0524 92569
Closed Tuesday and Wednesday
Open: dinner, lunch on Sunday
Holidays: variable
Seating: 70
Prices: 25-30 euros, wine excluded
Credit cards are not accepted, Bancomat

I DUE FOSCARI

3-Star Hotel
Piazza Carlo Rossi 15
Tel. 0524 930031-930039
Fax 0524 91625
E-mail: www.iduefoscari.it
Internet: www.iduefoscari.it
Open all year

Stefano Campanini, helped by his sister and his mother Maria in the kitchen, continues the family tradition in this small temple of cured meats that the Po mists give a special flavor to. Giuseppe Verdi's birthplace is a few miles away and the 18th century Sanctuary of the Madonna of the Meadows is just a few yards away from the trattoria, which opened in 1911 to offer refreshment to pilgrims. Meticulous service and modern surroundings with historic photos from the bassa parmense on the walls, especially of Antonio Guareschi, the local bard.

You have to start with the platter of cured meats and taste the **culatello di Zibello** produced and seasoned by Stefano (Slow Food Presidia), a very sweet **uncooked Parma ham** of more than 30 months seasoning, the other rare cured meats that are Slow Food Presidia: **mariola** and **raw shoulder** on the bone, **cooked shoulder from San Secondo** served hot: all served with an excellent **fried pie**. Then the hand drawn pastas: **tortelli with herbs**, caramelle agli asparagi, taleggio parcels with culatello, cappellacci with Treviso chicory, **anolini della bassa**. Among the main courses (if you get that far given the large portions): **veal cheek with rosemary, crusty duck** with potatoes, **botticella** (cooked salami that is halfway between a mariola and sauce salami) with mostarda. Among the homemade puddings we recommend the upside down chocolate cream and the semifreddo of Nonna Turivia.

The wine list also has a selection of champagnes, excellent to accompany the numerous cured meats (but you can also choose the rustic Fortana house wine). Booking is essential.

Located in the central square of Busseto, this hotel with its sign dedicated to Giuseppe Verdi was founded in the Sixties by the tenor Carlo Bergonzi; currently it's run by his son Marco and by Roberto Morsia. The rooms were refurbished in 1998 and are very comfortable and well-furnished, as are the communal rooms, neat and elegant. The buffet breakfast offers a selection of sweet and savory fare, such as croissants, butter, honey and jams, cured meats and cheeses. But there's also no lack of the traditional coffee, light refreshments and fresh drinks. The restaurant, which is open to non-residents, offers both half board and full board for hotel guests who stay for at least three nights. Alternatively the cost of a meal ranges from 40-45 euros per person, excluding wine.

• 9 single and 10 double rooms, with bathroom, air-conditioning, mini-bar, safe; 8 with balcony • Prices: single 62 euros, double 87 (26 euro supplement for extra bed); breakfast 8 euros per person • Credit cards: all, Bancomat • Off-street parking. Small pets allowed. Reception open 24 hours a da. • Bar, restaurant. Breakfast room. Conference room. Garden, terrace

CALESTANO
Fragnolo

CAMPOGALLIANO

LOCANDA MARIELLA

🍲 Trattoria
Frazione Fragnolo
Tel. 0525 52102
Closed Monday and Tuesday
Open: lunch and dinner
Holidays: variable
Seating: 90 + 50 outdoors
Prices: 28-30 euros, wine excluded
Credit cards are not accepted

LA BARCHETTA

🍲 Trattoria
Via Magnagallo Est 20
Tel. 059 526218
Closed Sunday
Open: lunch, Friday and Saturday also for dinner
Holidays: August 15-September 15
Seating: 40 + 40 outdoors
Prices: 25-30 euros, wine excluded
All credit cards accepted

There are at least three good reasons to take the road for the Parma hills which leads you first to Calestano, then Fragno and finally to the 700 meters of Fragnolo. The first is that you will find the 'old' members of the Gennari family, Adriana and Virginio, she at the bar and cash-desk, he in the kitchen. Custodians of the country ways of the Apennines, they have handed down the secrets of the cuisine, the pasta for the **cappelletti in broth** and the tortelli with herbs and potatoes, the perfectly cooked meat – **tripe alla parmigiana**, **guancialino of veal**, the roasts (duck, guinea fowl, lamb, veal), **boar stew**, the cake and tart recipes.

The second is the most important local product, **black Fragno truffles** that are gathered from 15 September to 15 February (the truffle fair is held between October and November, so it is best to book then), which is offered in numerous dishes, from the **soft polenta with cheese fondue**, risotto, potato gnocchi (from local potatoes) through to the classic fried eggs (for the rest of the year black truffles are replaced by the less precious scorzone with more than valid results). There are then the other local products, mushrooms and, above all the **cured meats**, starting with the **culaccia** and the Parma ham.

The third reason is Mariella, following in her parents' footsteps, who, with the help of husband Guido, has given her own taste to the inn – from the furnishings, the courteous efficient service, the choice of suppliers, the introduction of a large selection of Italian and French cheeses – and has added all her love for wine, which means a wine list of more than 1,500 labels from all over the world.

This trattoria is run by Giovanni and his wife Gianna, in the kitchen, and is surrounded by the lovely green Modena countryside. It takes its name from a bridge of boats that had once been built close by. Two small rooms – one on the ground floor and one upstairs – in simple but well kept surroundings (it is air conditioned and in the summer seating is available outside in the courtyard).

The menu changes with the seasons but you can start with, lardo, guanciale and pancetta di Colonnata, Parma ham, **culaccia**, marinated raw tuna with blue poppy seeds, smoked goose breast, zucchini flan with parmesan sauce. Among the first courses you will find **gramigna al torchio** with sausage or **pumpkin tortelloni with melted butter and balsamic vinegar**, **tortellini in broth**, **tagliatelle with ragù**, **maccheroncini al torchio** with ricotta, basil and tomatoes. Numerous different main courses: classic sliced fillet of horsemeat with garlic and rosemary, lamb chops served hot from the grill, **baked guinea fowl** breast of duck in salt and cardamom, cotechino with puree, **roast pork shank** and mixed boiled meats. You will also find grilled meat, cheeses and tuna. Homemade puddings: cinnamon semifreddo with plum sauce, chocolate mousse with chili cooked in the oven, **trifle** and semifreddo of zabaione, almonds and rum. The wine list presents a good selection of labels, with some excellent Lambruscos.

They cannot seat more than forty people at a time, so booking is essential if you want to find a table.

CARPINETI
Regigno

37 KM SOUTH OF REGGIO EMILIA

LE SCUDERIE

🔑Holiday farm
Via Regigno 77
Tel. 0522 618397
Fax 0522 718066
Open all year

Surrounded by the greenery of the Regigno estate, this vacation farm managed by Tiziana Campani and her husband Giancarlo Panciroli has been created in a recently renovated stone farmhouse. The comfortable rooms fitted with rustic furnishings are on the upper floor, while the communal areas are on the ground floor. For breakfast guests will be offered hot drinks, homemade jams, honey, bread and butter and homemade cakes. On request you can also have local cured meats and Parmesan cheese. The restaurant offers traditional Emilia mountain-style cuisine. Half board (40 euros per person) or full board (50 euros per person) is only available from the second day of your stay; alternatively a meal costs around 22-23 euros per person, including drinks.

• 2 double, 1 triple and 4 four-bed rooms, with bathroom • Prices: double room single occupancy 31 euros, double 52, triple 78, four-bed 104, breakfast included • Credit cards: major ones, Bancomat • Facility partly accessible to the mobility challenged. Off-street parking. Small pets allowed. Owners reachable until 10pm. • Restaurant. Reading and conference room (for 30 persons)

CASINA
Mulino di Leguigno

27 KM SOUTH-WEST OF REGGIO EMILIA ON SS63

MULINO IN PIETRA

🔑Holiday farm
Via Mulino di Leguigno 1
Tel. 0522 607503-339 8987592
E-mail: pinchio@aliceposta.it
Closed in January and February

In a beautiful hilly area only fifteen minutes by car from Canossa Castle, Luigi Pinchiorri and Cecilia Caletti provide hospitality in Leguigno's seventeenth-century flourmill built entirely in stone, and refurbished with great attention to detail. A wing of the building contains tools and objects from the past to show and evoke the way of life in a flourmill of those times. The rooms are charming and functional and are furnished with antiques. For breakfast you'll be able to taste excellent local jams made with wild fruit, fruit juices, honey – Luigi is also a beekeeper – homemade cakes and, on request, cured meats and cheeses. The farm has a restaurant that offers genuine cuisine with local traditional dishes at an average price of 19 euros per person, excluding wine. In addition to this they have a shop where you can buy wines, liqueurs, cured meats, honey and jams.

• 3 double rooms, with bathroom, TV • Prices: double room single occupancy 40-45 euros, double 55-60 (15 euro supplement for extra bed); breakfast 5 euros per person • Credit cards: none • Facility accessible for the mobility challenged, 1 room designed for their use. Off-street parking. Small pets allowed (not in the restaurant). Owners always reachable. • Bar corner, restaurant Garden, children's playground

CASTEL D'AIANO
Rocca di Roffeno

LA FENICE

🍲 Holiday farm
Via Santa Lucia 29
Tel. 051 919272
Fax 051 919024
E-mail: lafenice@lafeniceagritur.it
Internet: www.lafeniceagritur.it
Closed Monday, Tuesday, Wednesday, never in summer
Open: lunch and dinner
Holidays: January 7-February 7
Seating: 120
Prices: 25-30 euros, wine excluded
All major credit cards, Bancomat

Paolo and Remo Giarandoni breed the rare Mora Romagnola pig, today reduced to just a few specimens and therefore added to the Ark of the Presidia. Look for its meat in the dishes of La Fenice, which also offers accommodation (which must be booked in advance) and a swimming pool. The buffet breakfast is traditional, with savory foods on request.
The antipasti include a taste of: fried polenta, cured meat of venison and wild boar, **ciccioli** and **coppa di testa**, produced by a local pork butcher. The first courses include tagliatelle alla Fenice (dandelion, other herbs and stewed pancetta), the traditional **tortelloni of ricotta** (with butter and sage or chicory and asparagus), **tagliatelle with mushrooms,** gnocchi and risottos. The main courses include, **grilled meat,** rabbit in porchetta, breast of guinea fowl in traditional balsamic vinegar, melted cheese with cep mushrooms, **pork medallions in sweet and sour fondue.** To finish, homemade puddings, perhaps the least successful part of the menu, with macaroon cake, chocolate cake, creme brulée.
Good selection of wines of the Colli Bolognesi and of the region, with emphasis on organic production.

🔑 • 8 double rooms, en suite, minibar, TV • Prices: double single use 60 euros, double 80, breakfast included • Building partially suitable for the mobility impaired. Private uncovered parking area. Small pets welcome (not in common areas). Owners always available • Bar (reserved for those staying in the hotel), restaurant. Breakfast room. Park. Swimming pool

CASTELFRANCO EMILIA
Rastellino

IL GIOVANETTO

🔑 Bed and breakfast
Via Garzolè 41-43
Tel. 059 937344-335 6905060
Fax 059 937344
E-mail: info@ilgiovanetto.it
Internet: www.ilgiovanetto.it
Open all year

In this B&B competently managed by Cristina Bellodi, the guest rooms are on the second floor of a completely refurbished old building that at the end of the eighteenth century was inhabited by the musician Giovannetto. The rooms are elegantly furnished, mostly with antique family furniture. Every detail has been carefully thought out to ensure you have a pleasant stay: from the refined bed and bathroom linens to the generous breakfast, which is possibly the most attractive feature of the place. Coffee is placed directly on the table in the moka and there is no lack of milk, tea and fruit juices. Guests may help themselves from the buffet that offers sweet and savory fare, such as freshly baked bread rolls filled with local cured meats, savory cakes, a wide selection of cheeses, tarts and other homemade cakes, jams, rusks, yogurt and fresh fruit.

• 6 double rooms, with bathroom, air-conditioning, TV • Prices: double room single occupancy 80-90 euros, double 120 (40 euro supplement for extra bed), breakfast included • Credit cards: all, Bancomat • Facility accessible to the mobility challenged. Off-street parking, some covered. Small pets allowed. Owners always reachable • Breakfast room. Reading and TV room, billiard room. Garden, terrace

CASTELFRANCO EMILIA
Piumazzo

LA LUPA

☞—❂ Holiday farm
Via Cassola di Sopra, 22
Tel. 059 934384
Fax 059 935521
E-mail: lalupa@lalupa.it
Internet: www.lalupa.it
Open all year

The restructuring of this rural complex dating from the nineteenth century got underway in 1989. It's a 30-hectare farm cultivated with fruit trees (the area is famous for Vignola cherries) located between Castelfranco and Spilamberto, at the point where the River Panaro reaches the plain. The simply furnished rooms are in the main building that comprises the farmhouse and adjacent silos; the dining rooms are in a separate two-storey building (the restaurant is open for dinner from Thursday to Sunday; a meal costs 28 euros, wines excluded). There's lots of space outdoors so you can take relaxing walks in the grounds or enjoy the swimming pool. Breakfast is traditional Italian: coffee and light refreshments, fresh drinks, croissants, rusks and jams. The weekly rental for a double room ranges from 330 to 440 euros.

• 1 single and 5 double rooms, with bathroom, mini-bar, TV; 2 rooms with kitchenette • Prices: single 50-55 euros, double 68-77 (10-11 euro supplement for extra bed), breakfast included • 1 room designed for use by the mobility challenged. Off-street parking. Small pets allowed (not in the rooms). Owners always reachable • Restaurant. Garden

CASTEL MAGGIORE
Trebbo di Reno

ANTICA LOCANDA IL SOLE

☞—❂ 3-Star Hotel
Via Lame, 65
Tel. 051 6325381-6325298
Fax 051 702252
E-mail: info@hotelilsole.com
Internet: www.hotelilsole.com
Closed from 1-15 August and for 1 week at Christmas

At the beginning of the nineteenth century this building was a staging post for travelers to Bologna. Lying on the bank of the River Reno, this red brick-colored building has two storeys, with rooms on the upper floor under a mansard roof. The rooms are modern, comfortable and quiet; for some two weeks in the year the double room costs up to 160 euros (during this period double rooms are usually fully booked). Breakfast is buffet style and you'll often find small pastries on the table – in addition to yogurt, cereals, fresh milk and jams. Pastries are prepared in the restaurant below run by Guido Paulato and brothers Gianluca and Marcello Leoni. This is an ideal base for gastronomic and wine-tasting experiences, or for those visiting fairs and the city of Bologna.

• 4 single, 15 double and 4 triple rooms, with bathroom, air-conditioning, TV • Prices: single 65-98 euros, double 95-120, triple 130-210, breakfast included • Credit cards: all, Bancomat • 2 rooms designed for use by the mobility challenged. Off-street parking. Small pets allowed. Reception open 24 hours a day • Breakfast room, lounge. Garden with portico

CASTELNOVO NE' MONTI

IL CAPOLINEA

Restaurant
Viale Bagnoli 42 A
Tel. 0522 812312
Closed Sunday and Monday evening, never in August
Open: lunch and dinner
Holidays: first week in January
Seating: 50 + 20 outdoors
Prices: 28 euros, wine excluded
All credit cards accepted

Entrance to the National Apennine Park of Tuscany-Emilia, loved by rock climbers for the presence of the Pietra di Bismantova, Castelnovo ne' Monti is also worth visiting for its restaurants. At the Capolinea, the friendliness and expertise of Giancarlo Casoni and his wife Stefania will introduce you to wonderful cooking, made of carefully selected ingredients and recipes that are the best of Reggio mountain gastronomy. At lunchtime you will find "quick" menus, tasty but not so rich, while in the evening the restaurant becomes a shrine of gastronomic delights.
You must start with the excellent homemade **salami**, stuffed in soft gut, (available from January to the beginning of the summer). Fresh homemade pasta is another of the highlights on the menu, and varies with the seasons. In spring you will find **tagliatelle with prugnoli**, then the seasonal mushrooms, in winter served with boar, hare or pheasant sauces. **Maccheroncini made from chestnut flour** or spelt with ricotta and walnuts, **green tortelli with sheep's milk ricotta**, or with mushrooms and potatoes, and the cappelletti in broth are an excellent alternative. Meat prevails in the main courses: **roast lamb** from biological breeding farms, rabbit rolled in omelet and fine herbs and in the winter **mixed boiled meats**, with homemade cotechino. When they are on the menu, try the **mushrooms** in batter and fried and the selection of cheeses from the small dairies in the area, including the Reggiano Apennine sheep's' milk cheese (Slow Food Presidia). Puddings: house specialties are the cream and wild berry puffs and the peach and macaroon tart. The wine list offers a good selection of regional and national labels at the right prices.

CASTEL SAN PIETRO TERME

BORRO DI SOPRA

Rooms
Via Paniga 1870
Tel. 051 942444-333 3990972
Fax 051 942444
E-mail: cristinaverardi@libero.it
Internet: www.borrodisopra.it
Closed in January

Twenty or so years ago Cristina Verardi and her husband Alessandro bought a farmhouse in the countryside and made it their home. It's located a few kilometers away from Dozza, which is famous for its painted walls and for the castle that's the Emilia Romagna region's central wine store. A few years ago they restructured the barn to the same elegant architectural standard of the main farmhouse, creating four spacious rooms on the upper floor which were furnished with great attention to detail. On the ground floor there's a lounge with a beautiful fireplace where the guests eat breakfast by Cristina: tarts and other homemade cakes, jams and fruit juices. Often they lay on afternoon snacks on the splendid veranda facing onto the garden and occasionally jazz and classical music concerts, wine-tasting and regional cooking courses are organized.

• 4 double rooms, with bathroom, TV • Prices: double room single occupancy 50-60 euros, double 80-90 (20-25 euro supplement for extra bed), breakfast included • Credit cards: all except AE, Bancomat • Off-street parking. Small pets allowed. Owner always reachable • Breakfast room, reading room. Garden, veranda

CENTO

CESENA
San Vittore

25 KM SOUTHWEST OF FERRARA SS255

6 KM FROM THE TOWN CENTER

ANTICA OSTERIA DA CENCIO

Osteria-wine bar with kitchen
Via Provenzali 12 D
Tel. 051 6831880
Closed Monday, Saturday and Sunday lunch
Open: lunch and dinner
Holidays: 10 days after Carnival, August
Seating: 70 + 60 outdoors
Prices: 30-32 euros, wine excluded
All credit cards, Bancomat

CERINA

Restaurant-pizzeria
Via San Vittore 936
Tel. 0547 661115
Closed Monday evening and Tuesday
Open: lunch and dinner
Holidays: August and January
Seating: 150
Prices: 28-30 euros, wine excluded
All credit cards

Just a short walk from Guercino square in the heart of the old town, this osteria is a reminder of the past. You can stop and enjoy a good glass of wine and often, besides the wine, you can also try the typical dishes that follow the changing seasons and are prepared by Gabriele Ferri; Billy, Morena and Claudia will welcome you to a warm, comfortable dining hall in the winter while in the summer we suggest sitting in the cool garden at the back. Among the antipasti we would recommend the selection of sliced Romagna salamis, the **mortadella** (Slow Food Presidia), sottoli and pickles from the Dispensa di Amerigo di Savigno. The first courses are all fresh pasta and, in the best Emilia tradition, you can try more than one: tagliatelle, **pumpkin tortelli with meat ragù**, **maccheroncini** and **spaghetti al torchio**, **whipped rice** from the Po Delta. Among the main courses, **meat** triumphs with the Piedmont **fassone** (Slow Food Presidia) which is served **chopped with cep mushrooms,** asparagus or other fresh vegetables or as an excellent **roast beef.** The menu also offers a selection of Italian, French and English cheeses. The puddings are all homemade: fruit tarts, **sweet salami**, cream ice cream with balsamic vinegar, **hot focaccia with mascarpone**.
A rich, varied and interesting wine list, with a large section of it dedicated to regional wines.

In Via Fratelli Rosselli, the Sombrero homemade ice cream parlor offers excellent ice-cream: semifiore, chocolate and yoghurt flavors in particular. In Via Ugo Bassi, Macelleria Ceresi: cured meats, beef, pork and chicken; all of guaranteed quality.

At Cerina you will find a large car park, pleasant surroundings and a veranda in summer, a friendly welcome and good traditional dishes. All thanks to the sisters Dallara and Graziella with their son Vincenzo front of house and Rosanna with son Piergiorgio in the kitchen, who are able to satisfy all the different tastes of their guests.
The kitchen offers country dishes (**squacquerone and piadina**, **passatelli in broth**, **tagliatelle with ragù**, larded fillet, **grilled mutton**, seasonal vegetables, homemade **doughnuts** and biscuits and bread) or the à la carte menu which includes these and other dishes depending on the season: carpaccio di crudo with slivers of fossa cheese, **salumi di mora romagnola** (Slow Food Presidia), omelet with herbs, samples of local cheeses with homemade jams (cherries, figs including caramelized) which can also be bought by the jar; ravioloni, crepes and cappellacci, **pigeon al tegame**, cuts of Romagna beef (Slow Food Presidia). Traditionally on Fridays fish dishes: stewed baccalà, cuttlefish and peas, sardines. In summer cold dishes are also available; mushrooms and truffles in season. The puddings also vary with the seasons but they are always homemade. In short, although it is not the most attractive of places, the service and cuisine are still recommended.
A good selection of regional and national wines, also offered by the glass.

Near the Cathedral, in Corte Dandini 3, the Brancaleoni family has opened Casa Romagna, a shop offering all local and regional wine and food specialties.

CESENA

CESENATICO

MICHILETTA

🍲 Traditional osteria- trattoria
Via Fantaguzzi 26
Tel. 0547 24691
Closed Sunday
Open: lunch and dinner
Holidays: August 15-31 and
December 15-31
Seating: 45 + 30 outdoors
Prices: 25 euros, wine excluded
All credit cards welcome

OSTERIA DEL GRAN FRITTO LA BUCA

🍲 A recently opened Osteria
Corso Garibaldi 41
Tel. 0547 82474
Closed Wednesday
Open: lunch and dinner
Holidays: 20 days between September and October
Seating: 54
Prices: 30-33 euros, wine excluded
All major credit cards, Bancomat

The place: the heart of old Cesena. The restaurant: a 19th century atmosphere with the original reception desk and furniture. The owners: Rocco Angarola in the kitchen with his brother Giovanni; wife Johanna front of house. The cuisine: unquestionably Romagna, with the right balance of traditional recipes, new ideas and a personal touch. This sums up the features of this traditional osteria in Cesena, where you can enjoy the pleasure of flavors of the past, dictated by the season (ask them to list the dishes of the day, that are not on the menu). Among the antipasti **frittatina with stridoli**, artichokes with olives, **croutons** with seasonal vegetables, flan with broccoli and herbs. Tasty but delicate first courses, usually made with vegetables. We would also mention the **tagliolini with green shoots**, **risotto with seasonal vegetables**, spelt maccheroni with eggplant sauce, cappellacci with sweet peppers and salt ricotta. If they are to your taste, we recommend the **fegatelli con la rete** and grilled laurel; good **local rabbit in porchetta**. The meal closes with a good selection of cheeses or the traditional **trifle**, with panna cotta, honey sponge or spelt tart with fruit jam.
The wine list offers the best Romagna labels and a good choice of carefully selected national labels. You can also choose a good house wine or various types offered by the glass.

🍷 In **Gambettola** (13 km) Il Buongustaio, piazza Cavour 5, offers excellent cheeses: sheep's cheese ripened in terracotta amphoras with walnut leaves, cheeses ripened in pits or caves.

Stefano Bartolini has thought up a winning formula for his restaurant overlooking the port of Cesenatico: the left hand door leads to the Buca, a very refined restaurant, while the right hand door takes you into the osteria, which is more affordable and casual (but why use those horrible hand-helds for serving, given that there aren't that many seats?). In the middle a single kitchen. You can order just one dish or a whole meal: in the first case we recommend the **great fish fry** or the more simple fried squid and prawns. The fried nibbles (soft cheese, cherry mozzarella, vegetables, artichokes, Ascoli olives, etc.) complete the offer. If you wish to continue the menu offers excellent **bean and clam soup**, **risotto as they used to make it** (with four types of fish: paganelli, swordfish, zanchetti and angler fish heads), tagliolini with fish ragù and mezzamaniche pasta with mackerel. And again: **poverazze alla marinara**, baby squid in fresh tomato sauce, grilled **squid and prawn skewers** and **sardines sautéed with oil and lemon**. An inviting variety of puddings. The wine list is not very long but it is well mixed, not only white but also a few good reds, and a good number of labels are available by the glass.
In short, such a success that Stefano decided to repeat the formula – same dishes, same quality and same warm welcome – on the beach in Milano Marittima, in viale Boito 11.

🍷 In Cesenatico, in via Baldini 6, da Marconi offers excellent homemade pasta: tagliatelle, passatelli, lunghetti, potato gnocchi, stuffed pasta. In piazza Fiorentini 10, 'Giardino dei Sapori Perduti', homemade cakes, biscuits and jams.

52 KM SOUTH-EAST OF FERRARA ON SLIP-ROAD TO A 13

AL PONTICELLO

Bed and breakfast
Via Cavour 39
Tel. 0533 314080-347 7262449
E-mail: resca@libero.it
Internet: www.alponticello.it
Holidays vary

In the historic center of Comacchio, just a short distance from the cathedral, stands this pleasant, friendly, family-run B&B that has recently been refurbished. Located on the Canale Maggiore, it's managed by Riccardo Rescazzi with help from his mother, who prepares delicious cakes for morning breakfast. Cakes aside, we can safely say that guests will be offered all kinds of food, even marinated eel with a nice glass of red wine. The rooms are quiet, comfortable and furnished with great attention to detail; on arrival you'll find a beautiful basket of the season's fresh fruit waiting for you in your room. Riccardo organizes pleasant canoeing excursions for his guests and he'll also be pleased to provide bicycles and maps for excursions in the environs. This, in addition to helping you book tickets for any event in the Comacchio and Po delta areas.

• 3 double rooms, with bathroom, air-conditioning, mini-bar, safe, TV, modem connection • Prices: double room single occupancy 54-85 euros, double 75-85, breakfast included • Credit cards: DC, Bancomat • Facility accessible to the mobility challenged, 1 room designed for their use. Off-street parking. No pets allowed. Owners always reachable • Breakfast room

52 KM SOUTHEAST OF FERRARA A13 LINK-ROAD

DA VASCO E GIULIA

Trattoria
Via Muratori 21
Tel. 0533 81252
Closed Monday
Open: lunch and dinner
Holidays: January 7-31
Seating: 40
Prices: 28-32 euros, wine excluded
Credit cards are not accepted

Between the square of Comacchio and Trepponti, along one of the roads on the canal side, you will find this trattoria, one of the most traditional in Comacchio, serving the excellent dishes prepared by Mamma Giulia (helped by her daughter Elena) and served by Irene and the waiting staff.
The menu is mainly fish, especially **eel**, and built around seasonal availability. If you are lucky you will find the truly delicious small fried eel. During the year, the eel is prepared with **savoy cabbage**, marinated, **a becco d'asino**. However there are a lot of other interesting dishes too. Among the antipasti the local clams, the **clam soup** and fish antipasto. Among the first courses the classic spaghetti and clams (without tomatoes), **maccheroncini** home style, **garganelli di pesce**; we recommend the **seafood risotto** with its classic red color, which is eaten with a squeeze of lemon juice and a sprinkling of black pepper in Comacchio. Among the main courses, we recommend the **freshly caught grilled fish** and the excellent **fried fish**. Among the puddings you will always find the sorbetto and, if you can manage it, try the **trifle**. However, you should know that the Comacchio people finish a fish dinner, especially if they have eaten eel or fried fish, with a sliver of Parmesan.
Irene will help you choose from the labels they have stored in the cellar, but we recommend choosing the traditional Sabbia red wine, excellent with eel. If you are with children or people who do not like fish, there is an alternative menu. The inn is very well known and has an excellent quality-price ratio, so it is advisable to book.

CORNIGLIO
Ghiare

FAENZA

DA VIGION

LA BAITA

🍲 Trattoria/2 Star Hotel
Via Provinciale 21
Tel. 0521 888113
Fax 0521 888116
Closed Monday and Tuesday
Open: lunch and dinner
Holidays: variable
Seating: 60
Prices: 20-25 euros, wine excluded
All major credit cards, Bancomat

🍲 Wine-shop with kitchen
Via Naviglio 25
Tel. 0546 21584
Closed Sunday and Monday
Open: lunch and dinner
Holidays: January 1-15, one week in August
Seating: 55 + 55 outdoors
Prices: 30-33 euros, wine excluded
All major credit cards, Bancomat

The Rabaglia family has been managing this charming hotel restaurant since 1947 and the ambience and the cuisine have always remained those of an authentic trattoria. The breakfast is traditional. There are chairs and tables in the courtyard where you can read or chat. Half-board in a double room at 35 euros per person.
Here you must start with antipasti of cured meats: from the traditional to the not so common **spallaccio** and **gola**. In season, excellent cep mushroom salads. The pasta is drawn by hand, from the **tortelli of herbs** (pumpkin or potato), to the **tagliolini with cep mushrooms** and the filling **cappelletti soup**. The main courses start with goose and **roasted duck**, **baked shank of pork**, roast coppa, braised foal meat, hare and game in the hunting season. To finish home-made puddings: fruit tarts, **trifle**, ricotta cake with chocolate and "dolce amor", made with butter, chocolate, coffee and dipped savoiardi biscuits.
The cellar has a selection of local wines and some national labels. Booking recommended, especially for the weekend.

🔑 • 7 double rooms, en-suite, TV • Prices: double single use 23, double 46 euros (12 euro supplement for additional bed); breakfast 4 euros per person • External free public parking. Small pets welcome (not in the bedrooms). Owners available from 7 am to midnight • Bar, restaurant. Al fresco

🍴 At **Albareto** (22 km), at km 49 along the road leading to the Cento Croci pass, you will find the Maloberti Dairy which produces organic cheese. Taste and purchase the excellent Pangerlaio.

This historic delicatessen in the heart of Faenza, run by the same family for generations, has recently been converted into a wine-shop with kitchen, managed by Robertone. As you go in you will find cured meats and cheeses from all over Italy and the rest of Europe, together with other high quality products. There are three plain dining rooms with wooden tables, where you can sample the good food on offer, whether you want a full meal, just one dish, or a selection of **cheeses** and **cured meats** served with jam or caramelized figs and honey.
Some of the salads and cold meat dishes are menu staples – carne salada from Trentino, river shrimp salad and duck breast in balsamic vinegar – while the chef also offers a selection of dishes which vary almost daily. To start with, **tagliatelle** with fresh **mushrooms**, tagliatelline with seafood and vegetables, maccheroncini with prosciutto, shallots and peas, **spoia lorda with pineta sauce**, **curzul with ragù** and risotto with asparagus. As for the main courses, beef tagliata, **roulade with sauce** served with beans, pulpet a la mi manira, tre ov con la panzeta, **braised veal** with mushrooms and when in season **tripe**, baccalà and **giblet ragù**. The puddings are all homemade and vary every day.
Since last year Fabio has been running the courtyard area, which is open all year round offering aperitifs, or after-dinner drinks with cured meats, selections from the cheese board and a few cold dishes. Mainly frequented by the younger crowd, it is an opportunity to present wines and traditional produce from many parts of Italy. The wine list is extensive, with Italian and foreign labels, and all the wines made in Romagna.

LA CURBASTRA

Holiday farm
Via Cesarolo 17
Tel. 0546 32089-338 6102275
Fax 0546 32089
E-mail: info@agriturismolacurbastra.it
Internet: www.agriturismolacurbastra.it
Open all year

LOCANDA DELLA FORTUNA

Rooms
Via San Mamante 146
Tel. 0546 642318
Fax 0546 694413
E-mail: info@locandafortuna.it
E-mail: www.locandafortuna.it
Closed from beginning of January to end of March

This vacation farm was named for mathematician-physicist Gregorio Ricci Curbastro, who stayed here in the early 1900s. The one hundred year-old farmhouse surrounded by 26 hectares of orchards has been restructured to create comfortable, tastefully furnished rooms. It is an ideal place if you want a mix of relaxation, gastronomic and wine-tasting experiences, cultural tourism and physical activity. In the grounds there's a large swimming pool and if you so wish you can even have a poolside breakfast; otherwise it's served in the spacious dining room that was once a cattle shed. Here you'll also have dinner, tasting and savoring traditional Romagnola cuisine. The restaurant is open to non-residents and offers a menu for 15 euros, while for half board the cost ranges from 40-50 euros per person, depending on whether you're alone or a couple staying in a double.

• 16 double rooms, with bathroom, TV • Prices: double room single occupancy 35 euros, double 50 (10 euro supplement for extra bed), breakfast included • Credit cards: all, Bancomat • 1 room designed for use by the mobility challenged. Off-street parking. Small pets allowed. Owners always reachable. • Restaurant. Breakfast room. Grounds. Pool

Susanna Samorè's locanda is located in Oriolo dei Fichi, in the hilly area just outside Faenza. It is quiet and peaceful, and the five airy rooms are very well furnished – a sixth room will soon be ready. Breakfast – homemade tarts and ciambelloni, honey and jams, tea, coffee and milk – is served in the pleasant kitchen or in the large garden that surrounds the facility. Dinner is also served in the garden, where a swimming pool is being built. A meal at the restaurant – for residents only – costs from 25-30 euros per person, excluding wine. Instead for those who want to stay in the center of Faenza there's Paradiso Inn that has 12 rooms available at a lower cost. In this case, however, you'll not be served a full breakfast: in the morning coffee and a light snack will be brought to your room.

• 5 double rooms, with bathroom, TV • Prices: double room single occupancy 52 euros, double 72 (10 euro supplement for extra bed), breakfast included • Credit cards: all, Bancomat • 1 room designed for use by the mobility challenged. Free external public parking. Small pets allowed. Owners reachable from 8am to 11pm • Restaurant. Breakfast room, lounge. Garden

FAENZA

MARIANAZA

☕Trattoria
Via Torricelli 21
Tel. 0546 681461
Closed Wednesday
Open: lunch and dinner
Holidays: July 15-August 15
Seating: 50
Prices: 27-32 euros, wine excluded
All major credit cards

Every small to medium sized town in Italy should have a place like this, bang in the center (in a little alley just round the corner from piazza delle Erbe), and an honest-to-goodness spot for refueling at affordable prices. And it is no co-incidence that the Marianaza has many regulars who come for lunch and dinner every day (booking is recommended). It is entirely female-run: Luana and Natascia work front of house ably looking after both the clients and the meat roasting on the open fire which dominates the dining room. Their mother Mariangela takes care of the rest.

You can start with a selection of cured meats accompanied by a hot **piadina** and tasty pickled shallots, or with bruschettas with a variety of toppings. Then it is time for soup – including pasta and bean soup and the excellent **passatelli in broth** – or pasta: we recommend **tagliatelle with prosciutto and peas** or ragù (the pasta is handmade), or **tortelloni with ricotta** and garganelli with seasonal sauces. As for the main courses, the **mixed char-grilled meats** are a must, and the lamb chops, mutton, sausage and bacon sizzling over the fire are pretty tempting. The stuffed rabbit, **baccalà with leeks** and tripe in sauce are worth trying too. Round off with a traditional **zuppa inglese**, a good panna cotta or robiola cake.

There is a good selection of wines (with fair mark-up), offering the best of Romagna and some important labels from the rest of Italy.

FANANO
Canevare

AGRITURISMO DEL CIMONE

🛏Holiday farm
Via Calvanella 710
Tel. 053 669311
Fax 053 666631
E-mail: info@agriturismodelcimone.it
Internet: www.agriturismodelcimone.it
Open all year

In 1991 Anna Maria Tonielli and Sergio Lodi bought an old abandoned farmhouse that comprised two separate buildings, the Capanna dell'Acquila and the Palazza, in which they created rooms and apartments for guests. These buildings are on an approximately 50-hectare farm, mostly pastureland; the remaining part is covered with larch and beech woods, is used to grow vegetables or is planted with fruit trees. The vegetables, fruit, meat, milk and cheeses they make are certified as organically produced and can be bought directly on the farm. The rooms are simple and fitted out in rustic style. The wholesome breakfast consists of coffee, milk, tea and homemade bread, cakes, cookies and jams. There are many activities for those who love nature: walks through the Apennines and excursions by bike or on horseback. A meal at the restaurant – at lunchtime open to non-residents subject to booking – costs approximately 25 euros, wines excluded.

• 6 double, 4 triple and 2 four-bed rooms, with bathroom; 3 apartments (4 persons) with kitchenette • Prices: double room single occupancy 30-50 euros, double 55-80, triple 75-120, four-bed 100-160, breakfast included; apartments 70-115 euros; breakfast 8 euros per person • Credit cards: MC, Visa, Bancomat • 1 room designed for use by the mobility challenged. Off-street parking. Small pets allowed. Owners always reachable • Bar (for residents only), restaurant. Grounds, children's playground. Horse-riding

FARINI
Groppallo

52 KM SOUTH OF PIACENZA SS 654

FRATELLI SALINI

Hotel trattoria
Viale Europa 46
Tel. 0523 916104
Closed Wednesday, but not in summer
Open: lunch and dinner
Holidays: 15 days in January
Seating: 80
Prices: 20-28 euros, wine excluded
All major credit cards except AE, Bancomat

The Salini family went into business as pork butchers in 1820 in Groppallo, a little tourist resort in the hills above Piacenza, at an altitude of almost 1000 meters. They continue to ply their trade in the present day, respecting traditional methods, and also run a hotel with trattoria where you can sample the food made by Anna Maria: traditional Piacenza dishes with an Alpine flavor.

The atmosphere is warm and rustic, service cordial and informal. The meal starts with toast and a particularly good **pistà ad gràss** (minced lardo with garlic and parsley), all prepared, dressed and seasoned in the adjacent butcher's shop, like the other **cured meats**: coppa, pancetta, salami and the excellent **mariola**, a Slow Food Presidia. The first courses, all featuring fresh homemade pasta, are classic traditional dishes: from **tortelli with herbs**, or pumpkin or chicory and cotechino sausage in fall, to **chicche della nonna**, **pisarei e fasò**, lasagne and tagliatelle, when in season prepared with **mushrooms** picked in the surrounding woods, which can also be sampled **fried** or char-grilled. While the cured meats are one reason that bring many people here up the steep, winding road, the **meat dishes** are no less tempting (including organic cuts) prepared in a variety of ways – **char-grilled**, braised or tartare.

The puddings include good tarts and country cakes like **sbrisolona**, as well as almond semifreddo or strawberry tiramisù, or mint whip with dark chocolate, all homemade. The wine cellar offers a good selection of labels from the Piacenza area, including the best local names. It is advisable to reserve a table, especially in summer.

FELINO
Casale

17 KM SOUTH OF PARMA

LA PORTA DI FELINO

Trattoria
Via Casale 28 B
Tel. 0521 836839
Closed Sunday
Open: lunch and dinner
Holidays: last week of June – first week of July
Seating: 50 + 40 outdoors
Prices: 22-27 euros, wine excluded
All major credit cards

The old trattoria on the road from Parma to Felino has rediscovered its personality and sparkle since being taken over by Ciccio Zerbini and his wife Paola. He works in the kitchen while she is front of house, offering up wonderful regional dishes made using seasonal produce and ingredients from specified areas and producers.

The antipasti kick off with **cured meats**: prosciutto di Parma matured for 30 months, matured coppa, spalla cotta di san Secondo, Felino salami, spallaccio, culacia and culatello di Zibello. For something completely different, do not underestimate the **warm ricotta**, served with artichokes and pecorino, or cherry tomatoes, basil and grana, depending on availability. Their wonderful fresh pasta, rolled out on wooden rollers, forms the basis for **pumpkin tortelli** (from September to March) and **anolini in brodo**. Then there are many other types of pasta (tagliolini, stricchetti, maltagliati), all served with seasonal sauces. The main courses revolve around meat: first and foremost **tripe alla parmigiana** and **stuffed breast of veal** with roast potatoes. The **guancialetti di vitello** and filettini di maiale with braised baby onions are a worthy second choice, while the rabbit with baby vegetables and boned guinea fowl with potato stuffing are also satisfying. As for the puddings, we recommend the sbrisolona.

The cellar contains 300 wines, including at least a dozen local labels, from Colli piacentini to the Modena area, and it is a real shame that the wine list does not do them justice, merely listing them by name. The coffee deserves a mention, from the Giamaica coffee company in Verona.

ANTICA TRATTORIA VOLANO

🍲Trattoria
Via Volano 20
Tel. 0532 761421
Closed Friday
Open: lunch and dinner
Holidays: vary
Seating: 70 + 30 outdoors
Prices: 28-32 euros, wine excluded
All major credit cards, Bancomat

BORGONUOVO

🔑Bed and breakfast
Via Cairoli 29
Tel. 0532 211100
Fax 0532 246328
E-mail: info@borgonuovo.com
Internet: www.borgonuovo.com
Open all year

When you talk to Maria Teresa Cenacchi you get a measure of the dedication she has put into running this trattoria for the last thirty years, offering up the best of traditional Ferrara cuisine. The trattoria, rustic but inviting, looks over the Po di Volano and is right by the centre of Ferrara.

You can start off with some good cured meats, particularly the **salame ferrarese**. A soft salami with a distinctive garlic flavor, it is served with crescentine fritte, crescents of fried bread dough known in Ferrara as pinzin. First courses include **cappelletti in broth**, which are larger, but no less delicious than the Bologna version. **Pumpkin cappellacci with ragù** are a traditional specialty, filled only with pumpkin and parmigiano. Then there are tortelloni with ricotta and taglioline with prosciutto; if you book you can also sample the renowned – and labor-intensive – Renaissance dish, 'pasticcio di maccheroni alla ferrarese'. Main courses include pan-fried pigeon, baked prosciutto and the generous, varied **mixed boiled meats** with sauces. When in season these include **salama da sugo** with mashed potatoes. Dishes which recall the poverty of days gone by, like herring or dried cod with polenta, are served in winter, while from the nearby valleys there are traditional specialties like **eel 'a becco d'asino'**. There is a limited selection of puddings, including zuppa inglese and **torta tenerina**, time-honored traditions, just like mandurlin dal Pont, little meringues made with almonds from Pontelagoscuro, a sweet touch to end the meal.

The wine list is rather meager – go for the labels from the Po delta.

Managed by Filippo Orlandini's family, this B&B in the old center of Ferrara, Europe's first modern city, is located in a former convent dating from the seventeenth century. The big comfortable bedrooms and elegant communal rooms are all fitted out with period furnishings. For breakfast you'll be served (during winter in a room with paintings, carpets and a fireplace, in summer in the charming garden) homemade cakes, jams and yoghurt, fresh fruit, local bread (Ferrara is the home of the protected 'coppia' variety), cured meats and cheeses. On request, they can organize laundry and ironing services, cut-price tickets for major exhibitions and sports centers, excursions – also on horseback – to the valleys of Comacchio and in the Po delta Park. Bicycles are available free of charge, as well as the passes needed to enter the pedestrian area.

.

• 2 single, 2 double rooms and 2 suites (2-5 persons), with bathroom, air-conditioning, mini-bar, safe, TV, modem connection • Prices: single 55-65 euros, double 85-105 (25 euro supplement for extra bed), suite 85-215, breakfast included • Credit cards: all except DC, Bancomat • Public and private parking nearby (3-5 euros per day). Small pets allowed. Owners always reachable • Breakfast room, reading room with small library. Conference room. Garden

FERRARA

FERRARA

IN OLD CITY CENTER, BETWEEN THE ESTENSE CASTLE AND PIAZZA TASSO

IN OLD CITY CENTER, BETWEEN VIA GARIBALDI AND VIA RIPAGRANDE

DE PRATI

DOLCEMELA

🗝️3 Star Hotel
Via Padiglioni 5
Tel. 0532 241905
Fax 0532 241966
E-mail: info@hoteldeprati.com
Internet: www.hoteldeprati.com
Closed from 21-26 December

🗝️Bed and breakfast
Via Sacca 35
Tel. 0532 769624
Fax 0532 711007
E-mail: b&b@dolcemela.it
Internet: www.dolcemela.it
Open all year

The building that currently accommodates the hotel was already used for this purpose in the early days of the twentieth century, when Alfonsa Brandani offered lodgings for artists and performers from the opera and theater. This love of the artistic in whatever form is still evident in the communal areas and in the bedrooms, which are often decorated with paintings by contemporary artists. Recently refurbished and equipped with all modern comforts, the hotel is fitted with period furniture that preserves the charm of the place. The buffet-style breakfast is set out in a communal dining room or can be served in your room at no extra cost. You'll be able to try fresh products such as brioches, bread, cakes, yogurt, cured meats and dry cookies. The location of the hotel is particularly favorable, given that it's on a quiet road on the edge of the pedestrian area. From here you can comfortably reach all places of interest on foot.

• 6 single 9 double rooms and 1 suite (2-4 persons), with bathroom, air-conditioning, mini-bar, satellite TV, modem connection; 1 apartment (2-4 persons), with kitchenette • Prices: single 55-75 euros, double 90-110 (16 euro supplement for extra bed), suite and apartment 110-140, breakfast included • Credit cards: all, Bancomat • 1 room designed for use by the mobility challenged. Paid public parking (3 euros per day). Small pets allowed. Reception open from 7 am to midnight • Bar (for residents only). Breakfast room, lounge with reading corner

This B&B is in a building displaying many features peculiar to minor Ferrara architectural style. The Gothic arch still visible out front indicates that here in the distant past there used to be an old workshop. The entrance leads to the inner court that gives access to two rooms, while the other four are on the first floor. The rooms are named for particular varieties of apple and are spacious, comfortable and very well furnished. They are also very quiet and close to a number of important buildings, such as the Estense Castle and the cathedral. In the pleasant breakfast room you'll be able to help yourself to jams, cakes, cookies and brioches, yogurt, milk and coffee. Emanuela and Mark, owners of this charming facility, will rent you bicycles for 10 euros a day to visit Ferrara and the surrounding area.

• 6 double rooms, with bathroom, air conditioning, mini-bar, TV • Prices: double room single occupancy 80 euros, double 100 (10-30 euro supplement for extra bed), breakfast included • Credit cards: major ones, Bancomat • Garage (10 euros per day). No pets allowed. Owners always reachable • Breakfast room, lounge. Garden

L'OCA GIULIVA

Wine shop with kitchen
Via Boccacanale di Santo Stefano 38
Tel. 0532 207628
Closed Monday and Tuesday lunch
Open: lunch and dinner
Holidays: last 3 weeks of June, last
week of August, Christmas-Epiphany
Seating: 30 + 15 outdoors
Prices: 35 euros, wine excluded
All major credit cards

This is an elegant, splendidly balanced eatery: two dining rooms and tables laid in a refined, informal style, attentively waited on by Leonardo Marzola and Luca Bergamini, two of the partners. The food, made with flair and immense skill by the third partner Gianni Tarroni, is modern and presented with contemporary taste, but at the same time makes the most of traditional Ferrara ingredients and recipes.

As befits what once used to be a simple osteria, the menu is dedicated to traditional dishes: this is one of the reasons why we recommend the Oca giuliva, one of the few places in town which offers up the key specialties of Ferrara cuisine, from **cured meats** to **roast pigeon** and wild misticanza salad leaves with grapes, from an outstanding **pasticcio di maccheroni** in a sweet crust to the classic **cappelletti in capon broth** and **pumpkin cappellacci with ragù**. Main courses include traditional **salama da sugo with mashed potatoes**, Ferrara boned stuffed rabbit and warm **soused valley eel with onions**.

Then there is "Gianni Tarroni's dish of the day": varied, often original ideas which change from month to month and feature a lot of fresh fish, lamb, goose and duck dishes inspired by classic Jewish cuisine, of which Ferrara is one of the capitals.

The traditional puddings include **pampapato**, served cold with rum sauce in summer, chocolate tenerina cake with egg custard, and zuppa inglese. There is a great, extensive wine list, with particular focus on regional labels. Wines are also served by the glass, which means you can accompany each course with a different wine.

PIAZZA NOVA

Rooms
Corso Porta Mare 133
Tel. 0532 757614
Fax 0532 750292
E-mail: info@piazzanova.com
Internet: www.piazzanova.com
Open all year

Not far from Palazzo dei Diamanti in the historic center, the young couple Emanuela Zaia and Ruggero Calabria manage this comfortable vacation home – a recently renovated late nineteenth-century Ferrara cassero – with professionalism and courtesy. The rooms are fitted with antique furniture, have parquet floors and ceilings with wooden beams. The generous breakfast is served in a small room on the first floor and consists of bread, butter and jam, cookies, sbrisolona, homemade tarts and ciambellone, yoghurt, freshly squeezed juices, coffee, tea, milk and, on request, savory fare. There's a shuttle service to and from the train station, and you can also rent bicycles (5 euros per day) for excursions either to visit the city or the surrounding area. An interesting itinerary is to follow the city walls that surround the center and measure nearly ten kilometers.

• 4 double and 2 triple rooms, with bathroom, mini-bar, safe, satellite TV, modem connection; 5 rooms with kitchenette • Prices: double room single occupancy 50-70 euros, double 70-100 (15 euro supplement for extra bed), triple 90-110, breakfast included • Credit cards: all except AE, Bancomat • Parking out front, garage (1 space, 5 euros per day). Small pets allowed (30 euros). Owners always reachable • Breakfast room

FIDENZA
Tabiano Castello

IL TONDINO

🛏️Holiday farm
Via Tabiano 58
Tel. and fax 0524 62106
E-mail: info@agriturismoiltodino.it
Internet: www.agriturismoiltondino.it
Open from 8 March to 8 December

This vacation farm was created by re-structuring an old farmhouse that was once used by the Tabiano Castle's sharecroppers, while its name was inspired by the corral where colts were broken in. The facility is surrounded by wide open spaces where forests alternate with cultivated fields and makes the ideal place for those looking for a totally relaxing vacation. The rooms are comfortable and simply furnished, while the buffet breakfast offers homemade bread and cakes, jams and hot drinks. The restaurant is open to non-residents (a meal costs approximately 20 euros per person, wine excluded) and will prepare gluten-free dishes if requested. Recently a classroom has been organized for use in wine-tasting courses. Among the activities available, there are excursions by mountain bike or on foot, archery and fishing from the banks of the little lake.

• 6 double, 2 triple, 1 four-bed rooms and 1 suite (3 persons), with bathroom, air-conditioning, TV; some with balcony • Prices: double room single occupancy 70 euros, double 80-100, triple 130-150, four-bed and suite 160-200, breakfast included • Credit cards: major ones, Bancomat • Off-street parking, some covered. No pets allowed. Owners reachable from 7am to 10pm • Restaurant. Breakfast room. Classroom and wine-tasting room, conference room. Garden, solarium. Pool

FIDENZA
Santa Margherita

TRATTORIA DEL SOLE

🍲Traditional osteria-trattoria
Via Tabiano 76
Tel. 0524 63131-63324
Closed Wednesday
Open: lunch and dinner
Holidays: August 15-30, 7 days at the beginning of February
Seating: 60
Prices: 25-30 euros, wine excluded
All major credit cards

Just a few minutes by car from Fidenza, on the road to Santa Margherita, takes you into hill country, and a chance to stop off at the Trattoria del sole. For years this historic trattoria has been offering its guests tasty nibbles, good wine and a place to play cards, and its relaxed atmosphere will make you feel at home. Owner Luca will take you into one of the two dining rooms, while his wife Roberta is in the kitchen.

The menu changes frequently, according to seasonal availability. Luca also makes some excellent **cured meats** (coarse-grained salami, coppa, well-seasoned pancetta and culatello) which can be sampled in winter, while there is a good selection of cured meats that he ages in the cellar, including prosciutto, culatello and salami, which make a tasty antipasto served with baby onions in balsamic vinegar, baby artichokes or cep mushrooms preserved in oil. Then it's time for the first courses, and house specialties like **panzarotti** and gratin of pinwheel crepes filled with ricotta and herbs. Then there are **tortelli with potato** or herb filling, **tagliatelle with mushrooms** or, when in season, with local **truffles, or cappelletti in broth** with a cheese filling. The main courses include a good **fillet steak with balsamic vinegar**, or green peppercorns, or mixed grill. Equally good are the **roast duck** and guinea fowl, and in winter the trolley of **boiled meats** with cooked salami and pig's head. Puddings include a wonderful zabaglione semifreddo, tarts, panna cotta and **zuppa inglese**.

You can accompany your meal with the house wine or choose a bottle from the selection of local and national labels on the wine list.

FINALE EMILIA
Massa Finalese

FIORANO MODENESE
Salse di Nirano

ENTRÀ

Trattoria
Via Salde Entrà 60
Tel. 0535 97105
Closed Monday and Tuesday
Open: dinner only
Holidays: 13 August-mid September
Seating: 40 + 40 outdoors
Prices: 22-25 euros, wine excluded
No credit cards

PRA' ROSSO

Holiday farm
Via Nuova 5
Tel. 339 5958617-335 5620874
Internet: www.paginegialle.it/prarosso
Open all year

The drive up to this trattoria evokes some powerful atavic sensations: the wide open spaces of the Po valley, and the homely light shining out into the night, recalling the houses where most of us spent our childhood. In winter you can dine in one of the three plain dining rooms adorned with photos and mementoes of the beginning of the last century, while in summer you can eat al fresco in the courtyard, serenaded by a chorus of bird song.

The dishes on offer follow the seasons and the ingredients reflect local traditions and produce. The influence of the Ferrara area comes through in the salami, laced with generous helpings of garlic.

First courses include **tagliatelle** or short maccheroni with **meat ragù**, quadretti and **passatelli in broth**, potato gnocchi, and only when in season and if you are lucky enough to find it, **caciuf** (corn flour polenta with a stew of beans and ragù) served both hot and cold, or spaghetti with tuna, anchovies and mackerel, a popular local dish in days gone by. The main courses include **roast guinea fowl** and **mallard** and **spatchcock alla cacciatora**. From fall to Easter you will find **baccalà**. Then there is char-grilled meat and some wonderful **roast potatoes**. The puddings include **mascarpone** cream with a different flavor every day: chocolate, coffee, pineapple or wild berries. Then there is apple pie (when it's not too hot), **zuppa inglese** and a sumptuous **torta tenerina** (the Ferrara influence coming through once more).

If you go for local wines you can keep the price down and enjoy a meal that is fantastic value for money.

Emilio Storti manages this farm that grows fruit and vegetables, and also runs the vacation facility, with help from his family, in an old refurbished farmhouse. The big rooms have rustic-style furnishings; some have air-conditioning and three of them have a kitchenette. Breakfast is traditional and offers milk, coffee, tea, bread, butter, homemade tarts, as well as the honey and jams that they make themselves. The restaurant is open to non-residents and can seat approximately 50 (meals range from 20-25 euros, including wine; the supplement for half board is 15 euros per person). Guests may rent a van to carry up to nine people for excursions in the environs (among the many sites, we recommend a visit to the Palazzo Ducale di Sassuolo), while ecological guides are available if you are visiting the Salse di Nirano Nature Reserve.

• 1 single, 6 double rooms and 1 mini-apartment (2-4 persons), with bathroom, TV; some with air-conditioning, terrace, kitchenette • Prices: single 38 euros, double 55 (15 euro supplement for extra bed), mini-apartment 60-80, breakfast included • Credit cards: none • 1 room designed for use by the mobility challenged. Off-street parking. Small pets allowed. Owner always reachable. • Bar corner, restaurant. Breakfast room, TV room. Conference room. Garden, terrace

DON ABBONDIO

Wine store-restaurant
Piazza Guido da Montefeltro 16
Tel. 0543 25460
Closed Saturday lunch and Sunday
Open: lunch and dinner
Holidays: August 10-20, first week of January
Seating: 50 + 25 outdoors
Prices: 30-35 euros, wine excluded
All major credit cards

LA CASA RUSTICALE DEI CAVALIERI TEMPLARI

Restaurant
Viale Bologna 275
Tel. 0543 701888
Closed Sunday and Monday
Open: lunch and dinner
Holidays: last week of July-August
Seating: 70 + 70 outdoors
Prices: 32-35 euros, wine excluded
All credit cards, Bancomat

Once upon a time this was known as Osteria della trippa. It opened its doors at first light, to cater for night workers coming off their shifts. Located next-door to the former San Domenico monastery, now a cultural center, this wine-store-restaurant – run by Nicola in the kitchen and Alessandro and Simone front of house – presents an exploration of Romagna cuisine.

Just a stone's throw from the Adriatic riviera, in the plains at the foot of the Apennines, the area offers a wide range of high quality produce, from cold fillets of smoked baccalà, to sliced mackerel with cream of chick peas; from **culatello di Zibello** to toasted polenta; from stuffed rabbit to potato pie with leek sauce. First courses include **passatelli** served with chicory and bacon, **tagliatelle al ragù** and tortelli with herbs and pecorino. Once summer is over the passatelli are served in capon broth, the tagliatelle with cep mushrooms and the **tagliolini with lamb** and rosemary sauce, alongside **zuppa all'antica**, a soup with grains and pulses, and strozzapreti with white meat ragù.

Winter main courses start off with **tripe alla romagnola**, or **stuffed rabbit with potatoes** and duck breast with glazed baby onions. The rest of the year you can choose between fillet of perch in a potato crust or lamb or beef tagliata. All year round there are the **cured meats** and cheeses of Romagna, which are ideal for a late evening snack too. Don't miss out on the puddings: chilli-flavored chocolate mousse and hot apple pie with Sangiovese sauce.

There is a respectable, carefully-researched wine list which reveals good connections with the local area.

What was once the house of the Order of the Knights Templar has now been renovated and turned into a restaurant of great charm, ten minutes from the historic center of Forlì. Three inviting dining rooms and a garden for al fresco dining in summer, an elegant setting for the cuisine of Piera and her daughters Licia and Lucilla, whose husbands Stefano and Fabrizio work front of house and see to the fresh pasta and puddings.

Diners can choose between a range of different options à la carte or from well-structured set menus – local specialties, seafood, vegetarian, the seasons, or themed menus (the **baccalà** menu is an interesting choice, served steamed with Quarantine potatoes, oven-baked, and as a filling for tortelli).

Picking and choosing from the various menus (but mostly from the traditional one), memorable antipasti included some interesting cured meats, vegetable flans and quiches. Then **tagliatelle 'al sugo matto'**, **cappelletti in capon broth**, passatelli with pecorino served with bacon and mushrooms (in winter), and artichoke tortelli with lamb sauce (in spring). Leaving aside the fish and concentrating on the meat, we recommend the **shank of pork** with Sangiovese, stuffed saddle of rabbit or **cotechino sausage** with lentil sauce and **chestnut purée**.

Then there is an Italian **cheese board** served with jams and to finish off some creative puddings (sbrisolona with hot custard sauce, walnut semifreddo with fruit sauce, chocolate cake or a traditional **zuppa inglese**): all well-presented, like the other dishes on offer.

There is a good wine list and a wide selection of coffees.

FORLÌ

SALUMÈ

🍲Osteria with shop
Piazza Cavour 42
Tel. 0543 36400
Closed Sundays and Mondays
Open: 10am-11pm
Holidays: 15 days in August
Seating: 30 + 16 outdoors
Prices: 25-30 euros, wine excluded
All credit cards, Bancomat

Arriving from the motorway you can't go wrong – just take the main road towards the historic center and follow the signs for the Cavour carpark. On your way to the osteria take a look at piazza Saffi and the abbey of San Mercuriale with its belltower, the most important historic monuments in Forlì. After that owner Ritano Cavassi and his daughter Sofia will be waiting to welcome you into the Salumè.

The osteria is small but inviting and on entering you will notice the 1950s counter displaying cheeses and cured meats, and shelves loaded with tasty specialties on sale, including spirits, homemade biscuits and jams. The kitchen is on view, the domain of the talented Milena Cavassi who offers up a blend of tradition and seasonal produce. The menu is written on a board hung on the wall, while you can count on Ritano, who is passionate about the subject, to help you choose the right wine. The high quality **cured meats** and cheeses can be accompanied with **piadina** if you are needing a light snack, but also make an excellent antipasto to lead into tagliatelle with asparagus, **tortelli ai rosolacci** or a seasonal risotto (try the shrimp one). Then it's time for some **mutton in sauce** (cooked in pieces), **sliced beef**, or simple stuffed zucchini. For pudding there are tarts, zuppa inglese, strawberry bavarese, **mascarpone with caramelized figs** or tiramisù.

The wine list features a good selection of Italian labels, with special attention for local producers. There are also some international wines and a vast range of spirits. You are warmly recommended to reserve a table.

FRASSINORO
Fontanaluccia

ALLA PESCHIERA

🍲Traditional osteria-trattoria
Via Ponte Volpi 1
Tel. 0536 968275
Closed Monday
Open: lunch and dinner
Holidays: none
Seating: 90
Prices: 20-25 euros, wine excluded
No credit cards, Bancomat

This was originally a little kiosk on the banks of the Diolo river, a clean waterway offering rich pickings for fishermen, which runs through the stunning Abetina valley, a wonderful place for woodland walks. Then little by little Franco, a hardworking local man of few words, began extending it, creating an attractive, welcoming wood and stone building which blends in beautifully with the surrounding landscape.

A visit to the Peschiera could start off with a selection from the wide range of **cured meats** Franco makes from the free-range pigs he keeps. Prosciutto, lardo, salami and pancetta arrotolata, as well as good pecorino produced by local shepherds, and the ubiquitous **gnocco fritto**: a meal in itself if you wish. The first courses include some fabulous **tortellini in broth** (like all the other pasta dishes, made by local women), **ricotta tortelloni** and **tagliatelle with ragù** or game sauce. When it's the right time of year, the pasta dishes and the meat dishes (yard-reared chicken and rabbit) are served with **mushrooms**, then in the hunting season there is **game**, and in winter **maize or chestnut polenta**. Naturally, as the name of the place indicates (as do the tanks beside the building), there is also fresh **trout**, served in an unusual but tasty fried version, with herbs and spices. When booking we recommend you ask about what is on offer and if you so wish you can agree on a menu. Homemade cakes and fruit tarts are a perfect end to the meal, and can be followed by homemade infusions and liqueurs. Service is prompt and courteous, and the wine list, though limited, is honest and satisfactory.

GAZZOLA
Rivalta

CROARA VECCHIA

🗝️ Holiday farm
Frazione Rivalta
Tel. 0523 977153
Fax 0523 957628
E-mail: gmilanopc@tin.it
Internet: www.croaravecchia.it
Closed from November to February

The Vecchia Croara's rooms and apartments are in what was once an old convent. The facility is surrounded by a vast estate, in part dedicated to growing crops while the rest is pastureland for cows. A conservative approach to the renovation has preserved the special features of the buildings. The rooms are big and very well furnished: high ceilings with old wooden beams, antique furniture, precious curtains and linens in warm colors, all of which contributes to making the rooms pleasant to stay in. Breakfast comprises sweet and savory fare: cakes, bread, butter and jams, focaccia, cured meats and local cheeses, hot and cold drinks. Those who love riding can use the riding school facilities for guided or unaccompanied excursions on horseback.

• 1 single, 4 double and 2 triple rooms, with bathroom, air-conditioning, TV, some with fridge; 4 mini-apartments with kitchenette • Prices: single 80 euros, double 90, triple and mini-apartment 110, breakfast included • Credit cards: all except AE, Bancomat • 1 room designed for use by the mobility challenged. Off-street parking. Small pets allowed. Owners reachable from 7am to 9.30pm • Breakfast room, lounge. Garden. Pool, horse-riding

---

GAZZOLA
Rivalta

LOCANDA DEL FALCO

🍲 Restaurant with shop
Località Rivalta
Tel. 0523 978101
Closed Tuesday
Open: lunch and dinner
Holidays: in December and August
Seating: 80 + 50 outdoors
Prices: 35 euros, wine excluded
All credit cards

Val Trebbia is one of those places to visit in the slow lane. It should be explored at a relaxed pace to enjoy the scenery, with houses and villages that appear on the horizon from time to time, or suddenly from round a bend. And as you travel slowly down the road you will notice this tiny, picturesque Medieval hamlet, which contains a trattoria frequented by regulars and passing trade. On entering you are drawn to an old door on the left which opens onto a wonderful food shop, completely done up in dark wood, with a cornucopia of cured meats, vegetables, oils, wines and spirits. It is an attractive setting, which blends in well with the surrounding landscape. The restaurant itself has three dining rooms, the walls of which are adorned with English and Italian ceramics.
Once seated, it's time to start with a selection of mixed **cured meats** accompanied by homemade sweet and sour baby vegetables and sturgeon in olive oil. The subsequent courses feature the unmissable traditional **pisarei e fasò**, and good ricotta or pumpkin **tortelli**. When in season you can have: **anolini in broth** or tagliolini with mushroom sauce.
The main courses are tasty and well-made: roast duck or goose, served with apple; baked shank of veal with potatoes, **stuffed breast of veal** and fried lamb cutlets. When the weather turns cold it's time for **mixed boiled meats**, and in summer fillet steak and chargrilled chops. The puddings are definitely worth trying: mention should be made of the pear pastry and nougat semifreddo. The wine list is well thought out, with a good variety of local and national labels, and there is an excellent range of spirits.

GUIGLIA

OSTERIA VECCHIA ⊘

◡ Trattoria
Via Michelangelo 690-694
Tel. 059 792433
Closed Monday and Tuesday
Open: dinner, open for lunch on Sundays and holidays
Holidays: February and September
Seating: 80
Prices: 30 euros, wine excluded
All major credit cards, Bancomat

As time goes by this is one restaurant that continues to merit inclusion, even just for the chance for a frank discussion with Giovanni Montanari. This passionate supporter of the organic cause – rest assured you will not be served anything not produced or grown according to the dictates of certified organic farming – is convinced that food quality means more than just natural production, because together with respect for the environment there has to be sensory quality, safeguards for biodiversity, and respect for tradition and toil. Only organic food which also meets these criteria can be deemed of quality.

In the middle of the big dining room there is a buffet groaning with antipasti, where together with rice and mixed grain salads you will find a wide choice of raw and cooked vegetables, an excellent range of **cured meats** and above all a good range of **cheeses**, starting from **parmigiano reggiano** and various types of pecorino, burrata, goats' cheeses and mozzarella, which you can sample accompanied with hot **crescentine**. This is followed by a few first courses and main courses, all traditional, made by Giovanni's niece Simonetta: **tortellini in broth**, tagliatelle with ragù, **ricotta tortelloni**, mixed grain, rice and bean soup; then **roast guinea fowl**, chicken or rabbit 'alla cacciatora', and if you are in luck a **stew of vacca bianca modenese beef**, an indigenous breed at risk of extinction which is a Slow Food Presidia.

The puddings include savor tart (made with traditional cooked grape must) and other homemade cakes.

IMOLA

E' PARLAMINTÉ

◡ Trattoria
Via Mameli 33
Tel. 0542 30144
Closed Sunday evenings and Monday, May-August also Sunday lunch
Open: lunch and dinner
Holidays: 15/7-23/8, 15 days over Christmas and Epiphany
Seating: 40 + 20 outdoors
Prices: 25-30 euros, wine excluded
All major credit cards, Bancomat

This characteristic family-run trattoria in the center of Imola is a haunt for students, office workers, sales reps and politicians, who come to savor the meals prepared by the friendly Dal Monte family and enjoy a good discussion. To some extent, though it has changed over time, the trattoria has not lost its original role as a meeting place and venue for the heated debates that the name implies. The bar counter at the entrance, the old grocery store furniture, the well-spaced tables and the little courtyard out back are all emblematic of the warm, informal style of the place. The kitchen is a male domain, with father Raffaele and son Massimo, while the front of house is governed by mother Marta, courteous and pleasant.

The traditional local cuisine is complemented with a good number of fish dishes, some of which are unusual and interesting, springing from Raffaele's passion for the subject, and the desire to tempt the palates of the regulars. You will find a **salad of shrimp, potatoes and beans**, caponata of egg plant and shrimp, raw French oysters, spaghetti with tuna, **umbrine** from Camillona (a Slow Food Presidia) **baked in a salt crust**, **baccalà** – always a winner – both **char-grilled** and **mantecato**. When it comes to meat, there is salad with hot prosciutto, **pappardelle with duck ragù**, **stricchetti with sausage and peas**, beef tagliata with Sangiovese sauce and fried artichokes, and a cheese board served with honey and caramelized figs. To finish off there is a wonderful crème caramel and other homemade puddings.

There is a set menu at 25 euros for four courses, and an original wine list which includes wines served by the glass.

33 KM SOUTH EAST OF BOLOGNA SS 9 OR A 14

HOSTARIA 900

Restaurant
Viale Dante 20
Tel. 0542 24211
Closed Thursday and Saturday lunch
Open: lunch and dinner
Holidays: 15 days in August
Seating: 75 + 50 outdoors
Prices: 30-32 euros, wine excluded
All credit cards

Hostaria 900 is in an art-nouveau style building and features three dining rooms with large tables. Front of house are Orazio and Domenico, while Giorgia and Andrea work in the kitchen, ably plying their trade with high quality ingredients.
The food is all seasonal, but not always linked to local traditions. We started off with a hot flan of asparagus, prosciutto di Parma and culatello dell'Antica Corte Pallavicina di Zibello, squid in tempura with vegetables and cinta senese salami. First courses include some excellent **maccheroncini al torchio with pancetta and saffron**, then cappelletti 900, tortelli with a potato filling served with fondue of mortadella Antica Bologna, **tagliatelle with cep mushrooms**, green tagliolini al torchio with clams, zucchini and zucchini flowers, and **tortellini in chicken broth**. As for the main courses, there is a good range of **meat** for **grilling**, from mutton to chops, and from Tuscan fiorentina steak to beef fillet; or **sliced beef with Modena balsamic vinegar**, or lamb scottadito. All the main courses are served with chargrilled vegetables or potatoes with sea salt and rosemary. The dish of four cheeses with jams and honey is also good. Puddings include a coffee cream, **zuppa inglese** with alkermes sauce, chocolate salami with Amedei white chocolate, and mascarpone semifreddo with shavings of dark chocolate.
There is no shortage of fish dishes (one example: swordfish in a saffron fondant with Pachino tomatoes) and in summer you can eat in the garden which surrounds the villa. They offer reasonably-priced business lunches. There is a good wine list with fair mark-ups, and wines served by the glass.

IMOLA

33 KM SOUTH EAST OF BOLOGNA SS 9 OR A 14

OSTERIA DEL VICOLO NUOVO

Wine shop with bar and kitchen
Via Codronchi, 6
Tel. 0542 32552
Closed Sundays and Mondays
Open: lunch and dinner
Holidays: 10 July-August 20
Seating: 70 + 40 outdoors
Prices: 32-34 euros, wine excluded
All major credit cards, Bancomat

This osteria, run with great dedication by Ambra and Rosa for over twenty years, is in an attractive building in historic downtown Imola. It has one room at the entrance and another smaller dining area on the lower floor, with a stone vaulted ceiling.
You will be given a friendly welcome and made to feel at home. The dishes blend local traditions and produce with a sprinkling of creativity, using high quality ingredients. The menu changes with the seasons and according to availability of produce, and a few fish dishes are also offered.
You can start off with octopus and beans, vegetable and cheese flan, **zucchini flowers with ricotta and herbs**, **culatello** and **lardo di Parma**. The homemade pasta dishes go from **tortellini in chicken broth** to squid ink tagliolini with shrimp, from fresh pasta strichetti with peas and ham to **hand-rolled tagliatelle with rabbit sauce**, to lasagnetta gratin with zucchini and provola cheese. As for the main courses, there is **local rabbit in Sangiovese**, roasted sausages with potatoes, beef tagliata with rosemary, warm chicken salad with raisins and pine nuts, **squacquerone cheese with piadina** and jams and a good quality **cheese board** (including some Slow Food presidia). The puddings are also excellent: caramelized crema catalana, panna cotta with fresh fruit and zabaglione semifreddo with melted chocolate.
There is an extensive, well thought out wine list at reasonable prices. At lunch time you can opt for a single course for 11 euros.

LAMA MOCOGNO
La Santona

MIRAMONTI

⌂ Restaurant
Via Nazionale 207
Tel. 0536 45013
Closed Tuesday, but not in summer
Open: lunch and dinner
Holidays: second half of September
Seating: 40 + 12 outdoors
Prices: 20-25 euros, wine excluded
All major credit cards, Bancomat

At one of the highest points of highway 12 through Abetone and Brennero, which was built by the Estensi in the second half of the eighteenth century to link up with their lands in Emilia and Tuscany, lies the hamlet of La Santona, a scattering of houses on the slopes of Mount Cantiere. The Miramonti, which was also a hotel up to ten years ago, has been run by Vittorio and Lidia Galli for almost thirty years, and they continue to put the same passion into their consummate brand of simple cuisine.
To start off, **gnocco fritto** and the **salami** that Vittorio commissions from a local pork butcher. There are only four first courses but they are all high quality, and Lidia makes the pasta by hand. The **tortelloni with butter and sage** are filled with ricotta from a nearby dairy and the **tagliatelle with mushrooms** are made with ceps from the woods in the valley. Sample the tagliatelle with ragù, and if you taste a hint of nutmeg in the **beef and capon tortellini in broth**, remember that it is traditional in these parts. The daily selection of main courses includes tagliata with rosemary, **mixed grill** of white and red meats, and some simple, delicious escalopes with ceps, lemon or balsamic vinegar. When you book (which we would advise) ask them to make you **guinea fowl with truffle stuffing**, or their exquisite roast lamb with potatoes, or lamb or pork chops. This is a land of woods and forests, and it is worth trying the **wild boar with polenta**, and if the pickers have been lucky, mushroom salad, with **fried** or grilled **mushrooms**. The puddings are homemade: zuppa inglese and cassata. The wine list, which is not extensive, offers a selection of local and national labels.

LANGHIRANO
Torrechiara

TAVERNA DEL CASTELLO

⚷ Locanda
Strada del Castello 25
Tel. 0521 355015
Fax 0521 355849
E-mail: info@tavernadelcastello.it
Internet: www.tavernadelcastello.it
Closed for 15 days in January

The locanda lies within the walls of the medieval village of Torrechiara and was created by renovating an old building in 2003. The rooms are big, tastefully furnished and organized so that a third bed can be added. The typical Italian-style breakfast offers brioches, homemade bread, butter and jam, yogurt, cereals, cappuccino and, on request and free of extra charge, you can also opt for savory fare such as cured meats and cheeses. The garden at the foot of the castle walls is beautiful and offers a glorious view, in short, a great place to sit and chat and enjoy pleasurable evenings. Among the communal areas inside there are two small rooms on the first floor, while on the upper floor there's a spacious living room that can accommodate up to sixty people. The restaurant offers seasonal meat and fish dishes, revisited in a modern key (the cost of a meal ranges from 25-35 euros per person, excluding wine).

• 5 double rooms, with bathroom, TV • Prices: double room single occupancy 65 euros, double 95 (25 euro supplement for extra bed), breakfast included • Credit cards: Visa, AE, Bancomat • Free external public parking. Small pets allowed. Reception open from 7.30am to 1am • Bar, restaurant. Breakfast room, reading room. Conference room. Garden

LESIGNANO DE' BAGNI
Rivalta

LESIGNANO DE' BAGNI
San Michele Cavana

31 KM SOUTH OF PARMA

31 KM SOUTH OF PARMA

CAPELLI

LOCANDA DEL SALE

Trattoria
Via Fossola 10
Tel. 0521 350122
Closed Thursday
Open: lunch and dinner
Holidays: vary
Seating: 50
Prices: 26-32 euros, wine excluded
Credit cards: DC, Visa, Bancomat

Trattoria
Località La Maestà 11
Tel. 0521 857170
Closed Monday and Tuesday, but not in summer
Open: lunch and dinner
Holidays: 15 days in January
Seating: 35 + 20 outdoors
Prices: 25-30 euros, wine excluded
All major credit cards, Bancomat

It will be a surprise to reach this trattoria in the yard of the farm which the Capelli family has been running for decades, amidst the cows that provide the milk to make parmigiano reggiano, and the hens, chickens and rabbits that contribute to the menu.

The food is simple but based on ingredients of outstanding quality, and respecting local traditions. The talented Cristina, in the kitchen, and her husband Vincenzo, front of house, offer a range of well-prepared traditional dishes. Quite rightly the antipasto is based on cured meats: we sampled an exceptional **prosciutto** aged for 36 months, a well seasoned, sweet **guanciale**, good salami and **culaccia**. All accompanied with crispy fried polenta, baby onions in balsamic vinegar and creamed lardo with vegetables. They have made an appreciable choice to show prices and weights on the menu. There is an imaginative range of first courses: **tortelli** with herbs or made from green pasta, **filled with potato and spalla cotta** or pumpkin; **tagliolini with game**, mushrooms or sausage ragù. There is also a tasty rice savarin with mushrooms, and classic **cappelletti in broth**. The trattoria's signature main courses include meat prepared 'alla cacciatora': spatchcock, rabbit, duck, wild boar and roe deer. Then there is the classic **roast breast of veal**, roast brisket, and in the right season, mixed boiled meats. As for puddings there are cakes, a good sorbet, an excellent **zuppa inglese**, tiramisù and the wittily named "tiramigiù". There is a good range of wines, with a few important labels. House digestif and some renowned spirits.

To get to this trattoria you go up into the hills around Parma and take the 'prosciutto road' up to Langhirano, then Lesignano and then follow the signs for Cavana abbey, which dates back to 1111 (and is worth visiting). Then continue up the road for another two kilometers and you will come to the village of La Maestà, and the sign of the Locanda del Sale.

The trattoria is plain, minimal, in smart country style, with two dining rooms with terracotta floors and wooden beams. There is a huge Berkel slicing machine dominating the entrance, a clear message that cured meats are the order of the day here. The menu is varied: there are two set menus, for 27 or 32 euros. On the table the bread basket contains some wonderful white and wholemeal bread, as well as focaccia, all made by Angela, a great accompaniment for the Felino salami, **culatello**, **spalla cotta**, but above all the delicious **prosciutto crudo**. Then you can sample the classic **ricotta and herb tortelli** served with melted butter and parmigiano, **anolini in broth**, risotto with fresh salami paste, or potato and pumpkin gnocchi with pine nuts and basil. In summer there are also a few lighter dishes. As for the main courses, to stick to the traditional, there is stuffed roast breast of veal, **donkey stew** with char-grilled polenta, and **tripe 'alla parmigiana'**. Before you go on to pudding, you must sample the **parmigiano stravecchio**.

The puddings are all homemade and include tarts, sbrisolona, a range of semifreddo desserts, and **pear and chocolate cake**. The wine list is not lengthy, but does offer some good regional labels. The choice of spirits is more interesting, with homemade nut liqueur or bargnolino.

LONGIANO

IL RISTORANTE DEI CANTONI

☞Restaurant
Via Santa Maria 19
Tel. 0547 665899
Closed Wednesdays
Open: lunch and dinner
Holidays: February 15-March 20
Seating: 80 + 70 outdoors
Prices: 26-28 euros, wine excluded
All major credit cards, Bancomat

In the green hills which overlook via Emilia, between Cesena and Rimini, lies the town of Longiano, which boasts a fascinating history and monuments such as the Teatro Petrella, the Medieval district and the Castello Malatestiano, which houses the art collection of the Tito Balestra Foundation. Right beside the castle is this restaurant, where you will be welcomed by Danilo Bianchi and his wife Teresa and taken into one of the two dining rooms with arch vaults, or out into the garden.

The mainly traditional food benefits from the experience of pasta chef Rosanna, who makes all the pasta and the **piadina**. The menu is seasonal, with fish served on Tuesday and Friday lunch, as well as **mushrooms** and **truffles** (with a corresponding price hike). You can start with one of the dishes from the menu: "Lo sfizio" – hot pastries filled with vegetables, salad of char-grilled cep mushrooms – or with an antipasto, before going on to the fresh or filled pasta dishes. **Pappardelle with duck ragù**, tomato and bladder campion, **passatelli**, or cappellettoni filled with ricotta and caciotta cheese, served with sautéed fresh cep mushrooms. The main courses include some good roasts, **fillet steak with mushrooms**, or balsamic vinegar, or green peppercorns, a tasty fiorentina steak and tagliata of scottona. Cheese fans will be able to sample **formaggio di fossa** from Sogliano served with savor, sweet and sour Volpina pears and quince jam. To round off, home-made puddings and a glass of passito.

There is a good selection of wines: regional, with Sangiovese first and foremost, and some labels from further afield.

LUGO

SAN MARTINO ♭

☞Recently opened Osteria
Via Magnapassi 22
Tel. 0545 281928
Closed Tuesday, in summer evenings and Sunday
Open: lunch and dinner
Holidays: the mid-August and New Year
Seating: 80 + 80 outdoors
Prices: 30-33 euros, wine excluded
All major credit cards, Bancomat

This friendly, lively osteria near piazza Baracca in the historic city center is the ancient Colleggiata granary (1832), with a wonderful fire place in the main dining room and views of the atmospheric cloisters. The young owners Samuel, Simone and Claudio believe in blending tradition and innovation, backed up by their mother Tiziana, who represents the traditional part. The menu varies according to the seasons and the market availability of ingredients, and is the work of chef Omar Nannini.

You can start with a selection of **Romagna cured meats**, accompanied with shallots and vegetables preserved in oil, made by Tiziana using produce from her garden. Among the first courses, **strichetti with fresh Romagna salami** and spinach, **tagliatelle with a ragù of sausage**, pork and beef, and **passatelli in broth**. Main courses include **roast rabbit with aromatic herbs**, **chicken alla diavola**, lamb chops, char-grilled meat and **friggione**. The cheese board comes with jams and home-made caramelized figs. As for puddings, there are biscuits, crema catalana, icecream with caramelized figs and double chocolate terrine.

Brisighella oil and an extensive wine list, with a good range of local labels and different wine on offer by the glass every day. In winter there are wine tasting sessions and themed evenings.

♟ Le delizie del buongustaio at via Foro Boario 33 is a shop which makes and sells its own fresh sausages, salsiccia matta, cotechino, coppa di testa, soft pork crackling, and a range of Romagna salami including mora romagnola. At vicolo del Teatro 18, Bottega della natura, offers excellent organic produce.

MERCATO SARACENO
Montesorbo

MERCATO SARACENO
Montecastello

33 KM SOUTH OF CESENA SS 71 OR E 45

29 KM SOUTH OF CESENA SS 71 OR E 45

ALLEGRIA

DA ELENA

🍲 Osteria-trattoria
Via Ciola 321
Tel. 0547 692382
Closed Sunday for dinner and Monday, except in summer
Open: lunch and dinner
Holidays: 15 days at Christmas
Seating: 45
Prices: 20-25 euros, wine excluded
No credit cards accepted

🍲 Trattoria
Via 30 Aprile 104
Tel. 0547 91565
Closed on Monday
Open: lunch, and dinner on Friday,
Saturday, Sunday
Holidays: two weeks in middle of January, July
Seating: 70
Prices: 23-26 euros, wine excluded
Credit cards: all except DC, Bancomat

Instead of taking the easy road down to the town center, take this more demanding climb up provincial road 53 towards Ciola, and about ten kilometers after the lovely church of Montesorbo in the shape of a Greek cross (8th century, open on Sundays and holidays), you will find this isolated but welcoming trattoria. Even if you have to pass through the bar to find a seat in the small dining-room near to the kitchen, or even in the family breakfast room, the welcome you receive from Anna will make you feel at home. She will list the day's specials, which are always varied, prepared by her mother Bianca and her brother Massimo, and will be ready to offer advice and explanations about where the ingredients come from and how they are prepared. The enjoyment of the food itself will be accompanied by that of the company, in the century-old tradition of the osteria.

Start with the **cured meats**, cured by a friend who raises pigs, and local **cheese** made with cow's and ewe's milk, **croutons** with mushrooms, truffles and woodcock. The first courses include tortelloni, **tagliatelle** and **pappardelle** with traditional sauces, but also other types of pasta and sauces with vegetables in season. Then grilled meat, **game**, with wild birds cooked on the spit or fried (when available, it is best to book, and there will be a reasonable enough surcharge), **wild boar in wine**, **pigeon** and cockerel.

The puddings also follow the inspiration of the day, but they always include crostata and **ciambella**, which are a must. Only local wine.

A traditional osteria in a small village in the green Savio valley, a few miles from Mercato Saraceno. A large dining-room in a building constructed in the 1960s that looks like a family home. Which is what it is. The osteria has been family-run for forty years, the great-grandmother used to prepare piadina, crescioni and cured meats in the Republican Club, with portraits of Mazzini and Garibaldi on the walls, a long counter along one wall, and a large stove at the center. The enthusiastic stories told by granddaughter Giulia bring the atmosphere to life, even if the club and the party have vanished and the restructured house now belongs to Elena, the talented soul. But the passion for local cooking has not changed, nor has the pride of still being a friendly meeting place.

The recipe for **piadina** is still the same, the dough is made by hand, the mushrooms and truffles come from the surrounding woods, and the meat from nearby Tuscany. The menu is not rich but all the fare is traditional. Croutons, cured meats, **sautéed mushrooms** or mushrooms in oil, and fagiolata are among the antipasti. **Tagliatelle**, small **cappelletti**, tortelli with herbs, and potato gnocchi with various sauces, among the first courses. **Mutton**, **sausage** and **grilled pancetta**, grilled T-bone steak, pork chop, mixed vegetables au gratin, and cheese among the main courses. To order, **roast** veal, **pigeon** and lamb, **pan-fried rabbit** and, only in Winter, **cotechino with beans and baccalà**.

And to finish, panna cotta, mascarpone, **ciambella** and the famous "**porcospino**" (not in summer). Trebbiano, Albana and Sangiovese wines from two local cellars.

ALDINA

🍲 Trattoria
Via Albinelli 40
Tel. 059 236106
Closed Sunday and holidays
Open: only for lunch
Holidays: July 10-August 31
Seating: 70
Prices: 16 euros, wine excluded
No credit cards accepted

ERMES

🍲 Trattoria
Via Ganaceto 89-91
No telephone
Closed on Sundays
Open: only for lunch
Holidays: July and August
Seating: 30
Prices: 15-18 euros
Credit cards: no

The Aldina trattoria offers you a chance to enjoy the best of Modena: the historical center, in the winter fog or the summer heat. Find time to visit the covered market in Via Albinelli, opposite the trattoria, but also the nearby Piazza Grande, with its magnificent medieval cathedral. Stroll down Via Emilia, or take a look at the imposing military Academy, built as the palace of the Dukes of Este in the 17th century, when Modena was the capital of the Duchy. The city is all in this small space, and there is a clear thread that links the life of the past with that of today.

The Aldina has never changed either, during the years it has been in this guide, or even before. You will find a real trattoria, in simple premises on the second floor, where the welcome is quick but warm and genuine, and the food is perfectly prepared. **Tortellini in consommé** (some people ask for an entire tureen), ravioli with a "vecchia Modena" meat filling (cream and pancetta), **tortelloni of pumpkin** (typical of this area), tortelloni of ricotta and spinach, cannelloni au gratin, **tagliatelle with a meat** or mushroom sauce. Meat is traditionally served for the second course: **roast guinea-fowl** and ham, **mixed boiled meats, escalope of veal with balsamic vinegar** or mushrooms, pork shank, and mixed roasts. The side dishes are generous, as they were in the trattorias of the past.

The puddings include panna cotta, mascarpone, crème caramel, and apple cake. The wine on offer is genuine Lambrusco and other local wines, and there is no reason to drink anything else.

The main problem is finding a seat, particularly if you arrive at peak time: but if you trust Ermes, sooner or later, in spite of his rough inhospitable appearance, he will courteously offer you a table in the busy dining-room where the atmosphere is always cheerful and down-to-earth. Then you can place all your trust in the cooking skills of Bruna, Ermes' wife, and you will not regret it.

The quality of the food is guaranteed by the fact that everything is made fresh: the number of guests is always more or less the same, and ten years of experience have taught them not to overbuy. Early every morning, the fresh produce is delivered to the kitchen and the limited number of lunch dishes are prepared. The prices are reasonable because, although the raw materials are all good and expensive, the careful economies that you find in any careful household are used in the kitchen. The minced meat is used to make the meat sauce, which is served with the hand-made **tagliatelle** (flour, eggs and water do not cost much, what is priceless is the skill and speed needed to make them!) or in the lasagna. Beef and a good fowl make the consommé for the excellent **tortellini**, and the meat is then served with the **mixed boiled meats**, or used to make tasty **meatballs**. The first courses also include **tortelloni di magro**, while **veal escalopes with balsamic vinegar**, **roast veal** and stewed meats are among the main courses. The menu is always similar, tried, tested and guaranteed: it might look easy, but a growing number of restaurateurs have forgotten how to do it.

And since it is daunting to eat tortellini in consommé and boiled meats in the summer heat, Ermes closes.

MODENA

MONGHIDORO
Campeggio

STALLO DEL POMODORO

🍲 Wine center with meals
Largo Hannover 63
Tel. 059 214664
Closed Saturday and lunch Sunday
Open: lunch and dinner
Holidays: from Christmas to January 6
Seating: 60 + 30 outdoors
Prices: 28-30 euros, wine excluded
Credit cards: Visa

BORGO DI SUMBILLA

Bed and breakfast
Via Sumbilla 20
Tel. 051 6551228-6551176-335 6571176
Fax 051 6551176
E-mail: info@borgodisumbilla.it
Internet: www.borgodisumbilla.it
Open all year

Largo Hannover is a square in the town center where there are several bars and restaurants, surrounded by historical buildings, and frequented by young people in the afternoon and well into the night. Lo Stallo, a wine shop that also serves meals, is the first or last of these bars, depending on which direction you are coming from. The architecture and the ambience are extremely appealing. Here you can enjoy a good bottle of wine, or a complete meal. The cooking is not strictly traditional, and several more creative dishes are also proposed, but all the raw ingredients are selected with care (nearly all from the province of Modena). There are also menus for vegetarians and for people with gluten intolerance (and it is recommended by the Italian Celiac Association).

You can start with the mixed antipasti of the house: flans, salads, pies, fritters, onion pie. The alternatives are also good: a selection of **cured meats**, cream of parmigiano reggiano, caramelized balsamic vinegar on mixed vegetables. The first courses include **tortelli from Modena with nettles and provola** and the less familiar gnocchi of ricotta and buckwheat flour with a tomato sauce. As a main course: **breast of duck with cherry sauce** flavored with Lambrusco, **lamb chops** with minted beans and tomato compote, fillet of beef with nettle cream, **grilled lamb chops**. People who do not enjoy meat can choose from a selection of **raw-milk cheeses**, accompanied by preserves and mostarda. And pudding to finish: chocolate cake with custard, semifreddo with limoncello and pumpkin cream with liquorice. The wine list contains over 400 Italian labels, about twenty of which sold by the glass.

This B&B is in a peaceful area of the Apennines, near the watershed that divides the Sàvena from the Sambro valley. Here Silvia and Maurizio Naldi have recently restructured the remains of a medieval tower, creating a refined atmosphere using a variety of styles and materials: sandstone and massive wooden beams combined with period furniture and other antiques. The architectural refurbishment is made even more original by touches of bright color and the modern design of some of the furnishings. The rooms have been designed with great attention to detail that guarantees a sense of tranquility and the same applies to communal areas where between 8 and 9.30am they serve breakfast comprising specialties of the house. In the adjacent Monti restaurant, which has always belonged to the Naldi family, you'll be able to savor the hospitality that Emilia is famous for and enjoy the taste of local specialties (meals range from 25-30 euros per person, excluding wine).

• 3 double rooms, with bathroom (jacuzzi showers), safe, satellite TV (sound available through headphones only), modem connection • Prices: double room single occupancy 60 euros, double 80, Breakfast included • Credit cards: all, Bancomat • Covered off-street parking and external public parking 50 meters away. No pets allowed. Owners always reachable. • Self-service bar corner. Breakfast room, reading room. Garden, solarium.

MONTECCHIO EMILIA   MONTEVEGLIO

LA GHIRONDA   ABBAZIA

🍲 Restaurant
Via XX Settembre 61
Tel. 0522 863550
Closed Sunday for dinner and Monday
Open: lunch and dinner
Holidays: first week in January, July 15-31
Seating: 35
Prices: 30-35 euros, wine excluded
Credit cards: all major cards, Bancomat

🗝 Bed and breakfast
Via San Rocco 7
Tel. 051 6701024-340 7236508
Fax 051 6701835
E-mail: clcandel@tin.it
Internet: www.monteveglioatavola.it/bb_abbazia.html
Holidays vary

This delightfully friendly restaurant is located right where the Enza river divides the provinces of Parma and Reggio Emilia, and it serves dishes that are typical of this borderland. We are in the lands of Matilda of Canossa, where there are numerous picturesque castles, and Canossa itself is close by and well worth a visit. Camillo Fochi will welcome you to La Ghironda with impeccable courtesy and will describe in great detail all the ingredients and products that chef Daniele Stragapede uses in the kitchen. You must start with **cured meats** which include Bologna sausage (a Slow Food Presidia), culaccia from Langhirano, hand-made Felino salami, and traditional cured shoulder of ham, accompanied by gnocco fritto and a small giardiniera of vegetables in oil. The first courses include tiny, delicious **cappelletti in consommé** which are filled with fried pork, raw veal, boiled fowl, bread, parmigiano reggiano, eggs and nutmeg. June 24 traditionally marks the celebration of St. John's Day with a "tortellata", and numerous tasty varieties of **tortelli** are prepared: with greens, pumpkin, potatoes, beetroot and aged ricotta. The bigoli al torchio with guanciale and pepper are also excellent. The main courses include **tripe stew** alla reggiana, sautéed kidney with warm croutons, **potatoes and seasonal mushrooms au gratin** and **baccalà all'emiliana** with cherry tomatoes and onions. A cappuccino ice cream with coffee caramel will complete your meal perfectly, or you might prefer a bowl of zabaione with crushed almonds or traditional pastries with an excellent mixture of Jamaican coffee. The wine list is carefully selected, and includes numerous local producers and a good choice of national wines.

Monteveglio is a small village on a hill to the west of the main town. Its past is linked to Matilde di Canossa, who inherited the place in 1076 and subsequently founded the abbey, initially assigning it to the canonical order of San Frediano, then to the Lateran order and finally, to Franciscan monks. This small B&B located in the heart of the medieval village is dedicated to the abbey. The four rooms are spacious and airy, fitted with local handmade furniture. The communal areas consist of a large breakfast room and a terrace, particularly suitable for moments of relaxation. In the morning you'll be served hot drinks and juices, cookies from local pastry shops, homemade jams, bread and fresh fruit. If instead you would like savory fare, you need to agree this beforehand with the managers, Liviana Balestra and Claudio Candeli.

• 1 single and 3 double rooms, with bathroom (2 with shared bathroom), TV • Prices: single 25 euros, double 60-73, breakfast included • Credit cards: none • Free external public parking. Small pets allowed. Owners reachable from 9 am to 8pm. • Breakfast room. Terrace

MONTICELLI D'ONGINA
Isola Serafini

NEVIANO
degli Arduini

ANTICA TRATTORIA CATTIVELLI

Trattoria
Via Chiesa 2
Tel. 0523 829418
Closed Tuesdays for dinner and Wednesdays
Open: lunch and dinner
Holidays: July
Seating: 250
Prices: 35 euros, wine excluded
All credit cards

TRATTORIA MAZZINI

Restaurant
Via Ferrari 84
Tel. 0521 843102
Closed on Thursday
Open: lunch and dinner
Holidays: October
Seating: 50 + 40 outdoors
Prices: 28 euros, wine excluded
All credit cards, Bancomat

The Trattoria Cattivelli, which is very popular with people from Piacenza who have frequented it for many years, has been modernized on the inside, but retains its original architecture, so that it seems to have been born with this difficult but beautiful land. The Cattivelli family has been running it for eighty-seven years, always preparing local cuisine and selecting their raw ingredients carefully. In spite of its size, once seated you will not feel lost amid the many tables that furnish the two large dining-rooms.

The kitchen, where Cesira works with her daughters Manuela and Claudia, turns out the antipasti: **salad of smoked eel** or soused trout, also smoked. Or cured meats: **culatello from Zibello**, coppa and salami from the Piacenza hills. Then go on to **ravioli of river crawfish**, **tagliolini with eel sauce**, the ever-present **pisarei e fasò**, or tagliolini of emmer with crawfish. Then the main courses: crisp **fried freshwater fish** (catfish, ambola azzurra, eel), **roast sturgeon**, stewed snails alla piacentina. And for meatlovers: **braised donkey with polenta**, fillet of duck breast with shallots, roast stuffed guinea-fowl, **pig's trotters**.

For dessert, various soft puddings and excellent crostata; we also recommend the **spongata**. The wine list is substantial.

In Monticelli, Via Martiri della Libertà 75, Carlo Migliorati's baker's shop produces and sells spongata, biscuits and bread from the Piacenza plain. On the same street, at no. 20, is the Raiola bar and ice cream parlor: real ice cream made to a traditional recipe.

Before you even try the food, you will appreciate the pleasant surroundings, both the summer terrace, with its balcony of flowers and espaliers of ivy and jasmine, where you can enjoy the hill breeze, and the dining-room, also full of flowers and colors, where in winter the lit fireplace underlines the discreet atmosphere enhanced by the well-spaced tables. The rest rooms, with a large number of colored ornaments, reveal the same attention to detail. And we must not overlook Roberto's discreet, courteous service. And last but not least, Maria's cooking, which respects local traditions.

Start with **Parma ham** accompanied by squares of torta fritta. If you book first, you can order an antipasto of seven starters which will leave you practically replete. The menu offers plenty of variety, and you can choose well-balanced **pappardelle with duck sauce** or soft vegetable lasagna. But why not **anolini in consommé**, potato tortelli with cep mushrooms, bombetta of barley with fresh tomato and sausage, or the ever-present **tortelli d'erbette**. The main courses include fillet of beef served on a delicate cheese sauce, fagottini of pork fillet and crisp **breaded rabbit cutlets** or **horse-meat steak**. Among the puddings we recommend the apple cake with warm cream sauce, semifreddo with amaretto and peaches in syrup and fruit compote with fruit ice cream.

The wine list includes some wines sold by the glass, but is not very extensive. However, the mark-up is reasonable and there are plenty of good labels. If anything, it needs more wines from Emilia.

NONANTOLA
Rubbiara

NOVELLARA

OSTERIA DI RUBBIARA

🍲 Traditional osteria
Via Risaia 2
Tel. 059 549019
Closed on Tuesday
Open: lunch, Friday and Saturday dinner
Holidays: December 15-January 15 and August
Seating: 35 + 40 outdoors
Prices: 25-30 euros
Credit cards: Visa

LA STURLONA

🗝 Holiday farm
Via Sturlona, 12
Tel. 339 2907492
E-mail: annaferrari@balsamic.it
Internet: www.lasturlona.it
Closed from December to February

Ask someone to show you the way to Rubbiara because it's worth going there to visit Italo Pedroni and his historic restaurant. Don't bother to look for the sign of the osteria, because the owner removed it some time ago, but the references to local traditions, written in dialect on wooden tablets outside the osteria, will help you find it. There are only a few dishes, but they are all linked to the local territory with its wholesome flavors. Let yourself be guided by the advice that Pedroni hands out in his rough but friendly manner. In 1862, Giuseppe founded the osteria that Italo runs today with his family: his wife Franca in the kitchen, daughter Antonella in the dining-room and kitchen, and son Giuseppe Terzo in the dining-room (although his main responsibility is the family's ancient vinegar and liqueur production).

Sit down in one of the three delightful dining-rooms or, in summer, in the quiet garden, and leave everything to your host. Try the handmade **maccheroni al pettine** with delicious meat sauce flavored with chicken livers. Or the **tortelloni of ricotta** with butter, tagliatelle or **strichetti al ragù**. Until May, you can try the **tortellini in consommé**. The main courses include: roast pork, **guinea-fowl**, pork ribs and **chicken with Lambrusco** served with roast potatoes, salad or spring onions with balsamic vinegar. In addition to the homemade puddings, try the **ice cream with traditional balsamic vinegar**.

At weekends the menu and the price are set – two first courses, two main courses, pudding, and homemade liqueurs and wines for 31 euros. Make sure you have a good appetite, because you will not be served your next course until your plate is empty.

Anna Ferrari's vacation farm is in Novellara, one of the small 'capitals' of the Lower Reggio area that still retains signs of the past in its historic center. The farm offers four spacious apartments that can accommodate up to six people each. All of them are simply furnished and have a kitchen and independent access from the garden. The communal areas are spacious, as is the room where you'll be served a filling breakfast consisting of hot drinks, homemade cakes, bread, butter and jams. Another room, usually used for reading, can accommodate small groups for conferences and teaching. The restaurant, which can also be used by non-residents with a reservation, offers simple dishes at a cost of approximately 30 euros, local wines included.

• 4 apartments (2-6 persons), with bathroom, TV, kitchen • Prices: 2-person apartment 60 euros, 4-person apartment 90, breakfast included • Credit cards: none • Facility accessible to the mobility challenged, 1 room designed for their use. Off-street parking. Small pets allowed. Owners always reachable • Restaurant. Reading room, Conference room. Garden

31 KM SOUTH-EAST OF FERRARA

LOCANDA DELLA TAMERICE

Rooms
Via Argine Mezzano 2
Tel. 0533 680795
Fax 0533 681962
E-mail: info@locandadellatamerice.com
Internet: www.locandadellatamerice.com
Closed for 15 days in November and 15 in January

ANTICA CERERIA

Trattoria-osteria
Borgo Rodolfo Tanzi 5
Tel. 0521 207387
Closed Monday
Open: dinner, and lunch on Sunday and holidays
Holidays: two weeks in August
Seating: 100 + 35 outdoors
Prices: 30-35 euros, excluding wine
All credit cards

It can almost be said that the Po delta, with its high-water bed, channels and banks populated by fauna and flora is part of the structure. You're in one of the most isolated corners of the area to which your hosts Pia and Igles Corelli dedicate all their energies. The rooms are next to the famous restaurant, a school of haute cuisine, but also a place in which to relax in contact with nature. There are boat, bicycle and horseback excursions to explore the vast labyrinth of the delta; in the immediate vicinity there's a sports facility and an observatory. Breakfast is served in the communal room in large bowls: hot and cold drinks, cakes, mousse, yoghurt, custard cream, fruit, but also savory fare directly from Igles' kitchen.

• 4 double rooms and 2 mini-suites (2-3 persons), with bathroom, air-conditioning, mini-bar, satellite TV, modem connection. • Prices: double room single occupancy 78 euros, suite single occupancy and suite 93 (16 euro supplement for extra bed); breakfast 15 euros per person • Credit cards: all, Bancomat • 1 room designed for use by the mobility challenged. External parking nearby. Small pets allowed. Staff always reachable • Restaurant. Breakfast room. Garden

Dishes proposed by the kitchen (a meal costs from 65 euros, excluding wine) are creative, with a wealth of personal touches.

This attractive restaurant, very close to the Parco Ducale and the central Via D'Azeglio, is decidedly "slow" where environment, welcome and cuisine are concerned. Two small rooms with the kitchen in full view, and implements from rural life on the walls, give Antica Cereria a pleasantly rustic tone. Close to the cured meat counter, an amazing array of spirits is laid out on old tables. And what about the wines? There is no wine list, just the pleasant habit of taking guests down to the vaulted cellar to choose from a fair selection of labels with the price in full view (and decidedly reasonable).

Cinzia is in the kitchen, and Matteo, front of house, will skillfully guide you through a meal based on traditional Parma fare. To start with, do not miss the excellent **mountain ham** that is cured for 30 months. The array of seasonal antipasti is also enjoyable. But the restaurant's strong points are its first courses: **tagliatelle al culatello**, excellent baked gnocchi of ricotta, soups, saccottini of ricotta, **bomba di riso with pigeon**, and tagliolini. The main courses include a classic **breast of veal**, **vecia con caval pist**, a typical local dish, **goose with vegetables** and rabbit with herbs. And in winter, the classic **mariola**, a Slow Food Presidia, a good **tripe alla parmigiana** and diced braised wild boar.

There is an amazing array of puddings (Matteo is the pastry cook: coffee cream, baskets of strawberries with marsala mousse, beignets with chantilly cream and hot chocolate, mousse of yoghurt with berries. The restaurant is open until late, even just for a good bottle of wine and a snack.

PARMA
Gaione

PARMA
Botteghino

7 KM FROM THE CITY CENTER

6 KM FROM THE CITY CENTER

ANTICHI SAPORI

DA ROMEO

🍲 Trattoria
Strada Montanara 318
Tel. 0521 648165
Closed Tuesday
Open: lunch and dinner
Holidays: January 1-15, 3 weeks in
August
Seating: 100 + 80 outdoors
Prices: 25-30 euros, excluding wine
All credit cards

🍲 Trattoria
Via Treversetolo 185
Tel. 0521 641167
Closed Thursday
Open: lunch and dinner
Holidays: August and September
Seating: 60 + 160 outdoors
Prices: 28-32 euros, wine excluded
All major credit cards, Bancomat

An old country trattoria, which is now just outside Parma, which has been carefully and tastefully renovated. The ambience is pleasant and familiar, and even when it is full, the owner Davide keeps everything under control. The alfresco summer eating area is spacious and friendly.

The trattoria serves traditional food, but also some more creative dishes to offer the local public some novelties. Everything is prepared skillfully and the raw ingredients are chosen with care. You must try the antipasti: classic **cured meats from Parma**, which include culatello di Zibello and shoulder of San Secondo ham, caramelized **onion tart**, flan of ricotta and roast pumpkin, soft baccalà with fried bread and a sweet-sour sauce, asparagus with butter, spring black truffle and shallots. For a first course, the real party pieces, classic **tortelli with greens**, **anolini in consommé**, and tortelli of pumpkin, or other more innovative proposals: risotto with spugnole mushrooms, balsamic vinegar and slivers of grana cheese, fresh pasta with basil pesto and green beans, malfatti of ricotta, spring onions and greens. For a main course we recommend **stuffed breast of veal**, **fricassee of poussin** with spring onions and balsamic vinegar, beef guanciale or **roast shank**, with side dishes that vary with the seasons, or a classic **tripe alla parmigiana**. There is a good selection of cheeses, and some excellent cakes and soft puddings.

The wine list is extensive, with a good selection of Italian and foreign labels, and the mark-up is reasonable. The selection of local sparkling wines could be enlarged.

Located just outside Parma, this trattoria is managed by the Zanichelli family, and has changed with the times. It was opened in the Fifties, and like so many others in the villages nearby or city suburbs, it was at one and the same time a flourishing trattoria, a café, a tobacconist's, a food store and a petrol station. The furnishings are rustic, the atmosphere familiar, and the food continues to be traditional Parma fare.

After starting with a rich choice of traditional **cured meats** – prosciutto crudo, shoulder of San Secondo ham, salami from Felino, accompanied by fried polenta – you can go on to **cappelletti in consommé**, pasta and beans and rich **stuffed pasta**, with fillings that change with the season (greens, potatoes, pumpkin). If you order in advance, they will even prepare **bomba di riso with pigeon**. Then, to continue, **rabbit chasseur**, **roast guinea-fowl** and excellent **stuffed breast of veal**. In the Winter the menu also includes **wild boar with polenta**, braised beef and cotechino in a bread crust.

Homemade puddings and a good selection of wines and spirits, with interesting bottles to choose from off the list, possibly right from the cellar, all proposed at reasonable prices. Booking is recommended.

☕🏠 Torrefazione Gallo, Piazzale San Bartolomeo: visit Gianluca and Alberto for one of the best coffees in town.

PARMA

PIACENZA

TRATTORIA DEL TRIBUNALE

Trattoria
Vicolo Politi 5
Tel. 0521 285527
Closed Tuesday, and Monday in summer
Open: lunch and dinner
Holidays: Christmas period, 3 weeks in August
Seating: 80 + 40 outdoors
Prices: 30-35 euros, wine excluded
Credit cards: all, Bancomat

SAN GIOVANNI

Trattoria
Via San Giovanni 36
Tel. 0523 321029
Closed Monday lunch, and Sunday lunch in summer
Open: lunch and dinner
Holidays: one week in July, two weeks in August
Seating: 25
Prices: 28-33 euros, wine excluded
Credit cards: all except AE

The Trattoria del tribunale is in Parma's historical center, right behind the central Law Courts. It has several small dining-rooms on two floors, pleasantly and attractively furnished. In the summer the restaurant overflows onto tables set up on the lively pedestrian Via Farini. You are courteously welcomed by Ida, who coordinates the large staff. Husband Francesco is in the kitchen, where he prepares local dishes with some clever innovative touches, and he has succeeded in making the trattoria one of the magnets for good food in Parma.

You can start with the excellent local cured meats – well-aged **prosciutto crudo**, shoulder of boiled ham of San Secondo, **strolghino** salami, culatello – and grilled **cep mushrooms** when in season. Among the top quality first courses we recommend the **tortelli filled with greens**, or the trio of tortelli – with greens, pumpkin and potatoes – **anolini in consommé**, tagliolini with culatello and potato gnocchi. Meat predominates among the main courses, but there are also dishes with mushrooms and seasonal vegetables. The **stuffed breast of veal** and tender **guancialetto of veal**, the tripe alla parmigiana, **pork rind with beans** and **stracotto di asina** are all excellent. There is a wide choice of puddings, including semifreddo and ice creams prepared by Francesco: the crunchy semifreddo, the **apple cake** and the tiramisu are all wonderful.

The wine list is well assorted, with a good choice of local and Italian wines. There is also a good selection of spirits and liqueurs.

This delightful trattoria is located in the premises where the Da Giuan trattoria was located in the Twenties. Perhaps to link up to that time, or perhaps out of personal conviction, the proprietor, Roberto Zanetti, proposes a number of hard-to-find historical Piacenza specialties alongside some more modern dishes. The atmosphere is warm and friendly, with a retro note given by the antique furniture and the lovely embroidered tablecloths. Roberto's wife Carla welcomes you into the dining-room, with discreet courtesy.

The cuisine is traditional. Start with the **cured meats** (lardo, pancetta, salami and coppa all cured at home, culaccia from Val D'Arda served with home-made giardiniera of vegetables), and then go on to enjoy the rare **risotto** della Primogenita **with a sauce of three meats and mushrooms**, panzerotti alla piacentina, the excellent **pisaréi e fasò** or **tortelli con le code** filled with greens or pumpkin. In the summer you must try the pisaréi còi vartis (hops) and old-fashioned nettle soup. For a main course, we can recommend the **braised donkey-meat with polenta**, **picula ad caval**, coppa or pork in a salt crust, tripe alla piacentina with beans, **snails alla bobbiese** or a flan made with bertina pumpkin and robiola cheese. For puddings you will find sbrisolona with zabaione, soft nut brittle, a melting chocolate pudding and above all, **stracchino**, a traditional ice cream cake (who makes it any more?) in several different layers: almond, coffee, vanilla, zabaione and chocolate.

The wine list is good, with some good local and national labels, and different wines are proposed by the glass every week.

PIEVE DI CENTO

HOTEL DELLA PIEVE

3 Star Hotel
Via Matteotti 30 A
Tel. 051 6861786
Fax 051 6867960
E-mail: hoteldellapieve@libero.it
Internet: www.hot, dellapieve.it
Closed for 15 days in August

This hotel is the result of the conversion of an old aristocratic house located in the heart of the historic center. Since November 2003 it's been managed by Ferruccio Pozzati, who has put a lot of effort into modernizing the rooms. These (two of the single rooms have a French style bed) are simply furnished but fitted with all comforts. Among other things the buffet breakfast offers rusks on which you may spread butter and jam, freshly baked cakes, brioches and cereals. If you choose the half-board option supper will cost you 15 euros and lunch 12. In Pieve you can visit the collegiate church of Santa Maria Maggiore that has a Romanesque-Gothic bell tower and apse of the original construction, while in Cento you should visit the piazza del Guercino with the town hall and clock tower. Modena, Ferrara and Bologna are all reasonably close, approximately 25 kilometers away.

• 5 single and 7 double rooms, with bathroom, air-conditioning, mini-bar, TV, modem connection • Prices: single 65-78 euros, double 90-108 (32-38 euros supplement for extra bed, breakfast included • Credit cards: all, Bancomat • 2 rooms designed for use by the mobility challenged. Off-street parking (6 places). Small pets allowed. Staff always reachable. Breakfast room. Conference room

PONTE DELL'OLIO
Biana

BELLARIA

Osteria-restaurant
Località Biana 17
Tel. 0523 878333
Closed Thursday
Open: lunch and dinner
Holidays: first week in September
Seating: 50 + 30 outdoors
Prices: 25-27 euros, wine excluded
All major credit cards, Bancomat

In the days when automobiles began to be an affordable commodity, and economic well-being began to increase the purchasing power of the Italians, the Sunday drive into the countryside, stopping for lunch in a small restaurant, was a regular pastime. The habit lives on, and numerous visitors frequent the delightful Bellaria, which has been managed by the Trecordi family since 1972. It is located in a 19th century building that has been renovated, maintaining the original architectural structure. Exposed beams, prints on the walls, period photographs and checkered cloths on the tables all help to create the pleasant atmosphere. You will appreciate the hospitality, the simple, wholesome cuisine and the reasonable prices.

To start from the beginning: **burtléina** (only prepared in the evening), a sort of crisp omelet made with water and salt, an essential accompaniment to the typical **Piacenza cured meats**, including the ever-present lardo. There is a generous choice of first courses: **pisarei e fasò**, excellent **tortelli con la coda** or anolini in consommé, and tagliolini served with sauces that vary with the season. In the summer, **rigatoni al torchio** with zucchini, leeks and fresh basil, or bucatini with pesto made of celery and local pecorino. The main courses are also traditional: **picula ad caval**, **roast coppa**, roast duck with potatoes, **breast of duck with spring onions**.

The excellent home-made puddings will tempt the sweet-toothed: semifreddo with hot chocolate, crostata, zabaione with Port, three types of panna cotta. The cellar offers a large, interesting variety of local wines.

PORTICO e SAN BENEDETTO
Portico di Romagna

35 KM SOUTH-EAST OF FORLÌ ON SS 67

PORTOMAGGIORE
Quartiere

24 KM SOUTH-EAST OF FERRARA ON SP 495

AL VECCHIO CONVENTO

3 Star Hotel
Via Roma 7
Tel. 0543 967053
Fax 0543 967157
E-mail: info@vecchioconvento.it
Internet: www.vecchioconvento.it
Closed from 10-31 January

LA CHIOCCIOLA

Rooms
Via Runco 94 f
Tel. 0532 329151
Fax 0532 329151
E-mail: info@locandalachiocciola.it
Internet: www.locandalachiocciola.it
Closed from 7-17 January, 1-10 June and in September

Portico di Romagna, the main town of Portico and San Benedetto, is a small medieval village located at the foot of the Apennines, immersed in the greenery of the Casentinesi Forest National Park. Run by the Caneli family, the hotel is in a nineteenth-century building that once belonged to one of the area's most renowned families. The rooms are provided with all modern comforts, but at the same time have that feel of times gone by, thanks to the beautiful walnut and cherry wood furniture, wrought iron bedsteads, embroidered draperies and hand-decorated ceramics. The buffet breakfast (set out in the tavern or in the garden during summer), includes jams, homemade cakes, cured meats, cheeses and fruit. A meal at the restaurant – also open to non-residents – will cost you approximately 30 euros per person, wines excluded. Half board and full board cost 74 euros per person and 82 euros per person respectively. Your hosts will provide you with mountain bikes for excursions in the environs.

• 3 single, 11 double and 1 triple rooms, with bathroom, mini-bar (if requested), TV • Prices: single 59 euros, double 90, triple 82; breakfast included • Credit cards: all except DC, Bancomat • 3 rooms designed for use by the mobility challenged. Free external public parking. Small pets allowed (not in the restaurant). Owners reachable from 7am to 11pm. • Bar, restaurant. Breakfast room, Reading and TV room. Garden, solarium.

The B&B is in a recently restructured building that in the past was used for storing grain harvested in the surrounding countryside. It's run by the Migliari family, who also manage the restaurant of the same name next door. The six rooms are comfortable, airy and simply furnished. In the morning you'll be offered a wholesome, filling breakfast: coffee, milk, homemade cakes and jams, and for anyone who wishes, even sandwiches. Portomaggiore is a good base for visiting the Po delta and for taking excursions in contact with nature. Alternatively you can visit the 'delights' of the Este family court in Gambulaga and Voghiera, or play golf on the local course.

• 4 double and 2 triple rooms, with bathroom, air-conditioning, mini-bar • Prices: double room single occupancy 50 euros, double 75, triple 95, breakfast included • Credit cards: all, Bancomat • Facility partly accessible for the mobility challenged. Off-street parking. No pets allowed. Owners always reachable • Restaurant. Breakfast room. Garden

The restaurant (average cost of a meal is 45 euros, excluding wine) has nice first and main course dishes, among which specialties based on eel, frogs and catfish.

POVIGLIO
San Sisto

19 KM NORTH WEST OF REGGIO EMILIA, 20 KM NORTH EAST OF PARMA

CASA MOTTA

Trattoria/3 Star Hotel
Località Casa Motta 4
Tel. 0522 960764
Fax 0522 969392
E-mail casa.motta@virgilio.it
Internet: www.paginegialle.it/casamottasas
Closed Tuesdays and Sundays for dinner
Open: lunch and dinner
Holidays: August
Seating: 80 +200 outdoors
Prices: 28-33 euros, wine excluded
All major credit cards AE, Bancomat

In this old renovated farmhouse, deep inside a large tree park, the breakfast is traditional and with a supplement of 15 or 30 euros per person, you can enjoy half or full board accommodation. The cuisine is based on the local food of the lowland area of Reggio Emilia presented in a seasonal menu.
The excellent local cured meats (including **culatello** and **strolghino**), the traditional **erbazzone al prosciutto**, the cured meat fried in Lambrusco and, in winter, the polenta roasted with pancetta or with saraca (dried herring) are the antipasti. The first courses include **cappelleti soup**, tortelli of herbs or pumpkin, excellent **risottos** with pumpkin or with **black bullhead**. The main courses include roast rabbit, **fillet with balsamic vinegar**, grilled meat, **cotechino in crosta**, **trippa all'Emiliana** and fried black bullhead in cubes. It is possible to lunch with the **fried gnocco** (crescentine) and as much cured meat as you can eat. The sweets include hot zabaione with macaroons, **torta sbrisolona** with raisin wine and trifle.
The wine list includes a selection of Lambrusco, the Bianca di Poviglio and a small selection of labels from other regions.

• 2 single rooms, 4 doubles and 1 triple, en-suite, air conditioning, fridge bar, sat TV, modem socket; 3 with balcony • Prices: single 35 euros, double single use 42, double 60, triple 80, breakfast included • 1 room specifically designed for the mobility impaired. Private uncovered parking area. No pets allowed. 24/24 porterage service • Restaurant. Breakfast room, TV room. Conference room. Park, children's playground

QUATTRO CASTELLA

15 KM SOUTH-WEST OF REGGIO EMILIA

LA MADDALENA

2 Star Hotel
Via Pasteur 5
Tel. 0522 887021-887022
Fax 0522 888133
E-mail: lamaddalena@interfree.it
Internet: www.albergolamaddalena.it
Closed 1 week in August and from
27 December to 10 January

The hotel was founded back in 1936 when Maddalena Burani, grandmother of the current owners, opened a grocery store with locanda at the foot of Bianello Hill. In the Fifties the hotel was passed on to Maddalena's son, Ero, who constructed a new building alongside the old one. Today the hotel is managed by brothers Emilio and Emiliano who have done much to ensure the rooms are fitted with all modern comforts. The traditional breakfast is served in the communal room and consists of fresh bread, butter and jams, croissants, tarts, hot drinks and fruit juices. The restaurant is also open to non-residents and the cost of a meal ranges from 25-35 euros, wine excluded. The hotel is ideally located to visit places of naturalistic interest, such as Italy's bird protection oasis, and historic sites like the castles of Bianello, Canossa and Rossena.

• 3 single and 14 double rooms, with bathroom, air-conditioning, TV, modem connection; some with balcony • Prices: single 40 euros, double 58, breakfast included • Facility accessible to the mobility challenged, 2 rooms designed for their use. Off-street parking. No pets allowed. Reception open from 7am to midnight • Restaurant.

RAVENNA
Marina di Ravenna

13 KM FROM THE TOWN CENTER

ALMA

Trattoria
Via della Pace 468
Tel. 0544 530284
Closed Monday
Open: lunch and dinner
Holidays: Christmas, New Year and one month in winter
Seating: 60 + 60 outdoors
Prices: 20-25 euros, wine excluded
Credit cards: Visa, Bancomat

This simple trattoria which does not serve fish is located in one of the liveliest seaside towns in Romagna, on the coastal road that runs alongside the pinewood near the sea. In summer you can choose to eat alfresco in the courtyard under the wooden awning, or inside in the air conditioned dining-room. You will be welcomed by Massimo, who manages the restaurant that once belonged to aunt Alma, with his brother Michele in the kitchen.
Start with the **cured meats** and **squacquerone**, eaten with the piadina that you will always find on the table with the bread. The pasta is homemade: we recommend the **garganelli al pettine with zucchini flowers**, stridoli or tagliatelle with a meat sauce. But you could equally well choose the **strozzapreti with sausage** or with a mutton sauce, cappelletti with meat sauce, tortelli with butter and sage or nastrini with peas. In winter, try the passatelli and the **cappelletti in consommé**. The main courses always include **grilled meats**, with pancetta, mutton and sausage. The **stewed guinea-fowl** with potatoes, capers and olives, the **rabbit and tomato casserole**, and the pork or veal shanks are all excellent (the latter must be ordered in advance). The main courses are accompanied by grilled or roast vegetables, or potatoes with garlic and rosemary.
There is a selection of excellent homemade preserves and caramelized figs, which are served with some cheeses. The puddings are few in number but all good: trifle, crostata, mascarpone. The wine cellar offers a few regional labels, but they are among the best around. Booking is recommended.

RAVENNA
Sant'Alberto

16 KM FROM THE CENTER OF TOWN

IL MAGO DEL PESCE

Trattoria
Via Sant'Alberto 404
Tel. 0544 529048
Closed Sunday for dinner and Monday, summer Monday only
Open: lunch and dinner
Holidays: August 16-September 4
Seating: 40
Prices: 30-35 euros, wine excluded
All credit cards, Bancomat

Sant'Alberto is a district of Ravenna in the direction of the Comacchio valleys. There is still a ferry in operation across the Reno river to the oasis of Bosco Forte. This small trattoria is run with great passion by Bruno Bezzi, helped in the kitchen by Damiano Proni, and serves products from the surrounding valley and the sea all year round: eel, bluefish and lowland game.
Start with mackerel or marinated anchovies, and small portions of **eel a brodetto** with savoy cabbage and pinoli, clams and mussels. The first courses range from risotto with eel to **strozzapreti with a mackerel sauce**, **passatelli in fish consommé**, pasta with anchovies, and tagliolini with a fish sauce. As a main course, the ever-present fried eel, mixed grill of sardines, sardoncini and saraghini served on a small grill, sole, mazzola, **mixed fried fish**, and **brodetto dell'Adriatico**. From mid October to February, you can also eat **lowland game**: croutons of chicken liver, risotto with coot, tagliatelle with wild duck, duck, and stewed teal. From the end of May to July, you will find **frogs' legs**, once a typical dish in this area but which is becoming hard to find.
The puddings are good: **trifle**, apple pie, semifreddo with pinoli and honey, mascarpone. Choose your wine from a number of regional and national labels.

RAVENNA
Mezzano

LE FAVOLE

☞Restaurant
Via Reale 440
Tel. 0544 523204
Closed Tuesday and Wednesday
Open: dinner, also for lunch on holidays
Holidays: 10 days in January, 15 in July
Seating: 36
Prices: 33-35 euros, wine excluded
Credit cards: none, Bancomat

The fish cuisine of this little restaurant on the main Ravenna-Ferrara road, in an area where the staple fare seems to be anonymous mixed grills doused in breadcrumbs and second-rate oil, is quite outstanding, because it brings out the naturalness and flavor of the fish. The credit goes to the cook, Giampiero Benelli and his wife Sabrina, who carefully select and prepare the raw ingredients (book in advance to enjoy an evening dedicated to crudités). There is only one dining-room, and you will also be offered dishes not on the menu, depending on what the market offers that day.

A few suggestions: for antipasti, **coccio of shellfish and mollusks**, fantasia di mare and scallops; **strozzapreti with squill, gnocchetti of ricotta with pink scampi**, and homemade orecchiette with clams and broccoli. For seconds: **Fritto di mare** and vegetables, fillet of John Dory, local sole, but also turbot, bass and orata alla mediterranea (with potatoes, cherry tomatoes and white wine). Fish is the star of the menu, but there are alternatives: lombino of veal and seasoned lardo, for example. Or, for a first course, tortelli with asparagus and chives; **tagliatelle with mushrooms**, pinewood truffles, or **hare sauce**. Then, **leg of pork** in porchetta, fillet of beef with artichokes and Pinot, or tagliata of beef with prugnoli mushrooms and grana cheese. But the dishes vary frequently.

There are numerous puddings, not all local. The wine list offers a good choice of local and national labels. A word of advice: the adjacent car park is not very convenient, but there is a large square only a few minutes away.

RAVENNA
Camerlona

USTARÌ DI DU' CANTON

☞Traditional osteria
Via Piangipane 6
Tel. 0544 521490
Closed Monday evenings and Tuesday
Open: lunch and dinner
Holidays: 15 days at the end of July
Seating: 70 + 20 outdoors
Prices: 25-27 euros, wine excluded
All credit cards, Bancomat

If you take the road from Ravenna to Ferrara, after a few miles, on the corner of the road for Piangipane (hence the name of the osteria, du' cantun, two corners), is a rural house where the place has been located for decades. It is run by Michele in the kitchen and Susanna front of house, a husband and wife team who propose a traditional menu that focuses in particular on homemade first courses, served in the traditional way in a small frying-pan, and top quality grilled meat.

The meal starts with cured meats, mixed croutons, **filled zucchini flowers**, **salad of fresh mushrooms and parmesan**, then the excellent first courses mentioned above: **tagliatelle with meat sauce**, **strichetti with artichokes**, strozzapreti with bell peppers and sausage, **garganelli with chicory**, cappelletti with asparagus and ham, tagliatelle of emmer with fresh tomato and fossa cheese, and numerous other proposals that vary with the seasons. Among the main courses we can recommend the **grilled meat** – mutton, sausage, fillet of beef, T-bone steak – but also the **roast lamb**, breast of duck with pioppini mushrooms, roast **pork shanks**, rabbit cooked in beer.

The home-made puddings include **trifle** (the Ravenna version, without chocolate), semifreddo with amaretti, and panna cotta. The wine selection is not of the same high standard as the food, either for the number of labels or for the quality of the bottles proposed.

🍴 Spiedomania, Via Bassano del Grappa 30: a delicatessen with a wood-fired oven serving all types of meat kebabs, all certified and the fruit of constant research.

A MANGIARE

Restaurant
Viale Montegrappa 3 A
Tel. 0522 433600
Closed Sunday, also lunch Saturday in summer
Open: lunch and dinner
Holidays: one week in June, August
15-31, Christmas-New Year
Seating: 45
Prices: 28-33 euros, wine excluded
All credit cards, Bancomat

TRATTORIA DELLA GHIARA

Restaurant
Vicolo Folletto 1 C
Tel. 0522 435755
Closed Sunday and Monday
Open: lunch and dinner
Holidays: August and 10 days at Christmas
Seating: 35
Prices: 33-35 euros, wine excluded
Credit cards: Visa, Bancomat

There is a pleasant atmosphere in this osteria, which serves both traditional Reggio Emilia fare and innovative dishes created by Gianni Braglia. The other proprietor, Donatella Donati, a competent sommelier, is in charge of the dining-room.
The antipasti include one of the restaurant's strong points, **parmigiano reggiano mousse** with mostarda of pears, **cured meats with gnocco fritto**, **culatello from Zibello** aged at least 16 months, and carpaccio of duck breast with fattened liver flavored with Brachetto. The first courses (of homemade pasta) include classic **cappelletti in consommé**, green tortelli, tortelli of renette apples in a pistachio cream, gnocchi with gorgonzola, tagliatelline with julienne of culatello, risotto with pears, gorgonzola and traditional balsamic vinegar. Main courses: rabbit salad with slivers of parmesan and drops of traditional balsamic vinegar, beef fillet in red wine, **fried lamb chops**, zucchini flan with cream of taleggio and crispy guanciale, fillet with cep mushrooms. In winter, **gnocchi with pigeon sauce**, mezzelune with fossa cheese, **ganassino of horsemeat with polenta**, **suckling pig ribs**, breast of duck with traditional balsamic vinegar and borrettane onions. The menu also includes a number of fish dishes in summer.
There is a generous pudding menu: mousse of zabaione with Marsala, semifreddo with nut brittle and hot chocolate, hazel-nut pastries with vanilla ice cream and hot berry sauce, ginger ice cream, yoghurt pudding with melon sauce. The wine list is also generous, including more than 160 local and national labels and some foreign wines, with reasonable mark-ups, also served by the glass.

A welcoming, elegant restaurant in the town's historical center, which focuses on the cuisine and products of the Reggio Emilia area. Antonio Giordano, the discreet, competent proprietor, will meet you front of house, while his wife Marilena Braglia shows off her skills in the kitchen. There are no special effects, just top quality food, which conveys the quality and flavors of the raw ingredients, all strictly local and seasonal.
We went there in spring, and tried a cup of minute **cappelletti in consommé**, excellent **cured meats**, a soufflé of pears and fondue of parmigiano reggiano (which here is proudly known as grana reggiano). Then the pasta (which is hand-made): **green tortelli with butter**, **pappardelle with a vegetable ragù**, stracci of fresh pasta with a lamb sauce, and **tagliatelle with ham**. Then the main courses: **rabbit in a sweet-sour sauce**, chicken breast alla duchessa with stewed peas, **hot shoulder of San Secondo ham**, frittata with onions and traditional balsamic vinegar, **barzigoli of lamb** with zucchini flan. The selection of regional cheeses is limited but interesting. And finally, the puddings, with an unmissable **trifle**, home-made cakes, strawberry sherbet, semifreddo of zabaione with nut brittle and hot chocolate.
The wine list includes 130 labels and focuses on cellars in the region and in the center-north of Italy.

5 KM FROM TOWN CENTER

CASE MORI

🔑 Holiday farm
Via Monte l'Abbate 9
Tel. and fax 0541 731262
E-mail: agriturismo@casemori.it
Internet: www.casemori.it
Closed from 15-31 October

OSTERIA DË BÖRG

🍲 Osteria with meals
Via Forzieri 12
Tel. 0541 56071-56074
Closed Monday
Open: dinner, also lunch on Sundays and holidays
Holidays: variable
Seating: 90 + 40 outdoors
Prices: 30-34 euros, wine excluded
All credit cards, Bancomat

Silvia and Nicola Pelliccioni completed the refurbishment of one of the four cottages on their 22-hectare farm in 1999. The result is a splendid two-floor building with wooden beams and brick walls. The facility has two dining rooms dominated by an old fireplace and large kitchen, while on the upper floor there are the bedrooms (3 of them have a mezzanine floor with 2 additional beds) completely furnished in imitation antique. In one of the two communal rooms, protected by glass, you'll be able to admire the ancient ditch where grain was once stored. Outside there's a portico, an extensive garden and grounds where you can take pleasant walks. Breakfast is served in the communal rooms or, during summer, in the garden and comprises milk, coffee, tea, brioches and homemade cakes, plus a variety of jams. A meal at the restaurant – open to non-residents – costs 25 euros per person, including the house wine.

• 3 double and 1 four-bed rooms, with bathroom, TV • Prices: double room single occupancy 60-70 euro, double 70-80 (10-30 euro supplement for extra bed), four-bed 80-140, breakfast included • Credit cards: Visa, MC, Bancomat • Facility accessible to the mobility challenged. Off-street parking. Small pets allowed. Owners always reachable • Restaurant. Patio, garden, children's playground

Take time off to wander through the lanes and streets of the hamlet of San Giuliano: small houses painted with warm colors, close to the monumental Tiberio bridge. Luisa was born in one of these houses, right in the center of the district where she and her husband Veniero now manage this picturesque osteria, concentrating their enthusiasm on the local cuisine. You can watch as they prepare **piada** or grill meat in the fireplace, and the pasta for the first courses is all hand-made. On Fridays (or by booking in advance on other days) you can enjoy an all-fish menu, purchased fresh from the local market, and in this case, the price is considerably higher.
The day's specialties are listed orally, but they'll give you a menu if you prefer. Start with the mixed antipasto: an assortment of excellent **cassoncini with wild herbs**, pumpkin and potatoes, croutons, frittatina, vegetable pie, a selection of cured meats or cheese and vegetable soups. Choose your first course from the **tagliatelle** or **strozzapreti with an old-fashioned meat** or vegetable sauce; or cappelletti with carrots or spaghetti alla chitarra with fillet and vegetables. The main courses include **roast lamb**, fillet or tagliata of beef, **roast rabbit**, in porchetta or boned and stuffed, flavored with balsamic vinegar and ginger, and grilled vegetables.
The desserts are simple cakes or soft puddings, plus semifreddo of fruit in the summer. Sangiovese predominates on the wine list, with several good Romagna labels, but there are also some good bottles from the rest of central Italy.

RIMINI

OSTERIA DEL VIZIO

� Osteria-restaurant
Via Circonvallazione meridionale 41 A
Tel. 0541 783822
Closed Tuesday
Open: only for dinner
Holidays: July-August
Seating: 135
Prices: 30-35 euros, wines excluded
All credit cards, Bancomat

A short walk from the center of Rimini, behind the Arch of Augustus, is Palazzo Ghetti, once a match factory and now a welcoming osteria. Careful restructuring has brought to light the beautiful interior, with its wooden beams and terracotta floor, now tastefully furnished. Claudio Carlini, the talented proprietor, has succeeded in the difficult task of creating a restaurant for everyone: a young public that is always in a hurry, lovers of good food, or just people wishing to pass an enjoyable, relaxing evening.

The common denominator that links the motley clientele is the food, based on Romagna traditions and seasonal products. Although it is by the sea, the cuisine is inland: homemade pasta and good grilled meat. You can start with a mixed antipasto, four or five samples that vary with the season, but always include **cured meats** and mixed **cheeses**. The first courses are nearly all traditional and include **tagliatelle al ragù**, pasta e fagioli, **cappelletti** and passatelli **in consommé**, **green tortelli with fossa cheese**, strozzapreti with sausage and **stridoli**. Then try the **meat**, which is excellent **grilled** (chops, sausages, ribs, pancetta), **fillet** with green peppercorns or **balsamic vinegar**, or tagliata with herbs. And there are always numerous seasonal side dishes.

The puddings include tiramisù, panna cotta and catalan cream. The wine list is extensive, and includes numerous labels from Romagna.

RIOLUNATO

LA TAVERNETTA

⌒ Trattoria
Strada Statale 324, 29
Tel. 0536 75085
Closed Wednesday
Open: lunch and dinner
Holidays: 2 weeks in June and 2 in October
Seating: 60
Prices: 18-25 euros
All credit cards, Bancomat

Riolunato is a picturesque little town in the Apennines near Modena, not far from Abetone and Sestola, towns which attract skiers in the winter. It is quite a distance from Modena, but, with the right "slow food" mentality, the journey is a pleasant one, even landscape-wise.

La tavernetta, which becomes a pub with after-hours music in the evening, is extremely simple, and a pleasant place to eat with friends: the single large dining-room seats 60. The dishes are wholesome and well-prepared, as you would expect from a real trattoria, without frills. The bill prepared by proprietor, Guerrino Piacentini, is also without frills, and he still prepares it in lire and then translates it into euro, a habit that is becoming less common.

The menu is listed orally and the first courses always include perfectly prepared **tortelloni**, with butter, butter and sage or ragù, **tagliatelle al ragù di funghi**, risotto with mushrooms, and **tortellini**, of course. The main courses include pork chops, **fried chicken**, grilled meats, chicory salad, small onions in a homemade sweet-sour sauce, **polenta** and **game**. In the right season, there will be plenty of **mushrooms**, fried, sautéed or with polenta. And to finish, a sublime semifreddo (like tiramisu), torrone mousse and the typical local **trifle**. Local wines and a small selection of other wines – unfortunately there is no list – particularly from Veneto, at reasonable prices.

You will see that several regulars, mainly men, walk into the trattoria on their own and sit at the common tables in different parts of the room: a tradition that is still alive in certain mountain provinces.

18 KM SOUTH OF PIACENZA SS 45

18 KM SOUTH OF PIACENZA

CAFFÈ GRANDE

Osteria-trattoria
Piazza Paolo 9
Tel. 0523 958524
Closed Tuesdays
Open: lunch and dinner; in summer dinner only, Sunday and holidays also lunch
Holidays: 15 days in January, 10 in September
Seating: 50 + 50 outdoors
Prices: 28-30 euros, wine excluded
All credit cards

LA CASA ROSSA

Bed and breakfast
Località Casa Rossa
Tel. 0523 957613-348 8021119
Fax 178 2255235
E-mail: info@casarossapiacenza.it
Internet: www.casarossapiacenza.it
Open all year

Rivergaro is in the Trebbia valley, an area popular for horseback riding, on the border of Emilia and Liguria. Caffè Grande is in the main square, an old meeting point for a good meal. If you come in the spring or fall, the menu will be made up almost exclusively of traditional local fare, whereas in the summer there are often some digressions into seaside cuisine, but these, we have to admit, are often not exceptional.
Cured meats provide the classic openers: coppa from Piacenza, lardo, salami and pancetta, accompanied by a crisp frittatina of water and flour which is known locally as **burtlèina**, and is usually prepared on evenings when the restaurant is not crowded (if you want to be sure of finding it, we recommend booking). Otherwise culatello with pork rind, pan brioche and butter, salad of chicken perniciato with herb sauce, flan of goats' cheese, eggplant and zucchini. The first courses: **tortelli con le code**, which has always been the restaurant's strong point, **pisarei e fasò**, and **anolini**. Or tagliatelle of emmer with a sauce of vegetables and ricotta, tagliolini with vegetables and fonduta of parmesan, gnocchi of potatoes and turnips with gorgonzola and walnuts. There are plenty of meat dishes among the main courses, including **picula ad caval**, **roast veal shank**, and **lamb chops**.
The puddings are all typically homemade: **crostata** with jam or fruit, sponge cake with mascarpone cream, zabaione with strawberries, chocolate cake, steamed peaches with vanilla ice cream and chocolate, almond cream with cherry preserve. There is a fair selection of local wines. Booking is recommended.

This pleasant B&B surrounded by vineyards has been created in a renovated farmhouse that has lost none of its original architectural appeal. Given the setting, absolute peace and quiet are guaranteed. The rooms are all spacious and very well furnished. Guests staying in the elegant suite, which is particularly suitable for important occasions, will receive special treatment. During the summer, breakfast is served under the portico; alternatively, a buffet will be organized in a dedicated area in your own room and will consist of coffee, tea, milk, homemade cakes, cookies and fresh seasonal fruit. The B&B makes an excellent base for walks in the environs to discover the castles of the dukedoms of Parma and Piacenza or to visit the village of Bobbio.

• 2 double rooms and 1 suite (2 persons), with bathroom, mini-bar, TV • Prices: double room single occupancy 70 euros, double 90, suite 130, breakfast included • Credit cards: none • Off-street parking. Small pets allowed. Owners always reachable. • Portico

ROCCA SAN CASCIANO

RONCOFREDDO

25 KM SOUTH WEST OF FORLÌ SS 67

19 KM SOUTH OF CESENA, 38 KM FROM FORLÌ

LA PACE

L'OSTERIA DEI FRATI ⊗❚

⌒Trattoria with rooms
Piazza Garibaldi 16
Tel. 0543 951344
Closed Monday evening and Tuesday
Open: lunch and dinner
Holidays: none
Seating: 80
Prices: 25 euros, wine excluded
No credit cards

⌒Osteria recently opened
Via Comandini, 149
Tel. 0541 949649
Closed Monday and Tuesday, never in Summer
Open: evening, October-May also Sunday lunch
Holidays December 22-January 14
Seating: 40 + 50 outside
Prices: 25-30 euros – wine excluded
All credit cards, Bancomat

Rocca San Casciano is a small, quiet town in the Tuscan-Romagnolo Apennines, with old houses on the banks of the River Montone. The feeling of being in a place where time has stood still becomes even stronger in the main square, with its nineteenth century buildings, the tower and its fine clock, the few shops and a bar. The old Theatre building is now a bar with an old sign and, on the first floor, the Trattoria La Pace. The story of this place and the family – going back five generations – is told by the owner, Gino Garzanti, a tale backed up by the stuffed straw animals and birds, the period postcards and documents on the walls, the earthenware stove and the wine flasks on every table. Pasta is rolled out and ravioli with fresh ricotta cheese are prepared in a corner at the back of the main room.

Antipasti: **cured meats** home-made by Gino, pecorino cheese and honey, with delicious Tuscan bread. Tuscan **croutons** or **game** if you book. First courses include **tagliatelle** with prugnoli (in May) or **mushrooms**, excellent **ravioli of ricotta** with butter or meat sauce (not exceptional), cappelletti and **pasta and beans**. Main courses include excellent **grilled meat** and acceptable roast pigeon and guinea fowl prepared by Gino's wife, Palmira. Seasonal dishes include **spit-roast game**. If you book: roast lamb, goat and rabbit, **tripe**, cuttlefish with peas or baccalà (Friday). Fine pecorino cheese and excellent, truly fresh **ricotta**, served **with savor** and homemade fruit conserves.

Puddings include fruit tarts and cantucci. The Sangiovese house wine is served in flasks. Numerous grappas and spirits of various vintages.

Turning south towards Longiano on State Road 9 (Via Emilia), at Savignano coming from Rimini or at Case Missiroli coming from Cesena, and following the road signs for the town and then for the osteria itself, brings us to this place with its delightfully cool summer garden and exceptional view. Renato Brancaleoni and his family uphold country traditions, knowledge and flavors.

A fine example is the **cheese board**: Renato, who got to know about cheese as a child in the family shop, selects and matures local and national cheeses. A special favorite is the fossa **pecorino** cheese made by the family, enjoyed alone or with asparagus, artichokes and cardoons, or with passatelli, gnocchi, cappelletti and risottos; pecorino cheese made with mixed or dairy milk is also served with walnut leaves or hay and aromatic herbs; black or ash cheese is grated or proposed to close a meal. More than 180 types every year, served with conserves, honey, jam and marmalade. The **cured meats** include: prosciutto, lardo and capocollo, or coppa magra, soaked in wine and matured in hay. Antipasti also include croutons with vegetables, including the famous Roncofreddo asparagus; first courses include **legume soups**, cereals, vegetables and wild herbs, lasagne with cep mushrooms, **pappardelle with duck sauce** and potato gnocchetti. Second courses include **pollastrino al tegame** and **rabbit with aromatic herbs**. Home made **ciambella**, tarts and biscuits for dessert, moka coffee and a fine selection of spirits.

The wines: carefully chosen and well identified in the list that ranges more or less all over Italy, with a few international labels.

RONCOFREDDO
Montecodruzzo

19 km south of Cesena, 38 km south east of Forlì

OSTERIA DI MONTECODRUZZO

☞Traditional osteria
Piazza Ferretta 12
Tel. 0547 315091
Closed Monday
Open: dinner, also at lunch on holidays
Holidays variable
Seating: 90 + 40 outdoors
Prices: 16-22 euros, wine excluded
All major credit cards, Bancomat

Leave the E 45 highway at the Borello exit in the direction of Sorrivoli-Montecodruzzo. Here, there is a unique view of the entire Savio Valley as far as the distant Adriatic. In the village, next to the Malatesta tower, lies one of the oldest osteria in the region, located in a sixteenth century building in local stone, with a small cobbled square outside that is used in summer. The big windows ensure a breathtaking view at sunset. The cozy setting includes a fireplace in the main room and another at the entrance where meat is grilled. The counter, furniture and period objects all recall the food shops of Romagna in the 1950s. Roberto and Beatriz ensure a friendly welcome; Signora Benita in the kitchen prepares piadina and pasta; Lucio, the chef, ensures a personal touch for other dishes. Local, seasonal cuisine is exclusively based on fresh produce at very honest prices. Once a week, there is a menu based on Adriatic fish. Start with **cured meats**, mora romagnola and Cinta Senese, and cheese from local producers including – in season – **raviggiolo** (Slow Food Presidia). First courses include **tagliatelle al ragù**, **passatelli** and cappelletti **in chicken broth** and, in season, ravioli with wild herbs picked locally. The main courses include: **lamb chops**, soft and tasty, roast shank of veal, **rabbit al tegame**, galletto alla contadina with tomatoes and potatoes, grilled meat and, if you book, **allodole allo spiedo**. Camillona salt is used (Slow Food Presidia). Homemade puddings include fruit tarts and **chocolate salami**. Almost all wines from Romagna are available. The set menu at lunchtime costs 18 euro.

RUSSI
Ponte Vico

15 km south west of Ravenna

DA LUCIANO

☞Trattoria
Via Montone 1
Tel. 0544 581314
Closed Monday evening and Tuesday
Open: lunch and dinner
Holidays August 15-31
Seating: 100 + 30 outdoors
Prices: 15-25 euros, wine excluded
All credit cards

Ponte Vico, close to the River Montone, on the provincial road from Russi to Forlì: an old country trattoria mentioned as early as 1525 as Osteria del Vico and cited in the regulations setting out customs duties between Forlì and Ravenna. Country folk and dealers have stopped here for food for four centuries. Luciano is a singular character and has run the trattoria for forty years with his wife, Mina, in the kitchen – now helped by daughters Nadia front of house and Sandra in the kitchen. The homely rustic furnishings – wood-panelled walls, old straw chairs and very simple table settings – make this a popular and traditional trattoria with local workers. Absolutely everything is homemade – pasta, piadina, conserves – and utterly traditional. There is no written menu – dishes of the day are described orally. The seasonal menu focuses on old-time dishes. Antipasti include **piadina, squacquerone and caramelized figs** or a fine local salami; followed by **tagliatelle al ragù**, tortelli with wild herbs, **passatelli** and **cappelletti in broth**, **risotto with stridoli** picked on the banks of the river. Main courses include free range roast chicken and **rabbit** with potatoes, meat balls and **roast pigeon**. **Grilled** dishes include sausages, mutton, T-bone steaks and vegetables. The fine "fossa" cheese is served with a sublime **water melon conserve**. Homemade puddings: jam tarts, **trifle** and, in summer, semifreddo with zabaione or amaretti. Good Sangiovese house wine or one or two local labels.

Salsomaggiore Terme

Cangelasio

32 KM WEST OF PARMA, 8 KM FROM FIDENZA

San Giovanni in Marignano

68 KM SOUTH EAST OF FORLÌ, 20 KM FROM PESARO A 14

Antica Torre

☞❶ Holiday farm
Via Case Bussandri 197
Tel. and fax 0524 575425
E-mail: info@anticatorre.it
Internet: www.anticatorre.it
Open from March to November

Il Granaio

🥘 Restaurant
Via Fabbro 18
Tel. 0541 957205
Closed Tuesday
Open: lunch and dinner
Holidays always open
Seating: 70 + 25 outside
Prices: 30-33 euros, wine excluded
All credit cards, Bancomat

Active since 1988, this facility offers guests a pleasant, relaxing vacation in direct contact with nature. The rooms furnished in arte povera style have been created in the ancient tower and in some rural buildings. In the morning guests will be offered locally made honey and jams, tarts, doughnuts, fresh fruit, yogurt, various types of beverages and, on request, savories. The restaurant is for residents and is only open for dinner: it offers traditional dishes prepared with the farm's own produce at an average price of 20 euros per person. Those who enjoy physical activity will be able to cycle the paths of the Salsomaggiore hills. There are tennis courts and golf courses in the vicinity. Well worth visiting are Torrechiara Castle, the medieval villages of Castell' Arcuato and Vigoleno, the fortress of Bardi and the Stirone Palaeontological Park..

• 5 double, 1 triple and 1 four-bed rooms, with bathroom. • Prices: double room single occupancy 48-60 euros, double 80-100, triple 100-125, four-bed 120-150, breakfast included • Credit cards: none • Off-street parking. Small pets allowed. Owners always reachable • Restaurant. TV room, reading room, billiard room, wine-tasting room. Conference room. Portico. Pool, table tennis, 5-a-side soccer pitch and volleyball court

Maurizio Magnanelli has managed this delightful restaurant in the centre of the old town passionately since 1987 – following the restoration of a building used in the times of the Malatesta family as a granary. Diners are shown into a small room with fireplace, or a room on the first floor (air conditioned) or, in summer, to one of the tables in the lane to enjoy fine dishes prepared with quality ingredients in the kitchen run by Maurizio's mother Anna. The menu combines local flavors with fish specialties and traditional dishes from other regions.
Antipasti include **Parma ham**, lardo di Colonnata, finocchiona and **gnocco fritto**, a cheese board, croutons with sardines or omelet with vitalbe and sausage. First courses include **cappelletti in broth**, tagliatelle al ragù, **pappardelle al ragù di cinghiale**, tagliolini with clams, prawns and basil, tortelli with wild herbs and ricotta cheese with black truffle, mezzelune with sheep ricotta, fresh tomato and basil, lasagne all'ortica e pancetta stufata and **risotto with stridoli and sausage**. There is also a wide choice of excellent main courses: roast **rabbit with stuffing**, **baked shank of veal**, fillet of beef grilled with pancetta and bay leaves, beef fillet medallions, jugged venison with polenta. If you book – and sometimes "off menu" – red veal tripe and **stewed baccalà** with potatoes. A good cheese board.
Puddings include a delicious **cream of mascarpone**, cream and ricotta cake, chocolate cake. The cellar has a fair variety of regional and national labels, and some wines are also served by the glass. Booking is recommended.

SAN MAURO PASCOLI

15 KM SOUTH-EAST OF CESENA, 12 KM NORTH-WEST OF RIMINI

LOCANDA DEI FATTORI

🗝 Locanda
Via Due Martiri 29 A
Tel. 0541 933315-337 256631
Fax 0541 933315
E-mail: fattori@locandadeifattori.it
Internet: www.locandadeifattori.it
Holidays vary

This locanda lying within the grounds of Villa Torlonia – in what was once the estate managed by poet Giovanni Pascoli's father – is just a few kilometers from the beaches of Romagna and very near to the hills dotted with villages that historically were under the sway of the Malatesta family. A careful restoration process completed a few months ago has brought the original structure back to life. The facility comprises a restaurant (seats 90, revisited local cuisine at an average price of 30 euros, excluding wine) and a splendid locanda. While there are only three rooms, they are stylishly furnished with great attention to detail. There's also a children's playroom, and a lounge with TV for the grownups. In summer, the generous buffet breakfast, offering sweet and savory fare, and dinner can be served in the garden if you wish.

• 3 double rooms, with bathroom (2 rooms with bathroom next door), air-conditioning • Prices: double room single occupancy 50 euros, double 100, breakfast included • Credit cards: all, Bancomat • Facility partly accessible to the mobility challenged. Off-street parking and adjacent external parking. Small pets allowed. Staff always reachable. • Bar, restaurant. Lounge, children's playroom. Garden, grounds.

SAN PIETRO IN CASALE
Rubizzano

20 KM NORTH OF BOLOGNA

TANA DEL GRILLO

🍲 Trattoria
Via Rubizzano 1812
Tel. 051 811648-810901
Closed Monday dinner and Tuesday, July also Sunday
Open: lunch and dinner
Holidays 25 days in August, one week in January
Seating: 30
Prices: 35 euros, wine excluded
All credit cards , Bancomat

This small town, on the border between the provinces of Bologna and Ferrara, saw Giovanni Mazzali (from Bologna) and Susanna Pocaterra (from Ferrara) meet halfway, to take over the management of this trattoria, right opposite the church of Rubizzano, in 1994. Two small rooms, one with a fireplace, filled with a great many objects in different styles, on the walls and on the furniture. The environment is cozy and homely, thanks not least to the jovial Giovanni, who welcomes and serves guests, discreetly and professionally, during meals.
His previous experience as a director in a cured meat company explains the large selection of seasoned cured meats: various kinds of salami and ham, as well as **culatello** and Spanish pata negra – not to mention **ciccioli**, galantina and lion (mortadella packed in soft lining by Pasquini & Brusiani, Bologna). First courses include: taglioline del Grillo (with Parma ham and poppy seeds), **cappellacci of pumpkin** butter and sage, **gramigna with guanciale**, gnocchetti with chicory and balsamic vinegar. There are also **snails** and, in season, mushrooms, truffles and **game**; other main courses include: boned rabbit with cream of thyme, **rosa di Parma** (beef fillet with Parma ham and Parmesan cheese), padella del Grillo (with mixed meats and vegetables). The area is renowned for **asparagus** and, indeed, Susanna in spring prepares many asparagus dishes.
All puddings are home made: Ferrara "tenerina" with chocolate, latte portoghese, rice cake, fruit tarts, orange semifreddo, malaga ice cream. The small wine list offers interesting labels.

SAN PIETRO IN CASALE

24 KM NORTH OF BOLOGNA

TUBINO

⌂ Trattoria
Via Pescerelli 98
Tel. 051 811484
Closed Friday and Saturday at lunch
Open: lunch and dinner
Holidays; 10 days between June and July
Seating: 40
Prices: 28-35 euros, wine excluded
All credit cards

Anyone looking for something old-fashioned and substantial with a focus on quality ingredients (many of them Slow Food Presidia), and prompt, pleasant and friendly service should stop off at Tubino: Daniela front of house and Pigi in the kitchen will make you feel perfectly at home. Let them guide you. But if you really want to choose your own menu, try the excellent local **cured meats** as antipasto (or the specialties sometimes available from Friuli or other parts of Italy) accompanied by **fried crescentine**.

You can choose from the dishes of the day or classic first courses – such as the superb **tortellini in brodo** di cappone e manzo di razza romagnola, **gramigna with mora romagnola** sausage, **potato gnocchi with salmerino** del Corno alle Scale sauce, green tagliatelle with meat sauce. Main courses include **trippa alla parmigiana** (in season), meat cooked on oil stone, **steamed rabbit** and, when available, lamb chops; other reliable specialties include **snails** and **frogs' legs**.

Before enjoying the puddings, you must try the carefully chosen **cheese board**, served with honey and conserves; then try the semifreddo al torrone or the desserts that Pigi prepares from time to time. The wine list is extensive and detailed, with appropriate mark-ups; some wines are also served by the glass.

🍴 Via Matteotti 223-225: Palladino bakery-confectioner sells various kinds of traditional bread, including coppietta ferrarese, made without chemical additives.

SAN PROSPERO

19 KM NORTH EAST OF MODENA SS 12

BISTRÒ

⌂ Trattoria-pizzeria
Via Canaletto 38 A
Tel. 059 906096
Closed Wednesday
Open: lunch and dinner
Holidays August andHolidays Christmas
Seating: 100
Prices: 28-32 euros, wine excluded
All credit cards except AE, Bancomat

Trattorias in small towns are often centers of social activity and – in order to survive – must sometimes extend their menus to include other kinds of cuisine. Many such trattorias – like the Bistrò – also serve pizzas. And yet in spite of the fact that it is a pizzeria, the Bistrò is also able to serve really well prepared traditional meals. Signora Rita Malaguti has made her own pasta every day for the last twenty years. The **cured meats** are made and seasoned by Franco Fregni (only in late-fall and winter) and open the delicious menu: salami, coppa, coppa di testa, guanciale and ciccioli.

The first courses are superb and typical of Emilia: **tortellini in brodo** (the exquisite stuffing is made with pork loin, veal, pasta di salame, mortadella, cured ham, parmigiano reggiano and eggs); **tagliatelle with meat** or duck sauce, tortelli with ricotta, maccheroni al pettine with ham and peas, green tortelli with parmigiano reggiano filling. In season **pumpkin tortelli with sausage**. Main courses: in winter **cotechino** or fillet of pork with traditional balsamic vinegar. Other typical meat dishes include **stracotto di somarino** served with puree of potatoes or baked vegetables, as well as **steamed tripe**, braised beef, baccalà, various roasts and, in summer, veal with tuna sauce and roast beef. Cep mushrooms and truffles (in season) are the sublime ingredients of several dishes. Puddings are all traditional and home-made: trifle, **torta di tagliatelle**, chocolate salami, fruit tarts and biscuit mascarpone.

The wine list is simple with local Lambrusco di Sorbara labels.

SANTARCANGELO DI ROMAGNA
Montalbano

ANTICHE MACINE

Holiday farm
Via Provinciale per Sogliano 1540
Tel. 0541 627161
Fax 0541 686562
E-mail: macine.montalbano@tin.it
Internet: www.antichemacine.it
Closed for 20 days in January

SANTARCANGELO DI ROMAGNA

LA SANGIOVESA

Osteria-restaurant
Piazza Simone Balacchi 14
Tel. 0541 620710
No closing day
Open: dinner
Holidays: Christmas and 1 January
Seating: 240 + 50 outside
Prices: 30-35 euros, wine excluded
All credit cards, Bancomat

The building housing the vacation facility is a farmhouse that was used as an olive oil press at the end of the seventeenth century. Immersed in a wood of olive and walnut trees and surrounded by vineyards, it has a large swimming pool and seated around it you can admire the Romanesque parish church of Santarcangelo and, in the distance, the sea. The rooms are all different with some organized as junior suites and others structured over two floors with a large mezzanine and single beds. They all have beautiful wooden floors and elegant furniture. For breakfast you'll be able to try the farm's products, such as jams and fruit juices, served in the dining room in winter and on the veranda in spring and summer. A meal at the restaurant, which is also open to non-residents, costs from 25-32 euros per person, beverages excluded. Mountain bikes are available for excursions in the surrounding area.

• 2 single, 8 double rooms and 3 suites (1-4 persons), with bathroom, air-conditioning, mini-bar, safe, TV • Prices: single 50-55 euros, double room single occupancy 55-70, double 90-110 (15 euro supplement for extra bed), suite 110-130, breakfast included • Credit cards: all, Bancomat • Facility accessible to the mobility challenged, 1 room designed for their use. Off-street parking. Small pets allowed. Owners reachable from 8 am to midnight • Restaurant. Breakfast room, reading and TV lounge. Garden, veranda. Pool

Next to the Collegiata, at the foot of the staircase leading to the Clock Tower: that is where you will find the sign of La Sangiovesa, an evocative place set in the cellars of the noble Palazzo Nadiani. Four of the ten rooms are reserved for the osteria, for which bookings are not accepted; some of the dishes can also be found in the menu of the restaurant. At the entrance, a small shop sells selected local produce, and behind this the arzdore, to the sound of rolling pins, prepare and cook **piadina**.
The menu, created with strict emphasis on quality local produce by chef Massimiliano Mussoni assisted by Gianni Giorgini and Andrea Marconi, changes at least four times a year on a seasonal basis. **Cured meats**, omelets, **squacquerone**, cassoni, anchovies and preserves in olive oil to start. First courses – all pasta is made by hand – include excellent tagliatelle della Minghina, with fresh seasonal vegetables and tomatos, or old-style **pasta and beans**, **strozzapreti with Carpegna ham**, chick peas and aromatic herbs, **ravioli with cep mushrooms**, a fresh salami sauce and stridoli, baked green lasagne. Main courses include **trippa di scottona** alla contadina, scortichino of beef fillet, scottona steak cooked with Cervia rock salt (Slow Food Presidia) and grilled tomino of Montefiore Conca with vegetables and saba. Delicious puddings include **pesca cotta ubriaca** from Albana and tarts with fruit, ricotta and squacquerone and amarene (dark cherries). As well as the house pudding, **the ciambella** and rustic desserts.
The wine list is impressive, with the best labels from Romagna; wines are also served by the glass.

SANTA SOFIA

OSTERIA DEL BORGO DA FISCHIO

Osteria recently opened
Via Gentili 4
Tel. 0543 970417
Closed Tuesday
Open: lunch and dinner
Holidays 2 weeks in June, 1 in October
Seating: 50 + 20 outside
Prices: 25 euros, wine excluded
All major credit cards , Bancomat

Local people in Santa Sofia still all have nicknames. Fischio is the one attributed to Franco and then to his son Fabio who, together with mother Fiorella and Chiara, manage this friendly osteria located in an ancient palazzo. In summer, five tables are set on the terrace overlooking the River Bidente and they have a fine view of buildings with Tuscan-style architecture and the flight of wild ducks and geese. The interior is very pleasant and furnished in good taste; there are paintings by a local lady artist on the walls. Signora Fiorella is amiable; many of her recipes she has collected from the old people in the area and she serves them up suitably adapted to modern tastes, using seasonal produce, most of which she purchases from good local producers.
The menu changes every day in accordance with the season. Antipasti include: **piadina e raviggiolo** (Slow Food Presidia), croutons with pancetta and smoked cheese patè, fried sambuco and acacia flowers (in spring), cured meats, meat balls, **tortelli alla lastra** (in winter on Wednesdays). First courses include **tagliatelle with rabbit sauce** (although pigeon, duck, shallot and tomato sauces are also used), tortelli with meat and ricotta, **cappellacci with butter and sage**, scorsette (broad tagliatelle of durum wheat) with gorgonzola and wild asparagus, soups with cereals or mushrooms. The main courses include fillet or liver of pork, lamb and grilled meats, **ciavar** (salsiccia matta), boar, **cotechino**, Parmesan tripe (on Thursday), **baccalà with leeks** or grilled on Friday – with beans in summer. Excellent local cheese and ricotta. Tarts, doughnuts and scroccadenti for dessert. Fabio recommends wine from a selection of 300 labels in his cellar.

SARSINA

AL PIANO

3 Star Hotel
Via San Martino 23
Tel. 0547 95400
Fax 0547 698139
E-mail: info@alpiano.it
Internet: www.alpiano.it
Open all year

This hotel on the outskirts of Sarsina in the Savio valley was once a residence of the Counts Bernardini. The Ministry for Cultural Heritage ensured that the frescoes, furniture, doors, etc. were very carefully restored, while at the same time providing all modern comforts. The rooms are spacious and fitted with perfectly restored furniture. There are four historic rooms, two suites and eighteen modern rooms. Moreover there's a sixteenth-century alcove (260 euros per night) decorated with paintings by Vincenzo Giovannini dating from the eighteenth century. Breakfast offers sweet fare (and savories, on request), fresh fruit, yoghurt, cereals and a variety of drinks. In a refined and elegant setting, the restaurant offers a menu containing both international and typical Romagnola cuisine – also some gluten-free dishes – at an average price of 30 euros per person.

• 24 double rooms and 2 suites, with bathroom (suites have jacuzzis), mini-bar, safe, TV, modem connection • Prices: double room single occupancy 55-80 euros, double 80-120, suite 170, breakfast included • Credit cards: all, Bancomat • Facility accessible to the mobility challenged, 1 room designed for their use. Off-street parking. Small pets allowed. Reception open from 7am to 1am • Bar, restaurant, wine cellar. TV room. Conference room. Grounds

SAVIGNANO SUL RUBICONE

TRATTORIA DELL'AUTISTA

Trattoria
Via Battisti 20
Tel. 0541 945133
Closed Sunday, Friday and Saturday evening
Open: lunch and dinner
Holidays 3 weeks in August, 2 at the end of December
Seating: 50 + 35 outdoors
Prices: 20-25 euros, wine excluded
All credit cards, Bancomat

In the heart of the old town center, between Piazza Borghesi and Piazza Oberdan, this genuine trattoria has been managed with great passion by the Gobbi family since 1932. On entering, the furnishings and simplicity of the place will strike you: the impression is of going back in time. You will be given a friendly welcome in the dining room by Mauro and his son Nicola, while his wife Valentina and mother-in-law Agostina (an expert pasta-maker) run the kitchen, preparing traditional Romagna dishes.
At this stage, it is virtually impossible not to start with a basket of **piadina romagnola** accompanied by a classic dish of selected cured meats and cheese (could be improved, though), including the ever-present **squacquerone**. Then come the first courses: **tagliatelle al ragù**, **tortelloni with ricotta** tossed in butter and sage, passatelli in broth. Main courses include roast veal or rabbit, **a mixed grill** accompanied by grilled vegetables and, in winter, add cotechino, **tripe** and **baccalà**.
Home made puddings range from trifle to ricotta cake with **mascarpone** and crème caramel. House wines are joined by good local bottles at very fair prices – just like the bill at the end.

SAVIGNO

DA AMERIGO

Trattoria/Rooms for rent
Via Marconi 16
Tel. 051 6708326
Fax 051 6708528
E-mail info@amerigo1934.it
Internet: www.amerigo1934.it
Closed Monday, January-May also Tuesday
Open: dinner, Sunday also for lunch
Holidays: 20 days January-February, 20 August-September
Seating: 50 +30 outdoors
Prices: 33-35 euros, wine excluded
All major credit cards, Bancomat

Da Amerigo is a perfect combination of innovation and tradition. The restaurant is furnished in Thirties style, but the ambience is fresh and informal. Five bedrooms have been converted in the adjacent premises (available all week) furnished with both classic and modern furniture. Breakfast is served in a private room of the nearby café, where you can taste the products of the Dispensa di Amerigo, selected or produced by the manager Alberto. The cuisine on offer uses only the choicest ingredients. Three set menus are available: "Giorno di festa in paese" offers traditional cuisine including **calzagatti roasted with lardo and herbs**, tigelle with parmesan ice cream and balsamic vinegar, tortellini soup, ravioli of ricotta with parmesan and scallion, **guancia di vitella braised** with Barbera. "Ricordi d'acqua dolce", with dishes using the char of the Corno alle Scale, **eel** and **frogs**. "Scoperta e natura" is centred on seasonal products: **mushrooms, truffles** and asparagus of Altedo. But individual dishes can also be chosen. The **cheese board** offers a great selection and the puddings and home-made ice cream are excellent.
The wine list is extensive and detailed, with particular emphasis on regional products.

• 1 single room, 2 doubles, 1 with 4 beds and 1 mini suite (2-4 persons), en-suite, sat TV, modem socket • Prices: single 50-60 euros, double single use 60-75, double 75-90, with 4 beds 110-130, breakfast included • 1 room specifically designed for the mobility impaired. Free public parking nearby. Pets welcome. Owners available from 10am to midnight in the trattoria • Restaurant

SCANDIANO

OSTERIA IN SCANDIANO

🍲 Restaurant
Piazza Boiardo 9
Tel. 0522 857079
Closed on Thursday, June-July also Sunday
Open: lunch and dinner
Holidays: August and 12/24-01/6
Seating: 45
Prices: 30-33 euros,wine excluded
All credit cards, Bancomat

The entire family of Contrano Medici has managed this very pleasant restaurant at the foot of the medieval fortress, since 1985. Contrano looks after the dining rooms on two floors together with his son Simone, who has inherited his father's kindness and wisdom. Wife Nadia and the other son Andrea in the kitchen prepare dishes enhanced by quality ingredients.
Hereabouts, you have to try the **cured meats**. So, start with ham cut with a knife and a local salami served with fried gnocco. First courses usually include **green tortelli** with butter and sage (as well as pumpkin in winter) and tagliatelle with ham or duck sauce. Soups include the truly delicious **cappelletti in chicken broth** and maltagliati with beans. Main courses include **guinea fowl with balsamic vinegar**, musk duck with orange and onion sauce, rabbit roast with Scandiano white wine and, above all, **prosciutto di maialino** with flavorings. In summer you'll find dishes such as breast of chicken with a fine tuna sauce, which are lighter. There is also a special side dish: **baby onions in balsamic vinegar**. Traditional gold balsamic vinegar highlights the flavor of a **parmigiano reggiano** cheese seasoned for 36 months – and the cheese board includes selected other Italian varieties. The **trifle** is superb, and you must try the hot chocolate cake, the Catalan cream or one of the cakes of the day.
The excellent wine list has more than 300 quality labels and an interesting selection served by the glass.

SISSA
Gramignazzo

LAGHI VERDI

🍲 Trattoria
Via Co' di Sotto
Tel. 0521 879028
Closed Monday and Tuesday, never in August
Open: lunch and dinner
Holidays: December-February
Seating: 90 + 60 outdoor
Prices: 20-25 euros, wine excluded
All credit cards, Bancomat

From the top of the landfill of the Gramignazzo embankments, the view takes in the many small, dark lakes and their wonderful birdlife: grey herons, night herons, wild ducks and dwarf herons. The square building of this trattoria is on the right, a small place welcoming guests to a simple, neat environment. The hospitality is typically Emilian, although things are sometimes a bit rushed when the trattoria is very busy.
The small lakes are home to what was once considered the king of fish in the Po area – the catfish – prepared here in many delightful ways. Yet diners must also try the excellent cured meats of the lowlands: **culatello di Zibello**, salami, spalla cruda. **Marinated catfish** is the other excellent antipasto. Let your curiosity guide you in your choice of first courses: spaghetti with catfish, **tortelli with perch**, **pisarei e fasò** (a dish from Piacenza), tortelli d'erbetta. Then comes the triumph of fresh-water fish: **fried catfish** (truly superb), catfish with balsamic vinegar or baked, then **baked sturgeon** and **fried eel**, and even fried cod in the fall. If you book: deep-fried frogs' legs and the local triatto – fried lake ambolina (a fish rather like a sardine). The meal ends with puddings to dig your spoon into and an excellent **almond cake** resembling sbrisolona, thin and crunchy, served with Marsala zabaione.
Wines are mostly local but there are also several national labels and good still reds. Digestifs include nocino, bargnolino or canarino, all made and sold by the owners of the trattoria. In March, April and November the trattoria is also closed on Wednesday and Thursday.

SOGLIANO AL RUBICONE
Savignano di Rigo

SORAGNA
Diolo

DA OTTAVIO – IL RAGGIO

🍴 Restaurant/Holiday farm
Via Savignano di Rigo 3–Via Ca' Raggio 33
Tel. 0547 96000 – 0547 970002-338 3875699
Fax 0547 970002-328532
Closed Tuesday
Open: lunch and dinner
Holidays: 8-31 January
Seating: 110 + 12 outdoors
Prices: 22-27 euros, wine excluded
Credit cards none

OSTERIA ARDENGA

🍴 Traditional osteria-trattoria
Via Maestra, 6
Tel. 0524 599337
Closed Tuesday dinner and Wednesday
Open: lunch and dinner
Holidays: January 1-15, last 3 weeks of July
Seating: 60
Prices: 30-33 euros, wine excluded
All major credit cards

In the village of Savignano di Rigo, Tiziana Bernardini runs the restaurant Da Ottavio and the holiday farm Il raggio, which, being located in different areas of the town, have different telephone numbers. The rooms are modest and quiet and the breakfast offers some exquisite desserts. The cuisine is traditional. The antipasti are spianate of onion, eggplants and zucchini; **bread bustrengo,** eggs and cheese; an excellent **fossa cheese** with marmalades and, in season, with apricots and peaches cooked in wine. The first courses include exquisite **cappelletti, minestre matte** with countryside herbs, **tagliatelle with ragù** (and in season, mushrooms), gnocchi with fossa cheese, **grateti**. The second courses, **lamb chasseur** with aromatic herbs, **guinea fowl** with fruit or **al savor**, pork loin with almonds, **rabbit in porchetta**. The puddings include **lattaiolo, donut,** pagnotta di Pasqua. The wines are mainly of the area, with some national labels. Booking advisable.

🗝️➊• 2 single rooms and 3 doubles, with bathroom, TV • Prices: single 35 euros, double 65-67, breakfast included • Credit cards: none • Building accessible to the mobility impaired, 1 room specifically designed for the mobility impaired. Internal uncovered parking area. Pets welcome. Owners always available • Corner bar, restaurant. Breakfast room, reading room and TV. Park, terrace, veranda

🍷 For the fossa cheese at Sogliano al Rubicone go to: Rossini (via Pascoli 8), Venturi (via Roma 67), Pellegrini (via Le Greppe 14) or to the local tourist office (piazza Matteotti) for information on the November food festival.

This traditional old trattoria immersed in the lowlands around Parma faithfully proposes the environment and cuisine of a place of times gone by: broad counter, old tables, open beams. Everything contributes to forming a very convivial atmosphere.
Start with the superb **culatello** (this area is truly the homeland of the most noble cured meats); then try coppa, **spalla cotta di San Secondo** or the sweet pancetta – all accompanied by fried polentina and preserves in vinegar. First courses with pasta of various kinds and various stuffings: tortelli di erbette, **tagliatelle with salami sauce, anolini in capon broth, maccheroncini al torchio with duck sauce**. An excellent alternative is **rice bomb with wood pigeon** or, in season, pumpkin or chestnut gnocchi with truffle and mushroom sauces. The main courses are substantial: culatello with mushrooms, stewed guancialini of pork, **roast duck**, sautéed spring chicken, **boned goose stuffed with salami** and, to finish, in winter, **mariola** (Slow Food Presidia) and mixed boiled meats and traditional pickles.
Puddings include semifreddo with amaretto and Bavarian cacio. The wine list is extensive, with national and international labels. Traditional local digestifs: bargnolino, sburlon or nocino. German is also spoken.

🍷 Località Chiavica 61, Diolo: Massimo Pezzani of Antica Ardenga produces and sells culatello di Zibello, salami, cured hams, mariole and lowland pickles in jars.

SORAGNA

STELLA D'ORO

🛏️Locanda
Via Mazzini 8
Tel. 0524 597122
Fax 0524 597043
Internet: www.stelladoro.biz
Open all year

You'll find this family-run locanda in an alley very close to the main square of this small village in the Bassa Parmense area, one that offers a wealth of cultural and gastronomic experiences. Created in a little old palazzo, the facility has been organized with great attention to detail: the small arched loggia that faces onto the inner courtyard and the exposed entablatures that are a feature of the ceilings in most of the communal rooms contribute to creating a very particular atmosphere. All rooms are spacious and airy, elegantly furnished and equipped with all the necessary comforts. Breakfast is served in a pleasant room and offers exquisite croissants, jams and rusks, fruit juices and the usual hot drinks.

• 6 single, 7 double rooms and 1 suite, with bathroom, air-conditioning, TV • Prices: single 50 euros, double 80, suite 100; breakfast 4 euros per person • Credit cards: CartaSi, Visa, Bancomat • Free external public parking. No pets allowed. Owners always present • Restaurant. Breakfast room. Internal courtyard

🍲 The restaurant next door is run by Marco Dalla Bona who proposes revisited local dishes (a meal costs around 50 euros, excluding wine).

SPILAMBERTO

DA CESARE

🍲Trattoria
Via San Giovanni 38
Tel. 059 784259
Closed Sunday dinner, Monday and Tuesday
Open: lunch and dinner
Holidays: May 15-30, July 20-August 20
Seating: 32
Prices: 25-35 euros, wine excluded
All credit cards except DC, Bancomat

This trattoria is celebrating forty years in its first floor premises in the center of Spilamberto, the capital of traditional Modena balsamic vinegar. Cesare Roncaglia opened L'osteria del Ponte in 1966; in 1970, his daughter Marica and her husband Giancarlo Sola turned it into a traditional trattoria, beginning an adventure that still today sees her in the kitchen and him in the dining room.
Once seated, you are served diced mortadella to while away the time waiting for **omelets with traditional balsamic vinegar** and flakes of parmigiano reggiano cheese. Unless you ask for another menu, Giancarlo – a big, jovial man – begins serving the first courses (at least three): **tortellini in broth**, tortelloni with ricotta and erbette (pumpkin stuffing in season), **stricchetti with meat sauce** or mushrooms (depending on the season and availability) and **maltagliati with beans**. Meat courses include an excellent **baked guancia di vitello**, pork stew, **rabbit chasseur**, or **sweet and sour mixed fry** or tripe. Lastly, try the traditional puddings proudly on show at the entrance to the dining room: peach with alchermes and chocolate, **crunchy almond cake**, amaretto di Spilamberto, fruit tart, chocolate and coffee cake and many others. Only if you manage to enjoy all these delightful dishes will the bill come to around 35 euros, but you will pay much less for a less substantial meal.
Dishes can be accompanied by the best local Lambrusco but the wine list also has many other good Italian labels. Close with the excellent house Nocino.

TORRIANA

21 KM SOUTH-WEST OF RIMINI

LOCANDA DEL POVERO DIAVOLO

🍲 Rooms
Via Roma 30
Tel. 0541 675060
Fax 0541 675680
E-mail: povero.diavolo@libero.it
Internet: www.ristorantepoverodiavolo.com
Closed for 15 days in June and 10 in September

Stefania Arlotti and Fausto Fratti's locanda is just a few kilometers from the sea, on the hills overlooking Rimini. Their family home has been transformed to create a restaurant and five bedrooms, in part featuring early 1900s' furniture and for the rest, furniture purchased recently but in the same style. The rooms are unpretentious and while there's no TV you'll find notepads and a small selection of novels and books on local history. Breakfast is served in the bar or, during summer, in the courtyard. You'll be offered homemade sweets and cakes, five types of bread, jams, milk, tea and coffee.

• 3 double, 1 triple and 1 four-bed rooms, with bathroom, modem connection • Prices: double room single occupancy 60 euros, double 90, triple 110, four-bed 120, breakfast included • Credit cards: all except DC, Bancomat • Free public parking next door. Small pets allowed. Owners always reachable • Bar, restaurant. TV and music room, library. Conference room. Garden

🍲 The restaurant proposes a partially revisited local cuisine (a meal costs 45 euros, excluding wine).

TORRIANA
Montebello

18 KM SOUTH WEST OF RIMINI SS 258

PACINI

🍲 Trattoria
Via Castello 5
Tel. 0541 675410
Closed Wednesday, never in summer
Open: lunch and dinner
Holidays 15 days in January
Seating: 120 + 25 outside
Prices: 23-27 euros, wine excluded
All major credit cards , Bancomat

The delightful Valmarecchia area with its castles and delightful towns deserves a climb to the Montebello fortress. Rocca dei Guidi is still intact and can be visited day and night. But before your visit, stop off at Pacini, straight after the gate built by the Malatesta. The trattoria has been run by the same family for about forty years and Maria Elide and Paolo continue the traditions established by father Narciso. The furnishings are simple, the environment friendly and homely; prices are honest for seasonal menus focusing on local produce. Roberto ensures a warm, kindly welcome. Start with hot **croutons**, cured meats and homemade vegetable preserves in olive oil. Pasta first courses are also homemade: ravioli with herbs and cheese or **tagliatelle with meat sauce**, potato gnocchi with fossa cheese from Sogliano al Rubicone or **strozzapreti agli stridoli** and excellent cappelletti in broth. Main courses include **piccioni di nido al tegame** or **rabbit in porchetta**. There are also mutton, grilled Florentine tagliata with cep mushrooms, guinea fowl or **mixed grill**. There is also a good **piadina** which is served up immediately, accompanied by the classic **squaquerone** cheese or other fine local cheeses.
To close, try the traditional **porcospino** (always available); or the trifle, fruit tart, **scroccadenti** or ciambella. The wine list has several good regional labels. It is advisable to book in advance, especially at weekends. The first weekend in September you are likely to run into the Honey Festival, with local producers of honey and cheese.

TRECASALI

19 KM NORTH OF PARMA

NONNA BIANCA

🍲 Trattoria
Via Nazionale 38
Tel. 0521 878363
No closing day
Open: lunch, also in the evening on
Friday, Saturday and Sunday
Holidays: variable
Seating: 50 + 50 outside
Prices: 25-28 euros, wine excluded
Credit cards: CartaSi, Visa, Bancomat

The new premises next to the Town Hall
see Enrico continue to dispense his impressive wine and food culture in typically friendly style, while Franca in the
kitchen skillfully prepares traditional
dishes using excellent ingredients. So,
traditional cuisine of the Parma lowlands
in a landscape characterized by hazy
summers and foggy winters.
Cured meats obviously open the menu:
culatello of Zibello, prosciutto crudo of
Parma, **salami of Felino**. First courses
include the excellent ragù with **gnocchi**
or **tagliatelle**. Then the typical **ravioli
d'erbette** alla parmigiana. Ravioli are
also served with potato or pumpkin fillings, while mostarda recalls the traditions of the Mantua region – on the opposite bank of the great river. There are
also various risottos, including one with
a salami sauce. Traditional main courses
include the delicious **spalla cotta** and
tripe. There's more: braised guanciali,
punta di vitello ripiena and **mariola**
(Slow Food Presidia). High-quality free
range goose, rabbit, guinea fowl and
duck are supplied by a nearby farm.
Puddings include: **trifle**, chocolate salami, sbrisolona, baked cream and a
black teacake. Good list of wines and
spirits at reasonable prices; dessert
wines are also served by the glass.

🍴 Nearby: **Busseto**, Via Roma 76: la
Salsamenteria Storica Verdiana, a folklore
museum-workshop with mementos and
memories, culatello, coppa piacentina and
spalla cotta, also served on the premises.

VERGHERETO
Alfero

63 KM SOUTH WEST OF CESENA SS 71

LANZI

🍲 Restaurant with rooms
Via Don Babini 10
Tel. 0543 910024
Closed Wednesday
Open: lunch and dinner
Holidays: February
Seating: 60
Prices: 25-30 euros – wine excluded
All credit cards, Bancomat

Alfero is a little town in the Tuscan-Romagnolo Apeninnes bordering on Tuscany, nestling in woods of chestnut trees
and close to the source of the River
Tiber. It can be reached by leaving the E
45 at Bagno di Romagna, after a dozen
or so kilometers of evocative, winding
panoramic road. The Lanzi is in the center of the town – a restaurant founded
fifty years ago by Signora Enrica, mother of Giovanni Maria, who continues to
uphold traditional cuisine. The restaurant, in 1960s style, seems to have halted the passing of time and the atmosphere is truly familiar.
Meals begin with cured meats (excellent
prosciutto seasoned for at least 18
months by the local butcher), croutons
with lardo fuso or **cep mushrooms**. First
courses include the typically very thin
local **tagliatelle**, ravioli and **potato tortelli** (always available – sauces change with
the season) served with sauces of **mushroom**, truffles, vegetables, butter and
sage, or the classic Romagnolo meat
ragù with the addition of sausage. Then
try the **guinea fowl with juniper**, rabbit
with mushrooms, the classic **mixed grill**;
the hallmark dish is **grilled or sautéed
lamb** with rosemary and garlic. In season, if you book: **game** in abundance.
Exquisite side courses: roast potatoes,
gratin or grilled vegetables and fried cep
mushrooms.
Puddings include fruit tarts, trifle and
crème caramel; alternatively, try the fine
fossa cheese or the local pecorino with
caramelized figs. The wine list has a
good selection of wines from Romagna
and Tuscany. Lastly, the **nocino** digestif
is aged for three years by the owner in
person.

VERUCCHIO
Villa Verucchio

VETTO

LE CASE ROSSE

Holiday farm
Via Tenuta Amalia 107
Tel. and fax 0541 678123
E-mail: info@tenutaamalia.com
Internet: www.tenutaamalia.com
Open all year

ANTICA TRATTORIA DEL SOLE

Trattoria
Via Sole Sopra 45
Tel. 0522 815194
Closed Wednesday
Open: lunch and dinner
Holidays variable
Seating: 50 + 15 outside
Prices: 22-25 euros, wine excluded
All credit cards

This vacation farm is located within the vast Amalia estate, in the center of the splendid Marecchia valley, famous for its production of quality wine. One of the old farmhouses on the estate has been harmoniously refurbished and painted externally in the traditional reddish color, also used for the main villa nearby. There are seven spacious rooms that have been pleasantly furnished with antique pieces; from October to March rooms can only be rented in the weekend. From the beautiful portico, where during summer you can have breakfast and relax, you enter a comfortable living room. At other times breakfast is usually served inside and what stands out in the generous buffet are the homemade tarts and cakes baked by Lucia Gattei. Just a few hundred meters away, in addition to three restaurants, you'll find the attractive Gea wine cellar where you'll be able to taste the estate's wines. Bicycles are available for excursions in the surrounding area and there is a golf course right next to the estate.

• 1 single, 5 double and 1 triple rooms, with bathroom, mini-bar, TV, modem connection • Prices: single 55 euros, double 75, triple 85, breakfast included • Credit cards: all, Bancomat • Facility partly accessible to the mobility challenged. Off-street parking. Small pets allowed. Owners reachable from 7.30am to 9pm • Breakfast room, reading room. Garden, veranda

The road that rises from Montecchio to Castelnovo ne' Monti, Località Sole, overlooking the enchanting panorama of Val d'Enza comes to this simple, genuine hillside trattoria. The small bar opens on to a larger room, with many paintings and old photos on the walls, some of which recall the Festivaldenza, a song contest for osteria choirs and popular songs handed down from times gone by in these valleys, where singing was part of the local identity.

In the middle of the dining room, a large service window opens on to Paola Zanichelli's kitchen; she and her husband Sergio Gatti have run this typical trattoria for a number of years. Family management is reflected in the informal, no-frills service. There is no written menu and the very local dishes are described vocally. Start with the typical **erbazzone** reggiano or a reassuring antipasto of **cured meats** accompanied by mushrooms preserved in olive oil. First courses include delicious **tagliatelle with mushrooms** (plentiful) and the more delicate **tortelli di erbette**. Appetizing pappardelle and **risotto with pigeon giblets** complete the offering. Then come seasonal **fried mushrooms** and meat for all tastes: **roast coppa**, rabbit with potatoes, tripe, fried lamb chops, **guinea fowl with balsamic vinegar**. Close with trifle and **chocolate salami**.

The house wine is joined by several good Lambruscos and a few bottles from other regions: more than enough to adequately accompany this tasty cuisine. The bill is absolutely honest.

VIGNOLA

VIGNOLA

23 KM SOUTH EAST OF MODENA SS 623

OSTELLO CITTÀ DI VIGNOLA-CASALE DELLA MORA

Youth hostel
Via Tavoni 20
Tel. 059 776711
Fax 059 7702930
E-mail: info@cittacastellicilegi.it
Internet: www.cittacastellicilegi.it
Open all year

TRATTORIA BOLOGNESE

Trattoria
Via Muratori 1
Tel. 059 771207
Closed Friday dinner and Saturday
Open: lunch and dinner
Holidays August and Christmas
Seating: 40
Prices: 28-30 euros, wine excluded
All major credit cards, Bancomat

The Vignola hostel is in a recently built farmhouse inaugurated in 2004. The facility is managed by the Strada dei Vini Association that has created a showroom in the hostel to sell wines and gastronomic products originating in the territory between the hills of Modena and Bologna. The rooms are spacious, furnished in rustic style and have beautiful ceilings with wooden beams. For breakfast you help yourself from the buffet where you'll find products that are part of the Association. Outside there's a jogging track while just a short distance away there's the swimming pool, fitness center and an indoor tennis court; all have a special agreement with the Association. There are also bicycles for rent to visit the surroundings, and management organizes guided tours of all of their member companies.

• 1 triple, 3 four-bed and 2 five-bed rooms, with bathroom, TV • Prices: single 30 euros, double 50, triple 66, four-bed 80, five-bed 100, bed in shared room 18 euros, breakfast included • Credit cards: Visa, MC, Bancomat • Off-street parking (6 places) and free public parking 50 meters away. No pets allowed. Management present from 8am to 7pm from Monday to Friday; from 9am to 12.30pm and 2.30-6-30 pm on Saturday and Sunday. • Breakfast room, reading room. Grounds with jogging track.

It is well worth visiting the Panaro Valley in springtime to admire the spectacular blooming of the cherry trees or when the freshly picked cherries are being sold by the roadside.

This trattoria is close to the walls of the imposing castle that dominates Vignola and is run by the Franchini sisters – the family originates from Bologna (hence the name) and has managed it for more than 50 years. The menu focuses on typical Bolognese cuisine and dishes from the nearby Modenese Apennines. The Bolognese tradition does not usually include an antipasto but you may order an excellent ham and flakes of Parmesan cheese with drops of traditional balsamic vinegar. Yet the pasta dishes are excellent: all homemade and all of superb quality. Start with an excellent – and plentiful – dish of **tagliatelle col ragù** (depending on how hungry you are, half portions can also be ordered); you also have some excellent **tortellini in broth**, tortelloni di ricotta and **potato gnocchi with gorgonzola**, butter and tomato and a good pasta and beans. Main courses include guinea fowl or **rabbit (roast)**, scaloppine with lemon or balsamic vinegar, liver alla veneziana and **baked ham**; sometimes, the cook is prepared to serve an excellent **Bolognese cutlet**. As for puddings, don't miss the **fiordilatte** or tarts with seasonal fruit. Meals traditionally end with cherries preserved in spirits.

The Lambrusco is a little rustic but honest; there are also a few Colli Bolognesi labels.

ZIANO PIACENTINO
Casabella

ZIANO PIACENTINO
Vicobarone

CASABELLA

🍲 Restaurant
Località Casabella
Tel. 0523 862840
Closed Tuesday, in winter also Monday
Open: dinner, Saturday and Sunday also at lunch
Holidays 3 weeks in January, 10 days in July
Seating: 70 + 40 outdoors
Prices: 20-30 euros, wine excluded
All credit cards except AE

PODERE CASALE

🔑 Holiday farm
Via Creta
Tel. 0523 868302
Fax 0523 840114
E-mail: info@poderecasale.it
Internet: www.poderecasale.com
Closed from mid-November to Easter

The wine route from Castel San Giovanni to Vicobarone passes through the village of Casabella: the restaurant of the same name has a fine view over vineyards in the Val Tidone. Staid but elegant on the upper floors, the environment becomes more rustic in the tavern set in the old, refurbished cellar. The owners, Paola and Roberta, focus their cuisine on local dishes, traditions and ingredients.

To start, you must try the **fried gnocco** and the cured meats: salami, pancetta and coppa seasoned by the owners themselves, an excellent prosciutto crudo and an excellent **culatello**. Traditional first courses include tortelli and **pisarei e fasò** all year round; in winter, the emphasis is on **pappardelle with mushrooms**, gnocchi au gratin, onion soup and **pumpkin ravioli**. In summer, creativity has its day with bucatini in cream of capsicum peppers, olives and pecorino cheese, raviolini with cream of Parmigiano. The main courses include **roast of culatello with milk** but the huge selection also offers **boar stew with polenta**, braised meat and **picula 'd caval** (in winter); **baked Prague ham**, grilled lamb chops and sliced duck with Tropea onions are part of the summer menu. The puddings are also very good, especially the lemon and rosemary tart, semifreddo of chestnuts, the soft chocolate cake and the superb **latte alla portoghese**.

The fair house wines (white and red) are joined by the best bottles from the local area and several labels from the most celebrated Italian wine-making regions. The restaurant also has an area for the tasting and sale of Piacenza DOC wines; it is possible to purchase typical products selected by the owners.

The village of Vicobarone has a long history: in the IXth century it belonged to the monks of San Colombano who intensified the cultivation of vines, and then at the end of the seventeenth century the castle was converted into a refined home by the marquises Malvicini Fontana. The vacation farm managed by Daniela Carugati is located in the castle's old stables. The new owners began the restructuring works in 1991 and the wing where rooms are located was completed in 2000. Fitted out with rustic wooden furniture, the rooms are cozy and comfortable: many still feature the antique stone walls and wooden beams. The buffet breakfast is served in the wine-tasting room: you'll be offered homemade cakes, cookies, bread and jams, honey, cereals, yogurt, milk, tea and coffee. Outside there's a large garden and swimming pool.

• 6 double rooms, with bathroom, air-conditioning, satellite TV; 2 apartments (4 persons) with kitchen • Prices: double room single occupancy 65 euros, double 90-120, apartment 120-150, breakfast included • Credit cards: major ones, Bancomat • Facility partly accessible to the mobility challenged. Off-street parking. Small pets allowed. Owners reachable from 8.30am to 12.30pm and from 2 to 6pm. • Breakfast room. Conference room. Garden. Pool

Zocca
Missano

Zocca
Monteombraro

48 KM SOUTH EAST OF MODENA SS 623

45 KM SOUTH-EAST OF MODENA ON SS 623

CANTACUCCO

TIZZANO

🍲 Restaurant
Via Montalbano 5500 b
Tel. 059 987012
Closed Thursday
Open: lunch and dinner
Holidays; June 15-30, September 1-15
Seating: 60
Prices: 26-30 euros, wine excluded
All credit cards, Bancomat

🚜 Holiday farm
Via Lamizze 1197
Tel. and fax 059 989581
E-mail: agriturismo.tizzano@libero.it
Internet: www.agritizzano.it
Holidays vary

To get to Cantacucco you have to negotiate the steep twists and turns of the road that from the Panaro valley floor takes you to Zocca: some way before Zocca itself we find the medieval village of Missano; the restaurant-bar of the family of Roberto Biagioni enjoys a panoramic position. Roberto gives a friendly, professional welcome to guests in the dining room, while his wife Carla looks after the kitchen (and its various pasta-making machines).

The menu here is based on seasonal ingredients: the classic dishes on the main menu are joined by dishes of the day that Roberto is only too happy to describe. It is a good idea to start with **cured meats** (pork and game) accompanied by **tigelle** (focaccine made with flour, water and salt cooked on stone) and perhaps even the cep and galletti mushrooms preserved in olive oil by Carla; in winter, try the classic **borlenghi**. There are also some excellent first courses: **tortellini in broth**, tortelloni with various stuffings, cappellacci of wild boar, cordonetti (similar to spaghetti al torchio) with sausage and **tagliatelle with cep** mushrooms, meat sauce or other seasonal condiments. There are various quality cuts of grilled beef, as well as beef fillet with cep mushrooms, roast shank of pork, **stewed boar with black olives**, rabbit chasseur and wild **duck** with **orange** sauce. In season, fresh **mushrooms** are grilled, fried or sautéed; in the fall, the menu focuses on **chestnuts**, from the soup through to the sweet polenta. There are some excellent homemade puddings to finish: crème caramel, baked cream and ricotta and wild fruit mousse.

Excellent and wide-ranging wine list, selected with great care and knowledge.

The vacation farm managed by Stefano Fogacci, helped by his mother Nilde, is in the heart of Emilia's Apennines. It's a great location from which to visit cities of artistic interest, such as Bologna, and also to explore this corner of the province of Modena, with its many castles, abbeys and Romanesque churches. Moreover, there are also recreational and sports facilities in the vicinity. On the ground floor of the facility you'll find the restaurant (a meal costs 20 euros, excluding wine) and upstairs are the bedrooms, furnished in rustic style. The filling breakfast includes coffee, tea, fresh milk and some locally made products, such as the delicious cherry jam, ricotta, bread, cookies, butter and cream. After breakfast you'll be able to visit the surrounding countryside or alternatively you can participate in one of the courses organized by the farm.

• 7 double rooms and 2 apartments (2-4 persons), with bathroom • Prices: double room single occupancy 26 euros, double 44 (22 euro supplement for extra bed), breakfast included • Credit cards: none • Facility partially accessible to the mobility challenged. Off-street parking. Small pets allowed (on request). Owners always reachable • Restaurant

TOSCANA

Mar Ligure

Mar Tirreno

Mar Tirreno

A15

Pontremoli

Bagnone

Villafranca
in Lunigiana

Pieve
Fosciana

Abetone

Careggine

Castelnuovo
di Garfagnana

Cutigliano

Carrara

Gallicano

Barga

Massa

Bagni
di Lucca

S. Marcello
Pistoiese

Villa
Basilica

Monta

Camaiore

Pistoia

Pietrasanta

Borgo a
Mozzano

Pescia

Buggiano

Capannori

Massarosa

Lucca

Montecatini
Terme

Quarrata

A11

Montecarlo

Vinci

San Giuliano
Terme

Cerreto Gui

A12

Pisa

Castelfranco
di Sotto

San
Miniato

Livorno

Certaldo

Volterra

Cecina

Montescudaio

Bibbona

Sassetta

Castagneto
Carducci

Monterotondo
Marittimo

Campiglia
Marittima

Suvereto

Massa
Marittima

ISOLA DI CAPRAIA

Piombino

Gavorrano

Marciana
Marina

Portoferraio

Castiglione
della Pescaia

Marciana

Rio Marina

Porto Azzurro

Capoliveri

ISOLA D'ELBA

ABETONE
Le Regine

46 KM NORTHWEST OF PISTOIA SS 66 A 12

ANGHIARI
Scheggia di Montauto

21 KM NORTHEAST OF AREZZO

LA LOCANDA DELLO YETI

Trattoria
Via Brennero 324
Tel. 0573 606974
Closed Tuesday
Open: lunch and dinner
Holidays: in June and September
Seating: 20 + 20 outdoors
Prices: 20-30 euros, wine excluded
All major credit cards, Bancomat

Whether you're going up the Brennero road to reach the Abetone ski resorts or to enjoy the cool climate of the woods in summertime, this trattoria is the place for a pleasurable culinary stop-off. Vittorio in the kitchen and Elisabetta, front of house, will take good care of you and give you the chance to taste some very interesting dishes where ingredients are of the utmost importance.

The antipasti change with the season: **polenta** is served in a nest with cep mushrooms and numerous other versions, while the local **cured meats**, **savory pies** and crostoni are always on the menu.

When in season, the Abetone **cep mushrooms** feature in the home-made: other first courses include taglierini with speck, potato **gnocchi** with mint pesto, **tortelli** filled with pecorino from Pienza and pine nuts and served in a basil pesto sauce, red onion soup and, in summertime, **Garfagnana spelt** soup with mushrooms or zucchini flowers. Among the main courses, **loin of venison**, fillet steak all'alpina, grilled tagliata and tasty and tender **supreme of pigeon in Chianti sauce**. Worth trying is the grilled **raw-milk Pecorino** (Slow Food Presidium) with char-grilled vegetables. There's a good selection of desserts: chocolate and pear cake, blueberry tart and chocolate semifreddo, Recioto wine or local wild berries.

The wines on the list, well thought out and reasonably priced come from all over Italy and will be explained to you, with expertise and enthusiasm, by Elisabetta.

I CAPRIOLI DI SIGLIANO

Bed and breakfast
Sigliano di Sotto, località Montauto
Tel. 333 4640612-338 4919013-335 374310
E-mail: info@icapriolidisigliano.it
Internet: www.icapriolidisigliano.it
Open all year

The B&B is located on a hill overlooking the Tiber valley, on the border between Tuscany and Umbria, close to the ancient convent of Montalto: it's completely surrounded by fields and woods that stretch away as far as the eye can see. The farm building dates back to the 15th century and has been restored with carefully selected materials. Rooms are named for famous movies, as owners Giusy and Andrea are great cinema fans. Breakfast offers anything from homemade focaccia to cookies. Lunch can be arranged on prior request and offers frittata, soups and game dishes (15 euros per person, wine excluded). We also recommend you take a walk to the beautiful swimming pool in the middle of the countryside.

• 4 double, 1 triple and 1 four-bed rooms, with bathroom • Prices: double room single use 52-60 euros, double 70-80, triple 90-120, four-bed 110-160, breakfast included • Credit cards: none • Off-street parking. Small pets allowed. Owners always present • Restaurant, Reading, music and TV room. Grounds. Pool

ANGHIARI

NENA

🍽️Restaurant
Corso Matteotti 10-14
Tel. 0575 789491
Closed Monday
Open: lunch and dinner
Holidays: variable
Seating: 50
Prices: 28-35 euros, wine excluded
All credit cards, Bancomat

"And in a battle which lasted 20-24 four hours, only one man died, and he, not from wounds inflicted by hostile weapons, or any honorable means, but, having fallen from his horse, was trampled to death." This is how Machiavelli ironically recalls the Battle of Anghiari, fought and won by the Florentines against the Milanese army, on June 29 1440. It is here, within walking distance from the medieval historic center, that the restaurant dedicated to its original founder is located. A portrait of Nena hangs in the main dining room as if to point out the continuity of tradition in the good food proposed today by Palmira Alberti. Front of house Sergio Cappetti and Paolo Severi wait on the tables ably and professionally.

The wide array of antipasti available covers cured meats, excellent **black bread crostini** with mushrooms or tomato, cep and ovoli mushroom salad (when in season), and smoked duck breast, a traditional Jewish dish. The delicious **pappardelle** are served with **wild boar**, wild goose or venison sauce. Other first courses include: **Tuscan bread soup**, **pappa col pomodoro** and a traditional family recipe **bringoli con il sugo finto**. Main courses feature the classical Chianina steak, fillet of beef with cep mushrooms or truffles, fried or char-grilled lamb, seasonal vegetable flans, and, in winter, **game**. All the puddings are homemade: pumpkin jam tart, the ubiquitous **cantucci** and torcolo spongecake served with Vin Santo.

There is an excellent selection of local wines: around 200 labels with good value for money.

ARCIDOSSO
Bivio Aiole

AIUOLE

🍽️Restaurant-hotel
Località Bivio Aiole
Tel. 0564 967300
Closed Sunday for dinner and Monday
Open: lunch and dinner
Holidays: in November
Seating: 100
Prices: 28-30 euros, wine excluded
All major credit cards, Bancomat

For almost 40 years (since 1967) the Quattrini family have been running this little hotel at the beginning of the road that leads to the summit of Monte Amiata, with dedication, competence and professional skill. On the ground floor of the building, reminiscent of a mountain chalet, the restaurant welcomes hotel guests and passers-by. The secret of the restaurant's success is its combination of tradition, seasonal produce, and a culinary heritage which deserves to be preserved. Courteous, prompt service and a desire to keep the past alive ensure good food with real, authentic flavors.

To start, local cured meats and various kinds of crostini. Noteworthy first courses include 'snow flakes' (**potato and ricotta gnocchi**), **nettle tortelli** and **soups**, including chickpea. There are many well-made main courses: **lamb stew, suckling pig with Brunello**, jugged venison, **rabbit with herbs** (as many as 22 different types) and wild boar with chocolate. As side dishes there are vegetable flans that vary with the season. The puddings are simple and tasty: walnut or chocolate cake, homemade tarts and ricotta with chestnut cream.

There isn't a wine list: as well as the good house wines, a Rosso di Montalcino and a white, there are a few Tuscan labels.

ANTICA TRATTORIA DA GUIDO

Trattoria
Via Madonna del Prato, 85
Tel. 0575 23760
Closed Sunday, except the first Sunday of the month
Open: lunch and dinner
Holidays: second and third week of August
Seating: 40
Prices: 25-30 euros, wine excluded
All credit cards, Bancomat

Once you have admired the frescoes by Piero della Francesca inside the church of San Francesco you can continue your visit along one of the oldest and most characteristic roads of Arezzo, Via Madonna del Prato. Here, at number 85, you will find the Antica trattoria da Guido, just a few tables and a family atmosphere. Teresa, the life and soul of the restaurant, will welcome you and guide you through the various culinary options that are always in keeping with the seasons and Tuscan traditions; with a few Calabrian touches here and there linked to the Stilo family's origins. Along with the restaurant the family also runs the delicatessen down the road, dedicating to it the same level of care and attention.

The menu starts off with different types of bruschetta and a Tuscan classic: **spleen crostini** and Tuscan **cured meats**. The first courses are all fresh pasta dishes: tagliatelle, **pappardelle**, **potato gnocchi**, ravioli filled with ricotta and spinach, spinach tortelli, which can all be accompanied either with white (without tomato) **duck sauce**, wild boar or hare sauce or with seasonal vegetables and in fall cep mushrooms. Also excellent are the traditional soups: ribollita, pappa al pomodoro, **chickpea** or spelt and in summer the panzanella soup. The classic **steak** and tagliata are Tuscan Chianina. Alternatively, you can go for **duck in porchetta** or **rabbit roasted with wild dill**, served with excellent vegetable flans. The homemade puddings are very good too.

The interesting wine list improves year after year, focusing particular attention on local labels.

AREZZO

2 KM FROM CITY CENTER

CASA VOLPI

3-Star Hotel
Via Simone Martini 29
Tel. 0575 354364
Fax 0575 355971
E-mail: posta@casavolpi.it
Internet: www.casavolpi.it
Closed for 9 days at beginning of August

Casa Volpi is a hotel that still retains the appearance and atmosphere of a nice private home, where the Volpi family will welcome you with polite professionalism. This 20th-century building houses 15 guestrooms, all en-suite and with air-conditioning. The décor is elegant, with attention to detail and boasts furniture from the late 19th century. One of the winning features of the hotel is certainly its buffet breakfast, consisting of cakes, pastries, fresh fruit, fruit salad, local prosciutto and cheeses, freshly baked bread and jams. The restaurant offers typical local dishes prepared with selected ingredients like the excellent olive oil (25-30 euros, wine excluded). In summer guests can dine on the veranda overlooking the garden.

• 1 single, 11 double rooms and 3 suites, with bathroom (1 with jacuzzi shower), air-conditioning, mini-bar, safe, satellite TV, modem connection • Prices: single 65 euros, double room single use 65-90, double 90, suite 125 (10-15 euro supplement for extra bed); breakfast 8 euros per person • Credit cards: all except DC, Bancomat • 1 room designed for use by the mobility challenged. Off-street parking. No pets allowed. Owners always present • Bar, restaurant. Breakfast room. TV room. Grounds.

AREZZO

LA TORRE DI GNICCHE

🍲 Wine shop with food
Piaggia San Martino 8
Tel. 0575 352035
Closed Wednesday
Open: midday-3pm/6pm-1am
Holidays: 2 weeks in January, 1 in July
Seating: 30 + 20 outdoors
Prices: 18-25 euros, wine excluded
All major credit cards, Bancomat

Wooden tables, straw-backed chairs and a pleasantly informal atmosphere characterize this little osteria, named for Federigo Bobini, nicknamed Gnicche, a 19th-century brigand transformed by folklore into a romantic hero. The wine shop (which has one room that in the summer extends to the terraces of Palazzo delle Logge across the road) is just round the corner from the splendid Piazza Grande. Run with great dedication by Lucia, who has good help front of house from Stefano, the kitchen offers characteristic traditional dishes. You can get a taste of it straight away with the wide assortment of croutons and crostoni (including an unusual combination of beans and botargo) served as antipasti. The first courses mainly consist of **ribollita**, **onion soup au gratin** and other seemingly simple soups: the **pappa al pomodoro** for instance, follows a recipe which borders on ritual: the skin that forms on the surface has to be broken and stirred seven times. The rare **grifi all'aretina** (calf's muzzle stew) stands out among the main courses, alongside **meatloaf**, **tripe** and **stewed baccalà**. The cheese board revolves around pecorino cheeses from the Apennines and some fresh goat's cheeses, served with homemade preserves; the selection of extravirgin olive oils is also excellent. The puddings, prepared by Lucia, include **mascarpone and chocolate cake**, ricotta mousse with lemon cream and chocolate shavings, **pear and ricotta tart** and rice pudding.
There are over 800 labels selected with special care and a wide choice of locally produced wines, also served by the glass.

BAGNI DI LUCCA

27 KM NORTH-EAST OF LUCCA ON SS 12

CORONA

🗝 3-Star Hotel
Via Serraglia, 78
Tel. 0583 805151
Fax 0583 805134
E-mail: info@coronaregina.it
Internet: www.coronaregina.it
Closed from mid-January to mid-February

This hotel managed by Michela and Roberto Marino Merlo – with assistance from their parents – is located in an early 19th-century building overlooking the small waterfalls of the Lima river. Both the communal areas and rooms are spacious, comfortable and well furnished. Breakfast is certainly worth getting up for: a buffet of cured meats, cheeses, yoghurt, cereals, eggs, fresh fruit, homemade jams (Roberto is particularly proud of his creations, especially the orange marmalade), cookies and cakes is set up either in the lounge or the rose garden. The restaurant offers an à la carte menu starting from 35 euros, wine excluded, while half board is available for 55-66 euros.

• 3 single and 17 double rooms, with bathroom, mini-bar, TV, modem connection; 2 with terrace • Prices: single 45-60 euros, double 70-85 (34 euro supplement for extra bed), breakfast included • Credit cards: all except DC, Bancomat • 2 rooms accessible to the mobility challenged. Parking out front. Small pets allowed. Reception open from 7 am to midnight. • Bar, restaurant. Breakfast room. Garden.

BAGNO A RIPOLI
Bigallo

ANTICO SPEDALE DEL BIGALLO

☞—⚷ Youth hostel
Via Bigallo e Apparita 14
Tel. 055 630907-340 4123101
Fax 0577 996947
E-mail: info@bigallo.it
Internet: www.bigallo.it
Open from April to September

The Antico Spedale del Bigallo, a shelter for pilgrims in the Middle Ages and a Benedictine nunnery in the 16th century, now offers basic but comfortable accommodation. The beautiful rooms, with no television, air-conditioning or internet connection, are all named for the nuns who lived here in 1502: Scolastica, Fragia, Orsina, Badessa, Pippa, Lena, Simona, Lubecca. Badessa, Simona and Lubecca have beautiful views over Florence. Really cheap and very basic shared accommodation is also available. Buffet breakfast offers bread, butter, jams, yogurt, fruit, muesli, cereals, cured meats and cheeses. A restaurant service is available for groups and subject to booking: lunch is a very reasonable (10 euros per person), and packed lunch can be arranged (7 euros per person). Various courses, guided tours on foot or on horseback are also available.

• 3 double rooms and 1 suite, with bathroom, 1 triple and 1 five-bed room, with shared bathroom, 1 dormitory with 10 beds and 1 with 12 wooden cabins, each with 2 beds, with external shared bathrooms • Prices: double room single use 48 euros, double 66, triple 60, suite 132, bed in dormitory or cabins 22 euros per person, breakfast included • Credit cards: Visa, MC, Bancomat • Facility partly accessible to the mobility challenged. Adjacent parking. No pets allowed. Reception open 6am-11 pm • Restaurant. Hall for parties, concerts, meetings, exhibitions

BAGNONE

LA LINA

☞—⚷ Rooms
Piazza Marconi 1
Tel. e fax 0187 429069
Open all year

Francesca Ruzzi named this classic old-fashioned locanda in the center of Bagnone for her mother Lina, and has managed it since 1989. Located in a lovely aristocratic building restored in the 1980s, it makes an ideal base for people wishing to explore the natural beauties of the Lunigiana area or taste the local cuisine (15-30 euros). Rooms are simply furnished but with great attention to detail. A supplement of 6 euros is charged for breakfast (bread, butter, jams, hot and cold beverages) served in the restaurant dining room. For lunch and dinner mamma Lina prepares traditional Lunigiana dishes, like testaroli mushroom and vegetable pie. A wide selection of wines is available and as Francesca's husband, Walter Pigoni, is a sommelier he'll be happy to advise you on wines from Tuscany or other Italian regions.

• 5 double rooms, with bathroom; 2 with TV • Prices: double room single use 40 euros, double 55 (12 euro supplement for extra bed); breakfast 6 euros per person • Credit cards: Visa, Bancomat • Public parking in the immediate vicinity. No pets allowed. Reception open from 7am-midnight • Bar, restaurant

BARBERINO VAL D'ELSA

Cortine

32 KM SOUTH OF FLORENCE, 36 KM NORTHWEST OF SIENA

LA CHIARA DI PRUMIANO

🍲 Rooms
Strada di Cortine 12
Tel. 055 8075727-8075583
Fax 055 8075000
E-mail: info@prumiano.it
Internet: www.prumiano.it
Closed in January and February

BARGA

39 KM NORTH OF LUCCA SS 445

L'ALTANA

🍲 Trattoria
Via di Mezzo 1
Tel. 0583 723192
Closed Wednesday
Open: lunch and dinner
Holidays: February
Seating: 30 + 18 outdoors
Prices: 20-25 euros, wine excluded
All credit cards, Bancomat

La Chiara di Prumiano run by Gaia Mezzadri offers rooms in an 18th-century villa and in two adjacent buildings. Rooms are comfortable and some have a kitchenette. There's no television in the rooms or commonl areas but the reading room has a wide selection of books available for guests. For breakfast you can enjoy jams, bread, yogurt and muesli. You need to make a reservation for the restaurant, which offers vegetarian menus (20 euros, wine excluded). Music and meditation courses are available and guests can enjoy the nearby swimming pool, riding school and other sports facilities.

• 7 double and 5 triple rooms, with bathroom; 1 with kitchen, 1 with kitchenette • Prices: double room single use 60 euros, double 80, triple 90-100, breakfast included • Credit cards: Visa, MC, Bancomat • Parking out front. Small pets allowed. Reception open from 9.30am-1.30pm, owners always reachable. • Restaurant. Reading room with library, lounge. Garden

In the old part of the medieval village of Barga, just round the corner from Porta Reale, lies the cozy Altana trattoria, where, not so long ago, regulars used to stop by for a game of cards, a glass of wine and a tasty bite to eat. Now it's Angela and her mother Camilla who welcome us to the present-day trattoria, seating us in the dining room with its trompe l'oeil of a beautiful mountain panorama in the Garfagnana valley. The menu is based on traditional dishes and varies with the season.

For antipasti, cured meats, potato bread crostini and olives. Noteworthy first courses are the homemade pasta dishes: hand-cut **maccheroni** with meat or tomato sauce is excellent. Alternatively, **soup alla frantoiana** or the delicious **spelt soup** from Garfagnana. The main courses range from **meat stew** served with formenton (maize) polenta, to **roast** rabbit, pork and veal. Sometimes they also do baccalà and excellent **tripe**. In summer, vegetables stuffed with ricotta, grated pecorino, egg and herbs are on the menu too. To finish off: a slice of pecorino from the mountains surrounding Barga or some very good homemade dessserts: ricotta and walnut or chocolate cake and fresh fruit tarts, plus, in winter, **castagnaccio** and fritters made with Garfagnana chestnut flour.

The wine list includes a choice of good, not over-priced labels from the Lucca hills and Montecarlo.

🍴 At Via della Repubblica 162, in **Fornaci di Barga** (5 km), La Gastronomia di Massimiliano Luti sells cured meats and cheeses from Garfagnana and the Serchio Valley, soups, fresh pasta, tripe, roast meats and other dishes, including marinated trout.

BIBBONA

VILLA TOSCANA

🔑 Bed and breakfast
Via della Repubblica 41
Tel. 0586 671936-335 6852353-339 5070881
Fax 0586 636887
E-mail: info@lalocandadivillatoscana.it
Internet: www.lalocandadivillatoscana.it
Open all year

This charming B&B, just a few minutes drive from the Costa degli Etruschi, is located in Bibbona, a village high in the Maremma hills surrounded by olive groves and vineyards. A few rooms are available, tastefully decorated and with some antique furniture chosen by the owner who runs an antiques shop in the nearby town of Cecina. A small kitchen is available for guests to use. Another strong plus for Villa Toscana is that breakfast is served in your room or in a nice lounge with fireplace and offers hot and cold beverages, homemade cakes, Tuscan bread and jams, while cheeses and cured meats are available on request. This is a good base for those who enjoy days by the sea, good food and wine or who wish to visit places of artistic interest.

• 1 single, 3 double rooms and 2 suites, with bathroom, air-conditioning, satellite TV; suite has a garden • Prices: single 90 euros, double 120, suite 175, breakfast included • Credit cards: all except DC, Bancomat • Parking out front. No pets allowed. Staff always reachable • Breakfast room. Reading room

BORGO A MOZZANO

OSTERIA I MACELLI 🍾

🍲 Recently opened Osteria
Via di Cerreto
Tel. 0583 88700
Closed Wednesday, Saturday for lunch
Open: lunch and dinner
Holidays: 2 weeks in ooctober
Seating: 35
Prices: 18-25 euros, wine excluded
All credit cards

In an area with a strong tradition of live-stock farms and pig butchers this little wood-lined osteria is in what was once a butcher's shop. Just round the corner from the picturesque Maddalena bridge (more commonly known as the 'devil's bridge'), it is run by Alberto Lena and Patrizio De Servi, with the help of Samuele Martelli and Lara Ondati.
The menu, written on a blackboard and read out loud (sometimes a bit wearily), consists of a few classic local dishes, alternating with some more creative options. To start with the typical cured meats of Garfgnana are a must: **biroldo**, lardo, mezzina and **mondiola**. Then, **spelt soup**, legume soup and the home-made pasta dishes – **tortelli** and maccheroni. In line with the picture on the sign and the traditions of the Serchio Valley, main courses include a wide selection of meats: **veal stew**, **roast leg of pork**, **chicken** or **rabbit alla cacciatora** and guinea fowl. Fish will be well represented, with **trout** and **baccalà** cooked with leeks, **slow cooked** or steamed. Baccalà is very popular in these parts, so much so that in Anchiano, a hamlet of Borgo a Mozzano, there is even a yearly fair celebration dedicated to baccalà from Ny Alesund in Norway. Potato bread is another Garfagnano specialty and the puddings, including **castagnaccio**, are exquisite.
We didn't think the offerings on the wine list, which includes wines served by the glass, did justice to the food: go for the house wine.

🍯 In Via della Chiesa, **Pian di Coreglia** (9 km), the Nutini and Regalati pork butchers offer the Slow Food Presidium biroldo, as well as giallorini beans, ottofile corn flour, neccio (chestnut) flour and spelt from Garfagnana.

Borgo San Lorenzo

27 km northeast of Florence on SS 551

Locanda degli Artisti

🔑 3-Star Hotel
Piazza Romagnoli 2
Tel. 055 8455359
Fax 055 8450116
E-mail: info@locandaartisti.it
Internet: www.locandaartisti.it
Open all year

This cozy hotel is located in a pedestrian area in the old center of the capital of the Mugello area, Borgo San Lorenzo, a village dating back to the mid-19th century. 20 years ago the owners decided to close it down and rent out the restaurant, but later went on to renovate the building and fit the Art Nouveau-style interior with antique furniture. Breakfast is generous and consists of genuine, high quality products. You can set out from the hotel to explore this not so well known part of the Apennines on foot, by bicycle or on horseback or enjoy canoeing, sailing and windsurfing on Lake Bilancino. Car enthusiasts can visit the Mugello international circuit. When major sporting events are being held the cost of accommodation increases accordingly.

• 2 single and 5 double rooms, with bathroom, air-conditioning, satellite TV, fast Internet connection • Prices: single 60-80 euros, double 100-120, breakfast included • Credit cards: major ones, Bancomat • Parking nearby, garage parking at special rates. No pets allowed. Reception open 7am-11 pm. • Bar, terrace

Borgo San Lorenzo
Ronta

34 km from Florence on SS 551

Tre Fiumi

🔑 3-Star Hotel
Località Madonna dei Tre Fiumi 16
Tel. 055 8403015-8495705
Fax 055 8403197
E-mail: trefiumi@virgilio.it
Internet: www.albergotrefiumi.com
Closed in December

The hotel, mentioned in a 1710 edict of the Grand Duke of Tuscany, was once a stop-over place for travelers. It stands at an altitude of 360 meters, where it's cool in the summer and mild in winter. Guests can enjoy the countryside and explore the paths that lead into the Apennines between Tuscany and Emilia-Romagna. Those interested in history and architecture will want to visit the nearby Medici villas and old convents, churches and chapels. Sports fans can easily reach the Mugello circuit, the Borgo San Lorenzo Sports Center for a swim or a game of tennis or the Scarperia center for a spot of golf. The hotel-restaurant has been family run since 1947 and offers homely, traditional cuisine (around 25 euros, wine excluded). Rooms are spacious and cozy, and though they are simply furnished, some boast ceiling frescoes and original fireplaces.

• 2 single and 20 double, triple or four-bed rooms, with bathroom, TV • Prices: single 50 euros, double room single use 70, double 80, triple 95, four-bed 110, breakfast included • Credit cards: all, Bancomat • 3 rooms designed for use by the mobility challenged. Off-street parking. No pets allowed. Reception open 7am-midnight. • Bar, restaurant. Breakfast room, TV room. Garden

BUGGIANO
Colle di Buggiano

ANTICA CASA
LE RONDINI

Bed and breakfast
Via Pierucci 21
Tel. 0572 33313
Fax 0572 905361
E-mail: info@anticacasa.it
Internet: www.anticacasa.it
Open from March to November

This small B&B is located on top of a hill planted with olive trees, in a charming, fortified medieval village dating back to 1238, with cobbled streets and houses built of stone. Fulvia Musso's house dates back to the 16th century and has been carefully restored to retain original architectural features: terracotta tile floors, vaulted ceilings and various frescoes dating back to the late 18th century. Rooms are fitted with antique furniture and have beautiful views of the village and the hills thickly covered with cypress and olive trees. Rooms on the second floor have original frescoes. Breakfast of coffee, tea, croissants, bread, jams, honey and fruit is served in the garden, protected by a wall. In summer the limonaia (a winter garden used to protect citrus trees from the cold) doubles up as a kitchen that guests are free to use. A swimming pool is only 1 km away, riding stables 2 km and a golf course 8 km.

• 5 double rooms and 1 apartment (2-4 persons), with bathroom • Prices: double room single use 60 euros, double 75-115, breakfast included, apartment (minimum stay 3 nights) 65-80 euros • Credit cards: none • Public parking 300 meters away. Small pets allowed. Owners always reachable. • Kitchen. Reading room. Garden

CAMPIGLIA
MARITTIMA

LOCANDA
DEL CANOVACCIO

Bed and breakfast
Via Vecchio Asilo 1
Tel. 0565 838449-333 1646020
Fax 0565 838226
E-mail: locandadelcanovaccio@terra-toscana.com
Internet: www.terra-toscana.com/locandadelcanovaccio
Closed in January and February

A few years ago Davide and Laura D'Onofrio decided that the lovely old center of Campiglia Marittima was just the place to open their little restaurant, where guests can enjoy a creative cuisine consisting mainly of fish dishes (30 euros, wine excluded). Last year the couple decided to renovate the apartment above the restaurant and can now also offer accommodation. The three rooms are bright, nicely furnished, with original wooden beams and overlook a charming little 13th-century piazza. Breakfast offers toast, butter, homemade jams, fresh fruit, freshly baked pastries, hot beverages and orange juice. The beach at San Lorenzo is only a short distance away and guests can also visit the Etruscan archeological sites.

• 2 double rooms and 1 suite, with bathroom; suite with kitchenette • Prices: double room single use and double 90 euros, suite 110, breakfast included • Credit cards: major ones, Bancomat • Free public parking 200 meters away. No pets allowed. Owners always reachable. • Restaurant

CANTAGALLO

BEATRICE

Restaurant
Via della Rasa 10
Tel. 0574 933125
Closed Tuesday, Sunday and festivities for dinner
Open: lunch and dinner
Holidays: three weeks after August 15
Seating: 50 + 25 outdoors
Prices: 25 euros, wine excluded
No credit cards, Bancomat

Leaving the Chianti and Brunello vineyards behind you, deep in the solitude of woods crossed by a small tributary of the Bisenzio river, tower the Tuscan Apennines with their hidden valleys. The woods yield mushrooms and chestnuts, the streams trout and other fish from the salmon family, but apart from that, there are only a few villas with gardens to remind us that we are in the rich province of Prato. To reach Beatrice's restaurant, you need to keep going for another three kilometers after the town of Luicciana until you reach the scattered houses that form the village of Cantagallo. Be sure to reserve a table in advance, as this place is well off the beaten track.

This is plain establishment, with a bar at the entrance and a few tables outside in summertime, which comes into its own during the **mushroom** season: Beatrice knows all the local pickers and can cook up their findings any way you like.

Needless to say the menu is more limited at other times of year. To begin with you have cured meats, crostini, frittata and herb **fritters**. Then **potato tortelli**, nettle **ravioli**, **tagliatelle** and pesto or artichoke **lasagne**. For your main course, **roast shank of veal**, **fillet steak** and other char-grilled meats, accompanied by potatoes from the mountains or, season permitting, zucchini flowers, chicory and wild herbs. To finish off, home-made puddings: wild berry cake, marengo and in winter **castagnaccio**, made with chestnut flour from Cantagallo.

There's not a great deal of choice in the wine list, but the house wine is decent.

CAPALBIO
Ghiaccio Bosco

GHIACCIO BOSCO

Holiday farm
Strada della Sgrilla 4
Tel. and fax 0564 896539
E-mail: info@ghiacciobosco.com
Internet: www.ghiacciobosco.com
Holidays vary

Ghiaccio Bosco is an early 20th-century farmhouse that has belonged to the Olivi family for generations and Monica and Filippo started running it in 1995 after university. Rooms, created by renovating the old stables, are tastefully decorated and feature the colors of different local flowers. The four bigger rooms, that can be accessed from the portico and are fitted with valuable furniture, are priced between 80 and 125 euros depending on the length of stay. Buffet breakfast offers four different types of cake, two savory pies, cured meats, pickles, cheeses, fresh ricotta, bread, Italian omelets, cereals, jams and fruit. The restaurant is for residents only and is open during specific periods of the year (20 euros, wine excluded).

• 14 double rooms and 1 suite (3 persons), with bathroom, air-conditioning, safe, TV • Prices: double room single use 50-70 euros, double 75-115, suite 100-130, breakfast included • Credit cards: all except AE, Bancomat • Facility accessible to the mobility challenged, 2 rooms designed for their use. Off-street covered parking. No pets allowed. Owners always present. • Restaurant. Garden, veranda. Pool

CAPANNORI
Camigliano

CAREGGINE
Isola Santa

I DIAVOLETTI

DA GIACCÒ

🍴 Recently opened osteria
Via Stradone di Camigliano 302
Tel. 0583 920323
Closed Monday
Open: dinner, lunch on booking
Holidays: variable
Seating: 40 + 40 outdoors
Prices: 26-30 euros, wine excluded
All major credit cards, Bancomat

🍴 Restaurant
Via Provinciale di Arni 2
Tel. 0583 667048
Closed Tuesday, summer only for dinner
Open: lunch and dinner
Holidays: three weeks in November
Seating: 100
Prices: 25-30 euros, wine excluded
Credit cards: CartaSi, Visa

This simple, pleasant Tuscan osteria, run by the Bosi sisters, is located in one of the finest villas in the Lucca area: Villa Torrigiani in Camigliano. On the menu are traditional Lucca dishes, prepared with local produce and presented without too many innovations.

Start with Slow Food Presidium Tuscan cured meats, which include **biroldo** from Garfagnana and lardo di Colonnata accompanied with neccio (chestnut flour) bread, frittata with seasonal vegetables and mushroom croutons. Distinctive first courses include: spelt straccetti pasta served with broccoli and anchovies, **tortelli Lucchesi** with meat ragù, buckwheat tortelloni (filled with ricotta, herbs and red chicory) with leeks, **pappardelle with hare ragù** or wild boar sauce, or, when in season, with zucchini flowers, pistachio nuts and Parmesan shavings. Plus, **garmugia,** a Lucca soup of spring onions, asparagus tips, artichokes, peas, broad beans, minced beef, bacon and meat stock, that dates back to the 17th century. To follow, **fried chicken and rabbit** with seasonal vegetables or a tasty beef tagliata with cep mushrooms (which also often feature in the excellent side-dishes). Then Pecorino cheese from Garfagnana with honey, followed by ricotta mousse or pudding accompanied with melted chocolate or wild berry sauce.

As an alternative to the unpretentious house wine, the wine list offers several important, reasonably priced, Lucca labels.

Along the road from Castelnuovo to Massa, connecting Garfagnana with Versilia, you come to Isola Santa, a village that looks like a nativity scene with little stone houses built around a picturesque man-made lake (there's an ancient water mill at the bottom which can only be seen when the lake is emptied). In this setting Gabriele Mazzei serves you the specialties of the Garfagnana area, mostly made with produce from the surrounding woodlands and local area.

The spelt and wheat flours of the Garfagnana area are used to make the homemade pasta: hand-cut **maccheroni**, tagliatelle and tortelli which are served with mushrooms or truffles, when in season. The **mushrooms** (ceps or the rarer royal agaric) from the nearby woods, can also be ordered grilled, in salads and with herbs. To follow, excellent **grilled meats**, especially the locally-bred **lamb** and **kid**. Fresh trout from the lake below and nearby rivers is also often on the menu. Home-made desserts with wild berries and the traditional **castagnaccio** with ricotta.

There are around 50 quality labels on the well-planned wine list. It's also possible to purchase many local products.

🧀 In **Pontardeto di Pieve Fosciana** (15 km from Isola Santa) the Bertagni dairy produces and sells raw milk cheeses made from ewe's, goat's and cow's milk, singly or blended, as well as exquisite ricottas.

CARMIGNANO

CARRARA
Marina di Carrara

12 KM SOUTHWEST OF PRATO

6 KM FROM THE TOWN CENTER

SU PE' I CANTO

Wine shop with food
Piazza Matteotti 25-26
Tel. 055 8712490
Closed Monday
Open: lunch and dinner
Holidays: in August
Seating: 30
Prices: 25-30 euros, wine excluded
Credit cards: Visa, Bancomat

EFFE

Bed and breakfast
Via Garibaldi 27
Tel. 0585 780455-335 6818299
Fax 0585 780433
E-mail: va.endriz@tim.it
Open all year

On the slopes of Monte Albano, Carmignano lies in the heart of the main farming area of the province of Prato, famous for its quality wines, extra virgin olive oil and figs, that are dried and prepared using artisan techniques dating back to the 14th century (Carmignano dried figs are a Slow Food Presidium). In the main square of the village, just a short distance from the town hall and the museum dedicated to grapes and wine, is the renovated charcoal kiln which hosts the wine shop-osteria run by the Alderighi family. In this cozy country-style setting you will be able to sample the most traditional dishes of Tuscan cuisine, many of which are reproductions of ancient local recipes.

Among the cured meats that open the menu, together with various croutons, the **mortadella di Prato** (a Slow food Presidium) deserves a mention. The most popular first courses include: **ribollita**, **pappardelle with duck sauce**, **maltagliati with partridge sauce** and garganelli with vegetables. There is a wide range of meat dishes: **rabbit** della nonna, **braised beef al Carmignano**, **tripe alla fiorentina**, **sweet and sour tongue with onions and chocolate**. We also recommend the **baccalà with raisins** and the artichoke pie. To finish off, there are various puddings, cantuccini, castagnaccio and, when in season, schiacciata bread with grapes or cherries cooked in wine.

The wine cellar is well stocked with a wide range of wines from Carmignano (Rosato or Vin Ruspo, Barco Reale, Vin Santo) and a good few regional and national labels.

Floriana Castellini's B&B is part of her home, an old building completely refurbished in 2003. Guestrooms are comfortable and tastefully decorated, each identified by a specific color scheme and much use is made of the precious marble this area is famous for (the Apuan marble quarries are only a few kilometers away). Breakfast consists of coffee, milk, tea, fruit juices, focaccia, cookies and jams. Floriana is always available and will be more than happy to suggest places to visit. Guests can enjoy trips to the marble quarries, take a boat to the Bocche di Magra or the Cinque Terre, or visit Pisa and the other towns of artistic interest in northern Tuscany.

.
• 3 double rooms, with bathroom, terrace, air-conditioning, TV • Prices: double room single use 40 euros, double 60, breakfast included • Credit cards: none • External public parking. Small pets allowed. Owner always reachable. • Breakfast room with reading corner. Garden.

LOCANDA APUANA   ⊗

Trattoria
Via Comunale 1
Tel. 0585 768017
Closed Sunday for dinner and Monday
Open: lunch and dinner
Holidays: in January
Seating: 55
Prices: 25-28 euros, wine excluded
All major credit cards, Bancomat

OSTERIA GLORIA

Trattoria
Via Covetta 92
Tel. 0585 53876
Closed Sunday and festivities
Open: lunch and dinner
Holidays: 1 week between August 10-15 and Christmas
Seating: 50
Prices: 12-25 euros
No credit cards

Lardo di Colonnata is pork fat seasoned with salt and aromatic herb, and aged in special Apuana marble containers. This cured meat become famous in recent years, triggering a proliferation of mediocre imitations. In order to defend and promote the authentic product, a Slow Food Presidium was created to which a dozen or so producers adhere. One of these is Fausto Guadagni, whose sister Carla runs the Locanda Apuana with her companion Dario. This renovated grocery store has two dining rooms with marble floors and wooden tables; one with an open fire in winter and the other with a corner equipped for slicing the famous lardo and cheeses.

Service is polite and prompt, and you'll be able to sample traditional Carrara dishes with a few seasonal variations at very reasonable prices. Start with a taste of **lardo di Colonnata**, accompanied by seasonal vegetables, crostini, panizze and focaccia. The first courses include **taglierini with beans** (a local dish made with Borlotti beans), tordelli with tomato and basil, **chestnut flour** or wholemeal **tagliatelle** and testaroli with pesto. To follow: tagliata with lardo, wild boar (in winter), **stuffed boned rabbit**, zucchini strudel, spelt and ricotta and other savory pies, and meat carpaccio in brine. The **potatoes cooked in lardo** are also excellent. There's a wide selection of **Pecorino** and other cheeses served with home-made mostarda. Noteworthy desserts include: **Carrara rice cake**, chestnut flour crêpes with orange sauce and ricotta cake with pear sauce.

The wine list offers a wide, carefully assembled range of Tuscan labels. The selection of spirits is good too.

Don't be fooled by the apparent simplicity of this trattoria on a main road into downtown Carrara near the highway exit. Inside you can sit in the large dining room on ground level, with photos of Carrara at the beginning of the 20th century hanging on the walls, where a bar stays open from early morning till evening. A small staircase takes you up to another smaller dining area. It is a family-run business: the mother, Signora Gloria, works in the kitchen with the help of her daughter, while one of her sons and a son-in-law look after the grill, and her children and children-in-law take it in turns to wait on the tables.

On the list of traditional first courses are both the home-made **taglierini on beans** and **tordelli with ragù**: delicious. The vegetable soups and lasagnette with fish sauce are also worth trying. The **tripe**, when on the menu, is excellent, and so are the **cuttlefish with potatoes**, **paranza mixed fried fish** and anchovies, crispy and extremely fresh. The char-grilled meat, including the **Florentine T-bone steak**, is excellent as are roast beef with potatoes and **chine of pork** with steamed chickpeas or beans, and boiled or sautéed vegetables. On Friday and Saturday you'll often find a mixed grill of fresh fish.

For dessert, there's **rice cake**, traditional in these parts. The house wine, both red and white, is from Montecarlo of Lucca and eminently drinkable. The atmosphere is pleasant and informal, the hosts kind and attentive and the bill (house wine included) will make you want to come back.

CASTAGNETO CARDUCCI

DA UGO

Restaurant
Via Pari 3 A
Tel. 0565 763746
Closed Monday
Open: lunch and dinner
Holidays: in November
Seating: 50
Prices: 28-32 euros, wine excluded
All credit cards, Bancomat

CASTEL DEL PIANO
Montenero

ANTICA FATTORIA DEL GROTTAIONE

Osteria
Via della Piazza 1
Tel. 0564 954020
Closed Monday
Open: lunch and dinner
Holidays: January
Seating: 40 + 60 outdoors
Prices: 30-35 euros, wine excluded
All major credit cards, Bancomat

In terms of decor, service and presentation, this restaurant is firmly stuck in the 70s, but has a way of treating its customers, and offers an array of flavors and aromas that recall a traditional osteria. It has been run for over three decades by the 80-year old-Ugo, with the help of six family members and two employees. The food is unquestionably and decidedly local and continues to attract loyal customers from all over the world.

The meal begins with the classic Tuscan antipasti of cured meats and crostini or with **vegetables in olive oil**. If you like pasta, you can choose from the justifiably famous **tagliatelle with wild pigeon sauce** and pasta dishes with seasonal sauces such as fettuccine with mushrooms, **pappardelle with wild boar sauce**, cannelloni stuffed with ricotta and spinach with ragù; or, alternatively, **vegetable soup alla castagnetana**, which is excellent. To follow, **wild boar alla maremmana**, **wild pigeon al pentolo**, cooked in an infusion of herbs and red wine, and various types of grilled meats. From Easter to September they also cook fish dishes. Desserts include jam tart, panna cotta and a special tiramisù.

The cellar is really well stocked; the wine list deserves a note of merit for its attention to detail: the entry for each bottle includes name, producer, type, grape varieties, vintage and price (always reasonable). The evocative view over the Bogheri plains to the sea can be enjoyed from the dining room windows. It's worth booking in advance, especially in summer

Montenero d'Orcia is situated on the slopes of Monte Amiata. In this small, charming village, Flavio Biserni works with with a team captained by the pretty, professional Amanda Centurelli. This well-kept, inviting country-style osteria also features a terrace for use in fine weather. You can see what pleasure Flavio takes from playing host, providing the best for his customers with warmth and simplicity.

The menu begins with a good choice of antipasti from which we chose Cinta Senese cured meats, grilled vegetables and fresh goat's cheese and then, moving on to the first courses, **Arcidosso soup** with spinach and ricotta, **pappa al pomodoro** and **tortelli**, always on the menu in both summer and winter versions. Main courses go from classic braised wild boar al Montecucco, **peposo** stew, cooked according to an ancient recipe (book in advance), **stockfish** with tomatoes and onions, and if you book, bistecca alla fiorentina. We recommend the mixed vegetables fried in the fantastic local extra virgin olive oil. There's always a great selection of local Pecorinos on the cheese board, especially. The meal ends with traditional **caffè in forchetta**, **ricotta cake** and other specialties that vary with the seasons.

The wine list is tended with dedication and skill, featuring lots of labels from Tuscany and further afield. Flavio is an oil connoisseur and serves many Tuscan and other regional labels to accompany the appropriate dishes.

There are two good places for making purchases just round the corner from the osteria: the Perazzeta farm (wines and oils) and the Franci oil mill (oils).

CASTELFRANCO DI SOTTO
Orentano

CASTELLINA IN CHIANTI

DA BENITO ⊛

Trattoria
Via Martiri della Libertà 2
Tel. 0583 23155
Closed Wednesday, never in August
Open: lunch and dinner
Holidays: 3 weeks in November, 1 in April
Seating: 80
Prices: 23-25 euros, wine excluded
All major credit cards

COLLE ETRUSCO SALIVOLPI

3-Star Hotel
Via Fiorentina 89
Tel. 0577 740484
Fax 0577 740998
E-mail: info@hotelsalivolpi.com
Internet: www.hotelsalivolpi.com
Open all year

Run for over 15 years by Andrea with the help of a partner, this historic trattoria is renowned locally for its good food and value for money. It is situated on the main Pontedera-Altopascio road, on the border of the province of Lucca, around 20 kilometers from the main town Castelfranco. The menu changes with the seasons and the dishes are strictly traditional, free from frills or outside influences.

To start the meal there is a classic platter of **cured meats** from the best pork butchers in Tuscany, meat and tomato **croutons**, **fettunta**, baked olives, and sweet and sour onions. Very tasty first courses: **ribollita**, **spelt soup** with Lucchese beans, **pappardelle pasta with meat ragù**, spicy spaghetti (specialty of the house) and, when in season, pasta with white or marzolo truffles. The mixed grill of meat is char-grilled in a wood-fired oven and the steaks are served on a chopping board as per tradition. Other main courses are **beef braised in Chianti**, **wild boar stew** or hare stew and **tripe alla contadina**, a local variation of tripe alla fiorentina. There is an extensive and well thought out selection of **cheeses** served with mostarda and fruit preserves.

The selection of Tuscan wines is excellent though the wines from the other regions are less inspiring. There is a notable range of spirits, Andrea's passion. It's a good idea to book in advance.

Colle Etrusco Salivolpi is a peaceful oasis close to Castellina, a medieval village famous for its quality wines. The stone building, typical of the Chianti region, is surrounded by a splendid garden where guests can chill out or swim in the pool on a hot summer's day. Rooms are basic but spacious and well-fitted, and boast wood paneled ceilings, antique furniture and wrought iron bedsteads. Bathrooms are also comfortable. Buffet breakfast is varied and plentiful. Thanks to its spacious and relaxing communal areas this is the ideal place to read, enjoy a good glass of Chianti or an aperitif. This is a family-run business managed in a reserved yet professional way and your hosts will be happy to advise you on both cultural and food and wine-related trails.

• 1 single and 18 double rooms, with bathroom, satellite TV • Prices: single and double 95 euros (33 euro supplement for extra bed), breakfast included • Credit cards: all except DC, Bancomat • Off-street parking. No pets allowed. Reception open 8 am-midnight • Bar, breakfast room. Lounge. Garden. Pool

🖑 At Via del Confine 4, in Orentano, Boutique della Carne Due Mila offers game and meat and game ragù.

CASTELLINA IN CHIANTI

VILLA CRISTINA

🔑Rooms
Via Fiorentina 34
Tel. 0577 741166
Fax 0577 742936
E-mail: info@villacristina.it
Internet: www.villacristina.it
Holidays vary

CASTELNUOVO BERARDENGA
Corsignano Vagliagli

CASA LUCIA

🔑Bed and breakfast
Località Corsignano 4-5
Tel. 0577 322508-288574-335 6665921
Fax 0577 322510
E-mail: info@casalucia.it
Internet: www.casalucia.it
Open all year

This beautiful Art Nouveau-style villa, built in the early 20th century and now a quiet, friendly locanda, is located in the heart of the Chianti Classico region, just half an hour's drive from Siena. Rooms are spacious and bright, with all modern comforts and rustic furniture. Views over the vineyards are stunning, especially from the tower where the suite is located. Breakfast is in tune with the surroundings: homemade cakes and jams and toasted Tuscan bread. Villa Cristina is a good base for those wishing to visit the Tuscan towns of artistic interest but also for those whose purpose is simply to enjoy the food and wine. Food lovers can dine at the Albergaccio restaurant which offers excellent Tuscan dishes and is located just opposite the villa.

• 4 double rooms and 1 suite, with bathroom, mini-bar, safe, TV • Prices: double room single use 57 euros, double 73 (20 euro supplement for extra bed), suite 77, breakfast included • Credit cards: MC, Visa, Bancomat • Off-street parking. Small pets allowed. Owners always reachable • Bar corner. Breakfast room. Garden, terrace

The buildings forming part of an old kiln were completely renovated a few years ago, and now house the lovely Casa Lucia B&B, run by Lucia Formisano assisted by her kind and attentive staff. Rooms and apartments, all quiet and spacious, are located in three separate buildings but enjoy pleasant communal areas fitted with comfortable sofas and antique rugs and furniture. Breakfast is continental and offers home-made cakes, fresh fruit and jams, with savory items available on request. Guests can also enjoy the garden. The B&B's location close to Siena and other places of interest makes it an even more enjoyable holiday destination.

• 12 double rooms, with bathroom, TV; 3 apartments (2-4 persons) with lounge, kitchenette • Prices: double room single use 64-73 euros, double 76-84 (18 euro supplement for extra bed); breakfast 4 euros per person • Credit cards: major ones, Bancomat • Off-street parking. Small pets allowed. Owners always reachable. • Bar corner, tavern. Breakfast room, lounges. Grounds, solarium

Castelnuovo di Garfagnana

49 KM NORTH-WEST OF LUCCA SS 45

Vecchio Mulino

Wine shop with snacks
Via Vittorio Emanuele 12
Tel. 0583 62192
Closed Monday
Open: 7.30am-8pm
Holidays: variable
Seating: 20
Prices: 13-20 euros, wine excluded
All major credit cards, Bancomat

It is a truly special place, this old wind-mill within the walls of the pretty village of Castelnuovo. Try to imagine a larder piled high in a quaintly haphazard fashion with all manner of goodies: cured meats, cheeses, bottles, jars of preserves and all the other treasures that Andrea Bertucci has picked up on his travels round Italy. On the left is the wine shop counter and snack bar area, and in the little free space not occupied by shelves and crates, there are a few tables laid with paper tablecloths. There is also another little room with walls covered in awards and photographs of celebrities. They don't do any hot food, but the standard of the products on offer guarantees satisfaction.

The portions and variety of the **cured meats** and **cheeses** is enough for a hearty lunch: you must try the biroldo from Garfagnana (a Slow Food Presidium), prosciutto Bazzone, giant mortadella from Bologna and the Apennine pecorino cheeses aged by dad Mauro. Mamma Rosa prepares the **vegetables preserved in oil**, the toppings for the croutons, the **savory pies**, and jams and desserts (**castagnaccio**, wild berry tarts) that, like the summer platters of crudités, can round off your sumptuous snack. Andreone takes it in turns with his sister Cinzia to slice the cured meats by hand, entertaining regulars with tales of his latest f & w discoveries and the projects aimed at promoting them.

Among the treasures of the Vecchio Mulino there is an excellent selection of wines from Tuscany and the rest of Italy. All the products – including spelt, beans, chestnuts, flours, pasta and traditional biscuits from the mountains around Lucca– are also available for purchase.

Castiglione d'Orcia
Poggio Rosa

64 KM SOUTHEAST OF SIENA ON SS 2 AND SP 323

Aiole

Holiday farm
Strada Provinciale della Grossola
Tel. and fax 0577 887454
E-mail: paolo&noella@agriturismo-aiole.com
Internet: www.agriturismo-aiole.com
Closed from mid-January to mid-February

This lovely agriturismo, run by Noella and Paolo Duma, is a 10-minute drive from the village of Castiglione d'Orcia in the Crete Senesi area. Rooms are in a typical Tuscan farmhouse with wooden beams, terracotta tile floors, wrought iron bedsteads and other rustic but elegant furniture and fittings (the apartment can sleep 8-12 guests and can be rented for 1,200-2,400 euros per week). Surrounded by a large garden with a swimming pool for adults and one for children as well as a playground, the farm is ideal for families as well as for guests wanting to visit towns of cultural interest, like Pienza, or sample wines like the local Brunello di Montalcino. Breakfast is served in a lounge and offers cured meats, cheeses, home-made cakes and jams, hot beverages and fruit juices. Dinner is available on request (20 euros).

• 6 double rooms, with bathroom • Prices: double room single use 50 euros, double 65 (15 euro supplement for extra bed) breakfast included • Credit cards: none • Off-street parking. No pets allowed. Owner always present • Restaurant (residents only). Breakfast room. Reading room, lounge. Garden. Children's playground, boules court, pools

Castiglione d'Orcia
Vivo d'Orcia

62 KM SOUTHEAST OF SIENA

Castiglione d'Orcia
Campiglia

51 KM SOUTHEAST OF SIENA ON SS 2, SS 323 AND SP 18

IL CASTAGNO 🐱🍷

Traditional osteria/wine shop
Via Amiata 129
Tel. 0577 873508
Closed Monday
Open: lunch and dinner
Holidays: in June and September
Seating: 50 + 50 outdoors
Prices: 17-20 euros
All major credit cards, Bancomat

I TRE RIONI

Rooms
Via Campotondo, 3-corner Via Fiume
Tel. 0577 872015
Fax 0577 872693
E-mail: itrerioni@aruba.it
Internet: www.itrerioni.com
Closed for 10 days in January and 10 in December

The village of Vivo d'Orcia, surrounded by beautiful beech and chestnut woods, lies on the Siena side of Monte Amiata. In the center of the village, in the shade of a big chestnut tree, lies this osteria. It is family run: Seriana works in the kitchen, while husband Rossano and son Niccolò are front of house. The food is hearty, genuine fare, served up in generous portions.

Following the classic crostini and cured meats, you can try **tortelli** filled with ricotta and spinach served with **ragù di locio** (goose), or veal or wild boar, or go for **pici** served **all'aglione** or with bread crumbs, **mushroom soup**, schiacciatelli with truffles and cep mushrooms in a cream sauce, or **zuppa del carbonaio**, a recently rediscovered traditional winter recipe, made with various herbs, pulses and sausages. The main courses revolve around meat stews (wild boar, venison, **lamb**). Also worth trying is the **cappone incapponato**, capon roasted with potatoes, onions and tomatoes, and **scottiglia alla vivaiola**, a hearty meat stew, sometimes also prepared with game. In season you will find cep mushrooms served fried, grilled or with meat.

To round off the meal there is an excellent **cheese board**, dominated by the **Pecorino** aged by Rossano in the dairy opposite.

There are around 300 wine labels in the cellar, all very reasonably priced. At weekends it's a good idea to book.

At Via delle Sorgenti 36, in **Bagno Vignoni** (4 km), a medieval village and spa resort near San Quirico d'Orcia, we recommend stopping off at Loggiato, a wine shop serving snacks (and hot food too).

Campiglia is a tiny early medieval village high up on Mount Amiata where it's a real pleasure to stroll through the alleyways and up and down the steps that lead to the bell tower, with its magnificent views of the valley below. In the village center you will find Stefano Arrivati's restaurant which offers typical local dishes (a three course meal costs 30 euros, excluding beverages). Above the restaurant are four cozy, well-furnished rooms with basic comforts. Guests can enjoy a rich breakfast of toast, homemade jams, cheeses (including fresh ricotta), local cured meats, fruit juices, coffee and cappuccino.

• 4 double rooms, with bathroom, minibar, TV, modem connection • Prices: double room single use 40 euros, double 60 (15 euro supplement for extra bed); breakfast 5 euros per person • Credit cards: all, Bancomat • Restaurant accessible to the mobility challenged. Free external parking alongside. Small pets allowed. Owners always reachable. • Restaurant. Reading room. Garden, terrace.

CASTIGLIONE DELLA PESCAIA
Tirli

CAVRIGLIA
Aia

LA LUNA

Trattoria/2-Star Hotel
Via del Podere 8
Tel. 0564 945854
Fax 0564 945906
E-mail: info@locanda-laluna.it
Internet: www.locanda-laluna.it
Open Friday, Saturday and Sunday in winter, every day in summer
Open: dinner, Sunday lunch and dinner
Holidays: January 6-February 6
Seating: 80 + 25 outdoors
Prices 35 euros, wine excluded
All credit cards except AE, Bancomat

On the hill (400 mt) overlooking the magnificent beaches around Punta Ala, Signora Lina, her son Emilio and daughter-in-law Tiziana run this Tuscan-style inn. The hotel is open all week and offers a breakfast buffet with homemade preserves, ciambellone ring cake, Tirli flat bread, and local prosciutto.
The cuisine is typically land-based, the ingredients mainly sourced from small local farmers. An unusual start to the meal is the **pappa al pomodoro,** as an alternative to the more traditional Tuscan croutons, and deer or wild boar carpaccio. To follow, **maltagliati pasta** in a wild boar sauce or **with pigeon**, **tagliolini with summer truffle**, ravioli in hare sauce, **acquacotta**, black cabbage, and ribollita soups. For your main course stuffed pigeon is recommended, **wild boar Maremma-style** or with apples and fried polenta, grilled **steak**, **shank of pork in red wine sauce**. Some excellent varieties of mushrooms grow in autumn in the surrounding woods, becoming part of the menu's ingredients. The puddings, all prepared by Tiziana, include pear turnovers, crème brulée flambé, ricotta cheesecake and panna cotta.
Very thorough wine selection, with many regional, Italian, and a few French labels.

• 7 doubles, en-suite, air conditioned, satellite tv • Prices: double single use 40, double 60-100 euros, breakfast included • 1 room with access to the mobility challenged. Outdoor public parking. Small pets welcome. Porter available from 8 to midnight • Restaurant. Breakfast room. Reading lounge, tv room. Garden, sunbed

LA LOCANDA CUCCUINI

Rooms
Località Aia
Tel. and fax 055 9166419
E-mail: cuccuini@val.it
Internet: www.locanda-cuccuini.com
Closed from beginning of January to mid-February

La Locanda Cuccuini is located in the vast hilly area between the Chianti Senese, the upper Valdano and the Pratomagno areas. After working all around the world and also managing a famous Italian restaurant in Paris, Stefano Cuccuini decided to return home and dedicate himself to a new business venture, this beautiful B&B in the Cavriglia countryside surrounded by olive groves. Rooms are spacious, bright and comfortable, fitted with basic furniture. In summer breakfast is served outside and offers many quality homemade items. You won't fail to be impressed by Stefano and Anna Maria's kindness and hospitality. The restaurant offers traditional Tuscan dishes with the addition of some more elaborate creations (conveniently priced at 20-23 euros, wine excluded, half board 48 euros).

• 8 double rooms, with bathroom, TV (on request) • Prices: double room single use 45 euros, double 55 (18 euro supplement for extra bed); breakfast 5 euros per person • Credit cards: Visa, Bancomat • 1 room designed for use by the mobility challenged. Off-street parking. Small pets allowed. Reception open from 8 am to 11 pm • Restaurant. Garden, terrace

CECINA
San Pietro in Palazzi

LA CINQUANTINA

Restaurant-wine shop
Villa Guerrazzi-Località La Cinquantina
Tel. 0586 669004
Closed Tuesday and Wednesday for lunch, never in summer
Open: lunch and dinner
Holidays: none
Seating: 120 +120 outdoors
Prices: 32-35 euros, wine excluded
All credit cards, Bancomat

The latest addition to this establishment is a basement wine bar that serves reasonably priced cured meats, cheeses and a few hot dishes in the evenings; it also offers a three-course menu on Wednesday and four courses on Thursday, including wine and coffee, for 18 and 24 euros respectively. In the restaurant the set menu costs 30 euros, while choosing à la carte will cost you more. The Tirreno Promo Tour consortium, which manages the catering services in the Villa Guerrazzi complex and organizes a range of events, relies on the talents of chef Umberto Creatini, a dedicated foodie who remains faithful to the traditions of the Alta Maremma area.
You can start with **pelamyd** (a cheap but delicious member of the tuna family from this part of the Tyrrhenian Sea), seafood crudités (prawns, scampi and oysters) or **cured meats** and farm vegetables preserved in oil or with an **inzimino** vegetable sauce. As a first course, try the excellent **tortelloni with country ragù** or **zuppa di fosso** (a soup made with eel, snails, fresh water shrimp – now farmed – frogs' legs and meadow herbs). Or **gnocchi with razor clams**, **spaghetti with anchovies** or 'zighe' clams, or linguine with clams. The traditional **cacciucco** fish stew is a meal in itself. Second courses include rare **wild boar head alla castagnetana**, **stoccafisso alla livornese**, and tuna tagliata with vegetables. Then there's a good range of Italian cheeses. All the desserts are worth sampling.
The wine list focuses on labels from the Etruscan coast (Bolgheri, Montescudaio, Val di Cornia) and Tuscany in general, though it also includes good bottles from Italy and abroad.

CERRETO GUIDI
Stabbia

MUSIGNANO

Holiday farm
Via Poggio Tond, 12
Tel. 0571 957220-349 4085019-349 6446966
Fax 0571 957220
E-mail: agriturismo@musignano.it
Internet: www.musignano.it
Open all year

The agriturismo is located on a small hill not far from the center of Stabbia, easily reachable from Florence. After a five-minute drive along a quiet road you come to the well-restored, typical Tuscan rural building. Rooms are fitted with rustic furniture and apartments have a well-equipped kitchen. For breakfast you'll be able to enjoy hot beverages and sweet fare produced and sold by Alessandro and Roberta Borgiol's farm. Guests can relax and enjoy the fresh air under the gazebo in the garden or visit the Fucecchio oasis, one of the region's most important nature reserves.

• 4 double rooms, with bathroom, minibar, TV; 6 apartments (3-6 persons) with kitchen • Prices: double room single or double usey 50 euros, apartment 130-150; breakfast 5 euros per person • Credit cards: all, Bancomat • 1 room and 1 apartment accessible to the mobility challenged. Off-street parking. No pets allowed. Owners always present • Recreation room with reading area. Garden, solarium. Pool

CERTALDO
Castello

CHIANCIANO TERME

44 KM SOUTHWEST OF FLORENCE

80 KM SOUTHEAST OF SIENA ON SS 146

OSTERIA DEL VICARIO

PALAZZO BANDINO

🔑 Bed and breakfast
Via Rivellino 3
Tel. 0571 668228-668676
Fax 0571 668228
E-mail: info@osteriadelvicario.it
Internet: www.osteriadelvicario.it
Holidays vary

🔑 Holiday farm
Strada Stiglianese 3
Tel. 0578 61199
Fax 0578 654456
E-mail: gabrielevaleriani@libero.it
Internet: www.valerianigroup.com
Closed from January 7 to March 1

Located in the quiet medieval village (not open to traffic) where Boccaccio lived and was probably born, close to the Palazzo del Vicariato, built over the ruins of an ancient castle, is the 13th-century monastery which houses the Osteria del Vicario. This restaurant with accommodation has been in operation for 50 years and is enjoyable for its location and professional management. Rooms are situated in the old monks' cells and are elegantly fitted and furnished. Common areas are also well turned out and open onto a romantic cloister where the restaurant tables are set in summer (prevalently creative cuisine priced at 40 euros, wine excluded). Breakfast offers sweet items (croissants, jams, fruit juices), while savory fare is available on request.

• 4 double rooms, with bathroom, TV • Prices: double room single use 60 euros, double 90 (20 euro supplement for extra bed), breakfast included • Credit cards: all, Bancomat • Public parking in the immediate vicinity. Small pets allowed. Reception open 7am-midnight. • Restaurant. Reading room, lounge. Outside space, garden, terrace

Located in the hills of Valdichiana, not far from Chianciano Spa and towards Chiusi, is the estate belonging to the Valeriani family, comprising a manor house and surrounding buildings and reachable by an unmade road. Guestrooms and apartments have all modern comforts and are fitted with rustic furniture in arte povera style. Buffet breakfast offers yogurt, toast, cakes, their own honey (they also produce the oil and wine for the restaurant), cured meats and cheeses. Gabriele, who lives nearby, will be happy to provide you with information about places to visit in the area.

• 4 double rooms, with bathroom, minibar, satellite TV, some with terrace or garden; 9 apartments, with 1-2 bedrooms, lounge, kitchen • Prices: double room single use 68-78 euros, apartments 500-800 euros per week; breakfast 6 euros per person • Credit cards: major ones, Bancomat • Off-street parking. Small pets allowed. Reception open from 8 am to 8 pm, owners always reachable • Restaurant. Reading and TV room, Internet point. Conference room. Garden. Pool

77 KM SOUTHEAST OF SIENA ON SS 326

77 KM SOUTHEAST OF SIENA EXIT A 1 OR SS 326

LA CASA TOSCANA

LA SOLITA ZUPPA

Rooms
Via Baldetti 37
Tel. 0578 222227
Fax 0578 223812
E-mail: casatoscana@libero.it
Internet: www.valerianigroup.com
Open all year

Trattoria
Via Porsenna 21
Tel. 0578 21006
Closed Tuesday
Open: lunch and dinner
Holidays: January 10-March 10
Seating: 40
Prices: 28-32 euros, wine excluded
All credit cards, Bancomat

Located between the town hall and church of San Francesco is the late 18th-century building which houses this elegant locanda. Particularly attractive features are the beautiful stone stairway, airy entrance hall, rooms with wooden beams and coffered ceilings fitted with good quality handcrafted furniture and wrought iron bedsteads. Some rooms have their own courtyard. Buffet breakfast is included in the price (higher rates apply in peak season: New Year's Eve, Easter and in August-September) and offers tea, coffee, yoghurt, toast, cakes, cured meats and cheeses. This ancient Etruscan capital is an important road and railway junction and is an ideal base for those wanting to visit southern Tuscany and Umbria.

•1 single, 4 double and 1 triple rooms, with bathroom, mini-bar, satellite TV • Prices: single 80-115 euros, double 110-120, triple 120-135, breakfast included • Credit cards: CartaSi, MC, Visa, Bancomat • meter parking in immediate vicinity, free parking 300 meters away. Small pets allowed. Reception open 8am-8pm, owners always reachable. • Breakfast room. Reading and TV room, Internet point. Terrace

Here it's the owner Roberto Paccheri who will select the food and wines for you. Some people don't care for this type of service because it runs counter to the spirit of an osteria, where you can usually order just one course if you wish. However, this place is very attractive, well-appointed and inviting, and the food prepared by Luana, Robert's wife, is truly traditional, though a little lighter on cooking times and sauces.
The range of antipasti includes **crostini** with liver and spleen, **Cinta Senese cured meats**, **Cacio** (fresh Pecorino from Pienza) **with pears**, **baccalà alla fiorentina**, lamb offal, **beef tongue in piquant green sauce** and, in summer, cold ribollita soup. There are at least 15 different ingredients used for the **soups**, the house specialty, which vary according to the whims of the chef and the season: onions, beans, Tuscan kale, cauliflower, egg plant, potatoes, leeks, zucchini, peas, chickpeas, lentils, spelt, barley, mushrooms and chestnuts. First courses, made with home-made pasta, include **pici all'aglione** or with nana (duck), **spelt tagliatelle with peppers** or cep mushrooms, **tagliolini in ginger sauce**, **gnudini**, potato gnocchetti with herbs, and lasagne with wild boar ragù. Main courses include **Chianina beef** roasted in a wood-fired oven, **scottiglia mixed meat stew**, **agnello al buglione** (lamb stew), jugged wild boar, pork with apples, **tripe** alla fiorentina, **duck with prunes**, spicy spatchcock and rabbit with peppers. There's a good selection of raw milk cheeses and home-made dessert.

CIVITELLA IN VAL DI CHIANA

CIVITELLA IN VAL DI CHIANA

11 KM SOUTHWEST OF AREZZO

11 KM SOUTHWEST OF AREZZO

L'ANTICO BORGO

Trattoria with room
Via di Mezzo 35
Tel. 0575 448160
Closed Tuesday
Open: lunch and dinner
Holidays: none
Seating: 35
Price: 26-30 euros, wine excluded
Credit cards: all except AE

L'ANTICO BORGO

Bed and breakfast
Piazza Don Lazzeri 22
Tel. 0575 448160-339 7951674
E-mail: info@antborgo.it
Internet: www.antborgo.it
Open all year round

In the medieval village of Civitella, overlooking the Valdichiana and the Valdarno, this trattoria is housed in a beautifully restructured old oil mill which still conserves the original olive grindstone. The owners, Francesco Sabbadini and Vito Andrea Molaro, serve dishes that enhance local produce with all the savoir faire the former has picked up working at the best restaurants in Tuscany. Here you can either eat à la carte or choose one of two tasting menus (28 euros each): dishes change every two months.

Antipasti include cured loin of pork with extra virgin olive oil, raisins and walnuts, crostone with Pecorino, walnuts and honey and a classic mixed board of cured Cinta Senese pork: Firsts: **trippa in bianco** (without tomato), home-made **pici con sugo di nana** (duck sauce), cornflour **gnocchi with gravy and sausage**, fusilli with vegetables and **soups**. Second courses: roulade of rabbit with herbs and mushrooms, **frittata con gli zoccoli** (sliced salty bacon), beef tagliata with potatoes and rosemary sauce, **chine of pork with Chianti** and **sweet and sour hare**. When available from the butcher's, it's also possible to order a steak of certified Chianina beef (50 euros per kilo). Close with a platter of sheep and goat cheese and/or chocolate cake or baked cream.

The wine list offers a good choice of Tuscan labels plus a few distinguished 'outsiders'. With dessert, passito wine is served by the glass.

L'Antico Borgo is a pleasant B&B in a 19th-century building incorporated in an older complex, part of the Civitella town walls. The spacious, bright rooms are fitted out with furniture by local artisans and decorated with beautifully chosen fabrics with an eye to effective color combinations. The buffet breakfast is made by the owner, Maria Grazia, and served either in a special room (which also doubles as a small conference room) or in bedrooms. It includes home-baked cakes and cookies, sandwiches, honey and jam, plus al the classic hot beverages.

• 4 double rooms and 1 suite, with bathroom, mini-bar, satellite TV, some with balconies; 1 apartment with 2 rooms, 2 bathrooms, living room, kitchenette, terrace • Prices: double single use 90 euros, double 105 euros, suite 115 euros, apartment 140 euros, breakfast included • Credit cards: Visa, Mastercard, Bancomat • Free public parking. Small pets allowed. Owners available 9am-10pm • Restaurant. Breakfast room, reading room

CORTONA

CORTONA

28 KM SOUTH OF AREZZO SS 71

28 KM SOUTH OF AREZZO SS 71

OSTERIA DEL TEATRO

 Recently opened Osteria
Via Maffei 2
Tel. 0575 630556
Closed Wednesday
Open: lunch and dinner
Holidays: two weeks in November
Seating: 70 + 10 outdoors
Prices: 30-35 euros, wine excluded
All credit cards

TAVERNA PANE VINO

Wine shop with food
Piazza Signorelli 27
Tel. 0575 631010
Closed Monday
Open: lunch and dinner, January-Easter only for dinner
Holidays: January
Seating: 30 + 50 outdoors
Prices: 19-27 euros, wine excluded
All major credit cards, Bancomat

This elegant, inviting osteria is situated in a 16th century building, in the historic downtown, not far from the Signorelli theater. Owner Emiliano Rossi, with the help of the vivacious Ylenia, offers flavorsome, aromatic local specialties.
Both the Tuscan antipasti, with classic cured meats and local cheeses, **black bread crostini** and tomato crostini, and the house antipasti, with cured meats, vegetable omelets, spelt salad, truffle-flavored ricotta flan and fried flowers, are good. The traditional soups are good too: **acquacotta**, **ribollita**, **spelt and cep mushroom soup**. If you prefer filled pasta, you can choose from ravioli filled with zucchini and zucchini flowers, green tortellini with cream of truffle, potato gnocchi served with cep mushrooms and truffle or duck sauce and dill, or Savoy cabbage cappelletti in a truffle sauce. When in season, it's worth trying **pappardelle with hare sauce**. To continue, **Chianina fillet** cooked in various ways, duck breast with black olives, rosemary lamb chops, guinea fowl with cep mushrooms, rabbit chasseur, or **wild boar stew with polenta**. Side-dishes include tasty **zolfini beans**, seasonal vegetable flans, char-grilled vegetables or spinach. The menu ends with cantucci and Vin Santo, chestnut and rosemary pastries, plums cooked in Sangiovese and raisins, pears with melted chocolate and in summer semifreddo.
The wine list carries many labels from Tuscany and other regions, at good value for money.

Cortona is a town with a considerable history, and its architecture bears traces of its Etruscan, Roman, Medieval and Renaissance past. The osteria owned by Debora and Arnaldo Rossi, located in the cellars of an old building, lies in the historic downtown, in front of the Signorelli theater. Over the years Arnaldo has built up a monumental wine list, paying special attention to high quality small producers. A varying selection of wines is served by the glass; and on Thursday, during the cooler seasons, they organize wine tasting sessions featuring great vintages and important labels.
You can start with pinzimonio, or bruschetta with garlic and extravirgin olive oil, tomato, lardo di Colonnata, pecorino and truffle cream, or Tuscan kale, or **local cured meats**: lardo di Colonnata, capocollo, gota, prosciutto and Cinta Senese salami. Carpaccio of Chianina beef or Chianina tartare can be served as antipasti or as a main course. First courses include a good **chickpea and spelt soup**, or spelt and cep mushroom soup, **ribollita** and **pappa al pomodoro**. For a while now there has been a hot second course on the menu, that changes weekly, usually featuring Chianina beef: fillet cooked in lardo, braised meat, or **stew with potatoes**. The raw milk goat and sheep cheeses from different areas, aged for different lengths of time, are painstakingly selected by Arnaldo and often include some authentic rarities, with special attention to small producers from Valdichiana.
The desserts are truly delicious: seasonal fruit pies, cantucci, chocolate cake and various different kinds of chocolate made by a famous local artisan, to accompany with excellent distilled passito wines and Vin Santo.

CUTIGLIANO

DA FAGIOLINO

☞—○Rooms
Via Carega 1
Tel. 0573 68014
Fax 0573 68210
E-mail: luigiinnocenti@tiscali.it
Internet: www.dafagiolino.it
Closed in November

Following a quiet side-road on the way to Abetone, through the woods in the Apennines around Pistoia, you come to the picturesque medieval village of Cutigliano. An ancient building, now restored, houses the Innocenti family's trattoria with accommodation – a comfortable base for anyone wanting to enjoy the various activities available in the area: excursions, trekking, mountain-biking, horse-riding, fishing, paragliding and year-round skiing. Rooms are comfortable and fitted with modern furniture. Buffet breakfast offers hot and cold beverages, home-made bread, jams, yoghurt, cakes, fruit juices, prosciutto and cheeses. For those wanting a change from the food served in the trattoria (local cuisine, 20-35 euros, wine excluded, 10% discount for residents), the osteria next door serves good wine, cured meats, cheeses and traditional Tuscan dishes.

• 4 double, triple or four-bed rooms, with bathroom, mini-bar, TV, modem connection • Prices: double room single use 55 euros, double 75, triple 110, four-bed 135, breakfast included • Credit cards: all, Bancomat • Public parking in immediate vicinity. Small pets allowed. Owners always reachable • Bar, restaurant

CUTIGLIANO
Piano degli Ontani

FATTORIA LA PIASTRA

◁▷Holiday farm
Località La Casetta 19
Tel. 0573 68443
Open: lunch and dinner, October and January-April only Saturday and Sunday for lunch
Holidays: November 1-December 20
Seating: 40 + 50 outdoors
Prices: 25 euros
All credit cards

Deep in the lush countryside of the Apennines, this farm offers accommodation if you decide to stay overnight (there are three bedrooms and three apartments) and the surrounding mountains and woodlands are great for trekking or bike rides. You need to book in advance, especially in off-peak seasons, to be sure to sample the long list of specialties, prepared by signora Licia using meat from estate-reared livestock and produce from the farm and surrounding woodlands.
The menu usually opens with the typical Tuscan antipasti of croutons and cured meats, but also with mini omelets, marinated vegetables and mushrooms. First courses include **Tuscan bread and vegetable soup** (served with a drop of organic extra virgin olive oil from the Pistoia hills), **pasta and beans**, **maccheroni** made with marzolo corn (a local variety cultivated on the farm) with ragù, **bread and ricotta gnocchetti** and green ravioli with a ricotta and nettle filling. In the hunting season there are some wonderful pappardelle with wild boar or venison sauce. The **meats** are **roasted** or char-grilled and served with potatoes and seasonal vegetables. A good way to finish off is to sample a taste of the cheese board, which includes the **raw milk Pecorino** from the Pistoia mountains (a Slow Food Presidium), or one off the excellent home-baked cakes that vary according to season.
As for wine, there's a small selection of labels, and the house wine is a respectable Chianti from the Certaldo area.

40 KM NORTHWEST OF PISTOIA SS 66

36 KM NORTHWEST OF PISTOIA ON SS 12

L'OSTERIA

ROMA

Traditional osteria
Via Roma 6
Tel. 0573 68272
Closed Monday and Tuesday for lunch
Open: lunch and dinner
Holidays: January 7-21
Seating: 30
Prices: 25-27 euros, wine excluded
All credit cards

2-Star Hotel
Via Pacioni 43
Tel. and fax 0573 68121
E-mail: info@pensioneroma.it
Internet: www.pensioneroma.it
Open all year

It's really worth coming up here (just a few kilometers from Abetone) and getting lost among the beautifully restored medieval houses of Cutigliano. The osteria owned by Luigi Ranieri is just round the corner from the town hall. The dining room is well kept and inviting, and the walls are adorned with pictures of Zeno Colò (the much-loved ski champion) and a collection of mountain tools and utensils. The food benefits from the painstaking care that Luigi puts into selecting his ingredients every day.

In **mushroom** season he'll show you his pickings and recommend the best way to eat them: as antipasti, raw or on crostini, in soups, with pasta, in risotto, with a fillet steak or tagliata all'alpina, sautéed as a side-dish or, best of all, fried. Another delicacy is local **Fario trout**, which Luigi offers in various versions. Other dishes include **tortelli** filled with **herbs and ricotta**, **kid a scottadito**, **roast meatloaf**, **baccalà in sauce with leeks**, and **tripe** alla fiorentina. When in season, there's excellent **game** (venison, roe deer and wild boar). The cheeses rightly include **raw milk Pecorino** (a Slow Food Presidium) aged for various lengths of time. The menu ends with home-made tarts and, in summer, with ice-creams accompanied with wild berries.

The cellar offers a good selection of national labels, predominantly reds. Markup is average.

This small family-run hotel/restaurant located close to the cableway leading up to the Doganaccia ski slopes (open all year round) and the Croce Arcana peak is a comfortable place and offers a warm, elegant atmosphere. Rooms are tastefully furnished and common areas are welcoming and smart. Breakfast consists of coffee, tea, cocoa, home-baked bread, jams, honey and cereals. In the restaurant, thehostess Cristina Nesti offers traditional local dishes (half board for two people sharing 45-60 euros, full board 55-67 euros per person). Many activities are available for guests: gastronomic and cultural weekends, skiing holidays and various courses. Worth visiting in Rivoreta, about 10 kilometers away, is the Museo della Gente (People's Museum) dell'Appennino Pistoiese and the Torri di Popiglio archeological site. The train station (Pracchia) is 25 kilometers away.

• 1 single and 8 double rooms, with bathroom, TV • Prices: single 46-58 euros, double 60-74, breakfast included • Credit cards: all, Bancomat • Public parking next door, garage for motorbikes and bicycles. Small pets accepted. Reception open 7.30am-11.30pm. • Bar. Restaurant (for residents only). Reading room, TV room. Garden, terrace

CUTIGLIANO
Pianosinatico

41 KM NORTHWEST OF PISTOIA

SILVIO
LA STORIA A TAVOLA
🍲 Restaurant
Via Brennero 181-183
Tel. 0573 629204
Closed: Tuesday
Open: lunch and dinner
Holidays: 15 days in May, 15 in October
Seating: 40
Prices: 25-28 euros, wine excluded
All major credit cards, Bancomat

Pianosinatico is a little village perched on the mountainside along the road up to the Abetone pass. The restaurant is in the center. Here regulars know they can count on the experience and dedication of the chef, Silvio Zanni, who manages the restaurant with Nadia, Lidia and Andrea. There are two plain, tastefully decorated dining rooms, and the menu varies with the seasons.

To start with you can choose from **crostini with mushrooms** (when in season), knuckle of beef with oil and balsamic vinegar, carpaccio of cured pork tenderloin, or new potatoes with a truffle sauce. Enticing first courses include: ravioli filled with pecorino and pear, **tortelli del Melo** (named for a nearby village) made from marzolo corn flour, sheep ricotta from the Pistoia Mountains and Swiss chard, served with melted butter and wild mint, **spaghetti with onion sauce** (one of Silvio's legendary recipes), potato gnocchi with San Miniato truffle, **dormienti mushroom soup** (a local variety of mushroom found in spring) and **pancotto** with mushrooms. To follow there is a good beef tagliata, served with mushrooms or truffle, escalopes with coriander and steak with pink peppercorns. In season, they offer an entire menu based on local mushrooms. To finish, Slow Food Presidia **raw milk Pecorino cheeses** aged for different periods, custard and wild berry tarts, chestnuts au naturel with chocolate sauce and cream and homemade strudel.

Andrea's wine list is extensive and commendable and he'll recommend suitable accompaniments.

ELBA
Marciana Marina

FERRY FROM PIOMBINO THEN 24 KM FROM PORTOFERRAIO

AFFRICHELLA
🍲 Restaurant
Via Santa Chiara 7
Tel. 0565 996844
Closed Wednesday, 15-10/31-01
open Friday and Saturday
Open: evenings only
Holidays: February-Easter
Seating: 30 + 50 outdoors
Prices: 33-35 euros, wine excluded
All major credit cards

Marciana Marina remains one of the most characteristic spots on Elba. The church piazza opens up in front of the quay where fishermen land in their small boats and where you can buy very fresh fish. Continuing right you find Fulvio and Fiorella's restaurant, which has been a benchmark for seafood for 25 years. Here everything depends on the day's catch in the magnificent sea surrounding the island.

During our last visit we ate antipasti comprising **octopus salad**, cauliflower and shrimp flan with cuttlefish ink sauce, fish crouton, bianchetti cooked with sage; **linguine alla granseola** (crab) and **maltagliati al capone (capon)**; **stuffed mussels** and lastly, crema alla catalana. But there's a much wider choice and it varies continuously depending on the season and the day's catch. For antipasti, apart from the mixed platter, there's smoked swordfish, fish salad and **stuffed anchovies**. For firsts, spaghetti with clams, **tagliolini with shrimp**, **stringoli with lobster**, gnocchi al pesto and vegetable minestrone. There's also a wide choice for your main course: **stuffed squid**, oven-baked fish of the day, grilled fish platter, **cuttlefish with chard**, **shellfish soup**, grilled prawns, **angler fish all'isolana**, and for those who can't go without meat, tagliata or filet steak. To finish off, home-made puddings: tarte tatin, semifreddo with pine nuts, panna cotta.

There's a good choice of regional and other Italian wines, even though the list isn't always up to date and service tends to be, let's say, rather unorthodox. Considering the location, prices are fair, although expect to pay more if you order dishes made with shellfish.

ELBA
Rio Marina

DA ORESTE ALLA STREGA

🍲 Restaurant
Piazza Vittorio Emanuele 6
Tel. 0565 962211
Closed Tuesday, never in summer
Open, lunch and dinner
Holidays: January 10-March 10
Seating: 20 + 60 outdoors
Prices: 30-32 euros, wine excluded
All major credit cards

When Rio Marina was an important mining center this place stocked food and served as a store for miners. The owner at that time was the grandfather of Oreste Cecchini, who has been running the place since 1973. He turned it into a restaurant serving simple dishes based on local cuisine right from the start. With time, while remaining true to its origins, the cuisine has become more interesting and varied thanks to Claudio, the owner's son, who after attending hotel school and learning the trade in important Italian restaurants, brought passion and competence to the kitchen.

The place has two nicely furnished rooms and Flavio is responsible for the service. Among the antipasti we can recommend the **tonnina alla riese** (old-style fisherman's food), **palamita sott'olio**, anchovies marinated in lemon, cuttlefish in sweet and sour sauce, **Elba-style warm octopus**. For firsts: spaghetti of the chef, **linguine with fish roe and clams**, risotto with cuttlefish ink sauce, gnocchetti with octopus sauce, spaghetti with anchovies spiced with wild fennel. Among the main courses **fried** puntine, mixed fish platter, squid, octopus with potatoes, **sburrita di baccalà**, stoccafisso alla riese, **squid alla diavola** or oven-baked with potatoes, oven-baked fish of the day.

Homemade puddings feature **schiaccia briaca** and various others to get your spoon into. The wine list is fine for the food provided, the bread is homemade. From June to September Oreste never closes.

ELBA
Porto Azzurro

LA BOTTE GAIA

🍲 Osteria
Viale Europa 5-7
Tel. 0565 95607
Closed Monday never in summer
Open: lunch and dinner
Holidays: January 10-March 10
Seating: 40 + 20 outdoors
Prices: 30-35 euros, wine excluded
All major credit cards except AE

La Botte Gaia is just a few meters from Porto Azzurro's central piazza, pedestrian precinct and parking facilities, in an old building that was once part of a church before, in the early 1900's, being converted into a cellar in which wine to be shipped to Liguria was stored. Riccardo and Antonella Nelli, after earlier careers in tourism, took over the place and restructured it. They've created an osteria furnished with antiques, with a nice bar counter where they serve excellent aperitifs, two small dining rooms and a garden for eating outside in summer.

Antonella runs the kitchen and uses mostly local products, especially fish from the day's catch; Riccardo takes care of the tables and wines. To start with there's a cured meat board (the selection, as for the cheeses, is excellent), **palamita sott'olio** with boiled onions and beans, octopus salad. Worth trying among the firsts, **black tagliolini with seafood ragù**, maltagliati with Medici ragù, tondarelli with rocket, Pachino tomatoes and smoked ricotta cheese or octopus, **fresh pasta with anchovies**, gnocchetti with octopus sauce. You can continue with angler fish with artichokes, **pastry-wrapped tuna fillet** spiced with herbs, oven-baked fish of the day with vegetables, fried anchovies, palamita, **Elba-style fish soup**, **stockfish with potatoes**; for 'carnovires', beef stew with vegetables and **Elba-style tripe**.

Desserts: homemade **schiaccia briaca**, semifreddo al limoncello, chocolate flan, cantucci all'Aleatico. The wine list matches the cuisine.

ELBA
Portoferraio

LA CARRETTA

🍲 Restaurant-pizzeria
Località Magazzini 92
Tel. 0565 933223
Closed Wednesday, never in summer
Open, only evenings
Holidays: mid-October to mid-January
Seating: 80 + 50 outdoors
Prices: 25-30 euros, wine excluded
All major credit cards

The restaurant is on the road leading from Portoferraio to Bagnaia. Before the tourist invasion this was part of the countryside and used to produce fruit, vegetables and wine. Farmers lived in the 'magazzini' (this explains the name of the area), rural homes now mostly transformed into villas. In 1980 Roberto and Giovanna Olivari opened a pizzeria in an old farmhouse, but then, as enthusiasts of quality cuisine, they gradually introduced Elba dishes and soon became a benchmark for those who appreciated traditional recipes.
Roberto is front of house with his children, Pietro and Marta, assisted by Antonio, while Marcella runs the kitchen and makes the desserts. Apart from bruschetta with tomato and basil, some of the other very pleasant antipasti are **Elba-style polpetti affogati**, a mixed seafood platter and **island-style mussels**. First courses are also seafood-based: **spaghetti with rock-fish sauce**, **gnocchetti with gurnard**, black linguine with frog-fish sauce, spaghetti with anchovies; but also risotto with wild chicory and sausage and Elba vegetable soup. Among the main course dishes, **baccalà in sweet and sour sauce**, stockfish all'elbana, **inzimino of squid and chard**, oven-baked fish of the day with vegetables. Alternatively there's barbecued meat and a wide range of pizzas baked in a wood-fired oven.
The trolley of home-made desserts features apple tart with ice cream, and **cantuccini con l'Aleatico**. A good wine list offers local and other Italian labels. Dessert wines are served by the glass.

ELBA
Marciana Castello

OSTERIA DEL NOCE

🍲 Trattoria
Via della Madonna 27
Tel. 0565 901284
No weekday closing
Open: lunch and dinner
Holidays: from October to March
Seating: 30 + 60 outdoors
Prices: 30-35 euros, wine excluded
All credit cards except DC, Bancomat

On the western side of Elba at the foot of Mount Capanne is Marciana, one the oldest inhabited spots on the island. Near the Pisan fortress and municipal museum, Alberto Capelio and Rita Chiappara run this nice little trattoria, with just a few tables inside and also outside on a flowery terrace under the shade of a walnut tree, to which the name on the sign alludes. The cuisine is almost entirely based on seafood and a blend of and tribute to combined Ligurian and Elba traditions.
The menu depends on sea conditions and availability in the market, and as it changes often daily dishes are written up on a blackboard. To open there may be **pilchards in scabeccio** (fried with onions and pine nuts then soused in vinegar), **anchovies marinated with lemon**, sauté of mussels, octopus salad with potatoes and beans and antipasto al leudo (tomatoes and mosciame), named after an old type of Ligurian sailboat. Then, linguine with fish ragù, **trofie all'arsillo** (homemade pasta with a mixed seafood condiment), **linguine con sconcigli** (murex) or patelle (other small mollusks), **testaroli with clams and vegetables**, mussels and bean soup. For those who prefer an alternative to fish, Ligurian corzetti in walnut sauce. For your main course, **pesce capone** or **palamita all'elbana** (with tomatoes, potatoes and wild fennel), **stuffed squid** or mussels, **fried fish platter**, hake with shallots and onion grass, excellent **anchovies cooked Ligurian style**, grilled tuna or swordfish steak, and oven-baked fish of the day. Puddings, like the bread, are home-made: try the walnut cake.
The wine list offers quite a good selection of above all Tuscan and Ligurian wines.

ELBA
Capoliveri

FIESOLE
Pian di San Bartolo

FERRY FROM PIOMBINO + 17 KM FROM PORTOFERRAIO

5 KM NORTHEAST OF FLORENCE

SUMMERTIME

☞Restaurant
Via Roma 56
Tel. 0565 935180
No weekday closing
Open: lunch and dinner
Holidays: November 5-March 31
Seating: 30 + 20 outdoors
Prices: 30-35 euros, wine excluded
All major credit cards, Bancomat

TREMOTO

☞Trattoria
Via Bolognese 16
Tel. 055 401108
Closed Wednesday
Open: only for lunch
Holidays: August
Seating: 50
Prices: 25 euros, wine excluded
All credit cards, Bancomat

Maurizio Tosi opened this small restaurant, after various experiences in Italy, Europe and North America, in Capoliveri, a medieval village in the southwest corner of the island. Like most other places on Elba it's a fish restaurant, but there are also well prepared meat dishes. Maurizio has a good eye for ingredients and always manages to get hold of very fresh fish, which Tiziana Olivares then cooks according to island tradition. While the menu depends on what's available in the market, your obliginh host will almost always be able to offer you various combinations of marinated fish for antipasti, a seafood carpaccio and a **fried bread and fish platter**. Among the more frequent first courses, **linguine with shellfish, strozzapreti with local squid**, fidelini with anchovies, potato gnocchi alla Margherita, al cacio e pepe, with vegetables and smoked ricotta cheese, or with tomato and basil sauce. Among the main courses, **grilled sardines and anchovies and vegetables, guazzetto all'elbana**, fried or **stuffed anchovies**, tuna steak cooked with citrus fruit or poppy seeds, **swordfish** with vegetables. Fish from the day's catch is mainly cooked in the oven or grilled. You can round off the meal with homemade desserts: semifreddo all'amaretto, with pine nuts or chocolate, ricotta mousse with jam, cantucci with Aleatico or Moscato dell'Elba.
The wine list contains a good number of sound local and other Italian labels, some also served by the glass.

Equidistant between Florence and the center of Fiesole along the old road to Bologna (a road that offers some magnificent views), this spartanly furnished trattoria right next to a grocers transmits the idea of a place where you can have a meal that will satisfy even the most demanding palates without emptying your wallet. You enter from the bar-store where the typical local products on show on the large counter increase your desire to sit down at one of the tables in the back room to taste dishes prepared in a pleasant, unpretentious manner by the Fabiani family.
The menu never changes, opening with the classic Tuscan antipasti of salami, **finocchiona**, raw ham and **crostini with liver pâté** or tomato or, when in season, mushrooms. Among the first courses, tortelli al ragù, **pappardelle with wild boar sauce**, penne alla carrettiera, ravioli with butter and sage or a tasty **pasta and beans**. For seconds there's a really delicious **tripe alla fiorentina, arista al forno**, roast beef, a classic **steak** and a dish that may not be typical but certainly shouldn't be missed – roast suckling pig with crunchy crackling. Portions are very generous and don't leave much room for other treats, even though it seems a crime to give the puddings a miss: **blackberry tart** (fabulous) or apricot tart, grandma's cake, a refreshing zuccotto and the ever-present cantuccini of Prato biscuits served with Vin Santo.
There isn't a wine list although you'll spy some interesting, reasonably priced Tuscan labels (and some non-Tuscan ones too) on the shelves of the store. And in addition there's a more than acceptable house wine.

AL TRANVAI

Trattoria
Piazza Torquato Tasso 14 R
Tel. 055 225197
Closed Saturday and Sunday
Open: lunch and dinner
Holidays: August
Seating: 50 + 15 outdoors
Prices: 22-25 euros, wine excluded
All credit cards

DA BURDE

Trattoria
Via Pistoiese 6 R-154 N
Tel. 055 317206
Closed Sunday
Open: lunch, dinner if you book
Holidays: variable
Seating: 120 + 30 outdoors
Prices: 25-30 euros, wine excluded
All credit cards, Bancomat

This small, pleasant trattoria is in the working-class quarter of San Frediano, celebrated in the books of Vasco Pratolini, and local artisans still come to eat here. Elbow to elbow at tables with paper tablecloths and paper napkins, you'll taste really traditional Tuscan dishes.

The meal starts with crostini and cured meats. To follow, classic **ribollita** and **pappa al pomodoro**, tortelloni with ragù, taglierini with asparagus, orecchiette with tomato and ricotta, tagliolini with hot spicy tomato sauce, tagliatelle with vegetables, rigatoni all'arrabbiata. The main courses are more traditional with a predominance of offal: **lampredotto (tripe)** or boiled beef with green sauce, **tripe alla fiorentina** and, sometimes, budellina in umido (stewed calf's intestines). In addition, fried meatballs, **boiled beef with onions**, stewed chicken giblets, diced chicken cooked with sage and boiled meat salad. Dishes are accompanied by healthy portions of mixed salad, boiled vegetables, boiled beans or fagioli all'uccelletto (baked beans). When it's time for pudding there are fruit cakes with flavors that change with the season. This trattoria alos serves a gluten-free menu and is recommended by the Associazione Italiana Celiachia. You can finish off with home-made moka coffee served in enamel cups.

The bottled wine s available are all on the shelves and there are some acceptable labels, but you won't go wrong if you just stick to the Chianti house wine.

At Hemingway Caffè, Piazza Piattellina, 9 r, pralines, mousse and creams from Italy's top chocolatiers.

Going into da Burde you'll be welcomed (and probably taken off your guard) at the entrance by shelves stacked with razors, soap, paper and goods of all kinds, one of the places that for three generations has been offering simple, uncompromising Florentine cooking . The place is run by the Gori family, specifically by the brothers, Mario, Fabrizio and Giuliano. It's quite normal to find students and workmen rubbing shoulders with businessmen and professional people, all treated in the same straightforward manner by the fast, competent staff: we'd recommend you leave yourselves entirely in their hands to discover the dishes of the day.

After the croutons and cured meats the choice will be between spelt and bean soup, farinata gialla with red cabbage, **ribollita**, pasta and beans or **minestra di pane**. A must is the **bollito misto** made with chicken, beef, pig's trotters and tail, accompanied by pickled vegetables and homemade sauces. The **boiled beef** is also proposed 'rifatto' with onions. Alternatively there's **pig's liver**, beef stracotto, stew, meat loaf, **tripe alla fiorentina**, arista al forno and, of course, steak. Among the puddings, strawberry tart, apple pie, crème caramel and their own version of trifle.

Thanks to Andrea's efforts the wine list has improved considerably and now offers a wide choice of Tuscan labels and dessert wines, also available by the glass. Although the trattoria is not in one of the central areas it's easily reached by taking the road to Pistoia. On their web site – www.burde.it – you'll find information on which days they're open in the evening for dinner.

DA NERBONE

Trattoria
Mercato Centrale di San Lorenzo
Tel. 055 219949
Closed Sunday
Open: 7am-2pm
Holidays: in August
Seating: 30
Prices: 10-15 euros
No credit cards

DA SERGIO

Trattoria
Piazza San Lorenzo 8 R
Tel. 055 281941
Closed Sunday and festivities
Open: only for lunch
Holidays: August
Seating: 70
Prices: 20 euros, wine excluded
All major credit cards, Bancomat

A short way from the church of San Lorenzo in the very heart of old Florence lies the San Lorenzo covered market: colors, aromas, vendors crying out to habitual customers, passing visitors. In this picturesque context from 1872 (as the sign tells you) you'll find this unique eatery that's almost an institution for visitors to the market.

Right from early morning da Nerbone serves up classic Florentine dishes, starting with **sandwiches of lampredotto** (beef tripe) or **boiled beef in green sauce**. At lunchtime Italy's longstanding fast food tradition kicks in: you order, pay, get served in real-time and eat standing up at the counter or, if you're lucky, sitting at one of the tables out front sharing the space with other customers. The menu never changes and is strictly traditional Tuscan: **minestrone, penne strascicate, pappa al pomodoro, stracotto alla fiorentina, tripe al sugo**, peposo alle olive, roast beef. In summer, panzanella or boiled beef salad. On Friday there's always a few fish dishes, like baccalà or cuttlefish in inzimino. You can't expect anything more than an honest house wine, unpretentious yet drinkable, and a total check that never exceeds 15 euros.

The central market next to the Basilica San Lorenzo with its splendid Medici chapels is one of the best known corners of Florence, and at the same time a melting pot of races and a happy combination of daily Florentine life and cosmopolitan tourism. The trattoria, founded by Sergio Gozzi, has been in existence since 1915 and has a lively, friendly and very laid back atmosphere. Furnished in a simple, essential but at the same time really friendly manner, it's an ideal place to take a break after visiting San Lorenzo or after strolling among the crowds making their way along the two rows of 'barrocci', colorful market stalls.

The menu is ideal for lovers of Tuscan popular cooking. You start right in with the first course – you'll find a bigger choice of dishes in winter – **ribollita, minestra di farina gialla, pasta and beans**, whereas in summer the choice is likely to be between stuffed cannelloni and pasta with ragù or tomato sauce. When we last visited, on a Friday, there was a generous portion of baccalà alla livornese, accompanied by chickpeas dressed with olive oil, salt and pepper, plus a really wide choice of classic dishes for meat-lovers: **steak, mixed boiled meat**, roast beef, **pork chop alla livornese**, roast ham, **arista al forno**. In summer more fish appears on the menu: fried shrimp and squid, grilled tuna steak or bass. Vegetable side plates – try the eggplant alla parmigiana – can be a filling substitute for either a first or main course for those who have to get back to their tour of museums or monuments. The only dessert is the classic cantuccini with Vin Santo.

Apart from an honest house wine there are a few good regional and other labels.

Inside the central market (every morning except Sunday), Baroni sells Italian and foreign cheeses, cured meats and other quality gastronomical specialties.

DEL FAGIOLI

⌣ Trattoria
Corso de' Tintori 47 R
Tel. 055 244285
Closed Saturday and Sunday
Open: lunch and dinner
Holidays: August
Seating: 50
Prices: 22-25 euros, wine excluded
No credit cards

Strolling through Piazza Santa Croce and its environs you'll find that many restaurants and wine bars have sprung up in response to a growing demand created by tourists who flock to Florence throughout the year. In many cases these places are best avoided because of their second-rate menus, high prices or poor service. But not far from the piazza and the National Library the Del Fagioli restaurant offers typical Tuscan cuisine with a menu that does not compromise with new fads or improvisation.
The atmosphere's informal, the presentation homely, and there's a good number of tables and friendly waiters. The cured meats and classic **crostini** (with lardo or liver pâté) star among the antipasti; **ribollita** and **tortelli al sugo finto** (a tomato sauce without any meat, and defined as 'false' by popular tradition) are just some of the many first courses. Main courses include boiled, stewed, roast or grilled meat so there's a good choice: and you'll always find **Chianina beef steak** (with this the price indicated above will be higher) and **mixed boiled meat in parsley sauce**. Seasonal side plates accompany the main dishes.
To round up, fresh fruit, a limited choice of homemade puddings and the ever-present **cantuccini with Vin Santo**. The wine list isn't bad and consists mainly, though not exclusively, of Tuscan wines at reasonable prices. The cover charge is 1.50 euros.

HOSTERIA DEL BRICCO

⌣ Trattoria
Via San Niccolò 8 R
Tel. 055 2345037
Closed Monday
Open: lunch and dinner
Holidays: 15 days in summer
Seating: 50
Prices: 30 euros, wine excluded
Credit cards: MC, Visa, Bancomat

Just a stone's throw from Ponte Vecchio, in one of the historic quarters of the city that's still spared the invasion of mass tourism, lies this little trattoria where you will find simple, carefully prepared traditional Florentine dishes. It's located in a picturesque setting dating from the 1300s when it's said today's trattoria was the storeroom of a convent.
Daniele, young but already a veteran of the restaurant trade, offers dishes cooked by mamma Maria. The antipasti are really appetizing, served with various kinds of toasted bread: everyone can prepare their own **crostoni** by dipping into the bowls full of sauces made with liver, peppers, mushrooms and other seasonal variations. And to complete the tray there are cured meats, among which we should mention the rare **mortadella di Prato**. A vegetarian option is available made up of savory vegetable flans.
For your main course you can choose from the **peposo alla fornacina**, beef stew, or **suckling pig in porchetta**, tagliata with rocket and crackling, spatchcock chasseur and the truly classic **arista al forno**. If instead you want to try Tuscan first courses there's always **ribollita**, pappa al pomodoro, **crespelle alla fiorentina** and penne strascicate. As they serve very large portions don't be surprised if at a certain point Daniele refuses to take additional orders. Among the homemade puddings the chocolate and hazelnut cake is certainly worth trying.
As for wine, you can pick and choose from the unusual 'help-yourself' wine cellar that contains a large number of labels, and not only from Tuscany. Or you can trust whatever Daniele recommends as he's a very competent sommelier.

IL CIBREO

⬯Recently opened Osteria
Via dei Macci 122 R
No telephone
Closed Sunday and Monday
Open: lunch and dinner
Holidays: end July-beginning September, New Year
Seating: 30
Prices: 25-30 euros, wine excluded
No credit cards accepted

Il Cibreo was created by Fabio Picchi 20 years ago and is a kind of citadel for gourmets with its osteria, restaurant, bar and theater. The osteria has recently been refurnished with antique tables and a late 19th-century counter, and continues to be popular with the numerous diners who are prepared to face long queues for one of the few tables available in the dining room. In fact you can't book and that's why we haven't given a phone number: if you do try to book by phone you're put through to the restaurant, but it's in a different price bracket.

For antipasti, you'll find crostini al pâté, tomato in aspic, tripe and mozzarella, Pecorino and walnut salad and **ricotta flan**. Among the first courses, as if to emphasize Florentine habits in times gone by, there's no pasta: instead, you have polenta with herbs and cheese, leek, pepper or mushroom soup and, of course, **pappa al pomodoro** and **ribollita**. There's a particularly varied choice of main course: vitello tonnato, **stuffed chicken's neck** with mayonnaise, veal meatloaf, **chicken and ricotta meatballs**, sausage and beans, melanzane alla parmigiana, **cimalino with green sauce**, zampa alla parmigiana, cuttlefish or squid inzimino. Side plates arrive automatically so you don't have to order them. You can finish with delicious desserts, like vanilla bavarese with chocolate sauce, panna cotta or orange cheesecake.

There's a wide choice of wines, some available by the glass, but you can happily settle for the house red served in a Bordeaux bottle.

FLORENCE
San Salvi

INGRID

🗝Rooms
Piazza San Salvi 13
Tel. and fax 055 667646
E-mail: ingrid.florence.rooms@tin.it
Internet: www.ingridaffittacamere.it
Closed in August

The 'soccer stadium quarter' is the ideal place to stay for visitors wishing to enjoy one of the few truly 'Florentine' areas remaining in the city. You'll be welcomed and well looked after by Ingrid Krueger and Giovanni Fattori who will accommodate you in one of the tastefully furnished rooms where you can rest or set out in exploration of the alleyways that lead from Piazza San Salvi to the historic center. The facility isn't far from the Campo di Marte train station and is only a short bus ride from Fiesole and its famous hillside vineyards. Breakfast can be taken in the bar on the ground floor where you'll find excellent cappuccinos and delicious croissants.

• 3 double rooms, with bathroom, air-conditioning, TV; 1 apartment (6 persons) with two double rooms, small lounge with kitchenette, little garden • Prices: double room single use 50-80 euros, double 65-95, apartment (minimum 3 nights) 180-200; breakfast not included (bar underneath the facility) • Credit cards: major ones, Bancomat • 1 room designed for use by the mobility challenged. Free parking in the immediate vicinity. No pets allowed. Owners always reachable

I RIFFAIOLI

Trattoria
Via del Ponte alle Riffe 4 R
Tel. 055 5088070
Closed Sunday and festivities
Open: 10am-3.30pm, dinner if you book
Holidays: July or August
Seating: 35
Prices: 20-25 euros, wine excluded
All credit cards, except AE

JOHANNA II

Rooms
Via Cinque Giornate 12
Tel. and fax 055 473377
E-mail: cinquegiornate@johanna.it
Internet: www.ingridaffittacamere.it
Open all year

You'll find this trattoria in the Piazza delle Cure area, well off the beaten tourist track, in a decidedly family atmosphere both in terms of the warm welcome you get and the food served – simply prepared but very tasty. They serve traditional Tuscan fare and particular care is taken over choice of ingredients and suppliers, who are mainly local. So the menu changes with the season, apart from the classic croutons served with cured meats. Among first courses, we recommend **pici with 'plain' sauce of pork and sausage**, otherwise snails with zucchini, flowers and pine nuts or home-made **ravioli stuffed with ricotta and spinach**. Moving on to the main course, you'll probably find **chicken and rabbit** with vegetables, beef tagliata, a potato and ricotta flan; on Friday the menu also includes some fish dishes. The home-made puddings include a fresh tiramisù and cream cake.

The wine selection is interesting, mainly Tuscan wines at prices ranging from 10 to 15 euros, though some are available by the glass and, if you prefer, there's a choice of three or four house wines. I Riffaioli is only open for lunch but they have a generous idea of what lunch time means: in the evening they only accept bookings for group dinners, a pleasant way to pass an evening with friends with the whole place to yourselves.

Johanna I and II, Johlea I and II and Antica Dimora Firenze are five establishments under the same management, all located in quiet parts of the historic center. Of the five, Johanna II enjoys the added advantage of having a small garden and parking area, plus it's within walking distance of the train station. Your hostess and her friendly, courteous staff will welcome you into this warm, elegant place. Rooms are big and one of them also has a small terrace. The lack of communal areas means that guests can help themselves to the buffet set up in the reception area and enjoy breakfast in the comfort of their own room. Excellent value for money for accommodation in Florence.

• 7 double rooms, with bathroom, air-conditioning, fridge, TV • Prices: double room single use and double 85 euros (18 euros supplement for extra bed), basic breakfast included • Credit cards: none • Off-street parking (5 spaces). No pets allowed. Reception open from 8.30am-7pm • Garden

MARIO

⌒Trattoria
Via della Rosina 2 R
Tel. 055 218550
Closed Sunday
Open for lunch only
Holidays: August
Seating: 50
Prices: 18 euros, wine excluded
No credit cards

In the heart of Florence in front of the central market (also known as the San Lorenzo market) stands this trattoria Mario opened in 1953 and that today is run by his sons Romeo and Fabio, well-known Fiorentina soccer fans. In a piazza now packed with tourist-traps this simple, traditional trattoria is still easy to recognize by the crowd waiting outside for a table. From 11 a.m. onward you can have a glass of wine, bread and cured meats at the counter, while service at tables starts at midday and continues until 3 in the afternoon. The waiters will tell you where you can sit at the refectory-style tables and you'll find it's unusual to get up without having chatted to your neighbors.

Dishes of the day will be called off to you. You can start with seasoned pecorino, cured meats and croutons, or move on to the first course straight away: red cabbage or **bean soup**, **ribollita**, **pappa al pomodoro**, pasta with a meat or tomato sauce, **potato tortelli**, ravioli and, in summer, panzanella. Among main courses there's always arista, **steak**, roast beef, boiled meat. Depending on the day you'll also find either **tripe alla fiorentina** or tripe salad, ossobuco, **fried rabbit**, **braciola rifatta**, pancooked fish. The side plates are also very good: **beans dressed with olive oil**, fried potatoes (authentic, not frozen chips), mushrooms when in season. To end, a good choice of the season's fruit or cantuccini with Vin Santo.

The house wine is not bad although there are always a few labels too. Just ask one of the Colzi family, they'll always be happy to oblige.

RUGGERO

⌒Trattoria
Via Senese 89 R
Tel. 055 220542
Closed Tuesday and Wednesday
Open: lunch and dinner
Holidays: mid-July to mid-August, Christmass
Seating: 40
Prices: 25 euros, wine excluded
All credit cards

This typical trattoria is halfway along the road leading up from Porta Romana to the Certosa, a cozy place where your hosts will give you a warm welcome. A really pleasant place that the Corsi family have been running for more than 25 years. Testifying to the quality of their cuisine is the large number of visitors who flood into the restaurant, especially at lunchtime. While you may find a few tourists, it's mainly Florentines who get together here. Front of house is Daniele, while the kitchen is run with passion by Ruggero Corsi and his son Riccardo. As there aren't many tables in the small room out back, plus those in the entrance where there's a counter serving wine, it's always best to book. Specialties are traditional Tuscan dishes offered keeping a careful eye on what ingredients are in season.

To start, we recommend the mixed antipasti with cured meats and crostini or possibly the tasty stuffed vegetables. Among the wide choice of first courses, some of the trattoria's star turns are **pappa al pomodoro**, **ribollita**, pasta with ragù and **vegetable soup**. For main course. we recommend the pork and rabbit **roasts**, **mixed boiled meats**, **stracotto**, plus grilled meats in the evening (try the **pigeon**).

To wind up there are always home-made puddings or a glass of the classic Vin Santo served with biscuits. An acceptable choice of wine, including a house wine, mainly focusing on Tuscan labels.

TRE SOLDI

Trattoria
Via D'Annunzio 4 R-A
Tel. 055 679366
Closed Friday evening and Saturday
Open: lunch and dinner
Holidays: August
Seating: 30 + 30 outdoors
Prices: 30-35 euros, wine excluded
All credit cards

VILLINO IL MAGNIFICO

Rooms
Via Orcagna 24-26
Tel. 055 6266053
Fax 055 674283
E-mail: info@villinoilmagnifico.com
Internet: www.villinoilmagnifico.com
Open all year

A place with a really long tradition, much appreciated by the people living in the area although little known to the rest of the city. This is a real pity because of the atmosphere in the two small, tastily furnished dining rooms, and because of the quality of the cuisine.
You start with croutons, **soprassata**, lardo di Colonnata, or with two large boards of Siena or Calabria cured meats. First courses vary with the season: passatelli with fresh cherry tomatoes, **ravioloni with buffalo ricotta and herbs** in summer, fagottini with black Norcia truffle, yellow pumpkin and salted ricotta goat's cheese gnocchetti, **maltagliati with chicory**, penne alla diavola, homemade straccetti with meat and cep mushrooms. After all these gastronomic delights it's quite complicated to choose a main course, but a true Florentine would certainly plump for a **costata di cinta senese, coccio di manzo al pepe** or local tagliata. For a side plate, spinach, **beans dressed with olive oil**, Treviso chicory or rocket. Those who love cheese will find scamorze, burrate, erborinati varieties, in addition to a fair number of pecorinos: di fossa, alle vinacce, with walnut leaves, in botte or with fig leaves. Numerous excellent puddings: among these, chocolate and cinnamon fondue, wholemeal pancake with toasted pine nut chantilly, warm apple and almond pie, three-chocolate pyramid.
There's an extensive, well-described wine list of about 270 labels from various regions of Italy and there's also a good house red on tap. Service is attentive and efficient.

This locanda is proof that you can still find reasonably priced accommodation in Italian art towns. Il Magnifico is a typical late 19th-century Florentine building with large, tastefully furnished rooms and is the ideal place for anyone wanting to stay in the center close to the city's monuments and museums. All rooms are en-suite, comfortable and decorated in style with period furniture. Breakfast is buffet style. The centrally-located Locanda dei Guelfi (Via Guelfa 45, same telephone number) is under the same management and offers accommodation only (75-85 euros for a double room) in comfortable rooms just five minutes from the Santa Maria Novella train station.

•1 single and 5 double rooms, with bathroom (for 1 room, next door), air-conditioning, mini-bar, safe, satellite TV • Prices: single 50-75 euros, double room single use 65-85, double 65-110 (15-20 euro supplement for extra bed), breakfast included • Credit cards: all except DC, Bancomat • 2 rooms designed for use by the mobility challenged. Paid off-street parking (2 spaces) and paid external parking (3 spaces). Small pets allowed. Owners always reachable. • Breakfast and reading room. Patio

GAIOLE IN CHIANTI
San Regolo

GAIOLE IN CHIANTI

26 KM NORTHEAST OF SIENA SS 408

28 KM NORTH OF SIENA

IL CARLINO D'ORO

Trattoria
Via Brolio
Tel. 0577 747136
Closed Monday
Open: for lunch only
Holidays: last week in July
Seating: 60
Prices: 15-20 euros, wine excluded
No credit cards, Bancomat

LA FONTE DEL CIECO

3-Star Hotel
Via Ricasoli 18
Tel. 0577 744028
Fax 0577 744407
E-mail: info@lafontedelcieco.it
Internet: www.lafontedelcieco.it
Open all year

The tiny village of San Regolo near Gaiole is hidden away among the vineyards and olive groves in one of the most beautiful parts of the Chianti area. And among the houses is a trattoria that's also a store, a real functioning store that, as in the past, sells a bit of everything – bread , cigarettes, soap and wine. Carlino and his family have been running it since 1961. Towards lunchtime he and his son Fabrizio become hosts and serve visitors to the trattoria: in the kitchen their respective wives Marisa and Roberta prepare simple dishes based on traditional Tuscan recipes.

For antipasti you'll find the ever-present **black bread crostini** with spleen and cured meats. Moving on to the first course it's worth trying the tagliatelle with ragù, lasagna, **pappardelle with wild boar** or hare sauce, ravioli with ricotta and spinach, **panzanella** in summer and **ribollita** in colder months. Then there's mixed roast, **costoleccio**, **fried chicken and rabbit**, arista, duck in porchetta served with turnips or pan-fried herbs. To round off this simple but very satisfying meal, homemade tarts and cakes.

The short wine list proposes some good Chianti labels or alternatively there's a nice house wine on tap. There's a friendly atmosphere and the check is very reasonable.

The hotel – named for an ancient spring – is located in an early 20th-century villa overlooking Gaiole's main square. The building has been carefully restored and still maintains its original atmosphere whilst offering guests a comfortable, friendly stay. Each room is named for a flower and decorated with the corresponding color. In summer breakfast is served under a beautiful pergola and offers local sweet pastries as well as savories if you ask for them. Guests can explore the surroundings on foot, by bicycle or on horseback. Worth visiting on the way to Siena is Meleto Castle, with its circular towers overlooking the Chianti vineyards, and Brolio Castle, famous for its wine cellar.

• 1 single and 7 double rooms, with bathroom, mini-bar, satellite TV • Prices: single 65 euros, double 85-100 (25-30 euro supplement for extra bed), breakfast included • Credit cards: all, Bancomat • Public parking in the immediate vicinity. Small pets allowed. Reception open from 7 am to midnight, owners always reachable. • Bar. Breakfast room, TV room. Terrace. Garden

In **Gaiole** (10 km), some good addresses to buy extravirgin olive oil: Castello di Ama, Castello di Cacchiano, Badia a Coltibuono and Rocca di Castagnoli.

GAIOLE IN CHIANTI
Starda

28 KM NORTHEAST OF SIENA

OSTERIA DI STARDA

Traditional osteria
Castello di Starda
Tel. 0577 734100-339 7384363
Closed Monday
Open: dinner, June-October also lunch
Holidays: mid-January to end of February
Seating: 65+10 outdoors
Prices: 25-30 euros, wine excluded
All credit cards, Bancomat

An osteria in a village dating from 1100 that first belonged to the Guidi Counts and then the Malaspina family, located in a position where the Chianti area borders on the Valdarno. It lies within the Castello di Starda farmstead that produces wines, Vin Santo and olive oil (you'll taste them during your meal) and offers hospitality in apartments scattered around the village. Gabriella and her son Alessandro Dell'Acqua work in this fascinating environment. Alessandro had previous experience in New York, at the Enoteca Pinchiorri and at the osteria Cibreo in Florence, after which he decided to move to the Chianti area and run this osteria. The hands of a chef with this background bring out all the special flavors of traditional Tuscan cooking.
Pici alle briciole (or allo stracotto di vitello), **potato tortelli with wild boar sauce**, garganelli allo stracotto, **lampredotto (tripe) and cabbage soup** (sometimes, in winter), tripe salad, **peposo alla fornacina**, caramelle d'anatra al lardo di Colonnata in Vin Santo are just some of the dishes you'll find. Without forgetting antipasti like veal pâté on homemade pan di ramerino and, as a side plate, the classic beans dressed with olive oil. For pudding, a delicate chocolate soufflé, in winter castagnaccio and **angolucci di Starda** made according to an old farmhouse recipe. Note that there's also a fixed-price popular Tuscan menu at 18 euros (including cover charge and service).
Just a few words about opening times: from June to October Starda is open for lunch and dinner; in November and December, for lunch or dinne,r but only if booked beforehand. All other months it's only open in the evening.

GALLICANO
Ponte di Campia

39 KM NORTH OF LUCCA SS 12 AND 445

AL RITROVO DEL PLATANO

Trattoria and hotel
Via Provinciale 8
Tel. 0583 766142-766039
Closed Wednesday
Open: lunch and dinner
Holidays: November
Seating: 30
Prices: 20-25 euros, wine excluded
All credit cards, except AE, Bancomat

A trattoria under two huge plane trees near a lovely rose-colored house dating from the late 1800s, which is linked to a nice little hotel run by the Da Prato family. In a dining room that seems part farming museum and part landowner's home, with exposed beams and a grand piano used during musical evenings, you eat at tables of various styles, periods and sizes, set with sober good taste. The cuisine is based on local products in season and offers a good round-up of traditional Garfagnana recipes, with some small adaptations in a modern key and tributes to Giovanni Pascoli, who spent many afternoons here in the company of his friend Lemetti (there are several photos of the two of them in the dining room).
Among the first courses an excellent **spelt minestrone**, **vegetable soup** or your host's tortelli. Well worth a mention, the **trincetto**, an artisan-produced pasta made from chestnut flour. For your main course, some outstanding dishes made using **trout** caught in local streams. For those who prefer meat there's **rabbit stew** with polenta and **roast guinea-fowl** or chicken. Varied and very filling is a dish they've called 'pascoliano', which includes cured meats, cheeses and savory flans. The tarts, cakes and ice cream served for pudding are all homemade.
Gabriele is responsible for the carefully selected wines: it's a pity there's no wine list and that some of the bottles carry a rather high markup. There are also two good quality wines – a red and a white both called Melograno – that the Da Prato family produce from grapes grown on their land, with assistance from wine expert Saverio Petrilli. Service is courteous and attentive.

GAVORRANO
Bagno di Gavorrano

38 KM NORTH OF GROSSETO, 14 KM FROM FOLLONICA

LA VECCHIA HOSTERIA

Trattoria
Via Marconi 249
Tel. 0566 844980
Closed Thursday in winter
Open: lunch and dinner
Holidays: end of January
Seating: 70 + 70 outside
Prices: 25-30 euros, wine excluded
All credit cards, Bancomat

La Vecchia Hosteria is on the hill leading up to the village of Gavorrano in the hamlet of Bagno, a place that's also easy to access for the mobility challenged. Roberta front of house and Alberto in the kitchen will give you a pleasant welcome to this warm family environment, where evidently a lot of thought has gone into the furnishing and table settings.

The menu is typically Tuscan and follows the seasons; ingredients are all local and they produce their own olive oil. To start with, apart from the **cured meats** and **crostini**, worthy of note are the mixed farmhouse and **game** platters accompanied by quality preserves under oil. Among the firsts there are various types of homemade pasta (tortelli, gnocchi, tagliolini, **pappardelle**) also served with **wild boar** or cep mushrooms (for one euro more you can order a taste of three pasta dishes), and a good choice of soups, one of which is a well-prepared **acquacotta**. Main course dishes we particularly like include rabbit alla Vecchia, cooked in milk with white wine and olives, and the **mixed fried platter of chicken, rabbit and lamb** prepared in extra-virgin olive oil (and you can tell). Going up the price ladder there's also beef tagliata and **Florentine steak**. Every evening you'll find homemade puddings: mention must be made of the delicate tiramisu and **cantuccini** made by the village bakery and served with Tuscan Vin Santo, Moscato or Passito.

The wine list is good with over 100 labels – all the local DOC wines, a good selection of Chiantis, Brunellos and other excellent Tuscan wines offered with honest markups and a whole lot of useful information.

GREVE IN CHIANTI
Strada in Chianti

20 KM SOUTH OF FLORENCE SP 222

DA PADELLINA

Trattoria
Corso del Popolo 54
Tel. 055 858388
Closed Thursday
Open: lunch and dinner
Holidays: August 10-28
Seating: 80 + 30 outdoors
Prices: 25-30 euros, wine excluded
All credit cards except AE, Bancomat

The large village of Strada in Chianti is 10 kilometers from Greve along the road linking Florence with Siena that runs through Tuscany's most famous vineyards. It won't be difficult to spot this old-style trattoria arranged on two floors and with a beautiful terrace where you can eat outside in summer. The setting is a kind of temple to the memory of Dante: hanging from the ceiling are six beautifully worked glass lamps with scenes from the Divine Comedy and rare editions of the work are on show in one of the dining rooms. Host Alvaro Parenti has always loved Dante and enjoys reciting verses from the poem, almost all of which he knows by heart.

The cuisine is traditional Tuscan, starting with cured meats, crostini and home-made preserves. For firsts, **penne sul gallo**, **pappardelle with rabbit sauce**, classic **ribollita** or, in winter, **pasta and beans**. Main courses: **bistecca alla fiornetina** (the price goes up but it's well worth it), **peposo alla fornacina** (beef stew), pig's liver, **roast duck**, chicken in **Vin Santo**. The more traditional side plates are **beans in olive oil** and, in summer, fried zucchini flowers. In season, there's also game (must be booked). For pudding there's what is considered a must in Tuscany, **zuccotto**, cassata ice cream or Prato biscuits to dip in Vin Santo.

There are 180 labels, most of which are Chianti Classico, but there's also a good selection of wines from other regions.

GREVE IN CHIANTI
Lucolena

GIOVANNI DA VERRAZZANO

🗝️3-Star Hotel
Piazza Matteotti 28
Tel. 055 853189
Fax 055 853648
E-mail: info@verrazzano.it
Internet: www.verrazzano.it
Closed for 1 month between January and February

LOCANDA BORGO ANTICO

🍲Trattoria with rooms
Via Case Sparse 115
Tel. 055 851024
Closed Tuesday, 1/11-31/3 open Friday evening, Saturday and Sunday for lunch
Open: lunch and dinner
Holidays: between January and February
Seating: 60 + 60 outdoors
Prices: 30-35 euros, wine excluded
All credit cards, Bancomat

This hotel with restaurant is located in the beautiful central square of Greve, birthplace of explorer Giovanni da Verrazzano. It is managed by Rossella Rossi and Luciano Vienni, assisted by their families, and has been recently renovated. Rooms are large and well turned out with simple yet distinctive furnishings. All rooms are different and some have views of the square. In summer, guests can dine on the beautiful terrace which also looks onto the square. Just a few minutes drive away are the famous Chianti wine areas and so the hotel is the ideal location for those wanting to indulge in local wine and gastronomy. An excellent buffet breakfast is available to guests and the restaurant offers traditional cuisine for 30-35 euros, wine excluded.

• 9 double and 1 triple rooms, with bathroom (2 rooms with bathroom next door), mini-bar, TV • Prices: double room single use 86 euros, double 105, triple 133, breakfast included • Credit cards: all, Bancomat • Public parking in the immediate vicinity. No pets allowed. Reception open 7am-midnight, owners always reachable • Bar, restaurant. Terrace

Lucolena lies under the lee of the ridge of chestnut covered hills that separate the Rivers Arno, Greve and Pesa, a village with noble traditions. The Borgo Antico is at the top of the village in Località Dimezzano: a trattoria with rooms, frequented above all in summer, has been created from a group of refurbished old houses. In a pair of well furnished rooms, or on the terrace in good weather, you'll be greeted by kind and competent Stefano Fissi who will tell you about the dishes prepared by his wife Patrizia.
You can start with cured meats, **crostini**, fettunta, or goose ham sliced there and then. To follow are some good fresh homemade pastas: riccioli rustici, penne alla pecoraia, **pappardelle with duck ragù** or wild boar ragù. Alternatively, **vegetable and spelt soup**, pear and Gorgonzola cheese risotto or ricotta cheese and spinach ravioli with a hot tomato sauce. In season, pasta with either cep mushroom or truffle sauces are exceptionally good. Among the most popular main courses, **grilled meat** (Chianina beef, rosticciana, guinea-fowl), but it's certainly worth trying the excellent **grand Tuscan fried platter**, **wild boar in sweet and strong sauce**, **arista with beans** or oven-baked pecorino or scamorza cheese. For side plates there's fried vegetables, spicy baked potatoes or, as a tribute to nearby Valdarno, **zolfini beans dressed with olive oil**. To finish there are a few homemade puddings and a glass of liqueur: among these, the laurel-flavored one they make themselves.
As for the wines, you can have an excellent house wine or choose from the extensive list where Chianti reds are clearly much in evidence.

GREVE IN CHIANTI

30 KM SOUTH OF FLORENCE SP 222

MANGIANDO MANGIANDO

☞ Recently opened osteria
Piazza Matteotti 80
Tel. 055 8546372
Closed Monday
Open: lunch and dinner
Holidays: variable
Seating: 25 + 35 outdoors
Prices: 20-25 euros, wine excluded
Credit cards: MC, Visa, Bancomat

GREVE IN CHIANTI
Montefioralle

30 KM SOUTH OF FLORENCE SP 222

TAVERNA DEL GUERRINO

☞ Trattoria
Via Montefioralle 39
Tel. 055 853106
Closed Monday, Tuesday and Wednesday for lunch
Open: lunch and dinner
Holidays: in January-February and November
Seating: 40 + 40 outdoors
Prices: 30-32 euros, wine excluded
No credit cards

You'll find this tiny osteria under the portico of Greve's beautiful central piazza. It only has one room, dominated by the open-plan kitchen, and a few rather closely grouped tables set with paper tablecloths, while in summer there's a pleasant space for eating outside in the piazza. In this unpretentious, informal atmosphere Mirna will tell you about the dishes cooked by her husband Salvatore.

Although the menu is seasonal it hardly ever changes: traditional Chianti area pasta and excellent local meat dishes. To start don't miss the classic Tuscan **crostini**, **fettunta** (dressed with an excellent extra virgin olive oil), local Greve and Siena cured meats. In warm months they also serve generous, appetizing salads. For firsts there are mainly pasta dishes (**garganelli su sugo di cinta senese**, **chioccioloni with a Chianina beef ragù**, spaghetti alla carrettiera, **pappardelle with wild boar sauce** or hare sauce), but also some grain or vegetable soups. The highlight of the cuisine here is the excellently prepared meat dishes: Chianina beef fillet lardellato alla cinta senese, **roast arista di cinta senese**, farmhouse-style **wild boar stew**, **stuffed guinea-fowl**, **steak**. As an alternative to the dessert of the day you can try pecorino or other Tuscan cheeses.

Above all you drink Chianti, but there are also a few Supertuscans and some bottles from other Italian regions.

A short detour from the Chiantigiana leads to Montefioralle, a fortified village surrounded by vineyards two kilometers from the center of Greve. In one of the buildings constructed on the foundations of the village walls is the Taverna del Guerrino, run for decades by the Niccolai family. There are two small dining rooms furnished simply and with good taste and a stone stairway leads from inside up to an arbor where in summer you can enjoy the shade and admire the view over the surrounding countryside. In the kitchen is mamma Gabriella, while her son handles the tables with help from his father.

Simplicity and good taste are features of the menu too, which doesn't offer a wide choice or much variety although it does attempt a significant review of traditional Tuscan cuisine. In winter you'll start with the classic **fettunta**, **crostini** and Grevi **cured meats** (also made from game); in summer, a fresh **panzanella**. For firsts there's often **spaghetti with meat sauce**, either beef or wild boar stewed for a long time as prescribed by peasant tradition; alternatively, **minestra di pane**, **ribollita**, **bean soup**. While the choice of main courses is limited it does include a grilled platter (**rosticciana**, pork chop, sausages and an exquisite **steak**) of top quality meat cooked to a turn. For pudding, Prato biscuits with Vin Santo, torta della nonna and a few other homemade delicacies.

You can drink either the house wine or choose one of the labels (above all Chianti Classico and Montepulciano) from the short but well thought out wine list.

IL CANTO DEL GALLO

OSTE SCURO

Osteria-trattoria
Via Mazzini 29
Tel. 0564 414589
Closed Sunday
Open: dinner, lunch if you book
Holidays: variable, in February or November
Seating: 28
Prices: 25-30 euros, wine excluded
Credit cards: Visa, Bancomat

Recently opened Osteria
Via Malenchini 38
Tel. 0564 324068-339 8781794
Closed Monday evening and Tuesday
Open: lunch and dinner
Holidays: variable
Seating: 20 + 10 outdoors
Prices: 24-32 euros, wine excluded
Credit cards: CartaSi, Visa, Bancomat

Located in the heart of the old town, this little trattoria exploits the passageway leading through the ancient Medici walls. The place is very well maintained even though there's little space for customers, and the crowing cock theme is reproduced on all the furnishings and tableware. This logo as used in Nadia Svetoni's trattoria has a symbolic meaning aptly explaining what you'll find on the premises: the reawakening of a cuisine linked to the Maremma and its traditions. A reawakening that combines respect for the past with a modern sensitivity: Nadia uses only organic products even though the recipes she draws on are those used in the past by families of Maremma cowboys and woodcutters. The antipasti – **crostoni**, bruschetta, flans – are a tribute to local olive oil and vegetable production. Among the first courses, **spelt** or bean soup, **acquacotta**, wholemeal flour **gnocchi**, **pici**, **tortelli maremmani**, plus an inventive 'duet' of cheese-flavored crespelle and vegetarian lasagna. A must for the main course is **pullet alla diavola**, together with **spiced guinea-fowl** and, in winter, an excellent **wild boar stew** or **peposo**, a traditional hot spicy Tuscan beef stew. Nadia also makes the tarts that normally round off the meal.
As an alternative to the house wine there are around 30 Maremma labels.

In the old town, just a stone's throw from Porta Vecchia, at Via San Martino, 47, Alessandra Tonini has extended the range of fresh and preserved products on sale in his store, where you can also buy rare imported specialties and some Italian Slow Food Presidium products.

A new osteria ('winosteria'), a tastefully furnished modern environment enhanced by photos taken by owners Ida and Ezio. The cuisine is a pleasant blend of traditional and modern interpretations while ingredients – whether meat, vegetables or fish – are carefully selected.
The menu changes often, based on the season and availability of ingredients in the market. However, you'll always find a platter of traditional **cured meats** with homemade preserves under oil, a savory flan with capocollo, and Cantabria anchovies. Of the first courses, **old-style potato gnocchi with meat sauce** (Chianina ground beef ragù and dried Amiata cep mushrooms), bucatini with Tuscan pecorino cheese fondue and truffles, mezze maniche with a rock-fish ragù and cherry tomatoes. Continue with **diced beef stewed** in Morellino di Scansano wine, boiled beef, **tripe**, or **nana** (duck) **with red cabbage**, **roast leg of lamb** with local olives, herbs and chicory, and beef tagliata in a Marsala sauce. Special mention must be made of the **cheese board**, a selection of the best Tuscan farmhouse cheeses, in addition to other Italian and foreign specialties, always accompanied by mostarda or honey. The homemade puddings are very well prepared: tarts, panna cotta, crema catalana, semifreddi, creams.
There's an extensive wine list with over 200 labels, some of which are available by the glass; and also a wide choice of liqueurs. Worthy of note, the olive oil list, with particular emphasis on single cultivar oils.

IMPRUNETA

CASA BARTOLINI

☎—⚿Bed and breakfast
Via Volterrana 5
Tel. and fax 055 2047493-339 8599037
E-mail: aeo@casabartolini.it
Internet: www.casabartolini.it
Open all year

Albeit located on the outskirts of Florence, this is not a typical Tuscan house: no wooden beams, no aged terracotta-tiled floors, no four-poster beds. It's actually a small white house dating from 1970 and built according to the principles of 'radical architecture' (an architectural style developed in Florence at the time), with bright, colorful spaces, minimalist furniture, designer pieces and installations in progress by host, Dario Bartolini, architect and sculptor. His wife, Lucia Morozzo, an architect and agronomist, looks after the vegetable garden and prepares the food: Italian breakfast served at the old round table inherited from grandparents in the loggia is included in the price – if you want more of a brunch there's a supplement of 10 euros per person. The surroundings are typically Tuscan: olive and cypress trees and the monastery of Galluzzo with the Falterona and Fumaiolo mountains in the background. The artistic masterpieces of Florence are easily reachable by bus.

• 1 double room and 1 suite (2-5 persons), with bathroom; suite with mini-bar, terrace • Prices: double room single use 60 euros, double 75-82, suite 120-143, breakfast included • Credit cards: major ones, Bancomat • Off-street parking. Small pets allowed. Owners always present • Garden, veranda

LASTRA A SIGNA
Calcinaia

VILLA CIPRESSI

☎—⚿Rooms
Via Leonardo da Vinci 28
Tel. 055 8723149-347 1632049-346 0132450
Fax 055 8720002
E-mail: info@florencehouserental.com
Internet: www.florencehouserental.com/italiano/villaicipressi.html
Closed in January

The villa, which previously belonged to the Altoviti family, was purchased and renovated about fifteen years ago by the present owners, Paola Cei and Maria Cinelli. It's part of an old farmhouse with adjacent barn that can now boast spacious rooms fitted with antique furniture. Each pair of rooms shares a communal area with a kitchen-cum-lounge which doubles as a reading and relaxation room. Breakfast is traditional Italian style with tea, milk, coffee, jams and homemade cakes. A nice garden with swimming pool adds to the already attractive setting. The owners are available to organize guided tours to the main tourist attractions in the area.

• 4 double rooms, with bathroom, air-conditioning, mini-bar, TV, modem connection; 1 apartment with kitchen • Prices: double room single use 50 euros, double 65-100, apartment 100-200; breakfast 5 euros per person • Credit cards: major ones, Bancomat • Off-street parking. Small pets allowed. Owners always present • Breakfast room, reading and TV rooms, lounge. Garden. Pool

CANTINA NARDI

Wine shop with bar and food
Via Cambini 6-8
Tel. 0586 808006
Closed Sunday
Open: only for lunch
Holidays: 2 weeks in August
Seating: 35 + 20 outdoors
Prices: 25-30 euros, wine excluded
Credit cards: AE, Visa

GHINÈ CAMBRÌ

Osteria-wine shop
Via di Quercianella 263
Tel. 0586 579414
Closed Monday and Tuesday, never in summer
Open: dinner, in winter also for lunch on Sunday
Open: two weeks in January
Seating: 70 + 70 outdoors
Prices: 28-30 euros, wine excluded
No credit cards, Bancomat

The wine shop of the Nardi family (Nadio at the bar, Marco front of house and their wives in the kitchen) is a fixed part of the traditional Livorno scene. A small, discreet inn in the heart of town, wooden furnishings, a warm, friendly atmosphere. The tables are laid with simple checkered tablecloths and are divided in two rooms, with the walls lined with bottles and glasses. There is a small garden to eat in during the summer.

The menu changes often, depending on the season and the day's catch, so the dishes we list here are just a few examples of what you might find. Everything is scrupulously prepared and the result is tasty dishes with the typical seafood and land recipes that best express local cuisine. When you enter you can try the nibbles at the bar, accompanied by a glass of wine (a number are recommended) or you can choose something more substantial, to be enjoyed quietly sitting down.

Among the first courses we suggest the seafood carbonara, the **zerri in pesto** (small fried fish marinated in vinegar), **pappa al pomodoro**, vegetable, chickpea or spelt soup, **spaghetti** and other pasta dishes garnished with the day's catch (**squill, telline, mussels**). For main course, you'll find **baccalà sotto pesto, anchovy flan, octopus with potatoes, boiled peppers and eggplants**. You can also try a very good fish soup, but booking is required. Good puddings: chocolate biscuits and fruit tarts, fresh fruit salad.

There is a very wide choice of wines and the prices are very reasonable. A good choice of Tuscan labels, together with a selection from other regions.

A multi-ethnic town since the 16th-century Medici gate was built, Livorno is a linguistic melting pot and here the most colorful Tuscan dialect is spoken. This is confirmed by the sign and names of a lot of the dishes in this osteria in the hamlet of Castellaccio, at the foot of the hills inland from the city. Run by Barbara and Alessandro Prima, it has been a must for years for those who don't necessarily want to eat fish. Its strong points are its meat dishes, especially tagliata and fillet, cooked on the open grill in one of the rooms (there is also a pleasant terrace for the summer). The menu is rich, however, and will satisfy any taste.

For antipasti, **croutons**, cheese fondue, spelt, mussels, platter of **cured meats** and, in summer, mussel and clam soup and a cheese board. The most classic first courses are 'ghinè' (**pennette** with eggplant, peppers, tomato and buffalo mozzarella), 'artra robba' (tagliolini with cep mushrooms and zucchini), "ci vole i vaini" (**tagliolini with lobster**). Among the main courses, as we said, the excellent meat dishes of tagliate, **steak** and fillet with various garnishes (mushrooms, laurel, peppercorns etc.) but you can also find **mixed fish fry** and grilled seafood. A part of the menu is dedicated to salads and carpaccio for simpler and quicker meals, and the cep mushrooms stand out among the side dishes. Good desserts, including fantasy puff pastry, fruit in chocolate fondue and cheesecake.

The osteria-wine shop offers a very good wine list, with a particularly wide selection of reds, especially Tuscan, with very honest mark-ups.

Livorno

Il giro del cane

⌒ Osteria-trattoria
Borgo dei Cappuccini 314
Tel. 0586 812560
Closed Sunday
Open: dinner
Holidays: August
Seating: 35 + 20 outdoors
Prices: 30-35 euros, wine excluded
All credit cards except DC

Near to Borgo Cappuccini, one of the historic areas of Livorno, the new Gateway to the sea is being built, a great city council project to create a tourist port next to the new shipyards for luxury craft that have replaced the old Luigi Orlando naval shipyard. The Giro del Cane has decided to bravely pursue the traditional local cooking, with very few concessions to the advancing new times. Daniele Contini, owner and chef, and his trusted assistant cook Valerio, propose typical Livorno fish dishes, often called the poor man's dishes, in informally youthful surroundings, divided into two rooms plus a veranda for the summer. This year they have also decided to open in late afternoon to offer snacks, appetizers, sliced meats and cheeses together with a glass of good wine.

You can begin with an antipasto of mixed seafood – **acciughe alla povera**, octopus salad, fish timbale, puff pastry stuffed with shellfish or whatever the chef's fantasy suggests – to then continue with the first courses, the real highlight of the osteria: **spaghetti** with sea urchins, **ai datteri pelosi** or alle zighe, black rice, **linguine con totani**, **pappa al pomodoro with seafood,** penne with mullet. Among the main courses, freshly caught fish, which Daniele will list out loud: you can find gurnards, **mullet alla livornese**, traditional **fish soup** or shellfish soup, **fried paranza**, **stuffed mussels** and baccalà. The menu is enriched by a few meat dishes, which it is best to book, especially in the winter: steaks, fillet, pork and game. To close, a few appetizing homemade puddings: latte alla portoghese, sponge cake with stracciatella, panna cotta. Only a few wines, Tuscan whites and reds, are offered.

In caciaia

⌒ Osteria
Via dei Bagni 38
Tel. 0586 580403
Closed Monday and Tuesday
Open: dinner, Saturday and Sunday also for lunch
Holidays: variable
Seating: 60 + 40 out doors
Prices: 25-30 euros, wine excluded
All credit cards

The success of this osteria shows no signs of waning: thanks to the genuinely happy, cheerful atmosphere that all the staff, beginning with the stalwart Gangio, factotum patron, transmit to the guests. Solid reliable typical fish dishes, without flights of fancy but without any disappointments either ... that's what's offered at the Caciaia.

The chef Luciano and his assistants serve a variety of antipasti every day, including **anchovies alla povera**, **zerri** or baccalà sotto **pesto**, **sweet and sour agerti**, fish soup crostini. They continue with the **spaghetti alle cicale** or alle zighe, **tagliolini with fresh anchovies and wild fennel**, black rice (oe, with cuttlefish ink) and gnocchi al baffo. Among the main courses, traditional recipes like **stoccafisso alla livornese**, baccalà, stuffed mussels, often (but not always) **fish soup,** brochettes of totani and prawns, fresh fish caught daily prepared in various ways. Plus occasional meat dishes, like **tripe** or pork chops in tomato sauce. The choice of puddings is limited, but be sure to end with **ponce** alla livornese.

In the dining rooms and the covered veranda Federico offers friendly, informal service, suggesting both dishes and wines: there's no wine list but there are good Italian reds and whites. Booking is recommended, especially in summer. The osteria is listed by the Italian Celiac Association and has a gluten-free menu available.

LUCCA

BUATINO

🍲 Traditional osteria
Borgo Giannotti 508
Tel. 0583 343207
Closed Sunday
Open: lunch and dinner
Holidays: none
Seating: 70
Prices: 20-28 euros, wine excluded
All credit cards, Bancomat

This is one of the oldest trattorias in Lucca and a few years ago it was slightly renovated to make it more welcoming and to bring it up to current standards in terms of the elimination of architectural barriers. At lunchtime it serves the people who work nearby, with a quick meal which, however, preserves all traditional characteristics. In the evening it is calmer, in a friendly atmosphere often accompanied by good music. You can stay well into the night to drink a glass of wine, with a good offer of regional and national labels available at the bar.
All traditional dishes, some of which to be eaten crude with extra virgin olive oil from the Lucca hills. A few examples of the antipasti: hot focaccia and lardo, **cured Cinta Senese pork with liver pâté,** homemade bacon with Garfagnana pecorino, spelt salad, leek flan. Followed by soups (**farinata with black cabbage, frantoiana, pappa al pomodoro,** spelt soup), homemade **tordelli, tagliatelle with pigeon,** testaroli al pesto. Very typical main courses: **cioncia** (head of veal) **stewed, pork livers, roast pigeon, tripe alla lucchese;** or **mixed boiled meats with green sauce, stewed chicken,** roast lamb and potatoes, excellent roast-beef. Home-made desserts: latte alla portoghese, chocolate salami, candied fruit, pear tart and the classic **tart co' becchi.**
The wine list contains around 150 labels from Tuscany and the rest of Italy.

🍨 Gelateria Santini, Piazza Cittadella 1: excellent whipped cream, ice creams, zuccotti and semifreddi. Antica Bottega di Prospero, Via Santa Lucia: top quality pulses and stone ground flours.

LUCCA
Gattaiola

4 KM SOUTHEAST OF CITY CENTER

IL MECENATE

🍲 Restaurant-wine shop
Via della Chiesa 707
Tel. 0583 512167
Closed Monday
Open: lunch and dinner
Holidays: in November
Seating: 70 + 70 outdoors
Prices: 26-34 euros, wine excluded
All credit cards, Bancomat

This is definitely more of a restaurant than a trattoria, on the outskirts of Lucca where guests can sit late into the evening, for a snack and a good glass of wine. However, the traditional cuisine, warm welcome and reasonable prices have convinced us to include it among the osterias in our guide.
In the dining hall or, in summer under the arbor, you will be served by the owner, Stefano, helped by his young assistants who will present you with the dishes cooked by his wife, Sole. You start with some good Garfagnana **cured meats,** hot focaccia with lardo, vegetable pies. Followed by homemade pasta, the classic Lucca **tordelli** with meat (excellent), **pappardelle with pigeon** or hare, **straccetti with duck ragù,** malfatti with ricotta and spinach, testaroli lunigiani. In winter, there are also **soups** including the frantoiana with fresh oil. The highlight of the main courses is the excellent **roast pork,** but also the **roast pigeon,** stewed boar with polenta, **fegatelli with rapini, baccalà with chickpeas, stuffed artichokes,** and if you book mixed fried meats and vegetables. A good choice of cheeses and traditional puddings, including the **torta co' becchi.**
A good wine list with labels from all over Italy, with a special regard for Monte Carlo and the Lucca hills, where the very interesting house wine comes from.

LUCCA
Old town

LUCCA
Lucca-Vignallaria
Sant'Alessio

SAN FREDIANO

☞—๐ Youth hostel
Via della Cavallerizza 12
Tel. 0583 469957
Fax 0583 461007
E-mail: ostello.san.frediano@virgilio.it
Internet: www.ostellolucca.it
Open all year

VIGNA ILARIA

☞—๐ Rooms
Via per Pieve Santo Stefano 967 c
Tel. 0583 332091
Fax 0583 331908
E-mail: info@locandavignailaria.it
Internet: www.locandavignailaria.it
Open all year

Opened in 2001, this hostel is located in the old Real Collegio next to the Basilica of San Frediano, close to the city walls, and managed by hotelier Renato Stasi. Though the hostel is part of the Italian association of youth hostels, guests of any age are welcome to stay in the dorms or in the basic but comfortable family rooms (Italian nationals pay 9-17 euros per person or 18 euros for family members; foreigners must also pay a membership fee which costs 3 euros per night for the first 6 nights, after which the guest has full membership for a year and is no longer required to pay the fee). The independently-managed La Cavallerizza restaurant opens for dinner while lunch is available for groups upon reservation. The restaurant lounge opens onto the garden and guests can enjoy local dishes for a small supplement of 9 euros (vegetarian menus, set menus for groups and packed lunches are available on request).

• 8 rooms or mini-apartments (2-6 persons), with bathroom, and 20 dorms with common inside and outside bathrooms • Prices: double 45 euros, triple 68, four-bed 90, six-bed 135, bed in dorm 17-18 euros; breakfast 2-5 euros per person • Credit cards: none • Facility accessible to the mobility challenged. Off-street parking. No pets allowed. Reception open 24 hours a day. • Bar. Lounge, TV room. Garden

Located in the hills on the outskirts of Lucca, this locanda with restaurant attached is managed by Ferruccio Pera and Pietro Nardi and has been open for three years. The area surrounding it in the midst of the 'via delle Pievi' (a must for a visit) is truly charming: all around are woods, vineyards and olive groves, and as a backdrop, the city walls. Rooms are fitted with locally crafted furniture. Breakfast consists of toasted Luccal bread, warm croissants, fruit juices and country-style frittatas, with other savory fare available on request. For lunch guests can enjoy a good selection of fish and meat dishes and choose a wine from the 400 available on the extensive list (40 euro, wine excluded). This is an ideal base for anyone wishing to visit Lucca or wanting to explore the province's hills and savor its gastronomic specialties, especially the olive oil and wines.

• 3 double rooms and 1 suite, with bathroom, TV • Prices: double room single use 65 euros, double 85, suite 110, breakfast included • Credit cards: all, Bancomat • Off-street parking. Small pets allowed. Reception open from 8.30am-1 am • Restaurant. Garden

MANCIANO

DA PAOLINO

Trattoria
Via Marsala 41
Tel. 0564 629388
Closed Monday
Open: lunch and dinner
Holidays: January or February
Seating: 40 + 40 outdoors
Prices: 28-35 euros, wine excluded
All credit cards except DC, Bancomat

Manciano is a medieval town in the Grosseto areaof the Maremma, halfway between the sea on the 'Silver Coast' and the tufa hills of Sorano and Pitigliano. The trattoria was reopened in 1992 after almost thirty years of closure and has been very tastefully refurbished. The entrance has an original bar which joins the two halls, very simply but meticulously furnished. The family management is coordinated by Sabrina Benicchi who helps Marino Pieraccini run the trattoria. The menu changes with the seasons; the dishes are prepared with passion by Paola Boscherini and Giuseppa Perugini.
You can begin with croutons, bruschette, cured meats and local **cheeses** (with goat's cheese and herb tomini in season), carpaccio of goose breast and very good **game fillets**. Among the first courses we recommend **gnudi with ragù**, lasagnette with artichokes and creamed cheese. Classic **tortelli maremmani**, pici alla campagnola, **acquacotta**. The cuisine is best expressed in the main courses: **boar Maremma style** or with wild fennel, **roast pork**, chicken chasseur. At Easter you must try the lamb in sauce with artichokes. Good side dishes: boiled beans, roast potatoes, vegetable flans. Among the homemade puddings, we recommend the cantuccini with Vin Santo and the good ricotta briaca, a delicate grappa mousse.
The wine list has been given a makeover compared to the past and includes around 60 local and regional labels, with fair mark-ups.

MANCIANO
Poderi di Montemerano

LE FONTANELLE

Holiday farm
Localita' Le Fontanelle
Tel. and fax 0564 602762
E-mail: le.fontanelle@tiscali.it
Internet: www.lefontanelle.net
Open all year round

This agriturismo is near a small lake and surrounded by secular trees. Rooms are individual units scattered around the countryside like chalets and are fitted with period furniture. In the grounds you can find deer, mouflons, wild ducks, herons, geese and even a mascot, Gina the donkey. In summer, breakfast and lunch are served on the patio. In the kitchen Giuliana and Milva prepare local dishes with a personal twist (about 20 euros). Musts to see are the walled village of Montemerano, the Church of San Giorgio with its many works of art and the fortress of Manciano. Ten kilometers away are the sulfurous waters of the spa in Saturnia and it's only a half hour drive to the sea at Argentario.

•10 double, 2 triple and 2 four-bed rooms, with bathroom, mini-bar, TV • Prices: double room single use 47 euros, double 78, triple 85, four-bed 90, breakfast included • Credit cards: all except DC, Bancomat • 2 rooms designed for use by the mobility challenged. Off-street parking. Small pets allowed. Owners always present • Restaurant (only for residents and only for dinner). Lounge. Patio. Garden

MANCIANO
Saturnia

MARCIANO
DELLA CHIANA

56 KM SOUTHEAST OF GROSSETO

22 KM SOUTHWEST OF AREZZO

VILLA CLODIA

HOSTERIA
LA VECCHIA RÒTA

🔑3-Star Hotel
Via Italia 43
Tel. 0564 601212
Fax 0564 601305
E-mail: villaclodia@laltramaremma.it
Internet: www.hotelvillaclodia.com
Closed from 8 January to 8 February

🍲Osteria-trattoria
Via XX Settembre 4
Tel. 0575 845362-335 5912812
Closed Monday and Tuesday
Open: dinner, Saturday and Sunday also for lunch
Holidays: two weeks in June
Seating: 60 + 40 outdoors
Prices: 30-32 euros, wine excluded
Credit cards: AE, CartaSi

This small 3-Star hotel, professionally managed by the Bonanni family, is located in a beautiful villa with a garden and swimming pool in the characteristic medieval village of Saturnia (previously an Etruscan and then Roman settlement) just two kilometers from the spa. The view of the Albegna valley is stunning as you walk to the spa along the Via Clodia. Rooms are elegant, comfortable, spacious and well furnished, as are the reading room with fireplace and the other common areas. Buffet breakfast is served in the lounge and offers local produce (cured meats, cheeses, Tuscan bread), as well as jams and homemade cakes.

• 2 single, 7 double rooms and 1 mini-suite, with bathroom, mini-bar, safe, satellite TV • Prices: single 60 euros, double 95, mini-suite 115, breakfast included • Credit cards: Visa, Bancomat • Public parking in the immediate vicinity. No pets allowed. Reception open 7am-11pm • Breakfast room, TV room, reading room. Terrace, garden. Pool

In the square within the walls of this lovely village in the Valdichiana, we find the osteria of Massimo Giovannini, a singular host for a place from another age, where you will receive a very warm welcome and will feel part of gastronomic history. Massimo will explain the menu to you, with dishes that change with the seasons and follow the customs of the past.
To start, an excellent hand-sliced ham served with black croutons; if you are lucky you will also find the delicious **vettaioli di poponi and water melon preserved in oil** and authentic specialties like **nana** (duck) or **turkey**. Among the firsts try the **tagliatelle with bacon, broad beans and wild fennel** or with finferli mushrooms, gnudi of borage with prugnoli and asparagus, cep mushroom soup, risotto with acacia flowers, **scottiglia**, **acquacotta** and pezze della nonna alle pere incantate, an old family recipe. Among the main courses you will find forgotten dishes like vine-leaves stuffed with meat, served with bunches of green beans tied by a bow of bacon, or **hen pheasant in sour grape sauce**; less unusual but delicious the **suckling pig** cooked in the wood oven, **stew of ocio** (goose, sometimes Massimo dedicates an entire menu to this farmyard animal), **stuffed rabbit**, **nana in porchetta**. With a little extra on the bill you can try an excellent **steak** or tagliata of certified Chianina beef. To close, fruit tarts, apple and raisin tarts, Florentine schiacciata, cantucci dipped in local Vin Santo. Don't forget to taste the excellent Nocino.
The good house wine is backed up a small wine list, characterized by Massimo's witty comments label by label.

MARRADI

MASSA

IL CAMINO

IL PASSEGGERO

Restaurant
Viale Baccarini 38
Tel. 055 8045069
Closed Wednesday
Open: lunch and dinner
Holidays: 1 week June, 1 beginning of September
Seating: 90 + 50 outdoors
Prices: 30 euros, wine excluded
All credit cards, Bancomat

Restaurant
Via Alberica 1
Tel. 0585 489651
Closed Sunday
Open: lunch, Friday and Saturday also for dinner
Holidays: two weeks in August
Seating 60 + 30 outdoors
Prices: 33-35 euros, wine excluded
All credit cards, Bancomat

Geographically we are still in Tuscany, but you breathe Romagna, given that we are at the foot of the Apennines on the road that links the two regions through the lovely Colla Pass. The restaurant is just outside the town center, close to the station, and offers a friendly rustic atmosphere that has remained unchanged in time, both in its furnishings and the menu, with popular recipes that reflect local traditions and the land itself. You can sit in the comfortable indoor rooms or, in summer, outside on the patio. The menu is displayed at the entrance; otherwise it will be recited to you.
To begin, **crostini with livers** or **crescentine** with ham and cheese. This is followed by the ever-present homemade pasta, the **tortelli** with butter, sage and Parmesan, **cappelletti in broth** or **tagliatelle sul cinghiale** or with mushrooms. Among the main courses you must try the highlight of the restaurant, the delicious Mediterranean style **lamb**, namely grilled lamb chops with cherry tomatoes and aromatic herbs. Otherwise, the **chicken and olives**, boar or a good fillet steak, not to forget the **mixed fry**, a decidedly rich offering. In season, **mushrooms.** Mainly soft, creamy desserts, including crème caramel, chestnut blancmange and the "bicchierino", a specialty made from a secret recipe.
As an alternative to the house wine, a Sangiovese from Romagna, there are other labels from all over Italy.

We are in the historic heart of Massa: going down a few steps below street level, we come to this restaurant in the basement of a period palazzo. It is a friendly place, divided in small rooms with modern wooden furniture and tables laid with paper place mats. Alessandra and Lorenzo Rustichi run it with the help of a few assistants. They offer typical Massa dishes, and as the town is on the border of two Regions they are a combination of Ligurian and Tuscan traditions.
The antipasti include local cured meats and vegetable croutons with pâté or mushrooms. The first courses include **tordelli massesi** with meat and mushroom sauce, lasagne tordellate, cream of vegetable soups, **spelt soup** and **ribollita**, but also fresh fish dishes like spaghetti with clams or seafood. There is also a wide selection of seafood among the main courses: **fried anchovies**, baccalà marinated or baked in the oven with potatoes, **stewed cuttlefish**, fried anchovies with roast potatoes. Among the meat dishes, we suggest the roast veal and beef cooked in the pan. All the puddings are homemade, crème brûlée, fruit semifreddo and the excellent **tenerina** (chocolate cake).
Besides the house wine on tap, the wine list recommends some good Tuscan labels.

Gastronomia Valeria, Via Fermi 1, sells excellent produce and takeaway meals. At Via Aurelia Ovest 42, Macelleria Daniele Galeotti specializes in horse and donkey meat, producing some excellent home cured meats.

MASSA

MASSA MARITTIMA

OSTERIA DEL BORGO

Restaurant
Via Beatrice 17-19
Tel. 0585 810680
Closed Tuesday
Open: lunch and dinner, July-August only for dinner
Holidays: September 15-October 15
Seating: 35 + 30 outdoors
Prices: 25-30 euros, wine excluded
All major credit cards, Bancomat

DA TRONCA

Osteria-trattoria
Vicolo Porte 5
Tel. 0566 901991
Closed Wednesday, never in August
Open: only for dinner
Holidays: in January-February
Seating: 50
Prices: 25-30 euros, wine excluded
All credit cards except AE

In a Renaissance building in the ancient heart of Massa, at the foot of the Fort, the restaurant founded years ago by Pier Rolando Carnevali, remains a benchmark for lovers of good wine and traditional cooking. The two rooms are furnished in wood and Apua marble, perfectly in keeping with the surroundings; in summer some of the tables are set outside in the patio by the road. Carla Giometti Carnevali runs the service with her efficient and cordial manner.

Marco Miniani works in the kitchen preparing dishes from ancient Massa and Lunigiano recipes, especially pasta, vegetables and meat. We start with bruschetta, panzanella, **baccalà fritters, torta d'erbi**, ham, lardo and other Tuscan cured meats. We continue with soup (spelt for example) or typical pastasciutta; try the **lasagne stornellate** (Massa tordello open, broken up and mixed with the ragù) **panigacci with extra virgin oil and Parmesan**, potato ravioli with peperoni sauce. Among the main courses, **suckling pig**, pork fillet in crust, sliced beef, **hot grilled lamb, fried rabbit** Tuscan style, warm baccalà with stewed cherry tomatoes and olives; fresh fish, especially in the summer, with a fragrant **mixed fry** and classic **seppie in zimino**. Simple tasty puddings, in line with the osteria: the Savoyard cream with red vermouth is excellent.

An extensive pondered selection of wines, not just from Tuscany.

The osteria is in a large warehouse overlooking a characteristic alley in the historic heart of Massa Marittima, with all the fascination you expect of a Tuscan locanda. Open stonework, chestnut beams and set on two levels, we feel as if we have stepped back in time in this medieval Maremma hamlet.

Simple, well-prepared dishes, made with carefully selected seasonal ingredients true to local traditions. Courteous and professional service, although sometimes rather cool. To begin you will have a lovely board of **crostini** (besides the classics, varieties with chives and Ravaggiolo and with Rigatino, walnuts and Stracchino), true Tuscan pecorino with pears or typical **cured meats** served with the ever-present bruschetta. Among the pasta dishes, the very good fusilli with broccoli and rigatino, and the **penne with cauliflower and sausage** or ragù, among the soups **acquacotta** and others made with seasonal vegetables. Among the main courses, a choice of classic **tripe** or **rabbit in porchetta** or with vegetables, wild boar (in winter), **roll of lamb with spinach**. Side dishes of beet, potatoes or – something we tasted during our last visit – a very good cardoon flan. Homemade puddings: trifle, panna cotta, homemade tart and **panpepato ai fichi**, to remind us of the ancient ties of this part of the Maremma with Siena.

Enoteca Il Bacchino, a short walk from the cathedral: 500 wines, including all the DOC Monteregio, cheeses, cured meats and other excellent food products (many included among Slow Food Presidium).

DOMUS BERNARDINIANA

Holiday home
Via San Francesco 10-12
Tel. 0566 902641-339 1541377
Fax 0566 904514
E-mail: seminario.massa@tiscalinet.it
Open all year

The Domus Bernardiniana is located in an old Franciscan convent dating back to the 13th century, heavily restored over the centuries. Its optimal location close to the city walls makes it a peaceful place to stay as well as a good base for visiting places of interest (the main square is only 300 meters away). The management, closely linked to the dioceses of Massa Marittima and Piombino, refurbished the guest rooms in 2003 and they now offer comfortable accommodation at very reasonable prices. Breakfast and meals (only available to residents) are simple (half board 40 euros per person). Common areas are well turned out and include a conference room that seats up to 200 people. The property is particularly suitable for religious tourism.

• 7 single, 15 double and 1 triple rooms, with bathroom, the majority with mini-bar, TV; 2 apartments with kitchenette • Prices: single 30 euros, double 60, triple 90, apartment 30 euros per person, breakfast included • All major credit cards, Bancomat • Common areas and some rooms accessible to the mobility challenged. Off-street parking. Small pets allowed. Reception open 8am-8 pm • Bar, restaurant (for residents only). Reading room, TV room. Conference room. Garden, veranda

DUCA DEL MARE

3-Star Hotel
Piazza Dante 1-2
Tel. 0566 902284
Fax 0566 901905
E-mail: info@ducadelmare.it
Internet: www.ducadelmare.it
Closed from January 15 to March 1

The Orlandi family has been in the hotel and restaurant business for over 40 years. The hotel, which is managed by brothers Mario and Roberto with sister Annamaria, has been open for decades but was renovated a few years back. Rooms are fitted with modern, practical furniture, often remotely controlled. Breakfast consists of coffee, milk, tea, cocoa, croissants, cookies, bread, butter, jams, fruit, yogurt, muesli, cured meats and cheeses. The beautiful medieval town of Massa Marittima (Touring Club orange flag) is of great artistic, archeological and sporting interest and boasts over 150 kilometers of paths for excursions by mountain bike. For those wanting to swim and sunbathe, Lake Accesa (10 kilometers away) and the beaches on the Tyrrhenian coast (the Golfo del Sole-Follonica is about 20 kilometers away) are only a short drive from the hotel.

• 4 single, 23 double rooms and one four-bed suite, with bathrooms, air conditioning, satellite TV, modem connection • Prices: single 50-60 euros, double 85-95, suite 130-145, breakfast included • Credit cards: all except DC, Bancomat • 2 rooms designed for use by the mobility challenged. Off-street parking, public parking nearby, garage for bicycles. No pets allowed. Reception open 7.30am-midnight • Bar, breakfast room. Reading room, TV room. Terrace. Garden, pool

Massa Marittima

Il pungolo

⌂ Restaurant
Via Valle Aspra 12
Tel. 0566 902585
Closed Wednesday
Open: dinner, Sunday also for lunch
Holidays: November 15-30
Seating: 35 + 35 outdoors
Prices: 22-33 euros, wine excluded
Credit cards: MC, Visa, Bancomat

Just outside the historic center of Massa, this restaurant – which has been open for four years now – is a simple but friendly place. There are two rooms (dug out of the old cellars), plus a closed-in veranda. Marco, the kind and helpful owner, runs a rather seasonal kitchen, which, given the position of Massa Marittima, means two menus – one tied to the land and the other to the sea. There are not too many dishes – never trust mile long menus anyway – but they are always freshly made and portions are generous.

Among the antipasti, besides the raw marinated fish, try the **panzanella di mare**, an excellent combination of land and sea, salad with octopus and chickpeas and – changing idea – the selection of Tuscan cured meats and pecorino, served with pears and honey.

As for the first courses, the pasta is homemade and the choice varies among potato gnocchi, tortelloni with truffles or meat or boar ragù, and we personally recommend the **agnolotti alla nana** (duck). Between land and sea we would mention the good **chickpea and scampi soup** and fettuccine with mussels. The main courses are very simple with fillet, rabbit, **boar, kidneys** and **pignatta with veal and potatoes** (a nice way of serving stew), king prawns, grilled fish, octopus and moscardini.

Some of the desserts, like the panna cotta and tiramisù, are home-made while others are bought from a small local producer.

A good choice of wines, with the focus on the local ones (remember the Monteregio) with honest mark-ups.

Massarosa
Piano di Conca

Da ferro

⌂ Trattoria
Via Sarzanese Nord 5324
Tel. 0584 996622
Closed Tuesday
Open: lunch and dinner
Holidays: in October
Seating: 150 + 150 outdoors
Prices: 25 euros, wine excluded
All credit cards, Bancomat

The name is a tribute to great-grandfather Ferruccio who, at the beginning of the 20th century, ran a small shop to which the Viareggio people would come by bike to have a snack. Today the families of Giuseppe and Vittoriano Ceragioli run this trattoria on the old road that leads from Montramito to Camaiore.

Despite the number of seats, the atmosphere is simple and friendly. There is no architectural refinement in the furniture or lighting, but the service is genuine and the smiles last throughout your meal. The food is based on simple ingredients and dishes (a few concessions are made to tourists, however), beginning with the countryside antipasti of excellent cured meats. The **lardo di Colonnata** is really excellent but the rest is equally good (try the mortadella from Camaiore and the **biroldo** from Garfagnino). We then move onto the Tuscan classics: **homemade tortelli**, vegetable soups, **maccheroni** and tagliolini served with everything from **game** to **mushrooms** (when they are in season, prepared in lots of different ways), depending on the season and availability. Among the meat dishes the **roast guinea fowl** and **rabbit, stewed** and roast, and also grilled lamb and **stewed boar with olives**. Very good classic **grilled steak**. Polenta is served with **stoccafisso**, mushrooms, boar, rabbit. Depending on the day, there is tripe, boiled meats and on Friday, stoccafisso and baccalà, grilled or boiled. Among the side dishes the fried fresh vegetables and, among the puddings, home-made tarts of pears, apple or chocolate with becchi.

The house wine is simple but good, the oil is made on the owner's farm in Buti.

MONTALCINO

41 KM SOUTHEAST OF SIENA ON SS 2

IL GIGLIO

🔑3-Star Hotel
Via Soccorso Saloni 5
Tel. and fax 0577 848167
E-mail: hotelgiglio@tin.it
Internet: www.gigliohotel.com
Closed from 7-31 January

The hotel is located in two separate buildings, one with views of the Brunello hills (one of the rooms also has a lovely terrace) and the other opening onto a quiet alleyway. The small hotel buildings have recently been restored and are managed by Michele Machetti and his family. Guests are very well looked after: on arrival you can hand your car keys to a member of staff who will park your car for you; in the morning you can choose between continental or Tuscan breakfast with cheeses and local cured meats. Half board is available for guests staying for over 2 nights (70 euros per person sharing; for non-residents a set menu is 32 euros, wine excluded). The town center is within walking distance.

• 3 single, 7 double and 2 triple rooms, with bathroom, mini-bar, satellite TV, 1 with terrace; in the annex, 1 single, 2 double and 2 triple rooms, with bathroom • Prices: single 60 euro, double 90, triple 115; in the annexe, single 45 euros, double 70, triple 80; breakfast 6.50-8 euros per person • Credit cards: all except DC, Bancomat • Free and paid public parking, private off-street parking 50 meters away, garage for motorbikes. Small pets allowed. Reception open 7am-midnight. • Restaurant. Breakfast room, hall with reading and TV corner

MONTALCINO
Sant'Angelo in Colle

50 KM SOUTHEAST OF SIENA

IL PODERUCCIO

🔑Holiday farm
Localita' Sant'Angelo in Colle
Tel. 0577 844052-348 6435394
Fax 0577 844150
E-mail: poderuccio.girardi@virgilio.it
Open from Easter to end of November

This agriturismo is located in a thoroughly refurbished farmhouse in that part of the territory of Montalcino closest to Mount Amiata. Rooms are cozy and elegantly decorated and guests receive a warm welcome. Buffet breakfast offers sweet and savory fare served in a charming lounge, or in summer, out on the terrace. Guests can purchase the farm's own produce, especially wines and olive oils. Places worth visiting in the area are the Parco della Val d'Orcia and the many wine cellars that produce Brunello. Art lovers can visit Sant'Antimo Abbey or explore medieval Sant'Angelo in Colle with its narrow alleyways, typical archways and the village's fortified gate and walls.

• 5 double and 1 triple rooms, with bathroom, mini-bar, TV • Prices: double room single use 80 euros, double 85, triple 110; breakfast included • Credit cards: major ones, Bancomat • Off-street parking. No pets allowed. Owners always present • Breakfast room, reading room. Grounds, terrace. Pool

41 KM SOUTHEAST OF SIENA

41 KM SOUTHEAST OF SIENA

OSTERIA AL GIARDINO

Recently opened osteria
Piazza Cavour 1
Tel. 0577 849076
Closed Wednesday
Open: lunch and dinner
Holidays: January 15-February 15
Seating: 40 + 45 outdoors
Prices: 25-32 euros, wine excluded
Credit cards: MC, Visa, Bancomat

PALAZZINA CESIRA

Bed and breakfast
Via Soccorso Saloni 2
Tel. and fax 0577 846055
E-mail: cesira@montalcinoitaly.com
Internet: www.montalcinoitaly.com
Closed for 1 month between January and February

In the square in front of the town hall, there is a nice park where the children meet and play and there is the osteria of Gianluca Di Pirro, who took it over four years ago and is leading it to new glory. You go in through a glass door and find a simple but warm atmosphere: pastel colors on the walls and tablecloths, straw covered chairs, elegant cutlery and antique items of peasant culture spread round the room. His wife Paola is front of house.

Gianluca prepares traditional dishes, which he loves to present with a touch of choreography, given his pastry cook vocation. Among the antipasti worth noting are the **cured Cinta Senese pork** (Slow Food Presidium), the mixed Tuscan special, with croutons and cured meats, **melted pecorino with Montalcino honey,** or the beef carpaccio with pecorino from the crete senesi, and fresh vegetables. Among the first courses we find very good **pici all'aglione** (or alla nana) and **pappardelle with boar** (or hare), and you will also always find **ribollita** and **panzanella**, straccetti with chickpeas and the more personal risotto with red chicory, Brunello and pecorino. Followed by **Florentine steak**, **scottiglia of boar**, **ossibuchi alla toscana,** saddle of cinta senese with mushrooms, roast pork shank with Brunello sauce; a good selection of main dishes served with haricot beans cooked with oil, sage and tomato sauce or roast potatoes. Not to forget the puddings, the chef's passion: on the menu he writes "delights of the garden" and they are indeed a lovely surprise every day. There are around 70 labels on the wine list, with lots of Brunello and Rosso di Montalcino.

Located in a beautiful 13th-century building in the historic center of Montalcino, this family-run B&B is managed by Lucilla Locatelli (from Rome) and her photographer husband, Roberto Berti. Rooms are good value for money, quiet and fitted with antique furniture. The common areas consist of a charming lounge where guests can read or listen to music, the cozy breakfast room where you can enjoy good quality produce, including jams and homemade cakes, and the lovely courtyard garden. Worth visiting are the nearby municipal and diocesan Museum, the town hall and the churches of Sant'Egidio and Sant'Agostino.

• 3 double rooms and 1 mini-suite, with bathroom, satellite TV • Prices: double room single use 80 euros, double 85, mini-suite 110, breakfast included • Credit cards: none • Public parking close by. No pets allowed. Owners always reachable • Breakfast room, music and reading room. Garden

MONTALE
Podere Pianaccio

MONTECARLO
Cercatola

IL PIANACCIO

DA BAFFO

Holiday farm
Via Maone e Casello 150
Tel. 0573 959875-338 9038436-335 1321635
Fax 0573 959875
E-mail: info@agriturismoilpianaccio.it
Internet: www.agriturismoilpianaccio.it
Closed January 10-February 10

Holiday farm
Via della Tinaia 6
Tel. 0583 22381
Closed Monday
Open: dinner, October-March Saturday
and Sunday also lunch
Holidays: from after Christmas until mid-January
Seating: 30 + 60 outdoors
Prices: 20 euros
No credit cards

This renovated farmhouse with its 16 hectares of land is managed by Cristiano Giannuzzi and his family who will give you a warm, friendly welcome. Rooms are fitted with period furniture and have views over the surrounding hills. Breakfast offers coffee, cappuccino, tea, croissants, jams and fruit juices with yogurt and savory dishes on request. The restaurant, open to residents only, offers a traditional Tuscan menu for 25 euros. The farm's own produce is available for purchase (olive oil, wine, honey and jams) and you can rent a mountain bike or participate in cooking lessons. Tennis courts and golf courses are 15 kilometers away. The farm is a good base to visit Florence and the region's art towns, reachable by train from Montale-Agliana station 6 kilometers away.

• 4 double and 1 triple rooms, with bathroom, TV • Prices: double room single use and double 70-80 euros , triple 80-90, breakfast included • Credit cards: all, Bancomat • Facility accessible to the mobility challenged. Off-street parking. Small pets allowed. Owners always reachable. • Bar corner, restaurant (for residents only). Reading and TV room. Terrace. Boules courts. Pool

The news was announced for Spring 2006: there's going to be breaded and fried steak on the menu. In any other eatery it would be quite normal, but in this agritourism farm of the Carmignani family it is almost a revolution, because here they have been serving the same dishes for years, in the same surroundings with the same owners' verve. The theatrical personality of Gino Carmignani, known as Fuso (Baffo is the nickname of his father Lorenzo) is a very good vine grower and a friendly host. To reach the farm you drive through a sea of vines, and risk getting lost in all the small roads that pass through them. There is a small dining room and a larger space outside, with wooden tables simply laid.

The fixed menu is recited out loud, with a choice only for the main courses, and is excellent traditional home cooking. The cheese board (mainly pecorino) and cured meats (salami, **mezzina**, ham, lardo) is put on the table with Altopascio bread, often still hot from the oven, with delicious olives and tasty **fettunta**. For first course, **spelt soup**, **tagliolini on white bean purée** from Lucca, at weekends an elaborate slowly cooked **frantoiana soup**. For main course, pending the breadcrumbed steak, you can try the **rabbit chasseur with olives, beans all'uccelletto with sausages** or a crisp **chicken fried** in extra virgin olive oil with hand cut potatoes. To close, cantuccini with homemade Vin Santo, like the other wines that the Carmignani family produces specifically for their holiday farm.

MONTECATINI TERME
Montecatini Alto

22 KM SOUTHWEST OF PISTOIA

MONTELUPO FIORENTINO
Turbone

25 KM SOUTHWEST OF FLORENCE

CASA ALBERTINA

Bed and breakfast
Via Fratelli Guermani 12
Tel. 0572 900238
Fax 0572 904298
E-mail: info@casaalbertina.it
Internet: www.casaalbertina.it
Open all year

OSTERIA BONANNI

Traditional osteria
Via Turbone 9
Tel. 0571 913477
Closed Monday
Open: lunch and dinner
Holidays: August
Seating: 40 + 40 outdoors
Prices: 20-26 euros, wine excluded
Credit cards: Visa

Once home to Ugolino Simoni, the 14th-century doctor who studied and codified the therapeutic properties of the spa waters, this B&B is located in the upper part of Montecatini close to the main square. Over the years the building has been renovated and modernized and is now a lovely B&B. Rooms are fitted with a mixture of antique family furniture, modern and ethnic pieces and the communal areas boast a variety of rugs, vases and plants. The most charming part of the building is the small garden planted with orange and lemon trees and aromatic herbs, where in summer your hostess will serve you a breakfast of sweet fare, hot and cold beverages and local cheeses.

• 2 single and 7 double rooms, with bathroom; almost all with TV • Prices: single 60 euros, double 90, breakfast included • Credit cards: none • Facility accessible to the mobility challenged. Free public parking. Small pets allowed. Owners always reachable • Breakfast room, reading and TV room, lounge. Garden

We are in the open countryside, in a district of Montelupo called Turbone. The Bonanni trattoria has a large room, with a bar at the entrance, a small room and a few tables outside when it is fine. Mauro Bonanni, known by everyone as Capounto ("greasy head"!)for all the brilliantine he uses on his hair, is permanently at the bar; front of house his lively son Maurilio is helped by his niece. Marisa, Bonanni's other daughter is in the kitchen. The fittings are simple and the menu is the same, winter and summer, because all customers want to find the dishes the osteria is famous for. You can begin with excellent antipasti of various cured meats and Tuscan **croutons**, but above all the preserves in oil (Empoli artichokes, tomatoes, mushrooms, shallots). For your first course **penne strascicate**, **spelt minestrone**, mushroom soup, **pappardelle with wild boar sauce, tagliolini with truffles** (in season). You are really spoilt for choice among the main courses: apart from the grilled meat, try the excellent **chops alla livornese** or **rabbit with potatoes, tripe Bonanni style** or stoccafisso alla Marisa, ossibuchi, **baccalà**, **beans all'uccelletto**, sautéed vegetables. You are bound to be full now and it doesn't matter if the choice of puddings is limited to a few homemade tarts (when there are any) and the ever-present cantuccini with Vin Santo.
The house Chianti is passable; the wine list is basic, with a few good labels.

MONTEPULCIANO

68 KM SOUTHEAST OF SIENA ON SS 2 AND 146

IL RICCIO

Rooms
Via Talosa, 21
Tel. and fax 0578 757713
E-mail: info@ilriccio.net
Internet: www.ilriccio.net
Closed for 3 weeks in January

This small hospitality facility is in the splendid old center of Montepulciano in a refined building known as Palazzo Pucci, which in the past was also a seminary and the headquarters of the Italian School of Mosaic Art. Then in 1949 the building was bought by the Caroti family who, in the early 1980s, decided to renovate it and dedicated part of it to hospitality. So this is how the Il Riccio was launched: six spacious rooms with a view over the medieval village and valley, carefully chosen period furniture, and an entire family (Giorgio and Ivana, their son Iacopo and companion Monica) always ready to help you. The excellent breakfast can substitute lunch: local salami and cheeses, homemade cakes and jams, Tuscan bread, freshly baked croissants, squeezed juices and fresh fruit.

• 1 single and 5 double rooms, with bathroom, air-conditioning, mini-bar, safe, satellite TV • Prices: single 75 euros, double 85 (16 euro supplement for extra bed); breakfast 8 euros per person • Credit cards: all, Bancomat • Reserved paid parking in the immediate vicinity. Small pets allowed. Reception open 7am-midnight • Bar. Reading room. Terrace

MONTEROTONDO MARITTIMO

69 KM NORTHWEST OF GROSSETO SS 398

LE LOGGE

Osteria-trattoria
Piazza Casalini 4
Tel. 0566 916397
Closed Tuesday, never in August and Christmas
Open: lunch and dinner
Holidays: none
Seating: 28 + 20 outdoors
Prices: 25 euros, wine excluded
No credit cards

Don't be misled by the name: Monterotondo Marittima is a village in the hills, on the road between Massa Marittima and Volterra, immersed in countryside famous for its geothermal energy phenomenon (boraciferous soffioni). This bar-osteria is the local hang-out, and is situated in the center of the village opposite the town hall. The osteria is very simply furnished and is cozy, friendly and warm. Young Susy Ranieri, who has been running it for three years, helps her mother Laura and father Stefano prepare both traditional and personal dishes.

The meal opens with the classic Tuscan antipasti (cured meats, bruschetta and croutons) with tomino cheese grilled with sage and onion or rolls of raw ham and goat's cheese. They are followed by **Maremma tortelli** with excellent ragù, very good **acquacotta**, **black bean soup**, **pappardelle with wild boar sauce**, and tortellacci of potatoes with broccoli sauce. A wide variety of roast and grilled meats (excellent classic **steak** and tagliata with truffles) are the main offers for main course; alternatively, there's **stewed boar**, ossobuco or **tripe Maremma-style, stuffed rabbit** and **chicken alla cacciatora**. All served with fresh vegetables, boiled, roast or fried, and, when in season, local **mushrooms**. The meal ends with a reasonable selection of tasty home-made puddings.

The wine list (all Tuscan labels) isn't very long but the house wine on tap is really very good.

Monte San Savino
Bano

Belvedere

🍲Restaurant
Località Bano 226
Tel. 0575 849588
Closed Monday
Open: lunch and dinner
Holidays: none
Seating: 80 + 80 outdoors
Prices: 28-30 euros
All credit cards, Bancomat

Just a few hundred meters from A1 exit 27 you reach Monte San Savino, a lovely Renaissance town; continue along the Sienna-Arezzo road, and after a few miles you find the signs for Bano. The Belvedere restaurant is in an isolated position, in the middle of a wood of oak, olive, cypress trees and dry stone walls. Expert in the wines, oil, ingredients and flavors of Valdichiana country cooking traditions, Massimo will welcome you in the dining hall or patio.

We recommend starting with the black croutons served with excellent local **cured meats,** or the bruschette. Slowly cooked sauces make excellent dressings for the handmade pasta: try the **pici al sugo di nana** (duck), rabbit or boar. Very good the **strozzapreti di farro with chickpeas and rigatino, ribollita** and **bean soup**. Excellent quality meat, in particular the chianina that Massimo buys personally: **steak**, rosticciana, sausage and other grilled meats are a real specialty. We also recommend the **pork livers, fried rabbit, boar chasseur**, pork fillets with cep mushrooms, **duck** and rabbit **in porchetta**. The meal ends with cheese made from local raw milk and an inviting selection of puddings: cream gnocchi, trifle, apple tart with pine nuts and raisins and the ancient **bread cake**.

The good wine list offers numerous labels, nearly all from Tuscany, with an excellent quality-price ratio: around ten different labels can be tasted by the glass.

🍴 The butchers in **Monte San Savino** continue the excellent Norcio traditions. Visit Aldo, Piazza Gamurrini, for his cured meats and fresh pork from organic farms.

Monte San Savino

Logge dei mercanti

🔑3-Star Hotel
Corso Sangallo 40-42
Tel. 0575 810710
Fax 0575 849657
E-mail: info@loggedeimercanti.it
Internet: www.loggedeimercanti.it
Open all year

This 3-star hotel, once a pharmacy, is located in a beautiful Renaissance building next to the town hall and opposite the Logge del Sansovino, for which it is named. The hotel is managed by very helpful Manuela and her husband Roberto Lodovichi. Rooms have exquisite ceiling frescos (they're individually decorated and fitted with valuable antique furniture) and there's an amazing brick-vaulted lounge dug out of the rock. For breakfast you can enjoy coffee, milk, tea, pastries, jams, honey and a good selection of cured meats and locally produced cheeses. The nearby restaurant offers traditional Tuscan dishes (22-25 euros, wine excluded). Worth visiting are the cattle farms (the Chianina breed is reared in this area) and the renowned butchers of Monte San Savino.

• 3 single and 7 double rooms, with bathroom, air-conditioning, mini-bar, safe, satellite TV; 3 suites with lounge, terrace • Prices: single 55 euros, double 90 (20 euro supplement for extra bed), suite 120, breakfast included • Credit cards: all except DC, Bancomat • 1 room designed for use by the mobility challenged. Free public parking nearby. Small pets allowed. Reception open 24 hours a day • Breakfast and TV room. Tavern

MONTESCUDAIO

62 KM SOUTH OF PISA SS 206, 10 KM FROM CECINA SS 68

IL FRANTOIO

Restaurant
Via della Madonna 9
Tel. 0586 650381
Closed Tuesday
Open: dinner, for lunch in winter on festivities
Holidays: January 10- February 10
Seating: 40
Prices: 30-32 euros, wine excluded
All credit cards, Bancomat

Thanks to the warm welcome of Giorgio Scarpa and his wife Barbara, you don't feel as if you are entering a restaurant but a family home. Built in an old mill, it's for all the world like a private lounge. Giorgio is the expert in the kitchen, but is also constantly present at the tables. Cooking offers the best of Val di Cecina traditions, both land and sea, and fresh fish is always fairly priced. The menu follows the seasons and begins with antipasti such as **anchovies in parsley sauce, chicken salad,** baccalà in carpione and Amiata cured meats. For first course, **tagliatelle,** served according to the season with cep mushrooms, truffles or boar ragù, spaghetti with octopus, tagliolini with prawns, **pappa al pomodoro,** cacciucco of chickpeas or **lentils al coccio.** There is more meat than fish in the main courses: **stracotto di chianina,** steak, **tripe,** cow's liver with turnips, **rabbit alla cacciatora,** roast pheasant, **sweet and sour pigeon, devilled octopus,** and stockfish. Giorgio sometimes gives his imagination free rein and his pigeon with prunes and pistachio is out of this world. The meal ends with an excellent selection of **cheeses** and delicious desserts made by Barbara.
Wines are carefully selected from the Etruscan Coast, the rest of the Tuscany and beyond.

MONTESPERTOLI
Montagnana

22 KM SOUTHWEST OF FLORENCE

IL GUGLIERALLO

Bed and breakfast
Via Castiglioni 18
Tel. 0571 671025-339 6183769
Fax 0571 671025
E-mail: info@ilguglierallo.it
Internet: www.ilguglierallo.it
Open all year

Il Gugliarello, a beautifully renovated 18th-century farmhouse with large garden and swimming pool, is located in the hills on the left bank of the River Pesa, not far from San Casciano and Florence (easily reachable by bus). The scenery is typically Tuscan with vineyards and olive groves (in Montespertoli you can visit the Wine and Oil Museum). The owner, Maria Grazia Pollacci, offers comfortable, elegant rooms and the grounds are also organized to accommodate three or four mobile homes. For breakfast you can enjoy coffee, fruit juices, croissants, cookies and homemade jams (following a family tradition, the lady of the house also makes Vinsanto).

• 1 double and 3 triple rooms, with bathroom (next door in the case of 2 rooms) • Prices: double room single use 40-60 euros, double 70-100, triple 90-130 (20 euro supplement for extra bed), breakfast included • Credit cards: none • Off-street parking. Small pets allowed. Owners always present. • Breakfast room. Garden. Pool

MONTICIANO
Tocchi

LOCANDA DI BEPPE

🔑 Rooms
Localita' Tocchi 3
Tel. and fax 0577 757811
E-mail: info@locandadibeppeatocchi.it
Internet: www.locandadibeppeatocchi.it
Closed from mid-January to end of February

Tocchi is a rural village in the woods, about 15 kilometers from the Abbey of San Gagliano and perfectly located for those wanting to visit Siena. After years in the restaurant business on the islands of Giannutri and Giglio, Giuseppe Russo and his wife Tosca purchased a 19th-century travelers' lodge and turned it into a small B&B. Rooms are each decorated with a unique color scheme and furnished in rustic style. Breakfast consists of croissants, jams, yogurt, hot and cold beverages and occasionally home-baked cakes. The owners also run a restaurant located 5 kilometers from the B&B where you can enjoy traditional Tuscan dishes (20 euros, wine excluded).

• 2 single and 3 double rooms, with bathroom • Prices: single 35 euros, double 60, breakfast included • Credit cards: MC, Visa, Bancomat • Free public parking. Small pets accepted. Owners always reachable • Bar. Garden

ORBETELLO
Ansedonia

LA LOCANDA DI ANSEDONIA

🔑 Rooms
Via Aurelia Nord, km 140.5
Tel. 0564 881317
Fax 0564 881727
E-mail: info@locandadiansedonia.it
Internet: www.lalocandadiansedonia.it
Closed 15 days in February and 15 in November

The locanda is located in a renovated farmhouse near Grosseto in the heart of the Maremma, close to the exit from the Via Aurelia for the Argentario. The 12 rooms are friendly and comfortable, all have views of the surrounding countryside and are fitted with antique furniture (the price of a room can reach 130 euros in August and during important holidays). Breakfast is varied and offers home-made sweet and savory fare, coffee and tea and fresh beverages. Among the common areas is a veranda that opens onto a large garden, where you can enjoy the shade of the maritime pines. The restaurant serves seasonal fish and meat dishes (set menu 43 euros, wine excluded). Worth visiting are the beach resorts and the archeological site at Cosa, a Roman colony dating back to 273 BC.

• 2 single and 10 double rooms, with bathroom, air-conditioning, mini-bar, TV • Prices: single 70-85 euros, double 90-120 (20 euro supplement for extra bed), breakfast included • Credit cards: all except DC, Bancomat • Off-street parking. Small pets allowed. Owners always reachable. • Bar, restaurant. Breakfast room, reading room. Garden

ORBETELLO

I PESCATORI

Trattoria
Via Leopardi 9
Tel. 0564 860611
Open for dinner; Saturday also for lunch, winter only weekends
Holidays: none
Seating: 200 + 250 outdoors
Prices: 25-28 euros, wine excluded
All credit cards, Bancomat

It's not easy to fit this trattoria in among the osterias in our guide: in summer the service is spartan, with plastic tableware and numerous customers every day; during the rest of the year though, the evocative setting of the stables in the Spanish fort can finally be appreciated to the full, together with a cooler climate and better service. The young people in the Orbetello Pesca Lagunare cooperative, with its Slow Food Presidium, put everything they have into the management, continuously making improvements and adjustments. One thing is certain, though, the fish they serve is really fresh, at a fair price and cooked according to local traditions.

The menu reflects the day's catch. The Presidium **bottarga di cefalo** (grey mullet roe) is offered on crostini as an antipasto, sliced very fine and seasoned with just oil and lemon, or grated with parsley, garlic and a pinch of chili as a sauce for spaghetti or gnocchetti. Other antipasti are the lagoon oysters, **eel scavecciata** and carpaccio of bass or bream; when available, it's also worth trying the lagoon shrimps. Among the first courses, agnolotti with bass, gnocchi or **pasta with bream**, bass or botargo, or Tuscan ravioli with vegetables and botargo. All followed by excellent **grilled fish**, **eel sfumata** and fillet of bass in white wine. At the end of the meal enjoy a glass of lemon sorbet.

The wine list is growing and is dominated by a good selection of local whites.

PALAZZUOLO SUL SENIO

LA BOTTEGA DEI PORTICI

Osteria-wine shop with bar and kitchen
Piazza Garibaldi 3
Tel. 055 8046580
Closed Monday
Open: lunch and dinner
Holidays: variable, in September
Seating: 30 + 50 outdoors
Prices: 25 euros, wine excluded
All credit cards, Bancomat

It is not easy to reach Palazzuolo sul Senio, a village on the border with Romagna, but when you finally get to the main square, you will be more than repaid for your fatigue. At first sight, the inn run by Francesco Piromallo from Calabria, resembles a normal food shop. In the dining room, which has period photos and calendars hung on the wall, there is a small corner bar and a few simply laid tables. During the summer you can also eat outside. Francesco will serve you in his kind and courteous manner while wife Luana prepares typical Tuscan dishes.

Lots of good antipasti: **croutons**, local cured meats or game, polenta pudding with mushrooms, eggplant and ricotta flan and, when in season, cep mushroom salad. You continue with **bread gnocchi** with mushrooms, **ribollita**, **pappa al pomodoro**, tagliolini with cep mushrooms, **potato tortelli with ragù**, gramigna with sausage and chicory. As an alternative to the classic T-bone steak, you can choose from roast pork shank, **sausage and beans cooked with oil, sage and tomato sauce**, **tripe Florentine style**. Delicious conclusion with a wide choice of **cheeses** (chosen from those displayed at the entrance bar) and the excellent desserts prepared by Luana: milk alla portoghese, biscuits, tarts and blancmanges with wild berries or with the famous local chestnuts.

There is a very long wine list with around 100 labels. The house Sangiovese is also excellent.

in **Lozzole di Quadalto** (2 km), Cristina and Francesco Lecca rear wild pigs, sheep and goats and produce excellent goat's cheese.

PELAGO
Diacceto

PELAGO

LOCANDA TINTI

🍲Rooms
Via Casentinese 65
Tel. 055 8327007
Fax 055 8327828
E-mail: info@locandatinti.it
Internet: www.locandatinti.it
Open all year

OSTERIA DELLA SCIÒA

🍲Osteria-trattoria
Piazza Ghiberti 30
Tel. 055 8326062
Closed Wednesday, in winter also Monday and Tuesday
Open: lunch and dinner
Holidays: January 10-February 10
Seating: 30
Prices: 20-25 euros, wine excluded
All credit cards except AE, Bancomat

This traditional locanda in the center of Diaceto, a hamlet near Pelago and close to Pontassieve, is managed by the Tinti family. In the recently renovated palazzo there are six rooms for those who want to enjoy a peaceful break away from traditional holiday destinations. Pelago is located at an altitude of 500 meters, at the mouth of the Mugello and Casentino valleys but also only 25 kilometers from Florence. Pelago is a good base for those wanting to explore the Chianti Rufina wine region. Rooms are decidedly Tuscan in style, with wooden beams, terracotta tiled floors and late 19th-century rustic furniture, but there are also all modern comforts, from air-conditioning to satellite TV. Continental breakfast offers cured meats, cheeses, bread, butter and jams.

• 6 double rooms, with bathroom, air-conditioning, safe, satellite TV • Prices: double room single use and double 80 euros (30 euro supplement for extra bed); breakfast 8 euros per person • Credit cards: major ones, Bancomat • Public parking in the immediate vicinity. No pets allowed. Owners always reachable • Bar, ice-cream parlor, tearoom. Terrace, solarium

The trattoria is in central Ghiberti Square, alongside an old arcade where the offices of the street music festival, for which Pelago is justly famous, are located. The dining room is furnished in wood with wrought iron lamps. The family-style service is attentive but discreet. Enzo and Aurelia, united in their life and work, offer good food in a friendly, comfortable atmosphere, highly recommended for a pleasant evening.
You can begin with various different **croutons**: with **Pecorino di fossa and honey,** aromatic herbs, tomato and herbs, hot cheese, tomato and cheese, livers, or alternatively mixed cured meats and on a monthly rotation, delicious dishes such as carpaccio with pears or boar sausage with cheese flan. Among the most common first courses the **tagliatelle** with meat sauce, **hare ragù** or cep mushrooms, Sardinian-style ravioli with ricotta and lemon, wholemeal rice with sautéed vegetables. The main courses delicate and balanced: grilled lamb, **steak**, tagliata, eggplant pie, **boar in white wine**, roast veal with lemon, **rabbit with wild fennel**. When in season, choose the cep mushrooms as a side dish. If you still aren't full, there are some good home-made desserts.
The regional wine list has a good choice of Chianti Rufina; honest markups. Booking is advisable in the summer.

PESCIA
Monte a Pescia

PIENZA
Monticchiello

28 KM SOUTHWEST OF PISTOIA SS 435

59 KM SOUTHEAST OF SIENA SS 146

MONTE A PESCIA
DA PALMIRA

☞ Restaurant
Via del Monte Ovest 1
Tel. 0572 476887
Closed Wednesday
Open: dinner, festivities also for lunch
Holidays: October
Seating: 80 + 80 outdoors
Prices: 27-35 euros, wine excluded
Credit cards: Visa, Bancomat

LA PORTA

☞ Recently opened Osteria
Via del Piano 1
Tel. 0578 755163
Closed Thursday
Open: lunch and dinner
Holidays: January
Seating: 30 + 35 outdoors
Prices: 30 euros, wine excluded
All major credit cards, Bancomat

You can look out over the whole of the Valdinove valley from this village, a few miles from Pescia. The Da Palmira restaurant lies here among the hills and olive trees, with a panoramic terraced garden that overlooks the valley. The ambience is rustic and the fireplace always lit. You will be met by Roberto and Patrizia, the owners and managers as well as the stars of the kitchen.

The antipasti, mainly a range of local **cured meats**, are rich and varied. They are followed by **malfatti** and other home-made pasta served with seasonal products: Pescia asparagus in spring, cep mushrooms in the summer and fall, and game in winter, when the typical local soups are particularly good. Roberto Chilardi shows his skills at the wood-burning grill: **steaks** (beef or pork), chicken, **pigeon**, **rabbit** and baccalà are all cooked to a turn. As an alternative, a **mixed fry of vegetables and white meat** and, in winter, **tripe alla pesciatina** and **ciancia of veal** (an ancient dish that the local hide tanners used to prepare). Side dishes that you should not miss include **fromagioli di Sorana** (a Slow Food Presidium), increasingly rare but very tasty cheeses. And to finish, some good local cheeses such as **raw-milk Pecorino** from the Pistoia mountains and, in the fall, traditional **necci** eaten with fresh ricotta.

The wine list includes a selection of the best Tuscan labels, but there are numerous everyday bottles at accessible prices.

The village of Monticchiello is renowned for its 'teatro povero' (poor theater) depicting rural traditions and customs, which is written and performed by the local inhabitants in July and August, and changes every year. It. The osteria is at the entrance to the village. Daria, the courteous, professional proprietress, will help you choose your meal in a small, welcoming environment, which is simple and elegant. There is a splendid terrace where you can eat in the summer, enjoying the wonderful view from Pienza to Monte Amiata. Moreno is in the kitchen, where he skillfully prepares traditional dishes, carefully choosing his raw ingredients from the surrounding territory.

You can start with carpaccio of game, **Cinta Senese cured meats**, vegetable pies with cream of Pecorino. The best first courses are the home-made pastas: **pici with a duck sauce** or with cacio cheese and pepper, **pappardelle with Chianina beef ragù**, and ravioli of potatoes with Pecorino. But the **risotto mantecato of emmer** and the classic Tuscan soups (emmer, chickpeas, small Trasimeno beans and **ribollita**) are all good. For a main course, we recommend the **braised wild boar** or venison, **pig's livers**, lamb chops, and **steak**. In the right season, you'll find plenty of dishes with truffles and wild mushrooms. To crown it all, chocolate cake, semifreddo and small home-baked biscuits.

Daria, an expert sommelier, is in charge of the wines; the list includes a wide choice of labels, mostly from Tuscany, some of which are also available by the glass.

PIENZA
San Pietro

PIETRASANTA

SANTO PIETRO

LA GIUDEA

Holiday farm
Strada statale 146, 29
Tel. and fax 0578 748410
E-mail: santo.pietro@libero.it
Internet: www.agritoursantopietro.it
Closed from mid-January to end of
February

Trattoria
Via Barsanti 52-54, corner vicolo dei Lavatoi
Tel. 0584 71514
Closed Monday, in winter also Sunday for dinner
Open: lunch and dinner
Holidays: 7 days in September, December 15–January 6
Seating: 40 + 20 outdoors
Prices: 24-28 euros, wine excluded
All credit cards, Bancomat

This agriturismo in Val d'Orcia was once an old convent built between the 13th and 14th centuries and renovated maintaining the original external structure. Woods, olive groves and vineyards occupy the 32 hectares of land where they also rear horses, goats, rabbits and chickens. Other specialties are their own-produced cured meats, jams and homemade pasta. Guests can enjoy the farm's produce for breakfast or in the restaurant (average price 25 euros). Rooms are welcoming, comfortable and furnished with taste with beautiful views of the valley. Must visits are Pienza and the old town of Corsignano that Pope Pius II Piccolomini commissioned architect Rossellino to build: the prototype of the ideal town as imagined by the humanists.

• 2 single, 5 double and 2 triple rooms, with bathroom; some with balcony • Prices: single 50 euros, double 85, triple 110, breakfast included • Credit cards: all except DC, Bancomat • Covered off-street parking. No pets allowed. Owners always present • Bar, restaurant (for residents only). TV room. Garden. Pool

By the time you read this guide, the trattoria should have moved to Vicolo dei Lavatoi 52-54, on the corner of Via Barsanti, only a few meters away. We took a look at the new premises while they were being refurbished and they looked very attractive, even without the furniture: slightly larger than the previous premises, with space to seat 45, in a building with large wooden doorways and a garden shaded by a large magnolia and a huge fig-tree. The kitchen will remain in full view and the cuisine will maintain the approach adopted successfully in Via Barsanti 4: simple, traditional dishes, all beautifully home-made. This is guaranteed by the Simonetti family who manage La Giudea, with Barbara in the kitchen, and her husband Antonio and daughter Letizia in the dining room. Start with cured meats, carpaccio of tuna and **vegetable pies** (the cuisine here in the Versilia area shows the influence of neighboring Liguria). Then **tortelli di magro with pesto**, fettuccine with anchovies, **lasagnette tordellate** (filled with tordelli, or mistle-thrushes, from Lucca), linguine with clams or alla pescatora, **soup with beans and black cabbage** or emmer. The main courses include an excellent **cacciucco of rabbit and chicken**, **beef stew**, **roast pork with potatoes**, filleted anchovies, and **baccalà in sauce** or in a salad with pine-nuts and cherry tomatoes. If they are on the menu, be sure to try the **Savoy cabbage rolls** stuffed with meat and vegetables. To close, pear and chocolate pie or other desserts prepared by Letizia.
You may choose to accompany your meal with a bottle of wine from Tuscany or Liguria, but the house wine is also good.

PIETRASANTA

SCI

Trattoria
Vicolo Porta a Lucca 3-7
Tel. 0584 790983
Closed Sunday and festivities
Open: lunch and dinner
Holidays: December 15-January 15
Seating: 40 + 20 outdoors
Prices: 20-25 euros
No credit cards

The Sci is a popular old trattoria, which some people might find even too simple and discreet for their tastes: the bar-cum-dining-room leads into the kitchen, the menu is short, service can be a bit abrupt (but on one of our visits, when the place was not crowded, we were treated with extreme, spontaneous courtesy). If you are looking for somewhere authentic, where a complete meal with a few important traditional dishes costs little more than 20 euro, including the house wine, this is the place for you.

Cured meats and Tuscan croutons, omelet, vegetables conserved in oil, sometimes **meatballs** with tomatoes (in doses that are occasionally too generous) make up the antipasti, which are only served in the evening. Then there is a choice of two or three first courses and as many main courses. Some examples: **pasta and beans**, **emmer soup**, **pappa al pomodoro**, green tagliatelle with a meat sauce, pasta with fish sauce (very flavorsome), risotto with cuttlefish and greens, **baked beef with vegetables**, stewed chicken or **rabbit**, **stuffed vegetables**. Friday is traditionally the day for baccalà, stewed with potatoes, or baked in the oven. You can finish with homemade cakes or baked fruit. A word of warning to people from Tuscany, or just passing through, who are accustomed to 'pane sciocco' (unsalted bread): in Pietrasanta the bread is salted, as it is in Liguria and the rest of Italy.

In **Forte dei Marmi** (7 km), L'Angolo del Forte, at Via Dallapiccola 27, produces eight types of fortini, biscuits that are wrapped up individually as they come out of the oven.

PIEVE FOSCIANA

AI FRATI

Holiday farm
Località ai Frati 19 A
Tel. 0583 65378-320 0864919
Fax 0583 65378
E-mail: aifrati@libero.it
Internet: www.agriturismoaifrati.com
Closed from mid-January to end of February

This agritursimo is located in the old convent of San Francesco at an altitude of 450 meters, close to the spring of the Pra di Luna spa and two kilometers from Pieve Fosciana. The building is surrounded by 5 hectares of chestnut and pine trees. The apartments, located in what were once the monk's cells, are furnished in a simple, restrained manner. On the ground floor there are large rooms where conferences and events are often organized. Guests can also enjoy a lovely swimming pool with sun deck. Breakfast is varied and offers honey, jams, cakes and potato bread (a local specialty), all homemade. The farm produces corn and chestnut flour, fruit, aromatic herbs and honey, all of which can be purchased.

• 1 double room and 5 apartments (2 persons), with bathroom; apartments with lounge, equipped kitchen • Prices: double room single use 40 euros, double 50-75, apartment 70-115; breakfast 7-10 euros per person • Credit cards: none • Off-street parking. Small pets allowed. Owners always reachable • Breakfast room, conference rooms. Grounds, solarium. Pool

PIEVE FOSCIANA

52 KM NORTHWEST OF LUCCA SS 445 AND 324

IL POZZO

🍲 Restaurant-pizzeria
Via Europa 2 A
Tel. 0583 666380
Closed Wednesday
Open: lunch and dinner
Holidays: none
Seating: 150
Prices: 25-28 euros, wine excluded
All credit cards, Bancomat

PIOMBINO

82 KM SOUTH OF LIVORNO SS 1

IL GARIBALDI INNAMORATO

🍲 Restaurant
Via Giuseppe Garibaldi 5
Tel. 0565 49410
Closed Monday
Open: lunch and dinner
Holidays: variable
Seating: 40
Prices: 28-30 euros, wine excluded
All credit cards, Bancomat

Simple, well-prepared food, using local produce even when it isn't easy to find; this is the philosophy of the restaurant run by Giordano Andreucci and Maurizio Romei in the Garfagnana area. Wild herbs, vegetables, emmer, pecorino, mushrooms and black truffles when in season, and meat from selected farms: these are the ingredients used by chef, Maurizio, in a number of traditional recipes. Giordano, the wine and oil taster, is also in charge of the spirits and vinegar, and tries to use Slow Food Presidium products whenever possible.
For antipasti, typical cured meats (hand-cut prosciutto, Presidium **biroldo** and **mondiola**) accompanied by various types of **bread**, including the **potato bread** (Slow Food Presidium) and **emmer flour** bread. Follow with **soup** – emmer, mushroom, bean and cabbage – or home-made pasta, such as **ravioli with ricotta and greens** or pappardelle with game sauce in the hunting season. For main course, **roasts** from the wood-fired oven, stew of **Podolico beef**, **lamb with potatoes**, **pork chops** and other grilled meats, tagliata with wild herbs picked by Maurizio, fillet with cep mushrooms baked in foil, fried or grilled **mushrooms**. In summer, black truffle accompanies the carpaccio of beef, the pasta, meat, eggs and cheese baked in the oven. To close, local and other Italian **cheeses** – raw milk and fossa Pecorino and goat's cheese of various levels of maturity – and home-baked cakes made with apples, ricotta with candied fruit and chocolate or bilberries.
There is an excellent selection of Tuscan and Italian wines.

The restaurant is close to the main road that leads to Piazza Bovio, a fantastic balcony overlooking the sea and the nearby Isle of Elba. The restaurant has been in the guide for years, and is a must for people who enjoy fish. It is located in what were formerly a wine bar and a butcher's shop, and some of the earlier equipment still remains, such as the meat hooks and marble tiles on the walls.
The dishes vary every day, depending on the day's catch and the imagination of the two proprietors: the only constants are the **Corsican fish soup** and the confectioner's custard with lingue di gatto biscuits. The generous mixed antipasti contains eight different dishes, which may include anchovies au gratin or with pesto and butter, boiled tuna fish with oil from the coast, carpaccio of tuna, **palamita** pie with ricotta mousse, croutons with pâté of octopus, excellent **baccalà** with vegetables or **alla livornese**, delicate scaloppini of fried sciabola, carpaccio of grouper, croutons with paté of octopus, **salad of octopus and cannellini beans** and occasionally **clams with a tomato sauce**. Then there is a choice of three or four first courses and as many main courses: try the spaghettini al nero di seppia, or the **tagliolini with tuna, green bell peppers and tomato**, followed by a slice of fried tuna, mackerel in bianco with chilies, swordfish alla marinara, **tuna briao** (ubriaco, or drunk, i.e. cooked in red wine) and **fried paranza** which is always excellent. Close with a soft pudding: bavaresi with fruit or chocolate mousse.
Over 150 local and national labels, with extremely honest mark-ups invite you to try more than one bottle. The restaurant is recommended by the Italian Celiac Association, and also offers a gluten-free menu.

PISA

OSTERIA DEI CAVALIERI

🍲 Osteria
Via San Frediano 16
Tel. 050 580858
Closed Saturday for lunch and Sunday
Open: lunch and dinner
Holidays: August
Seating: 60
Prices: 30-32 euros, wine excluded
All major credit cards, Bancomat

If you have an opportunity to visit the city, after seeing Piazza dei Miracoli, wander through the old center to Piazza dei Cavalieri, the home of the Scuola Normale. The restaurant is just round the corner. In the kitchen Giovanni Mori prepares the best traditional dishes with top quality raw ingredients, while Ettore Masi is front of house. The restaurant is well furnished and its service fast, particularly at midday when the restaurant is crowded. In the evenings, the atmosphere is more relaxed and 'slow', though it's always best to book, and other specialties join those on the lunch menu.

Start with **pasta fritta** and Tuscan cured ham, **pancotto bianco di mare**, small vegetable flans or cream of chickpea with mussels and clams. There is a choice of fish or meat for first courses: the **tagliolini** are served with scampi, razor clams, rabbit and asparagus or duck sauce. There's a good choice of main courses: **dried cod with potatoes**, **tripe alla pisana**, baccalà salad, grilled scamorza and vegetables, tagliata with beans and pioppini mushrooms, **ossobuco with beans**, or fish of the day baked with vegetables. In the autumn, cep mushrooms in various ways. There's a good selection of homemade puddings (crostata of pears and cinnamon, semifreddo with croccante) or home-made ice-creams.

The wine list is interesting with a good choice of labels from the Pisa hills and the rest of Tuscany, plus a selection of the best national wines.

🍴 At Via Borgo Stretto 44, the old Salza café and pastry shop offers an array of Piedmontese sweet specialties as well as numerous savories.

PISA
Coltano

6 KM FROM CITY CENTER

RE DI PUGLIA

🍲 Holiday farm
Via Aurelia Sud 7
Tel. 050 960157
Closed Monday and Tuesday, July-August only Monday
Open: dinner, Sunday also for lunch
Holidays: January
Seating: 80 + 70 outdoors
Prices: 28-30 euros, wine excluded
No credit cards

Located between Pisa and Livorno, in a farmhouse on the Via Aurelia, this farm restaurant opened in 1988 thanks to the passion and tenacity of a group of friends who formed the Avola Cooperative. You dine in a large room complete with fireplace and grill or, if the weather is fine, alfresco on the spacious verandah in front. Sergio Sperandeo and his other colleagues and staff serve at table with courtesy and helpfulness. The dishes are all traditional Tuscan and vary with the seasons, but the helpings are generous. The main strength of the cuisine is the meat: once it was all produced on the farm, but now it is supplied both by the partners and by small local cattle farmers.

The meal obviously starts with classic **crostoni** (with chicken livers, lardo, and olive pâté) and bruschetta, but also with emmer salad, flans, and pastries filled with ricotta. The fresh pasta is all homemade: try the **pezzacci with rabbit sauce and rosemary**, the tortiglioni of goat's cheese, **spaghetti with mutton**, and tagliatelle with seasonal sauces. In addition to the wide choice of grilled meats (**lamb**, mutton, **duck**, **pigeon**, pork, **rabbit**) there is also an excellent guinea-fowl flavored with poppy seeds. Careful use of the grill also brings out the flavor of cheeses and vegetables. There are numerous good homemade puddings, including a torta delizia with peaches, and crostata of pears and chocolate.

The wine list is quite good, even if it only offers Tuscan labels, some of which are also served by the glass. There is a good wine on tap from the Tuscan hills, produced by one of the partners.

BALDO VINO

Wine shop-restaurant
Piazza San Lorenzo 5
Tel. 0573 21591
Closed Sunday
Open: only for dinner
Holidays: August 15-31, first week of February
Seating: 30 + 20 outdoors
Prices: 25-30 euros, wine excluded
All credit cards

ENOTECA DAL MIZIO

Wine shop with food
Via dei Macelli 9
Tel. 0573 23229
Closed Sunday and Monday for lunch
Open: lunch and dinne
Holidays: August 15-25
Seating: 40
Prices: 25-30 euros, wine excluded
All credit cards, Bancomat

We like this restaurant more every time we go there. And the credit goes to the young cook Margherita Amidei, the owner Francesco Balloni and to their great passion for things done well. The restaurant opened a few years ago as a wine shop: the wine list has been prepared with care and now numbers 1100 labels, as well as offering a growing selection of interesting wines by the glass. You can follow Francesco's advice and suggestions with your eyes closed, where both the wine and the food are concerned.

To start with, enjoy the good local **cured meats** including an excellent prosciutto made from pigs reared by a small local farmer. The other antipasti include **cibreo** with bruschetta and chicken liver terrine wrapped in bell peppers. For a first course, try the panzanella of couscous, ravioli of pecorino on a cream of broad beans, **pappa al pomodoro**, **tortelloni of baccalà** with cibreo of cockerel, ravioli with onion fondente and a cream of cannellini beans, or ravioli of leg of veal with slivers of ricotta from Puglia. Follow this with an excellent **fried veal brains**, fried sardines and anchovies, baccalà with fricassee of potatoes, and roast carpaccio of suckling pig. The choice of cheeses is also growing: you can choose freely from the board or order samples. Do not miss the **raw milk pecorino from the Pistoia mountains**, a Slow Food Presidia, which is used in several dishes: in summer, try the risotto with pea pods and slivers of pecorino. There are numerous puddings, accompanied by the appropriate wine served by the glass; for example, a sherbet of wine and sugar on a bread wafer or semifreddo of chestnuts with chestnut honey. It is always advisable to book.

Mizio is Maurizio Niccolai, who manages this well stocked wine shop (about 800 Italian and foreign labels) with his wife Paola and daughter Barbara; wine tasting and sales were expanded a few years ago to include some excellent food, all prepared using top quality local ingredients. The **cured meats** with which you start your meal are supplied by the Savigni farm in Pavana, which raises free-range pigs of various breeds, including the Cinta Senese (a Slow Food Presidium). Other protected products include **raw milk Pecorino from the Pistoia mountains**, served in a salad with fillets of anchovy, beans from Sorana, which can be served with shrimp, and Parmigiano Reggiano made with the milk of red cows, slivers of which dress the girello of smoked beef. These summer antipasti alternate in winter with **croutons of chicken livers** and there is always a tasty bruschetta. The first courses range from spaghetti with shallots and castelmagno cheese to **linguine with fillet of cinta senese**, **reginette with duck sauce** and birilli with classic Bologna sausage (a Slow Food Presidium) and fresh pecorino. The main courses include tagliata of chianina beef, **roast leg of duck** and other excellent meats. In the right season you will find **wild mushrooms** from the Pistoia mountains and above all some fish dishes in summer. Close your meal with a seasonal pudding, small apple tarts or pastries with chestnuts, or chocolate pralines. The selection of **cheeses** is excellent and there is a wide choice of extravirgin olive oils, and a good, constantly changing selection of wines by the glass. Theme evenings are a regular feature, offering different local specialties.

LA BOTTEGAIA

🍲 Wine shop-osteria
Via del Lastrone 17
Tel. 0573 365602
Closed Monday and Sunday for lunch
Open: lunch and dinner
Holidays: 15 days mid-August
Seating: 30 + 50 outdoors
Prices: 23-26 euros, wine excluded
Credit cards: AE, MC, Visa

TENUTAE DI PIEVE A CELLE

🗝 Holiday farm
Via Pieve a Celle 158
Tel. 0573 913087-335 247839
Fax 0573 910280
E-mail: info@tenutadipieveacelle.it
Internet: www.tenutadipieveacelle.it
Open all year

La BotteGaia is managed by two young men, Carlo and Alessandro, and is located on a corner of one of the loveliest squares in Tuscany, the one in front of Pistoia cathedral. It is always very busy and we recommend booking. The menu includes a number of cold dishes for people who only want a generous snack, and varies at least twice a week; the cuisine is traditional Tuscan, with the inevitable influence of the surrounding mountains of Emilia.

The traditional **cured meats** prepared by two well-known local butchers make an excellent antipasti, then try the flan of morellini artichokes on a fondue of pecorino from the Pistoia mountains, culatello sambucano with potatoes flavored with dill, and **cioncia** (a classic dish once made by tanners) on rusks of bread. Among the traditional first courses we recommend the **maccheroni with ragù of musk duck** named for San Iacopo, the town's patron saint, **soup made of chestnuts from** Momigno and leeks, and **farinata with leghe** (black cabbage). **Beef pot roast with beans all'uccelletta**, **lampredotto trippato** and Massa lamb with herbs are just some of the enticing main courses. The mouth-watering pudding list features an excellent **castagnaccio** made very thin and cooked with very little oil.

The wine list is particularly well prepared, and includes several small new winemakers: there are about one hundred labels, fifteen of which are served by the glass on a rotation basis.

At the end of a long attractive driveway lined with cypresses lies a typical Tuscan manor house dating from the mid-19th century and surrounded by extensive grounds with old trees. The farm extends over 10 hectares of woodland, vineyards, olive groves and organically cultivated land. The interiors are a blend of the traditional austere Tuscan style with a shrewd choice of contemporary and ethnic art. Rooms are fitted with antique furniture restored by the husband of the owner, Fiorenza Ravagnoli, who also encourages guests to use the extensive library and large CD collection. Breakfast offers home-made jams and bread, cakes and cookies all freshly baked daily. The restaurant menu includes Tuscan cuisine and fish dishes at a cost of 30 euros, wine excluded.

• 5 double rooms, with bathroom, air-conditioning, TV • Prices: double room single use 110 euros, double 120, breakfast included • Credit cards: all except DC, Bancomat • Off-street parking. Small pets allowed. Owners always present. • Restaurant (only open for residents in the evening). Reading room, lounges. Garden, grounds, solarium. Pool

PISTOIA

PONTREMOLI
Orsola

56 KM SOUTHWEST OF MASSA ON SS 62 OR A 15

TRATTORIA DELL'ABBONDANZA

◁ Trattoria
Via dell'Abbondanza 10
Tel. 0573 368037
Closed Wednesday and Thursday for lunch
Open: lunch and dinner
Holidays: 15 days in May, 15 in October
Seating: 40 + 40 outdoors
Prices: 22-25 euros, wine excluded
All credit cards except AE, Bancomat

COSTA D'ORSOLA

━O Holiday farm
Localita' Orsola
Tel. and fax 0187 833332
E-mail: info@costadorsola.it
Internet: www.costadorsola.it
Closed in November and January

This place is in the old part of town in a small street that gave the restaurant its name; it's utterly unlike the stereotypical Tuscan trattoria, with a light-filled environment and unusual, warm interior decoration, set off by Art Nouveau décor. The owners, Rossella and Patrizio (Iccio) Menici, prepare traditional fare and attempt to revive forgotten recipes. The menu varies with the seasons, but you can always start with crostini, bruschetta and typical cured meats. The first courses include **pappa col pomodoro**, **ribollita**, soup of cep mushrooms and **farinata with leghe** (black cabbage). In the winter you'll find a real rarity, **carcerato**, an emblem of poor cuisine which uses up leftovers: stale bread, stockmade with the less noble parts of the veal, seasoning, pepper and grated Pecorino. In the summer, enjoy the small cuttlefish au gratin in a cream of chickpeas and fish lasagne. As a main course, on our last visit we enjoyed the **fried chicken and vegetables**, which was crisp and not at all oily; you will often find **roast rabbit** on the menu or **meatballs**, **stracotto alla fiorentina** and, in winter, mixed boiled meats with green parsley sauce. The traditional Tuscan fish dishes deserve a special mention: **baccalà alla livornese**, **octopus in galera** and soup of moscardini; plus **baccalà fritters**, if they're on the menu. For puddings, try the Vecchia Pistoia **blancmange** and salami of chocolate.
The wine list is good and the bill reasonable.

These stone houses in an old village in the Lunigiana countryside were once the dwellings of farmers who worked the surrounding fields. Now they have been renovated using raw materials typical of the area (chestnut, slate). The rooms situated in the old cattle sheds are unpretentious but comfortable, fitted with both rustic and antique furniture. A conference and meeting room is in the process of being built. The four partners who own the farm rear Zerasca sheep (Slow Food Presidium) and also produce olive oil, honey and jams that guests can enjoy for breakfast alongside home-made cakes. The restaurant is only open in the evening and offers traditional local cuisine to residents and non-residents at a cost of 28-30 euros, wine excluded. Half board is 58 to 72 euros.

• 8 double, 3 triple rooms and 3 suites, with bathroom, terrace or patio • Prices: double room single use 50-70 euros, double 86-114, triple 112-148, suite 146-194, breakfast included • Credit cards: major ones, Bancomat • Free parking 30 meters away. Small pets allowed. Reception open 7.30-midnight • Bar with TV corner, restaurant (dinner only). Reading room with library. Garden, terrace. Tennis court, 5-a-side soccer pitch, pool

PONTREMOLI

56 KM FROM MASSA, 40 KM FROM LA SPEZIA SS 330 OR A 15

DA BUSSÈ

☞ Traditional osteria
Piazza Duomo 31
Tel. 0187 831371
Closed Friday
Open: lunch, Saturday and Sunday also for dinner
Holidays: July 1-20
Seating: 45
Prices: 25-30 euros
Credit cards: CartaSì, Visa, Bancomat

It was 1930 when Pietro Bertocchi opened an osteria in Pontremoli's main square, serving soups and other simple dishes to the farmers and stallholders on their way to the local market, from the very early hours of the morning. Three quarters of a century have passed and the osteria is still there, now managed by Antonietta and Ida Bertocchi with the help of their brother Luciano. Although it has since been modernized and expanded, and no longer opens before dawn, the menu still serves strictly local fare from the Lunigiana district, a frontier land between Tuscany, Liguria and Emilia. The dishes are always the same, cooked by Antonietta from quality ingredients, many of which are grown by Luciano, and served, occasionally with a rather military approach, by Ida.
You will always start with cured meats and **Pontremoli vegetable pie**, which is also offered as a main course. As a home-made first course, we recommend the **testaroli with pesto**, but the **tordelli of greens and ricotta**, ravioli with meat sauce, and the **lasagna mes-cie** made with chestnut flour and dressed with oil and pecorino, are all excellent. The **soup with ragù and Parmesan**, which used to revive the early customers in the old restaurant, is another of Antonietta's specialties. The main courses include exquisite **meat rolls**, roast veal cooked in a terracotta casserole, **rabbit chasseur**, and mixed boiled meats. The puddings are homemade and delicious: **spungata**, and almond and raspberry or almond and hazelnut cake, served with homemade honey, which can be bought by the jar.
All these dishes are accompanied by a good local red or white wine on tap.

PONTREMOLI
Guinadi

64 KM FROM MASSA, 48 KM FROM LA SPEZIA SS 330 OR A 15 AND SP 63

DA RENATO

☞ Trattoria
Località Guinadi
Tel. 0187 834715
Closed Tuesday
Open: lunch and dinner
Holidays: none
Seating: 50
Prices: 25-30 euros
No credit cards

Eight miles of tortuous mountain roads from the center of Pontremoli are the price you have to pay to reach Guinadi and the trattoria run by the Marioni family … but it's worth it! People come here in particular at certain times of the year to eat the delicious **mushrooms** that grow abundantly in the woods, and which Renato's wife, Luiciana, cooks very well. Before you actually eat them, you'll see them everywhere: in boxes just filled by the pickers (who include the proprietor himself), drying in containers, or bottled in jars of oil. When fresh, cook puts them in a saucepan or frying pan or on the grill within 24 hours, so that you can appreciate their full flavor.
The owner's son Fabio will welcome you to the simple trattoria. Start your meal with excellent **prosciutto crudo** and other cured meats, and firm, meaty cep mushrooms in oil or raw, served with extravirgin olive oil and flavored with mint. For first course, **tagliatelle** or polenta **with mushroom sauce**, meat ravioli with meat sauce and the typical **testaroli** lunigiani **with pesto**. Mushrooms abound among the main courses: fried, sautéed and grilled (the cep caps are particularly good). As an alternative, **roast lamb**, grilled chops and **stewed boar**. If you still have room, close the meal with a slice of crostata with berries or buccellato, or ice-cream with bilberry sauce.
The wine is served in 2-liter bottles. Before paying the amazingly reasonable bill, you can also enjoy a glass of good grappa.

38 KM NORTHWEST OF AREZZO ON SS 70

CASENTINO

🔑 3-Star Hotel
Piazza della Repubblica 6
Tel. 0575 529090
Fax 0575 529067
E-mail: info@albergocasentino.it
Internet: www.albergocasentino.it
Closed in November

CIBBÉ

🍲 Trattoria
Piazza Mercatale 49
Tel. 0574 607509
Closed Sunday
Open: lunch and dinner
Holidays: August
Seating: 30
Prices: 24 euros, wine excluded
All credit cards except AE

Poppi is a medieval village perched on a hilltop and makes a good base for trips in the Casentino area. Only a few kilometers away are the hermitage of Camaldoli, the convent of Verna, castles and Romanesque churches and the Parco delle Foreste Casentinesi on the border with Emilia Romagna. This hotel is part of the Guidi castle complex, the most prestigious building in the village, a great place to relax and close to numerous places of interest. Rooms are big and friendly with rustic furnishings. The restaurant is in what were previously stables and boasts wooden beams and a large fireplace in typical Tuscan-style, as is the cuisine (18-20 euros, wine excluded). In summer you can enjoy breakfast – homemade cakes or nice pastries made locally – in the garden.

• 2 single and 25 double rooms, with bathroom, TV • Prices: single 50 euros, double 65 (10 euro supplement for extra bed), breakfast included • Credit cards: all, Bancomat • 2 rooms designed for use by the mobility challenged. Public parking in the immediate vicinity. Small pets allowed. Owners always reachable • Bar, restaurant. Breakfast room, reading room. Conference room. Garden

The restaurant takes its name from an ancient, popular game that children used to play in the large characteristic square in the center of Prato, where the friendly trattoria run by the Panerai family is located: the trattoria is very rustic and rather dark, but certainly discreet and comfortable, to be recommended to anyone who wishes to try the typical local cuisine. Spartaco, the proprietor, serves at the tables, helped by one of his two children, while the other helps his wife Giuseppina in the kitchen. Service is fast but not unpleasantly so.

The trattoria is clean and Spartan, and the food is down to earth and plain, not a vast choice but all well made. After trying some croutons and cured meats (including **Prato mortadella**, a Slow Food Presidium), depending on the season you will be able to choose between **pappa al pomodoro**, **ribollita**, **rice and lampredotto soup**, **pappardelle with duck innards**, and gnocchetti with zucchini flowers. The strong point among the main courses is the **boiled meat**, even in a summer version, **stewed ox tail**, chicken rolls or rabbit and livers, and **hare in salmi**. On Friday you will find baccalà, with raisins or alla livornese. Desserts all show Giuseppina's skillful touch: **cakes and pies made with emmer and walnuts** (delicious), apples or rice and castagnaccio in the right season.

As an alternative to the wine on tap, you can choose from a wine list that includes good Tuscan wines, even if the mark-up is not what you would expect in an osteria.

🏷 Bozza di Prato, a naturally leavened sciocco or unsalted bread, is sold by Loggetti, at Via Matteotti 11.

46 KM NORTH OF AREZZO SS 71 AND 310

LA VECCHIA CUCINA DI SOLDANO

Trattoria
Via Pomeria 23
Tel. 0574 34665
Closed Sunday and festivities
Open: lunch and dinner
Holidays: August
Seating: 70
Prices: 25 euros, wine excluded
No credit cards accepted

LA TANA DEGLI ORSI

Restaurant-wine shop
Via Roma 1
Tel. 0575 583377
Closed Tuesday and Wednesday
Open: only for dinner
Holidays: variable in April and November
Seating: 20
Prices: 28-34 euros, wine excluded
All credit cards except AE, Bancomat

The decidedly rustic ambience, with checkered tablecloths and very simple service, is a characteristic feature of the restaurant that the Mattei family (Aldo in the dining-room, and his wife Piera and daughter Lisa in the kitchen) manages along the medieval walls, near to Piazza San Marco and the Castello dell'Imperatore. It is a historical restaurant which, in spite of a few problems on one of our last visits, we think we should continue to recommend, for the choice of local dishes at competitive prices.

Start with the classic **crostini** and Tuscan cured meats (although the servings can be too small), **fettunta** with anchovies and tomatoes, and the antipasti of Grandad Oreste (slices of pork with olives and walnuts). The first courses include soups such as **ribollita** and **acquacotta**, **tagliolini on chickpeas**, **pici** with a venison or beef sauce, **toppe** (squares of fresh pasta) **sul papero**, and emmer salad in the summer. **Mutton**, a type of meat that is quite common in the Prato area, is among the most frequent main courses, as well as **francesina** (boiled meat 're-cooked' with onions), **mixed boiled meats with green sauce, chicken livers with rapini**; plus cuttlefish in zimino, **baccalà with olives** and occasionally stuffed celery. To close, homemade puddings or biscotti to dunk in Vin Santo.

A very small selection of Tuscan labels with honest mark-ups simplifies the choice of the best wine to accompany the tasty creations from the kitchen.

A great sense of hospitality is the key to this restaurant in the center of Pratovecchio, a lovely little town in the Casentino area, where you can stop for a quick snack (from the excellent selection of **cured meats** and **cheese**) or for a complete meal, choosing from a generous range of dishes. Caterina will welcome you to the dining room which is decorated with old vats from the family cellar, an immediate promise of good wine, and a promise that is kept by the choice of about 800 labels selected with care and offered at very reasonable prices. Simone workis in the kitchen, preparing traditional local dishes, mainly seasonal, with excellent ingredients, including Slow Food Presidium products.

A tasty winter starter is the **terrine of tripe with zolfini beans**, whereas in the summer, you could start with a carpaccio of chianina beef or small tarts of figs and Casentino prosciutto. Because the raw ingredients are so hard to find, if they are on the menu, try the **gnocchi** made with red Cetica potatoes; the borrage ravioli are also excellent, as are the **tortelli of pigeon and truffles with butter and sage**. For main course, we recommend **pigeon en croûte** with chicory, **diced rabbit** with cep mushrooms, venison with artichokes, potatoes and black truffles, and tagliata of venison with Chianti. To close, home-baked cakes and pies.

In addition to the wines we mentioned above, there's also a good selection of spirits.

Traditional cured meats typical of the Casentino area can be bought from Marcello Orlandi, Via Garibaldi 70; Aldo Orlandi, Via Circonvallazione 1; Salumi di Scarpaccia, Località Scarpaccia 51 B.

QUARRATA
Montorio

RADICONDOLI
Porcignano

13 KM SOUTHEAST OF PISTOIA ON SS 66 | 50 KM WEST OF SIENA

IL CALESSE

🍲 Holiday farm
Via Carraia 215
Tel. 0573 367578-339 3560810
Fax 0573 750828
E-mail: info@agriturismoilcalesse.it
Internet: www.agriturismoilcalesse.it
Open all year

BOSCAGLIA 🐌
OPIFICIO DEL BOSCO

🍲 Restaurant
Località Podere Porcignano 100
Tel. 0577 793134
Closed Tuesday, never in summer
Open: lunch and dinner
Holidays: February
Seating: 50 + 30 outdoors
Prices: 25-28 euros, wine excluded
All credit cards except AE, Bancomat

Montalbano is a small village in the hills between Pistoia and Prato. Nearby you can still see the remains of the walls that used to mark the boundaries of one of the Medici game reserves. The vacation farm belongs to the Giuntini family and is located in a mid-19th-century farmhouse renovated using local materials and elements salvaged from demolition. Two of the most interesting parts of the building are the small cellar and the 'vinsantaia' where Vinsanto was made. All around are woods, vineyards and olive groves where guests can go for walks and enjoy a picnic near the old quarry. The restaurant is open to residents only and subject to reservation (about 21 euros, wine excluded).

• 3 double and 2 triple rooms, with bathroom (2 rooms share a bathroom), TV • Prices: double room single use 48 euros, double 84, triple 127, breakfast included • Credit cards: major ones, Bancomat • Off-street parking. Small pets allowed. Owners always present • Restaurant (for residents only). Reading room. Grounds, terrace

A dirt road through the Boscaglia estate in the woods of the Carline hills, leads to this restaurant which is surrounded by tall trees; not far away, in the holiday farm of Querceti, are facilities for all types of outdoor sporting activities. The atmosphere is warm and informal: one large room, with a fireplace filling one wall, finished with stone and brick; when the weather is good, you can eat alfresco. Marilena Grosso, the proprietor, adores traditional cooking and knows a lot about Italian food.

The dishes tend to be Tuscan, from homemade pasta to soups, game and mushrooms, vegetables and wild herbs, followed by homemade puddings. Start with **cured meats**, vegetables in oil, pecorino from Tuscany, **panzanella**, and **croutons of chicken livers** with Vin Santo, then **pasta and beans** with zolfini beans, **pappardelle with boar**, fettuccine with bell peppers or mushrooms, tortelli with walnuts, ricotta and borrage, vegetable and emmer soup, **ribollita** and **pappa al pomodoro**. For a main course, there is a choice of grilled meats, **T-bone steak** and tagliata, but also **stewed boar with polenta**, roast pork with wild fennel, and **stuffed rabbit alla Boscaglia**. Then there is omelet with freshly laid eggs, sautéed vegetables and a board of organic pecorino. To close, panna cotta with bilberries, crostata, **cantucci** with Vin Santo, and stuffed peaches, to be enjoyed with Marilena's rosolio and Alchermes.

The house wine is good and the wine list, which Nicola is responsible for, offers about seventy labels from Tuscany. There are two set meals, the regular meal for 28 euros and the vegetarian choice for 25, including the house wine.

RAPOLANO TERME
Serre di Rapolano

RIGNANO SULL'ARNO
Rosano

31 KM SOUTHEAST OF SIENA

24 KM SOUTHEAST OF FLORENCE, 9 KM FROM EXIT INCISA A 1

PALAZZO BIZZARRI

LA BOTTEGA A ROSANO

☞ Bed and breakfast
Via Matteotti 5
Tel. 0577 704765-348 7848761
Fax 0577 704765
E-mail: civitellig@katamail.com
Open all year

🍲 Trattoria
Via I Maggio 10
Tel. 055 8303013
Closed Mon, in winter also Sun for dinner
Open: lunch, Friday, Saturday and
Sunday also for dinner
Holidays: 3 weeks in August, 10 days at Christmas
Seating: 60 + 40 outdoors
Prices: 15-25 euros, wine excluded
All credit cards except AE, Bancomat

Serre is an ancient village founded by the Byzantines to oppose the advance of the Longobards. Later it became the location of a grancia (a fortified barn used to store provisions for pilgrims) belonging to Siena's Ospedale della Scala. On one of the village's main streets is the lovely building which houses the B&B, a 13th-century tower-house with extensions built in the 18th century. The three-storey house still retains the original terracotta tiled floors, ceilings, chandeliers and antique furniture of old, and the guest rooms are located on the first floor, once considered the noble floor. Breakfast is served in a lounge with fireplace and offers local organic produce. Guests can relax in the outdoor loggia and secret garden.

• 2 double rooms and 1 suite, with bathroom, TV; suite with fridge • Prices: double room single use 50 euros, double 70, suite 80; breakfast 5 euros per person • Credit cards: none • Free public parking 50 meters away. No pets allowed. Owners always reachable. • Lounge, small library. Garden

The idea behind the Bottega a Rosano is that of a grocer's store with a kitchen, which was very fashionable in the Florence area a few decades ago. Romana Fantechi and her son Damiano have maintained this formula successfully, making it a point of strength and distinction in contrast to many super-modern but anonymous food stores. From the early morning, there is a constant stream of people. Customers have breakfast with cake and crostata, they read the paper and chat with the other customers (whether they know them or not, which is typical of the Florentines!), they do the shopping, choosing from the array of cured meats, cheese, pasta and other specialties. At midday, the Bottega fills up with workers looking for a good meal. You can eat a sandwich with a good choice of red or white wines by the glass. Or you can sit down in the trattoria and eat in a more leisurely manner. Lunch costs about 15 euros and dinner 25.
Start with typical Tuscan antipasti and then choose from the interesting first courses such as **pappardelle al ragù**, tagliolini with truffles, and penne with cherry tomatoes and pecorino. For a main course, choose between the generous **mixed fry** of white meats, brains, vegetables and mushrooms, or the **cibreo** and **rabbit stew** with beans. The meat dishes are always interesting: lombatina, **steak**, fillet, sausage and rosticciana.
The wine list has a wide selection of reds from the Rufina and Colli Fiorentini areas, but that is not all. You will find all the Tuscan wines and a few from other regions. At weekends, the Bottega is also open for dinner and there is a pleasant verandah for alfresco dining in the summer.

San Casciano dei Bagni

DANIELA

🍲 Resturant with rooms
Piazza Matteotti 7
Tel. 0578 58041-58234
Closed Wed, never in summer; Dec-Feb open weekends
Open: lunch and dinner
Holidays: end February
Seating: 80 + 40 outdoors
Prices: 33-35 euros, wine excluded
All major credit cards, Bancomat

The interior design of the restaurant presents a successful balance between old, rustic and modern. Daniela Boni, the owner, serves at table with great competence and courtesy, while her husband Silvestro works in the kitchen, preparing local dishes that he has personally revisited. There is a fixed specialty meal for 33 euros, a regular fixed meal (22 euros) and one for children (15 euros).

Start with bruschetta, fried vegetables, flans, crostoni, pâté, cured meats, carpaccio of beef with green sauce, and pecorino au gratin. Follow this with **tortelli of potato stuffed with pigeon**, green gnocchetti with cabbage and truffle, **correggioli all'aglione**, tagliolini with a summer sauce of fresh vegetables, or with cep mushrooms when in season. Those who prefer soup, will not be disappointed by the emmer or onion soups, the **pappa al pomodoro**, or the **ribollita**. There is a wide choice of main courses: **roast stuffed rabbit**, lamb alla Daniela, **lamb shanks baked with potatoes**, breast of duck with red onions and wild fennel, grilled fillet of Chianina beef and **sausages**; in the winter, try the tasty wild boar with chestnuts, raisins and pine nuts. There are also several fish specialties. And cheese lovers will enjoy a good pecorino accompanied by cotognata and late-harvest wine. You can close your meal with a slice of chocolate cake, panna cotta or various mousses, including one of marrons glacés, and ice creams in the summer.

There are about one hundred quality wines, both local and from other areas, sold by the glass and by the bottle. The house wine is very good.

San Casciano in Val di Pesa
Montefiridolfi

A CASA MIA

🍲 Trattoria
Via Santa Maria a Macerata 4
Tel. 055 8244392
Closed Monday and Tuesday
Open: dinner, Sunday also for lunch
Holidays: July or August
Seating: 20
Prices: 25-30 euros
No credit cards

Maurizio Simoncini is a jovial but occasionally brusque host, who has been cooking since he was 16, and has gained experience in restaurants all over the Chianti area. In 2003 he set up on his own, and opened this small osteria at Montefiridolfi: he deliberately chose it small because he likes to establish a direct rapport with his guests, as if they were guests in his own home. He is in the kitchen, but as soon as he can he goes into the dining-room, which seats about twenty people at wooden tables with straw paper napkins; the cutlery is in the table drawer.

Maurizio proposes the antipasti (grilled vegetables, **bruschetta**, salads and cured meats), and the diner chooses the rest. The most popular first courses are **tortelli of ricotta and spinach** (homemade, of course), tagliatelle with mushrooms, **pennette sul coniglio**, and **mushroom** or emmer soup. The host also prepares a dish known as **peposo** that is not often found in public restaurants but used to be prepared in private homes (and may still be in some cases), but he will also cook roast veal shank, smoked sausage with cheese and the aristocratic **duck with orange**.

The desserts are simple but wholesome: torta della nonna, apple cake, chocolate cake, fritters and **schiacciata alla fiorentina** at different times of the year

The only wine is the house wine produced by Fattoria Castelvecchio, which is served on tap and included in the cost of the meal. The opening hours are rather limited, but just relax, the host has his own speed. Remember that on Saturday from June 15 to September 15, the restaurant is only open in the evenings.

SAN CASCIANO IN VAL DI PESA
Calzaiolo

16 KM SOUTH OF FLORENCE SS 2 OR HIGHWAY EXIT

MAMMAROSA

Trattoria
Via Cassia per Siena 32
Tel. 055 8249454
Closed Monday
Open: dinner, Sunday also for lunch
Holidays: variable in winter
Seating: 50 + 60 outdoors
Prices: 28-32 euros, wine excluded
All credit cards except AE, Bancomat

The trattoria run by Francesca Cianchi, on the ground floor of an old refurbished farmhouse, is one of the most delightful stop-offs in the Chianti area. The ambience is rustic and simple, but tasteful; in the summer it is pleasant to eat alfresco in the large, shady garden.

The menu always proposes classic traditional dishes: **pappa al pomodoro**, **minestra maritata** (a soup made of bread with cep mushrooms and spinach), **pappardelle with rabbit sauce**, Tuscan **mixed fry** with chicken, rabbit or lamb and vegetables, **steak** and **baccalà** fried or alla livornese. The other dishes on the menu, whether simple or imaginatively garnished, vary with the seasons and the available ingredients which Francesca likes to buy locally. To start with, choose from a range of summer dishes such as cold pappa al pomodoro, fried zucchini flowers, or liver pâté with truffles in the colder season; then for a first course, trofie with zucchini and spring onions, fusilli with eggplant in summer, and **maltagliati with boar** or **tortelli of potatoes with a venison sauce** in winter. For a main course, choose between chicken al mattone, classic fried pork chops with tomato and basil, baccalà with leeks, and cuttlefish in zimino; diners who do not enjoy meat can order the grilled vegetables and bean and potato flan with tomato fillets. End your meal with cream catalana, chocolate or apple cake, or ice-cream.

The wine list offers a small selection of Italian wines, with particular emphasis on the Chianti Classico area. Conclude your meal with an excellent cup of coffee from Piansa, one of the best cafeterias in Florence.

SAN CASCIANO IN VAL DI PESA
Ponterotto

16 KM SOUTH OF FLORENCE SS 2 OR HIGHWAY EXIT

MATTEUZZI

Trattoria
Via Certaldese 8
Tel. 055 828090
Closed Tuesday and Sunday for lunch
Open: lunch, Sunday only for dinner
Holidays: August
Seating: 35 + 20 outdoors
Prices: 22 euros, wine excluded
All major credit cards, Bancomat

A typical trattoria that only the locals know about on the provincial road from San Casciano to Certaldo, before the bridge over the Pesa river. Once a staging post, it is now a popular eating place with passing truck drivers. You eat in the simple dining-room, behind the food and tobacconist's store, or under the pergola in the summer. The food is cooked by mother Leda and presented by her son Alessandro, who takes care of the guests with extreme naturalness. Start with classic Tuscan antipasti of excellent, tasty **crostini with chicken livers**. Follow this with **soups** made with vegetables from the garden or pasta with a sauce of meat and chicken livers. Here in the country, grilling food is a tradition: hence succulent **steak** (of veal or pork), pigeon (very popular, though not always available), **rabbit** (roast if you want it), or **rosticciana**. There are various stews, including veal and **baccalà** prepared in various ways: we recommend the baccalà **alla fiorentina** with potatoes or leeks. The desserts prepared with fresh eggs and seasonal vegetables are all good and an excellent alternative to the meat dishes. Fresh fruit, cantucci or creams and mousses conclude the meal.

The wine is not the trattoria's strong point, but the wine from Montespertoli on tap is acceptable.

The La Ginestra cooperative sells its own organic products in Località Bargino, Via Pergoleto 3, from honey to extra virgin olive oil and pasta, all of excellent quality.

SAN GIMIGNANO
Libbiano

SAN GIMIGNANO

FATTORIA DI VAGLI

🝳🔑Holiday farm
Località Libbiano 14
Tel. 0577 946025-329 6190310
Fax 0577 946025
E-mail: info@naturaesalute.it
Internet: www.naturaesalute.it
Closed in November

OSTERIA DEL CARCERE ◎ ⌀ ⌾

🥘Recently opened Osteria
Via del Castello 13
Tel. 0577 941905
Closed Wednesday and Thursday for lunch
Open: lunch and dinner
Holidays: January and February
Seating: 30
Prices: 30-35 euros, wine excluded
No credit cards

The Fattoria dei Vagli is a 320-hectare farm in the countryside around Siena and Volterra that belonged to the Gucciardini family from the 17th century. A four kilometer drive on a country road brings you to the farmhouse now owned by the Ferri family that offers accommodation to guests and also sells the farm's produce. Pigs, cattle and poultry are bred in the wild and the delicious cured meats produced on the farm are served in the restaurant (residents can enjoy a three course meal for 18 euros, wine excluded). Also available are honey, wine and spelt used to make delicious soups. Rooms are simple but comfortable and for breakfast you can enjoy coffee, milk, tea, yoghurt, homemade cakes, jams and honey.

• 7 double rooms, 1 suite, 2 adjacent rooms (4 persons), with bathroom (2 with shared adjacent bathroom), satellite TV • Prices: double room single use 65 euros, double 73, suite 90, adjacent rooms 130, breakfast included • Credit cards: none • 1 room designed for use by the mobility challenged. Off-street parking. No pets allowed. Owners always reachable • Restaurant (open to non-residents subject to reservation). Lounge. Grounds

The restaurant is small – in fact many of the tables are located in the gallery – but it's very friendly. It's in the old part of town, close to Piazza della Cisterna. A variety of products that you can enjoy when you are seated comfortably at the table are displayed on the counter as you enter: cured meats, cheese and other local specialties. We recommend booking, particularly in the summer. The dishes that Elena and Ribomar offer their guests are all prepared with local ingredients and products from workshops in the neighborhood; for example, fresh and **cured meats** come from the Antica Macelleria Cecchini. Neither of the two proprietors is actually from San Gimignano (she's from Milan and he's Brazilian), but they have decided to offer their guests the best local produce. The antipasti include an array of bruschetta and **crostoni**, from a classic bruschetta with garlic or tomato, to a crostone with cream of lardo, cream of goat's cheese and herbs, or goat's cheese and saffron. Try the terrines: Renaissance style with plums, **beef chiantigiana**, lamb and olives or vegetarian version. There are no pasta dishes on the menu, only soups: **ribollita** and **pappa al pomodoro**, **emmer and beans** and vellutata of chickpeas. The main courses include **guinea fowl with chestnuts**, turkey with pistachio and orange and dishes linked to particular seasons or festivities, such as Easter **lamb**. The **cheeses** are good and we recommend the numerous paper-wrapped goat's varieties
The wines are all Tuscan, and are also served by the glass.

SAN GIOVANNI D'ASSO
Montisi

LA LOCANDA DI MONTISI

3-Star Hotel
Via Umberto I 39
Tel. 0577 845906
Fax 0577 845821-06233237708
E-mail: info@lalocandadimontisi.it
Internet: www.lalocandadimontisi.it
Closed from 10-31 January

Montisi is a small village dating back to the Middle Ages. This 3-Star Hotel created in a typical stone house renovated in 2001 is managed by Roberto Crocenzi, already owner of an osteria in Scanno. The seven rooms all have modern comforts and views of the Tuscan countryside, the rooftops of other houses huddled together and, beyond, the gently rolling hills. The communal lounge has wooden beams and some antique furniture. Here guests can enjoy breakfast with milk, coffee, tea, fruit juices, herbal teas, yoghurt, croissants, freshly baked village bread, cookies, honey, jams and cereal. In summer breakfast is served on the terrace of the nearby restaurant. The half board supplement is 20 euros per person.

• 4 double, 2 triple rooms and 1 suite (2-4 persons), with bathroom, mini-bar, safe, TV, modem connection; suite with air-conditioning • Prices: double room single use 45-55 euros, double 60-75, triple 90-100, suite 110-120, breakfast included • Credit cards: all, Bancomat • Free public parking 150 meters away. Small pets allowed. Owners always present. • Restaurant. Breakfast room, bar corner. Tavern

SAN GIULIANO TERME
Arena-Metato

BELVEDERE L'OSTERIA DI PIAZZA PADELLA

Osteria-trattoria
Piazza Belvedere (Ho Chi Minh) 7-8
Tel. 050 810161
Closed Sunday
Open: only for dinner
Holidays: January, 1 week in August
Seating: 35 + 30 outdoors
Prices: 25-28 euros, wine excluded
All credit cards, Bancomat

The osteria is in the main square, and used to be the local café; in fact the old counter can still be found in the entrance, dominated by a large old meat slicer. The two small dining-rooms (about forty seats in all, so it is a good idea to book) are soberly furnished; in the summer you can eat alfresco, under the portico that looks onto the square.
Stefania and Michele Pardini, who are responsible for the kitchen and the dining-room, concentrate on typical Tuscan food. Start with good antipasti of typical cured meats and croutons, then a first course of homemade pasta: the **pappardelle with hare** and the traditional **pasta and beans** are excellent; and because the coast is so close, it is not unusual to find bavette with clams and a good cream of **fish soup** with croutons of homemade bread. The main courses – particularly meat with **steaks of mucco pisano**, tripe and **fry-up of cockerel and rabbit** with vegetables – also include some dishes made with fish caught on the nearby coast, but also a tasty **stockfish stew with potatoes**. To conclude, the desserts made by Stefania: apple pie and the inevitable **torta co' bischeri**, the typical local sweet.
There is a good selection of Tuscan wines (and the number is growing), as well as a few labels from the rest of Italy.

At San Giuliano Terme, Via XX Settembre 3, the Macelleria-salumeria Giusti sells excellent fresh and cured cuts of Mucco Pisano beef raised on the Parco farm.

SAN GIULIANO TERME
Rigoli

10 KM NORTH OF PISA ON SS 12

VILLA DI CORLIANO

🗝️Period residence
Strada Statale 12
Tel. 050 818193
Fax 050 818897
E-mail: info@corliano.it
Internet: www.corliano.it
Open from March 15 to November 15

This hotel is located in a 16th-century villa belonging to Count Ferdinando Agostini Venerosi Della Seta and offers comfortable rooms fitted with antique furniture. Breakfast is varied and offers sweet fare (fresh croissants, home-baked cakes and cookies), savory items (cured meats, cheeses, eggs), hot and cold beverages and seasonal fresh fruit. The villa's extensive grounds are ideal for relaxing walks. The hotel is not only a comfortable holiday destination but also an excellent location for those wishing to visit art towns such as Pisa, Lucca, Siena and Florence. The villa is also said to be haunted by the 'benign' ghost of a beautiful woman, Teresa Della Seta Bocca Gaetani, who, according to legend, sometimes visit its lounges and vaults.

• 9 double rooms and 2 suites (2-4 persons), with bathroom (3 doubles with shared bathroom) • Prices: double room single use 50-90 euros, double without bathroom 70, double with bathroom 80-110, suite 100-145; breakfast 10 euros per person • Credit cards: all, Bancomat • Off-street parking. Small pets allowed. Reception open 8am-7pm • Bar. Breakfast room, reading room. Conference room. Grounds, solarium

SAN MARCELLO PISTOIESE
Maresca

26 KM NORTHWEST OF PISTOIA

IL CAPANNONE

🗝️2-Star Hotel
Via Teso 3454 a
Tel. 0573 64198-648810
Fax 0573 648810
E-mail: ilcapannone@leonet.it
Open all year

This small hotel and restaurant managed by the Mascagni family is located in the heart of the Teso forest at an altitude of 1000 meters in the Apennines between Tuscany and Emilia-Romagna. Traveling on foot or mountain bike (bikes can be rented at the hotel) you can reach an altitude of 2000 meters. The Museum of industrial archeology with its examples of metal work (a 15th-century blacksmith's workshop is still in working order) and machines to produce ice is worth a visit. Breakfast consists of jams, honey, cured meats, cheeses and hot and cold beverages. The restaurant offers traditional cuisine for 20-25 euros, half board 50 euros and full board 55 euros. Maresca, which like San Marcello is three kilometers away, is the town where guests can find shops, restaurants, a swimming pool and tennis courts.

• 1 single and 11 double rooms, with bathroom, TV • Prices: single 35 euros, double 60, breakfast included • Credit cards: none • Facility accessible to the mobility challenged. Off-street parking. Small pets allowed. Reception open from 7 am to midnight, owners always present. • Bar, restaurant. Reading room, TV room. Garden

SAN MARCELLO PISTOIESE

29 KM NORTHWEST OF PISTOIA SS 632 AND SS 66

IL POGGIOLO

🍲 Hotel restaurant
Via del Poggiolo 52
Tel. 0573 630153
Closed Tuesday for dinner and Wednesday
Open: lunch and dinner
Holidays: variable
Seating: 70
Prices: 20-26 euros, wine excluded
All major credit cards

San Marcello is on the road from Pistoia to the Abetone ski resort and the shady woods on this side of the Apennines. Il Poggiolo, in the center of town, has for several years proposed a simple cuisine that highlights the raw ingredients, nearly all of which are found locally. With Giuseppina Coltri and Angela Santini in the kitchen and Gian Paolo Iori in the dining-room, but ready to give a hand in the kitchen when necessary, the restaurant proposes the various products of the Pistoia mountains with skill and passion.

In the right season, **cep** mushrooms cooked in a variety of ways: the soup is particularly good, and the flavor of the mushrooms is enhanced by the careful addition of herbs. The **tortelli of ricotta and spinach** (greens in summer) are very tasty, stuffed with sheep's milk ricotta made by the local producers of raw-milk pecorino. In the winter there are numerous **game** dishes (venison, hare, boar and deer), but also Massa lamb and **kid**, cooked simply to bring out the flavor of the excellent meat. The fried dishes are all perfect, and the mushrooms and seasonal vegetables crispy and flavorsome. And to finish, several types of **raw-milk Pecorino from the Pistoia mountains**, a Slow Food Presidium, and puddings: **castagnaccio** and fritters made with chestnut flour and served with ricotta, and crostata made with bilberries from the surrounding woods, which are also served on their own; in the summer, excellent home-made ice cream, also made with berries. The wine list is simple, and the mark-up is reasonable; the accent is on reds from Tuscany, due to the type of dishes.

SAN MARCELLO PISTOIESE
Maresca

23 KM NORTHWEST OF PISTOIA SS 632 AND SS 66

LA VECCHIA CANTINA 🌀 ❦ 🍷

🍲 Trattoria
Via Risorgimento 4
Tel. 0573 64158
Closed Tuesday, never in summer and Christmas
Open: lunch and dinner
Holidays: 3 weeks after November 2
Seating: 40 + 16 outdoors
Prices: 28 euros, wine excluded
All credit cards, Bancomat

A friendly, well-furnished restaurant managed by Alvaro, who receives the guests warmly, and his wife Maria Luisa who spoils them with her good traditional cooking. The menu includes numerous vegetarian dishes and others made with local and Slow Food Presidium products, particularly the cured meats and cheese from the Pistoia mountains. The cuisine follows the seasons and the cultural and agricultural traditions of the area.

On our last visit, we tried the golosità della Cantina (mixed antipasti with **cured meats**, **crostoni** and seasonal pies served on a wooden platter), hand-made tagliolini with a vegetable ragù, a **chicory pie with fondue of Pistoia mountain raw-milk pecorino** (Slow Food Presidium), an excellent **T-bone steak** and wonderful **beef marinated in Chianti**; to finish, some cheese and fresh 'brutti e buoni' biscuits with good Vin Santo from Valdinievole. There are numerous other dishes on the menu: green ravioli with goat's and other cheeses, tortelli of ricotta and spinach, and other types of home-made pasta served with sauces of meat, mushrooms or game, grilled beef, veal, lamb and pork. At the end of the meal, try pears in wine, Vin Santo jelly and apple and chestnut cake.

The wine list has been compiled with care and stands out for the excellent quality of the labels and the honest mark-up.

🍴 In Via Gavinana, close to the restaurant, the Pasticceria-Gelateria Gori sells excellent sweets and hand-made chocolate.

SAN MINIATO
Corazzano

42 KM EAST OF PISA SS 67

LA TAVERNA DELL'OZIO

Trattoria-pizzeria
Via Zara 85
Tel. 0571 462862
Closed Monday
Open: lunch and dinner, August only for dinner
Holidays: variable
Seating: 30
Prices: 22-26 euros, wine excluded
All credit cards except AE

MARRUCOLA

Holiday farm
Via Cadenzano 40
Tel. 0571 418306
Fax 0571 444032
E-mail: info@marrucola.it
Internet: www.marrucola.it
Holidays various times in winter

We recommend booking even if there is not that much passing trade, because there are only a few tables and some dishes require prior notice in order to find the ingredients. The cuisine is local and the raw ingredients always excellent.

Simone, an excellent cook who was born in San Miniato, prepares the cured cuts of **pisano pesante pig**, a breed that is still raised wild, which are offered as antipasti with **croutons** and seasonal marinated vegetables, homemade preserves in oil and plenty more. The first courses of fresh pasta, range from **pappardelle with sauce of duck**, hare or boar, to **penne al colombaccio** and ravioli filled with meat or vegetables; but there are also classic Tuscan soups and seasonal vegetable soup. The main courses include the traditional favorites: **pork livers with lardo**, **mamme di San Miniato** (giant white artichokes stuffed with meat and pecorino and baked), and **fried mallegato** (a blood sausage seasoned with lardo, salt, nutmeg, cinnamon, pine nuts and raisins, a Slow Food Presidia). There is plenty of game – but also **cacciucco di colombacci**, stewed or grilled boar, **hare in dolceforte** – chicken and **fried rabbit**. For most of the year, you will find truffles (the white and marzolo varieties) from the countryside near San Miniato, and always good raw-milk cheese aged by Simone. To finish, simple traditional Tuscan puddings skillfully prepared by Silvia.

There is a fair choice of Tuscan wines and a pleasant house wine at an extremely reasonable price.

This agriturismo is located in a picturesque area in the hills, behind what once used to be a Capuchin monastery and is now a study center with accommodation belonging to a bank. Claudio Cenni has renovated his old farmhouse and created lovely common areas, comfortable rooms (the larger ones have a lounge) and an independent apartment with its own entrance. Silvia looks after guests and is always polite and thoughtful. Continental breakfast offers milk, tea, cappuccino, hot chocolate, fruit juices, jams and home-made cakes: cured meats and cheeses are available if you ask and subject to a price supplement. The farm's own produce (vegetables, olive oil, wine) is also used for dinner (20 euros, half board 62-72 euros per person) and excellent quality meats, often Slow Food Presidia, come from other farms.

• 10 double rooms, with bathroom, air-conditioning; some with small lounge • Prices: double room single use 55-65 euros, double 84-104 (21-33 euro supplement for extra bed), breakfast included • Credit cards: Visa, Bancomat • 1 room designed for use by the mobility challenged. Off-street parking. No pets allowed. Owners always reachable • Restaurant (for residents only), breakfast room. Veranda. Pool, billiards, small table for children

SANSEPOLCRO

ENOTECA GUIDI

🍲 Wine shop with food
Via Pacioli 44
Tel. 0575 736587
Closed Wednesday, Saturday and Sunday also for lunch
Open: lunch and dinner
Holidays: July
Seating: 30 + 15 outdoors
Prices: 28-34 euros, wine excluded
All credit cards, Bancomat

The Enoteca Guidi is located in a 17th-century building, in a side street off the town's main street, not far from the museum where the works of Piero Della Francesca bear testimony to the cultural tradition of this land. As far back as 1955, the Guidi family had a shop selling excellent local produce: truffles, mushrooms, fossa cheeses and cured meats in oil. Their son Saverio, sommelier and wine enthusiast, and his wife Simona, expanded the shop in 1999, adding a vast, carefully selected range of wines and some dishes. Allowing every wine on the list to be tasted, even the dearest ones, but charging only for the actual wine drunk was a far-sighted idea.

You stop at the wine shop for a snack of excellent cheese, the Tuscan varieties with pears and the fossa varieties with honey, or French cheeses with jam and mostarda, or **cured meats** accompanied by a glass of wine, or a full meal. All the main courses of meat (**carpaccio of chianina beef**, breast of goose, angus beef, or bresaola) and fish (carpaccio of swordfish, tuna, salmon, or baccalà) are cold. Antipasti and first courses follow the seasons, focusing on local produce but also with a pinch of fantasy. We ourselves began with a salad with a blend of strawberries, goat's cheese, paté de foie gras with crispy bread and vegetable couscous with smoked swordfish and caper sauce. Noteworthy first courses include **ravioli of ricotta and spinach** with black truffles, with lardo, rosemary and cherry tomatoes, spaghetti alla chitarra with aromatic herb pesto and grilled vegetables, or **tagliatelle with prugnoli mushrooms**. To round off the meal, Simona's desserts with a broad selection of wines.

SARTEANO

DA GAGLIANO

🍲 Trattoria
Via Roma 5
Tel. 0578 268022
Closed Tuesday and Wednesday; in summer Tuesday and Wednesday for lunch
Open: lunch and dinner
Holidays: variable in winter
Seating: 20
Prices: 25-26 euros, wine excluded
No credit cards

In the square of the old town stands the simple, traditional Da Gagliano trattoria. It can only seat a few around old wooden tables on benches and straw-seated chairs, but sharing a table with strangers creates a pleasant convivial atmosphere. Giuliano, the enthusiastic young proprietor suggests the "works" of his partner Angela, who in the kitchen really knows where it's at.

The menu is a compendium of honest local flavors, beginning with the antipasti: **salad of tripe and chick peas**, pecorino al coccio, carpaccio di capocollo with valeriana and eggs, warm pecorino and truffle pie. The **stringozzi** pasta served with cinta senese pork sauce or with beans and artichokes is made by hand; then **ricotta roll** with asparagus or beetroot, various **spelts** and **risottos**, bread gnocchetti with beans and ham or with beetroot and pine nuts, lasagna with vegetables and cheese, **acquacotta alla maremmana** and other soups. The bounteous helpings have made us pretty full by the time the main course arrives but how can you resist the **suckling pig alla fiorentina** or **rabbit al Chianti**? Not to mention the stuffed meat loaf, the **baccalà with leeks**, and the **tripe**, cooked local style? And then **pork stew al buglione**, **rolled roast pancetta** and an array of seasonal vegetables. Then, to round off the meal, a piece of pie. The organic one with carrot jam served warm is excellent, country cakes with dried fruit or torta della nonna, ricotta mousse with Vin Santo, cantucci or brutti e boni with Muscatel.

The wines are the house variety and there is a selection of labels which although not extensive offers the essential local wines.

SASSETTA
Pian delle Vigne

LA CERRETA

🔑 Holiday farm
Via Campagna Sud 143
Tel. 0565 794352-338 1851877
Fax 0565 794352
E-mail: info@lacerreta.it
Internet: www.cerreta.it
Open all year

There's no TV on this farm, not in the rooms (organized in four old stone-built farmhouses) and not in the lovely lounge with fireplace. Nor is there any air-conditioning (the sea is a few kilometers away and a lovely breeze comes off the Apennines in summer). What there is, however, are large shared tables to encourage guests to socialize and also horse riding and courses in 'equestrian harmony'. Guests will truly enjoy a holiday immersed in nature. The farm produces organic wines, olive oils, fruit and vegetables and rears local breeds of pig (Macchiaioli and Cinta Senese), cows and horses from the Maremma, chickens and bees. Meals (half board 55-65 euros) are prepared using, in the main, the farm's own produce. For breakfast, bread and cakes baked in the wood-fired oven, fresh milk, butter, jams, honey, eggs and cured meats produced on the farm.

• 7 double 2 triple and 2 four-bed rooms, with bathroom; some with terrace or small patio • Prices: double room single use 75 euros, double 85-105, triple 95-115, four-bed 105-125, breakfast included • Credit cards: major ones, Bancomat • 1 room designed for use by the mobility challenged. Off-street parking. Small pets allowed. Owners always reachable. • Restaurant (for residents only). Lounge, reading room. Garden. Riding school

SCANDICCI
San Martino alla Palma

LOCANDA MONTAGUGLIONE

🔑 Bed and breakfast
Via Rinaldi 6
Tel. and fax 055 751181
E-mail: info@locandamontaguglione.it
Internet: www. locandamontaguglione.it
Open all year

This old fortress, converted into a noble residence and subjected to various extensions from the 15th century onwards, is the home of the Martelli family. It is located near Villa Antinori in the Florentine hills, amid cypresses, vineyards and olive groves. Guest rooms are on the ground and first floors, and have been recently renovated and are elegantly furnished. Breakfast (home-made sweet items and savory fare available on request) is served in a lovely lounge with fireplace and in summer in the garden (4,000 square meters with a sundeck and a BBQ area). Although it's only four kilometers from the Signa highway exit, the B&B is in a secluded area, perfect for a relaxing holiday.

• 8 double rooms, with bathroom (2 with jacuzzis), air-conditioning, TV, modem connection • Prices: double room single use 50-65 euros, double 70-90 (20 euro supplement for extra bed), breakfast included • Credit cards: all, Bancomat • 1 room designed for use by the mobility challenged. Off-street parking. Small pets allowed. Owners always reachable • Breakfast room, lounge. Garden, solarium

SCANDICCI
San Colombano

SCANSANO

7 KM WEST OF FLORENCE   29 KM SOUTHEAST OF GROSSETO SS 322

TRATTORIA DINO

LA CANTINA 🍾

☞ Trattoria with rooms
Via San Colombano 78
Tel. 055 790067-790005
No closing days, Sunday if you book
Open: lunch and dinner
Holidays: three weeks in August
Seating: 80
Prices: 22-28 euros, wine excluded
Credit cards: MC, Visa, Bancomat

☞ Wine shop with food
Via della Botte 1-3
Tel. 0564 507605
Closed Sunday for dinner and Monday
Open: lunch and dinner
Holidays: January10 -second Friday in March
Seating: 50
Prices: 35 euros, wine excluded
All major credit cards, Bancomat

This is a typical trattoria attached to a grocer's shop of the kind still occasionally to be found in some parts of Tuscany. Alongside the shelves stocked with what you need for the larder, there are wooden tables and straw-seated chairs – a basic but comfortable environment thanks to recent renovation (the air conditioning is a boon in summer). Giampiero Raveggi, increasingly helped by his son Paolo, is carrying on the work of his grandfather who would serve his customers a fry of small fish from the river Arno, and now, as then, offers a rich variety of good, traditional dishes. At the time of writing the upper floor is being renovated to create six bedrooms. You begin with the classic Tuscan **crostini** with chicken liver paté, finocchiona and **cured Cinta Senese pork**. Then there are excellent soups that vary with the season – **ribollita**, **pappa al pomodoro**, **pasta and beans** – and hand-made pasta: **pappardelle** with **hare** or wild boar, **penne strascicate** and taglierini with cep mushrooms in season. For main course, **T-bone steak**, **roast lamb** and **stracotto**. Soup with chicken livers and **mixed boiled meats** on Monday, **tripe** on Thursday and **baccalà** on Friday. Booking ahead, you can order **Tuscan mixed fry** with chicken, rabbit and seasonal vegetables, **peposo** (beef stew) and francesina (boiled beef re-cooked with onions). At the end of the meal, fresh fruit or fresh fruit salad and the classic biscuits with Vin Santo.
The flasks of local wine are good or, if you prefer, there are some Tuscan labels to choose from.

In the beautiful town of Scansano, the Cantina of via della Botte is at once a wine shop, an oil shop and a restaurant. It stocks typical local produce (wines, oils, mushrooms, cured meats and biscuits and various kinds of homemade breads) and simple dishes rich in flavor, prepared using genuine, seasonal ingredients. The vaulted brick ceilings and the big wooden tables set well apart help create a pleasantly informal atmosphere. To select your drink take a walk round the shelves, sampling some of the savories accompanied by a glass of wine. The choice is hard because there's such a wide choice: Morellino di Scansano first and foremost, then an extraordinarily rich selection of wines from Tuscany, some of which are old vintages, and also labels from Friuli and Sicily.
The dishes are traditionally Tuscan, although in some cases the chef's imagination has been given free rein. To begin with, typical croutons, vegetable flans which change with the seasons, **cured meats** and pecorino cheeses from Mount Amiata, with homemade bread and bread-sticks. Then, you can choose a soup – the classic **acquacotta** or a tasty **kale and bean soup** – or pasta: **tortelli maremmani** or tortelli stuffed with pumpkin, **maltagliati with wood pigeon sauce**, lasagne with rabbit or game sauce. For a main course we suggest wild boar casserole, roast pigeon with potato crust or chicken in pepper crust. Excellent side dishes with seasonal sautéed vegetables, **beans al fiasco**, celery flan. To finish your meal a range of tarts with homemade jams or the wonderful homemade biscuits.

60 KM EAST OF GROSSETO

LA PIEVE

🛏🗝3-Star Hotel
Via Societa' Operaia 3
Tel. 0564 987252
Fax 0564 987756
E-mail: lapieve@laltramaremma.it
Internet: www.laltramaremma.it
Closed in February

GROTTA DI SANTA CATERINA DA BAGOGA 🍾

🍲 Restaurant
Via della Galluzza 26
Tel. 0577 282208
Closed Sunday for dinner and Monday
Open: lunch and dinner
Holidays: first two weeks of February, last week of July
Seating: 60 + 24 outdoors
Prices: 28-30 euros, wine excluded
All credit cards, Bancomat

Patrizia Bevilacqua and Roberto Marni gave up their jobs (she was a communications expert, he an art director) and left Lombardy to pursue their true passion for food, wine and hospitality, opening this hotel in a small village in the Grosseto countryside. Extremely friendly, ever smiling, the couple will welcome you with enthusiasm. The hotel rooms (located on the first floor like the Il Giardinetto restaurant) are fitted with period-furniture and each room has its own distinctive features. The restaurant offers creative local dishes at a cost of 30-35 euros, wine excluded (Patrizia is in charge of the kitchen and also organizes cookery courses). Buffet breakfast offers cereals, jams, fruit juices, freshly baked croissants, home-made cakes and savory fare on request.

• 7 double and 1 triple rooms, with bathroom, air conditioning, TV, modem connection • Prices: double room single use 50-60 euros, double 88-98, triple 114-127, breakfast included • Credit cards: all except AE, Bancomat • Public parking nearby. Small pets allowed. Reception open 8am-11.30pm • Bar, restaurant. TV room. Terrace. Garden

Wandering through the fascinating labyrinth of narrow streets in Siena, you inevitably come to Via della Galluzza with its characteristic arches that enhance its beauty. It is here, in this 'olde world' setting, that you will find the Grotta. Bagoga is the nickname given to jockey Pierino Fagnani who had to stop riding in the Palio because of injury and dedicate himself while still very young to his other great passion, food. This restaurant, which Pierino has run since 1973, is Siena to the core. You can sit outside in the alleyway for your meal and enjoy a truly unique atmosphere. The menu has a wide selection and except for a series of seasonal dishes, it hardly ever changes; excellent cuisine with a Siena accent. ' clear as a bell'!
To start with, a sampling of local **cured meats**, bruschettas, **canapés**, then a list of thoroughly traditional first courses: **ribollita**, **pici with wild boar sauce** or other sauces depending on the season, **bean soup** and, in season, mushroom soup. The main courses include various meats (veal, pork, lamb) on the grill, **rabbit alle Crete Senesi** or with Vernaccia di San Gimignano, pheasant alla Tolomei and turkey (**turkey** cooked according to a 17th-century recipe with the spices normally used for panpepato, a typical Siena hard cake). End your meal with good cheeses (which Pierino ripens in the cellars), an enticing rice cake with wild fruit and classic Siena sweets (biscuits with Vin Santo and ricciarelli).
The wine list is excellent and many labels can be had by the glass. In addition to the tourist menu, there's a 30 euro alternative wine excluded that gives a broad panorama of the culinary traditions of the area.

HOSTERIA IL CARROCCIO

Recently opened Osteria
Via del Casato di Sotto 32
Tel. 0577 41165
Closed Tuesday for dinner and Wednesday
Open: lunch and dinner
Holidays: variable
Seating: 35 + 20 outdoors
Prices: 27-34 euros, wine excluded
Credit cards: Visa

ANTICA TRATTORIA DI' TRAMWAY

Trattoria
Via Pistoiese 353-357
Tel. 055 8778203-877144
Closed Sunday for dinner and Monday
Open: lunch and dinner
Holidays: in August
Seating: 75
Prices: 25-30 euros, wine excluded
All credit cards

In Siena, where mass tourism has spawned a spate of eateries, this small osteria, a stone's throw from Piazza del Campo is still to be recommended if you want to enjoy authentic Tuscan cuisine. The tiny single dining room extends into a sort of niche dug into the stone with small tables and one larger one, all set very simply.

The menu, on paper in the evening and read out at lunchtime, has a good selection of traditional dishes. In addition to the classic **cured meats** and Tuscan crostini with spleen, antipasti include **chicken liver salad**, **spicy lampredotto (tripe)**, potato and sausage pie and **curly kail roulades** with tomato sauce. Soups are more frequent in winter but **'Renata's ribollita'** (named for the owner Renata Toppi) is also served in summer; the pasta dishes include pici, **pappardelle with wild boar sauce**, **gnocchi** with red lettuce or other vegetables and spaghetti alla carbonara. There's a wide choice of meats: **stews** and ossobuco **alla senese**, **casserole of pork**, turkey in tarragon sauce, **duck Etruscan-style**, friselle of chicken and, of course, Chianina **T-bone steak**. Round off your meal with pear and chocolate tart, mascarpone tart, biscotti and **ricciarelli with Vin Santo**.

Set menus at 29 and 30 euros, the latter including the house wine. In addition to the latter (which is good) there are 120 excellent wines, mostly Tuscan.

This used to be the osteria of the tram station, and with the grocer's shop next door it was the classic place for travelers on the Florence to Pistoia line to stop for refreshments. People still come and go today to buy salamis, cheese or vegetables; some stop at the osteria for a full lunch or just a snack or even for a chat over a cup of coffee or a glass of wine. It gets crowded at lunchtime because of its good value for money and its fast service. The dishes are traditional and prepared using excellent raw materials. The start is first-rate with traditional **cured meats** and we recommend the finocchiona, and the classic **crostini** followed by **penne strascicate** or the regional specialty **tagliatelle with mutton sauce**; or again, pappardelle with wild-boar or hare sauce and then soups such as ribollita and pappa al pomodoro. Of the main courses we had a really good **roast rabbit** and **baccalà alla livornese**, usually served on Friday. Then there's **tripe** (on Tuesday), **kid cutlets** and a wide range of grilled meats. You end your meal with cookies dipped in Vin Santo but there are also homemade puddings.

In addition to the tobacconist and lottery counter that trattoria owner Paolo Bacchereti managed to get from recent extension work into what used to be the station, there is also a small but interesting wine shop containing major Tuscan labels (Carmignano first and foremost) and from the rest of Italy which grace the trattoria's wine list.

In Via del Casato di Sotto, close by the osteria, Cantina in Piazza stocks almost every wine from the five DOCG areas of the province of Siena.

SIGNA
Colli Alti

10 KM WEST OF FLORENCE ON SS 66

CASA NARDI

🔑 Bed and breakfast
Via dei Colli 390
Tel. 055 8963833-347 3380410
Fax 055 8963833
E-mail: info@casanardi.it
Internet: www.casanardi.it
Open all year

The Nardi family have lovingly renovated their 16th-century courtyard farmhouse and converted part of it into a B&B. It's located in the Florentine hinterland, at the crossroads between Via Pistoiese and the road that wanders up the Bisenzio valley. Rooms have all modern comforts and technologically advanced services, including broadband internet access, but still manage to retain their rustic look. Breakfast offers hot and cold beverages, croissants, homemade cakes and cookies. Florence can be easily reached by train or bus and there is also a cycling route that connects the Parco dei Renai to the Cascine.

• 4 double rooms, with bathroom, satellite TV, modem connection • Prices: double room single use 60 euros, double 75 (20 euro supplement for extra bed), breakfast included • Credit cards: all, Bancomat • Off street parking. No pets allowed. Owners always reachable • Breakfast rooms, lounge. Garden

SINALUNGA
Bettolle

50 KM SOUTHEAST OF SIENA

LA BANDITA

🔑 2-Star Hotel
Via Bandita 72
Tel. 0577 624649-335 6945920
Fax 0577 624649
E-mail: locandalabandita@inwind.it
Internet: www.locandalabandita.it
Closed from 10 January to 15 March

La Bandita is a tastefully restored 19th-century farmhouse surrounded by a large courtyard with pine trees and many, many olive trees. Since 1988 guests have been able to enjoy a quiet, relaxing holiday in Val di Chiana, one of the most beautiful parts of the Tuscan countryside. The nine rooms are simple and welcoming, fitted with rustic and antique furniture. Breakfast consists of both sweet and savory fare and includes home-made jams and cakes. The restaurant (under different management, Tel. +39 0577 623447), offers seasonal menus (30-35 euros, wine excluded) prepared with excellent local produce, such as Chianina beef and Cinta Senese cured meats. Many places of historic and cultural interest – Montepulciano, Pienza, Montalcino, Cortona, Siena, Arezzo – are within easy reach.

• 9 double rooms, with bathroom • Prices: double room single occupancy 75 euros, double 85-110, breakfast included • Credit cards: all, Bancomat • Off-street parking. Small pets allowed. Reception open 7am-10 pm • Restaurant. TV room. Grounds, pool

SORANO
Sovana

STIA

SCILLA

FALTERONA

1-Star Hotel
Via del Duomo 3
Tel. 0564 616531
Fax 0564 614329
E-mail: info@scilla-sovana.it
Internet: www.scilla-sovana.it
Open all year

3-Star Hotel
Piazza Tanucci 85
Tel. 0575 504569
Fax 0575 504982
E-mail: info@albergofalterona.it
Internet: www.albergofalterona.it
Open all year

Sovana is a secluded village, partly uninhabited, with a rich history of which there are traces dating back to Etruscan, Roman and medieval times. This is where you'll find the Scilla hotel, a small building with comfortable rooms. Although not officially a 3 Star Hotel yet, it has all the makings of one: excellent service and a welcoming, friendly atmosphere. Breakfast is served in the nearby Ristorante dei Merli and offers hot and cold beverages, homemade cakes, jams and some local savories. A must to see is the historic center with its tuff-stone buildings, the cathedral and the small Etruscan necropolis just a kilometer away. On request you can visit the wine cellars in the area, considered the new homeland of great Tuscan wines.

• 6 double and 2 triple rooms, with bathroom, air-conditioning, mini-bar, satellite TV • Prices: double room single use 70 euros, double 90, triple 110, breakfast included • Credit cards: all, Bancomat • Off-street parking. Small pets allowed. Reception open from 7am -11pm. • Reading and TV room. Garden

The porticoed square in Stia, an example of disordered harmony if ever there was one, is truly distinctive and was in fact chosen as a set for Leonardo Pieraccioni's movie Il ciclone. The hotel overlooks the square and is named for the mountain which provides the source of the River Arno. This 15th-century building was renovated in 1998 and offers beautifully furnished rooms with wood-paneled ceilings and curtains in warm colors. Plans to renovate the building across the road are in progress and will add rooms and a restaurant to the existing hotel. Buffet breakfast is varied and offers bread and cakes from the village bakery, local cured meats and cheeses. A must to see in the area is the Parco nazionale delle Foreste Casentinesi, the village of Pioppi, medieval churches and castles, the sanctuary of Verna and monastery of Camaldoli. Stia is well known for the production of casentino cloth and in the village you can purchase clothing made from this fabric.

•3 single, 9 double, 2 triple and 1 four-bed rooms, with bathroom, mini-bar, satellite TV • Prices: single 49-54 euros, double 67-80, triple 80-100, four-bed 90-110, breakfast included • Credit cards: all except DC, Bancomat • Facility partly accessible for the mobility challenged. Free public parking 100 meters away. Small pets allowed. Reception open 7 am-midnight. • Breakfast room. Reading room, TV room. Conference room

SUVERETO

77 KM SOUTHEAST OF LIVORNO

TERRANUOVA BRACCIOLINI
Badiola

34 KM NORTHWEST OF AREZZO SS 69 OR A1

IL CAMINETTO DA GHIGO

🍲 Trattoria
Piazza San Francesco 7
Tel. 0565 828118
Closed Monday
Open: lunch and dinner
Holidays: January-February
Seating: 30 + 30 outside
Prices: 28-30 euros, wine excluded
Credit cards: al except AE, Bancomat

COSTACHIARA

🍲 Traditional osteria-trattoria with rooms
Via Santa Maria 129
Tel. 055 944318
Closed Monday for dinner and Tuesday
Open: lunch and dinner
Holidays: in January and in August
Seating: 70 + 50 outdoors
Prices: 32 euros, wine excluded
All credit cards, Bancomat

Come in summer and dine out at one of the tables on the tiered terraces in this jewel of a Tuscan village. An atmosphere suspended in time, a true 'slow' experience. Add to this the obliging prompt service, copybook Marema cooking and a bill that is, as they say, 'more than reasonable', and you'll understand why Ghigo has earned himself our snail symbol.

On the menu consolidated classics of the area: typical, simple but characterized by high quality ingredients and preparation of uncommonly high pedigree. The menu starts with crostini, bruschetta and cured meats, followed by **tortelli maremmani**, **pappardelle with wild boar,** excellent soups, the **acquacotta** first and foremost, and home-made pasta with vegetable sauces. Mains are no less appetizing: **wild boar stew** and **rabbit 'Etruscan-style'**, accompanied by beans al fiasco and vegetable flans. The **Chianina beef** deserves a mention apart and comes in a variety of shapes and forms, all magnificently cooked: **bistecca alla fiorentina**, tagliata with herbs and **fillet steak with onions**, red wine and balsamic vinegar. For dessert, freshly home-baked cakes, the inevitable cantucci, tiramisù and panna cotta.

The intelligent wine list encompasses the local area and beyond.

Nestling in the Valdarno countryside, this osteria is within easy reach of the motorway exit of the same name and is housed in a splendid refurbished farm building. The cuisine reflects old Tuscan tradition and that of the Arno valley in particular. It has long been included in the Osterie d'Italia guide and makes extensive use of Slow Food Presidia, protected geographic indications and protected origin denomination produce. The setting is typically Tuscan; solid wood furniture and marble-top tables with the kitchen in full view yp allow you to see the cook at work. The menu is varied but there are a number of local specialties that can be enjoyed all year round.

Don't miss the dozen or so appetizers from cured meats, marinated anchovies, **panzanella** or **pappa al pomodoro** to tongue in green sauce, grilled vegetables and **zolfini beans** cooked in different ways. The first courses are traditional: **pici del fattore** or **with garlic, ribollita** and **potato tortelli with rabbit sauce**. Afterwards, classic cuts of chianina beef – tagliata with arugula and rosemary and **Fiorentine T-bone steak** – and the outstanding **chicken** of Valdarno with **celery rocchini**. The puddings are all home-made and in harmony with the rest of the menu.

The wine list contains some good Chiantis and other local wines. In summer, you can eat outside under the awning or in the garden. There are also a number of well-appointed rooms for those who want to extend their stay.

TERRANUOVA BRACCIOLINI
Penna Alta

IL CANTO DEL MAGGIO

🍲 Osteria-trattoria with rooms
Località Penna Alta 30 D
Tel. 055 9705147
Closed Monday, October-May also on Tuesday
Open: dinner, festivities also for lunch
Holidays: November
Seating: 40 + 40 outdoors
Prices: 30-35 euros, wine excluded
All credit cards, Bancomat

This beautiful osteria with overnight accommodation, which emerged from the refurbishment of a typical country building, is set in the medieval township of Penna Alta, halfway between Terranuova Bracciolini and Loro Ciuffenna. The second floor features wooden beams and a fireplace, while a garden redolent with the aroma of herbs and flowers is transformed into a particularly enjoyable dining area for summer evenings. The management involves the whole Quirini family: Mauro and Rosy, their daughter Simona, an excellent pudding chef, and her husband, the maitre d' and maitre chocolatier. Local produce is used, including zolfini beans (Slow Food Presidium), and great attention is paid to the quality and seasonality of the raw materials, and to the use of traditional recipes.
To begin with we suggest warm hen fillet salad, croutons with liver paté, typical cured meats and, as a first course, **pappardelle sull'ocio**, ravioli with garden herbs, **gnudi** (gnocchi stuffed with ricotta and spinach) dressed with seasonal meat sauce. To follow there is an excellent interpretation of the **peposo alla fornacina** – beef muscle cooked according to an ancient recipe with red wine and lashings of pepper – Tuscan **roast ham**, **wild boar Maremma style** and **Florentine T-bone steak**. For desserts, try the real seasonal specialty of rose petal pudding with chocolate.
The wine list presents a generous assortment of local wines and an intelligent selection from other areas, all at highly reasonable prices. Note also the liqueur sampling and the small artisan praline shop run by the owner's son-in-law, Michele.

TERRANUOVA BRACCIOLINI
Paterna

L'ACQUOLINA

🍲 Traditional osteria-trattoria
Via di Paterna 94
Tel. 055 977514
Closed Monday and Tuesday
Open: dinner, festivities and June 1-Aug 15 also lunch
Holidays: August 15-31
Seating: 40 + 60 outdoors
Prices: 30-35 euros, wine excluded
All credit cards, Bancomat

This is the archetypical Tuscan osteria: a renovated country house with a generous portico kept open in summer and closed in by glass in winter with a well-tended garden where you can dine on warm summer evenings. Inside, the dining room has wooden beams, old pillars and a big open fireplace. Managed by Paolo and his wife Daniela, the recipes are rooted in the land, where possible using produce in season and Slow Food Presidia. In the kitchen, expert cooks prepare pasta for the firsts and excellent pastry for the puddings.
The choice is generous. Begin your meal with **crostini with zolfini beans** or liver paté, seasonal vegetables dipped in batter and fried, eggplant parmesan, **panzanella** or an enticing **pappa al pomodoro**, cheeses and cured meats made from Cinta Senese pork. Follow that with good first courses: **bean soup** (zolfini or coconano) or curly kail soup, **ribollita** and **acquacotta** or pasta dishes such as **pici con sugo finto** (without meat) or **alla scamerita** (without tomato and with pork), **potato tortelli with rabbit sauce**, tagliatelle with meat sauce. There's a broad choice of main courses: **mixed fried meats** (chicken, rabbit, lamb) and vegetables, **duck in porchetta** or stewed, **boiled rifatto**, **baccalà**, meat balls, tripe and, if you book in advance, grilled Chianina beef. The seasonal side dishes are also good – onions, leeks and celery cooked to local recipes – and cheeses, especially local ones. Round off your meal with homemade jam tarts and various puddings.
The wine list comprises the local variety from the wine producer's cooperative of Parterna, as well as a selection from local wineries.

TORRITA DI SIENA
Montefollonico

TREQUANDA

51 KM SOUTHEAST OF SIENA, 6 KM FROM PIENZA SS 326

44 KM SOUTH EAST OF SIENA

LA BOTTE PIENA

Recently opened osteria
Piazza Cinughi 12
Tel. 0577 669481
Closed Wednesday
Open: lunch and dinner
Holidays: January 9-February 13
Seating: 40 + 25 outdoors
Prices: 18-25 euros, wine excluded
All credit cards except DC, Bancomat

CONTE MATTO

Restaurant-wine shop
Via Taverne 40
Tel. 0577 662079
Closed Tuesday
Open: lunch and dinner
Holidays: January, 10 days Nov or Dec
Seating: 50 + 40 outdoors
Prices: 35 euros, wine excluded
All major credit cards, Bancomat

Montefollonico is a picturesque little town nestling in the valleys of Pienza, Montepulciano and Torrita. At its heart stands La Botte Piena, an osteria where you can enjoy essential Tuscan cuisine. The setting is country: wooden tables, straw-seat chairs and pots, the fire lit on cold days and a carpenter's bench as a work top and another ten tables or so on the veranda overlooking the square. Simone is front of house and he also looks after the wines, while his wife Elena does the sourcing. Sandra, Simone's sister, is the cook.

Here, you can have a snack or enjoy a full meal from 10am to midnight (from All Saints to Palm Sunday, on weekdays from 5pm). To begin there's a broad selection of **bruschettas**, from the classics with choice olive oils to those with tomato, Cinta Senese lardo, beans and onion, pecorino and rigatino, truffle, sausage, pecorino with jam (made of green and red tomato, peppers, eggplant or yellow pumpkin). Many **cured meats**: pork, Cinta Senese, wild boar, game, turkey, goose, guinea fowl, ostrich. First courses: home-made **pici** with country sauce, **with sugo finto**, with breadcrumbs, **with garlic**; or **ribollita** and seasonal soups; **polenta with cep mushrooms** or with cheese and truffles. Continue with **tripe, sausage and beans**, pork fegatelli or **belly pork and beans**. The home-made dessserts are good and simple: tarts, hot chocolate cake with ice cream, ricotta with chocolate and hazelnuts, cookies and Vin Santo. The wine list comprises some 200 Tuscans, some served by the glass. The house wine is pleasant, and there's also a good selection of afrer-dinner wines and liqueurs.

Standing in the town square of Trequanda, you are a stone's throw from the Conte matto, a cozy restaurant housed in what was the grain store of the castle and run by the Arrigucci family. The menu comprises traditional recipes and subtle new interpretations of older dishes making use of everyday household produce: oils, cured meats, pasta, compotes and digestive liqueurs.

Begin your meal in traditional fashion – **croutons with liver paté,** cured meats of wild boar and cinta senese – as well as more sophisticated antipasti like terrine of duck liver with caramelized onions, potato, mushroom and truffle pie or flan of eggplant with cream of tomato and basil. Continue with **ribollita, pappa al pomodoro**, **soup of spelt and borlotto beans**, and cream of chickpea and cep mushroom soup; among the pastas try **pici with duck sauce, pappardelle with hare sauce** or the innovative ravioli with pecorino di fossa cheese and cream of saffron pistils. Then there is chianina beef prepared in a variety of ways, **pigeon** "the old way" (marinated in Vin santo for 24 hours and cooked in a casserole) and, following Renaissance recipes, **wild boar in dolceforte** and **lamb cutlets** wrapped in lardo di Colonnata with honey, white pepper and lavender. In season, there are specialties of game, white truffle and mushroom. Round off your meal with good **cheeses** – there is a good selection of Crete Senesi Pecorino cheeses – and sweets including tiramisù and almond parfait.

The wine list, compiled by David is varied, with a good selection served by glass.

VILLA BASILICA
Biecina

DA ALDO

⌒Trattoria
Via delle Cartiere 175
Tel. 0572 43008-43170
Closed Sunday
Open: lunch and dinner
Holidays: two weeks in August
Seating: 70
Prices: 23-25 euros
All major credit cards, Bancomat

If you're ever in Pinocchio country near the tourist resort of Collodi, it's worthwhile pushing on to the little outlying district of Biecina where there is an authentic family-run trattoria. Da Aldo gives onto the road and the entrance is between the café and the grocer's shop where you will find homemade produce including excellent olive oil and cured meats, which also feature in the dishes served at table. On the way in you see a table replete with seasonal produce and the kitchen where Raffaella and Mirco prepare the food under the watchful eye of host Aldo, the long-time owner of the trattoria, while Giorgio is front of house. The surroundings are family informal and simply furnished, and the menu consists essentially of seasonal dishes. Antipasti include typical Tuscan cured meats, a **mixed vegetable pickle** with an aroma of extra virgin olive oil, croutons with mushrooms and **fettunta** with tomato. Afterwards, the real specialty is pasta rolled by hand for the first courses which include **tagliatelle with meat** or **game sauce** (wild boar or venison). In season **mushrooms** (from the nearby woods) point up the flavor of the pasta in the **ravioli with butter and sage,** or combined with spelt. Again, among the main courses, **fried cep mushrooms** (in a light corn-flour batter) or an enticing raw **mushroom salad**. Then **wild boar stew**, often with **polenta,** and stewed or roast venison. The sweets are home made: cakes, biscuits and **fritters**. The house wine is worthwhile (the red is better), and to finish a pleasant evening, a good 'explosive' coffee with liqueur. All this is possible in the evening – the lunchtime menu is set for the many workers who stop in.

VILLAFRANCA IN LUNIGIANA
Mocrone

GAVARINI

⌒Restaurant-wine shop with rooms
Via Benedicenti 50
Tel. 0187 495504
Closed Wednesday, never in August
Open: lunch and dinner
Holidays: November
Seating: 200 + 30 outdoors
Prices: 22-28 euros, wine excluded
All credit cards except DC, Bancomat

The Lunigiana area is a melting pot of traditions from Tuscany, Liguria and Emilia, an interesting mixture reflected in the important dishes served in this restaurant which was established in 1909 as an osteria and grocer's shop and has evolved significantly since then. Today the building with its garden houses the restaurant and a wine shop with seating for an additional 100 (open on Thursday evening and on Sunday), as well as eight bedrooms.
Comfortably seated in one of the beautiful rooms, you can begin with antipasti of mixed specialties of the Lunigiana area, like **sgabei** (fried pasta) and **barbotta** (focaccia made of corn-flour), excellent **savory pies** and **stuffed vegetables**, vegetables preserved in oil and pickled and cured meats. For first courses, classic **testaroli with pesto**, **cazzotti** (**chestnut flour gnocchi**) **with sausage and onion sauce** and **chicchere** (small gnocchi of spinach and potato). There are also meat-filled ravioli with meat sauce or tagliatelle with cep mushrooms. The star main course is **bomba di riso**, a specialty from Piacenza which combines rice with wood pigeon, but there are also **stewed venison or veal**, **roast loin of veal**, **suckling pig with chestnuts**, **grilled lamb**, beef entrecôte with cep mushrooms and a couple of fish dishes. In season, you'll find lots of **mushrooms** as well. The **cheese board** is varied and there are many home-made desserts: walnut or apple or pear cake, tarts, cheesecake, tiramisu and panna cotta.
The wine list has varieties from all over Italy, all reasonably priced.

VINCI

43 KM WEST OF FLORENCE

IL NICCHIO

Restaurant
Via Fucini 16
Tel. 0571 56054
Closed Tuesday
Open: lunch and dinner
Holidays: January
Seating: 40 + 40 outdoors
Prices: 22-30 euros, wine excluded
All credit cards, Bancomat

The Nicchio restaurant-pizzeria has been located in the large building that houses the Casa del Popolo at the end of the town of Vinci for ten years. You enter the restaurant directly from the café by a sliding door on the left. The restaurant is furnished simply but with character. In warm weather you can sit outside under a large wooden awning. Front of house is Marilena Masi who manages the restaurant with her two daughters. The menu, which also lists some good pizzas, has land specialties as well as many seafood dishes, echoing the local cuisine, in portions which are truly generous.

To begin with, it is hard to choose among warm cuttlefish salad, seafood or meat carpaccios, cold roast loin of pork in oil plus typical Tuscan antipasti (salamis, ham, croutons) and fish soup. And in winter **fettunta alla frontoiana** made with toasted bread drizzled with oil and flavored with seasonal herbs and olives, is irresistible. Then the **soups** (spelt, cereals or onion), the **polenta flan with cep mushroom sauce**, spaghetti with seafood, little tricolor gnocchi with prawns, macaroni alla carbonara di mare. The land-based main courses include grilled meats (**steak**, fillet, lamb, pigeon, **chicken**, quail) or **tripe Florence style**. If, on the other hand you prefer seafood, try grilled sea bass or an excellent and generous portion of mixed fried fish. If you still have any room left, you can round off the meal with crema catalana, panna cotta, or tiramisù.

The house wines are acceptable. There are also some good whites and reds in equal numbers in a simple and essential wine list.

VOLTERRA
Mazzolla

73 KM SOUTHEAST OF PISA SS 68

ALBANA

Trattoria
Villaggio Mazzolla 71
Tel. 0588 39001-39050
Closed Tuesday
Open: lunch and dinner
Holidays: 10 days in January, 10 in November
Seating: 30 + 20 outdoors
Prices: 23-30 euros
All credit cards, Bancomat

This typical country trattoria is located in one of the townships of the so-called 'balze', or hills, of Volterra which has maintained all its Medieval charm intact; where time seems to stand still and life is conducted in a human dimension. The trattoria is imbued with the same spirit, and the family management of Diego and Mariana, who were both born into the restaurant tradition, is noteworthy for the care and attention they pay to taking full advantage of local dishes and produce. The cuisine follows the seasons and makes use of local know-how.

Begin your meal with **home-cured meats**, crostini both vegetarian and meat, classic **marinated herring** and raw milk cheeses from the Volterra hills. The first courses vary from ravioli made with chestnut flour and **spelt flour straccetti made with rabbit or meat sauce**, to the classic dishes with **game** such as pappardelle with wild boar, venison or wood pigeon; then there are the traditional Volterra specialties like spaghetti al rogo and **Volterra soup**. For main courses, game again from the surrounding area rich in almost impenetrable forests and caves – **wild boar stew**, roe and red deer venison and wood pigeon – or rabbit in white wine and the classic grilled steak. You can also order **tripe Volterra-style**, hare or wild boar in dolceforte, mixed fry of chicken and rabbit with seasonal vegetables, still done in an iron saucepan cooked with good local extra virgin olive oil. The sweets are home made or prepared by local bakers or pastry-shops; the wine list is rather short but the two house wines are good.

Your are advised to book in advance and try the menu of the day.

VOLTERRA

66 KM SOUTH EAST PISA SS 68 439

DA BADÒ

⬠Trattoria
Borgo San Lazzero 9
Tel. 0588 86477
Closed Wednesday
Open: lunch and dinner
Holidays: 15 days in June
Seating: 45
Prices: 26-35 euros, wine excluded
All credit cards, Bancomat

When Giacomo Nencini and Michele Gabellieri took over the management of this trattoria, they kept the name of the old owner on the signboard that reads 'Bar da Badò'. They have worked hard on bringing back to the people of Volterra the enjoyment of a meal like in bygone times. The setting is typical osteria with the café counter in the entrance and a couple of tables nearby for sitting and having a quick sandwich with excellent cured meats; then you enter the restaurant's two well furnished dining rooms, with wine bottles lining the walls.
Begin with **home-cured meats,** canapés and, in summer, fragrant **panzanella**. The pasta is home-made too; we suggest the excellent **pappardelle with hare sauce**, **Volterra-style soup** and **risotto with curly kail**. The main dishes include **wild boar stew**, **tripe**, pepato (a cut of meat near the marrow bone cooked in the pot with black peppercorns), **rabbit alla cascciatora**, duck and superb **baccalà rifatto**. Round off your meal with good cheeses, especially choice sheep's and goat's milk varieties made by small Tuscan producers, and the home-made sweets that change daily.
The wine list deserves a special mention; more than a hundred Tuscan labels from little known but very interesting wineries. Book in advance.

🍴 At Via Don Minzoni 30, La Vena di Vino is a wine shop with a vast selection of Tuscan and Italian wines to sample with the best local cheeses and salamis. At Via dei Marchesi 13, the Chic & Shock ice cream shop sells traditional and innovative flavors.

VOLTERRA
San Giusto

66 KM SOUTHEAST OF PISA ON SS 68 AND 439

FATTORIA DI LISCHETO

🚪Holiday farm
Localita' San Giusto
Tel. 0588 30403-30414
Fax 0588 30403
E-mail: lischeto@libero.it
Internet: www.agrilischeto.com
Open all year

This vacation farm in a recently renovated farmhouse belongs to the Cannas family. Don't let the presence of a swimming pool give you the wrong idea, this place offers authentic rural hospitality. Lischeto is an organic farm (furniture, shutters and walls are all painted with water-based organic paints) that has a flock of over 1,000 sheep and makes delicious cheeses. The olive oil is also excellent and can be purchased on the farm. Breakfast is really generous and consists of home-made pecorino cheeses, cured meats, cakes, honey and jams. Rooms are spacious and quiet, fitted with simple, modern, functional furniture. The restaurant offers local cuisine prepared with ingredients from the farm at a cost of 25 euros; half board in a double room is 55-62 euros. The farm also offers independent apartments with a kitchenette rented on a weekly basis, an ideal solution for longer vacations.

• 4 double rooms, with bathroom; 14 apartments, with bathroom, kitchenette • Prices: double room single use 47-52 euros, double 72-80, breakfast included; apartment 287-940 euros per week • Credit cards: all, Bancomat • Facility accessible to the mobility challenged, 2 rooms designed for their use. Off-street parking. Small pets allowed. Reception open 9am-7pm • Restaurant (open to non-residents, reservation required). Garden. Pool

VOLTERRA

66 KM SOUTHEAST OF PISA SS 68 AND 439

LA PRIMAVERA

☎—⚷ Rooms
Via Porta Diana 15
Tel. and fax 0588 87295
E-mail: info@affittacamere-laprimavera.com
Internet: www.affittacamere-laprimavera.com
Open all year

La Primavera, located in the old part of Volterra and just a short walk from the Roman theater, is managed by Silvia Paneschi and offers accommodation in a welcoming and comfortable environment. Rooms are furnished in a simple manner and are painted in different pastel colors reminiscent of springtime. Traditional breakfast offers coffee, milk, tea, croissants, homemade cakes, cured meats, cheeses, yogurt, jams and fruit juices. In Volterra, visit the Etruscan Museum, the Museum of Religious Art and the Civic Gallery. From the town you have beautiful views over the Val di Cecina with its churches, villages, rural buildings, cypress trees, calanchi, rivers and fauna. Guests can enjoy beautiful walks in the Berignone and Monterufoli-Caselli Nature Reserves.

• 4 double and 2 triple rooms, with bathroom • Prices: double room single use 50 euros, double 70, triple 80, breakfast included • Credit cards: none • 1 room designed for use by the mobility challenged. Off-street parking. No pets allowed. Owners always reachable • Breakfast room, reading and TV room. Garden

VOLTERRA
Rioddi

66 KM SOUTHEAST OF PISA

VILLA RIODDI

☎—⚷ 3-Star Hotel-Residence
Strada Provinciale Monte Volterrano
Tel. 0588 88053
Fax 0588 88074
E-mail: info@hotelvillarioddi.it
Internet: www.hotelvillarioddi.it
Closed November 3-December 5 and January 10-March 1

This small hotel in the Volterra countryside was opened eleven years ago and is managed by Luca Scudellari and his mother, Mirella, in a 15th-century building once used as a staging post. Rooms are spacious, offer all modern comforts and five of them can accommodate three to four guests. There's also a comfortable and well appointed independent apartment that's rented on a weekly basis. The buffet breakfast is set out in a communal lounge and consists of hot and cold beverages, fruit juices, cured meats and patéés, muesli, jams and home-made cakes. In summer you can enjoy breakfast out on the terrace with its beautiful views of Volterra, the Valcecina and its distinctive calanchi. The beautiful garden and two swimming pools (one for children) are ideal for relaxation and add value to this charming property

• 13 double rooms, with bathroom, air-conditioning, mini-bar, safe, satellite TV; 1 apartment (2-4 persons) with kitchenette • Prices: double room single use 50-83 euros, double 60-93 (15-17 euro supplement for extra bed), breakfast included • Credit cards: all, Bancomat • 2 rooms designed for use by the mobility challenged. Off-street parking. No pets allowed. Owners always present. • Bar. Breakfast room. Garden, terrace. Poolsa

UMBRIA

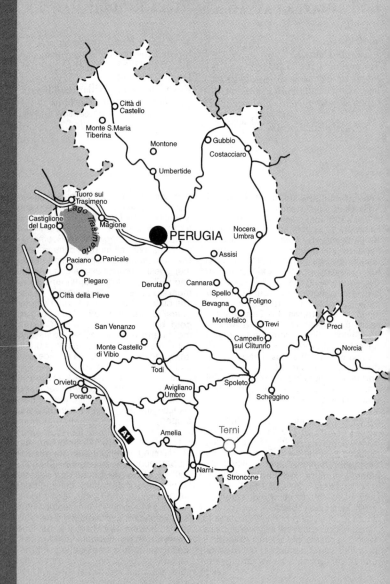

AMELIA

LOCANDA PODERE SAN GIUSEPPE

☛—o Holiday farm
Strada Amelia-Giove km 7,200
Tel. e fax 0744 981020
E-mail: info@locandasangiuseppe.it
Internet: www.locandasangiuseppe.it
Open all year round

The locanda, an old refurbished farmhouse, is about seven kilometers from Amelia on the road to Giove. It's surrounded by lush, green woods abounding with fauna and offers the possibility for a quiet and relaxing holiday. The rooms are spacious and tastefully furnished and the common areas, consisting of a hobby room, reading room with fireplace, restaurant and extensive outdoor spaces, are equally pleasant. In the immediate vicinity there are many tourist attractions: the Roman ruins of Carsulae, Lugnano in Teverina, Orvieto, the Marmore waterfall and the fossil forest of Dunarobba. The Cantamessa, Mariani and Benigni families also manage the restaurant, which is open to non-residents, and offers traditional Umbrian dishes and a wide selection of local game. Half board and full board are both available on request, the former at a cost of 60 euros and the latter at 70 euros per person.

• 6 double and 4 triple rooms, with bathroom, TV • Prices: double room single use 55 euros, double 90, triple 135 (10 euro supplement for extra bed, breakfast included • Credit cards: all, Bancomat • Facility accessible for the mobility challenged, 2 rooms designed for their use. Off-street parking. Small pets allowed. Owners always present • Restaurant. Games room, reading room. Garden, solarium. Pool

ASSISI
Biagiano

IL MANIERO

☛—o 2-Star Hotel
Via San Pietro Campagna 32
Tel. 075 816379
Fax 075 815147
E-mail: ilmaniero@ilmaniero.com
Internet: www.ilmaniero.com
Open all year round

The coat-of-arms of Count Ugolino di Pietro di Girardone showed two rampant lions and an oak tree. This symbol is now belongs the current owners of Il Maniero, Stefania and Massimiliano Generotti, who acquired the noble family's castle and transformed it into a hotel in 1990. The rooms are essential and simply furnished, while breakfast is nicely presented and includes a wide choice of sweet and savory foods. You'll be able to taste jams, local cheeses and eggs, but also cakes baked by the owners' mother, fruit tarts and the typical torcolo umbro. The restaurant is in the ancient wine cellar and offers typical Umbrian dishes with personal touches (a meal costs 25-35 euros, excluding wine, supplement for half board is 18 euros per person). The castle is surrounded by extensive grounds where guests can stroll or swim in the recently built swimming pool.

• 5 single and 12 double rooms, with bathroom, TV • Prices: double room single occupancy 52-62 euros, double 78-96 (16 euro supplement for extra bed), breakfast included • Credit cards: all except DC, Bancomat • Off-street parking. Small pets allowed. Reception open 7am-11pm. Owners always reachable. • Bar, restaurant. Breakfast room. Extensive grounds, terrace. Pool

24 KM EAST OF PERUGIA SS 147 AND SS 75

LA PIAZZETTA DELL'ERBA

Traditional osteria
Via San Gabriele dell'Addolorata 15 B
Tel. 075 815352
Closed Monday
Open: 12.30pm-2.30 pm/7.30pm-10.00pm
Holidays: mid-January/mid-February
Seating: 40 + 20 outdoors
Prices: 25-28 euros, wine excluded
All credit cards except AE, Bancomat

MALVARINA

Holiday farm
Via Pieve di Sant'Apollinare 32 – Località Capodacqua
Tel. and fax 075 8064280
E-mail: info@malvarina.it
Internet: www.malvarina.it
Open all year round

Anyone who thinks that you can only find mediocre food in Assisi, as you rush from one church to another, is mistaken. La Piazzetta is here to prove you wrong. In their search for new ideas, four friends (Stefano, Davide, Pier Paolo and Giulio) decided to turn their passion into a profession and opened a restaurant that represents the very best of tradition and local specialties. What's more, its excellent position in the center of Assisi, close to the temple of Minerva and the cathedral of San Rufino, gives a special feel to the osteria.

The menu, which changes regularly, depends on the availability of fresh seasonal ingredients and includes dishes of certain appeal. For instance, as an antipasto, you can choose a salad of pecorino, pears and walnuts with honey dressing or smoked breast of duck marinated in lemon juice. Among the first courses, the **ravioli rossi** with asparagus served with lemon and ricotta sauce are worth sampling for their interesting flavor, but don't miss **tagliolini with truffle,** when available. As a main course, you can choose from **piccione all'assisana** (pigeon sautéed in white wine and served with a sauce of its own liver) and **filetto alle erbe fini,** fillet steak with herbs or with balsamic vinegar and mosto cotto. Herbs are a common feature of all the dishes and are combined in the classic **torta al testo**. Having reached this stage, order a slice of chocolate cake on a bed of patisserie cream.

The wine cellar is managed by the jazz pianist Ramberto Ciammarughi, Davide's brother, who devotes all his artistic sensibility to its composition. The excellent house wine is also well worth a try.

Capodacqua is a small village a short distance from Assisi; following a typical country road you come to this peaceful farmhouse surrounded by secular olive trees. The agriturismo is managed by Claudio Fabrizi, helped by the members of his family, who are available to accompany guests on theme-based excursions, as well as showing them how to grow olives. The farm's organically grown products provide Claudio's mother with the necessary ingredients to prepare really filling breakfasts: honeys, jams, fruit tarts and typical local cakes. The farm's poultry is often the main ingredient for meals in the restaurant (25 euros, drinks included, also open to non-residents by reservation).

• 9 double, 2 triple and 1 four-bed rooms, with bathroom; 3 apartments (2-4 persons) with kitchenette • Prices: double room single use 52 euros, double 93, triple 105, four-bed 140, breakfast included; apartments 98 euros; breakfast 7.50 euros per person • Credit cards: all except AE, Bancomat • Facility accessible for the mobility challenged, 1 room designed for their use. Off-street parking. Small pets allowed (in the apartments). Owners always present. • Restaurant. Garden

ASSISI

ASSISI
Santa Maria degli Angeli

PALLOTTA

Restaurant – 2-Star Hotel
Via Volta Pinta 2 – Via San Rufino 6
Tel. 075 812649-812307
Fax 075 812307
E-mail: pallotta@pallottaassisi.it
Internet: www.pallottaassisi.it
Closed Tuesday
Open: lunch and dinner
Holidays: end of February-early March
Seating: 80
Prices: 25-30 euros wine excluded
All major credit cards, Bancomat

The Pallotta restaurant and hotel are close to each other in the proximity of the Palazzo dei Priori. Rooms (available all week) are located in a medieval building. The half-board supplement is 14 euros, and breakfast is both sweet and savory. The cuisine consists of local dishes prepared with home produce. You may start with typical regional cured meats and crostini with a variety of patés. Of the first courses don't miss the delicious **soup of Trasimeno beans** (Slow Food Presidia), **strangozzi** (egg-free tagliatelle) with truffle or with ricotta cheese and black olives, and **spelt soup**. The most successful main courses are **pigeon alla ghiotta**, **rabbit alla cacciatora with torta al testo**, barbecued meat with roast potatoes with wild fennel and roast suckling pig. The vegetarian menu is full of different choices. Finally, desserts include zuppa inglese and rice cake. It's possible to visit the cellar, which houses all the main regional wines and a good number of labels from other regions.

• 3 singles and 5 doubles, en-suite, television • Prices: single 40, double 65 euros (extra bed 10-15 euros), breakfast included • Restaurant access for the mobility challenged. Paid public parking 300 mt away. Small pets welcome. Porter available between 8am and 6.30pm, owners always on premises • Restaurant. Breakfast room, reading and TV rooms, living room

Opposite the basilica In **Santa Maria degli Angeli** (4 km), Brufani sells mature and fresh cheese from Umbria, as well as dairy products from other regions.

TERRA NATIA

3-Star Hotel
Via Berlinguer 5
Tel. e fax 075 8043318
E-mail: terranatia@libero.it
Internet: terranatia.cjb.net
Closed 24 and 25 December

Close to Assisi, in Santa Maria degli Angeli where the basilica of the same name watches over San Francesco's tabernacle, the Porziuncola, this hotel occupies a 15-century farmhouse that, albeit refurbished, still conserves its original charm. The hotel is a celebration of the colors of Umbria, and its ten rooms are dedicated to some of the region's most typical localities in the region. Hotel guests can dine in the restaurant – I vecchi tempi – and enjoy traditional local dishes cooked by chef Roberto Vitali (25-30 euros excluding wines, half-board 55-65 euros per person). The owner of the restaurant, Fabrizio Alzamira, bakes the typical cakes served for breakfasts personally: torcoli umbri, fruit tarts and other delicious fare. Graziano Baffi, art expert and restorer of antique paintings, will be there to give you a friendly, warm welcome.

• 7 double, 1 triple and 2 four-bed rooms, with bathroom, air-conditioning, TV • Prices: double room single use 40-55 euros, double 75-90, triple 90-105, four-bed 105-115, breakfast included • Credit cards: all, Bancomat • Facility accessible for the mobility challenged, 2 rooms designed for their use. Off-street parking. Small pets allowed. Reception open from 8 am to midnight. • Bar, restaurant. Conference room. Garden

Avigliano Umbro

La posta

Restaurant
Via Matteotti 19
Tel. 0744 933927
Closed Tuesday
Open: dinner, festivities for lunch
Holidays: variable
Seating: 40 + 30 outdoors
Prices: 30-35 euros, wine excluded
All major credit cards

By the time this guide is published, renovation work on La Posta will be finished or well on the way to completion. The work is the latest in a series of efforts made by Paola and Piero Venturini to make their restaurant, located in the middle of Avigliano, a perfect starting point for visits to cities of artistic interest or local nature sites, such as the fossil forest of Dunarobba and the grotto of Santa Restituta.

In the meantime, we can confirm that when we last visited nothing had changed in gastronomic terms and that the menu still focuses on traditional dishes and local produce. You can start with antipasti like **baccalà croquettes** in a delicate tomato sauce, **timbale of tripe and potatoes**, or a variety of vegetable flans, including one with zucchini and eggplant served with a pepper sauce. The menu continues with a selection of home-made pasta, including paccheri with tomato and crispy bacon sauce, and **ciriole** served with finferli mushrooms, when in season. As an alternative, soups, many of which combine barley with various other root vegetables.First courses also include occasional fish-based dishes. Main courses: **stewed rabbit** with roast potatoes, roast pigeon, also served with potatoes, and fried chicken with vegetables. You can end the meal with one of the home-made puddings, all of which excellently made.

The wine list is extensive and well constructed, comprising both local and non-local wines in a selection that highlights the search for small producers whose quality is on a par with the leading brands. Honest mark-ups.

Bevagna

Enoteca di Piazza Onofri

Recently opened osteria
Piazza Onofri 1
Tel. 0742 361926
Closed Wednesday
Open: dinner, Saturday and Sunday
also for lunch
Holidays: 15 days in August
Seating: 80 + 25 outdoors
Prices: 25-30 euros, wine excluded
All credit cards, Bancomat

Converted into a well-stocked wine shop, just a short walk from the center, this old oil mill blends into the medieval spirit that still characterizes the Umbrian village of Bevagna. Especially during the 'Gaite' celebrations held during the second week of June when ancient times are commemorated, indeed re-enacted, with a degree of participation rarely seen elsewhere. If you want to conjure up the gastronomic past, the Enoteca in Piazza Onofri is a good place to start and offers a pleasant way to explore Umbrian cooking —with special emphasis on traditional dishes.

Antipasti include a selection of cured meats and bruschetta with local oil, redolent of the fragrant produce of this old oil mill. Homemade **taglierini** with **cep mushrooms**, ravioli filled with potato and truffle and a wide choice of soups in winter serve as an introduction to the main courses, which mainly focus on game. It's not unusual to find partridge and woodcock cooked in the best local tradition; if not, you'll have to make do with **piccione alla ghiotta**, warmly recommended. Fillet of baccalà with tomatoes and peppers, rib of Chianina beef and **grilled lamb** are worthy alternatives. The dessert menu comprises a good selection of traditional pastries. The cheese board offers an extensive but balanced choice of Italian and foreign produce, including a good selection from France.

At the end of the meal, Sara and Angelo, the highly professional hosts, will remind visitors that this is a wine shop with over 500 bottles sourced from around the world, and including about 150 Umbrian wines. Wines can also be tasted by the glass.

BEVAGNA
Arquata

FONTE FULGERI

☞—❾ Holiday farm
Vocabolo Arquata 222
Tel. 0742 360044-360676-360541
Fax 0742 360541
E-mail: palini.nello@alice.it
Internet: www.fontefulgeri.it
Closed mid-January-mid-February

This agriturismo, managed by Nello Palini and his family takes its name from a spring found in the vicinity. The building is an Umbrian farmhouse with four rooms to accommodate guests, and is surrounded by vegetation, vineyards, orchards, vegetable gardens, fields planted with cereals and legumes. Apart from growing vegetables, the Palini family raises cattle and poultry, meat from which is often an ingredient in the dishes served in the restaurant, also open to non-residents by reservation (25-27 euros, excluding wine; residents 22 euros). The spacious, bright rooms are simply furnished. Breakfast is traditional and includes home-baked cakes and tarts, bread, butter, jam, milk, tea and coffee. Here you can relax outside in the fresh air or visiting the local art towns: Bevagna, Assisi and Spoleto.

• 1 double, 2 triple and 1 four-bed rooms, with bathroom • Prices: double room single use 40 euros, double 65, triple 75, four-bed 80, breakfast included • Credit cards: none • Off-street parking. Small pets allowed. Owners always present • Restaurant. Breakfast room. Garden

BEVAGNA

IL CHIOSTRO DI BEVAGNA

☞—❾ 2-Star Hotel
Corso Matteotti 107
Tel. 0742 361987
Fax 0742 369231
E-mail: info@ilchiostrodibevagna.com
Internet: www.ilchiostrodibevagna.com
Closed in February

This small hotel, managed by Stefania and Fabio. offers guests the opportunity to stay in one of the historic sites of the town center, only a short walk away from the main square. Here, in the cloister of the Dominican convent, with its dual order of arches decorated with original frescoes, peace and quiet are guaranteed. The rooms are simple, bright and with rustic furniture. Breakfast is served in a special room and includes traditional hot drinks, two or three types of fruit juice, rusks and jam, homemade cakes, cured meats and cheese. One of the most characteristic events in this town is the Mercato delle Gaite, a re-evocation of Bevagna's medieval past staged to welcome in the summer.

• 2 singles, 7 doubles, 3 triple and 2 four-bed rooms, with bathroom, TV • Prices: single 50 euros, double 75, triple 82, four-bed 90, breakfast included • Credit cards: all except AE, Bancomat • Facility accessible to the mobility challenged, 1 room designed for their use. Off-street parking. No pets allowed. Reception open 8 am-midnight • Breakfast room, reading and TV room. Cloisters

BEVAGNA

IL POGGIO DEI PETTIROSSI

🔑3-Star Hotel
Vocabolo Pilone 301
Tel. 0742 361740-361744
Fax 0742 369238
E-mail: info@ilpoggiodeipettirossi.it
Internet: www.ilpoggiodeipettirossi.it
Open all year

Il Poggio dei Pettirossi, managed by Livio Fancelli, is a harmonious group of refurbished and new buildings that blend in well with the unspoilt Bevagna hills. At an altitude of 325 meters, the hotel offers a splendid view over the valley below. The comfortable, spacious rooms are furnished with 'arte povera' furniture. The buffet breakfast offers a choice of coffee, milk, tea, croissants, tarts and other homemade cakes, jams, fresh fruit and juices and savory fare. The restaurant is open to non-residents and serves typical traditional Umbrian dishes (25 euros, excluding wine). Nearby you can visit towns like Assisi, Perugia, Spoleto, Spello and Montefalco. Amongst the many local events, we can recommend the Quintana in Foligno and the Festival of the Two Worlds in Spoleto.

• 27 double rooms and 2 suites (4 people), with bathroom, terrace, fridge, safe, TV, modem connection; 4 with kitchenette • Prices: double room single use 50-70 euros, double 70-80 (20 euro supplement for extra bed), suite 90-120 euros, breakfast included • Credit cards: all, Bancomat • Facility accessible for the mobility challenged, 2 rooms designed for their use. Off-street parking. No pets allowed. Reception open from 8 am to midnight • Bar, restaurant. Breakfast room, TV room. Conference room. Garden, terrace, solarium. Pool

CAMPELLO SUL CLITUNNO
Fonti del Clitunno

LA TRATTORIA

🍲 Trattoria
Strada delle Vene 7
Tel. 0743 275797
Closed Thursday
Open: lunch and dinner
Holidays: January
Seating: 70 + 70 outdoors
Prices: 25-28 euros, wine excluded
All credit cards, Bancomat

The River Clitunno is barely 15 kilometers long but was a source of inspiration in the past for both poets and painters, including Camille Corot. One of the reasons is the captivating beauty of the place, with springs rising to form a small lake, dotted with islets and surrounded by a lush vegetation of poplars and weeping willows. The trattoria, professionally run by Gabriele Checcarelli and his daughter Dalila, is quite close to the springs. Local dishes can be enjoyed in a choice of two possible settings, depending on the season: you can either eat in the well-decorated internal rooms or on the terrace outside.

To start, a range of local cured meats, delicately flavored **frittatas with truffle**, seasonal vegetables and sometimes fried anchovies. The first courses include a local specialty, **stringozzi** (short maccheroni made from flour and water), with asparagus and tomato, with seasonal vegetables – zucchini, peas or young beans – or with **crayfish**. Alternatively, you can opt for **rigatoni al rancetto** (a sauce made with lardo similar to amatriciana) redolent of peasant traditions on feast days. Meat features largely among the main courses: **rabbit 'in porchetta'**, guinea fowl 'in salmì', **stuffed pigeon** and, when in season, **stewed snails**. A slice of home-baked fruit tart provides a fitting end to the meal.

In addition to the house wine, you can choose a bottle from the wine list which, albeit not long, has been carefully selected to include labels from the region and elsewhere in Italy.

CANNARA

PERBACCO

🍲Recently opened osteria
Via Umberto I 14
Tel. 0742 720492
Closed Monday
Open: only for dinner
Holidays: August
Seating: 50
Prices: 28-30 euros, wine excluded
All credit cards, Bancomat

Here's an example of how the profile of a Slow Food Presidium can be raised so that the product in question becomes the main ingredient of dishes in a village like Cannara. The quality of the red onions grown in this sandy soil, aided by a damp climate, is undoubtedly excellent. Sweet, digestible and delicious to eat, even raw, they are used in soups and antipasti that have evolved directly from the peasant tradition.

In this pleasant osteria, just a short walk from the center, owner Ernesto serves 'poor' onion-based dishes to which he adds a personal touch without going over the top. You'll have the possibility of choosing schiacciata di patate with baked onions or **sformato of red onions** with Parmigiano-Reggiano cream sauce as an antipasto, or mixed cured meats with **torta al testo**, hot chicken liver paté, spelt salad and nervetti of veal. **Onion soup** is a must as a first course, but the **spaghetti Perbacco** served with onions and anchovies are also worth a try. Otherwise, choose from a selection of homemade pasta, such as bran tagliatelle with wild asparagus, when in season. As a main course, you can sample a dish now rarely cooked, namely boiled, rolled **calf's head** with **salsa verde**. Other excellent choices include lamb coratella and stuffed duck leg. You can round off your meal with a wonderful selection of traditional desserts.

The wine list is reasonable and includes regional and national labels, some of which can be tasted by the glass.

CASTIGLIONE DEL LAGO

L'ACQUARIO

🍲Restaurant
Via Vittorio Emanuele II 69
Tel. 075 9652432
Closed Wednesday
Open: lunch and dinner
Holidays: beginning January-end February
Seating: 50 + 10 outdoors
Prices: 30-33 euros, wine excluded
All major credit cards

This attractive restaurant on the main street in the old partr of Castiglione del Lago is run by Ilio and Tiziana, who will welcome you with professionalism and courtesy. Besidesw the inside rooms, furnished simply and decorated with dried-flower arrangements, the restaurant also has about a dozen outside tables looking onto Via Vittorio. The kitchen is in the accomplished hands of Irene and Vera who, with years of experience behind them, turn out perfectly cooked fish, vegetables and meat dishes, often with a touch of personal creativity (the dessert made from carp roe, for example).

As might be expected, the menu is dominated by a choice of freshwater fish: **caviale del Trasimeno** (pike roe) served on toast, eel marinaded with bay leaves, **smoked tench** or tench mousse; stracci with chive and truffle or **tagliatelle with carp roe** and fillet of perch. As main dishes, you can choose from **carpa regina in porchetta**, baked fillet of pike, roulade of tench with raisins and pine kernels, tegamaccio, stewed eel, or **brustico**, a classic local pike dish. The menu also includes a number of meat dishes, such as **pici with goose sauce** or, as a main course, fillet of duck accompanied by a selection of seasonal vegetables. The various types of pasta are all hand-made. You can end your meal with a choice of desserts, including a slice of torta della nonna with Vin Santo, fiadoncelli with apple and spiced wine, or the cooks' creations, such mousse flavored with mint and wild fennel.

The wine list includes mainly local and regional varieties, plus local Trasimeno labels, with a number of good wines from Orvieto, Montefalco and Torgiano, which are also available to take away.

CASTIGLIONE DEL LAGO
Petrignano

56 KM WEST OF PERUGIA RACCORDO A 1 OR SS 599

LA LOCANDA DI GULLIVER

🍲 Restaurant-pizzeria
Località I Cucchi
Tel. 075 9528228
Closed Monday
Open: lunch and dinner
Holidays: 7 January-mid-February
Seating: 80 + 80 outdoors
Prices: 25-30 euros, wine excluded
All credit cards, Bancomat

Petrignano is a small village on the border between Umbria and Tuscany, halfway between Castiglione del Lago and Montepulciano. After driving along country roads that meander through the rolling hills, you'll come to one of the most representative wineries in the area, the Fanini Estate. As well as the cellars that store the company's wine, rooms are available and, on the upper floor of the building, the restaurant is run capably by Manuela and Sauro. As might be expected of a border area, the house specialties are influenced by both regions.

Among the various antipasti, it's worth mentioning the smoked tench and trout salad, crostini of polenta with cep mushrooms and various kinds of bruschetta – the one with tomato and **Trasimeno beans** (a Slow Food Presidum) is well worth trying. The first courses are dominated by a choice of home-made pasta served with fish or meat sauces: **tagliatelle with smoked tench**, garganelli with wild boar or **pici with rabbit sauce**. A vegetarian alternative is penne al profumo di bosco, with cep mushrooms. If it's available, be sure to order **tegamaccio** (a freshwater fish stew whose sauce you mop up with bread), but the perch or eel kebabs and **grilled carp fillets** are equally delicious. The menu also caters for meat lovers: roast loin of lamb or **lamb stew with thyme**, breast of duck and chicken bits with rosemary.

Manuela is in charge of desserts, and the adequate wine list reflects Umbrian and Tuscan influences. The menu also includes a range of pizzas baked in a wood-fired oven.

CASTIGLIONE DEL LAGO
Pescia

44 KM WEST OF PERUGIA

PODERE PESCIA

🔑 Country house
Località Pescia 39 A
Tel. 075 951824-333 2226722
Fax 075 951024
E-mail: info@poderepescia.it
Internet: www.poderepescia.it
Open all year round

Podere Pescia is a beautiful farmhouse situated in Umbria between the border with Tuscany and Lake Trasimeno. The owner, Giancarlo Caponeri, also works on the restoration of old buildings and renovated this place while managing to preserve its special features, such as the stone masonry, large chimneypots, old door beams, dovecote and bell tower. The rooms and the apartment are spacious with antique furniture, and all of them have a little corner where you will find everything you need to prepare hot drinks. Breakfast is served in what was once the stable and consists of both sweet and savory fare, such as croissants, cakes and jams, ham and cheese. During August a half-board option is available at a cost of 60-70 euros per person. There is a large garden with a swimming pool.

• 5 double rooms, with bathroom, safe, TV; 1 apartment (3 persons) with kitchen • Prices: double room single use 70-100 euros, double 70-110, apartment 70-120 (20-30 euro supplement for third bed), breakfast included • Credit cards: none • 1 room accessible for the mobility challenged. Off-street parking. Small pets allowed. Owners always reachable. • Bar. Breakfast room. Garden, solarium, outdoor areas. Pool

CITTÀ DI CASTELLO

IL CACCIATORE

🍲 Traditional osteria
Via della Braccina 10
Tel. 075 8520882
Closed Tuesday
Open: lunch, dinner on booking
Holidays: September
Seating: 32
Prices: 20-25 euros, wine excluded
All credit cards

On entering you'll be taken by surprise and might even walk out again to check the sign – is this really an osteria? No, there's no mistake: this is the modern version of an osteria, namely a wine shop with a counter at the entrance and tables in a smaller room at the back. Perhaps this transformation is not wholly welcome in terms of appearance, but once inside, the warm reception makes you want to stay. The small dining room, with its beautiful vaulted brick ceiling, has a mixed clientele— a few elderly men, workers, students and foreign tourists – and is reminiscent of a Paris bistro:.

Each day Ivana produces a menu that is simple but well structured, in which traditional dishes alternate with a number of classier creations. Sandro, her son, works front of house and is an extraordinary source of information on fine food in Umbria's upper Tiber valley. Pasta is home-made three times a week and includes stuffed varieties, such as **agnellotti** (agnolotti) **al sugo** or, depending on the season, **maltagliati with chickpeas and potatoes**, passatelli and cappelletti in stock, and tagliatelle with a variety of sauces. The main courses feature **roast pigeon** and lamb 'a scottadito', whereas in winter you can opt for **pork shank imporchettato**, tripe, corata in guazzetto and **chicken livers with lardo**. Vegetables are available in season and the desserts feature a vast range of pastries. The wine list is short but with modest mark-ups. The house wine (Trebbiano or Sangiovese) is from nearby Romagna. One last thing to note: the osteria is only open for lunch … unfortunately!

CITTÀ DELLA PIEVE

MADONNA DELLE GRAZIE

🔑 Holiday farm
Località Madonna delle Grazie 6
Tel. 0578 299822
Fax 0578 297749
E-mail: info@madonnadellegrazie.it
Internet: www.madonnadellegrazie.it
Open all year round

In the early Nineties, restaurant experts Maria Teresa and Renato Nannotti pooled their efforts into this charming agriturismo overlooking the Tiberina and Chiana Valleys. Apart from the elegantly furnished common rooms, there's a very pleasant outdoor area with a swimming pool and riding school. Pets are not allowed directly onto the premises themselves, but there are covered fenced-in areas where they can be accommodated. The farm produces extra-virgin olive oil, wine, honey and meats that can be tasted in the restaurant, Le due valli, which is also open to non-residents by reservation (25-30 euros, excluding wine; half board 65-80 euros per person). There are many cities of artistic interest nearby, as well as Lake Trasimeno and signposted trails that can be completed on foot, on horseback or mountain bike. There's also a picnic area with a barbecue.

• 10 double rooms, with bathroom; 2 apartments (4 persons) with kitchen • Prices: double room single use 58-78 euros, double 90-120, breakfast included; apartment 600-850 euros a week • Credit cards: all except DC, Bancomat • Restaurant accessible for the mobility challenged. Covered off-street parking. Small pets allowed (not in rooms). Owners always present. • Restaurant. Breakfast room, reading and TV room. Pool, horse-riding, boules court

COSTACCIARO
Case Sparse di Villa

DERUTA

VILLA PASCOLO

IL BORGHETTO

🛏️ Country house
Case Sparse di Villa
Tel. and fax 075 9170770
E-mail: info@villapascolo.com
Internet: www.villapascolo.com
Open last Sunday in March-beginning of
October, first Sunday in December-Easter

🍲 Osteria
Via Garibaldi 102
Tel. 075 9724264
Closed Sunday
Open: only dinner
Holidays: variable
Seating: 30
Prices: 26-32 euros, wine excluded
No credit cards accepted

In 1998 three friends – Antonella, Paola and Norberto – gave up their jobs to realize a dream they had all had for a long time. They bought a 19-century villa immersed in a park of secular trees, they refurbished it respecting its original structure and equipped it to accommodate guests. The rooms, facing onto the peaceful grounds, are simple, with antique and arte povera furniture. Breakfast consists of healthy, genuine foods: bread, butter, jam, cake, rusks, yogurt, fresh fruit, milk, barley, chocolate, tea, coffee and fruit juices. In the restaurant, guests can enjoy traditional dishes (20-22 euros, excluding wine; half board 41-45 euros per person). Bicycles are available for excursions in the countryside or you can go on organized visits to nearby Mount Cucco. Sports facilities nearby.

• 2 double and 4 triple rooms, with bathroom, safe • Prices: double room single use 30-31 euros, double 50-56, triple 75-84, breakfast included • Credit cards: all except AE, Bancomat • Off-street parking. No pets allowed. Owners can be contacted up to 10 pm • Restaurant. Reading room. Conference room. Garden, terrace. Pool

Il Borghetto is at the bottom of the hill in the old part of town; it's an intimate setting in which the scant number of tables is offset by the great attention paid to clients and the fact that the owners cook more for pleasure than out of obligation. The osteria is run by Filiberto Guttuso, originally from Rieti, and his wife Franca, both of whom regularly journey all over central Italy to discover products, Slow Food Presidia and wines that can be included on the menu.
To start, you can choose the typical Umbrian antipasto of **cured meats** from Collazzone, filled focacce, coratella and nervetti, **ciauscolo** di Muccia, and excellent Pecorino and goat's cheeses from Monte Cucco and Sigillo. The first courses include hand-drawn fettuccelle and **tagliolini**, served with ham, duck and cep mushrooms, or with ragù of pheasant and mushrooms. Alternatively, you can opt for gnocchetti alla Provola, or **spelt** from Monteleone di Spoleto and cannelloni filled with cream of potato, lardo di maiale nero and sweet Pecorino. As a main course, you can play safe by ordering **tagliata di chianina** and sirloin with various types of stuffings, but other choices include stringhette di manzo alle erbette, **duck** with beans and Scamorza cheese with ham and truffle. The dessert list rotates about 30 or so recipes handed down by the proprietors' families: from torta della nonna to **crema di ricotta al caffè**.
The wine list relies on quality rather than quantity and deserves applause for its weekly selection of Umbrian wines, including relatively unknown labels, not to mention its modesti mark-ups. A small but intelligently chosen range of wines is also available by the glass.

FERENTILLO
San Pietro in Valle

FOLIGNO

20 KM NORTHEAST OF TERNI SS 209

37 KM SOUTHEAST OF PERUGIA SS 75

ABBAZIA DI SAN PIETRO IN VALLE

Historic residence
Via Case Sparse 4
Tel. 0744 780129
Fax 0744 435522
E-mail: abbazia@sanpietroinvalle.com
Internet: www.sanpietroinvalle.com
Open Easter-beginning of November

DA REMO

Restaurant
Via Filzi 10
Tel. 0742 340522-340679
Closed Sunday for dinner and Monday
Open: lunch and dinner
Holidays: August 1-15
Seating: 40 + 25 outdoors
Prices: 25-30 euros, wine excluded
Credit cards: Visa, Bancomat

It's rare to stay in a place so steeped in history as the Abbazia di San Pietro in Valle. Legend has it that it was erected by the Duke of Spoleto, Faroaldo II, who had a dream in which Saint Peter asked him to build a monastery in his honor. Since 1995, the abbey has been the property of the Costanzi sisters who, together with the National Heritage Office of Perugia, have restored it extensively. Every nook and cranny here contains a reminder of the past: from the rooms with their niches and vestibules, to the common areas with their frescoed walls and brick ceilings, ideal for conferences or, more simply, for a quiet read. In addition to the surrounding greenery, there's also a cloister that communicates with the church of the same name. Buffet breakfast includes home-made cakes, bread and jams, yogurt and cereals. The four double rooms located in the cloister cost 125 euros, other rooms only reach this price during the mid-August and Easter holiday periods.

• 19 double rooms and 2 suites, with bathroom, fridge, satellite TV, modem connection • Prices: double room single use 75-95 euros, double 105, suite 169-179, breakfast included • Credit cards: all except DC, Bancomat • Reserved external parking. Small pets allowed (in some rooms). Reception open 7am-11 pm• Restaurant (separate management). Breakfast room, reading and TV room. Conference room. Garden, cloister

The restaurant stands on a tree-lined boulevard close to the central station. With just a few tables, inside and outdoors, the restaurant has an elegant atmosphere, thanks mainly to the attractive furnishings and the classical background music. Considerable care has been taken to showcase the collection of Umbrian wines (including both Rosso and Sagrantino di Montefalco) and the trolley of PDO oils from the Foligno district, which can, on request, be sampled with garlic-flavored bruschetta.
The menu is limited but changes frequently, and is hand-written in old-fashioned calligraphy. Ennio, the great-grandson of the first proprietor, Remo, after whom the restaurant is named, is helped by his wife, who runs the kitchen, and his son, who waits at the tables. To start, an attractive selection of local **cured meats**, followed, as a first course, by **strangozzi** (similar to tagliatelle but made with flour and water) **with cep mushrooms** or agnolotti alla Piermarini with truffles. Grilled meats are a permanent feature of the main courses, which also feature an extremely tender pasticcio of veal and ham with cheese and cep cream sauce, and **baked suckling pig**. Dishes are always served with a selection of seasonal vegetables. The choice of desserts is never very varied but the semifreddo al caffè with whipped cream and the crème brûlée served with caramel and dusted with icing sugar are both worth a try.
Particularly noteworthy are a number of tasty dishes that aim to combine cured meats with local and other national cheeses (for example, salami casereccio served with a delicious Taleggio della Valsassina).

FOLIGNO

GUBBIO
Cima di Mengara

IL BACCO FELICE

IL PANARO

Wine shop-trattoria
Via Garibaldi 71
Tel. 335 6622659
Closed Tuesday
Open: 11.30am-3pm/5pm-midnight
Holidays: none
Seating: 30
Prices: 20-25 euros, wine excluded
All credit cards, Bancomat

Trattoria
Località Cima di Mengara
Tel. 075 920035
Closed Tuesday
Open: lunch and dinner
Holidays: in February
Seating: 60
Prices: 22-25 euros, wine excluded
All credit cards

Il Bacco Felice is the osteria to visit in Foligno. Not because it boasts an unusually old origin, or because it has been managed by a long line of local patrons. On the contrary, Salvatore Denaro, a Sicilian from Piazza Armerina, has only lived and worked in Foligno since the 80s.

The fact isthat the osteria is a key stopping point on the busy Via Garibaldi: people pause to exchange pleasantries in the morning, some come in to ask advice about an old bottle of wine they've found in the cellar at home and others linger at the tables to discuss the "magnificent destinies and progress of the world" until two in the morning. The osteria's clientele includes students, soldiers, intellectuals and journalists, professionals and penniless artists, as well as foodies; their visits are marked by thousands of scribbled comments on the walls. As well as being a great wine lover – here you'll find everything you've ever longed for – Salvatore is a convinced supporter of the produce of Slow Food Presidia, which he uses in all his dishes: from Nubia red garlic to Trasimeno beans, from Martinafranca capocollo to the Nebrodi black pig, whose pork he uses to make sausage. This is an osteria where you eat what's available, depending on the season. You might find the typical **panzanella**, regional cured meats and cheeses (carefully selected by Salvatore himself), soups, including not-to-be-missed lentil soup, **pasta with rabbit ragù**, pork fillet **al Sagrantino**, and **pollo alla diavola** with herbs. The main dessert is **rocciata** spoletina. Exquisitely fragrant 'brutti ma buoni' cookies are also served with your coffee.

In the rest of Umbria it's called torta al testo, a specialty of flour, water and salt that, in the past, was used as a substitute for bread but is now available with a variety of fillings, including local cured meats or vegetables, or served with stew. In Gubbio, they prefer to call it **crescia sul panaro**. The panaro, or testo, is the disk of pottery, terracotta, metal or cast iron that used to be heated and used to bake the focaccia, typical of popular, peasant cooking. There's a good place to taste crescia on the Strada Eugubina that links Gubbio to Perugia: Il Panaro, a historic trattoria that was already well known in the 30s, now run by partners Pietro and Elio, helped by the latter's wife.

Obviously, you start with crescia, which is served with cured meats, lonza and prosciutto crudo, together with vegetables served with local cheeses, rucola and stracchino. This bar-trattoria also serves other dishes, all cooked according to simple recipes and techniques. To start, mixed crostini usually followed by homemade pasta: **tagliatelle with goose sauce** or, when in season, pappardelle with cep mushrooms or black truffles. Excellent alternatives include tripe with tomato sauce or **zuppa di farro e cicerchie**. All the main dishes include meat: from chicken or **rabbit all'arrabbiata** to the traditional **friccò di pollo** (chicken cooked in a terracotta pot with herbs, tomatoes and white wine).

To end the meal, desserts such as zuppa inglese and tozzetti with Vin Santo. All accompanied by the house wine in a convivial setting where you'll meet new friends and hear their stories.

GUBBIO
Santa Cristina

MAGIONE
San Feliciano

30 KM NORTHEAST OF PERUGIA E 45 EXIT AT PONTE PATTOLI

20 KM NORTHWEST OF PERUGIA SS 75 BIS

LOCANDA DEL GALLO

ROSSO DI SERA

Country house
Località Santa Giustina
Tel. and fax 075 9229912
E-mail: info@locandadelgallo.it
Internet: www.locandadelgallo.it
Closed from Epiphany until Easter

Recently opened osteria
Via Fratelli Papini 79
Tel. 075 8476277
Closed Tuesday
Open: dinner, Sundays also for lunch
Holidays: January
Seating: 35 + 50 outdoors
Prices: 25-30 euros, wine excluded
All credit cards, Bancomat

The locanda is housed in a noble 12-century house that used to belong to the Marquis Caprinica del Grillo family, renovated with full respect for the original features of the building. Managing the place today are Paola Moro and Erich Brever, who have furnished it in an Oriental style that creates a pleasant contrast with the exterior. For breakfast they offer jams and honey bought from local producers, while cakes and bread are home-made and, on request, they also serve savory fare and fresh eggs. The restaurant, for residents only, serves Umbrian fare, though often with an oriental twist (25 euros, excluding wine). Completely surrounded by greenery and olive trees, this is just the place for a relaxing stay. Guests can use the private pool during summer and riding excursions are also organized.

• 10 double rooms, with bathroom • Prices: double room single use 84-92 euros, double 112-120 (28-31 euro supplement for extra bed, breakfast included • Credit cards: major ones, Bancomat • Off-street parking. No pets allowed. Owners always present • Bar, restaurant (for residents only). Breakfast room, reading and TV room. Conference room. Grounds. Swimming pool

You can admire spectacular sunsets from the terrace of this modern osteria on the shores of Lake Trasimeno. The osteria, recently repainted its furniture rearranged, offers a friendly welcome and obliging service. Federica Trovati has devised an appetizing menu that brings out the best of the ingredients, sourced locally with complete respect for seasonal variations. It's worth noting, however, that while still based on traditional recipes, some dishes have been influenced by a degree of creativity that might prove confusing to those in search of the authentic flavors of the past. Nonetheless, Rosso di Sera is still one of the most reliable addresses for good food in the Trasimeno area.
It isn't easy to list all the dishes due to the readiness and frequency with which Federica changes the menu: The first courses may include various kinds of home-made pasta served with **lake fish ragù** (maccheroncini al ragù bianco with perch and truffle or chitarrini with smoked tench, just to mention a couple of examples), or with rabbit sauce or vegetables. **Rabbit** is also offered as a main course, togerher with excellent **roast suckling pig** and **stew** or **loin of lamb**. Freshwater fish again feature in the **tegamaccio**, one of the best in the area and the iconic dish of Lake Trasimeno. The selection of cheeses and cured meats is comprehensive.
The wine list features numerous labels from Umbrian and national wine producers, as well as a few foreign wines. The mark-ups are modest.

MONTE CASTELLO DI VIBIO
Doglio

LA FATTORIA DI VIBIO

🗝 Holiday farm
Località Buchella 9
Tel. 075 8749607
Fax 075 8780014
E-mail: info@fattoriadivibio.com
Internet: www.fattoriadivibio.com
Closed from mid-January to mid-February

This agriturismo overlooks the valley dominated by Mount Peglia and is the result of the painstaking refurbishment of a group of farm dwellings. The Saladini brothers, Giuseppe and Filippo, will make you feel at home in a family atmosphere, advising you on excursions to nearby places of artistic interest. The rooms are spacious and comfortable, furnished in a classic style with wrought-iron beds. Breakfast is traditional and offers coffee, milk, tea, fruit, jams, tarts and other homemade cakes, as well as savory fare such as local cheeses and cured meats. Half board is available (85-105 euros per person). The cost of a double room may reach 130 euros during the months of May, July and September. In August a minimum stay of one week is required.

• 6 standard double and 4 superior double rooms and 3 suites, with bathroom, satellite TV; 2 apartments (4-7 persons) with kitchen • Prices: double room single use 85-100 euros, standard double 120, superior double 140-150, suite 150-160, breakfast included; apartment 800-1900 euros a week • Credit cards: all, Bancomat • Off-street parking. Small pets allowed (not in August). Reception open 8am-midnight • Bar, restaurant, wine cellar. Breakfast room, TV room. Conference room. Open-air and covered swimming pool, sauna, Turkish bath, massage center, fitness room

MONTEFALCO
Belvedere

B&B IN VILLA

🗝 Bed and breakfast
Località Belvedere di Montefalco 47
Tel. 0742 379338-328 9457576
Fax 0742 379338
E-mail: bbinvilla@libero.it
Internet: www.bbinvilla.com
Open all year round

The B&B built by the Valentini family is on a hill with a view of the valley that extends from Spoleto to Perugia. Guests are guaranteed peace and quiet as the villa is in a secluded position, albeit within easy reach of interesting places such as Assisi, Todi, Perugia and Spoleto. The rooms are simple, airy and nicely furnished; common areas, such as the lounge with its small library and the breakfast room by the kitchen, are spacious. This is where Mirella prepares the delicious cakes she serves along with jams, bread, fresh fruit and hot drinks. In the large, shady garden you can sit and chat at the tables or use the open-air pool from which you have views over the surrounding hills. Among the activities, visits to nearby wine cellars, famous for the production of Sagrantino.

• 7 double, 2 triple and 1 four-bed rooms, with bathroom, TV (on request); some rooms with air-conditioning • Prices: double room single use 60 euros, double 70-80, triple 90-100, four-bed 120, breakfast included • Credit cards: all, Bancomat • Facility accessible for the mobility challenged, 1 room designed for their use. Off-street parking. No pets allowed. Owners present from 8 am to midnight. • Breakfast room, 2 reading and TV rooms. Garden, solarium. Pool

MONTE SANTA MARIA TIBERINA
Petralta

PETRALTA

🗝Holiday farm
Vocabolo Petralta 15
Tel. 075 8570228-339 6836769
Fax 075 8570228
E-mail: agripetralta@libero.it
Internet: www.petralta.com
Open all year round

Petralta is one of the most popular holiday farms in Umbria and, arguably, in the whole of Italy. Taken over by the Parigi family, originally from Tuscany, it has been created from a carefully renovated farmhouse. Part of the facility is in an old stone tower, and while the owners live on the ground floor of the building, the three guest rooms are on the second. Another room and two apartments are located in front of the main building. The various rooms are decorated with rustic furnishings and antiques. Breakfast consists of organic products: honey, seasonal fruit, jams, cakes and toasted bread plus cvoffe, milk and so on. The restaurant is only open to residents and has a cuisine based on organically grown products (22-25 euros, wine excluded). Guests are free to use the pool, while Guido, one of the owners, organizes riding courses.

• 2 double and 2 triple rooms, with bathroom (2 rooms share the same bathroom); 2 apartments (4 persons) with kitchen • Prices: double room single use 65 euros, double and triple 50-60, apartment 65-94, breakfast 5 euros per person • Credit cards: all, Bancomat • Off-street parking. No pets allowed. Owners always present • Restaurant (for residents only). Garden, terrace. Pool

MONTONE

LOCANDA DEL CAPITANO

🗝3-Star Hotel
Via Roma 5-7
Tel. 075 9306521
Fax 075 9306455
E-mail: info@ilcapitano.com
Internet: www.ilcapitano.com
Closed January 10-February10

Once home to the swashbuckling Braccio Fortebraccio, this beautiful stone building lies in the heart of the medieval village of Montone, and since 1997 has been the home of Giancarlo and Carmen Polito, who have converted it into a small but very charming hotel. The rooms – bedrooms have every comfort and common spaces are delightful – have parquet floors and the furniture is 17-century Umbrian in style. The building is surrounded by gardens and terraces that create an even more evocative atmosphere (two of the rooms give directly onto the patio). Breakfast is buffet style and you can eat meals (around 30 euros per person, wine excluded, supplementary half-board 30 euros per person) in the adjacent restaurant, the wine cellar of which contains 400 labels from all over Italy. Activities include painting and cookery courses, trekking and horse riding and, in the autumn, truffle hunting with dogs. There are tennis courts six kilometers away and a golf course 25 kilometers away.

• 10 double rooms, with bathroom, fridge, satellite TV, modem connection • Prices: double room single use 80 euros, double 120, breakfast included • Credit cards: all, Bancomat • Facility accessible to the mobility challenged, 2 rooms designed for their use. Free public parking 70 meters away. Small pets allowed. Reception open from 7 am to midnight • Bar, restaurant. Reading and TV room. Terrace, hanging gardens.

NARNI

15 KM SOUTHWEST OF TERNI SS 3

IL PINCIO

☞ Restaurant
Via XX Settembre 117
Tel. 0744 722241
Closed Wednesday, never in summer
Open: lunch and dinner
Holidays: variable
Seating: 40
Prices: 25-30 euros, wine excluded
All credit cards, Bancomat

Ideally placed thanks to its vicinity to several major trunk roads, Narni is a good base for visiting Umbria's art cities and also for excursions to Rome, which is only 100 kilometers away. Narni itself also offers a number of interesting sights: the old town center enclosed by medieval walls, the underground city with all its chambers, tunnels and crypts, and the fortress of Albornoz, to name but a few of the most interesting.
Easily reached along the Belvedere, Cesare Passone's restaurant is in the highest part of the old town and is partly housed inside a grotto, which leads into a small but well-stocked wine cellar. The kitchen is the domain of Leonardo or, when he's away on special courses to perfect his trade, the excellent Rita. Both are responsible for devising a seasonal menu that prides itself on vegetables and meats bought from local producers. To whet your appetite, you'll be offered black bread bruschetta with warm ricottina and honey as a prelude to the **antipasto umbro**, which mainly consists of cured meats from Norcia. As first courses, you can choose between **manfricoli** (a typical pasta from Narni, made from just flour and water) served with garlic and tomato or truffle, **gnocchi with mutton** and **ravioli di ricotta**. Main courses include **agnello 'a scottadito'** or sautéed lamb flavored with truffle, pigeon and rabbit, as well as a hearty **selection of grilled pork cuts** served with seasonal vegetables. With a bit of luck (a phone call in advance might help), you'll also find game (thrush, boar, lark), when in season
All in all, the restaurant offers particularly value for money with minimum mark-ups on the wine list.

NOCERA UMBRA
Colle

55 KM EAST OF PERUGIA SS 75 AND SS 3

LA CANTINA DELLA VILLA

☞ Trattoria
Via Colle 141
Tel. 0742 810666-810329
Closed Wednesday
Open: dinner, Saturday and Sunday also for lunch
Holidays: one week at Christmas
Seating: 80
Prices: 18-22 euros
Credit cards: AE

The attractive Villa della Cupa, mentioned in an 18-century papal survey, is right in the heart of rural Umbria. Its well laid-out wine cellars now contain a number of rooms decorated in an appropriately country style with tables and benches and, as ornaments, the original wooden wine barrels. The 'professor', also known as Signor Rambotti, will take your orders from the menu written on paper napkins.
The cuisine is typically local, with dishes based on traditional country cooking; it's a pity that a tasty, age-old recipe like 'pecora e acquacotta' is only available if booked in advance for a minimum of six people. There's still plenty to choose from, however. Among the antipasti, excellent **crescia** served with different fillings. Among the first courses, it's worth trying the **gnocchi with mutton ragù** and home-made tagliatelle, not to mention the **onion**, **pasta and fennel soup**. The main courses are of similarly high standard, with beautifully **baked veal shank**, barbecued belly pork, mutton brochettes, **wild boar with honey** or simple but well prepared mixed grill. You can round off with a home-made pudding. The house wine on offer is good value for money.
The restaurant forms part of a complex (involving an agriturismo, self-catering apartments and camp site), all part of a project to integrate the management of the farm, tourism and other small business activities. Professor Rambotti will be pleased to provide fuller details, as well as recommend interesting trails to explore the surrounding area.

NORCIA
Castelluccio

ORVIETO

97 KM SOUTHEAST OF PERUGIA

72 KM NORTHWEST OF TERNI SS 71 EXIT A 1

TAVERNA DI CASTELLUCCIO

☕ Trattoria with rooms
Via Dietro la Torre 8
Closed Wednesday, never in summer
Open: lunch and dinner
Holidays: November-February
Seating: 60 + 30 outdoors
Prices: 20-25 euros, wine excluded
Credit cards: Visa, MC, Bancomat

L'ASINO D'ORO

☕ Restaurant
Vicolo del Popolo 9
Tel. 0763 344406
Closed Monday
Open: lunch and dinner
Holidays: variable
Seating: 45 + 45 outdoors
Prices: 25-30 euros, wine excluded
All credit cards except AE

Although administratively part of Norcia, Castelluccio is about 30 kilometers away from the town. As you approach the village, round endless bends, you can admire the beauty of this unspoilt corner of Umbria, with its mountains, uplands and lush pastures carpeted in spring with brightly colored flowers. Castelluccio, famous for its tiny lentils, is hidden away here, almost isolated from the rest of the world, Not that lentils are the only ingredients to feature at the Taverna di Castelluccio, stylishly managed by Miriam and Peppe.

The menu starts with an antipasto of cured meats, a tribute to the famous tradition of Norcia, served with ricotta and truffle fritters, or a threesome with **coratina** (lamb innards), lentils cooked in various ways and a classic of the Sibillini mountains, **farecchiata** (a light polenta made from wild pea flour served with an anchovy sauce). You can continue with lentil and spelt soup or an excellent choice of first courses, including **tortelloni di ricotta**, **stringozzi alla norcina** and chitarrini del Vettore, served with mushroom sauce, lentils and fresh ricotta. Then comes an ample selection of locally sourced meats, ranging from **sausage stew with lentils**, to grilled mutton and **lamb 'a scottadito'**. To round off, a good regional cheese board, including varieties flavored with local herbs by the proprietors, or, if you prefer a sweet, go straight for the **torta di ricotta**.

The wine list is first-class and features a good line-up of local labels.

The Asino d'Oro is a pleasant place to eat and provides an experience that gratifies almost all the senses …. Taste, first and foremost. The restaurant is located in the old town, in a narrow street that leads off the main street toward Piazza del Popolo. The setting is simple but well maintained and the atmosphere is often enhanced by background classical music.

The menu is full of well prepared traditional dishes (some – such as tegamaccio of eggplant and peppers served with melted chocolate, for example – are given interesting explanations in a footnote). Highly skilled maestro that he is, Lucio Sforza starts the ball rolling with a selection of crostini, followed by other appetizing antipasti: **baffo** (fried guanciale, or cheek bacon) **with sage and vinegar**, herring with apple budino and timbale of eggplant with goat's cheese. In the daytime menu, it's difficult to choose between soups and pasta dishes, such as **umbricelli** with ricotta, basil and lemon and **gnudi** with chard and goat's cheese. Moving on to the main courses, the roast silverside of Chianina beef and the **rabbit** with peppers, cherries and capers are both excellent. On the fish menu, we recommend **stewed baccalà** with raisins and fillet of whitefish with Onano lentils. Desserts vary according to Lucio's inspiration: mint blancmange with peach jelly, liquorice blancmange, hazelnut and coffee bavarois, or vellutata of dark chocolate, amaretti and chilli.

A good choice of regional wines, available both by the bottle and by the glass, embraces the best Umbrian production. A round of applause for the varieties of coffee on offer, and the excellent practice of not including children under 12 in the final bill.

LA GROTTA   ## LA PALOMBA

Trattoria
Via Signorelli 5
Tel. 0763 341348
Closed Tuesday
Open: lunch and dinner
Holidays: one week in July and in winter
Seating: 60
Prices: 30-32 euros, wine excluded
All credit cards, Bancomat

Trattoria
Via Manente 16
Tel. 0763 343395
Closed Wednesday
Open: lunch and dinner
Holidays: between July and August
Seating: 50
Prices: 22-24 euros, wine excluded
All credit cards, Bancomat

It's not every day that, just because you've chosen a first course (in this case **tagliatelle with chicken giblets**), you're enthusiastically led into the kitchen where the patron wants to show you the free-range chickens whose innards will soon be served on your plate. Franco Titocchia, the proprietor of La Grotta, is exuberant, confident and proud of how he runs his trattoria, which is regularly visited by the inhabitants of Orvieto, Italian and foreign tourists, and food enthusiasts and experts. His reputation rests on his experience and his trattoria is something of an institution since he's been in the business since 1945.

The menu offers an exciting range of gastronomic specialties. The antipasti include mixed crostini and bruschetta with Orvieto oil, ham and **cured boar**. Then you can choose from **umbricelli** or tagliatelle **with duck ragù** or all'arrabbiata, tagliolini with artichokes or zucchini, and excellent dishes made with locally grown chickpeas. The **chicken in tegame** with black olives is just one of many main courses, others being **pigeon in salmì**, **lamb cutlets**, grilled meats, wild boar stew or rabbit in parsley sauce. To end your meal you can choose between the cheese board, which assigns pride of place to local Pecorino, or a selection of home-made desserts: tiramisù, panna cotta, zuppa inglese and tozzetti with Vin Santo.

The wine list features an exhaustive range of Orvieto labels, as well as a good showing from the rest of Umbria and Italy.

For anyone wishing to have proof or confirmation of the excellence of Orvieto's local cuisine, we warmly recommend La Palomba, in the heart of the city next door to the 13-century Palazzo Comunale. This is just the right place to enjoy simple food with traditional flavors and soak up the atmosphere of the city. The trattoria is a family affair and each member shares in the general management with courtesy, friendliness and expertise. The kitchen is the realm of Giovanna, who for five decades, as if by magic, has transformed prime quality seasonal produce into delectable food that is now part and parcel of local gastronomic history. Clients can try her **crostini al salmì** and various types of bruschetta, including one with extra-virgin olive oil and truffle freshly grated at the table. Among the first courses, **tagliatelle al sugo di gallina** and **umbricelli all'arrabbiata** or with other seasonal accompaniments. On feast days, Giovanna cooks a fantastic pigeon dish, **palomba alla leccarda**, as well as **tripe** and lamb 'a scottadito', all well presented by the consolidated front of house team of Carla, Enrica and Giampiero. If you can still manage a pudding to round off your meal, try ordering one of the delicious home-made treats: wild berry pie, ice cream served 'caldo-freddo' or classic tozzetti with Vin Santo.

The wine list is well structured and includes both local and regional wines, as well as a few good labels from Tuscany.

72 KM NORTHWEST OF TERNI | 72 KM NORTHWEST TERNI EXIT A 1

LOCANDA ROSATI

🗝Holiday farm
Località Buonviaggio 22
Tel. 0763 217314-348 7466451
Fax 0763 217314
E-mail: info@locandarosati.orvieto.tr.it
Internet: www.locandarosati.orvieto.tr.it
Closed from January 7 to March 1
and December 24-25

In the hills of Orvieto, a few kilometers from Lake Bolsena, you'll find this late 19-century stone farmhouse out of which owners, Giampiero, Luisa, Alba and Paolo (the chef), have converted into an agriturismo. The three common rooms are basic and unpretentious as is the rest of the house. Breakfast is excellent and consists of coffee, tea, milk, orange juice, yogurt, cake, homemade bread and jam, and on request, bacon and eggs, ham and cheese. In the evening you can enjoy the local cuisine with its strong flavors in the restaurant, which is for residents only (around 30 euros, including wine). Near the dining room is a wine cellar dug out of the tufa and a space where they sell olive oil, jams and wines from Umbria and Tuscany.

• 1 single, 5 double, 2 triple and 2 four-bed rooms, with bathroom (1 with jacuzzi), modem connection; some rooms with air-conditioning • Prices: single 90-100 euros, double 110-120, triple 140-150, four-bed 170-180, breakfast included • Credit cards: Visa, MC, Bancomat • Facility accessible to the mobility challenged, 1 room designed for their use. Off-street parking. Small pets allowed. Owners always present. • Restaurant (for residents only). 2 lounges, Internet point. Grounds. Pool

TRATTORIA DELL'ORSO

🍲 Osteria
Via della Misericordia 18-20
Tel. 0763 341642
Closed Monday and Tuesday
Open: lunch and dinner
Holidays: July
Seating: 60
Prices: 30-33 euros, wine excluded
All major credit cards, Bancomat

The Trattoria dell'Orso is a good example of how there are still places in a tourist city like Orvieto that keep up the standards of traditional cooking. The osteria, managed by the friendly and competent Gabriele Di Giandomenico and Ciro Cristiano, is one of the oldest in the city. In the past, the clientele included country people, farmers and salesmen visiting the city on market days. Now, after appropriate restoration work, the premises have been tastefully decorated and decorated with wooden wall sculptures.The kitchen, however, continues to serve local dishes that reflect a seasonal use of prime ingredients.
The meal starts with vegetable dishes and mixed crostini, which are followed by excellent homemade **tagliatelle**, served with **mushrooms** or **truffles** – also used to dress other dishes – or with cherry tomatoes and Scamorza. There is also a variety of equally delicious **soups**, including classic **spelt** soup. All the main dishes feature some form of meat: from **guinea fowl with truffles** to **rabbit with spices**, lamb 'a scottadito' and **chicken alla cacciatora**. The dishes are always served with a selection of vegetables in season. To round off the meal, we recommend the selection of pastries or various types of puddings. There's a good wine list, obviously biased mainly on Orvieto labels.

🍨🍴 At Via Cavour 56, the Gelateria Pasqualetti sells ices, semifreddi and fruit filled with ice cream; at number 101, the Gastronomia Carraro stocks an extensive selection of local produce; at number 21, Bar Pasticceria Montanucci is the city's smartest café.

PACIANO

LA LOGGETTA

◔ Osteria
Piazza Santa Maria
Tel. 075 830144
Closed Tuesday
Open: lunch and dinner
Holidays: November and February
Seating: 30 + 50 outdoors
Prices: 25-27 euros, wine excluded
All credit cards, Bancomat

Paciano is one of Umbria's smallest municipalities. Encircled by 14-century walls, the village looks onto the oak-wooded slopes of Monte Petrella and Monte Pausilio. Fausto Santiccioli, the owner, gives you such a warm welcome you are immediately ready to enjoy a particularly pleasant stay. Once you've made yourself at home in one of the small rooms or on the wide terrace, you can savor the choice of dishes listed on original menus presented as newspapers containing pages of local history and tourist information.

The first page news concerns the bread and pasta: both are made daily, using stone-ground flour. Turning the page, you find details of antipasti, **bruschette with Trasimeno beans**, a selection of local lardo, grilled vegetables, **cured meats,** including cinta senese and fine pecorino, chicory with pears, orange and fennel and zucchini carpaccio with pecorino flakes. The page of the first courses announces hand-made **tagliolini with baccalà and chickpeas**, tagliatelle with black or white truffles, spelt with mushrooms and onions, **risotto with beans and white leeks**. The paper continues with **stewed wild boar**, tagliata di capocollo with salad, Trasimeno beans with red onions, celery and aromatic herbs, duck with prunes and dried tomatoes and terrine of eggplant with sheep's cheese and truffle. Vegetables are seasonal, and there is an excellent choice of puddings, such as semifreddo with coffee and nougat. A separate menu is dedicated to **freshwater fish**.
The wine list is extraordinarily long and carefully structured, with special attention to Umbria and Tuscany. Prices are honest.

PANICALE

LE GROTTE DI BOLDRINO

🗝 3-Star Hotel
Via Virgilio Ceppari 30
Tel. 075 837161
Fax 075 837166
E-mail: grottediboldrino@libero.it
Internet: www.grottediboldrino.it
Open all year round

Panicale is a characteristic medieval village on the border between Umbria and Tuscany. Not to be missed here is the church of San Sebastiano with Perugino's of the martyrdom of the saint. Right behind the village walls you'll find this small, pretty hotel that during summer welcomes guests under a pergola of sweet-scented wisteria. Laura Nicchiarelli has chosen to furnish the rooms – with all essential comforts – with original late 19^t -century furniture. Breakfast consists of croissants, tarts, rusks, yogurt, fresh fruit and hot drinks. The restaurant, which is also open to non-residents, completes the hotel's facilities. During the summer season you can eat outside in the garden (25 euros, excluding wine; half board with double room occupancy 58-63 euros per person, excluding wine).

• 9 double rooms and 2 junior suites, with bathroom, fridge, safe, TV • Prices: double room single use 58-62 euros, double 70-80, junior suite 100-110, breakfast included • Credit cards: all except AE, Bancomat • Facility and 1 room accessible to the mobility challenged. Free public parking out front. Small pets allowed. Owners always present • Restaurant. Lounge. Conference room. Garden

4 KM FROM CITY CENTER

STELLA

⛉Restaurant-wine shop
Via dei Narcisi 47 A
Tel. 075 6920002
Closed Tuesdays
Open: only dinner, festivities for lunch
Holidays: second and third week of July
Seating: 35 + 30 outdoors
Prices: 23-25 euros, wine excluded
All credit cards except AE, Bancomat

TRATTORIA DEL BORGO

⛉Trattoria
Via della Sposa 23 A and 27
Tel. 075 5720390
Closed Sunday
Open: only dinner
Holidays: in August
Seating: 75 + 40 outdoors
Prices: 25-32 euros
Credit cards: CartaSi, Visa

Arkadiusz is Polish by origin, but he trained as a sommelier here in Perugia. This becomes obvious as soon as you enter this restaurant-winery, whose list runs to over 350 national labels, including practically every Umbrian producer. What's more, there's a special room where you can taste wine by the glass. The mark-ups are extremely honest, by the way.

Even the menu is structured round the wines, with an appropriate wine being suggested for every dish. The antipasti are based on a selection of traditional **cured meats**: local prosciutto, guanciale and finocchiona, often served with a range of delicious savory pie. You can rely on the home-made pasta for the first course: **fettucine with cep mushrooms**, cappellacci al fiordilatte with tomato sauce, or gnocchetti with walnuts and cheese. The main courses include a wide variety of Umbrian specialties, all interpreted with elegance, and the **perch fillet** with capers and lemon reminds us that Lake Trasimeno is nearby. Other dishes are aromatic tagliata with juniper and rosemary and straccetti di vitello with cep mushrooms. The kitchen, run by Nicola and Silvia (the host's wife), also produces a selection of delicate, well-balanced fried dishes: **lamb chops**, pumpkin flowers and traditional **baccalà**. Parmigiana di melanzane, grilled vegetables and roast peppers with anchovy and caper sauce make up the list of vegetables.

There's an excellent cheese board (we recommend the raw milk Umbrian pecorino) and the puddings are delicious: cakes change from day to day or chocolate fondue with biscuits and fruit is always on the menu.

At this trattoria, in the old town just a short distance from Via dei Priori, you'll be guests of Emilio Cassioli, the former butcher and expert norcino, or pork curer, who runs the place with his wife Carla. You'll be bowled over by the couple's friendly welcome and their gastronomic knowledge. In summer, you'll be able to dine in the charming garden, surrounded by the old city walls.

To start, try the **mixed cured meats** – coppa del norcino, prosciutto, and salami – all home-made and often accompanied by **torta al testo**. The classic **torta con i ciccioli** is rarely found elsewhere, but here it features on the menu about twice a year. Among the home-made pasta dishes, you'll find excellent **pappardelle with wild boar** and ravioloni with cheese sauce. In winter, the choice includes **cappelletti in chicken stock** and **gnocchi with goose sauce**. Emilio's experience as a former butcher is the main guarantee for the prime quality of the meat, all sourced locally. Grilled **boar sausages** and lamb 'a scottadito' are the strong points, but **suckling pig alla perugina**, **chicken livers** and **barbozzo** (pig's cheek) alla contadina are equally delicious. If you order a steak alla fiorentina, you won't regret it. Alternatively, try the coratella or baked parmigiana di verdura (when in season, try the one with cardoons). Many dishes are flavored with truffle when it's the right time of year. The home-made puddings are simple, but delicious.

The wine list isn't very long, but includes the most important regional wines.

PIEGARO
Piazzola

34 KM SOUTHEAST OF PERUGIA

WINE BARTOLO HOSTERIA

⌒ Osteria
Via Bartolo 30
Tel. 075 5716027
Closed Wednesday
Open: only dinner
Holidays: August 1-25
Seating: 40
Prices: 23-30 euros, wine excluded
All major credit cards, Bancomat

PIAZZOLA ALLA QUERCIA

Holiday farm
Località Piazzola 48
Tel. 075 8358455
Fax 075 8359621
E-mail: info@piazzola.it
Internet: www.piazzola.it
Open all year round

Right in the historic heart of Perugia, just a few steps from Corso Vannucci, where the evening 'struscio' or promenade is still fashionable, close to the Fontana Maggiore, two young Perugians, Andrea at front of house and Umberto in the kitchen, have turned a smart restaurant, 'Il Bartolo' into an attractive osteria with an excellent regional wine list.

The service is friendly and the menu changes with the seasons, though some dishes are permanent. To start, you can enjoy delectable mixed bruschettas (the one with truffle and chickpeas is excellent) or first-class beef carpaccio Chianina (white Chianina cattle, known as giants on account of their size, have been bred in Umbria and Tuscany since ancient times). Standing out among the first course are **stringozzi with truffle and Pecorino** from Norcia, hand-made cappellacci with cep mushrooms and classic **lentil soup**. The **brasato al Sagrantino** with mashed potatoes is excellent, as is the stracotto of Chianina beef cooked in the region's humbler but equally delicious Sangiovese wine. Lamb is always present on the menu (try the **coratella** served with **torta al testo** and roast leg of lamb). The **boiled Chianina beef** is also excellent. Leave room for the desserts, all home-made, like the bread.

The impressive wine list includes many of the best Umbrian labels and a few interesting bottles from the rest of Italy: note also that a few wines are served by the glass.

Founded by the Romans in 290 BC, Piegaro was famous in medieval times for its glass production. Certain sites in the area are definitely worth a visit: the castles of Greppolischieto and Cibottola, the sanctuary of the Madonna di Mongiovino and Colle San Paolo parish church. After a day exploring historic villages or on the shores of Lake Trasimeno a little bit further north, you can relax in the warm, quiet atmosphere of this beautiful agriturismo. Guests may choose between rooms and apartments, both located in two simply furnished old stone buildings that have recently been renovated. Buffet breakfast consists of bread, jams, cheeses and cured meats that guests may eat either in the breakfast room or out on the terrace, with its view over the hills. Also on the terrace, you can end the day with a dinner at 15-25 euro, excluding wine.

• 7 double rooms, with bathroom; 5 apartments (2-5 persons) with kitchen • Prices: double room single use 31-38 euros, double 62-76, breakfast included; 2-person apartment 152-415 euros, 4-5 person, 163-630 per week • Credit cards: none • 1 apartment designed for use by the mobility challenged. Off-street parking. Small pets allowed. Owners always present • Restaurant. Breakfast room. Conference room. Garden, terrace

PORANO

IL BOCCONE DEL PRETE

Osteria
Via Bellini 12-16
Tel. 0763 374772
Closed Monday
Open: lunch and dinner
Holidays: none
Seating: 70 + 30 outdoors
Prices: 30-32 euros, wine excluded
All major credit cards

Porano is a small village on a tufa plateau, with a marvelous view of Orvieto cathedral just eight kilometers away in the distance. With its cluster of old buildings, steep narrow streets and succession of ancient buildings, it's well worth visiting. As is the Boccone del Prete, which adds considerably to the charm of the place. Outside you are welcomed by an attractive sign, while inside the tables are set in rooms converted from 13-century wine cellars, creating a particularly evocative atmosphere. In terms of the cuisine, the osteria has opted to follow what is now a frequent trend, combining traditional dishes with more innovative and creative options.

You'll find combinations like grilled bread with extra-virgin olive oil topped with carpaccio di coppa, lemon and mint, a **selection of local cheeses and cured meats**, and baffo served with vinegar and sage. To follow, Manola and Adriano propose **vegetable soups**, one with **Cannara onions** (Slow Food Presidium) or pasta dishes, such as **tagliatelle with duck giblets**. But always ask because the first courses often change, as do the main courses. Possible dishes might include **stewed baccalà cakes**, **coratella**, **roast pork** with apple and Seville orange, and various grilled meats. The vegetables are simple but beautifully cooked and always seasonal. Finish your meal with the classic choice of tozzetti and Vin Santo, or a dessert like zuppa inglese or custard with fruit purée.

The wine list is managed by Stefano, the owner, and includes a good selection of local wines, as well as top Italian producers.

PRECI

IL CASTORO

Restaurant-pizzeria
Via Roma
Tel. 0743 939248
Closed Thursday, never in summer
Open: lunch and dinner
Holidays: 10 days in November
Seating: 120 + 70 outdoors
Prices: 28-30 euros
All credit cards except AE, Bancomat

Built round a Benedictine oratory, Preci is a small town at the point where three valleys meet, on the border between Umbria and the Marche. Rita and Stefano Nardi opened their bar-trattoria in 1986 not far from the center, before moving to the current location. The substance here far outweighs the form. In fact, the restaurant-pizzeria is housed in a prefabricated building but, thanks to the quality of the food, in season it is literally besieged by food lovers.

Some people travel as far as 100 kilometers from Perugia to enjoy the menu based on mushrooms, game and black truffle from Norcia, the leitmotif of the place. The set menu at 28-30 euros (including house wine) is extremely popular. You start with the not-to-be-missed **fritta-ta al tartufo**, Umbrian bruschetta, **wild boar prosciutto** and, from Norcia, corallina salami, **ciauscolo**, capocollo and coppa di testa. These are followed by **strangozzi** with truffle or **alla preciana** (with ragù and truffle), pappardelle with wild boar or hare sauce without tomato, ravioli with cheese and truffle and fioretti (short egg pasta) served with various sauces. Meat features largely among the main courses: from excellent **tagliata di chianina** with cep mushrooms and slivers of truffle to wild boar alla cacciatora, lonzino, lamb coratella with onions, **lamb** 'a scottadito' or **fried**. Otherwise, you could order Scamorza with cep mushrooms and truffles or a dish of Pecorino and ricotta. Tiramisù or zuppa inglese round the meal off nicely. In the evening, the restaurant also serves pizzas.

Reasonable house wines and a good selection of liqueurs. Booking is recommended, especially at weekends.

SAN VENANZO
Collelungo

SCHEGGINO

LOCANDA SAN BARTOLOMEO

🔑 Country house
Vocabolo San Bartolomeo 30
Tel. and fax 075 8743990
E-mail: locsanbartolomeo@hotmail.com
Internet: www.locandasanbartolomeo.com
Closed from Epiphany until Easter

RISTORANTE DEL PONTE

🍲 Hotel restaurant
Via del Borgo 11
Tel. 0743 61131-61253
Closed Monday
Open: lunch and dinner
Holidays: 3-26 November
Seating: 100 + 50 outdoors
Prices: 25-30 euros, wine excluded
All credit cards except DC, Bancomat

This small locanda, managed by Roberto Ciccarelli, is set in a beautifully refurbished 18-century Umbrian country house at the end of a scenic road that winds its way round both sides of a hill. The rooms are simply furnished with antique pieces in harmony with the style of the building itself, and have been given names inspired by popular novels from 'Jane Eyre' to 'Room with a View'. The rooms don't have TV sets, but there is a small library and guests are welcome to make use of it. The home-made breakfast consists of milk, coffee, tea, cakes and jams. You can either relax beside the pool or take a refreshing swim. The restaurant is for residents only. Half board costs 70 euros per person.

• 5 double rooms, with bathroom • Prices: double room single use 70 euros (30 euro supplement for extra bed), breakfast included • Credit cards: none • Off-street parking. Small pets allowed. Owners always reachable • Restaurant. Lounge. Garden. Pool

The tunnel from Spoleto to Valnerina, the true gastronomic heartland of Umbria, allows you to reach to reach Scheggino, a village whose gastronomic heritage includes truffles, trout and crawfish, in just a few minutes. The restaurant, run by the Ronca family, lies close to the River Nera, and a wooden bridge leads to it from a convenient car park nearby. The spacious, well-lit rooms are furnished with sobriety and good taste with no sign of the fake country-style so popular in this area.

There are virtually two menus: with and without **winter black truffle**, You can choose from hand-sliced, fully matured local prosciutto and **crawfish in parsley sauce** as antipasti, before continuing with a range of home-made pastas, including tagliatelle and **pappardelle with wild boar** and spelt-flour tagliolini with wild asparagus, as well as delicate **risotto with black truffle**. This is Valnerina and the main courses inevitably include its specialties, such as grilled lamb or lamb alla cacciatora. Other dishes are crawfish and trout, served in countless different ways: with oil and lemon, grilled, fried, sautéed or with truffle. As a fitting end to your meal, we recommend the zuppa inglese.

The good wine list features many Umbrian producers. After eating so well at such honest prices (provided you don't choose too many truffle-based specialties), it's well worth stopping to see the trout swimming in the canal in front of the restaurant: a sort of natural aquarium in this beautiful corner of Umbria.

SPELLO

SPOLETO

ALBERGO DEL TEATRO

3-Star Hotel
Via Giulia 24
Tel. 0742 301140
Fax 0742 301612
E-mail: info@hoteldelteatro.it
Internet: www.hoteldelteatro.it
Variable holidays

OSTERIA DEL TRIVIO

Osteria
Via del Trivio 16
Tel. 0743 44349
Closed Tuesday
Open: lunch and dinner
Holidays: January
Seating: 45
Prices: 25-30 euros, wine excluded
All credit cards, Bancomat

Spello is a small village where you'll find reminders of a Roman past, such as the Porta Consulare and sites of great artistic interest such as the church of Santa Maria Maggiore, with the Baglioni Chapel, frescoed in the 16 century by Pinturicchio. It's also a good base from which to visit places such as Assisi and Perugia. This hotel, managed by Gioacchino Cruciali, is in an elegant 18-century building with spacious, well furnished rooms fitted with every comfort. The large terrace enjoys a view over the village roofs and valley below. Breakfast includes many local products, such as rocciata, home-made cakes, cookies and jams along with coffee, milk and so on.

• 1 single, 7 double and 3 triple rooms and 1 suite, with bathroom, fridge, safe, TV, modem connection • Prices: single 55-60 euros, double 90-95, triple 115, suite 200-220, breakfast included • Credit cards: all, Bancomat • Free public parking, garage (7 spaces). Small pets allowed. Owners always reachable • Bar. Breakfast room, reading room. Conference room. Terrace

This trattoria is run by the charming Umberto and Mirella husband-and-wife team with taste and enthusiasm. Both have always loved cooking and came back to Spoleto after travelling around the world for years, building up extensive catering experience. After restoring an old property in the city center, they opened this attractive osteria, The tables are set with checked tablecloths and the walls are decorated with black and white photos of Umberto and his family.
The menu, presented orally by the owner and cooked by his wife, follows the seasons and the availability of prime quality ingredients: at all events, the menu is full typical Umbrian dishes. To start, you can savor the classic antipasto of local cured meats, raw vegetables, artichokes preserved in oil, and Pecorino. For first courses, **strangozzi alla spoletina** – with wild asparagus or pecorino and broad beans – or **ravioli with chicory and fresh tomato**. The main courses feature an excellent **rabbit in white wine,** delicious **meat-filled zucchini**, pork fillet with balsamic vinegar or a mixed grill. Home-made desserts round off a satisfactory meal. The wine list is reasonable.

In **Strettura** (17 km from Spoleto, in the direction of Terni), Forno Vantaggi produces excellent pane di Strettura (bread which, thanks to a complex baking process, lasts well) and pizza di Pasqua.

STRONCONE

PORTA DEL TEMPO

☛❶Country house
Via del Sacramento 2
Tel. 0744 608190-333 3742957
Fax 0744 609034
E-mail: info@portadeltempo.com
Internet: www.portadeltempo.com
Open all year round

The eight tastefully furnished rooms are in a small noble 16-century palazzo, re-strutured but retaining all the features of the original structure. Carpeted floors, walls painted in warm colors, beautiful fabrics: all this makes the country house managed by Rosanna Russo a great place to chill out in the center of Stroncone. The breakfast provides real added value: it's made by Rosanna's partner and consists of several types of cake (chocolate or pear and cinnamon) cakes, fresh fruit pastries, lemon cookies, croissants and, on request, sweet and savory fare for those allergic to gluten. Guests are catered for in ever respect, and specific excursions area organized to allow them to discover lesser known parts of Umbria.

• 1 single and 6 double rooms and 1 suite (3 persons), with bathroom, fridge, TV • Prices: single and double room single use 50-70 euros, double 60-110, suite 70-130, breakfast included • Credit cards: all, Bancomat • 2 rooms designed for use by the mobility challenged. Both free and paid external public parking. Small pets allowed. Owners always reachable • Breakfast room

TODI
Pesciano

LA MASALE

☛❶Bed and breakfast
Strada Vicinale del Piano 17
Tel. 075 8947073-348 4901258
Fax 075 8947073
E-mail: lamasale@inwind.it
Internet: www.lamasale.com
Open all year round

Cristina from the Ticino area of Italy and Max from Paris fell in love with Umbria and decided to open a B&B in this completely renovated 19-century country house. The rooms are spacious and bright, with a mixture of antique and ethnic furniture and paintings by contemporary French artists. The room in the lofts and the suites are more spacious and a third bed can be added. The generous breakfast is served until mid-morning, which means guests can enjoy a lie-in. Bread and cakes are all home-baked and the jams are home-made too. The eggs come from the hens you'll see pecking around in the garden and the fruit is fresh. There's also the possibility to log on to the Internet in the reading room, while lovers of the outdoors have access to bicycles for excursions in the surrounding area.

• 2 double rooms, 2 suites and 2 lofts, with bathroom, TV (on request) • Prices: double room single use 80 euro, suite and loft 90 (25 euro supplement for extra bed), breakfast included • Credit cards: Visa, MC, Bancomat • Off-street parking. No pets allowed. Owners always present • Breakfast room, reading room with Internet point. Garden. Pool

TODI
Pian di San Martino

LA TORRIOLA

🗝Holiday farm
Località La Torriola
Tel. 329 6197626
Fax 075 8944747
E-mail: torriola@libero.it
Internet: www.torriola.com
Closed for 1 month after Epiphany

TODI
Pontenaia

LA MULINELLA

🍲Restaurant
Località Pontenaia 29
Tel. 075 8944779
Closed Wednesday
Open: lunch and dinner
Holidays: in November
Seating: 60 + 60 outdoors
Prices: 22-25 euros, wine excluded
Credit cards: CartaSi, Bancomat

This agriturismo, managed by Maurizio Giannini, is housed in a building that was refurbished in 2001, in a peaceful, panoramic hilly area, ideal for a totally relaxing vacation. Besides welcoming guests Maurizio also produces and sells wine and olive oil. The apartments, with small kitchenettes or fully equipped kitchens, are furnished in rustic style and can accommodate couples or larger family groups. Breakfast includes local honey and jams, bread and cookies, yogurt and cereals, coffee, milk and tea. Be sure to visit the Forello Gorge or Civitella del Lago. As an alternative, organized activities, olive oil tasting courses, horse riding and mountain bike excursions.

• 5 apartments (2-4 persons), with bathroom, fridge, TV, modem connection, kitchenette or separate kitchen • Prices: 2-person apartment 80-110 euros, 4-person 140-180; breakfast 5 euros per person • Credit cards: all except DC, Bancomat • Off-street parking. No pets allowed. Owners always reachable • Breakfast room. Lounge with reading corner and satellite TV. Garden, solarium. Pool

Situated just a few kilometers from Todi, close enough to see Bramante's church of Santa Maria della Consolazione on the hill opposite, La Mulinella still feels like a country trattoria where, in summer, you can enjoy a magical atmosphere as the night draws in, announced by chirping crickets. Even when the restaurant is crowded, it is still a pleasant place to visit, with its soft, measured and respectable atmosphere.
The choice of food follows the best Umbrian traditions and includes, to start, prosciutto with mixed bruschettas and crostini (the fineness and delicacy of the **chicken liver patè** are exceptional: ask for a separate serving). The menu then moves on to a selection of hand-rolled pastas: **tagliatelle with truffle**, vegetables and mushrooms, or **with goose sauce**. In winter, it's well worth trying the **zuppa** della nonna **with pulses and mushrooms**. The main courses are dominated by game: venison, **wild boar** (alla cacciatore or roulades), **pigeon 'alla ghiotta'** or roast. Alternatively, you can opt for lamb 'a scottadito', baccalà stewed with prunes and raisins, or 'stringhette' of pork. There's also an excellent beef fillet cooked in a variety of ways. Note the presence of several truffle-based dishes (which doesn't significantly add to the final bill. End with a homemade dessert: semifreddo, tiramisù or panna cotta with wild berries.
The wine list reveals a number of interesting Umbrian wines with honest markups.

45 KM SOUTH OF PERUGIA SS 3 BIS

45 KM SOUTH OF PERUGIA

PANE E VINO – LA LOCANDA DEL BORGO

Osteria-wine shop – Rooms for rent
Via Ciuffelli 33 – Via Santa Prassede 19
Tel. 075 8945448
Fax 075 8949931
E-mail: paneevinotodi@libero.it
Internet: www.panevinotodi.com
Closed Wednesday
Open lunch and dinner
Holidays: 12-30 November
Seating: 50 + 40 outdoors
Prices: 22-30 euros wine excluded
All major credit cards, except DC, Bancomat

SAN LORENZO TRE

Period residence
Via San Lorenzo 3
Tel. and fax 075 8944555
E-mail: lorenzotre@tin.it
Internet: www.todi.net/lorenzo
Closed in January and February

Loredana Angelantoni and Fabio Canneori's warm welcome creates a cozy atmosphere both in the locanda (open all week long) and in the osteria. The rooms, large and comfortable, have beautiful ceilings with exposed beams. Breakfast is abundant and filling.
The osteria serves a vast collection of regional and a few national wines, plus numerous varieties of grappa. The meal starts off with **cheese quiche**, local cured meats and cheese accompanied by walnut and olive bread. In winter, don't miss the **chickpea and cep mushroom soup** and in spring all the specialties using **wild asparagus**. In summer, truffle is the main ingredient on crostini and **strangozzi**, lamb and fillet steak. Booking ahead, it's possible to have famous **pigeon alla ghiotta**, a historic Todi dish. To end, we recommend **tozzetti** biscuits with Vin Santo and amor polenta, a pudding made with cornmeal and almonds with red fruit or chocolate sauce. Local regional wines and products are for sale and customers are even entitled to restricted traffic zone passes.

• 5 doubles en-suite (2 with shared facilities), television • Prices: double single use 40-50, double 60-70 euros (extra bed 15-30 euros), breakfast included • restaurant access for the mobility challenged. Paid parking. Small pets welcome. Owners always available • Restaurant. Breakfast room

This place, run in a courteous, friendly manner by Marzia Morena and her staff, is located on the second floor of an elegant building that's been in the family for seven generations. The interior is reminiscent of an upper-class home of the late 1800s and has undergone only conservative renovation (with the addition of bathrooms, first and foremost). There is evidence all round of great attention to detail: antique furniture that has belonged to the family for five generations, linen or hemp sheets and bath towels, and furnishings in common areas that recreate an atmosphere of yesteryear. The rooms are filled with books and three of them offer a view of the surrounding countryside. Breakfast includes a wide selection of herbal teas in addition to the usual hot beverages and home-made cakes, warm croissants, jams and various types of bread.

• 6 double rooms, with bathroom (2 rooms with a shared bathroom) • Prices: double room single use 50-65 euros, double 70-105, breakfast included • Credit cards: all except AE, Bancomat • Paid public parking, ticket for 2 reserved car spaces. Small pets allowed. Owners always reachable. • Breakfast room, reading room. Terrace

In **Pian di Porto** (3 km), the Montecristo dairy farm sells cow's milk or mixed milk Caciotta cheese (some flavored with wild thyme) and sheep's ricotta cheese.

TREVI
Bovara

TREVI
Bovara-Fondaccio

50 KM SOUTHEAST OF PERUGIA ON SS 75

50 KM SOUTHEAST OF PERUGIA SS 75

CASA GIULIA

⚷Country house
Via Corciano 1
Tel. 0742 78257-348 3604619
Fax 0742 381632
E-mail: info@casagiulia.com
Internet: www.casagiulia.com
Open all year round

I MANDORLI

⚷Holiday farm
Via Fondaccio 6
Tel. and fax 0742 78669
E-mail: mandorli@seeumbria.com
Internet: www.agriturismoimandorli.com
Open all year round

Casa Giulia is a 17th-century country house that has always belonged to Caterina Alessandrini Petrucci's family. The rooms are in the main two-story building situated in large grounds at the foot of Mount Serano, a strategic position for reaching many of Umbria's interesting historic and artistic sites. In front of the main building, another, which can accommodate up to 250 people, is used for parties and conferences. Rooms are furnished with great attention to detail in harmony with the outside appearance of the building. The owner of the house, who personally manages the whole complex, will welcome you upon arrival. Breakfast, served in a common room or, in summer, in the grounds with their tall trees and swimming pool, features bread and butter, jams, home-baked cookies, yogurt and cereals, hot and fresh drinks.

The holiday farm managed by the Zappelli Cardarelli sisters in the countryside close to Trevi consists of various rural buildings that have been tastefully refurbished. The atmosphere is very relaxing, and here, what with rooms with wrought-iron beds and the pleasant, comfortable reading room, it's almost like living in times gone by. A visit to the recently restored old olive oil press is a must. The guests can choose from a number of options for their stay: from small and large rooms to apartments, usually rented on a weekly basis, with private garden, tables and chairs. Breakfast is simple and filling: it includes coffee, milk, tea, jams, homemade cakes, local bread and cheese. The restaurant serves typical local dishes at an average price of 20 euros, drinks excluded. The garden is pleasant and includes a children's playground.

• 4 double and 1 triple rooms and 1 suite, with bathroom, TV, 4 rooms with air-conditioning; 2 apartments (2-4 persons) with kitchenette, air-conditioning • Prices: double room single use 70-85 euros, double 80-101, triple 100-131, suite 120-191, breakfast included; apartments 64-104 euros per day • Credit cards: all, Bancomat • 1 room designed for use by the mobility challenged. Off-street parking. Small pets allowed (only in the apartments). Owners always reachable. • Breakfast room, reading and TV room. Conference room. Grounds. Pool

• 3 double or triple rooms, with bathroom, TV; 3 apartments (2-4 persons) with kitchen • Prices: double room single use 40-50 euros, double 60-70, triple 80-90, breakfast included; apartments 65-145 euros • Credit cards: none • Facility accessible for the mobility challenged, 2 rooms designed for their use. Off-street parking. Small pets allowed (only in the apartments). Owners always reachable • Restaurant (for residents only). Reading room. Garden. Pool

TREVI

LA VECCHIA POSTA

☞ Recently opened osteria
Piazza Mazzini 14
Tel. 0742 381690
Closed Thursday
Open: lunch and dinner
Holidays: 15 February-5 March
Seating: 40 + 25 outdoors
Prices: 25-30 euros, wine excluded
All credit cards, Bancomat

The area around Trevi is renowned for its prime quality crops, including olives grown on terraces cleverly built with dry-stone walls, and black celery, which is grown in particularly damp soil, also known as canapine because it was formerly used to sow canapa, or hemp. Local oils and celery are among the prime quality products used at La Vecchia Posta, a small restaurant (from this year the proprietors have also made five rooms available inside a 16-century building) in the main town square, opposite the civic tower.

The antipasto is made up, as tradition dictates, of cured meats and mixed crostini, delicate frittatas with truffle or **bruschette all'olio** (the extra vergin oil is cold pressed and comes from the surrounding hills) accompanied by spelt salad. Moving on to the courses, you can choose between soups or various types of home-made pasta: **strangozzi alla trevana**, or with asparagus, tortellini or cappelletti with truffle, **pappardelle al cinghiale** or tagliatelle with beans and pecorino. As a main course, in addition to **fegatelli di maiale**, which are served in the traditional way, you can choose from wild boar stew, **lamb a scottadito**, beef carpaccio and pork fillet, all of which are served with black celery, cep mushrooms or wild asparagus. The puddings and ice-creams are all home-made.

The wine list obviously focuses on local wines, with a good choice of labels and vintages, but it also includes a reasonable number of national wines.

TUORO SUL TRASIMENO
Isola Maggiore

SAURO

☞ Hotel Restaurant
Via Guglielmi 1
Tel. 075 826168
No closing days
Open: lunch and dinner
Holidays: from November to February
Seating: 150 + 100 outdoors
Prices: 22-28 euros, wine excluded
All major credit cards, Bancomat

From the quay at Tuoro Navaccia, it only takes 10 minutes by ferry to reach Isola Maggiore. Since no cars are allowed on the island, the town has preserved its original structure and is well worth a visit to admire the interesting examples of religious and civil architecture. The Sauro, which is also a small hotel with a dozen or so rooms, is an excellent stopover if you want stay in this quiet, sheltered spot, and also offers an opportunity to sample typical lake dishes. The Scarpocchi family has run the hotel-restaurant for over 40 years, and you can either eat inside or, in fine weather, on the wide terrace outside.

Once you are seated, order the **antipasto misto di lago**, a delicate terrine of perch, whitebait, eel, carp roe tarts, smoked tench, and tench croquettes. The fish is either caught by Sauro himself or purchased from local cooperatives. The same species are also used in first courses such as **pasta with carp roe** and **taglierini with smoked tench**. Once you get to the main courses, you can choose from bass fillets with butter and sage, classic **carpa regina in porchetta** (larded and flavored with garlic, rosemary and wild fennel), or mixed preparations such as **fried lake fish** and **tegamaccio**, a typical local dish made with eel and perch. One of the best desserts is **salami al cioccolato**.

The wine list is limited to a few regional wines, such as Grechetto, Orvieto classico and the DOC wine Colli del Trasimeno.

UMBERTIDE
Niccone

24 KM NORTH OF PERUGIA ON SS 3 B

LA CHIUSA

🗝️🍲 Holiday farm
Frazione Niccone 353
Tel. and fax 075 9410848
E-mail: info@lachiusa.com
Internet: www.lachiusa.com
Closed from mid-January to mid-March

Claudio Rener, previously a computer technician in a large company, and his wife Dada, took the radical decision to abandon the frantic rhythm of city life to open La Chiusa in Umbria and lead a simple existence in contact with nature. Currently managed by the couple's daughter and son-in-law, Masha and Giovanni, the agriturismo has basic comforts and is furnished in a rustic manner, with plenty of outdoor spaces such as the shady garden with swimming pool for chilling out. The generous breakfast consists of yogurt, cakes and cookies, eggs, cheese, cured meats and fresh fruit. The restaurant (34 euros per person, wine excluded) is only open for dinner and Sunday lunch, and serves dishes using local products revisited by Dada, who often organizes cookery courses as well. For the first three weeks of August, Easter, and New Year's Day, half-board is compulsory: 85 euros per person.

• 1 double and 2 four-bed rooms, with bathroom, fridge; 2 apartments with kitchen • Prices: double room single occupancy 75 euros, double 100, four-bed and apartment 170; breakfast included • Credit cards: all, Bancomat • Common areas and 2 apartments accessible for the disabled. Off-street parking. Small pets allowed. Owners always reachable. • Bar corner, restaurant. Breakfast room. Garden, terrace, veranda. Pool

UMBERTIDE
Niccone

34 KM NORTH OF PERUGIA

LOCANDA DI NONNA GELSA

🍲 Trattoria
Via Caduti di Penetola 30
Tel. 075 9410699
Closed Tuesday
Open: lunch and dinner
Holidays: February
Seating: 50 + 80 outdoors
Prices: 22-30 euros, wine excluded
Credit cards: AE, MC, Visa

Niccone Valley is a natural corridor linking northern Umbria to the Trasimeno area and Cortona. The Locanda di Nonna Gelsa is a haven where you can stop to savor dishes with clearly defined tastes and flavors. It's run by Chiara, who's well accustomed to satisfying the requirements of the foreign visitors who frequently eat in the trattoria. Chiara also coordinates the two Marcos (her brother and husband) who ply back and forth between the dining room and kitchen, where Simone prepares food according to local traditions.
The specialties include meats, all locally sourced and mainly grilled: roast pork (pancetta, costicciole and sausages), pork liver and **Chianina beef steak**. If you fancy something different, you can order coratella of lamb or **rabbit all'arrabbiata**. As an antipasto, crostini with chicken livers are always on the menu, together with cured meats and **arvolto** (a sort of pizza fried in olive oil and seasoned with a spicy tomato and garlic sauce). The pasta dishes are all home-made, from the **tortelloni** served **with cep mushrooms**, with ragù or red chicory, to **tagliatelle with chicken giblets**. At the right time of year, a little grated truffle may be added to the strangozzi. The desserts, including the custard tart, are all home-made and reminiscent of childhood parties.
The wine list focuses on local products but also includes a respectable selection of Umbrian and Tuscan bottles.

MARCHE

ACQUALAGNA
Furlo

ACQUAVIVA

ABBAZIA DI SAN VINCENZO AL FURLO

🔑 Rooms
Via Pianacce 67
Tel. 0721 700016-338 1771031
E-mail: cesare.marte@lycos.it
Internet: www.lalocandadellabbazia.it
Open from March to mid-December

O' VIV

🔑 3-Star Hotel
Via Marziale 43
Tel. 0735 764649-765054
Fax 0735 765054
E-mail: info@oviv.it
Internet: www.oviv.it
Closed in November

Traveling on the via Flaminia between Fossombrone and Acqualagna (truffle town), close to the Furlo gorge, what strikes us is the simple beauty of the thirteenth century abbey of San Vincenzo, whose origins probably date back to the sixth century. The recently refurbished locanda of the same name, run by the ever smiling Cesare, is located in what used to be the monastery. The rooms, well furnished and comfortable, offer an intriguing view over the surrounding mountains. Breakfast is traditional and you can either have it in the tavern or on the large lawn in front of the entrance to the rooms. Worth a visit nearby, apart from Urbino and the many historic centers "not in the front line" (Urbania, Fossombrone, Cagli...), are Furlo's natural reserve, the Candigliano dam and the tunnels excavated more than two thousand years ago to make the transit of the consular road easier.

• 1 single room, 4 double and 1 suite (5 people), bathroom, mini-bar, television, modem connection • Prices: single 60 euros, double 100, suite 350, breakfast included • Credit cards: major ones, Bancomat • Off-street parking. No pets allowed. Reception open from 10am to 10pm • Breakfast room. Park

In Acquaviva, medieval stronghold and custodian to many important finds from the Picene age, you will come upon the O' Viv hotel (Acquaviva Frenchified), housed in an elegant noble building dating back to the eighteenth century that overlooks the ancient boundary wall. Rooms are comfortable and the hotel is a good stopping off place for tourists doing Picene itineraries or if you want to chill out in the quiet freshness of the hill, enjoying breakfast based on homemade confectionery such as ciambellone and fruit pies, or typical local savory products, like cured meats and cheeses. You will also find a restaurant in the cellars of the hotel. It is open every night except Monday and Tuesday during winter and offers Tuscan and Marche cuisine, with a menu that varies week by week (18 euros, wine excluded).

• 9 double rooms with bathroom, television • Prices: double room single use 40-55 euros, double 60-75, breakfast included • Credit cards: all, Bancomat • Public parking in the immediate vicinity. Small pets allowed. Reception open 24 hours a day • Restaurant. Reading room. Terrace

AMANDOLA

PARADISO

🗝️○3-Star Hotel
Via Umberto I 7
Tel. 0736 847468
Fax 0736 847726
E-mail: hparadiso@inwind.it
Internet: www.sibillinihotels.it
Closed from 15 November to 15
December

Inaugurated in the Sixties and recently modernized, the Curi family hotel is a comfortable starting point if you wish to visit the Sibillini Park. The refurbished rooms are fitted with finely crafted furniture, the others keep the original pieces. The well kept communal spaces extend, by way of a portico, to a big garden, which is connected by a path to the main square, adjacent to a public park with playground and baroque puppet theatre. In the summer, breakfast is served outside and Enrica prepares jams and cakes, as well as the main meals (homely regional cuisine, average price 20-25 euros excluding wines). At night in summer, piano bar under the arbor in the park. Cookery courses are organized as well as visits to the local wine cellars.

• 2 single rooms, 32 double, 2 suites and 2 apartments, bathroom, television; 30 rooms with safe • Prices: single 40 euros, double 62-72, suite 82, apartment 90-120, during the low season breakfast included; in high season, breakfast 5 euros per person • Credit cards: all, Bancomat • 1 room equipped for the mobility challenged. Off-street parking (2 places). Reception open from 7 am to 12 am • Bar, restaurant. TV and reading room on the veranda, internet point. Park. Tennis court, boules court

ANCONA
Montacuto

AIÒN

🍲 Holiday farm
Via di Montacuto 121
Tel. 071 898232
Closed Monday and Tuesday, never on holidays, in summer only on Monday
Open: only for dinner
Holidays: variable
Seating: 50 + 60 outdoors
Prices: 28-35 euros
All credit cards

For the last few years, the Moroder farm, which is famous for its wines, has been raising poultry, growing pulses, vegetables, olives, berries and herbs, and producing truffles. The latter, of the black Norcia variety, ripen late in the Cònero area, i.e. in early Spring. All these products are used in the food prepared at Aiòn, a vacation farm, which the passion, hard work and good taste of Serenella and Alessandro Moroder have turned into an elegant country osteria. When you get to Montacuto, a village on the slopes of Mount Cònero, a small road, signposted, leads down through the vineyards to a cluster of refurbished buildings.
The cuisine is traditional and relies on seasonal produce, particularly where the vegetarian choice is concerned. The menu is limited as to the number of dishes, but they are all strictly local: **emmer salad**, potato pie, dried tomatoes, and parmesan baskets with vegetables. Among the first courses we recommend the **ravioli of ricotta and spinach with truffles**, the **Cònero vegetable soup** flavored with a drop of extravirgin olive oil, **chitarrine con l'umido**, **gnocchi with duck sauce** and pappardelle with wild boar ragù. The main courses are all served with side vegetables prepared in a variety of ways, and include **chicken in potacchio** or with Rosso Cònero wine, **turkey with chestnuts**, salmì of boar, and duck with truffles.
Pancakes with berries, chocolate pie, and homemade crostata complete the meal before a good cup of espresso coffee. It goes without saying that the wines are produced on the farm.

ANCONA
Portonovo

ANCONA
Candia

12 KM FROM CITY CENTER

8 KM FROM CITY CENTER

DA MARCELLO

LA ROCCA VERDE

Restaurant
Via Portonovo
Tel. 071 801183
Closed Monday, never in summer
Open: lunch and dinner
Holidays: January 15-March 1
Seating: 80 + 50 outdoors
Prices: 32-35 euros, wine excluded
All credit cards, Bancomat

Holiday farm
Via Piantate Lunghe 76
Tel. 071 2906183
Closed Monday, Tuesday and Wednesday
Open: dinner, also midday in holidays but not in Summer
Holidays: February and end-August
Seating: 70 + 70 outdoors
Prices: 30 euros
Credit cards: Visa, Bancomat

On a bright evening in the spring or early autumn, it is difficult not to be affected by the beautiful Gulf of Cònero; the sheer chalk cliffs above the sea act as a natural setting for the sunset, and the color of the Adriatic changes slowly from intense green to dark blue. The restaurant run by Marcello Nicolini is always a good place to stop. The menu is very rich, occasionally too rich, particularly where the antipasti are concerned (they could be a meal on their own), and great care goes into the presentation. We recommend booking well in advance because the restaurant can be very busy, particularly at weekends.

The dishes are obviously based on local fare: fried calamaretti and zucchini, soft **marinated anchovies**, octopus with potatoes, piping hot grilled sardoncini, **stewed raguse** (a fish that is very popular in the Cònero area), sautéed mussels and seafood, green lasagnetta with mussels, risotto allo scoglio, **tagliatelle with chopped clams and mussels**, ciavattoni alla marinara, a **mixed fry of small fish**, freshly caught fish, boiled, grilled or baked. The puddings are certainly not the most interesting part of the menu: apart from the homemade ciambellone, there is a choice of citrus fruit sherbet or trifle.

The wine list is generous, and contains numerous regional labels which are given the right emphasis with reasonable mark-ups. Service is courteous and professional.

In town, Bontà delle Marche (Corso Mazzini) is a good place to find handmade gastronomic products: pasta, salamis, oil, cheese, wine and preserves.

Just one word of advice: if you aim to dine at this farm restaurant which is more than reliable for the quality of its raw materials (from organic vegetables to locally reared meat), make sure you book. It is always busy, but if you book in advance, you may also be able to choose a menu other than the one proposed by Marco Maurizi for that evening. The restaurant's success is not difficult to explain. The quality of the ingredients, many of which are produced on the farm, is set off by the painstaking cooking, all rounded off by the friendly character of the owners and the enjoyable atmosphere.

You can start with some vegetarian dishes – seasonal salads or vegetables cooked in various ways – and an assortment of cured meats and salamis, followed by excellent **smoked pork** and steamed capon breast. The pasta is all rolled by hand, and ranges from the classic **tagliatelle with duck** or guinea-fowl **sauce** to gnocchi and ravioli with a variety of sauces, and the excellent **pappardelle with boar sauce**, an animal that can be found wild all over the Cònero Park. The spit at the center of the room is used for the slow roasting of **suckling pig** or boar, while the tagliata of marchigiana beef is grilled. The **fabrianese lamb** is fried or baked, and the **rabbit**, flavored with **wild fennel** is cooked in a terracotta casserole. You can continue and conclude with a number of ewe's milk cheeses and simple puddings such as tiramisù, fruit crostata and biscuits.

The house Rosso Cònero or a number of labels from the Marche give any meal a truly local flavor.

APPIGNANO
Verdefiore

OSTERIA DEI SEGRETI

☞—◦ Country house
Contrada Verdefiore 41
Tel. and fax 0733 579786
E-mail: info@osteriadeisegreti.it
Internet: www.osteriadeisegreti.it
Closed in November

Having gone past Osteria Nuova on the way to Appignano, another two kilometers and you'll run into Verdefiore, a place surrounded by lush green countryside and hills. This is where the Lucamarini brothers have recently restored an old rural complex with barn and deposits to obtain rooms and apartments (rented also on a weekly basis at 350-420 euros) of various sizes, simple but well kept. Outside, the garden and swimming pool with deck-chairs and beach umbrellas. The buffet breakfast, includes drinks and juices, bread, cakes and home made tarts, jams and chocolate. The restaurant (run separately, tel. 0733 57685) offers dishes strictly from the local tradition (17-25 euros, wine excluded). Nearby, the historical sites of San Severino and Tolentino, as well as Macerata and its annual opera season.

• 4 double rooms with bathroom, television; 8 apartments (4-6 people) with kitchen • Prices: double room single use 35 euros, double 60, breakfast included; apartment 60-100 euros • Credit cards: all except DC, Bancomat • 1 apartment equipped for the disabled. Off-road parking. Small pets allowed. Owners always contactable • Restaurant. Garden. Swimming pool

APPIGNANO
DEL TRONTO

SANTA LUCIA   🍾

🍲 Restaurant
Valle Chifenti 93
Tel. 0736 817177
Closed Monday
Open: lunch and dinner
Holidays: variable
Seating: 50 + 200 outdoors
Prices: 25-30 euros
All major credit cards

The Monte dell'Ascensione is close by and its imposing bulk catches the eye. As a result, you might not notice the anonymous building that houses the Santa Lucia restaurant. It has been open since 1978, and reflects the fashions of those times: the straw-bottomed chairs, paintings on the walls, spartan restrooms and large function room recall noisy family outings to a restaurant on Sundays. It is only a brief impression: the dishes prepared by Giuseppina Troiani and Nazzareno Simonetti, and presented at the table by his brother Graziano, are modern rereadings of classic local recipes. The theme of the whole meal is a passion for quality raw materials – including an excellent extravirgin olive oil – which are sourced locally from small producers. The two set meals are very economical: 25 euros for the classic selection and 30 euros for a menu with **truffles**, both including three set wines.
The antipasti might include marinated carpaccio of beef, **prosciutto of lamb**, cured meats and different salamis. A pie of **broccoli with an anchovy sauce**, a marriage between the countryside and conserved fish that reaches the foothills of the mountains, makes way for the first courses which include several types of homemade fresh pasta: **campofiloni with meat sauce**, **tagliatelle with a pigeon sauce**, and gnocchetti with Savoy cabbage. Tagliata, fillet and **steaks** are cooked to a turn on the grill, but there is always a choice of white meats (rabbit, chicken), roast or sautéed. The puddings, although good, are not particularly original. The cellar on the other hand is a different matter: alongside the best that the Marche and Abruzzo have to offer, there are also numerous good foreign wines.

6 KM FROM CITY CENTER

C'ERA UNA VOLTA

Trattoria
Località Piagge 336
Tel. 0736 261780
Closed Tuesday
Open: lunch and dinner
Holidays: none
Seating: 40 + 40 outdoors
Prices: 20-23 euros, wine excluded
All major credit cards

CORSO

Trattoria
Corso Mazzini 277
Tel. 0736 256760
Closed Sunday for dinner and Monday
Open: lunch and dinner
Holidays: August
Seating: 26
Prices: 30-32 euros, wine excluded
All credit cards

There have been a few changes to the furnishings in the dining-room, but none in the kitchen, for this trattoria that has been in our guide from the start. It is easy to find, leaving the center of Ascoli by the road for Colle San Marco. You will be met by the proprietor Tonino who will show you to your table with spontaneous courtesy. It is worth asking if there is a table on the veranda, because from there you have a panoramic view over the city.
Start with the substantial local antipasti: diced **omelet with tripe**, with cep mushrooms, cured meats and salamis (pork loin, sausage and cjauscolo), the rare **cotica 'bbiturata** (slivers of pork rind boiled and served in small discs with pecorino, tomato and marjoram), or the equally tasty **tripe in bianco**, marinated vegetables and bruschetta with zampone or Savoy cabbage. The first courses change with the seasons, and those particularly worth mentioning are the white polentina with cep mushrooms, chopped meat, mozzarella and parmesan, **gnocchi filled** with meat, ricotta and spinach, **soup of emmer and chickpeas** and spaghetti primavera. The main courses are mostly meat: from a pan of **stewed lamb and pork** to **pigeon casserole** (also called "in arrosto morto") and guinea-fowl with cep mushrooms cooked in Rosso Piceno wine. As an alternative, try the **stuffed, fried olives** accompanied by lamb, cream cheese, and artichokes when in season. Davide, Tonino's son, is in charge of the kitchen, and he prepares different sweets every day that are accompanied by a glass of homemade mistrà.
The cellar features labels from the Piceno area and Abruzzo, but the house wine by the carafe is an excellent traveling companion.

A strange language is spoken between the tables, that sounds more Abruzzo than Marche. It does not even resemble the dialect of nearby San Benedetto del Tronto: in fact the only thing that comes from this seaside town, a proud enemy in the past, is the fish that goes on the table. We are listening to Ascoli dialect. The limited number of tables in the trattoria is soon taken by loyal customers, who all know each other and chat amicably in a familiar, intimate atmosphere, which is typical of the local culture that it helps to keep alive.
The cuisine runs along the same lines: no expensive seafood – except for some shellfish which is boiled and served with its marine humors intact – and a presentation that is pretty basic. It is the fresh raw ingredients that really make the difference: anchovies marinated in vinegar, boiled squill, a dense, tasty **soup of squid and beans**, a pan full of clams and mussels, **stewed sea snails**. The first course depends on what was in the market: **mezzemaniche with peeled shrimp** and fresh tomato, and spaghetti with cuttlefish ink. And risotto or linguine alla marinara. A dish of mixed fried fish or just calamaretti, **monkfish in potacchio**, grilled fish, **guazzetto of sole** or other small fish, for a main course. Lemon sherbet concludes the meal.
The wine list mainly features wines from the Marche, but includes some small producers from other regions, all with a good quality/price ratio. Because of the small size of the only dining-room, we recommend phoning ahead to check that there is a table.

DA MIDDIO

🥘 Trattoria
Via delle Canterine 53
Tel. 0736 250867
Closed Sunday and Monday
Open: lunch and dinner
Holidays: 15 days between June and July
Seating: 40
Prices: 15-18 euros, wine excluded
All major credit cards

LANGUAGE AND ART

🔑 Bed and breakfast
Via dei Soderini 16
Tel. 347 5312280
Fax 0736 255045
E-mail: info@bb-languageandart.com
Internet: www.bb-languageandart.com
Open all year round

Since the premature death of the trattoria's original owner, his young daughter has welcomed the guests. Elisa and her mother Gigliola, who still works in the kitchen, have decided to continue in Middio's memory, to the relief of the inhabitants of Ascoli Piceno and of the regular customers of one of the most popular local eateries. At Middio's you might find yourself sitting with perfect strangers. This is not just a fashionable gimmick, but has always been the custom, and the many regulars who are aware of this do not bat an eyelid.

The menu varies every day, but always focuses on local dishes that are prepared simply, with taste and a light touch that seems to betray their names: **vincisgrassi**, bucatini all'amatriciana, carbonara, **baccalà**, tripe, **beans with pork rind**, stew, **mutton alla callara** slow-cooked in the oven, lentil soup and plenty more, all accompanied by good wine, including the excellent organic wines produced by the Aurora cellar in Offida. To conclude your meal, you might find **trifle**, prepared by Gigliola with her usual skill, or cantucci with vincotto.

The prices are extremely economical. One amusing fact: the check will arrive on a normal cash register receipt decorated with a hammer and sickle (and the room itself flaunts pictures of Che Guevara and Lenin). Just as Middio would have wanted.

🍴 In Via Giudea, 10, a short walk from Piazza del Popolo, the Gelateria Veneta, which was opened 1923, produces an array of excellent ice cream, both classic flavors and fruit ices without added sugar.

Language and Art's premises are to be found in a fine medieval building, in a historical street of the city center. The exact location is an apartment with big, sunny rooms, and modern, functional bathrooms, fitted with period furniture and paintings. Breakfast includes jams and homemade cakes. Available for guests is the kitchen, where you have breakfast, and the washing machine for personal things. The host, Marilena Piccinini, a real expert on the artistic heritage of Ascoli Piceno and local gastronomy, offers some extra services, such as the use of bicycles, a jacuzzi, and the domestic computer. Together with a local cultural association, she also organises mosaic, ceramics, découpage, and embroidery courses, and she personally runs the cookery courses.

• 4 double rooms with bathroom, 1 with patio • Prices: double room single use 45 euros, double 70, breakfast included • Credit cards: none • Public parking nearby. Small pets allowed. Owners always contactable • Breakfast room. Living room, reading and television room

ASCOLI PICENO
Abbazia di Rosara

VILLA CICCHI

🗝Holiday farm
Via Salaria Superiore 137
Tel. 0736 252272
Fax 0736 247281
E-mail: info@villacicchi.it
Internet: www.villacicchi.it
Holidays variable

Surrounded by parkland of age-old trees, this historic late seventeenth century home refurbished with full respect for the original structure has lost none of its past charisma, without saying goodbye to modern comforts. The rooms, four of which have kept their original tempera decoration, are fitted out with authentic eighteenth century furniture. One of them, the superior, costs 140 euros a night. Attentively run by Laura Cicchi and her daughters Maria Elena and Alessandra, the structure (in the family since 1911) allows you to follow courses of typical local cuisine, decoration and handicrafts. The restaurant (for half board there's a supplement of 25 euros per person, wines excluded), is open to non-residents and offers recipes from Ascoli using produce from the farm. Aperitifs are served in the big cellar. Breakfast, served as a buffet in different places depending on the season, includes ciambelloni, tarts, chocolate cakes and homemade jams. Inside the farm complex there is a little church consecrated in 1734.

• 6 double rooms with bathroom, satellite television, • Prices: double room single use 80-95 euros, double 80-120, breakfast included • Credit cards: all, Bancomat • Facility partly accessible to the mobility challenged. Off-road parking. Small pets allowed. Owners always contactable • Restaurant, canteen. Breakfast room, television room with small library. Conference room. Grounds. Terrace. Swimming pool

ASCOLI PICENO
Piagge

VILLA SGARIGLIA

🗝3-Star Hotel
Frazione Piagge 295
Tel. 0736 42368
Fax 0736 352237
E-mail: info@villasgariglia.it
Internet: www.villasgariglia.it
Closed from 10 to 30 January

Villa Sgariglia lies on the road to colle San Marco, a ridge that dominates the city of Macerata. The hotel was inaugurated in 2001 after the meticulous restoration of the residence of the Sgariglia's, a noble family of Ascoli. Occupying two floors and the outbuilding, many of the rooms retain the original frescoes on the walls and ceilings and all have period furniture. In the restaurant lounge traditional Italian breakfasts are served and the average cost of a meal is about 25 euros, drinks excluded. The villa is surrounded by a big park of chestnuts and firs, great for long walks. The San Marco hermitage, a thirteenth century construction built over a sheer rock face by Benedictine monks, is worth visiting.

• 1 single room, 10 double and 2 with 4 beds, bathroom, mini-bar, safe, television, several rooms with balcony • Prices: single 40 euros, double 65, with 4 beds 80, breakfast included • Credit cards: all, Bancomat • Facility accessible to the mobility challenged, 1 room equipped for them. Off-road parking. Small pets allowed. Reception open from 7am to 12am • Restaurant. Park. Pool

CALDAROLA
Vestignano

CAMERATA PICENA

30 KM SOUTH WEST OF MACERATA

15 KM WEST OF ANCONA

IL PICCIOLO DI RAME

TAVERNA DEI GUELFI

Recently opened osteria
Castello di Vestignano
Tel. 348 3316588
No closing day
Open: dinner, Sunday for lunch
Holidays: September
Seating: 22
Prices: 30 euros
No credit cards accepted

Recently opened osteria
Piazza Vittorio Veneto 56
Tel. 071 7499899
Closed Sunday for dinner and Monday
Open: lunch and dinner
Holidays: between July and August,
10 days after Epiphany
Seating: 45
Prices: 25-28 euros, wine excluded
All credit cards

It might take more than one attempt to find a table at this minute osteria – so do not go to Vestignano without calling first! It only opens if at least six tables are booked and it soon fills up. When your table is confirmed, you will also be told what time you are expected. But it is really worth the trouble, and you will soon understand the efforts made by the proprietor Silvano Scalzini, and realize that what might seem to be an eccentric way of doing things at first glance is in fact justified. Silvano will explain his approach to cooking: only dishes prepared on the day, taken from old local recipe books. You do not choose: the 12 samples offered will take you back in time, thanks to the dining-room that was once a medieval oil mill, and well documented research that Silvano will explain as the meal progresses.

There is a choice of five antipasti: a taste of coroncina extravirgin olive oil on a crouton, pea soup, **black-eyed beans all'agro**, **quadrucci pilusi** (pasta made of flour and water) with **chopped lardo and peas**, and **lentil soup with herbs**. Three first courses: **cargiò** (giant ravioli with ricotta) with truffles, moccolotti with chopped tomato and herbs, and **vincisgrassi with chicken giblets**. The main courses are: a medieval contrast between ginger and anis that flavors a fillet of pork, baked guinea-fowl and vegetables, and a plate of **pecorino** and **ciauscolo**.

And to conclude, a cream pudding with a drop of bitter chocolate accompanied by mistrà, a typical liqueur made with anise. The house wine can be a bit off, but guests are free to arrive with their own wine.

You want to say: "Meat-eaters of the world unite!". The meat-eater's paradise exists, and it is in Camerata Picena. But such a claim may appear excessive or limiting. However, the osteria run by Maurizio Pergolini, with its attractive atmosphere, specializes in meat grilled over a wood fire. Steak, fillet and loin are cooked to a turn and – what is more important – made from the meat of selected cattle reared in the most important meat-producing areas of the world: Argentina, Canada, Ireland, Hungary, and Italy, of course.

But since you cannot live on protein alone, here are a number of proposals to make up a balanced meal: local **cured meats** or tasty cured ham to fill a hot **crescia** (the local name for the well-known piadina), vegetables au gratin, hand-rolled **green tagliatelle with mushrooms**, **fusilli and beans**, penne alla puttanesca, pies of ricotta and spinach flavored with seasonal vegetables, strozzapreti alla Tito (with delicately chopped sausage, tomato, rocket and a drizzle of light cream). The grill is used not only for veal and beef but also for lamb or **arrosticini of mutton** (kebabs that are common in Abruzzo) but for those who want an alternative, there is always pork shank, **pork rind with beans**, **tripe**, and veal steak in red wine. The puddings are simple: tiramisù, panna cotta, ciambellone, and some industrial ice cream.

To drink, there is a good house wine, and a small wine list mainly of Italian reds. The service is courteous and friendly. Bear in mind that the restaurant is small (and somewhat noisy) so that it is best to book in advance; portions are rather generous, and the grilled meat is paid by weight, so the price varies with your appetite.

CAMERINO
Polverina

CASTELDELCI
Gattara

LA CAVALLINA

Holiday farm
Strada Statale 77 km 49,00
Tel. 0737 46173
Fax. 0737 464500
E-mail: lacavallina@tin.it
Internet: www.lacavallina.it
Closed from 23 to 26 December

GATTARA

Restaurant with rooms
Via Gattara 18
Tel. 0541 915814
Closed Tuesday
Open: lunch and dinner
Holidays: variable
Seating: 80 1 0 outdoors
Prices: 25-30 euros
All credit cards

The stone cottage which houses the organic farm La Cavallina has been welcoming guests for about ten years now. The cottage itself is more than two centuries old and is located near the Parco dei Monti Sibillini, on a hill facing the lake of Polverina. From here it is easy to reach tourist attractions like Camerino, Visso, Caldarola, Tolentino, Sarnano, Serrapetrona, but also Fabriano, Assisi, Loreto, Norcia, Castelluccio and the Adriatic coast. The rooms, decorated with arte povera furniture, comfortable and spacious, have got independent entrances. Breakfast includes coffee, milk, tea, jams and homemade cakes, cured meats if you ask. In the restaurant (18-20 euros, wine excluded) you can taste dishes from the Marche tradition, prepared with seasonal raw materials from the farm or nearby.

• 4 double rooms with bathroom, television • Prices: double room single use 40 euros, double 60 (20 euro supplement for extra bed), breakfast included • Credit cards: all, Bancomat • Facility partly accessible to the mobility challenged. Off-road parking. No pets allowed. Owners always contactable • Restaurant. Garden. Boules court

It is not exactly easy to reach Gattara, and communications can be even more complicated in winter when the snow comes. If you take provincial road 258 from Rimini, at Ponte Messa you will find a sign for the trattoria; after a couple of miles, there is a sharp turn to the right across the Marecchia river, which takes you along a winding road full of potholes to this small village on the hillside. The trattoria, which offers a few tables in a room to the right of the entrance and a few more on a balcony overlooking the wood, is located at the highest point of the small group of sandstone houses.
You get the impression of somewhere very down-to-earth, almost removed from time, where you can also spend the night (there are six rooms, furnished for a relaxing rest). It is run by Edda in the kitchen and Settimio in the dining-room, helped by Valentina. The food is straightforward, without affectation, and the cook's skill is obvious from the delicious filling of the **agnolotti** with their aroma of nutmeg, the delicate meat sauce or the tasty lamb chops. The dishes are recited to you: mixed croutons, a **soup of chestnuts** and **cascioncini with potatoes**, tagliatelle, agnolotti and **gnocchi** – all homemade – served with a meat or **wild boar sauce**, or with mushrooms. Then there is grilled meat, sausages, lamb or T-bone steak. And for puddings, cantucci, homemade ciambellone and Vin Santo. Sometimes the menu stretches to lasagna, boar in salmì and mushrooms and truffles when in season.
The wine list only has a few labels in addition to a reasonable Sangiovese by the carafe.

CASTELRAIMONDO
Sant'Angelo

CINGOLI
Torre

43 KM SW OF MACERATA SS 361

25 KM NORTH-WEST OF MACERATA SP 502

IL GIARDINO DEGLI ULIVI

🖙 Holiday farm
Via Crucianelli 54
Tel. 0737 642121-338 3056098
Fax 0737 642600
E-mail: info@ilgiardinodegliulivi.com
Internet: www.ilgiardinodegliulivi.com
Closed: Tuesday, never in summer
Open: lunch and dinner
Holidays: variable
Seating: 60
Prices: 35 euros, wine excluded
All credit cards except AE, Bancomat

The Cioccoloni family has created an exemplary farm tourism facility in the charming hamlet of Sant'Angelo, the heart of a 35-hectare estate (cereals, olives, vineyards, horse breeding). The rooms are embellished with period furniture; a vast choice of excellent local and homemade produce is offered for breakfast.

The traditional, seasonal cuisine, gives ample scope for creativity. The use of aromatic herbs is well balanced and the dressings light, the results thus reaching heights that are difficult to find elsewhere. Local cold cuts, **fried bread with finely chopped liver,** delicate ricotta cheese ravioli with pea and asparagus sauce, **gnocchi with stracotto** stewed, **pencianelle** (pasta made with water, flour and a little yeast) all'amatriciana rivisitata, pan-fried chicken and potatoes, **pork and veal meatballs, lamb with lemon** and tarragon, cream pudding with sponge cake in fruit sauce, homemade tarts; these are just some of the delicacies on offer here.

Homemade pasta and bread, and the wine list with over 50 regional labels, complete an offer not to be missed.

🛏 • 5 double rooms, en-suite, TV (on request) • Prices: double single use 42-80, double 80-120 euros, breakfast included • Communal areas and 1 room suitable for the mobility impaired. Internal uncovered parking area. Pets welcome. Owners are always available • Restaurant. Breakfast room, lounge, reading room and TV. Garden, terrace.

GLI ULIVI

🛏 Holiday farm
Località Capovilla 41
Tel. 0733 603361-338 4727326
Fax 0733 603361
E-mail: gliuliviagriturist@tiscali.it
Internet: www.gli-ulivi.it
Closed from mid-November to Christmas

Very near Cingoli, "the balcony of the Marche", we find this late seventeenth century cottage entirely built in stone, Lauro Cherubini and Giuseppina Brunetti's farm. The farm vacation rooms have wooden ceilings, beds in wrought iron, simple furniture, basic bathrooms: everything is simple and low keyed. Bricks alternate with stone in the dining room with fireplace and in the lovely little cellar where you can have dinner in peace and quiet. The restaurant is open to non residents but you have to book (a meal costs 25-35 euros, including beverages). You can stay half-board at a price of 50-60 euros per person. Breakfast, served at the table, is abundant and no detail is ignored: apart from hot and cold drinks there are homemade jams and cakes that vary on a daily basis.

• 6 double rooms with bathroom, air conditioning, television (on request) • Prices: double room single use 35-40 euros, double 70-80 (20 euros supplement for extra bed), breakfast included • Credit cards: none • 1 room equipped for the mobility challenged. Off-road parking, garage for motorcycles (3 places). No pets allowed. Owners always present. • Restaurant. Living room, reading area. Kitchen for childrens' meals. Garden

CINGOLI
Colle San Valentino

CIVITANOVA MARCHE

24 KM NORTH-WEST OF MACERATA SP 502   27 KM EAST OF MACERATA SS 485

VILLA UGOLINI

🔑3-Star Hotel
Via Sant'Anastasio 30
Tel. 0733 604692
Fax 0733 601630
E-mail: raffaela.rango@tiscalinet.it
Internet: www.villaugolini.it
Open all year round

CHALET GALILEO

🍲Restaurant-chalet
Via IV Novembre 20
Tel. 0733 814993-817656
Closed Tuesday for dinner and Wednesday
Open: lunch and dinner
Holidays: variable in winter
Seating: 50
Prices: 32-35 euros, wine excluded
All major credit cards

In the quiet landscape of the Marche hills, this small hotel is located in a building constructed in the seventeenth century by the Ugolini family. Bought in 1991 by Pierino Angelucci and Raffaela Rango (who also run a restaurant in Cingoli called La Terrazza), a few years ago it underwent a complete restructuring. The rooms are simple, but big and bright; the ceilings on the third floor have kept their old beams. The room where a rich buffet breakfast is served, is very pleasant: homemade cakes and jams, local cheeses and cured meats. On display in the garden is the oil mill found during the restructuring works and a small swimming pool is currently being built; from here on the clearest days you can see as far as mount Cònero and the Adriatic.

• 2 single and 10 double rooms with bathroom, air conditioning, television, modem connection • Prices: single 32 euros, double 60 (20 euros supplement for extra bed), breakfast included • Credit cards: all, Bancomat • 2 rooms equipped for the mobility challenged. Off-road parking. Small pets allowed. Reception open 24 hours a day • Breakfast room. Garden with playground, patio

This restaurant is right on the beach, but is a vast improvement on the average eating place along the shore-line at Civitanova. Courtesy comes naturally and the experience and expertise of young Stefano Orso and his helpers are obvious: years of practice in the best restaurants in the Marche are an advantage, even more so when they are backed up by attention to the customer. The cuisine follows tradition, but does not ignore innovation. There is a written menu, but it is probably easier to trust in Stefano's impartial advice, both for the variety of fish on offer and for the choice of the right wine out of the small but satisfactory cellar.

After antipasti of salmon or **marinated anchovies**, crostone with squid and green beans, fried anchovies with balsamic vinegar, whitebait with greens, **salad** of seafood or **octopus**, or a soup of mussels and clams, there is a wide choice of first courses: **spaghetti al cartoccio**, **paccheri with calamaretti**, clams, scampi and cherry tomatoes, tagliolini of emmer flour with a fish sauce, passatelli alla Galileo (only in winter), gnocchi with scampi, tagliatelle alla marinara and **rigatoni with panocchie** and cherry tomatoes. All inviting, delicate dishes, thanks to Rosa's precious assistance in the kitchen. They are followed by boiled fish (with cider vinegar), **mixed fry** from the Adriatic or a fry of calamaretti alone, angler fish or **baked turbot** with potatoes, olives and cherry tomatoes, mixed grill or steamed dory. Each dish is accompanied by salad or fries. To conclude, a classic lemon sherbet or soft pudding, perhaps a yoghurt mousse with fresh berries.We recommend booking in advance because of the restaurant's popularity.

COMUNANZA

DA ROVERINO

☞ Hotel trattoria
Via Ascoli 10
Tel. 0736 844242-844549
Closed Sunday
Open: lunch and dinner
Holidays: in September
Seating: 100
Prices: 22-25 euros, wine excluded
All credit cards

Somewhere you can rely on. Founded straight after the war by the father and uncle of the current owner, Giuseppe Cutini, Roverino is an extremely reliable address, but also a good choice as a base for excursions into the Sibillini mountains. The mountains produce most of the raw ingredients that are used every day in the kitchen with great experience and skill.

The menu has the weekly cycle of an old-fashioned osteria: on Fridays, the traditional fast day, baccalà or **stoccafisso**, while **tagliatelle al ragù** (cooked very slowly, so that it is highly concentrated) are always on the menu, together with **lamb**, which is grilled in the open fireplace. The only whims on this unchanging and reassuring menu are the seasonal **omelet with mushrooms** or truffles (both white and good quality black truffles can be found in the Sibillini), **pigeon casserole** (when Giuseppe manages to find the right birds), and homemade **gnocchi** with tomato. There are few variations, but that does not matter: regular customers expect to find **fried chicken with peppers** in the summer, tasty **artisan pork sausages** in the winter, and occasionally **boar in salmì**. But we could say that the truly revolutionary are also the most conservative, who follow tradition with their hearts and souls.

The wine cellar is tiny but contains an amazing number of excellent labels, all with extremely reasonable mark-ups.

🍴 The Prosciuttificio Prosperi, in Via Dante, prepares, salts, seasons and sells traditional tasty prosciutto. The Salumeria Bruno Strada, in viale Dante 58, offers a selection of cured meats, cheeses and other products.

CUPRA MARITTIMA

OASI DEGLI ANGELI 🐌 🍷

☞ Holiday farm
Contrada Sant'Egidio 50
Tel. 0735 778569
Open Friday, Saturday and Sunday
Open: dinner, Sunday for lunch and in summer also for dinner
Holidays: in September
Seating: 25 + 15 outdoors
Prices: 35 euros, wine excluded
All credit cards

Driving along the Adriatic, if you turn inland when you come to the river that crosses Cupra Marittima, you can take a small winding road to this vacation farm in the quiet of the countryside. The restaurant is a small domestic paradise with a few well-laid tables, and is furnished with great attention to detail. If you want to try Eleonora Rossi's culinary proposals, you must book, because the restaurant is only open from Friday to Sunday. The cuisine is local, and most of the ingredients are produced right on the farm, a successful combination of tradition and refined creativity. Marco Casolanetti, father of the famous Kurni, waits at table.

There is a set menu, but it changes often with the seasons. To start with, after the local **cured meats**, let yourselves be tempted by the pea or artichoke flan with guanciale and scalded cherry tomatoes, vegetable mille-feuilles and tiny savory pastries with five cereals and sesame, or the marinated pumpkin. The best first courses are the **homemade pasta with duck** or pigeon sauce, ravioli filled with eggplant with cherry tomatoes or bronze-cut pasta with a vegetable sauce. As a main course, you might try the **fried rabbit with herbs**, roast chicken, lamb with potatoes, **stuffed pigeon** or guinea-fowl with sage. The puddings are also homemade: tiramisù, zabaglione with a hazelnut cream, custard with sour cherries and mille-feuilles with strawberries and mint.

The cellar is well stocked, and you will often find some interesting novelties among the better-known labels.

ESANATOGLIA

LA CANTINELLA

🍲Restaurant
Corso Italia 9
Tel. 0737 889585
Closed Thursday
Open: lunch and dinner
Holidays: variable
Seating: 100
Prices: 20-25 euros, wine excluded
Credit cards: Visa

Way off the beaten track, like all the mountain regions in the Marche, Esanatoglia offers the peace and quiet of uncontaminated areas, like the source of the river Esino or the wonderful view of the monastery of San Cataldo, not far from the medieval village, on the border of Marche and Umbria. Numerous enthusiasts frequent the area to visit the lands where Verdicchio di Matelica, one of the great Italian white wines, is produced, or to watch the motorcycle races on a famous local circuit.

In the old part of town, La Cantinella is a good place to enjoy the local cuisine in a spacious, quiet, relaxing environment. Giuseppa Barbarossa, the proprietor, makes all the food herself, from the hot and cold antipasti, including **crescia with ciauscolo**, a typical local salami to spread on bread, to an array of first courses such as **passatelli in consommé** and many types of homemade pasta – **tagliatelle with meat sauce** or with crawfish, **tortelli in chicken broth**, cappellacci with truffles and cep mushrooms, pancakes stuffed with ricotta and spinach, and pasta and beans in the cold season. As a main course, you can choose grilled lamb, beef or pork, a **mixed fry all'ascolana** or **crawfish** (common ingredient of the local cuisine) **in a brodetto** or alla diavola. To conclude, try one of the local cheeses in the small selection or one of the homemade puddings: trifle, fruit salad with ice cream or panna cotta.

The small list of mainly regional wines is looked after by Isabella, Giuseppa's daughter and a sommelier, who also performs front of house duties.

FALCONARA MARITTIMA

L'ARNIA DEL CUCINIERE

🍲Restaurant
Via della Repubblica 9
Tel. 071 9160055
Closed Monday
Open: lunch and dinner
Holidays: August
Seating: 50 + 30 outdoors
Prices: 30-35 euros, wine excluded
All credit cards, Bancomat

The best way to get to l'Arnia del cuciniere from the labyrinth of one-way streets in Falconara Marittima is to take the Via Flaminia, exit it at Via Trieste and then go back as far as Via della Repubblica, where the restaurant is located. The proprietor and chef is young Claudio Api, who manages it in a welcoming, relaxed way, while Marco Tinti is an impeccable front of house.

The menu is divided into "surf and turf" proposals, with a clear predominance of the former. The fish is bought every day at the fish market, particularly from the fishermen's Consortium of Ancona, which certifies the origin and freshness of the raw ingredients. Among the many, constantly changing, dishes, we should mention the antipasti of raw seafood, carpaccio of swordfish, fried bonito with vegetables, and **warm squid salad**. To follow, **chitarrine ai moscioli in porchetta**, **orecchiette with roast jumbo shrimp**, cannoli filled with rock fish, cavatelli with telline, zucchini and saffron pistils or, for people who do not like fish, maltagliati of potato with thyme and eggplant. Thursday is **fish soup** day, while **stoccafisso all'anconetana** is nearly always available, particularly in the winter (the proprietor is a member of the Accademia dello stoccafisso which is very well-known locally). Otherwise you can choose between perfect, golden **fried paranza**, grilled fish from the Adriatic or, on the meat front, between tagliata of beef and fillet in a bread crust. There is a good choice of sweets, and we can mention the Catalan cream and the chocolate flan in particular.

The cellar has more than 130 labels from the Marche, with reasonable markups, and a choice of various wines by the glass.

FALCONARA MARITTIMA

FANO

10 KM WEST OF ANCONA SS 16

12 KM SOUTH-EAST OF PESARO SS 16 OR EXIT A 14

VILLA AMALIA

3-Star Hotel
Via degli Spagnoli 4
Tel. 071 9160550
Fax 071 912045
E-mail: info@villa-amalia.it
Internet: www.villa-amalia.it
Closed 15 days in January and 15 in July

AL PESCE AZZURRO

Self-service restaurant
Viale Adriatico 48
Tel. 0721 803165
Closed Monday, never in summer
Open: lunch and dinner
Holidays: October 1-April 15
Seating: 400
Prices: 9.50 euros
No credit cards accepted

You stay in this hotel in a nice early twentieth century villa, because it's close to Falconara airport (but also near the sea) and, perhaps especially, because it's close to the well known restaurant of the same name, one of the Marche's best. Rooms are in the outbuilding and in the courtyard that the restaurant gives on to. Breakfasts, either sweet or savory, based on top quality products, homemade jams and sweets, are one of the strong points of the locanda which is relaxing and well served by its seven medium sized, simply furnished rooms. Hotel and restaurant have been owned by the Ridolfi family since 1980, the year it was opened.

• 4 single and 3 double rooms with bathroom, air conditioning, mini-bar, television, modem connection • Prices: single 75-90 euros, double 100-120, breakfast included • Credit cards: all, Bancomat • Off-road parking. Small pets allowed. Reception open from 7.30am to 12am • Restaurant. Breakfast room, Garden, terrace, patio

In the restaurant (seating 50) fish and meat dishes with the imprint of the Marche revisited with a personal touch. Cost about 50 euros excluding wines.

The Società anonima cooperativa tra marinai e pescatori – now known as Coomarpesca, with about 500 members – was founded in 1939, growing out of the 19th century Mutual Aid Association, and it is the oldest and most representative cooperative of local sailors and fishermen. In 1979, the members had the idea of promoting the consumption of local fish by opening a simple self-service restaurant, which would be open in the summer months near the port of Fano. In spite of considerable resistance in the first years of activity, time and public support have proved the cooperative right, and the cuisine has improved and become more specialized over the years, in step with the decision to concentrate mainly on blue fish.
The restaurant is extremely economical (9.50 euros for two antipasti, a first course and two main courses), but it offers carefully prepared traditional recipes, varying them every day. The antipasti include clams and cannellini beans, octopus or whitebait salad, **sardoncini a scottadito** or marinated in vinegar, mackerel with olives, small mullet, and shellfish such as garagoli and bombolini. They are followed by tagliatelle with chickpeas and mackerel, **tortiglioni with squid**, **penne alle sarde**, risotto alla pescatora, and spaghetti del marinaio. To conclude, excellent cuttlefish with peas, **a blue fish gratin**, cod in pizzaiola, **suri alla Sante**, grilled or sottovento, Fano fish soup and plenty more. Anyone who comes here must be prepared to share a long table with other people, attracted, as they are, by good value for money, and to drink a toast with a good Bianchello del Metauro, without asking for the wine list.

FANO

12 KM SOUTH EAST OF PESARO SS 16 OR EXIT A 14

DA MARIA

Trattoria
Via IV Novembre 86
Tel. 0721 808962
Closed Sunday, never in summer
Open: lunch and dinner
Holidays: Christmas and Easter
Seating: 30 + 20 outdoors
Prices: 35 euros, wine excluded
No credit cards accepted

DA TANO

Restaurant
Via del Moletto 10
Tel. 0721 823291
Closed Tuesday
Open: lunch and dinner
Holidays: November-February
Seating: 60 + 20 outdoors
Prices: 35 euros, wine excluded
All major credit cards

The sign saying "pesce fresco" (fresh fish) outside the trattoria is one indication. But you really have to taste that fish to understand that this is not just one of the many eating places on the coast that make such a claim, but a trattoria where the freshness of the raw ingredients is not only an act of faith, but stands for "today's fish, caught in the Adriatic and only by small fishing boats". We could add the names of the suppliers, each of whom has his own specialty: the squid and cuttlefish come from Ivan, Enrico provides the sole, turbot and angler fish, while another fisherman brings clams and telline. The ambience in the trattoria is more 1950s than new Millennium, with humble furnishings and a delicate aroma of shellfish and sole coming from the kitchen.

Domenica describes the various dishes and then serves sole, hake, bream or **steamed baby turbot**, grilled polentina with clams and calamaretti, **salad of cuttlefish and squid**, boiled razor clams and mussels, **small mullet with tomato**, squill and plenty more. This is followed by delicate **tagliatelle with clams**, grilled sole, or calamaretti plain or with a touch of tomato. The main courses always include the day's fish, grilled or steamed, which is amazingly light, and the typical local **guazzetto fanese**, a stew of boned fish cooked on the grill.

A few different wine labels, most of which come from the region, are stored in the naturally fresh cellar. You know you will not need anything to help you digest, but who could refuse a moretta, the strong fishermen's coffee? Maria avoids giving us her recipe and serves a glass of the smoking mixture, with a star anise flower.

A few miles from the old center, on the road from Fano to Pesaro, is the friendly little fish restaurant, which Daniele and Andrea have run with skill and courtesy for the last few years. The restaurant has recently been refurbished, and is quiet and hospitable, with room to eat alfresco in the summer.

The menu varies with what the local fish market has to offer, so we can only mention the dishes we found. For antipasti, mazzolina novella with vegetables and grilled polenta, **steamed nocchie**, octopus and potato pie, diced angler fish, and a **pan of shellfish and molluscs**. If you do not know what to choose, we recommend trying the set two or four samples of antipasti. The generous choice of first courses includes dried pasta and homemade fresh pasta, like the **cappellacci of fish with sauce of sole fillets** (something you must try), ravioli of ricotta and spinach with shellfish, tagliatelle al mattarello with the aromas of the Adriatic, passatelli with clams and gallinule, but also **paccheri ai cannelli e pendolini**, tagliatelle with Mediterranean lobster and pendolini, egg maccheroncini with nocchia meat. The main courses include **mixed grill from the Adriatic**, angler fish with artichokes, **baked sea bass** with vegetables and **turbot with roast potatoes**, which we recommend. The fish is not all caught in the Adriatic, but its origin is always indicated on the menu.

The puddings are all of a high quality, particularly the chocolate pie. The wine list is varied, with plenty of regional products.

FERMO

FRONTONE

L'ENOTECA BAR A VINO ☖❚

Wine cellar and wine bar with food
Via Mazzini 1 at the corner of piazza del Popolo
Tel. 0734 228067-348 9035257
Closed Monday, never in August
Open: 12.00pm-12.00am
Holidays: variable
Seating: 35 + 35 outdoors
Prices: 30 euros
All major credit cards

IL DAINO ❚

Hotel restaurant
Via Roma 19
Tel. 0721 786101-786441
Closed Monday
Open: lunch and dinner
Holidays: in October
Seating: 120
Prices: 25 euros, wine excluded
All credit cards, Bancomat

The Wine Store is located under the Loggiato di San Rocco, in one of the most picturesque corners of the town center. It is small, but perfectly decorated, from the candles on the tables right down to the background music and the tables placed outside in the summer. Here Peppe, the host and proprietor, guides his guests knowledgably through the menu, proposing simple, straightforward dishes. The great emphasis put on the quality of the ingredients means that the menu always presents seasonal and typical local products. And driven by passion and expertise, his constant research also takes in ideas from other parts pf Europe. The cheese, wine and champagne are selected carefully with an expert eye.

Open from midday to midnight, at lunchtime the kitchen can prepare an enjoyable snack of cured meats and cheese, accompanied by wine by the glass or a label chosen by Peppe.

After an aperitif, for dinner you have a choice of two set meals at different prices. As an antipasto, you can try croutons with cherry tomatoes, a pie of vegetables, ewe's milk ricotta and zucchini, breaded fried anchovies with cherry tomatoes, **ciauscolo** and excellent mixed **cured meats** by Passamonti. This is followed by lasagna or **risotto with fresh cep mushrooms**. The meat dishes include **roast rabbit with mushrooms** or roast shoulder of pork. There is an excellent **cheese board**, which boasts local, French, British and Spanish cheeses. Apple pie and a small delicate **crostata** conclude the meal. The wine cellar also sells a range of typical products, local oils, pasta and jams from the Marche.

We recommend this restaurant warmly because it will be a surprise. From outside, and probably even from the entrance, you would probably expect anonymous chain-gang cuisine, but once you sit down, you will feel the sincerity of the local specialties, a friendly warmth, the excellent raw ingredients, most of which are sourced locally, and a well balanced choice of wines, that invite you to try imaginative combinations. On our visit, we ordered **omelet with black truffles**, **cappellacci of pumpkin**, and **grilled kid and lamb**. Simple dishes that recreate precise flavors. You have to accept it, here the lamb tastes of lamb, and if you are looking for sensationalism, food design or fusion cuisine, you have come to the wrong place. The menu is rich and based on products bought from local suppliers; in addition to the dishes already mentioned, the menu includes croutons with truffles (which are present all year round, either white, black, bianchetto or scorzone), mixed cured meats, omelet with mushrooms, **potato gnocchi with duck sauce**, ravioli or tagliatelle with meat sauce, **cappelletti in consommé** (always available, so ask for them even if they are not mentioned), filled pasta, **rabbit in porchetta**, tagliata of beef (unfortunately in the predictable version with green peppercorns and rocket) and numerous puddings which, like the fresh pasta, are all homemade.

As we said earlier, the wine list is quite generous and the prices reasonable. Do not be put off by the seating capacity: 120 diners do not worry the kitchen or dining-room staff, who deal with large numbers without problems, ensuring prompt service and good quality food.

FRONTONE

LOCANDA DEL CASTELLO

🛏 Rooms
Piazza della Rocca 5
Tel. 0721 790661–335 6242213
E-mail: info@locandadelcastello.it
Internet: www.locandadelcastello.it
Open all year round

A refuge in a quiet quarter dominated by the fortress that soars up massively over everything and that has an all round view over a landscape that goes from the hills of Pesaro to the massive counterforts of Catria and Nerone, as far as Montefeltro. But the attraction of the place run by Giorgio Giuliacci and his wife isn't limited to these logistic details. Breakfast is traditional with hot drinks, orange juice, butter, jam, croissants, tarts, biscuits and homemade fruit cakes. Easy parking space right by the entrance, big rooms provided with every comfort and well fitted bathrooms, terracotta tiled and wooden floors everywhere to give an impression of intimacy. You couldn't ask for more if you want to have a relaxing holiday interspersed with excursions nearby.

• 6 double rooms and one apartment (4 people), bathroom, air conditioning, mini-bar, television • Prices: double room single use 55 euros, double 70, apartment 100, breakfast included • Credit cards: all except AE, Bancomat • Facility partly accessible to the mobility challenged. External parking close by. Owners always contactable • Bar (only for guests). Terrace

GENGA
Pierosara

DA MARIA　　　　　　　🍷

🍲 Restaurant
Frazione Pierosara 67
Tel. 0732 90014
Closed Thursday, never in spring and summer
Open: lunch and dinner
Holidays: January 10-30
Seating: 90
Prices: 25-30 euros, wine excluded
All credit cards except AE, Bancomat

The small town of Genga is on the road from Ancona to Fabriano, inside a Nature park that contains beauties such as the Red Gorge and the caves of Frasassi. As you climb up to the hamlet of Pierosara, you can enjoy the beautiful view of the surrounding mountains, and stop in the trattoria run by Claudio and Gabriella Bruffa who continue to make traditional, simple dishes that are all prepared perfectly and with absolute dedication. The restaurant is in an old building, but it is friendly and well furnished, and the service is prompt and professional.
In a fairly complex menu, which also contains a few commonplace and international dishes, you will have no trouble choosing those that represent the surrounding area, highlighting the local flavors, the seasons, and the excellence of the raw ingredients (mushrooms and truffles are always on the menu when in season). To start with, we recommend the cured meats or the carpaccio of veal, but it is the first courses in particular that are in tune with tradition: large ravioli or **tagliatelle with scorzone truffles**, delicate **tagliolini with galletti mushrooms and cherry tomatoes**, orecchiette with fava beans in porchetta, passatelli with cep mushrooms, or **pappardelle with a sauce of wild boar**, hunted in the surrounding woods. Going on to the main courses, try the **lombata of Marchigiana beef** (also served as tagliata), the **grilled lamb chops**, pork kidneys, **wild boar chasseur** or **boned rabbit in porchetta** with wild fennel. And finally, fresh fruit or puddings such as cantuccini or fruit crostata. The wine list is Claudio Bruffa's department; he is a sommelier, and he proposes a wide selection of regional labels together with some other Italian wines.

GENGA

Genga Stazione

FRASASSI LE GROTTE

🗝🛏 3-Star Hotel
Via Marconi 33
Tel. 0732 905003
Fax 0732 905914
E-mail: info@hotelfrasassi.com
Internet: www.hotelfrasassi.com
Open all year round

Owned by the body that manages the biggest grottos in Europe and inaugurated in 1999, this hotel is about 300 meters from the ticket office, in the middle of the Parco Naturale della Gola della Rossa. With no architectural barriers for the mobility challenged, it has 35 very friendly, comfortable rooms. The restaurant offers typical regional dishes together with quite a good wine selection (half board 48-55 euros per person) and it will also provide an equipped meeting room with 150 seats and a big private parking area. Apart from the not to be missed visit to the grottos and the church of San Vittore delle Chiuse, with the Speleocarsico Museum attached, the place is an ideal staging post for rafting, caving, mountain bike riding, trekking and sport climbing.

•5 single and 30 double rooms with bathroom, air conditioning, mini-bar, television • Prices: single 38-50 euros, double 60-80 (10 euro supplement for extra bed), breakfast included • Credit cards: all, Bancomat • Facility accessible to the mobility challenged, 2 rooms equipped. Reserved external parking. Small pets allowed. Reception open 24 hours a day • Restaurant. Living room, reading, room, television room. Conference room

GROTTAMMARE

A CASA DA ANGELO

🍲 Holiday farm
Contrada San Giacomo 26
Tel. 0735 631730
Closed Tuesday, in winter open
Saturday and Sunday
Open: dinner, on festivities also for lunch
Holidays: variable
Seating: 70 + 60 outdoors
Prices: 25 euros
All credit cards

From the Grottammare exit on the motorway you have to go a few miles back up the Tesino valley on the south side of the river, taking care not to miss the small sign that indicates the road to this traditional vacation farm. When you get to the old farmhouse immersed in the hills, you will be welcomed with great courtesy by the Cencetti family, and you will savor a range of wholesome seasonal dishes. The dining-room is full of light and decorated with restraint; in summer you can eat alfresco and enjoy the peace and quiet of the garden.

The menu proposes traditional Umbrian fare (reflecting the proprietors' origins) as well as dishes from the Marche, and makes ample use of the vegetables produced on the farm (most of the ingredients are in fact home grown). Start with **prosciutto crudo** cut by hand, pecorino, marinated vegetables, fried zucchini flowers, flans of potatoes and peas or other vegetables, and chicory tarts. The home-rolled pasta includes **ciriole** (typical of Terni, and made with flour and water) **with wild asparagus** or eggplant and cherry tomatoes, Savoy cabbage and sausage, or artichokes and mushrooms, and **tagliatelle with a duck sauce**; and now there is a novelty: **maltagliati**, made with a dough of durum wheat flour and parsley and served with vegetables or a creamy cheese sauce. If you order it in advance, you can enjoy the exquisite **stuffed duck**, but the **rabbit in porchetta**, ham baked in the wood-fired oven, guinea-fowl with grapes, grilled chicken and lamb are equally good. The puddings are simple and homemade.

The wines are the house wine by the carafe, and bottles from two well-known local cellars.

GROTTAMMARE

VILLA HELVETIA

🗝3-Star Hotel
Via Salvi 1
Tel. 0735 631293
Fax 0735 735491
E-mail: villahelvetia@libero.it
Internet: www.grottammare.it/villahelvetia
Open all year round

In the center of this delightful seaside resort whose charm derives from the beautiful cluster of houses in the upper part of the town and their contrast with the palm-lined promenade, especially the part that hosts a line of turn of the century buildings, this small hotel retains its original nineteenth century character. The interiors are Art Nouveau style: the refurbished, air-conditioned rooms are simple but comfortable, with frill-free furniture, and walls and curtains in pastel shades. The welcome makes you feel at home and service is courteous and attentive. You can have what you want for breakfast, ranging from sweet to savory.

• 3 single and 13 double rooms with bathroom, air conditioning, television • Prices: single 55-85 euros, double 80-110, breakfast included • Credit cards: all except DC, Bancomat •. Outside public parking in front of hotel. No pets allowed. Reception open from 7 am to 11 pm • Breakfast room, living room

ISOLA DEL PIANO

LOCANDA ALCE NERO-MONASTERO DI MONTEBELLO

🗝Holiday farm
Via Montebello 1
Tel. 0721 720334-720126
Fax 0721 720326
E-mail: fondazionealcenero@alcenero.it
Internet: www.alcenerocooperativa.it
Closed January

The Alce nero is a big cooperative known for its work in organic agriculture and for its products: pasta, cereals, flours, legumes and more. Inside this enormous property there are two structures given over to farm tourism: the Alce nero hotel, created in a visible stone country house and the Montebello Monastery, dating back to the fifteenth century. Two options are offered: rooms, especially those in the Monastery, are very big and some of them can host up to four people. Apartments are rented for a minimum of three days and, as they have a kitchen, guarantee maximum freedom of movement for guests. The restaurant is in the same building as the locanda (half board 45-50 euros) and breakfasts are genuine and traditional. Many possible cultural visits in the environs.

• 10 double rooms with bathroom (2 rooms with shared bathroom); 2 apartments with kitchen (6 people) • Prices: double room single use 45-50 euros, double 60-70, apartment 65-130, breakfast included • Credit cards: major ones, Bancomat • Off-road parking. No pets allowed. Owners always present • Bar, restaurant. Reading room, television room. Conference room. Garden, park. Swimming pool

26 KM SOUTH OF ANCONA

VILLA TETLAMEYA

🔑 4-Star Hotel
Via Villa Costantina 187
Tel. 071 978863
Fax 071 976639
E-mail: info@loretoitaly.com
Internet: www.loretoitaly.com
Open all year round

DA ROSA

🍲 Trattoria
Via Armaroli 17
Tel. 0733 260124
Closed Sunday
Open: lunch and dinner
Holidays: Christmas
Seating: 40
Prices: 28-32 euros, wine excluded
All credit cards

The hotel is in Loreto on the upper floors of a Marche villa dated 1873. The rooms are elegant and furnished with antiques, and they enjoy all comforts. In the park opposite, private parking is available if required. Continental breakfast includes croissants, cappuccino, yoghurt, sliced meats, bread and jams. Downstairs large rooms are specially equipped for business meetings and conferences. Special attention is paid to the food and wine tourist, and dinners with recipes from the Marche tradition can be organized in the large dining room. In the same complex and run by the same people the Zi' Nenè restaurant (average price 40-50 euros, drinks not included, set menu 18 euros).

• 2 single, 4 double rooms and 2 suites, bathroom, air conditioning, mini-bar, safe, satellite television • Prices: single 75 euros, double 115, suite 135, breakfast included • Credit cards: all except DC, Bancomat • Facility accessible to the mobility challenged, 1 room equipped for them. Off-road parking. No pets allowed. Reception open 24 hours a day • Breakfast room, lounge, television room. Conference room. Winter garden, park

The trattoria run by Elio Vincenzetti in this attractive inland town in the Marche region is a must for lovers of good food. Located in the old town, it proposes traditional dishes from Macerata and the rest of the region, as well as others that are the fruit of careful re-interpretations that focus on the quality of the raw ingredients. The menu contains meat dishes but also some fish when this is available.

The springtime menu that we were offered included small omelet of asparagus and scorzone truffles, a **Macerata mixed fry in foil**, chicory tips with anchovies, **coratella of lamb with artichokes**, flan of fava beans and pecorino or a plate of local cured meats as antipasti. Going on to the first course, you will have to choose between trying the **vincisgrassi**, tagliolini of Campofilone, **gnocchi with a sauce of rabbit** and saffron, or **risotto with red wine and truffles** or mantecato with fava beans and pecorino. The main courses are interesting: **pork liver in rete** with bay leaf, **lamb chops grilled** or fried with fava beans and cherry tomatoes, **stuffed pigeon** (known as pistacoppi), tagliata of Marchigiano beef, chicken in potacchio (with tomatoes and herbs), and **suckling pig with a sauce of vincotto**. To conclude, fresh fruit or, as a pudding, soufflé with mistrà ice cream, green apple sherbet, bavarese with passion fruit, strudel or crostata of orange and chocolate.

There are numerous local labels in the wine list and some interesting Italian wines; certain wines may be ordered by the glass.

5 KM FROM CITY CENTER

62 KM NORTH OF ASCOLI PICENO

LE CASE

4-Star Hotel
Località Mozzavinci 16
Tel. 0733 231897
Fax 0733 268911
E-mail: ristorantelecase@tin.it
Internet: www.countryhouselecase.it
Closed 7-31 January and 15 days in August

OSTERIA DELL'ARCO

Recently opened osteria
Piazza Gramsci 27
Tel. 0734 631630
Closed Thursdays
Open: dinner, festivities or on booking also for lunch
Holidays: January
Seating: 35 + 35 outdoors
Prices: 30-35 euros, wine excluded
All major credit card, Bancomat

Sunk in the green of the Macerata hills, this hotel was born out of an old rural settlement consisting of various outhouses surrounding two large cottages. Carefully refurbished, the complex today offers friendly rooms and independent apartments, all furnished with authentic period pieces and craft articles. It's surrounded by a big park and boasts a wellness center with large swimming pool that gives on to the countryside (the use of swimming pool, sauna, jacuzzi and gym is included in the price). Buffet breakfast includes hot drinks, juices and fresh fruit, bread, croissants, focaccia, tarts and sweets made at home every morning, plus jams, honey, cured meats and cheeses.

• 14 double rooms and 1 suite (4 people), bathroom, air conditioning, minibar, safe, television; 4 apartments (4 people) with kitchen, • Prices: double room single use 90 euros, double 125 (20 euro supplement for extra bed), suite 210 euros, breakfast included; apartment 300 euros per week• Credit cards: all, Bancomat • Facility accessible to the mobility challenged, 1 room equipped for them. External parking with reserved spaces. No pets allowed. Reception open from 9 am to 10 pm • Restaurant, wine shop. Breakfast room, reading room. Garden, terrace. Fitness center with indoor swimming pool

The restaurant offers local dishes at 30-40 euros, wine excluded, the taverna is engaged in research cooking (60-70 euros).

In the small, quiet square in the country town of Magliano, L'Arco is a precious stopping off place that fits perfectly into its context. Giulio Polci is in charge in the kitchen, while his wife Cristina manages the dining-room skillfully. The seasons decide the menu, as well as the suppliers of the raw ingredients: Romanina from Piane di Montegiorgio for the vegetables, Peppe Dell'Orso from Loro Piceno for the beef and cured pork, Cameli for the lamb, Eros Scarafoni from Belmonte for the cow's milk cheese, and the L'Una Rosa wood-fired oven, also in Belmonte, for the bread.
The first thing to be served is antipasti of **boiled marchigiana meat**, mixed cured meats, carpaccio of smoked baccalà and misticanza di campo. This is followed by homemade **tagliatelle with a sauce of coxcombs and sinews**, **cream of cicerchia** and guanciale, pappardelle of emmer with sausage and a sauce of cavoli strascinati, and tortelli filled with oxtail. The quality of the meat is brought out in classic recipes like grilled medallions of scamone, **rabbit in the manner of Val di Tenna**, **roast suckling kid**, and roast lamb.
The Polcis are helped in the kitchen by Bukurije, a lady from Macedonia who has settled in Magliano. They also select the **cheeses**, oils and wines: the wine list looks to the South, as well as to the Marche and the crucial wine producing areas, and they know how to choose products that are not well known, but good, and inexpensive. Thanks to the intelligent way the cellar is managed, the restaurant has grown, building up a loyal clientele, which rewards the efforts made to combine research, constantly high quality and low costs.

MALTIGNANO

L'ARCO

☞ Trattoria
Via IV Novembre 63-65
Tel. 0736 304490
Closed Wednesday
Open: lunch and dinner
Holidays: August 15-30
Seating: 60
Prices: 20-25 euros
Credit cards: CartaSi, Visa

The character of this little restaurant does not change over the years, and it continues to pull in the crowds on Fridays, thanks to the appeal of a menu based entirely on baccalà. The trattoria is on the road through the village of Maltignano, on the inland border between Marche and Abruzzo. It is family-run, and Maria Cesira is assisted by her sons, Piero and Stefano, and by her sisters-in-law.

The meal usually starts with salamis, different types of pecorino and fried cream cheese, zucchini and **olives all'ascolana** (homemade); the traditional autumn antipasti of a salad of cep mushrooms is replaced in summer by a selection of grilled vegetables. As a first course, we recommend the **ceppe** (tapered pasta typical of nearby Civitella d'Abruzzo, prepared using a knitting needle) served with a tomato, meat or mushroom sauce, **rigatoni with sausage**, **timbale**, which is always available on holidays, gramigna alla norcina with sausage, truffles and pecorino. The main courses are a strong point: succulent **veal shanks** or roast saddle of veal with cep mushrooms; but also grilled lamb chops and **stewed kid**. But the real specialty, as we mentioned, is the **baccalà**, which is prepared every Friday (from October to March), or to order on other days: it may be boiled with various sauces, with polenta, spaghetti or mezzemaniche with tomato, stewed with chickpeas, or roast. As a pudding, there is a popular trifle.

In addition to the local house wine, there are some good bottled wines, from both sides of the Marche-Abruzzo border.

MATELICA
Pianné

IL CAMINO

☞ Restaurant
Contrada Pianné
Tel. 0737 786035
Closed Monday
Open: lunch and dinner
Holidays: none
Seating: 60 + 40 outdoors
Prices: 20-30 euros, wine excluded
All credit cards

In the capital of Verdicchio wine production, the excavation of important Picene and Roman archeological sites is progressing rapidly, and you can admire some of the items found (including some grape seeds that are over two thousand years old) in the Civil Museum in Palazzo Finaguerra. The Piersanti Museum, one of the most important in the Marche region, contains paintings and objects from different periods, as well as a stone globe engraved with astronomical coordinates, that is over 2500 years old.

Il Camino is located in this special valley, the only one in the Marche region that runs parallel to the sea and enjoys an almost continental climate. The restaurant rightly continues to respect local gastronomical traditions, preparing **crescia with cured meats** and local types of cheese, pasta handmade by Fabio and Ivana, which may be **tagliatelle with fava beans**, with a duck sauce or with truffles, **pappardelle with boar sauce** or with mushrooms, tagliolini, ravioli or **vincisgrassi**. In winter you will often find **pulse soups**, pasta and beans, and polenta with cream or tomato sauces. Grilled meats are the specialty of the restaurant: beef, **lamb** and pork sourced from local farmers, but also **rabbit in porchetta** and, occasionally, game served with vegetables au gratin. In the fall and winter, the homemade puddings include a **cresciafogliata**, which we recommend.

The wine list focuses primarily on Verdicchio and some regional labels.

MONDAVIO

39 KM SOUTH-EAST OF URBINO SS 73 BIS

LA PALOMBA

☞Hotel restaurant
Via Gramsci 13
Tel. 0721 97105
Always open, Oct-Apr closed Sunday
for dinner and Monday for lunch
Open: lunch and dinner
Holidays: 1 week end-September
Seating: 80 + 30 outdoors
Prices: 30 euros, wine excluded
All credit cards, Bancomat

La Palomba is a restaurant and hotel with about fifteen bedrooms, in the center of town, opposite Francesco Giorgio Martini's mighty tower, and there is one dish that everyone there will recommend, and for which it is worth traveling even hundreds of kilometers to enjoy, at any time of the year: the **cappelletti in brodo** prepared by the skillful hands of the ladies who work in this restaurant will remain an indelible memory of a gratifying gastronomic experience. There is nothing excessive, sophisticated or reinvented about the cappelletti of La Palomba, only the taste of a delicate, spicy filling, wrapped in a thin veil of hand-rolled pasta and cooked in a tasty meat consommé skimmed of any excess fat. Absolute perfection, a dish that becomes pure essence and aesthetics, and that would have appealed to Brillat-Savarin, the theorist of the osmazome. In addition to this unmissable dish, the restaurant run by the Cerisoli family offers a vast choice of other delights: croutons with mushrooms or truffles, homemade **cured meats**, **cheese** ripened in walnut leaves, tagliatelle with meat sauce, **tacconi allo sgagg** (a pasta made of fava bean flour with lardo and garlic), passatelli in consommé, and **gnocchi with duck sauce**. Grilled meat is one of the main courses, but there is also **fried lamb** and vegetables, pasticciata alla pesarese, and cheese and vegetable omelets. There are several homemade puddings, crostata, **trifle**, panna cotta, jelly roll, small spumoni with almonds, and ammonia biscuits (don't worry, it's only a type of yeast). The extensive wine list includes numerous regional labels. The restaurant is always open on holidays.

MONDAVIO
Cavallara

39 KM SOUTH-EAST OF URBINO SS 73 BIS

MARIA

☞Trattoria
Via Cavallara 2
Tel. 0721 976220
Closed Monday, in winter also on
Sunday for dinner
Open: lunch and dinner
Holidays: in July and March
Seating: 80 + 20 outdoors
Prices: 28-32 euros, wine excluded
All credit cards

"Actually it has always been my dream to be able to dance well." If you come here on a Saturday evening in winter, the sight of couples moving to the notes of a small orchestra, might make you think of a scene from Nanni Moretti's film Caro diario. The Cerisoli family has not changed the custom begun many years ago when it introduced dancing after dinner, as a way of increasing satisfaction and loyalty among the clientele. Dancing is now limited to one evening a week, but the food is always of the same high standard.
The team of mothers, wives and sisters who work in the kitchen is too well trained. Too good to forget the traditional methods, intelligently making them lighter to account for modern taste. And maintaining an integrity of flavors that has become rare, like the courtesy of Gabriele Cerisoli, who works front of house. Depending on the season, the menu offers a choice of pecorino mousse with herbs, **carpaccio of marchigiano beef**, **chicken livers** with truffles, and cold vegetable soup. The first courses are always excellent, mainly homemade pasta: **tacconi of fava beans with guanciale and pecorino**, potato gnocchi with duck sauce, tagliolini with white truffles and **passatelli asciutti** served with an opulent sauce of **cep mushrooms and fossa cheese** or, in spring, with peas, asparagus and mushrooms. The main course is a triumph of meat, often from domestic animals: **rabbit in porchetta** (flavored with wild fennel) or fried, guinea-fowl with black truffles or in an olive crust, and **roast goose**.
The puddings are one of the restaurant's main attractions, so make sure you keep some space. The wine list is more than satisfactory, with a wide regional choice.

MONTECICCARDO

17 KM SOUTH-WEST OF PESARO

IL CONVENTINO

Recently opened osteria
Via Conventino 1
Tel. 0721 910588
Closed Monday and Tuesday
Open: dinner, festivities for lunch on booking
Holidays: January
Seating: 60 + 120 outdoors
Prices: 30-35 euros, wine excluded
All credit cards

The magic evoked by certain places seems to spring from the skills of an able stage designer. As here, in the Conventino dei Servi di Maria di Monteciccardo, where the austerity of a perfectly restored religious building, endless views over well-groomed countryside and the silence of a quiet hamlet ensure authentic emotions. These premises, five years ago, encouraged Roberto Bartolucci to turn the three rooms below the former convent into a hospitality center that, in summer, spreads out into the enchanting exteriors.

His wife Bruna looks after cuisine and recipes, for the most part based on local ingredients, with a delicate approach to traditional dishes. Such as: panzanella with tomatoes, basil and local ham, fresh ricotta with strips of guanciale and **Marchigiana carpaccio with green beans** to start. First courses follow the balanced style of vegetables-meat-cheese offered with the antipasti: **ravioli with ricotta and wild herbs** and seasoned pecorino cheese, **passatelli asciutti with quail sauce** or gnocchi with duck sauce, **tagliolini with wild dill**, chitarrine with artichokes and dry ricotta. White and red meats alternate in the main courses on offer: **rabbit wrapped in lardo** with roast potatoes, roulades of scamone in an asparagus sauce, fillet of pork cooked in orange with leeks and green peppers, **goose in porchetta**. Close with the cheese board or delicious homemade creations such as savarin with vanilla sauce, bavarese with strawberries, millefeuille with wildberry cream.

The wine list is interesting, and the selection of labels is unusual.

MONTECOSARO

21 KM EAST OF MACERATA

LA LUMA

3-Star Hotel
Via Cavour 1
Tel. 0733 229466
Fax 0733 229457
E-mail: info@laluma.it
Internet: www.laluma.it
Open all year round

Born out of the former palazzo Garulli, La Luma is a nice hotel with some very original interiors. In some rooms you are struck by the bare stone walls and the ceiling vaults, the niches hollowed out of the walls and the period furnishings. In the rooms, with their panoramic views of the Chienti valley and all comforts, traditional furnishings and beds with wooden or wrought iron bedheads. And in the hotel basement, you can still see the tuff grottos. Buffet breakfast offers tarts, doughnuts and homemade grape bread, as well as the typical cafeteria products and fresh drinks. The restaurant, run by the same owners, is 100 meters from the hotel, and is also open to non-residents. A meal costs around 30 euros, excluding wine.

• 9 double, 1 triple room and 1 suite with bathroom, air conditioning, minibar, safe, several rooms with terrace • Prices: double room single use 62 euros, double 77, triple 100, suite 124, breakfast included • Credit cards: Visa, Bancomat • Facility accessible to the mobility challenged, 2 rooms equipped for them. Outside public parking, garage (3 places, 10 euros per day). Reception open from 7am to 2am • Bar, restaurant. Breakfast room, reading and television room. Terrace

MONTEFALCONE APPENNINO

42 KM NORTH-WEST OF ASCOLI PICENO

DA QUINTILIA MERCURI

🍲 Trattoria
Via Corradini 9
Tel. 0734 79158
Closed Wednesday
Open: lunch and dinner, in summer also for dinner
Holidays: Christmas and Easter
Seating: 20
Prices: 25 euros
No credit cards accepted

For some time now, the best trattoria in the province has been in Montefalcone. The much-loved Quintilia Mercuri, tireless "mistress" of ceremonies, still smiles on guests who almost always arrive from afar just to enjoy the pleasure of a meal here. She almost exclusively confines her attention to guests who book, so it is a good idea to book in advance to ensure that everything goes according to plan; there is no menu and it should come as no surprise that you have to explain your preferences in advance by telephone. Put it this way, all of these details are part of the experience. The setting has remained unchanged for years: meals are served at home, surrounded by antique furniture, everyday objects and unfashionable windows.
Cured meats, cheese and **croutons** with chicken livers, vegetables or truffles are followed by **campofiloni with traditional** meat sauce, **potato gnocchi** or **ravioli** with meat and vegetables – all homemade and topped with a meat sauce or tomatoes with basil. Just as the stomach begins to feel satisfied, up come generous helpings of **pan-fried white meat** with garlic, rosemary and a dash of vinegar or roast meats. The typical **mixed fried side course** with creamed vegetables and Ascoli stuffed olives is well worth trying. Close with homemade puddings including tarts, doughnuts or trifle.
There is no wine list as such – only house white or red on tap. It doesn't matter: the magic of this trattoria doesn't involve wine and the more demanding clients can always bring a good bottle with them. The bill is still only – and hopefully for a long time to come – 25 euros all included.

MONTEFELCINO
Fontecorniale

22 KM SOUTH-WEST OF PESARO, 26 KM NORTH-EAST OF URBINO

COSTA DELLA FIGURA

🍲 Holiday farm
Strada Costa della Figura 30
Tel. and fax 0721 729428
E-mail info@costadellafigura.com
Internet: www.costadellafigura.com
Always open
Open: lunch and dinner
Holidays: variable
Seating: 30
Prices: 25-30 euros, wine excluded
No credit cards accepted

This farm tourism facility is nestled among the hills of the Pesaro hinterland. Mother Zaira draws out the pasta by hand and prepares simple dressings with the products of her organic vegetable garden. The father Enrico prepares the meats and cured meats. Marco is the host. On the upper floor there are four comfortable bedrooms and a spacious lounge, and a beautiful swimming pool graces the terrace. At breakfast time, honey and jams from the farm can be found on the menu.
The meals follow the seasons: fresh vegetables are served as antipasti with an exquisite **crescia**, alongside delicious omelettes and homemade **cured meats.** In summer, the **pumpkin flowers in batter** are a must. The few cheeses offered are purchased from the neighboring shepherd Delà. Among the first courses you will find **tagliatelle**, gnocchi and ravioli all handmade and served with vegetables or meat sauce. The main courses feature free-range meat: to be tasted are the **rabbit in porchetta** and the **oven-baked suckling pig**. The meal ends with house puddings that range from the ring cake to the tarts with Zaira's homemade jams. The wines of the Fattoria Mancini of Pesaro, served in a jug, accompany the courses. Booking is advisable.

🛏️ 4 double rooms, en-suite, fridge-bar, safety deposit box, satellite TV • Prices: double single use 40, double 80 euros, breakfast included. Entire building is suitable for the mobility impaired. Internal uncovered parking area. Pets welcome. Owners are always available • Restaurant. Reading room. Garden, terrace, solarium. Swimming pool

MONTEMONACO
La Cittadella

ORTEZZANO

42 KM NW OF ASCOLI PICENO SS 4 AND 78

45 KM NORTH OF ASCOLI PICENO

LA CITTADELLA DEI SIBILLINI

Restaurant-country house
Località La Cittadella
Tel. 0736 856361
Fax 0736 844262
E-mail informa@cittadelladeisibillini.it
Internet: www.cittadelladeisibillini.it
Always open, lunch and dinner
Holidays: October-March open only at weekends, Christmas and Easter
Seating: 60 + 20 autodoors
Prices: 23 euros, wine excluded
Credit cards: Visa, Bancomat

I PICENI

Restaurant with rooms
Piazza Savini 1
Tel. 0734 778000
Closed Tuesday
Open: dinner, Saturdays and festivities also for lunch
Holidays: January and last week of September
Seating: 35 + 20 outdoors
Prices: 26-32 euros, wine excluded
All credit cards except DC

Located in the heart of the Parco dei Sibillini, with a quite unique panorama, La Cittadella organizes pork butchery courses, visits to artisan workshops, and also provides mountain bikes for guests. There is no porterage service, but the guests are awaited until the agreed arrival time.
The cuisine on offer is seasonal. Among the antipasti you will find prime local **cured meats**, local sheep's cheeses, vegetable omelets, polentina with wild boar sauce, beans with cotiche, **soups of cereals and pulses**, eggplant alla parmigiana. Pasta like the excellent gnocchi al sugo rosso, **tagliatelline with cep mushrooms**, **pappardelle al ragù**, polenta al sugo, is all handmade. Among the main courses you can try lamb, pork or chicken roasts, **coniglio in porchetta**, **roasted pigeon** and barbecued lamb. To finish, homemade desserts, coffee and mistrà liqueur.
The wine list favors the regional labels and Silvio Antongnozzi, one of the owners, is always present in the dining area, to advise on the wines.

10 double rooms, 6 triple rooms and 2 with 5 beds, en-suite, TV (on request) • Prices: double single use 45-50, double 60-70, triple 75-90, with 5 beds 130 euros, breakfast included. 2 rooms suitable for the mobility impaired. Open air free parking. Pets welcome. Owners always available • Restaurant. Tavern. TV room. Swimming pool

At **Montemonaco**, Corona Carni, viale Stradone 26: rustic cured meats and mutton and pork. In the hamlet of **Ferrà di Sotto** Aldo and Augusto Fortuni pick mushrooms and truffles including white ones.

The River Aso flows placidly from the Sibillini mountains down to the sea, creating a small valley that is intensely cultivated with fruit trees. The villages hereabouts, built to exploit the agricultural potential, are all recent. For a touch of history you have to climb the slopes and rediscover the small towns dotting the hills. One of these – the ancient Urticinum, now Ortezzano – stands out for the conservation of its buildings and the beauty of its streets. A house overlooking a tiny square is home to I Piceni, once a small restaurant and today a locanda thanks to the rooms available on the upper floor.
Cuisine ranges from turf to surf and includes local flavors with a personal touch: **cold beef** flavored with bay leaf and aged pecorino, selected cured meats with rosemary focaccia or a salad of fennel, oranges, olives and dill seeds are just some of the antipasti. **Fettuccine with rabbit sauce**, rigatoni with broccoli and guanciale, **ravioli with duck sauce** and black truffle – not to mention **campofiloni with clams and turnip tops** and bean soup with croutons and garlic – all with delightfully pleasant flavors. There is a huge selection of main courses: the succulent fillet steak wrapped in spiced lardo, breast of goose cooked in Piceno red wine or **Sibillini lamb scottadito**, **fried baccalà**, slices of fresh tuna with fennel. Alternatively, there is a small selection of cheeses and preserves. The puddings are superb: the very popular **semifreddo di mistrà** with a barley and pear sauce and saffron with chestnut honey and hot chocolate topping.
Small but competent wine list. The place is small, so it's best to book.

ORTEZZANO

45 KM NORTH OF ASCOLI PICENO

LA ROSA DEI VENTI

🍲 Traditional osteria
Via Leopardi 17
Tel. 0734 778016
Closed Monday and Tuesday, never in summer
Open: lunch and dinner
Holidays: variable
Seating: 30 + 20 outdoors
Prices: 25-30 euros, wine excluded
All credit cards

Ortezzano is reached along the Val d'Aso on the road that, near Pedaso, leaves the Adriatic coast behind and moves towards the hinterland and the Sibillini mountains. Driving amidst intensely cultivated orchards, we reach a delightful little town. The same adjectives could well be used to describe the osteria, seemingly cut out of a grotto, where every detail speaks of welcoming simplicity.
Cured meats are the pride of Ortezzano, beginning with **ciauscolo**, the soft salami eaten spread on bread. Naturally, it is among the antipasti served in the osteria together with one of those traditional dishes – **chicken galantina** – that is worth the trip on its own. The dish is accompanied by delicious fried and stuffed **Ascoli olives**. Antipasti also include wild asparagus and artichokes preserved in olive oil purchased from a small local company, as well as pecorino cheese. Then come **ravioli** filled with **ricotta and spinach** and topped with vegetables, tagliatelle with Sibillini truffle, **Abruzzo-style scrippelle 'mbusse** with pecorino, **lamb a scottadito**, or breaded and roast lamb, **sweet and sour rabbit** and sautéed vegetables. The menu changes in summer to include fresher, lighter dishes: strozzapreti with green tomatoes, home-made pizzicotti (similar to ravioli) with tomatoes and basil, tagliatelle with vegetables. Second courses focus on excellent lamb dishes.
Finish the meal with syruped fruit or homemade puddings. The wine list is mostly regional labels.

OSTRA

38 KM WEST OF ANCONA

LA CANTINELLA

🔑 3-Star Hotel
Via Amendola 5
Tel. 071 68081
Fax 071 68290
E-mail: lacantinella@libero.it
Internet: www.lacantinella.net
Open all year round

Ostra is a nice little town with a medieval stamp to it which lies inland, a few kilometers from the popular beaches of Senigallia. The historic center is largely surrounded by the boundary wall with its nine towers. This small family run hotel isn't far from the historic area and was created in a completely restructured building from the Seventies. On the ground floor are two dining rooms, one in the hotel, the other 20 meters away; meals, at an average price of 30 euros excluding wine, offer local cuisine. The buffet breakfast includes sweet fare such as stuffed croissants, tarts and doughnuts, plus a good selection of savories, including cured meats, pork sausage and cheeses. A swimming pool has been available since last summer.

• 15 double and 6 triple rooms with bathroom, balcony, television • Prices: double room single use 34-40 euros, double 54-58, triple 70-74; breakfast 4 euros per person • Credit cards: all, Bancomat • Communal areas accessible to the mobility challenged, 3 rooms equipped for them. Off-road open air parking. No pets allowed. Reception from 8am to 12am • Bar, restaurant. Lounges. Conference room. Garden. Swimming pool

Il Covo

Trattoria
Via Colombo 32
Tel. 0734 933152
Closed Monday
Open: lunch and dinner
Holidays: variable
Seating: 30
Prices: 27-32 euros, wine excluded
All major credit cards

Locanda del Faro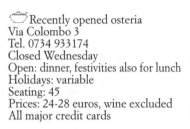

Recently opened osteria
Via Colombo 3
Tel. 0734 933174
Closed Wednesday
Open: dinner, festivities also for lunch
Holidays: variable
Seating: 45
Prices: 24-28 euros, wine excluded
All major credit cards

This honest sea-food trattoria in the village of Pedaso has become a landmark. Small-scale fishing has always been one of the main sources of income for local inhabitants and recently, in response to the problems threatening this livelihood, a cooperative was set up with the dual purpose of ensuring the safety of fishermen and the greatest transparency for consumers. Toto, the owner of Il Covo, buys his fish from this cooperative every day. The trattoria with its small, frill-free rooms, is managed with help from the family; it is only a short distance from the railway station, the sea front and the main road.
Sea-food salad, oysters and sea truffles, octopus salad with celery, **marinated anchovies**, sea squills, mussels and **lumachine in umido** provide a fine start to a meal that continues with first courses which are changed daily: **mezzemaniche** with octopus or **with squill and dill** flavored with mistrà Varnelli, **linguine with creamed anchovies** or blue fish pesto, conchiglie with cuttlefish and peas, pennette with scampi sauce, white chitarrine with mixed fish and risotti. The main courses, obviously, depend on the day's catch. Dishes may include **angler fish in guazzetto** (or baked with potatoes), baked sea bass (also in a potato crust), excellent **mixed grills** and mixed fried fish (zanchette, calamaretti, mullet, hake), cuttlefish and beetroot, at times (or if you book) the **brodetto** fish soup.
These fine meals are accompanied by several, essentially regional wines.

Just a few yards from Pedaso railway station, what was once the tiny jail in the Carabinieri barracks, is now home to the restaurant of Luigi Nocera, born in Campania but Marchigiano by adoption. In this small restaurant the vaulted ceilings help to create a warm, welcoming and comfortable atmosphere. The menu, that changes with the seasons and available products, is essentially local with occasional references to Neapolitan gastronomy superbly prepared by chef Pigi.
Antipasti and first courses are generally set for the day, while main courses and puddings offer more choice. Start with savory local **cured meats** accompanied by hot focaccia. Follow with tacchinella or pork salads with wild herbs, flans with ricotta and vegetables or escarole strudel. First courses include excellent home-made **lasagne with rabbit sauce** or (a Neapolitan dish) pork sauce, ricotta and crumbled boiled egg. Alternatively, try the scrigno di tagliatelle with wild boar, wrapped in Colonnata lardo. Only Gragnano, for the **dry pasta dishes** topped **with meatball sauce**, artichokes and potatoes, mushrooms and vegetables. The main courses include the classic **sautéed rabbit** with preserves in vinegar, black olives and capers, as well as guinea fowl with grapes and chestnuts and **shank of veal** or pork, roast or casseroled, always accompanied by seasonal vegetables. There is a good selection of local and other cheeses. Puddings include home-made dishes such as trifle, millefeuille and bavarese with chestnuts or oranges, as well as typical Neapolitan puddings like pastiera and babà.
The wine list (fairly priced) is extensive, with special emphasis on local labels.

PESARO
Santa Marina Alta

PESARO
Casteldimezzo

DA GENNARO

LA CANONICA

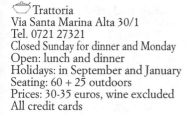

Trattoria
Via Santa Marina Alta 30/1
Tel. 0721 27321
Closed Sunday for dinner and Monday
Open: lunch and dinner
Holidays: in September and January
Seating: 60 + 25 outdoors
Prices: 30-35 euros, wine excluded
All credit cards

Recently opened osteria
Via Borgata 20
Tel. 0721 209017
Closed Monday
Open: dinner, festivities also for lunch
Holidays: January
Seating: 42 + 42 outdoors
Prices: 35 euros, wine excluded
All credit cards

Sitting at one of the few tables at this fish and seafood trattoria, located on the San Bartolo panoramic road climbing from Pesaro into the hills, guests are very conscious of how equable family management, polite, friendly service and the relationships that the owners enjoy every day with local fishermen make for an enjoyable meal without risking unpleasant surprises. The menu depends on the day's catch and follows the seasons with a distinct local character – on the border between the Marche and Romagna – tasty, appetizing, immediate and fresh.

Try starting with **boiled canocchie** with a dash of extra virgin olive oil, cod Catalan-style and mazzola, seafood salad with typical **Adriatic baby cuttlefish**, **clam and mussel soup**, **marinated anchovies** and calamaretti. But the other antipasti are equally good – very fresh scallops, tasty **lumachini (small snails) in a delicate guazzetto** and delicious crab. The first courses are plain but delightful: gnocchi with crustaceans, **tagliatelline with red fish sauce** and, especially, Adriatic sole, **tagliolini with seafood** and crustaceans, risotto. Main courses, always depending on the catch, focus on the characteristic **Adriatic arrostita**, as well as delicate mixed fried fish or (if you book at least one day in advance), the rich **brodetto**. Close with puddings such as tiramisù and home-made tarts.

The wines are mostly from the local area and region but are very carefully selected.

Isolated but still at the center of the world: the tiny home of the parish priest, in a tiny hamlet seemingly suspended over the Adriatic, is the attraction that takes us away from the coast to drive up the short, twisting road to the San Bartolo Regional Park. Quite apart from the peace and quiet, the fresh sea breeze and the beauty of the tiny square, guests find superb cuisine here. This is all due to Andrea Rignoli and Andrea Ventura who have combined fair prices, a courteous but informal welcome in the two small dining rooms and an impressive menu including both meat and fish, with opening times from mid-morning snacks to after-dinner drinks.

Everything is open to view – from the wine list selected through personal research to the list of suppliers helping to orchestrate the menu. Cuisine usually moves between restrained creativity and echoes of ancient recipes: **tortino of bread**, pears and pecorino, lasagne with fresh cep mushrooms, **fricassee of local lamb**, semifreddo with chestnuts, coffee and dates in the turf menu. The surf menu includes creamed beans with mullet and raw cep mushrooms, **fish sausage**, **baked canocchie**, marinated gray mullet with pumpkin and potatoes, **tagliolini with angler fish sauce**, slices of grilled tuna, chocolate pie with ginger ice-cream.

Three carefully chosen wines add 9 euro to the final bill. You can also get away with ordering just one prepared dish: **fried paranza**, with cured meats, **non-pasteurized cheese** or a pudding enjoyed with a glass of Passito wine.

PESARO

PETRITOLI

OASI SAN NICOLA

🔑 3-Star Hotel
Via San Nicola 8
Tel 0721 50849
Fax 0721 390428
E-mail: info@oasisannicola.it
Internet: www.oasisannicola.it
Open all year round

OSTERIA DE LE CORNACCHIE

🍲 Traditional osteria
Via del Forno 10
Tel. 0734 658707
Closed Tuesday
Open: dinner, festivities in winter also for lunch
Holidays: variable
Seating: 70 + 10 outdoors
Prices: 20 euros
All credit cards, Bancomat

Once a thirteenth century monastery (the surviving church continues to function even today), the Oasi San Nicola is in a fortunate position between the hills and the sea, a few minutes from the center of Pesaro, but far from all the chaos and noise. The furniture of the rooms and of the big communal spaces is warm and elegant, the management highly professional. You can stop in one of the beautiful historic rooms, take a stroll in the park, or have a swim in the pool. In summer time guests can use stretches of sandy beach a few kilometers away (shuttle available on request). The buffet breakfast served from 7.30 to 10.30, includes coffee, milk, croissants, fruit, yoghurt. The restaurant, also equipped for banquets and receptions, offers traditional menus at 20 euros excluding wines; half board costs 50-70 euros, full board 55-75 per person.

• 24 double rooms and 4 suites with bathroom, safe, satellite television, modem connection • Prices: double room single use 50-70 euros, double 70-90, suite 90-200, breakfast included • Credit cards: all, Bancomat • Facility partly accessible to the mobility challenged, 2 rooms equipped for them. Off-road parking. Small pets allowed. Reception open 24 hours a day • Bar, restaurant. Reading room. Conference room, Park, garden. Swimming pool, sports field. Beach

In the historic center of Petritoli, pass through a small arch overlooking the Aso Valley and enter Sergio Federici's osteria. On summer evenings, a few tables outside ensure you will dine in the fresh breeze from the valley. Inside, the small room has large barrel vaults where rural tools hang together with aging cured meats. There is also a corner fireplace, wooden benches and shared tables – already set with a fine selection of **cured meats**, including lonza and lonzino, ciauscolo, larded salami and liver sausage which guests themselves can slice up! Antipasti also include **tripe with tomatoes** and mushrooms mixed with scrambled eggs, together with several side plates such as wild chicory with potatoes, **beans 'ngreccie** (boiled and flavored with a mint sauce), creamy beans. There is also a seasoned, sapid and spicy pecorino.

The menu – unless otherwise agreed when booking, normally set by the owner – continues with a tasty **polenta with sauce and spare ribs**, sometimes followed by gnocchi or pasta with a traditional meat sauce. Main courses include **roast shank of veal**, very tender after long cooking and highly aromatic, while meals close with rustic sweets like ciambelloni and tarts.

Only the local house table wine is served. Don't miss a taste of the famous mistrà (anise liqueur), made by the owner on the basis of the traditional recipe or aromatized with ruta, a wild rock herb with digestive properties.

PORTO SAN GIORGIO

PORTO SANT'ELPIDIO

69 KM NORTH-EAST OF ASCOLI PICENO SS 4 AND SS 16 OR A 14

69 KM NORTH-EAST OF ASCOLI PICENO SS 4 AND SS 16 OR A 14

DAMIANI E ROSSI

PAPILLON

Trattoria
Via della Misericordia 7
Tel. 0734 674401
Closed Monday and Tuesday
Open: dinner, on festivities also for lunch
Holidays: January
Seating: 50 + 70 outdoors
Prices: 35 euro, wine excluded
No credit cards accepted

Restaurant
Viale Trieste 1
Tel. 0734 900203
Closed Monday
Open: lunch and dinner
Holidays: January
Seating: 60 + 20 outdoors
Prices: 35 euros, wine excluded
All major credit cards, Bancomat

Although far from the stereotypical checkered table-cloths, carafes of house wine and set menus every day, Aurelio Damiani has achieved a modern interpretation of the essence of the trattoria. While the past is reflected in the diverse clientele – young couples and families, for example – and the limited menu, the difference lies in the sensitivity of a chef who has prepared delicious dishes for twenty-five years.

Seasonal and local produce are used with great skill in lighter versions of traditional preparations. This balanced creativity is set off by the passion that the owner communicates to clients: wine, cheese, cured meats, mushrooms and truffles. The short menu or the set menu (six dishes at 35 euros) include: sweet and sour breast of duck with citrus fruit, **pumpkin flowers with a sapa** sauce, broccoli flan in anchovy sauce, winter **soup with tripe and marjoram**, semolino gnocchi with cherry tomatoes, wild herbs and guanciale, **paccheri with rabbit** flavored with thyme, summer maccheroncini with eggplant, fresh tomatoes and basil. Other excellent dishes include **mixed fried fish all'ascolana, saddle of rabbit in porchetta, suckling pig stuffed with sweetbread** and black truffle, Sibillini veal with truffle, porchetta baked in a wood oven. Lastly, the noteworthy **cheese board** and home-made jams (the one made from soft Ascoli olives is a personal invention) or various cream and chocolate puddings.

The excellent and extensive wine list includes three wine "pairings" with the dishes of the day.

Bar Ciferi, Viale Don Minzoni 4 – excellent home-made ice cream.

On the sea-front at Porto Sant'Elpidio, the Papillon is an excellent example of what's new in catering on the Riviera. The restaurant is cool and bright and very close to the sea. The cuisine focus is on very fresh produce: fresh fish cleaned immediately and cooked quickly.

Try the **squid** (or cuttlefish) salad with steamed vegetables, steamed or gratin mullet with vegetables and tomato sauce, sautéed scampi or panocchie (sea squills), **sardines scottadito**, the very delicate **stuffed squid, tuna in porchetta** and wild fennel, accompanied by caponata di verdure. An excellent first course decision includes the proposal of inland Maceratese pasta, **tajulì Pelosi,** which elsewhere has practically disappeared from view. These tagliolini are made exclusively with water and flour and are ideal for delicate fish and vegetable condiments. Moreover, **spaghetti with creamed blue fish** or moscardini, **mezzemaniche** with squill and cherry tomatoes or **with red fish sauce** or sardines, fennel and cherry tomatoes. Main courses depend on the catch of the day but may include **turbot al tegame with potatoes**, pan-fried passera with potatoes and pendolini tomatoes, steamed or baked dory, **fried paranza**. Good puddings, such as crunchy almonds with creamed pistachio nuts.

Carefully chosen wines at fair prices. Prices may increase depending on what – and how much – diners select but are fair in relation to quality.

POTENZA PICENA

OSTERIA DEL VICOLO

🍲 Recently opened osteria
Via Battisti,1
Tel. 0733 672340
Closed Monday
Open: lunch and dinner
Holidays: variable
Seating: 35
Prices: 21-25 euros, wine excluded
All major credit cards, Bancomat

Riccardo Carestia is the prototype chef coming to the fore in a scenario where few young people have clear ideas: the generous daily set menu (the complete article includes samples of two main courses) focuses on simple dishes characterized by delicate pairings, top quality ingredients (home-made preserves in olive oil and bread), a very pleasant atmosphere, and last but not least, an excellent selection of wines at fair prices. The restaurant has two small communicating rooms plus a private room with a single table (on request when booking).
As for the food, bear in mind that the competitive prices of the two menus include dishes satisfying small and large appetites alike. A starter based on cured meats, possibly accompanied by pecorino made from non-pasteurized milk, and jam may be followed by: omelet with broccoli, **baked baccalà** in a vegetable guazzetto (or creamed with cress in a green sauce), cream of pumpkin with finferli mushrooms, broccoli flan with fondue, **turkey and fava beans in porchetta**, chicken terrine with cream of pumpkin and quail eggs. The two first course samples include ravioli with ricotta and cep mushrooms, **tagliatelle with duck sauce** or hare sauce. Main courses include **stuffed pigeon** and polenta, **grilled lamb**, fillet of veal in a curry sauce or fillet of pork in a sauce among the many red and white meat dishes. Diners can end the meal with a pudding – usually a single serving with several tastes: mousse of chestnuts or strawberries and baked cream, vanilla cream and jelly with wild fruit – and a selection of cheese.
Meals are accompanied by fine wines at fair prices or the reasonable house wine on tap.

RIPE

A CASA DI FABIO

🍲 Holiday farm
Via Matteotti 13
Tel. 071 7957107
Closed Wednesday and Saturday for lunch
Open: lunch and dinner
Holidays: variable
Seating: 50
Prices: 23-30 euros, wine excluded
All credit cards

Fabio Landi is, if nothing else, a food and wine freak. After lengthy tours taking in a plethora of Italian restaurants for pleasure and information, he decided to open his own place in October 2004. All fruit and vegetables are organically grown on his farm inland from Ancona, while the menu is virtually a showcase of the most authentic cuisine of the Marche region. Almost everything is cooked in the wood-fired oven or on the grill, looked after by Giovanni. Stefano and Alessio do the wines.
Meals start with home-made cured meats, omelets with seasonal vegetables, **porchetta** baked in the wood oven and **cheese pizza**. Depending on the season, first courses include **homemade** tagliatelle **with a typical meat** sauce (**meat and chicken**) or tomatoes, fresh ricotta and basil, **vincisgrassi** with meat sauce and truffle (in season), sauceless lasagna with vegetables, pasta with Savoy cabbage and speck, vegetable or legume soups; the carbonara is excellent. Main courses include casseroled (or roast) chicken with olives and capers, roast or jugged boar (from October), other game, **goose cooked in the wood oven** – one of the most classic festive dishes of the Marche countryside – **baked stoccafisso**, rabbit chasseur, tripe (if you book); not-to-be-missed – and one of the most frequently available dishes – is the fine **mixed grill with lamb**. Lastly homemade tarts, ciambellone and trifle.
The wine list includes some of the most interesting labels from the Marche and several major Italian reds.

SAN BENEDETTO DEL TRONTO

CASERMA GUELFA

🍲 Recently opened osteria
Via Caserma Guelfa 5
Tel. 0735 753900
Closed Monday
Open: lunch and dinner
Holidays: between August-September, during the fishing break
Seating: 65 + 35 outdoors
Prices: 35 euros, wine excluded
All credit cards

The ancient via Salaria, built to service the Roman troops on the Adriatic, terminated here, on the border between the Marche and Abruzzo. The former customs house has seen something of a gastronomic resurgence over the last ten years or so – fish cuisine distinctly inspired by sea-faring fishermen. This cult is interpreted by Federico Palestini, paragon of loyalty for purely biographical reasons: before opening this restaurant, he spent thirty years as a fisherman. Over and above the dining room and patio in the courtyard, "La Caserma" recently added an area which is used as a fish bar: from late afternoon, it is possible to nibble at molluscs and anchovies (preserved in salt in glass jars and, to a limited extent, also available for purchase) accompanied by a glass of wine.

Apart from the main menu (with detailed indications of the prices of every antipasto and not the entire series), it is also possible to opt for a 30 euro menu or another, more expensive menu with more variety and a greater quantity of fish. The main dishes include **mullet marinated** with olive oil, lemon and cipollotto, **sautéed calamaretti, mackerel in sauce** and olives with fish stuffing; **pasta** homemade by Federico's assistant is served **with angler fish pesto**, crustaceans or sea bass stuffings; fish such as turbot or angler fish are baked, boiled with vegetables, cooked in guazzetto, fried or roasted. **Fish brodetto** (soup) is available if you book.

Federico's son and fiancée serve at table, Marino looks after the fish bar and the young Japanese chef completes the personnel at La Caserma.

SAN BENEDETTO DEL TRONTO

33 KM NORTH-EAST OF ASCOLI PICENO SS 4 AND 16

DA VITTORIO

🔑 Rooms
Via della Liberazione 31
Tel. 0735 81114
Fax 0735 789199
E-mail: info@davittorio.net
Internet: www.davittorio.net
Open all year round

A brand new locanda completes the diversified catering complex (wine bar and fish restaurant with 900 labels on the list) conceived by Vittorio Cameli in a new San Benedetto del Tronto residential quarter, reachable from the center down via Silvio Pellico. The rooms, provided with all comforts (the minisuite can easily accommodate three people), are each distinguished by a prevalent color and personalized furnishings. Breakfast can also be personalized, sweet and/or savory, great attention paid to the raw materials.

• 3 double rooms and 1 minisuite, bathroom, air conditioning, mini-bar, television, modem connection • Prices: double room single use 80 euros, double 85, minisuite 100, breakfast included • Credit cards: all, Bancomat • Facility accessible to the mobility challenged. Off-road parking. Small pets allowed. Owners always contactable • Restaurant, wine bar. Portico, terrace

🍲 Vittorio and wife Licia offer one of the best fish menus on the Piceno coast at 50 euros a head excluding wine, while a lunch break at the wine bar will set you back about 15 euros.

LOCANDA DI PORTA ANTICA

Historic residence
Piazza Dante 8
Tel. 0735 595253-576632
Fax 0735 576631
E-mail: info@locandadiportaantica.it
Internet: www.locandadiportaantica.it
Open all year round

PROGRESSO

3-Star Hotel
Lungomare Trieste 40
Tel. 0735 83815
Fax 0735 83980
E-mail: info@hotelprogresso.it
Internet: www.hotelprogresso.it
Open all year round

In an old, out of the way little square, close to the thousand year old Torre dei Gualtieri, in the old town of San Benedetto del Tronto, there's this sixteenth century building whose façade has been embellished by portals of ancient travertine from Ascoli. Inside you will find the Locanda di Porta Antica, established in the early Nineties following the patient restoration work instigated by the husband and wife team Paolo and Annamaria Magni. Interiors are embellished by terracotta floors and late eighteenth century doors: the five big, sunny rooms are furnished with authentic antiques. Breakfast, served in the room, is rich and personalized, with homemade sweets and croissants coming straight from the pastry-shop; in a few rooms in the summer you can have breakfast on the terrace. Two free tickets for parking space are available for guests.

• 1 single and 4 double rooms with bathroom, safe, television, modem connection; 2 rooms with terrace • Prices: single 62 euros, double room single use 88, double 104, breakfast included • Credit cards: all except AE, Bancomat • Facility accessible to the mobility challenged, 1 room equipped for them. Public parking space close by. Small pets allowed. Owners always contactable

Apart from a little restoration work a few years ago, the hotel hangs on to the Art Nouveau appearance of when it was inaugurated in 1925. At that time it was right on the southern border of the town. Today viale Trieste – and this gives you some idea of how much San Benedetto grew in the twentieth century – is bang in the middle of the palm-lined promenade of this Marche resort, the most popular tourist attraction in the region. Big rooms with high ceilings, lounge and decent bar corner in a Fifties atmosphere, pleasant veranda on which to have lunch (seafood cuisine, about 20 euros excluding wines). Satisfactory buffet breakfast. Full board in double room (minimum 3 days, including beach service) 51-83, half board 47-78 euros. From this year a refreshment point has been set up by the sea.

• 2 single and 32 double rooms with bathroom, air conditioning, balcony, mini-bar, safe, satellite television, modem connection • Prices: single 47-60 euros, double 78-100 (15 euro supplement for extra bed), breakfast included • Credit cards: all, Bancomat • Facility accessible to the mobility challenged, 2 rooms equipped for them. Parking space available outside. Small pets allowed. Reception open 24 hours a day • bar, restaurant. Television room. Meeting room. Garden, patio. Beach

SAN BENEDETTO DEL TRONTO

33 KM NORTH-EAST OF ASCOLI PICENO SS 4 AND 16

TRE BICCHIERI

Wine bar-recently opened osteria
Via Todaro
Tel. 0735 84489
Closed Mondays
Open: lunch and dinner
Holidays: none
Seating: 40
Prices: 20-25 euros, wine excluded
All credit cards

Along the Adriatica State Road, just after the San Benedetto hospital driving south, a well-refurbished building is home to the creation of restaurateur Vittorio Cameli: the ground floor contains the historic restaurant with sea cuisine Da Vittorio, then four rooms on the first floor, while below, entering from Via Todaro, is the Tre Bicchieri wine bar. Here, the owner, helped by his son Marco, has created an informal atmosphere where – at fair prices – the excellent cellar sells wines from all over the world; wines are served by the glass and, last but not least, simple but delicious foods are on offer. In short, there is something of everything to attract a varied clientele, especially young people.

The small menu includes meat and fish, and dishes of the day described when ordering are often added. A few examples: marinated salmon and **anchovies**, sea-food salad, **soft Ascoli olives** stuffed in two versions (with meat or fish), fried olives, mixed bruschette, **local cured meats** of high quality with croutons. There is always a good selection of first courses: **potato gnocchetti** (homemade) **with white fish sauce**, **orecchiette with squid and broccoletti**, spaghetti alla carbonara. Main courses reflect local traditions: fish kebabs, generous portions of **fried squid**, **hake and zanchette**, **cuttlefish with peas**, mixed roast fish (sole, mazzolina, kebab and cuttlefish), grey mullet baked or with a salmoriglio sauce. Land dishes may include roast shank with potatoes, **rabbit in porchetta**, beans with pork rind. Puddings include several homemade cakes or pastries stuffed with cream.

SAN LEO

73 KM WEST OF PESARO

CASTELLO

2-Star Hotel
Piazza Dante 11-12
Tel. 0541 916214
Fax 0541 926926
E-mail: albergo-castello@libero.it
Internet: www.hotelristorantecastellosanleo.com
Holidays variable

The hotel run by the Sacchetti family lies at the heart of the San Leo quarter, in the beautiful piazza Dante which is surrounded by impressive buildings of historic interest. The building that houses the premises dates back to the sixteenth century and some of the rooms come with nineteenth century furniture. The rooms face either the square, the pre-Romanesque church or the valley of the Marecchia river. You can have breakfast in the bar or, when the weather's fine, in the patio out in the square. On offer are sweets and croissants, jams and bread, fruit juice and hot drinks. The restaurant holds a big room that can be used for conferences. An average meal costs around 20 euros excluding drinks. Apart from the center of San Leo, about a kilometer away you can visit the Sant'Igne monastery, founded by San Francesco.

• 9 double and 5 triple rooms or 4-bed rooms, bathroom, television • Prices: double room single use 45 euros, double 55-70, triple 65-80, with 4 beds 80-85, breakfast included • Credit cards: all, Bancomat • Free public parking at 50 meters. Small pets allowed (not in August). Owners contactable from 7.30am to 11pm • Bar, restaurant. Television room. Patio.

SAN LEO

73 KM WEST OF PESARO, 26 KM SOUTH-WEST OF RIMINI SP 258

LA ROCCA

🍲 Hotel restaurant
Via Leopardi 16
Tel. 0541 916241
Closed Monday, never from July15-September 15
Open: lunch and dinner
Holidays: December 9-25 and
January 8-February 3
Seating: 80
Prices: 30-35 euros, wine excluded
All credit cards except DC

San Leo, like so many history and art cities, does not always offer catering to match – and it is hard to understand the reason for such inadequacy, since good food and love of art go hand in hand, and both are included in the baggage of the cultured tourist. Such shortcomings, however, do not apply to this restaurant, located beneath the construction from which it takes its name: careful sourcing of ingredients, traditional dishes and a large wine list focusing on the Marche and Romagna regions ensure an enjoyable break while visiting the city that saw the last days of Count Cagliostro.
You will be welcomed into a dining room furnished with simplicity and offered a menu which changes with the seasons. Except for a dish named pasticciata alla Cagliostro and the vaguely devilish appearance of the chef, nothing in the atmosphere or the menu recalls the life of the unfortunate necromancer. Start with a selection of local **cured meats**, especially the Carpegna prosciutto dop, and various home-made preserves in olive oil. Then come **tortelloni** of San Leo– filled with beet, ricotta and Parmesan cheese – **with meat sauce**, **cappelletti in brodo**, tagliatelle with mushrooms or **passatelli with truffles**. Main courses – also seasonal – include **lamb with thyme** or Sangiovese red wine and ginger, local beef tagliata and pasticciata, a steamed dish seasoned with cloves. The **cheese** selection is very extensive. First and foremost, seasoned pecorino – which is also used in several dishes.
Close the meal with good puddings, such as the home-made tart with spelt flour, quince and figs, iced soufflé with fondant chocolate and a sauce of strawberries or vincotto (cooked wine).

SAN SEVERINO MARCHE

30 KM SOUTH-WEST OF MACERATA

DUE TORRI ☉

🍲 Hotel restaurant
Via San Francesco 21
Tel. 0733 645419
Closed Sunday for dinner and Monday
Open: lunch and dinner
Holidays: one week for Christmas, 20-30 June
Seating: 100
Prices: 28-30 euros, wine excluded
All credit cards

The lament for the demise of typical, local catering risks becoming a ragbag of commonplaces – tradition, territory, quality – which rarely give rise to any real changes in direction. Too often, owners seem to adopt an image or an idea without actually truly raising the profile of the territory and without making it clear what kind of clientele they are targeting. This restaurant in the medieval heart of San Severino, owned by the same family since 1932, forms an exception to this comment in the person of chef Paolo Severini, also a sommelier and a true admirer of tradition (he has the ideas and, more than that, he knows the facts); it is Paolo himself who selects the raw materials and ingredients from top quality small producers, such as local and Visso cured meats. These and other local specialties, as well as some interesting wine labels, are on sale in the Bottega dell'Africano next to the restaurant.
His wife Secondina Bellini works in the kitchen, preparing seasonal menus with substantial dishes which could never be accused of frivolity: omelet with truffles, **pappardelle with boar sauce**, canne d'organo filled with ricotta, tagliolini with wild pigeon sauce, **cicerchia soup**, chicken galantina, gran fritto with vegetables and meat, **snails in porchetta**, **roast pigeon** and, to close, sopravvissana ricotta tart, apple and walnut tart and cuore di latte with black cherries. Yet there's much more: if you like offal, don't miss the **salad with tripe** and preserves in olive oil, **roast head of lamb**, mutton coratella flavored with onion and lemon, quinto quarto of pork with fennel. The wine list is exclusively regional and table service is always courteous.

SANT'ANGELO IN VADO

PALAZZO BALDANI

3-Star Hotel
Via Mancini 4
Tel. 0722 818892-810101
Fax 0722 819322
E-mail: info@palazzobaldani.it
Internet: www.palazzobaldani.it
Open all year round

Palazzo Baldani, a plain building in neo-classical style, dates back to the end of the Eighteenth century; after a period of steady decline the building underwent meticulous refurbishment and the beauty of old times has been recaptured. The rooms, on two floors, are characterized by fine furnishings, and pastel shades dominate walls and fabrics. Breakfast offers a good variety of sweet and savory products and hot foods, all homemade. The same building contains the Taddeo e Federico restaurant, also run by Mario Beccari (a meal costs around 32 euros excluding wine). In summer tables are set in the building's internal courtyard. Bicycles are available to guests for excursions in the environs and there is also a wellness center with sauna.

• 2 single, 11 double rooms and 1 suite, bathroom, air conditioning, mini-bar, television, modem connection; 1 apartment with kitchenette (4 people) • Prices: single 50-60 euros, double 80-100, suite 100-120, apartment 120-180, breakfast included • Facility accessible to the mobility challenged, 1 room equipped. Free public parking. Small pets allowed. Managers always contactable • Bar, restaurant. Breakfast room, living rooms, reading room. Conference room. Indoor courtyard. Sauna

SASSOCORVARO

LA VINERIA RISTORANTE 2000

Restaurant-wine bar
Via Puccini 9
Tel. 0722 76274
No closing days
Open: lunch, dinner only on booking
Holidays: August
Seating: 120
Prices: 25-30 euros, wine excluded
All major credit cards

Two souls characterize this place: the space available is divided to ensure distinct separation between the restaurant as such and the wine bar, while the menu is characterized by simple dishes targeting a particular glass of wine chosen from the impressive list. The gastronomic boundaries of this osteria are less precise, since it is located where three regions meet: the Marche, Romagna and Tuscany.
Inspired by the best artisan producers of the environs, this is a fine example of the cross-influences already seen in the past, although dishes are more delicate and interpreted intelligently. **Crostolo with cured meats** – Carpegna and its renowned hams is close by, as well as the delicious Mercatale lardo – and cheese (ricotta, ambra di Talamello, fresh pecorino) join the delicate beef carpaccio or very fresh vegetable dishes such as eggplant timbale. **Cannelloni with ragù**, ravioli with ricotta and spinach or **tortellini in broth** are first courses prepared with great care and enhanced by the distinct flavor of fossa cheese. Main courses focus on meat: the best cuts are carefully and skillfully chosen and prepared as tagliate enhanced by Cartoceto extra virgin olive oil or baked in crusty bread. Not to mention **rabbit in porchetta**, **lamb cooked in wine** and, when available, jugged boar. Desserts are all homemade: fruit tarts, chocolate cake, ice cream and strawberries, trifle.
The wine list has personally selected labels, as well as some of the best known national names, with particular emphasis on central Italy. Service is young, timely and friendly.

SENIGALLIA

26 KM NORTH-WEST OF ANCONA SS 16 OR EXIT A 14

OSTERIA DEL TEATRO

🍲 Osteria with bar and food
Via Fratelli Bandiera 70
Tel. 071 60517
Closed Saturday for lunch and on Sunday
Open: lunch and dinner
Holidays: 115 days in June
Seating: 50 + 20 outdoors
Prices: 20-30 euros, wine excluded
All credit cards, Bancomat

SENIGALLIA
Cesano

26 KM NORTH-WEST OF ANCONA SS 16 OR EXIT A 14

PONGETTI

🍲 Trattoria
Strada Statale Adriatica Nord 94
Tel. 071 660064
Closed Monday and Tuesday
Open: lunch and dinner
Holidays: 3 weeks in January
Seating: 60
Prices: 35 euros, wine excluded
All credit cards, Bancomat

The assortment of wines and cheeses are the main attraction of this osteria near the Teatro la Fenice. And there are also hot dishes, changed every week, with special emphasis on seasonal produce. Marco Pasqualini and Caterina Pajalunga go for the complete service: from simple a aperitif to evening snacks accompanied by a fine glass of wine, to full dinners.
Start with croutons with scamorza and Parma ham, local pork guanciale, lardo di Colonnata or Alto Adige speck with rye bread, then taste the sautéed seasonal vegetables or **local cured meats** from small producers, perhaps served with piadina. The menu always includes two first courses with homemade pasta: such as **cresc' tajat** (a kind of maltagliati) **with tomatoes and lardo**, **pappardelle with rabbit sauce** and fresh tomatoes, gnocchetti with various condiments, **legume soups** in winter, pasta with vegetables in summer. Main courses always include beef tagliata and **veal in tuna sauce**. Otherwise, try the seasonal **cheeses** from all over Europe and every Italian region. Special mention can be made of local pecorino varieties made from non-pasteurized milk as well as goat and cow cheeses from French and pecorino from Spain. Lastly, puddings include semifreddi, cream sfogliatine, syruped fruit with ice cream.
As we mentioned, one of the main attractions of this osteria is its wine list: more than 100 labels are available, with a fine showcase of the best local wines alongside numerous wines from other regions.

Driving north on State Road 16, before reaching the Cesano suburb of Senigallia, we come to the Pongetti where the name restaurant in reality hides the atmosphere and style typical of a trattoria. Family management (the mother, even after sixty years in the kitchen, still cooks the food), homemade pasta, efficient service, a simple environment and evident professionalism and conscientiousness are all the hallmarks of a true trattoria. The menu focuses on fresh fish, prepared in a simple manner, cutting a fine line between middle-class city cuisine and the popular seafood tradition. Cold antipasti include **boiled canocchie**, seafood salad with squid, cuttlefish and preserves in olive oil, scampi and prawns of incomparable freshness. The hot antipasti include sautéed mussels and clams and **steamed sea snails** flavored with wild fennel. First courses include consolidated classics: home-made tagliatelle with clams, risotto alla marinara, **tagliatelle with angler fish**, Gragnano spaghetti with scampi and clams. Main courses always include **mixed fry of paranza**, as well as grilled and boiled fish, all prepared from the catch of the day. Close with panna cotta, crema catalana or the industrial puddings that are available.
The wine list – essentially whites – is limited but well-chosen, with labels matching the dishes. The price of a meal is at the upper limit set for this Guide but, as we all know, there are no standard prices for fish.

SERRA DE' CONTI

COQUUS FORNACIS

☞Restaurant
Via Fornace 7
Tel. 0731 878096
Closed Manday and Tuesday
Open: lunch and dinner
Holidays: variable
Seating: 60
Prices: 30-33 euros, wine excluded
All credit cards, Bancomat

A superbly intelligent restoration of industrial archeology has saved from ruin and neglect a splendid kiln on the road from Serra de' Conti to Arcevia. In one of the buildings belonging to the complex, Marco Giacomelli – an experienced chef – has set up a bright restaurant on the ground floor and a locanda with several rooms on the first. Modern furnishing in minimalist style, with well-separated tables (some of which informally set in the American style), is joined by cuisine that truly raises the profile of local produce through finely interpreted traditional dishes.

At mid-day, the restaurant only serves brunch, combining various dishes – hot and cold – hallmarked by lightness and speed, but of impressive quality. In the evening, the menu offers around twenty dishes – in harmony with the seasons – including fantasy antipasti: chicken breast with herbs and spices, crostone with guanciola and sage in vinegar, Venus rice pie with melted Parmesan cheese. First courses are a triumph of tradition, with **cresc tajat in an unusual sauce**, **passatelli** with seasonal vegetables, **gnocchi with duck sauce**, ravioli with potatoes and asparagus and a rabbit sauce. The main courses include the classic **rabbit in porchetta**, perfumed lamb, **tagliata alla marchigiana** and quails in potacchio. Excellent puddings include almond millefeuille with mascarpone, apple sfogliata with sapa cream, trifle.

The wine list is essentially regional, with the best labels from the Marche.

SERRAPETRONA

LA CANTINELLA

☞Trattoria
Piazza Santa Maria 3
Tel. 0733 908112-908310
Closed Tuesday
Open: lunch, festivities and August also for dinner on booking
Holidays: variable
Seating: 80
Prices: 20-23 euros
All credit cards, Bancomat

Vernaccia di Serrapetrona (the first docg wine in the Marche region) – a sparkling red wine that is fermented repeatedly to ensure an unusually full fragrance – has made this small inland town not far from the Sibillini mountains famous. In a corner of the little square, a bar leads up to a large, warm and friendly dining room, where Adriano personally describes the dishes of the day inspired by tradition and local customs. The antipasti always include croutons with local cold cuts and cured meats – we especially recommend the soft **ciauscolo**. Tasty first courses include the traditional **tagliatelle with chicken giblet sauce**, ricotta ravioli with tomatoes or truffle, medallions of meat and spinach and **pappardelle with hare sauce**. The mixed grilled meat is generous and includes kebabs, pork and liver with bay leaf. The **fried lamb** and **jugged boar** are both excellent; moreover, if you book, Nadia and Roberta will prepare testarelle of roast lamb. Puddings include tiramisù, trifle and tozzetti accompanied by sweet Vernaccia.

The wine cellar has several regional labels but it is preferable to drink the local dry Vernaccia, ideal for the entire meal. The place opens for mid-morning snacks of which a roll and a glass of wine are the essential ingredients.

🍷 Just before entering the town (Via Colli 1), the Quacquarini pastry shop has Vernaccia ciambelle, anise tozzetti and exceptional torroni in fall and winter, as well as Vernaccia docg.

SERRAPETRONA
Borgiano

SERRA SAN QUIRICO

OSTERIA DEI BORGIA ⊘▮

LA PIANELLA

Traditional osteria
Via Cameraldo 3
Tel. 0733 905131
Closed Monday, in winter also on Tuesday
Open: only for dinner
Holidays: mid-June/first week in July
Seating: 60 + 60 outdoors
Prices: 18-25 euros, wine excluded
All credit cards

Restaurant
Via Gramsci 31
Tel. 0731 880054
Closed Monday
Open: lunch and dinner
Holidays: January
Seating: 50 + 20 outdoors
Prices: 28-33 euros, wine excluded
All credit cards

Borgiano, a piece of Serrapetrona over-looking the reservoir of the same name, does not have the benefit of a major trunk road in the vicinity but it is well worth making a detour to enjoy Stefania's cuisine and the warm welcome from Sandro and Maurizio in this osteria that, from the very first visual impact, smacks of excellent wine and superb food. We are still pleased with the intelligent idea of a single set menu – changed every week and on a seasonal basis – thanks to which you can enjoy – only in the evening, and only if you book – three antipasti, two first courses and one second course of impressive quality for just 17 euros. Alternatively, on Sunday afternoon, you can order tasty snacks based on local cured meats, selected **cheese**, home-made preserves in olive oil and bruschette.

We were served: cream of zucchini with robiola and fried bread, chicken strudel with capsicum peppers and spelt salad, eggplant alla parmigiana, **wholemeal tagliatelle** with fresh tomatoes, olives and capers, **braised shank of pork** cooked in Cònero red wine accompanied by green beans and baked potatoes. You might also be served pumpkin flowers with ricotta and fresh tomatoes, **spelt polentina with pork spare ribs** and wild fennel, a flan with zucchini and melted seasoned pecorino. Puddings (not included in the price of the set menu) include bavarese cake with coconut and pistachio sauce, white chocolate coffee mousse as well as the typical lattacciolo.

The wine list, with reasonable mark-ups and also served by the glass, includes many regional labels and a good selection of national products.

Furnished in a pleasing country style, the restaurant is surrounded by pine woods that in the 1960s were home to a well-known summer dance hall. Raul Ballerini's cuisine, to some extent unique in the panorama of regional cooking, upholds seasonal produce and local traditions – and the chef uses his expert eye to pick wild mushrooms and aromatic herbs. Raul is a true connoisseur of the surrounding mountains and knows exactly when and where to find his ingredients, which he selects and cooks with great skill.

The menu usually opens with **crescia** accompanied by cured meats and fresh vegetables, homemade preserves in olive oil or vinegar, followed by homemade pasta such as **tagliatelle, with a traditional meat sauce** or mushrooms, **gnaccheragatti** (semola pasta, chestnut flour and water) **with cicerchia and potatoes**, gnocchi with seasoned pecorino, **risotto with silene herb**, tortelli with borage and tagliolini with cep mushrooms. For the main course, try **guanciale** of veal **braised with Cònero red wine, shank of pork**, lamb with mint or suckling pig with fennel. All meat dishes are accompanied by seasonal vegetables, especially **fava beans in porchetta** and various kinds of mushroom – when in season, don't miss the char-grilled cep mushrooms.

Puddings are homemade and the house wine is joined by valid regional labels. Service is attentive and courteous, enlivened by Raul's enthusiastic and cultured descriptions.

SERRA SAN QUIRICO

LE COPERTELLE

Restaurant with rooms
Via Leopardi 3 A
Tel. 0731 86691
Closed Tuesday, never in summer
Open: lunch and dinner
Holidays: none
Seating: 70 + 30 outdoors
Prices: 25-30 euros, wine excluded
All credit cards

We are in the foothills of Verdicchio dei Castelli di Jesi, almost on the border with the territory where the other Verdicchio – Matelica – is produced. The restaurant has a few rooms and takes its name from the defensive passageways that still characterize the medieval walls of this well-preserved town. Located where the town begins, near the entrance arch to the piazza, the restaurant has four small, discreet and comfortable dining rooms. Combining local history and gastronomy is a matter of pride for Felice Orazi, who presents a menu worthy of being framed which includes, for example, the detailed description of the composition of **calcione**, the typical Easter sweet-savory dish made from flour, eggs, pecorino and lemon. It is perhaps perplexing at first taste but becomes utterly captivating as you progress.

Start the meal with good cured meats, crescia with herbs, **omelet with garlic and mentuccia** (a traditional Easter dish together with lamb livers); first courses include home-made **tagliatelle** with truffle or **mushrooms**, **legume soups**, tagliolini with Serra San Quirico lardo. **Roast kid** or lamb with aromatic herbs, **stuffed pigeon** and veal prepared in many different ways are occasionally joined by snails with wild fennel or **marchigiana veal tripe**. Close with the selection of local cheeses, fig lonzino and home-made puddings.

Good choice of regional wines with special emphasis on Verdicchio from the two production zones, Lacrima di Morro d'Alba and Vernaccia di Serrapetrona, as well as some carefully selected national labels.

SERRUNGARINA

DA LUISA

Restaurant
Via Roma 8
Tel. 0721 896120
Open from Monday to Friday for lunch,
Saturday for dinner and Sunday in winter
Holidays: between January and February
Seating: 50 + 30 outdoors
Prices: 22-27 euros, wine excluded
All credit cards

Has time come to a standstill (in a positive sense, of course) in this restaurant? This is the impression made by the bill which, unlike many other places, does not reflect the price increases that followed the introduction of the Euro. Yet – we think – for a bill to be reasonable is only a question of correct family management and careful monitoring of the budget. The impressive menu focuses almost exclusively on local cuisine enlivened by creative touches here and there; the wine list is short but prices are very competitive; last but not least, the puddings – evidently the chef's passion – include a selection of pastries worthy of a confectionery boutique in a big town.

On the evening when we dined in this restaurant, we were welcomed with a glass of Prosecco and an artichoke pie served as antipasti. The menu included omelet with croutons al guanciale, cream of onion and **tortelli with pigeon filling**, chickpeas and brusco bread, **cresc'taiat with chickpeas**, passatelli with melted seasoned cheese and cep mushrooms, **tacconi** (pasta made with bean flour and water) **with bacon and pendolini tomatoes**, gnocchi with meat sauce, **rabbit in porchetta**, **snails in guazzetto** flavored with fennel, guinea fowl with rosemary – all served in generous portions and accompanied by a variety of seasonal side dishes.

As already mentioned, there is an impressive list of puddings. We were treated to the debut of era buono, a semifreddo with white, milk and fondant chocolate. The name will be explained by one of the many waitresses ensuring delightful service in the dining room.

SERRUNGARINA
Bargni

SIROLO

VILLA FEDERICI

LOCANDA ROCCO

☛🔑Country house
Via Cartoceto 4
Tel. and fax 0721 891510
E-mail: info@villafederici.com
Internet: www.villafederici.com
Holidays variable

☛🔑3-Star Hotel
Via Torrione 1
Tel. e fax 071 9330558
E-mail: info@locandarocco.it
Internet: www.locandarocco.it
Open from April to December

"By all means prepare a room for me, so that my stay will bring me contentment and joy ..." So said Cardinal Ranuzzi in 1683, referring to the Villa dei Pini built by abbey Domenico Federici. After more than three centuries we find no change in the atmosphere of this historic dwelling, with its simply and practically furnished rooms; the management has changed though, Mirco has been replaced by Virginio Baldelli, helped by his wife and parents. Breakfast is excellent, everything is homemade, from the donuts to the tarts, cookies to jams and omelets; plus ricottas and local cured meats. Ask to have a look at the cellar and the various grottos it consists of and try the typical dishes from the area in one of the wicker-furnished lounges set up in the grounds.

This locanda, right in the heart of Sirolo, was built in 1300 on the ancient walls of the city above the entrance gate, to host wayfarers. Restructured in 1998, the rooms are comfortable, with nice wooden ceilings and stone floors, furnished with antique pieces alternating with modern detailing. Buffet breakfast includes hot and fresh drinks, with bread, sweets, cakes and jams, all homemade, as well as artisan-produced cured meats and cheeses. The beautiful Conero beaches – easily reachable by shuttle – are close by. On festivities and in August the double room price with breakfast rises from 145 to 150 euros.

• 4 double rooms and 1 suite with bathroom, suite with television • Prices: double room single use 60-75 euros, double 75-93 (37-46 euro supplement for extra bed), breakfast included • Credit cards: all, Bancomat • Off-road parking. Small pets allowed. Owners always contactable • Restaurant. Reading room and tv. Park

• 5 double and 2 triple rooms with bathroom, air conditioning, mini-bar, safe, satellite television • Prices: double single occupancy 100, double 115, triple 173 euro, breakfast included • Credit cards: the main ones, Bancomat • 1 room equipped for the mobility challenged. Private outside parking at 500 meters (1 space per room). Pets not admitted. Owners always contactable • Restaurant. Breakfast room, lounge. Terrace

🍲 The restaurant is of great interest. Seats 30 and the average price of a meal is 30 euros.

🍲 A small restaurant serving local fish dishes, revisited in a modern key (set menu 39-49 euros).

TREIA
Chiesanuova

VILLA CORTESE

🔑 Country house
Contrada Sterpare 32
Tel. 0733 216891-380 5197117
Fax 0733 215844
E-mail: info@villa-cortese.it
Internet: www.villa-cortese.it
Closed 15 days in January

Villa Cortese belonged to Count Pignotti in the late Eighteenth century, and he used it mainly for meetings and parties. Entirely renovated in the early Nineties, the complex, run by Ines Laubbichler and Robert Ortolani, now has three not particularly big rooms, elegantly finished. The terracotta floors and wooden beams stand out, and well restored period furniture alternates with modern pieces. Breakfast includes a wide choice of beverages, fresh fruit, jams, homemade cakes and tarts, eggs, cured meats and cheeses. The restaurant (no half board available) offers original dishes at an average price of 40 euros excluding. The cypress park and tall trees outside are very pleasant.

• 3 double rooms, with bathroom, tv • Prices: double single occupancy 45, double 70 euros; breakfast 5 euros per person • Credit cards: all, Bancomat • Communal areas available to the mobility challenged. Internal covered parking. Small pets accepted. Owners present till midnight • Restaurant. Park, veranda

URBANIA
Mulino della Ricavata

MULINO DELLA RICAVATA

🔑 Holiday farm
Via Porta Celle 51
Tel. and fax 0722 310326
E-mail: info@mulinodellaricavata.com
Internet: www.mulinodellaricavata.com
Open all year round

The mill on the banks of the river Metauro, restored in 1997, is nearly a thousand years old and is linked to the history of the dukes of Urbino (first Montefeltro, then Della Rovere), who had a hunting lodge, il Barco, on the other bank of the river. The complex is now a vacation farm run by Anna Faggi and her husband, helped by their daughter. There are four nice rooms, one of which, with mansard roof, can hold up to four guests; they all have a bathroom, but in the case of one of them you have to leave the room and go down a few steps to get to it. In the morning you can have coffee, milk, yoghurt, fruit, bread and homemade cakes. In the restaurant (open to non-residents provided they book, dinner 28 euros excluding wine), Anna uses ingredients 80% of which are organically cultivated.

• 4 double rooms, bathroom (1 close by) • Prices: double room single occupancy 40 euros, double 60-70 (10 euro supplement for extra bed), breakfast included • Credit cards: none • Off-road parking. Small pets allowed. Owners always contactable • Restaurant. Breakfast room, living room. Garden.

URBANIA

OSTERIA DEL CUCCO

Traditional osteria
Via Betto de' Medici 8
Tel. 0722 317412
Closed Monday
Open: lunch and dinner
Holidays: in February and in June
Seating: 24
Prices: 35 euros, wine excluded
No credit cards accepted

The Cucco in the name of the osteria is in fact Dodi, who gives us a truly friendly welcome before serving up her sublime dishes. It is her job in fact to look after the kitchen and the cozy dining room which is open for both lunch and dinner. You will find here the atmosphere of an old osteria, with long benches instead of chairs, just three large, plainly set tables, which you share with other diners, photos, paintings and decorations including the typical tools of country culture.
Together with her aunt, Dodi prepares bread using local organic flour. This bread accompanies delicious antipasti: **fava bean salad**, zucchini and santoreggia, cow's cheese with vegetal rennet, polentina with truffle, crostatina di ratatuia, baked crespelle with ricotta and mint, and various omelets with seasonal vegetables. Homemade pasta is traditional but sometimes includes creative condiments and fillings: special mention must be given to **ravioli**, passerotti (pasta filled with ricotta and wild herbs), **tagliolini with wild fennel, bread crumbs and tomatoes**. Meat dishes are essentially white, such as **rabbit** (served on or off the bone) **in porchetta** or cooked with favas, guinea fowl with juniper and **sautéed spatchcock**. Puddings are all homemade: we would also mention the vanilla cake, sour cherry cream and cassata with candied citron.
Meals are accompanied by a local, organic house wine as well as several regional labels.

URBANIA
Pieve del Colle

PIEVE DEL COLLE

Holiday farm
Località Pieve del Colle 1
Tel. 0722 317945-347 9144820
Fax 0722 317945
E-mail: info@pievedelcolle.com
Internet: www.pievedelcolle.com
Open all year round

The nice stone complex was built in 1734 by the Dean of San Severo as a home for the parish's tenant farmer. The estate is now cultivated – cereals but also olives, vines and organic vegetables – by the Silvestrini family, which has restored the farm to its former glory, assigning part of it to farm tourism. Isabella welcomes you, her mother Ave Torcolacci looks after the kitchen (a meal 12-25 euros, excluding wine). Beam ceilings and terracotta floors give warmth to the two dining rooms and the rooms themselves, which are big, well furnished and have independent heating. Breakfast includes coffee, milk, bread and homemade sweets and jams. On the farm a museum to the threshing season has been set up, a moment in the farming calendar that the vacation farm still celebrates in August with a goose menu. Some of the farm products are on sale.

• 5 double rooms with bathroom, television; 1 apartment (4 people) with kitchen • Prices: double rooms single occupancy 40 euros, double 60 (15 euro supplement for extra bed), breakfast included; apartment 104 euros; breakfast 5 euros per person • Credit cards: major ones, Bancomat • Restaurant accessible to the mobility challenged, apartment equipped. Off-road parking. Small pets allowed. Owners always contactable • Restaurant. Living room

URBINO
Gadana

VISSO

CA' ANDREANA ⊗

Holiday farm
Via Gadana 119
Tel. 0722 327845
Closed Monday
Open: dinner, lunch on booking
Holidays: January-February
Seating: 32
Prices: 25-30 euros, wine excluded
All credit cards

DA RICHETTA

Trattoria
Piazza Garibaldi 7
Tel. 0737 9339
Closed Monday
Open: lunch and dinner
Holidays: between September and October
Seating: 50
Prices: 22-27 euros, wine excluded
All credit cards

The Gadana area, outside Urbino, on the road from San Marino to Rimini, offers a beautiful landscape that, in certain respects, recalls the backgrounds of many Renaissance paintings: woods, fields, hamlets and isolated farms. One such, superbly renovated and set in the lush green of the Urbino countryside, is Ca' Andreana – now a vacation farm. The welcoming rooms have essential, well-chosen furnishings which create a pleasant, family atmosphere. Cuisine is essentially local, with extensive, skillful use of wild, aromatic herbs (basil, nettle, borage, field herb, fennel/dill, asparagus) and a delicate use of condiments. On our visit, we enjoyed the springtime menu which included ricotta flan with melted cheese and saffron, **cappelletti in brodo** (a cult dish in this area and served every day), ravioli filled with ricotta and nettle, **roast leg of suckling pig** with apple sauce, medallions of **rabbit in porchetta**, local beef tagliata, guinea fowl in balsamic vinegar, grilled vegetables or mixed field herbs. Puddings include tarts, moresca tart with chocolate, coffee and toasted dry fruit, apple pie and baked cream.
There is a huge selection of **cheeses**, many of which produced locally; the wine list is balanced in its selections and prices. In summer, we recommend dining outdoors, in the refreshing shade of the perfumed wisteria.

Via Gadana 114, Ca' Bianchino farm: organic, free-range rearing of cinta di Siena pigs and production of meat/cured meats. Urs Abderhalden, Località **Montecalende** 73 (6 km): excellent, small-scale production of natural and caciotte goat's cheese.

The now historic Richetta's, managed today by Orazio Blanchi, is a not-to-be-missed stop-off serving the typical cuisine of the Upper Macerata. Friendly service, more or less original furnishings and typical Sibillini mountain cuisine ensure the typical enchantment of the 1950s trattoria.
Antipasti include typical cured meats – especially local ciauscolo and ham – Visso pecorino and caciotta cheese with black olives and preserves in olive oil. The list of first courses is an authentic summary of the history of the place: **spaghetti alla carbonara** or **all'amatriciana** (white and tomato versions), **cappelletti with sauce**, tagliatelle with cep mushrooms, **vincisgrassi**, baked cannelloni and sometimes lentil soup. The main courses focus on local meat: **lamb** – grilled, fried or alla Richetta (sautéed) – **Sibillini mutton**, slices of veal or beef and mixed grills of pork, lamb and mutton (costarella, sausage and fegatello). The menu also includes a number of side dishes and a limited choice of puddings, such as tozzetti served with Moscato di Pantelleria. For just a few euros more – even so the bill rarely exceeds 30 euros, wine included – you can enjoy dishes like tagliatelle, eggs and omelets flavored with **Norcia black truffle**.
The wine list reflects the character of the typical trattoria: a few labels at fair prices and a selection of quality bottles. Booking is advisable, especially for Sunday lunch when two shifts are the rule.

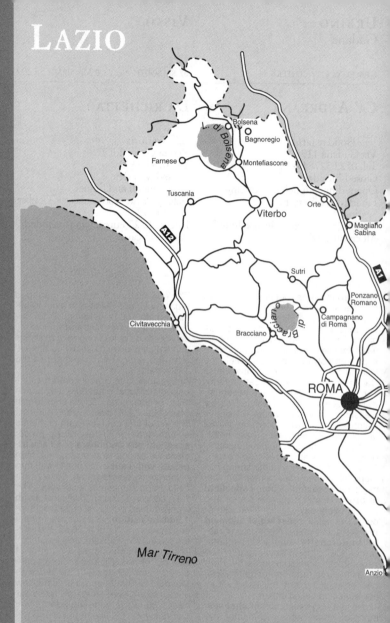

LAZIO

Lago di Bolsena
Bolsena
Bagnoregio
Farnese
Montefiascone
Tuscania
Viterbo
Orte
Magliano Sabina
A12
Sutri
Ponzano Romano
Civitavecchia
L. di Bracciano
Campagnano di Roma
Bracciano
A1
ROMA
Mar Tirreno
Anzio

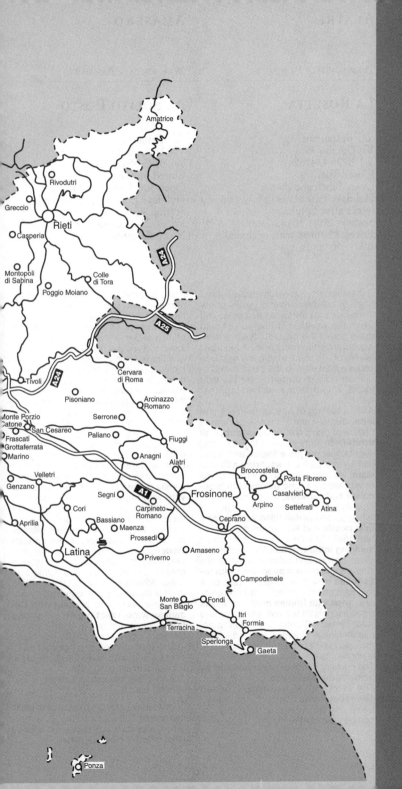

ALATRI

LA ROSETTA

Restaurant
Via Duomo 39
Tel. 0775 434568
Closed Tuesday
Open. lunch and dinner
Holidays: two weeks in July, two
weeks after Epiphany
Seating: 120 + 30 outdoors
Prices: 25 euros, wine excluded
All credit cards

This traditional, family-run restaurant has
been situated for about 50 years under
the immense, pre-Roman acropolis, and
when the weather is fine you should
make use of the beautiful terrace looking out over the roofs and historic bell
towers of the town. Mauro will help you
choose from among the traditional Ciociarian dishes prepared by his wife
Paola, who runs the kitchen together
with Rita.

After a tasting of little appetizers and
local cured meats, there's an ample
choice of good first courses: **zuppa di
urtuti** (with eight kinds of legumes and
vegetables), **sagne e fagioli** and fresh,
homemade pasta: **maccaruni alla ciociara**, fettuccine with porcini mushrooms
or with lemon, **sagne pelose with broccoletti and sausage**, mazzacrocchi with
chicory and basil salsa verde, gnocchi
with ragù and **ravioli filled with sheep's
milk ricotta and Roman mint** with fresh
tomatoes. To follow there's the classic
suckling lamb a scottadito; rabbit with
olives, capers and sultanas; chicken alla
ciociara; **coratella d'abbacchio with artichokes** or with Alatri red onions, pork
loin saccottino with provola and radicchio; **tripe with Roman mint**; and **snails**
(in season) with tomato, wild mint and
wild fennel. Ricotta and fruit pies,
ciambelline al vino and, around Christmas, an excellent pampepato, constitute
a worthy finale.

The culinary offerings are completed by
homemade ratafià and local liqueurs.
The selection of reasonably priced
"everyday" wines correctly prioritizes
Lazio and provides a satisfactory accompaniment to the food.

AMASENO

AL SOLITO POSTO

Restaurant
Via Auricola 8 A
Tel. 0775 65428
Closed Monday
Open. lunch and dinner
Holidays: first week of September
Seating: 40 + 30 outdoors
Prices: 21-23 euros, wine excluded
No credit cards

If you exit the autostrada at Frosinone
and continue towards Latina, driving
through fields filled with buffalos, you'll
come across Amaseno, the splendid
church of Santa Maria rising above the
town roofs. Follow the signs for Auricola,
and finally for the restaurant, a few kilometers beyond the little village. Outside
there's an elegant pergola, to be used
during the long summer, and inside
three small, attractive dining rooms.

In the kitchen, Cinzia prepares simple
and authentic dishes which make the
most of seasonally changing ingredients
from local farms. Homemade bread,
often made with walnuts, olives, rye or
corn, will be brought as soon as you sit
down. Then start with the **stuffed mozzarella di bufala** or the **fava bean puree
with wild fennel**, savory pies, sautéed
vegetables and locally made cured
meats. To follow, simple but tasty first
courses: **tagliolini with chicken giblets**,
**ravioli filled with ricotta and squash
flowers**, potato gnocchi with pine nuts
and shallots and seasonal vegetable
pappardelle with saffron and buffalo bresaola. Among the main courses **buffalo
meat** is always present, prepared in various ways, as well as **brasato with Cesanese wine**, **roast piglet** and **spring
lamb** with potatoes and artichokes.
Desserts include sour-cherry pie, buffalo's-milk-ricotta torta, ginger biscuits,
ciambelline with wine, fruit mousse,
tiramisù and zuppa inglese.

The short but interesting wine list is reasonably priced.

In **Patrica** (23 km) on the SS 156 Monti
Lepini at km 9, the Cooperativa Stella offers
Ciociaria mozzarella di bufala and different
kinds of buffalo meat and salumi.

AMATRICE
Conca

ANAGNI

PICCOLO LAGO

LO SCHIAFFO

Holiday farm
Località Conca
Tel. 0746821041-339 5721978
E-mail: scandarello@mail.inet.it
Internet: www.lagoscandarello.com
Open all year

Restaurant
Corso Vittorio Emanuele 270
Tel. 0775 739148
Closed Monday
Open: lunch and dinner
Holidays: last week of July
Seating: 60
Prices: 32-35 euros, wine excluded
All credit cards

This facility, managed by the Rosati family, is in Conca, a village on the banks of Lake Scandarello near Amatrice. Hospitality is offered in various buildings: the recently renovated farmhouse dating from 1870 that has rooms for rent, a more recent stone building with rooms and apartments (B&B), and a newly-built villa (the actual vacation farm) that can accommodate up to six people. There's also a small restaurant under separate management that's open to non-residents. The buffet breakfast is set out in communal rooms in the room rental and B&B buildings, though on request you can have room service. There's a small organized bathing-beach on the lake that guests are free to use.

• 1 single and 7 double rooms, 1 suite and 6 apartments (2-4 persons), with bathroom; some apartments with kitchen • Prices: double room single occupancy 50-70 euros, double 70-90, breakfast included; 4-person apartment 95-105 euros, breakfast 3 euros per person • Credit cards: Visa, MC, Bancomat • 1 room designed for use by the mobility challenged. Off-street parking. No pets allowed. Owners always present. • Reading and TV room. Gardens. Beach

The name of this restaurant, located in the historic center of Anagni near the Romanesque cathedral and the Palazzo dei Papi, recalls an infamous affront against Pope Boniface VIII, when he received a slap (schiaffo) from the French king's soldiers. Its premises, recently renovated and enlarged, are simply decorated and well-kept, giving the restaurant a pleasant ambience.

The chef-owner, Guido Tagliaboschi, is skilled at interpreting Anagni's culinary traditions, using local ingredients and creating seasonal menus, and shows a tendency to interpret rustic recipes with a gentle creativity. There's an ample choice of antipasti to start: carpaccio of buffalo and wild Priverno artichokes, squash flowers stuffed with favas and pecorino, eggplant millefeuille, caciotto primo sale and gratinéed tomatoes, **salt cod and potato timbale with pecorino romano**. Then the excellent first courses, such as cannoli of Ciociaria fini-fini with ricotta and Campoli truffles; ravioli with mozzarella di bufala; **zuppa of dried tomatoes, Atina cannellini beans and chicory**; and wild-herb maltagliati with asparagus, buffalo speck and goat's milk cheese. Mains include **rack of local lamb with herbs** and a potato flan, the **deboned rabbit with wild fennel**, beef tagliata with Cesanese del Piglio sauce, **grilled salt cod** with sautéed potatoes and **guinea fowl in porchetta** with chestnuts and Marsala sauce. Bread gelato, ricotta torte and tiramisù with berries provide a happy finish to the meal.

The mark-ups on the excellent wine list are very reasonable.

APRILIA

DA ELENA

🍲 Restaurant
Via Matteotti 14
Tel. 06 92704098
Closed Sunday
Open. lunch and dinner
Holidays in August
Seating: 40
Prices: 33-35 euros, wine excluded
All credit cards except AE, Bancomat

Like many cities of the Agro Pontino (the reclaimed Pontine marshes), Aprilia doesn't have much history, and as such, not many long-standing culinary traditions either. In the past the local cuisine has been very influenced by recipes from regions such as the Veneto or the Marches, from where many of the settlers arrived during the Fascist era. This is the case with Silvano Favero, whose family (orginally from the Veneto) has owned this restaurant for over 50 years. However after all those years Lazio has left its own indelible mark, as is evident from the menu.
After a tasting of antipasti – tasty battered, fried vegetables, mozzarella di bufala and sheep's milk ricottina sourced from local shepherds, typical castelli Romani cured meats – come the unmissable dishes of the local cuisine: **pasta e fagioli** enriched (in the right season) with mushrooms or truffles, **rigatoni with oxtail alla vaccinara**, **bucatini all'amatriciana** and **chickpea and lentil zuppa** with wild greens. Among the main courses we would note the abbacchio alla cacciatora and the **suckling pig in porchetta**, as well as the **fried fish di paranza** and the **involtini of swordfish**, fished from the nearby sea at Anzio. Finish with good homemade desserts and ciambelline al vino.
Silvano's sons and Silvana the sommelier will help you choose the right wine to pair with your food, choosing from an careful list focussed on local wineries.

🍷🍴 Marco Davi's enoteca perBacco, via Marconi 8, for wines and spirits to taste and buy. The cold and hot plates offered as accompaniments are steadily improving.

ARCINAZZO ROMANO
Altipiani di Arcinazzo

DA SILVANA

🍲 Trattoria
Via Sublacense (at the turn for Piglio)
Tel. 0775 598002
Closed Tuesday
Open: lunch only, dinner also in the summer
Holidays: none
Seats: 80 + 20 outdoors
Prices: 20-25 euros excluding wine
All credit cards except for DC, Bancomat

Set among the grassy meadows and ancient forests of the beautiful Altipiani Arcinazzo, this family-run trattoria is housed in an early-20th-century farmhouse. The atmosphere is warm and welcoming, and mamma Silvana's cooking is pure and authentic. Her daughter Giovanna, courteous and professional, will guide you through the menu and wine list.
Begin with a tasting of local cheeses and cured meats: Guarcino prosciutto, smoked guanciale with balsamic vinegar and salumi made with venison or wild boar. Move on to **fettuccine with ragù**, **strozzapreti with porcini mushrooms**, gnocchi with Pachino tomatoes and pecorino romano, **pasta e fagioli**, or if you're really hungry, "piatto unico della nonna", a dish of white polenta, wine-braised beef, pallocco (a small, sweet, local chicory) and ciabattoni (typical large white beans). Among the main dishes Silvana's specialty is **rabbit alla cacciatora**, but you could also opt for the lamb chops a scottadito, the baked veal roll, **chine of pork with Cesanese wine**, or various dishes with **snails**, when they're in season. There's a good selection of local cheeses to finish – there's always gran cacio Morolo and Amaseno marzolina – as well as homemade desserts such as fruit pies and cakes, small cookies and ice cream in flavors like chestnut or fior di latte with rose.
The wine list is well chosen, primarily centered on the surrounding area, and there's also a special coffee list, with different kinds of arabica and robusta.

🍷 In **Affile** (10 km) the Azienda Elis, Via Santa Croce 11, sells organically raised snails.

ARPINO

CAVALIER D'ARPINO

☞—◑3-Star Hotel
Via Vittoria Colonna 21
Tel. e fax 0776 850060-849348
E-mail: info@cavalierdarpino.it
Internet: www.cavalierdarpino.it
Closed 15 days in November

32 KM EAST OF FROSINONE

In the River Liri valley, just two kilometers separate Arpino, an ancient medieval village, from the hamlet of Civitavecchia, the imposing stone walls of which guard traces of Volsci, Samnite and Roman civilizations. Here, in a former 19ᵗʰ-century wool factory that's been completely renovated, is a hotel surrounded by grounds with palms and age-old trees. The rooms on the three upper floors are functional and fitted with arte povera furniture. On the ground floor are two large dining rooms (half board ranges from 45-57 euros, full board, from 55-68 euros per person), which are also used for meetings and conferences. Buffet breakfast is set out there and among other things includes homemade cakes baked using typical local products.

• 3 single and 25 double rooms, with bathroom, air-conditioning, mini-bar, safe, TV • Prices: single 34-55 euros, double 50-85 (25 euro supplement for extra bed), breakfast included • Credit cards: all, Bancomat • Facility accessible to the mobility challenged. Off-street parking. No pets allowed. Reception open from 6.30 am to 1 am, owners always reachable. • Restaurant. Conference room. Grounds

BAGNOREGIO
Buonasera

BUONASERA

☞—◑Holiday farm
Località Buonasera 18
Tel. 0761 792397-349 3513581
Fax 0761 792397
E-mail: info@agribuonasera.com
Internet: www.agribuonasera.com
Open all year

30 KM NORTH OF VITERBO

This seven-hectare farm is just a few kilometers from Civita di Bagnoregio, a beautiful medieval village in the peaceful setting of the Carbonara reserve. The vacation farm is in an old stone farmhouse surrounded by a beautiful enclosed garden and has been refurbished, while respecting the original architectural style. The rooms are pleasant and fitted with stylish furniture. And in addition, if you are planning to stay for at least two nights, there are two small apartments available, with a jacuzzi, refrigerator and TV. In the morning Stefano Agugliaro and his wife Stella, who live in the farmhouse, will offer you doughnuts, tarts, honey and jams or, on request, a continental breakfast. If you wish there's a half board option; this way you'll get to eat in their little restaurant that uses products they grow themselves and animals raised on the farm. Not very far away is Lake Bolsena, Europe's largest volcanic lake

• 4 double, 1 triple rooms and 2 apartments (4 persons), with bathroom • Prices: double room single occupancy 55-60 euros, double 70-84, triple 90-100, breakfast included; apartment 90-105 euros • Credit cards: all, Bancomat • 1 room designed for use by the mobility challenged. Off-street parking. Small pets allowed. Owners always present. • Restaurant. Breakfast room, reading and TV room. Garden with play area, grounds. Pool

BOLSENA
Montesegnale

BRACCIANO

31 KM NORTH OF VITERBO SS 2

39 KM NORTH OF ROME SS 493

LA TANA DELL'ORSO... BRUNO

🍲 Trattoria
Località Montesegnale 162 I
Tel. 0761 798162-798730
Closed Thursday and Friday lunch
Open: lunch and dinner
Holidays: three weeks in January
Seating: 25 + 25 outdoors
Prices: 20-28 euros, wine excluded
All major credit cards, Bancomat

VINO E CAMINO

🍲 Enoteca with bar and kitchen
Piazza Mazzini 11
Tel. 06 99803433
Closed Monday
Open: lunch and dinner
Holidays: the week of Ferragosto (August 15)
Seating: 60 + 45 outdoors
Prices: 35 euros, wine excluded
All credit cards, Bancomat

Bruno and Rossella live on a little hill with a great view of the lake, just over a kilometer outside the center of Bolsena. This is where they decided to move their trattoria La Pietra, which they had run for years; the location, name and number of covers changed, but not the reliably excellent ingredients (particularly those from the lake), local cooking and friendly warmth.

The inviting choice of antipasti includes **roast sand-smelts with sage**, marinated whitefish fillet, bruschetta with extra-virgin olive oil and beans del purgatorio. The first courses are heavy on sauced pastas and soups, all well-made: **linguette di passera with fish sauce**, **tench minestra**, **spatatata** (soup with potatoes, egg, wild mint and bread), gnocchetti with broccoli and pecorino. If ordered in advance there's also the **sbroscia**, a soup that combines vegetables with lake fish (tench, pike, whitefish, lasca and others). Continue with **whitefish with aromatic herbs** and, unusually, the restuarant's own wild strawberries; **eel alla cacciatora** and perch fillets. There's meat on the menu too – sausages with lentils, **tegamaccio** (potatoes, artichokes, wild mint and lamb), involtini of mortadella and cheese – or frittata with potatoes, onions and (when in season) wild asparagus. The interesting **cheese board** includes about 20 different types from the area and the rest of Italy, and there are also homemade desserts based on cream, ricotta or homemade jam.

The wine list is adequate, containing both local and national bottles.

It's always a pleasure to return to this restaurant run by the Baroni siblings: Massimo in the dining room and Cristina in the kitchen. In the summer you can eat outside, with a view of the Odescalchi castle, but it's equally pleasant inside: simple, with wooden furnishings and well-spaced marble tables.

The menu brings together the traditions of Lazio with a broader perspective, always maintaining the greatest respect for the ingredients. That's why sheep's and goat's milk **cheeses** from a small Cerveteri producer coexist among the antipasti with mussel soup with pecorino and spelt salad with mackerel fillet, mint and chives. There's a similar contrast in the first courses: on one side **tonnarelli cacio e pepe**, **fettuccine with abbacchio ragù and pecorino**, bucatini all'amatriciana, **pasta e fagioli** with pecorino maltagliati and **zuppa with onions** (or leeks or chestnuts), and on the other, couscous salad with "true" octopus and cherry tomatoes; **fava bean puree with sautéed chicory**; scorpionfish passata with squid-ink maltagliati pasta; and **potato ravioli with tomato, mint and pecorino**. All the pastas are homemade. The menu continues with porchetta, pork in caul fat with apple puree, **shank** in salsa verde with oil-preserved vegetables, grilled tuna fillet, lettuce wraps filled with pike and Colonnata lardo or grouper-stuffed peppers. We recommend the espresso millefeuille with Chantilly cream and chocolate drops for a fitting finish to your meal.

The excellent wine list will please all tastes and budgets; there's also a good selection of spirits.

BROCCOSTELLA

LA PESCA

☎⚲Holiday farm
Via la Pesca 12
Tel. 0776 891427-333 4129913
Fax 0776 887141
E-mail: agriturismolapesca@libero.it
Open all year

The vacation farm is located in the Lake Posta Fibreno Nature Reserve, a lake that features a kind of island made of peat-like intertwined vegetable matter that floats on the lake, continuously shifted around by the wind. Many birds nest in trees and bushes growing around the lake, where scuba diving excursions are also organized. The facility, managed by Miriam Moscardi, offers lodging in two old refurbished farmhouses and guests will be able to practice sports such as canoeing, fishing and archery. Breakfast includes homemade jams and cakes, while the restaurant offers traditional cuisine at a price ranging from 25-28 euros per person, and is also open to non-residents at weekends and on public holidays. In the surrounding area we would recommend a visit to Montecassino Abbey, the old center of Sora and the National Park of the Abruzzi.

• 5 double and 1 triple rooms, with bathroom, TV • Prices: double room single occupancy 40 euros, double 80, triple 120, breakfast included • Credit cards: major ones, Bancomat • Off-street parking. Small pets allowed. Owners always reachable. • Restaurant. Breakfast room. Garden. Pool

CAMPAGNANO DI ROMA

LA RISERVA DI MARTIGNANELLO

☎⚲Holiday farm
Strada Valle di Baccano 29
Tel. 06 9041081-335 7321261-339 1433591
E-mail: martignanello@yahoo.it
Internet: www.martignanello.it
Open all year

Martignano is a volcanic lake with hardly any buildings on its shores as it's part of the regional Due Laghi Nature Reserve. The vacation farm is organized in two low buildings, which include seven spacious, comfortable and tastefully furnished rooms. In order to reach the facility you pass through a gate on the Valle di Baccano road and proceed for about one kilometer on an unmade track. The restaurant is in a restructured old farmhouse and has a pergola with view of the lake. It's open to non-residents and a meal costs from 28-35 euros per person, wine excluded. For breakfast, guests will be able to have cakes, homemade jams and honey, milk, tea and coffee. There's a small private beach on the banks of the lake.

• 7 double rooms, with bathroom, minibar; some with jacuzzis, kitchenette • Prices: double room single occupancy 55-70 euros, double 70-90 (15-20 euro supplement for extra bed, supplement for use of kitchen 15 euros), breakfast included • Credit cards: none • 1 room designed for use by the mobility challenged. Off-street parking. Small pets allowed. Owners always contactable • Restaurant. Breakfast room. Garden. Beach

CAMPODIMELE
Taverna

CARPINETO ROMANO

LO STUZZICHINO

LA SBIRRA

Restaurant-pizzeria
Via Taverna 14
Tel. 0771 598131-349 3678486
Closed Wednesday
Open: lunch and dinner
Holidays: variable
Seating: 50
Prices: 25 euros, wine excluded
All major credit cards, Bancomat

Trattoria
Via Verdesca 24
Tel. 06 9798635
Closed Tuesday
Open: lunch and dinner
Holidays: two weeks in July
Seating: 90
Prices: 20 euros, wine excluded
No credit cards accepted, Bancomat

Campodimele, in the Aurunci mountains, has come to be known as "the village of 100-year-olds" for the unusual longevity of its inhabitants, and it's also home to this welcoming restaurant, run by the Capirichio family. Mamma Pina is in the kitchen with Francesco, the former a faithful follower of the local cuisine, the latter providing a touch of creativity. In the dining room the other son, Roberto, greets guests under the watchful eye of his father, Fioravante. Finally there's grandmother Romilda, responsible for the bread and biscottini baked in the wood-fired oven, used in the evening for pizza.
To follow the spirit of this guide, we'll mention the more traditional choices from the menu, leaving other publications to fetishize deconstructed dishes adorned with veloutés and juliennes. Instead, we recommend starting with the brined Itrana olives, sausages, seasonal vegetable fritters, marzolina cheese fresh or in oil with pepenella or the veal with scorzone truffle, oil and lemon. Don't forget to taste the **cicerchie**, a traditional local legume which the Capirchios grow themselves and use for various dishes such as classic zuppe and rissoles. From the pastas, the **laina** and **gnocchetti** with goat or wild boar ragù are worth noting. Follow with a mixed grill of free-range Campodimele pork, **goat** and lamb prepared in various ways and **wild boar stew**. Desserts are good, particularly the lemon and fig mousse, the orange tortina with amaretti, pistachio bavarese, zuppa inglese with sugared pine nuts and chocolate mousse.
The selection of wines is continually growing, and provides a suitable accompaniment to the food.

This historic trattoria can be found in the historic center of Carpineto Romana, almost facing the piazza della Collegiata. Run continuously by five generations of the Calvano family, it's currently in the hands of Luca, with experienced assistance provided by his mother Immacolatina in the kitchen. The original two dining rooms, with simple and homely decor, have been recently joined by a third in the renovated cellar, with a central fireplace and stone walls. On some quiet evenings you might happen across a pile of fresh, handmade pasta resting on one of the wooden tables – evidence of the kitchen's strong point.
After a selection of cured meats, local cheeses and **bruschetta** – try the ones topped **with lamb coratella** – move on to that handmade pasta: **fettuccine with porcini mushrooms** or ragù, **gnocchi with coda di soreca**, ricotta ravioli, lasagne, **polenta with pork spareribs** or mushrooms. Main courses come with vegetables, potatoes or beans either in vinegar or gratinéed in the oven, and we particularly recommend the **suckling lamb**, **rabbit alla cacciatora** and **kid** alla carpinetana. Steaks, pork chops and sausages, **trippetta alla romana** and salt cod also feature. If ordered in advance, there can be interesting **game** on offer, prepared with truffles and mushrooms from the Lepini mountains. Tarts with almonds, blackberries or sour cherries; ricotta cakes; ice cream; and Carpineto dolcetti secchi provide a suitable finish to the meal.
The local wine is available on tap, or you can choose a bottle from the short but interesting list compiled by Luca.

LA STRADANOVA

Recently opened osteria
Via Matteotti 6
Tel. 06 9719083
Closed Monday
Open: lunch and dinner
Holidays: 10 days in September
Seating: 44 + 20 outdoors
Prices: 23-25 euros excluding wines
No credit cards

VILLA OLIMPIA

Rooms
Piazza Regina Margherita 10
Tel. e fax 06 9710007
E-mail: villaolimpia@tin.it
Internet: www.villaolimpia.com
Open all year

This osteria is strategically located at the axis of Piazza Regina Margherita and Via Matteoti (formerly Strada Nova), created by Pope Leo XIII at the start of the 20th century as a symbolic link between the old and the new: the maze of medieval alleys and the main road to Rome. There's no sign outside, just a discreet brass plate to indicate the front door. Inside, Barbara offers a courteous and warm welcome. In the kitchen mamma Stefania guarantees experience and a rich understanding of local produce.
Apart from some confused missteps (rocket and strawberries in some first courses) which are easily forgivable, in general the menu offers dishes firmly rooted in tradition. Start with the **prosciutto di Bassiano**, tuna and cucumber panzanella and croutons with various toppings. Then **zuppe** (with beans and maltagliati pasta, chestnuts and spelt, or chickpeas); **ravioli with chestnuts, broccoli and sausage**; and panzerotti filled with ricotta and spinach. In the right season there's tagliolini with shrimp and artichokes or **ravioli filled with ricotta and spinach**. Move on to meat from the family farm – piglet, **roast pork, abbacchio a scottadito** and scaloppine with cep mushrooms – or game sourced by father Luciano, such as an excellent **wild boar with juniper**. The **abbacchio porchettato with artichokes** is a speciality, but has to be ordered beforehand. Sides include sautéed chicory, broccoli affogati, and **puntarelle with anchovy sauce**. To finish, ciambelline with wine, homemade pies, strawberry mousse, ricotta ciambella in mocha sauce and stregata pears.
The shrewd list of regional wines boasts retail prices, and includes some spirits..

Villa Olimpia is an ancient medieval palazzo located in the center of the village of Carpineto Romano, where Pope Leo XIII was born. Many narrow alleys that still bear witness to the past, start off from here: portals portraying events, flag doors, mullion windows and the many churches in Romanesque, Gothic and Baroque style. The palazzo was acquired and restructured in 1999 by Cleonice Panetti, who manages it with her husband. The few guestrooms are pleasant, functional and equipped with arte povera furnishings. Breakfast, served in the small communal room, in your own room or on the small balconies that look over the village roofs, offers tarts and other homemade cakes, bread, butter, jams and the classic bar fare. For lunch and supper the B&B has an agreement with two nearby restaurants that offer a set menu at a fixed price.

• 1 single, 2 double, 2 triple and 1 four-bed rooms, with bathroom, TV; 3 with air-conditioning • Prices: single 30 euros, double 50, triple 65, four-bed 80, breakfast included • Credit cards: major ones, Bancomat • Public parking in the immediate vicinity, garage (2 spaces, 12 euros per day). Small pets allowed. Owners always present. • Breakfast room, reading room. Terrace

CASALVIERI

OSTERIA DEL TEMPO PERSO

🍲 Recently opened osteria
Piazza San Rocco
Tel. 0776 638039-340 2532207-329 4031223
Closed Monday
Open: dinner, Sunday and festivities also for lunch
Holidays: variable
Seating: 60
Prices: 20-25 euros, wine excluded
All major credit cards, Bancomat

A year ago we considered this osteria a welcome new arrival, and since then it's become one of the best destinations for food and wine in the Valle di Comino and beyond, and highly deserving of the snail symbol. The love for local products, the consistent quality and the passion of mamma Sabrina and her two sons, Marco and Matteo, have led to such success that you have to book well in advance to get a table. But once you're there and sat down, it's like being at the home of a friend.

The wide choice of antipasti changes often, depending on what's in season and at the market. You might find **cionce** (fried) **pizzas**, savory pies, rustici, vegetable flans, cured meats and local cheeses like San Donato Val Comino pecorino alla marzolina from Campoli Appennino. First courses worth ordering include **maltagliati with Atina cannellini beans** and **ricotta ravioli**, as well as various kinds of pasta with wild chicory, classic lasagna and **fini-fini** with tomato and basil or Campoli Appennino truffles; in the winter months try the pasta with potatoes, **pappardelle with wild boar** or sausage, **fettuccine with classic ragù**, polenta and various minestras. Follow with **roast abbacchio with potatoes**, straccetti with wild rocket and grilled meats. **Stewed wild boar** and stracotti are good in the colder months. Puddings are homemade, from semifreddo to creams to dig your spoon into, panna cotta, lemon tart, warm zabaione, chocolate soufflé and apple pie.

The continuously evolving cellar is Marco's domain and his passion, and he's put together a comprehensively original list.

CASPERIA

LA TORRETTA

🗝 Bed and breakfast
Via Mazzini 7
Tel. e fax 0765 63202
E-mail: latorretta@tiscalinet.it
Internet: www.latorrettabandb.com
Open all year

The B&B is in a building dating from the fifteenth or sixteenth century in the historic center of Casperia, a beautiful twelfth-century village. The rooms and communal areas offer a clear expression of the current owners' – Maureene Donovan and Roberto Scheda – passion for creating an attractive, charming environment. Roberto took charge of renovating the building himself, salvaging the old wooden ceilings and frescoes, and furnishing it with antiques and some modern pieces. Maureene, on the other hand, will be happy to advise you on possible visits and excursions, and sometimes may even accompany you to towns of artistic interest reachable in one day. During the summer breakfast is served on the panoramic terrace and offers fresh fruit, jams, yoghurt and cereals, ricotta and other local cheeses, homemade and pastry shop cakes, and a wide choice of teas and coffees.

• 1 single and 5 double rooms, with bathroom; 1 apartment (2-4 persons) with kitchen • Prices: single 60 euros, double 80 (15 euro supplement for extra bed), breakfast included; apartment (minimum 3 nights) 90 euros • Credit cards: Visa • Free external public parking. No pets allowed. Owners always present. • Breakfast room, lounge. Terrace

CEPRANO

ENOTECA FEDERICI

Wine shop with bar and kitchen
Piazza Martiri di via Fani 8
Tel. 0775 914048
Closed Tuesday
Open: lunch and dinner
Holidays: variable
Seating: 20
Prices: 23-26 euros, wine excluded
All credit cards

The Federici siblings run this small restaurant, attached to the family's well-stocked wine shop and pasticceria, located in the main square of Ceprano, once the ancient Latin colony Fregellae and now an important archeological site. However in the summer and for special occasions the whole restaurant is transferred to another spot, La Vignola, in the countryside. The market and the seasons dictate the menu, devised by Luca in the kitchen, while Pietro is in charge of hosting and the wines. Priority is given to regional labels, with many available by the glass.

You could start with fritto di verdurine, a seasonal vegetable timbale, **fried sheep's milk ricotta** or the **soups** of **chickpeas with baccalà fillets** or of Atina cannellini beans with pecorino di fossa and truffles. The well-put-together selection of first courses includes **pappardelle** alla manfrediana (**with lardo, cep mushrooms and chestnuts**) or with artichokes and guanciale, **ricotta ravioli**, tagliolini with wild asparagus or cherry tomatoes, **fettuccine with mutton sauce**, risotto with sausage and fava beans, zuppa with spelt and **minestra over bread**. Moving onto the mains, don't miss classics like **chicken with peppers** or tomatoes, abbacchio lamb chops with aromatic herbs, **mutton al sugo** and **chicken straccetti with Cesanese wine**, or you could choose tagliata, beef bollito, or more creative dishes like oxtail timbale in a cacao sauce with crispy celery.

There's a good selection of puddings – pies, homemade biscottini, tozzetti and briachelle – and an excellent Chantilly cream.

CERVARA DI ROMA

FERRARI

Trattoria
Via XX Settembre 20
Tel. 0774 828720
Closed Mondays
Open: lunch and dinner
Holidays: none
Seating: 75
Prices: 25 euros, wine excluded
All credit cards, Bancomat

If you're driving from Vicovaro towards Arsoli on the via Tiburtina, at a certain point trees start lining the road, and a few kilometers further still you'll find yourself in the center of Cervara di Roma. This is the heart of the Monti Simbruini park, which dominates the Aniene Valley. A well-preserved ancient village, Cervara was built by Benedictine monks on the top of a mountain. Its narrow streets are only negotiable on foot, and have been decorated with sculptures in the rocks, murals and poetry by contemporary artists. In one of these narrow streets you'll find the palazzotto which since 1954 has housed the Ferrari family's trattoria, once managed by the grandparents of the current owners, and now by Eugenio, front of house, and Maria and Francesco, in various roles in the kitchen. Start with a sampling of local pecorino and ricotta and bruschetta with truffles or cep mushrooms, which abound in the surrounding beech and chestnut forests. Then move on to homemade pasta with meats and local products such as **gnocchi with mutton sauce**, **strozzapreti with truffles**, **ravioli with sheep's milk ricotta** and fettuccine with mushrooms. In the colder months try the **polenta with pork spareribs**. More meat, for the most part cooked over an open fire, once you reach the mains: pork sausages and steaks, beef steaks and fillets, **mutton spiedini**, **lamb chops** and smoked provola cheese, paired with sides of potatoes or seasonal vegetables. To finish, panna cotta, various biscuits and cookies, tiramisù and wild berries.

To accompany your meal try the fairly good local red, or choose from a selection of local and national labels. Reservations are recommended.

CIVITAVECCHIA

LA BOMBONIERA

Restaurant
Corso Marconi 50
Tel. 0766 25744
Closed Monday
Open: lunch and dinner
Holidays: variable
Seating: 40 + 40 outdoors
Prices: 35 euros, wine excluded
All credit cards

Civitavecchia is one of Lazio's most important ports, the base for a fleet of fishing boats which provide a daily supply of highly prized fish from the Tyrrhenian Sea. It's this seafood that dominates the menu at the Bomboniera, opened in 1981 by the Sardinian Giulio Bussu. He's still running the place, assisted by his wife Maria Giovanna in the kitchen and daughters Michela and Eleonora. In the summer months it's very pleasant to eat outside with a view of the sea.

To begin we recommend the misto di mare, a selection of different seafood including **anchovies all'ammiraglia**, a terrine of white fish and salmon, sautéed mussels and clams, marinated tuna, mussels alla marinara, oysters and burridda. First courses include **spaghetti with carpet-shell clams**; **gnocchi allo scoglio**; risotto alla pescatora; **ravioli with seafood**; fettuccine with clams, mussels and asparagus; risotto with langoustines and pumpkin flowers; and **spaghetti with mullet bottarga**. Continue with a mixed fry of shrimp, squid and merluzzetti, gilt-head sea bream fillet with tomatoes and peppers, **grilled** langoustines or **giant shrimp**, the daily catch cooked over charcoal and, if preordered, the highly recommended **zuppa di pesce**. Seafood alternatives include veal fillet and grilled tagliata. The small selection of cheeses includes a Slow Food Presidia, **Casizolu** from Santu Lussurgiu. Puddings include **sebadas** with honey or semifreddo with amaretti and Anghelu Ruju chocolate.

Giulio's grand passion for wine is reflected in a vast and exhaustive list.

CORI

DA CHECCO

Trattoria
Via della Repubblica 174
Tel. 06 9678336
Closed Thursday
Open: lunch and dinner
Holidays: variable
Seating: 70 + 30 outdoors
Prices: 20 euros, wine excluded
All credit cards, Bancomat

Near the Temple of Hercules, this osteria is the oldest in Cori. Its origins date back to the prewar period, when it was known as La càttara; in the 1960s it was taken over by Checchino, who preserved the tradition of guests sitting around for hours, idly chatting and drinking, and offered dishes that are still cooked today by the current owner, Luca Zerilli. He's been here since 2000, and has focussed on the traditional gastronomy of Cori, making the most of the local wine and olive production.

Among the antipasti, along with traditional **prosciutto cotto di Cori**, diners can try the excellent Itrana olives in brine or flavored with aromatic herbs. Moving on, there's fettuccine or **cellitti** (a kind of pasta made only with water and flour) **with chanterelles** or porcini; maltagliati with garlic, lardo and pecorino; and gnocchi with sausage, rucola and mushrooms. Equally good alternatives include scafata from the Lepini mountains and **spaghetti with wild asparagus** (available in season, if ordered in advance). The main courses are centered on meat: we recommend the **abbacchio alla scottadito**, as well as the fillet in a porcini crust or ai dioscuri and the spiedini with mutton or mixed meats, all accompanied by wild chicory or **artichokes alla giudìa**. To finish there's cheeses from the shepherds of Cori and Giulianello or traditional sweets like the Christmas mostaccioli with honey, biscotti al vino and the ciambelle scottolate. The well-put-together wine list has all the best local labels.

CORI

DA ZAMPI

🍽️ Restaurant
Via Leopardi 17
Tel. 06 9679688
Closed Monday
Open: lunch and dinner
Holidays: variable
Seating: 60 + 30 outdoors
Prices: 20-22 euros, wine excluded
All credit cards, Bancomat

There's no doubt that ancient Cora is worth a stop to visit its fine monuments: the polygonal walls (the oldest part dating back to the 5th century BC), the Temple of Hercules and the church of Sant'Oliva, full of frescoes and with a Renaissance cloister where for several years symphony concerts have been performed. Many excellent oils, wines and cheeses are produced in the surrounding countryside, and Da zampi owners Ottavio, Gina and son Luca have taken full advantage of this fact.

To begin there's always a sampling of **prosciutto cotto di Cori,** made by Ottavio according to the traditional local recipe. For a first course try the fettuccine with **chanterelles** or fresh cep mushrooms, gathered in the nearby Lepini forests. When it's in season don't miss the **scafata**, a soup based on new favas (scafo being the local name for the beans), artichokes and peas. Between February and April you will also find wild asparagus, in an omelet or a sauce for spaghetti. Among the mains the lamb is worthy of attention, sourced (as are most of the cheeses) from the shepherds of Cori, Giulianello, Artena and Roccamassima. Try the **coratella** di abbacchio, the **abbacchio al forno with potatoes** and the roast veal shank. The puddings, like ciammellette and ciammelle scottolate, are typical of the town.

There's a good selection of local wines, including a red produced only from the native varietal nero buono. There's also a list specifically dedicated to the excellent local oils.

FARNESE

LA PIAZZETTA DEL SOLE

🍽️ Traditional osteria
Via XX Settembre 129
Tel. 0761 458606-333 8996520
Closed Wednesday
Open: dinner; Friday, Saturday, Sunday and festivities also for lunch
Holidays: variable
Seating: 35
Prices: 28-30 euros, wine excluded
All credit cards, Bancomat

Farnese is a pretty village in the Lazio Maremma, less known than the Tuscan Maremma but equally picturesque. Just as pleasant is a visit to this restaurant, located on the second floor of an old palazzotto. The small, welcoming dining room is up a short flight of stairs, and is furnished with just a few well-spaced tables. Front of house is Miriam Maraschi; Antonella Ferrari is in the kitchen.

The menu varies depending on what's in season, and welcomes happy incursions from nearby Tuscany. You can start with mixed croutons, **cured meats**, pancetta salad with balsamic vinegar, herring on beans del purgatorio and bruschetta with Tropea anchovies. Then move on to cream of carrot soup with grape croutons; **zuppa of chickpeas and baccalà**; maltagliati with ricotta, zucchini and fresh tomatoes; **fettucine with pumpkin flowers** and lasagne alla parmigiana. Good mains include **wild boar in buione** and **rabbit in porchetta** or in sweet-and-sour, as well as tagliata al pistachio, lamb chops and roast pork. Make sure to leave room for the excellent puddings, such as millefeuille with Chantilly cream, almond and apricot bavarese, ricotta cream with peach sauce and the ever-present tozzetti with Vin Santo.

For wine, you could choose the house red or white, or a bottle from a list which focuses on wines from Lazio and Tuscany.

🍯 In **Piansano** (18km), in Fiocchino, the Il Fiocchino farm sells sheep's milk ricotta and pecorino of different ages from the Alta Tuscia, all made artisan fashion with the milk from their own flocks.

FIUGGI
San Lorenzo

FONDI
Madonna degli Angeli

33 KM NORTHEAST OF FROSINONE

56 KM SOUTHEAST OF LATINA SS 7

SAN LORENZO

Holiday farm
Via Prenestina 96-SS di Fiuggi 155 km 29,400
Tel. 0775 505514-515389-347 7217828
Fax 0775 505514
E-mail: san_lorenzo@libero.it
Internet: www.italiaagriturismo.net/san_lorenzo
Open all year, October-March only at weekends

LA MAGNATORA

Restaurant-pizzeria
Via Fossella 5
Tel. 0771 500252
Closed Wednesday
Open: lunch and dinner
Holidays: 10 days in November and the end of January
Seating: 80 + 60 outdoors
Prices: 30-33 euros, wine excluded
All credit cards except AE, Bancomat

This vacation farm is one kilometer away from Fiuggi, on the Via Prenestina, and was built over the remains of a complex of cisterns dating from the age of the Roman Empire. George Koch, his wife Maria Pia and their son Francesco, and a relaxing family atmosphere will welcome you in what is said to have been a monastery that according to tradition was built by the Templars. The rooms are simple and furnished with great attention to detail. Meals are served on the veranda with garden-style tables and chairs that fit in well with the atmosphere, or in summer, on the terrace. The generous breakfast consists of their own organically produced food: homemade tarts and cakes, various types of jam, yoghurt, cereals and savory fare. Guests can have a simple meal in the restaurant, mainly based on local products, at a price of 25 euros for residents or 28-30 euros for non-residents.

• 7 double rooms, with bathroom; 2 apartments (2-4 persons) with bathroom, kitchenette • Prices: double room single occupancy 50 euros, double 70, apartment 77-120, breakfast included • Credit cards: all, Bancomat • Off-street parking. Small pets allowed. Owners always present. • Restaurant. Breakfast room. Garden, terrace, veranda

Fabio and Antonio Locolle's restaurant is nestled in the green countryside around Fondi, near the remains of the abbey of San Magno. On first entering the large central dining room this doesn't feel at all like the typical osteria, crowded as it is with large groups, young people and big families, all ready to order the excellent pizza from the wood-fired oven. But there are smaller, quieter dining rooms, and the kitchen is ready to please anyone ready to try well-prepared, traditional Fondi dishes.
In addition to the local ricottina, you could start with antipasti based on ingredients from fresh or salt water: **fried sand-smelts**, river frogs and crawfish, stuffed sardines a beccafico. The flavorful and substantial first courses include **zuppa of chanterelle mushrooms and cannelloni, strozzapreti with asparagus and guanciale, tonnarelli with lamb ragù**, gnocchi with wild boar sauce. Wild boar reappears in the main courses, alongside other prized **game** (woodcock, thrush and hares from the area between Lenola and Itri), and grilled meats and sausages; there are also some very traditional dishes such as **whipped baccalà with pine nuts and raisins** or with dried peppers. More coastal options include fried totani and squid, depending on what the catch is like from the nearby sea at Sperlonga. Puddings are homemade: a tart of fragola grapes, tozzetti, orange or almond cakes.
The constantly growing wine list means you can always find the right match for the dishes.

FONDI

VICOLO DI M'BLO

🍲 Restaurant
Corso Appio Claudio 11
Tel. 0771 502385
Closed Tuesday
Open: lunch and dinner
Holidays: at Christmas
Seating: 40 + 25 outside
Prices: 35 euros, wine excluded
All credit cards, Bancomat

Enzo Simonelli has an incredibly youthful energy, even though he's been working as a restaurateur together with Maria Loreta for more than 40 years. One sign is the bed and breakfast he's opened in the historic center of Fondi – not, however, at the expense of the Vicolo. In the summer you can eat in the courtyard, and admire the Catalan style of the Palazzo Caetani, while in winter the dining room is warm and friendly.
Ingredients are sourced from Lake Fondi, the sea at Sperlonga and the mountains that divide the city from nearby Ciociaria. Prices are reasonable as long as you don't choose certain fish and shellfish, and seasonal **game** such as wild duck, coot, woodcock and lark. But it's easy to be satisfied with less costly dishes, such as **fried frogs** or jambarej (lake shrimp), **whitebait zuppa** and **sauté of clams and sea truffles**. For your first course, the soups are particularly good: **zavardella** with seasonal vegetables and beans or **zuppa ciociara** with mushrooms, chickpeas, chicory and cornbread. Alternatively there's lasagne, paccheri with octopus and Gaeta olives, maccheroncini with artichokes and **seafood ravioli**. **Zazzicchie** (dried sausages) from Fondi and **abbacchio chasseur** are among the meat choices, while fish lovers can try the ever-changing selection of traditionally prepared seafood such as sea bream, turbot, pandora and gurnard. **Tarts with figs**, sour cherries or oranges, cream gelato with wild blackberries and amaretti round out the meal.
The wine list has been intelligently put together, and includes both big names and off-the-beaten-track discoveries by owner Enzo.

FORMIA

IL GATTO & LA VOLPE

🍲 Restaurant
Via Abate Tosti 83
Tel. 0771 21354
Closed Wednesday, never in summer
Open: lunch and dinner
Holidays: between Christmas and New Year's
Seating: 70 + 50 outdoors
Price: 35 euros
All credit cards

Tonino and Giancarlo Simeone's slogan is "Dishes from long ago for the gourmets of today," and their success has come from following the traditions of the gastronomy of Formi and the Gulf of Gaeta. The good wine list and pleasant atmosphere of their restaurant, both inside and out, haven't hurt.
There's always at least one set menu for meat and one for fish, both paired with wines by the glass, or you can choose à la carte, beginning with some of the numerous small antipasti. From these we recommend the fried capetroccole (very small octopi), **marinated anchovies** or anchovies in tortiera, **gratinéed** little fish called **cicinielli** and stuffed sardines a beccafico. For some time now the best first courses have been those with handmade pasta: gnocchetti with razor clams and eggplant, **linguine with capetroccole**, spaccatelle with murex, or meat-based dishes like **rigatoni with tripe ragù**. The attention paid to often-underappreciated seafood continues in the main courses, with **sugli alla scapece**, little cuttlefish di rezzella and **stuffed calamaretti** (little squid), plus whatever else might happen to be in the daily catch. In the meat category you'll find traditional, substantial dishes, such as **tripe tegamino**, lamb chops and **fritto all formiana**, mixed fried offal.
For the proper finish, pair a little glass of limoncello or loquat liqueur made by Giancarlo with a dessert like strawberry mousse, a tart made with two kinds of sour cherries or figs, or a delizia made of sponge cake and lemon cream.

LAZIO

FORMIA

SIRIO

🍲 Restaurant
Viale Unità d'Italia
Tel. 0771 790047-772705
Closed Monday dinner and Tuesday, in summer Tuesday and Wednesday at lunch
Open: lunch and dinner
Holidays: 20 days between December and February
Seating: 50 + 35 outdoors
Prices: 35 euros, wine excluded
All credit cards, Bancomat

It may be located on the busy main road that connects Formia and Gaeta, but all you have to do is pass through the gate of the small park that leads to the restaurant and suddenly you're in another world of peace and relaxation. In the warmer months there are also tables outside (though the number of covers remains the same). Claudio Ferrari welcomes diners with his usual courtesy and expertise while his brother Stefano will be in the kitchen, preparing dishes which betray the Tuscan origins of the family and offer a perfect harmony between the land and the sea.
Chicken-liver crostini, sausages in lard and cured meats such as lardo, guanciale, pancetta and lonzino from **Cinta Senese** pigs represent some of the earthy antipasti, while from the sea there's shrimp, squid and murex salad or the **fried capetroccole** (the dialect name for a kind of tiny octopi). The first courses also play between coastal and inland influences: tagliolini with gurnard and pecorino, **amberjack ravioli with lupini** (gray clams), **pappardelle with hare ragù**, no-egg maccheroni in a Tuscan ragù. Main courses from the sea include Ponza pezzogne, a stew of bluefish with porcini mushrooms, fillet of amberjack with eggplant and the humble but exquisite **anchovies with escarole**, while from the land there's tagliata, chops and **roast stinco**. Preceded by an ever-large choice of **cheeses**, the meal finishes with sweets, ice creams and jams made in-house: cakes with apples and blueberry jam, panna cotta with lemon marmalade or gianduia gelato with orange marmalade. The ample wine list boasts honest mark-ups and is also careful to put local wineries to the fore.

FRASCATI

CACCIANI

🔑 3-Star Hotel
Via Armando Diaz 13-15
Tel. 06 9401991
Fax 06 9420440
E-mail: info@cacciani.it
Internet: www.cacciani.it
Open all year

Located in the old town center, this charming, comfortable hotel is owned by the hard-working Cacciani family, who are also proprietors of the popular restaurant next door. Many of the rooms have a terrace with views of Rome and the nearby Aldobrandini Villa; the most spacious and elegant ones are those of the 40 series, created in a period apartment. The location is excellent both for excursions in the Castelli Romani area and for transport services to Rome. The buffet-style breakfast offers top-brand coffees and teas, jams, fruit, yoghurt and homemade traditional cakes. Hotel guests get a 10% discount on meals eaten in their restaurant.

• 1 single and 21 double rooms with bathroom, mini-bar, satellite TV; almost all with terrace • Prices: single and double room single occupancy 78 euros, double 95 (20 euro supplement for extra bed), breakfast included • Credit cards: all, Bancomat • Facility accessible for the mobility challenged, 1 room designed for their use. Public parking in the immediate vicinity. No pets allowed. Reception open 24 hours a day • Restaurant. Breakfast room. Conference room.

🍲 The restaurant is also open to non-residents and offers both traditional and creative dishes: a meal costs about 45 euros, excluding wine.

COLONNA

ZARAZÀ

3-Star Hotel
Piazza del Gesù 12
Tel. 06 94018088
Fax 06 94018730
E-mail: hotelcolonna@hotelcolonna.it
Internet: www.hotelcolonna.it
Open all year

Restaurant
Via Regina Margherita 45
Tel. 06 9422053
Closed Monday, Sunday dinner October-May
Open: lunch and dinner
Holidays: in August
Seating: 50 + 30 outdoors
Prices: 24-26 euros, wine excluded
All credit cards except DC

This Fifties building in the historic center of Frascati became a hotel after a complete refurbishment in 1999: today it has good quality furnishings and a variety of services. Guests can take advantage of a number of interesting possibilities, such as bicycle rental, guided tours of the Castelli Romani, laundry, ironing and baby-sitting services, use of nearby sport facilities, tourist assistance with maps and all kinds of informative material. The Cavassini family focuses closely on hospitality: proof is the breakfast that includes coffee-bar beverages, a variety of breads and cakes from the best local bakeries, yoghurt, excellent jams and cereals, fresh fruit and, on festivities, typical cakes. During Christmas, Easter, New Year's Eve and August 15 the price of double rooms is 140 euros.

• 17 double, 2 triple and 1 junior suite, with bathroom, air-conditioning, safe, mini-bar, satellite TV, modem connection • Prices: double room single occupancy 85-100 euros, double 110, junior suite and triple 150-180, breakfast included • Credit cards: all, Bancomat • 1 room designed for use by the mobility challenged. Garage (9 spaces). No pets allowed. Reception open 24 hours a day. • Bar. Breakfast room

The outlook opposite this restaurant offers a striking view of the Italian capital, an evocative sight particularly at night when it sparkles with thousands of lights. Zarazà has been here for half a century, though a few years ago it transferred from a few steps away into the current, more comfortable premises.
Bruno Bronzini has been diligent in following the footsteps of his father Gino. For example he observes the tradition (which, it must be said, is not universally appreciated) of bringing antipasti to the table even if they haven't been ordered. But as long as you're not tormented by hunger, keep your appetite for the following dishes, all of which are worth trying: **pasta with chickpeas**, **bucatini alla amatriciana**, **spaghetti cacio e pepe**, tagliolini or **gnocchi with oxtail ragù** are expertly prepared with a light hand in the saucing. As is the custom, a **skate soup with pasta and broccoli** is served only on Fridays. Traditionally "lean" Fridays also mean **anchovy tortino** and **stewed salt cod**, while Sunday is the day for **roast lamb's head**. There are also innovative main courses, but we find the cornerstones of Lazio cooking more convincing: tripe alla romana, **oxtail alla vaccinara**, **coratella d'abbacchio**, spring lamb al tegame or a scottadito and vignarola with guanciale, fava beans and artichokes. The restaurant's own extra-virgin olive oil is used on mixed field greens, chicory, broccoletti and other vegetables.
Wines are generally local, and the wine on tap from the restaurant's own vineyards is simple and pleasant. No wines by the glass, but the mark-ups are admirably reasonable, sometimes close to the retail price.

DIVINO AMORE

⌣ Trattoria
Via Sacra Famiglia 3
Tel. 0775 290325-340 5834612
Closed Sunday
Open: lunch and dinner
Holidays: three weeks in August
Seating: 35
Prices: 32-35 euros, wine excluded
All credit cards, Bancomat

SELLARI

⌣ Trattoria
Via del Cipresso 28
Tel. 0775 852715
Closed Saturday
Open: lunch and dinner
Holidays: July 15-31
Seating: 80
Prices: 22-25 euros, wine excluded
All credit cards, Bancomat

Opposite the Sacra Famiglia church, this family-run trattoria is a faithful interpreter of Ciociarian culinary traditions. You'll find Pietro welcoming guests in the dining room and expertly helping them navigate the seasonally changing menu put together by Simonetta in the kitchen, while Enzo's job is sourcing ingredients from small, local producers.

You can start with a fresh ricottina, flavored with herbs or walnuts; the selection of cured meats or a buffalo carpaccio. Move on to Ciociaria minestrone, various **zuppe** – chicory and cannellini beans, ovoli (Caesar's mushrooms) in broth with vegetables, chestnut and cicerchia, maltagliati and beans – or homemade pasta such as **fini-fini** alla ciociara (**with tomato, mozzarella di bufala and basil**), tortellini all'opera (with ricotta, truffles and walnuts), Gragnano paccheri with bresaola, spaghetti alla chitarra with wild asparagus, fava beans and artichokes and **green nettle gnocchetti with snails**. Passing on to the mains, there's the house speciality, **mattarellum** (strips of buffalo flavored with 18 herbs and rolled around small wooden pins), as well as **brasato with Cesanese wine**; **roast lamb with pecorino di fossa**, or deboned and paired with artichokes; beef fagottino with seasonal vegetables; **salt cod breaded** with cornmeal and grilled. Round off the meal with local cheeses – marzolino, Amaseno mozzarella di bufala and pecorino ciociaro – served with jams or mostardas made in-house, or one of the many homemade desserts.

The fairly good wine list dedicates particular attention to the local area without forgetting the most important Italian wine regions; or choose from the good selection of artisanal beers.

This historic trattoria in the higher part of the town is always filled with passing tourists as well as regulars, who appreciate a restaurant which has stayed true to itself, in terms of the simple cooking, authentic ingredients and honest prices. Family-run, you'll find owner Giacinto welcoming you in the dining room and mamma Elena bustling about in the kitchen.

A sampling of cured meats and grilled vegetables accompanied by very good bread could be followed by **fini-fini** (a typical hand-made Ciociaran pasta) with fresh tomatoes, timballo alla ciociara, **bucatini all'amatriciana**, **fettuccine with mushrooms**, vegetable soups or **rattattuglie**, prepared according to tradition with a mix of different kinds of pasta. There's also **bread zuppa**; **sagne** with sausage, fresh tomatoes and wild herbs; and gnocchi with seasonally changing sauces. Then there's **buffalo spezzatino**, **chicken alla pietra**, rabbit alla cacciatora, liver with Alatri red onions, **lamb a scottadito** or breaded, **stewed salt cod** with potatoes (on Tuesdays), and, if pre-ordered, baked lamb meatballs with herbs. To finish there's a tasting of local cheeses, **tozzetti** and homemade ciambelline, accompanied by ratafià.

In addition to the local wine on tap, the wine list includes the most important local wines like Cesanese and Atina Cabernet plus a few from outside Lazio; there's a good selection of liqueurs and spirits.

🍷 Enoteca Celani, via Aldo Moro 401: wines, spirits and gourmet specialties. Wine and Champagne tastings paired with oysters and little snacks..

80 KM SOUTHEAST OF LATINA ON SS 148 AND 213

69 KM SOUTHEAST OF LATINA SS 148

GAJETA

🔑 3-Star Hotel-residence
Lungomare Caboto 624
Tel. 0771 45081
Fax 0771 4508237
E-mail: gajeta@gajeta.com
Internet: www.gajeta.com
Open all year

MEDITERRANEO

🍲 Recently opened osteria
Via Bausan 42
Tel. 0771 461212
Closed Tuesday, never in August
Open: only for dinner
Holidays: 20 days in February
Seating: 70
Prices: 30-35 euros, wine excluded
All credit cards, Bancomat

The Gajeta hotel is in a well-refurbished old palazzo overlooking the bay. In addition to rooms (during August and at New Year a double room costs 141 euros) you can also stay in a studio apartment with kitchenette. Many rooms have private terraces with a beautiful view. The buffet breakfast offers sweet and savory fare. Although the hotel is in a paid parking area, guests are given free passes. The nearby NATO base means that they have many foreign guests, but also customers who are so fond of the place they come back year after year. There's a wine bar and tavern – Il Gringo – that's part of the hotel although under separate management and open to non-residents. It serves Tex-Mex dishes and traditional Mediterranean fare for approximately 15 euros, wine excluded (the Gajeta hotel guests get a 10% discount). In addition to this, the hotel also has a special rate agreement with a tennis club.

• 5 double rooms and 14 suites (2-4 persons), with bathroom, air-conditioning, mini-bar, satellite TV • Prices: double room single occupancy 63-89 euros, double 80-120, suite 79-184, breakfast included • Credit cards: all, Bancomat • Facility accessible to the mobility challenged, 2 rooms designed for their use. Parking in the immediate vicinity. Small pets allowed. Reception open 24 hours a day. • Wine bar. Breakfast room. Terrace, solarium.

After a day on Gaeta's splendid beaches, in the evening it is worth taking a stroll through the Medieval village as far as the port of Punta Stendardo, where you will find this osteria, housed in an old warehouse where fishermen used to store their nets and preserve anchovies in salt.
The cuisine is traditional Gaeta fare, with the fish of the day as the main attraction on a constantly changing menu. Put yourselves in Roberto Nocca's hands, and as the perfect host he will explain and recommend the various enticing dishes prepared in the kitchen by Ruggero. First of all, you should not miss the Gaeta **tiella** and its many variations, ranging from baccalà to anchovies, octopus, sconcigli, onions and vegetables. To follow this, try the fish cannelloni (we recommend the delicate fresh home-made pasta) and the **spaghetti with tiny balls of fried anchovies**, but also the linguine flavored with lemon and squid, shells with baby cuttlefish, mussels and cannellini beans, or rigatoni with rocket pesto and mussels with tomatoes. Then make way for grilled fish and shellfish from the gulf, or **baccalà** with escarole lettuce, black olives, raisins and pine-nuts, pesce sciabola alla marinara and roast **angler fish** in a sweet-sour sauce.
The wine list has expanded and now contains about one hundred national wines. Where the price is concerned, it is in the highest bracket of this guide, but you have to pay the price for fresh fish, and we think that in this case – helped by the view over the gulf that will provide a backdrop to your dinner – you will not regret it.

GAETA

VILLA FANTASIA

🛏️ Bed and breakfast
Via Roma 96
Tel. 0771 464743-349 5324129
E-mail: fabiofan@tin.it
Internet: www.villafantasia.it
Open from March to October

Serapo beach, a famous beauty spot, is only 50 meters from the refined villa refurbished with great care and opened as a B&B by Fabio Fantasia in 2003. The rooms of this friendly place are quiet and simply furnished; the shady garden is made even more appealing by the large gazebos used for breakfast and outdoor reading, the solarium and the pool with jacuzzi. In the morning, to get your day off to the best possible start, you'll be offered a selection of sweet and savory fare, with croissants, bread, butter and jam, pastries, accompanied by fruit juices, milk, tea and coffee. In the environs you can visit the Mount Orlando urban park with the cleft mountain that, according to tradition, split at the time of Christ's death. In front of the park there's the WWF blue oasis that organizes educational and recreational activities.

• 3 double rooms, with bathroom, air-conditioning, TV • Prices: double room single occupancy 40-80 euros, double 60-120, breakfast included • Credit cards: none • Off-street parking. No pets allowed. Owners always present. • Breakfast room. Garden, terrace, solarium. Pool with jacuzzi

GENZANO DI ROMA

PIETRINO E RENATA

🍲 Restaurant
Via Cervi 8
Tel. 06 9391497
Closed Monday
Open: lunch and dinner
Holidays: variable
Seating: 80
Prices: 25-28 euros, wine excluded
All credit cards except AE

This restaurant is one of the most reliable in the hodge-podge of eating places in the Castelli Romani district. Which explains why Renata and Pietrino – respectively in the kitchen and in charge of raw materials and recipes – have been successful for over forty years. It is also reassuring to see that their two young daughters, Claudia and Giorgia, who have been breathing in all this experience since they were children, now run the dining room with great confidence.
The antipasti are generous and varied, comprising numerous different samples, the most interesting of which are the **stewed beans**, fried zucchini flowers and **stuffed friggitel**i. These are followed by excellent homemade first courses, such as **pappardelle with a hare sauce**, **pasta e ceci**, classic pasta all'amatriciana, **linguine with artichokes and guanciale** and a vast selection of seasonal **soups**, which may be emmer, dry pulses or cep mushrooms. As a main course, try the **abbacchio alla svinatora**, belly of beef with sweet cicely, tagliata of rib, or cep and **galletti** mushrooms when available, cooked in various ways. Conclude with a pudding made by Claudia who has recently added a good Catalan cream and a range of interesting semifreddos to the classic local sweets.
The prices of the small wine list chosen by Pietrino are extremely reasonable.

🍞 Genzano traditional bread is the only type to have received IGP designation; you can buy it from the wood-fired ovens of Bruno Ripanucci, in Corso Don Minzoni 29, or from Panificio Tosca run by Iacoangeli, in Via Italo Belardi 45.

GRECCIO
Spinacceto

GROTTAFERRATA

HOSTERIA DI NONNA GILDA

🍲 Traditional osteria
Via Limiti sud 85-87
Tel. 0746 753144
Closed Sundays
Open: lunch and dinner
Holidays: 15 days between July and August
Seating: 25 + 10 outdoors
Prices: 24-26 euros, wine excluded
All credit cards, Bancomat

LA BRICIOLA DI ADRIANA

🍲 Restaurant
Via D'Annunzio 12
Tel. 06 9459338
Closed Sunday for dinner and Monday
Open: lunch and dinner
Holidays: variable
Seating: 35 + 15 outdoors
Prices: 30-35 euros, wine excluded
All credit cards, Bancomat

The restaurant is at the crossroads of the turn-off to the Franciscan Sanctuary of Greccio. It was once a typical country inn with a shop, but now Ellidia Cipriani has transformed it into a reliable eating place for lovers of good food and wine, who choose to stop for a complete meal, or to enjoy a glass of wine and a snack at the wine bar.
The service is friendly and informal, with rough paper napkins; the daily menu is recited and is only available in full in the evening, or if you order in advance. Homemade pasta, game, truffles and mushrooms are the strong points of the cuisine, which is all traditional. Start with **prosciutto di Norcia** and a selection of local and national cheeses, accompanied by rough pizzas with greens, roast and preserved vegetables. Follow with first courses that vary with the seasons, from **tagliolini with cep mushrooms** or truffles, to a **soup of emmer and mixed pulses** with maltagliati, while classic **pizzicotti** (small gnocchi of water and flour) with tomato, fagottini al formaggio and **ravioli with goat's ricotta** are always available. The **roast duck** is the pride of the restaurant, and there is even a duck painted on the sign outside. As an alternative main course, try the **hare chasseur** or **sautéed pheasant** with Marsala, accompanied by vegetables dressed with sabine extravirgin olive oil. The raspberries served with the panna cotta and the quince for the jams used for the crostata prepared by Ellidia's mother, all come from the family garden. The wine list sets off the meal perfectly, with wines from all the best producing areas in Italy; the mark-up is reasonable.

La Briciola is never a disappointment; it is always a pleasure to visit Adriana Montellanico again, as she confirms her skill both in the kitchen and in the affable way she welcomes customers, an approach adopted by all the members of the family who serve at table. There are a number of regular items on the menu, but also numerous novelties in which the cook's imagination and experience play an important part.
Start with the classic **zucchini alla velletrana**, misticanza with anchovies or sinews, or **vignarola** in springtime (a stew of young fava beans, artichokes and peas). Follow this with the ever-present **broccoli and arzilla** soup (made with the chiodata or petrosa species) or **bean soup with wild fennel**, but the pappardelle with ragù of galletti mushrooms and a sauce of mixed meats with tomato, or farfalle with green tomatoes, oil and herbs, flavored with parmigiano reggiano and pecorino in summer, are equally outstanding. There is a wide choice of main courses, including a **pan of small anchovies and endive**, stuffed rabbit, **cep mushrooms alla velletrana**, **boned abbacchio**, fagottini of veal with scamorza cheese, and seasonal dishes such as salad of young tuna and moscardini with fresh borlotti beans. Conclude with mille-feuilles with zabaglione and cream, fresh berries, peach, blueberry, pear or chocolate crumble and numerous versions of fruit cremolato.
The wine list contains regional and national products, and is in the hands of Adriana, who will also offer a homemade fruit liqueur at the end of the meal.

20 KM SOUTHEAST OF ROME SS 511

20 KM SOUTHEAST OF ROME

L'OSTE DELLA BON'ORA

Traditional osteria
Via Vittorio Veneto 133
Tel. 06 9413778
Closed Monday
Open: lunch and dinner
Holidays: two weeks in August
Seating: 25 + 15 outdoors
Prices: 30-33 euros, wine excluded
All credit cards, Bancomat

VERDEBORGO

3-Star Hotel
Via Anagnina 10
Tel. 06 945404
Fax 06 94546193
E-mail: info@hotelverdeborgo.it
Internet: www.hotelverdeborgo.it
Open all year

At the entrance to this new restaurant is the sign painted by illustrator Pablo Echaurren, and inside you are met by two small, cozy rooms that are pleasantly and tastefully decorated (seats are also available outdoors). After several jobs in Rome, the owners Massimo and Maria Luisa – now helped by their sons, Marco in the dining-room, and Flavio who specializes in puddings – moved to Grottaferrata, where they now propose traditional dishes, prepared with quality ingredients, with some successful and intelligent ideas of their own.

To start with, we can recommend the antipasto dell'oste which includes coppiette (strips of dried, spiced meat), cured meats, guanciale and lonza di testa or cream of zucchini with crispy pancetta, or pearls of pear with parmesan. The first courses include the classic pasta **cacio e pepe**, but also a convincing **amatriciana** served in a shell of pecorino, calamarata with an onion sauce, and handmade fettuccine alla boscaiola and gnocchi. This is followed by impeccably prepared **oxtail alla vaccinara**, **chicken alla romana**, **rabbit chasseur**, brasato of gaffo (veal cheek cooked with herbs and red wine) and several fish dishes. All the main courses are accompanied by **ramolacci** (a vegetable that grows wild locally), misticanza with poppy and orange, sweet-sour or sautéed vegetables. And to finish, the puddings of the house, Maria Luisa cream or espresso mille-feuilles.

The wine and spirits list is good, with a selection of labels from Lazio, all with reasonable mark-ups. At the end of the meal, ask the proprietor to tell your fortune: when he is in the mood, Massimo likes to read the tarot cards to his guests.

This hotel was opened in 2000 in a restored, early-1900s villa near the old center of Grottaferrata, a small village in the Castelli Romani area, famous for the splendid Abbey of San Nilo. It has elegant rooms and is surrounded by small, well-kept grounds where breakfast is served in summer. The atmosphere is relaxed and young Giada Giuliodori is always happy to try and meet the various needs of her guests. There's a generous buffet breakfast that offers a variety of sweet and savory fare: fresh fruit, fruit salads, yoghurt, cereals, traditional coffee-bar food and typical cakes during the festivities. The prices are only just within the limits laid down by our guide and remain fixed throughout the year. They include many comforts, for example, the free drinks left for you in your room's mini-bar. Other services, such as laundry, ironing and guided tours are arranged by the management on request.

• 4 single, 12 double rooms and 2 suites (2-4 persons), with bathroom, air-conditioning, mini-bar, TV, modem connection • Prices: single 105 euros, double room single occupancy 115, double 125, suite 155-200, breakfast and drinks from the mini-bar included • Credit cards: all except DC, Bancomat • 1 room designed for use by the mobility challenged. Off-street parking. No pets allowed. Reception open 24 hours a day. • Bar. Breakfast room. Grounds

FEOLA

3-Star Hotel
Via Roma 4
Tel. 0771 80205
Fax 0771 80617
E-mail: hotel.feola@libero.it
Internet: www.hotelfeola.com
Open from April to November

MARI

3-Star Hotel
Corso Pisacane 19
Tel. 0771 80101
Fax 0771 80239
E-mail: albergo.mari@tin.it
Internet: www.hotelmari.com
Holidays in winter at various times

The hotel is located near the port, directly behind the small square in the historic center. Originally an old fishermen's home that was later used as the political police headquarters during the Fascist era, the building has now been restructured and enlarged to create this family-run hotel managed by Maria Feola, with help from her husband Salvatore and their son Angelo. Breakfast is Italian style, with homemade cakes and tarts prepared by Maria, tea, coffee, milk, jams, bread and butter. It's served in the garden where the guests can also have dinner and enjoy some local specialties. The restaurant is only open from early June until the end of September, while during the months of July and August the price of a double room may go up to as much as 150 euros.

• 3 double, 6 triple and 2 four-bed rooms, with bathroom, air-conditioning, TV • Prices: double room single occupancy 55-80 euros, double 75-98 (27-32 euro supplement for extra bed), breakfast included • Credit cards: all except AE, Bancomat • Public parking in the vicinity. Small pets allowed. Reception open from 7 am to midnight. • Restaurant. Garden, solarium

Ponza is an island of volcanic origin, famous for its beautiful beaches, coves and charming natural bays. Tourists are attracted because it is reputed to have the cleanest water in the Mediterranean. Hotel Mari is on Corso Pisacane, the island's busiest street; the most attractive rooms are those that give the guests the feeling of entering the belly of an ancient sailing-vessel, but that also have a view of the sea. In the high season the price goes up. From the hotel you have a view over the entire port, dominated by the red lighthouse that was built in Bourbon times. The rooms are all nice and variously furnished. The buffet breakfast offers a variety of sweet fare, yoghurt, tea, milk and coffee. A few steps away from the hotel is Ponza's small main square that during the evening bustles with life.

• 1 single and 17 double rooms, with bathroom, mini-bar, air-conditioning • Prices: single 55-80 euros, double 85-120, breakfast included • Credit cards: all, Bancomat • Public parking in the immediate vicinity. No pets allowed. Reception open 24 hours a day. • Breakfast room

Island of Ponza

Silvia

🔑 1-Star Hotel
Via Marina Santa Maria
Tel. 0771 80075
Fax 0771 80742
E-mail: pensionesilvia@libero.it
Internet: www.wel.it/silvia.html
Open from March to October

Facing out onto the bay of Santa Maria, the Silvia Hotel welcomes you to premises with a simple but comfortable atmosphere. This is the ideal choice for those who love the sea and good food. The hotel is in an historic building directly facing the beach and the quiet rooms with a view reflect those of island-style houses. Tables in the restaurant are sheltered by a cane-roofed veranda and seem to intermingle with the boats drawn up on the sand. The kitchen mainly focuses on fish dishes and the price of a meal averages 30-35 euros, beverages included. Breakfast is served at your table and offers sweet fare along with tea, milk and coffee. On the beach guests can rent a boat to go and explore the island's reefs and many bays.

• 10 double rooms, with bathroom; 5 with balcony • Prices: double room single occupancy 49-70 euros, double 70-100, breakfast included • Credit cards: all major ones, Bancomat • Parking in the immediate vicinity. No pets allowed. Reception open from 8 am to midnight. • Restaurant. Veranda

Itri

Mandrarita

🔑 Holiday farm
Strada Provinciale Itri-Sperlonga km 4,800
Tel. 0771 729186-329 4276035
E-mail: info@mandrarita.it
Internet: www.mandrarita.it
Open from April to October

The Itri-Sperlonga road is quite a challenge with its succession of hairpin bends, although it rewards those who choose to take it with a splendid panorama and a relaxing sense of isolation. The vacation farm belongs to Marisa Ruggieri and her brother Giancarlo, who respectively take care of hospitality and managing the farm. Guests are guaranteed silence, the coolness of the grounds and hills and the pleasure of using the swimming pool. The rooms are furnished in arte povera style and all of them have a mezzanine floor so a third bed can be added. For breakfast you'll be offered fresh fruit, jams, homemade cakes, yoghurt and fruit juices. The restaurant serves dishes based on traditional recipes, enhanced by the use of excellent ingredients such as fruit, vegetables, olive oil and wine produced on the farm. The famous beach of Sperlonga is only ten kilometers away.

• 6 double rooms, with bathroom, terrace • Prices: double room single occupancy 55 euros, double 90 (35 euro supplement for extra bed), breakfast included • Credit cards: all, Bancomat • Off-street parking. Reception open from 7 am to 10 pm. • Restaurant. Breakfast room, TV room. Grounds, solarium. Pool

10 KM FROM CENTER OF LATINA

HOSTERIA LA FENICE

🍲 Recently opened osteria
Via Bellini 8
Tel. 0773 240225
Closed Sunday for dinner and Wednesday, in summer Wednesday for lunch and Sunday
Open: lunch and dinner
Holidays: 7 days variable, 4 in December
Seating: 50 + 20 outdoors
Prices: 33-35 euros, wine excluded
Credit cards: CartaSi, Bancomat

IL CASALE CORTE ROSSA

🗝 Holiday farm
Strada Provinciale Borgo Sabotino 49
Tel. e fax 0773 645766
E-mail: corterossa@tin.it
Internet: www.corterossa.it
Closed in November

The sound traditional skills of Graziella and Sandra, combined with the dynamism of the young but expert Emiliano Caggiari front of house, create a winning combination that continues to draw satisfied crowds to this restaurant. The menu does occasionally include less usual proposals, but the references to local tradition – for both the raw ingredients and the recipes – remain deep rooted. This is underlined by the selection of antipasti, which let you sample a range of antipasti including **prosciutto from Bassiano**, savory rustic pies, baked ewe's milk ricotta with Campoli truffles, and homemade pickles. The first courses vary with the seasons, but we can recommend the **spaghettoni of flour and water with broccoli and marzolina cheese**, tagliolini with Campoli truffles, **ravioli of vegetables and ewe's milk ricotta**, or the **soup of emmer, chickpea and cannellini beans**, pasta e fagioli and **scafata**, a soup from the Lepini mountains made with artichokes, fava beans and potatoes. Truffle lovers can grate some on a tagliata of beef with fava bean purée, or simply on a fried egg. The other main courses exploit the local meat, such as **stewed kid** with white wine, rabbit stuffed or cooked in Marsala, **roast veal shank** and **pork loin with chestnuts**; and you will always find **stewed snails** and **stewed frog's legs**. The meal is brought to a close with homemade puddings: mille-feuilles with buffalo ricotta, crème caramel and crostata with sour cherries.
The wine list is well stocked and it is always possible to order wine by the glass, even prestigious varieties.

Although the sea is only two kilometers away, if you choose to stay here it will be mostly to enjoy the peaceful, green surroundings of the 100-hectare estate. Parts of the original structure of this farmhouse built in 1929 have been adapted (like the cattle sheds that have been transformed into comfortable suites), but the agricultural activity continues to this day – they raise cows, sheep, goats and show-jumping horses. The tastefully furnished rooms offer adequate levels of comfort; the suites, which are more spacious, have an entrance from the garden area. Products from the estate are used in the kitchen to produce traditional farmhouse-style dishes served in the restaurant, which is also open to non-residents (average price 25 euros per person). The interesting botanical garden of Ninfa, Park of Circeo, the temple of Hercules at Cori and the town of Anzio are all within easy reach.

• 9 double rooms and 1 suite, with bathroom, air-conditioning, mini-bar, TV • Prices: double room single occupancy 50-70 euros, double 55-85, suite 70-100 (20 euro supplement for extra bed), breakfast included • Credit cards: all, Bancomat • 1 room designed for use by the mobility challenged. Off-street parking. No pets allowed. Owners always present. • Bar, restaurant, refreshment rooms. Grounds with small lake. Pool

Latina

Borgo Fàiti

8 KM FROM CITY CENTER

LA LOCANDA DEL BERE 🍷

Restaurant
Via Foro Appio 64
Tel. 0773 258620-618620
Closed Sunday
Open: lunch and dinner
Holidays: 15 days in August
Seating: 50
Prices: 33-35 euros
All credit cards, Bancomat

One of the small group of houses along the Via Appia near Latina, that make up the hamlet of Borgo Fàiti, bears the sign of the restaurant run by Maurizio and Antonella Mangoni; it has a number of regular customers who enjoy an aperitif and a snack in the lower dining-room, or a complete meal in the restaurant itself. In both cases the result is more than satisfactory, partly because of the choice between meat dishes and fish brought in from Terracina which is not far away.

The best way to start is with the selection of antipasti, where you are spoilt for choice between turf (carpaccio and buffalo mozzarella, hot croutons, vegetable pies, small omelet) and surf (**marinated anchovies**, pressed octopus, fillets of bass). As a first course, we must mention the tagliolini al coccio and the **spaghetti with lucerna and tomatoes**, which are almost a meal in themselves, but you will also find trofie with totani and smoked provola, **pasta and beans** with Campoli truffles, gnocchetti with wild asparagus and classic **strozzapreti with wild boar sauce**. Guinea-fowl stuffed with cep mushrooms, **veal shank**, baccalà with truffles, **cep mushrooms with polenta** – plus various dishes with the day's catch – make up the wide choice of main courses which lead up to the locanda's traditional pudding: plates of fruit, ice cream and sweets that vary constantly, which are good to look at even before you discover how good they are to eat.

The choice of wines is broad and correctly priced, as you would expect from a restaurant that is also a wine shop.

Latina

LA TABERNA DEI LARI 🍲

Recently opened osteria
Via Leopardi 21
Tel. 0773 411061
Closed Monday
Open: only for dinner
Holidays: in August
Seating: 40 + 20 outdoors
Prices: 33-35 euros, wine excluded
All credit cards, Bancomat

Roberto Faraglia, the proprietor and chef of this simple, down-to-earth osteria, returned to his native Latina a few years ago, and now dedicates all his passion to the delightful restaurant he runs with his wife Isabella. In the small dining-room in winter and on the veranda in summer, the atmosphere is always pleasant and you can be certain of finding something to enjoy at all times of the year.

A few legitimate creative inventions of Roberto's do not exclude the traditional proposals which, on the contrary, seem to be more numerous than in the past. To start with, **croutons with buffalo mozzarella from Fossanova**, eggplant pie and **sautéed mussels, clams and razor clams**; we must also mention the antipasto dei Lari, a selection of cold cuts and cheese, which could also be served at the end of the meal, and which Roberto puts together from an assortment of almost forty different types. The first courses include a classic, **pici** of flour and water with Pachino cherry tomatoes, but you should also try the sedanini cacio e pepe, **spaghetti with bass and salted ricotta** and the **calamarata with anchovies, zucchini and anchovy colatura**. The main courses may be meat – sucking pig with fresh beans and wild fennel – or fish from the Circeo area, particularly in the summer: mixed grills but also jumbo shrimp alla marinara, **turbot with potatoes** and **olives of swordfish and eggplant**. We have already mentioned the wide choice of cheeses, after which you can finish with one of the many puddings: mille-feuilles, cremolata of strawberries and raspberries, chocolate mousse and granita of figs.

There are over a hundred wines on the list, with a good assortment of local and Italian labels.

36 KM NORTHEAST OF LATINA

54 KM WEST OF RIETI

CASAL DEI LUPI

LA PERGOLA

🔑⚬3-Star Hotel
Strada Provinciale Farneta km 0,850
Tel. 0773 952800
Fax 0773 951969
E-mail: casaldeilupi.latina@libero.it
Internet: www.casaldeilupi.com
Open all year

🔑⚬3-Star Hotel
Via Flaminia km 64
Tel. 0744 919841-2-3-4
Fax 0744 919142
E-mail: info@lapergola.it
Internet: www.lapergola.it
Open all year

Leave main road 156 at the junction for Maenza-Carpineto, maybe after having visited the archeological site that's right on the corner. After only a couple of kilometers you'll find yourself in a peaceful oasis: greenery, silence, a lovely shaded garden and a beautiful swimming pool. Then a charming restaurant comprising two private rooms with a beautiful patio where you'll be able to lunch for a price starting at 20 euros per person. Last but not least, the rooms are all furnished with antiques but at the same time equipped with every modern comfort, from air-conditioning to satellite TV and an Internet connection. Breakfast offers cappuccino, tea, brioches and other cakes, bread, butter and jam. The XIIIth-century baronial castle of Maenza and Cistercian Abbey of Fossanova are both well worth a visit.

La Pergola is on the Via Flaminia, on the border between Latium and Umbria, at the foot of the hill that leads up to the village of Magliano Sabina. Property of the Massoli family, in the old days the hotel was a staging post where mail coach horses were changed. There are extensive outdoor spaces and a beautiful view of the Tiber valley, while the spacious rooms with their brick arches are comfortable and tastefully furnished. The buffet breakfast consists of coffee, milk, tea, butter, jams and homemade cakes. The restaurant has a nice menu that mainly focuses on somewhat revisited, though typical local dishes, along with an interesting wine list. A meal costs an average of 35 euros per person. A wine cellar has recently been added – open from Wednesday to Saturday – that offers a few warm dishes and a variety of cured meats and cheese platters.

• 4 double rooms, with bathroom, air-conditioning, mini-bar, satellite TV, modem connection; 5 apartments (3 persons) with kitchenette • Prices: double room single occupancy 35-50 euros, double 60-90, breakfast included; apartment 60-90 euros, breakfast 6 euros • Credit cards: all, Bancomat • 1 apartment designed for use by the mobility challenged. Off-street parking. Small pets allowed (only in apartments). Reception open 24 hours a day • Bar, restaurant. Breakfast room. Garden. Pool

• 1 single, 21 double and 1 triple rooms, with bathroom, air-conditioning, mini-bar, TV • Prices: single and double room single occupancy 56 euros, double 87, triple 110, breakfast included • Credit cards: all, Bancomat • 2 rooms designed for use by the mobility challenged. Off-street parking. Small pets allowed. Reception open 24 hours a day. • Restaurant, wine cellar. TV room. Conference room. Garden, covered terrace.

Magliano Sabina
Madonna degli Angeli

Marino

Ristorante-
Locanda degli Angeli

⌒ Restaurant/3-Star Hotel
Località Madonna degli Angeli 1
Tel. 0744 91892-91377
Fax 0744 91892
E-mail: rh.angeli@libero.it
Internet: www.hoteldegliangeli.it
Closet Sunday dinner and Monday
Open: lunch and dinner
Holidays: in August
Seating: 100 + 50 outdoors
Prices: 30-35 euros wine excluded
All credit cards, Bancomat

Cantina Colonna

⌒ Restaurant
Via Carissimi 32
Tel. 06 93660386
Closed Wednesday
Open: dinner, Saturday and Sunday also for lunch
Holidays: 15-20 days in August
Seating: 50
Prices: 27-30 euros, wine excluded
All major credit cards, Bancomat

The Marciani family runs a restaurant and a number of rooms full of charm and comfort (available all week) with spectacular views of the hills. Breakfast includes a vast array of pastries, but also cured meats and cheeses.
At mealtime you are spoilt for choice. We recommend sheep's milk **ricotta-filled zucchini flowers**, black truffle and Parmesan, and eggplant pie with shallot sauce. Among the first courses, fresh strozzapreti pasta with speck and zucchini, fresh square-shaped pasta with vegetable ragù, outstanding homemade **tagliolini al guaciale**, **Swiss chard tortelli**, chickpeas and ricotta, served with potato polenta al rosmarino. Main courses are meat-based, as per the area's tradition: **lamb a scottadito**, **roast kid**, guinea-fowl alla leccarda or glazed with fruit. However, **oven-baked baccalà** in a bread crust or scamorza with cep mushrooms are appetizing alternatives. The homemade pudding and **cheese boards** are well-assorted, including panna cotta with warm chocolate sauce. The quality and length of the wine list is remarkable, the home wine is exceptionally good.

🛏• 7 double rooms and 1 suite (4 people), en-suite (jacuzzi), air-conditioned, terrace, mini-bar, television, modem connection • Prices: double single use 67, double 83, suite 109 euros, breakfast included • 1 room suitable for the mobility-impaired. Private outdoor parking. No pets. Porter on duty from 7am to midnight • Restaurant. Reading and tv rooms. Park, patio

The formula adopted by the restaurant run by the Mari family in the center of Marino, has always been to offer dishes of strong tradition, with the result that over the years it has become a benchmark for the cuisine of the Castelli Romani district. For many people who run restaurants in this area, it would be easy to give into the folkloristic appeal of huge quantities, flirting waitresses, and rivers of wine on tap (an early 20th century poem mentioned fountains of wine) without worrying about the quality. But not here, where the atmosphere and the cooking maintain a sobriety that translates into precise flavors and respect for the traditions of the past, although the recipes themselves are somewhat lighter than they would have been once. Everything is offered with generosity, starting from the antipasto of small omelets, cold cuts and preserves in oil. The first courses are a sort of guide to local culinary history: various shapes of pasta served all'**amatriciana**, alla carbonara, alla **gricia** or **cacio e pepe**, **rigatoni with an oxtail sauce**, **fettuccine** with a hare sauce or **with chicken giblets**, and soups of vegetables and pulses. The main courses are equally reassuring: roast or grilled **abbacchio**, or chicken with bell peppers, **tripe alla romana** and **oxtail alla vaccinara**, game when in season, and breast of veal alla fornara with potatoes. As a pudding, we recommend avoiding the more banal proposals and trying a classic homemade crostata.
In addition to the best wines from Lazio, there are also several labels from outside the region, all proposed with honest mark-ups.

MARINO

LA CREDENZA

🍲 Trattoria
Via Cola di Rienzo 4
Tel. 06 9385105
Closed Sunday
Open: lunch and dinner
Holidays: August and Christmas
Seating: 30
Prices: 33-35 euros, wine excluded
No credit cards accepted

The restaurant is close to the historical Palazzo Colonna and consists of just one room, rather like the sitting-room in a private home, decorated with a beautiful dresser. A small number of tables are the stage on which Massimo Lauri, an architect who has turned his attention to food, successfully performs his role as a rough and ready but appealing inn-keeper from the Castelli Romani. His wife Maria D'Annunzio, is completely different, and she produces dishes inspired by the traditions of the Castelli Romani and Abruzzo.
A specialty from Abruzzo to start your meal with, if you are there at the right time of year, is an **omelet of orapi** (a sort of spinach picked on the Gran Sasso when the snow melts) accompanied by different croutons with eggs and truffles, or with **coratella di abbacchio**. This is followed by a long list of first courses, which includes **fettuccine with meatballs and veal olives**, rigatoni with an oxtail sauce, **pasta and broccoli with arzilla consommé, a soup of baccalà and chickpeas** and various types of risotto. Tradition also influences the main courses, and you can choose between a good **tripe alla romana** and **oxtail alla vaccinara**, but also rabbit with olives and beans with pork rind. You can opt for a fish menu, if you arrange it in advance (but this will obviously raise the price somewhat).
For the wine, to start with, try some of the house Marino served by the carafe, but then ask your theatrical host to tell you what he knows about wine: the cellar is sure to have some surprises in store.

MONTEFIASCONE

URBANO V

🗝 3-Star Hotel
Corso Cavour 107
Tel. 0761 831094
Fax 0761 834152
E-mail: info@hotelurbano-v.it
Internet: www.hotelurbano-v.it
Open all year

Although this is a modern facility, it's located in a beautiful old palazzo in the historic center of Montefiascone, a village that is famous for its Est! Est!! Est!!! wine. The rooms are airy, simply though elegantly furnished and equipped with all modern comforts. On sunny days, the large terrace offers guests a beautiful panorama that stretches from the Cimini Hills over the wide Etruscan plain, to the Tyrrhenian Sea, Lake Bolsena and Mount Amiata. The hotel periodically organizes excursions and wine-tasting visits to nearby wine cellars for groups of at least ten people.

• 16 double rooms and 6 suites, with bathroom, air-conditioning, mini-bar, safe, satellite TV, modem connection • Prices: double room single occupancy 60-80 euros, double 70-100, suite 110, breakfast included • Credit cards: all, Bancomat • 1 room designed for use by the mobility challenged. Public parking in the immediate vicinity, garage (2 spaces, 8 euros per day). No pets allowed. Reception open 24 hours a day. • Bar. Meeting and conference room. Terrace

Monte Porzio Catone

I TINELLONI

☞Restaurant
Via dei Tinelloni 10
Tel. 06 9447071
Closed Wednesday
Open: lunch and dinner
Holidays: between July and August
Seating: 75 + 20 outdoors
Prices: 25-30 euros, wine excluded
All credit cards, Bancomat

The wine shops in the old towns in the Castelli Romani used to be called "tinelli". Tina Intreccialagli and her husband Enzo Pompei began their culinary adventure in one of these just over fifteen years ago. She works in the kitchen, preparing traditional local dishes, while he is an enthusiastic sommelier, and searches constantly for quality raw ingredients.

A taste of local cured meats, which include an excellent guanciale, accompanied by bruschetta and seasonal vegetables grilled or preserved in oil, will prepare you for the substantial first courses which range from classic **bucatini all'amatriciana** to **spaghetti cacio e pepe**, **mezzemaniche with galletti mushrooms** and the delicious seasonal soups. The menu continues with dishes that it is difficult to choose between: guinea-fowl with brandy and black olives, **pork loin with milk**, and delicate stuffed chicken parcels, although we still prefer the classic Roman dishes like **oxtail alla vaccinara**, **coratella with artichokes** and the excellent **grilled abbacchio chops** (all the meat comes from farms in the Carpineto area). The puddings range from crostata with jam made by your hostess, to crème brûlée, which we recommend, a perfect balance of flavors, and baked ciambelline. The cellar is run by Enzo and offers a reasonable selection of labels that accompany the meal very well.

🍴 The Antico Panificio Egidi, in Piazza Porzio Catone, makes many different types of bread and traditional local products: ciambelle al vino, serpette all'uovo and tozzetti biscuits with nuts.

Monte San Biagio

HOSTARIA DELLA PIAZZETTA 🐌

☞Trattoria
Viale Littoria 13
Tel. 0771 566793
Closed Tuesday
Open: lunch and dinner
Holidays: none
Seating: 50
Prices: 30 euros, wine excluded
No credit cards accepted

Flaviano and Luisa Rizzi will welcome you to their pleasant restaurant, close to the old center of Monte San Biagio, with its attractive but little known old lanes, where you can enjoy the best traditional dishes from the town and nearby Lago di Fondi, prepared with unchanging passion.

Start with a classic mixed antipasto, where it is the raw ingredients that make the difference: marzolina made with the milk from a native species of goat that risked extinction, or dried sausage (protected by the DOP designation) made from the outstanding local black pig. On your journey of discovery of ancient flavors and recipes, choose a first course from among the soup with erba santamaria, **pettl e fasuol**, **frascatejell with milk**, zippi with broccoli and sausage or **linguine with ambariegl** (shrimp). The Lago di Fondi serves up its treasures, unfortunately scarcer every year, but with a little luck, you might find **soup of frog's legs**, **fried eel**, **stewed snails** and fried ambariegl. Apart from the excellent **grilled baccalà**, it is the local meat that dominates the main courses: coratella of lamb, **abbuot alla fressor** (fried lamb gut), **stewed fellata mutton** and local sausage. The puddings – mostaccioli, ciambelline al vino, crostata of sour cherries and amaretto cake – are simple and homemade and bring the meal to a pleasant conclusion, washed down by the many liqueurs that Flaviano makes from local berries and plants: cetrangole, olive leaves, wild fennel and jujube.

A small wine list accompanies the meal satisfactorily.

Montopoli di Sabina

43 km southwest of Rieti SS 4

Casale del Farfa

🍽 Restaurant
Via Ternana 53
Tel. 0765 322047
Closed Tuesday
Open: lunch and dinner
Holidays: between July and August
Seating: 60 + 30 outdoors
Prices: 25-28 euros, wine excluded
All major credit cards, Bancomat

Located halfway between Rome and Rieti, a few miles from the 5th century Abbey of Farfa, this restaurant is actually a farm, with an annexed restaurant inside an old farmhouse. The building also has a veranda which is very popular in summer, while indoors there is a large room with lovely wooden beams and tables laid in the manner of an old fashioned country trattoria. Alessio Moroni looks after the farm, while his wife Cristina runs the restaurant. She will help you to choose from among the traditional dishes, which are now prepared by Massimo Pigliaceli.
You can start with the antipasto misto del Casale, which includes cheese, olives and good homemade pickles. The list of first courses is a compendium of different types of homemade pasta, **gnocchetti of ricotta and spinach** with tomato, **stringozzi cacio e pepe**, **pappardelle with a mutton sauce** and fettuccine with asparagus and saffron. The meat from the farm or from local breeders is the strong point of the main course, like the mixed grill, diced pork with cep mushrooms, chicken with lemon or **coratella of abbacchio alla romana**. As an alternative, there are cheese dishes, such as honeyed pecorino with pears or grilled homemade cheese. Each dish is accompanied by a rich mixed salad, grilled eggplant or French fries.
There is a good selection of homemade puddings, and a choice between the house wine on tap, and the labels on the small wine list.

🛢 The shop alongside the restaurant sells oil, cheese, vegetables and seasonal fruit produced on the farm. Telephone first at weekends to check that it is open.

Orte
Seripola

30 km northeast of Viterbo

Locanda della Chiocciola

🍲 Rooms
Loclità Seripola
Tel. 0761 402734-348 5108309
Fax 0761 490254
E-mail: info@lachiocciola.net
Internet: www.lachiocciola.net
Closed for 20 days in December and 15 between January and February

Follow the road from Orte to Amelia, take a left in the direction of Penne in Teverina and after two kilometers you'll find the Locanda della Chiocciola, on the borders of Latium and Umbria. A farmhouse dating from the fifteenth century, with an old annex surrounded by greenery and efficiently managed by Roberto and Maria Cristina de Fonseca Pimentel. The eight rooms are all different from one another, furnished with antiques and equipped with every comfort (the double superior room can cost up to 126 euros). The buffet breakfast offers cakes, cookies, homemade ciambelloni and savories. For your leisure you can use the outdoor swimming pool. The area is just right for excursions on foot or bicycle and also for guided tours. The restaurant is open for non-residents from Thursday evening to Sunday lunchtime and offers typical local dishes accompanied by wines from central Italy, at an average price of 27 euros per person.

• 4 double, 3 triple and 1 four-bed rooms, with bathroom, mini-bar, TV • Prices: double room single occupancy 70 euros, standard double 100-110 (35-55 euro supplement for extra bed), breakfast included • Credit cards: Visa, Bancomat • 1 room designed for use by the mobility challenged. Off-street parking. No pets allowed. Reception open from 7 am to midnight. • Restaurant. Breakfast room, billiard room. Garden, Pool, fitness center

PALIANO

TAVERNA COLONNA

⬭ Restaurant
Via Lepanto 5
Tel. 0775 571044
Closed Sunday for dinner and Monday
Open: lunch and dinner
Holidays: 1 week in January and 1 in July
Seating: 60 + 40 outdoors
Prices: 27-30 euros, wine excluded
All credit cards, Bancomat

The Taverna is located inside Palazzo Colonna; it is a pleasant, relaxing environment, and in summer you can eat alfresco in the courtyard. The cellar, which is Francesca's department, is also a wine shop and has an excellent variety of labels, all sold at acceptable prices, some of which can also be tasted by the glass.

The kitchen is Enzo's realm, and he revisits recipes and products from Ciociaria with imagination, but does not forgo a few experiments with fish. There is a satisfactory set meal, or you can choose à la carte, starting with the steamed Mediterranean shrimp with basil mayonnaise, **panzanella with fried zucchini flowers**, eggplant flans with ricotta and carpaccio of mozzarella with oil. As a first course we recommend the **patac-cacce with vegetable ragù**, the **soup of mad herbs**, **fini-fini** with veal olives, **tagliatelle** with jumbo shrimp and zucchini, and spaghetti alla chitarra with rabbit, fresh vegetables and Gaeta olives. Then try the combination of turbot and salmon with seasonal vegetables, **kid with thyme**, aromatic saddle of veal, grilled buffalo steak and **artichokes alla giudia**. A broad selection of Italian **cheeses** leads to a good choice of puddings, including a crispy wafer with fresh fruit and vanilla ice cream, trifle and cream of cherry and green apple.

We have already mentioned the well-stocked cellar, and we confirm our appreciation for a restaurant which certainly deserves our little snail, for the food, but also for the friendly welcome and the excellent service.

PISONIANO

BACCO

⬭ Trattoria
Via Piagge 16
Tel. 06 9577224-9577005
Closed Monday and Sunday for dinner
Open: lunch and dinner
Holidays: 15 days in September
Seating: 60
Prices: 20-22 euros, wine excluded
No credit cards accepted

The upper Aniene Valley, between Tivoli and Subiaco, maintains its strong rural identity, practically unaffected by the vicinity of the Rome-l'Aquila motorway. Pisoniano is surrounded by olive trees and pastureland (but do not forget to visit the Hemp Museum), at the foot of the green Mount Mentorella, the highest peak in the Prenestini mountains, where a famous sanctuary, now very popular with excursionists, used to connect the transhumance routes from Abruzzo and Lazio.

The old inn was taken over thirteen years ago by Augusto, a retired teacher, who now welcomes you into two spotless rooms, offering traditional dishes prepared by his wife Rina. The antipasto is simple, but you will appreciate the quality of the raw ingredients, including the bread: homemade prosciutto and cured meats, olives and croutons with mushrooms. This is followed by the first courses, particularly small tunas with vegetables, **pasta and beans**, gnocchi longhi, **fettuccine with cep mushrooms**, **sagne with baccalà** and **ricotta ravioli**. The main courses feature meat from local farms: the **roast suckling pig** is the highlight, but the **grilled abbacchio**, sausages and pork loin are almost as good. Each dish is accompanied by seasonal vegetables, mainly homegrown: green beans, tomatoes, and broccoli sautéed or in a tart sauce. A good pecorino may conclude the meal perfectly or introduce the puddings, such as strudel with strawberries, ciambelline with aniseed or tozzetti with almonds.

You can trust the local red, which is honest and drinkable, but there are also some good bottles that will not weigh too heavily on the check.

Poggio Moiano

Da Maria Fontana

Trattoria
Viale Manzoni 13
Tel. 0765 876169
Closed Monday
Open: lunch, dinner on booking
Holidays: 1 week in August and 1 in January
Seating: 70
Prices: 25 euros, wine excluded
Credit cards: Visa, Bancomat

Founded in the fourteenth century, Poggio Moiano lies in the Sabine Hills near to the Via Salaria, one of the old Consular roads. If you are there in the last weekend in June, you can take part in the Infiorata, when the local inhabitants celebrate the holiday of the Sacro Cuore di Gesù. The trattoria is still named after the mother of Anna Rosa and Rodolfo, the current proprietors, who continue her work. It looks like so many other trattorias, with no particular attraction, but it is worth stopping there to taste what it has to offer.

Once you are sat down, start with an antipasto, which gives the kitchen time to prepare the rest of the meal that is cooked on the spot. You will be offered cured meats, omelet, local types of cheese and vegetables in oil, possibly accompanied by some hot **coratella**. The homemade pasta is rough and crisp: **capelli d'angelo**, **fettuccine**, tagliatelle with chestnut flour or **ravioli filled with greens and ricotta**, served with a **mutton sauce**, or tomato and basil, pork ribs or a simple white sauce of asparagus or cep mushrooms. Another first course that we recommend is the **lasagna with spinach and mushrooms**. The meat is simple and tasty, mainly grilled, and all from organic farms in the Sabine hills: sausages, steak and pork chops to start with, but there are also some more elaborate main courses, such as **straccetti with cep mushrooms** and truffles. If you are still hungry, finish your meal with a pudding, and we recommend the sour cherry crostata in summer, and the panna cotta with chocolate in winter.

The cellar is limited to a few local labels, as well as carafes of the house wine.

Ponzano Romano

Monterone

Holiday farm
Contrada Monterone
Tel. e fax 0765 338019
E-mail:
agriturismo.dipillo@flashnet.it
Internet: www.dipillo.it
Open from April to December

This vacation farm lies on a hillside that rises up from the right-hand bank of the River Tiber and is surrounded by countryside. After having spent most of his life traveling around the world, a few years ago Nunzio Di Pillo decided to refurbish two of his properties: rooms are located in the old medieval watch-tower and adjacent buildings, while the old farmhouse has been transformed into an apartment, with two bathrooms and a kitchenette that's rented out to groups of at least six people. The furnishings are restrained and Nunzio decided not to put a TV in the rooms. The farm practices organic agriculture and produces jams and honeys that are offered to guests for breakfast, along with homemade pastries, coffee and light refreshments. Other products such as eggs, meat, olive oil, legumes and vegetables are used in the restaurant (there's a fixed price menu at 25 euros per person).

• 4 double rooms and 1 suite, with bathroom; suite with mini-bar • Prices: double room single occupancy 45 euros, double 75, suite 95 (20 euro supplement for extra bed), breakfast included • Credit cards: all, Bancomat • Facility partly accessible to the mobility challenged. Off-street parking. Small pets allowed. Owners reachable from 7 am to midnight. • Restaurant. Breakfast room. Grounds

POSTA FIBRENO

IL CASALE

🚜Holiday farm
Contrada La Pesca 5
Tel. 0776 871744-333 1352593-335 6110510
Fax 0776 871744-890478
E-mail: info@agriturismoilcasale.it
Internet: www.agriturismoilcasale.it
Open in August and at weekends

Located within the Lake Posta Fibreno Nature Reserve, this vacation farm overlooks the river Fibreno which is populated by much sought-after species of fish, such as the spotted trout and the rare carp. The farmhouse itself is surrounded by greenery and has recently been restructured. Rooms are spacious, simply furnished and offer the guests the possibility of a truly relaxing vacation. Owner, Antonietta La Pietra, offers a traditional-style breakfast, with milk, tea, tarts and coffee. The restaurant, which is open to non-residents, has a set menu of dishes made from the farm's products (vegetables, eggs, wine, olive oil, fresh meats) at an average price of 27 euros per person (half board costs 60 euros). The lake offers many opportunities for sports as do the facility's organized outdoor areas that include a volleyball court and a space to practice archery.

• 1 single and 5 double rooms, with bathroom, TV • Prices: single 40 euros, double 80, breakfast included • Credit cards: all, Bancomat • 1 room designed for use by the mobility challenged. Off-street parking. No pets allowed. Owners always reachable. • Restaurant. Garden

PRIVERNO
Ceriara

ANTICA OSTERIA 🐌🏆🍾
FANTI

🍲Restaurant
Strada Statale 156 km 29,300
Tel. 0773 924015
Closed Thursday
Open: lunch and dinner
Holidays: October 20-30, Christmas and 26 December
Seating: 40 + 15 outdoors
Prices: 33-35 euros, wine excluded
Credit cards: DC, Visa, Bancomat

For the last eight years, our snail, bottle and cheese symbols have rewarded one of the best restaurants in the province of Latina, where the merit goes equally to Annunziata Fanti in the kitchen and Tommaso De Massimi in the dining-room (with the precious assistance of their children). The result of their efforts is a restaurant where guests like to return, where tradition is respected and revered, but also intelligently reinterpreted.

The set meal comprises five courses, but there is also a rich à la carte menu that changes with the seasons. To start with, **flan of Priverno artichokes** with a cream sauce of fava beans and calamint, rabbit terrine with cannellini beans and **fishcakes of baccalà** with purée of chickpeas. And you must try the **bazzoffia** (a soup typical of Priverno with artichokes, peas, greens, egg and pecorino, which was once a meal in itself) or the **chiacchetegli soup**, while for a traditional dish of pasta, we recommend the millerighe with buffalo speck and salted ricotta, trucioli of flour and water with sausage and marzolina cheese, or egg spaghetti with sausage and broccoli. As a main course, **stewed buffalo** with cabbage in white wine, rabbit with rosemary and **black Carpineto pig** with cannellini beans from Atina. End your meal with a classic mille-feuilles, a crostata with orange marmalade, and custard, or the tortino di ciambella cresciuta (a typical Priverno pudding) with cream, pears and chocolate.

The selection of cheese and wines is always extensive, with the focus on local production.

PRIVERNO
Fossanova

PROSSEDI

35 KM EAST OF LATINA ON SS 156

36 KM EAST OF LATINA, 16 KM FROM FROSINONE SS 156

ANTICO BORGO

OSTERIA PERSEI

3-Star Hotel
Via dell'Abbazia 9
Tel. e fax 0773 939110
E-mail:
albergoanticoborgo@gmail.com
Internet: www.albergoanticoborgo.it
Open all year

Traditional osteria
Vicolo del Montano 3
Tel. 0773 957351
Closed Monday through Wednesday,
in August Monday only
Open: dinner, Sunday also for lunch
Holidays: 1 week in November, 10 days for Christmas
Seating: 50 + 40 outdoors
Prices: 28-30 euros, wine excluded
All major credit cards, Bancomat

This is a unique hotel, in so far as it welcomes guests in a hall with a glass floor, under which you can see the remains of an ancient Roman villa. The hotel is in the medieval village of Fossanova, famous for its abbey which contained the cells of San Tommaso d' Aquino and other Cistercian monks. In addition to the natural charm of the place itself, the rooms are really attractive, fitted with classic furniture that caters well for today's requirements. Breakfast is served in a cozy room and includes milk, rusks, coffee, tea, croissants, bread, butter and jams, but also savory fare and seasonal fresh fruit. In spring and summer the village and the abbey are livelier as there are a number of quality cultural and musical events, adding to the attractiveness of this beautiful place.

• 10 double rooms, with bathroom, TV • Prices: double room single occupancy 55 euros, double 80; breakfast included • Credit cards: all, Bancomat • Facility accessible to the mobility challenged. Public parking in the immediate vicinity. Small pets allowed. Reception open 24 hours a day. • Bar. Breakfast room. Garden

Daniela and Mirko will be pleased to welcome you to the lovely room that was once an oil mill, or to the large garden where you can eat alfresco in summer.
The kitchen is entrusted to the capable hands of mother Concetta, who prepares dishes that are part of local tradition without too many frills. You can start with **buffalo mozzarella from Amaseno**, homecured prosciutto and a good selection of Italian cured meats accompanied by various types of bruschetta and croutons. This is followed by convincing **soups** (pulses, bread and vegetables, and in summer, fava beans, peas, artichokes and biede) and a whole variety of homemade fresh pastas: mezzemaniche alla pecoraia, **pappardelle with a musk duck sauce**, tagliolini with wild asparagus, **long fusilli with minced buffalo meat** and a sauce of basil and toasted almonds, and gnocchi with lamb sauce. Then try the **fried breaded lamb**, boar steak, buffalo chasseur, **stewed boar with chestnuts and honey**, fillet, T-bone steaks and **ciambella di Morolo** (a local cheese) **al coccio with vegetables**. All the dishes are served with sautéed cep mushrooms or vegetable flans. There is a good choice of puddings prepared by Daniela at the end of the meal, and we recommend the tiramisù with peaches, almond cake with bitter orange marmalade, crostata with green tomato jam and the good fresh cherry cake.
The wine list is Mirko's department, and it continues to improve; the attention to local labels and the honest mark-up, have won it one of our bottles.

729   LAZIO

11 KM NORTH OF RIETI ON SS 521

L'OSTERIA

TENUTA DUE LAGHI

Trattoria
Vicolo Fra' Fedele Bressi 4
Tel. 0746 496666
Closed Saturday for dinner and Sunday
Open: lunch and dinner
Holidays: variable in summer
Seating: 25
Prices: 20-22 euros, wine excluded
No credit cards accepted

Holiday farm
Località Campigliano 29
Tel. 0746 685206-347 7705131
Fax 0746 685206
E-mail: info@tenutaduelaghi.it
Internet: www.tenutaduelaghi.it
Closed in November

Close to Rieti station, right next to the gate into the old town set in the austere stone walls, is the restaurant opened by Sergio Mancini in 1994. The excellence of the Romanesco cuisine, the low prices, the simple decor and the cordial welcome given to guests made it an immediate success. Today Sergio is no longer there, but his teaching is followed by his three daughters, Francesca, Cristina and Mariasole, who take turns in the kitchen and in the one, rustically decorated dining-room.

The day's menu is written on a sheet of rough paper that is passed around the tables, and depending on the season, it proposes antipasti such as panzanella, **salad of nervetti** and beans, or "poisoned" bruschetta (with a sauce of fresh chili peppers and black olives). The first courses always include **bucatini cacio e pepe**, but you might also find **spaghetti all'amatriciana**, gnocchi with meat sauce, **fettuccine with cep mushrooms**, pulse soup with croutons, pasta and chickpeas, **pasta and beans**, **pappardelle with a boar sauce** and tonnarelli with sausage, chicory and pecorino. Then try the **boiled meat alla picchiapò** or in a green sauce, **tripe alla romana**, **oxtail alla vaccinara**, roast veal shank, brasato with red wine and stewed baccalà. And to conclude, tiramisù and crostata of strawberries.

A carafe of the house white or red is quite acceptable, but you will also find a wine list of about thirty wines that go very well with the food.

This vacation farm is just two kilometers away from the remains of the Roman villa of patrician Quinto Assio, a friend of Cicero who was a guest there on a number of occasions. The 19th-century farmhouse has been refurbished by the Vincenti Mareri Tosoni family, who have always been landowners in this area, and sits on a hill that dominates the plain of Rieti. Rooms and suites are furnished with antiques but are fitted with all modern comforts. All rooms have exceptional views stretching from Mount Terminillo to the Franciscan sanctuaries and the Lake Lungo and Ripasottile Nature Reserves. The suite, which is located in the tower of the villa, has an independent entrance and features a jacuzzi. The restaurant is in the estate's former cattle sheds and dishes are prepared with their own organically grown produce. Breakfast is inviting and generous, offering sweet fare and, on request, savory fare too. This is an excellent base for walks to explore the local natural surroundings.

• 6 double rooms and 1 suite, with bathroom, TV • Prices: double room single occupancy 40-50 euros, double 70-100, suite 140-180, breakfast included • Credit cards: all, Bancomat • 1 room designed for use by the mobility challenged. Off-street parking. Small pets allowed. Owners always reachable. • Bar, restaurant. Conference room. Grounds. Pool

DA ARMANDO AL PANTHEON

🍲 Trattoria
Salita de' Crescenzi 31
Tel. 06 68803034
Closed Saturday dinner and Sunday
Open: lunch and dinner
Holidays: August
Seating: 35
Prices: 30-35 euros, wine excluded
All credit cards, Bancomat

DAL CAVALIER GINO

🍲 Trattoria
Vicolo Rossini 4, corner of Piazza del Parlamento
Tel. 06 6873434
Closed Sunday
Open: lunch and dinner
Holidays: August
Seating: 45
Prices: 25-30 euros, wine excluded
No credit cards

Just a few steps from one of the best-known Roman monuments, this historic trattoria promises authentic food in an area increasingly dominated by super-touristy restaurants. Armando Gargioli opened the place in the 1960s and now his sons Claudio and Fabrizio run the kitchen and dining room respectively. The family's success comes from knowing how to bring together top ingredients in traditional dishes (with some minor reinterpretations), while maintaining a good price/quality ratio. The atmosphere is welcoming, and the service informal but attentive.

To start, we recommend the herring with beans and onions and the **bruschetta alla vignarola** with chicory, olives and sausage, or for stronger palates the spicy indiavolata with Calabrian 'nduja. Among the first courses the tagliolini with asparagus tips and pecorino di fossa is worth a mention, as are the linguine with grouper and cherry tomatoes and the **spaghetti alla gricia**, both flavorful and delicate. The main courses are meat-based and follow Roman tradition, often using historic recipes for the "fifth quarter," i.e. offal: from **coda alla vaccinara** to **coratella**, without forgetting other classics like **spring lamb a scottadito,** and more unusual offerings like spelt and gorgonzola rissoles and duck with prunes. The home-made desserts change seasonally; in the late spring we tried a ancient Roman torta, made with ricotta and strawberry jam; strawberry savarin and tiramisù with berries.

For those who aren't content with the Castelli on tap the wine list is exhaustive and top-quality.

A discreetly lit sign indicates the entrance to this old-fashioned trattoria, located in a little street next to Palazzo Chigi. Inside the decor has remained unchanged for 50 years, and contrary to every marketing strategy priority goes to the quality of the product instead of the image. There are no fancy wine glasses or other frills, and instead of a menu with elaborate descriptions you'll find a blackboard by the entrance with a schematic list of the day's choices. But the simplicity itself which appeals and makes the atmosphere welcoming. The restaurant is always packed, also because of the decidedly good value. Service, coordinated by Cavalier Gino himself together with his son, is both attentive and laid-back.

The food is traditionally Roman, apart from a few successful reinterpretations, like the **pasta and chickpeas in a brodo d'arzilla** (a broth made with skate, cooked until it almost dissolves) with the legumes taking the place of the more classic broccoli. Alternatively there's **tonnarelli cacio e pepe**, carbonara or **amatriciana**. The main courses also have a marked Roman accent, from **cuttlefish with peas** to **oxtail alla vaccinara**, cooked for a long time with lots of flavorings, as well as **involtini alla romana**, **abbacchio** and **salt cod with potatoes** (not always available). To finish there are spoon sweets like crème caramel and tiramisù.

To pair with the food try the house wine, or choose from a few recently added regional labels.

ROME
Campo de' Fiori

ROME
Ardeatino

DA SERGIO

� Trattoria
Vicolo delle Grotte 27
Tel. 06 6864293
Closed Sunday
Open: lunch and dinner
Holidays: August
Seating: 70 + 35 outdoors
Prices: 28-30, wine exlcluded
All credit cards, Bancomat

DA VITTORIO 🍾

⌣ Restaurant-enoteca
Via Musco 29-31
Tel. 06 5408272
Closed Saturday and Sunday
Open: lunch and dinner
Holidays: August
Seating: 40
Prices: 25-28 euros, wine excluded
All credit cards, Bancomat

The area around Campo de' Fiori is crowded with many eateries with an international flavor packed with office workers at lunch and tourists in the evenings, this trattoria is classic and straightforward. It's been run for almost 30 years by Sergio Mariotti's family; son Sandro is responsible every day for sourcing quality ingredients, while his sisters skilfully prepare them, presenting some of the traditional dishes of Roman cuisine. The service is no-frills, but still attentive and courteous, and the menu is usually described by voice, even though a printed menu is available on request.
Start with the mixed antipasti made up of grilled vegetables, cured meats and boiled potatoes; the outstanding first courses include various kinds of pasta – fettuccine, **tonnarelli** or spaghetti – sauced with **amatriciana**, carbonara, **gricia**, puttanesca, arrabbiata or **cacio e pepe**. Among the mains you'll always find next: grilled steak and sausages, **abbacchio a scottadito**, straccetti with arugula, **tripe al sugo** and kebabs, made with quality meat. If you want something lighter, in the summer there's always fresher options like caprese or salads. On Thursdays you can count on the **gnocchi**, while on Tuesday and Friday you can try fresh fish, which varies depending on what's in the market. To finish there are some desserts and good seasonal fruit.
To go with your meal you can choose the house wine on tap, either red or white, or one of the regional bottles on the list.

Some recent renovations have made this place even more welcoming. The entrance hall now includes an enoteca, with shelves packed with bottles and the possibilty to taste and buy wines. However it's still the headquarters of the Alberto Sordi Fan Club, and the rudder of the restaurant remains firmly in the hands of Giovanna Dorigo in the kitchen and her son Roberto Sassaroli in the dining room. They offer a menu focussed on the typical dishes of Roman cuisine, with an substantial wine list and a cordial and relaxed atmosphere.
Once sat down, you could skip the antipasti (a course without much history in Roman restaurants) in order to dive into the firsts without delay: **spaghetti all'amatriciana**, carbonara, **gricia** or **cacio e pepe**; gnocchi al sugo; pasta and potatoes; **pasta and beans**; pasta and lentils and lasagna. The abundant and flavorful main courses, following true Roman tradition, include **spring lamb a scottadito** or roasted with potatoes, bollito misto, salt cod, chicken and peppers, tripe, **coda alla vaccinara**, **coratella**, meatballs, Roman saltimbocca, stewed cuttlefish with peas, veal stew alla cacciatora and **polenta with spareribs and sausages**. Close with some decent spoon sweets.
The wine list, put together with passion and competence by Robert, boasts over 400 labels, Italian and foreign, with honest prices.

🍷 The Antica Enoteca Manzoni in Piazzale Ardigù 27 offers a wide selection of wines from Italy and abroad and a good choice of oils, jams, artisanal pastas and sweets; in Piazza Accademia Antiquaria 14, Pugliapasta is an artisanal producer specializing in Puglian pastas.

FELICE

Trattoria
Via Mastro Giorgio 29
Tel. 06 5746800
Closed Sunday
Open: lunch and dinner
Holidays: 3 weeks in August
Seating: 90
Prices: 25-28 euros, wine excluded
All major credit cards, Bancomat

This famous trattoria deserves an affectionate "welcome back!" as it reopens after an attractive restoration. You'll find it just steps away from the Testaccio market, one of the capital's most authentic. Felice, the owner, still appears in the dining room for lunch but now the day-to-day management is taken care of by a trustworthy group, composed of son Franco in the kitchen together with the talented Salvatore and Loredana, and Flavio De Maio, who runs the dining room with skill, experience and the help of some young recruits. For the rest little has changed; the kitchen still prepares the most classic of Roman specialties, the glory of this place for decades.

The portions are often enormous. Here you come to eat without scruples, without hesitation, accompanying everything with a good bread made with natural yeasts. Skip the generally meager antipasti, and dedicate yourself immediately to the sumptuous first courses: **tonnarelli cacio e pepe** or withan involtini sauce, linguine with tuna, **potato gnocchi** al sugo on Thursdays, fettuccine alla vignarola in the spring, **skate broth with broccoli** or peas, **pasta e fagioli** and the two unmissable Roman pasta sauces, **gricia** and **amatriciana**. The mains are just as good and include **baccalà**, **roast lamb** with potatoes, tripe, **coda alla vaccinara**, **coratella**, fried spring-lamb chops, legendary **involtini with meatballs al sugo**, breaded cutlets, ossobuco with peas, **fritto di paranza** and moscardini with peas. Don't miss the **artichokes alla romana** when they're in season. The most common dessert is tiramisù served in a glass. There's a small but careful selection of bottles from which you can choose a regional wine to pair with your meal.

GNEGNO

Trattoria
Via Prati della Farnesina 10
Tel. 06 3336166
Closed Sunday
Open: lunch and dinner
Holidays: first half of August
Seating: 70 + 20 outdoors
Prices: 25-35 euros, wine excluded
All credit cards, Bancomat

The Ponte Milvio has become a hub of Roman nightlife, particularly following a series of events organized at the Olympic stadium, which is right behind this restaurant. You'll find in a narrow street, away from the chaos of the piazza. There are some outside tables, two dining rooms and wood-paneled walls, and the family atmosphere and friendly service mark it as a typical neighborhood trattoria, frequented mainly by regulars but also by many young people who come for the honest home cooking. The antipasto buffet of grilled vegetables, various frittatas, mozzarella and a good prosciutto crudo will warm you up for some top first courses with a solid Roman stamp, **spaghetti alla carbonara** and three kinds of **bucatini**, all'amatriciana, gricia or cacio e pepe; or alternatively there are flavorful minestras with beans, chickpeas and lentils. The main courses also reflect the city's traditions, with **tripe**, **abbacchio**, **coratella**, rabbit alla cacciatora, **roast pork with potatoes** and the highly recommended **grilled salt cod**. Finish with homemade desserts like pies, crema catalana and chocolate and coffee semifreddo.

It's a shame that the only wine choice is between a red or white Pitigliano, as it doesn't really do justice to the quality of the food.

Gianfornaio, Piazzale di Ponte Milvio 36, for various kinds of bread, biscotti, baked sweets, slices of pizza and fresh pasta. Mondi, Via Flaminia Vecchia 468, for well-made pastries and ice cream.

ROMA
Monteverde

ROME
Montecitorio-Colonna

Between Via Aurelia Antica and Villa Doria Pamphili

IL CASTELLETTO

🗝🔑2-Star Hotel
Via dei Carraresi 27-29
Tel. 06 66166573
Fax 06 66148182
E-mail: info@il-castelletto.com
Internet: www.il-castelletto.com
Open all year

MATRICIANELLA 🍷

🍲Trattoria
Via del Leone 4
Tel. 06 6832100
Closed Sunday
Open: lunch and dinner
Holidays: 3 weeks in August
Seating: 60 + 20 outdoors
Prices: 30-35 euros, wine excluded
All credit cards, Bancomat

Located in the Via Bravetta area near the consular road that leads to the Tyrrhenian and Ligurian coast, Il Castelletto is a sound option for those who want to stay in Rome but don't want to pay over the odds for the privilege. Although the area is sometimes heavily trafficked, this disadvantage is offset by its good connections with the city center: it takes 20 minutes by bus to get to St Peters. Owner, Fabiano Accatino, who has recently renovated this small, early 1900s villa, is always ready to supply guests with maps of the city, and informative material on tourist attractions and transport services. While the rooms are not very large, they are pleasant, cozy and offer many comforts. Breakfast in the communal dining room will comprise coffee, milk, tea, fruit juices and croissants.

• 17 double rooms, with bathroom, air-conditioning, mini-bar, TV, modem connection • Prices: double room single occupancy 60 euros, double 90 (10-15 euro supplement for extra bed), breakfast included • Credit cards: all, Bancomat • Facility accessible to the mobility challenged. Off-street parking. Small pets allowed. Reception open 24 hours a day. • Breakfast room

Matricianella is in the heart of Rome, between the piazzas of San Lorenzo in Lucina and Fontanella Borghese: a typical trattoria where you can sample all the classic dishes of authentic Roman cuisine. The interior is simple and functional, with the possibility during the city's long stretch of good weather to use the pleasant outside area, and the service is relatively quick and professional, notwithstanding the nearly constant crowds.
We recommend moving straight to the canonical Roman firsts, without antipasti – **bucatini all'amatriciana**, **spaghetti cacio e pepe** or alla carbonara, **rigatoni with pajata** (young lamb intestines) and **rigatoni with oxtail sauce**. There's also a seasonally changing dish of the day like green gnocchi with tomatoes and basil, **fettuccine with porcini** and chicory or various seafood-based options. The main courses are also firmly traditional, from those based on offal, like **coratella di abbacchio**, grilled sweetbreads, **fried brains**, tripe and **coda alla vaccinara**, to the grilled meats, saltimbocca alla romana and eggplant Parmesan. Roasted fish are sometimes available. Instead of a main, or as a side, you can choose from a wide variety of fried things, like apples, zucchini, carrots and mushrooms, as well as golden potato skins and the traditional fried **artichokes alla giudia**. The homemade desserts are well-prepared.
The wine list deserves a special mention, as it presents a selection of labels from Italy and abroad rich in quantity and quality. The mark-ups are fair and there's a good choice by the glass.

ROME
Testaccio

NE ARTE NE PARTE

Recently opened osteria
Via Luca della Robbia 15
Tel. 06 5750279
Closed Monday
Open: lunch and dinner
Holidays: variable
Seating: 75 + 18 outdoors
Prices: 30-32 euros, wine excluded
All credit cards, Bancomat

After various managments and some ups and downs, this restaurant has now been taken over by three partners from the world of showbusiness. They've entrusted the day-to-day running to Massimo Di Castro, who now supervises the kitchen. The cooking is inspired by pure Roman tradition, and the osteria has two dining rooms and a small outdoor space to be used in nice weather. The decor is rustic and minimal, the service courteous and efficient.
A series of antipasti are laid out on two tables to start: vegetables au gratin or in vinegar, potatoes, peas, **marinated anchovies** and other constantly changing options. Unusually for a Roman restaurant the selections are fresh and appetizing. But don't eat too much; make sure you save room for the delicious Roman first courses: **spaghetti alla gricia**, amatriciana, carbonara or **cacio e pepe**; **rigatoni with pajata** or involtini sauce and **pasta e fagioli** and pasta e ceci. Move on to **oxtail alla vaccinara**, **tripe** alla romana, **coratella** with artichokes, **spring lamb** a scottadito or roasted, saltimbocca alla romana, chicken with peppers, stewed **salt cod**, involtini al sugo, sweetbreads or spezzatino with peas, all accompanied by roast potatoes and vegetables in vinegar or sautéed. Sometimes you'll also find fresh fish cooked over charcoal. Desserts include tiramisù, testa di moro and pies with visciola cherries, figs or fruit and cream.
There's a short wine list for those who want something more than the house wine on tap.

ROME
Trionfale-Piazzale Clodio

OSTERIA DELL'ANGELO

Trattoria
Via Bettolo 24
Tel. 06 3729470
Closed Saturday for dinner, Sunday and Monday lunch
Open: lunch and dinner
Holidays: August
Seating: 120 + 40 outdoors
Prices: 25-30 euros
No credit cards

Angelo Croce has built up his reputation over 15 years of honorable service, and his restaurant guarantees satisfaction to those looking for the true taste of traditional Roman cooking. The evening menu is fixed price (30 euros), and opens with a tasting of antipasti including **pesce finto**, salsicette, bruschettas and **green beans all'uccelletto**. To follow you can choose from the city's classic first courses, like **tonnarelli cacio e pepe**, **rigatoni all'amatriciana** or alla carbonara, gnocchi with different sauces and **broccoli and skate soup**. If you love grilled meat you'll be happy with the mains, with maremmana, liver, **abbacchio** and pork, as well as traditional dishes like **spezzatino alla picchiapò**, rabbit with white wine and olives, **coda alla vaccinara**, **tripe** alla romana, **baccalà** and anchovy tortino. Everything is accompanied by roast potatoes, puntarelle, chicory, artichokes and whatever else is in the market depending on the season. The ciambelline with Cesanese make for a safe conclusion.
For drinks there's nothing much apart from an acceptable Castelli on tap. The owner is convinced that wine, particularly in times of crisis, shouldn't have too much of an impact on the final bill. "La ggente vié wui pe' fassi 'na bella magnata": the people come for good food. In our opinion a good wine wouldn't hurt. Particularly in times of crisis.

La Tradizione, Via Cipro 8, has one of the city's best selections of cheeses and cured meats; the Pasticceria Antonini, Via Sabotino 21-29, is a good source for sweets and ice cream; the Emporium Naturae in Via delle Milizie 7 is a historic location for organic foods and herbalist products.

OSTERIA DEL VELODROMO VECCHIO

Recently opened osteria
Via Genzano 139
Tel. 06 7886793
Closed Sunday
Open: lunch; Thursday, Friday and Saturday also dinner
Holidays: August
Seating: 38 + 20 outdoors
Prices: 26-32 euros, wine excluded
All credit cards, Bancomat

PALATIUM

Restaurant
Via Frattina 94
Tel. 06 69202132
Closed Sunday
Open: lunch and dinner
Holidays: 2 weeks after August 15
Seating: 100
Prices: 30-35 euros, wine excluded
Credit cards: all, Bancomat

Matteo and Alessandra Ballerini have been managing this small osteria for 10 years now. Located between the Appio and Tuscolano neighborhoods, it's on the site, as the name implies, of an old velodrome. The Ballerinis' work begins with sourcing ingredients in the city's markets and specialty shops, and the result is good honest Roman cooking, somewhat lightened. The pleasant atmosphere is also key, with a quiet dining room from which you can see the kitchen and a small space outside with some tables for when it's warm. And while it's true that on the busiest evenings the service might slow down, it's compensated for by the warm hospitality.

The mixed antipasto varies depending on the season, what looks good in the market and Matteo's inspiration – fried anchovies, grilled vegetables, mozzarella di bufala – and warms up the appetite for the well-prepared traditional firsts like **pasta with beans** or **with broccoli in skate broth**, gnocchi (also available made with semolina, a rarity) allo stracotto, **tonnarelli cacio e pepe** or all'amatriciana and **rigatoni with oxtail sugo**. Continue with **roast abbacchio**, meatballs, **tripe**, cuttlefish with peas, **salt cod with raisins and pine nuts**, bollito alla picchiapò and **anchovy and endive tortino**. Alessandra runs the dining room and also prepares the desserts, from which we recommend the crème brûlée, the almond or strawberry bavarese and the fruit pies.

The wines are served at the right temperatures and the list has correct mark-ups and is constantly being updated with some really excellent wines. But it's still perfectly possible to settle for the more than acceptable house wine on tap.

It looks easy on paper! All you do is fit out a window with Lazio food products in the heart of Rome. Then, with the expert consultancy of a great local chef, you sell exclusively wines, oils, honeys, liqueurs and preserves from the region – and the die is cast. Yet, if you enter Palatium you'll realize just how much work, care and attention go into an initiative of this kind. Two floors, an immaculate yet informal atmosphere, a place for stopping off for an aperitif or for sitting down to a full meal, choosing from a comprehensive seasonal menu – the Lazio Regional Authority has believed in the project right from the start. Start by choosing from the mindboggling selection of **cured meats** – coppa viterbese, mortadelline di Campotosto, porchetta di Ariccia, prosciutto di Bassiano or prosciutto di Guarcino – and cheeses. Then come roulades of eggplant with ricotta romana, **char** in basil sauce, **tiella di Gaeta**, soup of Anguillara Sabazia broccoli and Atina beans, stracci di pasta with baccalà and fresh peas, **pappardelle with lamb ragù** and Leonessa potatoes, timballo of zite and Roman courgettes, tonnarelli with veal and pecorino, **maccheroncini with duck and artichoke**, gnocchi of ricotta **with courgette flowers and pecorino**, Otello chickpea cream and baccalà. Mains are also very much Lazio-oriented with Monte San Biagio sausage, **Viterbo rabbit alla cacciatora**, **fried baccalà** with escarole and Gaeta olives, **tripe alla romana** and **chicken with peppers**. To end, Terracina strawberries, chocolate cake with Monti Cimini hazelnut cream and Sermoneta lemon cake.

PRISCILLA

🍲 Traditional osteria
Via Appia Antica 68
Tel. 06 5136379
Closed Monday, October-May also
Sunday for dinner
Open: lunch and dinner
Holidays: in August
Seating: 50
Prices: 15-22 euros, wine excluded
All credit cards, Bancomat

ROMANO

🔑 2-Star Hotel
Largo Corrado Ricci 32
Tel. 06 6795851
Fax 06 6795851-6786840
E-mail: info@romanohotel.it
Internet: www.hotelromano.com
Open all year

This traditional osteria, with over a century of history behind it, can be found in one of the most fascinating streets of Rome, in front of the little church of Quo Vadis and a few steps from the Priscilla catacombs and the Caffarella park. Outgoing owner Alessandro Ratini runs the two (air-conditioned) dining rooms on his own, with the help of two women in the kitchen. They put a distinctly housewifely stamp on the cooking, with flavorful dishes prepared without frills.
There's just one "apristomaco" to whet your appetite, a bruschetta with tomatoes, so you can move without delay on to the city's traditional first courses: **gnocchi all'amatriciana**; **tonnarelli cacio e pepe**, alla carbonara or with anchovies and pecorino; **pappardelle with wild boar**; pasta and chickpeas; **pasta and beans**. In the summer you might find some variations from further afield: linguine al pesto or Abruzzo-style rigatoni with eggplant, capers, peppers and cherry tomatoes. The main courses, accompanied by the classic sides – roast potatoes, broiled peppers and eggplants, vegetables in vinegar or sautéed – include **tripe alla romana**, spezzatino with potatoes, **bollito alla pichiapò**, brisket alla fornara, **roast pork in tegame**, beef straccetti, **stewed meatballs** and traditional involtini. The homemade tiramisù and crème caramel make for reliable desserts.
The red and white house wine from the Castelli offers a more than adequate pairing, or there's a selection of some good Italian labels.

🍴 The Cellini pasta-maker in Via Odescalchi 39 sells a wide variety of fresh pastas and ready-made food to take away.

This small hotel is located near Largo Romolo e Remo, at the junction between Via Cavour and Via dei Fori Imperiali. In the heart of the ancient city, just a stone's throw from the Colosseum and Piazza Venezia, therefore, an ideal base for visiting Rome. Basic and unpretentious, it has a small hall and rooms furnished in a reserved manner, some with a view of the Forum. While the hotel itself doesn't have a communal lounge it has an agreement with the bar next door that serves breakfast inside or outside when the weather is good. The enviable location, friendly welcome and availability of a wealth of useful tourist information make the Romano a great address for those wanting to visit the city from a base located right in its bustling center. In peak tourism months the cost of double rooms can be as high as 150 euros.

• 5 single and 11 double rooms, with bathroom, air-conditioning, safe, TV • Prices: single 60-85 euros, double 90-120 (20-45 euro supplement for extra bed), breakfast included • Credit cards: all, Bancomat • Garage parking at special rates (26 euros per day). Small pets allowed. Reception open 24 hours a day

ROMA
Porta Pia

SAN MICHELE A PORTA PIA

Bed and breakfast
Via Messina 15
Tel. 06 44250596-349 2644505-338 6402775
Fax 06 44235575
E-mail: sanmichele2000@yahoo.it
Internet: www.bbsanmichele.com
Closed in August, 15 days in both January and February

In the center of Rome, just a few hundred meters from Via Veneto and Termini train station, you will find this B&B run by the Ruschioni family, inaugurated for the Jubilee Year. It's organized in an elegant apartment on the fifth floor of a 1940s building. The rooms face onto a large entrance hall: on the right there's a communal room where breakfast is served: tea, coffee, milk, yoghurt, croissants, sealed portions of jam and butter, and delicious homemade cakes and soft ciambelloni prepared by your hostess. This room can be used by guests throughout the day. In summer you can use the spacious terrace. The rooms are functional and tastefully furnished. The same family also has another B&B called Le tue Vacanze in an adjacent building, with 3 double rooms and a triple.

• 2 double and 2 triple rooms, with bathroom, (2 of them next door), air-conditioning, TV • Prices: double room single occupancy 55-70 euros, double 75-90, triple 100, breakfast included • Credit cards: none • Garage at special rates in the immediate vicinity (15 euros per day). No pets allowed. Owners always present. • Breakfast room. Terrace

ROMA
Aurelio

SANTA EMILIA DE VIALAR

Vacation home
Via Paolo III 16
Tel. 06 39366528
Fax 06 6371207
E-mail: sja.roma@suoresangiuseppe.191.it
Closed in August

If you don't mind forgoing the pleasures of Roman nightlife (the front desk closes at 11:00 pm and guests aren't given keys to the building), but are looking for peace and quiet, then this facility run by the nuns of San Giuseppe dell'Apparizione is the ideal place for you. Located in an imposing building surrounded by a garden with palms and pines, it offers an amazing view of the dome of St Peters. The rooms are furnished very basically without TV (there are TVs in two communal rooms), but they are spacious and airy, and almost all of them offer a view of Michelangelo's dome. Breakfast is quite traditional: tea, coffee, milk, bread, butter, jams and savory fare. The extremely competitive price by Rome standards and its location in the heart of the eternal city make it a place to be recommended.

• 8 single and 21 double rooms, with bathroom (singles with shared bathroom) • Prices: single 35 euros, double room single occupancy 45, double 75, breakfast included • 1 room designed for use by the mobility challenged. Off-street parking. No pets allowed. Reception open from 7 am to 11 pm. • Kitchen. Breakfast rooms, TV room. Conference room. Garden, 2 terraces.

TABERNA RECINA

Enoteca with bar and kitchen
Via Recina 22-26
Tel. 06 7000413
Closed Sunday
Open: lunch; Friday and Saturday dinner also
Holidays: August 12-September 5
Seating: 35
Prices: 28-30 euros, wine excluded
Credit cards: MC, Visa, Bancomat

TRAM TRAM

Traditional osteria
Via dei Reti 44-46
Tel. 06 490416
Closed Monday
Open: lunch and dinner
Holidays: 1 week in August
Seating: 45 + 15 outdoors
Prices: 30-35 euros, wine excluded
All credit cards, Bancomat

Around a year ago this charming place opened where there used to be a neighborhood café/dairy, not far from San Giovanni. It's kept the small sign and also serves a similar purpose, opening at 7am for breakfast and then becoming an enoteca and wine bar during the day, with wines by the glass with little homemade snacks. The food is typically Roman, with some intelligent Mediterranean incursions, and is the fruit of the experience of Matteo Ballarini (also at the Osteria del Velodromo Vecchio) and the passion of Antonio Piermarini.

On the simply laid tables you'll find good rustic bread from Genzano (an IGP) and extra-virgin olive oil. Start with lonza and mozzarella di bufala, **anchovies with endive** and potato tortino with onions and tomatoes. The first courses are varied and tasty, with classic amatriciana, **gricia** and **cacio e pepe** as well as **linguine with salt cod**, winter soups of chickpeas or **broccoli in skate broth** and spaghetti with swordfish and eggplant. The skill of young chef Antonio Cornacchia is confirmed with the mains, with **involtini al sugo**, eggplant alla parmigiana, **meatballs al sellero** (celery), roast brisket, salt cod with raisins and pine nuts and many other seasonally changing dishes. Finish off with good homemade desserts: pies, ricotta and apple cakes.

For wine you can choose from the many selections by the glass or select the bottle of your choice from the open shelves. The bottles are sold at retail prices.

This small and typical little restaurant in San Lorenzo gets its name from the tram which passes right in front. The kitchen is supervised by mamma Rosanna, who moved here from Puglia, and it turns out seasonally changing dishes which reflect the high quality of the ingredients used. Her daughter Fabiola, who used to help out, is no longer here, having opened her own cocktail bar/bookshop directly opposite.

Start with spiced vegetables and giant shrimp or **coratella**, and for a first choose between the classic **rigatoni with pajata** (lamb intestines); **minestra of broccoli and skate**; delicate pappardelle with tomato, lamb and peppers; gnocchetti with grouper or salt cod and Puglian dishes like orecchiette all'ortolana or with broccoli and clams and tiella of rice, potatoes and mussels. The mains show the influence of both the land and the sea, with **abbacchio alla scottadito**, **grilled sweetbreads** and pajatina, **coda alla vaccinara** (not always available), swordfish involtini, **salt cod with potatoes**, **anchovy and endive tortino** and veraci octopi alla luciana. The side dishes are numerous: fava puree with chicory, **artichokes alla romana**, **puntarelle with anchovies**, chicory all'agro, roast potatoes, mixed salad. To finish there's crema with zabaione, lemon or strawberries; panna cotta; chocolate mousse and crème caramel.

The ample wine list includes the best labels from around the country at reasonable prices, and there's also a selection of spirits and dessert wines available by the glass.

TRATTORIA CADORNA

TRATTORIA MONTI

☞Trattoria
Via Cadorna 12
Tel. 06 4827061
Closed Saturday and Sunday lunch
Open: lunch and dinner
Holidays: August
Seating: 50 + 30 outdoors
Prices: 32-34 euros, wine excluded
All credit cards, Bancomat

☞Restaurant
Via di San Vito 13 A
Tel. 06 4466573
Closed Sunday dinner and Monday
Open: lunch and dinner
Holidays: August, 1 week at Christmas and 1 week at Easter
Seating: 45
Prices: 30-32 euros, wine excluded
All credit cards except AE

This trattoria has been open for almost sixty years and offers a typically Roman menu. Run by Giovanni and Gabriella Tudini, now helped by their sons Marco and Giuseppe, it is frequented by a loyal clientèle, and is the ideal place if you want to try typical dishes prepared with top quality ingredients.
You start with a wide range of nibbles: burrata, buffalo mozzarella, bread fritters with tomato and basil, breadsticks with pecorino, grilled rissoles, eggplants and ham. Then you can choose from **rigatoni with pajata**, pappardelle Cadorna with a sauce of bacon, eggs, peas, mushrooms and parmesan, **spaghetti cacio and pepper** carbonara or **gricia**, **bucatini all'amatriciana** and **gnocchi** on Thursday, true to custom. If you are looking for something lighter, go for spaghetti with clams or rigatoni with fresh tomato and basil sauce. There are also various soups, such as vegetable soup with buffalo mozzarella and toasted bread or **pasta and beans**. The main courses are traditional too: **oxtail**, tripe, saltimbocca or **ossobuco alla romana**, **abbacchio a scottadito**, roast lamb cubes and fish dishes, mixed grill, anchovies alla pizzaiola and a mixed dish of "poor" fish with mackerel, cod, anchovies, mullet and tuna. Vegetable dishes are always available, like eggplant parmigiana or **Roman artichokes.** Very good home-made puddings.
Besides the house wine, there is a small selection of national labels.

Ⓘ Enoteca Marchetti, via Flavia 28: great selection of wines and oils: Macelleria De Angelis, via Flavia 74: meat from all over the world, cheese and gastronomic dishes.

Spread over three rooms, which are now much brighter and welcoming for the recent refurbishment, the Camerucci family trattoria offers a genuine anthology of Marche cooking, sometimes revisited with style and without excess just for the sake of it. Warm welcome, great attention to details, top quality ingredients are all factors that have earned this trattoria our snail this year.
Among the antipasti you will find red onion tart with gorgonzola sauce, stockfish carpaccio and classic **Marche mixed fry**, with stuffed olives, pumpkin flowers and Ancona style cream. Among the first courses, we recommend the wide choice of **soups** – pumpkin and leek, fava bean and chicory, or bean – or **tagliolini with anchovies**, **fossa euwe's cheese and raisins** and the splendid **tortello with egg yokes**, perfumed with precious touches of truffle. Local recipes dominate, without monopolizing, the main courses, where you will find classic **rabbit with pork** and **Ancona style stockfish** but also brains with zucchini and lamb chops. If you prefer vegetarian dishes, you should try the various tarts, such as zucchini with carrot sauce or parmesan in lettuce sauce. The puddings provide a worthy finished note, to be eaten with a glass of passito: we recommend the pear jelly in orange sauce or mango with peaches, semifreddo with macaroons and nougat with chocolate sauce or apple tart with zabaione.
The wine list offers the best national wines, from the cult labels to bottles of everyday table wine, with a varied selection of Verdicchio marchigiano.

ROME
Ostiense-San Paolo

SAN CESAREO

ZAMPAGNA

SAN CESARIO

Trattoria
Via Ostiense 179
Tel. 06 5742306
Closed Sunday and festivities
Open: only for lunch
Holidays: August
Seating: 40 + 12 outdoors
Prices: 18-20 euros, wine excluded
No credit cards

Osteria/Bed and breakfast
Via Filippo Corridoni 60-62
Tel. 06 9587950
E-mail: info@osteriasancesario.it
Internet: www.osteriadisancesario.it
Closed Sunday dinner and Monday
Open: lunch and dinner
Holidays: August 15-30
Seating: 40 + 30 outdoors
Prices: 35 euros, wine excluded
All major credit cards except DC, Bancomat

A trattoria that has been offering home-made Roman cooking since 1924, with no frills or changes: if you are looking for a genuine inn where traditions, simple dishes and good ingredients are served with a warm family welcome, then Zampagna is the place for you. A lot of regular customers but also tourists who are visiting the nearby Basilica of S. Paul, or families out for lunch on their day off.
Maria and her brother Alvaro will settle you at the few tables inside – or in the internal courtyard – and tell you about the menu. After quick antipasti, move onto the excellent firsts, with the classic pasta dishes – **spaghetti all'amatriciana** or carbonara, **fettuccine alla gricia** or roulade sauce, **tonnarelli cacio and pepper** – and the traditional soups, **pasta and bean** or chickpea. The main courses are also traditional, and you can choose from saltimbocca and **tripe alla romana**, **coda alla vaccinara**, veal chasseur, roulades in sauce, **boiled meat picchiapò**, **chicken and sweet peppers** or, on Fridays, **baccalà**, accompagnied by sautéed vegetables or vinegar or lemon, asparagus tips or artichokes. You finish with fruit, sour black cherry tart or apple pie.
A limited choice of wines, with draft Marino, an honest Montepulciano d'Abruzzo or a sweet Lambrusco.

This osteria is enthusiastically run by the Dente and Ferracci families. The rooms (available all week) are quiet and well furnished, facing the small inside patio and garden, where it is possible, in the warmer season, to enjoy meals and the homemade pastry-based breakfasts.
Made up of regional dishes, but with a touch of creativity, the menu boasts excellent seasonal ingredients. Among the antipasti we recommend broad beans with offal and pecorino cheese, **fried artichokes with sweetbreads** and **tripe with green sauce** with capers and anchovies. To follow, a mouth-watering array of fresh, homemade pasta: **fettuccine with mutton sauce**, **rigatoni with pajata**, **gnocchetti a coda de soreca alla matriciana** and lane der pecoraro with baccalà or with mutton sauce and pecorino cheese. Apart from tripe, other main course choices are coda and Roman-style **quinto quarto**, braised beef guanciola al Cesanese, rabbit chasseur and catfish. To close off the menu, the cheese selection is courtesy of small local producers and the delicious home-made puddings are baked, like the bread, in the house oven.
The extensive wine list introduces a number of distinguished labels, whether already reputed or emerging, with particular importance given to regional wines, such as the Malvasia puntinata and the Cesanese.

Quadrozzi Wine Bar (via Ostiense 34) for wines, spirits, distillates and more besides; Emporio del gusto (via Chiabrera 58 a) offers a good choice of cut meats, cheeses, wines, oil and other quality products.

• 4 double rooms, en-suite, mini-bar, television • Prices: double single use 60, double 70-90 euros, breakfast included • Adjacent public parking. Pets welcome. Porter available in the osteria from 9 am to midnight • Restaurant. Breakfast room, small lounge. Garden

Segni

58 km southeast of Rome A 1 o SS 1

La Saracena

Trattoria
Via Porta Saracena 7
Tel. 06 9769062
Closed Monday, never in August
Open: lunch and dinner
Holidays: 2 weeks between August and September
Seating: 42 + 25 outdoors
Prices: 20-25 euros, wine excluded
All credit cards, Bancomat

Segni is a village on the Lepini slopes, at the gateway to Ciociaria. The main attractions are the cyclopic polygonal walls and the characteristic medieval hamlet with all its enchanting views. The Saracena trattoria is situated on the edge of the ancient hamlet, and since 1998 has been enthusiastically and expertly run by Giuliano Iannucci. The search for quality ingredients that respect the seasons and traditional cuisine is a fundamental feature of the patron's work. Equally fundamental is the service, which is extremely courteous and informal in these simple surroundings.
You can start with a mixed platter of cheeses and local cut meats, served with rosemary foccaccia, or pleasant ravioli with bresaola and truffles. Among the first courses you find the **infrascati** (typical local pasta made with water, yellow and white flour) in a sauce of cherry tomatoes, artichokes and rocket, delicate **tagliolini with asparagus tips and truffles** (when in season) or, more rustic and filling, cavatelli with broccoli and sausage. When it is cold you will always find polenta and **cep mushroom and chestnut soup**. The main course is mainly meat, including shredded meat with rocket and grana padana cheese, classic **rabbit chasseur**, saddle of pork and artichokes and **grilled lamb chops**, cooked as tradition dictates. Among the homemade puddings, we recommend an unforgettable flaky creamy pastry and coffee mousse.
The well thought out wine list concentrates on quality rather than quantity: otherwise you can choose the honest house wine.

Serrone

42 km northwest of Frosinone

Belsito

Hotel-restaurant
Via delle Rimembranze 29
Tel. 0775 523106
Closed Wednesday, never in summer
Open: lunch and dinner
Holidays: 10 days in November
Seating: 50 + 40 outdoors
Prices: 23-25 euros, wine excluded
All credit cards, Bancomat

The restaurant is in the higher part of Serrone, with a wonderful view of the Sacco Valley, and the Lepini and Ausoni mountains. Inside there is a typical farmhouse feel about things, which is confirmed in the menu prepared by brothers Gabriele and Carlo, with their passion and spirit to source the best ingredients that Serrone has to offer.
Antonietta, Gabriele's wife, turns out dishes that best set off Ciociara traditions. Starting with ciammella and lardo from Mount Scalambra, we would recommend the **mutton and cereal soup** in Serrone rolls, platter of local cured meats, pork livers wrapped in bay leaves and mixed fried vegetables. You continue with a rustic choice of first courses: **patacche with mutton ragù, frascatelli with chicory and guanciale, fettuccine with cep mushrooms,** ravioli with local euwe's ricotta and the opulent **long gnocchi with ragù of cinta and wild strigoli**; in summer you will find parmigiana of zucchini and eggplants, tomatoes stuffed with rice and potatoes roasted in the wood oven. Among the main courses we recommend the **suckling pig** with aromatic herbs, **boiled veal and hen** in green sauce, roast kid or **lamb**, and also Cesana beef stew, roast ham with wild myrtles and **cinta sausage** a punta di coltello. Before choosing from the rich selection of puddings, leave some space for the sheep's and goat's cheeses personally ripened by Gabriele on Mount Scalambra, served with the cooked must from Cesana or different types of honey.
The wine list is Carlo's concern. He rightly prefers the local wines, but also includes other Italian regions. Honest markups.

SETTEFRATI
Massarella

SPERLONGA

VALLE DELL'AQUILA

TRAMONTO

Country house
Località Massarella
Tel. e fax 0776 695247
E-mail: info@valledellaquila.it
Internet: www.valledellaquila.it
Open all year

Restaurant-pizzeria
Viale Colombo 53
Tel. 0771 549597
Closed Thursday lunch and
Wednesday, never in summer
Open: lunch and dinner
Holidays: December 8-January 6
Seating: 90 + 90 outdoors
Prices: 32-35 euros, wine excluded
All credit cards except AE

Valle dell'Aquila is a resort inaugurated in 2004 after completion of the renovation of two old farmhouses on bio-architectural lines. The facility is in Val Comino, an area of the Ciociaria in lower Latium that is still not very well known. It's located on a large piece of land, in part cultivated with fruit trees and partially forest, where if you're lucky you'll catch a glimpse of deer and hawks. The buffet breakfast includes many organic products and homemade cakes, while the restaurant – also open to non-residents – mostly offers traditional dishes (half board ranges from 55-70 euros per person). Currently the owners are setting up a fitness area with sauna, gym, tennis court and also a beauty center, while last year a swimming pool was built. There's also a fenced area for large dogs.

• 7 double rooms and 2 suites, with bathroom, TV, modem connection • Prices: double room single occupancy 60-65 euros, double 80-90, suite 100-110, breakfast included • Credit cards: all, Bancomat • Communal area and some rooms accessible to the mobility challenged. Off-street parking. Small pets allowed. Owners always reachable. • Bar corner, restaurant, wine-tasting room. Reading room. Conference room. Garden. Fitness area. Pool

The formal requisites are all there: a lovely terrace overlooking the sandy beach of Sperlonga, where you can eat with the sun setting before you. The substance is guaranteed by the Ferrante family who have been running this restaurant for years with all their enthusiasm and now with the new drive given by young Fausto.
With the sea below, fish had to dominate the menu, but there are also the family's homegrown products and, if you can't go without, meat as well (not to mention the good pizzas in the evenings). Anna works in the kitchen with the chef Antonio Carannante and will suggest you start with **sautéed mussels and clams**, or octopus salad, **anchovy tart** or crunchy mullet fillets on creamed potatoes and pesto. Followed by **vegetable ravioli and grouper ragù**, calamarata with seafood and fresh tomatoes and **spaghetti with clams**. The daily catch varies considerably in type (and cost), but the **octopus soup**, fillet of blue fish Sicilian style and **fried paranza** are nearly always available. Fausto looks after a very good **cheese** board with more than twenty varieties to choose from, which proudly lead you onto the puddings. We would mention the pleasant ice water white celery from Sperlonga (a real rarity and about to receive IGP certification) and crumbly apple tart with almonds and vanilla ice cream.
A fair wine list with labels from all over the country.

Pasticceria-gelateria Fiorelli, in via San Rocco 15, deserves its fame, but the price to pay is the queue and unavoidable waits in the summer.

LA LOCANDA DI SATURNO

Restaurant
Via Agneni 37
Tel. 0761 608392
Closed Monday
Open: dinner, Saturday and Sunday also for lunch
Holidays: variable
Seating: 45 + 35 outdoors
Prices: 30-35 euros, wine excluded
All credit cards, Bancomat

L'ENOTECA DEL CAMINETTO

Wine store with food
Via Marconi 22
Tel. 0773 702623
Closed Monday
Open: dinner
Holidays: 1 week in September and 4 in January
Seating: 30
Prices: 32 euros, wine excluded
All credit cards, Bancomat

In the center of Sutri a winding alley leads you to a hidden corner where you will find the restaurant. You enter through the attractive external courtyard, where it is nice to eat in the summer, and go into the inner room, with exposed brickwork and a high ceiling with wooden beams.

The menu prepared by Fabio Calcagni and Marisa Faraoni changes with the seasons and with what the market offers. Therefore besides the dishes on the menu you will find others as well.

Among the antipasti we would mention the croutons with scapicollata (similar to capocollo), hot bread with creamed vegetables, boar carpaccio and platter of local **cured meats**. Followed by **strappatelli** (fresh, irregular shaped pasta made from water and flour) **all'amatriciana**, risotto with asparagus, saffron, pine nuts and fresh euwe's cheese, **tagliolini with mushrooms**, various soups – the summer coral soup made with coral beans is good – and **acquacotta viterbese**, very smooth and rich with beet and spinach. Among the main courses, besides **baccalà with onion and tomato**, there are mainly meat dishes, including tagliata of beef, straccetti with aromatic herbs or fillet of pork with plums. The cheese board completes the offer served with honey and homemade puddings: strawberry crêpes; ricotta tart, flaky pastry basket with cream and chestnuts from Mount Cimini, coffee tiramisù.

Choose the wine from the Morellino di Scansano on tap and the fifty or so mainly regional labels on the wine list.

Originally a mere offshoot of the Caminetto, one of the most famous restaurants in Terracina, today the Enoteca has found its own place in the rankings. This, thanks to Nazzareno Fontana's decision to diversify the type of cuisine (in fact fish, which is the main player in the restaurant, is almost completely absent here, apart from a few dishes where it's offered raw or smoked). The place is run by Nazzareno's son, Biagio, who has grown more and more enthusiastic about his role and is by now your perfect host. Given that **cheese** and **cured meat** lovers have a great variety to choose from, we prefer to focus on the various warm dishes that will enable you to compose a full meal. You can begin with a **timbale of potatoes and mushrooms**, rice polenta with Gorgonzola cheese or the sfogliatine with ricotta and spinach. Following this you can opt for a classic, such as **bucatini all'amatriciana**, although the **fettuccine with finferli mushrooms** or the calamarata with bacon and eggplants are just as good. Among the local meats pork really stands out – from sausages to **spare ribs** – and buffalo, which you'll find in the timbale with eggplants and mozzarella. Often you'll also find Chianina beef, mainly barbecued. Ice-creams and sorbets are a good alternative (or intro) to the puddings, which include millefoglie, tartelle di ricotta on English coffee sauce and amaretto cake.

There's a wide choice of wines with honest markups. You can have wine by the glass, and they change the wine every day.

RIFUGIO OLMATA

Trattoria
Via Olmata 88
Tel. 0773 700821
Closed Wednesday
Open: lunch and dinner
Holidays: December 20-January 5
Seating: 40 + 20 outdoors
Prices: 32-34 euros, wine excluded
No credit cards

SAINT PATRICK

Wine shop with bar and food
Corso Anita Garibaldi 56
Tel. 0773 703170
Closed Tuesday
Open: only for dinner
Holidays: 3 weeks in winter
Seating: 45 + 30 outdoors
Prices: 26-34 euros, wine excluded
All credit cards, Bancomat

For nearly twenty years now mushroom lovers have been able to count on the Rifugio Olmata: they have a wide choice – of course what's available depends on the season – finferli, mazze di tamburo, galletti and chiodini, and all at reasonable prices, even if you choose more sought-after varieties such as royal agaric or cep mushrooms. Basically Giovanni Di Bartolo and his wife Franca know how to keep their customers coming back. The antipasti consist of tastes of cured meats, omelets, mushrooms and artichokes preserved in olive oil, mozzarella and local cheeses. But if it's available try the cep or **royal agaric mushroom salad**, it's an unforgettable treat. First courses are also dedicated to mushroom lovers: **strozzapreti with galletti**, **cep mushroom and chickpea soup**, fusilli with mixed mushroom, eggplant and zucchini sauce. Alternatively try the strozzapreti with pesto sauce or the ravioli filled with ricotta cheese and spinach. The restaurant's classic dish is **oven-baked cep mushroom heads**, but it would be a mistake not to taste the **stewed snails** or the various types of meat: **tripe alla romana**, beef roulades and eggplants, buffalo or **goat stew**.
The owner is of Sicilian origin and he often brings back forms of top-quality Ragusano cheese and a few bottles of Cerasuolo di Vittoria, available in addition to other wines like Merlot del Circeo or Moscato di Terracina.

Originally a wine bar, in recent years Massimo and Ivana Masci's place has become a restaurant proper, due also to the fact that the kitchen area has been enlarged. They have created a setting and atmosphere that respects the original architectural beauty of this medieval house located in the historic center, and where the wine cellar has been created in an underground Roman cistern. It's a pleasant place to stop off if you just want to taste the wide selection of **cured meats** and **cheeses** personally selected by Massimo, or if you want a full meal. In this case you can start with the cold lamb gigot with herbs, veal carpaccio, polenta flavored with cheeses and truffles or the crostone with melted caciocavallo. The **soups** made by Ivana are a good way to continue your meal: with mushrooms and potatoes, with vegetables, with onions and groviera cheese croutons or with beans and herbs. There's no lack of pasta dishes either: for example, **lasagna with eggplants and mozzarella** and rice timbale with mushrooms and sausage. Meat for your main course varies from sausages and broccoletti to **porchetta al forno**, from **wild boar in salmì** to **spare ribs and polenta**. As mentioned above, Massimo selects the cheeses, but when it comes to puddings this is Ivana's realm: semifreddo all' amaretto, bread pudding, moretto and ricotta cheese cake.
All these dishes can be accompanied by a wide choice of wines, including top local and regional labels.

Vineria Cesare 1963, Via San Francesco, 3: you both taste and buy excellent wines here, accompanied by cold and warm dishes proposed by Massimo and Simona Cappellanti.

TIVOLI
Villa Adriana

25 KM EAST OF ROME

ADRIANO

🗝️3-Star Hotel
Via di Villa Adriana 194
Tel. 0774 535028
Fax 0774 535122
E-mail: info@hoteladriano.it
Internet: www.hoteladriano.it
Always open

TUSCANIA

24 KM WEST OF VITERBO

MIRANDOLINA

🗝️Bed and breakfast
Via del Pozzo Bianco 40-42
Tel. e fax 0761 436595
E-mail: info@mirandolina.it
Internet: www.mirandolina.it
Open all year

This hotel, run by sisters Gabriella and Patrizia Cinelli, who inherited the business originally set up by their grandfather, is close to Villa Adriana and only a few kilometers from Villa d' Este. It's in an old farmhouse surrounded by grounds, and while Patrizia enhances the place with her works of art, Gabriella, chef and sommelier, takes care of the managerial side of things, including establishing the menu. Both sisters teach in the cooking school called 'Le memorie di Adriano' alongside chef Emilia Di Carlo. The rooms are spacious, comfortable and furnished in a modern style. There's much demand for suite 14 where writer Marguerite Yourcenar once stayed. The hotel is great if you want to relax as the only noise will be the blackbirds singing in the grounds. The buffet breakfast offers genuine food: coffee, milk, tea and their own production of pastries. In the restaurant, seasonal dishes made using quality ingredients (including some Slow Food Presidia) – a meal costs from 30-32 euros per person, excluding wine.

• 2 single, 5 double rooms and 3 suites (2-4 persons), with bathroom, satellite TV; suites with air-conditioning, mini-bar, safe, modem connection • Prices: single 80-95 euros, double 100-115, suite 110-200 (25 euro supplement for extra bed), breakfast included • Credit cards: all, Bancomat • Off-street parking. Small pets allowed (12 euros per day). Reception open 24 hours a day. • Bar, restaurant. Breakfast room, conference room. Garden. 2 tennis courts

Tuscania is one of the most beautiful little towns in upper Latium and the historic center proudly displays traces of the past, with monuments, churches and testimony of the Etruscans and Romans who once inhabited the area. The B&B is in a palazzo that looks out over the surrounding countryside and has recently been refurbished by the new owner, Susanna Lukowski. Two breaches in the town walls enable you to enjoy a view of the Torre di Lavello Park. As you enter there's a small room where breakfast is served: hot drinks, fruit juices, fresh bread, butter, honey, homemade jams, yogurt, ricotta (typical of this area) and homemade cakes. In the summer season you can use the patio. The nearby restaurant, also managed by Susanna, offers seasonal dishes (the average price of a meal is 25 euros per person, excluding wine), with a few Sicilian touches.

• 5 double rooms, with bathroom • Prices: double room single occupancy 40 euro, double 65 (10 euro supplement for extra bed), breakfast included • Credit cards: Bancomat • External parking reserved for guests. Small pets allowed. Owners always reachable. • Restaurant. Outside space

VELLETRI

LA VECCHIA TAVERNA

Trattoria
Via San Girolamo Miani 6
Tel. 06 9637926
Closed Monday
Open: lunch and dinner
Holidays: two weeks in August
Seating: 45
Prices: 25-30 euros, wine excluded
All credit cards, Bancomat

Rino Borro can safely say he's won the bet he made (with himself) in 2001, namely, that he would be able to convince a large number of people to appreciate quality food. You'll find this friendly trattoria at the end of the alley that runs through the village's central market place where he buys some of the vegetables used in the kitchen. His suppliers are the so-called vignarole, smallholders who sell what they've gathered each day from their small plot of land. Once you're seated at your table you can begin with a selection of cured meats accompanied by several types of bruschette and a generous plate of vegetables, either grilled or au gratin. To follow, nice homemade pasta – the **fettuccine** are excellent – all' **amatriciana, with cacio and pepper**, alla **gricia** or with artichokes when they're in season. But also worth trying are the ravioli with zucchini and potatoes or with guinea-fowl ragù and wild asparagus. Meat is widely used in main course dishes: Rino gets his meat in Poggio Mirteto from Stefano Facioni: he orders Chianina and Apennine white calf that are then served as tagliate, bocconcini and T-bones. However, there's no lack of more traditional dishes like **abbacchio allo scottadito** or **rabbit chasseur**, hot spicy rabbit leg and **pan-cooked guinea-fowl**. Rino's wife Daniela prepares the puddings: millefoglie, tiramisu and seasonal jam tarts.
The wine cellar is Salvatore's domain, and he has put together a wine list that offers a good selection of regional and high quality national labels, available at reasonable prices.

VELLETRI
Colle Ionci

L'ELCE E IL CASALE

Bed and breakfast
Via Acqua Lucia 27-74
Tel. 06 9638414-333 7875046
Fax 06 96152618
E-mail: info@colleionci.com
Internet: www.colleionci.com
Open all year

A short distance from the old center of Velletri are these two recently refurbished buildings located in the attractive setting of grounds boasting chestnut trees, Mediterranean pines and olives. The B&B is run by Valeriano Bottini (the owner is his wife Daniela) and it has airy rooms that are simply yet tastefully furnished. Breakfast may be eaten inside or in the grounds and includes fruit juices, milk, coffee, cookies, jams, croissants and, on request, savory fare. Thanks to an agreement with the Colle Ionci Cultural Association, visits can be organized and tickets booked for nearby museums. Your hosts also manage a restaurant that has a menu based on traditional dishes revisited in a more personal key and with touches of Abruzzi cuisine as a tribute to the owners' origin, all at an average price of 25 euros per person.

• 4 double, 2 triple and 4 four-bed rooms, with bathroom, terrace, TV • Prices: double room single occupancy 40 euros, double 66, triple 80, four-bed 95, breakfast included • Credit cards: Visa, MC, Bancomat • Off-street parking. Small pets allowed. Owners always reachable. • Restaurant. Reading and TV room. Conference room. Grounds

VITERBO
San Martino al Cimino

VITERBO

7 KM FROM CITY CENTER

IL MODERNO ⊗

Restaurant-pizzeria
Piazza Buratti 22
Tel. 0761 379952
Closed Tuesday
Open: lunch and dinner
Holidays: June 15-30, December 24-January 3
Seating: 70 + 70 outdoors
Prices: 30-35 euros, excluding wine
All major credit cards, Bancomat

LA TORRE

Osteria-wine store
Via della Torre 5
Tel. 0761 226467
Closed Sunday for dinner and Monday
Open: lunch and dinner
Holidays: mid-July to end-August
Seating: 30
Prices: 20-25 euros, excluding wine
All redit cards, Bancomat

Anna and Graziella will welcome you to this restaurant, which is in San Martino al Cimino's central piazza in front of the 13th-century Cistercian abbey, and will describe for you the list of inviting dishes prepared by Aldo. The menu centers on local products and varies as the seasons change. You can begin with a wide selection of cured meats, many of which they produce themselves, borage roulades or acacia fritters with pecorino romano. To follow there are homemade pastas such as umbricelli (made with flour and water) flavored with tomatoes and wild fennel, or **chestnut flour gnocchi with mushrooms**, but also **soups** made with chestnuts, or artichokes, or lettuce and potatoes, or Etruscan style (with beans and wild turnip tops), or chickpeas and spelt. Another of their specialties is polenta, of which there are many versions, including chestnut and chickpea polenta served with mutton ragù sauce. Among the main courses, in addition to the barbecued meats there's **roast suckling pig seasoned with wild fennel**, wild boar stew, lamb with artichokes and turkey with chestnuts, often accompanied by garden salads flavored with an anchovy and caper pesto or by side dishes focusing on local produce (**Onano lentils** and purgatorio beans). There's a very good selection of **cheeses**, some of which they refine and modify themselves (with chestnut or fig leaves, with ash, or grape must) accompanied by honey, compote and mustards. To finish, puddings made by Graziella, or tarts with ricotta and chestnuts or with pears, ricotta and chocolate. The wine list assembled by Maurizio includes wines from all parts of Italy, but with a focus on wines from Latium.

Up until last year we covered La Torre restaurant; this year's entry concerns the adjacent wine store of the same name – once called the Arcigola club, founded in 1985 – that in the meantime has become an osteria proper. In the kitchen chef Noda prepares traditional local dishes using seasonal ingredients and products acquired from local farms, with a menu that varies each month. The menu is simple and inviting, starting with antipasti of bruschetta flavored with local extra-virgin olive oil, and then **Lake Bolsena lattarini in carpione** and mixed cured meats from the Tuscia area, that among others includes cooked Viterbo salami. Among the first courses, dishes that deserve a special mention are the **lombrichelli with ewe's milk ricotta and fava beans**, orecchiette flavored with tomatoes and fish from Lake Bolsena and the pan-cooked **Onano lentils** (a Slow Food Presidia). You can continue with oven-baked coregone with sauce of gurgulestro (a herb some people think tastes like fennel), rabbit with olives, oven-baked lamb and grilled calf's liver seasoned with wild fennel. To end your meal, some local cheeses and homemade puddings, such as ciambellone with ricotta, Mount Cimini hazelnut cake and Tuscia tozzetti.
To accompany your meal, wines from the restaurant's very well-stocked cellar. Wines are personally selected by your host, Carlo Zucchetti, and over fifty labels can be tasted by the glass. One last thing worthy of note: when you get the check you'll see that they don't include a cover charge.

'L RICHIASTRO

Trattoria
Via della Marrocca 16-18
Tel. 0761 228009
Closed from Sunday evenings to Wednesday
Open: lunch and dinner
Holidays: from July to September
Seating: 60 + 20 outdoors
Prices: 24-30 euros, excluding wine
No credit cards, Bancomat

PORTA ROMANA

Trattoria
Via della Bontà 12
Tel. 0761 307118
Closed Sunday
Open: lunch and dinner
Holidays: August 1-18, December 25-31
Seating: 48
Prices: 25-28 euros, excluding wine
Credit cards: BA, Visa, Bancomat

This rustic-style trattoria is simply furnished and has a wooden roof and a large peperino stone fireplace, while food is served in earthenware dishes. Located in a richiastro (that is, an inner courtyard of a medieval house), it's managed by Giovanna who offers dishes based either on typical local cuisine or sometimes on Renaissance recipes that are modified to give them a more contemporary taste. Her husband Cesare manages to reconcile his professional duties with his natural convivial manner, and being a good host he'll be pleased to suggest and explain the dishes of the day. You can begin with the **crostini** topped with a variety of sauces: egg and rocket salad, pig's liver, red cabbage or peppers. To follow the **soups**, which are an ever-present feature of the menu: depending on the season you'll find soups made with chickpeas and chestnuts, lentils and mushrooms, spelt, beans and broccoletti, fava beans and endive or strigoli and hops. Alternatively there are good homemade pastas, among which **lombrichi** alla vitorchianese (**tomatoes, wild fennel and pecorino**), **fettuccine** all'uccelletto pazzo, **gnocchi 'ncotti** (with tuna or with thyme and pecorino) and pizzicati with zucchini. Then there are the main course meat dishes: roast beef with dried figs or with red wine and raisins, chicken with wild fennel and a dish we really recommend, capomazzo (a delicate **lamb pajata with potatoes**) or **pork skewers with tredura sauce** (ginger, saffron, bay leaf, eggs and local pecorino flavored with honey). To end your meal, home-made puddings. The wine list still hasn't changed from previous years: there are a bunch of quite good labels and a house wine.

We're always happy to return to this trattoria as we can be sure there won't be any change in the fare, which is based on a traditional menu cooked using local ingredients. Annunziata will describe the dishes that her mother, a likeable, lively 84-year-old named Brandina, prepares with great dedication. You can start with bruschetta and follow it with legume and vegetable **soups** – onion, bean, chickpea or lentil soups – but perhaps the best is the soup made with **mixed herbs** (with ramoraccio, sugamele, spinacella and other herbs) collected in the family's fields. The homemade pastas are very good: for instance there's **gnocchi with ragù**, oven-baked lasagna or **tortelli** with several fillings (pumpkin, broccoli and walnuts, mushrooms, ricotta, pears and cheese). And if ordered in advance you can have **spaghetti with anchovies**. Meats served for main courses all come from the family butchers shop: **grilled liver, beef roulades in tomato sauce, lamb coratella**, stuffed bantam, mixed roast (with stuffed quail, sausage, spare ribs and potatoes), sausages and broccoli in a wine sauce, meatballs and, on request only, **pignattaccia** (mixed meat dish oven-baked in the pignatta). Alternatively you can have **baccalà stew with raisins** and, when they're in season, oven-baked cep mushrooms with potatoes. The meal ends with tozzetti and wild cherry jam tart accompanied by a glass of Aleatico wine.
The wines available are mostly local, reasonably priced and go well with the dishes.

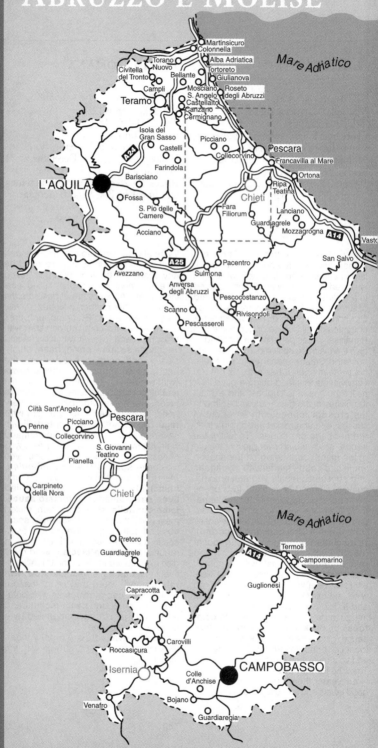

ABRUZZO E MOLISE

Mare Adriatico

Martinsicuro
Colonnella
Torano
Nuovo
Alba Adriatica
Civitella
del Tronto
Bellante
Tortoreto
Campli
Giulianova
Mosciano
Roseto
Teramo
S. Angelo
degli Abruzzi
Castellalto
Canzano
Cermignano

Isola del
Gran Sasso
Picciano
Pescara
Castelli
Collecorvino
Francavilla al Mare
Farindola
Ortona
L'AQUILA
Barisciano
Ripa
Teatina
Fossa
Chieti
S. Pio delle
Fara
Lanciano
Camere
Filiorum
Guardiagrele
Mozzagrogna
Acciano
A14
Vasto
San Salvo
A25
Pacentro
Avezzano
Anversa
degli Abruzzi
Pescocostanzo
Scanno
Rivisondoli
Pescasseroli

Città Sant'Angelo
Pescara
Picciano
Penne
Collecorvino
S. Giovanni
Teatino
Pianella
Chieti
Carpineto
della Nora
Pretoro
Guardiagrele

Mare Adriatico

Termoli
A14
Campomarino

Capracotta
Guglionesi

Roccasicura
Carovilli

Isernia
CAMPOBASSO
Colle
d'Anchise
Venafro
Bojano
Guardiaregia

ACCIANO

San Lorenzo

ALBA ADRIATICA

39 KM SOUTHEAST OF L'AQUILA ON SS 261

34 KM NORTHEAST OF TERAMO ON SS 80 AND 16 OR A14

LOCANDA LA CORTE

HOSTARIA L'ARCA   ◓

Hotel-restaurant
Frazione San Lorenzo 1
Tel. 0864 799191
Closed Monday
Open: lunch and dinner
Holidays: December 10- February 13
Seating: 70 + 40 outdoors
Prices: 27 euros, wine excluded
Credit cards: CartaSi, Visa, Bancomat

Osteria
Viale Mazzini 109
Tel. 0861 714647
Closed for lunch on Tuesday and Saturday
Open: lunch and dinner
Holidays: variable
Seating: 50 + 20 outdoors
Prices: 25-30 euros, wine excluded
All credit cards

Set in the beautiful, unspoilt surroundings of the Subequana Valley in Velino-Sirente Regional Park, you'll find the restaurant in the village of San Lorenzo di Acciano where brother-and-sister team Anna and Tonino Cercarelli have converted rooms inside the old Palazzo Lattanzi. Once seated, you'll be offered a range of special dishes, reinterpretations of traditional recipes, sometimes with an updated twist. The service is friendly and the menu draws its inspiration from local produce.

Delicious **ricotta** is used from springtime onwards when the pastures are at their lushest: it is served alone or baked with chili peppers, in a salad with mushrooms and arugula, in ravioli with endives, leeks and walnuts, with rigatoni, speck and zucchini or aged and grated on **chitarra al sugo di agnello** and in **crespella with zucchini and mint sauce**. Other first courses include a spelt salad, saffron giuncata, cured meats and smoked mozzarella with lardo. Main coursesL **coniglio porchettato** with wild fennel, round of veal with onions, carrots and almonds, **guinea fowl stuffed with truffle** and lamb in pastry. Save room for desserts like the chocolate cake or hot **bocconotto** with a filling of honey and pine nuts in cooked grape must.

The wine list includes many Abruzzo wines as well as a handful of bottles from other regions. A special place is reserved for spirits and liqueurs, including some homemade varieties.

Don't be put off by the Spanish-looking sign: this osteria run by Massimiliano Capretta has strong local roots. Capretta or his brother Marco will describe the menu to you in an informal and friendly manner. They still do this despite the fact that (at long last) a written menu is now available, as well as a list of the various coffees, bottled waters and foreign beers served. There is quite a wide choice, including a traditional set menu and a vegetarian one. The source of the ingredients is given for almost every dish. Seasonal antipasti include cream of tomato soup and marinated zucchini in summer or **spelt polentina with guanciale**, cream of potato or mushroom soup, sautéed spelt with guanciale or sausage in winter. Among the first courses, you can confidently select a classic dish from Teramo, **chitarrina al sugo di polpettine di carne** or **ceppe** (another traditional type of pasta) **with porcini mushrooms**, or you can opt for maltagliati with asparagus or **soup made from organic vegetables and pulses**. Alternatively, you could choose dishes from outside the region, like pumpkin tortelli, supplì di riso or vegetable soups with croutons. There is also an excellent **selection of grilled meats** like beef filet, tagliata or succulent local **lamb chops**. A serviceable cheeseboard rounds off the meal before you conclude with desserts, including a frothy zabaglione with Marsala, chocolate tart or the local specialty of scrucchijata made with Montepulciano grapes.

The wine list is predominantly regional with a few labels from farther afield.

ANVERSA DEGLI ABRUZZI

78 KM SOUTHEAST OF L'AQUILA, 15 KM FROM SULMONA ON SS 479

LA FIACCOLA

Trattoria
Via Duca degli Abruzzi 12
Tel. 0862 49474
Closed Thursday
Open: lunch and dinner
Holidays: none
Seating: 70
Prices: 18-20 euros, wine excluded
Credit cards: CartaSi, Visa

This small osteria in the historic center of Anversa – an attractive place not far from the Cocullo exit off motorway 25 – is named for Gabriele D'Annunzio's tragedy La fiaccola sotto il moggio, which the Abruzzo poet set in this very village. You'll be given a warm welcome by patron Gino Di Cesare. The menu is dominated by the local sheep-farming tradition: among the antipasti you'll find excellent **smoked sheep's ricotta** served on juniper leaves, a variety of pecorino cheeses, including brigantaccio (matured using an old method of hiding the cheeses under a covering of bran to prevent them being stolen by robbers), sheep salami, and delicious **salami of liver and honey** served with homemade preserves.
The strong link to the local economy is also evident from the first courses like **gnocchi del pastore** (served with a sauce made from pecorino cheeses at different stages of maturity, fresh and smoked ricotta, walnuts and basil), **risotto with saffron and cream of ricotta**, chitarrina with ricotta and truffle or **tagliatelle with lamb ragù**. For the main course, you can choose roast or lamb **porchettato**, roast rabbit, arrosticini and, to order, mutton al cotturo. Alternative main courses include grilled scamorza and melted pecorino served with honey.
Ricotta also plays a leading role in the desserts, either sweetened and dusted with cocoa or coffee, or served with jam, honey and chopped almonds. Alternatively, you can opt for pan dell'orso or an apple cake made by a nearby bakeshop. The whole meal can be accompanied by the house wine or a bottle from a limited selection of regional wineries.

BARISCIANO

18 KM SOUTHEAST OF L'AQUILA

CONVENTO SAN COLOMBO

3-star hotel
Via Provinciale, km 4,200
Tel. 0862 899017 or 0862 899022
Fax 0862 899016
E-mail: info@sancolombotur.com
Internet: www.sancolombotur.com
Open all year round

This hotel is in an enviable location, situated in a wood, in a panoramic position at the foot of the Gran Sasso and majestic Campo Imperatore plain, close to Rocca Calascio and the splendid medieval village of Santo Stefano di Sessanio. The original cells, refectory, stables and wine cellars of the convent of San Colombo – where there were monks up until 1809 – have been preserved and renovated to provide pleasant rooms with every modern comfort. For breakfast you'll be served homemade cakes and sweet fare such as ferratelle, apple and jam tarts. Nature-lovers can hire mountain bikes, while outings on horseback and other excursions are organized too. This is definitely an ideal place to relax in Franciscan surroundings with all the comforts of a modern hotel. The restaurant offers local dishes and the average price of a meal is 22 euros, excluding wine; half board ranges from 48-58 euros per person.

• 1 single, 7 double rooms and 1 suite, with bathroom, mini-bar, safe, TV • Prices: single 36-46 euros, double room single occupancy 46-56, double 72-92, suite 87-107, breakfast included • All major credit cards, Bancomat • Facility accessible to the mobility challenged. Free public parking in the immediate vicinity. Small pets allowed. Reception open from 8am to 12am. • Restaurant. Conference room. Garden

BELLANTE
Scalo

BOJANO

IL CASALE

Restaurant
Via De Luca 1
Tel. 0861 611925
Closed Tuesday
Open: lunch and dinner
Holidays: none
Seating: 45 + 45 outdoors
Prices: 30 euros, wine excluded
All credit cards, Bancomat

DA FILOMENA

Trattoria
Località Limpilli 199
Tel. 0874 773078
Closed Monday
Open: lunch, Sat. also for dinner if you book
Holidays: in July
Seating: 70
Prices: 30 euros, wine excluded
All credit cards, Bancomat

It is easy to find this small farmhouse surrounded by a well-tended garden, just a hundred meters or so off the main road leading from Teramo to Giulianova. The all-female waitstaff are very polite. The atmosphere is very pleasant with comfortably spaced and elegantly set tables, accompanied by quiet background music. The cellar is respectably extensive and almost entirely from Abruzzo, combined with a suitable variety of wines sold by the glass.

After closing for a short period and then starting up again, Franca Di Giacomo continues to work on her own. She is a solid traditional cook who does not balk at experimentation. Many of the dishes on the list are still firmly anchored in Abruzzo tradition, particularly those from Teramo. Start with cured meats and cheeses made in the Gran Sasso and Monti della Laga Park (ham, loin, **smoked ricotta with juniper**), classic **mazzarelle** from Teramo (chicken livers and coratella wrapped in chicory), **scrambled eggs with peppers** (a typical peasant supper dish). Follow this with **zuppa di ceci di Navelli**, gnocchetti with asparagus, saffron and crisply fried pancetta, **pappardelle with duck sauce** or **pappicci** made from water and flour with guanciale and pecorino. For your main course, choose lamb with artichokes, **turkey alla canzanese, baccalà with cream of peppers**, capocollo di maiale with sweet 'n' sour vegetables. Unfortunately, the puddings are not so inspiring, with the overused threesome of panna cotta, tiramisu, strawberries and cream. However, there is an excellent cheeseboard to round off your meal.

In the heart of historic Sannio, at the foot of Mount Matese, Bojano lies partly on the vast plateau known as Piana di Bojano and partly on the outlying foothills of Mount Mates at the southern end of Mount La Gallinola, the second highest peak of the massif that marks the boundary between Campania and Molise. Once you reach the town, ask for directions: Filomena is on the outskirts and without directions you might get lost.

The trattoria offers a selection of local dishes, which vary according to the seasons. A number of **paste e legumi** occupies the place of honor on the menu, with flavors that are distinctly different, almost forgotten. As you would expect in a restaurant of this kind, the hearty selection of antipasti includes plain but tasty **local cured meats** like soppressata, prosciutto and variations of pork, as well as good **cheeses** and **dairy products** (the latter are also offered as an alternative sweet course). Apart from various combinations of pasta with chickpeas and beans, there are other types of **pasta** (filled and plain) **served with meat sauce** and, when in season, the delicious **orecchiette with turnip tops** or **tagliatelle with porcini mushrooms**. If you are still hungry, the main courses prominently feature the splendid local meat. **Roast mutton** and mixed meats, **sausages**, steak – all grilled; or if you want an alternative, you could opt for the excellent **roast scamorza**.

There are only a few desserts, some of which, like the wine list, could use a little work. The latter is limited to a good house wine and a few bottles, mainly from the region.

CAMPLI

CAMPOBASSO

LOCANDA DEL POMPA

Locanda-Trattoria
Bivio Campli 5
Tel. 0861 569011
Closed Wednesday
Open: lunch and dinner
Holidays: two weeks in February
Seating: 60
Prices: 30 euros, wine excluded
All credit cards

DA NONNO CECCHINO

Trattoria
Via Larino 32
Tel. 0874 311778
Closed Sunday for dinner
Open: lunch and dinner
Holidays: first week in november
Seating: 80 + 30 outdoors
Prices: 25 euros, wine excluded
All credit cards

The Pompa family are an institution in the history of Teramo catering, having run various restaurants in the city itself in the second half of the last century. They now manage this pleasant, isolated country inn halfway between Teramo and Campli.

Whether in the cozy dining room or under the outside porch, here you'll get a comprehensive idea of the wealth of the local cuisine. To start, antipasti which, depending on the season, feature ricottina with saffron and courgettes, cured pork and game, vegetables fried or preserved in oil, **ciffe e ciaffe** (lamb offal with aromatic herbs and peppers) and **potato millefeuille** with black truffle and cheese fondue. On to first courses with **saragolla wheat spaghetti with guanciale**, organic emmer soup with ham and beans and chitarrine with porcini mushrooms, ragù or tomato, fresh basil and juniper-smoked ricotta. Plus **cuzztil** with courgette flowers and saffron, and on May 1, the not-to-be-missed **virtù teramane**, a sort of minestrone combining 40 or so herbs and vegetables. Standing out among the mains are **lamb with herbs** or with saffron, Marchigiana beef tagliata and fillet of rabbit with basil. An excellent **cheeseboard** brings together mainly central Italian varieties. Desserts include semifreddo of ricotta with woodland fruits, chocolate mousse, wholemeal **crostata with cream and sheep's ricotta** and classic **pizza dolce**.

The carefully assembled wine list covers the whole of Italy with a focus on Abruzzo labels. Mark-ups are reasonable.

Older inhabitants of Campobasso nostalgically remember the days when the trattoria run by Cecchino Cerone was the best place to enjoy traditional local food in the entire regional capital. Unfortunately the old patriarch is no longer with us, but the new Cecchino is in an attractive, rustic venue, with a large tunnel vault. The new trattoria makes only a small dent in the enormous heritage of recipes collected by Cerone but is run with a sure hand by Gianfranco and Michele Corsillo, the former attending to guests while the latter oversees the kitchen. They do their best to uphold the reputation by serving simple, farmhouse dishes in line with local tradition.

Antipasti include local **cured meats** and **preserves**, traditional **trippette** and **mussillo**, which are dishes that have nearly disappeared. There is a wide choice of pasta dishes such as tasty **cavatelli** served, depending on the time of year, with mushrooms and truffles, or peppers and onions and **pasta con gli spigatelli** or with **pulses**. There are also occasionally **soups** made with potatoes, zucchini and celery or beans and celery. On Wednesday and Friday, you'll usually find **baccalà** on the menu, sometimes accompanied by **friarelli and peperoni**, but also by cherry tomatoes or **mollicato al forno.** Other original and particularly tasty dishes include **allulur'** (an old recipe for stuffed lamb's tripe), **agnello cace 'e ova** and **roasted lamb's head** with potatoes. Flavorful **meat** preparations and **grilled sausages** are always available.

Choose from a selection of delicious desserts. There is also a praiseworthy wine list, with numerous good wines offered at very reasonable prices.

CAMPOBASSO

CAMPOMARINO

69 KM NORTHEAST OF CAMPOBASSO ON SS 647

LA GROTTA (DA CONCETTA)

Trattoria
Via Larino 9
Tel. 0874 311378
Closed Saturday, Sunday and festivities
Open: lunch and dinner
Holidays: variable
Seating: 50
Prices: 20-22 euros, wine excluded
No credit cards

NONNA ROSA

Trattoria
Via Biferno 41
Tel. 0875 539948
Closed Tuesday
Open: lunch and dinner
Holidays: 10 days in October
Seating: 25
Prices: 30 euros, wine excluded
All credit cards, Bancomat

This is perhaps the most popular trattoria in the city, a place that for over 20 years has remained faithful to the style of Concetta Cipolla, herself a cook for half a century. She is perfectly at ease in the role of the classic hostess and occasionally ventures into the dining room to serve at table or to talk about what she has cooked. Concetta has created an informal, rustic atmosphere that is very friendly, with paper-covered checked tablecloths.

The first thing you'll be offered is fiadone, a hot cheese dish, while you wait to order. The menu changes daily and reflects the seasonal nature of the ingredients. For antipasti there is a tasty **pizza e minestra**, a typical dish from the mountain areas of Molise made using cornmeal and vegetables (mixed greens in summer, broccoletti in winter), followed by **pasta and beans**, a polenta, eggplant and tomato pie, chickpea soup with toasted bread, and an excellent **grilled eggplant filled with smoked provola**. As an alternative to the platter of grilled meats (sausage, lamb cutlets, veal and pork escalopes, chicken livers, and scamorza molisana), you can opt for the cold sliced **porchetta**: this is an entire pork filet that is slowly roasted with aromatic herbs for an entire day and then served with delicious carciofini in oil.

A selection of first-rate homemade pastries offers a lovely conclusion to your meal and you won't be able to resist the **mandorle atterrate**, almonds roasted with white wine and sugar, but no coffee. You will be served quickly and with a smile, and the wine list includes a satisfactory choice of local wines from Molise. Book ahead, especially for lunch.

This charming little trattoria is hidden away up a narrow street. Inside, it resembles a private drawing room with its attractive wooden furnishings and an open hearth for grilling. Giuseppe L'Abbate runs the place and has cooked here for the past 10 years, much to the delight of those who enjoy fine meat. He is a passionate chef and frequently comes to chat with guests and also personally selects all the ingredients used here from trusted suppliers. These include the excellent hand-sliced prosciutto, the cured meats and vegetables preserved in oil, the local cheeses (caciottine with chili pepper and dried buffalo mozzarella with cuore di pomodorino pachino), as well as the eggs for herb frittatas. These dishes are served with hot bruschette and lardo. Next you can choose from the excellent **puréed fava beans with chicory** or a wide variety of fresh pasta with different sauces, including chitarra served with meat sauce, **orecchiette with turnip tips** or **ragù di braciolette**. But Giuseppe's real skill and passion comes to the fore with the main courses and the **grilled meats**. There's a perfectly cooked selection of top quality meats from the best herds. The **fiorentina T-bone** is outstanding (it's worth visiting just for this) and is served by Giuseppe on a hot serving plate before being cut with reverence and expertise. But there are also other cuts like scottona filet, **lamb** from the Molise mountains and pork sausages. You can also choose **grilled cheese** as an alternative. Save room for a delicious dessert to end your meal.

The wine list includes a good selection of local wines and others from Italy's best known wine-producing areas.

CANZANO

LA TACCHINELLA

Trattoria
Via Roma 18
Tel. 0861 555107
Closed Sunday for dinner and Monday, not in summer
Open: lunch and dinner
Holidays: variable
Seating: 50
Prices: 22-24 euros
Credit cards: MC, Visa, Bancomat

This trattoria is steeped in history. Four generations have cooked here and it's worth it to visit the neviera, or snow house, a natural refrigerator dating from the 13th century that was built below the restaurant. Snow was carried here by mules in order to preserve meat. Here, you'll also find many delicacies on offer, including the elaborate and refined **turkey alla canzanese**, an iconic dish which gives the restaurant its name: meat from a turkey hen is boned, seasoned and cooked slowly before being allowed to cool in gelatin.
Dario will help guide you through the menu, which includes an interesting range of first courses, including tricolored fettuccine with mushrooms and truffles, **scrippelle m'busse** (small crepes served in broth with pecorino), **chitarrina with small meatballs** and the "lacrima", a spicy pasta. Moving onto the main courses: the menu keeps to tradition with mutton alla callara or **mazzarelle** (roasted lamb entrails wrapped in endive leaves) and – on Friday – a rich array of **baccalà** dishes. Lastly, it is worth succumbing to the temptation of homemade desserts like bacio di dama or chocolate tart with gelato, served either hot or cold. If you're lucky, you'll be able to taste the **tisichelle** (anise-flavored ciambelline). These days, the snow house is a cleverly lit basement: here you can enjoy another magical moment as you listen to Dario's stories while enjoying cantuccini and vin cotto.
There is a reasonable wine list featuring mainly regional wines, but the house wine served in bottles stands up well to the competition.

CAPRACOTTA

L'ELFO

Restaurant
Via Campanelli
Tel. 0865 949131
Closed Monday
Open: lunch and dinner
Holidays: May 5-20, November 5-20
Seating: 50 + 20 outdoors
Prices: 22-26 euros, wine excluded
Credit cards: CartaSi, Visa, Bancomat

Capracotta is one of the most attractive corners of Molise, an ideal destination for anyone wishing to find a quiet spot with unspoiled natural scenery as well as the chance to walk along woodland paths. In the center of the village, you'll be welcomed by a young couple, Franca and Michele, to this restaurant housed in the wine cellar of an old aristocratic palazzo.
The meal starts with the classic choice of cured meats (soppressata and sausages), local **dairy produce** including stracciata and ricotta and traditional zuppe and minestre like **voccarusc'** (mountain spinach), **bleta m'paniccia** (chard with stale bread and bacon) and **foglie e patan'** (cabbage with potatoes). Also try **quail eggs al tegamino** served with truffles in season. These are followed, in season, by tagliatelle served with prugnoli and wild asparagus, ravioli filled with ricotta, nettles and grated truffle, classic **lentil soup from Capracotta** with cicoria or leeks, cannoli filled with vegetables and fresh sheep's cheese or lasagnette with potatoes and orapi. In addition to the delicious local grilled meats, you can choose pork with Moscato del Molise, **wild boar shank with finferli mushrooms** or roast lamb bocconcini. If you book ahead, you can get the "**pezzata**", which are boiled mutton bocconcini with a variety of flavorings. Desserts include a choice of delicious tarts (with ricotta, almonds and chocolate or with walnuts and wild berries).
There is a good wine list featuring about 80 labels – most from Molise and Abruzzo.

CAROVILLI

LA GRANDE QUERCIA

🗝️Holiday Farm
Contrada Fonte Curelli
Tel. 0865 838712
E-mail: info@altavia-hrh.com
Internet: www.altavia-hrh.com
Closed for 15 days after Epiphany

This small farm is situated in the hills of upper Molise, not far from Isernia, with its exceptional historic center and the other medieval sites in the environs. The stone farmhouse managed by Eutimio Falasca offers a family atmosphere and is dominated outside by the very old oak tree which has given the place its name. The rooms are simple and comfortable, with terracotta floors and arte povera and period furniture. The mansard rooms have wooden beams, while the railing alongside the stairs leading up to them was previously a manger. Breakfast consists of bread, butter, jams and homemade cakes. The restaurant offers good cured meats and dairy products, pasta with truffles and mushrooms, lightly fried lamb offal, poultry and cuts of veal. The average price of a meal comes to 20-25 euros. They also organize horseback treks.

• 2 single and 3 double rooms, with bathroom, TV • Prices: double room single occupancy 37 euros, double 52 (10 euro supplement for extra bed), breakfast included • Credit cards: none • 1 room designed for mobility challenged. Off-street parking. Small pets allowed (not in rooms). Owners always present • Restaurant. Garden

CASTELLALTO
Castelnuovo Vomano

VILLA GOBBI

🗝️3-star hotel
Via Nazionale 323
Tel. and fax 0861 57326
E-mail: info@villagobbi.it
Internet: www.villagobbi.it
Open all year round

An ancient farmhouse and stables were completely restructured to create this hotel lying midway between the Adriatic coast and the mountains. Each of the spacious, airy rooms has a different color scheme and all of them are comfortable and outfitted with modern furniture. There are tapestries and ceramics on the walls and attractive carpets on the floors. The generous buffet breakfast is served in a cozy room and offers croissants, bread, jams, cakes, ham and cheese, dried and fresh fruit, yogurt, cereal and hot and cold drinks. The hotel is an ideal base for visits to San Clemente al Vomano, famous for the rich ciborium believed to be the oldest in the Abruzzo region; Teramo with its beautiful cathedral and Roman amphitheater; and Atri's cathedral with its splendid portals.

• 5 single, 6 double rooms and 2 suites, with bath (shower or jacuzzi), A/C, minibar, TV, modem connection • Prices: single 55 euros, double 85, suite 105, breakfast included • Credit cards: all, Bancomat • Facility accessible to the mobility challenged, 2 rooms designed for their use. Off-street parking. No pets allowed. Reception open 24 hours a day • Bar. Breakfast room, TV room

CASTELLI
Colledoro

41 KM SOUTH OF TERAMO ON SS 491

DA LUISETTA

☞Restaurant
Contrada Colledoro 1
Tel. 0861 979100
Closed Tuesday
Open: lunch and dinner
Holidays: in September
Seating: 90
Prices: 20-25 euros, wine excluded
All credit cards

Although not far from Castelli, a beautiful town renowned for its ancient ceramic tradition, this restaurant actually stands on top of a hill further south. If you are driving through Val Vomano, you'll find the way to Colledoro between the road for Castel Castagna and the one to Castelli. This small hamlet boasts a bar and restaurant where Donna Luisetta used to cook until just a few years ago. Today, her sons Vitaliano, Raniero and Lanfranco, as well as her daughters-in-law and grandchildren, continue to offer authentic preparations of the local cuisine.
There is no written menu for the dishes. For antipasti you might taste pecorino at various stages of maturity, perhaps accompanied by local prosciutto and vegetables in oil. First courses include handmade pasta, such as the excellent **tagliatelle with porcini mushrooms** and truffle sauce and **gnocchi in duck sauce**, whereas what is regarded as the highlight, a risotto with mushrooms, mixed vegetables and cream, is less interesting. These are followed by **roast or grilled meat**, such as lamb, pork and beef steaks, or kid when available. Many clients choose to come on Friday and on the last Sunday in the month when the entire menu is dedicated to **baccalà** (also available if booked at least three days in advance): raw or marinated, with potatoes, in tomato sauce, roast, grilled or fried. For dessert choose from panna cotta (flavored with caramel, chocolate or forest fruits) and coffee cream tart.
There is only a limited choice of wine from Teramo and its province, but the local house wine is satisfactory.

CERMIGNANO
Montegualtieri

29 KM SOUTHEAST OF TERAMO

CAPODACQUA

🗝Holiday farm
Contrada Scanzature 17
Tel. 0861 66678
Fax 0861 413754
E-mail: aziendacapodacqua@virgilio.it
Internet: www.agriturismocapodacqua.it
Open all year round

Annamaria Di Furia and her family have worked meticulously to restructure a rural building dating from the late 1800s to create this farm holiday spot near the River Vomano. The brick and stone walls of the original structure are still visible and the wooden floors and ceilings have been retained too, everything perfectly complemented by the period furniture and wrought-iron bedsteads. The facility also has three rooms used for activities such as cooking courses. In the workshop they produce the tasty jams that are served for breakfast, as well as the bread, tarts and various vegetables preserved in olive oil. From Thursday to Sunday you can again find these preserves on the lunch and dinner menus, plus other typical dishes from the Teramo area. The price of a meal ranges from 20 to 25 euros, (half board runs 37 to 40 euros per person).

• 4 double rooms, with bath, TV • Prices: double room single occupancy 30-32 euros, double 45-50 (15 euro supplement for extra bed), breakfast included • Credit cards: none • Restaurant accessible to the mobility challenged. Off-street parking. Small pets allowed. Owners always present • Restaurant. Classrooms. Terrace, garden

CITTÀ SANT'ANGELO

CIVITELLA DEL TRONTO

17 KM NORTH OF PESCARA ON SS 16

18 KM NORTH OF TERAMO

OSTERIA DELL'ANGELO

Restaurant
Via Diaz 8
Tel. 085 9699023
Closed Monday
Open: dinner, for lunch if you book
Holidays: 2 weeks in February
Seating: 35
Prices: 30 euros, wine excluded
All credit cards.

ZUNICA

4-Star hotel
Piazza Pepe 14
Tel. 0861 91319
Fax 0861 918150
E-mail: tremonelle@zunica.it
Internet: www.hotelzunica.it
Closed in January

This beautiful medieval town, with all its palazzi, alleys and small squares, is only a few minutes from the motorway exit for Pescara Nord. You can see the entrance to the restaurant from Piazza Garibaldi: you'll be welcomed by the exuberant hospitality of Mimmo Marcella, who returned to his hometown after acquiring years of experience on cruise ships. The setting is pleasantly cluttered with prints, lamps and a number of old tills from various periods and countries collected by the owner. The menu is determined by what ingredients are purchased that day. Two blackboards at the entrance show the dishes of the day with their respective prices, all good value.
There's a tempting choice of antipasti: raw oysters and **scampetti** or a rare **papalina** with oil and lemon, **spicy moscardini**, half a lobster in tartare sauce, pepata di cozze and **totanetti with onions**. In the fish fry you'll find pumpkin flowers filled with scampi, **borage filled with prawns and mozzarella** and caramella di scampi lined with lardo. If you want to taste the chitarra pasta with shellfish, tagliolini with prawns or **gnocchi di patate with scampi**, remember that the portions are generous, or if you're persuaded by the owner's chatty friendliness, you might feel tempted by the **John Dory in guazzetto**, the excellent roast or a crisp **frittura**. The desserts are all homemade and quality makes up for variety. The two standouts are the traditional Abruzzo **pizza doce** and the chocolate mousse. When we last visited there was no wine list, so it's worth asking for recommendations or choosing a bottle from the limited selection of Abruzzo wines.

This facility is in an attractive 17th-century palazzo that has been operated as a hotel and managed by the same family since 1880. It's in an enviable location, situated in the main square of Civitella del Tronto, one of the last Bourbon bastions at the time of the unification of Italy. The view of the valley below and the Gran Sasso above has made it popular with guests, who also appreciate the quality of the recently refurbished rooms. These are furnished in a tasteful, elegant manner. The buffet breakfast offers a variety of sweet and savory fare, such as croissants, jams, butter, cheeses, ham and hot and cold beverages. The bar, wine shop and communal areas in general are pleasant, as is the restaurant (average price for a meal is 35 euros; half board ranges from 55-70 euros per person for a minimum stay of three days), where they organize tastings and themed dinners.

• 14 double and 6 triple rooms, with bath, mini-bar, TV, modem connection • Prices: double room single occupancy 40-70 euros, double 70-110, triple 90-140, breakfast included • Credit cards: all, Bancomat • Facility accessible to the mobility challenged. Free parking outside the historic center. Small pets allowed. Reception open 24 hours a day • Bar, restaurant, wine shop. Reading and TV room. Conference room

COLLECORVINO

IL FOCOLARE

🍲 Restaurant
Contrada Campotino 43
Tel. 085 4471382
Closed Monday
Open: dinner, for lunch on Sunday and holidays
Holidays: variable
Seating: 70 + 70 outdoors
Prices: 25 euros, wine excluded
All credit cards

Under the cool wooden pergola of Il Focolare, you can enjoy the aromas and flavors of the surrounding area thanks to the cooking of the Mazzocchetti family. Inside, the restaurant is divided into two rooms (one is reserved for smokers), but the setting is quite rustic and suitable for those who like spending the evening in good company.
Start with a plentiful range of hot and cold antipasti: homemade **giardiniera**, pecorino served with honey, local prosciutto and sausages in oil, roasted eggplant, **mushroom salad** and stuffed mushrooms, and excellent **cipollata** and coratella d'agnello. Among the first courses, choose from a number of hand-rolled pasta dishes, including pasta alla chitarra with mushrooms and black truffles, **ravioli with saffron and asparagus**, gnocchi alla contadina (with bacon and broccoli) or ragù, **anellini del Focolare**, a variation on the classic pasta alla pecorara, with ricotta and artichokes and fettuccine with asparagus and truffle or sagnette served without tomato but with chickpeas and rosemary. These are followed by predominantly meaty main courses. Inevitably there is **roast leg of lamb**, carrè of lamb, grilled meat, tagliata and fiorentina, but it is important to mention the excellent **arrosticini**, mutton kebabs which are cut by hand and then threaded onto skewers. There is a top-notch selection of homemade desserts, including cannoli alla crema and sfogliatine with crema all'Aurum.
The wine list is good and features the main regional producers with a few good national or international labels, all proposed at modest mark-ups.

COLLE D'ANCHISE

LA PIANA DEI MULINI

🔑 Locanda
Fondovalle del Biferno, Strada
Statale 647 km 7.00
Tel. 0874 787330
Fax 0874 776825
E-mail: info@lapianadeimulini.it
Internet: www.lapianadeimulini.it
Open all year round

Michele Lucarelli's locanda is located near the center of Campobasso on the banks of the Biferno River. Built in the early 1800s, it was originally a water-driven flour mill with an adjacent farm and wool-dyeing center. It's built around a courtyard and has two floors. On the ground floor there are stone arches that support the overhanging balconies where the rooms are located; all have access to the terrace. This architectural style is not seen frequently in the Molise countryside. The rooms have beautiful terracotta floors and wrought-iron beds and are tastefully furnished. Breakfast consists of jams, homemade cakes, fresh fruit and also savory fare. The restaurant offers traditional Molise dishes (a meal runs 20-25 euros, excluding wine).

• 7 double rooms, with bath, A/C, TV (on request) • Prices: double room single occupancy 40 euros, double 60 (20-euro supplement for extra bed), breakfast included • Credit cards: CartaSi, Bancomat • Facility accessible to the mobility challenged, 1 room designed for their use. Off-street parking. Small pets allowed. Owners always present • Restaurant. Reading room. Conference room. Garden, terrace

COLONNELLA
Rio Moro

46 KM NORTHEAST OF TERAMO, 10 KM FROM SAN BENEDETTO DEL TRONTO

ZENOBI

🍲 Restaurant
Contrada Rio Moro
Tel. 0861 70581
Closed Tuesday, never in August
Open: lunch and dinner
Holidays: in January
Seating: 80 + 60 outdoors
Prices: 28-30 euros, wine excluded
All credit cards

You get to Colonnella by leaving the A24 at Val Vibrata. Just before you reach the village, follow the signs and enjoy the views of the rolling hills of olive trees that lead down to the azure sea. For years, in this pleasant country house (where eating outside in summer is always a delight), Patrizia Corradetti and her three children have made the most of the area's wonderful ingredients, preparing them with utmost respect according to traditional recipes.

You'll be offered a delicious range of antipasti: local cured meats, **coratella d'agnello** served with sweet or hot peppers, homemade preserves and pickles, beans and cabbage, vegetable pies. First courses: **ceppe al ragù** (a delectable dish from nearby Civitella del Tronto, this is homemade bucatini prepared by wrapping the pasta around a knitting needle), ravioli in green tomato sauce, classic chitarra teramana and **scrippelle 'mbusse**. But save some room for **capra alla neretese**, the masterpiece of Abruzzo cooking, which is prepared to perfection here, or for **roast goose**, grilled mushrooms in season or sauteed free-range chicken. On Friday, there's an excellent menu featuring **baccalà** or stockfish. The usual desserts and good homemade cookies offer a satisfying end to your meal. The service is excellent and the atmosphere homey.

The wine list continues to grow: it is well structured and extensive, ranging beyond Abruzzo as well.

🍷 The Corradetti family also runs a farm where you can purchase a variety of products. We particularly recommend the wine and oil.

FARA FILIORUM PETRI

16 KM SOUTH OF CHIETI ON SS 81

L'ANTICO TRATTURO

🔑 Holiday Farm
Località Piana Masseria 2
Tel. 0871 706066 or 340 3341518
Closed in November

This agriturismo is definitely worth a visit. The refurbishment carried out on the old stone farmhouses here included the restoration of furniture, beds and chandeliers. Interiors are pleasantly decorated in natural colors, and each of the rooms bears the name of a different district in the area. Owner Nicolino Ciavolini's passion for tradition can be seen from the museum he has set up. It is dedicated to the bundle of cane that the districts of Fara burn every year in January to celebrate a historic event in this village's history. Breakfast consists of cakes, jams and hot drinks. The kitchen prepares local dishes using meat and vegetables produced on the farm (a meal costs 20 euros, excluding wine). Given the location of the facility a reservation is highly recommended.

• 5 double rooms, with bath • Prices: double room single occupancy 40 euros, double 50-60 (20 euro supplement for extra bed), breakfast included • Credit cards: all, Bancomat • Off-street parking. No pets allowed. Owners always present • Restaurant. Garden, grounds. Horseback riding

FOSSA

OSTERIA DEL MELOGRANO

🥘 Trattoria
Piazza Masci 3
Tel. 0862 751484-347 7559438
Closed Monday
Open: dinner, for lunch on Sunday
Holidays: variable
Seating: 40
Prices: 25 euros, wine excluded
Credit cards: CartaSi, Visa, Bancomat

This trattoria is housed in an aristocratic palazzetto in the middle of a tiny village steeped in history and charm under the ruins of Castle d'Ocre and watched over by the convents of Sant'Angelo and Santo Spirito. There are three comfortable, attractive rooms: two on the first floor and another smaller one on the ground floor, all with sober, pleasant furnishings. Gianluca Carrozzi, a young self-taught chef, helms the kitchen, while Rita Mucciola manages the front of the house.
The osteria is gradually building up good relationships with small producers and suppliers from L'Aquila and the nearby Subequo valley. This translates to antipasti that include cured meats and local cheeses as well as samples of other seasonal products like **coratellina d'agnello** and a salad of spelt and vegetables. Among the various **soups**, we recommend spelt soup with porcini mushrooms and saffron and the autumn chickpea and chestnut soup. The **pappardelle with cream of chickpeas and porcini mushrooms** or wild boar ragù are excellent, and the pasta alla **chitarra** can be served with **lamb sauce** or with cream of zucchini and saffron from L'Aquila. The local **lamb cutlets** with rosemary are particularly notable, but there are other meaty offerings like costata, tagliata of beef, roast scamorza, rabbit, wild boar and **stracotto al Montepulciano**.
The homemade desserts are quite ambitious and the wine list offers a good range from throughout Abruzzo.

FRANCAVILLA AL MARE

VILLA ANTONELLA

🔑 Bed and breakfast
Via Valle Anzuca 14 a
Tel. 085 4910650
E-mail: a.mancinelli@cartorange.com
Internet: www.villaantonella.it
Open all year round

Antonella Mancinelli comes from a local family that is very well known in the restaurant trade. Her B&B is a beautiful villa in the upper part of Francavilla with five rooms furnished English-style. It's located just a short distance from the place where Francesco Paolo Michetti and Gabriele D' Annunzio used to meet and converse and is also not far from the Michetti Museum, which contains the works of this Abruzzo artist. Breakfast consists of croissants, jams, bread, milk, cappuccino, teas, homemade cakes and, on request, gluten-free items as well. The Mancinelli family also manages the nearby La Nave restaurant, which specializes in fish dishes (B&B guests get a 10% discount). During the day you can go to the beach or, if you like, head to the Maiella, which is less than half an hour away by car.

• 4 double, triple or quadruple rooms, with bath, A/C, mini-bar, TV • Prices: double room single occupancy 47 euros, double 70, triple 81, four-bed 90, breakfast included • Credit cards: none • Facility accessible to the mobility challenged. Off-street parking. No pets allowed. Owners present until 1am. • Restaurant. Breakfast room. Garden. Tennis court

GIULIANOVA
Lido

OSTERIA DAL MORO

🍲 Trattoria
Lungomare Spalato 74
Tel. 085 8004973
Closed Tuesday and Wednesday; only Wednesday in summer
Open: lunch and dinner
Holidays: Sept. or Oct., Feb. or March
Seating: 55 + 10 outdoors
Prices: 30-32 euros, wine excluded
All credit cards

This trattoria, which is popular among residents and regular customers from the nearby Marche region or Pescara, is a great place to enjoy gastronomic dishes served in a family atmosphere. Paper napkins are perfectly acceptable with the generous helpings of antipasti, including excellent mezzanelli (small scampi) with cherry tomatoes, **fritturina di merluzzetti**, **stuffed mussels** and trancetto di pesce sciabola, **boiled scampi** and sauteed mussels, mackerel with herbs and **marinated anchovies**. Then come the first course: **chitarrina al sugo rosso di pesce and scampi** and orecchiette served with broccoletti and fish, **mezzemaniche al pesce azzurro** and risotto with shellfish and salmon, excellent gnocchetti with fish sauce and **maltagliati ai frutti di mare**. As befits a good fish restaurant, the main course depends on the sea's offerings, as well as the skill of the fishing boats from Giulianova. There is a crisp **frittura** with small cod and zanchette, squid and scampi or prawns, a variety of **roasted** fish, with an excellent pesce sciabola and mackerel, as well as the ever-present scampi, with monkfish, plaice and sole. There is a limited choice of desserts and gelato. The wine list includes a few good local labels (Trebbiano d'Abruzzo) as well as some wines from other regions.

The bill will come as a pleasant surprise for its particularly good value. The service can be a little slow at peak times, and it is worth booking well in advance if you want to eat on Friday or Saturday evening. The Osteria dal Moro is a reliable place to eat superb fish at very reasonable prices – something that is all too rare today.

GIULIANOVA
Lido

25 km east of Teramo on SS 16 or exit A 14

OSTERIA DELLA STRACCIVOCC

🍲 Restaurant
Via Trieste 159
Tel. 085 8005326
Closed Sunday evening and Monday
Open: lunch and dinner
Holidays: October or November
Seating: 80
Prices: 30–35 euros, wine excluded
All credit cards except AE

Consistently excellent and always featuring fresh ingredients, honest prices and good teamwork: this restaurant has much to recommend it. Fabio, Emiliano and Federico take care of the tables, while Mamma Maria and his wife Monia take care of the kitchen. Behind the scenes, Papà Francesco is responsible for sourcing the fish. The restaurant is often crowded with tables of young people and families, and it's no wonder, what with the quantity and quality of the antipasti and other preparations.

The fish dishes start with a delicious series of unusual antipasti, including oysters, **raw scampi** and **boiled stracciavocc** (squill), sautéed mussels and clams, insalata di mare, marinated anchovies, **cod with peppers** and spelt soup with mazzolina, gratinéed mussels and razorshells. This is followed by a series of first courses that vary according to the seasons: there may be **tagliatelle nere with calamaretti and bass**, a delicate risotto with sole, **maccheroncini di Campofilone with red scampi sauce** or maltagliati with scampi, calamaretti and asparagus. If you've not overestimated your appetite, you might have room to taste a **guazzetto** that still smells of the sea, **roast turbot with potatoes and olives** or a crisp **frittura di paranza** and other main courses depending on the fish available at the market.

The quality of the desserts doesn't quite live up to the rest of the menu and deserves a little more attention, apart from a tasty homemade tiramisù. The wine list is reasonable, including the best of the region and a few national labels with fair mark-ups.

SANTA CHIARA

Restaurant
Via Roma 10
Tel. 0871 801139
Closed Tuesday
Open: lunch and dinner
Holidays: variable
Seating: 70
Prices: 30 euros, wine excluded
All credit cards

Gino Primavera's confidence and skill have given him much success in promoting the special recipes and produce local to Guardia. These include pasta, mutton and wild greens gathered from the Parco della Majella, his own home-reared pigs, as well as preserves and local cheeses.

This comfortable, well-furnished restaurant not only offers an exceptional gastronomic experience, but a bit of culture too, thanks to an extensive menu that provides detailed information about the source and history of the recipes and raw ingredients used. You can try the **terrine of pig's head with fennel**, **snails alla guardiese**, pecorino cream served with a semolina flan and crisp leeks, the farmhouse tart with prosciutto di Orsogna, **corde di chiochie** (an old variety of mountain wheat) served with wild greens gathered from La Majella, **crioli** (a large pasta alla chitarra rolled by hand) with lardo, spelt linguine with salted cacio, pennoni al sugo di torcinello (roulades of lambs entrails), **braciole di cavallo** and **d'asino**, meat tiella, **lamb from the Park**, pork cif e ciaf and a tagliata of Aberdeen Angus beef.

There is a wide choice of desserts, including **ciotola di sanguinaccio**, spumone Villese, gnocchetti with cherry ragù and various semifreddi. The wine list is well chosen, with predominantly regional bottles stored in the attractive open-plan wine cellar.

Don't forget to visit Lullo, via Roma 99, or Pasticceria Palmerio, at number 69: both places offer **sise delle monache**, the classic Guardagrele pastry.

GUARDIAGRELE

25 KM SOUTH OF CHIETI ON SS 81

VILLA MAIELLA

Restaurant/3-Star Hotel
Via Sette Dolori 30
Tel. 0871 809362-809319
Fax 0871 809319-809662
E-mail: info@villamaiella.it
Internet: www.villamaiella.it
Closed Sunday evening and Monday
Open: lunch and dinner
Holidays: 2 weeks in July
Seating: 60 + 20 outdoors
Prices: 32-35 euros, wine excluded
All credit cards, Bancomat

The atmosphere here is always pleasantly informal thanks to Angela and Peppino Tinari's warmheartedness. Rooms are bright and well-furnished. Breakfast offers delights like ricotta with honey and walnuts, taralli biscuits, fresh fruit juices, cured meats, prosciutto and pancetta.

In the kitchen, expert, innovative hands are hard at work. Here they use excellent ingredients to produce seasonal and local dishes like outstanding **traditional cured meats** (homemade), all the Presidia in the Abruzzo region (Vastese-style Ventricina, Campotosto mortadella, Farindola pecorino cheese among them), **pallotte cac'e ove**, **taccole with rabbit ragù and saffron** from l'Aquila, **lamb ragù**; free-range **chicken cooked in wine** and **rack of lamb** Pennapiedimonte-style. Tantalizing desserts include simmered must with ricotta, cream puffs and chocolate 'delizie'.

The cellar will satisfy the greatest wine enthusiasts with its quality labels at a good price. They offer year-round accommodation.

4 single, 6 double, 2 triple rooms with 2 to 4 beds, en-suite, A/C, mini-bar, cable tv, modem connection • Prices: single 47, double 90, triple 119, with 4 beds 150 euros, breakfast included • 2 rooms designed for the mobility impaired. External reserved parking for guests. No pets allowed. Porter available until midnight, owners always present • Bar, restaurant. Conference room

GUARDIAREGIA

LE COCCOLE

🍲Holiday farm
Contrada Riponi
Tel. 0874 60787-340 4954937
Fax 0874 60787
E-mail: info@agriturismolecoccole.it
Internet: www.agriturismolecoccole.it
Closed 15-30 November, January-
March only open at weekends

This vacation farm is located at an altitude of 750 meters, at the foot of Mount
Mutria. The rooms in a well-renovated
old farmhouse are simply furnished yet
comfortable. Francesco De Michele and
his wife Tania Tallarino run the facility
and live not too far from it. In summer
breakfast is served on the large communal terrace and consists of bread, butter
and jams, rusks, homemade tarts and ricotta cheese cakes. In winter, they use
the dining room in the restaurant, where
you can also enjoy a typical Molise meal
for 20 euros, including house wine (half
board is 42 euros, and full board 50
euros per person). Places to visit in the
vicinity are the WWF Oasis of Guardiaregia, the Altilia archeological site and the
sanctuaries of Castelpetroso and Santa
Lucia.

• 1 single, 1 double, 2 triple and 3 four-
bed rooms, with bathroom, TV • Prices:
single 29 euros, double 46, triple 59,
four-bed 72, breakfast included • Credit
cards: none • Restaurant and 1 bedroom accessible to the mobility challenged. Off-street parking. Small pets allowed (not in communal areas). Owners
reachable from 8.30 am to 11 pm. •
Restaurant. Reading and TV room. Garden with children's playground, terrace.
Boules court

GUGLIONESI

IL PAGATORE

🍲Restaurant
Corso Conte di Torino 71
Tel. 0875 680550
Closed on Sunday, never in August
Open: lunch and dinner
Holidays: first week of Oct., after Epiphany
Seating: 30 + 20 outdoors
Prices: 25-28 euros, wine excluded
No credit cards

Located not far from the coast and on
top of a hill with a splendid view,
Guglionesi looks down on the Biferno
river valley. The town is steeped in history and it's worth taking time to visit its
historic ruins. Don't forget to visit the
church of San Nicola, an eleventh century gem which is only a few meters
from the entrance to the restaurant. The
strange name on the sign for this rustic
restaurant derives from Giorgio's nickname, "the Payer". In fact, he's the
spontaneously generous man who will
serve at your table.
Inside "Il Pagatore" is countrified but
comfortable, with a few, well spaced tables and wooden benches. You can sample reliable cooking based on local traditions, enriched by a few well-balanced innovations and an expert choice of raw
ingredients. The place is run by Rolando
Colavitti, the chef, who is Giorgio's brother, helped by his bustling mother. Start
with the generous portions of delicious
antipasti, consisting of **preserves** and
local cured meats. The first courses include a wide range of **fresh pasta**, both
with and without fillings, accompanied by
a variety of sauces, mainly (but not solely)
based on meat. The main courses also
reveal a similarly "carnivorous" tendency,
with the classic **roast lamb**, tagliata and a
good **fillet of beef**. Special credit should
be given for the reinterpretation of the
torcinello, which is offered in an usual
and highly successful light version.
To sum up, we are pleased to note the
new additions to the pudding menu
(alongside the usual good **tiramisù**);
however, the choice of wine is still limited to a good house wine and a handful
of well hidden bottles, mainly from local
producers.

GUGLIONESI
Petriglione

56 KM NORTH-EAST OF CAMPOBASSO ON SS 483

LA MASSERIA

🔑 Holiday farm
Contrada Petriglione, 11
Tel. 0875 689827-689409
E-mail: mariele90@postino.it
Open all year round

Thanks to its position, this facility, carved out of a country house that has undergone basic refurbishment, is the ideal place for a relaxing vacation. Surrounded by olive trees and vineyards, it lies between the River Biferno and Lake Liscione, while only a few kilometers to the east there's the beautiful beach of Termoli. The rooms are comfortable, quiet and simply furnished; for breakfast Giuseppe di Cesare offers tarts, jams, typical cakes and the usual hot drinks. The communal lounge with its open fireplace and bookshelves is very cozy. You can organize a number of excursions in the surrounding area, take a boat trip to the Tremiti Islands from nearby, or you can follow embroidery and knitting courses organized at the farm.

• 1 single, 1 double, 1 triple and 2 four-bed rooms, with bathroom • Prices: single 30 euros, double 52, triple 78, four-bed 84 (16 euro supplement for extra bed), breakfast included • Credit cards: none • Facility accessible to the mobility challenged, 1 room designed for their use. Off-street parking. No pets allowed. Owners always present • Breakfast room. Lounge. Garden with children's playground.

ISOLA DEL GRAN SASSO D'ITALIA
San Pietro

40 KM SOUTH OF TERAMO SS 81, 150 AND 491

IL MANDRONE

🍲 Trattoria
Frazione San Pietro
Tel. 0861 976152
Closed on Tuesday, never in August
Open: lunch and dinner
Holidays: 2-3 weeks in Jan. or Feb.
Seating: 50
Prices: 20-22 euros
No credit cards

The road that climbs up to Isola del Gran Sasso, with its countless hairpin bends overlooking the Gran Sasso-Laga Park, continues to offer a fascinating prologue to a stopover capable of refreshing and comforting the most reluctant customer. You'll be welcomed by Loredana and Nada Canuti who used to work at Il Mandrone.
The house is still the same, a stone and wood construction like many other mountain dwellings. The cooking is also unchanged, and the trattoria continues to propose the same hearty but delicious dishes, which are nonetheless balanced and easily digestible. The main source of inspiration is the local cuisine from Teramo, with a few digressions that don't stray far from Abruzzo. You start with the antipasti, consisting of cured meats (including a memorable **ventricina di Crognaleto**), preserves, local pecorino or **crocchette di melanzane**. Then, moving on to the first courses, the strong points continue to be **strongole alla barcarola** (homemade spaghettoni in a sauce of meat and mushrooms but no tomato, flavored with herbs from the Gran Sasso) but it is also worth trying the classic **chitarra with meatballs** or the "sorprese" (a sort of ravioli). Among the main courses, grilled meats feature in addition to **pecora alla callara** and **fried lamb cutlets**.
And to finish, a selection of tasty homemade puddings. A local house wine is served together with a number of good Abruzzo labels.

LANCIANO

TAVERNA DEL MASTROGIURATO

� Restaurant-wine shop
Corso Roma, Vico 11
Tel. 0872 712207
Closed Tuesday and Wednesday for lunch
Open: lunch and dinner
Holidays: in July
Seating: 40
Prices: 30 euros, wine excluded
All credit cards

We're in the Borgo di Lanciano neighborhood, right in the old town, just a few steps from Piazza Plebiscito between the churches of San Francesco and Santa Lucia. In what was once a priest's residence is the Taverna del Mastrogiurato, named for a medieval character who during important festivals would take over the city, and is still commemorated each year during the Settembre Lancianese.

The young owners, Gianni Vinciguerra front of house and Costanza Esposito in the kitchen, are ready to serve you traditional cooking as well as more common dishes whose quality is just as high. Here you'll find antipasti of Abruzzo cured meats and cheeses as well as warm plates, like the **pallotta cac' 'e ove** which is particularly good. Among the firsts we recommend the **frascarielli with beans**, a historical Lanciano preparation; **chitarrina with black truffle** from Sangro; **raffiche** (a kind of large potato gnocchi made with tomatoes and vegetables) sauced with cherry tomatoes and pecorino flakes; or chestnut gnocchi with cep mushrooms. There's a good choice of meats to follow, from veal fillet to grilled tagliata flavored with citrus oils from the Colline Teatine (dop). Or there's tasty grilled lamb, **roast pork capocollo** and local cheese baked with truffle shavings. To follow a **semifreddo with mostocotto** (or with almonds or chocolate), warm apple pie fragrant with cinnamon, or tiramisù with amaretti. Try the homemade infusion of herbs and spices. The wine list includes the best regional wines and a well chosen selection of bottles from around the country.

L'AQUILA

CASALE SIGNORINI

🔑 3-Star Hotel
Strada Statale 17, km 27.600
3 Star Hotel
Tel. 0862 361184
Fax 0862 361182
E-mail: info@casalesignorini.it
Internet: www.casalesignorini.it
Open all year round

The hotel is on a small hill from which you enjoy a beautiful view. It was previously a farmhouse that has recently been refurbished and is surrounded by extensive grounds and gardens. The hotel is only 5 minutes by car from the city center, on the Via Salaria that leads to Rieti and Rome, and so is an ideal base for those who want to visit the city but prefer to stay in a place offering peace and quiet. The rooms are modern, well-furnished and comfortable. In addition, the buffet breakfast is carefully prepared and offers both sweet and savory fare, together with coffee, milk and tea. The restaurant next to the hotel specializes in seafood dishes and you can enjoy a good meal for an average price of 35 euros, excluding wine.

• 5 double and 5 triple rooms, with bathroom, mini-bar, TV • Prices: double room single occupancy 60 euros, double 80, triple 90, breakfast included • Credit cards: all, Bancomat • Communal areas accessible for the mobility challenged. Off-street parking. No pets allowed. Reception open 24 hours a day • Bar, restaurant. Garden

L'AQUILA

DUOMO

☞—🔑3-Star Hotel
Via Dragonetti 6-10
Tel. 0862 410893-410769
Fax 0862 413058
E-mail: info@hotel-duomo.it
Internet: www.hotel-duomo.it
Open all year round

L'AQUILA
Camarda

ELODIA

🍲Restaurant
Strada Statale 17 bis 37
Tel. 0862 606219
Closed Sunday dinner and Monday
Open: lunch and dinner
Holidays: two weeks at the end of July
Seating: 45
Prices: 30-35 euros, wine excluded
All credit cards

The hotel is in a beautiful eighteenth century palazzo that has been completely refurbished. It is located in the heart of the city in a place where there used to be an eatery. The restoration was carried out respecting the original structure, and furnishings of the rooms and communal areas are in keeping with an atmosphere permeated by art and history. The buffet breakfast offers sweet and savory fare. This is an ideal place to stay during business trips since guests have a conference room equipped with an Internet connection at their disposal. On the other hand it's also a great place to be for tourists as they will find that places of historical and artistic interest within the city are all in the vicinity.

• 4 single, 18 double, 5 triple rooms and 3 suites (4 persons), with bathroom, TV • Prices: single 55-65 euros, double room single occupancy 65-75, double 80-92, triple 95-115, suite 140, breakfast included • Credit cards: all, Bancomat • Garage (5 euros per day). No pets allowed. Reception open 24 hours a day • Bar. Breakfast room, reading and TV room. Conference room

To find the Elodia, either drive out of the city towards Paganica on state road 17, which continues on up to the Gran Sasso; or exit the A24 at Assergi and do the few kilometers that separate you from Aquila. Once here you'll be welcomed by the Moscardi family: Antonello, Nadia and Vilma, with their mother, Elodia herself, in the kitchen. Their attractive restaurant boasts attentive service and gives diners the opportunity to take a tour of the best of Abruzzo cuisine, with a particular focus on two typical products, saffron and truffles, often used in creative ways.
Before the antipasti there's a sampling of Aquila cured meats (don't miss the Slow Food Presidia **mortadella di Campotosto**) and artisan fresh cheeses like variously aged pecorinos and ricotta; or beef carpaccio with fennel and raspberry vinegar or some little lamb preparations. Then **timbale of ricotta with eggplant**, cherry tomatoes and smoked ricotta; gnocchi with zucchini and saffron, **chitarra pasta with lamb sauce**; and various vegetable soups and veloutés. The varied, flavorful mains include **lamb with saffron**, duck breast with a citrus and Montepulciano d'Abruzzo marinade, **mazzarelle** (rolls of lamb offal) in tegame with fresh tomatoes, rabbit in a crunchy pastry crust and vegetables or the three-part sampling of baccalà.
To finish there's dark-chocolate wafers with hazelnut mousse, warm coffee and chocolate tortino, pear bavarese with saffron and almonds or the traditional **dolcetti** of the day, perhaps with a cocoa cru, herbal infusion or tea. The cellar is well-stocked with many Abruzzo wines and some noted labels from the rest of the country.

L'AQUILA

LORETO APRUTINO
Fiorano

LA CONCA
ALLA VECCHIA POSTA

⌒ Trattoria
Via Caldora 12
Tel. 0862 405211
Closed Sunday dinner and Monday
Open: lunch and dinner
Holidays: end of January and beginning of August
Seating: 50
Prices: 23-28 euros, wine excluded
All credit cards, Bancomat

LE MAGNOLIE

Holiday farm
Contrada Fiorano 83
Tel. 085 8289804-335 7787622
Fax 085 8289534
E-mail: lemagnolie@tin.it
Internet: www.lemagnolie.com
Open from March to December

From Piazza Duomo and up a pretty flight of stairs overlooked by historic palazzos, you reach Porta Bazzano, which opens onto a view of this ancient farmhouse which once served as a staging post, just a few steps from the beautiful Romanesque basilica of Santa Maria di Collemaggio.

Here Gregorio and Rosalba have created a haven for the culinary traditions of Aquila; courteous and kind, they'll be happy to guide you towards dishes full of the fragrances and flavors of the past. Antipasti arrive with seasonal vegetables and cured meats (including Campotosto mortadella and Vasto ventricina); the **turkey alla canzanese**, spelt salad, and omelets with mountain herbs are also worth noting. First courses range from **gnocchi with dried ricotta** from Castel del Monte and Novelli saffron to crêpes with lamb and vegetables, excellent **chitarrine** with wild herbs, and, in the right season, the notable tagliatelline with mushrooms and truffles. The **surgitti**, fricelli pasta made with flour and water and cooked in vegetable soup, is a historical dish which derives from the seasonal migration of Abruzzo shepherds and their sheep towards neighboring Apulia. Sheep are the basis for the main courses: **sautéed lamb cacio e uova** (with cheese and egg); muscisca (dried mutton cooked and held together with eggs); **marriddi**, lamb giblets from Castel del Monte with rosemary; pallotte del pastore; ricotta and cheese rissoles in a tomato sauce. Puddings include pies, ricotta with coffee and chocolate and crêpes with chestnut cream.

The wine list is a work in progress, but does represent most of the principal regional labels.

This vacation farm stands on 27 hectares with olive groves and kiwi plants. Apart from being in a peaceful location the facility is halfway between sea and mountains. For a few years now the Tortella family have combined agricultural activities based on a passion for research, with the hospitality that fits in so well with the characteristics of this place. It's organized in three farmhouses, one of which has a large arbor and also houses the restaurant. The rooms and apartments (studios and with two-bedrooms), which are spacious and furnished in a rustic style, are located in the other buildings and so allow guests complete freedom to enjoy their stay. For breakfast there are homemade cookies, cakes and jams. The restaurant, mainly open for residents, offers cooked vegetables, but also lamb and rabbit dishes (a meal costs 25 euros, excluding wine).

• 2 double rooms, with bathroom, fridge; 9 apartments (2-5 persons) with kitchen • Prices: double room single occupancy 50 euros, double 60-70, breakfast included; apartment 85-120 euros; breakfast 3 euros per person • Credit cards: all, Bancomat • 1 apartment designed for use by the mobility challenged. Off-street parking. Small pets allowed. Owners always contactable • Restaurant. Reading and TV room. Grounds. Swimming pool

MARTINSICURO
Villa Rosa

35 KM NORTHEAST OF TERAMO SS 80 AND 16

MOSCIANO SANT'ANGELO

25 KM NORTHEAST OF TERAMO A 14, SS 80 E 262D

IL SESTANTE

Trattoria
Lungomare Italia
Tel. 0861 713268
Closed Sunday for dinner and Monday
Open: lunch and dinner
Holidays: in August, Christmas
Seating: 60
Prices: 33-35 euros, wine excluded
All credit cards, Bancomat

BORGO SPOLTINO

Restaurant
Strada Selva Alta
Tel. 085 8071021
Closed Monday and Tuesday
Open: lunch and dinner
Holidays: variable
Seating: 50
Prices: 30 euros, wine excluded
All credit cards

Located between the Marches and Abruzzo, Il Sesante is a good seafood restaurant that looks out over the Adriatic. Here the menu is based on the seasonally changing catch of the day, using exclusively local products prepared with simplicity and celebrating the true flavors of the shellfish and fish. The set menu offers a vast array of sea flavors, with large and small antipasti such as **boiled langoustines**, anchovies a scottadito, sautéed giant shrimp and **fried magnana** (tiny baby sardines). You can also find rare **angler fish tripe**, cod cazòle (egg sacs), raw langoustines and mantis shrimp, oysters and mollusks like bomboletti, **flavorful little sea snails**. Firsts are generally abundant portions of bronze-die-cut Gragnano pasta with sauces of fish and shellfish: **mezze maniche with crustaceans**, gnocchetti with clams, Campofilone spaghetti with zucchini and panocchie, **seafood ravioli.** Then boiled or roast scamponi, alla catalana or in guazzetto (optionally spicy), an outstanding **roast turbot** and **frittura**. If available, don't miss the raw or fried calamaretti, little squid, as they are quite rare these days. The pudding list includes sorbets, crema catalana, pies and fruit creams. Among the wines Trebbiano gets prime billing, with a good selection of wines from well-known producers, as well as bottles of Chablis, some good sparklers and other national wines with honest mark-ups. We appreciate the presence of half-bottles and the well-chosen local Trebbiano on tap. The service is courteous and speedy, though it can slow down on particularly busy days; always book for Friday or Saturday dinner.

You can spend a pleasant evening in Borgo Spoltino, which has its own ancient little church, dining in a tranquil room where even if they happen to be holding a banquet next door you won't be disturbed.
You can look into the kitchen, where'll you see Gabriele Marrangoni bustling about. He's a talented, self-taught chef, and he's put together a two-part menu, one half dedicated to traditional dishes, the other to more creative inventions which are nonetheless based on seasonal and local ingredients. Among the traditional dishes you'll find a salad of barley and garden vegetables, stuffed and fried pumpkin flowers and asparagus omelets to start. Then **spelt soup with beans and vegetables**, **pappardelle with mutton ragù** and herbs or with lamb, **white tripe with marjoram**, shepherds' meatballs and **mutton steaks**. There are also dishes based on local white meats, pigeon and pork. From the creative offerings you could choose a millefeuille of liver, a pumpkin veloutè with grape must, pumpkin pappardelle with chicory and guanciale, linguine with baccalà, beef tagliata and pork with chocolate and chili pepper sauce with a port wine reduction.
The puddings are good, with an excellent **pizza teramana**, and you'll find a good selection of regional and national wines. The check reflects good value for money.

MOZZAGROGNA
Sette Castle

ORTONA
Caldari

49 KM SOUTH-EAST OF CHIETI

33 KM EAST OF CHIETI

CASTELLO DI SEPTE

AGRIVERDE

🔑4-Star Hotel
Località Castello di Sette 20
Tel. 0872 578940-578635
Fax 0872 578645
E-mail: casteldisepte@tin.it
Internet: www.castellodisepte.it
Closed from 24-26 December

🔑Holiday farm
Via Stortini 32
Tel. 085 9032101
Fax 085 9031089
E-mail: agriturismo@agriverde.it
Internet: www.agriverde.it
Open all year round

Sette Castle is perhaps the most famous of the Frentani castles and has Lombard origins according to the few existing historical sources. It seems that the Counts Teatini used it as both an armory and a residence. Later it was occupied first by the Normans and then by the Swabians, but a slow decline got underway in the early 1300s and continued up to just a few years ago when the structure was completely rebuilt thanks to a grant from the Ministry for Cultural Affairs. Today it's a lovely hospitality facility with a panoramic view over the Val di Sangro, 41 rooms fitted with all modern comforts and a spacious restaurant area that is often used for banquets and wedding receptions. Half board is available starting from a two-night minimum stay and costs 70 euros per person based on double room occupancy. Outside there's a large garden with swimming pool for the use of guests.

• 14 single, 24 double rooms and 3 suites, with bathroom, air-conditioning, mini-bar, satellite TV • Prices: single 65 euros, double room single occupancy 75, double 90-100, suite 140, breakfast included • Credit cards: all, Bancomat • Facility accessible to the mobility challenged, 1 room designed for their use. Off-street parking. No pets allowed. Reception open 24 hours a day • Restaurant. Breakfast room, lounges. Garden. Swimming pool

Agriverde is one of the region's elegant facilities, famous for the production of wines, organic oil and other products. The spacious rooms (classified as either standard or superior) are in a nineteenth-century farmhouse that has been completely refurbished. Nearby there are the wine cellar, built according to bio-architectural principles, and the fitness center where various types of treatment are carried out, from wine-therapy to honey compresses. The vacation farm is managed with professionalism by Giannicola Di Carlo and offers many activities, among which the possibility to make use of the nearby stables. The day begins with a classic breakfast consisting of coffee, milk, jams, rusks and cakes. The cuisine centers on the use of organic products (meals cost 25 euros, wine excluded, and there's a 20 euro supplement per person for half board).

• 12 double rooms, with bathroom, air-conditioning, TV • Prices: double room single occupancy 43-50 euros, double 66-90 (26-31 euro supplement for extra bed), breakfast included • Credit cards: all, Bancomat • Restaurant accessible to the mobility challenged. Off-street parking. Small pets allowed. Reception open from 9 am to 8 pm. • Restaurant, wine-tasting room. Reading room. Conference room. Garden, terrace. Swimming pool, fitness center

ORTONA

AL VECCHIO TEATRO

Restaurant
Largo Ripetta 7
Tel. 085 9064495
Closed Wednesday, never in August
Open: lunch and dinner
Holidays: November
Seating: 35 + 30 outdoors
Prices: 30-32 euros, wine excluded
All credit cards, Bancomat

The walk east by the port to the attractive Aragonese castle, dating from 1445 and currently under renovation, is very pleasant, and nearby there's lots more to see, like the 13th-century Torre dei Baglioni, the Tostiano Musical Institute and the regional wine store in Palazzo Corvo d'Abruzzo, the museum-gallery, Palazzo Farnese, the library of the sea and the old Sant'Anna theater.

Right next to the theater is this typical restaurant run by Armando Carusi front of house with his wife Daniela and daughter Eleonora in the kitchen. In summer you can sit on the terrace looking out over the port, and eat a seafood-based cuisine. However there are also some dishes based on well-selected earthy ingredients: meats, cured meats and cheeses. Start with the excellent **raw fish**, the octopus soppressata with potatoes and eggplant, fish marinated in the **scapece** (with vinegar and saffron) and langoustines, squid and cuttlefish on the grill as antipasti. The **fisherman's "richiamata"** is delicious, a mix of short pasta with a delicate brothy sauce of crustaceans, but so too are the **spelt tubetti with bummalitt'** (sea snails); the **chitarra with mixed fish** with or without tomatoes; **tacconetti with pumpkin and beans**, shrimp and mussels; and potato and borage gnocchi with a langoustine sauce. Whole fish, caught locally, are usually grilled, roasted with vegetables or prepared all'acqua pazza, or there's a light **fritto misto** and the fish soup called **brodetto**.

Puddings are homemade, with two extraordinary specialties: the **nevole ortonesi** (with cooked grape must) and the **bocconotto frentano** stuffed with almonds and chocolate. Choose from among the best Abruzzo wines.

PACENTRO

TAVERNA DE LI CALDORA

Restaurant
Piazza Umberto I 13
Tel. 0864 41139
Closed Sunday for dinner and Tuesday
Open: lunch and dinner
Holidays: variable
Seating: 100
Prices: 35 euros, wine excluded
All credit cards

The charming village of Pacentro, protected by Mt. Morrone, overlooks the scenic Peligna Valley, and for some time now it's been possible to enjoy the view from the Taverna's elegant veranda. Carmine and Teresa Cercone have restored the interior and the kitchen, but they've stayed faithful to the style which for years made this restaurant one of the best-loved in the region.

We recommend diving right into the genuine but refined rustic cooking with a series of antipasti beginning with a sublime **sheep's milk ricotta** served in its own little basket, followed by seasonal dishes like **Savoy cabbage strascinate with pieces of wild-boar sausage**, mushroom and Parmesan salad, Paganica beans with cardoncelli mushrooms or a selection of local cured meats and fresh **cheeses**. Then there's **sheep's milk ricotta ravioli with tomato sauce**, one of the house specialties, chitarra with bianchetto truffles and saffron, **gnocchi with venison ragù**, tagliatelle with a tomato-less rabbit **ragù** and **carrati with mutton sauce**. Don't miss the **grilled lamb**, the kid with cacio cheese and egg, the mutton al cotturo and the **grilled marro**, an unusual lamb offal dish. Alternatives to meat include baccalà with potatoes, Castel di Sangro scamorza and mountain pecorinos of different origins and ages.

Close with Sulmona confetti or homemade puddings: cantuccini, sfogliatina with cream and **chocolate cake**. The list of wines and spirits is broad and well-chosen, and offers good value.

ACQUAPAZZA

Recently opened osteria
Via Flaiano 37
Tel. 085 4514470
Closed Saturday for lunch, Sunday
Open: lunch and dinner
Holidays: variable
Seating: 40
Prices: 32-35 euros, wine excluded
All credit cards

LA LUMACA

Recently opened osteria
Via delle Caserme, 51
Tel. 085 4510880
Closed Tuesday
Open: for dinner only
Holidays: variable
Seating: 40 + 10 outdoors
Prices: 25-30 euros, wine excluded
All credit cards, Bancomat

The old town of Pescara, normally noted for containing the residences of writers Ennio Flaiano and Gabriele D'Annunzio, changes character when night falls and the narrow little streets become a seething stew of humanity. This small seafood restaurant is on the relatively tranquil Piazza Garibaldi (enter from a nearby side street), and over the years has earned a sound reputation, thanks to the calm, unobtrusive style of Ernesto Vianello and Paola Cetrullo.

The name derives from a cooking method for medium-sized fish which uses water, oil, cherry tomatoes, white wine and various aromatic herbs. It's one of the restaurant's best dishes, but there are others equally good, prepared with a balance between simplicity and creativity by the talented chef Andrea Di Buò, a Marches native. For lunch there's a short set menu, while at dinner you'll find antipasti like **raw calamaretti**; marinated mackerel, anchovies or swordfish; a **sauté of mixed seafood** or of langoustines with artichokes or Catalan-style; langoustines shelled or with tomatoes and guazzetto of mussels and clams. Fresh pasta is used for **tagliatelle with langoustines**, chitarrina with seafood, **orecchiette with broccoli and mantis shrimp**, garganelli with pumpkin and shrimp or with zucchini and langoustines. Depending on the catch, apart from the **fish all'acquapazza**, there might be angler fish either with potatoes, grilled or sautéed with tomato and oregano; turbot with lemon or a delicate **frittura di paranza**. The few puddings and ice creams are recommended.

The wine list runs from Abruzzo to many other Italian regions.

La Lumaca, in the old part of Pescara, has changed management: Severino Forcone, a culinary institution in the city, has now handed over the business to his young partner Luca Filippini, though the kitchen is still in the capable hands of chef Nicola Di Sabatino. New tableware and cutlery have been introduced along with a few new dishes, prepared as ever with select local ingredients.

Start with local cured meats and cheeses, omelets with seasonal vegetables and **vegetable flans**, or the delicate zucchini and basil terrine with wild-mint oil. Severino will advise on the choice of firsts, among which there's the excellent **farrotto with mixed greens**, maltagliati with eggplant and tomato, **chitarra with Bussi shrimp**, maccheroncini with peppers and spicy ventricina or a **timbale of scrippelle** with asparagus. The main courses are dominated by meat: roast pork with apricots, **mutton alla callara**, mamma Lilia's stew and beef fillet alla piastra are some of the summer options. Or there's the lighter **stewed baccalà with olives** or a plate of cheeses with jams and honey. Puddings could be a **crostata with peaches, figs and amarene cherries**, semifreddo al parrozzo or the panna cotta with strawberry sauce. The cellar boasts a wide selection of national and international labels, many also available by the glass.

Thanks to a collaboration with the Italian Celiac Assocation, several gluten-free dishes can be served.

LOCANDA MANTHONÉ

🍲 Recently opened osteria
Corso Manthoné 58
Tel. 085 4549034
Closed Sunday
Open: for dinner only
Holidays: variable
Seating: 45 + 25 outdoors
Prices: 31-33 euros, wine excluded
All credit cards

TAVERNA 58

🍲 Trattoria
Corso Manthoné 46
Tel. 085 690724
Closed Saturday for lunch, Sunday and festivities
Open: lunch and dinner
Holidays: August
Seating: 60
Prices: 30-32 euros, wine excluded
All credit cards

An osteria with a pleasant, informal atmosphere, the Locanda Manthoné offers good value for money. Despite its having become successful and rather fashionable, Luca Panunzio has managed to keep his place from either falling into the trap of trendy cuisine or the temptation to compromise on the quality of raw materials, tricks others use to keep prices low. The only reproach one might make to skilled chef Enzo D'Andreamatteo would regard the heavy puddings, perhaps a little too much after a series of courses generous in size and seasoning. The sober elegance of the decor and the cellar rich in well-chosen bottles complete the picture.

The menu, with four or five options per course, changes seasonally and might include tondini Tavo beans with cacigni and crispy peppers, **timbale di sfoglia** with ciabbotto all'abruzzese (sautéed vegetables), **cep mushrooms and pecorino salad** and a selection of **cured meats from Aquila**. The classic chitarra al sugo with little meatballs is well-executed, and the potato gnocchi with artichokes, saffron and shavings of salt ricotta and ravioli with Andria burrata and black truffles are also good. Next to **grilled meats** like lamb and beef from Chianina and Abruzzo-raised Marches cattle there's **stewed Scanno kid**, excellent baccalà with potatoes and black olives and **sautéed spatchcock** with capers and peppers.

Then there's cakes, sfoglie and meringate, as well as simple and delicious toasted almonds covered in good-quality chocolate, plus choice coffees, chocolate crus, spirits, cigars and herbal infusions.

When this restaurant opened in 1980 it was one of the first in old Pescara, which today is the center of Pescara nightlife. Giovanni Marrone, capable and ironic, will look after you in a friendly atmosphere which reflects a real link to the land. The kitchen finds the right balance between tradition and innovation and turns out a varied, original menu. The antipasti include river fish (**trout** and **shrimp**), tripe with shavings of pecorino, **Castelvecchio chickpea polenta and baccalà** with sweet rosemary, pâté of Muscovy duckling, Torano prosciutto, Teramo ventricina, coppa and **ventricina vastese** (a Slow Food Presidia). Notable firsts include makaira (square spaghetti made from barley) with chopped vegetables and delicate oil from Chieti; crespelle with cheese and fresh salad greens and fregnacce with prosciutto sfrigoli and tomatoes. The strong ties with local tradition can be seen in the main courses like Majella mutton al tegame, baccalà al cartoccio with onion jam, **land snails** in spicy tomato sauce, young chicken in porchetta with thyme honey (an Abruzzo revisiting of lacquered duck), **Prati di Tivo rabbit with black olives and red Sulmona garlic**, **brodetto with trout** from the River Tirino and a good selection of cheeses including some top Abruzzo pecorinos.

There's a rich pudding cart, with the semifreddo al parrozzo and the warm **zabaione with Marsala** particularly recommended. The cellar has a wide selection of wines from the region and the rest of Italy.

DUCA DEGLI ABRUZZI

Bed and breakfast
Piazza Duca degli Abruzzi 5
Tel. 0863 911075
Fax 0863 911762
E-mail: ducadegliabruzzi@pescasseroli.net
Internet: www.pescasseroli.net/ducadegliabruzzi
Open all year round

This B&B is in a recently refurbished palazzo next door to the house where philosopher Benedetto Croce was born in the historic center of Pescasseroli. As the town is also the headquarters of the Abruzzo National Park, the B&B is an ideal base for nature excursions and relaxing winter sports vacations. The pleasant rooms have attractive wooden floors and fixtures, soft colors and furniture made by local craftsmen, in addition to all the usual comforts. Breakfast consists of typical homemade cakes, organic jams, milk, tea, coffee, juices and savory fare. If you wish, you'll also be able to dine in the restaurant (a meal costs 26 euros, excluding wine) that's managed by Lella, with menus focusing on typical local products and traditional dishes.

• 8 double rooms, with bathroom, satellite TV, modem connection • Prices: double room single occupancy 48-52 euros, double 60-88 (15-20 euro supplement for extra bed), breakfast included • Credit cards: all, Bancomat • Restaurant accessible to the mobility challenged. External parking with reserved spaces. No pets allowed. Owners always present • Restaurant

PLISTIA

Restaurant/3-Star Hotel
Via Principe di Napoli 28
Tel. 0863 910732
Fax 0863 911741
E-mail: info@albergoristoranteplistia.it
Internet: www.ristorantealbergoplistia.it
Closed Monday, never in summer
Open: lunch and dinner
Holidays: two weeks in May
Seating: 45
Prices: 25-30 euros, wine excluded
All credit cards

Authentic mountain-inn atmosphere, simple and down-to-earth. Pets are not allowed in the rooms (available all week). Requests taken for breakfast. Lunch starts off with local cured meats, delicate **ricotta, zucchini flowers and elderflowers in batter** or mozzarella wraps with rocket and prosciutto. Good main courses: **gnocchi with asparagus and saffron, lasagne in broth with small meatballs and scamorza**, salatielli with cep mushrooms, pasta with potatoes and salted ricotta, **bean soup with spelt**, tagliolini with zucchini and saffron. Apart from the traditional **roast lamb** or **kid** and barbecued sausages, main courses include patate maritate, roast pig shank, **roll of lamb with lardello** or local cheeses. Lastly, **ricotta pie**, crème caramel, with whipped cream and coffee, and spumette, lemon-flavored meringue with custard cream and raspberries. Satisfactory wine labels from Abruzzo including a few renowned spirits. Reservations recommended.

• 10 doubles, en-suite, mini-bar, television • Prices: double single use 54-60 euros, double 76-86, breakfast included • Restaurant access for the mobility-impaired. Outside resident and non-resident parking. Free garage (3-4 spaces). Pets welcome. 24hr porter • Bar, restaurant. Reading and tv rooms. Courtyard, patio

In piazza Vittorio Emanuele II, the Antico Forno sells delicious pastries, breads and pizzas. In piazza Municipio, Sapore di Vino is a customer attraction for its aperitivo, which boasts local delicacies, or for those who wish to purchase regional and national wines or liquor.

95 KM SOUTH-WEST OF L'AQUILA ON SS 17

95 KM SOUTH-WEST OF L'AQUILA ON SS 17

ALBERGO DELL'OCA

☎Hotel
Via Santangelo in Piazza 16 (ex via dell'Oca)
Tel. 0864 642600-642530
Fax 0864 642600
E-mail: info@cameredelloca.com
Internet: www.cameredelloca.com
Open all year round

MASSERIA CERASELLA

☎Rooms
Strada Regionale 84 Frentana, km 6
Tel. 0864 641520–347 6287760
Fax 0864 641520
E-mail: info@masseriacerasella.it
Internet: www.masseriacerasella.it
Closed from 20 September to 10 October

The picturesque mountain center of Pescocostanzo, with its old palazzos and narrow paved roads, is one of the best preserved villages in this area. Josephine Curry must have fallen in love with the place too, as after meeting her Abruzzo-born husband in London, she now manages this small hotel with her daughter in a caring, discreet manner. The rooms are in a recently refurbished building and have country-style furnishings. The owner also prepares breakfast that consists of homemade ciambelloni, chocolate cakes and tarts, along with traditional hot drinks and fruit juices. The village center is well worth visiting, with its thirteenth-century church, craft shops famous for making lace, wooden items and jewelry. If you have the chance, buy some of the local cheeses – first and foremost, caciocavallo.

• 1 single and 4 double, triple or four-bed rooms, with bathroom, mini-bar, TV • Prices: single 30-40 euros, double 47-70, triple 65-95, four-bed 78-115, breakfast included • Credit cards: all, Bancomat • Free public parking. Small pets allowed. Owners always contactable • Bar. Reading and TV room

Located in the Park of the Maiella and only a short distance from the Roccaraso skiing facilities, Pescocostanzo is one of the best-preserved and beautiful villages in Abruzzo, with a wealth of monuments and a tradition for outstanding craftwork. The ideal place to stay for a Nature or sport related vacation, this farmhouse has been carefully renovated to create comfortable rooms painted in bright colors and furnished country style. You'll find it has a warm, family atmosphere, with invitingly cozy communal areas; your pleasant hostess lives in the facility and will delight you for breakfast with exquisite homemade cakes and other sweet fare and hot drinks. Outside there's a large garden that has a stone barbecue for grilling tasty local meats.

• 2 double, 2 triple and 1 four-bed rooms, with bathroom • Prices: double room single occupancy and double 55-80 euros, triple 70-95, four-bed 85-110, breakfast included • Credit cards: major ones, Bancomat • Off-street parking. No pets allowed. Owners always present • Breakfast room, reading and TV room. Garden

PICCIANO

FONT'ARTANA

🍲 Trattoria
Piazza Duca degli Abruzzi 8
Tel. 085 8285451
Closed Tuesday
Open: dinner, Sunday also lunch
Holidays: first half of August, second half of February
Seating: 50 + 15 outdoors
Prices: 23-26 euros, wine excluded
Credit cards: CartaSi, Visa

The Font'Artana is located in the cellar of an old house in the center of town, carefully renovated and boasting cross vaulting and exposed brick walls. The sincere warmth of host Antonio Di Giovacchino and the authentic, hearty cooking of his mother Concetta and wife Cristina add to the appeal of this trattoria inland from Pescara.

Ingredients and dishes vary with such frequency that in this case the absence of a menu is justified. There are always **pizz'onte**, fritters (which can be used instead of bread) with an array of antipasti, fresh cheese, ricotta, pecorino and typical cured meats, prosciutto in oil, **sautéed vegetables** (depending on the season it could be cacigni with beans, Savoy cabbage with sausage or wild spinach), mixed vegetable soup, cac'e ove rissoles and lamb livers or stew. Then polenta with peppers and **pork cif e ciaf** (a stew cooked in a pan). First courses include green chitarrina with goat's cheese and sausage, **ricotta ravioli with artichokes**, strapizz (maltagliati) with fresh favas and tomatoes, spelt soup with vegetables, **chitarra** or **gnocchi with duckling sauce**. Then **lamb cacio e uovo** or grilled, on its own or as part of a mixed roast, pork fillet, veal tagliata with herbs and **rabbit stuffed** or al tegame chasseur.

The sweets are good, like the classic pizza doce and the delicate latteruolo, a kind of crème caramel, and pies. Homemade infusions to round off, and your choice of the best regional wines from a cellar you can visit.

RIPA TEATINA

LA CAPEZZAGNA

🔑 Holiday farm
Contrada Santo Stefano 64
Tel. 0871 398040-347 8584768
Fax 0871 398040
E-mail: info@lacapezzagna.it
Internet: www.lacapezzagna.it
Open all year round

A highly service-oriented facility: this is how you could describe this place that Mauro and Sandra Lovato opened a few years ago. First it's in a beautiful location, surrounded by vineyards and olive groves in one of the province's most productive areas. Second, the quality of the various sized apartments furnished in a commendably restrained manner, and lastly, the generous breakfast, with jams, fresh fruit, cakes, hot drinks and fruit juices (on request, you can also have an English breakfast). As an added service, for example, you can use the organized beach located only eight kilometers away, and you'll be given a voucher for the swimming pool on the nearby golf course, all free of charge. Meals in the restaurant – open for residents only – consist of traditional meat and vegetable dishes (half board ranges from 51-61 euros per person).

• 3 suites (2-4 persons), with bathroom, terrace, TV, modem connection • Prices: double room single occupancy 40 euros, double 62-80, triple 93-120, four-bed 120-140, breakfast included Credit cards: all, Bancomat • Facility accessible to the mobility challenged. Off-street parking. No pets allowed. Owners always present • Restaurant. Reading and TV room. Garden, terrace. Free use of organized beach 8 km away

GIOCONDO

Restaurant
Via Suffragio 2
Tel. 0864 69123
Closed Tuesday
Open: lunch and dinner
Holidays: second half of June
Seating: 40
Prices: 25-30 euros, wine excluded
All credit cards, Bancomat
Formaggio e bottiglia

In the Maiella National Park, not far from the renowned ski runs at Roccarase, stands this restaurant, one of the most reliable in the area for the consistent quality of its food. The kitchen respects the culinary traditions of inland Abruzzo, so you'll find lots of pork and lamb, sausages, cheeses and beans. In fact it's with a plate of local cured meats and cheeses, including an exquisite ricotta served with vegetables in oil and coratella, that you should start your meal. Then move on to the many pastas, all made in-house, which include, along with the classic **cazzariell' with beans** and cordicelle with sausage, gnocchi with mutton sauce, polenta with broccoli and sausage or with pork spareribs, **pappardelle with goat's milk ricotta and broccoletti** and, when in season, **pancotto with wild spinach**. Among the mains there's lots of grilled meats, but the **breaded and roast rabbit** is well worth a taste, as is the lamb allo scottadito, **kid cac'e ove**, turkey roulades stuffed with field greens or, if booked in advance, **mutton al cotturo**. There's also a fairly good **cheese board** with pecorino, scamorza, caciocavallo and fresh and salted ricotta, some baked and served with mountain honey, making an excellent non-meat option.
The homemade puddings shouldn't be missed, particularly the cannoli alla crema and the **semifreddo** with custard, cream and almonds **covered in melted chocolate**. To pair with the food there's a good choice of wines from Abruzzo and the rest of the country.

RIVISONDOLI

96 KM FROM L'AQUILA, 32 KM SOUTHEAST OF SULMONA SS 17

LA PORTELLA

Restaurant-pizzeria
Via Sulmontina 44
Tel. 0864 69372
Closed Wednesday, never in high season
Open: lunch and dinner
Holidays: variable
Seating: 70
Prices: 30-32 euros, wine excluded
All credit cards, Bancomat

A little outside the historic center of Rivisondoli, this family-run restaurant offers a very long menu (maybe a little too long). Start with a first-rate selection of cured meats, cheeses, and vegetables in oil: knife-cut prosciutto, goose speck, salami, **Campotosto mortadella** (a Slow Food Presidia), liver sausages, pecorino, formaggio ubriaco, the delicious trecce from a nearby cheesemaker and **ricottina** in a wicker basket. Everything is accompanied by hot bread baked in the restaurant's big wood-fired oven. The pastas, handmade in-house, are simple but tasty: **annellini alla pecorara**, pappardelle with hare sauce, tagliatelle or ravioli with truffles or the **timbale of cep mushrooms**; the polenta with broccoli and sausage is also worth a try, as are the **soups of Savoy cabbage, potatoes and beans** or lentils and chestnuts. Then meat, which dominates the mains: grilled tender fillet, with gorgonzola or green peppercorns; pork or veal steaks; **roast lamb** and **arrosticini** (kebabs), which also appear in the arrosto misto. Alternatively there's baked local cheeses or pecorino with honey.
There aren't many puddings, but you could choose a pear and dark-chocolate cake, apple pie or the delicious **hazelnut and chocolate confetti** from nearby Sulmona, which go with coffee. The decent wine list includes some labels from the rest of Italy. To finish you could try a house infusion, like one with gentian. The service is courteous and always helpful. The restaurant gets very busy during high season, and reservations are recommended.

RIVISONDOLI

96 KM SOUTH-EAST OF L'AQUILA ON SS 17

LE CERNAIE

📞 Hotel
Via Regina Elena 107
Tel. 0864 640016
Fax 0864 69543
E-mail: albergolecernaie@cheapnet.it
Internet: www.albergolecernaie.it
Closed May and June

Rivisondoli is a small center famous for its parish church with spectacular baroque altar, but above all because it's near the Roccaraso skiing facilities. The hotel managed by Niko Romito is in a small, recently renovated palazzo not too far from the center of the village. The rooms are furnished with Abruzzo artisan furniture, wrought iron bedsteads and false ceilings with wooden beams that contribute to making the atmosphere pleasant and friendly. In the communal room you'll be served a generous breakfast of coffee, milk, tea, orange juice, croissants, butter, jams, yoghurt, and homemade tarts and ciambelloni.

• 6 single and 7 double rooms, with bathroom, TV; 4 with terrace • Prices: single 65-85 euros, double 75-100 (34-45 euro supplement for extra bed), breakfast included • Credit cards: major ones, Bancomat • Restaurant accessible to the mobility challenged. Free external public parking. No pets allowed. Reception open from 8 am to 8 pm. • Bar, restaurant. Breakfast room.

🍲 50 meters from the hotel is the Reale restaurant managed by the same family, which offers both traditional and innovative dishes (a meal costs 40 euros, excluding wine).

ROCCASICURA
Friscialete

33 KM NORTH OF ISERNIA

IL TRATTURO

📞 Holiday farm
Località Friscialete
Tel. and fax 0865 837151
E-mail: info@iltratturo.com
Open all year round

You'll find this farm on one of Molise's ancient sheep tracks where former cattle sheds have been converted into rooms and a dining area. Littorio Vannuccini, who loves to chat and is an expert on the surrounding area, has created a facility with warm, pleasant rooms, and a dining room lunchroom that is just as cozy, dominated by a large stone fireplace topped by an oak beam. Breakfast is inviting, and consists of fresh ricotta, blackberries and bilberries, quince tarts, jams, honey, cured meats from pigs fed exclusively with acorns, granone maize and bran. The kitchen offers dishes prepared with vegetables, legumes and meats either produced on the farm or sourced from local producers. A meal costs about 30 euros, excluding wine; half board is 50 euros per person. You must make a reservation if you want to stay or eat here.

• 6 double rooms, with bathroom • Prices: double room single occupancy 50 euros, double 80 (28 euro supplement for extra bed), breakfast included • Credit cards: none • Off-street parking. Small pets allowed (not in the rooms). Owners always present • Restaurant. Reading and TV room. Grounds, terrace. Horse-riding

Roseto degli Abruzzi

Vecchia Marina

🍲 Restaurant annexed to hotel
Lungomare Trento 37
Tel. 085 8931170
Closed Sunday evening and Monday
Open: lunch and dinner
Holidays: variable
Seating: 35 + 25 outdoors
Prices: 33-35 euros, wine excluded
All credit cards

One of the most pleasant experiences we had while researching this guide was in this peaceful restaurant by the sea. The building, which also houses a family hotel, is rather anonymous, but a pretty garden, with some tables for diners and holidaymakers, adds considerable appeal. The simply decorated dining room is connected directly with the kitchen, from which arrive reassuring signs of domestic industriousness and mouthwatering aromas of fish and shellfish. Seafood arrives at the table revealing its unmistakable freshness and is prepared with respect for its quality. The **crudo of shrimp, langoustines and mullet** is particularly notable, as are the boiled mantis shrimp and langoustines, **marinated anchovies** and little fish of the day in a tomato sauce.

The care over ingredients is also shown in the use, finally, of extra-virgin olive oil, both in the kitchen and at the table, using two Abruzzo oils of considerable quality in appropriately different ways. Gragnano **pastas** with delicate **calamaretti, sole and langoustines** are notable among the firsts, as are **linguine alla pescatora**, chitarrine with seafood and risotto with fish. Not to be missed among the mains (and almost always available, thanks to good relationships with local fishermen) is the **guazzetto di pesce**, which in our case included skate, small squid, a langoustine and star-gazer (little-known but full of flavor): The assortment was well-balanced and cooked perfectly. The roasts and fries are also good. The service is informal, friendly and punctual, in harmony with the family-run atmosphere. There are some good wines available, on a par with the quality of the food.

San Pio delle Camere

La cabina

🔑 2-Star Hotel
Via Principe Umberto 1
Tel. 0862 931010-93567-339 2717613
Fax 0862 931121
E-mail: khdeb@tin.it
Internet: www.ristorantelacabina.it
Open all year

Once you come to the Navelli plain driving along state road 17, you'll be astonished by the number of towers, fortified villages and rural churches you see. This is where the hotel is located, on what was the site of a small locanda in the 1920s that used to be a point of reference for carters on their way to L'Aquila. The rooms are simple but comfortable; breakfast consists of milk, coffee, tea, croissants, butter, jams and homemade sweet fare. The hotel also has a wine shop where cheese and wine-tastings are organized. Small and medium-sized pets are welcome to stay in a space of their own, close to the facility. In the adjacent restaurant there's a wide use of genuine local produce, such as Santo Stefano lentils and the renowned saffron grown in this area (meals cost 25 euros, beverages excluded).

• 7 double rooms and 1 apartment (6 persons), with bathroom, TV • Prices: double room single occupancy 30 euros, double 60 (10-15 euro supplement for extra bed), apartment 25 euros per person, breakfast included • Credit cards: all, Bancomat • 1 room designed for use by the mobility challenged. Free external public parking. Pets allowed. Owners always reachable • Bar, wine cellar, restaurant

SAN SALVO
San Salvo Marina

SAN SALVO

AL METRÒ

🍲 Restaurant
Via Magellano 35
Tel. 0873 803428
Closed Suday for dinner, Monday
Open: lunch and dinner
Holidays: variable
Seating: 40
Prices: 30 euros, wine excluded
All credit cards, Bancomat

OSTERIA ✏
DELLE SPEZIE

🍲 Recently opened osteria
Corso Garibaldi 44
Tel. 0873 341602
Closed Wednesday
Open: lunch and dinner
Holidays: in September
Seating: 45
Prices: 30 euros, wine excluded
All credit cards

The Metrò in San Salvo Marina, which specializes in seafood prepared using the best fresh ingredients, keeps getting better and better. Loads of room, cordial service and well-set tables are the icing on the cake of the pleasant dining experience which awaits you in this restaurant run by the Fossaceca family.
Let them guide your choices from the recited menu, which varies depending on what's available in the market. Few antipasti but well-prepared, giving you an idea of the kitchen's skill. For example: cod carpaccio with pappa al pomodoro, cuttlefish tagliata on fava and pecorino cream, filleted mullet on a potato fondue with crunchy fried artichokes, traditional classics like **bummalitt** (sea snails), or the shellfish guazzetto; it's also possible to order great plates of crudità. **Pastas** of various kinds follow, both traditionally sauced – with local fish and **frutti di mare** – or more creatively, for example with artichokes and shrimp. They are often served directly from copper saucepans. Seconds involve different fish prepared in a variety of ways: roast, all'acqua pazza, the ever-present **brodetto** and also **frittura di paranza**, really very good and quite light.
The family's pasticceria, next door, predates the restaurant and guarantees excellent fresh pastries and cookies. The wines have been intelligently chosen, and are served in the correct glasses.

In a small town near the Molise border, this restaurant, with a low-key entrance and sign, stands out for its attractive interior. A gentle pace, intelligently prepared food, quality music at the right volume and discreet service complete the picture. Contrary to the name, the use of spezie (spices) is not at all invasive. Here everything is carefully calibrated to point up the potentiality of a cuisine deeply rooted in the land, which finds new vitality in some unusual flavor combinations.
Start with the good selection of seasonally changing antipasti. The **chicory impazzita** (battered and fried) is delicous in its simplicity; the classic **ventricina vastese**, correctly presented in small pieces, is not to be missed if available. Moving on to the firsts, some dishes like **pennoni with almonds and saffron** are by now classics, but the tasty **stuffed pastas** with different fillings are just as good: they use walnuts, chestnuts and some very good meats. The main courses vary from traditional to innovative. The **lamb abbottonato** is recommended, as is the **suckling pig with honey**, the beef fillet and the **grilled Molise scamorza**. Fish used to appear on the menu, but no longer, and thanks to the superlative meat preparations it's not much missed.
To finish, excellent puddings: the owner, talented Giancarlo Cilli, is the son of a confectioner and it shows. The wine list is not very long but it's put together well, with sensible choices, generally local, and with very reasonable mark-ups.

SAN SALVO
San Salvo Marina

RISTORANTE MARINA

Restaurant
Via Pigafetta 70-Strada Statale 16, Piazzale Agip
Tel. 0873 803142
Closed Sunday and Monday dinner
Open: lunch and dinner
Holidays: in December
Seating: 50
Prices: 28-35 euros, wine excluded
All credit cards, Bancomat

Even though it's along the main Adriatic state road, in a town which livens up only in the summer, you can tell right away that this restaurant isn't just for tourists. The sign isn't particularly obvious, but you will spot the restaurant right behind the Agip gas station. The majority of the clientele are regulars of all stripes who come regardless of the season. The interior is modern, simple and informal, as it has been for over 15 years. In the dining room Michele Raspa is solicitous and cordial while mamma Adele in the kitchen prepares ever-changing dishes, always based on the fresh, local catch of the day.

There's no menu on the table, but you'll be given a choice between the day's specialties, which often include scampetti al tegamino, **battered whitebait**, a **baked anchovy timbale**, stuffed medalions of squid on a bed of zolfini beans, as well as excellent raw fish and carpaccios. All the pastas are good, including **fusilli caserecci with amberjack**, cavatelli with langoustines and **linguine ruvide alla marinara**, while the most popular dish among the mains is the **mixed grill**, cooked over charcoal. Depending on availabilty there might also be an acquapazza of white fish or a **brodetto**, which are two of the most characteristic stews of this coastal zone. The use of only Abruzzo oils, brought to the table in their own bottles, is praise-worthy, and the small selection of pecorino cheeses is also local, as are most of the wines from the 50-strong list. To finish there are some cookies and biscuits baked in-house.

SCANNO
Dente San Nicola

IL RIFUGIO DEL LUPO

2-Star Hotel
Viale del Lago
Tel. 0864 74397–333 3340650
Fax 0864 74397
E-mail: info@ilrifugiodellupo.it
Internet: www.ilrifugiodellupo.it
Open all year round

From Anversa degli Abruzzi, skirting the spectacular Sagittario Gorge (nature reserve, like Mount Genzana that rises above it) you come to Lake Scanno. This is where you'll find the Rifugio del Lupo, in one of the most beautiful and popular places in Abruzzo, not too far from the eastern borders of the National Park. This small family-managed hotel is in a very peaceful area surrounded by greenery, just 500 meters from the lake and 10 minutes from the charming old center of Scanno. The comfortable, spacious rooms have rustic and mountain-style furniture and bunk beds for children. In the restaurant, which is also open to non-residents (the cost of a meal ranges from 20-25 euros, excluding wine), you'll be able to taste traditional Scanno dishes and often lake fish such as coregone and perch. In summer and on bank holidays they normally apply half board or full board terms (ranging from 45-65 euros per person).

• 9 double rooms, with bathroom • Prices: double room single occupancy and double 40-60 euros, breakfast included • Credit cards: all, Bancomat • 1 room designed for use by the mobility challenged. Off-street parking. No pets allowed. Owners always present • Restaurant. Lounge, TV room. Garden

SCANNO

LA CASA DI COSTANZA

Bed and breakfast
Via Napoli 27
Tel. 0864 747821-368 511473
Fax 0864 747821
E-mail: info@lacasadicostanza.com
Internet: www.lacasadicostanza.com
Closed from mid-November to mid-December

La casa di Costanza is a recently opened B&B located in a villa built in the Sixties close to the center of the village. The facility is on three floors with an apartment and fully fitted kitchen on the ground floor. The rooms – a third bed can be added in some – are on the first and second floors. The communal area includes a terrace with tables and umbrellas, the lounge where guests can engage in conversation or read a book close to the fireplace, and adjacent breakfast room. A buffet breakfast offers various types of beverages, bread, butter and organic jams, freshly baked cakes and other sweet fare.

• 5 double rooms, with bathroom, balcony, TV, modem connection; 1 apartment (4-6 persons) with kitchen • Prices: double room single occupancy 35-50 euros, double 50-80 (15 euro supplement for extra bed), breakfast included, apartment 80-120 euros; breakfast 3 euros per person • Credit cards: all, Bancomat • Apartment accessible to the mobility challenged. Off-street parking. Small pets allowed (in the apartment). Owners always reachable • Restaurant. Reading and TV room. Garden, terrace.

200 meters from the B&B Costanza runs an osteria that offers a combination of traditional and creative dishes (a meal costs from 20-30 euros, excluding wine).

SULMONA

CLEMENTE

Restaurant
Vico Quercia 5
Tel. 0864 52284
Closed Thursday
Open: lunch and dinner
Holidays: end of June, mid-July
Seating: 60
Prices: 25-28 euros, wine excluded
No credit cards

For years, talented and passionate chef Clemente Maiorano has been preserving the culinary traditions of this pretty little Paelignian town. The quality of his ingredients and authenticity of the preparations are beyond reproach, but we do have some minor criticisms about the welcome and the service, which on recent visits were not exactly impeccable.
In the absence of a written menu you have to rely on the server's descriptions of the antipasti, which reflect the local shepherding traditions: **mutton salami**, smoked ricottina with juniper and fresh grilled pecorino, and the **thresher's breakfast**, a series of preparations based on eggs, greens and garden vegetables; depending on the season you might also be offered polenta, **lamb livers** or baked eggplant with tomato. The first course sauces are also seasonal: **chestnut fettuccine with forest mushrooms**, strozzapreti with Savoy cabbage and guanciale, **pappardelle with a tomato-less lamb and saffron ragù**, paccheri with eggplant and cacioricotta and minestra del pastore, made with maltagliati, potatoes and a spoonful of warm ricotta. There are some baccalà dishes (on winter Friday there's a special menu that has to be pre-ordered), as well as **pork fillet with cooked grape must** or peaches, lamb fillet with mushrooms, casseroled rabbit with mushrooms and lamb bocconcini with cacio and egg. Homemade cakes provide a sweet finish: almond and chocolate, ricotta with rum and white chocolate or peach with cinnamon.
The wines, still unlisted, are from Abruzzo and the rest of Italy, and some are available by the glass.

63 KM SOUTH-EAST OF L'AQUILA ON SS 17

SANTA LUCIA

Bed and breakfast
Corso Ovidio 13
Tel. 0864 210616-348 7053850
Fax 0864 207586
E-mail: info@bebslucia.com
Internet: www.bebslucia.com
Open all year round

ENOTECA CENTRALE

Wine shop with bar and kitchen
Corso Cerulli 24-26
Tel. 0861 243633
Closed Sunday
Open: lunch and dinner
Holidays: two weeks between August and September
Seating: 30 + 25 outdoors
Prices: 25-30 euros, wine excluded
All credit cards, Bancomat

Initially a Benedictine monastery, the building was taken over and transformed by the Celestine monks into a grancia, that is, a formal meeting place. Currently the building is a B&B that retains all the features of the old structure. Entering the pleasant internal cloister delimited by four arches and a portico that has a loggia above it, you get to the four rooms furnished with great attention to detail by the owner, Antonio Donatelli. The most attractive suites are the fra' Tommaso room (with open fireplace) and the Badessa, a double room refurbished using salvaged wood and embellished by family antique furniture, a parquet floor and caisson ceilings. The other two rooms are under a mansard roof and are more modern, with a predominance of light-colored woods and pastel colors. The communal room where homemade cookies and tarts are served is equally attractive.

• 2 double rooms, 1 triple and 1 suite (4 persons), with bathroom, air-conditioning, mini-bar, TV, modem connection; 2 with terrace • Prices: double room single occupancy 65 euros, double 90-100, triple 130, suite 130-180, breakfast included • Credit cards: all, Bancomat • Free public parking 50 meters away. No pets allowed. Owners present from 8 am to 11 pm. • Reading and TV room. Cloister

We've been singing the praises of Marcello and Pietro Perpetuini for years. With their attention to quality ingredients, insistence on good service and emphasis on educating diners' palates, they're truly ideal interpreters of the Slow Food philosophy. The Centrale is an always-pleasant destination for an aperitivo or a meal, which at lunch could be a quick bite, perhaps sat at the long bar. The cellar is well-stocked with a wide range of wines available by the glass. Once at a table, start with a selection of **cured meats** and **cheeses**, vegetable flans and omelets and the delicate **Teramo-style tripe in bianco**. Then classic dishes with strong identities but correctly lightened: **timbale of scrippelle**, scrippelle 'mbusse, **mazzarelle**, sweet ravioli, **virtù del Primo Maggio** (a kind of soup with vegetables, beans, spices, pork gristle and offcuts of homemade pasta), as well as **chitarra with meat pallottine**, salted ricotta ravioli with cherry tomatoes and basil, gnocchi with zucchini and summer truffles and veal genovese and linguine with chicory and cep mushrooms. From the main courses there's Angus beef in various preparations, as well as the good **turkey alla canzanese**, snails al tegame, **chicken alla contadina** with peppers and herbs and the ever-present **Monti della Laga lamb** (fried cutlets, with cheese and egg or roasted). Finish with a baverese, which depending on the season could be with hazelnuts, coffee, chocolate or mint, or with the classic Abruzzo sweet pizza or a cake with cream and fresh fruit.

In Via Riccitelli 25, at Alberto il Fornaio, excellent bread and typical sweets.

TERAMO
Acquachiara

TERMOLI

RIFUGIO DELLE AQUILE

🍲 Trattoria-rifugio
Località Acquachiara
Tel. 0861 286279
Closed Wed., in winter opened from Fri. to Sun.
Open: lunch and dinner
Holidays: none
Seating: 130 + 120 outdoors
Prices: 25 euros, wine excluded
All credit cards, Bancomat

LOCANDA ALFIERI

🛏➊ Rooms
Via Duomo 39
Tel. e fax 0875 708112
E-mail: info@locandalfieri.com
Internet: www.locandalfieri.com
Open all year round

This is a genuine rifugio, a mountain hut which has been completely renovated and which you'll find at an altitude of over 1,000 meters once you've turned onto the Laga provincial road 51 from the Teramo-Ascoli highway, near the junction for Campli. There are some rooms available as well as several hundred hectares of land, from where many of the restaurant's ingredients come.

Vincenzo and Pacifico, always cordial, will welcome you with **stuffed olives**, battered and fried vegetables and homemade cured meats and cheeses. There's a wide choice of first courses, from **pappardelle with wild boar** or venison to gnocchi alla caprese (with goat's milk ricotta, recommended), as well as **tagliatelle with cep mushrooms** or truffles and **cappelli del prete** (ricotta-stuffed ravioli **with cheese and truffle**). Ceppe are typical of the area around Teramo, a long pasta made using a knitting needle. For seconds, don't forget the constantly turning spit, which produces a memorable **skewered lamb**. But there are plenty of other dishes which draw on local traditions, like suckling wild boar or **kid**, both of them **roasted with potatoes**, lombatina (also of wild boar) with mushrooms or truffles and **goat alla castellana** (flavorful and light). To go alongside there's seasonal vegetables from the fields round the restaurant. The homemade puddings include the ubiquitous tiramisù alla riccia with coffee, a **crostata with goat's milk ricotta and chocolate** and cookies and biscuits to nibble on at the end. Choose the right pairing for your meal from around 200 wines from Italy and abroad, with Abruzzo naturally enough in prime position, and close with Vincenzo's own gentian liqueur.

In a recently refurbished four-floor house in the heart of the medieval quarter of Termoli, Manuela and Rino are ready to give you a very warm welcome. From this year, moreover, a new room is available in the nearby annexe. All rooms are cozy, comfortable and tastefully furnished: a pity there's no elevator. The beautiful room where breakfast is served also doubles as a reading room where you'll find daily newspapers. Unfortunately this room isn't accessible to the mobility challenged, although room service is provided. The buffet breakfast offers homemade and other typical local products. During the summer period you'll be able to take advantage of various services provided by the locanda: purchasing tickets to the Tremiti Islands, (45 minutes away by hydrofoil) booking boat excursions, fishing trips, a guide who will take you to visit the old village: laundry, ironing and baby-sitting services are also available.

• 2 single, 4 double and 3 triple rooms, with bathroom, air-conditioning, minibar, satellite TV, modem connection • Prices: single 40-45 euros, double 60-100, triple 75-110 (15 euro supplement for extra bed), breakfast included • Credit cards: major ones, Bancomat • Public and paid private parking nearby. No pets allowed. Owners always present • Breakfast-cum-reading room

68 KM NORTHEAST OF CAMPOBASSO SS 647

68 KM NORTH-EAST OF CAMPOBASSO ON SS 647B AND 647

NONNA MARIA

RESIDENZA SVEVA

Trattoria
Via Oberdan 14
Tel. 0875 81585
Closed Monday
Open: lunch and dinner
Holidays: November 1-15
Seating: 35 + 40 outdoors
Prices: 32-35 euros, wine excluded
All credit cards

Hotel
Piazza Duomo 11
Tel. 0875 706803
Fax 0875 709526
E-mail: info@residenzasveva.com
Internet: www.residenzasveva.com
Closed from 25-27 December

You'll be guaranteed a good meal at this little trattoria, the interior barrel-vaulted, simple and comfortable, with an unusual view of the old freshwater storage tank. The number of covers doubles in the summer, when you can eat outside in the street, which is pedestrians only. The kitchen shows the strong influence of regional traditions and seasonal ingredients and with care and delicacy does justice to excellent fish, almost exclusively sourced from the restaurant's own two fishing boats.

The antipasti are typical of Termoli cooking: crouton with mussels all'antica, **little cuttlefish al coccio with red onions**, stuffed cuttlefish with bell-pepper sauce or with peas and **whitebait fritters**, all prepared simply but well. Crudo-lovers shouldn't miss the fish and shellfish carpaccios, always local and very fresh. The trattoria's classic first courses – tubetti in fish broth and spaghetti with a sauce of stuffed cuttlefish – have seasonal variations. The homemade **maccheroni alla chitarra with asparagus, seafood and sun-dried tomatoes** are very good, as are the egg tagliolini with fresh fava puree, tasty little cuttlefish with salted ricotta, and if you're lucky in the summer, **cavatelli with sea urchins and cherry tomatoes**, a true delight. In addition to the inevitable **brodetto alla termolese** and a good **frittura di paranza**, there's always local fish either grilled, roasted or all'acqua pazza, prepared simply so as to showcase the quality of the original ingredients.

To finish there's a selection of homemade pasticceria secca and fruit pies. The service is friendly and efficient, and the cellar offers a good selection of Molise wines.

The historic center of Termoli is like a spur of rock overlooking the sea, a medieval quarter that's surrounded by walls and is marked by its typical winding alleys. It is precisely in this part of the village that Fabrizio Vincitorio, who previously owned a bathing establishment, has acquired and refurbished some buildings and created a rambling hotel offering numerous hospitality ideas. The rooms have an atmosphere of yesteryear, but at the same time offer all modern comforts. During the busiest period from June to mid-September the hotel offers additional services, such as the restaurant (a meal costs 30 euros, wine excluded) and use of an organized beach. In high season larger rooms with a sea view cost up to 109 euros.

• 1 single and 13 double rooms, with bathroom, air-conditioning, mini-bar, TV • Prices: single 34-49 euros, double 59-109 (16 euro supplement for extra bed), breakfast included • Credit cards: major ones, Bancomat • 1 room accessible for the mobility challenged. Paid garage parking 200 meters away. Free public parking. No pets allowed. Reception open from 7 am to midnight, staff always reachable • Restaurant. Breakfast room. Organized beach

TERMOLI

SAN GIORGIO

🔑 2-Star Hotel
Corso Fratelli Brigida 22
Tel. e fax 0875 704384
E-mail: info@pensionesangiorgio.it
Internet: www.pensionesangiorgio.it
Open all year

The San Giorgio Hotel is a small place located in a palazzo built in the 1800s that, after suffering damage in World War II, was completely renovated by the Pipoli family who now manage it. It's in the historic center, a few minutes away from the sea and from the quay where you can board a ferry for the Tremiti Islands, 45 minutes away. The rooms are furnished simply in modern style and have all essential comforts. The buffet breakfast includes a good choice of cured meats and local organic cheeses, jams and bread, cream-filled croissants and cookies. One of the communal areas is a small restaurant, also open for non-residents (a meal costs approximately 18 euros, excluding wine; there's a 15 euro supplement per person for half board), plus there's a garden and a room for moments of relaxation.

• 2 single, 4 double, 2 triple and 1 four-bed rooms, with bathroom, air-conditioning, satellite TV • Prices: single 35-45 euros, double 55-65, triple 70-85, four-bed 80-90, breakfast included • Credit cards: all, Bancomat • Communal areas accessible for the mobility challenged, 1 room designed for their use. Paid public parking 400 meters away. Small pets allowed. Reception open 24 hours a day • Bar space, restaurant. Relaxation room. Garden, terrace

TORANO NUOVO

LA SOSTA

🍲 Trattoria
Via Regina Margherita 34
Tel. 0861 82085
Closed Tuesday
Open: lunch and dinner
Holidays: 3 weeks after August 15
Seating: 75
Prices: 20-25 euros, wine excluded
All credit cards

The old-time atmosphere of this historic restaurant, run by friendly, dedicated Francesco and Serafino Luciano, has been updated in terms of the service, the welcome and waiting times. However the attention to ingredients and the respect paid to culinary traditions remain unchanged, as does the setting: two comfortable little rooms, with a cupboard and a sideboard full of oil, bread, spices and other typical aromas.
Here Teramo cuisine reigns supreme: that will be abundantly clear to you after you try the antipasti of local cheeses and cured meats, **lamb coratella** with tomato and chili pepper, tripe and seasonal vegetables al tegame. Continue with the sumptuous **crêpe timbale** (revealing the influence of the aristocratic influx and French grande cuisine), **maccheroni alla chitarra** with rissoles, gnocchi, tagliatelle with mushrooms (cep in the right season), or the not-to-be-missed **spaghetti alla pecorara**, with sausage sauce. There are some real stars among the main courses: **goat spezzatino alla neretese** (stewed, with onions and peppers), roast kid, **mazzarelle** (stewed lamb offal), fritto misto (fried stuffed olives, pecorino, cream and lamb), chicken and rabbit chasseur, lamb a scottadito, pork with mushrooms, veal shank.
Then on to homemade puddings such as grape jam tart, **ricotta pie** and pizza casereccia (spongecake, alchermes liqueur, cream and chocolate). About a hundred wines, mostly from Abruzzo, make choosing the right pairing easy for a memorable meal.

TORTORETO
Lido

VASTO

DELFINA & GIOVANNI

Restaurant
Lungomare Sirena 378
Tel. 0861 786578
Closed Monday
Open: lunch and dinner
Holidays: second half of September
Seating: 70
Prices: 35 euros, wine excluded
All credit cards

ALL'HOSTERIA DEL PAVONE

Restaurant
Via Barbarotta 15
Tel. 0873 60227
Closed Tuesday
Open: lunch and dinner
Holidays: between January and February
Seating: 45
Prices: 35 euros, wine excluded
All credit cards

On the promenade of Tortoreto, this simple restaurant is a great place to enjoy fresh fish. For years now, mother Delfina Stuardi has cooked in the kitchen, while her son Alfonso serves in the dining room. The ambience is modern and the service cordial, lively and simple – like the cooking. No over the top sauces or condiments here: just extra virgin oil from the Teramo hills to recreate old-fashioned flavors. As in the spaghetti with fish **guazzetto** served in the frying pan, the traditional one-off dish of local fishermen. The numerous starters include **marinated mackerel** and **anchovies**, boiler baby scampi and calamari, **anchovies scottadito** and clams en papilotte. Firsts feature **linguine with sole and scampi** and splendid spaghetti alla pescatora. For mains, **anglerfish**, **turbot**, John Dory and sole, roasted or **all'acquapazza**. If you're lucky you'll also find **frittura di paranza**, fresh mixed fry.
The cellar is very well stocked with wines for every pocket. The place is invariably packed, so we advise you book ahead. Also, the check obviously increases in price if you order particularly prized crustaceans and fish.

Once in the beautiful historic center of Vasto take a walk along the pedestrian street which leads to the splendid Palazzo d'Avalos. Just before it a street to the right takes you to a parallel piazzetta where you'll see Nicolino Di Renzo's restaurant, on the first floor of a 17th-century house. It still contains original features like exposed-brick vaults and arches, and care has been taken over the decor as well as the cellar, which houses many regional and national bottles.
The seafood cuisine is no less interesting, starting with the varied antipasti, particularly if the market permits a choice of crudità, served before **tuna carpaccio**, **octopus soppressata**, scampetti with tomato, sautéed mussels and clams, gratineed scallops and langoustine-stuffed pumpkin flowers. The first courses, based on fresh or artisan-produced pasta, are sauced generously and sometimes in a creative way: you'll find pennoni with yellow pumpkin, mussels and clams; **fusilli in fish broth; maccheroncini with langoustines and cherry tomatoes** and borage ravioli with ricotta, langoustines and truffles. Then there's fish cooked in the oven or al tegame: salt-baked sea bass, John Dory with potatoes, **angler fish with tomato and capers** and inevitably **brodetto alla vastese** and **frittura di paranza**.
Among the homemade puddings the warm puff pastry fazzoletto with cream and apple is worth a try.

In **Scerni**, a few kilometers from Vasto, is the Fattoria dell'Uliveto, headquarters of the Accademia della Ventricina del Vastese (a Slow Food Presidia), a salami made with great artisan knowledge.

Vasto
Marina di Vasto

Venafro

Villa Vignola

☎—❶5-Star Hotel-residence
Strada Statale 16, Località Vignola
Tel. 0873 310050
Fax 0873 310060
E-mail: villavignola@interfree.it
Internet: www.villavignola.it
Closed during Christmas season

Dimora Del Prete di Belmonte

☎—❶Bed and breakfast
Via Cristo 49
Tel. 0865 902769-900159
Fax 0865 902769
E-mail: info@dimoradelprete.it
Internet: www.dimoradelprete.it
Open all year round

Not far from the village is a beautiful villa set in a bay right by the sea. It's just a few kilometers from Vasto and the Palazzo Avalos, home of the Civic Museum, the castle dating from the XVth century that overlooks Piazza Rossetti and the church of Santa Maria Maggiore which contains works by Titian and Veronese. Affable Guido Mazzetti offers hospitality in airy and tastefully furnished rooms with all modern comforts (those with a sea view are obviously a little more expensive at 130 euros). The buffet breakfast offers sweet and savory fare, along with hot and cold drinks. Guests may use the private beach for relaxing days by the sea. The restaurant is good and offers mainly seafood dishes – the average price of a meal is 45 euros, excluding wine.

• 4 double rooms and 1 suite, with bathroom, air-conditioning, mini-bar, satellite TV, modem connection • Prices: double room single occupancy 75 euros, double 120 (42 euro supplement for extra bed), suite 130, breakfast included • Credit cards: all, Bancomat • Off-street parking. Small pets allowed. Reception open 24 hours a day • Restaurant. Reading and TV room. Garden, terrace. Free private beach

The B&B run by Dorothy Volpe Del Prete is in an old dwelling in the heart of the historic center, built by incorporating buildings dating from the 16th century and completely refurbished in 1860. The rooms have high frescoed vaults and neoclassic-style antique furnishings. Communal areas are fascinating: the Pompeian room with grand piano that guests are free to use, the internal courtyard with the old palms, the rose garden containing some rare botanical species, and the terrace that dominates the entire valley, where guests can dine in summer. Breakfast is varied, with homemade cakes and jams, fresh fruit, local cured meats and cheeses. The restaurant (average price for a meal is 30 euros), exclusively for residents and their guests, uses products from the family-owned farm.

• 4 double rooms, 1 suite, with bathroom, balcony: 1 apartment (2-5 persons) with kitchenette, air-conditioning, terrace • Prices: double room single occupancy 95 euros, double 110, suite 150 (30 euro supplement for extra bed), breakfast included; apartment 500 euros a week • Credit cards: all, Bancomat • Free public parking. Small pets allowed. Owners always present • Restaurant (only for residents). Reading and TV room. Conference room. Garden, terrace

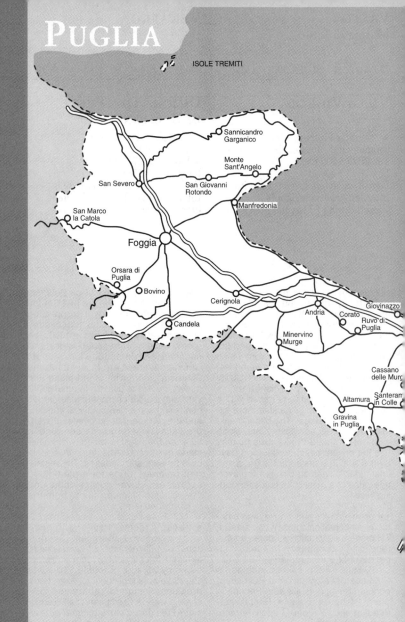

PUGLIA

ISOLE TREMITI

Sannicandro Garganico

Monte Sant'Angelo

San Severo

San Giovanni Rotondo

Manfredonia

San Marco la Catola

Foggia

Orsara di Puglia

Bovino

Cerignola

Giovinazzo

Andria

Corato

Ruvo di Puglia

Candela

Minervino Murge

Cassano delle Murg

Altamura

Santeram in Colle

Gravina in Puglia

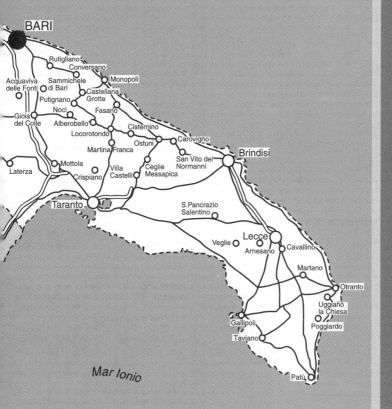

Mar Adriatico

BARI

Rutigliano
Conversano
Acquaviva
delle Fonti
Sammichele
di Bari
Monopoli
Putignano
Castellana
Grotte
Gioia
del Colle
Noci
Fasano
Alberobello
Locorotondo
Cisternino
Martina Franca
Ostuni
Carovigno
Laterza
Mottola
Villa
Castelli
Ceglie
Messapica
San Vito dei
Normanni
Brindisi
Crispiano
Taranto
S.Pancrazio
Salentino
Veglie
Lecce
Arnesano
Cavallino
Martano
Otranto
Uggiano
la Chiesa
Gallipoli
Poggiardo
Taviano
Mar Ionio
Patù

LA CANTINA

☞Restaurant
Vico Francesco Lippolis 8
Tel. 080 4323473
Closed Tuesday, never in August
Open: lunch and dinner
Holidays: 10 days in February, 3
weeks of June-July
Seating: 32
Prices: 25-30 euros, wine excluded
All major credit cards, Bancomat

L'ARATRO

☞Restaurant
Via Monte San Michele 25
Tel. 080 4322789
Closed Monday
Open: lunch and dinner
Holidays: January
Seating: 70 + 50 outdoors
Prices: 30 euros, wine excluded
All major credit cards

Alberobello is well worth a visit, whether you spend your time wandering through the narrow streets of the old center or enjoying its beautiful views. This tiny restaurant can be found in the attractive commercial part of town, which borders the 'trulli' area without clashing with it. Four steps take you into a simple room with a few tables and an open kitchen at the back. Here, the Lippolis family has been serving up culinary delights for almost half a century. Antonio has been retired for some time, but Francesco – who had long worked as apprentice to his father – has able taken over the reins.

It's easy to be overwhelmed by the hot and cold antipasti that arrive at your table: capocollo and cured sausages, **dairy produce**, home-made oil-preserved vegetables, exquisite **boiled oroblanco** (a wild herb found in fava and lupine fields) **with oil and lemon**, fried lampascioni (wild onion-like bulbs) and gratinéed vegetables. The first courses include classic dishes such as **orecchiette with cime di rape** (turnip tops) or horsemeat ragù and maccheroncini with tomatoes and cacioricotta cheese. The main courses are meat-based: grilled sausages and kebabs, horse diaphragm and traditional **brasciole** (horsemeat steaks) with ragù. Try the almond dolcetti for dessert. You can choose from a small selection of Puglia wines.

One of the prime tourist destinations of the region, Alberobello is famous for its 'trulli'. These traditional conical stone houses are found throughout the Val d'Itria, one of the most beautiful parts of Puglia. Alberobello has the highest concentration: there are around a thousand of them, all protected as national monuments since 1930. It's not surprising then that crowds of tourists fill the street that climbs steeply through Monti, the most attractive quarter. Several years ago Domenico Laera opened this restaurant in a group of 'trulli' halfway up the ascent. While some dishes are meant more for tourists, overall he's stayed faithful to local traditions.

The antipasti are typical of the area, with ricottine, **vegetable flans** (try the eggplant), burrata, hot focaccia, baked vegetables and stewed tripe. Local cuisine also figures largely in the first courses with dishes like **cavatellucci with beans and seafood**, for example, or **orecchiette with turnip tops** and fricelli with sausage and tomatoes. Choose from main courses such as horsemeat and **roast lamb with potatoes and lampascioni** or with wild chicory. There's a broad selection of desserts: don't miss the **almond mousse** or the cookies.

The dependable cellar offers all the best regional wines with an emphasis on reds. Expect a bigger bill if you order fish.

🏺 At Via Due Macelli 5, you'll find PMC, where you can purchase pasta cut with old-fashioned bronze dies.

🏺 At Via II Traversa Colucci, the Artelat cheesemakers produce bocconcini, mozzarella, burrata, Scamorza, ricotta, Cacioricotta and Caciocavallo silano. In Viale Einaudi, the Tarallificio dei Trulli bakes taralli with olive oil, wine and spices.

ALBEROBELLO

TRULLI
DEL CENTRO STORICO

🗝️Rooms
Via Indipendenza 4
Tel. 080 4325103-336 692408
Fax 080 4327581
E-mail: info@ristoranteterminal.it
Internet: www.ristoranteterminal.it
Open all year round

Staying in a trullo is a uniquely fascinating experience thanks to the history behind these extraordinary structures, recently added to the UNESCO world heritage list. You can forgo a served breakfast and choose to prepare it yourself in the kitchenette available in each trullo, or alternatively you can have breakfast in one of the many cafés in the old center of Alberobello. The trulli are pleasantly decorated and practical places to stay and provide the ideal way to take part in the life of the town. Michele Cardone has always believed in the value of this form of hospitality and manages the rooms in partnership with Sergio Pugliese. The pair also run the Terminal restaurant-pizzeria which serves a local menu at 25-30 euros and at 18 euros for guests staying in the trulli.

• 2 single rooms, 7 doubles and 2 rooms with 10 beds, with bathroom, air conditioning, mini-bar, television, kitchenette • Prices: single 50-60, double 75-90 (supplement of 20 euros for an extra bed), ten-bedded room 250 euros, including breakfast • Credit cards: all, including Bancomat • Free public car park, garage (5 euros per day). No animals are allowed. Owners always available • Restaurant

ALTAMURA
Guro Lamanna

MADONNA
DELL'ASSUNTA

🗝️Holiday farm
Strada Provinciale 35 km 17,00
Tel. 080 3140003-3103328
Fax 080 3103328
E-mail: taniadibenedetto1@virgilio.it
Open all year round

When you reach Altamura, take the main road to Corato and then the provincial road to Ruvo di Puglia until you come to this agriturismo, set in the rooms of an old 17th-century monastery, complete with a consecrated church where weddings are still held. The accommodation comprises a number of apartments furnished in rustic style and a large restaurant, which is also open to the public for lunch and on holidays (30 euros). Breakfast consists of sweet and savory dishes, including bread, butter and jam, ricotta, cheese and other home-made preserves. The estate is used to grow organic crops and to breed farmyard animals and horses. Guests can hire horses for trekking. Alternatively, they can go on bicycle trips or visit local attractions, such as Castel del Monte.

• 3 double rooms and 1 four-bedded room, with bathroom • Prices: double for single use 30, double 46, four-bedded room 92 euros, including breakfast • Credit cards: all, Bancomat • Outside car park on premises. Small pets welcome. Owners always present • Bar space, restaurant. Park. Horse-riding

ANDRIA
Montegrosso

ARNESANO

ANTICHI SAPORI

VILLA FALCONI

Trattoria
Piazza Sant'Isidoro 9
Tel. 0883 569529
Closed Saturday dinners and Sunday
Open: Lunch and dinner
Holidays: 3 weeks in July, 1 in
December
Seating: 40
Prices: 30 euros, wine excluded
All major credit cards

Bed and breakfast
Via Falconi 15
Tel. 0832 326926-347 6086095
E-mail: info@villafalconi.it
Internet: www.villafalconi.it
Open all year round

Pietro Zito continues to earn considerable praise for his trattoria, well known for being a good deal, and for its kitchen, which produces food that serves as an expression, in its simplicity, of the local culinary heritage and traditional gastronomy. Eating here, you'll really appreciate the quality and freshness of the raw ingredients that are used.

Antipasti include fresh **goat's milk ricottina**, Venosa sausage and vegetable-based dishes, such as **baked sponsali** (long leek-like onions), roast artichokes and eggplant with dried tomatoes and Scamorza, accompanied by excellent bread baked in a wood-fired oven, and sesame-seed taralli. The first courses are characterized by the winning combination of fresh homemade pasta and various kinds of vegetables: **burnt-grain strascinati** (very typical of this area) **with baby broccoli and breadcrumbs**, **potato gnocchetti with cima di rape** (turnip tops) and troccoli with eggplant, tomato, basil and hard ricotta. Follow with main courses such as **grilled rib of Podolico beef**, **tiella of roast lamb** with potatoes, mushrooms and sun-dried tomatoes or donkey meat fillet over coals (you have to book). The proper finish to your meal? Ricotta and candied fruit **cassata**, sugared orange peel or cave-aged Pecorino with dried figs and vincotto.

The cellar offers mainly regional wines and the two in-house labels are serviceable.

Set in a park of secular trees, Villa Falconi is an aristocratic 19th-century residence where guests can enjoy the well-tended gardens, large reception rooms and welcoming bedrooms whose terraces overlook the citrus orchard and swimming pool. The apartments have either one or two bedrooms and also a kitchenette. Breakfast, which consists of bread, butter and jam, brioches, orange juice, milk and coffee, is served in a special room or, in fine weather, outside in the park. It's worth visiting the excavations at Rudiae, a Messapican and, later, a Roman town, and the Cesine wildlife oasis at Acaia, a wetland area of over 600 hectares; there's also a golf club nearby for keen golfers.

• 4 double rooms, with bathroom, air conditioning, some with terraces; 2 apartments (2-4 persons) with kitchenette • Prices: double for single use 35-45, double 70-90, apartment 35-45 euros per person (supplement of 20 euros for extra bed), including breakfast • Credit cards: none • Outdoor car park on premises. No animals allowed. Owners always present • Breakfast room. TV room, music room, library, billiard room. Park. Swimming pool

The Galleria Enogastronomica, Via Castel del Monte 27, offers typical products from the best Puglia producers.

AL FOCOLARE DA EMILIO

☞Restaurant-pizzeria
Via Principe Amedeo 173
Tel. 080 5235887
Closed Sunday for dinner and Monday
Open: lunch and dinner
Holidays: August
Seating: 60
Prices: 30-35 euros, wine excluded
All major credit cards

ANTICHI SAPORI

☞Restaurant-pizzeria
Piazza Vittorio Veneto 5
Tel. 080 5431267
Closed Wednesday
Open: lunch and dinner
Holidays: last week of August, first week of September
Seating: 70 + 70 outdoors
Prices: 30-33 euros, wine excluded
All major credit cards

When you've had enough of the chaos and frenzy of this lively city, put yourself in the hands of the Veronoli family, who run their pleasant restaurant right in the business and financial heart of the place.

Dorotea watches over the kitchen, while in the front of the house Enrico and Sergio move around with the mastery and savoir faire of those who have been doing their job for a long time. The decor, simple but attentive to detail, takes a back seat to the excellent cooking here. The menu is based on traditional dishes, revived and modernized while still retaining familiar flavors. Antipasti include **mussels au gratin**, **raw seafood**, grilled vegetables, frittatas and mozzarella. For a first course (usually pasta with vegetables, beans and/or fish) you would do well to choose the **tagliatelle with seafood**, which is always good. The main courses faithfully follow Puglia tradition; fish features largely here and is prepared simply (the daily catch is fried or baked). However, meat, which can be even better than the fish, is also present in **torcinelli, barbecued lamb** and the platter of grilled meats. There's not a huge selection of desserts, but they can include chocolates from the Pasticceria Berardi (in winter) and **sporcamusi**.

The choice of wines is somewhat limited, though there are admirable regional labels. In the evening you can opt for an excellent pizza, if you don't want a full dinner.

A few kilometers south of the center of Bari, this small former fishing village is now a residential zone of villas and condominiums, many providing second homes for city-dwellers who want easy access to the beach. You'll find this restaurant in the center of town, in the little square round the marina. It's a 'safe haven' for those who love fresh fish but don't want to pay too much for it.

Michele Buono and his son Raffaele have brusque voices but friendly smiles and run the restaurant with professionalism, serving simple, tasty food. Freshness is the key, so the menu is likely to change with the daily catch.

As soon as you sit down, the table fills with raw and cooked antipasti from sea and land, a delight to the eye and the tastebuds. You might have octopus salad, **timbale of rice, grains and seafood**, stuffed mussels, musci (a kind of mollusk that looks like a stone but gives off extraordinary iodine aromas) opened over the fire, fava purée with shrimp and croutons or **trionfo di crudo** (raw sea urchins, oysters, noci, black mussels and bearded mussels). First courses include green or red tagliolini, homemade pasta with seafood, **cavatelli with chickpeas and mussels** and **tiella alla barese** (rice, potatoes and mussels). The main courses vary with what fish have come in, but look out for the langoustines. Everything cooked over the charcoal grill (always for just the right amount of time) is also good. The fish soup is excellent but must be ordered in advance.

Get the sporcamusi for dessert. There's a limited, but not uninteresting, choice of wines.

BARI

BOVINO
Scalo

LA LOCANDA DI FEDERICO

⌣ Osteria
Piazza Mercantile 63-64
Tel. 080 5227705
Closed Monday
Open: lunch and dinner
Holidays: August 16-30
Seating: 50 + 60 outdoors
Prices: 30 euros, wine excluded
All major credit cards

LA PERGOLA

⌣ Restaurant
Strada Statale 161
Tel. 0881 961503
Closed Wednesday
Open: lunch and dinner, November-May dinner only
Holidays: September 1-15
Seating: 50 + 40 outdoors
Prices: 25-30 euros, wine excluded
All major credit cards, Bancomat

A pleasant stroll through the city takes you to the entrance of this osteria, now a benchmark for traditional cuisine in Bari. From the seafront by the Teatro Margherita (now undergoing a long overdue restoration), walk along the first boulevard of the Murattiano quarter (Corso Vittorio Emanuele) to Piazza Ferrarese, skirting the traditional fish market, which then leads you to the elegant Piazza Mercantile.

You're welcomed to the osteria by Gianluca Spagnuolo, who manages the charming restaurant with professionalism and discretion. The cooking has a strong local imprint and no frills, starting with raw and cooked antipasti: grilled vegetables, fresh dairy products, rustic savory pies, **onion calzone** and **raw seafood**. Among the first courses are fava purée and chicory, fusilli with eggplant-mint pesto and Cacioricotta, **rice with potatoes and mussels** and orecchiette with cime di rapa (turnip tops) or ragù. The mains are also in line with tradition and include baked **stuffed cuttlefish**, pork shank cooked with Primitivo di Manduria wine, **horsemeat brasciole in ragù** and various seafood dishes. Depending on the catch, there might be mullet en papilotte or sea bass baked in salt. Desserts include **sporcamusi** with pastry cream, torta della nonna and ricotta-chocolate flan.

The wine cellar is improving and includes an ample selection of Puglia labels, plus some good bottles from outside the region.

Bovino Scalo lies at the crossroads of the Bari-Naples and Foggia-Naples state roads. It was once a land of brigands and coach stations for travelers to stop at on their journey. There used to be many locandas around here, but then the autostrada replaced the old roads and many of the establishments closed their doors. Yet some have stayed on, such as Pasquale De Angelis, owner of La Pergola. De Angelis has a great passion for searching out high-quality local products and his restaurant reflects his commitment to quality.

The menu is varied and ranges from dishes featuring produce from the inland as well as fresh fish from nearby Manfredonia. You can begin with the gran fantasia di mare, with **crustaceans** and **mollusks** served raw and cooked. The **octopus salad** is excellent, as are the shrimp, mussels, cockles, cuttlefish au gratin, octopus alla luciana and mussels with mint and lemon. Local **cheeses** and cured meats are selected with care. Continue with paccheri with clams and artichokes, **cavatelli with shrimp and peas** and **orecchiette with mussels, porcini mushrooms and saffron** or with fresh sausage, Cacicavallo cheese and scorzone truffle. Preparations can be somewhat elaborate – this is true of the main courses, which might include gilt-head **sea bream fillets in a potato crust** with cherry tomatoes and fresh rosemary, roast monkfish with chickpeas, an excellent **frittura mista**, and for those who don't like fish, sausage in a Cacicavallo crust, **kid with herbs** and **braised wild boar** with thyme and oregano. To finish try the berry semifreddo or the fig soufflé. The ample wine list has more than 80 labels from the area and from all over Italy.

BRINDISI

CANDELA
Canestrello

PANTAGRUELE

🍽 Restaurant
Via Salita di Ripalta 1-3
Tel. 0831 560605
Closed Sunday for dinner and Monday, in summer Saturday and Sunday
Open: lunch and dinner
Holidays: none
Seating: 60
Prices: 35 euros, wine excluded
All credit cards

MASSERIA CANESTRELLO

🔑 Bed and breakfast
Contrada Canestrello
Tel. 0885 660792-338 9520641
Fax 0885 660792
E-mail: giorgio@masseriacanestrello.it
Internet: www.masseriacanestrello.it
Open from Easter to September,
in winter subject to booking

In a city that's long been a gateway to the east, bustling with sailors and tourists, this restaurant is always a reliable port of call. Right in the center of the city, it's just a few steps from the Duomo and the port. Simply appointed yet pleasant, the restaurant is run by Armando Brenda with competence and courtesy. Here you can eat the freshest seafood, its original flavors and aromas unsullied: the local culinary traditions prize the skillful but minimalist preparation of top quality raw ingredients. The seafood is complemented by well-executed dishes that use the land-based bounty of meats, mushrooms, cheeses and other dairy products.

There is a rich selection of antipasti, such as anchovies marinated with green onions, fried seasonal vegetables, fish mousse, shrimp with arugula, octopus tartare with vegetables and **mussels au gratin**. Among the first courses: laganari with spiny lobster or langoustines; strozzapreti with creamy pumpkin, porcini mushrooms and guanciale; **orecchiette with clams and zucchini**; and risotto with shrimp and seasonal vegetables. To follow there's fish, which vary depending on what's available at the market: perhaps boiled langoustines, **rockfish soup**, cuttlefish, bass, dentex or sea bream cooked on the grill. Or among the some meat options: excellent **young horsemeat fillet with wine**. Desserts are top-notch and include mint bavarois and **babà crumble with caramel** over chantilly cream.

The ample wine list pays particular attention to local labels. Service is professional and cordial, meeting the expectations of any Slow diner, Brindisi native or not.

The whitewashed building of the Masseria Canestrello lies close to Ofanto, a few kilometers from the Candela motorway exit. A sheep farm in the 19th century, its main crop is durum wheat. The rooms are named for local varieties of wheat Arcangelo, Creso, Svevo, Bronte and Simeto – and are spacious, comfortable and elegant, as well as being tastefully furnished. The kitchens in each apartment are fully equipped and allow you to prepare meals in complete independence. At breakfast you can choose from sweet or savory foods, including a range of typical local produce. Minibus and coach trips and excursions are often organized to nearby sights. A shuttle bus can also be organized on request to and from Naples and Bari airports.

• 5 double rooms, with bathroom, air conditioning, TV (on request); 2 apartments (2-4 persons) with kitchenette • Prices: double for single use 45-65, double and apartment 75-110 euros (supplement of 20-30 euros for extra bed), including breakfast • Credit cards: none • Covered car park on premises. Small pets welcome. Owners always present • Kitchen, reading room, TV room, billiard room. Garden. Swimming pool

CAROVIGNO

27 KM NORTH OF BRINDISI ON SS 16

IL CASTELLETTO

Restaurant-pizzeria
Contrada Morandi
Tel. 0831 990025
Closed Monday
Open: lunch and dinner
Holidays: vary
Coperti: 50 + 50 outdoors
Prices: 25-30 euros, wine excluded
All major credit cards

Restaurant owners Giuseppe and Maria welcome their guests to this fortified farmhouse surrounded by an age-old olive grove. In summer the roomy patio allows alfresco dining, while during the rest of the year you'll be seated in one of three charming dining rooms, formed from the same number of caseddhe (a kind of trullo), with an adjacent wine bar. Here you can sample some first-rate wines, choosing from Giuseppe's selection of over 300 labels from Puglia and the rest of Italy. The tables are spacious and carefully set, providing an ideal stage for Maria's modern and creative cooking.

Just-baked grissini, taralli and bread rolls with onions, walnuts, almonds, tomatoes or sesame accompany a splendid farmhouse **ricottina** with sesame seeds, anchovy salad, tuna prosciutto with fennel and Caciocavallo podolico. Among the first courses there are **fava purée with chicory**, red onions and sweet peppers; **orecchiette mollicate with turnip tops**; tubettini with chickpeas and raw oil; and homemade ravioloni stuffed with artichokes and chicory. To follow, try **capocollo of wild boar**, lamb cutlet with herbs, stewed rabbit with mushrooms, stuffed zucchini alla poverella and when available, fresh fish from the Adriatic. There's a good selection of local cheeses and cured meats. Desserts include an almond semifreddo with fig jam and a bauletto of dark chocolate.

In **San Vito dei Normani** (6 km) at Via Errico 33, a community of cheese producers from the Alto Salento produce Campanella, Giuncata, Burrata, Cacioricotta and fresh and aged cheeses from goat's, cow's and sheep's milk.

CASSANO DELLE MURGE
Cristo Fasano

30 KM SOUTHWEST OF BARI SS 271

AMICIZIA

Holiday farm
Strada Statale 271 per Santeramo, km 32,900
Tel. 080 763393
Fax 080 763556
E-mail: info@ristoranteterminal.it
Internet: www.amicizia.it
Open all year round

The agriturismo run by the Caponio family is housed in a farmhouse in the Murgia barese area, surrounded by a large estate that grows olives, almonds, fruit and vegetables. The proprietor Pietro, his wife Vita Maria and their two daughters also rear animals, run the restaurant (open to the public by reservation, 25 euros, excluding wine), and provide farm hospitality. An appropriate number of rooms are provided for this purpose, furnished in rustic style and suitable for use by couples or small family groups. Hot drinks, butter, jam, cheese, jam tarts and freshly baked biscuits are served for breakfast. Of the various outdoor activities available, don't miss the chance to do some horse trekking.

• 4 double rooms, 7 triple rooms and 2 four-bedded rooms, with bathroom, fridge, TV • Prices: double for single use 35-45, double 55-65, triple 70-85, four-bedded rooms 85-105 euros, including breakfast • Credit cards: all, including Bancomat • Access to mobility challenged. Outdoor car park on premises, free garage (space for 2 cars). No animals allowed. Owners always present • Bar, restaurant. TV room. Conference room. Garden. Horse-riding

CASTELLANA-GROTTE

MASSERIA TORRICELLA

🔑 Holiday farm
Strada Canale di Pirro, 19
Tel. 080 9309994-333 3968173
Fax 080 9309994
E-mail: masseriatorricella@libero.it
Internet: www.masseriatorricella.it
Open all year round

From the farm, the view spans the whole of the karst formation known as the Canale di Pirro. Back in the 15th century, Franciscan monks decided to establish themselves here, a place particularly suited to meditation. Over the centuries, a succession of owners altered the original layout of the structure, turning it into a large masseria or farmhouse; the Consoli family recently purchased the property and, after thoroughly restorating it, have revived interiors, large halls, spaces and, above all, the bedrooms, which are now sure to guarantee a comfortable stay. Guests can stroll through some 50 hectares of woodlands and fields, where they will meet goats, sheep and donkeys grazing freely. The farm also has a small restaurant where traditional dishes can be enjoyed at an average price of 25 euros. Minimum stay of two nights over holiday weekends, at Easter and at Ferragosto, the mid-August national holiday.

• 11 double rooms, with bathroom • Prices: double for single use 44-55, double 60-72 euros, including breakfast • Credit cards: all, including Bancomat • 2 rooms with facilities for the mobility challenged. Outdoor car park on premises. Small pets welcome. Owners always available • Restaurant. Park

CAVALLINO

OSTERIA DEL POZZO VECCHIO

🍲 Osteria-pizzeria
Via Silvestro 16
Tel. 0832 611649
Closed Monday
Open: lunch and dinner, in the summer only dinner
Holidays: none
Seating: 100 + 100 outdoors
Prices: 22-25 euros, wine excluded
All credit cards, Bancomat

The old pozzo (well) which gives this osteria its name is in the middle of a citrus orchard. Here, particularly on summer evenings, food lovers from near and far come to enjoy good traditional dishes or well-made pizzas in a pleasant setting.
In the small Norman town of Cavallino, not far from Lecce, Fernando Carlà, a true admirer of traditional cuisine, manages his restaurant with a strong emphasis on the quality and seasonal nature of his ingredients. Antipasti, heavy on vegetables, open the way to classic Salento first courses such as 'ciceri e tria' (pasta and legumes), **fava purée with chicory**, cecamariti, **sagne 'ncannulate al sugo** with mature ricotta, and less typical dishes, just as good, such as risotto with Scamorza, chicory and pancetta or pappardelle with hare. The main courses are varied: mixed roasted and grilled meats, horse fillets and chops, **turcinieddi** (kid or lamb offal), tripe with potatoes, **horsemeat stew** and the classic **octopus a pignatu**. Finish with exquisite pasticciotto cake or traditional spumone from Lecce.
The wine selection is good, showcasing all the best labels from Salento and Apulia in general, as well as many from the rest of the country. There's also a special list dedicated to oils and vinegars selected by the proprietor.

CEGLIE MESSAPICA

CERIGNOLA

38 KM WEST OF BRINDISI ON SS 16 AND 581

37 KM SOUTHEAST OF FOGGIA ON SS 16 OR A 14

CIBUS

'U VULESCE

Restaurant
Via Chianche di Scarano 7
Tel. 0831 388980
Closed Tuesday, never in summer
Open: lunch and dinner
Holidays: 10 days in July
Seating: 80
Prices: 30-32 euros
All credit cards

Osteria
Via Battisti 3
Tel. 0885 425798
Closed Thursday for dinner and Sunday
Open: lunch and dinner
Holidays: 15 days in August
Seating: 40
Prices: 22-27 euros, wine excluded
All major credit cards

Ceglie has had a reputation for years as a good place to eat, with even the street maps produced by the local authorities for visiting tourists promoting the town's gastronomy. Lillino Silibello is one of the standard-bearers of local food and wine. He is an expert in finding prime raw ingredients, none of which come from further than 20 or 30 km away from his restaurant. The Caciocavallo podolico, though typical of another part of the region, comes from a nearby producer, the only one in the lower Val d'Itria. This commitment to local sourcing is also reflected in the meat (fresh and cured), vegetables, the fantastic oil and the wine. It stands to reason that the cooking, entrusted to Silibello's mother and sister, follows the local traditions, though the menu can include some unusual dishes and personal interpretations.
The menu changes frequently, but particularly memorable are the antipasti of cheese, vegetables and cured meats, including Slow Food Presidia such as **Caciocavallo podolico** and **Martina Franca capocollo**. Among the first courses, try the tagliolini with rabbit ragù and seasonal vegetables and **eggplant stuffed with baked pasta**. Among the main courses: the not-to-be-missed **fillet of Podolica beef**, braciolette of young horsemeat al sugo and **gnummerieddhi** cooked on the charcoal grill. Conclude your meal with some traditional Ceglie cookies or a delicious hot ricottina with vincotto. The carefully considered wine list boasts some real rarities, such as Primitivo di Attanasio. The restaurant is run by the owner, who, together with the fine waiters, provides service that's never less than cordial and always with great attention to detail.

An important agricultural hub of the Tavoliere plain, Cerignola has long been known for excellent produce like the Bella di Cerignola olive, which is the biggest on the market. The Di Donna family are long-standing interpreters of local culinary traditions. The father, Nicola, used to be in the kitchen, but he's been replaced by Pina and her skilled cooking. Friendly Rosario and Pierluigi work front of house and are on hand to help you satisfy 'u vulesce', the craving for something good and tasty.
There's an antipasti buffet to begin, featuring seasonal vegetables: **stuffed eggplant**, flans of garden vegetables, baccalà fritters and **lampascioni battered and fried** or with a touch of olive oil. Among the best local dishes are the **cicatelli di grano arso with white fava purée**, the **orecchiette with horsemeat ragù** and buffalo milk ricotta, pancotto with turnip tops and spunzoile onions and the excellent **laganelle with beans, chard**, fresh tomatoes and basil. There's a good selection of main courses: stuffed guinea hen (not always available), **stuffed cuttlefish al sugo**, roast piglet with potatoes, roast stuffed faldina lamb, **egg soup with spunzoile onions**, baked baccalà with potatoes and **roast lamb** with lampascioni and potatoes.
The puddings are those traditional during festival time in Cerignola: seven-layer pizza, cartellate, calzoncelli made with vincotto, mostaccioli, chiacchiere and spoonable sweets like chocolate soufflé. The cellar has a good selection of regional wines.

CISTERNINO

TAVERNA DELLA TORRE

🍲Restaurant
Via San Quirico 3
Tel. 080 4449264
Closed Tuesday
Open: lunch and dinner
Holidays: January
Seating: 45
Prices: 30-35 euros, wine excluded
All major credit cards

Cisternino overlooks the Val d'Itria, perched on a plateau dotted with white houses, trulli and woods. One of the most beautiful of Puglia's historic towns, it's an incredible labyrinth of narrow streets and one bleach-white house after another, interrupted by the typical fornelli, butcher shop-cum-trattorias where you can find delicious grilled meats. This rustic restaurant is in the heart of town, near the main church dedicated to San Nicola. Spread over two floors, the dining rooms are decorated tastefully and feature unfinished stone walls. Service is courteous and attentive. Owner Mario Lo Russo offers a creative and rich menu that showcases the bounty of both land and sea. The antipasti are good and flavorful: there's marinated beef with raw mushrooms and grana cheese, octopus with mint, **tempura shrimp**, the **house antipasto** (seasonal vegetables prepared in different ways) and a plate of local cured meats. First courses include handmade **orecchiette with fresh tomato sauce and Cacioricotta,** pasta with eggplant ragù and buffalo mozzarella, potato gnocchetti with a fresh pecorino and chive fonduta and creamy risotto with leeks, shrimp and saffron.
The predominantly meaty main courses might include **roasts**, **horsemeat tagliata** with arugula and local cheese or wild boar filet with herbs. There are also seafood mains with fresh fish prepared in a number of ways. To finish, try the panna cotta with berries, hazelnut and chocolate flan with zabaglione foam or the 'coppa taverna' (vanilla gelato with honey croccantini and chocolate fonduta).
The cellar offers a good selection of Italian wines, with a particular focus on regional labels.

CONVERSANO

CORTE ALTAVILLA

🔑4-star hotel
Via Goffredo Altavilla 8
Tel. 080 4959668
Fax 080 4951740
E-mail: info@cortealtavilla.it
Internet: www.cortealtavilla.it
Open all year round

The hotel is right in the center of Conversano, a small town known for its elliptical street plan and a series of religious and civic buildings that testify to successive historical and artistic eras. Following restoration, what used to be the residence of the Counts of Conversano in the 13th-century now contains elegant rooms and apartments, decorated with paintings and capable of satisfying a variety of logistic requirements. The common areas are warm and attractively furnished as are the breakfast room and the sun patio, with its tables and large sunshades, where you can start the day in fine weather with a choice of hot drinks, ricotta, jams, doughnuts, tarts, freshly baked croissants filled with crème patisserie, cheeses and locally cured meats.

• 10 double rooms, 7 triples and 3 suites, 3 mini-apartments, with bathroom, air conditioning, mini-bar, safe, television, modem connection, kitchenette • Prices: double for single use 49-86, double 65-115, triple and suite 110-140, mini-apartment 140-170 euros, including breakfast • Credit cards: all, including Bancomat • 1 room with facilities for the disabled. 2 private car parks off the premises (1 with attendant). Small pets welcome. Concierge service 7am-midnight • Bar space. Breakfast room. Conference room. Terrace

Conversano

Montepaolo

MONTEPAOLO

Holiday farm
Contrada Montepaolo 2
Tel. 080 4955087-335 1331586
Fax 080 5217221
E-mail: info@montepaolo.it
Internet: www.montepaolo.it
Closed in November

A country house that dates back to the 16th century, Montepaolo was the hunting estate of the Counts of Acquaviva d'Aragona. In 1830 it was purchased by an ancestor of the Ramunni family who have now turned it into an agriturismo. The rooms and common spaces are furnished in a simple but practical style. Traditional dishes, enhanced by the proprietor's creative touches, are served in the three rooms used as a restaurant, at 20 euros a head for guests. On Sundays, the restaurant is also open to the public by reservation (average 25-30 euros). Courses are held on various subjects and, during the fruit harvest, guests are also invited to help with jam-making. The surrounding countryside offers numerous opportunities for trips; the grottos of Castellana and the trulli of Alberobello are both only a short distance away. Bicycles are available for guests to use on short rides. Minimum stay of three nights in August.

• 6 double rooms, 3 triple rooms and 1 four-bedded room, with bathroom, mini-bar, safe, television • Prices: double for single use 52-90, double 79-121, triple 100-150, four-bedded room 116-173 euros, including breakfast • Credit cards: all, Bancomat • Covered car park on premises. No animals allowed. Owners present 8am-8pm • Restaurant. Reading room. Garden, sun patio. Swimming pool

Corato

LA BOTTEGA DELL'ALLEGRIA

Osteria
Via Imbriani 46
Tel. 080 8722873
Closed Sunday dinner
Open: lunch and dinner
Holidays: vary
Seating: 20
Price: 25 euros
All major credit cards

This osteria is located in the historic center of Corato, a city of Byzantine origin that's known for the many dolmen (prehistoric stone monuments) in its environs. Recently opened, it adheres strictly to local traditions. As indicated by the name, it's also a little bit of a bottega, with wines, pastas, and gourmet specialties for sale on the shelves at the entrance. A hearty invitation to conviviality is provided by the fireplace in the main dining room, which pleasantly warms the tables in the winter months. Glowing embers are also key to the preparation of several flagship dishes from this part of Puglia, such as **kid with cardoons**, which acquires an unmatchable flavor from slow, careful cooking in a terracotta vessel placed over charcoal. Even the simple bruschettas have a great flavor, topped with delicious cherry tomatoes, garlic and chili. Other recommended appetizers and first courses are typically of the Murge district: dairy produce and Caciocavallo of different ages; Martina Franca cured meats; **eggplant with cherry tomatoes, Caciocavallo and pancetta**; baked fennel with breadcrumbs; **bean soup with wild greens** and **pasta with cardoncelli mushrooms**.
Owners Savino and Cinzia are assisted in the kitchen by Maria, a passionate cook who is an expert and scrupulous interpreter of local recipes. These include **horsemeat braciole al sugo** (cheese, parsley, garlic and lardo in addition to the pieces of meat). The menu is completed by cheeses (Pecorino, Caciocavallo, Canestrato) and a good selection of wines.

CORATO

45 KM WEST OF BARI

TRIPOLI

🛏️Diffuse hotel
Via Monte di Pietà 21
Tel and fax 080 8986828
E-mail: info@albergotripoli.com
Internet: www.albergotripoli.com
Open all year round

Some historians date the origins of Corato back to the Second Punic War, whereas other findings appear to go even further back, to the 8th and 7th centuries BC. Corato subsequently formed part of different dominions, including those of the Swabian and Anjou rulers, but most of the buildings and the town's economic development only date from the end of the feudal epoch. The rooms in this 'diffuse hotel', furnished with 'arte povera' furniture, are located in two neighboring 14th-century buildings that were recently refurbished. The largest rooms spread over two or three levels and the mini-apartment, which also has a kitchenette, is ideal for larger groups. Breakfast is served in a small breakfast room, and consists of hot drinks, fruit juice, freshly baked croissants, butter and jam.

• 6 double rooms and 4 suites (3-4 persons), with bathroom, air-conditioning, fridge, TV; 1 mini-apartment (6 people) with kitchenette • Prices: double for single use and double 50, suite 70, mini-apartment 90 euros, including breakfast • Credit cards: all, Bancomat • Free public car park 50 meters away. No animals allowed. Concierge service 7 am-2 pm, 4 pm-midnight • Breakfast room

FASANO
Speziale

44 KM NORTH OF BRINDISI SS 16 AND SS 379

MASSERIA DI PARCO DI CASTRO

🍲Holiday farm
Strada Statale 16 km 868,400
Tel. and fax 080 4810944
E-mail: infotiscali@masseriaparcodicastro.it
Internet: www.masseriaparcodicastro.it
Closed Monday and Tuesday
Open: dinner, Saturday and Sunday also lunch
Holidays: 3 weeks in January
Seating: 100
Prices: 25-28 euros, wine excluded
All major credit cards, Bancomat

The 18th-century cattle sheds, hayloft and fold have been converted into three lovely dining rooms and four bedrooms that overlook the large internal courtyard. The greater part of the ingredients used in the kitchen are produced on the farm, as are all the breakfast pastries and jellies. The cuisine is seasonal, faithful to the land and local traditions, starting with the antipasti: grilled vegetables, **dairy produce** and local cured meats, fava purée with chicory and peppers, **buckwheat with cherry tomatoes and cheese**, bruschettas with mature ricotta. The first courses contain fresh homemade pasta with a variety of dressings: **orecchiette with chicory and anchovies** or with strong mature cheese and rocket leaves, **tagliolini with cardoncelli mushrooms** and gnocchetti alla poveraccia. Among the main courses are **mixed meat grill** and **roast rabbit with olives and lampascioni onions** or with bay leaf, as well as guinea fowl, chicken with Primitivo wine and beef straccetti with vegetables. The meal comes to an end with almond pastries, tarts and other traditional puddings served with sweet wines and home-made liqueurs. The wine list is made up entirely of regional labels.

🛏️• 4 doubles, en-suite • Prices: double single use 40-50, double 60-80 euros (extra bed 15-25 euros), breakfast included • Restaurant access for the mobility challenged. Private outdoor parking. Small pets welcome (not in common areas). Owners always on premises • Restaurant. Living room. Conference room. Courtyard

FASANO
Speziale

FOGGIA

NARDUCCI

🔑 Holiday farm
Via Lecce 144
Tel. 080 4810185-080 4810049
Fax 080 4810185
E-mail: agriturismo_narducci@yahoo.com
Internet: www.agriturismonarducci.it
Open all year round

CHACAITO L'OSTERIA 🐌 ⊘ 🍶
DELLO ZIO ALDO

🍲 Osteria
Via Arpi 62
Tel. 0881 708104
Closed Sunday
Open: lunch and dinner
Holidays: 2-3 weeks in August
Seating 40
Prices: 33-35 euros, wine excluded
All major credit cards

Originally a staging post in the late 19th century, the main house on this farm, whose estates stretch over 15 hectares, has been fully refurbished while adhering scrupulously to the features of the typical Puglia masseria, or farmhouse. The spacious bedrooms, tastefully but simply furnished, are housed where the stables used to be. The kitchen serves typical country dishes at an average price of 20-35 euros (half-board 50-60 euros a head). The restaurant (open to the public on Saturday evenings and for Sunday lunch, subject to booking) is housed in an old building that was once the oil mill, but is now a splendid large room with a star ceiling. Guests can buy the farm produce, including rosolio, tomato sauces, jams and preserves, vegetables and extra virgin olive oil. The area offers numerous opportunities for excursions, and it's also possible to hire bicycles from the farm; public beaches and lidos are within a radius of three or four kilometers. Minimum stay of six days in August.

• 4 double rooms, 1 triple rooms and 4 quadruple rooms, with bathroom, air-conditioning, TV • Prices: double for single use 50-60, double 70-90, triple 105-135, four-bedded rooms 140-170 euros, including breakfast • Credit cards: all main cards, including Bancomat • Access to mobility challenged. Covered car park on premises. No animals allowed. Owners always present • Restaurant. Reading room, TV room. Garden, sun patio. Boules

At the begining Aldo's passion was just a hobby: 'I wasn't a pro yet, just cooking for friends. And then at home there would be 10 to 15 of us at the table, every day for generations'. His osteria is located on a street in the old town, close to the civic market. It's a lively place, where youth and community traditions come together. This – plus the creativity of an interpreter who can be both faithful and inventive – influences the restaurant's cooking, which is local and traditional but never static. This is how food with popular origins should be, used to dealing with the restrictions and opportunities of the market, limited by dependence on farmers and gatherers and catering to consumers without deep pockets. The very best of the countryside, the fallow fields, the woods and the local pastures, the waterways, lakes and the sea, comes to the fore in Aldo's dishes.

This makes it difficult to describe his menu, which may include peppers all'acqua, **salsicciata** (pork, wild boar and horse sausage) with herbs and spices, tagliata with shavings of cacio-cavallo (both the meat and the cheese from podolico cows), **fava purée** and **cicerchie with baccalà, pappardelle spezzate with porcini mushrooms and snails**, troccoli with horse ragù, **meat and onion alla genovese** or fish from the Gulf of Manfredonia.

The serious wine list, with labels from Puglia and the rest of Italy, serves as a good starting point for evaluating the positive signs coming from Capitanata winemaking. Homemade desserts, a selection of liqueurs, cigars, herbal teas and friendly service all contribute to an always intriguing meal.

DA POMPEO

ZIA MARINELLA

🍲 Restaurant
Vico al Piano 14
Tel. 0881 724640
Closed Sunday
Open: lunch and dinner
Holidays: August 15-31
Seating: 60
Prices: 23-30 euros, wine excluded
No credit cards accepted

🍲 Osteria
Via Saverio Altamura 23
Tel. 330 654510
Closed Sunday
Open: lunch and dinner
Holidays: the week of Ferragosto
Seating: 60
Prices: 25-30 euros, wine
All credit cards except AE, Bancomat

This friendly restaurant in the old town (near the Teatro Umberto Giordano) is regularly packed, particularly at lunchtime, so we recommend making reservations. The crowds come for confidently prepared seasonal delicacies at the peak of freshness and the easy professionalism of the Pillo family. The large, well-ordered kitchen is on view, and helps whet the appetite for dishes that derive from land traditions as well as the catch brought into the nearby port of Manfredonia.

You can begin with delicious little **moscardini** (or totanetti when available) with **lentils**, **anchovies au gratin** (the little anchovies from the gulf available only in springtime) or potato purée with shrimp. The seasonal vegetables prepared in different ways are also delicious. Continue with cavatelli with peas; **chicory and fava purée** with toasted homemade bread and the restaurant's own extra virgin olive oil, fava bean, artichoke and pea soup and the not-to-be-missed homemade **orecchiette with tomatoes and Cacioricotta**. For main courses there's excellent meat – not necessarily local – usually cooked on the grill, or **brasciola** (stewed roulades). The baked **lamb with mushrooms and potatoes** is also worth a taste.

The cheeses and local cured meats are top quality. Delicious desserts include pineapple semifreddo, pear flan with chocolate, strawberries, various sponge cakes with pastry cream and plain and almond cookies, all accompanied by a good Moscato from Trani.

The adequate selection of regional and national wines would benefit from a proper list.

The old part of Foggia has benefited from intelligent restoration by the town authorities and contains pleasant surprises for those seeking authentic cooking. This osteria is right in the heart of town, located in a building dating from the early 20th century, with tufo arches and brick vaults and a warm, friendly atmosphere. While it may not have a long history – it opened just a few years ago – you'll still find all the elements of a traditional osteria.

The name comes from Aunt Marinella, who oversees the kitchen with energy and creativity, while in the front of the house you'll find the Furores, a father-and-son team. The menu is distinguished by the freshness and quality of the raw ingredients, which follow the changing seasons, and are cooked according to the traditional canon. Among the pastas, all home-made, you can choose from **cavatelli di grano arso** with tomatoes and ricotta marzotica, **Zia Marinella's orecchiette al verde** with cherry tomatoes au gratin, pappardelle with zucchini and smoked scamorza, cicatelli with beans and classic fava purée with wild chicory. Main courses not to be missed are the **roast suckling pig** with potatoes and lamb 'scottadito' with cardoncelli mushrooms and artichokes. For dessert we particularly recommend the **zeppole di San Giuseppe** or the babà with wild berry cream.

The various local and Italian wines are reasonably priced.

🍷 Enoteca Nuvola, Via Trento 5 b, has an excellent selection of local and Italian wines.

34 KM SOUTHWEST OF LECCE ON SS 101

34 KM SOUTHWEST OF LECCE ON SS 101

ANGOLO BLU

LE PURITATE

Trattoria
Via Muzzio 45
Tel. 0833 261500
Closed Monday
Open: lunch and dinner
Holidays: November
Seating: 80
Prices: 30-35 euros, wine excluded
All credit cards

Restaurant
Via Sant'Elia 18
Tel. 0833 264205
Closed Wednesday, never in summer
Open: lunch and dinner
Holidays: October
Seating: 45 + 50 outdoors
Prices: 32-35 euros, wine excluded
All major credit cards, Bancomat

The tortuous, narrow white streets of Gallipoli's old town are filled, year after year, with improbable restaurants for passing tourists, pubs, sandwich places and all the worst the food-service world has to offer. Negotiating this labyrinth of alleyways and signs is not easy if you don't take advantage of certain stand-outs, such as this little restaurant just a few steps from the beautiful cathedral of Sant'Agata (one of the best examples of the Salento baroque). Here, at highly competitive prices, you can find an alternative to other restaurants which might be more lauded, but are also more expensive and less authentic.

You can begin with marinated gobetti (local shrimps) or totanetti, **raw seafood**, fried paddlefish with cherry tomatoes, pine nuts and rosemary, sweet and sour cod or **pittole, fritters of cuttlefish and shrimp**. Then move on to first courses like **linguine with sea urchin, fish soup**, fresh tagliolini with seafood and orecchiette 'panza ricca'. The mains include violetti (crustaceans typical of Gallipoli) or **angler fish alla gallipolina**, roast Mediterranean yellow-tail steak, and stewed cuttlefish with peas. Finish off your meal with desserts accompanied by a China Calissaia liqueur prepared using an ancient local recipe. You might choose from fruit pies, **cupeta** (made with almonds and sugar) and divini amori.

The wine selection is very modest.

Those who live in the old part of Gallipoli call it 'the island'. Until a few years ago, it was noted for its high number of churches with respect to the population – some, such as the cathedral and San Francesco, well worth visiting. There haven't been any new churches put up recently, but a lot of new restaurants have opened, by no means all equally good. Of those, this one definitely deserves a mention, and not just because of its enchanting view of the Purità bay, which gives the restaurant its name. However the gazebo (which seems to be a necessary appendage to every restaurant in town) doesn't really add to the charm.

As one would expect, the kitchen is heavily influenced by the sea, with regular antipasti including stewed octopus, octopus salad, gratin or **fried mussels**, **sea urchins** (jewels of the Gallipoli rocks) and some unexpected rarities, like **scapece gallipolino** (oily fish such as sardines or anchovies marinated in vinegar, saffron and breadcrumbs) and marinated mackerel. Among the firsts: **tubettini with fish sauce**, tagliolini with shrimp and lemon and sometimes risotto with mussels. For mains, there's a wide choice of fish prepared in all the classic ways (grilled, boiled, baked, salt-baked) or alternatively, the **mixed fried fish**, or salt-baked jumbo shrimp. The desserts are generally bought in, with the exception of the spumone gallipolino. The cellar is limited and the service can be a bit patchy on busy days.

GIOIA DEL COLLE

GIOVINAZZO

39 KM SOUTH OF BARI ON SS 100

18 KM NORTH OF BARI SS 16

OSTERIA DEL BORGO ANTICO

⌒ Osteria
Via Cavour 89
Tel. 080 3430837
Closed Wednesday
Open: lunch and dinner
Holidays: variable
Seating: 60 + 35 outdoors
Prices: 25-30 euros, wine excluded
All major credit cards, Bancomat

SAN MARTIN

🗝 4-Star Hotel
Via Spirito Santo 46
Tel. 080 3942627
Fax 080 3901238
E-mail: info@smartinhotel.it
Internet: www.smartinhotel.it
Open all year round

Gioia del Colle is located halfway between the coastal cities of Bari on the Adriatic and Taranto on the Ionian Sea. Thanks to its flourishing livestock, wine and cheese industries it's an important agricultural center, renowned not only for its unrivaled mozzarella and other dairy products, but also for the cultural and architectual wealth of its historic center, including Frederick II's Castello Svevo and the Casa Torre. The surrounding countryside is dotted with ancient fortified farmhouses and archeological sites.

If you want to get to know the gastronomical treasures of the area, Gianni Antonicelli is ready to help you. He's the friendly host of this osteria, located in the old town in a peaceful courtyard where in the summer you can dine al fresco. The kitchen uses many excellent ingredients from nearby farms, and the menu changes depending on what's in season. Don't skip the antipasti, which always include a selection of local **dairy produce** such as burrata and mozzarella; an eggplant millefeuille and the unusual **parmigiana di boragine (borage).** Among the first courses we recommend the **zuppa di legumi di Sarconi**, the spaghettoni with asparagus and langoustines, the **orecchiette alla poveraccia** with fried bread and the local fagottini (rolls of chard leaves stuffed with cavatellini in meat sauce). The main courses, which don't follow the seasons quite as strictly, include horsemeat **brasciolette**, grilled meats, beef tagliata with arugula and Parmesan shavings and stuffed fillet. To finish, don't miss the traditional **sporcamusi with vincotto**. The cellar offers a selection of the best regional labels, as well as carafes of a fairly good, well-chosen Primitivo from Gioia.

In the center of Giovinazzo, the hotel managed by Nicola Dolciamore, an architect, is housed in a monastery that underwent a series of alterations between the 11th and 16th centuries, and was completely restored in 2003. The spacious rooms offer all the comforts typical of a 4-Star hotel and are furnished in period style. The buffet breakfast includes croissants, cereals, pies, cookies, crisp breads, jam, honey, yoghurt and hot and cold drinks. The restaurant offers local recipes and more creative dishes (20-25 euros, excluding wine; half-board supplement 18 euros per person). Large terraces on the top floor provide panoramic views and allow guests to enjoy the sun. If you want to go to the seaside, the staff will tell you where the best beaches are.

• 3 single rooms, 11 doubles, 3 triples, 1 four-bedded room and 2 suites, with bathroom, air-conditioning, mini-bar, television • Prices: single 100, double 120, triple 150, quadruple room 160, suite 150 euros, including breakfast • Credit cards: all, including Bancomat • 1 room with facilities for mobility challenged. External public car park, garage (5 euros per day) 1 km away. 24-hour concierge service • Bar, restaurant. Reading room, conference room. Terraces, sun patio

58 KM SOUTHWEST OF BARI ON SS 96

Osteria ☺🗡️
di Salvatore Cucco

🥘 Trattoria
Piazza Pellicciari 4
Tel. 080 3261872
Closed Sunday for dinner and Monday
Open: lunch and dinner
Holidays: August 15-31
Seating: 50
Prices: 30 euros, wine excluded
All major credit cards except AE

Alle Due Corti

🥘 Osteria
Via Leonardo Prato 42
Tel. 0832 242223
Closed Sunday
Open: lunch and dinner
Holidays: July 27-August 19
Seating: 65
Prices: 25-28 euros, wine excluded
All major credit cards except AE, Bancomat

On the edge of the Murgia district, almost in Basilicata, the arid landscape is characterized by irregular limestone formations. The countryside is rich in pastures and a source of cardoncelli mushrooms and wild greens. Olive trees and grapevines abound and many big wineries from the north have invested here, buying up acres of land and planting both indigenous and international varietals. In Gravina, located on the edge of a deep, picturesque gravina (gorge), Salvatore Cucco's osteria has become an institution for fans of traditional local cuisine.

Plenty of local vegetables appear in the antipasti: **roasted cardoncelli mushrooms**, delicate lampascioni, cabbage flan, zucchini omelet, an excellent **eggplant millefeuille** and artichoke heart carpaccio, plus a fairly good selection of local cured meats and **dairy** produce, the highlights of which are tasty cured Basilicata pork sausage, sheep's milk ricotta, bocconcini and stracciatella. The veal fillet tortino with zucchini is also worth noting. Among the first courses we recommend the **timbale of cardoncelli** with fava purée and the **home-made taglioline** with wild asparagus, cherry tomatoes and Cacioricotta, or with cicerchia puree. Among the notable main courses is the **lamb** (sourced from local farms), roasted and served with a small timbale of wild chicory. It's also very good grilled over charcoal and acquires a distinctive taste cooked in a pot with wild herbs, when it's known as u calaridde. To finish, try the almond dolcetti with bay-leaf liqueur or classic tiramisù. Local wines dominate the cellar, as they should in a DOC zone, but there's also a good selection of wines from the rest of Italy.

Lecce's splendid baroque churches and monuments have made it an essential tourist destination, and now the city is looking to satisfy the growing demand from visitors who want to sample traditional local cooking. Among the restaurants which offer dishes inspired by local recipes, simple service and a good value, we don't think twice about recommending this osteria located in the middle of the historic center. You'll find it between the magnificent Porta Napoli and the church of Santa Croce, a masterpiece of Lecce baroque. The restaurant has three soberly furnished dining rooms. Given the high influx of diners, it's advisable to reserve well in advance. The menu changes every 15 days, depending on what's in the market. You can begin with **cocule** (eggplant rissoles), **monicedde** (small snails) sauteed with wine and onions or peppers or stuffed eggplant baked in the oven. Among the classic first courses the **ciceri e tria** (pasta with legumes), **sagne 'ncannulate with horsemeat ragù**, orecchiette or another homemade pasta baked with mozzarella and cacioricotta are particularly noteworthy. Among the mains, try the traditional **turcinieddi** (lamb offal roulades), either grilled or stewed; the lamb, roasted or with artichokes; or the Spanish-influenced **taeddha** with potatoes, onions, tomatoes and black mussels. You can finish your meal with homemade desserts or traditional spumone. Wines are mainly from the Salento area.

🍞 For breads, pizza and pucce, visit these two bakeries: Osvaldo Conte, Via Cosatadura 28, and Furnu de Petra, Via Casetti.

CUCINA CASERECCIA

🍲 Trattoria
Via Costadura 19
Tel. 0832 245178
Closed: Sunday for dinner and Monday
Open: lunch and dinner
Holidays: beginning of September
Seating: 50
Prices: 20-25 euros
All major credit cards except AE

OSTERIA DEGLI SPIRITI

🍲 Osteria
Via Battisti 4
Tel. 0832 246274
Closed Sunday for dinner
Open: lunch and dinner
Holidays: last 2 weeks in July
Seating: 50
Prices: 25-30 euros, wine excluded
All major credit cards, Bancomat

Dishes firmly rooted in Salento traditions, attentive service and good value make this trattoria (located just outside the city center near the Villa Comunale) a place to return to again and again.

The simple decor is in tune with the food, which highlights seasonal produce from the surrounding fields and vegetable gardens, and Anna Carmela Perrone's welcome is typical of the informal management. Let her be your guide in choosing dishes and condiments, such as an extra virgin olive oil that's excellent on the many vegetables on the menu.

In the winter, don't miss the **wheat and mixed vegetable soup**, while in the spring, order the artichoke soup with fresh broad beans, peas and mint. At other times of the year you'll find a **taieddra of zucchini with potatoes and mussels**, cannelloni with ricotta and cardoons, **rianata** (barley maccheroncini with potatoes, zucchini and pecorino cheese, baked in the oven), **orecchiette** or sagne 'ncannulate pasta with fresh tomatoes or **vegetables and beans** cooked in a clay pignata, or pot, fava purée with wild chicory or ciceri e tria, pasta with legumes. For a main course, try the horsemeat stew and **horsemeat roulades in sauce**, lightly spicy spareribs, beef polpettoni filled with cheese and cooked with white wine, pork sausage or grilled horse chop. If you're not into meat, there's always a good **octopus in pignata** or stuffed calamari. The side dishes are (unusually) regular features: paparine (tender poppy shoots) with olives, chard and roast potatoes.

Red wine by the carafe (though there are also several good bottles of local Vino Salentino) and a final selection of biscuits and cookies should not be ignored.

This osteria, near the public park in the center of the city, seems to get better with every visit and aims to be a point of reference for the Lecce restaurant scene. Pietro and Tiziana welcome you to their simply decorated dining room, the tables laid with care. Professional and cordial, they will guide you towards dishes that combine simplicity with respect for the seasons. Here, you'll find good, honest cooking that follows local traditions.

You can start with abundant antipasti, including **pittule**, caponata, **arancini**, potato croquettes, sautéed mushrooms, wild chicory sauteed with tomatoes, fried or **stuffed artichokes** and other seasonal vegetables enhanced by good extra virgin olive oil. Among the firsts there are classic dishes such as **ciceri e tria** (pasta and legumes), **fava purée with wild chicory** and **orecchiette with turnip tops**; also good are the fresh maccheroncini with pecorino and pepper and the orecchiette with chickpeas and clams or with eggplant and shrimp. To follow, try the lamb, either roast or with artichokes, lamb **turcinieddi** (offal roulades) and sausage, rissoles al sugo, **horsemeat stew al sugo**, **octopus alla pignata** and fried anchovies. Round off the meal with a delicious Lecce **pasticciotto** cake, the typical spumone with a sponge-cake center or walnut or orange-chocolate cake.

The wine list is fairly long, and includes all the best local bottles plus a good number of well-chosen wines from the rest of Italy.

LECCE

PRESTIGE

🚪Bed and breakfast
Via Santa Maria del Paradiso 4
Tel. 0832 243353-349 7751290
Fax 178 2215006
E-mail: info@bbprestige-lecce.it
Internet: www.bbprestige-lecce.it
Open all year round

The well furnished rooms of this elegant B&B right in the city center are welcoming and comfortable, ensuring a relaxing stay for guests. In fine weather, breakfast, which consists of croissants, biscuits, bread, butter and jam, fruit juice, coffee, milk or tea, is served on an attractive terrace with a panoramic view of the old town. Guests can also use the sunbeds and sunshades on the terrace to relax and improve their suntan. Renata Merola, the hospitable proprietor, is always on hand to give her guests useful tips on the most interesting itineraries to follow round the city and its environs. On request, a shuttle bus can be organized to and from Brindisi airport. Clients are offered free parking in front of the B&B. Minimum stay of one week in August.

• 3 suites, with bathroom, air-conditioning, mini-bar, safe, television, wireless connection • Prices: suite for single use 60-70, suite 80-90 euros (supplement of 30 euros for extra bed), including breakfast • Credit cards: none • External parking nearby, authorized garage (7 euros per day). Small pets welcome. Owners always available • Breakfast room, reading room, internet connection. Terrace, sun patio

LOCOROTONDO

LA TAVERNA DEL DUCA

🍲Osteria
Via Papadotero 3
Tel. 080 4313007
Closed Sunday for dinner, never in summer
Open: lunch and dinner
Holidays: November 15-30
Seating: 30 + 30 outdoors
Prices: 30 euros, wine excluded
No credit cards accepted

This area offers numerous delights both cultural and scenic: the trulli of Alberobello, the Castellana caves and the unique Val d'Itria. The Locorotondo public park offers a panorama of trulli and vineyards, a magical landscape that's as beautiful in the evening as it is during the day. The old-timers who still tend the vines are often responsible for preserving the local country culture and many food traditions live on unaltered.
This small, friendly osteria is particularly worth noting because, despite Antonella's youth, her cooking respects the history of this part of Puglia. Among the antipasti, in addition to delicious **fried polpette**, the vegetables are outstanding, whether fried, roasted or preserved in oil: the **fried artichokes** and the zucchini pie are just two examples. In addition to the classic **white fava purée** with wild chicory there are several handmade pastas, such as **orecchiette with donkey ragù** (simmered for at least five hours), **strascinate with turnip tops** or beans in the winter, cavatelli with beans or chickpeas and troccoli (a long pasta) with tomatoes and cacioricotta in the summer. The main courses include the famous **fornello** di gnumarieddi, sausages and bombette; donkey braciole (stewed roulades) and the excellent **tripe suffuchèt** (pieces of tripe with lots of onions, cooked for hours with various seasonings).
A sweet finish is provided by almond dolcetti and homemade rosolio liqueurs (try the wild fennel or the bay leaf), but if you're really lucky you'll find 'apple surprise' (enclosed in puff pastry, filled with pastry cream and baked) on the menu. The wine offered is an unassuming Primitivo.

MANFREDONIA

MARTINA FRANCA

39 KM NORTHEAST OF FOGGIA ON SS 89

30 KM NORTH OF TARANTO ON SS 172

IL BARACCHIO

🍲 Trattoria
Corso Roma 38 (corner of via De Florio)
Tel. 0884 583874
Closed Thursday
Open: lunch and dinner
Holidays: 10 days in July
Seating: 70
Prices: 25-35 euros, wine excluded
All major credit cards

AL RITROVO DEGLI AMICI

🍲 Restaurant
Corso Messapia 8
Tel. 080 4839249
Closed Sunday for dinner and
Monday; all Sunday also in summer
Open: lunch and dinner
Holidays: variable
Seating: 40 + 18 outside
Prices: 35 euros, wine excluded
All credit cards accepted

The sea plays a major role in the cuisine of this coastal town, nestling at the foot of the Gargano on the shores of the Gulf of Manfredonia. Fiorenzo makes the most of this resource as the basis of the dishes served in his trattoria, without ever lapsing into banality or obviousness. Look to your left as you enter and you'll see his wife Nella in the kitchen, assisted by her friend Giulia.

Guests are welcomed with courtesy, and as soon as they are seated good local bread and olives are served, followed by antipasti such as seafood salad with octopus and cuttlefish or marinated anchovies. One of the best first courses is the **zuppetta alla marinara** (with crustaceans and mollusks), a huge portion which is best shared with fellow diners. Other firsts include home-made **troccoli with cuttlefish** or mixed seafood, **pasta with chickpeas and clams** and orecchiette with shrimp and arugula, or more earthy dishes like various pastas with ragù or tomato and cacioricotta. Fish also figures prominent among the main courses: worth noting is the **gallinella (gurnard) all'acquapazza** served with wild asparagus in the spring, and we also recommend the **mullet with lemon and oregano**, the grilled fish and the mixed fried fish. You'll almost always find grilled crustaceans.

Traditional baked dolcetti conclude the meal, or try the good ricotta roulade. The light white wines on offer accompany the food perfectly.

🫒 On the road to San Giovanni Rotondo (10 km) in **Contrada Miscillo**, km 3, D'Apolito makes excellent extra virgin olive oil from ogliarola olives.

Martina dominates the Val Itria in a countryside dotted with trulli, caves and woods. It's a noble, elegant town in which airy, restrained examples of baroque architecture triumph, as seen in the numerous palazzos and the gate that gives access to the old town. In the months of July and August the historic center becomes the stage for the Festival of the Valle d'Itria, which hosts prestigious international opera singers.

Just a few steps from the center is this restaurant housed in a gracious home dating from the late 1800s. Both elegant and comfortable, here you'll be able to enjoy the main attraction of the Ritrovo: the wholesome local cuisine. Anna Ancona, owner and chef, is truly enthusiastic about a job she has been doing for years. Start with warm olive bread and inviting antipasti like capocollo and lardo di Martina Franca, meatballs, crêpes with cardoncelli mushrooms, cheese soufflé, zucchini and eggplant flan. To follow, there's **broad bean purée with vegetables**, laganari with zucchini, maritati with fresh tomatoes and flakes of cacio cheese, **cream of chickpeas with cardoncelli mushrooms**, **orecchiette with turnip-tops** and bucatini all'amatriciana. Mains are meaty: there may be **leg of lamb**, **lamb cutlets a scottadito**, beef tagliata or straccetti. For dessert, you must taste the **bocconotto martinese**, made with puff pastry and confectioner's cream.

There's a good wine list with a thoughtfully considered selection of regional and other Italian labels.

CIACCO

Restaurant
Via Conte Ugolino 14
Tel. 080 4800472
Closed Sunday for dinner and
Monday, in summer Monday only
Open, lunch and dinner
Holidays: variable
Seating: 45 + 20 outside
Prices: 35 euros, wine excluded
All major credit cards

Martina Franca has every reason to be considered the capital of the Val d'Itria: it has one of the area's most interesting old centers and organizes top quality classical music festivals. Furthermore the trulli-dotted land around it offers magnificent views of the sea. It has a longstanding tradition, without equal in this area, for the preparation of cured meats. All of this makes for a pleasantly stimulating visit, particularly when accompanied by a meal at the place Cristina has set up in one of the narrow streets of the old quarter. Just go up the stairs leading to the second floor and take a seat in the spacious, elegant dining room or, in summer, on the adjacent terrace. Then you'll be ready to enjoy a memorable gastronomic experience in true Puglia or, more precisely, Martina Franca tradition.

Begin with **bread with pepper and lard**, **fried meatballs**, stuffed peppers, vegetables preserved in olive oil, fresh cheeses and cured meats typical of the area, like **capocollo** (Slow Food Presidium). First courses are also traditional, particularly the fresh pastas (mainly **orecchiette** and cavatelli) with vegetable or **meat sauces**. Main courses include roast leg of pork, **barbecued meats** and lamb ribs. To round off your meal there's nothing better than **bocconotto alla martinese** or a fruit bavarois.

The wine list includes quite a good selection of mostly regional wines.

FASCINO ANTICO

Bed and breakfast
Strada statale 172 Alberobello-Locorotondo, km 0,500
Tel. and fax 080 4325089
E-mail: info@fascinoantico.com
Internet: www.fascinoantico.com
Open from April to November

Michele Greco, who has managed this place for the past few years with his wife Giuseppina, was previously a restaurateur and he has also built trulli in his time. The B&B is to be found inside a number of trulli, which Michele has restored to their original splendor (the farmyard is particularly attractive). The rooms are plainly furnished but fitted with all the essential comforts, and other services are available in the commonl spaces. Breakfast, which includes hot drinks, bread, home-made jams, croissants and, on request, savory food, is served in the bar. The B&B is located in a peaceful area, close to interesting places to visit, such as Alberobello and Martina Franca.

• 2 double rooms, 1 triple room, and 2 quadruple rooms, with bathroom, air conditioning, TV; 1 double and 1 quadruple room with kitchenette • Prices: double for single use 45, double 65, triple 90, quadruple 120 euros, including breakfast • All main credit cards, including Bancomat • 1 room with facilities for mobility challenged. Outdoor car park on premises. No animals allowed. Owners always present • Bar corner. Reading room and TV. Garden

MARTINA FRANCA

MARTINA FRANCA
Monti del Duca

IL GALLO FELICE

☞—o Bed and breakfast
Via Crispiano 101
Tel. 335 8248622-349 6411981
Fax 099 375992
E-mail: alexandrovic@inwind.it
Open from Easter to September and at Christmas

LABBRUTO

☞—o Bed and breakfast
Via Monti del Duca 52 G
Tel. and fax 080 4838553
E-mail: labbruto@motolese.net
Internet: www.motolese.net/labbruto
Open all year round

On the outskirts of Martina Franca, on the road that leads to the village of Crispiano, Emira Leccese and her son Alessandro run this attractive B&B, housed in three expertly restructured ancient trulli, set in 7,500 square meters of farmland. Two of the trulli contain four double rooms furnished with 19th-century Puglia furniture, large bathrooms complete with bath, and also a kitchen; the third, which originally acted as the mill where wine and oil were made, has been turned into a spacious sitting room with solid walnut furniture and an attractive fireplace. Breakfast includes savory fare, home-made cakes and jams. Cooking, flower pressing and papier-mâché courses are held during the summer.

• 4 double rooms, with bathroom • Prices: double for single use 35-45 euros, double 50-80 (supplement of 10 euros for extra bed), including breakfast • Credit cards: none • Access to mobility challenged. Outdoor car park on premises. Small pets welcome. Owners always present • Rest and TV room. Garden

Donna Rosellina's B&B is housed in a fully restored historic farmhouse dating from 1643. The complex consists of a manor house surrounded by trulli and old stables now used as mini-apartments which are extremely comfortable and stylishly furnished, complete with kitchenettes or fully-fledged kitchens. In some of the rooms you can admire frescoes painted by Rosellina to brighten up the atmosphere, while others are notable for their bare stone walls. In the common spaces, it's worth mentioning the café, which is open 9am-midnight, where you can enjoy a hearty buffet breakfast with cakes. Savory food, including locally sourced cheese and cured meats, is also available on request. Outside, there is plenty of space for guests to enjoy the swimming pool, organize barbecues or simply chill out on the lawns or stroll through the woods.

• 4 single rooms and 2 four-bedded rooms, with bathroom, air conditioning, fridge, television, kitchenette or kitchen • Prices: double for single use and double 100 euros, four-bedded rooms 140-160, including breakfast • All major credit cards, including Bancomat • Uncovered car park on premises, free garage. Small pets welcome. Owners always present • Bar. Breakfast room, TV room. Conference room. Garden. Swimming pool

LA TRADIZIONE CUCINA CASALINGA

Trattoria
Via Imbriani 11
Tel. 0833 691690
Closed Thursday
Open: lunch and dinner
Holidays: last week of February, September 1-15
Seating: 50
Prices: 25-30 euros, wine excluded
All major credit cards accepted

This trattoria's address is one you'll want to pass on to your best friends. Minervino Murge is a village where the roots of a farming tradition are still strong, to an almost overwhelming degree, as testified by its cuisine and agricultural pride, a potential that has still to be completely explored. And so the efforts of the Dinoia brothers are most commendable, given that they play a small but important part in helping people get to know the gastronomy of the Upper Murgia area.

The environment is unpretentious and the food served draws on all the features of age-old farmhouse traditions put to new uses and with a certain creative touch. After the antipasti, including **fried zucchini balls**, **sausage and peppers**, lampascioni, snails and other seasonal delicacies, you move on to a first course of home-made pasta. Particularly good are the **troccoli alla murgese** (odd-shaped pasta with Marzotica ricotta and cherry tomatoes), strascinati with cime di rape and **ulivi alla minervinese** (pasta in the shape of olive leaves with sausage and tomato sauce). Among the main courses, try the large **grilled meat platter** with lamb, goat and mutton, stewed **pork sausage** or cardoncelli mushrooms cooked over a charcoal fire. The really outstanding dish is the **cutturid con cime di rape** (lamb stew with turnip tops), delectable, well-balanced and chock-full of bold flavors.

There's a limited choice of desserts (though the **ricotta tart** is nice) and the selection of wines, which includes the place's own and a few regional labels, isn't particularly exciting.

MASSERIA BARBERA

Holida farm
Strada Statale 97 km 5,850
Tel. 0883 692095
Closed Sunday evening and Monday
Open: lunch and dinner
Holidays: July 1-15 and in January
Seating: 100
Prices: 30 euros, wine excluded
All major credit cards accepted

Masseria Barbera is a farm in Upper Murgia, a few kilometers from Castel del Monte, that offers the warmth and friendliness of farm hospitality. Just outside Minervino you'll come to the Barbera family's property (they've owned it for five generations), which covers an area of about 50 hectares, with vineyards, olive groves, orchards and pasture land. Riccardo, who has a passion for the land, abandoned the legal profession to manage the farm. In the 1800s the rooms that now house the restaurant and hotel were the nucleus of a typical fortified Murgia-style farmhouse.

The cuisine is closely tied to the territory and often uses produce grown by the farm as ingredients. You start with a long sequence of antipasti, so many that you may not be able to handle them all: **ricotta with vincotto**, **vegetables fried in batter**, vegetable omelets, bread polpette, zucchini flowers stuffed with ricotta and mozzarella, capocollo, focaccia made with scorched grain. The latter is also used to make the popular **orecchiette**, that with the soups made with the season's vegetables and **pancotto with cime di rape**, a soup of stale bread and turnip tops, are just a few of the first courses. For your main course the focus is on local **grilled meat** accompanied, in season, by cardoncelli mushrooms and lampascioni. There's a good selection of homemade puddings with fruit tarts, ricotta flan and **glazed citrus fruits**.

The wine list has grown and now includes a good choice of the region's major producers together with a few other Italian wines. We can recommend the house wine. Also there's a rather good extra-virgin olive oil that's produced on the farm.

MONOPOLI

MONTE SANT'ANGELO

46 KM SOUTHEAST OF BARI

55 KM NORTHEAST OF FOGGIA ON SS 272

LA PORTA VECCHIA 2004

Bed and breakfast
Via Peroscia 21
Tel. 080 802690-339 8491175-349 7766042
Fax 080 9371489
E-mail: bed&breakfast@laportavecchia.it
Internet: www.laportavecchia.it
Open all year round

MEDIOEVO

Restaurant
Via Castello 21
Tel. 0884 565356
Closed Monday, never in summer
Open: lunch and dinner
Holidays: February 15-28 and November 15-30
Seating: 60
Prices: 26-35 euros, wine excluded
All major credit cards

This B&B run by Mina is in the center of Monopoli, just a stone's throw from the sea and a stretch of public beach. It is located in a 17th-century building, which was once housed the curia of the nearby church of San Leonardo. After being fully restored last year, the B&B now consists of four guest rooms, a small lounge on a mezzanine floor and two terraces overlooking the coast below. Depending on the time of year, breakfast is served either in the small room or on the terraces. Breakfast includes fresh fruit juices and hot drinks, doughnuts, cakes and homemade jams. You can benefit from the place's central position to visit a number of the town's historical buildings, such as the church of Santa Maria degli Amalfitani and the Aragonese castle.

• 2 double and 2 triple rooms, with bathroom, air conditioning, television; 1 with balcony • Prices: double for single use 35-45 euros, double 60-80, triple 70-100, including breakfast • Credit cards: none • Free public car park 150 meters away. No animals allowed. Owners present 8am-1pm • Breakfast room, sitting room and reading room. Terrace

Pasquale Mazzone, owner of the Medioevo, does it the hard way by painstakingly sourcing the best local products. The menu – actually prepared by chef Tonino Palumbo – begins with vegetable antipasti and the superb **cured meats**, produced from the meat of free-range pigs. The line-up of firsts is varied and wide-ranging, focusing particularly on the local territory. To start, choose a fresh pasta like **orecchiette al ragù paesano** (but also with cime di rape, turnip tops, or zucchini flowers), troccoli (**'ndruccele**) **with a tomato and Cacioricotta cheese sauce** – but sometimes with cuttlefish ragù spiced with wild fennel – fettuccine (lajine) with chickpeas and baccalà ragù (with porcini mushrooms in season). Don't miss the soups like the fava and wild chicory, or **pancotto with cabbage, potatoes and fava beans**.
Continue with **grilled lamb** or lamb al profumo del Gargano, goat stew and roulades (**turcinieddi**) alla Medioevo. When the sea is generous there's excellent stuffed cuttlefish, fritto misto or a platter of grilled seafood. The cheese board offers a good selection from local producers. You can try the **Caciocavallo** grilled. The village's traditional desserts are divine. There are **almond-filled wafers**, mostaccioli, peperati, dried figs with almonds and walnuts doused with rum served with artisan gelato.
There are a few home-made liqueurs (with pomegranate peel, walnuts, apple seeds, olive and orange leaves) and a wine list that includes a pleasant Montepulciano they make themselves and some good Puglia wines and other Italian labels.

MOTTOLA
Contrada Pandaro

NOCI

MASSERIA COLOMBO

L'ANTICA LOCANDA

Holiday farm
Strada Statale 377 Noci-Mottola km 38,800
Tel. 080 5242431-348 3434178
Fax 080 5242431
E-mail: info@masseriacolombo.it
Internet: www.masseriacolombo.it
Closed from 1 February to Easter

Osteria
Via Santo Spirito 49
Tel. 080 4972460
Closed Sunday evening and Tuesday
Open: lunch and dinner
Holidays: none
Seating: 60
Prices: 28-30 euros, wine excluded
Credit cards: MC, Visa

Benedetto Siciliani has been running this 17th-century farm, a sprawling complex consisting of the main residence and some recently restored trulli which are now used to offer B&B accommodation, for some years now. All the rooms, which have bare stone walls, have a day zone complete with kitchenette. Another distinguishing feature of the farm is its herd of Podolic cattle, used for beef and dairy production. Hunters can shoot quail, woodcock and game on this 650-hectare estate, or alternatively search for mushrooms and aromatic herbs. There is no common breakfast room which is served individually in your trullo from 7.30-10am as requested. Breakfast consists of the usual hot drinks, homemade ricotta, jams, cakes and biscuits.

• 4 double rooms and 1 four-bedded room, with bathroom, fridge, television, kitchenette • Prices: double for single use 45-50 euros, double 80-100 (supplement of 30 euros for extra bed), including breakfast • Credit cards: all, except for DC, Bancomat • 1 room with access to the mobility challenged. Outdoor parking on premises. Small pets welcome. Owners always present • Park, veranda

Noci is halfway between Bari and Taranto, on a hill in a part of the Murge area much visited by tourists coming to see the trulli and caves. The oldest part of the village is clustered around the Chiesa Madre, an area characterized by narrow, tortuous streets with their old farmers' homes, historic noble palazzos marked by a unified elegance and numerous religious shrines. Pasquale Fatalino's commendable osteria is located in this fascinating setting. A lot of thought has gone into the furnishings, the service is good and the cuisine is respectful of traditions and everything the region has to offer.

To start, a taste of the local cured meats and fresh cheeses selected by the owner is almost mandatory, punctuated by various types of preserves in oil and **fried lampascioni onions al vincotto**. But the dried horsemeat straccetti and meatballs are interesting too. First courses are **orecchiette with cime di rape** (turnip tops), lampascioni soup with cheese, parsley and whipped egg, fava purée and chicory or **cicorielle a'zise** (boiled in meat stock). Various types of meat take pride of place for the main course and all dishes undergo a long and very careful preparation: there's tripe stew, **oven-roasted lamb** with artichokes and lampascioni, **boned rabbit** cooked with Murgia herbs and, in summer, mutton cooked in the pot. There isn't a wide choice of desserts but they are all very well made.

The wine list offers a carefully considered selection of mainly regional labels.

NOCI

ORSARA DI PUGLIA

50 KM SOUTHEAST OF BARI SS 634

44 KM SOUTH OF FOGGIA ON SS 90

MASSERIA ABATE

PEPPE ZULLO

4-Star hotel
Strada Provinciale for Massafra, km 0,300
Tel. 080 4978288
Fax 080 4978023
E-mail: info@abatemasseria.it
Internet: www.abatemasseria.it
Closed in January and February

Restaurant with rooms
Via Piano Paradiso
Tel. 0881 964763
Closed Tuesday
Open: lunch only
Holidays: January 15-31 and in November
Seating: 60 + 40 outside
Prices: 26-35 euros, wine excluded
All credit cards

This is an 18th-century farm with trulli, surrounded by the countryside of the Alta Murgia only about 30 kilometers from the beaches of Polignano and Monopoli. It took two years to finish the restoration project: spaces that were previously farmyards and stables are now used to serve breakfast (yogurt, bread, cakes, homemade biscuits, coffee, tea, fruit juice, freshly squeezed juice, seasonal fruit) and as lounges. The rooms are situated partly in the old mangers and partly in the trulli. The restaurant, also open to the public, serves exquisite local dishes (average 30 euros, excluding wine; half-board supplement 25 euros per person) and excellent pizzas. The Tinelli family will guide you on walks through the woods of the estate where you can meet wild horses and enjoy the tranquility of the countryside. Minimum stay of one week in July and August.

• 8 double rooms, with bathroom, air-conditioning, small garden or terrace, fridge, satellite TV, modem connection • Prices: double for single use 45-72 euros, in the trulli 70-115, double 70-112, in the trulli 110-186 (40-60 euros supplement for extra bed), including breakfast • Credit cards: all, Bancomat • 1 room with facilities for the mobility challenged. Outdoor car park on premises. No animals allowed. 24-hour concierge service • Bar, restaurant. Sun patio. Swimming pool, tennis court

Located in the mountains and woods of the southern part of the Daunia area, Orsara is known for its agriculture, its production of excellent cured meats and, in recent years, for its summer jazz festival. Peppe Zullo is the dynamic owner of this restaurant whose cuisine reflects local traditions (this is an area influenced by nearby Campania). Hence extensive use of meat and vegetables and a lot of room for creativity. In addition to the restaurant, Peppe runs the wine cellar, the five guest rooms, the display of products (the highlight: 30 heirloom varieties of apple that have been saved from exinction) and the herb garden. He also puts the final touches on the selection of cured meats and cheeses, which might include Cacioricotta, Caciocavallo, Pecorino and Caciopuleo (goat's milk cheese spiced with mint).
Wild asparagus with mint, **roulades of eggplant with Cacioricotta** and lamb livers spiced with bay leaf are the most common antipasti. First courses are **orecchiette with chickpeas and borage**, cavatelli with baccalà and artichokes, **paccheri with cotechino** and wild fennel and fusilli with wild boar sauce. Among the main courses we'd suggest the **roast kid and potatoes** cooked under hot ashes, lamb spiced with thyme or millefoglie of wild boar or veal with Caciocavallo and vegetables. To finish, try **pastiera orsarese**, tarts (with wild berries and cuccuzzare apples) or pupatielli (short pastry biscuits). The wine list is excellent, with all the top Puglia and other southern Italian labels, other prestigious Italian wines and a wide selection of liqueurs.

35 KM NORTH OF BRINDISI

MASSERIA LAMACAVALLO

MASSERIA RIENZO

🔑 Holiday farm
Strada Provinciale Ostuni-Torre Pozzella km 4
Tel. 0831 330703-333 4143105
Fax 0831 330703
E-mail: vacanze@lamacavallo.com
Internet: www.lamacavallo.com
Open all year round

🔑 Holiday farm
Contrada Rienzo 8
Tel. and fax 0831 304548
E-mail: info@masseriarienzo.com
Internet: www.masseriarienzo.com
Open from March to October

This is a typical Brindisi farm, surrounded by olive groves and run by Etta and Cosimo Putignano. Like all the other houses in the area, it is whitewashed, its architecture a blend of Baroque and Saracen. It offers a choice of accommodation, ranging from the lamie, typical single storey buildings, to apartments with tasteful, practical furnishings. Each apartment has a wide terrace with a pergola and prices depend on the size and the number of occupants. The farm is only five kilometers from the sea and has an old oil mill where you can still see the ancient equipment used to produce the extra virgin olive oil that guests can buy from the farm, together with all kinds of preserves, pickles, vegetables and olives in brine, dried oven-baked figs, almonds and fruit. In the summer, special barbecues are organized for the guests in the courtyard of the farm with grilled meat and fish. Minimum stay of one week in July and August.

• 7 apartments (2-4 persons) with bathroom, fridge, television, kitchenette • Prices: double for single use and double 65-120 euros, four-bedded rooms 120; breakfast 3 euros per person • Credit cards: none • 2 apartments with access to the mobility challenged. Covered car park on premises. Small pets allowed. Owners are always present • Bar. Sitting room, reading room, TV room. Park

Situated halfway between Ostuni and the sea, the farm was an oil mill in the 18th-century but was later rebuilt and converted into an aristocratic residence. The property, which is surrounded by fields growing olives, fruit and vegetables, was bought by the Zizzi family. The rooms are tastefully decorated with extensive use of fine materials, furniture and fabrics. The same can be said for the common spaces, including the conservatory which is decorated with a late 19th-century tapestry. Outside, guests can relax in the garden or enjoy the sun beside the pool. Breakfast is served in the restaurant or on small tables outside and includes an excellent choice of home-baked cakes. The restaurant serves traditional local dishes (about 20 euros for guests and 30 euros for visitors). Minimum stay of one week in July and August.

• 4 double rooms and 1 suite, with bathroom • Prices: double for single use 60 euros, double 90-120, suite 150, including breakfast • Credit cards: none • Outdoor car park on premises. No pets allowed. Owners always present • Restaurant. Sitting room. Garden, sun patio. Swimming pool

OSTUNI
Tolla

OTRANTO
Porto Badisco

35 km NORTH OF BRINDISI SS 16

50 km SOUTHEAST OF LECCE SS 16 OR 543 AND 611

MASSERIA TOLLA

Bed and breakfast
Contrada Tolla
Tel. 339 3332646-328 5324101
E-mail: info@masseriatolla.it
Internet: www.masseriatolla.it
Open in January, from April to
September, and in December

MASSERIA PANAREO

2-star Hotel
Litoranea Otranto-Santa Cesarea Terme
Tel. 0836 812999-338 3712326
Fax 0836 812999
E-mail: alessandro.zezza@tin.it
Internet: www.masseriapanareo.com
Closed in November

You reach this B&B by driving along the provincial road to Martina Franca and then turning onto the tree-lined private drive. It is housed in an early 19th-century farm which was bought by the Laveneziana family and recently restored. The rooms are furnished in a minimalist style, in harmony with the plainness of the exterior and the common spaces. In a small room, dominated by a period dresser, you will be served an abundant buffet-style breakfast, including hot drinks, cakes and jam. Guests can relax by walking in the countryside or visiting the nearby towns of Ostuni and Martina Franca. Do not be put off by the words written on the church opposite the B&B —'No shelter offered here' —because Giuseppe and Manuela are extremely hospitable. Minimum stay of five days in August.

• 4 double rooms, with bathroom • Prices: double for single use 40-55 euros, double 60-90 (supplement of 20-28 euros for extra bed), including breakfast • Credit cards: none • Structure with access to the mobility challenged. Outdoor car park on premises. No pets allowed. Owners always present • Breakfast room with TV corner. Garden

Surrounded by five hectares of Mediterranean maquis and by an orchard, Masseria Panareo is only a short distance from Otranto's beaches. Formerly a country house, it was turned into a hotel in 1987 by the Zezza family, who still run it today. The rooms are furnished in a sober style with arte povera furniture and wrought-iron beds; some have a splendid view of the sea. The attractive restaurant with its terracotta floor and stone ceiling serves a range of typical local dishes, served with a creative touch (average 25-30 euros, excluding wine). For breakfast there's a choice of home-baked cakes. Guests can explore the park around the farm and other nearby sites where they will discover grottos dating back to 4000 BC, a Messapic cemetery that is difficult to date, and the ruins of the monastery of San Nicola di Casole. Minimum stay of one week in July and August.

• 17 double rooms, with bathroom, television; some with balcony • Prices: double for single use 60-83 euros, double 80-110 (supplement of 28-38 euros for extra bed), including breakfast • Credit cards: all, Bancomat • 1 room with facilities for the mobility challenged. Outdoor car park on premises. No animals allowed. Owners always present • Bar, restaurant. Reading room, TV room. Park

PATÙ

POGGIARDO

RUA DE LI TRAVAJ

LA PIAZZA

Trattoria
Piazza Indipendenza
Tel. 349 0584531
Closed Wednesday, never in summer
Open: dinner, November-June
Sunday also lunch
Holidays: October
Seating: 35 + 40 outside
Prices: 20-22 euros
All major credit cards

Trattoria
Piazza Umberto I 13
Tel. 0836 901925-339 7777073
Closed Thursday, never in summer
Open: dinner, lunch only if reserved ahead
Holidays: variable in winter
Seating: 35 + 60 outside
Prices: 21-26 euros, wine excluded
All major credit cards

When you reach Capo di Leuca, the most southerly point of the heel of the Italian boot, you can make a detour to Veretum, once an important Messapic settlement. Today the only remaining monument, known as Centopietre, is a must-see. It's a small rectangular building, originally a tomb dating from the 9th century built with around 100 blocks of stone probably taken from a previous Roman building.

In the center of the village of Patù, in Piazza Indipendenza near the 17th-century church of San Michele, lies this delightful trattoria with two small dining rooms. In the room next to the kitchen there's an open fire to warm up the evenings in winter while in summer you can eat outside in the lovely inner courtyard.

In the kitchen is Fiorina, who was born in Cuneo but now prepares traditional Salento dishes with tremendous skill, while Gino De Salve organizes the impeccable service in the front of the house. He'll offer you a series of antipasti, like **tomato and pepper scattarisciati** (a hot pepper sauce you spread on bread), potato pitta, pizza rustica with onion, capers and olives, onion or spinach omelets. For firsts, there's **scurdijata** (peas, turnips and fried bread), **baked beans with fried peppers**, spelt and bean soup, home-made pasta – orecchiette and sagne 'ncannulate – with tomato sauce and Cacioricotta or ricotta 'scante. Main courses include **meatloaf with chicory**, horsemeat stew, **rabbit alla cacciatora**, baccalà with sponzali (onions) and braised beef al Negramaro. Normally you can finish off the meal with traditional cookies, a glass of Moscato and home-made liqueurs (bay leaf or blueberry). The wine list is acceptable and growing all the time.

Stefano Nuzzo and his wife Kledya run this trattoria in a lovely piazza in Poggiardo, just a few minutes drive from the splendid seaside resorts of Castro and Santa Cesarea. You go through the bar to get to the small dining room. It's a friendly place even if simply furnished and the tables are perhaps a bit too close together, but with a nice open fire that warms up the room in fall and winter.

The cuisine ranges from traditional to innovative, although the ingredients are always really top quality. There's a very wide choice of antipasti, **potato croquettes**, fennel au gratin and fried, chicory and pecorino rissoles, cauliflower au gratin with anchovies and cherry tomatoes, **Savoy cabbage roulades** stuffed with ground pork, fava purée with black mussels and ricotta rissoles with pomegranate jam. First courses are perhaps more traditional: impepata of mussels, **orecchiette alla salentina**, **sagne torte con ricotta scante**, maccheroncini with zucchini and tuna and **cecamariti** (a soup made from peas, turnips and pieces of fried bread). For your main course, choose from both meat and fish dishes like prawns cooked in fava purée, the **fried fish platter** from the day's catch, **roast lamb and potatoes** and meatballs in tomato sauce. There's semifreddo alla cupeta and homemade cookies for dessert.

The wine list offers a good selection of Puglia labels and mark-ups are reasonable.

PUTIGNANO

IL CANTINONE

Trattoria-pizzeria
Via Arco San Lorenzo 1
Tel. 080 4913378
Closed Tuesday
Open: lunch and dinner
Holidays: 2 weeks in July
Seating: 180
Prices: 25-30 euros, wine excluded
All credit cards

Putignano lies at the heart of an area with a strong vocation for tourism. It's very near to some of the prettiest villages in the Valle d'Itria but also a place with an outstanding entrepreneurial spirit in both the agricultural and textile sectors. There's a unique atmosphere in the town during Carnival – one of the most picturesque in Italy – when the entire population is involved in celebrations of what must originally have been a pagan rite. Inside the lovely historic center, just a stone's throw from the cathedral, is Antonello Romanazzi's place. Il Cantinone is furnished in a way that gives it a medieval atmosphere, with its cross-vaulted ceilings, dressed stone walls and rustic wooden tables in keeping with the setting. Of course, the food here is very closely linked to the region in terms of ingredients and attention to seasons.

As per tradition there are many filling and very tasty antipasti such as grilled vegetables, **Caciocavallo cheese** grilled over an open fire, grilled pork belly, local fresh cheeses and cured meats. Among first courses, **baccalà and potatoes**, **orecchiette with ragù** and spaghetti with olives, anchovies and fried breadcrumbs. In the right season there are also homemade pastas served with game sauces (wild boar or hare). **Meat** plays a starring role in main courses and is the real specialty here: horsemeat, pork, the typical **sausage** and lamb, all cooked on a fire right in front of you. Be sure to try the tripe or **donkey brasciole** too.

Desserts are prepared according to festive occasions and the places they are associated with. There are some made with almonds or dried figs at Christmas and **pettole** at Carnival time. The wine list has a good selection of regional labels.

RUTIGLIANO

LAMA SAN GIORGIO

Holiday farm
Strada Provinciale Rutigliano-
Adelfia, km 8,700
Tel. 080 4761609-348 3342889
Fax 080 5237535
E-mail: giovanniscianatico@tin.it
Internet: www.lamasangiorgio.it
Open all year round

The farmhouse, which was built in the early 19th century and completed in the first decade of the last, was purchased by Nicola Didonna in 1970 and returned to its ancient splendor following a meticulous restoration project that highlights the original characteristics of the structure. It is located on the Scianatico farm, which grows grapes for eating and wine-making, olives for oil-making and eating, and also cherries.

Furnished with period pieces, the farmhouse is a peaceful place to stay, and also offers excellent cooking, including rustic but refined dishes, enhanced by local produce (average 25-30 euros, 18 euros for farm guests). Wide choice of walks and trips in the vicinity, plus free beach only 7 kilometers away at Torre a Mare.

• 3 double rooms and 4 triples, with bathroom, television • Prices: double for single use 60 euros, double 70, triple 90, including breakfast • All major credit cards, Bancomat • Uncovered car park on premises. No animals allowed. Owners always available • Restaurant, TV room. Playground. Beach (7 km)

Ruvo di Puglia

RISTOR 🍾

Restaurant
Via Alberto Mario 36-38
Tel. 080 3613736
Closed Monday
Open: lunch and dinner
Holidays: July
Seating: 40
Prices: 30-32 euros, wine excluded
All major credit cards

At the foot of the Murge hills, Ruvo nestles among vineyards and olive groves. Once known for producing ceramics, Ruvo still hosts an impressive collection at the Jatta National Museum, which, along with the limestone Romanesque cathedral, warrants a visit.

For a pleasant break, go to this small, attractive restaurant run by the Saulle family: Teo services the dining room, while his brother Michele runs the kitchen with his mother and father. Their dishes bring out all the aromas of the Murge, a territory that provides some interesting ingredients. The antipasti are traditional: sheep's milk ricotta cheese, **burratine**, smoked horsemeat fillet, zucchini flowers stuffed with fresh sausage and Murgia cheeses, homemade **focaccia farcita**. Among the first courses are the classic **cavatelli with cardoncelli mushrooms**, orecchiette with tomato and wild asparagus, **fava purée with tender wild chicory** and fettuccine with duck ragù and smoked Scamorza cheese. After that come local meats cooked over an open fire, such as **roast leg of lamb** with Murgia herbs, or **horsemeat chops** with ragù. There are some interesting fish dishes, too. A successful Saulle family original is the **octopus rissoles**, browned and served with fresh tomatoes. For dessert, the caramelized zucchini flowers filled with ricotta cheese and the chocolate coated eggplant chips combine tradition and creativity.

The wine list features the best Puglia wines and an interesting selection of other Italian labels. Given the small number of tables, we recommend reservations.

U.P.E.P.I.D.D.E. 🍾

Restaurant
Via Sant'Agnese 2
Tel. 080 3613879
Closed Monday
Open: lunch and dinner
Holidays: between July and August
Seating: 60
Prices: 30 euros, wine excluded
All major credit cards

This restaurant is located alongside the splendid Aragonese walls, just steps away from the historic center, which is itself worth visiting for its beauty and its excellent state of preservation. What we especially like about it is its ambience and its wholesome traditional food. Owner Dino Saulle is an important figure in the restaurant trade in Puglia who knows how to give a friendly welcome and dish out simplicity with a touch of invention.

Have a seat in one of the small dining rooms, under a barrel-vaulted ceiling, and the antipasti will soon start to arrive: **parmigiana di melanzane**, cardoncelli mushrooms (cultivated) with pecorino and **Caciocavallo cheese grilled over an open fire**, vegetables either grilled or preserved in olive oil, local guanciale bacon with sweet corn and onions, fresh cheeses and warm terrines. Traditional Puglia dishes available for your first course include **orecchiette with a mixed meat ragù**, **cavatelli with mussels and beans**, fava purée and chicory, home-made pasta with cardoncelli mushrooms or **mushroom gnocchetti with fava bean purée**.

Broiled sausages, a **mixed grill** of excellent meats, **horsemeat brasciole** and **gnumeridd'** (roulades made with lamb giblets) are just a few of the main course dishes. After that come excellent **seasoned cheeses** or homemade desserts, and Dino knows best as far as these are concerned.

The wine cellar is expanding: the wine list includes interesting regional and other Italian labels, and the prices are very reasonable.

San Giovanni Rotondo

Antica Piazetta

⌒ Restaurant
Via al Mercato 13
Tel. 0882 451920
Closed Wednesday
Open: lunch and dinner
Holidays: July 1-15, January 15-31
Seating: 80
Prices: 25-30 euros
All major credit cards

The quality of the food offered in this area has inevitably been affected by tourism and the religious traffic that has increased even further since the beatification of Padre Pio da Pietralcina. And yet there are exceptions that prove the rule – for instance, this very unusual restaurant right in the historic center, housed in a cleverly restored old cinema. It's the brainchild of the Di Maggio and Petruccelli families, who have managed to create appropriate settings to enjoy traditional dishes in what were previously the seating and gallery areas. The quality and freshness of the ingredients are beyond dispute: the chefs use what is available that day in the market, products from local vegetable gardens and the nearby port of Manfredonia. So for antipasti you'll be able to choose from **fried vegetables**, cured meats, aged and **fresh cheeses**, really fresh **shellfish**, light fried fish platter and soups. The **fresh pastas** on the menu for first courses are homemade and served with **cime di rape (turnip tops) and beans**, meat ragù or braciole with local vegetables. For your main course don't miss one of the various **oven-roasted dishes** such as baccalà and potatoes, lamb, potatoes and onions or turbot, potatoes and herbs. Another dish to taste when it's available is **musciska**, spiced and dried mutton or horsemeat served grilled and cut up into strips. To finish, a few traditional desserts.

The wine list features some good regional and other Italian labels, plus there are various quality liqueurs and regional beers.

Sannicandro Garganico

La Costa

⌒ Restaurant
Via Magenta 11-15
Tel. 0882 471768-329 2098139
Closed Monday
Open: lunch and dinner
Holidays: none
Seating: 40
Prices: 25-30 euros, wine excluded
All major credit cards

Sannicandro is a medieval village sitting on a low hill overlooking the Lesina and Varano lakes. The center is dominated by the castle built for Federico II. The imposing square fortress has round or square towers at the corners. White-walled constructions line the center's quaint streets, paved with local stone, and in one of them stands a pleasant, friendly restaurant where Franchino Sticozzi oversees both the service and the kitchen.

The antipasti are drawn alternately from the land and the sea, with grilled vegetables, **sausage** spiced with wild fennel and bruschette. The bread used for the latter is made by a woman named Maria in the traditional manner using a starter and is cooked in a wood-fired oven. First courses include **pancotto with vegetables**, orecchiette with Garganico goat sauce (must be ordered in advance), farfalle with scampi and watercress, **linguine with Lesina eel sauce** (Slow Food Presidium), brodetto dell'Adriatico (fish soup) and fava purée with chicory. Apart from a few dishes, like the fried fish platter or seared prawns, the majority of main course dishes focus on local meat, mainly **lamb** cooked in various ways: with asparagus and wild fennel, oven-roasted or simmered in wine with mixed meats. Unusual specialties: veal **musciska** (traditional dried meat), torcinello with pancetta and pork and eel or **lake mullet alla pescatora**.

There's a good selection of local cheeses and only a few desserts, but all of them local favorites like pupurato, fig honey and ricotta cheese mousse.

The wine list offers mainly regional wines.

SAN PANCRAZIO SALENTINO
Torrevecchia

38 KM SOUTH OF BRINDISI

TORREVECCHIA

Holiday farm
Contrada Torrevecchia, provincial road for Avetrana
Tel. 338 8287360
Fax 0831 667522-667450
E-mail: info@torrevecchia.com
Internet: www.torrevecchia.com
Open all year round

This 14th-century farmhouse was lovingly restored ten years ago and stands beside a 7th-century crypt that contains the remains of Byzantine frescoes. The rooms are simply and tastefully furnished. The restaurant, which is also open to the public, offers typical regional dishes made using organic produce from the farm (average 20 euros, half-board 57-68 euros). There are endless opportunities for leisure activities, including walks and trips on bikes, on horseback or by gig. In addition, some of the best-known seaside resorts in Puglia, including Porto Cesareo, Santa Caterina and Gallipoli, are only about ten kilometers away. Minimum stay of one week in August.

• 7 double rooms and 2 suites (3 persons), with bathroom, air-conditioning, mini-bar, television • Prices: double for single use 42-52 euros, double 84-104, suite 126-156, including breakfast • Credit cards: none • Outdoor car park on premises. Small pets allowed. Owners always present • Restaurant. Reading room. Swimming pool, tennis court, five-a-side pitch, boules court

SAN SEVERO

29 KM NORTHWEST OF FOGGIA ON SS 16 OR A 14

FOSSA DEL GRANO

Osteria
Via Minuziano 63
Tel. 0882 241122
Closed Tuesday, Saturday and Sunday from July through August
Open: lunch and dinner
Holidays: none
Seating: 30
Prices: 25-30 euros, wine excluded
All major credit cards

San Severo is an example of how the big agricultural towns in the Tavoliere area have been centers of trade, culture, and population flows between the three sub-regions (which also include Gargano and Subappennino) of the Capitanata area. This is because of the complexity of the agricultural food chain. The osteria serves as the meeting place of wheat farmers, shepherds and winemakers, where ideas cultivated by the rich diversity of the land here can be gathered and transmitted. Here, water and land, plains and mountains intersect, and the resources of lakes and the sea coexist with excellent horticultural products and extraordinary specialties in animal husbandry.
The dishes that Gino and Carlo bring to the dining room and that Tonia and Giuseppe – part of the same family – prepare in the kitchen faithfully reflect the this region and its gastronomic tradition. There's classic **cicatelli di grano arso with arugula and toasted ricotta** and **pot-roasted leg of lamb**, dishes that are part of tradition or are linked to what the local market offers. All are presented with a creative touch. Examples include **bran with shellfish and saffron**, **squid soup with fava purée** and **Caciocavallo podolico pie**. Homemade pastas with the season's vegetables, homemade desserts, and the best labels from Daunia and the rest of Puglia complete a menu that is neither ordinary nor over-the-top.

La Mollica di Alfredo Mennelli, Via Soccorso 150, sells an excellent selection of cheeses and cured meats, including some Slow Food Presidia.

San Severo

29 km north of Foggia on SS 16 or A 14

Locanda di Bacco

🍲 Osteria
Via Soccorso 142
Tel. 0882 226121
Closed Sunday evening and Monday
Open: lunch and dinner
Holidays: August
Seating: 40
Prices: 25-30 euros, wine excluded
All major credit cards

As time has passed, the endless plain known as the Tavoliere has given more space to the cultivation of olives and table grapes. Particularly suitable for growing durum wheat, the variety used mainly to produce pasta, this area is changing, and the large silos still visible here and there are now vestiges of the past. Wheat has had a strong influence on local gastronomic traditions, which are based on the production of bread and various types of homemade pasta. These items feature prominently at this osteria, though it is best known for its meat dishes. Seafood also makes an appearance on the menu in antipasti like **octopus cooked in red wine** and stuffed mussels. This osteria's most famous dish, one that symbolizes the gastronomic wisdom of farmers who made a virtue of necessity, is without a doubt the **pancotto**, a vegetable and stale bread soup prepared in a number of ways depending on the season. Pastas here include **orecchiette with horsemeat ragù** and **cecatelli with mussels**, cherry tomatoes and wild fennel. You can choose fish (cooked in salt or baked in the oven), but we highly recommend a meat dish for your main course: tripe, **horsemeat roulades** or a platter of grilled meats. The desserts are good, as is the wine list, consisting of mostly regional labels.

San Vito dei Normanni
Deserto

21 km west of Brindisi

Tenuta Deserto

🔑 Holiday farm
Contrada Deserto
Tel. 0831 983062-347 9141045- 335 8135384
Fax 0831 983062
E-mail: info@tenutadeserto.it
Internet: www.tenutadeserto.it
Open all year round

Not far from San Vito dei Normanni, you come to the Tenuta Deserto, surrounded by 70 hectares of olive groves and woods of oak, ilex, pine and eucalyptus. The first building you see as you come up the drive leading to the estate is a small chapel, then you'll notice the 17th-century watchtower, the stables, the main house, the trullo and other recently restored residential buildings. Well furnished and characterized by their vault ceilings, the apartments are available in different sizes and sleep between two and eight people. They can also be rented for a single night, but the prices are much better value for weekly stays. Breakfast includes milk, tea, coffee, fruit juices, yogurt, jam, homemade pies and doughnuts, not to mention the cured meats and local cheeses. On the farm, you can buy extra virgin olive oil, preserves, wine and eggs.

• 12 apartments (2-8 persons) with bathroom, kitchen; some with air-conditioning • Prices: 48 euros per person, including breakfast • Credit cards: Visa, MC, Bancomat • A number of apartments have access to the mobility challenged. Outdoor car park on premises. Small pets welcome. Owners present 8am-midnight • Breakfast room, reading room and TV. Garden. Swimming pool

TARANTO

TRATTORIA GESÙ CRISTO

🍲 Trattoria
Via Battisti 8
Tel. 099 4777253
Closed Sunday dinner and Monday
Open: lunch and dinner
Holidays: none
Seating: 100
Prices: 28-30 euros, wine excluded
All major credit cards, Bancomat

Taranto is probably best known for its steelworks and its naval base, but the city also has a softer side. The National Archeological Museum, for example, houses exhibits on the art and culture of Magna Graecia, and you can find many other charms just by walking round the old part of the city, Pasquale and Alessandro Caso faithfully continue to operate the osteria their grandfather (nicknamed Jesus Christ... honestly!) opened about 60 years ago. The three dining rooms are festooned with representations of the Passion of the Christ, not so surprising given the place's name.

The best fare here is the seafood; and indeed, the fishmonger next door is owned by the same family. The antipasti start arriving as soon as you sit down: these include the classic octopus salad alla luciana, casseroled cuttlefish with tomato sauce and **mussels** au gratin (Taranto mussels are smaller than the norm). There's a very tasty **impepata of shellfish** and, when the catch permits, marinated anchovies. Among the first courses: **tubetti with mussels** in tomato sauce, linguine with clams and risotto alla pescatora. **Fish cooked over an open fire** stands out among the main courses, which also include white sea bream, bass and gilthead. The red mullet is good, either grilled or cooked in the oven, and the **mixed fried fish platter** is a must.

The choice of desserts varies, but the best among them are the fruit tarts with gelato and pralines. There are few wines offered; most people drink the house wine. In all honesty, the service could be improved, but given the quality of the food here, one can turn the other cheek.

TAVIANO

47 KM SOUTHWEST OF LECCE

A CASA TU MARTINU 🐌

🍲 Osteria with rooms
Via Corsica 95
Tel. 0833 913652
Closed Monday, never in summer
Open: lunch and dinner, in summer dinner only
Holidays: September 20-October 5
Seating: 70 + 60 outside
Prices: 20-25 euros, wine excluded
All major credit cards

You'll find this picturesqe spot inland of Gallipoli, just a few kilometers from the Lido Pizzo beach. Owner Vincenzo Portaccio renovated an 18th-century building to house his osteria, leaving many of the original features intact. The result is that diners can admire the star-vaulted ceiling, the sideboards built into the walls, the old-fashioned electrical system, and the enormous open fire in one dining room that burns all winter long. In the summer, the food is served in the shade of a small citrus grove in the courtyard of the inn that was added here two years ago.

The cuisine is traditional Salentine, with a menu that changes with the seasons. You start with a buffet of antipasti, with excellent **pettuline** served with vincotto, potato croquettes, rice arancini and meatballs. Next come the first course dishes, which include **pasta 'mmaritata with sauce and strong ricotta cheese**, 'ciceri e tria', minchiareddhi d'orzo, **sagne 'ncannulate**, vegetable-based dishes like pasta'e mugnuli, fava purée and chicory with fried bread or a tasty **chard and meatball soup**. Main courses are almost exclusively meat-based, with **turcinieddhi of lamb**, stewed horsemeat and a grilled meat platter with turnips and wild chicory on the side. In summer – catch permitting – and on Tuesdays and Fridays in winter, there's fish: tubettini with grouper sauce, **fried fish platter**, or fish soup, which must be ordered in advance. There's also a wide selection of traditional home-made desserts, such as almond cake, spumone, fruit and jam tarts and **torta pasticciotto**.

The wine list includes the best regional labels and quite a good selection of other Italian wines.

Uggiano La Chiesa

Masseria Gattamora

3-Star hotel
Via Campo Sportivo 33
Tel. 0836 817936
Fax 0836 814542
E-mail: masseriagattamora@libero.it
Internet: www.gattamora.it
Open all year round

Gattamora is a 19th-century farmhouse which was turned into a hotel in 2000. The rooms, furnished in sober, elegant style with period furniture and wrought-iron beds, now occupy what was formerly the oil mill. The reading room is very welcoming with a fireplace and comfortable armchairs. The restaurant is open to the public and is housed in what were once the stables and haylofts, which still feature their characteristic vaulted ceilings (about 28 euros, excluding wine; half-board supplement 25 euros per person): the menu includes both meat and fish dishes. The buffet breakfast is served in the restaurant in winter and under a pergola in summer: it includes both sweet and savory foods, many of which are home-made. The Masseria often organizes sailing trips along the Salento coast.

• 11 double rooms, with bathroom, air conditioning, television, modem connection • Prices: double for single use 40-60, double 70-100 euros (supplement of 20 euros for extra bed), including breakfast • Credit cards: all, including Bancomat • 2 rooms with facilities for the mobility challenged. Outdoor car park on premises. No pets allowed. Owners always present • Restaurant. Reading room. Garden, pinewood. Swimming pool

Veglie

Casa Porcara

Holiday farm
Strada provinciale Veglie-Monteruga km 2,5
Tel. 0832 326402-360 869074
Fax 0832 244085
E-mail: info@casaporcara.it
Internet: www.casaporcara.it
Open from March to end of October and at Christmas

In addition to the rooms and apartments for guests, the farm has set up a roomy education center in a building that once used to store dried tobacco. The rooms, which are all bright and soberly furnished, are inside the original farmhouse and in the dairies where cheese used to be made. Outside, you can explore the extensive property owned by the Costantini family, using the bicycles which are made available. Breakfast consists of fresh dairy produce, jams made from organic fruit, home-made bread and pies, and is served in the restaurant, with its beautiful wooden floors and brick vaults. The restaurant is also open to the public, evenings only (20 euros, excluding wine).

• 6 double and 3 triple rooms, with bathroom, fridge, television; 2 apartments (3-4 persons) with kitchenette • Prices: double for single use 27-32 euros, double 54-64, triple 69-82, apartment 90-110 per person (supplement of 17-20 euros for extra bed), including breakfast • Credit cards: all, Bancomat • Access to the mobility challenged, 2 apartments specially equipped. Outdoor car park on premises. Small pets allowed. Owners present 7am-9 pm • Corner bar, restaurant. Reading room. Conference room. Garden

CAMPANIA

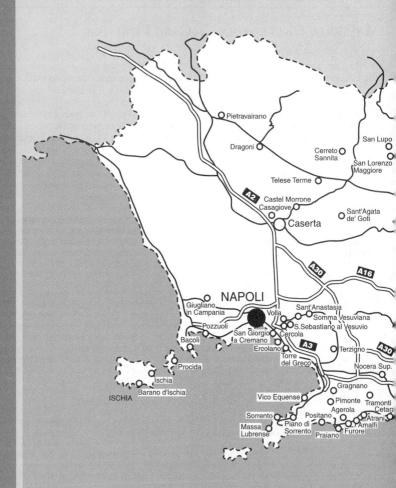

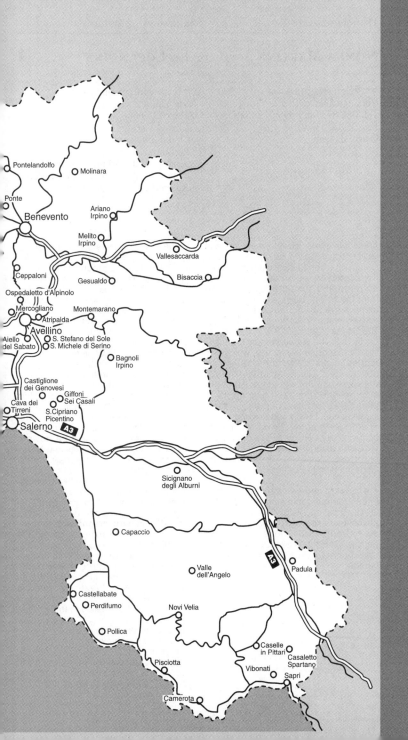

AGEROLA

NONNA MARTINA

Bed and breakfast
Via degli Ontanelli 3
Tel. 081 8731495-339 2724829
Fax 081 8731495
Open all year

Agerola is a true 'slow' town, in terms of its ties with the surrounding territory and its firm intention to keep traditions alive. It's located on the border between the Sorrento and Amalfi peninsulas and from the town, driving through Furore along a road with breathtaking views, you will reach Amalfi in just 20 minutes. The Nonna Martina B&B is in a small, recently built villa surrounded by greenery. Nicola manages the facility, which has four spacious rooms furnished in arte povera style. Nicola's mother Martina, will wake you up with the scent of her ciambellone ring cake and apple or pear cakes (pennate pears are a tasty local variety). Hiking and trekking fans – often guests at this B&B – will feel at home because Nicola is an expert guide for paths along the two coastlines: one of the most famous is the 'Path of the Gods' leading to Positano.

• 4 double rooms, with bathroom • Prices: double room single occupancy 35-45 euros, double 52-60 (12 euro supplement for extra bed), breakfast included • Credit cards: none • Off-street parking. Small pets allowed. Owners always present • Breakfast room. Garden, terrace.

AIELLO DEL SABATO

LA LOCANDINA

Restaurant-pizzeria
Via Vigna 9
Tel. 0825 666620
Closed Tuesday
Open: lunch and dinner
Holidays: in July
Seating: 120 + 30 outdoors
Prices: 28-35 euros, wine excluded
All credit cards, Bancomat

Just a few kilometers south of Avellino, Aiello, looking out over the Sabato valley is a small town, surrounded by mountains. The restaurant, ably run by Rita Mauriello, is spacious and well-appointed and stands out for food which reworks the classics of the Irpinia area. Thanks to the work of the tried and trusted staff, the menu has been considerably extended, but still remains faithful to its aim of promoting traditional local products.
The meal starts with a trolley of antipasti, including mixed cured meats, excellent **buffalo mozzarella** and seasonal vegetables roasted or served in flans. Then there are the skillfully-made first courses, among which we enjoyed the **calamarata** (a type of pasta which resembles calamari in shape) **with zucchini flowers** and fusilli with baccalà, peas and cherry tomatoes. As an alternative you will be offered scialatielli and ravioli with a variety of sauces or classics like **minestre maritate**, a soup of meat and vegetables, and **lagane and beans**. Main courses we enjoyed included some new dishes such as **baccalà alla perticaregna** and, as a detour from local traditions, steak alla fiorentina. Or you can go for local meats, both white and red, char-grilled, roasted or in sauce. The puddings made by the young chefs Enzo and Nunzia are also regularly updated. We recommend the chestnut tartufo and seasonal fruit pies. A separate mention deserves to be made of the **pizza**, where Nicola's talents really come to the fore.
As of this year the wine list is more extensive and has received more attention, and it now presents the best Campanian labels and a good range of national wines. There is also a selection of grappas and other spirits.

AMALFI

22 KM WEST OF SALERNO SS 163

CANTINA SAN NICOLA

🍲 Osteria-wine bar
Via Salita Marino Sebaste 8
Tel. 089 8304549
Closed Friday
Open: lunch and dinner, August only for dinner
Holidays: between January and February
Seating: 50
Prices: 20-25 euros, wine excluded
All major credit cards, Bancomat

Cantina San Nicola offers ... a glimpse into the soul of Amalfi. What you'll find here among the winding medieval alleyways can't be garnered neither from the port nor from the Duomo. The osteria lies on one of these lanes, left of the main street, in a Benedictine convent built in 1180. The sober décor creates a perfect setting for the locally-sourced produce – including Provolone del Monaco, bread baked in a wood-fired stove and the simple dishes prepared by Angelo and Gino.

The menu changes with the seasons and includes, in winter, various soups (with beans or chickpeas), while in summer we recommend **crespolini**, a roulade of pasta filled with ricotta. The **caponata** is a must – made with biscuits from Agerola, onions, olives and Cetara anchovies (a Slow Food Presidium) – just like the ricotta and fiordilatte cheese from the Lattari Mountains, the country cured meats, the **grilled Scamorza** served on lemon leaves and the **anchovy pie**. Their simple, no-frills style also comes through in main courses like **baccalà with black olives**, tomatoes stuffed with rice and anchovies and other meat and fish dishes. The homemade desserts we recommend are the **sfrucculata** (sun-dried figs filled with walnuts and wild fennel), a traditional winter goody, and the cookies. The wine list is rich and varied.

The osteria also organizes tasting evenings and events to promote local products.

AMALFI
Pogerola

28 KM WEST OF SALERNO SS 163

TRATTORIA DA RISPOLI

🍲 Traditional osteria
Via Riulo 3
Tel. 089 830080
Closed Thursday, never in summertime
Open: lunch and dinner
Holidays: none
Seating: 20 + 40 outdoors
Prices: 18-20 euros, wine excluded
No credit cards accepted

Although this is the Amalfi coast, what we have here is a typical village osteria, with a homey welcome, country-style food and a small grocery shop run on the side to bring in a little more money.

The restaurant, run by Enza and Marina Rispoli, inherited from their father over 30 years ago, is a no-frills kind of place with plain décor and no fancy tableware (in summer we recommend sitting on the little panoramic terrace). As for the food, they preserve authentic family recipes and a sense of rural hospitality, straightforward but never rude.

Don't be put off by the touristy style of the written menu, just ask Marina what the dishes of the day are: these are the most tempting, traditional offerings prepared by Enza, according to the availability of local produce. Watch out, though, because portions are on the generous side.

Among the first courses, we recommend **scialatielli with clams**, linguine with scampi and, on Saturdays and holidays, lasagne, **gnocchi with tomato** or **oven-baked pasta alla siciliana**. If you reserve in advance, you can also sample an impeccable rendition of pasta alla genovese. Main courses, both fish and meat, are well done: **mixed fry**, fried whitebait, shrimp, squid, **grilled** jumbo shrimp or swordfish, but also veal cutlets, pork chops, sausages and roast chicken. To round off, desserts from the De Riso di Minori pastry shop.

You can wash your meal down with house red or white as the wine list is virtually non-existent. The down to earth prices deserve a note of merit, though.

Ariano Irpino

La Pignata

🍲 Restaurant
Viale dei Tigli 7
Tel. 0825 872571-872355
Closed Tuesday
Open: lunch and dinner
Holidays: last two weeks of
September
Seating: 70
Prices: 30-35 euros, wine excluded
All credit cards, Bancomat

Guglielmo Ventre, the founder and heart and soul of La Pignata is actually a sociologist by profession. As well as being a gastronome, he's also a committed environmentalist. Not that this distracts him from his pursuit of traditional recipes.
The kitchen is run by his mother Rita and his wife Carmela, while Ezio looks after the wine list, which boasts almost 600 labels, with pride of place rightfully taken by local Avellino labels, as well as important national wines. This is a tried-and-tested team, as you'll be able to see for yourself when you sample the food, all seasonal, presented in a range of set menus.
The flavor of the ravece variety of olive oil comes through in dishes like pan-fried baccalà served with polenta or crostini, honey mushrooms and potatoes. First courses we sampled included chickpea, cep mushroom, truffle and baccalà soup and **paccheri with anchovy sauce**, potatoes and toasted breadcrumbs; depending on when you visit, you'll also be able to sample **tagliatelle lardellate**, **orecchiette alla pastora** and a range of different soups, including bean and chestnut. The hallmark mains are all meat-based: from roast **stuffed boned rabbit** with lampascioni (wild onions) to pork capocollo with annurca apples and cep mushrooms, from **mugliatielli** to **suckling pig with cooked grape must**. Or you could go for the **baccalà arrecanato** or baccalà fishcakes.
To finish off, something from the sumptuous **cheese board** or one of the good desserts. We were served buffalo milk yoghurt with ravece olive oil and chestnut mousse with quaresimali biscuits.

Arpaise

Buca dei Ladroni

🍲 Restaurant
Via Capone 1
Tel. 0824 46699
Closed Sunday for dinner and Monday
Open: lunch and dinner
Holidays: none
Seating: 40 + 40 outdoos
Prices: 25-28 euros, wine excluded
No credit cards accepted

A few months ago, the Buca dei Ladroni moved from its old home in Ceppaloni to the old part of the village of Arpaise, conserving the name its owner, Pino Pugliese, gave it when it first opened in 2001.
To start, **sheep's milk ricotta**, **Venticano prosciutto** and bean soup. Among the first courses, rigatoni (from the Benevento firm Rummo) in a meat and tomato ragù with meatballs, lightly pan-fried with Castelfranco in Miscano caciocavallo cheese; also the traditional **cavatelli with ricotta and sheep cheese**. Depending on the season, you'll find **maritata soup**, pizza made with polenta and black cabbage soup, **pettola and beans**. Among the main courses, **steak of marchigiana**, a common cattle breed in the Sannio area, and **oven-baked mugliatielli**. Rita also makes the puddings: plain chocolate and pear, **apple pie**, cookies with lemon icing. The extensive wine list has been very carefully selected and includes both regional and other Italian wines with honest mark-ups. The selection of spirits is excellent and Anthemis, a herb liqueur made by the monks of the nearby Montevergine Abbey, is a must.

ATRANI

'A PARANZA

Trattoria
Traversa Dragone 2
Tel. 089 871840
Closed Tuesday, never in summer
Open: lunch and dinner
Holidays: in December
Seating: 60
Prices: 35 euros, wine excluded
All credit cards, Bancomat

The houses and noble residences of Atrani, built in a tiny inlet wedged between rock faces which plunge directly down to the sea, are a wonderful example of Man's capacity to mold a rugged, often hostile natural environment to his own needs. Venturing into its intricate network of alleys, stairways and underpasses, you'll come to the main square, the hub of this little town, and just round the corner is 'A Paranza, one of the riviera's most popular eateries. When you get there, Massimo, one of the owners, and Alfonso, will soon show you that in these parts hospitality is not something they take lightly. The décor is simple, and the food straightforward and authentic, based on top quality fresh fish.
In the kitchen Roberto, the other partner, works with the local catch, offering dishes that are light and delicious. You can start with seasonally inspired treats such as
pizzelle di cicinielli, porpetiello (octopus) with peas, zucchini flowers stuffed with smoked Provola cheese, **pan-fried anchovies stuffed with fior di latte**, **marinated tuna** and carpaccio of hake. As for the first courses, we recommend spaghetti alla chitarra with squid and **calamarata with taratufi and turnip tops**. Main courses include various types of fish poached, baked in salt or oven-roasted, or in the right season, a sumptuous **frittura di fragaglie**, fried whitebait. The desserts are partly the work of a renowned local pastry shop, and partly prepared by the chef.
There's an extensive wine list, with the emphais on carefully-sourced Campania labels.

ATRIPALDA

VALLEVERDE

Trattoria
Via Pianodardine 112
Tel. 0825 626115
Closed Sunday and holidays
Open: lunch and dinner
Holidays: in August
Seating: 60 + 30 outdoors
Prices: 25-30 euros, wine excluded
All major credit cards, Bancomat

Valleverde is a historic restaurant in Atripalda, renowned for its traditional Irpinian cuisine, and represented in the eyes of connoisseurs and regulars by Zia Pasqualina, who opened it in 1953. Pasqualina passed away two years ago, shortly after her son Rino, who to all intents and purposes had taken over the running of the place, which is now in the hands of Enza, Sabino and Bruna. Despite these sad losses, the atmosphere of the Valleverde is as homely and welcoming as ever, and the food is still the same tasty, traditional fare we have know and loved for years.
Dishes are made of local produce, all selected with painstaking attention: cured meats, fasule and escarole, **boiled potatoes with friarielli and eggs**, orecchiette or **cavatielli with broccoli**, **minestre maritate** or with **accio** (celery), **baccalà and potatoes**, fusilli with escarole, rabbit and **chicken alla cacciatora**, meatballs in sauce, **loin of pork with pickled peppers** are just some of the dishes in the osteria's reliable, hearty repertoire. Then there's the **cheese board**, assembled by Sabino, who sources products such as Pecorino di Carmasciano, Caciocavallo podolico, Caciotta, Pecorino romano, Provolone del monaco and salted ewe's milk ricotta. As well as the wine list, which boasts around 400 local and national labels, there's an oil list and a good selection of grappas, signs of genuine care for the customer which is something of a rarity these days, and which originated with Pasqualina herself.

ANTICA TRATTORIA 🐌 ▮ MARTELLA

🍲 Trattoria
Via Chiesa Conservatorio 10
Tel. 0825 32123-31117
Closed Sunday for dinner and Monday
Open: lunch and dinner
Holidays: in August and during the Christmas vacation
Seating: 80
Prices: 30-35 euros, wine excluded
All credit cards, Bancomat

'O BARONE

🍲 Restaurant
Corso Umberto I 63-65
Tel. 0825 756040
Closed Wednesday
Open: lunch and dinner
Holidays: 10 days in July
Seating: 60
Prices: 25-30 euros, wine excluded
All credit cards, Bancomat

In the historic center of Avellino this trattoria, which has been in existence, for seven decades, can rightly lay claim to being the defender of the produce and flavors of the Irpinia area.

The place has come on since the days of its founder Ricuccio, when it operated as a locanda with a limited range of dishes, to those of current owner, grandson Enrico, who has modernized the decor and opened a catering company. But apart from the few, in part necessary, changes made to keep up with the times, the Martella is still the same as ever, rightly ignoring passing fads.

The trattoria is simple and homely, and the food genuine and of high quality. Dishes vary on a daily basis, and after traditional antipasti of vegetables, soppressata and ricotta, you could go for **bucatini al soffritto** (with pork offal and hot chili conserve), smoked fusilli and **cecatielli with broccoli**. In winter there is a wonderful range of **soups**: with potatoes and beans, Savoy cabbage and potatoes, barley and cep mushrooms or pumpkin. The main courses, some lighter than others, are mainly meat: from **tripe** to **pork livers**, from veal sirloin steak flavored with **mugliatielli** to **rabbit alla cacciatora**. To round off, a selection of local cheeses – Carmasciano, buffalo milk Caciocavallo and Moro – as well as other Italian products, and homemade puddings such as sbriciolata cake with ricotta and chocolate, chocolate mousse and babà.

The wine list includes local and national labels and mark-ups are fair.

Maybe it was the restoration of the 17th-century Bellerofonte fountain to its original splendor that gave Alfredo the idea of turning back the clock. The owner has in fact restored the original sign and the fresco which adorns the entrance, and has decided to restore the restaurant's original name. So it's O Barone once more, as Alfredo's grandfather had decreed, in the days when it occupied a different location. It is now situated in Corso Umberto I, just a stone's throw from the drinking trough that Francesco Marino I Caracciolo commissioned the architect Cosimo Fanzago to design in 1669 to create the landmark and symbol of the city of Avellino, fed by the waters of Monte Partenio.

Compared to the past, the quality of the food hasn't changed, based as it is on a successful combination of tradition and innovation. For antipasti, you can choose between grilled ricotta with lardo di Colonnata, **zucchini flowers stuffed with buffalo mozzarella** and ricotta, potato curls with cod and botargo, **zucchini and fried seppioline**, and vegetable millefeuille with anchovies or sardines. Vegetables and fish come to the fore in first courses like rigatoni with swordfish and egg plant, **gnocchetti with tub gurnard**, zuppa primavera, ravioloni with ricotta in a fava bean and artichoke sauce, and ravioli with zucchini and almonds. As for the main courses, you can opt for meat dishes such as **lamb with asparagus**, fish such as turbot or **baccalà**, or specialties like sweet bread with rocket, and crunchy ham and balsamic vinegar. To round off there are home-made desserts. You can accompany your meal with the house Aglianico or red or white wine from Irpinia.

BACOLI

A RIDOSSO

🍲Restaurant
Via Mercato di Sabato 320
Tel. 081 8689233
Closed Sunday for dinner and on Monday
Open: dinner, lunch on booking
Holidays: 13/08-28/08, 23/12-05/01
Seating 50 + 20 outdoors
Prices: 35 euros, wine excluded
All credit cards, Bancomat

The Phlegrean coast, which boasts many interesting historic and artistic sites to visit, such as the sibyl's ghrotto and Baia castle, is littered with restaurants that embody the worst in shabby standardized tourist eateries. In such a context, it's comforting to see that there are some pockets of resistance, where traditions are taken into account and 're-worked' with great creativity. This little osteria in Bacoli is adorned with works by important contemporary artists – Schifano, Fiume, Barisani, Di Ruggiero and Longobardi – and the esthetic taste of owner Gigi Palombo also come through in the food.

The menu, on display at the entrance and explained directly to customers inside the restaurant itself, includes bruschetta with cherry tomatoes al piennolo, **sauté of clams**, taratufi or razor clams, **pan-fried mussels**, raw tuna, carpaccio of baccalà and a delicate sea bass soufflé. Among the first courses, we recommend **gramigna a mare** (a particular type of pasta served with lobster, scampi and seafood, cooked in fish stock), classic spaghetti with seafood or **risotto alla pescatora**. As for main courses, you can choose one of the fishes of the day, which are sold by weight (take care though because here you could push up the check) or go for a **mixed fry** or grill. First and main courses always include a few local specialties. For dessert, we recommend the traditional millefeuille, mousse with chopped almonds and semifreddo (coffee, citrus fruit or hazelnut flavors).

The wine list, which offers a good range of regional labels, as well as national and foreign wines, is more than satisfactory.

BACOLI
Casevecchie

DA FEFÈ

🍲Restaurant
Via Miseno 125
Tel. 081 5233011
Closed Sunday for dinner and Monday, never in summer
Open: dinner, Saturday and Sunday also for lunch
Holidays: December 20-January 10
Seating: 40 + 80 outdoors
Prices: 30-35 euros, wine excluded
All credit cards except DC, Bancomat

This popular restaurant, run by Bruno Esposito, overlooks the port where the Roman imperial fleet led by Pliny the Elder was based, set in a sunny bay against the backdrop of the promontory named for the legendary trumpeter of Aeneas.

The location really comes into its own when the sea breeze blows during sultry summer evenings, but it is also an attractive spot in winter. The menu reflects the seasons and highlights the quality of locally caught fish. If you like oily fish and sea food such as the mussels farmed just off Punta Miseno, you'll get a taste of the genuine local specialties without going overboard price-wise.

The antipasti we recommend, apart from the house mixed platter, are fried zucchini flowers filled with ricotta, **pickled scabbard fish**, **'o purpo, octopus salad**, and piquant steamed mussels in the juice of Phlegrea lemons and the local Falanghina wine. First courses include **fettuccine with zucchini and mussels**, or with seafood, risotto alla pescatora, **spaghetti with anchovies**, onion and cherry tomato, or, when in season, with sprigs of wild fennel (increasingly rare) from the Miseno mountains. The main courses focus on seasonal oily fish, squid, octopus, baby cuttlefish, swordfish and tuna, marinated or char-grilled, **fried anchovies** or **whitebait**, with the addition of cuttlefish and squid, **purpetielli in cassuola** (stewed octopus) or octopus soup.

The desserts are nothing special, but the local Falanghina wine is delicious. Alternatively, you can choose from a good selection of other regional labels.

BACOLI
Miseno

MISENO

🚪🔑2-Star Hotel
Via Miseno 141
Tel. 081 5235000
Fax 081 5234651
E-mail: hotelmiseno@hotelmiseno.it
Internet: www.hotelmiseno.it
Open all year

The hotel is situated in what was once the Roman port of Miseno, a naval base on the Tyrrhenian Sea. It's managed by Annunziata Colutta and her daughter Maria Chiara, and has recently been modernized to offer unpretentious basic accommodation. The rooms are furnished simply and offer the minimum comfort necessary for a pleasant stay – the most attractive and comfortable offer a view over the small harbor. Breakfast is served at the tables and consists of traditional Italian fare: bread, rusks, fresh croissants or cakes, jams, butter, cappuccino, coffee and fruit juices. Management can offer special rates for hiring motor-boats or rowing boats. There's a hydrofoil service out to the islands and a shuttle service to and from the airport.

• 20 double rooms, with bathroom, terrace, TV; several rooms with air-conditioning • Prices: double room single use 50 euros, double 60-80 (10 euro supplement for extra bed), breakfast included • Credit cards: all, Bancomat • Public parking nearby, free garage. No pets allowed. Reception open 8am-midnight • Bar, restaurant. Breakfast room, reading and TV room. Terrace, solarium

BACOLI
Fondi di Baia

IL CASOLARE DI TOBIA

🍲 Holiday farm
Via Pietro Fabris 12-14
Tel. 081 5235193
Closed Monday, Sundays and holidays also for dinner
Open: dinner, lunch on booking
Holidays: August 16-30
Seating: 60 + 20 outdoors
Prices: 30-32 euros, wine excluded
No credit cards accepted

Thanks to its stunning position, the Baia area was the location of choice for the Roman aristocracy, but the lavish villas built here have all since been swallowed up by the sea due to the area's brady-seismic activity. Right next to the castle is the agriturismo run by Tobia and Elisabetta Costagliola, which can be reached on foot along a country path after leaving your car in the nearby parking lot. You'll immediately feel at home in this rustic but inviting eatery, whose two owners are committed to safeguarding the flavors of rural cuisine. There's a daily set menu which they change regularly. You can start with a rich selection of antipasti, from **goats' cheese** to homemade **cured meats** – do try the capicollo – all beautifully presented; depending on the season, there's a variety of raw and cooked vegetables, omelet made with freshly laid eggs, or chicken or **pork liver** with onion. The first courses revolve around soups – pasta and peas with ventresca tuna, **pasta and beans with belly pork, bean and escarole soup**, pasta and chickpeas – but there are also tagliatelle or gnocchi with ragù, pappardelle with zucchini flowers and tasty **bucatini with rabbit sauce**. The main courses consist of pork, lamb or kid char-grilled or roasted in the wood-fired oven, **rabbit alla cacciatora** and an unusual **chicken with stuffing**. The desserts are simple and homemade, just like the limoncello that accompanies them.
The extensive wine list featuring not only regional labels, but you can also opt for the wine made by local growers.

LA CATAGNA

⌒ Restaurant
Via Pennata 26
Tel. 081 5234218
Closed Monday
Open: dinner only, Sunday also for lunch
Holidays: between December and January
Seating: 20 + 4 outdoors
Prices: 30-35 euros, wine excluded
No credit cards accepted

VILLA OTERI

⟵● 3-Star Hotel
Via Lungo Lago 174
Tel. 081 5234985
Fax 081 5233944
E-mail: reception@villaoteri.it
Internet: www.villaoteri.it
Open all year

In Bacoli, go along the lakefront in the direction of Miseno, then turn left before the little bridge over the canal which joins the two lakes. Go up a narrow street and down the other side and you'll come to Via Pennata: turn right and after a few houses right again into a little alley, and you'll find this tiny restaurant, which boasts unbeatable views over the Campi Flegrei, from Punta Pennata to Miseno. The dining room is simple, with a few items of marine bric-à-brac. You will be welcomed by Crescenzo Della Ragione, a free-diving fisherman by profession, who after working in a number of different restaurants decided to open one of his own. His mother helps out in the kitchen and kitchen garden. The menu reflects the day's catch and the dishes are prepared in the kitchen which is exposed to view: the flavors of the ultra-fresh fish are enhanced by the fact that it's never overcooked, and in a few dishes is even served raw. To start, you can have bruschetta with anchovies, **sautéed clams**, **sea bass fillets** and **sweet and sour rice**, octopus salad, **sconcigli** or **white-spotted octopus alla genovese**. Then comes a slightly spicy **anchovy soup**. First courses include **linguine with crabs and baby cuttlefish**, pasta and beans and other pasta dishes, all featuring fish and/or seafood. The main courses are in keeping with the marine theme: **sea urchin with capers and olives**, poached white bream and exquisite **fried shrimp and baby cuttlefish**. To finish off, there are a few simple home-made desserts and, as for wine, a few labels from local winemakers. Booking is essential.
The name of the restaurant, La Catagna, refers to the crevice between the rocks where fish hide.

The hotel, an elegant neoclassical-style residence in an enviable position on the shores of Lake Miseno, was completely renovated in 2000. The rooms have been fitted out by the Faga husband-and-wife team to satisfy even the most demanding guests. The latter are pampered right from the early morning, starting with a generous buffet breakfast that includes jams, croissants and freshly squeezed juices, along with the traditional coffee, tea and milk. Furthermore, there are a variety of other services, such as access to a private beach and nearby spa, organized guided tours to the archeological site of the Campi Flegrei, and a shuttle service to and from the beach and the nearby airport. The cost of half-board ranges from 55-75 euros per person, whereas the supplement for full board is 10 euros.

• 9 double rooms, with bathroom (1 with jacuzzi), air-conditioning, mini-bar, safe, satellite TV, modem connection • Prices: double room single use 65-85 euros, double 80-120, breakfast included • Credit cards: all, Bancomat • Off-street parking. Small pets allowed. Reception open 24 hours a day • Bar, restaurant. Breakfast room. Terrace, solarium

BAGNOLI IRPINO
Laceno

39 KM SOUTHEAST OF AVELLINO

LA CASA DI TORNOLA

Bed and breakfast
Via delle Ginestre 2
Tel. 0827 68008-339 6395590
E-mail: lacasaditornola@cheapnet.it
Internet: www.lacasaditornola.it
Open all year

La Casa di Tornola stands at an altitude of about 1000 meters in one of the most unspoilt corners of Irpinia. Albina Meloro runs the B&B and restaurant with help from outside staff. This farmhouse was completely renovated in 2002 to create rooms with rustic-style furnishings that are unpretentious and quite comfortable. There are numerous nature trails that you can explore by renting a bicycle or booking a tour guide. Breakfast is good and consists of milk, coffee, tea, jams, cookies and home-baked panettone. The nearby restaurant, also open to non-residents, offers traditional, though sometimes 'revisited' dishes (28-30 euros, wine excluded).

• 3 double rooms, with bathroom, balcony, TV • Prices: double room single use, double 70 (15 euro supplement extra bed), breakfast included • Credit cards: all, Bancomat • Off-street parking. Small pets allowed. Owners always present • Bar corner, restaurant. Breakfast room, reading room. Garden

BAGNOLI IRPINO
Laceno

49 KM SOUTHEAST OF AVELLINO

LO SPIEDO

Restaurant with rooms
Via Serroncelli 25
Tel. 0827 68073-68074
Closed Tuesday
Open: lunch, weekends and summer also for dinner
Holidays: July 1-15
Seating: 150
Prices: 25-30 euros, wine excluded
All credit cards, Bancomat

The restaurant, ably run by Nicola Memoli, lies on the Laceno plateau inside the Parco Regionale dei Picentini. The area boasts the richest reserves of drinking water in southern Italy and two thirds of it is covered by beech groves and other woodlands. It is famed for high quality produce such as the chestnuts of Montella, the hazelnuts of Giffoni, annurca apples and prized cheeses such as Caciocavallo.The woods are also home to wild boar and prized cep mushrooms, which when in season form the backbone of the menu of Lo Spiedo.
As well as **mushrooms** – do try the soup with chanterelles, honey and cep mushrooms, creamed cep mushrooms or various salads – the antipasti include a number of dishes made with **black truffles** from Bagnoli, which are available from late fall to the end of winter. This delicacy is used to flavor ricotta and also in an unusual parmigiana. Then there are the tasty first courses: **pappardelle with wild boar ragù**, potato gnocchi with mushrooms and truffles, crepes and **tagliatelle with cep mushrooms** and ricotta-filled ravioli with tomato or truffle. As for the main courses, these are mainly based on locally-sourced meat, from wild or farmed livestock. There is a good **wild boar stew with cep mushrooms**, as well as chargrilled meats: veal or pork chops, sausages, **lamb** and white-meat brochettes. Alternatively, you can opt for oven-baked cep mushrooms or Scamorza cheese with truffle. To finish off, fruit salad or puddings with wild berries, babà alla crema or sweets made with chestnuts or fig preserves.
As well as local wines, you can order DOC and DOCG wines from the province of Avellino.

ALBERGO DELLA CORTE

🛏️ 3-Star Hotel
Piazza Piano di Corte 11
Tel. and fax 0824 54819
Open all year

COTTON CLUB

🍲 Osteria
Via de Vita 16
Tel. 349 3827226
Closed Tuesday
Open: dinner only
Holidays: August 10-25
Seating: 25 + 15 outdoos
Prices: 25-28 euros, wine excluded
No credit cards accepted

This hotel, managed by the Barbato brothers, is in an old quarter of Benevento, near interesting sites such as the church of Santa Sofia, Trajan's arch, the Roman theater and Rettori Castle, partially occupied today by the Museo del Sannio. We also suggest a visit to sculptor Mimmo Paladino's 'hortus conclusus' with works dating from 1992. The hotel was previously owned by Antonio and Gianluca's parents, who in 2001 had it renovated, refurnished and fitted with all essential comforts. The rooms are simple, with wrought-iron bedsteads and a few accessories in arte povera style. Simplicity is also the theme in common areas, such as the bar and breakfast room, where in the morning you'll be offered coffee, milk, tea, rusks, butter and jams.

• 2 single, 8 double, 1 triple and 1 four-bed rooms, with bathroom, TV; several rooms with balcony • Prices: single 38, double 50, triple 70, four-bed 80 euro, breakfast included • Credit cards: none • Free public parking, 20 meters away, paid garage parking at special rates. Small pets allowed. Owners always present. • Bar. Breakfast room

Downtown, not far from Trajan's Arch and the cathedral, this little establishment is slightly off the beaten track, on a road which runs perpendicular to Corso Garibaldi, the pedestrian precinct that splits the old town in two. It came about by chance: the young owner Ernesto Pietrantonio, a photographer by profession, opened a club for his musician friends in what was once his studio. Then he got his parents involved and gradually the place became an osteria, where you will be welcomed as one of the family. Mamma Maria Rosaria is in the kitchen, while Don Ottavio receives diners and enjoys regaling them with anecdotes of life in Benevento.
With just a few tables and offering a few dishes every night, the Cotton Club is recommended in the winter for its **pancotto with chicory sprouts** or broccoli (according to season), **zuppa contadina with bread and Savoy cabbage**, stuffed Savoy cabbage leaves, pasta with chickpeas and baccalà, and a soup of cardoons and meatballs (only in the Christmas period). You should try Maria Rosaria's spaghetti, flavored with Mediterranean spices and named 'Vucciria' in memory of a trip to Palermo. Main courses include **stuffed cuttlefish**, patate arrecanate (potatoes with tomatoes, onions and oregano), **baccalà with tomato**, and **polenta with pork ribs**. Cheeses and cold cuts are local (go for the Pietraroia cheese and ham).
Desserts, when on offer, are homemade. The few wines come exclusively from Benevento (Aglianico del Taburno and Falanghina).

OLD TOWN

LE STANZE DEL SOGNO

🔑 Rooms
Piazzetta De Martini 3
Tel. 0824 43991-338 4603359
Fax 0824 43991
E-mail: lestanzedelsogno@katamail.com
Internet: www.lestanzedelsogno.it
Open all year

NUNZIA

🍲 Traditional osteria
Via Annunziata 152
Tel. 0824 29431
Closed Sunday
Open: lunch and dinner
Holidays: August 10-25
Seating: 60
Prices: 20-25 euros, wine excluded
All credit cards, Bancomat

Le Stanze del Sogno now offer even more rooms than last year: rooms in three buildings very near to one another in the middle of the old town, where you'll be able to admire Trajan's arch and the monastery of Santa Sofia (where the Museo del Sannio is currently housed). There are rooms of various sizes and suites with kitchenettes, all simply furnished with wrought iron bedsteads, arte povera-style accessories and different color schemes. Recent restructuring work has also improved the level of comfort (all rooms now have air-conditioning and DVD players). The particularly economical price includes a small breakfast (coffee wafers and ready-made products); if you pay 8 euros more, you can have breakfast in a local bar.

• 7 double rooms, with bathroom, air-conditioning, terrace, TV; 3 suites with kitchenette • Prices: double room single use 40 euros, double 60 (25 euro supplement for extra bed), suite 80-100, breakfast included • Credit cards: all, Bancomat • 1 suite designed for use by the mobility challenged. Both free and paid external parking. No pets allowed. Owners reachable from 8am-11 pm • Breakfast room, reading room. Garden, terrace

Signora Nunzia is something of a culinary institution in Benevento. Her trattoria is just round the corner from the main square, and while her warm welcome, constant attention and a smile are the rule, the secret of her success resides in respect for the most authentic local, homely food traditions. Angelo buys the vegetables, cured meats, cheeses, oil, meat and raw materials directly from the suppliers, while Mario works front of house and serves.

The antipasti are traditional cured meats and **cheeses** from Taburno and Fortore. First courses which stand out include **cavatelli with beans**, lagane and chickpeas, **orecchiette with broccoli**, tagliatelle with artichokes, sautéed escarole and minestra maritatea (meat and vegetable soup). Two Benevento classics are almost always on the menu: **scarpariello** (a variety of fresh pasta similar to pasta alla chitarra) with a sauce made of cherry tomatoes, provola cheese and basil, and **cardone**, a traditional Christmas soup made of chicken stock, cardoons, meatballs, beaten egg and cheese. Main courses include **baccalà alla Nunzia** (with tomato, olives, capers, parsley and chili pepper), stuffed cuttlefish, tripe, **ammugliatielli**, a meat and potato stew, mutton kebabs, and an impeccable **eggplant parmigiana**. There are various side dishes made with broccoli, chicory, eggplant, peppers and mushrooms. The puddings – apple with Strega liqueur, cassatine and torroncini – come from the best artisan confectioners in town.

The meal is accompanied by the main local wines: Aglianico del Taburno, Falanghina, Greco di Tufo and Fiano.

BISACCIA

68 KM NORTHEAST OF AVELLINO

GRILLO D'ORO

⌒ Trattoria with rooms
Via Mancini 195
Tel. 0827 89278
Closed Monday
Open: lunch and dinner
Holidays: none
Seating: 35
Prices: 25-30 euros, wine excluded
No credit cards accepted

CAMEROTA
Marina

121 KM SOUTHEAST OF SALERNO SS 562

LA CANTINA DEL MARCHESE

⌒ Traditional osteria
Via del Marchese 13
Tel. 0974 932570
Always open June-September, October-May, weekends only
Open: dinner only
Holidays: November and February
Seating: 80
Prices: 18-25 euros
All credit cards, Bancomat

The town of Bisaccia, the oldest part of which is round the ducal castle, is just over 10 kilometers from the Lacedonia exit on the Naples-Bari motorway, or can be reached from road 303. Albeit without any great artistic merits, this is an attractive little town and there is one good reason to visit it: the chance to sample some of the area's traditional specialties as served by the Arminio family. After the death of the legendary 'Luis', the family has rolled up its sleeves and continues to offer a vast range of traditional dishes. The restaurant is plain and inviting, the service (by the men of the family – Vito, Franco and Luigi) is efficient and the food (prepared by the women – Flora and her daughter-in-law Lina) is the traditional fare of the upper Irpinia area.

The menu comprises the same tried and tested dishes as ever. You can start with local cured meats, seasonal vegetables, **fried liver** and fried **dried pumpkin** flavored with chili pepper. Then it's on to first courses such as **summer soup** with zucchini, potato, bread and eggs, **cavatielli** with chickpeas or **beans**, and **ciambotta** stew with tomatoes, peppers and potatoes. Then come pasta dishes like orecchiette and marcanalli served with meat ragù. Main courses include meat dishes like **stuffed pigeon**, **rabbit alla cacciatora** and **char-grilled lamb**. Sometimes they also offer puddings like ricotta cake or almond biscuits.

The wine list is currently being extended and features provincial and regional labels.

This is one place where the commitment to preserving local culinary traditions is self-evident. On offer here diners will find the flavors of the rural traditions of the Cilento area as they have been handed down through the ages. The Cantina del Marchese presents the same dishes year in year out, with the same high standard of quality, and in the philosophy of the guide this gets a high score.

The first courses, based on poor rural traditions from the inland area (there's no fish on the menu here, apart from anchovies), include specialties like **ciaurella** (a soup made of potato, fava beans, Swiss chard and wild fennel), **maracucciata** (polenta made of legumes and grains), **lagane and chickpeas**, bean soup, or **cicci maritati**, which according to tradition is a soup made to use up stores of seven different kinds of legumes and celebrate the beginning of the country summer, on May 1. The focus is on traditional flavors, so don't miss the **pizza rianata**, made with wholemeal flour and prepared with a variety of toppings, or simply with pieces of fresh tomato. Particular care goes into the cured meats – the soppressa, made personally by owner Francesco and his brother Andrea, is well worth a try – and there's a wonderful range of cheeses, both aged and fresh, including Provolone del monaco, Caciocavallo podolico and mozzarella with mortella (myrtle). To round off, a few local puddings such as **pastiera**.

The medium-range prices, the well-appointed dining room with wine barrels and beamed ceilings, and Malvasia and Aglianico wines on draft (there are also a few local labels on offer in the bottle) complete the charm of the place.

CAMEROTA

RIANATA 'A VASULATA

� Traditional osteria
Via San Vito 25
Tel. 0974 935427
No closing day
Open: only dinner
Holidays: from October to April
Seating: 25
Prices: 12-18 euros
No credit cards accepted

Coming to the town of Camerota, pretty much cut off from the fast routes to the Salerno riviera, feels a bit like going back in time. It's a place you have to make a detour along the old provincial road to visit. But the very fact that the town is off the beaten track means that some of the its inhabitants have effortlessly preserved memories of traditional local dishes. This is the case of the little osteria run by Milva D'Alessandro, daughter of the town's main baker, built by the old coach road paved with lava stone from Vesuvius.

There is a limited range of simple dishes, one type of wine, a red without a label which does not seem to have suffered for having been produced by local farmers…If you come here you simply must try the **pizza rianata** (with oregano), made with wholemeal flour and topped with oil, garlic, oregano and pomodoro schiattato (literally 'squashed' tomato) or tomato conserve. Other great dishes are pasta all'ortolana, with a variety of seasonal vegetables, **fusilli with mutton sauce**, **sausage and potatoes**, **ciambotta** (a mixed vegetable stew cooked in a terracotta pot called a pignatiello) and **sciambielli**, made with tasty local eggplant. Don't be surprised by the absence of a wine list or menu, which is written on a blackboard near the wood-fired oven. Both would be out of keeping with the down to earth spirit of the place and its straight-talking owners (Milva is assisted by her husband). What will surprise you, and pleasantly so, is the check: you'll feel like you're still paying in lire. It's incredible that places like this still exist!

CAPACCIO
Capaccio Scalo

LA PERGOLA 🐌 ▮

⌖ Restaurant
Via Magna Grecia 1
Tel. 0828 723377
Closed Monday, never in summer
Open: lunch and dinner
Holidays: September 15-30
Seating: 50 + 100 outdoors
Prices: 30-35 euros, wine excluded
All credit cards, Bancomat

Capaccio, the gateway to the Cilento Park, is where the Sele plains meet the last stretch of the gulf of Salerno. The nearby temple of Paestum increases the appeal of the area. The restaurant, run by the Longo family, lies behind the main road and boasts a spacious garden, which is as beautifully cared for as the inside of the restaurant. At the entrance is an area for tasting wines and the excellent local **cheeses** (look out for the ewe's milk ricotta and buffalo mozzarella).

The kitchen is run by Alfonso, while front of house to welcome the guests are his wife Silla and their son. Most of the dishes are local seasonal specialties, but creative innovations may also appear. The meal starts with a choice of six-seven antipasti, followed by the first courses: we recommend the **vermicelli with broccoli and anchovies**, sedani with zucchini flowers and buffalo ricotta (watch out for the massive portions though!) and **bavette with buffalo ricotta**, lemon and cinnamon, which originated as an alternative take on tagliolini with milk, a dish traditionally served on Ascension Day. Main courses include dishes which blend fresh produce with the day's catch: **roast tuna** with oregano and tomato, swordfish with Tropea onions, dentex in an eggplant sauce, and tuna with lemon – as well as meat dishes, with **buffalo** to the fore. For dessert, we recommend the **eggplant and chocolate cake**.

The wine list is well thought out, with labels representing the region and the rest of Italy.

CAPACCIO
Paestum

CASAGIOVE

SELIANO

Holiday farm
Via Seliano
Tel. 0828 723634-724544
Fax 0828 724544
E-mail: seliano@agriturismoseliano.it
Internet: www.agriturismoseliano.it
Open from 01/03 to 03/11 and from 27/12 to 07/01

LE QUATTRO FONTANE

Trattoria
Via Quartiere Vecchio 60
Tel. 0823 468970
Closed Sunday
Open: lunch and dinner
Holidays: August, Easter, 23-12/06-01
Seating: 80
Prices: 20-27 euros, wine excluded
All credit cards

At a short distance from the Paestum archeological site, the nobly descended Belelli family manages this agriturismo, growing vegetables organically and breeding horses and buffalos for the production of milk and meat. Guest rooms are located in the former stables of a mid-19th-century farmstead and are furnished with antique furniture belonging to the family. Breakfast is a comprehensive affair and consists of hot drinks and juices, plum and other cakes baked by your hostess, Cecilia, and also bread, butter and jam, rusks, cured meats and cheese. In addition, on request you may also have bacon and eggs, omelets, fruit juices and fruit salads. The restaurant, which is open to non-residents, serves regional dishes cooked using the farm's produce (25-30 euros per person; half-board ranges 58-80 euros per person). The management organizes periodic regional cooking courses.

• 8 double, 3 triple and 3 four-bed rooms, with bathroom, air-conditioning; 1 apartment with kitchenette • Prices: double room single use 50-100 euros, double 75-120, triple 95-140, four-bed 115-160, apartment 90-135, breakfast included • Credit cards: all except AE, Bancomat • Off-street parking. Small pets allowed. Owners reachable 7.30am-8.30pm • Bar, restaurant. TV room. Conference room. Grounds, swimming pool. Beach 5 km away

Casagiove lies just off the Caserta nord motorway exit. Once run by Francesco Russo, and originally a wine shop, it gradually evolved into a trattoria thanks to the success of the traditional dishes prepared by his wife. The chef herself, custodian of the historic memory of the trattoria and keeper of ancient local recipes, is still active, assisted by her son Michele, who has taken over the running of the place. Recent improvements have been made to the selection of oils and **cheeses**, such as Pecorino di laticauda and Conciato romano, on offer.
We recommend starting with the house antipasti, followed by first courses dictated by the seasons and festivities. You will be able to sample dishes like **minestra maritata** and **zuppa di soffritto**, escarole with potatoes or beans, various soups made of legumes or spring vegetables and **bread dough fritters made with beans** or chickpeas. Then **pork rind** and **baccalà** fried, boiled or dressed with oil and lemon, in insalata di rinforzo or **in cassuola** with capers, olives and tomato. In summer don't hesitate to order the **fried whitebait**, a simple dish of fried anchovies or the seafood soup. The puddings, sometimes bought in from a local confectioners, are always good.
The wine list presents the best regional labels and good national and international names: let Biagio, the experienced wine waiter who coordinates service front of house, be your guide.

By Caserta, in the hamlet of **Puccianiello** (2 km), at Via Santissimo Nome di Maria 2, Il Manicaretto produces fresh and filled pasta, as excellent brioche rustica.

Casaletto Spartano
Battaglia

Palazzo Gallotti

🗝Bed and breakfast
Via Nazionale 19
Tel. and fax 0973 374063
E-mail: info@palazzogallotti.it
Internet: www.palazzogallotti.it
Open from May to October or on request

The five rooms fitted with period furniture are in a wing of Palazzo Gallotti, built towards the end of the 15th century and inhabited ever since by the Gallotti barons (Roberto Simoni, who manages the B&B with his wife Bettina is a descendant of the Gallotti family). There's a superb view from the windows of the building, which stands at an altitude of 460 meters: the village is near the Cilento National Park, a UNESCO world heritage site since 1997. The tasty morning breakfast served in the lounge or in the garden includes quality local produce and homemade jams. The managers are happy to suggest and provide informative material on excursions in surrounding areas (on request they also prepare takeaway snacks). Guests can visit certain areas of the palazzo normally reserved for the family – the chapel and Art Nouveau-style dining room.

• 5 double rooms, with bathroom (4 with shared bathroom), balcony • Prices: double room single use 40 euros, double with shared bathroom 50, double with private bathroom 60, breakfast included • Credit cards: none • Free external parking. No pets allowed. Owners always present • Lounge. Garden.

Caselle in Pittari

Zì Filomena

🍲Restaurant
Viale Roma 11
Tel. 0974 988024
Closed Monday, never in summer
Open: lunch and dinner
Holidays: none
Seating: 100 + 20 outdoors
Prices: 23-30 euros, wine excluded
All credit cards, Bancomat

The restaurant lies in the vicinity of the Bussento gorge, part of the Cilento National Park. The recently revamped osteria (now on two floors, with a spacious dining room with stone walls and a lighter, airier feel) was originally run by Zì Filomena, the keeper of the village's culinary traditions for over 40 years. The restaurant itself has been in operation since the 30s, when it was a tavern which offered hospitality to passing travelers. Now the kitchen is run by daughter-in-law Grazie Fiscina, expert pasta-maker, assisted by Giuseppina and Angelina, while front of house are the nephews of the famous aunt.

The menu revolves around local traditions, starting with hearty antipasti of cured meats, char-grilled vegetables, **escarole and beans**, **pickled zucchini** with fresh mint, potato gattò, **eggplant parmigiana** and local goats' cheese served with bread baked in the wood-fired oven. Then there are the generous first courses, which recall traditional rural Sunday lunches, which were the one chance for a hearty meal after a week of meager rations. The pasta is home-made: fusilli and **cavatelli with mutton ragù** or tomato, **ravioli with ewe's milk ricotta**, **lagane and chickpeas**, pasta and beans, pasta and potatoes, and fettuccine, if reserved in advance. Main courses include lamb, kid, pork chops and barbecued sausages. The **free-range chicken with potatoes** is excellent. To finish off, home-baked fruit pies.

To drink, you can either go for the house wine, bottled with its own house label, or choose among a few good local reds. One word of advice: groups should book in advance to give staff time to source all the ultra-fresh produce.

CASERTA
Caserta Vecchia

GLI SCACCHI

Restaurant
Via San Rocco 1
Tel. 0823 371086
Closed Monday, November-February
also Tuesday and Wednsday
Open: lunch and dinner
Holidays: December
Seating: 80 + 40 outdoors
Prices: 30 euros, wine excluded
All credit cards

The restaurants of Caserta Vecchia have been under observation for a few years now, after criticism from various sources that many establishments were offering poor menus with few links to the local area. Eateries appeared to be targeted mainly at day-trippers, leaving an old town of enormous artistic and architectural appeal without adequate dining opportunities. Fortunately, things seem to be changing.

At Gli Scacchi, situated near the main parking lot, you'll be welcomed by owner Gino Della Valle, who will recommend traditional dishes rediscovered and skillfully interpreted by his wife Marilena, a chef passionate about her work. Of the seasonal antipasti, which revolve round local vegetables and cheeses, we recommend the spring zucchini and potato mold. There's a good choice of first courses: **stringozzi with mutton ragù**, legumes or vegetable soups, the traditional Easter dish **minestra maritata**, **tripe with potatoes**, **cianfotta** (a Caserta summer soup), chestnut and mushroom soup in fall, and excellent paccheri with baccalà, usually made in winter. To follow, pork ribs, **lamb in sauce** with artichokes and potatoes, char-grilled sausages and **baccalà in cassuola**, fried or boiled. You can round off with regional cheeses or a selection of local Pecorino cheeses, but do leave room for the jam tarts made with the fruit from the Della Valle orchard, the delizia al limone and hot chocolate tortino, minor masterpieces created by Signora Marilena.

The wine list is good with a prevalence of labels from Caserta and the rest of the region.

CASTELLABATE
San Marco

GIACARANDA

Boarding house
Località Cenito
Tel. 0974 966130
Fax 0974 966800
E-mail: giaca@costacilento.it
Internet: www.giacaranda.it
Open all year

The Giacaranda is down a short unpaved road just outside the seaside village of San Marco. Located on a farm with a number of buildings scattered about the grounds, rooms and apartments are furnished in typically 'feminine' style: antique bedside cabinets and chests of drawers, hand-embroidered sheets and curtains. Breakfast is either served in your room or in the garden of pomegranate trees and exotic plants. Varied and filling, it consists of milk, tea, coffee, cakes and fruit jams, yoghurt made with buffalo milk and locally produced butter. The restaurant, which is open to non-residents, offers traditional dishes with a few minor adaptations (the cost of a meal ranges from 35-40 euros per person, wine excluded). Apart from enjoying the peaceful atmosphere of this place and or the sea, within easy reach at places such as the oasis of Punta Licosa, guests may also take part in courses and seminars organized by the owner, Luisa Cavaliere.

• 7 double rooms, with bathroom, air-conditioning, TV, modem connection; 2 apartments with 1-3 rooms, kitchen • Prices: double room single use 50 euros, double 100, breakfast included; apartments 60 euros per person • Credit cards: all, Bancomat • Off-street parking. Small pets allowed. Owners always present • Restaurant. TV room. Conference room. Grounds. Tennis court. Beach 2 km away.

CASTELLABATE
Santa Maria

CASTEL MORRONE

LA TAVERNA DEL PESCATORE

🍲 Restaurant
Via Lamia 1
Tel. 0974 968293
Closed Monday, never in summer
Open: lunch and dinner, in summer
only for dinner
Holidays: December-February
Seating: 20 + 30 outdoors
Prices: 35 euros, wine excluded
All credit cards, Bancomat

IL FRANTOIO DUCALE

🍲 Restaurant
Via Altieri 50
Tel. 0823 399167
Closed Wednesday
Open: lunch and dinner
Holidays: two weeks in August
Seating: 100
Prices: 30 euros, wine excluded
All major credit cards

As well as its artistic heritage (the medieval old town is a UNESCO world heritage site), Castellabate is worth visiting for its typical wine and food. In the lovely seaside hamlet of Santa Maria, Franco Romano will welcome you into his restaurant, the legacy of a time-honored family tradition. Small and well-appointed, the dining room is adorned with wood and ceramics and the exterior is enhanced by Mediterranean plants.

Franco, assisted in the kitchen by his wife Andrea, offers dishes that are a well-made, creative but balanced revisitation of local ingredients. You can start, for instance, with **creamed Controne beans** cooked in rock fish stock with the tasty addition of mussels and croutons. One menu staple is **anchovies stuffed with provola**, or fried or alla parmigiana. Then there are the first courses, among which linguine with botarga, tagliolini with fava beans and clams, **spaghetti with raw anchovies** and **gnocchetti** of buffalo ricotta with **a sauce of sconcigli** (murexes). While the tuna in a herb crust is one great reason to come here, there are also others, in the shape of the **fish soup**, **totani with potatoes** and steamed sea bream with ciambotta vegetable stew. There's a vast range of dessert, from fruit creams and mousses to almond and wild berry cake, lemon cake or buffalo ricotta and pears. The wine list features around 140 labels, mostly from Campania. To finish off you can choose from the limited selection of spirits.

The nature walks, the two craters on the side of Monte Fioralito, the ruins of the Norman castle and the little mausoleum dedicated to Garibaldi's heroes led by Pilade Bronzetti are all good reasons for visiting Castel Morrone. If you want to refuel, resist the temptations offered by places in the village and head straight for the castle, where you'll find the restaurant run by the Leonetti family. The ever-professional Pietro will be waiting to greet you, while his mother and father are in charge of the kitchen, and guarantee that you a state of the best the local cuisine has to offer.

Don't pass up on the wonderful homemade antipasti such as char-grilled vegetables, fritters of various kinds, and the vegetables preserved in oil which make a great accompaniment for the local cured meats and delicate **Pecorino** cheeses. First courses include pasta and beans with wild asparagus, **bread dough fritters and chickpeas**, wonderful **ziti with mutton ragù**, soup of spolichini beans, pasta with baccalà and the particular Morrone version of **minestra maritata**. The main courses are also high quality: rabbit and **chicken alla cacciatora**, barbecued lamb, **pork chops** from the local **black Caserta pig**, served **with papaccelle**, baccalà, boiled or fried and, if booked in advance, mutton stew. During the summer, you'll also find fish dishes. The **cheese board** has been expanded, as has the range of desserts on offer, though our favorites are still the delizia al limone and the orange cake.

If you don't want to accompany your meal with the good house Aglianico, choose from the regional or national labels on the wine list.

CASTIGLIONE DEL GENOVESI

IL RICCIO

🍲Restaurant
Via Parrilli 29
Tel. 089 881641
Closed Monday, in winter also Sunday dinner
Open: dinner, holidays also for lunch
Holidays: 1 week after August 15,
between January and February
Seating: 140 + 40 outdoors
Prices: 23-25 euros, wine excluded
All credit cards, Bancomat

This village was the birthplace of philosopher and economist Antonio Genovesi. It lies in the hills behind the city of Salerno, surrounded by woodlands and chestnut groves, and is the place to come if you're looking for cool, fresh air. Here you can sample the hearty cooking of Fulvia Natella, who runs Il Riccio with her sons. A converted cattle shed, the place has been divided into a number of dining rooms with wood-beamed ceilings, brick arches and terracotta floors, and also has an outdoor area.

Dishes are traditional with occasional creative touches, revealing Fulvia's passion for her art. There's a wide range of antipasti: cold cuts such as soppressata, capocollo, pancetta and prosciutto, frittata, various dishes made with seasonal vegetables, **potato gattò** and **ewe's milk ricotta**. The chef's talents really shine through in the first courses, with handmade pasta, such as the signature dish of tagliatelle with pumpkin and smoked provola cheese; then there are **cavatelli with pepper and sausage**, lagane and chickpeas, and in season **scialatielli with cep mushrooms**. As for the main courses, various char-grilled meats – try the **lamb**, then steaks of varying thicknesses, or pork sausages with the classic side order of sautéed broccoli. The puddings include **zeppole**, fried to order, tossed in sugar and served piping hot, and in the fall calzoncelli with chestnuts. The wine list features around 230 labels, with several big Italian and foreign names and a good range of Campanian labels. As of this year, in two adjoining rooms a wine bar serves wines by the glass, cured meats, cheeses and a few ready-made dishes.

CAVA DE' TIRRENI
Arcara

L'ARCARA

🍲Restaurant-pizzeria
Via Lambiase 7
Tel. 089 345177-442341
Closed Monday
Open: dinner, holidays also for lunch
Holidays: three weeks in November
Seating: 130 + 80 outdoors
Prices: 25-28 euros, wine excluded
All credit cards

Cava de' Tirreni, a town of Roman origin, flourished economically thanks to the Benedictine abbey of La Santissima Trinità. Many of the merchants owned farmhouses in the hills around and came here during the hot season. One of these farmhouses, situated by the Molina river a few hundred meters from the main road to Vietri sul Mare (a staging post under the Bourbons), is now the Arcara restaurant. The place is beautifully kept and in summer you can enjoy the cool shade of the garden.

Fabio Senatore will welcome you in and talk you through the menu, which features a good number of **home-cured meats** (from capocollo to pancetta, from soppressata to guanciale, served with mixed seasonal vegetables). In summer, fish dishes come to the fore: Vietri and Cetara are a short distance away and high quality fish is a given, accompanied by seasonal produce: **totani with potatoes**, cuttlefish with peas and seafood with artichokes, to name but a few. As for the first courses, as well as summer dishes such as **paccheri with tuna** or tagliolini with shrimp and zucchini flowers, the rest of the year you can have **paccheri with pork ragù** and, depending on the season, hand-made pasta with mushrooms from the Lattari hills or asparagus risotto. While the poached or grilled fish is sure to please, the **meat** selected by the owner and served in **ragù** or grilled, is unbeatable. The desserts reflect local traditions and are beautifully made, from delizia al limone to chocolate tortino.

The wine list is well balanced and has something from all the regions of Italy (it's good value for money too).

CEPPALONI
Beltiglio

14 KM SOUTH OF BENEVENTO

LA RETE

Restaurant
Contrada Masseriol 11-13
Tel. 0824 46574
Closed Tuesday and Wednesday
Open: lunch and dinner
Holidays: 10 days in July
Seating: 80 + 80 outdoors
Prices: 30-35 euros, wine excluded
All credit cards, Bancomat

Located in the hamlet of Beltiglio in the hills near Ceppaloni, this restaurant is one of those places where the beauty of the landscape and good food come together. From the outdoor tables you can admire a view over the Sabato valley, while you'll be guided in this rewarding journey through the flavors of Sannio cuisine by Dionisio Mignone, son of owner Vincenzo, who launched the restaurant in 1978.
You'll start with mixed antipasti that include prosciutto and lonza, zucchini and eggplant medallions al parmigiano, small ricotta cheeses and bruschetta, then on to a wide choice of first courses mainly cooked using pasta freshly made by Dionisio's grandmother, Gerarda. You can choose from fusilli with cep mushrooms and cardarelle, sausage and parmesan, **cicatielli with wild boar** or sausage and tomato sauce, delicate lasagna with ricotta, basil and cherry tomatoes or with eggplant and walnuts, and again, **potato gnocchi** with black truffle and parmesan. Among the main courses, all inspired by local tradition, **oven-baked stuffed side of lamb** and veal shank cooked in Aglianico wine, which are only a few of the available dishes. To conclude, we must mention the desserts, all local: apple with Strega liqueur, quaresimali, babà and cassatine.
Afterwards, there's a nicely varied cheese board and a very long wine list with approximately 1,000 labels. There's also an olive oil list, a children's menu and a children's playground.

CERRETO SANNITA
Cerquelle

33 KM NORTHWEST OF BENEVENTO SS 372

LA VECCHIA QUERCIA

Restaurant with rooms
Via Cerquelle 25
Tel. 0824 861263-816217
Closed Tuesday
Open: lunch and dinner
Holidays: none
Seating: 150 + 50 outdoors
Prices: 25-30 euros, wine excluded
All credit cards, Bancomat

After leaving Cerreto, a typical little town in the Benevento area famous for its production of pottery, you continue towards Monte Coppe until you get to this restaurant managed by the Parente cousins. Outside there's a gazebo that can be used on warmer days, indoors there are classic-style furnishings. In the kitchen Aldo Meglio values tradition and the use of seasonal products. There's a wide variety of antipasti, among them, stuffed peppers and eggplants, zucchini flowers in batter, broccoletti preserved in olive oil, roast Provoletta cheese, cow's milk ricotta, local cured meats, zucchini soup with dried sausage and **ciaudella** (steamed fava beans with seasoned sausage, onions and bacon). The winter menu sees other dishes, like **pork rind with beans**, corn flour pasticchio and wild vegetable pie or pizza filled with chard. The selection of first courses is just as wide: **curiuli with wild asparagus**, orecchiette with eggplant and tomatoes, **pappardelle with wild boar ragù**, spelt flour stracciate and beans, tagliatelle alla leonessa (with peas, prosciutto and mushrooms), **pepper and eggplant soups**, beetroot fusilli with zucchini and Caciocavallo. On request you can have **carrati with lamb ragù**. For main courses, meats such as lamb and chicken cooked in a variety of ways: in spring virni mushrooms accompany the **chicken stew** or the stuffed turkey, while in winter we recommend the **lightly fried pork** with pickled peppers. There's a good selection of puddings.
To accompany your meal, locally produced wines, mostly Aglianico and Falanghina.

CETARA

CETARA

ACQUAPAZZA

Traditional osteria-trattoria
Corso Garibaldi 38
Tel. 089 261606
Closed Monday
Open: lunch and dinner
Holidays: variable in winter
Seating: 30 + 20 outdoors
Prices: 30-35 euros, wine excluded
All credit cards, Bancomat

The two Gennaros are a great team and they've have launched the restaurant business in Cetara, exploited the seaside village's vocation for fishing and processing mackerel, sardines and anchovies. One product unique to Cetara is 'colatura di alici' (Slow Food Presidium), an anchovy sauce. To get to Acquapazza you turn off the Amalfi coast road and take the street through the village center almost as far as the beach. Gennaro Castiello will give you a warm welcome to his beautifully designed and personally describe the seafood dishes meticulously prepared by his partner Gennaro Marciante. All dishes are based on market availability, starting from the antipasti, many of which raw: from beautifully sweet shellfish to delicate pezzogna and tasty mackerel, sardines and anchovies. The marinated dishes are excellent, as are the **tuna carpaccio** with pistachio nuts and the **red mullet** with pine nuts served on fig leaves. To follow, paccheri with botargo and figs, more traditional **spaghetti with anchovies**, cherry tomatoes and green chili peppers, and **linguine with colatura di alici**. The main courses are up to the same standard: from musdea with potatoes and botargo to **anchovy parmigiana** with zucchini and mozzarella. The choice of desserts includes pear ice-cream, Annurca apple cake and pear and ricotta nests. New regional labels are continuously being added to the already good wine list.

IL CONVENTO

Restaurant
Piazza San Francesco 16
Tel. 089 261039
Closed Tuesday, never in summertime
Open: lunch and dinner
Holidays: none
Seating: 80 + 40 outdoors
Prices: 25-30 euros, wine excluded
All credit cards

This restaurant in the center of Cetara on the Amalfi coast, run by the Torrente family (Pasquale and his wife in the kitchen, Luigi and his father Gaetano front of house), is located in a 17th-century convent. A place of historical interest, it offers a friendly atmosphere and good cooking.
The choice of dishes is halfway between tradition and creative cuisine: there's no lack of pesce azzurro – the mackerel, sardines and anchovies that are the stars of Cetara's economy – but you'll also find new recipes ivented by the chef. **Anchovies** are cooked in various ways and served as antipasti, lightly fried and **filled with smoked Provola**, marinated scapece-style, fried and grilled. Tuna also plays an important role. Aside from classic preparations, it's offered as a carpaccio and in a successful reinterpretation of **Genovese sauce**, with lots of oinion. In addition you can taste **colatura di alici** (Slow Food Presidium) used to flavor spaghetti, potatoes, cannolicchi (razor clams) or to add something extra to orecchiette with turnip tops. One of the new dishes is the home-made toasted wholemeal laganella made with mussels, wild fennel and lemon. For your main course, the catch of the day is served barbecued or grilled, and always accompanied by warm pizza. Don't forget to taste the **escarole pie** with raisins, pine nuts, dry bread and botargo.
For dessert, everything from excellent local pastries to home-baked cakes, from babà and chocolate eggplant to, mattonella, galletta pizza and warm chocolate cake with fruit sauce.
The wine cellar is very well stocked with a prevalence of regional labels.

CETARA

SAN PIETRO

Trattoria
Piazza San Francesco 2
Tel. 089 261091-333 8296251
Closed Tuesdays, never in summer
Open: lunch and dinner
Holidays: end-January-beginning-February
Seating: 40 + 35 outdoors
Prices: 35 euros, wine excluded
All credit cards except AE, Bancomat

The village of Cetara has a long tradition of fishing pesce azzurro (fish such as mackerel, sardines and anchovies) that has given rise to many small-scale, quality canning businesses. Generally speaking, restaurants in the area offer extremely good food and the San Pietro is no exception. Here you'll find traditional Mediterranean cooking using the very best fish, vegetables and local cheeses.
Owners Franco Tammaro and Bruno Milano will give you a warm welcome and the waiters will help you choose dishes from a menu that varies with the seasons. Great emphasis is placed on **pesce azzurro**, which you can taste **smoked** over aromatic wood fires (the restaurant prepares this dish itself) and other types of little known fish. A special mention should also be made of **Provola cheese with Cetara anchovies** in Amalfi lemon leaves, **raw pesce azzurro platter**, **spaghetti with colatura di alici** or mixed seafood, and tubettoni with rock-fish. For main course, the catch of the day comes oven-baked with potatoes, all'acquapazza (stewed), grilled or in a soup. The desserts are excellent: some of them are bought in from a famous local pastry shop, others are made by the restaurant.
A lot of thought has gone into the wine list, which includes unusual regional and other national labels (including sweet red wines).

At Corso Umberto I 64, Il Nettuno sells canned anchovies and tuna, colatura di alici and other seafood specialties.

DRAGONI

VILLA DE PERTIS

3-Star Hotel
Via Ponti 30
Tel. and fax 0823 866619
E-mail: info@villadepertis.it
Internet: www.villadepertis.it
Closed 10/01-10/03 and 12/11-30/11

Villa de Pertis is a small hotel in a 17th-century residence that has been restructured while retaining many of its original features. The elegant period furnishings of the rooms (al with en-suite bathrooms, except for one double room that has an adjacent bathroom) are all different, and the suites have spacious living rooms with a fireplace and comfortable couches. In the morning guests sit round the same table to enjoy bread baked in a wood-fired oven, jams and other home-made products. Guests can also choose a half board option (at a cost of 52 euros per person). This is a particularly nice place to relax and from the garden there's a view stretching from the Matese Mountains to the hills sloping down to the River Volturno.

• 4 double, 1 four-bed rooms and 2 suites, with bathroom; suites with TV • Prices: double room single use 63 euros, double 75, four-bed 124, suite 128, breakfast included • Credit cards: all except DC, Bancomat • Restaurant accessible for the mobility challenged. Off-street parking. Small pets allowed. Reception open until 11pm, owners always present • Restaurant. Breakfast room. Garden

ERCOLANO

9 KM SOUTH OF NAPLES A 3 EXIT TORRE DEL GRECO

VIVA LO RE

Osteria
Corso Resina 261
Tel. 081 7390207
Closed Sunday and Monday
Open: lunch and dinner
Holidays: August
Seating: 54
Prices: 25-30 euros, wine excluded
All credit cards, Bancomat

The entrance to this osteria is in Corso Resina, on what used to be the royal road to Calabria, just a short distance from the archeological site of Herculaneum. The road, built in Bourbon times, is still lined by baroque villas with pleasant gardens and terraces overlooking the sea.

Open since 1995, this osteria is very capably managed by Maurizio Focone, sommelier and cheese taster. His restaurant offers a cuisine based on seasonal produce and ingredients from the area around Vesuvius. The osteria comprises several rooms, all of them displaying bottles of wine (in total the place stocks more than 1,500 labels). The menu is written on a blackboard in the main room, but it will be repeated to you and explained by the waiter.

Antipasti change every week and consist of tastes of various dishes. Among the first courses, the bucatini, potato and provola timbale, **cream of potatoes and Vesuvian cep mushrooms**, **timbale of pasta alla Genovese** (with meat and onions), **tubettoni with spolchini beans and mussels**, cannelloni filled with ricotta and Provolone del monaco cheese and a cherry tomato al piennolo sauce, **lentil and sausage soup** or cicerchie (grass peas) with stewed stockfish. In summer: **vermicelli with clams and Schito artichokes** or green fettuccine with red mullet and fennel. Main courses feature good cuts of beef, **rabbit** stuffed with eggplant and bacon, **carrè of Benevento lamb** with potato and lardo pie, grilled tuna, and fried baccalà on cream of cabbage. End with a good Annurca apple pie or a chocolate and ricotta flan.

FURORE

31 KM WEST OF SALERNO

SANT'ALFONSO

Holiday farm
Via Sant'Alfonso 6
Tel. and fax 089 830515
E-mail: info@agriturismosantalfonso.it
Internet: www.agriturismosantalfonso.it

To stay in this agriturismo, leave your heavy baggage behind, park the car and tackle the steep climb (500 meters) up from the main road below. This was once a convent and a place for meditation (the chapel is still extant); today, it is an ideal place for chilling out and enjoying the magnificent view. The bedrooms are furnished with restraint; buffet breakfasts include a selection of home-made cakes, jam & marmalade, fruit and preserved fresh and hot beverages. Excellent meals are also served to non-residents on holidays (25-30 euros; 20 euro supplement per person for half-board).

• 10 double rooms with bathroom, air-conditioning, TV • Prices: double room single use 50 euros, double 60-80 (20 euro supplement for extra bed), breakfast included • Credit cards: all, Bancomat • Free external public parking. Small pets allowed. Owners always present • Restaurant. Reading room. Garden, terraces with views

GESUALDO

LA PERGOLA

⌒ Trattoria
Via Freda
Tel. 0825 401435
Closed Wednesday
Open: dinner, lunch by reservation
Holidays: November
Seating: 70 + 30 outdoors
Prices: 27-32 euros, wine excluded
All credit cards, Bancomat

Guarded by the Castle of Carlo Gesualdo, this restaurant offers a pleasant atmosphere and good food. It's managed
by two young people, Franca and Antonio De Filippis, who deserve to be con-
gratulated for the way in which they've
defended and revitalized local flavors by
salvaging their grandmothers' recipes.
Franca works front of house, while Antonio is in the kitchen helped by Antonio
Ferrante. They still take advantage – and
who can blame them? – of the precious
advice of Antonio's mother, Concetta. The
menu, seasonal and mainly based on
vegetables from the garden, aims to promote local tradition. You'll taste dishes
such as the zucchini, cheese and pumpkin flower flan, **fresh garlic soup and
egg a sciuscella**, chickpea and broccoli
soup with pork meatballs. Among the
classic winter dishes, **Materdomini bean
and chestnut soup** or **potato**, mushroom and Caciocavallo podolico **pie**. The
various pasta sauces feature vegetables:
in spring, **maccaronara with wild asparagus** and fresh peas, in summer, ravioli with creamed eggplant and salted ricotta cheese or maccheroni with string
beans, walnuts and pine kernels. Plus
chitarrine or gnocchetti with ragù. Meat
from the Irpinia area – mainly poultry –
takes pride of place in main courses:
rabbit and peppers alla composta
(pickled), free-range chicken with gallinacci mushrooms, stuffed lamb and **leg
of lamb baked in hay** are just some of
the choices. To end your meal, cheese
accompanied by honey or fig jam and
puddings such as Annurca apple tart,
chestnut and chocolate flan, zuccotto di
torrone and sheep's milk ricotta.
The wine list offers the area's best reds
and whites.

GIFFONI SEI CASALI
Sieti

IL BRIGANTE

⌒ Traditional osteria
Via Andoli 2
Tel. 089 881854-328 9592987
Closed Tuesday
Open: dinner, festivities also for lunch
Holidays: Christmas period
Seating: 50 + 20 outdoors
Prices: 18-23 euros, wine excluded
All credit cards, Bancomat

Sieti is a medieval village just a few kilometers from Salerno. In the center is this
osteria, opened in what were once the
cattle sheds of an old noble home by
Guido Brancaccio, a former painter, and
his wife Rosaria, whose passion is cooking. In summer you can eat outside in
the courtyard. The style of the cuisine is
simple and unpretentious with lots of
local ingredients: from the Giffoni hazelnut and the olive oil of the Salerno hills,
both protected products, to wine, chestnuts and wild mushrooms.
The antipasti consist of a selection of
local cured meats and dishes prepared
using seasonal vegetables, such as
green stewed pumpkin with beans and
sausage, Savoy cabbage with beans,
eggplant and smoked Provola roulades
and salad of **Senerchia beans**. Among
the first courses: **lagane and chickpeas**,
strascinati with eggplant, cortecce with
cep mushrooms, **pasta with chestnuts
and sausage**. Barbecued meats, lamb in
particular, make a nice main course. Alternatively, you can have **wild boar with
potatoes and chiuchiarole** (pickled red
peppers) or **stuffed hen** (available on request and only during certain periods) as
it's a dish that requires cooking for many
hours. The stock obtained from this last
dish is served with hand-made tagliolini.
To end your meal, desserts made with
hazelnuts, best accompanied by wild
fennel or Annurca apple liqueur. The
wine list focuses on reds from the Campania region.

GIUGLIANO IN CAMPANIA

14 KM NORTHWEST OF NAPLES

FENESTA VERDE

Restaurant
Vico Sorbo 1
Tel. 081 8941239
Closed Sunday for dinner and Monday
Open: lunch and dinner, festivities only for lunch
Holidays: August, December 23–January 3
Seating: 80
Prices: 32-35 euros, wine excluded
All credit cards, Bancomat

LA MARCHESELLA

Restaurant
Via Marchesella 186
Tel. 081 8945219
Closed Wednesday
Open: lunch and dinner
Holidays: 15 days mid-August
Seating: 80 + 30 outdoors
Prices: 32-35 euros, wine excluded
All credit cards, Bancomat

The sign outside this restaurant, situated in the village center, close to the church of the Annunziata, reminds us that it has been open since 1948. What remains of the original restaurant are the color of the windows, the welcome you receive and the pleasant aroma that comes from the kitchen. Luisa and Laura Lodice, along with their husbands Guido and Giacomo, are now a benchmark for gastronomy in Campania and it's not easy to describe their skill in words. The excellent quality of the ingredients and local dishes, almost disarming in their simplicity, needs no additional comment. As there's no written menu, Guido will describe all the best dishes of the day. There's a wide choice of antipasti: in summer scampi with citrus fruit, smoked tuna and swordfish, marinated baccalà with botarga and pine nuts, king prawns and mussels in batter and **eggplant parmigiana without tomato**; in winter, you'll find **sausage and friarielli timbale**, pepper roulades with prosciutto and cheese, leek and cep mushroom soup, cultivated mushrooms filled with meat and cheese and **roast artichokes**. First courses may include **ziti alla Genovese**, **mezzanielli lardiati**, pasta and Villaricca beans, paccheri with peppers, eggplant and sausage, **minestra maritata** and tubettoni with mussels and broccoli. For main courses: fried baccalà and **mixed fried seafood**, beef or **pork chop** stuffed with pine nuts and raisins. For dessert pastiera, made during the Easter period, chocolate flan, semifreddo with cream and melon. The wine list offers more than 300 labels, including most of the wines produced in Campania and a selection of the best other Italian wines.

This is a place that never ceases to amaze for the quality of its food, the discreet atmosphere and, last but not least, Gena and Tommaso's kindness. Giugliano is in the Neapolitan hinterland, an area that like all suburban conurbations doesn't receive a very good press. In this specific case, any prejudices you may have will evaporate one by one. Dishes on the menu are a tribute to the local area but without being banal. Don't fail to taste antipasti such as **eggplant parmigiana without tomato**, potato gattò, sausage and friarielli greens, stuffed mushrooms or courgette flowers, eggplant fritters, **anchovies stuffed with provola**, octopus carpaccio, swordfish with lemon dressing, **marinated baccalà**, anchovy pie, buffalo mozzarella and fried calamaretti and eggplant tartar. For first courses in summer feature gnocchetti with clams, cherry tomatoes and pumpkin flowers, **tubetti with mussels and beans**, paccheri with scampi or angler fish, mussels and eggplant or cream of tomato soup. In winter the condiments change: gnocchi with Provolone del monaco fondue and cep mushrooms, **pasta and beans**, escarole soup with baccalà, clams, cabbage and pine nuts, **mezzanielli lardiati**. To follow, fillet of beef stuffed with bacon and Ragusano cheese, **baccalà**, turbot with potatoes. To finish, white chocolate and rum flan, ricotta tart, millefoglie, pear and ricotta cake, mousse of buffalo ricotta, Annurca apple pie. The wine list (there's also an olive oil list) offers an extensive collection of regional and other Italian wines.

AGLIO, OLIO E POMODORO

Restaurant
Spiaggia dei Maronti-Località Petrelle
Tel. 081 906408
No closing day
Open: lunch and dinner
Holidays: November-before Easter
Seating: 50
Prices: 30-35 euros, wine excluded
No credit cards, Bancomat

IL FOCOLARE DI LORETTA E RICCARDO D'AMBRA

Restaurant
Via Cretajo al Crocifisso 3
Tel. 081 902944
Closed Wednesday, never in summer
Open: dinner, weekends also for lunch
Holidays: December 9-27
Seating: 90 + 100 outdoors
Prices: 30-35 euros, wine excluded
All credit cards except DC
Chiocciola

South-facing Maronti beach is one of the most beautiful on the island and, on clearer days, Capri seems very close indeed. The lush vegetation and the thermal springs make it a very pleasant place to be and its beauty increases in the late afternoon and evening. On the beach and just steps away from the sea is this small restaurant in a cave owned and managed by Peppe. A barman and showman in Ischia's golden days, he'll welcome you with such politeness and warmth that you'll immediately feel at home.

The cuisine revolves round the freshest seafood from local fishermen. Obviously the menu varies daily according to the catch, but the result is always a triumph of color, aroma and flavor. We tasted stuffed courgette flowers, **clam and mussel sauté**, shrimp in light tomato sauce, **fried anchovies** and **grilled eggplants**. To follow there's always **spaghetti** with various types of **seafood** with fish in tomato sauce or seasonal vegetables. Then you'll be offered the catch of the day cooked however you want (grilled, fried or oven-baked). Home-made puddings among which caprese and fruit tarts, and liqueurs – limoncello, rucolino and a delicious cherry liqueur – make a perfect end to your meal.

The local house wine is good though you can also choose from among a few island and Friuli labels. In peak season, booking is advisable as there are so few tables.

Green is the island's dominant color, thanks to the vineyards, orchards, promontories with aromatic herbs and, above all, the distinctive tufa stone that gives the island its unique character. The D'Ambra family emphasizes local agricultural produce and flavors, bucking the popular image of an island famous for its blue sea and seafood only. It all began when Riccardo D'Ambra, his wife Loretta and numerous family members opened a restaurant where they created a menu of dishes different from those served in other eateries. Today the couple's sons, Agostino and Francesco, run the kitchen with help from their mother, while Silvia and her sisters serve front of house. Riccardo himself is a born actor who will entertain you with his colorful history of the island. Of the antipasti, we should mention **crostini with crushed wild garlic**, potato and scamorza flan served with pumpkin sauce (a typical dish in September) and the ever-present **eggplant parmigiana**. First courses include paccheri with wild garlic, **ravioli of escarole al vincotto**, mezzanielli with wild herbs or **soup with zampognari beans**. Main courses concentrate on meat dishes, such as the **lamb al mirto del Cretajo**, varies cuts cooked on a hot stone and, ordering in advance, **rabbit all' ischitana**, excellent with a side dish of french fries. For dessert, crème brûlée alla verbena and chocolate soufflé with geranium cream. The wine cellar offers many labels, mainly local.

ISLAND OF ISCHIA
Lacco Ameno-Fango

MASSA LUBRENSE
Sant'Agata sui Due Golfi

RESIDENCE VERDE

Holiday farm
Via Crateca 34
Tel. 081 995123-347 7820694
Fax 081 995123
E-mail: residenceverde@pointel.it
Internet: www.ischiatravelweb.it/residenceverde
Open from Easter to end-October

FATTORIA TERRANOVA

Holiday farm
Via Pontone 10
Tel. 081 5330234
No closing day
Open: lunch and dinner
Holidays: December 8-March 8
Seating: 50
Prices: 30 euros
All credit cards except AE, Bancomat

The strong point of this facility is its vineyard-orchard, little more than a hectare of land, that Francesco Verde, a retired doctor, has kept as it was handed down to him by his forebears. Local grape varieties, with singular names such as arrigghio and coglionara, are grown in rows between fruit trees. The farm offers guests two solutions for their vacation: hotel or residence. The bedrooms and apartments are furnished in a simple, functional manner. The panoramic position is further enhanced by the very quiet surroundings. Breakfast is served to hotel guests and includes the produce of the farm: fruit and excellent jam and marmalade. All guests can use the swimming pool and the tracks leading to the Epomeo crater.

• 9 double rooms with bathroom, terrace, mini-bar, television, several rooms with kitchenette; 1 apartment (4-5 people) with kitchen • Prices: double room single use 25-45 euros, double 50-90 (8-14 euro supplement for extra bed), breakfast included; apartment 66-160 • Credit cards: none • 2 rooms with facilities for the mobility challenged. Off-road parking. Small pets allowed. Owners always reachable • Breakfast room. Garden, terrace. Swimming pool

Fattoria Terranova is a farm in the remote hills of Sant'Agata sui Due Golfi, in the heart of what's known as the 'Terra delle Sirene', or Siren Land. The farm serves its own produce: wine, olive oil, vegetables and fruit, jams, lemon liqueur and rosolio. The atmosphere is rural, tables are arranged under a Sorrento-style pergola, and you'll be served informally but politely by three young people: Rossella, Luigi and Francesca Ruoppo. The chef is just as young though he's already very experienced.
Dishes on the menu are all traditional. The antipasti are so generous they can make a meal on their own – on your plate you'll find some seafood but mostly cured meats and vegetables. Following on, **shrimp and squid fried in green batter** is a must. The first course usually features two or three choices according to what's available in the vegetable garden and the shops. We tasted excellent **tubettoni con una finta genovese**, though you may also find eggplant timbale, delicate homemade **ravioli with zucchini flowers** or alla caprese. For main courses there are only meats: excellent **mixed grilled meat** cooked on the barbecue, but you can also have straccetti in red wine sauce or **oven-baked shank of pork**. There's an interesting variety of traditional Neapolitan and Sorrento puddings: caprese, **babà**, **fruit tart**, and with your coffee, a tasty warm puff-pastry.
To drink, the red or white house wine, or one of a dozen labels from the Campania region. To end your meal, **lemon liqueur** and risoli flavored with local aromatic herbs. The check is reasonable and booking is essential.

MASSA LUBRENSE
Villazzano

IL GIARDINO DI VIGLIANO

🔑 Holiday farm
Via Vigliano 3
Tel. 081 5339823
Fax 081 5339837
E-mail: info@vigliano.org
Internet: www.vigliano.org
Open all year round

The sign above the entrance to this vacation farm invites visitors to raise their gaze to take in the beauty of the place. Situated on the Sorrento peninsula. A narrow avenue beneath a pergola of scented lemon trees leads to a meticulously restored stone building on two levels that was once a look-out tower. Here guests are welcomed by Peppino, his wife Ida and their children. The bedrooms, with wood or brick floors and plain furnishings, have a fine view over the garden. A traditional breakfast of honey, jam and marmalade, bread and home-baked cakes is served in a common room. In the restaurant, residents only, meals (17 euros, wine excluded) are prepared by Ida using local or farm products.

• 8 double rooms with bathroom • Prices: double room single use and double 60-70 euros (30-35 euro supplement for extra bed), breakfast included • Credit cards: none • Off-road parking. No pets allowed. Owners always present • Restaurant. Breakfast room, reading and television room. Garden, terrace, solarium

MASSA LUBRENSE
Santa Maria dell'Annunziata

LA TORRE

🍲 Restaurant
Piazzetta Annunziata 7
Tel. 081 8089566
Closed Tuesday, in summer only for lunch
Open: lunch and dinner
Holidays: January 7-31
Seating: 80 + 80 outdoors
Prices: 28-30 euros, wine excluded
All major credit cards, Bancomat

In Santa Maria dell'Annunziata, vines and citrus and olive trees frame a view of the sparkling sea, clear blue sky and Capri, which seems so close you could reach out and touch it. All this is enough on its own to make the trip worthwhile, but if you're looking for more you'll find it at La Torre. The two owners of the restaurant are Tonino Mazzola and his wife Maria Aprea, true queen of the kitchen, while their daughters Amelia and Alessia help front of house. To start you can choose dishes that blend sea and land ingredients, such as cuttlefish with Sorrento walnuts and **octopus with artichokes** or potatoes. Lots of fish and vegetables also in first courses: **paccheri with mussels and potatoes**, ravioli with smoked Provola and rocket, flavored with a light local cherry tomato sauce; **eggplant timbale** and linguine stuffed with tomato sauce and mozzarella. But there are so many combinations: a wide variety of sauces can be the right condiment for homemade pastas, for instance, seafood or tomato and basil sauces. To follow, the catch of the day cooked on the barbecue, oven-baked, fried or all'acquapazza (stewed). When in season, **Crapolla shrimp** also appears frequently. Seasonal side dishes are tasty too, and the **eggplant parmigiana** is outstanding. Local cheeses include an excellent Provolone del monaco, and the delicious desserts are all home-made, from cold ricotta and pear cake to oven-baked cassatina with cow's milk ricotta, candied fruit and chocolate.
The wine list has expanded, focusing on Campanian labels plus a few good national wines. At the end of the meal, infusions and homemade rosolio.

MASSA LUBRENSE
Marina del Cantone

LE SIRENE

3-Star Hotel
Via Marina del Cantone 27
Tel. 081 8081027-8081771
Fax 081 8081027
E-mail: info@lesirenehotel.it
Internet: www.lesirenehotel.it
Closed January 10-February 10

The hotel is beautifully situated a short stroll from the sea, in a small fishing village in the Punta Campanella marine park, The building dates back to the late 17th century and was once a convent under the orders of the Certosa di Padula. Today, fully restored and modernized, it has bedrooms, common areas and a restaurant. The bedrooms are furnished in marine style and have view over the the sea or of the hill to the rear and are reasonably comfortable. Breakfast is served in a common room and consists of cakes, jam and marmalade made in the restaurant. The Sorrento peninsula and the Amalfi coast offer a vast range of excursions. We recommend hiring a boat to visit the inlets along the coasdt or walks along the well-marked paths. Half board 75-85 euros per person.

• 8 double rooms, 4 triple and 4 with 4 beds, bathroom, balcony, air conditioning, mini-bar, safe, satellite television • Prices: double room single use 100 euros, double 100-120, triple 130, with 4 beds 140, breakfast included • Credit cards: none • Outside parking on payment and free parking at 800 meters. Small pets allowed. Porter service 6am-1pm • Bar, restaurant. Private beach

MASSA LUBRENSE
Sant'Agata sui Due Golfi

LE TORE

Holiday farm
Via Pontone 43
Tel. 081 8080637-333 9866691
Fax 081 5330819
E-mail: info@letore.com
Internet: www.letore.com
Open from Easter to beginning November and at Christmas

Le Tore is a, agriturismo set in a late 19th-century building; the organic farm produces excellent olive oil, fruit and seasonal vegetables, as well as poultry and rabbits. Owner Vittoria Brancaccio is an expert agronomist. Helped by local workers, she has adapted facilities to meet the needs of people seeking a simple vacation in close contact with nature. Excursions on foot or bike are organized, as well as courses and stages. The superb breakfasts consist almost entirely of the farm's own produce: jams, honey, fruit, eggs, homemade sweets. Farm products are star in typical dinners and lunches (18-25 euros, wine excluded).

• 8 double rooms with bathroom; 1 apartment (5 people) with kitchen, garden, terrace • Prices: double room single use 60 euros, double 90 (30 euro supplement for extra bed), breakfast included • Credit cards: main, Bancomat • 1 room equipped for the mobility challenged. Off-road parking. Small pets allowed. Owners always present • Restaurant (only for resident guests or groups on prior booking). Breakfast room. Garden

MASSA LUBRENSE
Sant'Agata sui Due Golfi

LO STUZZICHINO

🍲Restaurant
Via Deserto 1
Tel. 081 5330010-333 3323189
Closed Wednesday, never in July and August
Open: lunch and dinner
Holidays: January 25 – February 20
Seating: 50 + 80 outdoors
Prices: 27-30 euros, wine excluded
All major credit cards, Bancomat

Originally a take-away food outlet, Lo Stuzzichino gradually grew into a restaurant whose food reflects the character of Massa Lubrense, a seaside town yet to be raided by mass tourism. It is run by the young but already expert manager and sommelier, Mimmo De Gregorio, whose wife helps front of house, while his parents put their experience to good use in the kitchen. The cuisine is based on local traditions and the use of quality ingredients, hence simple but very tasty dishes, with just a few minor adjustments to cater for foreign tourists with a stereotyped idea of Italian food.

The general menu is vast, and we suggest you choose from the menu of the day, based on the season and the daily market. Begin with **eggplant parmigiana pie**, the tasty mixed antipasti of the house, or **caprese** with tomatoes and local mozzarella. To follow, **pasta with beans and mussels**, pappardelle with clams and a scent of lemon, **calamarata with mussels and potatoes**, ravioli of borage or **cannelloni alla sorrentina**. For main course, there's excellent meat, but the real star is seafood: **stewed squid and potatoes**, baby octopus al pignatiello, **Crapolla shrimp** or grilled squid. You can also choose from the catch of the day cooked to your liking: oven-baked, grilled, fried or all'acquapazza (stewed). All mains can be accompanied by seasonal vegetables. To end your meal, Provolone del monaco cheese and diavoletti di Arola in lemon leaves. There's a good choice of home-made puddings, such as pear and ricotta cake or pizza della nonna with cherry cream and chocolate.

A very good wine list offers approximately 150 labels and a selection of grappas, whiskies and liqueurs.

MASSA LUBRENSE
Sant'Agata sui Due Golfi

MARGHERITA

🍲Restaurant
Via dei Campi 13
Tel. 081 8780321
Closed Monday, never in summer
Open: lunch and dinner
Holidays: none
Seating: 70 + 70 outdoors
Prices: 28-30 euros, wine excluded
All credit cards, Bancomat

Sant'Agata sui due Golfi and its immediate environs are one of the best areas for wine and food in Campania. While there are many world famous, but expensive restaurants, these have paved the way for more affordable places that offer an opportunity to taste local cuisine based on carefully selected ingredients. Margherita has carved out a niche for itself with cooking that has hardly changed since it opened nearly 50 years ago. The dining room is pleasant and in summer other tables are added in an outdoor area immersed in lush vegetation. The business involves the entire Tizzani family: in the kitchen, serving customers and managing the administrative side of things. The cuisine is based on local tradition, the seasons and what's available at the market. Fresh bread, meat, local cheeses and cured meats, vegetables from the family vegetable garden, freshly made pasta and home-made puddings and liqueurs: this is the restaurant's winning formula. Meat or seafood antipasti, including cured meats and local vegetable are followed by **freshly made pastas** served with a variety of **seafood** or fish sauces, or alternatively with tomatoes, eggplant and mozzarella or **alla Genovese** (meat and onions). For main courses, a variety of fresh fish cooked to your taste: oven-baked, fried, **all'acquapazza** (stewed) or in a soup. When available, don't miss the **salt and pepper Crapolla shrimp**. Otherwise there's an Italian-style mixed fried fish platter, **eggplant parmigiana** or stuffed peppers. The home-made puddings are good and the wine list, though not particularly extensive, offers a good variety of Campanian labels at reasonable prices.

Massa Lubrense
Villazzano

Melito Irpino

Villa Pina

🛏️ 3-Star Hotel
Via Partenope 40
Tel. 081 5339780–0878 2212
Fax 081 8071813
E-mail: info@francischiello.com
Internet: www.francischiello.com
Open all year round

Trattoria di Pietro

🍲 Restaurant
Corso Italia 8
Tel. 0825 472010
Closed Wednesday
Open: lunch and dinner
Holidays: in September
Seating: 90 + 15 outdoors
Prices: 30-35 euros, wine excluded
All credit cards, Bancomat

A small, peaceful, hotel immersed in the greenery on the road from Sorrento to Massa Lubrense. The plain, spacious rooms (some can sleep up to 3 or 4) are furnished with good taste and every comfort and offer views of the magnificent panorama with Capri in the background. The hotel is managed by the Gargiulo family, who also own the famous Antico Francischiello da Peppino restaurant. A warm welcome is assured by Signora Pina and her children, Firminia and Francesco. Breakfast includes coffee, milk, fruit juices, croissants, conchas, pastry, jams and preserves and fresh fruit. Half board 90 euros per person.

• 3 single rooms, 22 double, bathroom, air conditioning, mini-bar, satellite television • Prices: double room single occupancy 65 euros, double 95, triple 150, with 4 beds 200, breakfast included • Credit cards: all, Bancomat • Common areas accessible to the mobility challenged. Off-road parking. No pets allowed. Reception open 24 hours a day • Restaurant. Breakfast room, reading and television room. Solarium. Terrace

🍲 The Antico Francischiello da Peppino restaurant serves classic Neapolitan cuisine with seafood (50-70 euros, wine excluded).

Enzo Di Pietro's restaurant has been open since the 30s but is now to be found in new Melito, given that the village was entirely rebuilt after the earthquake of 1962. The building housing the restaurant is in the same anti-seismic style – square, white, two-floor constructions – as the rest of the village, But don't be put off by this, since memories of the atmosphere in old Melito – where the river ran through the town and locals swam in it in summer, the public square crowded during festivities and narrow alleyways buzzing with life – still live on in the sepia photoss on the walls and in the dishes served in this restaurant. In his cooking, Enzo, helped in the kitchen by his parents and wife Teresa, and by his children Anita and Pasquale in the dining room, conjures up memories by using spices and ingredients that draw on past tradition. There's a lot of emphasis on **pulieio**, a herb similar to mint with aromatic and refreshing properties, used in a sauce to flavor **cecatielli**. The fascinating list of dishes includes **stuffed escarole** and roasted eggplants, paccheri ai profumi dell'orto, **orecchiette with cherry tomatoes and ricotta**, **minestra maritata**, celery hearts with cardoncelli mushrooms, **fusilli a ciambotta** or with minced meat and tomato sauce, and cecatielli with broccoli, barbecued **lamb**, veal flavored with wild fennel, chicken and **rabbit alla cacciatora**, beef stew with egg, oven-baked **mugliatielli** and baccalà. If that's not enough, at the end of your meal, sample the Pecorino di laticauda or local Caciocavallo from the well-stocked **cheese board**, or try the almond and hazelnut croccante. The wine list offers a well balanced variet, and there's also a wide selection of grappas, whiskies and liqueurs.

MERCOGLIANO
Capocastello

MOLINARA

I SANTI

AL BORGO

Osteria
Via San Francesco 17
Tel. 0825 788776
Closed Sunday for dinner and Monday
Open: lunch and dinner
Holidays: 15 days between July and beginning August
Seating: 54
Prices: 27-30 euros, wine excluded
All credit cards except AE, Bancomat

Restaurant-pizzeria
Corso Umberto I 1
Tel. 0824 994004
Closed Monday
Open: lunch and dinner
Holidays: July 1-10
Seating: 70
Prices: 18-20 euros, wine excluded
All major credit cards, Bancomat

The osteria is in the medieval village of Capocastello, with its small alleys and hidden spots from which you can enjoy beautiful views. The inside is pleasant, enhanced by exposed stone walls, wooden beams and tables set in a refined manner. Owners Emilio and Federico, helped in the kitchen by Lino Di Bonito, are equally meticulous in taking care of their customers by offering a well-balanced menu of seasonal quality products such as fresh and cured meats and cheeses, mushrooms and local varieties of fruit (Annurca apples and Mastantuono pears).

The menu, which changes often, starts with schiacciata of smoked pork with pecorino, prosciutto with local ricotta and peppers, lettuce **roulades** with Scamorza and cured meats (or **with eggplants, local cheeses and basil**), oven-baked potatoes with Provola, cep mushrooms and local bacon. For first course, among the newly added dishes we suggest the gnocchetti made from bran and breadcrumbs with **pesto di friarielli greens**, basil and cherry tomatoes, **cordicelle** (hand-made flat pasta) **with courgette flowers** and bocconcini di pasta filled with provola and ricotta, and cep mushrooms. To follow you can have **veal steak in Aglianico** (wild boar is cooked the same way), veal fillet with peppers and **pork shank with lampascioni** (wild onions). To end your meal, croccantino with hazelnuts, cream and chocolate, semifreddo, mousse and other puddings, all created by the chef.
To accompany your meal, a bottle of Aglianico or wines from other regions. Plus, locally made liqueurs.

For those visiting Pietrelcina (the village where Padre Pio was born) we suggest they venture into the Fortore, a country area where you'll be surrounded by nature as far as the eye can see. Molinara is an isolated on the border between the Campania and Puglia regions. You'll find this restaurant in the old center, currently undergoing restructuring work. It's by no means typical in terms of its interior designs, but it's certainly authentic. Rocco Matteo, proud of this world apart, has been the owner of the restaurant for over 20 years. In the kitchen works Antony, who has always shared the owner's philosophy and gastronomic aims.

The cuisine has a definite personality. Start with **grilled ricotta** and **cauliflower fritters**, then move on to local firsts, such as **quagliatelli and beans**, **paccozzelle and chickpeas**, or a dish that may seem rather run-of-the-mill but is not to be missed since it's made using top quality ingredients: **cavatelli with cherry tomatoes and basil**. For main course, only meat (but excellent!) grilled on the barbecue.

As an alternative, the pizzas, which attract lots of customers: not to be missed are **pizza with chicory and mozzarella** and, when in season, pizza with sausage and turnip. The local cheeses are good (there are two cheese producers in the area) and, among the desserts, worth a try is the cassatina di San Marco dei Cavoti, made by a famous local pastry shop that exports its torroncini all over the world. The choice of wine is limited to a few labels from the Benevento area.

MONTEMARANO
Ponteromito

32 KM EAST OF AVELLINO

IL GASTRONOMO

Restaurant
Via Nazionale 77 A
Tel. 0827 67009-67059
Closed Wednesday and Sunday for dinner
Open: lunch and dinner
Holidays: in July
Seating: 90
Prices: 30-35 euros, wine excluded
All credit cards, Bancomat

The Pisaniello family restaurant is well known by tourists who ski in the Picentini mounts. Here brothers Massimo and Franco are helped by their mother Anna Maria is a great help in the kitchen, while the well-trained staff always serve you quickiy and efficiently. The Pisaniellos continue to serve dishes that emphasize local traditions, introducing just a few changes and creative touches. The basis for their cooking is top quality local ingredients like Laceno mushrooms and truffles and Podolico beef. The house antipasti, generous and very well presented, include **Venticano prosciutto** and **Montella ricotta**, though there are also more elaborate dishes such as cream of beans with polenta and crispy bacon, and savory potato pie, cep mushrooms and Ravece olive oil. Among the first courses: **ravioli of cow's milk ricotta** with turnip tops and smoked Provola, **cecaluccoli** (handmade gnocchetti) with lardo di Colonnata, cherry tomatoes and ricotta cheese, **maccaronara all'antica** and other creative dishes invented by the chef. To follow, Podolico beef cooked in different ways, lightly seasoned **veal chop** on the bone cooked in Fiano d'Avellino wine or **Carmasciano lamb**. The selection of local cheeses is excellent and includes Pecorino carmasciano produced in Rocca San Felice.
The wine cellar has a large number of local quality wines and some excellent national labels.

NAPLES

DIMORA SANT'ELIGIO

3-Star Hotel
Via Rota 36-38
Tel. 081 268165-202785
Fax 081 5637544
E-mail: info@dimorasanteligio.it
Internet: www.dimorasanteligio.it
Open all year round

Opened little more than a year ago, the hotel is located in an old but completely renovated building. Occupying two floors, the spacious, bright rooms all have well-appointed bathrooms. The entire building is furnished in 19th-century style: the ground floor has a small lounge with library for guests. The top floor has a big terrace with tables and chairs and a view over the roofs and the bell tower of the old town. The continental breakfast can also be served in the rooms, while the reception has charming personnel and a hostess happy to solve any problem and provide information. The price of the rooms includes manned parking.

• 12 double rooms with bathroom, air conditioning, mini-bar, satellite television • Prices: double room single use 95 euros, double 120 (15 euro supplement for extra bed), breakfast included • Credit cards: all, Bancomat • 2 rooms equipped for the mobility challenged. Safe parking in the immediate vicinity. Small pets allowed. Reception open 24 hours a day • Restaurant (managed separately). Breakfast room, reading and television room, internet point. Terrace

EUROPEO

⌒ Ristorante-pizzeria
Via Marchese Campodisola 4
Tel. 081 5521323
Closed Sunday
Open for lunch, also dinner Thursday,
Friday, Saturday and before holidays
Holidays: 15 days after Ferragosto
Seating: 65
Prices: 35 euros, wine excluded
All credit cards, Bancomat

HOSTERIA TOLEDO

⌒ Traditional Osteria
Vico Giardinetti 78 A
Tel. 081 421257
Closed Tuesday for dinner
Open: lunch and dinner
Holidays: never
Seating: 70
Prices: 25-30 euros, wine excluded
All credit cards, Bancomat

Europeo, a relaxing place with an oblig-ing family atmosphere, is situated in the center of Naples, near Piazza Borsa. The two dining rooms – one large, the other reserved – are decorated with paintings and antique prints of the city. In charge is Alfonso Mattozzi, a worthy follower of his family's tradition. It's he who wel-comes you and explains the typical local dishes on the menu.
The meal begins with **focacce filled with sausage**, friarielli (local meadow greens) and escarole, tortano napoletano, **croc-chi (croquette potatoes)**, fried courgette flowers, wonderful **mozzarella di bufala** campana and sautè of clams.
First courses: tubettoni with seafood, lin-guine with langoustine, pasta, potatoes and Provola, **ziti alla genovese** (with beef and onions), **bean and escarole soup**, chickpea soup and **fagioli alla maruzzara** (bean soup) ... and in the winter don't miss the minestra maritata. Mains are ... mainly fish: fried or stuffed anchovies, **polpo alla luciana** (classic Neapolitan octopus dish) and mixed fries from the daily catch. But if you're meat-inclined, go for the finanziera or beef stew. Plus vegetable dishes such as eggplant parmigiana, stuffed peppers and cianfotta. And don't overlook the pizza option.
The home-made desserts include great babà and zeppoline, and the mind-bog-gling wine list includes virtually every-thing Campania has to offer. Plus the best from the rest of Italy.

The restoration and upgrading of the Quartieri Spagnoli, the neighborhood that climbs from Via Toledo up the hill, is the result of the dynamic revival of social life that got underway long before urban-planning projects were launched. The re-vival was partly encouraged by eateries that attract tourists and locals to an area of the city that used to be considered off-limits. This two-storey osteria, which opened a few years ago, reflects the tra-ditional aspects of Neapolitan cuisine. The menu starts with **sautéed mussels** or clams, octopus salad, then moves on to **ziti in tomato sauce** or **alla Genovese** (boiled beff and onions), **spaghetti** or other pastas with **seafood**, pasta with chickpeas or seafood risotto. Main cours-es: **chops**, **beef in ragù**, sausage with Provola, **fried fish platter** with a spectac-ular side plate of fried spaghetti, or bar-becued fish (sea bass, gilthead and squid), depending on what's available.
Other excellent side dishes include egg-plant parmigiana, zucchini a scapece and fried peppers in tomato sauce. Classsic local desserts: babà, pastiera and caprese.
The wine list continues to expand, with good Campanian and other national la-bels.

HOTEL DES ARTISTES

🗝3-Star Hotel
Via Duomo 61
Tel. 081 446155
Fax 081 2110403
E-mail: info@hoteldesartistesnaples.it
Internet: www.hoteldesartistesnaples.it
Open all year round

I VISCONTI

🗝Bed and breakfast
Via Pasquale Scura 77
Tel. 081 5529124
Fax 081 4202752
E-mail: info@napolibandb.it
Internet: www.napolibandb.it
Open all year round

Like all downtown lodgings, the main attraction of this hotel is that it's within easy walking distance of all the city's monuments and cultural sites: it's only a short stroll to the Cathedral, the Decumani, the popular Vergini and Sanità quarters and the National Archeological Museum. The hotel is on the main floor of a well-kept old palazzo (access by elevator). The bedrooms, of various dimensions, are of two main types: standard rooms overlook the inner courtyard, while deluxe rooms overlook Via Duomo itself. They are all spacious and furnished in a restrained, basic manner. The common areas such as the hall, bar and small breakfast room are immaculate. Tourist information and assistance are available at reception.

• 8 double rooms, 2 triple and 1 with 4 beds, bathroom, air-conditioning, television • Prices: double room single use 70-90 euros, double 90-110, triple 120, with 4 beds 140 (30 euro supplement for extra bed), breakfast included • Credit cards: all, Bancomat • 1 room equipped for the mobility challenged. Garage available for hotel guests at 100 meters (15 euros/day). Small pets allowed. Reception open 24 hours a day • Bar. Breakfast room, lounge

In a strategic position between the subway in Piazza Dante and the Montesanto cable car, this B&B is ideal for people who want to see the city without having to drive. I Visconti is on the second floor of an 18th- century aristocratic palazzo, with four rooms for guests, furnished with great care and elegance, as well as common areas. An inside staircase with 70 steps leads to the terrace with chairs and small tables, where guests can enjoy tea or aperitifs (and breakfast, which is included in the price of the room). Kind, charming personnel will happily provide all information guests may require and serve a generous traditional breakfast.

• 1 single room, 3 double and 1 triple, bathroom, air conditioning, TV • Prices: single 45-55 euros, double room single use 65-76, double 95-99, triple 124-130, breakfast included • Credit cards: all except AE, Bancomat • 1 room equipped for the mobility challenged. Garage for guests at 500 meters (18 euros/day). Small pets allowed. Owners present 8am-9pm • Breakfast room. Fitness center. Solarium. Terrace

LA CHITARRA

Osteria-trattoria
Rampe San Giovanni Maggiore 1 bis
Tel. 081 5529103
Closed Saturday for lunch, Sunday and Monday for dinner
Open: lunch, dinner on booking
Holidays: August
Seating: 32 + 6 outdoors
Prices: 22-27 euros, wine excluded
All credit cards, Bancomat

L'ALLOGGIO DEI VASSALLI

Bed and breakfast
Via Donnalbina 56
Tel. 081 5515118
Fax 081 4202752
E-mail: info@bandbnapoli.it
Internet: www.bandbnapoli.it
Open all year round

The Chitarra osteria-trattoria is located in the area of the most prestigious faculties of Naples's Federico II university. The Maiorano brothers manage the place with passion and considerable skill: Giuseppe is front of house while Luigi runs the kitchen. In this cozy, informal atmosphere, at midday you can have lunch consisting of a choice of two first courses and two main courses and a side dish for a very reasonable price; in the evening, instead, there are many more dishes to choose from. The menu is always inspired by tradition and consists of simple, unpretentious dishes. Antipasti include excellent **crocchè**, risen pasta with cicinielli, focaccia with escarole and friarielli greens, **marinated anchovies** and eggplant parmigiana. Among the first courses there are two sauces Neapolitans like to use on their macaroni to celebrate festivities: **ragù** and **Genovese** (boilede beef and onions). Plus **tubettoni with beans and mussels** and, in winter, traditional minestra maritata and **soup 'e suffritto**. Main courses: fish dishes such as fried **breaded bandiera fish** and anchovies cooked in various ways, or pork ribs with papaccelle (pickled peppers) and stuffed peppers. The **baccalà with chickpeas** deserves a special mention. For dessert, you'll find classics like **babà**, pastiera and sfogliatellona frolla.
The growing wine list includes the best Campanian wines. At the end of your meal, locally made nocillo or limoncello.

Opened a few years ago, this B&B on the first floor of the 18th-century Palazzo Donnalbina is currently undergoing renovation. The bedrooms, with fine wooden false ceilings, are not all that large but are furnished with excellent taste and every comfort. The ancient flooring is a delightful aspect of almost the whole building. The owners pamper their guests with afternoon tea, snacks, aperitifs and even loans of DVDs. A good breakfast is served in a common room or in bedrooms: it includes tea, milk, coffee and traditional Neapolitan pastries. The very central position means that you can reach most of the monuments in Naples on foot.

• 4 double rooms and 1 triple, bathroom, air-conditioning, television • Prices: double room single use 65-76 euros, double 95-99, triple 124-130, breakfast included • Credit cards: all except AE, Bancomat • 1 room equipped for the mobility challenged. Garage available for guests nearby (18 euros/day). Small pets allowed. Reception open from 8am-9pm • Breakfast room. Fitness center

NAPOLIT'AMO

☛—◖3-Star Hotel
Via San Tommaso d'Aquino 15
Tel. and fax 081 4977110-4977142
E-mail: albergonapolitamo@virgilio.it
Internet: www.napolitamo.it
Open all year round

NEAPOLIS

☛—◖3-Star Hotel
Via Del Giudice 13
Tel. 081 4420815
Fax 081 4420819
E-mail: informazioni@hotelneapolis.com
Internet: www.hotelneapolis.com
Open all year round

Right in the center of Naples, close to the Vomero cable car station and Piazza del Plebiscito, this hotel occupies the third floor of a modern building. The comfortable rooms have fine bathrooms and functional furnishing. The continental breakfast is served in a large, bright room. The kind and helpful management is part of the Napolit'amo Tourist Centre, that organizes visits to the city and excursions to the environs and places of major interest in the region, with professional multi-lingual guides. Its head office is in Palazzo dei Principi Tocco di Montemiletto, Via Toledo 148, alongside another small hotel with 13 rooms.

• 17 double rooms with bathroom, air conditioning, safe, television • Prices: double room single use 65-75 euros, double 90-115, breakfast included • Credit cards: major ones, Bancomat • 1 room equipped for the mobility challenged. Garage for guests nearby (13 euros per day). Small pets allowed. Reception open 8am-midnight • Breakfast room, lounge, internet point

Right in the center, at the entrance to Decumano Maggiore and in the limited traffic/pedestrian zone: an ideal starting point for artistic itineraries in Naples. The hotel is on the third floor of a renovated period palazzo with access by private elevator. The bedrooms are large – some can be set up with 3 or 4 beds – and furnished in an essential yet tasteful style. The comforts made available to guests include – in every room – a computer with free internet access and software specifically created to optimize your stay in the city. A traditional breakfast is served in a common room with croissants, jams, milk, coffee and tea. 15 euro supplement per person for half board.

• 5 single rooms and 13 double, bathroom, air conditioning, mini-bar, television, pc • Prices: single 55-85 euros, double 80-125 (20 euro supplement for extra bed), breakfast included • Credit cards: all, Bancomat • 1 room equipped for the mobility challenged. Garage (10 euros / day). Small pets allowed. Reception 24 hours a day • Bar, restaurant. Breakfast room, television room

SANSEVERO DEGAS

🗝2-Star Hotel
Calata Trinità Maggiore 53
Tel. and fax 081 7901000
E-mail: prenotazioni@albergosansevero.it
Internet: www.albergosansevero.it
Open all year

SOGGIORNO SANSEVERO

🗝Residence
Piazza San Domenico Maggiore 9
Tel. and fax 081 7901000
E-mail: prenotazioni@albergosansevero.it
Internet: www.albergosansevero.it
Open all year

Located in the city center on the third floor of an 18th-century building with a majestic portal, the hotel owes its name to the celebrated impressionist painter, Edgar Degas, who usually stayed in this palazzo when he came to Naples. The rooms are all doubles, though the larger ones can become triples, and all are fitted with antique-style furniture. The view from most rooms is truly remarkable: Piazza del Gesù with the spire of the Chiesa dell'Immacolata, the Chiesa del Gesù with its splendid 15th-century ashlaring, the Basilica of Santa Chiara and Spaccanapoli. You'll get a warm welcome from the partners in the hotel, who also own other facilities in the city center. Breakfast consists of coffee, milk, tea, fresh bread, croissants from the pastry shop, but also fruit juice, butter, jam, honey and cheese.

• 9 double rooms with bathroom, air-conditioning, TV, modem connection • Prices: double room single use 55-75 euros, double 70-110 (20 euro supplement for extra bed), breakfast included • Credit cards: all, Bancomat • Facility accessible to the mobility challenged. Paid public parking in the immediate vicinity. Small pets allowed. Reception open 24 hours a day • Breakfast room

Located right in the old center of Naples, this residence is on the first floor of the Princes of Sansevero's distinguished palazzo with its beautiful baroque portal and entrance hall with precious stucco bas-reliefs. The furnishings vary from room to room: some have beautiful hand-made furniture in antique style, while others have more modern pieces that make for a lighter atmosphere. The common areas have ethnic-style furnishing accessories. All rooms face onto the palazzo's two large courtyards, which are so monumental that no one will regret the lack of a view over the beautiful square outside. One thing you can be sure of is a warm, friendly welcome here. For breakfast you'll be offered hot drinks and fruit juices, croissants from the pastry shop, honey, jams, cheeses and fresh bread.

• 6 double rooms, with bathroom, TV, modem connection • Prices: double room single occupancy 55-75 euros, double 70-110 (20 euro supplement for extra bed), breakfast included • Credit cards: all, Bancomat • Paid public parking in the immediate vicinity. Small pets allowed. Reception open from 7.30 am to 10 pm • Breakfast room, reading room

TAVERNA DELL'ARTE

Traditional osteria
Rampe San Giovanni Maggiore 1 A
Tel. 081 5527558
Closed Sunday
Open: only for dinner
Holidays: three weeks in August
Seating: 42 + 15 outdoors
Prices: 30 euros, wine excluded
All credit cards except DC, Bancomat

VADINCHENIA

Restaurant
Via Pontano 21
Tel. 081 660265
Closed Sunday
Open: only for dinner
Holidays: August-first week of September
Seating: 70
Prices: 30-32 euros, wine excluded
All credit cards, Bancomat

The osteria is located in the Aragonese quarter of Naples, near Mezzocannone, the center of university life. An ancient phrase mentioned on the osteria visiting card reminds us that in the past eating and drinking were separate activities: the first took place in taverns while the latter was done in wine cellars. The menu is pinned up at the entrance and varies with the season and what's available at the daily market.

Start with antipasti of **sciurilli** (courgette flowers) **filled with ricotta**, or prosciutto and salted ricotta accompanied by homemade olive pâté or, when in season, escarole stuffed with baccalà. Firsts: **tagliatelle allo scammaro** (capers, anchovies and olives) or with artichokes, or **beans alla maruzzara**, **paccheri** alle due Sicilie, flavored with eggplant pesto, or menaica **anchovies** with tomato, pine nuts, raisins and pecorino. For your main course, fish and meat specialties: **cuttlefish and squid**, baccalà and anchovies, sweet and sour baccalà, **fried fish platter**, **baccalà with potatoes** (the osteria's signature dish), 'mbuttunata sausage, mixed barbecued meat, scorzetta of beef and sweet and sour pork with cep mushrooms. At the end of your meal you'll be offered a **basil sorbet** that precedes the traditional puddings: caprese or pastiera, blancmange and orange cream. To close, a glass of Malvasia or grappa.

The brief wine list offers reasonably priced labels from Campania with a description of the grapes they are made from. Given the limited seating, it's advisable to book ahead.

This small restaurant is in a central location (the area close to Piazza Carità) in a two-storey building furnished simply and informally. The service offered by the staff and owner is equally informal. The true protagonists here are dishes prepared daily in the kitchen that, apart from a few where creativity dominates, are a good combination of Campania and the nearby Basilicata regional cuisine. There are two antipasti: one of **baccalà** with baccalà mousse, baccalà with peppers, carpaccio and mussillo croquettes; the second of **misto Vadinchenia**, which offers cheeses and vegetables (eggplant flan and stuffed ricotta). The first courses include **Gragnano paccheri alla genovese** or **with anchovies and Pecorino** or with angler fish sauce, **ferricelli** or other types of pasta with **caciato ragù**. Ask if they have any dishes not shown on the menu: there may be interesting surprises in store. Mains include **squid** stuffed with vegetables and Moliterno sausage (the same sausage is served on its own with a side plate of potatoes), **stuffed escarole**, fillet of beef in wine sauce and sea salt, and a few other fish dishes. To close, a good selection of cheeses and home-made puddings. The wine list offers a wide variety of Italian regional labels, plus a selection of national and foreign liqueurs.

NAPLES

NOCERA SUPERIORE
Materdomini

VECCHIA CANTINA

🍲 Trattoria
Vico San Nicola della Carità 13-14
Tel. 081 5520226
Closed Sunday and Tuesday for dinner
Open: lunch and dinner
Holidays: in August
Seating: 46
Prices: 22-25 euros, wine excluded
All major credit cards

TERRA SANTA

🍲 Osteria
Piazza Materdomini 46
Tel. 081 933562
Closed Tuesday
Open: lunch and dinner, Saturday and
Monday only dinner, Sunday only lunch
Holidays: in August, 23/12-05/01
Seating: 50
Prices. 28-35 euros, wine excluded
All credit cards, Bancomat

The Vecchia Cantina trattoria, which opened over 40 years ago, is close to the Pignasecca market, where it sources many of its ingredients, just a stone's throw from the city center. Don't be fooled by the name (old cellar): there's nothing old about this restaurant. Husband-and-wife Nunzia and Franco are the true depositaries of traditional recipes, the only thing that's ancient about the place: Monday, pasta and legumes, and so on until Sunday, pasta with ragù. Every dish is linked to seasonal products available at the market. These flavors will live on and be handed down to the couple's son, Gianni, who serves at table and also sells wines from selected Campania producers, and Maria, the daughter-in-law, who runs the kitchen. The place has two small, simply furnished rooms while to liven up the atmosphere there are many bottles displayed on the various shelves and racks. From the all-Neapolitan menu, we reccomend the dishes that are Maria's favorites: **stuffed sciurilli** and risen pastas, **tubettoni with beans and mussels, ziti alla genovese, mezzanelli lardiati**, mixed fried fish platter, **golden fried anchovies**, pork chops and meatballs in ragù, **escarole 'mbuttunata**, zucchini a scapece ... After a selection of Pecorino and Podolico cheeses, you can end your meal with desserts such as such as caprese and babà.

The Campania Felix of Roman times was the Nocera-Sarno plain, an area that once saw an exceptional concentration of crop cultivation. Today much has changed as a result of an inappropriate use of the land and lack of planning, which means that agricultural production is very low indeed. However, the Terra Santa restaurant still offers the possibility to taste flavors of the past. The restaurant is on the road from Nocera Superiore to Roccapiemonte, in what was once the ossuary of a 12th-century abbey. Alfredo and Rosario will give you a warm Neapolitan-style welcome, while in the kitchen Giuseppe Stanzione deploys his top quality ingredients, many of which are Slow Food Presidia from Campania and other parts of Italy. Start with **baccalà fritters** on cream of broccoli or with escarole in puff pastry with capers and olives. The first courses are made with fresh or Gragnano pasta and flavored with seasonal sauces: cannelloni with finely-sliced buffalo mozzarella, tomatoes and Provola, spaghettoni with San Marzano tomatoes and **calamarata with seafood**. Main courses: seared tuna, superb **baccalà** and organic Chianina beeft cooked on lava stones. The **cheese board** and puddings (gianduia semifreddo, cold chocolate cake with almond ice cream) are also very good (among the puddings:
There's no wine list so you can choose a bottle from the small but well-stocked cellar next door: all are very reasonably priced.

Novi Velia

La Chioccia d'Oro

🍲 Restaurant
Via Bivio di Novi Velia
Tel. 0974 70004
Closed Friday
Open: lunch and dinner
Holidays: first week in March and
September
Seating: 70 + 80 outdoors
Prices: 22 euros, wine excluded
All credit cards, Bancomat

The restaurant is named after a local legend, a fact that indicates the owner's desire to remain in touch with traditions and with the land. Giovanni Positano has quite rigid rules on two aspects: the selection of ingredients, which he only buys from farmers he trusts, and the use of seasonal products from the vegetable garden and woodland. As there's no written menu, the waiter will introduce you to dishes typical of the inland Cilento area. You'll start with antipasti of vegetables in olive oil or v pickled and cooked in different ways, capocollo, salami and soppressata and the **mozzarella in mortella** (Slow Food Presidium: cow's milk mozzarella bound in myrtle-wood sticks). Afterwards, **oven-baked conchiglioni**, stuffed paccheri, nidi di chioccia (tagliatelle rolled up with prosciutto, mozzarella and béchamel sauce, then topped with ragù) and pappardelle with ragù. Then super mains such as wild boar prepared in various ways, barbecued pork, **oven-baked lamb**, **boned rabbit with herbs** and veal steaks, all dishes often accompanied by cep mushrooms. The selections of local cheeses and desserts, some bought in from pastry shops in the village, are highly impressive. To accompany your meal you can choose between the red house wine or one of the Italian labels (mark-ups are honest). If you choose the set menu, bear in mind that portions are abundant.

🍶 To buy good olive oil, go to Oleificio Emilio Conti, at Massa di Vallo della Lucania (3 km), Via Nazionale 11.

Ospedaletto d'Alpinolo

Osteria del Gallo e della Volpe 🐌 ⊘ 🍷

🍲 Osteria
Piazza Umberto I 11-13
Tel. 0825 691225
Closed Monday
Open: dinner only
Holidays: two weeks at the beginning
of July, 10 days at Christmas
Seating: 45
Prices: 30-35 euros, wine excluded
All credit cards, Bancomat

Chef-owner Marisa is the heart and soul of this osteria, which she runs together with her husband Antonio. A true champion of local cuisine, she promotes an understanding of and link to the land, taking typical products – mushrooms, chestnuts, black truffles – and exploiting them with a mastery which brings diners to the restaurant in increasing numbers. Among the dishes we tried during our visit were a delicate **salt cod mousse** served with a vellutata of cicerchie (grass peas) and an eggplant flan with Piennolo tomato cream, followed by **lasagnetta with porcini mushrooms** and chestnuts and hand-made tagliatelle with a vegetable carbonara. The main courses included successful pairings like pork fillet with Annurca apples and veal sirloin with Tropea onions. You may also find **Cetara anchovy tortino with garlic and oregano**, **timballo of cheese-filled paccheri** with meat ragù, **lamb with wild mint and pecorino**, crespelle (crêpes) and eggplant parmigiana. The excellent selection of cured meats and **cheeses**, both local and from around Italy, includes a semi-aged Cilento goat's cheese, Pienza, aged Monteleone caciocavallo and many more. Close with desserts like ricotta cake, castagna del prete, peach and amaretti roll and panbiscotto with pears. The comprehensive wine list includes good Avellino wines, plus many distinguished national labels.

🍶 In Via Chiusa di Sotto and in the little alleyways of the center, numerous artisan bakers making castagna del prete, pantorrone and nougats.

FATTORIA ALVANETA

TAVERNA IL LUPO

⌒Holiday farm
Contrada Pantagnoni
Tel. 0975 77139-328 7046591
Closed Tuesdays
Open lunch and dinner
Holidays: none
Seating: 40
Prices: 20-25 euros
All credit cards and Bancomat

⌒Osteria
Largo Municipio 8
Tel. 0975 778376-347 8295374
Closed Sunday dinner and Monday
Open: lunch and dinner
Holidays: variable
Seating: 60
Prices: 25 euros, wine excluded
All credit cards

It's not easy to reach Francesco Barra's agriturismo, but the journey, which takes you on a road that climbs up through the woods, is well worth it. The restored farmhouse, surrounded by fields of cereals, fruit trees and vegetable gardens, has a beautiful setting and lots of outdoor space and even a children's playground. Recently we've noticed encouraging signs of growth: one such is the notably improved wine list – in the past there wasn't much on offer beyond the house wine.

The women in the family run the kitchen, skilfully cooking the farm produce and meat from their own animals. To start, there's a choice of grilled vegetables and **home-cured meats** (sausage, sopressata, prosciutto, capocollo and lardo), followed by first courses, either soups or pastas, also made in-house. Try the **cavatielli** or the fusilli **with pork**, flavored with mushrooms or truffles when in season; **ricotta ravioli with ragù**; lagane with chickpeas or beans; and various **soups**. Particularly recommended are the wild chicory soup with annoglia (a sausage made with pork rind and other offcuts) and the soup with bread polpette. In winter expect to find soffritto of pork or lamb; **stuffed belly pork**, stewed or in a salad; **tripe with peas**; and **pork livers with bay leaf**. Pork is grilled, while chicken and rabbit are sautéed or roasted with potatoes, and there's also a wealth of vegetarian dishes like **ciambotta**, eggplant, sautéed mushrooms and stuffed peppers.

Honey and jams from the farm are also used make crostatas, alongside other desserts like **panzerotti di sanguinaccio** and traditional **cream pizza**.

Padula, at the far south of the Vallo di Diano, is known above all for the imposing Carthusian monastery of San Lorenzo, an immense amalgamation of 14th-century, Renaissance and Baroque architecture. From there it's a climb up to Padula's historic center, through a labyrinth of narrow little streets to the Sant'Agostino convent, now the town hall. In the same piazza you'll find Michele Cartusciello's osteria, conceived as a kind of museum of times gone by, the walls covered with old photos, letters from American emigrants and historic objects. There are several different dining rooms, some tiny (with just one table), others larger.

The food also lets you discover the past, through the excellent traditional cooking of Michele's mamma. On the menu, all in dialect, you'll find dishes that represent the cultures of Campania and nearby Calabria and Basilicata. After starting with a more-than-adequate cheese board (including cheeses aged in hay, in caves or in marc), you could try, for example, **lagane and beans**, ravioli with egg, ricotta, pecorino and parsley, **cavatelli with fava and green beans**, **bread polpette in tomato sauce**, stuffed artichokes and peppers and **stuffed eggplant**. Desserts range from fig tart and lemon or orange preserves to cookies with fragola grapes.

The wine list has around 40 labels from all over Italy. The courteous service deserves a special mention.

Perdifumo
Vatolla

Piano di Sorrento

Il Vecchio Casale

🗝Holiday farm
Via Vigna
Tel. 0974 845235-339 2598687
Fax 0974 821296
E-mail: vecchiocasale@libero.it
Internet: www.ilvecchiocasale.it
Open from 15/06 to 15/09, festivities and weekends

Le Tre Arcate

🍲Restaurant-pizzeria
Piazza Cota 9-10
Tel. 0831 5321849-339 2837856
Closed Wednesday
Open: lunch and dinner
Holidays: January
Seating: 45 + 60 outdoors
Prices: 30-35 euros, wine excluded
All credit cards, Bancomat

This farm, run by Anna Maria Malandrino, is on a hill, just outside the village of Vatolla. It is an interesting example of early 18th-century Cilento architecture comprising a stone-farmhouse and small towers that have recently been renovated. The rooms are spacious and simply furnished, with all essential comforts and accessible from within the facility or from the terrace reserved for guests. Common areas include a bar, where you'll be served a traditional breakfast with good home-made jams and cakes, and a restaurant that serves dishes made with the farm's organic produce (half board costs 50 euros per person). Outside guests can relax in the many shady green areas or enjoy the swimming pool bordered by olive trees.

• 1 single, 4 double rooms and 1 suite, with bathroom, TV; several rooms with balcony • Prices: single 35-40 euros, double 70-75, suite 140-145, breakfast included • Credit cards: none • Restaurant accessible to the mobility challenged. Off-street parking. No pets allowed. Owners always present • Bar, restaurant. Reading and TV room. Garden, terrace. Swimming pool

This restaurant traditionally bases its food on the daily catch and fresh seasonal vegetables. The menu varies on a weekly basis and features simple mostly traditional dishes of oily fish and Mediterranean vegetables. This is the philosophy that has always inspired Lucio Russo, who runs the place with the help of his son Alessandro and chef Gennaro Esposito.
The antipasti we enjoyed included rolled fish with scamorza and lemon, **anchovy and escarole pie**, and marinated or fried fish. As for the first courses, you are spoilt for choice: as well as gnocchi sorrentini, cavatelli and **scialatielli** – all hand-made – there's pasta from Gragnano **shrimp and zucchini** or squid and Provolone del monaco. To keep the final check down, go for **oily fish** for main course, grilled or cooked in a stew with capers, olives and tomatoes. Other mains include **anchovies stuffed with smoked provola**, tuna with onions, squid with potatoes, or grilled, cold or au gratin. There are also a few meat dishes. Lucio's desserts, go from cakes to babà and delizie, but the one which really stands out is **isolotto**, Caprese cake with a hot dark chocolate center.
Alessandro's wine list is well thought out and the man himself is on hand to offer valuable advice whenever needed.

🍴 The Caffè Gelateria Cota (Piazza Cota 11-12) offers traditional Sorrento sweets such as delizie al limone, caprese and babà with creamy lemon sauce. It also makes exquisite almond petits fours and a wide range of artisan ice-creams.

Pietravairano

La Caveja

🍲Restaurant/Locanda
Via Santissima Annunziata 10
Tel. 0823 984824
Fax 0823 982977
E-mail: albergoristorantecaveja@virgilio.it
Closed Sunday dinner and Monday
Orario: lunch and dinner
Holidays: none
Seating: 40
Prices: 30-35 euros, wine excluded
All major credit cards, Bancomat

The tastefully restored farmhouse, at the entrance to the village, houses the restaurant of Bernardino Lombardo. The hotel rooms (available all week) have beautiful majolica floors. At breakfast you can enjoy the produce of the farm, including excellent jams.
The meal opens with nibbles of mozzarella and ricottina a latte crudo, **pancotto soup with beans**, tripe and potatoes, **cherry tomatoes arreganati** and **uovo a suscella**. The first courses include pasta and paprika, **ziti allardiati**, **minestra maritata** in the Easter period, soups of legumes in winter and fresh vegetables in spring. Alternatively, pettole e ceci dressed with the robust fruity oil of the house. Meat dominates the main courses: stuffed guinea fowl, **baked black Casertano piglet**, capon with aromatic herbs and **boned Matese lamb**. A large selection of local and national cheeses and, for dessert, jam tarts, pastiera pasquale and lemon cake.
The wine list features the best regional and national labels.

🛏• 7 single rooms, 7 doubles and 1 suite, with bathroom, air conditioning, fridge bar, TV • Prices: single 60, double 80, suite 120 euros. Premises accessible to the mobility impaired, with 2 suitably equipped rooms. Private uncovered parking. Pets not welcome. Owners present 8am-1 am • Restaurant. Breakfast room. Garden

🍴 At **Casanova di Carinola** (20 km) the De Ruosi farm produces and bottles an excellent extra virgin olive oil with the Monte dei Greci label from local cultivations.

Pimonte

Lo Scoiattolo

🍲Restaurant
Via Santo Spirito 1
Tel. 081 8792674
Closed Wednesday, never in August
Open: lunch and dinner
Holidays: 10 days in November
Seating: 80 + 40 outside
Prices: 25-30 euros, wine excluded
All major credit cards, Bancomat

On the way to Agerola, in the heart of the Lattari Mountains, you'll find Pimonte, a little town not far from the Gulf of Naples and Monte Faito. The restaurant is on the hill of Monte Croce, just a few steps from the town's main piazza. Chef Paolo Durazzo is young but already highly skilled (it runs in his family!), and you'll find his wife Marianna welcoming guests in the dining room.
The menu is based on local, seasonal produce from the sea and the mountains, prepared with just a touch of innovation without ever obscuring the ingredients' essential qualities. The antipasti are typical of the area, with local cured meats and **Agerola cheeses**, plus vegetables, in oil or in fritters. First courses to look out for include **ravioloni with eggplant and local fiordilatte** in a sauce of cherry tomatoes from the hills and fragrant basil and paccheri di Gragnano (a nearby town famous for its pasta) with artichokes and seafood. In the winter you'll find **farinaccio with ragù** made with pork rinds, tracchie and beef. Moving on to the main courses, there's **octopus with escarole** or chickpeas, battered artichokes with **fried squid** or **stockfish parmigiana** with eggplant and fiordilatte. The **grilled fish**, totani with potatoes and the **mixed fry** are all excellent. If you don't like fish, the local **beef tagliata** or the various preparations of seasonal vegetables will keep you happy. The traditional desserts are all home-made.
There's a good selection of wines, starting with those from around Pimonte, Gragnano and Lettere, moving on to the rest of Campania, the Amalfi Coast in particular, and finishing with top bottles from other regions. Reservations recommended.

PISCIOTTA
Marina

ANGIOLINA

🍲 Restaurant
Via Passariello 2
Tel. 0974 973188
Open every day
Open: dinner
Holidays: November-Easter
Seating: 20 + 30 outside
Prices: 25-28 euros, wine excluded
All credit cards, Bancomat

Taking a seat in Angiolina's intimate dining room or on the open-air terrace, enjoying the warm, sincere welcome and sampling dishes prepared with care and simplicity: all this will help you forget – at least while you're having dinner – the ugly buildings that have spoilt this strip of Salerno coastline. Angiolina herself has been cooking here for over 40 years, tirelessly recreating genuinely traditional dishes. She's been joined by her son Rinaldo, who provides a counterbalance of creativity, and has also devoted himself to promoting Menaica anchovies, a Slow Food Presidium, and organizing excursions for tourists to see traditional fishing techniques.
The anchovies appear alll over the menu: in **cauraro** (a spring minestrone with wild herbs), stuffed **'nchiappate**, marinated, breaded or used to sauce **spaghetti**. Alongside are traditional dishes such as **stuffed eggplant** with pasta, mozzarella, olives, capers and pine nuts; ricotta ravioli; **paccheri with mixed fish** (the selection varies from day to day); grilled pesce azzurro like anchovies and sardines; and marinated amberjack, as well as modern creations like risotto with shrimp and orange or albacore carpaccio. Home-made desserts include fresh fruit mousses, cream puddings and Cilento fruit salad with figs, pears and lemon zest and juice.
The good wine list focuses on Campania but also includes labels from further afield.

PISCIOTTA

CASA PIXOS

🛏 Vacation home
Via Canto del Gelso 22
Tel. 0974 973792–349 6076795-333 2710349
Fax 0974 973647
E-mail: casapixos@libero.it
Internet: www.casapixos.supereva.it
Open all year

Casa Pixos is a group of three residences dating from the seventeenth century in which there are now two studio apartments and a two-bedroom apartment that can accommodate from two to five people. All the apartments have private bathrooms and a kitchenette, and have been renovated while respecting the original structure of the buildings. In the rooms every space – difference in levels, niches, sloping roofs and ancient wooden beams – has been utilized to enhance the interiors. The furnishings have been chosen with great attention to detail, with a pleasant combination of modern and antique pieces. Large windows face onto the garden which is an apotheosis of Mediterranean vegetation – hibiscus and bougainvillea – while from the terraces there's a view over the gulf. At the time you book you'll be asked to say whether you want the breakfast option: if you do, for a cost of 5 euros more the fridge will be loaded up with everything necessary and you'll also find a basket of bakery products in your room.

• 2 apartments (2-3 persons) and 1 apartment (4-5 persons), bathroom, terrace, kitchen • Prices: apartment for 2-3 persons 60-90 euros, apartment for 4-5 persons 75-110; breakfast 5 euros per person • Credit cards: none • Free external public parking. Small pets allowed. Owners always reachable.

99 KM SOUTHEAST OF SALERNO

96 KM SOUTHEAST OF SALERNO SS 447

LA LOCANDA DEL FIUME – 'A MACHINA

Holiday farm
Contrada Fiori
Tel. 0974 973876-335 8119175-335 5326132
Fax 0974 973703
E-mail: sonjadamato@libero.it
Internet: www.amachina.it
Closed January and February

PERBACCO

Osteria-wine shop
Contrada Marina Campagna 5
Tel. 0974 973889
Always open between June and September, in spring weekends only by reservation
Open lunch and dinner
Seating: 50
Prices: 25-35 euros, wine excluded
All credit cards and Bancomat

Sonja D'Amato's well-managed agriturismo is in the middle of an olive grove surrounded by approximately one hectare of land cultivated with fruit trees. Accommodation is in a former water mill dating from the 18th century that has been completely refurbished while respecting the local architecture. The rooms, from this year are even more spacious, are tastefully furnished: antique furniture, olive wood parquet floors, freshly painted walls and wrought iron bedsteads. Common areas are just as pleasant: the restaurant room containing the ancient oil press, the hall with its wooden ceilings and the beautiful terrace. For breakfast you'll be offered jams and wholemeal bread made by the owner, cakes, cookies and cold and hot drinks. The restaurant, which is open to non-residents by reservation, serves local cuisine (20 euros per person, excluding wine).

• 2 double, 7 triple and 2 four-bed rooms, with bathroom; several rooms with balcony, 2 with air-conditioning • Prices: double room single use 54-81 euros, double 80-120, triple 120-180, four-bed 160-240 • Breakfast included • Credit cards: all, Bancomat • Off-street parking. Small pets allowed. Owners always present • Restaurant. Breakfast room, reading and TV room. Terrace, garden

Perbacco, a historic osteria and wine bar, had a major impact on the local gastronomic scene when it was founded in 1987. Management has now been taken over by Vito Puglia, a national Slow Food leader. A good wine list, expertly sourced ingredients – today including almost all the Slow Food Campania presidia – proper wine glasses and a convivial ambience are now easier to find, but when Perbacco first opened they were rare indeed.
The change of kitchen staff – Mario Postiglione, a real maestro, is now in charge – has brought the menu back on to a traditional track, one which allows room for originality but is always firmly rooted in the idea that ingredients are of primary importance.
For antipasti, fillet of scabbard fish gratin on lemon leaves, **menaica anchovy tortino**, **friarielli greens in a cherry-tomato salad** and eggplant roulades with ricotta and basil sauce. The many pastas change every day but might include **scialatielli with gurnard**, paccheri with San Marzano tomatoes, n'duja and cacioricotta cilentana or **mafalde with green chilies, anchovies and cherry tomatoes**. Follow with mixed fried fish or **grilled fish**, which varies with the day's catch. The **Campanian cheese board** is very good as is the marvellous **torta caprese.**
The backdrop is a landscape of ancient olive trees set against a shining turquoise sea, luminous even at night. This is Perbacco and Vito intends to make it even better: restoration work is currently going ahead to create rooms and new spaces. Welcome back, Perbacco!

POLLICA
Celso

PONTE

COSTANTINOPOLI

☞Restaurant
Contrada Costantinopoli 6
Tel. 0974 901134
Open weekends, always in summer
Open: lunch and dinner
Holidays: October-Easter
Seating: 80 + 100 outside
Prices: 25 euros, wine excluded
All credit cards, Bancomat

ANTICA OSTERIA FRANGIOSA

☞Trattoria
Via Ocone 12
Tel. 0824 874054
Closed Wednesday
Open: lunch and dinner
Holidays: first week of September
Seating: 80 + 30 outside
Prices: 18-20 euros, wine excluded
All credit cards and Bancomat

Halfway between Agropoli and Palinuro, strategically located Pollica is a small town clinging to the Cilento coast which enjoys both as yet uncontaminated sea and jealously preserved mountain traditions. The easily accessible restaurant is just outside town and offers a children's play area as well as stunning views from the terrace. Simplicity, honesty and good taste are all evident, as is the joie de vivre of the Marano family women who have run the restaurant for many years. All in all, it's a pleasant place to come, where diners can sample the true flavors of Cilento cuisine.

Antipasti include local cured meats, vegetables preserved in oil, cracked olives and fresh goat's cheese. The first courses favor fresh handmade pastas: **cannelloni**, ravioli, **fusilli** and excellent **cavatelli with clams or beans**. The main courses generally involve grilled meats, particularly the locally raised chicken, or, if bought fresh that day, swordfish steak. Meanwhile vegetables grown by local farmers are used for **pizza rustica**, **eggplant parmigiana**, the classic vegetarian stew, **ciambotta**, stuffed eggplant alla cilentana, zucchini flower fritters, escarole pizza and eggplant rolls. The wood-fired oven is used to bake excellent bread, while the olive oil used is made by the owners' uncle and aunt. The simple desserts include cannoli with cream and chocolate, coffee and chocolate cake and sweet pizza with lemon frosting.

The limited wine list features local labels.

At the foot of the Taburno, near the freeway exit for Caianello, Ponte is a small village just 15 kilometers from Benevento. The restaurant here, run by the friendly Frangiosa husband-and-wife team, has attracted local food-lovers for more than 30 years. They've now been joined by their son Giovanni (an expert sommelier who will help you find just the right pairing of local wine and food), but you'll still find Concetta in the kitchen. She has a light hand with salt, seasonings and sauces, a skill which helps her prepare local recipes in the best way possible.

You'll start with **crostini with beans** flavored with a prized extra virgin olive oil from the area, but the rich selection of antipasti also includes cured meats, ricottine and local cheeses, **grilled eggplant** and fried zucchini fl.owers, all accompanied by good focaccia. Then you can choose from dishes unique to the Benevento area, or homemade fresh pastas: soup with salt cod, potatoes and cauliflower; **stuffed escarole in chicken broth**; chicory and fava zuppa; **cavatelli tomato and pork spareribs**; fusilli baked with meat sauce and mozzarella; scialatielli with tomato and basil. Then move on to casseroled salt cod with cherry tomatoes, olives and capers, or various meats: rabbit, pigeon, **lamb tripe**, ammugliatielli (lamb offal) and **soffritto**. Recommended desserts: home-made sbriciolata cake with ricotta, chocolate and almonds, or crostata with fruit.

Wines can be chosen from a selection that covers the best-known wineries from Taburno, Solopaca, Guardiolo, Sant'Agata dei Goti and Sannio.

POSITANO
Nocelle

CASA CUCCARO

🗝️●Bed and breakfast
Via Nocelle 28
Tel. and fax 089 875458
E-mail: info@casacuccaro.it
Internet: www.casacuccaro.it
Open all year

Nocelle is a little village perched on top of a hill in the Lattari Mountain Regional Park, just a few kilometers from Positano. There are many options for people looking for a relaxing vacation by the sea or keen to explore the mountains, including hiking along the famous 'Paths of the Gods'. In Nocelle, Gerardina and Giuseppe Cuccaro have renovated a rural property to create the rooms for their B&B. The comfortable, simply furnished rooms all face the sea and offer a magnificent view, which can also be enjoyed from the common terrace. Breakfast is traditional and consists of coffee, milk, tea and home-baked cakes. The only slight drawback is that Nocelle doesn't have roads so you'll have to leave your car in the free public parking place, just a three-minute walk from the B&B.

• 7 double rooms, with bathroom, air-conditioning, terrace, mini-bar, TV, modem connection • Prices: double room single use 35-40 euros, double 70-80 (20 euro supplement for extra bed), breakfast included • Credit cards: none • External public parking before entering the village. No pets allowed. Owners always present • Breakfast room, TV room. Terrace, solarium

POSITANO
Montepertuso

IL RITROVO 🍾

🍲Trattoria
Via Montepertuso 77
Tel. 089 812005
Closed Wednesday, never in the summer
Open: lunch and dinner
Holidays: January 7-March 1
Seating: 60 + 70 outside
Prices: 35 euros, wine excluded
All credit cards, Bancomat

We're not going to dwell on Positano's beaches or its center, all crowded with tourist restaurants. In Montepertuso, instead, you'll find places like Il Ritrovo, that serve reasonably priced dishes that respect local culinary traditions. Here the wooden beams are hung with spunzilli, bunches of the little local tomatoes; in summer, you can eat outside under a leafy arbor or, in the winter, enjoy the warmth of the fireplace in the middle of the dining room. Salvatore Barba cooks in the kitchen, while Teresa serves in the dining room. Many of the ingredients – vegetables and white meats – come from their own land, farmed by father Domenico.
The antipasti buffet is dominated by vegetables in many guises: eggplants, onions, grilled pumpkin, zucchini alla parmigiana, pumpkin flower fritters. Among the firsts, we recommend the **spaghetti with piennolo cherry tomatoes** and cavatelli with zucchini and scamorza, and of the mains the sautéed nassa shrimp and the **frittura di fragaglie** (a mixed fry of tiny fish that have got stuck in the nets) or the rich **zuppa saracena**, with rock fish, sea bream, squid, cuttlefish, flying squid, giant shrimp, langoustines and other seafood, a meal in itself. Meat lovers will always find rabbit and **chicken, alla cacciatora** or grilled. Home-made puddings include excellent little biscuits and cookies and warm chocolate cake, paired with blueberry or wild fennel liqueurs. The decent wine list ranges beyond Campania.

POZZUOLI
Lucrino

ABRAXAS ⊘▮

▱ Osteria
Via Scalandrone 15
Tel. 081 8549347
Closed Tuesday
Open: dinner, lunch on Sunday only
Holidays: August 10-28 and December 24-January 4
Seating: 80 + 70 outdoors
Prices: 30-35 euros, wine excluded
All credit cards, Bancomat

The picture windows offer beautiful views, the restaurant being on a promontory between the Averno and Lucrino lakes. In summer the terrace provides a pleasant place for dinner. The restaurant is run with skill by Nando, who personally sources seasonal ingredients to prepare family recipes and promote the local cuisine.

The winter menu includes, among other dishes, ricotta and local cured meats, sausages with Savoy cabbage and chestnuts and **potato gattò** with rosemary sauce. Among the firsts, **ziti** or paccheri **with pork ragù**, fresh pastas with walnut cream or piennolo cherry tomatoes and shavings of Provolone del monaco. Then **pork with pappaccelle**, Avellino sausage and beef from select cow breeds. In summer the focus shifts naturally to vegetables: **parmigiana di zucchini** or potatoes with escarole, sausage and provola; eggplant stracciata; zucchini flan with bell-pepper sauce. Also **fresh pastas** of various kinds with zucchini or eggplant sauces; try the lasagne with zucchini and provola. Among the desserts, we recommend the chocolate flan and **caprese** and the panna cotta with strawberries or chocolate.

You can see into the attractive wine cellar, which contains a good number of wines, some served by the glass, and different spirits.

🍶 In **Pozzuoli**, at Via Pergolesi 86, the L'Arcante wine shop presents a rich selection of Italian wines, with many from the Phlegrean area, plus select oils and gourmet foods.

POZZUOLI
Arco Felice

LA TRIPERGOLA

🔑 3-Star Hotel
Via Miliscola 165
Tel. 081 8042120
Fax 081 8042124
E-mail: info@latripergola.it
Internet: www.latripergola.it
Open all year

This hotel in Arco Felice, just behind the coastal area of Lucrino, takes its name from the ancient spa resort of Tripergole, submerged as a result of the eruption that in 1538 created Monte Nuovo. The surrounding area is rich in history and natural, archeological and cultural resources. The spacious rooms of this hotel managed by Ferdinando Testa have recently been refurbished, with the addition of marine-style furnishings, and are pleasantly comfortable. Half the rooms have a sea view. Common areas are unpretentious and well kept. The generous buffet breakfast consists of bread, rusks, freshly made croissants, jams, butter, fruit juices, cappuccino and coffee. The supplement per person for half board is 15 euros.

• 19 double, 5 triple and 6 four-bed rooms, with bathroom, air-conditioning, mini-bar, satellite TV, modem connection • Prices: double room single use 65 euros, double 85, triple 100, four-bed 115, breakfast included • Credit cards: all, Bancomat • 4 rooms designed for use by the mobility challenged. Off-street parking. Small pets allowed. Reception open 24 hours a day. • Bar, restaurant. Breakfast room, reading and TV room. Conference room. Terrace

30 KM WEST OF SALERNO

35 KM WEST OF SALERNO SS 163

COSTA DIVA

LA BRACE

🔑 3-Star Hotel
Via Roma 12
Tel 089 813076
Fax 089 8131217
E-mail: info@locandacostadiva.it
Internet: www.locandacostadiva.it
Closed in November and January 7 to February 7

🍲 Restaurant-pizzeria
Via Capriglione 146
Tel. 089 874226
Closed Wednesday, never spring and summer
Open: lunch and dinner
Holidays: November
Seating: 75
Prices: 32-35 euros
All credit cards except AE, Bancomat

This hotel stands in a truly enviable position, perched on the edge of a cliff overlooking the sea at Praiano. The original old farmhouse has been meticulously restored with great attention to detail, as can be seen from the walls and floors, decorated with beautiful majolica tiles. The spacious, airy rooms have been given the names of the movie actresses who frequent the Amalfi coast. All the rooms have different color schemes and, above all, all of them have a private garden and terrace with a view of the Saracen watchtowers and fishermen's homes. Owner Filippo Milo will be there to welcome you and will ensure you have a pleasant, interesting stay. He'll be pleased to organize fishing trips, guided walks along the various paths or visits to the Punta Campanella area. The traditional-style breakfast offers home-baked cakes and hot and cold beverages.

• 8 double rooms and 5 suites, with bathroom (some with a jacuzzi), air-conditioning, terrace, mini-bar, satellite TV, modem connection • Prices: double room single use 70-110 euros, double 80-120, suite 130-160 (40 euro supplement for extra bed), breakfast included • Credit cards: all, Bancomat • Off-street parking. Small pets allowed. Reception open 24 hours a day • Bar. Breakfast room, reading and TV room. Garden, terrace. Organized beach

Giannino Irace's restaurant is blessed with a large terrace facing Positano, from which you can make out Punta Campanella and the faraglioni of Capri. After various experiences abroad and at hotels in the area, Irace opened this place in 1975 with his wife Martine, and since then he's neither significantly changed the decor, nor given in to any temptation to tamper with the menu. Overseen by chef Bartolomeo Cuomo, it's based on Mediterranean cuisine and pairs the daily catch of fish with seasonal vegetables.
Particularly worthy of note are the **totani with potatoes**, **vermicelli with fresh anchovies and cherry tomatoes** or Amalfi pesto (with parsley and anchovy extract), and for mains, the grilled or salt-baked fish and the **frittura mista,** or mixed fry. Though there's a strong focus on the sea, in the winter you'll also find 'land' dishes like pappardelle with rabbit, good **ravioli of ricotta and potatoes with ragù**, and, on request, the typical peasant dish **migliaccio salato**, a kind of baked timbale of pasta, semolina, mozzarella and sausage. The pizzas, served only in the evening, are not bad, though they always seem to be made by a different pizzaiolo. Martine bakes reliably good desserts such as seasonal fruit pies, almond and lemon cake, ricotta cake and pastiera.
To drink, regional wines, mainly whites.

SALERNO

HOSTARIA IL BRIGANTE

Traditional osteria-trattoria
Via Fratelli Linguiti 4
Tel. 089 226592
Closed Monday
Open: lunch and dinner
Holidays: August 5-20
Seating: 60
Prices: 15-20 euros, wine excluded
No credit cards accepted

LA VECCHIA QUERCIA

Holiday farm
Via Montevetrano 4
Tel. 089 882528-335 7843018
Fax 089 882010
E-mail: info@lavecchiaquercia.it
Internet: www.lavecchiaquercia.it
Open from March to the Epiphany

Il Brigante has been around for 20 years, but it seems newer. The spirit of the owner, Sandrino Donnabella, helped by his tireless wife Antonia in the kitchen, is the same as it was the day they opened, and they display a verve that unites innovation and tradition. They host presentations of little known books, exhibitions of local artists and historical recreations of ancient recipes. Apart from pictures of brigands, the walls also display quotes from Benedetto Croce and the whole place feels like the headquarters of some secret society.
The cooking is quintessentially local, starting with **sangiovannara** – found only here – **pasta with zucchini flowers** and **caponata** with olives, capers, eggplant and zucchini, but without the traditional biscotto di grano. In addition to such traditional plates, the menu also tangles with more unusual affairs such as couscous with angler fish. Other typical dishes include **stuffed Savoy cabbage**, **genovese di mollame** and **anchovies** in various preparations. Among the sometimes innovative desserts the most classic is **pastiera.**
The house wine is always the same, no more than passable, though there are some local labels for which you'll have to negotiate carefully (not for the price, but just to get them onto your table!) with the owner, who, good traditionalist that he is, has never served a Coca-Cola in his life.

At Via Dei Mercanti 75, the historic Pasticceria Pantaleone makes traditional Campanian sweets: pastiera, babà, millefoglie and their exclusive specialty scazzetta, based on sponge cake, pastry cream and wild strawberries.

Just a few kilometers from Salerno this beautiful early 20th-century country house, surrounded by the Montevetrano vineyards, has been tastefully renovated. The facility is managed by Anna Imparato, who welcomes her guests to an old-world atmosphere, rarely found elsewhere nowadays. The rooms have essential furnishings; 2 suites share a fully equipped kitchen and can be combined to create an apartment suitable for six people. The outdoor areas are charming: for instance, the portico is like an outside lounge and then, of course, there's the swimming pool. For breakfast, delicious home-made cakes and jams. In the adjacent restaurant – open to non-residents by reservation – the excellent cuisine focuses on local traditional dishes (35 euros per person, excluding wine; half board 23 euro supplement per person).

• 3 single, 2 double rooms and 3 suites (3 persons), with bathroom, terrace, TV (on request), modem connection • Prices: single 50-55 euros, double 90-100, suite 95-110, breakfast included • Credit cards: major ones, Bancomat • Off-street parking. No pets allowed. Owners always reachable • Restaurant. Breakfast room, Reading room. Garden. Swimming pool

San Lorenzo Maggiore

La Vecchia Trainella

☞❶Holiday farm
Contrada San Marzano 14
Tel. and fax 0824 815065
Open all year

This agriturismo is set in a really fantastic setting dominated by Monte Taburno, locally renamed 'the sleeping woman of Sannio' because the shape of the mountain resembles just that. Here you can be sure of a peaceful vacation, perhaps going for walks in the surrounding countryside in real contact with rural life. But it's also nice to take a short break here during a longer journey, whether on your way to or from places nearby like Benevento and Pietrelcina, or more distant like Naples and Caserta. The place is simply yet elegantly furnished, creating a pleasant, familiar, cozy atmosphere; on the upper floor there's also a small apartment with kitchen that can accommodate up to five people. Breakfast consists of a variety of home-made jams and cakes. Half board costs 35 euros per person.

• 3 double rooms, 1 apartment (2-6 persons), with bathroom, TV; • Prices: double room single use 20 euros, double 40 (10 euro supplement for extra bed), apartment 40-105, breakfast included • Credit cards: none • Off-street parking. Small pets allowed. Owners always present. • Restaurant. Breakfast room, TV room. Garden, children's playground

San Lupo

L'Oliveto

☞❶Holiday farm
Contrada Campopiano
Tel. and fax 0824 811194
Open all year

San Lupo is a small village in the upper Benevento area, on the slopes of Monte Petroso. Just a short distance from the village itself, from this agriturismo, there's a superb view over the tops of age-old olives and out to the Sannio hills. Olives are this farm's major crop and the local variety produces a top-quality extra virgin olive oil. The farm is family-run and offers comfortable, nicely furnished rooms that will ensure you have a pleasant, relaxing stay. The outdoor area has a children's playground and there's also an organized camping site. Maria Guerrera will be there to welcome you: for breakfast she provides traditional coffee and light refreshments, homemade cakes and jams. Maria also cooks meals using the estate's own products. Half board 30-35 euros per person.

• 4 double rooms, with bathroom, TV • Prices: double room single use 25 euros, double 40-50 (10 euro supplement for extra bed), breakfast included • Credit cards: none • Off-street parking. Small pets allowed. Owners always present. • Restaurant. Breakfast room, Entrance hall with TV. Grounds

SAN MICHELE DI SERINO

TAVERNETTA MARINELLA

Restaurant
Via Cotone 1
Tel. 0825 595128
Closed Sunday dinner and Monday
Open: lunch and dinner
Holidays: August 16-31
Seating: 95 + 40 outdoors
Prices: 27-30 euros, wine excluded
All credit cards

This restaurant, currently run with great success by Giovanni Romana, is housed in a former locanda and named after its original owner, Marinella. It has chosen to recall the past with the present name, just as the flavors of the past are recalled and renewed with gusto in the cooking. Giovanni is helped by his father Michele in the dining room, while his mother Nellina and Pasquale Berritto work in the kitchen.

The menu follows the changing seasons and pays tribute to the strong flavors of the land round Avellino. During our visit we tasted a triptych of turnips and potatoes, a green bean and wild mint flan and **macaroni frittata** with balsamic vinegar and olive oil, then paccheri di Gragnano with lardo, cherry tomatoes and caciocavallo podolico and a tasty **zuppa di cicci e baìne** (cannellini and green beans) and veal tagliata alla serinese. Inevitably the dishes change constantly, depending on the availability of ingredients. In the winter, you could try chestnut and mushroom or **escarole and bean soup**, ravioli with cep mushrooms and black truffles or **schiaffoni with wild boar ragù**. There's almost always an interesting selection of cured meats and local cheeses, and reliable seconds like roast pork shank with potatoes and **veal braciola with ragù**. Giovanni's family has been making sweets and ice creams for many years, so the puddings, all home-made, are highly recommended.

There are around 100 labels in the cellar, with particular emphasis on Campania.

SANT'AGATA DE' GOTI

MUSTILLI

Holiday farm
Via dei Fiori 20
Tel. 0823 717433
Fax 0823 717619
E-mail: info@mustilli.com
Internet: www.mustilli.com
Open all year

Palazzo Rainone is an 18th-century noble residence situated in the center of Sant' Agata de' Goti, in a small quiet square close to a convent. The rooms for the vacation farm are on the second floor overlooking the village rooftops and are all furnished differently with family furniture or more modern pieces. There's a spacious common reading room with a vaguely retro atmosphere (high ceiling and velvet-upholstered armchairs and couches). This family-run agriturismo is managed by Marilì Mustilli, who for breakfast serves traditional coffee and light refreshments, yogurt, home-baked cookies and fresh fruit. On request you can also have savory fare. The restaurant is only open for residents (25-30 euros). The facility organizes courses on various topics, from wine-tasting and gastronomy to music.

• 4 double rooms and 1 suite (4 persons), with bathroom, air-conditioning, TV • Prices: double room single use 55 euros, double 80, suite 140 (15 euro supplement for extra bed), breakfast included • Credit cards: all, Bancomat • Off-street parking. Small pets allowed. Owners always reachable • Restaurant (residents only). Breakfast room, reading room, lounges. Conference room. Terrace

SANT'AGATA DE' GOTI   SANT'ANASTASIA

PIAZZA DUOMO   ## 'E CURTI

Restaurant-pizzeria
Piazza Duomo 6
Tel. 0823 717683
Closed Tuesday
Open lunch and dinner
Holidays: last week of August and first week of September
Seating: 50 + 30 outdoors
Prices: 22-27 euros, wine excluded
All credit cards, Bancomat

Traditional osteria
Via Padre Michele Abete 6
Tel. 081 8972821
Closed Sunday
Open: lunch and dinner
Holidays: August
Seating: 40
Prices: 30-35 euros, wine excluded
Major credit cards

Sant'Agata de' Goti, built on the ruins of ancient Saticula, is a big tourist attraction. The village forms a semi-circle on the edge of a tufa cliff, with a maze of narrow alleys leading to the cathedral on the piazza in front of which you'll find this well-kept, friendly restaurant. The cooking respects local traditions and seasonal ingredients, but is also influenced by the flair of owner Carmine De Rosa, assisted by his son Vincenzo, front of house.

The **cured meats**, like soppressa and sausage, are well worth trying, as is the Campania **mozzarella di bufala** sourced from nearby Caserta cheesemakers, grilled cheeses with vegetables in oil or cheese flavored with chili peppers. Vegetable dishes include delicious eggplant parmigiana, **fried green peppers**, green beans with tomato, **viticielli** (a wild asparagus-like plant found in the spring), fried and combined with fresh cheeses. Among the firsts: **pacche with beans**, **cavatelli al sugo**, ravioletti with mushrooms and walnuts, **scialatielli** with Taburno black truffles. For main course, we recommend **grilled lamb**, though the brochettes and sausages are also good. Plus every evening there's pizza cooked in the wood-fired oven.

The selection of local wines and spirits is good.

Founded in 1924, this restaurant has been run by the same family for over 50 years. Thanks to its welcoming ambience, friendly owners – Carmine front of house and Angela in the kitchen – and excellent local cooking, it's a standard-bearer for Vesuvian restaurants.

The ingredients are selected with care and the dishes prepared according to traditional recipes. The meal begins with mozzarella; **squid stuffed with mozzarella, pecorino and parsley**; olives alla napoletana; pumpkin flower fritters; eggplant roulades with little piennolo tomatoes. In winter you'll find zuppe, like bean and mushroom and **minestra maritata**, and pastas like Gragnano spaghetti with walnuts, raisins, pine nuts, capers and olives; **paccheri with lamb ragù**; or fettuccine with pecorino and pancetta. Meat dishes like **soffritto**, **tripe** and **roulades of lamb intestines** ('ndruglietielli), leg of lamb with peas and grilled lamb chops dominate the main dishes. In summer you could have rice with mussels and potatoes, **gnocchi with limpets and mussels** and various dishes with spolichini (fresh beans). Dishes often showcase fish like anchovies and sardines, as well as the ever present **stoccafisso** (stockfish) either **stewed** or with olives and capers, and sometimes also fried baccalà. Finish with ricotta cake, pizza di crema, pastiera and il Nucillo, made to an ancient family recipe and today sold by the owners' children.

The cellar contains a selection of wines from Campania and the rest of Italy, plus the house wine, Catalanesco, made with Vesuvian grapes.

Under the portico of the cloistered nuns' convent, Panetteria Frogiero sells 'nfrennula and tarallini. At the Gelateria Mario Perna Baratta, Piazza del Carmine, the coffee is excellent, as is the ice-cream at the Bar Gelateria Normanno, Via Roma 65.

SANTO STEFANO DEL SOLE
San Pietro all'Olio

10 KM SOUTHEAST OF AVELLINO

SAPRI

159 KM SOUTHEAST OF SALERNO

TABERNA VULGI

Restaurant
Via Casino 6
Tel. 0825 673664
Closed Sunday dinner and Monday
Open lunch and dinner
Holidays: first two weeks of September
Seating: 50 + 50 outside
Prices: 28-35 euros, wine excluded
All credit cards except AE, Bancomat

LOCANDA DEI TRECENTO

3-Star Hotel
Piazza Regina Elena
Tel. 0973 603160
Fax 0973 603349
E-mail: locandadeitrecento@libero.it
Internet: www.golfodipolicastro.it/locandadeitrecento
Closed between September and November

In reality, this restaurant is more sophisticated than its name suggests, recalling the inns of the common people of Ancient Rome, may suggest. Run by two partners, Giovanni and Gennaro, it's friendly and serves reliably good food, striking a balance between tradition and thoughtful innovation and giving prominence to local ingredients. Everything here is chosen with care – from the meat and the vegetables to the oil and even the salt – and prepared with skill.
In summer you can start with a carpaccio of Sorrento tomatoes and smoked tuna and a successful reworking of **Caprese** salad, consisting of pastry filled with mozzarella and served on a bed of San Marzano tomatoes. Follow with **lagane with Crotone beans** and tuna bottarga, paccheri with baccalà and zucchini, burnt-grain **fettuccelle with rabbit ragù**, grilled shoulder fillet, **pork fillet in caul fat** with green onions, **roast lamb** with dried tomatoes and fennel and, for dessert, caramel panbagnato with mint sauce. The dishes change constantly according to new discoveries, suggestions and reinventions. In winter, for example, don't miss the minestra maritata or the sumptuous **maialata**, and also the soppressata to start. Seasonal vegetables are used for soups, side dishes and flans of various kinds.
The wine list promotes Irpinian wine makers, without ignoring worthy national labels. There's a good selection of grappas and a vintage rum to sip with a cigar.

This small hotel in the southernmost part of the Campania region, south of the gulf of Policastro, owes its name to the revolutionary expedition led by Carlo Pisacane and Giuseppe Nicotera that landed at Sapri. This hotel is organized in a recently built farmhouse managed by Osvaldo Balbi, located right in front of where the landing took place. It has eight comfortable double rooms fitted with functional modern furnishings. In addition, there are two mini-apartments with kitchenette that can accommodate up to four people and can be rented for a minimum period of seven days. Breakfast is served in a cozy common room and offers a variety of products produced in the nearby Parco del Cilento: jams, honey and preserves cakes and fresh and hot drinks. On request, you can rent bicycles or participate in excursions to nearby historical and art towns and seaside resorts. High season prices apply for two weeks during the month of August.

• 8 double rooms, with bathroom, air-conditioning, mini-bar, TV, several rooms with terrace; 2 apartments (4 persons) with kitchenette • Prices: double room single use 45-95 euros, double 60-125 (15-30 euro supplement for extra bed), breakfast included • Credit cards: all, Bancomat • Apartments accessible to the mobility challenged. Off-street parking. No pets allowed. Owners always present • Bar. Breakfast room, terrace. Organized beach

SICIGNANO DEGLI ALBURNI

LA TAVERNA DEI BRIGANTI

Traditional osteria
Via Convento 25
Tel. 0828 973808
Closed Monday
Open: dinner, lunch also on holidays
Holidays: variable in the winter
Seating: 35 + 20 outside
Prices: 20-25 euros, wine excluded
No credit cards

Sicignano, at the foot of the imposing Alburni massif, is about 12 kilometers from the Salerno-Reggio Calabria highway exit. The reference to brigands in the restaurant's name recalls the area's past, which the owners help to promote with their traditional dishes. The osteria is run by Raffaele Polito, and the friendly interior is warmed by a fireplace and features a baby grand piano. Raffaele is front of house while his wife Marianna is in the kitchen, using locally sourced ingredients as a source of inspiration for a series of tasty dishes.

The wide range of antipasti includes soppressata, sausage, grilled polenta with **pig's lung sausage** and **sheep's milk ricotta with dried peppers**. Pastas are handmade: fusilli, ravioli and **cavatielli** with **lamb ragù**; pappardelle with wild boar or, in season, cep mushrooms; **lagane with chickpeas** or beans. When the cold weather arrives, so do heartier dishes like **minestra maritata** (with wild greens and various cuts of pork) or Savoy cabbage soup with pork. Pork also features in the mains like **sfrionza** (veal sautéed with potatoes and pickled red peppers), typical of the Alburni, and there are also fillet and sirloin steak or **sausages with sweet roast peppers**. We also recommend the free-range chicken stuffed and cooked in ragù, which must be pre-ordered.

Finish with sponge cake with chocolate, chestnuts or wild strawberries. There aren't many wines; the reds that go best with the food are mainly from the south.

SOMMA VESUVIANA

LA LANTERNA

Restaurant-pizzeria
Via Colonnello Aliperta 8
Tel. 081 8991843
Closed Monday
Open: lunch and dinner
Holidays: August
Seating: 60 + 30 outside
Prices: 28-35 euros, wine excluded
All credit cards, Bancomat

La Lanterna is in the Vesuvius National Park, at the foot of Monte Somma, near the ancient Casamale, still surrounded by Aragonese walls. For some time now, this area has sought to protect and promote its typical products, and in Luigi Russo's restaurant there's even a showroom dedicated to them: from various kinds of apricots (pellecchiella, cafona, monaco bello, palummella) to the little Slow Food Presidium Piennolo tomatoes. Once seated at the table, let yourself be guided by the chef-owner, Vincenzo Nocerino, who will suggest the best dishes. On our visit we particularly enjoyed the antipasti of octopus carpaccio, **marinated salt cod** (Somma Vesuviana has developed a whole culture of salt-cod cooking, based on its historical role as an importer), and **parmigiana of scabbard fish**. If ou book ahead, you can also try the tegamino di baccalà, with bread, potatoes and Piennolo tomatoes. Among the summer first courses, we recommend the penne with stockfish and eggplant and the **tubetti with mussels and zucchini flowers**; in the winter, the **bean and escarole soup**, the **zuppetta of chickpeas and pioppo mushrooms** and the penne with escarole, provola and walnuts. Among the mains, there's a good choice of meats, like wild boar, **rabbit stuffed** with friarielli greens and porcini mushrooms and, of course, the salt cod, either grilled or in rissoles. The desserts are so good, they seem to have been made by a pasticceria.

The wine list could do with some revising and organizing, above all in the dessert wine and spirits section, but there are some decent options and mark-ups are reasonable. Pizza is available only in the evening.

SORRENTO

CASA ASTARITA

🗝Bed and breakfast
Corso Italia 67
Tel. 081 8774906-348 2627325
Fax 081 8071146
E-mail: info@casastarita.com
Internet: www.casastarita.com
Open all year

Casa Astarita is a nice B&B that two sisters, Rita and Annamaria, opened after modernizing their old family palazzo. Three of the rooms face onto Sorrento's main street, the others face the inner courtyard. Each is marked by different color schemes and furnishings – antique family furniture or more modern pieces – but all have been designed with great attention to detail. The only common area – called 'grandmother's room' – is in the center of the building and has terracotta floors, a majolica fireplace, an old sewing-machine and the table where breakfast is served. Guests have free Internet access. The day begins with jams, cakes, brioches and warm croissants prepared by a bakery located a few meters away. The choice of possible excursions and tour is very wide indeed – all you need is a plenty of time to cover them all!

• 6 double rooms, with bathroom, air-conditioning, safe, satellite TV, modem connection • Prices: double room single use and double 75-95 euros (15 euro supplement for extra bed), breakfast included • Credit cards: major ones, Bancomat • 1 room designed for use by the mobility challenged. Garage parking at special rates (10 euros per day). Small pets allowed. Owners always present • Breakfast room, lounge

SORRENTO
Borgo dei Pescatori
Marina Grande

SANT'ANNA DA EMILIA

Trattoria
Via Marina Grande 62
Tel. 081 8072720
Closed Tuesday, never March-August
Open: lunch and dinner
Holidays: November
Seating: 30 + 40 outside
Pricesi: 25-28 euros, wine excluded
No credit cards

The trattoria is situated in a restructured monazzero, a fishing boat repair shop, to the extreme left of the pier of the Marina Grande. The atmosphere is simple, even a tad d'antan. Not for nothing, since the place has been around for a long time and used to serve meals to the crews of postwar Italian neorealist mpvies (Sorrento was a popular location in those days). Not much has changed since then, not even the outside terrace on stilts where you can dine in summer. Nonna Emilia, daughter of the founder, runs the kitchen with her nieces Irene and Teresa. The daily menu is written on a sheet of paper and its contents depend on the daily catch and the produce available at the daily vegetable market. Antipasti include **marinated and fried anchovies** grilled vehetables, **caprese** with Sorrento tomatoes and **mussels with lemon** or tomato. For first course, **spaghetti** with mussels or **clams, gnocchi alla sorrentina** (with tomotato and mozzarella) and so on. Afterwards, don't miss the **frittura di paranza**, fried calamari, and the grilled fresh fish. There are also a few meat dishes.
To drink, we recommend the house wine, but you can also choose from four or five regional labels. The place is always crowded summer for dinner, so be ready to stand in line.

28 KM NORTH OF BENEVENTO

27 KM SOUTHEAST OF NAPLES, 8 KM FROM POMPEI

LA LOCANDA DELLA PACCHIANA

🍲 Hotel-restaurant
Viale Minieri 32
Tel. 0824 976093
Closed Friday dinner
Open: lunch and dinner
Holidays: none
Seating: 70
Prices: 20-22 euros, wine excluded
All credit cards except DC, Bancomat

THE PINK GARDEN

🍲 Restaurant-pizzeria
Via Sant'Antonio 232
Tel. 081 8283624
Closed Tuesday
Open: lunch and dinner
Holidays: two weeks around mid-August, Christmas and Easter
Seating: 80 + 100 outside
Prices: 30-35 euros, wine excluded
All credit cards, Bancomat

Visitors come to Telese for the beneficial sulfurous waters of its spa, but also to enjoy the Sannio landscape of vineyards and olive groves and to spend pleasant days visiting the surrounding medieval villages, archeological sites, artisan workshops and wineries. Their stay will be even more pleasant, if they plan a stop at this restaurant, run by the young Piero and Franco, serving dishes that reflect Sannio traditions and seasonal produce. Passing through the area with the counter and small bar tables, you reach the two comfortable, friendly dining rooms which, save for some bizarre ceiling decorations, are simply furnished.

Start with the antipasti buffet: seasonal vegetables – grilled, marinated, or in oil – cured meats and the most representative local cheeses, like Caciocavallo silano and **Pecorino laticauda**. Move on to a wide choice of home-made first courses, like tortellaccio with woodland flavors, **strigoli with virni** (St. George's mushrooms) **and cherry tomatoes**, spaghetti with wild asparagus, **strettine with zucchini**, paccheri with herbs, **fili d'angelo all'olio santo** and diavoletti cacio e pepe. In winter, the menu is bulked out with flavorful soups, like **pane cotto with beans and broccoli** and minestra maritata. The mains are based on meats like roast veal from Podolico cows, **grilled Laticauda lamb**, rabbit in porchetta and also beef from Ireland and Argentina, also grilled. To finish, the home-made desserts include sbriciolata with Strega liqueur, panna cotta and amarena cherry delizia.

The cellar offers a decent selection of the best wines from the province and the region.

Don't be deceived by the English name – the cooking is 100% Neapolitan – or the fact that to reach this restaurant you have to follow the road that runs inland to Vesuvius, because here you'll find lots of fish. Easily reached from the nearby archeological sites of Herculaneum and Pompei, this restaurant is run by the Ascione brothers, Salvatore, Antonio, Giuseppe and Luigi, some in the kitchen and some front of house in the simply decorated dining room. At weekends and other busy times, their sisters come to help out.

Chef Salvatore is responsible for sourcing ingredients, taking particular care over the fish that comes from the nearby coast and local markets. The daily catch, of course, dictates the menu, as does tradition. Among the antipasti, we recommend the giant shrimp in lemon leaves, **fried cicinielli** (whitebait), various kinds of marinated fish, seafood sauté and ricotta-stuffed fritters. The pasta – both traditional dry shapes and fresh – is served with different seafood-based sauces, from the classic **spaghetti with clams** to **paccheri with angler fish sauce** to fresh pastas with mussels. In summer, the sauces are enriched with greens and vegetables, as in fettuccine with clams and zucchini or **spaghetti with mussels and cannellini beans**. Among the mains, you'll find the **frittura mista** or various kinds of fish cooked in the oven or stewed all'acquapazza, or salt-baked. Finish with home-made desserts like pies with Annurca apples or Vesuvius apricots and chocolate semifreddo.

There's no wine list; you're offered a choice of a few local wines and some from the rest of Italy.

TRAMONTI

Gete

OSTERIA REALE

🍲 Trattoria/Rooms
Via Cardamone 75
Tel. 089 856144
Fax 089 853232
E-mail: info@osteriareale.it
Internet: www.osteriareale.it
Closed Wednesday, except in August
Open: dinner, Saturday, Sunday and public holidays also for lunch
Holidays: 20 days in February and in November
Seating: 45 + 30 outdoors
Prices: 30-32 euros, wine excluded
All major credit cards, Bancomat

Luigi Reale has recently put his father's vineyards of Tintore and Per'e Palummo back into production, and has renovated a farmhouse belonging to the family, creating a small number of rooms (available all week) and an osteria, with a delightful outdoor pergola. The cuisine is a balance between tradition and creativity, and respects seasonal local produce. The meal opens with **fiordilatte**, lemon-scented ricotta, timbale of anchovies and potatoes, puff pastry cakes with ricotta of Tramonti and, in winter, timbale of minestra maritata and spicy sausage. The first courses include **taccole with dried cherry tomatoes and ricotta**, cappellacci in salsa di pesce bandiera and lemon, ricci (fresh pasta similar to fusilli) with mussels, crayfish and pumpkin flowers. Often there are first courses made of chickpeas or beans. To follow, meat and fish: **kid baked** with potatoes and black olives, **boned rabbit stuffed** with vegetables, **millefoglie di pesce bandiera** with mozzarella and cherry tomatoes. Try the **pizza** of Tramonti, different from the Neapolitan variety, but just as good. The meal ends with goat's ricotta cream with chocolate flakes, almonds and lemon, pear and chocolate or cream tarts. Cardamone or Getis wine produced by the owner and other good labels, mostly from the Campania region, are served with the meals.

🛏️ 3 double rooms, en suite, balcony, TV • Prices: double single use 40, double 65-75 euros (supplement for additional bed 15 euros), breakfast included • 1 room suitably equipped for the mobility impaired. Private outdoor free parking area. Pets not welcome. Owners always available • Bar, restaurant. Garden, terrace

VALLE DELL'ANGELO

OSTERIA LA PIAZZETTA

🍲 Osteria with rooms
Piazza Canonico Iannuzzi 2
Tel. 0974 942008
Always open
Open: lunch and dinner
Holidays: one week in September
Seating: 24
Prices: 25-28 euros, wine excluded
No credit cards

To reach this tiny village of fewer than 100 inhabitants, you have to penetrate deep into the remotest heart of the Cilento visit. But it's worth it to visit this osteria in the center of Valle dell'Angelo, run since 1999 by Angelo Coccaro, known to his friends as Alì, and his wife Carmela. Inside, the typical pastel colors of a village square have been painted on the walls, together with ceramic signs and stone doors. Carmela learned her cooking skills from her mother and brilliantly exploits the local ingredients supplied by a small community of farmers. Angelo serves in the dining room and will happily chat about the mountains – he's full of suggestions for anyone planning an excursion to nearby Monte Cervati.
To start, local **cured meats** and **cheeses**: capocollo, sausage, soppressata, fresh and aged sheep and goat cheeses and an excellent **Caciocavallo podolico** from nearby Piaggine. The traditional Cilento pastas are hand-made and include **ravioli filled with ricotta**, fusilli and **cavatielli with** wonderful **meat or boar ragù**. In the fall, the menu includes **tagliolini with cep mushrooms and chestnuts and**, soups with vegetables and legumes, such as **escarole and regina bean**. Continue with the meats used for the ragù, above all pork chop and belly pork, **wild boar stew** with vegetables or pork fillet with cep mushrooms. Around Easter, you'll find **stuffed pizzas** with toma, chard, broccoli or borage.
Finish with the sponge cake with cream. The small but quality choice of wines includes Campanian reds and some Tuscan labels. Reservations are essential.

VALLESACCARDA

60 KM NORTHEAST OF AVELLINO ON 16 OR SS 90 AND 91

MINICUCCIO

Hotel-restaurant
Via Santa Maria 24-26
Tel. 0827 97020-97454
Closed Monday
Open: lunch and dinner
Holidays: at Christmas
Seating: 350
Prices: 23-27 euros, wine excluded
All credit cards

The large capacity of this restaurant may not accord completely with the spirit of the classic osteria - usually small and intimate - but the cooking certainly does. Owner Franco Pagliarulo's years of research have led him to discover many typical dishes, and the menu changes seasonally, even weekly. A stop at the Minicuccio will guarantee you a satisfying tour of the gastronomy of Irpinia.
Now for the dishes themselves. In spring and summer it's all about vegetables, cooked in many different **soups** – **new fava bean**, green bean, pea, zucchini and potatoe – and in the classic **ciambotta**. In winter there's the **minestra maritata** with Savoy cabbage and pork, bean soup with pork rind and pork soffritto. The dry and fresh pastas with different sauces are all good: **lagane** with cicerchie, chickpeas, beans or pork tongue, **cavatelli with ragù**, ricotta or broccoli, tacculecchi often come with a sauce of cocozza (zucchini) shoots and oil of Ravece. There's a huge number of main courses to choose from, like **sausage with pickled peppers**, kid and veal stews, **lamb** in different guises (with rosemary, baked with potatoes, with peppers, **pan-roasted**), rabbit or chicken alla caxcciatora and **baccalà**, either roasted or **alla pert'caregna** (with dried peppers). For sides there are peppers fried, stuffed or cooked with toasted breadcrumbs, potato croquettes and various salads. Close with sweet ricotta pizza, zeppole with honey, susamielli (sweets with honey and vincotto), taralli and cookies.
To go with your meal there's the local Aglianico or good DOC wines from Irpinia and the rest of Campania.

VIBONATI
Villammare

149 KM SOUTH OF SALERNO A 3

TAVERNA PORTOSALVO

Osteria
Corso Italia, 77
Tel. 0973 365474-338 5617963
Closed Monday, never in summer
Open: lunch and dinner
Holidays: January 7-25
Seating: 24
Prices: 28-35 euros, wine excluded
All credit cards except AE, Bancomat

Not far from the main square in Vibonati is a little alley that takes you to a former warehouse. Following careful restoration, the premises have been converted into a charming osteria run by Gerardo Menza, who's from Basilicata and has a straightforward but courteous manner. He takes great care over sourcing his ingredients, and given that we're in one of Italy's many seaside towns, it's all about the local fish, which you'll find everywhere on the menu, from antipasti to seconds.
If they're in season, you should start with the **cicinielli** (whitebait) either in a **tortino** (pie), fried or cooked all'acquapazza (ie, stewed); marinated amberjack, **squid stewed with potatoes** and wild fennel, octopus with vegetables or squid with artichokes. The reliable first courses include various kinds of hand-made pastas with fish sauces made from the daily catch. We tried the **ravioli of pasta and potatoes stuffed with fish**, **tubetti with angler fish** and black tagliatelle (made with squid ink) with langoustine sauce. There's an embarrassment of riches for the mains, as you can choose your fish from a display: maybe an amberjack so fresh that it needs the absolute minimum of preparation, a scabbard fish to be chopped into cutlets, a forkbeard, or a **shellfish stew**. Finally there's almond or **prickly pear blancmange,** a homage to nearby Sicily.
The wine list gives prominence to wines from Campania and the rest of southern Italy, with sporadic 'incursion' from Trentino. It's not huge but you'll always find something to go with your meal.

VICO EQUENSE
Preazzano

46 KM SOUTH OF NAPLES

CASSIOPEA

🛏️🔑 Bed and breakfast
Via Bosco 772
Tel. 081 8024527-339 7462336
Fax 081 8024771
E-mail: cassiopea.bb@libero.it
Internet: www.anbba.it/bb/cassiopea
Closed from November to February

This peaceful B&B, run by Caterina and Ignazio Esposito, both active environmentalists, is in the hills near Vico Equense, a place famous for its cheese, Provolone del monaco. The 18th-century residence has recently been restructured to create three bright and airy rooms on the ground floor, all simply furnished; one room has a mezzanine floor and can accommodate up to four people. Breakfast is set out in a cozy common room and consists of coffee and light refreshments, bread and local produce, honey and jams. Guests can spend their time on the beach at Seiano or Positano, or explore the mountains in organized excursions to the nearby Parco dei Monti Lattari. Just 50 meters from the B&B is a bus stop on the route that departs from the railway station.

• 3 double rooms, with bathroom, minibar, satellite TV • Prices: double room single use 35 euros, double 50-55 (15 euro supplement for extra bed), breakfast included • Credit cards: none • 1 room designed for use by the mobility challenged. Off-street parking. Small pets allowed. Owners always reachable • Breakfast room, lounge. Garden. Terrace

VICO EQUENSE
Arola

38 KM SOUTHEAST OF NAPLES, 7 KM FROM THE CENTER OF TOWN

TORRE FERANO

🍲 Trattoria
Via Bosco 810
Tel. 081 8024786
Closed Tuesday in winter, Monday and Tuesday lunch in the summer
Open: lunch and dinner
Holidays: January 10-February 10
Seating: 50 + 50 outdoors
Prices: 30-35 euros
All credit cards, Bancomst

The road to Arola is off the state highway for Sorrento, past the turnoff for Vico Equense. Here you're in the Lattari Mountains, homeland of Fior di latte and Provolone del monaco. In winter, the dining room is warmed by a fireplace and in summer you can enjoy the view of the Gulf of Naples and the Sorrento peninsula from the terrace. The owners are Antonio Staiano, who sources the ingredients, and Camillo Sorrentino, who oversees the kitchen and the dining room. The final result of their joint efforts is a traditional interpretation of quality ingredients: copper pots are used, the meats are grilled over real charcoal, not on a flat-top, and potatoes are actually cooked in the ashes.
The menu turns on seasonal offerings from the sea and the land. In spring and summer, you can start with tuna croquettes and fried sage leaves or fior di latte roll with wild rocket and cherry tomatoes, followed by **artisan spaghetti with fresh tomato** and basil, **malfatti with murex and seaweed** or Gragnano fusilli with Mastantuono pears. Among the seconds, there's breaded tuna, **frittura di paranza** and aromatic herb tart. In the fall and winter, try calzoncelli with ricotta and salami, local cured meats, **tripe soup** Equense-style, **fresh pasta with soffritto**, soup with chestnuts and cep mushrooms from Faito, ziti with baccalà and potatoes, chicken stuffed with chestnuts, **porchetta** roasted in a wood-fired oven, local beef tagliata and various dishes based on Provolone del monaco. Finish with tortino of Sorrento lemons, blackberry bavarois, Sorrento walnut strudel and bacetti with Faito chestnuts. A good local wine is included in the price and there are also some Campania labels.

889   CAMPANIA

VICO EQUENSE
Pacognano

VILLA GIOVAN BATTISTA DELLA PORTA

🍲⦿Locanda
Via San Bernardino 1
Tel. 081 8029243
Fax 081 8799055
E-mail: info@villadellaporta.it
Internet: www.villadellaporta.it
Open all year round

Surrounded by the green hills of Vico Equense, this residence, once the home of writer and scientist Giovan Battista Della Porta, has been tastefully refurbished with total respect for the original architectural structure. Today it accommodates the locanda run by Peppe Guida's family with the indispensable support of Eduardo Buonocore. The apartments and rooms are spacious and comfortable, furnished with pieces reminiscent of those of the bourgeois homes of the area. The common areas are especially charming. For breakfast, you'll be offered locally made products such as croissants, jams, fruit, milk, the famous butter and a selection of delicious petite patisserie. The supplement per person for half-board is 25 euros.

• 2 double rooms, with bathroom (tub or jacuzzi shower), air-conditioning, mini-bar, satellite TV; 6 apartments (2-6 persons) with kitchenette • Prices: double room single use and double 70-85 euros (10 euro supplement for extra bed), apartments 70-140, breakfast included • Credit cards: all, Bancomat • Off-street parking. No pets allowed. Owners always present. • Restaurant. Breakfast room. Garden, terrace

🍲 In the restaurant next door, Peppe Guida serves stylish seafood and meat dishes with a personal touch (35-50 euros, excluding wine).

VOLLA

IL SEBETO

🍲Restaurant
Via Rossi 65
Tel. 081 7743872
Closed Sunday dinner and Monday
Open: lunch and dinner
Holidays: two weeks in August
Seating: 60
Prices: 25-30 euros, wine excluded
All credit cards and Bancomat

Over the last decade this area has been subject to rapid economic growth and a building boom, so it's good to see this restaurant in the forefront of an attempt to claw back some of the memory of how things used to be. This can be seen in the name – the Sebeto was a river, partly subterranean, which made the zone fertile – and, above all, the attention to local cuisine, with a particular focus on ingredients (green Volla chili peppers , for example). The decor is simple in the extreme – we'd prefer it without the TV set that reigns on high, but each to their own.
Owner Innocenzo Manfellotti will help you choose from the menu which, under antipasti, includes **fiorilli stuffed with ricotta and pepper**, pizza bread bruschettas, stuffed escarole and **sautéed friarielli**. Notable first courses are orecchiette alla Sebeto with beans and pancetta, penne with eggplant and provola or asparagus and ricotta, **spaghetti with fresh tomato and basil** (don't let the apparent simplicity deceive you, it's exactly this kind of dish that heightens flavors), gnocchi with potato puree gratinéed in the oven, **cianfotta** (stewed vegetables), **pasta and beans**, pasta and chickpeas and **pasta with potatoes**. Among the seconds, **pork chop** with basil or fish, which Innocenzo buys every day from a trucker friend from Mazara del Vallo. The desserts, like babà or caprese, are home-made.
The limited wine list consists mainly of Campanian labels.

🍷 In **Cercola** (3 km), the Pastificio Leonessa, at Via Don Minzoni 335, makes pasta with traditional bronze dies and excellent fresh pasta.

BASILICATA

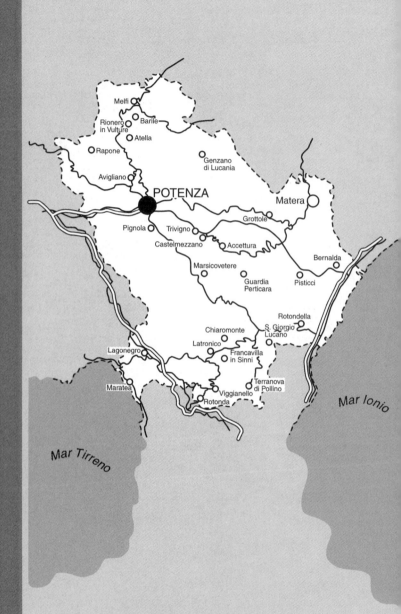

Melfi
Rionero in Vulture
Barile
Atella
Rapone
Genzano di Lucania
Avigliano
POTENZA
Matera
Pignola
Trivigno
Grottole
Castelmezzano
Accettura
Marsicovetere
Bernalda
Guardia Perticara
Pisticci
Rotondella
Chiaromonte
S. Giorgio Lucano
Latronico
Lagonegro
Francavilla in Sinni
Maratea
Terranova di Pollino
Viggianello
Rotonda

Mar Ionio

Mar Tirreno

PEZZOLLA

🍲Restaurant with
accommodation
Via Roma 21
Tel. 0835 675008
Closed Friday, never in summer
Open: lunch and dinner
Holidays: none
Seating: 40 + 20 outdoors
Prices: 23-25 euros, wine excluded
All credit cards, Bancomat

Zia Isa, who runs the Pezzolla with her son Mario, is one of those legendary characters from the Italian culinary world who prefer to shy clear of the spotlight. Yet her commitment to her work, long experience and knowledge of the products she uses has made her place one of the most appreciated gastronomic stop-offs in the region. Entering the restaurant's small dining room, the visitor immediately feels at home.

You can either order à la carte or choose a rich set menu at 25 euros. In either case, you start with home-made antipasti preserved in oil, cured meats and local cheeses. First courses include fresh pasta dishes such as **orecchiette**, cavatelli, pappardelle and **manate**, a special form obtained by constant kneading and breaking by hand.The most typical dressings are the tasty **mushrooms** and **truffles** which proliferate in the Gallipoli-Cognato woods in the surrounding mountains. Second courses consist mainly of barbecued meats, mainly sourced from the local pig, wild boar, lamb and **Podolico cattle** farms. For those who don't like meat, Scamorza, Pecorino and Caciocavallo are the alternatives.

To end the meal, try the home-made tarts, hot honey **zeppole**, ricotta sweets and almond biscuits. The wines in the cellar are few but excellent.

LA VALLE DEI CAVALLI

🔑Holiday farm
Contrada Piani di Carda
Tel. 0972 716240-338 2228005
Internet: www.agriturismolavalledeicavalli.it
Open all year round

This farm tourism facility, run by the Summa brothers and situated out in the country, is ideal lovers of nature and sport, with instructors available for western riding courses and guides for horse riding along the valley trails at the foot of Mount Vulture. The spacious, comfortable rooms are simply furnished. Breakfast, served in the 40-table dining room, includes coffee, cappuccino, milk, tea, jams, homemade tarts and, if you ask, savories too. The cooking is traditional. In the hot season you can eat outside under a wooden arbor.

Half board costs 45 euros per person, full board 55.

• 1 double and 2 triple rooms with bathroom, television • Prices: double room single use 30, double 60, triple 80 euros, breakfast included • Credit cards: all, Bancomat • Open inside parking. Small pets accepted. Owners always contactable • Restaurant. Horse-riding

AVIGLIANO
Frusci-Monte Carmine

BARILE

PIETRA DEL SALE

☞Restaurant
Contrada Pietra del Sale
Tel. 0971 87063
Closed Monday and Sunday for dinner
Open: lunch and dinner
Holidays: none
Seating: 80 + 30 outdoors
Prices: 25-30 euros, wine excluded
All credit cards, Bancomat

LA LOCANDA
DEL PALAZZO

⚫4-Star Hotel
Piazza Caracciolo 7
Tel. and fax 0972 771051
E-mail: info@locandadelpalazzo.com
Internet: www.locandadelpalazzo.com
Closed two weeks in July and one in January

Situated at an altitude of 1100 metres, this Doria guard house is home to the Pietra del Sale, which lies at the foot of the Madonna del Carmine sanctuary opposite Lagopesole Castle, the ancient manor house of Frederick II of Swabia.

The restaurant is just one part of the business of the Samela brothers, who produce lamb and wild boar, wild berries, and **cured meats** (sausage, soppressata, ham, capicollo) and **cheeses** (fresh caprini, seasoned or aromatized, Filiano pecorino, Caciocavallo silano and Podolico), which appear in the restaurant's mixed hors-d'oeuvre along with fried or baked eggplant and peppers, zucchini a scapece and excellent ricottina cheese with honey. First courses are made with fresh hand-made pasta: **cauzuni** (ricotta cheese and mint), tagliatelle with caprino and truffle, **cautarogne** (that's what strascinati are called in Avigliano dialect) dressed with wild boar ragù or goat Cacioricotta and meat. Meat prevails in the main courses: **stewed or grilled boar**, **mugnulatieddi** (lamb innards), grilled lamb, and (if you book) **cutturieddu** (a very spicy lamb stew). Also typical of the area is **baccalà**, stewed or **fried with crusch peppers**. Finish off with wild berry tarts and homemade ice-cream.

The wine list features several Aglianico del Vulture producers and other Italian labels.

After 25 years running a restaurant in Cremona, Rino Botte decided to return to his place of origin. Here, in August 2001, on the premises of the old family wine company that had been closed for more than 30 years, he opened this pleasant restaurant-hotel.

All the rooms bear the name of one of the local Aglianico vineyards (Gelosia, Macarico, Titolo, Rotondo...) and each is different from the next in terms of fabrics and colors. The furnishings are simple and scrupulous.

The restaurant area has been developed from the 16th-century part of the building, where the cellar and the mill of the noble palace of the Caracciolo-Torella families used to be situated. The dishes served by Lucia Giura are typical of the local cuisine. Tours of the Aglianico vineyards can also be organized.

• 2 single and 9 double rooms with bathroom, air conditioning, mini-bar, satellite television, modem connection • Prices: single 67, double room single use 80, double 98 euros; breakfast 5 euros, per person • Credit cards: all, Bancomat • Building accessible to the mobility challenged. Public parking in the immediate vicinity. Small pets accepted. Owners always present • Restaurant

🍯 At **Pietragalla** (21 km), in the San Nicola district, Gerardo Possidente's Timpa del Cinghiale company produces tasty locally bred pork and wild boar sausages. The borzillo, made with pork, wild boar and Senise peppers, is excellent.

BERNALDA

LA LOCANDIERA

🍲Restaurant
Corso Umberto I 194
Tel. 0835 543241
Closed Tuesday
Open: lunch and dinner
Holidays: none
Seating: 80
Prices: 22-25 euros, wine excluded
No credit cards, Bancomat

This cozy little restaurant, opened a few years ago, is situated a few kilometers away from Metaponto and the Ionian beaches. The open kitchen is run by women: Clara makes dishes from recipes that she has picked up in the family, while sister Mary and her daughter provide courteous service in the dining room, which has a plain brickwork ceiling.
The various antipasti, mainly based on seasonal vegetables from the Metaponto plain, include homemade pickles, omelets, pepper and egg ciambotto, hot **cialledda** (traditional country dish made with stale bread) and **crapiata**, made of pulses and cereals. First courses vary with the season: tripoline with fried breadcrumbs, cavatelli with beans and mussels, **ferricelli with horsemeat ragù**, bucatini with beans and Cacioricotta, Sarconi bean soup, pumpkin soup… Second courses include tasty horsemeat or veal **braciola**, stewed **calf's tripe**, roast lamb or kid, and **pastorale** (traditional braised mutton with vegetables and spices). If you prefer cheese, try the Pecorino di Moliterno and Caciocavallo lucano. End with a slice of tart (especially the one with acinata, the grape jam) or ricotta cake and peaches and, in the summer, semifreddo al torroncino with cotto d'uva and ricotta cream, accompanied by homemade rosolio.
The cellar stocks the best Aglianico labels and a few national wines.
Good value for money.

CASTELMEZZANO

AL BECCO DELLA CIVETTA

🍲Hotel trattoria
Vico I Maglietta 7
Tel. 0971 986249
Closed Tuesday, never in August
Open: lunch and dinner
Holidays: variable
Seating: 80
Prices: 25-30 euros, wine excluded
All major credit cards, Bancomat

Castelmezzano, a very popular place with lovers of the mountains and mountaineering, is situated in the regional park of Gallipoli Cognato and the Dolomiti Lucane. In this recently refurbished trattoria, Antonietta works tirelessly, cooking, coordinating the service and personally picking the herbs that flavor her dishes.
The fixed menu is read out, not printed. The house antipasti include typical local cured meats, crusch peppers, ricotta, omelettes, vegetable soup with bread croutons al finocchietto and **zuppa maritata**. First courses are all based on fresh pasta: strascinati, made with a mixture of four different types of flour abd dressed with vegetable ragù, **caserecce with crusch peppers** and **Cacioricotta**, orecchiette with meat sauce. The second courses feature: **lamb with herbs and potatoes,** roast pork and **Podolico veal with Scamorza and scarola**. The cheese selection is interesting, and if you book in advance, Antonietta will let serve you sheep and goat cheeses and ricotta from small farms in the area. In season, an entire menu is dedicated to mushrooms. Local desserts, such as crostl, cartellate and **calzoncelli** melfitani, are accompanied by ricotta mousse with chocolate flake and fresh fruit tegolino.
The wine list presents a wide choice of Aglianicos, plus a few labels from adjacent regions, not to mention Piedmont and Friuli. A good variety of spirits is also available. For visitors who wish to stay overnight, a small hotel has been created in the same building.

CHIAROMONTE

132 KM SOUTH OF POTENZA SS 598 AND SS 92

COSTA CASALE

☖ Holiday farm
Contrada Vito
Tel. and fax 0973 642346
Closed Wednesday
Open: lunch, dinner on booking, August lunch and dinner
Holidays: none
Seating: 50 +50 outdoors
Prices: 22 euros
No credit cards

Surrounded by 40 hectares of land which dominate the valley of the Sinni River, the Costa Canale holiday farm stands in the Parco Nazionale del Pollino, downstream from Chiaromonte. In addition to the owners' home, the restaurant and five apartments – available all week and furnished with 19th-century iron beds – the farm includes 10 hectares of orchard, two hectares of olive grove, stables for horse-riding, a deer park and pig, sheep and cattle farm. The farm produce, which can be bought on the premises, provides the basis for the cuisine prepared in the restaurant.

The fixed price menu is explained orally. The antipasti include a selection of excellent cured meats and **cheese**, **soffritto**, stuffed peppers, mushrooms, potato timbale. Next come two samplings of the fresh homemade pasta: the **fusilli with boar** or venison **sauce** and the **strascinati with peppers and breadcrumbs** are very good. The home-raised (**lamb**, kid, venison, **boar**, pork, veal) are usually prepared in the oven or grilled. For dessert, **ricotta cake** or cake made with homemade jam, plus, according to season, apricots, plums, peaches and figs from the orchard.

The good quality local wine is served in carafes.

🛏–❶• 5 apartments (1-4 people), ensuite, TV • Prices: apartment 25-100 euros, breakfast included • Private uncovered parking area. Pets welcome. Owners always available • Restaurant. Garden. Horse-riding

FRANCAVILLA IN SINNI
Scaldaferri

135 KM SOUTH OF POTENZA SS 92 AND 653

LA FONTANA DEL TASSO   ◎ᵛ

☖ Holiday farm restaurant
Contrada Scaldaferri 40
Tel. 0973 644566
Closed Tuesday
Open: lunch and dinner
Holidays: variable
Seating: 50 + 10 outdoors
Prices: 28 euros, wine excluded
No credit cards accepted

Leave the Sinnica, the highway that links the Tyrrhenian to Ionian, at Francavilla in Sinni and climb Mount Caramola. In a pretty stone structure hidden in the greenery, Maria and her husband Prospero, real experts of the food products of the Parco del Pollino, will serve you excellent dishes, often flavored with local aromatic herbs.

The countless antipasti include: cured meats and cheeses, **minestra impastata** (made with green beans, potatoes, pumpkin and dried peppers), ricotta-filled pumpkin flowers, potato crocchette, **gniummarielli** (lamb intestines stuffed with chicken livers), potatoes and fried peppers, **bread stuffed with ciambotta**, and kid soffritto. While you wait for the first courses, you'll be served a hot herb liqueur. The meal then proceeds with **rascatielli** dressed with **salted ricotta and dry Senise peppers**, cep mushrooms, fresh tomato or local truffle, fusilli or cavatelli served with potatoes, pancetta and rosemary, excellent **sausage and ricotta ravioli**, and **mischiglio** (flour mixed with beans, chick-peas, barley and wheat) and dressed in various ways. The lamb and kid, barbecued or roasted in the wood oven are excellent, as are the chicken and rabbit. To finish off, ricotta and wild berry mousse, with walnuts or hazelnuts, peach and pear yogurt ciambella, cake with confectioner's custard and wild berries or seasonal fruit tarts.

A good selection of regional wines is available and the home-made **rosolio** is excellent.

GENZANO DI LUCANIA
Spinazzola

CARRERA DELLA REGINA

🔑 Holiday farm
Strada Provinciale 169 km 48.800
Tel. 0971 774470-349 7611453
Fax 0971 774470
E-mail: postmaster@carreradellaregina.it
Internet: www.carreradellaregina.it
Open June-September, in fall and
weekends in spring

Surrounded by secular woods, with a view that extends from the Vulture hills to the plains of nearby Puglia, this holiday farm is run with friendliness and courtesy by the Cosentino family. The farm boasts 70 hectares of woods that you can visit on horseback or mountain bike, corn fields and fruit and vegetable gardens. It also breeds sheep, goats and farmyard animals are bred here. Facilities range from a beautiful swimming pool to a camp site. The rooms, furnished in rustic style, are comfortable and each has a bathroom and a TV set. Breakfast is traditional, with savory dishes available on request. In the large, old-fashioned dining room, a variety of traditional dishes, based on old country recipes, are served.

• 4 double rooms and 2 with 4 beds, bathroom, television • Prices: double room single use 30-35, double 50-74, with 4 beds 100-128 euros, breakfast included • Credit cards: all, Bancomat • Internal parking covered and uncovered. Small pets accepted. Owners always contactable • Restaurant. Swimming pool, riding

GROTTOLE

LA BUFALARA

🔑 Holida farm
Contrada Bufalara
Tel. 338 9617714-347 1456985
E-mail: hilde.leone@tin.it
Internet: www.bufalara.it
Open all year round

This farm, run by the enthusiastic young Hilde Leone, helped by her mother Hedda Seeliger, lies close to the historic sanctuary of Sant'Antuono. The rooms have been are situated alongside the central building and six of the seven rooms can be paired to form mini-apartments. The old structure has been skilfully restored, and enhanced by Hilde's commendable taste (it was she, for example, who decided to decorate the rooms with local antiques). A rich, varied breakfast caters for Italian and foreign tastes (especially German, given Hedda and Hilde's background). The large lounge is a place to sit back and relax. Visitors can make a number of interesting walks in the area and the one to the sanctuary of Sant'Antuono is particularly recommended.

• 7 double rooms with bathroom, television, living room, cooking range • Prices: double room single use 35, double 70 euros, breakfast included • Credit cards: none • Uncovered internal parking. Small pets allowed. Owners always contactable • Living room

GUARDIA PERTICARA

73 KM SOUTHEAST OF POTENZA

VECCHIO MULINO

☞Trattoria
Via Roma 36
Tel. 0971 964010
Closed Monday
Open: lunch and dinner
Holidays: one week in September
Seating: 30 + 60 outdoors
Prices: 15-20 euros, wine excluded
No credit cards accepted

Guardia, a fairytale village whose streets, houses and monuments are all made of stone, is the perfect place to go to combat the stress of ther big city and the effects of fast, sophisticated food. The restaurant, run by Nicola and Maria, really was a mill, as its name suggests, and the reserve of internal spring water is still used today.

Nicola is not just a first-class, passionate chef, he is also constantly on the look out for genuine, tasty products, such as local cheeses and **cured meats**: soppressata, sausage, capocollo and also the excellent **pezzente**, a Slow Food Presidium, are usually served as antipasti together with vegetables preserved in oil and seasonal fresh vegetables. Pasta plays an important part in the menu, and Maria is an expert at preparing the different shapes. Try the **cavatelli with cruschi peppers**, the orecchiette al ragù, the ferricelli with wild mushrooms, **lagane and chick peas** or pasta with Sarconi beans. Second courses star barbecued meats, especially lamb, and the tasty **salsiccia al peperone di Senise**. If you book in advance, you can order **pastorale**, stewed mutton with vegetables, a traditional dish in this part of the Apennines. In summer, tables are set in the nearby square and the meal always ends the right way with Maria's homemade desserts: **sanguinaccio tart** (made with pig's blood, sugar and chocolate), ricotta cake, chickpea and chocolate panzerottini and zeppole.

The local Grottino di Roccanova wine is also served by the glass, and other regional labels are also available.

LAGONEGRO
Monte Sirino

100 KM SOUTH OF POTENZA SS 585 EXIT A3

AZIENDA VALSIRINO

☞Solida farm
Contrada Aniella
Tel. 338 8158496-368 7557703
Closed Tuesday
Open: lunch and dinner
Holidays: October
Seating: 80 + 40 outdoors
Prices: 20 euros
No credit cards accepted

This farm, run by Mario Civale, is situated on Mount Sirino, at an altitude of 1200 meters, among the tall pines and the broom that turns this lovely landscape yellow in June. The large rooms, simply furnished and decorated with traditional rural objects, make guests feel at home immediately. The fresh air that you breathe here even on clammy August days will stimulate your appetite and prepare you to savor the 18 antipasti that might even turn out to be all you need to eat (and they only cost 14 euros). They include **vegetable and cereal soup** (beans, spelt, corn), eggplant ammollicate with tomatoes andPpecorino cheese, olives, **tripe with potatoes,** liver with raw peppers, **ciambotta**, potatoes and baby onions, frittata with peppers, zucchini and asparagus, sliced pork and wild boar, potatoes stuffed with ricotta cheese, sheep ricotta. At this point, if you still have room left for a first course, you can choose from ravioli, cavatelli, fusilli, tagliatelle dressed with ricotta and cheese or **local mushrooms and truffles**. Second courses consist of barbecued meats: wild boar, lamb, kid, **Podolico veal** and **pork**. For dessert, excellent home-made cakes with wild strawberries, jams, ricotta, and pears.

The only wine on offer is the house Aglianico. The home-made digestive liqueurs are also worth tasting.

🍴 At **Rivello** (12 km) the grocer Luigi Martino, Via Garibaldi 5, is the only artisan who still produces soperzata, delicately spiced pork fillet, a local specialty.

LATRONICO

MARATEA
Massa

124 KM SOUTH OF POTENZA

133 KM SOUTH OF POTENZA A 3 AND SS 585

LA TAVERNA DEI GESUITI

Restaurant
Via Lacava 6
Tel. 0973 858312
Closed Monday, never in August
Open: lunch and dinner
Holidays: 15 days in September
Seating: 56 + 60 outdoors
Prices: 25 euros, wine excluded
All credit cards, Bancomat

IL GIARDINO DI EPICURO

Restaurant
Località Massa
Tel. 0973 870130
Closed Wednesday, never in summer
Open: lunch and dinner
Holidays: November
Seating: 50 + 50 outdoors
Prices: 25-35 euros, wine excluded
All credit cards except AE, Bancomat

Latronico is on the Sinnica trunk road, 10 kilometers from the Lauria Nord motorway exit. The restaurant, opened by a group of friends and entrusted to chef Franco Tucci, is situated at the entrance to the village. The name on the sign reminds us that there were Jesuits in the village in the 18th century and that they had a reputation as gourmets. The restaurant has two floors, with a number of simple little rooms decorated with lovely period photographs. In summertime, you can dine in the garden.
Start with the local cured meats (**sausage**, fresh or preserved in lard, soppressata, ham), vegetable omelettes, bruschette, sheep and goat cheeses . In the kitchen, Maria Antonietta that prepares the fresh pasta: **rasc'atieddi** with traditional **mixed meat sauce**, tomatoes or vegetables. Plus **lagane and chickpeas** with the intoppo di baccalà, **lagane and broad beans** with guanciale and pecorino, **miskiglio with broccoli and Pecorino**, orecchiette, maccheroni or fusilli with the local mushrooms or with mollica fritta and puparul'crusch. Rich second courses: roast lamb and pork, **tripe** all'arrabbiata or with beans and sauce, **gliummarieddi** (lamb's intestines rolled in spices and aromas), stewed **baccalà alla trainiera** with parsley and crunchy peppers. Some nourishing side dishes: **ciambotta**, potatoes and cep mushrooms, grilled eggplant and zucchini. Everything is accompanied by excellent wood-baked bread.
The cellar stocks a selection of good local Basilicata labels from and a few significant national wines.

Maratea is famous not only for its old town, its beaches and the Gulf of Policastro, but also for the beautiful mountain woods that surround it. This is where Massa is to be found, perched on a peak that dominates the enchanting blue of the most beautiful of Tyrrhenian coastlines. To reach the Bocchiglione family restaurant, you have to face a long hard climb, but the pleasures of the journey's end will repay your efforts. Michele, a figure straight out of a story of satyrs, a cross between Bacchus and Pan, will welcome you to dining room or terrace and explain what his mother Milena has prepared in the kitchen.
You start off with local cured meats (capicollo, ham, soppressate), vegetables, home-pickled or preserved in oil, **ricotta and honey Pecorino** and, on request, tasty Massa mozzarella. For first course, pappardelle with **mutton sauce** or cep mushroom cream, **lagane and chickpeas**, gnocchetti with truffle or asparagus cream, **ravioli with ricotta and truffle**. Veal, lamb, kid and pork are barbecued along with Pecorino and Caciocavallo. In season, don't miss the **mushrooms** and **truffles** from the surrounding woods. In summer, you need to order the fish soup. The meal ends with various homemade cakes: walnut and ricotta, lemon, tangerine, fruit pies.
House wine by the carafe is fair, but you'll also find a few good regional and national labels. The many home-produced liqueurs —sweet basil, myrtle, citron, lemon, tangerine, strawberry, fennel – never disappoint.

BASILICATA

MARSICOVETERE
Villa d'Agri

MATERA
Rioni Sassi
Old town

47 KM SOUTH OF POTENZA SS 598 AND 276

OSTERIA DEL GALLO

Recently opened osteria
Largo Nazionale 2
Tel. 0975 352045
Closed Tuesday
Open: lunch and dinner
Holidays: none
Seating: 200
Prices: 18-20 euros, wine excluded
All credit cards

CAPRIOTTI

Bed and breakfast
Via Gradoni Duomo 23-28
Tel. 0835 333997-329 613757
Fax 0835 333997
E-mail: capriottibb@yahoo.it
Internet: www.capriotti-bed-breakfast.it
Open from March to December

Villa d'Agri, dominated by Mount Volturino (an extinct volcano), is a symbol of the profound changes that have taken place in the upper Agri valley in recent decades. It is in this area that two gastronomic delights are produced: Moliterno casieddu (Slow Food Presidium) and Sarconi beans. The aim of the D'Andrea brothers when they set up this place a few years ago was to promote the typical flavors of the area: hence the invaluable collaboration of excellent cooks and impeccable staff.
For antipasto, don't miss the tagliere del gallo, a board of mixed local cheeses, ham, game and bruschetta. You then move on to a wide choice of first courses (**soups**, pasta dishes and risottos), among which **cuccia** (mixed soup of pulses and cereals), black truffle risotto, strascinati del Gallo, agnolotti al profumo di bosco, paccheri dell'oste and orecchiette with wild boar sauce. The best main courses are **grigliata mista del pastore** (grilled lamb, pork and sausage), barbecued free-range spatchcock, and **baccalà with dried peppers.**
The wine list offers a wide selection of Italian and local wines, including the omnipresent Aglianico del Vulture.

At the foot of the Cathedral and its panoramic square, a cobbled street takes you to the heart of the ancient Sassi neighborhood. This is where Olivio, Cicci to his friends, and his wife have restructured two establishments hewn out of the rock, turning them into comfortable places for a pleasant holiday in Matera. The generous, tasty breakfast includes home-made jams, honey, fresh fruit and local bread. Not far away you will find many of the towns artistic attractions – rock churches, Byzantine paintings – against the breathtaking backdrop of the River Gravina.

• 3 mini-apartments (1-4 people), bathroom, television, fridge, kitchen range • Prices: single 50, double 67 euros (15 euros supplement for an extra bed), breakfast included • Credit cards: none • Low-cost garage space available (10 euros per day). Small pets accepted. Owners always contactable • Breakfast room, living room

At the Giocoli butcher's shop, at Via Mario Pagano 3: Marsicovetere ham, typical cured meats from Basilicata and other local specialties. In **Paterno** (7 km), the Pasticceria Masi at Via Castagne 1 has sold excellent sweets for over 30 years.

IL CANTUCCIO

⌂ Trattoria
Via delle Beccherie 33
Tel. 0835 332090
Closed Monday
Open: lunch and dinner
Holidays: September 1-15
Seating: 37 + 20 outdoors
Prices: 23 euros, wine excluded
All credit cards, Bancomat

LA CASA DI LUCIO

⚷ Hotel-residence
Via San Pietro Caveoso 66
Tel. 0835 312798
Fax 0835 318685
E-mail: info@lacasadilucio.com
Internet: www.lacasadilucio.it
Open all year round

Il Cantuccio is in Matera old town, near Piazza Vittorio Veneto, a square where every year, on July 2, a re-enactment of the 'assault on Bruna's cart' is re-enacted, an event enjoyed for the whole township and for the many tourists who come to watch. A welcoming, well-kept trattoria, it is run by Micha (from Matera despite the unusual name), who prepares traditional, country dishes.

The mixed antipasti vary according to season: cured meats, cheeses and **cruschi peppers** mainly in winter; vegetables, frittelle, fried bread balls and broccoli especially in summer. The first courses feature all the typical forms of hand-made pasta: **orecchiette with lamb ragù**, with broccoli, or with fresh sheep's ricotta, grated lemon and cinnamon, **cavatelli with broad beans and chicory** or alla frantoiana. If you book ahead, you can alwso savor **baked pasta alla materana**. The cheese fagottini and Pollino truffle with cep mushroom sauce are also well worth a try. For second courses, the excellent **braciolette al ragù**, **lamb alla contadina** (cooked on the hot plate with Tropea onions and baby tomatoes), **tortiera di agnello alla materana**, fillet steak with red wine and mushrooms and, if you book, **gnumarieddi** (barbecued lamb's innards). The choice of local cheeses is interesting: cellar seasoned Caciocavallo podolico, Canestrato di Moliterno, and goats' cheeses.

To close the meal, you can choose between **strazzate** and mostaccioli served with the house limoncello. The cellar stocks a good number of regional and a few national labels.

A few meters from the panoramic square of San Pietro Barisano, a cobbled street leads to this completely restored hotel-residence: from spaces hewn out of the tufa, Lucio has managed to create elegant suites and welcoming, comfortable rooms with restored furniture. The lounge and reading room are tastefully furnished.

After a lovely breakfast of cakes and biscuits baked in the open kitchen, local Matera bread, home-made jams and cured meats and cheeses from Basilicata, guests can take a walk through the narrow streets of the small town, visit the many archaeological and artistic sites in the area, and enjoy the sweeping panoramas of the Murgia materana.

• 8 apartments (1-4 people) and 2 suites, bathroom, air conditioning, minibar, satellite television • Prices: single 90, double 120, triple 140, with 4 beds 160, suite 250-500 euros, breakfast included • Credit cards: all, Bancomat • Parking lot close by. No pets allowed. Reception open 24 hours a day • Bar, restaurant. Breakfast room, lounge, reading and television room. Terrace

LE BOTTEGHE

Trattoria
Piazza San Pietro Barisano 22
Tel. 0835 344072
No closing day
Open: lunch and dinner
Holidays: in January
Seating: 95 + 50 outdoors
Prices: 30-35 euros, wine excluded
All credit cards, Bancomat

LE MONACELLE

Holiday home-hostel
Via Riscatto 9-10
Tel. 0835 344097
Fax 0835 336541
E-mail: lemonacelle@hotmail.com
Internet: www.lemonacelle.com
Open all year round

In front of the big oven inside the Le Botteghe trattoria, so called because it used to house craftsmen's workshops, you'll always find Angelo Giannella, nicknamed 'Il Rosso', busy at work, putting his experience as a butcher at the service of the restaurant. And he's always ready with advice to help you choose the best cut of meat for your meal. Front of house, Pino will take care of you with courtesy and professional skill.
You start with Caciocavallo podolico cheese, Murgia Park sheep's cheese, Gorgoglione goats' cheeses, and cured meats from Grottole, as well as assortments of stuffed mushrooms, **fried lampascioni**, eggplant rissoles, stuffed zucchini and eggplant. For first course, we recommend fusilli with fried breadcrumbs and bran, cavatelli with tomatoes, basil and Cacioricotta cheese, **strascinati with sausage and cardoncelli mushrooms**, tagliatelle and chickpeas with fried breadcrumbs and the excellent **broad beans and chicory**. The generous helpings of **kid**, **lamb**, beef, are personally chosen by 'Il Rosso', and invariably come from the Murgia area. If you're not in a rush, don't miss the **pignata**, a very elaborate dish made of lamb, celery, potatoes, onions, bits of cured meat and Pecorino cheese, all cooked in a pot with a lid made of bread. The traditional desserts include excellent chocolate and ricotta cakes.
The cellar stocks an excellent selection of regional wines and a number of reliable national labels, plus a choice of oils, all from the province of Matera, for which a list is being prepared.

This 'pilgrim's house' is located in a position that reflects the age-old history of Matera. Not far away you'll find the impressive 13th-century cathedral. The conservatory of Santa Maria della Pietà was built in 1594 above the monastery, just beside the crypt of Sant'Eustachio. The view from the house's large great panoramic terrace and rooms is spectacular. The complex was restored in 2000 and is now one of the most interesting tourist accommodation facilities in the south of Italy. It contains two large dormitories and simple but comfortable, well furnished rooms, as well as congress and reading rooms. On the walls of the building are spectacular walkways and panoramic terraces overlook the sheer drop down to the River Gravina and the Murgia plateau beyond. Only groups are allowed in the restaurant and booking is essential.

• 9 double rooms, triple or with 4 beds, bathroom, air conditioning, television, modem connection; 2 dormitories (14-16 people) with shared bathroom • Prices: double room single use 55, double 86, triple 105, with 4 beds 135, bunk bed in the room 16 euros, breakfast included • Credit cards: all, Bancomat • Structure accessible to mobility challenged. Small pets accepted. Reception open 24 hours a day • Bar, restaurant. Living room, reading room, television room, internet point. Conference room, meeting room. Garden, terrace, solarium

---

LOCANDA DI SAN MARTINO

3-Star Hotel
Via San Martino 22
Tel. 0835 256600
Fax 0835 256472
E-mail: info@locandadisanmartino.it
Internet: www.locandadisanmartino.it
Open all year round

LUCANERIE

Restaurant
Via Santo Stefano 61
Tel. 0835 332133
Closed Sunday for dinner and
Monday
Open: lunch and dinner
Holidays: in August
Seating: 40
Prices: 28-30 euros, wine excluded
All credit cards, Bancomat

Thanks to Dorothy Zinn and Antonio Panetta, areas once used for a variety of other functions (housing, deposits, workshops and even a small church) have been meticulously restored and converted into comfortable rooms. Each room, identified by a name taken from its original function or from a particular detail, is literally hewn out of the rock and furnished with taste and simplicity. The rooms are independent and each looks over the unique Sassi panorama, with its artistic and historic sights. Breakfast offers coffee, milk, tea, fresh local bread, some of which baked in a wood-fired oven, and jams.

• 1 single room, 19 double rooms and 8 suites, bathroom, air conditioning, minibar, satellite television, • Prices: single 68, double 86-99, suite 105-160 euros, breakfast included • Credit cards: all, Bancomat • Structure accessible to the mobility challenged. Free external public parking. No pets allowed. Reception open 24 hours a day • Bar. Breakfast room, Reading room. Solarium

One of the busiest restaurants in Matera – simple traditional cuisine in a comfortable, informal environment – competently managed by Enza Leone and Franco Abbondanza. The two owners come from the upper Matera hills where, in an unspoilt environment, which belongs more to the past than the present, it has been possible to preserve traditions and recipes from times gone by.
The menu includes a number of substantial antipasti: Gorgoglione sausage, pezzente, goats' cheese accompanied by various fruit jams, bread croutons with Sarconi beans, **barley soup with broad beans and cep mushrooms**, and Senise **cruschi peppers**. The fresh pastas, handmade in a variety of shapes (ferricelli, **raschatielli**, cavatelli), are dressed with **cardoncelli mushrooms and sausage**, cruschi peppers and fried bread crumbs, ceps and Pollino black truffle. Great attention is dedicated to the choice of meats: barbecued Basilicata **lamb**, **gn'mmridd**, **manzo podolico** stew with beans, barbecued pork with cooked figs deserve. You can end with ricotta cheese cake or with goat's cheese mousse, replaced in summer by wild berry chocolate semifreddo; not to be missed, during the Christmas holidays, the **cartellate** al miele or al vin cotto.
The cellar contains almost all the labels of Basilicata and a few from the rest of Italy at good value for money. Booking is recommended.

🍴 A few meters from the restaurant you can stop at the Antico forno a legna Perrone, where you can buy bread, taralli, dolcetti and other cakes and biscuits.

SAN PIETRO BARISANO

Hotel-residence
Rione San Biagio 52-56
Tel. and fax 0835 346191
E-mail: info@residencesanpietrobarisano.it
Internet: www.residencesanpietrobarisano.it
Open all year round

A neighborhood once full of women busy at their daily chores and children noisily playing has now become a series of pleasant squares where you can sit out in the sunshine or simply idle away the time in the cool summer nights. With this conversion old stone caves and grottoes, Vincenzo and Rosa have created an original environment of comfortable rooms fitted with all mod cons. Every corner has been occupied in a creative way, and the original light-filled bathrooms are particularly impressive. The furniture in the spacious rooms is modern but in keeping with the historic atmosphere of the place. Each apartment has its own gas ring, but if guests opt bto sample the delights of the local cuisine, they can also eat at the restaurant overlooking the square, which is part of the residential complex.

• 5 apartments (2-4 people), bathroom, air-conditioning, mini-bar, satellite television, • Prices: double room single use 60-75, double 80-110, triple 110-140, with 4 beds 145-170 euros; breakfast 8 euros per person • Credit cards: all, Bancomat • Public parking close by. Small pets accepted. Owners always contactable • Restaurant. Terrace

SASSI SAN GENNARO

Bed and breakfast
Via San Gennaro 24
Tel. 338 8608686
E-mail: info@bbresidenzasassi.it
Internet: www.bbresidenzasassi.it
Open all year round

Recently enlarged, the b&b run by Franco Di Benedetto is set in an old monastery dedicated to San Gennaro, not far from the beautiful 13th-century cathedral, in the heart of Matera old town. The rooms are furnished traditionally, with taste and class, and breakfasts are abundant and varied, in true Matera style: bread baked in wood-fired ovens, tarts and other home-made cakes and local jams. In the surrounding neighborhood, it is possible to visit important rock churches and other well preserved art treasures. In summer you can enjoy the cool evening air in the courtyard in front of the hotel. A reading room is also available.

• 3 double rooms and 8 mini-apartments, bathroom; 5 with kitchen range • Prices: double room single use 55 euros, double and mini-apartment 70 euros, breakfast included • Credit cards: none • Parking close by. No pets allowed. Owners always contactable • Breakfast room, reading room, television room. Terrace.

MELFI

NOVECENTO

Restaurant
Contrada Incoronata
Tel. 0972 237470
Closed Sunday for dinner and Monday
Open: lunch and dinner
Holidays: 15 days end-July
Seating: 40 + 40 outdoors
Prices: 30 euros, wine excluded
All credit cards, Bancomat

This attractive, friendly restaurant is run by the Lamorte family on the way into to Melfi, a city that deserves a visit if only for the castle, which houses an archeology museum. Husband-and-wife team Maria and Alessandro look after the kitchen, while sons Alfredo and Arturo are front of house. The dishes, prepared with local ingredients, vary with the season according to local tradition.
Antipasti include ricotta, buffalo mozzarella, egg and sausage, grilled or fried vegetables, vegetable pie, **burratina** and typical Basilicata cured meats. First courses are made of fresh pasta: tagliatelle with truffles, **maccheronata alla trainiera**, pappardelle with lamb or wild boar sauce, **sweet ricotta ravioli** (with cinnamon and sugar), meat ravioli with vegetables, frascinelli with tomatoes, basil and Cacioricotta. Outstanding second courses include stewed wild boar, **pork with peppers in vinegar** or with wild fennel, brasato all'Aglianico with mosto cotto, barbecued **lamb** and, if you're lucky, **agnello a cutturiedd**, the local lamb stew. The home-made extra-virgin oil, made with ogliarola olives from Mount Vulture, is excellent. The **cheese board** features Filiano sheep's cheese, Moliterno canestrato, Caciocavallo podolico and a few local goats' cheeses. You can end with ricotta mousse with hazelnuts and chocolate, sfogliatine with wild berries, or traditional calzoncelli, mustacciuoli and 'Melfi cake'.
The wine list is not only comprehensive but also reasonably priced.

PIGNOLA
Lago Pantano

LA FATTORIA SOTTO IL CIELO

Holiday farm
Contrada Petrucco 9 A
Tel. 0971 420166-486000
E-mail: fattoriasottoilcielo@libero.it
Internet: www.lafattoriasottoilcielo.it
Closed Wednesday
Open: lunch and dinner
Holidays: none
Seating: 80 + 80 outdoors
Prices: 25-30 euros, wine excluded
All credit cards, Bancomat

This farm, surrounded by the WWF reserve of Lake Pantano, owes its fame to the fine cooking of the Di Lorenzo family. The rooms, available all week, are each personalized with a different color.
The seasonal antipasti include parmigiana di melanzane, timbales of zucchini or potatoes, eggplant roulade with fresh tomini, and the 'cinque portate del fattore', five mini-servings of omelets, **cured meats** and mushroom and vegetable dishes. The fresh home-made pasta is flavored with simple tasty dressings: **caserecce with wild turnips and crusch peppers,** scialatielli alla mediterranea, **lagane and chickpeas**, **strascinati ammollitati** or with cacioricotta cheese. Moving on to second courses, don't miss the **agnello arraganato** (stuffed with capers and peppers), the braised veal with polenta, and the **loin of pork with apple sauce**. The meal closes with typical local desserts such as ricottina del massaro, **'ncartellate**, babà, and cannoncini with hazelnut cream.
The wine list includes the finest labels of Basilicata and 300 national and foreign bottles.

• 6 double rooms, en suite, air conditioning, fridge bar, TV • Prices: double single use 38, double 56 euros (supplement for additional bed 15 euros), breakfast included • Private uncovered parking area. Pets not welcome. Owners always available• Restaurant. TV room, conference room. Tennis court, horse-riding, birdwatching hut, archery, trekking trail

PISTICCI
Marconia

POTENZA

59 KM SOUTH OF MATERA

SAN TEODORO NUOVO

⊨—0 Holiday farm
Contrada San Teodoro
Tel. 0835 470042
Fax 0835 470132
E-mail: uff.santeodoronuovo@libero.it
Internet: www.santeodoronuovo.com
Open all year round

ISUCCIO

⌒ Trattoria
Via Appia 198
Tel. 0971 471312
Closed Sunday
Open: lunch and dinner
Holidays: 10 days in August
Seating: 50
Prices: 18-23 euros, wine excluded
All credit cards, Bancomat

This farm, which has belonged to the Doria family for years, is the headquarters of an organic farming company that makes oil and grows citrus fruit, grapes, wheat and vegetables. This once noble residence contains apartments that, albeit differing in furnishing, size and position, possess all the main comforts. Breakfast includes jams and homemade cakes, as well as cured meats and local cheeses. The restaurant serves dishes from the regional cuisine which, in summer, you can enjoy outside on a romantic patio. The swimming pool is hidden away among the fruit trees, while the beaches of the Ionian Sea are just five kilometers away. Close at hand are two 18-hole golf courses (shuttle service provided), a tennis court and a riding stable.
Numerous sites of artistic and archeological interest are nearby.
Half-board supplement 25 euros per person.

• 10 mini-apartments (2-4 people), with bathroom, air conditioning, fridge-bar, television; 5 mini-apartments with kitchen • Prices: double apartment single use 50, double 100 euros (33 euro supplement for extra bed); breakfast 10 euros per person • All major credit cards, Bancomat • Uncovered internal parking. Small pets allowed. Owners always contactable • Restaurant. Breakfast room, living room, television room. Garden. Swimming pool

Strategically positioned not far from the east-side exit of the Basentana highway, this trattoria is still the traveler's stop-off that its founder, Isuccio, intended it to be, and today it serves traditional Basilicata and Potenza dishes prepared by Maria Rocchina. The meal starts with good cheeses and local cured meats: ricotta, scamorza, Caciocavallo podolico di Accettura, Pecorino di Filiano, Canestrato di Moliterno, sausage, soppressata, and ham. First courses feature fresh pasta: **lagane and vegetables** (beans or chickpeas), **strascinati with Cacioricotta and crusch peppers**, orecchiette with 'Basilicata ragù' (prepared with different types of meats), and ricotta ravioli. Not to be missed the **manate with breadcrumbs and toasted walnuts in oil**, a dressing that used to be considered the Parmesan of the poor. The second courses often include mixed barbecued meats, **roast kid, lamb, cheese and eggs, kid and potato tortiera**, stewed tripe. Especially in winter, excellent **baccalà a ciauredda** or fried with crusch peppers appears on the menu. If you book ahead, you can also savor the famous **cutturiedd** (mutton stew with spices and a lot of chili peppers).
The wine list offers regional wines and several Italian labels. Booking is advisable, especially during weekends.

🍷🍴 At the Laboratorio di Vino wine shop at Via Scafarelli 20, it is possible to buy typical food products and Slow Food Presidia items, as well as great wines (more than 600 labels).

LA TETTOIA   ## ZI MINGO

🍲Restaurant
Via Due Torri 1
Tel. 0971 24123
Closed Sunday
Open: lunch and dinner
Holidays: 15 days between August and September
Seating: 80 + 15 outdoors
Prices: 25-35 euros, wine excluded
All credit cards, Bancomat

🍲Trattoria
Contrada Botte 2
Tel. 0971 442984
Closed Monday
Open: lunch and dinner
Holidays: 1 week in mid-August
Seating: 80 + 30 outdoors
Prices: 15-20 euros
All credit cards, Bancomat

This friendly place, its walls decorated with autographed photos of the showbiz personalities and politicians who have eaten over the years have eaten there, is right in the middle of Potenza old town, behind the Town Hall. It's run by the Lo Russo family, with wife Liliana supervising the cooks and husband Vito waiting in the dining room.

You can choose from three menus: Basilicata, vegetarian and fish. Try the local antipasti: mixed fry, cured meats and local sausage, Burrata cheese, ricotta, stewed mushrooms and the ever-present **prosciutto alla carrettiera**. First courses feature fresh home-made pasta: **lagane and chickpeas**, **strascinati cu lu n'truppc**, cavatelli alla moda del casaro (bacon, mushrooms, fresh cheese and cherry tomatoes cooked in Aglianico wine), **fusilli with breadcrumbs**, trittico lucano (orecchiette, strascinati and fusilli with meat sauce). For second course: **lamb chop alla contadina** (with crusch peppers, cherry tomatoes and grated bread), **u' cutturiedd** (traditional mutton stew, which needs to be ordered in advance), **baccalà** with crusch peppers or **a ciauredda** (stewed with fresh onions). Equally delicious are the **mushroom and potato tortiera** and stuffed eggplant. The small selection of regional cheeses is very good: Caciocavallo podolico, Pecorino di Filiano, Canestrato di Moliterno, scamorze and ricotta. **Mustazzuol** and **stozze**, typical sweets from Avigliano, can end the meal as an alternative to the fried zeppoline with cream and cherry jam, maybe in combination with a nice glass of dessert wine.
A rich selection of Italian wines.

One of the few places that keeps alive the gastronomic tradition of Potenza. Founded by Zi Mingo, 'Uncle Domenico', after his death it was taken over by his grandchildren Maria Grazia and Michele, keen to carry on his simple, tasty way of cooking local produce. Maria Grazia, has picked up and cooks family recipes, while Michele serves diners in the spirit of friendliness and familiarity that has always characterized the place. Especially in summer, it's a pleasure to enjoy the cool air eat in the new outside dining area.

The menu starts off with Abriola bread bruschetta, **ciambotta** of peppers, bacon and eggs, cheeses from Ruoti and cured meats from Picerno (ham, capocollo, sausage). The first courses, all variations of handmade **fresh pasta**, include **strascinati with mixed mushrooms**, with turnip tops or with ragù and mozzarella, as well as ricotta-filled ravioli with ragù. The best second courses are **brasciole** (rich veal rolls with meat sauce) and **pork with peppers in vinegar.** Barring the the Carnival period, desserts are conspicuous by their absence.

The cellar isn't exactly well stocked either, but the house wine is decent and good value for money. Booking is advisable especially at weekends.

🍷 In Via Verdi 12, the Pizzeria Montesano bakes wonderful oss di mort (salted taralli with fennel seeds), as well as pizzas and panzarotti. Booking is essential.

RAPONE

RIONERO IN VULTURE
Monticchio Bagni

VALLE OFANTO

☞⚷Holiday farm
Strada Statale Ofantina km 23.380
Tel. 0976 96314-335 1362128
E-mail: info@valleofanto.it
Internet: www.valleofanto.it
Closed 15 days in November

IL CASALE DELL'ACQUA ROSSA

☞⚷Holiday farm
Frazione Monticchio Bagni
Tel. and fax 0972 731072
E-mail: leo.telesca@libero.it
Internet: www.ilcasaledellacquarossa.3000.it
Open all year round

The Tornillo family has been working this farm for some time now, cultivating vineyards, vegetables and fruit trees and breeding hens, guinea-fowl and rabbits. The decision to let part of the house to tourists was taken in 2004, when three rooms were specially refurbished to accommodate families. The rooms are simple and comfortable, as are the common spaces, bar and restaurant. Breakfasts comes with fruit tarts and doughnuts, honey, jam, hot drinks and fruit juices. Available outdoor activities include swimming, riding, walking and cycling. Alternatively, the owners will be glad to give provide information of sites in the area of natural beauty and historic interest.

• 1 double room and 2 rooms with 4 beds, bathroom, air-conditioning, mini-bar, television, modem connection • Prices: double room single use 35, double 55, triple 70, with 4 beds 85 euros, breakfast included • Credit cards: all, Bancomat • Structure accessible to the mobility challenged. Manned external parking. No pets allowed. Owners always contactable • Bar, restaurant. Television room. Garden, playground, swimming pool, horse-riding, five-a-side football pitch

This agriturismo, a pleasant, relaxing place to stay, two kilometers away from the volcanic lakes of Monticchio, at the foot of Mount Vulture, is run by the Telesca family. The simply furnished rooms all have private bathrooms and televisions. Half or full-board are both available. The cooking is done by the owners and is mainly local in inspiration. The traditional breakfast consists of home-made tarts and sweets, but savories are also available on request. Book is advisable and, if you arrive at night, it's a good idea to warn the owners in advance.

• 1 single room, 3 triples and 2 with 4 beds, bathroom, television • Prices: single 35, double 50, triple 60, with 4 beds 75 euros, breakfast included • Credit cards: all, Bancomat • Internal uncovered parking. No pets allowed. Owners always contactable • Restaurant. Garden

ROTONDA

DA PEPPE   @y☺

⌂ Restaurant
Corso Garibaldi 13
Tel. 0973 661251
Closed Monday, never in summer
Open: lunch and dinner
Holidays: none
Seating: 70
Prices: 25-28 euros, wine excluded
All credit cards

Peppe Di Marco's restaurant, situated in the old center of Rotonda, in the beautiful natural setting of the Parco Nazionale del Pollino, has been revisiting typical local cuisine for years now. The whole family is on the books: Peppe in the kitchen, assisted by Carmine Signore, his wife Angela and daughters Flavia and Antonella in the dining rooms, of which there are two, a larger one downstairs, a smaller one upstairs.

To start off, try insalata di paddraccio (a local cheese) with crunchy vegetables or the ricotta cheese bauletto with wild asparagus. For first course: **tagliatelle with wild boar**, **lagane and beans** or ravioli with nettle tips. Most of the seconds are barbecued; we recommend the **lamb with potatoes and peppers** and the coniglio al profumo del Pollino, rabbit with mushrooms and aromatic herbs. Peppe only uses extra virgin olive oil to dress his creations, and the side dishes of seasonal **mushrooms** and local **cheeses**, including Caciocavallo podolico, are excellent. Desserts are all home-made: be sure to ask for the special **Rotonda red eggplant cake**.

The cellar is stocked with a selection of labels from Basilicata and nearby Calabria.

🍯 Opposite the restaurant, Peppe has a shop that sells local produce and crafts. In the main village square, on market days, you can buy white poverelli beans, dry red peppers and Rotonda red eggplant.

ROTONDELLA

LA MANGIATOIA

⌂ Restaurant
Via Giotto 23
Tel. 0835 504440-504137
Closed Monday
Open: lunch and dinner
Holidays: none
Seating: 90 + 20 outdoors
Prices: 18-25 euros, wine excluded
No credit cards accepted

Thanks to its enviable geographical position, Rotondella, a quiet, friendly hillside village, is known as the 'balcony over the Ionian Sea'. You can reach it from the Taranto-Reggio Calabria state highway or from the Sinnica road which links the Tyrrhenian to the Ionian. La Mangiatoia is a two-floor family-run establishment: downstairs you find a pizzeria-wine shop, on the first floor the restaurant whose traditional and homely kitchen is run by Signora Cosima and her son Giuseppe.

The menu is rich starting from the antipasti: **pastizzi** (calzoni stuffed with meat), **falagoni** (calzoni with legumes, onions, spinach, chard and zucchini) and **Arab bread** stuffed **with vegetables in oil** or Pecorino and cured meats from Basilicata. Rightly famous are the **frizzuli**, a type of long fresh pasta prepared by Cosima with a special needle: the pasta is dressed with either **mixed ragù** or lamb ragù and further flavored with fried breadcrumbs and powdered red pepper. Vegetable dishes vary with the seasons, and the the green bean soup and **lagane with chickpeas** are especially noteworthy. Meats are selected by Cosima's husband: try the delicate **suckling kid**, excellent both roasted or barbecued, the roast or stewed rabbit, or the **coratella with peas and peppers**.

You can end with the fragrant seasonal fruit from the family garden or a home-made dessert: cannoli di ricotta, small fancy cakes and, at festivities, **pastizzotti** and **ricotta tart**. The wine selection is limited to a few regional labels and the house wine.

SAN GIORGIO LUCANO

TERRANOVA DI POLLINO

121 KM SOUTH WEST OF MATERA

154 KM SOUTH OF POTENZA SS 653 AND 92

MASSERIA D'ELIA

LUNA ROSSA

🗝Holiday farm
Contrada Scorrano
Tel. and fax 0835 815979
E-mail: robernardo@libero.it
Open all year round

🍵Restaurant
Via Marconi 18
Tel. 0973 93254
Closed Wednesday, never in summer
Open: lunch and dinner
Holidays: in October
Seating: 60 + 50 outdoors
Prices: 25-30 euros, wine excluded
Credit cards: all, Bancomat

San Giorgio Lucano lies at the foot of the Pollino massif. Here you can enjoy the peace and quiet of rural life, take excursions round the national park, visit important nearby cultural centers, or bathe on the not too distant Ionian beaches. In this recently refurbished, family-run agriturismo, the rooms are furnished in a mixture of rustic and modern styles. Breakfast includes homemade jams and tarts, butter, milk and biscuits. The restaurant, also open to non-residents, serves local dishes at a price of 25 euros, wines excluded. Cookery courses are run periodically. For sports lovers, facilities include a swimming pool, a 5-a-side football pitch and boules and tennis courts.

• 3 mini-apartments (1-5 people), bathroom, air-conditioning, fridge, television, kitchen space • Prices: apartment 100 euros, breakfast included • Credit cards: none • Internal uncovered parking. Small pets accepted. Owners always contactable • Bar, restaurant. Television room, living room. Swimming pool. Horse-riding, five-a-side football pitch, boules court, tennis court

At the Luna Rossa restaurant, right in the middle of the Parco del Pollino, you'll have no problem making friends with chef and owner Federico Valicenti, who's been promoting the local area, its products, dishes and natural beauty for years.

Choosing à la carte or from a varied set menu, you can begin with Pollino cured meats and cheeses, bruschetta, tripe salad, fried bread with tomato, potato pie, sausage and cruschi peppers, **mushroom soup** on oregano and maize flour bread. To follow, **cavatelli zinn zinn** (tiny tiny), ferrazzuoli with sultanas and breadcrumbs, **foglie d'ulivo**, literally olive leaves, a kind of green pasta, with fresh ricotta cheese and spices, tapparelle with fried herbs, **mischiglio** (cavatelli of flour of chick-peas, barley, bran and oats) with cherry tomatoes and laurel or walnut sauce. The second courses are all meat-based: **capicollo with peppers**, lamb with Pecorino cheese or wild onions, **kid with herbs**, and saddle of pork with cream of asparagus. Also excellent is the **ingrattonato**, minced tripe with eggs, cheese and meat stock. If you book ahead, you can savor **coscia della sposa**, the 'leg of the bride', larded leg of kid cooked on hot bricks. End with Pecorino accompanied by orange honey, Scamorza with chestnut cream or, moving on to the desserts, cream of cooked figs, chestnut mousse, or baskets of walnut cream with cinnamon and chocolate.

The cellar stocks an excellent selection of regional wines, including the emerging Aglianico, and a smaller but interesting selection of other Italian labels. Also worth a try are the Pollino herb liqueurs.

TRIVIGNO

LA FORESTERIA DI SAN LEO

🗝️ Holiday farm
Contrada San Leo 11
Tel. 0971 981157-335 6452487
Fax 0971 442695
E-mail: mariagiovanna.allegretti@tin.it
Open from April to November

This agriturismo is located in a former Benedictine hermitage, inside of which the remains of the 14th- century monastery of San Leone are still visible. Rooms and apartment, fitted with all modern comforts, have independent entrances and are all decorated in different colors. The restaurant consists of a number of welcoming rooms with plain stone walls and serves Basilicata food and wine specialties. For budding cooks, courses in traditional cuisine are also organized periodically. Nature lovers can walk, ride or cycle in the woods round the farm, while a playground is available for the kids.

• 2 double rooms and 1 with 4 beds, bathroom; 1 apartment (4 people) with kitchen • Prices: double room single use 40-55, double 62-76, triple 75-95, with 4 beds 90-110 euros, breakfast included; apartment 80 euros • Credit cards: CartaSì, Bancomat • Mobility challenged catered for. Open inside parking. Small pets welcome. Owners always contactable • Restaurant. Living room. Park with playground

VIGGIANELLO

LA LOCANDA DI SAN FRANCESCO

🗝️ 3-Star Hotel
Via San Francesco 4
Tel. 0973 664384
Fax 0973 664385
E-mail: vinc.romeo@libero.it
Internet: www.locandapollino.it
Open all year round

This family-run hotel is located in the heart of the Basilicata side of the Parco del Pollino, in a recently refurbished 19th-century building in the old town of Viggianello. The building is on four levels, with a small tavern in the basement, a restaurant on the ground floor, and rooms on the first and mansard floors. Up to four beds can be fitted into the large rooms, which stand out for their solid wood furniture. The hotel is surrounded by a thick wood and from it you can admire the peak of Mount Pollino. This is an ideal base to visit the park from as the trails start only six kilometers away. Domenica, mother of owner Vincenzo, works in the kitchen of the excellent restaurant and uses only local produce.

• 16 double rooms with bathroom, television • Prices: double room single use 31-36, double 52-62 euros, breakfast included • All major credit cards, Bancomat • Public parking in the immediate vicinity. Small pets accepted. Reception open 24 hours a day • Restaurant. Tavern

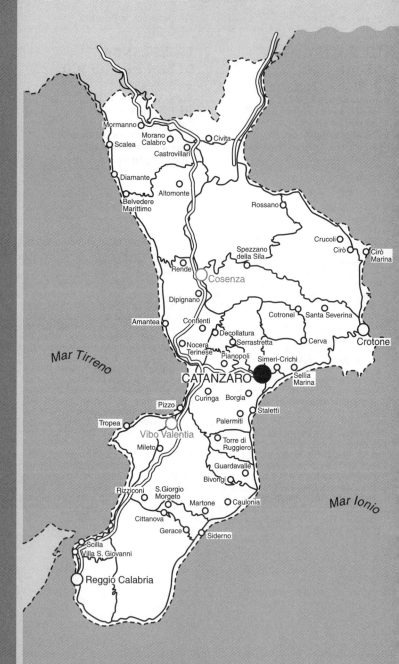

ALTOMONTE
Sant'Anna

61 KM NORTHWEST OF COSENZA

LE FARNIE

Holiday farm
Contrada Sant'Anna
Tel. 0981 948786-349 7252009-347 8822687
Fax 0981 948786
E-mail: info@agriturismolefarnie.it
Internet: www.agriturismolefarnie.it
Closed in January and February

The five rentable rooms of Carlo Piragine's farm are on the third floor of an old country house built in the 18th century which has been completely renovated. The rooms are simple and bright and face on to a wide communal terrace shaded by a pergola. One of the rooms also has a bunk bed. Guests take breakfast in the restaurant (also open to non-residents, a meal costs around 22 euros including beverages), where hot drinks are served along with apple pies and other homemade pastries. Local cheeses and fresh eggs are available on request. At the farm you can purchase a very good, locally produced extra-virgin olive oil, various vegetables preserved in oil, jams and bitter-orange marmalade. The village of Altomonte is about a kilometer away, with charming private houses and religious buildings dating from medieval times.

• 5 double rooms with bathroom • Prices: double room single occupancy 50-60 euros, double 70-80 (20 euros supplement for extra bed), breakfast included • Credit cards: none • Communal areas accessible to the mobility challenged. Covered off-street parking. Small pets allowed (not in the rooms). Owners always present • Restaurant. Garden, terrace

AMANTEA

43 KM SOUTHWEST OF COSENZA

ENOTECA DUE BICCHIERI

Restaurant-enoteca
Via Dogana 92
Tel. 0982 424409
Closed Sunday dinner and Monday, never in summer
Open: dinner, Sunday only for lunch
Holidays: last 2 weeks of September
Seating: 40 + 40 outdoors
Prices: 20-26 euros, wine excluded
All credit cards, Bancomat

Gianluca Ganci had a good idea last year when he decided to transform his well-stocked wine store into a restaurant. The change was gradual, as first he added some small snacks, then some cold dishes and finally arrived at a rare thing in Calabria – a wine shop offering a complete menu. He's been successful, with food that is never ordinary, using quality ingredients and with support from an excellent wine list. Gianluca is always on hand to advise customers (he's a professional sommelier), while his wife Marta runs the kitchen with two assistants.
Start with marinated anchovies, porcini mushroom flan, **marinated zucchini with mint and anchovies**, raw shrimp and roast red onion with ewe's milk ricotta. First courses offer a mix of dishes from the land and the sea with homemade ricotta and porcini mushroom-filled agnolotti with a red onion and walnut sauce, or **paccheri with Sila wild boar ragù**. You'll appreciate the aroma of the sea in the **calamaretti** (Gragnano pasta) **with fish soup**. Moving on to the main course there's **oven-baked anchovy flan**, **grilled swordfish** with capers and olives, pan-sautéed rabbit, **roast lamb** and an excellent sirloin steak. For cheese lovers there's always Monte Poro pecorino (a Slow Food Presidium).
Marta is in charge of puddings and the traditional **mostacciolo with honey** is a real treat, but also nice are the apple purée tart caramelized with red wine, tiramisù with seasonal fresh fruit and ewe's milk ricotta cheesecake.

43 KM SOUTHWEST OF COSENZA

43 KM SOUTHWEST OF COSENZA SS 18

LOCANDA DI MARE

MEDITERRANEO

Trattoria
Via Stromboli 20
Tel. 0982 428262
Closed Monday, never in summer
Open: lunch and dinner
Holidays: none
Seating: 60 + 70 outdoors
Prices: 22-25 euros, wine excluded
All credit cards, Bancomat

3-Star Hotel
Via Dogana 64
Tel. 0982 426364
Fax 0982 426247
E-mail: info@mediterraneohotel.net
Internet: www.mediterraneohotel.net
Open all year round

Protected by two promontories that have preserved it from all attempts at illegal construction, Amantea still boasts unspoilt cliffs and beaches and a clean sea, the same waters which provide the fish (especially the anchovies, sardines and swordfish), the main ingredient in the local diet. The entrance to this trattoria is shaped like the prow of a boat, which tells you what to expect here: Nothing but fish, cooked by Maurizio according to traditional local recipes.

Once you're seated ask Maurizio's wife, Maria, what's on that day. We recommend the mixed antipasti, which includes **anchovies** either marinated or **arriganate, piticelle di rosamarina** (spicy fritters made with tiny baby fish), the classic seafood salad and monacelle (fritters with a filet of anchovy inside). Then there's a good selection of first courses, which include delicate ravioli stuffed with grouper and served with a ground shrimp and crab sauce, **pasta with anchovies** in a tomato sauce, spaghetti with mussels and clams, risotto alla marinara and **tubettini with rosemary**. **Anchovies** are a constant presence in the main courses: You can eat them **stuffed**, roasted or fried. Alternatively, go for the **swordfish al tappeto** (slices of fish roasted with herbs and potatoes) or mixed grills. If they have it, don't miss the **Belmonte tomato salad**, an ideal accompaniment for the various fish dishes. To end, chocolate-coated dried figs purchased from local producers or tiramisù, which is Maria's specialty.

You can accompany your meal with the house white or a bottle from the region.

This hotel just 200 meters from the sea and located in a refined, mid-19th century building has a friendly atmosphere that will guarantee you a pleasant stay, thanks also to the hard work and hospitality of Enzo. The rooms are spacious and comfortable. The restaurant, also open to non-residents, offers interesting local cuisine (average price 22 euros, wine excluded; half board 47-82 euros per person). There's a laundry and ironing service available on request and a shuttle to and from Lamezia airport. On the hotel's private beach a diving school organizes excursions to the nearby protected marine reserve. You can rent a bicycle from the hotel to explore the surroundings: the fish, fruit and vegetable markets and many artisanal workshops specializing, among other things, in dried figs and preserved fish. The entrance to the hotel parking lot is off the Statale 18.

• 2 single, 14 double and 11 triple rooms, bathroom, air-conditioning, minibar, safe, satellite television • Prices: single 35-60 euros, double 60-80, triple 70-100, breakfast included • Credit cards: all, Bancomat • 1 room designed for the mobility challenged. Off-street parking. Small pets allowed (not in the dining room). Reception open 24 hours a day • Bar, restaurant, tavern. Television room. Conference room. Playground for children. Private beach

Belvedere Marittimo

69 KM NORTHWEST OF COSENZA SS 107 AND 18

Sabbia d'Oro

🍲 Restaurant
Vai Piano delle Donne
Tel. 0985 88456
Closed Tuesday, never in summer
Open: lunch and dinner
Holidays: December-January
Seating: 100 + 200 outdoors
Prices: 30-32 euros, excluding wine
All credit cards, Bancomat

Calabrian food is defined by the peper-oncino (chilli pepper). A few kilometers north of Belvedere Marittimo, at diavolil-lo, there's an academy and festival dedicated to the spicy peppers, promoting an ingredient that's ubiquitous in traditional local food.
The cuisine at Sabbia d'Oro is no exception. Here you'll find the classic **piti-celle di rosamarina**, as well as **devil's tart** (with a hot-pepper and orange marmalade with the addition of almonds).
Of course not everyone likes spicy dishes, so out of the restaurant's kitchen, capably run by Anna Maria Monetta, and onto tables inside or directly overlooking the beach, come dishes like octopus with Tropea onions, sardine or **anchovy raganelle di fragaglia** (tossed in the frying pan with bread crumbs and sweet dried peppers). To follow, tagliatelle gial-lomare, with fish and zucchini flowers; **spaghetti** alla pescatora, **with shellfish**, with scampi or with clams and **gnocchetti Sabbia d'oro**, with shrimps, tomatoes and arugula. For main courses go for the **swordfish arreganato**, tuna steak served with seasonal vegetables, nidi di mare (grouper filets in a potato crust), mixed grills, the **fried paranza platter** and roasted baby cuttlefish. If booked ahead you can also have lobster alla catalana – but this will push up your final bill. To end your meal there's the tart we've already mentioned or babà with a lime-flavored cream.
As you would expect the wine list is mainly regional, but there are also wines from the rest of the country.

Bivongi

150 KM NORTHEAST OF REGGIO CALABRIA SS 110 OR A 3 EXIT LAMEZIA

La Vecchia Miniera

🍲 Restaurant
Contrada Perrocalli
Tel. 0964 731869-338 5761250
Closed Monday
Open: lunch and dinner, in winter only for lunch
Holidays: 10 days at the end of September
Seating: 150 + 60 outdoors
Prices: 19-22 euros, excluding wine
Credit cards not accepted

To reach Bivongi, a small village in the far north of the province of Reggio, you take the Ionian coast road as far as Monasterace and then provincial road 110. The restaurant is in what was once the wash-house of a now-abandoned mine. Its rooms are decorated in a restrained manner and can cater for a large number of people both in winter and summer. The women of the Capo-rale family are in charge – Laura front of house, Ilenia and her mother Vincenza in the kitchen – and they offer dishes based on authentic ingredients.
For antipasti you have preserves in olive oil (olives, sun-dried tomatoes and egg-plants) and local cured meats such as capocollo and **soppressata**. Then move on to the **scilatedde** made in the traditional way using a knitting needle, **with a goat sauce**, very tasty and cooked for many, many hours; or the excellent **penne with mushrooms** picked in the surrounding woods. When it comes to the main course you can opt for **trout** (caught in a nearby lake or River Stilaro) either **arriganata** (cooked in foil with marjoram and hot peppers) or grilled; alternatively there's **grilled lamb**, pork fillet with mushrooms, sausages served with roast potatoes and goat's meat cooked in various ways. In the hunting season, there might be **wild boar chops**. There's a small selection of desserts that normally includes home-made tiramisù.
To accompany your meal there's a homemade red wine, Bivongi DOC wines (red, white and rosé), other labels from Calabria and some from the rest of Italy.

BORGIA
Roccelletta

15 KM SOUTH OF CATANZARO

IL PERO SELVATICO

🍴⬤Holiday farm
Via Scylletion km 0.950
Tel. and fax 0961 955153-721708
E-mail: info@ilperoselvatico.it
Internet: www.ilperoselvatico.it
Open all year round

Managed by Gregorio Mazza, the Li Donnici estate comprises 60 hectares of land planted with citrus, fruit and olive trees, and chickens, turkeys and black pigs are also raised. The setting retains the feeling of the original 18th-century stables, renovated to draw attention to the stone walls, wooden ceilings and false ceilings made of canes. The rooms, which are located on the first floor, are furnished in modern style and give onto an internal courtyard. The traditional breakfast includes homemade cakes and excellent freshly squeezed citrus juices when in season. The communal areas are spacious as is the restaurant where non-residents are welcome for lunch at a cost of approximately 30-35 euros, wine excluded. Guests can make use of the beaches that lie about one kilometer away from the estate; the adjacent Scolacium archeological site is worth visiting.

• 10 double rooms with bathroom, air-conditioning, television • Prices: double room single occupancy 45-55 euros, double 75-85 (25-30 euro supplement for extra bed), breakfast included • All major credit cards, Bancomat • Facility accessible for the mobility challenged, 1 room designed for their use. Off-street parking. Small pets allowed. Owners always contactable, staff always present • Restaurant. Lounge. Conference room. Park. Equipped beach 1.5 km away

CASTROVILLARI

75 KM NORTHEAST OF COSENZA

LA LOCANDA DI ALIA

🍴⬤4-Star Hotel
Via Jetticelle 55
Tel. 0981 46370
Fax 0981 46522
E-mail: alia@alia.it
Internet: www.alia.it
Open all year round

The building that houses the hotel and restaurant belonging to Gaetano, Antonio and Pinuccio Alia is surrounded by typical Mediterranean plants and land cultivated with olive and fig trees. Guests can reach the garden and swimming pool directly from their rooms, which are all furnished in a modern, simple manner and feature frescoes by a local artist. There are different types of room, the most spacious with a small living room, patio and jacuzzi. The breakfast is typically Italian, with seasonal fruit, biscotti made by a local bakery, and fruit salads and cheeses available on request. At the Madia di Alia you can purchase locally made products like Tropea onion jam, elderflower jam or liqueurs prepared according to ancient recipes.

• 3 single, 6 double rooms and 5 suites, bathroom, air-conditioning, mini-bar, television, modem connection • Prices: single 80 euros, double 100, suite 120 (20 euro supplement for extra bed) breakfast included • Credit cards: all, Bancomat • 2 rooms designed for the mobility challenged. Covered off-street parking. Small pets allowed. Reception open 24 hours a day • Bar, restaurant. Breakfast room, reading and television room. Conference room. Garden. Swimming pool

🍲 Famous for its traditional (30-35 euros, wine excluded) and creative (40-45 euros) menus.

DA SALVATORE

Trattoria-pizzeria with rooms
Salita I del Rosario 28
Tel. 0961 724318
Closed Monday, July-August also Sunday
Open: lunch and dinner
Holidays: August 8-31
Seating: 75
Prices: 20-22 euros, excluding wine
All major credit cards, Bancomat

SANTAROSA

Holiday farm
Viale Europa, turn-off for San Floro
Tel. 0961 746963
Fax 0961 61855
E-mail: info@agriturismosantarosa.it
Internet: www.agriturismosantarosa.it
Open all year round

You'll find Salvatore's restaurant in a little narrow street which crosses Corso Mazzini just a stone's throw from the cathedral and Politeama Theater. For years it's offered reliably good food in the center of Catanzaro. Currently it's in the hands of Francesco, the son-in-law of the man who gave his name to a place often frequented by actors and musicians.

The menu offers a real taste of Calabrian cuisine in just a few dishes. Start with vegetable fritters, pickled vegetables and samples capocollo, pecorino and soppressata. Then on to a first course or if you wish a main course which is hard to find these days. It's called **morzeddu**, and was once a common street food, consisting of soft pitta filled with tripe and veal offal cooked with herbs and hot peppers. A good alternative is baccalà, but you can also have **scilatelle with pork ragù**, **cavatelli with mussels and beans**, gnocchi alla casereccia, maccheroncini, pappardelle and lasagna with seasonally changing sauces. Another famous dish here is **tiana di capretto**, kid cooked slowly in a pan together with artichokes, potatoes, peas and spiced bread. Other main courses include stuffed chicken, **fried** or stewed **baccalà** with potatoes and zucchini or eggplant parmigiana. Fish is often available too, either grilled, in guazzetto, all'acquapazza or fried. Finish with fruit cakes and chestnut or walnut truffles.

There's quite a good selection of Calabrian labels on the wine list or you can accompany your meal with the red house wine.

The farm run by Maria Teresa Corporale and her husband Aldo Pegorari is more or less halfway between Catanzaro and the sea, and is surrounded by 100 hectares of cultivated land. The structure is an ancient stone house, with the old oil mill converted into two large rooms which house the restaurant (a meal costs 18-30 euros; half board is 65 euros per person). Recently their guest facilities have been expanded to include ten spacious guest rooms equipped with all mod cons, and a reception hall. The furnishings and the linens have been chosen with great attention to detail; one of the rooms features a mezzanine floor and can accommodate up to five people. There are many activities available for guests: from cookery courses to horseback riding, from trekking to helping with farming chores.

• 10 double rooms with bathroom, air-conditioning, mini-bar, television, modem connection • Prices: double room single occupancy 55-65 euros, double 95 (30 euro supplement for extra bed), breakfast included • All major credit cards, Bancomat • Facility accessible to the mobility challenged. Off-street parking. Small pets allowed (not in the rooms). Owners always contactable. • Restaurant. Conference room. Garden. Horse-riding

CAULONIA
Marina di Caulonia

110 KM NORTHEAST OF REGGIO CALABRIA S 106

TRATTORIA DEL PESCE FRESCO

Trattoria
Contrada Canne, Via Lepanto
Tel. 0964 82746
Closed Monday, never in summer
Open: lunch and dinner
Holidays: Christmas
Seating: 40 + 20 outdoors
Prices: 25-30 euros, excluding wine
No credit cards

Marina di Caulonia is only six kilometers from Roccella Jonica, the most important port on the stretch of sea between Crotone and Reggio. Every day fishing boats dock here laden with their catch, and every day Felice comes to find the best ingredients for his restaurant. With assistance from his wife Rosa, the seafood is transformed in the kitchen of this typical seaside trattoria into dishes served in the indoor dining room or outside in the garden.

Helped by their son, the Marrapodi family propose mixed seafood antipasti featuring **marinated anchovies**, or alternatively, small portions of vegetables – crushed olives, eggplants and sun-dried tomatoes preserved in olive oil – and cured meats such as the **capocollo** they produce themselves. Firsts and mains focus almost entirely on seafood: **linguine with squid ink**, risottos and **spaghetti with wolf-fish** or scorpionfish are always available, but if you want their magnificent **fish soup** – you can have it as a first or main course or even make it your entire meal – accompanied by croutons, you must book it in advance. It's not easy to find a sufficient variety of seafood to ensure a well-blended, harmonious taste. But even if you don't book this dish there are many others to keep you happy: grilled **cuttlefish** and **shrimps**, wolf-fish and **gurnard** are all reliable choices. Lastly, chocolate or fruit cakes, or during the Easter period a sweet pizza with candied fruit and vincotto.

Felice makes his own wine or there's a choice of a few Calabrian and Sicilian bottles.

CERVA

45 KM NORTHEAST OF CATANZARO SP 109

MUNDIAL 82

Trattoria-pizzeria
Via Daniele 221
Tel. 0961 939481-939510
Closed Tuesday, never in summer
Open: lunch and dinner
Holidays: July 1-20
Seating: 55
Prices: 21-23 euros, wine excluded
All major credit cards, Bancomat

Located in the Sila Piccola area, Cerva offers numerous opportunities for nature walks, along the banks of the River Crocchio with its waterfalls and pools, or exploring the dense beech, oak and chestnut woods. And it's here that the mushroom hunters find **porcini mushrooms** and, the rare royal agarics that for years now have been the top dish at Mundial 82.

Mushoom lovers will find this place a real treat as Maria is an artist when it comes to preparing fresh mushrooms, preserving them in olive oil or drying them so that they're available throughout the year. Mushrooms are the basis for the menu – from the antipasto to the main course. They might be served fresh in salads, used to flavor risottos and pastas (even together with shrimps), or grilled, roasted, breaded or fried, in which case they are also a good accompaniment for escalopes and rabbit. There are also some – though not many – tasty alternatives, ranging from homemade cured meats to **tagliatelle with goat ragù**, **cavatelli with beans** cooked in a pignata, **rabbit alla cacciatora** and even goat stew (which must be ordered in advance). To end the meal, local cheeses (Sila caciocavallo and pecorino from Crotone), tarts, **cuzzuppe** at Easter and **pitte 'nchiuse** at Christmas.

To drink there's a good selection of regional wines, and the natural water from local springs is worth trying. This place has a great atmosphere, and the service provided by owner Giuseppe Masciari is courteous and efficient. It's best to book.

CIRÒ
Cappellieri

CIRÒ
Sant'Elia

33 KM NORTH OF CROTONE ON SS 106

38 KM NORTH OF CROTONE SS 106

IL MEDITERRANEO

L'AQUILA D'ORO

Restaurant-pizzeria
Strada statale 106-Casello 191
Tel. 0962 32118-338 9936631
Closed Wednesday
Open: lunch and dinner
Holidays: two weeks in November
Seating: 45 + 60 outdoors
Prices: 23-28 euros, wine excluded
All credit cards except AE, Bancomat

Trattoria-pizzeria
Via Sant'Elia 7
Tel. 0962 38550
Closed Monday
Open: lunch and dinner
Holidays: variable
Seating: 40 + 25 outdoors
Prices: 20-23 euros, wine excluded
No credit cards accepted

Lucia and Salvatore Santoro continue to focus on the wine list in addition to offering quality food. The restaurant is lined with cupboards containing many bottles of wine, not only Calabrian but also wines from the rest of the country which offer the widest panorama possible. So you can be sure you'll find just the right wine to accompany the seafood and meat dishes on the menu.

Antipasti include **whitebait fritters**, croutons with sardines, squid lightly fried in olive oil and lemon juice, monkfish soup with tomato and basil, octopus with peppers or balsamic vinegar and **anchovies scattiate**. Often the first course dishes use a combination of seafood and vegetables: **scilatelle with mussels, potatoes and hot chilli peppers**; cavatelli with clams and chickpeas or spaghetti with cuttlefish ink, scampi and cauliflower for instance. As an alternative we can recommend the **tagliolini with anchovies and noci di mare** in a crisp batter. To follow there are excellent **mixed fries** or various soups, **baked turbot with porcini mushrooms and potatoes**, shrimp in tomato sauce, needle fish (alternatively also white bream can be prepared in the same way) cooked in the oven and served with toasted bread and spinach. If you prefer meat you can opt for **roast kid** with broccoli or **sausages with turnips** and dried chilli peppers.

To finish, a taste of smoked ricotta or pecorino and homemade cakes like sponge cake with fig jam, Sila chestnuts cooked in wine or dried fruit tart.

Sant'Elia is only four kilometers from Cirò and not much further from the sea. If you happen to be in these parts don't miss this little trattoria – which also has some outside seating under an arbor – run by Elisabetta and Salvatore Vizza, who will offer you both traditional seafood and meat dishes.

The generous antipasti include **pitta with pork crackling** or with elderflowers, **cipollata**, stuffed eggplants, peppers under salt with potatoes or accompanied by anchovies, wild onions in olive oil, crushed or pickled olives. The rustic cuisine continues in the same vein for first courses, with **scilateddi** in a vegetable sauce, **with sausage meat** or mushrooms; **cavatelli alla cirotana** (with a pork sauce and veal meatballs) and oven-baked pasta stuffed or with beans. The few seafood dishes, like **anchovies scattiate** (lightly fried with herbs and vinegar) and cuttlefish with potatoes, are decent alternatives to the meat: wild boar stew, **barbecued kid** and **rabbit alla cacciatori**. The **cheese board** is always well-stocked and so you'll be able to taste the best regional products like giuncata, ricotta, goat's milk cheeses and pecorino. You can end the meal with desserts associated with holidays or the changing seasons, but throughout the year you'll always find lemon-flavored cakes, tiramisù, tarts and sweet crespelle. They also serve pizza every evening in summer and at weekends in winter.

You can choose from the local Cirò wine on tap or other good Calabrian wines (there are around ten labels on the list).

CIRÒ MARINA

33 KM NORTH OF CROTONE SS 106

MAX

🍲 Trattoria-pizzeria-enoteca
Via Togliatti
Tel. 0962 373009
Closed on Monday, never in summer
Open: lunch and dinner
Holidays: second half of September
Seating: 120-200 outdoors
Prices: 22-25 euros, excluding wine
All credit cards, Bancomat

The varied menu here is of the reasons for Max's success. The excellent wine list, with the best Cirò and Melissa DOC wines and other regional and national bottles, is another draw, as is the well-chosen range of **cheeses**, with over a dozen kinds focussing particularly on aged and fresh ricottas served with cinnamon, chocolate or grape mostarda; in winter the selection includes some blue cheeses. In the evenings they also serve good pizzas, and the wood-fired oven also gets used for meat, soups and potatoes cooked in the ashes.

The menu is based on seasonal ingredients and changes each month, even though some dishes are always available. So you can start with homemade **sardella** served with peppers or red onions, fried whitebait, the excellent **soppressata**, peppers with anchovies and various samplings of seasonal vegetables. In addition to tagliolini with grouper ragù and pasticcio of **pasta and potatoes alla cirotana** (gratinéed with local pecorino), we can recommend the **cavatelli** made with red wine and a sauce of **tomato-less fish ragù** or **bean and shellfish soups** cooked in the opening of the oven. Then you can move on to **grilled pesce azzurro** (anchovies, sardines or mackerels), fried mixed seafood and **roast meats** with fresh salads.

Ricotta is the star ingredient in desserts like the mousse. But alternatively there are also fried cannoletti with tangerine-flavored cream, chocolate cakes, biscotti, crustuli and crêpes.

CITTANOVA

66 KM NORTHEAST OF REGGIO CALABRIA

LA MAMMA

🍲 Trattoria
Via San Giuseppe 33-corner of Via Roma
Tel. 0966 660147-655849
Closed Tuesday
Open: lunch and dinner
Holidays: July 15-31, Sept. 15-30
Seating: 60 + 70 outdoors
Prices: 20-25 euro, excluding wine
All credit cards, Bancomat

This classic trattoria is located inland from Reggio, and can be reached by taking the main Statale road 111 running from the Tyrrhenian to the Ionian coast. The place is run by Maria, helped by her children, and she's responsible for simple but tasty dishes representative of the best of Calabrian home cooking.

Vegetables, cured meats and baccalà are the stars of the antipasti, among which you may also find various kinds of fritter and crocchette, **raw stockfish salad**, oil-preserved and fried vegetables, capocollo, salami and also fresh **ricotta** and local pecorino. Among the first course dishes, there's a tasty red-bean soup alongside pasta with various sauces: **linguine with baccalà**, fettuccine with porcini mushrooms, penne with eggplants and the always recommended **pasta 'ncasciata al forno**. Then move on to the meats: roast lamb or **kid** with potatoes, the mixed platter of grilled fish or breaded swordfish cooked with herbs (especially in summer). Among the main courses there's **baccalà** again prepared in many different ways: **alla ghiotta, a mulinara**, fried or roasted. Then with the offal they prepare a stew of **stuffed ventriceddi**. Sesame bread is homemade as are the desserts: cassata di ricotta (lighter than the similar Sicilian variety), cannoli, babà and lemon cake.

The wine list contains some 200 regional and national labels – with a rotating selection available by the glass. There's also an excellent selection of grappa, rum, calvados, armagnac and cognac, selected by Girolamo.

CIVITA

AGORÀ

☕Restaurant
Piazza Municipio 30
Tel. 0981 73410
Closed Monday, never in August
Open: lunch and dinner
Holidays: none
Seating: 160
Prices: 24-26 euros
All major credit cards, Bancomat

For some years now the Nicoletti family has been running a butcher's shop in the center of Civita, which has proved a good way to get to know the farmers and shepherds who supply the rabbit, beef and mutton used every day in the kitchen at the Agorà. As a result there are many meat-based specialties like **veal tripe**, chops and meatballs, various cuts cooked in a wood-fired oven, **pork rind and beans**, **kid testoline** and meat kebabs flavored with Pollino herbs.
But the restaurant, which has three cozy, simple rooms, has many more dishes that are worth trying, often drawing on Calabrian-Albanian tradition. Start with **mixed antipasti**, fritters made with seasonal vegetables and tasty homemade preserves under oil served together with local cured meats and fresh ewe's milk ricotta. Then move on to handmade pasta, such as **rrashkatjël** (like fusilli, shaped using a knitting needle) **with kid ragù**, lagane with various beans and cavatelli or **strangulet** (handmade gnocchetti) with vegetable sauces. As a good alternative there are chickpea, wild chicory or bean soups. If you don't want meat then it's worth remembering that every Friday there's a menu dedicated entirely to **baccalà**. To end your meal, try one of the homemade desserts, like the tart with a sheep's milk ricotta filling, fruit-flavored semifreddi or the ring-shaped dolce della sposa.
Both regional and other Italian bottles are on show in one of the dining rooms. Otherwise there's a house wine that's included in the price of the menu.

CIVITA

LA KAMASTRA

☕Restaurant
Piazza Municipio 3-6
Tel. 0981 73387-22182
Closed Wednesday, never in August
Open: lunch and dinner
Holidays: December 22-January 2
Seating: 80
Prices: 25-30 euros, excluding wine
All credit cards, Bancomat

Civita – Cifti in arbëreshe dialect – was one of the first places in Italy where immigrants from Albania began to settle just after 1450. Here the traditions of this ancient Albanian population are so deeply rooted that they have influenced many aspects of the local culture – from music to language to gastronomy. Kamastra is the place to come to learn more about these Balkan influences, as will be clear when you consult the bilingual menu.
Giuseppe Bloise, one of the owners, will advise you to start with the mixed antipasti, where in addition to preserves in oil, pancetta and ricotta there's excellent **Pollino prosciutto**. Then get ready to taste the dishes prepared by the other partner, Giuseppe Zaccaro, who's specialty is fresh pasta: **bakalla me tumac** (pasta with baccalà sauce), ndul kothra e nenes (pork rind, sausage and wild vegetable soup), **tumacme qiqrat** (lagane and chickpeas), strangule me neneze (cavatelli with nenesa, a Pollino herb) and **dromesat**, a dish that provides a lesson in gastronomic archeology. Then there's **wild boar alla bracconiera** (stewed with herbs), **pancooked Civita kid** served with potatoes, or grilled pork, veal and sausages. Finish with typical krustuli soaked in cooked grape must.
Apart from the red and white house wines you can choose one of the Calabrian wines on their list. These can also be purchased in the shop next to the restaurant, where you'll also find local artisanal products.

921   CALABRIA

CONFLENTI
Muraglie

COTRONEI
Santa Venere

55 KM NORTHWEST OF CATANZARO SS 19 AND A 3   45 KM NORTHWEST OF CROTONE

LE MURAGLIE

☞Holiday farm
Contrada Muraglie
Tel. 0968 64367
Closed Monday for dinner
Open: lunch and dinner
Holidays: none
Seating: 50 + 20 outdoors
Prices: 18-22 euros, wine excluded
No credit cards accepted

SANTA VENERE

☞Restaurant-pizzeria
Via San Francesco
Tel. 0962 44241
Closed Monday, never in August
Open: lunch and dinner
Holidays: none
Seating: 150 + 60 outdoors
Prices: 20-22 euros, wine excluded
No credit cards accepted

Situated more or less halfway between Conflenti and Martirano, this peaceful little oasis of a farm is run by Matilde and Armando Roperti, with lots of help from their children. Inside there's a rustic dining room, while the outside tables can seat about 20 diners. The warm, friendly welcome and the few well-prepared dishes available each day give the place a feel of authentic rural hospitality. To start you can have generous **homemade antipasti** including the farm's own cured meats, local cheeses and various vegetables preserved in olive oil or pickled. Then on to the homemade **scilatelle** or strozzapreti that, depending on the occasion, will be cooked in pignata **with beans**, frittule (pork rind) and peas or fava beans, fresh porcini mushrooms in autumn or **with soppressata and black olives**. Beans are used in winter soups (the one with beans and pork rind is particularly good). Meat is mainly poultry or rabbit and pigs raised on the farm: so there's free-range chicken and **rabbit alla cacciatora**, **barbecued sausages** and, especially during the early months of the year, **pork roasted** or prepared in other ways. You can also always count on the season's vegetables, like early fava beans (try them with pecorino) and peas, French beans, eggplants, tomatoes and zucchini. A handful of good biscotti – mostaccioli made with honey and bocconotti with grape must – accompanied by a nocino or homemade limoncello make an ideal end for your meal.

As an alternative to the few bottled wines available, there are also red and white house wines.

Cotronei is one of the most important centers in the province of Crotone. Its narrow winding streets, arches and craft workshops make it well worth a visit. Then there's the excellence of its produce – extra-virgin olive oil, the porcini mushrooms which abound in the surrounding woods and sun-dried figs flavored following age-old recipes. Fedelina and Severino Caligiuri, ably assisted by their son Rosario, run this restaurant a few kilometers from the center of town. Given the beautiful panoramas, pleasantly furnished dining rooms and the well-prepared, genuine dishes, it's a place that's always a pleasure to return to.

Antipasti show how good the local vegetables are, from eggplants stuffed with tomato to small pizzas, crostini with various condiments, fritters and meatballs, depending on the season. You can continue with **tagliatelle alla pecorara** (with a tomato sauce, smoked ricotta and pancetta), risottos, **soups** with mixed vegetables in the summer and **chestnuts and porcini mushrooms** in the fall. In season porcini are also used in a sauce for **chickpea-flour cavatelli** or as a topping for crêpes, in addition to being roasted together with pancetta, or breaded and fried. In season there's also plenty of game – hare, guinea fowl, woodcock, wild boar – or alternatively they prepare a good **roast kid**. Every evening there's also tasty pizzas cooked in a wood-fired oven. As for desserts they have various mixed fruit or jam tarts, almond pastries and crustoli.

The house wine is included in the price but if you want to branch out they have some good Calabrian and Tuscan labels.

CROTONE

CRUCOLI
Torretta

54 KM NORTHWEST OF CROTONE SS 106

SPARVIERO DUE

☝Restaurant
Via Interna Marina 37-39
Tel. 0962 25009
Closed Monday, never in summer
Open: lunch and dinner
Holidays: none
Seating: 80
Prices: 25-33 euros, excluding wine
All credit cards, Bancomat

POLLO D'ORO

☝Hotel-restaurant
Corso Garibaldi 87-89
Tel. 0962 34005
Closed Sunday, never in summer
Open: lunch and dinner
Holidays: December 20-January 5
Seating: 60
Prices: 24-28 euros, wine excluded
All credit cards, Bancomat

If you're passing through Crotone, visit the majestic castle, whose extensions and refurbishments bear witness to historical events long past, and don't miss the opportunity to visit this restaurant which is very close to the port. Maria runs the kitchen and is an expert in preparing the fish from the day's catch that her husband Alfredo brings back from the sea every day on his boat. Whitebait or **scrine** (small local molluscs) are used to prepare tasty fritters served as antipasti as an alternative to other simple dishes, for instance, **octopus roll**, anchovies cooked in a variety of ways, cuttlefish with peas or mussels au gratin. Seafood also stars in first course dishes, among which you'll find tubettini with a monkfish ragù, cavatelli or ricotta and spinach-filled ravioli with a shrimp sauce, **maccheroncini with anchovies**, **lasagna with whitebait** or **linguine alla Sparviero** (with shellfish). The really traditional dish in Crotone's cuisine is **quadaru**, a mixed fish soup cooked in a ceramic pan and served allo Sparviero, as either a first or a main course. Otherwise to round off your meal you can choose from the day's catch (red mullet, white sea bream, dentex or gilthead) either grilled, baked or all'acquapazza, or lightly fried sea bass and **anchovies arriganate**. Maria almost always prepares tarts and tiramisù for dessert.
As for wine, you can rely on quite a good selection of Cirò and Valdineto wines.

☝ You can buy fresh fish at the Pescheria del Tarantino in Via Porto Vecchio. In Contrada **Poggio Pudone**, Alfonso Maria Maiorano raises sheep and produces pecorino canestrato and an excellent smoked ricotta.

Located just a stone's throw from the main road, the name of Raffaele and Natalia Parilla's restaurant is an invitation to stop and try some of their chicken and other specialties. Not only the **pan-fried chicken** served with fried potatoes but everything that precedes it, like capocollo, sausages, hot spicy **soppressata** served as antipasti together with preserves in oil from the vegetable garden and Sila woods (sun-dried tomatoes, porcini mushrooms and eggplant). Not forgetting the first courses: **lasagna** with a wealth of juicy ingredients (ragù, soppressata, provola cheese and eggs) that remind you of the generosity of this region. Other dishes linked to the land include **cavatelli with beans**, orecchiette with mushrooms and sausage, **tomatoes stuffed with rice** and many meats for the main course: veal scallops with mushrooms and **roast kid** with potatoes. However the pictures on the walls and the very air you breathe in Crucoli are reminders that the sea isn't far away. And it's best represented by the **sardella**, a hot spread made from baby sardines, spiced with chilli pepper and wild fennel, as well as other types of fish, depending on what's available on the day. The mixed fried fish; grouper cooked in tomato sauce, grilled or with lemon and roast swordfish are just a few examples. And you can end in great style with figs stuffed with walnuts and almonds and coated with chocolate, chestnuts with cooked grape must pudding and the typical **pitta impigliata**.
The wine cellar is small but well-stocked, with some interesting local and regional labels. To close you can choose from a selection of whiskeys and liqueurs.

CURINGA

ANTICO FRANTOIO OLEARIO BARDARI

Holiday farm
Contrada Trunchi 1
Tel. 0968 789037-338 4288954
Fax 0968 789037
E-mail: info@agriturismobardari.it
Internet: www.agriturismobardari.it
Open: every day, lunch and dinner
Holidays: none
Seating: 50 +100 outdoors
Prices: 23-25 euros, wine excluded
All credit cards, Bancomat

Patrizia Bardari manages a beautiful agriturismo surrounded by land planted with vegetable fields, olive groves and orchards, with poultry, sheep and pigs are bred to prepare excellent **cured meats**. The rooms are bright and inventively furnished. At breakfast you can taste some of the farm produce, which is also available for sale. Half-board costs 55 euros per person and booking is essential.
The menu changes often and includes a rich **mixed antipasto**, two first courses, two second courses and a selection of desserts. The meal opens with cured meats, smoked ricotta, pizza rustica, **eggplant cannoli** stuffed with prosciutto or tuna, fritters and timbales and **stuffed cherry tomatoes**. Hearty first courses like **baked pasta** with meatballs, salame, ricotta and tomato sauce or bean and porcini mushroom soup give way in summer to lighter dishes like the tagliolini with cream of zucchini and peppers or the **scilatelli all'ortolana**. The main courses include mixed grills, **roast kid** with potatoes, **chicken with peppers** and pork involtini. To finish, bocconotti made with jam, crostate with Morello cherries, quince or with pastry cream, pear and chocolate.
To drink, there's the house wine on tap and an interesting selection of regional wines. Reservations are essential.

• 5 double rooms and 1 quadruple, en suite, TV • Prices: double room single occupancy 50, double 100, quadruple 200 euros, breakfast included • Restaurant accessible to the mobility challenged. Private uncovered parking. Pets not allowed. Owners always available • Restaurant. Reading room and TV. Garden, veranda

DECOLLATURA
Sorbello

LA VECCHIA FATTORIA

Holiday farm
Contrada Sorbello
Tel. 0968 61815-349 8179563
Fax 0968 61815
E-mail: talaricoangela@libero.it
Open June-September, also public holidays; rest of the year at weekends

Angela Talarico, assisted by her husband Giovanni Costanzo, manages this agriturismo located on approximately 10 hectares of olives, vines and fruit trees. They also rear pigs and poultry, the meat of which is often served in the restaurant, along with homemade pasta and seasonal vegetables (half board is 35-40 euros per person). An old brick farmhouse and a more recent building provide the accommodation. In addition to the rooms there are three small apartments equipped with kitchenettes, and two one-bedroom apartments with living rooms, all furnished in a simple yet functional manner. Breakfast includes homemade fruit and jam tarts, and also cured meats produced on the farm. We highly recommend a visit to the nearby sanctuary of Conflenti.

• 4 double rooms with bathroom; 5 apartments (2-4 people) with fridge and kitchenette • Prices: double room single occupancy 25-35 euros, double 50-70, apartment 50-140, breakfast included • Major credit cards, Bancomat • Facility accessible to the mobility challenged, 1 room designed for their use. Off-street parking. Small pets allowed. Owners always present • Restaurant. Television room. Garden with children's playground. Swimming pool

DIAMANTE

76 KM NORTHWEST OF COSENZA SS 18

LA GUARDIOLA

🍲 Restaurant-pizzeria
Lungomare Riviera Blu
Tel. 0985 876759-338 6466713-340 3053801
Closed Tuesday, never in summer
Open: lunch and dinner
Holidays: November 1-February 28
Seating: 60 + 80 outdoors
Prices: 26-32 euros, wine excluded
All major credit card, Bancomat

The owners of this beach restaurant, the Perrone brothers, are both fishermen. The location is evocative but the sea air has also aged the structure and this winter restructuring work will have to be undertaken.
Here the daily catch is cooked simply and often flavored with diavolilli, the local red chilis. The round red and green ones are stuffed with tuna and anchovies, preserved in oil and served as an antipasto, the fierier one used to dress octopus in **polpetti affogati** and in pasta sauces (**spaghetti alla lucifero** with whitebait and chili pepper is the place's signature dish) and in crostatas and ice-cream. More in general, antipasti include seafood salad, whitebait, **algae fritters** and marinated **anchovy fritters**. First courses: **linguine with sea-bass**, with seafood or with cuttlefish and ravioli stuffed with fish. For mains, sea-bass, bream and other fish grilled or stewed, swordfish 'sausage' (a new entry this year) and two typical local dishes: **anchovy stew** and **baccalà alla diamantese** (with potatoes, tomatoes and chili). Besides chili, another important ingredient in crostatas and ice-cream is lime.
If you don't want to drink the dry or fizzy house wines, the wine list offers a few good Calabrian labels and a small selection of spirits and liqueurs.

🍴 L'Accademia del Peperoncino, or Chili Pepper Academy is at Via Amendola 3. At Piazza XI Febbraio 17, Peccati di Gola sells typical Calabrian delicacies. On the promenade, Gelateria Pierino sells chili ice-cream and wonderful granitas.

DIPIGNANO
Tessano

12 KM SOUTH OF COSENZA

LIVIO

🍲 Restaurant
Via Pulsano 63
Tel. 0984 445506
Closed Monday
Open: lunch and dinner
Holidays: August
Seating: 140 + 60 outdoors
Prices: 18-25 euros, wine excluded
All major credit cards, Bancomat

Tessano is a small village close by Dipignano, a place famous in the past for its copper pots, which were exported to towns and villages throughout Italy. Livio Massaro's restaurant – which he runs with the invaluable assistance of his wife, Sabrina – is in a modern building and is subdivided into dining rooms of various sizes. Compared with previous years we're pleased to say there's been a positive change in the way the kitchen operates and in the menu. This is because Livio himself has decided to pay closer attention to both these areas. So there's been a slight reduction in the number of dishes offered but an increase in overall quality.
The antipasti and a good number of the first courses focus largely on vegetables: tubero alla calabrese (hollowed out potatoes, seasoned with rosemary and baked in the oven), baked rice timbale with fried pumpkin, **zucchini fritters** and **eggplant involtini**. Then large squared spaghetti with zucchini, squash blossom and prosciutto; **spaghetti with fresh anchovies** and cherry tomatoes; **orecchiette alla tessanese**, with chicory, sausage, fresh ricotta and tomato; tagliatelle with porcini mushroom sauce and baked pasta with pancetta and onions. To follow, meat dishes like sausages with cime di rapa and served in hollowed-out bread, and **pig's liver with caul fat**; alternatively there's **baccalà alla cosentina** or mixed baked cheeses like caciocavallo, pecorino and smoked scamorza. For dessert we'd suggest one of the several **fig specialties**: dried then stuffed with almonds and walnuts, covered with chocolate or soaked in fig honey.
Apart from the house wine, there's a selection of bottles from Calabria and the rest of Italy.

GERACE

LA CASA DI GIANNA

🔑 4-Star Hotel
Via Paolo Frascà 4
Tel. 0964 355024-355018
Fax 0964 355081
E-mail: info@lacasadigianna.it
Internet: www.lacasadigianna.it
Open all year round

The Casa di Gianna, a refurbished building that once belonged to a noble family, is located in the heart of the old center of Gerace. The rooms are furnished with great attention to detail: refined linens and draperies that vary from room to room, old-fashioned writing desks, early 20th-century furniture and also rooms with visible wooden beams. Communal areas, such as the small lounges where guests can listen to music or read (there's a well-stocked library), the restaurant (a meal costs around 15 euros, wine excluded) and the terrace used for the restaurant in summer are all attractive, well-designed and cozy. Breakfast consists of local products such as bread, jams and croissants. Also in Gerace, Aurelia Fimognari manages the Casa del Borgo located in an elegant building typical of the village as well as Palazzo Sant'Anna, originally a 14th-century convent.

• 1 single and 8 double rooms and 1 junior suite, bathroom, air-conditioning, mini-bar, satellite television, safe, modem connection; several rooms with balcony • Prices: single 60-80 euros, double room single use 80-96, double 100-120 (30 euro supplement for extra bed), suite 150-180, breakfast included • All credit cards, Bancomat • Facility accessible to the mobility challenged. External parking with reserved spaces. Small pets allowed. Reception open 24 hours a day • Bar, restaurant. Breakfast room, reading room. Terrace

GERACE
Azzurria

LA TAVERNETTA

🍲 Trattoria
Strada Provinciale Locri-Antonimina 112
Tel. 0964 356020-349 6162254
Closed Tuesday
Open: lunch and dinner
Holidays: variable
Seating: 60 + 60 outdoors
Prices: 18-20 euros, wine excluded
No credit cards

La Tavernetta is a small place (reservations are essential, especially in winter) not far from the old center of Gerace, on the road leading to Antonimina and its famous spa. During the winter there's open fire in the dining room, while in summer you can eat on the veranda under an arbor – just the right setting for a typical Calabrian meal.
Pasquale will be happy to describe the dishes prepared by his wife Rossella, using seasonal products and focussing on traditional dishes from the area. The **mixed antipasti** is filling and can include capocollo, salami and local pecorino cheeses, potato fritters, grilled or stuffed vegetables, sun-dried eggplants or tomatoes preserved in olive oil. Then there might be **bucatini with stucco sauce**; homemade **maccaruni** with tomato, eggplants, salted ricotta, capocollo and basil; tagliatelle with vegetables or anchovies; chickpea and bean soups with leafy greens; or **linguine** with shrimp and cherry tomatoes, **ventresca sauce**, wild boar or **goat ragù**. When you come to the main course opt for the grilled meat (pork, wild boar, lamb); in winter, **tripe with beans and potatoes** or **stocco** cooked with olives and potatoes or roasted with chilli peppers, tomatoes and onions. But there's also something to whet the appetite of vegetarians: **eggplants** cooked **alla parmigiana** or in involtino, whereas peppers and tomatoes are usually stuffed with breadcrumbs, capers, olives, garlic and parsley. Apart from desserts served during specific holiday periods you'll usually find fruit tarts and a good homemade tiramisù.
You can either drink the house wine or there are some good bottles of Cirò and Bivongi wines to choose from.

GUARDAVALLE
Marina

MARTONE

MAMMA ASSUNTA

⌒Trattoria
Via Pietro Nenni
Tel. 0967 86121
June-September open every day, in
winter by reservation only
Open: lunch and dinner
Seating: 40 + 80 outdoors
Prices: 15 euros
No credit cards accepted

LA COLLINETTA

⌒Trattoria-pizzeria
Via Colacà
Tel. 0964 51680-338 8550930
Closed Tuesday
Open: lunch and dinner
Holidays: variable in autumn-winter
Seating: 75
Prices: 20-22 euros, wine excluded
No credit cards

It's always a pleasure to visit the coast at Guardavalle, a place that's not yet been overtaken by the chaos of mass tourism, because here you can still enjoy the benefits of the seaside without suffering today's drawbacks. But while this trattoria is right on the seafront and has a lovely pergola under which you can get your fill of fresh sea air, you'll not find a trace of fish on the tables. Assunta Cosentino made this decision and instead she serves up excellent local specialties at what can only be defined as truly popular prices. For just 15 euros you can have antipasti, two first courses, two main courses and a side. Not bad for a hearty meal right beside the sea.

The antipasti include local cured meats, among which the ever-present **soppressata** and samplings of various vegetables of the day (sun-dried tomatoes, artichokes in olive oil, olives, pickled vegetables). Every day you'll find **scilatellì** shaped with a knitting needle and served **with meatballs in tomato sauce**, **with goat's meat ragù** or simply with tomato and basil. The other first course dish will either be pasta and beans, **potato gnocchi** or vegetable soup, depending on the day. Then comes **meat** either **stewed** or grilled, **chicken alla cacciatora**, roast pork and **goat stew**, all served with sides of peppers, eggplants or fried artichokes. To end there's fresh fruit and, if available, a glass of mint liqueur or homemade limoncello.

To drink there's only the house wine. Remember that Assunta only cooks if she has bookings: be sure to call at least one day in advance so she can do the shopping and get organized for your visit.

Holm oak, beech and chestnut woods guarantee that the agricultural village of Martone has a reserve of mushrooms and game. Giuseppe Trimboli makes the most of this local bounty, assisted in the Collinetta kitchen by his mother Rosa and wife Lucia. If the mushroom hunt has been successful then you'll have **porcini** prepared in several different ways: roasted, in salad, breaded and fried, alla martonese (with bread and potatoes), as a sauce for pasta or on the side of sausages.

But there's no lack of alternatives, as you can see from the wide choice of antipasti: **warm ricotta**, beans cooked in a terracotta casserole, capocollo and **soppressata**, eggplant parmigiana, lightly fried vegetables and crushed olives. Continue with the handmade pastas – stuffed or otherwise: **panzerotti with meat and caciocavallo** from Sila with cherry-tomato sauce or caciocavallo and basil, or cavatelli with turnip tops and anchovies, **bucatini with stockfish** or **maccaruni with wild boar sauce**. Sometimes you'll also find potato gnocchi or a hearty bean soup. The most typical main course dishes are **leg of lamb cooked in clay** and **oven-baked salt cod au gratin**. Otherwise you can have barbecued steaks or fillet or, in season, venison, wild boar or guinea fowl cooked in various ways. There's local pecorino and homemade desserts to round off your meal. You'll find tiramisù, apple or berry tarts, fruit gelatos and Gioiosa tartufo, accompanied by their homemade liqueurs. Good pizzas cooked in a wood-fired oven are available every evening.

To drink there's the house wine or a few regional or other Italian bottles. Choose the carafe of water instead of bottled!

MILETO

MORANO CALABRO

12 km SOUTHWEST OF VIBO VALENTIA SS 18

80 km NORTHWEST OF COSENZA

IL NORMANNO

LA LOCANDA DEL PARCO

Trattoria-pizzeria
Via Real Badia 37
Tel. 0963 336398
Closed Monday
Open: lunch and dinner
Holidays: September
Seating: 50 + 30 outdoors
Prices: 18-22 euros, wine excluded
All credit cards, Bancomat

Holiday farm
Contrada Mazzicanino
Tel. 0981 31304-30326
Fax 0981 31304
E-mail: info@lalocandadelparco.it
Internet: www.lalocandadelparco.it
Open all year round

This trattoria in Mileto, around 30 kilometers from Tropea's celebrated beaches, is truly unpretentious. Inside there's wood-paneled dining rooms and tables set in a casual, homely manner, and through an opening in the wall to the kitchen you can get a glimpse of Clementina sliding pizzas into the oven. Outside, but protected by the courtyard walls, there's a small area where Gianni serves customers in his usual friendly manner.

The antipasti, which like the other dishes follow the seasons, will be brought out on a tray and diners help themselves to as much as they want. You'll probably find fresh ricotta and an excellent **pecorino del Poro** (a Slow Food Presidia) served between April and May with raw fava beans. You'll always find **sautéed vegetables** and 'nduja, other local cured meats and homemade preserves in olive oil (sun-dried tomatoes, eggplants and zucchini). In summer there are many fresh vegetable dishes, among which we can recommend the zucchini flower fritters. Handmade **fileja** pasta, tagliatelle and gnocchi are served with meat sauces (pork or **goat ragù**) and fresh porcini mushrooms, possibly mixed with sausage or peppers. Then pasta and beans, pasta and chickpeas and **tripe in tomato sauce** – obviously the latter are winter dishes. For main courses, mixed grills, **sausage and cime di rapa, roast kid with potatoes**, fried, roast or oven-baked baccalà with potatoes and peppers, stockfish and stews. A good alternative in summer are the generous portions of vegetables. To finish up there are homemade tarts or the classic Pizzo tartufo.

To accompany your meal there's the red house wine or a few regional labels from the cellar.

The inn is located in the National Park of Pollino, just a few kilometers from the old center of Morano. The rooms are located in the main building and an annex, surrounded by a beautiful garden with a swimming pool. The rooms are all peaceful, spacious and tastefully furnished. Adriana Tamburi will be there to welcome you and cater to all your needs, while her breakfast menu includes homemade sweet and savory fare with jams, butter, cheeses and cured meats. The restaurant is also open to non-residents who book in advance, and offers locally produced foods and traditional Calabrian dishes (meals cost 20 euros, house wine included; half board is 45 euros per person). Guests can participate in nature walks or, alternatively, can visit historical sites such as the center of Morano and ruins of Sibari.

• 7 double rooms with bathroom, terrace; 2 chalets, 2 annexes • Prices: double room single occupancy 35 euros, double 60 (30 euro supplement for extra bed), breakfast included • Credit cards: major ones, Bancomat • Off-street parking. Small pets allowed. Owners always present • Restaurant. Reading and TV room. Conference room. Garden. Swimming pool.

MORANO CALABRO

VILLA SAN DOMENICO

☞❶4-Star Hotel
Via Paglierina 13
Tel. 0981 399881-399991
Fax 0981 30588
E-mail: info@albergovillasandomenico.it
Internet: www.albergovillasandomenico.it
Open all year round

Hugging the sides of a cone-shaped hill, Morano is a late-medieval village known for its Collegiate Church of Maddalena and Norman castle. Hotel Villa San Domenico, managed by Pasquale Vacca, is located in the historical center in a 16th-century house. The renovation has managed to preserve the building's original façade intact; the rooms, which face onto the internal garden, are comfortable and furnished with antiques to create a cozy atmosphere. The suites have a mezzanine floor which allows extra beds to be added, whilst the cottage has an independent entrance and a small private garden. The buffet breakfast offers an ample choice of sweet and savory fare as well as hot and cold drinks. Half board ranges from 60-70 euros, full board from 80-90 euros.

• 7 double rooms, 1 cottage and 3 suites, bathroom, terrace, mini-bar, satellite television, modem connection • Prices: double room single occupancy 70 euros, double 103, cottage and suites 135-160 (40 euro supplement for extra bed), breakfast included • Credit cards: all, Bancomat • 1 room designed for the mobility challenged. Off-street parking. Small pets allowed. Reception open 24 hours a day • Bar, restaurant. Reading and television room. Conference room. Garden, terrace.

MORMANNO
Procitta

PARCO VILLA ELENA

☞❶Holiday farm
Contrada Procitta
Tel. 0981 80254
Fax 0981 81350
E-mail: info@parcovillaelena.it
Internet: www.parcovillaelena.it
Open all year round

This agriturismo is located in the middle of the countryside, in a well-restored early 20th-century farmhouse. Communal areas such as the bar and restaurant, which can seat up to 100 people, are very spacious (a meal costs 20 euros, including house wine, half board based on double room occupancy averages from 47-51 euros per person). Its main attraction is the versatile outdoor space that can be used for various activities: the riding school offers nature excursions on horseback, available also for beginners; in addition there's a children's playground and dedicated areas for archery as well as jogging and cycling. Alongside a typical Italian breakfast, Francesco Donnici serves cakes, jams and locally produced dairy products. The Donnici family can provide groups with a villa (5 bedrooms, kitchen and services) located 12 kilometers from Parco Villa Elena.

• 4 double rooms, 6 triples and 2 quadruples, bathroom, terrace, mini-bar, television, modem connection • Prices: double room single occupancy 35-40 euros, double 54-60, triple 81-90, 4-bed 108-120, breakfast included • Major credit cards, Bancomat • Restaurant accessible to the mobility challenged. Off-street parking. Small pets allowed. Owners always present. • Bar, restaurant. Reading and television room. Conference room. Garden with playground. Horse-riding.

NOCERA TERINESE
Vota

PALERMITI
Nucifero

VOTA

MEZZALUNA

☞—◑Holiday farm
Contrada Vota 3
Tel. 0968 91517-347 3184181
Fax 0968 91517
E-mail: infomail@agrivota.it
Internet: www.agrivota.it
Open all year round

☞—◑Holiday farm
Contrada Nucifero
Tel. 0961 917130-333 6844641
Fax 0961 917130
E-mail: info@agriturismomezzaluna.it
Internet: www.agriturismomezzaluna.it
Open all year round

Giovanni and Marisa Mauri's place is located in 35 hectares of olive groves, vineyards, fields and gardens overlooking the Savuto valley. The hamlet, once the home of peasant farmers and old farm buildings, has been refurbished and transformed into a holiday destination, with rooms and apartments located in three separate structures. Every room has a view of the Tyrrhenian Sea with a glimpse of the Stromboli volcano in the distance. Hearty breakfasts include homemade pies as well as cakes, jams, eggs, toast and cured meats. The farm restaurant, also open to non-residents, features homemade products from pasta to vinegar (a meal costs from 15-25 euros, excluding wine; half board is 46-55 euros per person and full board 71 euros). Use of the kitchen is available on request and there are discounts for children under the age of eight.

Umberto Ranieri's farm is located two kilometers from Squillace, a short distance from some of the most famous seaside resorts on the Ionian coast, like Copanello and Soverato. The rooms are located in a group of recently renovated 18th-century farmhouses. The furnishings are simple yet tasteful and the choice of colors together with exposed stone walls contribute to creating a rustic and friendly atmosphere. Breakfast is served in a separate room from the restaurant area and is usually personalized in order to satisfy each guest's requirements. For example, those with a sweet tooth can opt for typical Calabrian pastries or the usual croissants. The extensive outdoor spaces will ensure you have a relaxing stay, while the cost of a meal in the restaurant (also open to non-residents) averages 16 euros, excluding wine.

• 5 double and 3 triple rooms and 3 apartments (4 people), bathroom, fridge and television (on request) • Prices: double with single occupancy 35 euros, double 62, triple 93, apartments 31 per person; breakfast 4 euros per person • Major credit cards, Bancomat • Off-street parking, some places covered. Small pets allowed (not in the rooms). Owners always present • Restaurant. Reading and TV room. Playground, terrace. Swimming pool, boules court

• 13 double or triple rooms with bathroom, television (on request) • Prices: double room single occupancy 40-47 euros, double 62-72, triple 93-108, breakfast included• All credit cards, Bancomat • Facility accessible to the mobility challenged, 3 rooms designed for their use. Off-street parking, some of which covered. Small pets allowed. Owners always present • Restaurant. Breakfast, reading and TV room. Garden, terrace. Horse-riding, 5-a-side soccer pitch, volleyball court

PIANOPOLI
Gabella

LE CAROLEE

➡ Holiday farm
Contrada Gabella
Tel. 0968 35076-24076-200714
Fax 0968 35076
E-mail: lecarolee@lecarolee.it
Internet: www.lecarolee.it
Open all year round

As the crow flies the sea is just a few kilometers away, while in the other direction are the chestnut and alder forests covering the Mancuso and Reventino mountains. Surrounded by 42 hectares of olive groves, the two ancient farmhouses were fortified in the early 19th century and adjoining the main unit is a private chapel. The bedrooms are in one of the two buildings and feature antique furnishings. The living area is cozy and warm, and there's also a grand piano and a small library of interesting books on regional subjects that guests are free to consult. Breakfast includes hot drinks, croissants, jams, yogurt, cured meats, cheeses and toast. The restaurant offers traditional cooking, and there's a special emphasis on the use of seasonal products (meals cost 30 euros, wine excluded).

• 7 double rooms with bathroom, television, modem connection; 1 apartment (5-6 people) with kitchen • Prices: double room single occupancy 50-60 euros, double 75-95 (10 euro supplement for extra bed) breakfast included; apartment (minimum 7 nights) 1046 euros; breakfast 5 euros per person • All credit cards, Bancomat • Restaurant accessible to the mobility challenged. Off-street parking. Small pets allowed. Owners always present • Restaurant. Reading and television room, library. Garden. Swimming pool

PIZZO
Contrada Mangano

GO

🍲 Restaurant
Strada Provinciale Sant'Onofrio
Tel. 347 1137854-335 8173379
Closed Sunday dinner an Monday,
never in summer
Open: lunch and dinner
Holidays: variable between November and February
Seating: 70
Prices: 35 euros, wine excluded
All major credit cards, Bancomat

This restaurant opened recently but has already become well-known in the area, thanks to its pleasant setting and interesting food prepared with carefully selected ingredients. This, at least in part, justifies the significant increase in prices compared with those indicated last year. The restaurant is in a pleasant farmhouse, the refurbishment of which has done nothing to detract from the original features, with a terrace overlooking the Tyrrhenian Sea. The owner, Vittorio, will be your host and quite often he entertains guests with traditional Calabrian songs; there's also Massimo in the dining room and Amalia preparing the dishes – often with a personal touch – in the kitchen.
For antipasti you'll find samplings of sardines or anchovies cooked in various ways, **tuna or** spatola **bottarga** and whitebait fritters; apart from seafood there's cured meats and **fresh ricotta**. The first courses also reflect both the land and the sea, for instance **scilatelli with fish ragù**, with chopped tuna or **mutton sauce, spaghetti with neonata** or flavored with nothing more than Tropea onions, pasta with beans and potatoes or, when in season, fresh porcini mushrooms. For a main course we recommend the **mixed seafood platter** (in addition to sardines and anchovies here they mainly serve spatola and forkbeard) or meat (fillet, tagliata and fiorentina), mainly grilled. If you don't feel like either fish or meat then the **eggplant parmigiana** is always an excellent alternative. A choice of homemade tarts, cakes and Pizzo tartufo ice cream can round off your meal. The wine list includes quite a number of reasonably priced bottles from the region and the rest of Italy.

8 KM FROM CITY CENTER

AL FOCOLARE

☞ Trattoria
Via Anita Garibaldi 203
Tel. 0965 373661-349 8082577
Closed Monday
Open: dinner only
Holidays: end August
Seating: 50
Prices: 25 euros, wine excluded
Credit cards: Visa

BAYLIK

☞ Restaurant
Vico Leone 1-5
Tel. 0965 48624-338 7876375
Closed Monday
Open: lunch and dinner
Holidays: variable during summer
Seating: 80
Prices: 30-32 euros, excluding wine
All credit cards, Bancomat

There's an all-male team managing the Focolare, which was launched by three friends – Pietro in the kitchen, Basilio and Valentino running the front of house – who are traditional food enthusiasts and have also founded a cooperative, the Paleofaghi. The trattoria, just a few minutes from the center of Reggio, is pleasant and has been well designed, with a large glass panel that lets you see what's going on in the kitchen, and a veranda outside.

Dishes are basic and simple, offering quite a broad panorama of the cuisine of the Aspromonte foothills. You start with antipasti that can include **cured meats** like capocollo, soppressata, salami and guanciale; but also zucchini-flower or **baccalà fritters**, pecorino cheeses of different ages, eggplants in sweet-and-sour sauce and **bread and cheese rissoles**, prepared according to a longstanding tradition that calls for the use of stale bread. To follow, **maccaruni** made with just flour and water and in winter served with **pork crackling and toasted breadcrumbs** or, during the rest of the year, with a tasty lamb ragù. But the **zucchini and potato soup** and pasta and beans are very good. Main course meat dishes change with the season. We can recommend the **leg of lamb 'mbuttunatu**, flavored with parsley, garlic and rosemary; the involtini stuffed with smoked caciocavallo cheese; roast pork shank and **pancetta stuffed with mushrooms** served with onions in sweet-and sour-sauce. The desserts are simplicity itself: either fruit pies or chocolate or vanilla pudding.

The wine list focuses on Calabrian and Sicilian wines, although it also includes some of the top labels from other parts of southern Italy.

Here at the Baylik, continuity of management is synonymous with the high quality of the food. Take a seat in this recently renovated restaurant that Giovanni Zappia opened back in 1950 – today he's assisted by his sons Nato and Enzo – and, ignoring the non-traditional tourist menu, have a look at the regular menu. Even better, let the staff tell you what the dishes of the day are, dependent as they are on the generosity or otherwise of the sea.

The warm and cold antipasti include marinated stockfish or anchovies, swordfish carpaccio, anchovy or **spatola fritters**, **fish parmigiana** or fish polpettine either fried or with tomato sauce, mussels au gratin and **anchovy tortiera**. Among firsts, apart from some creative dishes like spaghettini with swordfish and melon, there are traditional choices like **spaghetti** with shellfish, **squid ink** or bottarga; risotto alla pescatora; **linguine alla Baylik** (with anchovies, breadcrumbs, garlic and chilli peppers) and fish soup. Mains involve various types of fish, either roast, grilled or fried. Just to give you an idea, they prepare a tasty **fritto misto**, roast swordfish or cuttlefish, amberjack with 'nduja sauce, **swordfish alla palermitana** (breaded and cooked on a red-hot slab) and skewered mussels. There are also a few meat selections.

To finish, homemade gelato and sorbets. There's an extensive wine list with about 150 labels from all over the country.

🍶 In Via Santa Caterina 87, Torrone Pasticceria Giuseppe Malavenda: mandarin and almond torroncino covered with white or bitter chocolate and traditional pignolata.

REGGIO CALABRIA
Bocale Secondo

RENDE

LA BAITA

⌒Restaurant
Viale Paolo Renosto 5
Tel. 0965 676017
Closed Tuesday, never in summer
Open: dinner, Sunday also lunch
Holidays: October-November
Seating: 60 + 80 outdoors
Prices: 22-32 euros, wine excluded
All credit cards, Bancomat

HOSTARIA DE MENDOZA

⌒Trattoria
Piazza degli Eroi 3
Tel. 0984 444022
Closed Wednesday
Open: lunch and dinner
Holidays: 3 weeks in August
Seating: 45
Prices: 25-30 euros, excluding wine
All major credit cards, Bancomat

In the past it might have seemed very strange indeed to find a mountain chalet-style building on a beach. Today it's been modified: the small bathing-beach and terraced veranda have given it more of a seaside look. There's also a award-winning pizzeria – with a separate entrance – which gives those looking for somewhere to eat here an additional option. The Riggio brothers' restaurant (where they are ably assisted by their wives and two cooks) continues to be a reliable place to stop for a well-prepared seafood meal cooked with fresh fish of the day, traditional local recipes and a level of service that is becoming more and more professional.

You'll taste local **shrimp di nassa**, either raw or lightly pan-fried, octopus alla luciana, wheat and fish salad, **neonata fish fritters** and filleted raw tuna. Among the homemade pastas, we recommend the **maccheroni with swordfish** and wild fennel, scilatelli with octopus sauce and **gnocchi al cartoccio** with mussels, clams and cockles. Fish dominates the main courses too: grouper stewed with olives and capers or baked in the oven, grilled amberjack, **spatola involtini** with sun-dried tomatoes. In winter, when fish is much harder to find, they have the maialata, a menu dedicated to pork, with grilled **pork rinds**, chops and sausages and the excellent **pork ragù** used as a sauce for the maccarruni 'i casa. Desserts are traditional: chocolate salami, dried figs dusted with cinnamon and stuffed with ricotta.

Herb-flavored breads (cooked in the pizza oven), cured meats and typical cheeses complete the offer. There's a nice list of olive oils, Italian wines and liqueurs.

Rende is divided into two parts that clearly reflect the two stages of its existence. Up on a hilltop and reachable by elevators and escalators is the old village, dominated by the Norman castle: in the plain below there's the new town. It's in the historic center, in a well-restored 16th-century palazzo, that you'll find the recently inaugurated Hostaria de Mendoza, now in our guide for the second year. It is making a name for itself and continues to be managed by Ettore and Elisa, both of whom have considerable experience as he was a chef on cruise ships and she was a hotel manager. Overall there have been few changes in the meat- and vegetable-based menu, although there's now a wider choice of first courses. The antipasti are rather basic and include **prosciutto with Crotone pecorino**, goat's milk cheese with honey, artichoke hearts and truffle fonduta. For firsts you can have homemade pasta filled with pumpkin and prosciutto with cream of pumpkin and, also handmade, **tagliatelle** with black truffles or **Sila porcini mushrooms**, **pappardelle with wild boar ragù** and **mezzelune with a game filling**. You can then continue with either Italian or some Argentinean meat dishes, such as **bocconcini of wild boar**, **herb-flavored breaded lamb chops** and pork fillet with mashed potatoes. In addition to millefoglie with a cream or hazelnut filling and tarts with homemade jams, in autumn you can also find stuffed figs.

The wine list continues to focus on wines from the region and the rest of Italy.

62 KM NORTHEAST OF REGGIO CALABRIA   88 KM NORTHEAST OF COSENZA

OSTERIA CAMPAGNOLA DELLA SPINA

Trattoria
Contrada Audelleria 2
Tel. 0966 580223
Closed Monday
Open: lunch only
Holidays: August 16 – September 15
Seating: 40 + 20 outdoors
Prices: 24 euros
No credit cards accepted

LE COLLINE DEL GELSO

Holiday farm
Contrada Gelso Mazzei 18
Tel. 0983 569136-335 5366452-338 4289504
Fax 0983 569136
E-mail: info@lecollinedelgelso.it
Internet: www.lecollinedelgelso.it
Open all year round

To welcome you to this authentic trattoria, open only at lunchtime and mainly frequented by workers from the surrounding area, you'll find Carmelo Rosina, helped in the dining room by her brother-in-law. Once you're seated inside, or better still under the shady pergola, you'll be ready to taste the genuine seasonal dishes prepared by Domenica.

Start with a plate of homemade **cured meats**, such as capocollo and soppressata, and fresh **ricotta** served fresh in its basket. But there are certainly many alternatives: eggplant rissoles, pieces of **fried baccalà**, stuffed chilli peppers, friselle with sun-dried tomatoes, fried zucchini flowers, anchovies with lemon. In winter try the **cime di rapa and bean soup** with its slightly bitter taste, cooked in a clay pot just like the chickpea soup also. Instead in summer we can recommend the rigatoni with zucchini and squash flowers. Often you'll find penne alla campagnola with provola and vegetables and handmade **maccaruni** with porcini mushrooms or an artichoke, eggplant or tomato sauce. The **stockfish**, either **stewed** or roasted, is served every day, whereas if you want **stuffed ventricelle** with breadcrumbs, olives, capers and pecorino you'll have to go on a Friday. Otherwise opt for the grilled sausages, pork chops and **pig's livers**. Lastly, there's fresh fruit or almond cookies to dip in Vin Santo.

In addition to your antipasto, first and main course and desserts, the modest price also includes house wine and a digestivo glass of nocino or limoncello.

This farm located in a peaceful country setting conveniently close to the Ionian coast. The rooms and suites are in a country house built in the 18th century and in a few rustic buildings refurbished utilizing quality materials. Some of the rooms have a little private garden, but there is also a communal garden perfect for relaxing. The interiors are tastefully styled: terracotta floors, freshly painted walls, wrought-iron beds and beautiful furniture with a dark wood finish; the living rooms are decorated with carpets, plants and paintings. Breakfast offers a good variety of sweet and savory fare, with the aim of promoting local products. A half-board option is available (62-75 euros per person). The cost of a suite ranges from 36-56 euros per person, and the minimum stay in August is one week.

•4 double rooms and 5 suites (4 people), bathroom, mini-bar, television; 2 rooms with air-conditioning, suites with kitchenette • Prices: double room single occupancy 43-65 euros, double 68-104, breakfast included • Major credit cards, Bancomat • Facility accessible to the mobility challenged. Off-street parking. Small pets allowed. Owners always contactable • Restaurant (residents only). Lounges. Garden, fitness course. Horse-riding

ROSSANO
Scalo

SAN GIORGIO MORGETO

88 KM NORTHEAST OF COSENZA

75 KM NORTHEAST OF REGGIO CALABRIA, ON A 3 OR SS 118, 111 AND 536

PARIDÒ

LA SCALETTA

◯ Trattoria
Via dei Normanni
Tel. 0983 290731
Closed Sunday
Open: lunch and dinner
Holidays: variable
Seating: 80
Prices: 24-27 euros, wine excluded
All credit cards, Bancomat

◯ Trattoria
Via Florimo 14
Tel. 0966 946390
Closed Tuesday, never in summer
Open: lunch and dinner
Holidays: end September to mid-October
Seating: 80 + 40 outdoors
Prices: 20-22 euros, wine excluded
All credit cards, Bancomat

You'll find Paridò only when you leave the Byzantine part of Rossano, with its churches of San Marco and the Panaghia, and move on to the modern section overlooking the sea. The trattoria is capably managed by Pietro Giovanni Rizzuti, who is constantly occupied with a search for old recipes, whether for dishes served at aristocratic tables or popular traditional ones, which he then reinterprets in a respectful manner.

The **battered and fried ricotta** makes a good starter or alternatively there's a sampling of seasonal vegetables cooked in any way Pietro feels like that day (one specialty worth trying is the **eggplant rissoles**) or seafood antipasti like marinated anchovies and **baby cuttlefish in cassuola** (with peppers and onions). There's almost always a new dish among the firsts like gnocchi with a pumpkin and porcini mushroom sauce in the fall. Often the pasta dishes have a mix of seafood and vegetables for a sauce (for instance, farfalle with swordfish and eggplants, with shrimp and rocket, or winter **soups with shellfish and beans**). In other dishes seafood stars alone, as in **spaghetti with anchovies** or gnocchi with shellfish. To follow, fish soup, **spatola involtini**, fillets of various types of fish cooked with citrus fruit, **anchovies scattiate** and baccalà with potatoes. The desserts are always special, whether the orange- or peach-flavored tiramisù, Christmas treats like crustuli pastiera at Easter.

In addition to the house wine, the cellar contains some good Calabrian, Sicilian and Campanian bottles to accompany your meal.

Certain interesting changes have brightened up the menu at this typical trattoria in San Giorgio, run in a capable friendly manner by the Ligato brothers. While the location is well inland from Reggio, in the northwestern corner of the Parco dell'Aspromonte, you'll sometimes find simple but tasty seafood dishes on the menu.

These could include seafood salad and marinated anchovies, in addition to the already numerous dishes based on **stockfish**. As for the latter, it's the star ingredient in La Scaletta's cuisine and a theme menu running from the antipasti through to the main course. You can have it **raw in a salad**, as a sauce for linguine and, as a main course, **alla ghiotta** (with tomatoes, capers, black olives, parsley and oregano), cooked **with garlic and amareii** (turnip tops), fried and accompanied by peppers. But you can also count on other authentic dishes that faithfully represent the territory. Fritters of seasonal vegetables, sun-dried tomatoes and eggplants in olive oil, capocollo and **fresh ricotta** are all common antipasti. Then pasta and beans or homemade **maccaruni with a goat ragù**, followed by barbecued **lamb** and **kid**. To close, a slice of local pecorino or simple homemade desserts like fruit tarts and tiramisù. Pizzas cooked in the wood-fired oven are served every evening.

Included in the price there's a more-than-acceptable house wine produced from local grapes. Otherwise you can choose one of cellar's bottles from Calabria or elsewhere in Italy.

SANTA SEVERINA
Puzelle

SCALEA

LE PUZELLE

LA RONDINELLA

🗝️⚬ Holiday farm
Località Puzelle, SS 107 bis
Tel. 0962 51004-338 1834387-338 9281377
Fax 0962 23983
E-mail: lepuzelle@libero.it
Internet: www.lepuzelle.it
Closed for 15 days in November

🍲 Restaurant with rooms
Piazza Principe Spinelli 1
Tel. 0985 91360
Closed Sunday, never in summer
Open: lunch and dinner
Holidays: none
Seating: 50 + 15 outdoors
Prices: 28-30 euros, wine excluded
All credit cards, Bancomat

This agriturismo is surrounded by a vast estate planted with olive trees, vineyards, citrus trees and vegetables. The farmhouse was built at the beginning of the 20th century and the original barn and stables have been converted to form seven differently sized rooms and two spacious dining areas. The rooms, with beautiful terracotta floors, wooden ceilings and rustic furnishings, all share a common balcony that overlooks the peaceful countryside. Breakfast is very filling and includes freshly squeezed juices, fresh fruit, croissants, jams and homemade cakes, in addition to hot drinks. The restaurant mainly focuses on ingredients produced on the farm itself (a meal costs 17 euros, wine excluded). During their holiday guests may relax in the swimming pool area or even decide to go for an excursion on horseback; don't skip a visit to the village of Santa Severina, with its Byzantine and Norman architecture.

• 4 double rooms and 3 quadruples, bathroom, several rooms with balcony, television • Prices: double room single occupancy 28-35 euros, double 56-70, triple 70-85, quadruple 90-110, breakfast included • Credit cards: CartaSi, MC, Visa • Communal areas accessible to the mobility challenged. Off-street parking. Small pets allowed. Owners always present • Bar, restaurant. Reading and television room. Garden, terrace. Swimming pool, horse riding

After restructuring a room adjacent to the restaurant, the Rondinella has doubled its internal capacity – a change that Anna's regular customers appreciate. As ever she's assisted in the dining room by her husband Ciriaco and daughter Francesca and the formula remains the same: mixed antipasti (15 to 20 different kinds) two first courses and a mixed platter with five or six deserts. There's no main course, unless it's booked in advance, but with all of the other delicacies served no one really seems to miss it. And as the dishes change daily all that we can give is an indication of what might be available.
As mentioned, the antipasti are very generous: a serving of cured meats (capocollo, soppressata and prosciutto), local cheeses and **tartine** with a pumpkin and fennelseed sauce, arugula or hot spicy neonata. Then trays will be brought to the table and you just help yourself: peppers with anchovies, potatoes or baccalà; fritters; mushrooms; vegetables in olive oil; **baccalà with Savoy cabbage** or **fried with dried peppers** and roasted eggplants. You might feel that at this point you've had enough. However, the first courses are not to be missed: **fusilli** with cacioricotta or **with 'nduja**; **tagliolini** with chickpeas, beans or **tender fava beans and shavings of pecorino**; **parmigiana of eggplant** or Savoy cabbage; pasta grattata and many more treats. If you wish you can phone them to book a roast, but make sure you save room for desserts like **lime-flavored tiramisù**, stuffed figs and panna cotta with lime or chestnuts.
The wines and liqueurs are homemade, and if you wish you can stay overnight in one of the ten rooms they have in the center of Scalea.

SCILLA

ALLA PESCATORA

🍲 Restaurant
Lungomare Colombo 32
Tel. 0965 754147
Closed Wednesday, never in August
Open: lunch and dinner
Holidays: mid-December to the beginning of February
Seating: 75 + 30 outdoors
Prices: 30-33 euros, wine excluded
All credit cards, Bancomat

In the waters between Scilla and Cariddi fishermen still go out in their traditional feluche (boats with a long gangplank extending from the bow where a crew member stands ready to harpoon a fish) to capture swordfish. This very old and exciting form of fishing is an important factor in the local economy. But Michele Donato, the long-term host at this famous restaurant on the seafront, doesn't just get his ingredients from them, he also buys from all kinds of other fishing boats that land their catch – with fish to suit every taste – on Scilla's beaches.

For antipasti you'll find a seafood salad, with octopus, mussels and shrimp; **buccuni** (similar to sea snails) flavored with a spicy tomato sauce; **mussels au gratin** and shrimp cocktail. There will also be some types of smoked fish sourced from local producers. Then it's the turn of their tasty **linguine alla pescatora** (with mussels, clams, squid and swordfish) or linguine with a swordfish sauce, excellent **tagliatelle with red shrimp**, **risotto alla ghiotta** or with shrimp and arugula. For a main course you can choose from a crispy fritto misto, a fish from the day's catch either baked or grilled and, of course, **swordfish** that can be cooked a bagnomaria, roasted or **in involtini**. Lastly, homemade desserts such as tiramisù and lemon mousse.

The wine list offers a wide selection with a special focus on southern Italian labels.

🍯 **Bagnara Calabra** (9 km) is the regional capital of nougat, which you can buy in all of its forms, including chocolate, from Cardone (Via Don Minzoni) or Careri (Via Nazionale, 264), two pastry shops that also have a number of other Calabrian specialties.

SELLIA MARINA
La Petrizia

ALLA VECCHIA OSTERIA U NOZZULARU

🍲 Trattoria
Località La Petrizia, SS 106
Tel. 0961 969854-328 2630784
Clodes Monday, never in summer
Open: dimmer, festivities and in summer also for lunch
Holidays: 20 days in October
Seating: 80 + 60 outdoors
Prices: 18-25 euros, excluding wine
All credit cards, Bancomat

Agriculture is important in and around Sellia Marina: pastures that feed cows and, above all, sheep and goats; peach orchards; citrus fruit orchards and vegetable gardens provide the ingredients for a cuisine that, despite the nearness of the sea, draws very heavily on the flavors of the land. The olives are not to be missed, whether eaten straight or in the form of oil. And it's in an old storehouse for olive husks and nozzuli (olive stones) that the Camastra family (Peppino front of house, Antonia and Adolfo in the kitchen) have created their trattoria. A trattoria that's changing in terms of structure – this year they've added an outdoor area for use in good weather – but not in terms of concept. In fact the Camastras continue to rely on local produce, often enhanced by their own olive oil.

Fish has, however, elbowed its way into the menu, as can be seen by the **whitebait fritters** and toast with Calabrian caviar (sardella). Still for antipasti (but also as a main dish) there are the focaccias and **pizze pizzicate** cooked in a wood-fired oven. For first course try the handmade **scilatelle** normally served with a **ragù calabrese**. Main courses are usually local meats: rabbit, sausages, **kid alla tiana**, **roast lamb**, goat. But vegetables and beans are always present: **chickpeas flavored with wild fennel**, beans, fava beans and cicerchie cooked slowly in a clay pot. There's a small selection of homemade desserts Take your pick from the bottles on display in a refrigerated cabinet or on the racks; there's a good regional selection.

SERRASTRETTA

34 KM NORTHWEST OF CATANZARO

PARCO PINGITORE

🍲 Restaurant
Contrada Monache
Tel. 0968 81071
Closed Tuesday
Open: lunch and dinner
Holidays: none
Seating: 80 + 40 outdoors
Prices: 20-25 euros, wine excluded
No credit cards

The walls of this popular eating place are decorated with photographs, farming implements and bottles of wine from all over Italy. Who knows if these decorations will remain at the new address, Contrada Tavernisi 1, where Delfino Maruca, his wife Annarita and their two children will move at the end of 2006. The place will change its name to Vecchio Castagno, but the number of covers, rustic style and telephone numbers will stay the same.

The owners promise the cooking won't change either. Antipasti: olives, **ricottina nella fuscella**, local Pecorino, 'gelatina' and home-cured meats, such as **soppressata di Decollatura** (Slow Food Presidium). First courses: **tagliatelle with nettles and porcini mushrooms**, linguine with wild fennel and walnut pesto, **chestnut flour tagliolini** with ricotta and walnuts, tagliolini with elder and broccoli, pumpkin and pulse soup. The finest mains feature pork: sausage with potatoes, chops with chestnuts and, in winter, **frittole**. Or alternatively, **breaded lamb cutlets with herbs**, lamb with walnuts and **baccalà du zucculiare** (a dish which used to be made in the fall for peasants engaged in crushing chestnuts with their wooden clogs, 'zoccoli'), mixed grill and **trout 'al cartoccio'**. Side dishes include **patate 'mpacchiate**. At the end of the meal, fruit crostatas, chestnut pralines with chocolate and rum, granulata of prickly pears or arbutus, and chestnut mousse. Try the home-made infusions too.

SIDERNO
Siderno Superiore

101 KM NORTHEAST OF REGGIO CALABRIA, 14 KM FROM LOCRI SS 106

ZIO SALVATORE

🍲 Trattoria
Via Annunziata 1-3
Tel. 0964 385330
Closed Tuesday
Open: lunch and dinner
Holidays: variable
Seating: 100 + 50 outdoors
Prices: 16-20 euros, wine excluded
All major credit cards, Bancomat

If it weren't for the fact that this place seats around 100 diners, plus another 50 on the veranda, you might think you were eating in a private house. No frills, dishes inspired by the day's fresh ingredients, genuine flavors and a magnificent view over the Ionian Sea with a panorama stretching from Cape Bruzzano to Stilo Point. Present owner Giuseppe Fragomeni continues in the tradition established by his uncle Salvatore, who founded this trattoria. Giuseppe has done nothing to change the philosophy laid down by his uncle.

Start with eggplants, either roasted, in olive oil, pickled or stuffed; salami and hot spicy soppressata; pecorino cheeses at various points of maturity from their home store; anchovies arriganate; eggplant or zucchini-flower fritters and stuffed peppers. As a first course there's **maccaruni 'i casa**, with a pork meatball ragù, **goat**, **schiocca cherry tomatoes** (the ones hung up in bunches) lightly grilled and flavored with fresh extra-virgin olive oil or **soppressata and eggplants**. The meat-based seconds – **goat stew**, roast **pork** or **al sugo with meatballs**, roast lamb – are accompanied by side plates of green vegetables, potatoes, chickpeas and beans or fresh salads. Although the **roast stockfish** flavored with olives and chilli pepper isn't always available, it's not to be missed if you do happen to see it on the menu. Desserts are homemade, and can vary from tarts and Christmas sanmartine to **zeppole** with sugar or honey.

In the cellar they have a house wine made from a local grape variety. This is the only wine available and it's included in the price of your meal.

SIMERI CRICHI

Apostolello

6 KM NORTHEAST OF CATANZARO

LA BOTTEGACCIA

🍲 Trattoria
Contrada Apostolello 43
Tel. 0961 799185-339 3321764
Closed Sunday dinner, in August
Sunday for lunch
Open: lunch and dinner
Holidays: variable
Seating: 70 + 20 outdoors
Prices: 15-20 euros, wine excluded
All credit cards except DC, Bancomat

This trattoria run by Anna Guarnieri – with help from her family – has figured in our guide for a number of years. This is because the food is always reliable, focusing on traditional Calabrian family-style dishes and especially dishes based on products from the family vegetable garden. It seems the restaurant has recently attracted a new type of public, mostly local youngsters who often forgo the habitual pizza to taste a few old-style dishes, all at very reasonable prices.

To start, antipasti comprising vegetables cooked in many different ways, cured meats like **capocollo** and soppressata, pecorino cheese and preserves in olive oil, among which we can recommend the **wild artichokes** and round chili peppers stuffed with tuna and herbs. All of this accompanied with durum wheat bread they make themselves in a wood-fired oven. Anna is an expert 'knitter' and for years now has been making large quantities of **scilatelli**, which can be served with a pork ragù, a rich **meatball sauce** or other seasonal condiments. But the soups are just as tasty; among them the star is **fagiolata alla pignata**, where the taste of the beans is enhanced by sausage with chopped heart and lung in the pork mix. Then a dish that's an icon of Catanzaro-area cuisine, **morzello** (giblets lightly fried then cooked slowly for a long time in a spicy tomato sauce) that you eat in pitta bread. This dish alone makes a filling meal. Good alternatives are the eggplant or zucchini parmigiana (very rich, with tomatoes, provola cheese, eggs and soppressata) and **'a tiana**. Lastly, tarts, tiramisù and a selection of homemade liqueurs. You can either drink the red they produce themselves or one of the regional wines on offer.

SPEZZANO DELLA SILA

Camigliatello Silano

31 KM EAST OF COSENZA SS 107

LA TAVERNETTA

🍲 Restaurant
Contrada Campo San Lorenzo 14
Tel. 0984 579026
Closed Wednesday
Open: lunch and dinner
Holidays: November 20 – December 10
Seating: 80
Prices: 30-35 euros, excluding wine
All credit cards, Bancomat

The owner of this well-established restaurant on the northern slopes of the Sila Grande, Pietro Lecce, is certainly not resting on his laurels. As well as a capable restaurant owner we could also say he's an all-round businessman, given the ongoing investments he is making to improve his premises. Recently he's bought a hotel near the restaurant that's been closed for some time and, while waiting for completion of the restructuring, he's extended the kitchens and cellar with an adjacent wine-tasting room. Here, surrounded by about 750 Italian labels and 250 foreign ones, you can enjoy an aperitivo accompanied by warm grissini before taking your seat in the dining room (there's one room reserved for smokers).

The various types of Sila **wild mushrooms** (porcini, finferli and, now rather rare, royal agarics) play an essential role in the antipasti: in addition to good salads, **porcini mushroom soufflé** with crema di moro (a medium aged cow's milk cheese), pancotto with cherry tomatoes and porcini mushrooms. To follow, **fratto di fave** with finferli and pesto, **chestnut-flour sfogliatine with finferli ragù**, tagliolini with finferli flowers, saffron and porcini mushrooms and, as an alternative to pasta, bean and porcini soup. For your main course there's meat cooked in various ways: **roast suckling pig**, leg of lamb stuffed with guanciale and pecorino, blackcurrant-flavored stewed venison and **boccone reale** (fillet steak with porcini mushroom caps). **Porcini** also feature roasted, **breaded** or with garlic.

A special mention goes to the desserts, which are often based on the figs known as **fico dottato cosentino** (Slow Food Presidia).

STALETTÌ
Copanello

TORRE DI RUGGIERO
San Basile

27 KM SOUTH OF CATANZARO

53 KM SOUTHWEST OF CATANZARO

HAMILTON

I BASILIANI

🗝️ 3-Star Hotel
Piazzetta Falcone 8
Tel. and fax 0961 910808
E-mail: hotel.hamilton@tiscalinet.it
Open all year round

🗝️ Holiday farm
Contrada San Basile
Tel. 0967 938000-349 3675463
Fax 0967 938000
E-mail: info@ibasiliani.com
Internet: www.ibasiliani.com
Open from Easter until end of October

Copanello lies on the Ionian coast of Calabria to the south of the bay of Squillace: the rocky coastline boasts a multitude of grottos and coves, uncontaminated waters and a headland exuding the aromas of Mediterranean vegetation. The Hamilton is located on the main Ionian coast road in this charming setting and is exactly the right spot to relax in tune with nature and an enchanting marine landscape. The rooms are comfortable and equipped with modern furnishings, and all have a view of the bay. From the terrace there's a view that sweeps from Punta Alice to Monasterace. Breakfast is traditional and includes coffee, tea, milk, fresh drinks, croissants and jams.

•7 double rooms with bathroom, air-conditioning, mini-bar, television, several rooms with terrace • Prices: double room single occupancy 55-100 euros, double 80-100, breakfast included • Credit cards: all, Bancomat • Adjacent free public parking. No pets allowed. Reception open 24 hours a day • Breakfast and reading rooms. Terrace. Beach 400 meters away.

This facility run by Marina Martelli lies in 35 hectares of woods and organically cultivated gardens and orchards, and offers guests the choice of two options for their stay. Double rooms are in the farmhouse, an old building with two floors, whilst the apartments are located in more modern buildings in the village. Breakfast consists of locally produced fare such as fruit, jams and pastries, as well as ricotta and other local cheeses. There are many ways to relax: guests can use the swimming pool, formerly an irrigation basin, or make use of the extensive communal areas. The restaurant offers regional vegetable and meat dishes (meals range from 25-35 euros, including beverages, and the cost for guests is 25 euros).

• 8 double rooms with bathroom, several rooms with fridge; 5 apartments (2-4 people) with kitchenette or separate kitchen • Prices: double room single occupancy 40-60 euros, double 54-76 (16-20 euro supplement for extra bed), breakfast included; apartments 250-700 euros a week; breakfast 3 euros per person • All credit cards, Bancomat • 1 room designed for use by the mobility challenged. Off-street parking. Small pets allowed. Owners always present • Restaurant. Reading and television room. Garden. Swimming pool

OSTERIA DEL PESCATORE

Trattoria
Via del Monte 7
Tel. 0963 603018-347 5318989
No closing days
Open: dinner, in summer also for lunch
Holidays: end-October to end-March
Seating: 36 + 12 outdoors
Prices: 20-24 euros, wine excluded
No credit cards

ANTICA OSTERIA VECCHIA VILLA

Trattoria-pizzeria
Via Garibaldi 104-piazza della Stazione
Tel. 0965 751125-795670
Closed Sunday
Open: lunch and dinner
Holidays: 15 days in August
Seating: 70 + 25 outdoors
Prices: 21-25 euros, wine excluded
All credit cards except AE, Bancomat

Although the name of this trattoria in the center of Tropea refers to a fisherman – Gaetano to be exact – in fact it's run by sisters Anna, Rosalba and Francesca. However their father's contribution to the success of the place can't be overlooked, In fact, it's Gaetano who supplies the ingredients every day, which are then transformed in the kitchen and served up on the few tables in this unpretentious trattoria. While the sea certainly dominates, there are also some good local vegetables and a few meat dishes that make an appearance on the blackboard which details the day's menu.

The **'nduja**, a very hot, spicy sausage spread and a symbol of Calabrian cuisine can make a good antipasti, but also a tasty sauce for pasta. But if you just want to eat fish, start with **octopus salad** or shellfish salad, then continue with **spaghetti with sardine sauce** or a swordfish and tomato sauce. The **sardine soup** fried and then mixed with a sauce containing garlic, red pepper and marjoram can either be your first or main course. Good alternatives are the mixed grilled or fried platters that include less refined fish such as anchovies and **spatola**. Otherwise start with **spaghetti with Tropea red onions** or **alla tropeana**, with peppers, zucchini and eggplants. Then roast or stuffed eggplants and peppers or a rich **Tropea-style salad**. Among the few desserts usually available you can try the hazelnut tartufo and the mostaccioli, very crunchy cookies to be dipped in Zibibbo wine.

You can drink either the red or white house wine, or one of the few regional and Sicilian wines in the cellar.

In addition to the pleasantly furnished rooms inside, decorated with old photos of the straits separating Calabria from Sicily, this trattoria has recently added a small outdoor space. Outside there's now also room for barbecuing fish or meat. Apart from these pleasant innovations, the menu, with a bilingual description of the dishes, remains true to itself. Owners Angelo and Francesco place a lot of emphasis on seasonal vegetables – especially eggplants, using even the skins, which are pickled – which they use to prepare typical local dishes.

The buffet of antipasti includes various kinds of fritters, olives preserved in oil, stuffed peppers, **eggplant involtini** (stuffed with capers, olives, stale bread and grated pecorino), **caponata** and stockfish either raw or in salad. Then it's the turn of the **maccaruni a sipala**, with a vegetable and salted ricotta ragù, cooked in the oven in a clay pot covered with pizza dough, or pacchiri (like rigatoni, but wider and longer) chi cacciofuli and **schiaffittuni a viddota** (rolls of fresh pasta stuffed with eggplant or, in winter, with sausage). Then you continue with grilled dishes: the typical **stockfish alla trappitara**, cooked with olives, potatoes, capers and tomatoes or, if you prefer meat, the cosciottu 'i porcu.

You can accompany your meal with one of the local and regional wines on the list, although the house wine served in a carafe makes a valid alternative.

In **Reggio Calabria** (11 km), in the hamlet of Catona, Sol.Mar. produces Bergamino, an excellent liqueur made with bergamot.

SICILIA

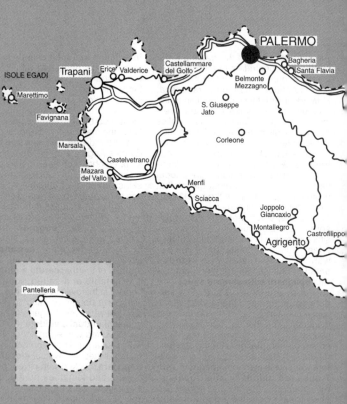

ISOLE EGADI

Marettimo

Favignana

Trapani
Erice Valderice

Castellammare
del Golfo

PALERMO

Bagheria
Santa Flavia

Belmonte
Mezzagno

S. Giuseppe
Jato

Corleone

Marsala

Castelvetrano

Mazara
del Vallo

Menfi

Sciacca

Joppolo
Giancaxio

Montallegro

Castrofilippo

Agrigento

Ustica

Pantelleria

MAR MEDITERRANEO

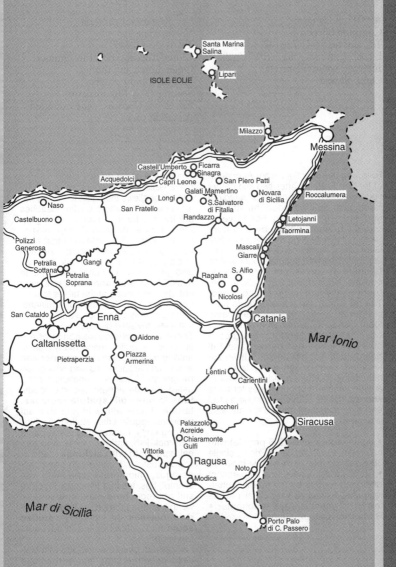

ACQUEDOLCI

VILLA NICETTA

🔑Holiday farm
Contrada Nicetta
Tel. and fax 0941 726142
E-mail: agriturismovillanicetta@virgilio.it
Internet: www.villanicetta.it
Open all year

Following the directions from Acquedolci for San Fratello, after two kilometers you'll reach this agriturismo, situated in a farmhouse built between the late 17th and early 18th centuries. For 11 years now it's been managed by Salvatore Salmeri, his wife Nina and their children Gabriella, Cettina and Gerry. The rooms are furnished with antique country-style furniture. Breakfast consists of jams, cookies, home-made ciambellone, Nebrodi honey and home-baked bread. The restaurant, which is open to non-residents by reservytion, offers tasty local dishes. Guests can make use of two shared refrigerators; half board costs 55 euros per person and full board, 65 euros per person. Given the location, guests can enjoy both the mountains and the seaside, and there's a wide variety of opportunities for tours and excursions. Bicycles can be rented and excursions on horseback are also organized

• 6 mini-apartments (2-6 people) with bathroom; 2 with kitchen • Prices: single 38 euros, double 76, breakfast included • Credit cards: none • 1 mini-apartment designed for use by the mobility challenged. Off-street parking. Small pets allowed. Owners always reachable. • Restaurant. Lounge. Garden

AEOLIAN ISLANDS
Lipari
Pianoconte

LE MACINE

🍲Restaurant-pizzeria
Via Stradale 5
Tel. 090 9822387
Closed Tuesday, never in summer
Open: lunch and dinner
Holidays: in February
Seating: 80 + 150 outdoors
Prices: 33-35 euros, wine excluded
All credit cards

The largest of the Aolian Islands, Lipari offers visitors many itineraries of cultural interest or allows them just to admire nature in a setting where pristine beaches are the outstanding feature. Going up the hill, near the San Calogero spa, you'll come to this restaurant that happens to house an interesting collection of traditional farm implements. You can also get here on the free transport made available by the owner, Giovanni, who coordinates service at the tables together with his wife Tina and son Emiliano. The cuisine is based on seafood with just a few revisited dishes.

There's a surprising selection of antipasti in the buffet: many, many dishes, among which marinated grouper and swordfish carpaccio spiced with green pepper and luvaro and anchovies marinated in apple vinegar, sliced octopus, **tuna in olive oil**, **spatola roulades**, tartare of tuna with wild fennel, roast peppers, eggplant flan, stuffed zucchini. Among firsts, outstanding is the pasta with rock-fish, shrimp, olives, wild fennel; **spaghetti with alalunga**, capers, dried tomatoes; bavette with clams, asparagus, onion grass; spaghetti with scampi, figs, toasted almonds. If you've still got room for a main course then worth trying are the grilled **luvaro imperiale roulades**, the Lipari-style **stuffed squid** and, when booked in advance, fish soup.

For dessert, peach semifreddo with Malvasia or with orange and bergamotto cream. A nice selection of Sicilian labels, including quite a good wine they produce themselves from local grape varieties.

AEOLIAN ISLANDS
Lipari

41 KM FROM MESSINA + FERRYBOAT

AEOLIAN ISLANDS
Santa Marina Salina
Lingua

41 KM FROM MESSINA + FERRY

ORIENTE

3-Star Hotel
Via Marconi 35
Tel. 090 9811493
Fax 090 9880198
E-mail: info@hotelorientelipari.com
Internet: www.hotelorientelipari.com
Closed in November and December

'A CANNATA

Restaurant
Via Umberto I 13
Tel. 090 9843161
No closing day
Open: lunch and dinner
Holidays: none
Seating: 120 + 200 outdoors
Prices: 30-33 euros, wine excluded
All credit cards

The Oriente Hotel is in a quiet central area, in the archeological park of Contrada Diana, 50 meters from the main road and 300 from the port. The rooms are airy and all have private bathrooms. There's a generously varied continental-style buffet breakfast that can be eaten in a Mediterranean garden. The spacious veranda is equipped with a maxi-screen TV, cable TV and a video recorder. Further facilities are a large, panoramic solarium and a snack bar that offers cold snacks. Although the hotel doesn't have its own restaurant it has agreements with some local eateries in the vicinity.

• 2 single and 30 double rooms, with bathroom, air-conditioning, balcony or terrace, fridge, safe, television • Prices: single 40-80 euros, double 60-130 (25-40 euro supplement for extra bed), breakfast included • Credit cards: all, Bancomat • Off-street parking. Small pets allowed. Reception open 24 hours a day • Bar. Reading room, TV room. Conference room. Veranda. Garden, solarium

Of the seven islands in the Aeolian group, declared a world heritage site by UNESCO, Salina is richest in terms of vegetation, with woods that go right up to the craters of its extinct volcanoes. The island's name, which derives from the salt beds closed long ago in the hamlet of Lingua, is where the Ruggera family have been running their restaurant for over twenty years. Concetta and her daughters Angela and Franca take care of the kitchen while her son Santino handles the tables, which in summer are also set in a large outdoor space.
Among the antipasti we can suggest the **octopus salad**, marinated anchovies, botargo with figs, mussels alla marinara and various preserves in olive oil they make themselves, including cucunci, that is, capers (a Slow Food Presidia). In the selection of first courses we should mention the **pasta alla cucunciata**, **spaghetti all'eoliana** with a tuna, eggplant, caper and olive sauce, linguine with dried tomatoes, baked ricotta and onion, spaghetti del 'postino', a tribute to the film 'Il postino – The postman' starring Massimo Troisi that was shot on the island. Depending on the day's catch, if available try the **paddlefish cutlet**, **sea urchin in sweet-and-sour sauce**, stewed grouper, **stuffed squid** alla Malvasia. For side plates there are tasty peppers with breadcrumbs and apple, grilled eggplant with finely chopped capers, chard with raisins, black olives, pine nuts and capers.
For dessert, almond semifreddo and, sometimes, the traditional cookies – spicchitedda and sfinci d'ova. The collection of labels available includes typical wines produced on the island, among which the famous Malvasia.

AGRIGENTO
San Leone

AIDONE

LEON D'ORO

🍲 Restaurant
Viale Emporium 102
Tel. 0922 414400
Closed Monday
Open: lunch and dinner
Holidays: variable in winter
Seating: 90 + 110 outdoors
Prices: 35 euros, wine excluded
All credit cards

CASALE BELMONTINO

🔑 Holiday farm
Contrada Belmontino Soprano
Tel. 348 2590132
Fax 348 2502229
E-mail: info@casalebelmontino.it
Internet: www.casalebelmontino.it
Open all year

After a must visit to the Valley of the Temples, we suggest you take a break in this restaurant near San Leone beach. Opened in 1981, it's managed by brothers Vittorio and Totò Collura with sound support in the kitchen from chef Calogero Fortunato. Take a seat in the pleasant rooms indoors or in summer outside and you'll find a menu that has both traditional dishes and some interesting new creations.

Among the antipasti we can recommend the mussels with tomato sauce and parsley, marinated red mullet and anchovies, tuna roulades and vegetable pesto, moscardini and sea snails. Moving on to your first course, nice fresh Agrigento-style **pasta with pilchards**, **caserecce with swordfish and pistacchio nuts**, **bavette with red mullet ragù**, wild fennel and fava bean macco. Other suggestions are the spaghetti with clams, risotto alla marinara, rotolini with a prawn, vegetable and aged pecorino sauce. Depending on what's available in the market, the choice of main courses can include **stuffed swordfish chops**, **hake with anchovy sauce**, sardines and anchovies alla vastedda, excellent fresh fish cooked in sea salt or grilled aiole, prai, red mullet or dentex. Among the few meat dishes, a nice veal fillet with carrube pesto.

There's quite a good selection of Sicilian cheeses and delicious home-made puddings, like Ribera orange cream cake, Sicilian cassatina, almond and basil-flavored semifreddi. The wine list is excellent too.

Inland from Enna is this old, completely restructured farmhouse with well furnished rooms that include Caltagirone chandeliers and ceramics. The facility has a swimming pool and guests can also try their hand at archery and ride on horseback up to the nearby Lake Ogliastro. This makes an ideal base for excursions to the Roman villa in Piazza Armerina and the Morgantina archeological site. Mellina Dani, manager of this vacation farm where they speak fluent English and French, will be happy to provide information and suggest visits in the environs. In the spacious common dining room you can taste traditional dishes prepared with vegetables from the garden and meat from the animals they raise on the farm. For breakfast, you'll also be offered organic jams, fresh ricotta and other cheeses (you can visit their dairy if you wish). Half board costs 55 euros and full board 70 euros per person.

• 3 single, 10 double, 3 triple rooms and 7 with four beds, with bathroom, air-conditioning, mini-bar, safe, TV • Prices: single 40 euros, double 80, triple 120, four-bed 160, breakfast included • Credit cards: major ones, Bancomat • Facility accessible to the mobility challenged, 1 room designed for their use. Off-street parking. Small pets allowed. Owners always reachable. • Restaurant. TV room, reading room. Pool, archery, horse-riding

BAGHERIA

BELMONTE MEZZAGNO

16 KM SOUTHEAST OF PALERMO EXIT A 19

17 KM SOUTHEAST OF PALERMO

DON CICCIO

ITALIANO CIBUS

Trattoria
Via del Cavaliere 87
Tel. 091 932442
Closed Wednesday and Sunday
Open: lunch and dinner
Holidays: August
Seating: 80
Prices: 25 euros, wine excluded
All major credit cards

Trattoria
Piazza Martiri d'Ungheria 14
Tel. 091 8720397
Closed Tuesday
Open: lunch and dinner
Holidays: August
Seating: 50
Prices: 28 euros, wine excluded
All credit cards

Bagheria, a largish town not far from Palermo, is famous for its many old noble country villas: Villa Butera, Villa Valguarnera and the mysterious Villa Palagonia, famous for its countless statues depicting monsters, continue to fascinate visitors. In addition to its artistic merits, another reason to visit Bagheria is the interesting, wide-ranging gastronomic experience it offers. This celebrated, down-to-earth trattoria first opened 50 years ago is the high point. It's comforting to know that it's still run by family members who inherited it from the founder, the legendary Don Ciccio Castronovo: his son Santino and his grandchildren Francesco and Salvatore. The cooking remains anchored to tradition, though lately some small innovations have been introduced.

After the only antipasto, hard-boiled egg with salt and zibibbo, come **bucatini with sardines**, or meat ragù, or garlic, or swordfish. Among the main courses, the delicious **sardines a beccafico**, tasty meat roulades, **tuna ammuttunatu**, meat-loaf and 'u **bruciuluni** (falsomagro). Of the wide choice of side plates, **artichokes alla villanella** are a must, as are the eggplant caponata. The meal ends with fresh fruit, banana or orange with Marsala, cannoli or cassata di ricotta.

A small wine list of Sicilian labels or a robust house wine can accompany your meal.

The road that takes you in about half an hour from Palermo to the quiet little farming village of Belmonte Mezzagno offers some unforgettable views. When you get there you'll find the Italiano family's trattoria, a place that has managed to resist changing fashions and has proposed the same formula for years now: a set menu that changes daily and includes three first course dishes (always very filling), two main courses and a dessert. In true Sicilian osteria tradition there are no antipasti. Ingredients are all sourced from local farmers.

You can start with **rigatoni with tomato sauce, fried eggplant and salted ricotta**, fresh ravioli filled with ricotta and served with pork sauce or, when in season, **rigatoni with broccoli arriminati** (tossed in the pan). Portions are generous but try to leave some room for the main course: **falsomagro, stuffed pork chop** and, in winter, magnificent **roast kid** with potatoes. To finish, **sweets** with **ricotta filling** and exquisite cannoli. The wine list is always interesting and contains a good selection of Sicilian and other Italian labels: there's also a well-balanced selection of liqueurs.

Gelato In, Via Libertà 2° Edificio, sells excellent ice-cream, zuccotto, cakes and hard cookies. A must is the original 'stuffed ice-cream': flavors available are hazelnut, coffee, strawberry, oven-baked cassata and chocolate.

In **Piana degli Albanesi** (14 km), in contrada Ponte Rosso, Aura bakes bread made with durum wheat flour, cookies, among which mostaccioli, tegolini and quaresimali, and sfinciuni topped with tomato, onion and seasoned Caciocavallo cheese.

BUCCHERI

56 KM WEST OF SIRACUSA

U LOCALE

🍲 Trattoria
Via Dusmet 14
Tel. 0931 873923
Closed Tuesday
Open: lunch and dinner
Holidays: in July
Seating: 50 + 16 outdoors
Prices: 19-22 euros, wine excluded
No credit cards, Bancomat

In a narrow street in the mountain village of Buccheri stands the trattoria Sebastiano and Giuseppe Formica opened in 1990, transforming an old storeroom and fitting it out with the furniture and nick-nacks you used to find in farmhouses. A place that gets really full on weekends and that proposes a cuisine in step with the seasons based on quality local ingredients, including those grown in their own vegetable garden and cooked to a treat by Sebastiano.

Many antipasti: olives, dried tomatoes, **pork in aspic**, black pig salami, ricotta, mushrooms, **piscirovu** (omelet) with asparagus or ricotta, breaded wild fennel, friscalutu (bread with mushrooms and flakes of pecorino). Also good are the olive, tomato and chilli pepper pâtés they make themselves. Then tasty homemade pasta: tagliolini with cime di sinapa, asparagus and wild fennel, taglierini with **fava bean macco**, pasta with fresh mushrooms and zucchini, cavatelli and **ricotta-filled ravioli with pork sauce**, tagliatelle with roast peppers and tomatoes, **arricciata ca lumia** (a lemon and mint sauce). Always appetizing are the roast shank of pork, tripe in a tomato or plain sauce, **leg of pork with almonds**, roast lamb and potatoes, filling steaks. Almost impossible to find elsewhere are the **mutton brochettes** and **lattuchedda**, filleted underbelly of veal. To accompany the food there are a few, but appropriate Sicilian wines.

To finish, exquisite **cannoli di ricotta** and funciddi, dry almond and hazelnut cookies.

🍴 In Piazza Roma, 25, the Giangravè butchers shop has good local cured meats and cheeses.

CALTANISSETTA
Old town

PIAZZA GARIBALDI

🛏️ Bed and breakfast
Piazza Garibaldi 11
Tel. 0934 26436–340 3795803
Fax 0934 26436
E-mail: info@piazza-garibaldi.it
Internet: www.piazza-garibaldi.it
Open all year

Giancarlo Ciulla and his wife Mariella Di Falco opened this pleasant B&B after renovating one wing of Palazzo Salamone, of which the facade is now also being restored. They live on the first floor, while the guest rooms are on the upper floor, two of them with a terrace overlooking the main street. The rooms have tiled floors, wooden ceilings with frescos portraying colorful landscapes that give them a lighter air. Furnishings consist of tables, chairs, bedside tables, wooden chests, large mirrors on the walls and some pieces of antique furniture. Bathrooms have been furnished with great attention to detail too. Breakfast is served in rooms and offers a choice of coffee, milk, barley, chocolate, tea, bread, toast, croissants, orange juice, homemade jams, cookies and oven-baked doughnuts.

• 1 single, 1 double and 1 triple room, with bathroom, air-conditioning, TV • Prices: single 40 euros, double 60, triple 80, breakfast included • Credit cards: none • Public parking in the immediate vicinity. No pets allowed. Owners always reachable.

CALTANISSETTA
Serra dei Ladroni

CAPRI LEONE

SERRA DEI LADRONI

ANTICA FILANDA

Bed and breakfast
Contrada Serra dei Ladroni
Tel. 0934 568688-333 1630938
E-mail: info@serradeiladroni.it
Internet: www.serradeiladroni.it
Holidays variable

Restaurant/3-Star Hotel
Contrada Raviola
Tel. and fax 0941 919704
E-mail info@anticafilanda.it
Internet: www.anticafilanda.it
Closed Monday
Open: lunch and dinner
Holidays: January 15-February 25
Seating: 130
Prices: 33-35 euros, *f* wine excluded
All credit cards

This old renovated, very well furnished stone farmhouse is surrounded by olive trees and overlooks the bed of the Niscima river. Run by Adriana Venniro and her husband Salvatore Petix the B&B has two rooms with an independent entrance. Each room has a double bed, terracotta floors, wooden beams and a mezzanine floor where, if needed, two extra single beds can be added. A relaxing place and the ideal base for many possible excursions in the surrounding area and the neighboring provinces. You'll be able to explore Nature and places of artistic interest about which the owners will be happy to provide you with useful information. In the morning you'll have breakfast on the beautiful panoramic veranda, choosing from coffee, milk, tea, fruit juice, yogurt and home-made jams.

• 2 double rooms, with bathroom, TV • Prices: double room single use 35 euros, double 45 (15 euro supplement for extra bed), breakfast included • Credit cards: none • Off-street parking. Small pets allowed. Owners always reachable • Veranda, portico

The place offers a sweeping view of the Tyrrhenian Sea and sometimes a glimpse of the Aeolian islands. The rooms are tiled in Sicilian terracotta and furnished with solid cherry wood. Annexed to the charming hotel (open all week), the restaurant serves traditional cuisine and new permutations always rooted in local tradition. The antipasti include baked potatoes with pancetta, mushroom pie on cheese spread, frittata, cardoons and sage leaves fried in batter. The local cheese board and the **cured black Nebrodi pork** are excellent. The pork, from farms comprised under the Slow Food Presidium, is used in dishes like **pappardelle with ragù** and roast pork shoulder. The menu also offers artichoke ravioli with lamb ragù, **pennette with Bronte pistachio pesto**, ravioli of ricotta with mushrooms, grilled sausage and rabbit and **baked** or pan-fried **lamb**. The home-made puddings include **ricotta parfait** with orange jam and iced prickly pears.
The carefully chosen wine list has over 400 Sicilian and national labels with a small selection of imports.

• 1 single room, 7 doubles, 6 triples and 2 suites, with bathroom (shower or hydro massage), balcony, air-conditioning, mini-bar, safety deposit box, sat TV, modem socket • Prices: single 45-60, double single use 60-70, double 90-110, triple 125 -145 euros, breakfast included • 1 room specifically designed for the mobility impaired. Internal open parking area. Pets welcome. Owners always available • Bar, restaurant. Breakfast room, reading room, conference room. Garden, swimming pool

CARLENTINI

CASTELBUONO
Bergi

TENUTA DI ROCCADIA

☛—❶Holiday farm
Contrada Roccadia
Tel. and fax 095 990362
E-mail: info@roccadia.com
Internet: www.roccadia.com
Open all year

BERGI

☛—❶Holiday farm
Strada Statale 286, km 17,600
Tel. 0921 672045-368 7102848
Fax 0921 676877
E-mail: agriturismobergi@agriturismobergi.com
Internet: www.agriturismobergi.com
Open all year

This agriturismo between Catania and Siracusa in a low hilly area that faces Brucoli Bay, was opened after the restructuring of some early 20th-century farmhouses. The rooms have a pleasant view and are fitted with rustic furnishings. Around the facility there are many hectares of citrus groves and in addition the farm produces almonds, cheeses, jams and preserves that can be purchased there. Some of these products, such as the cheeses and the jams, are offered for breakfast, along with fruit juices, cookies, milk and coffee. Pietro Vacirca assists owner Maria Nunziata Ferrauto and he'll be happy to suggest tours of the surrounding area and provide information on the best beaches, excursions inland from Siracusa, to Etna and the archeological site of Lentini.

• 20 double rooms, with bathroom, air-conditioning, TV, mini-bar • Prices: double room single use 47-57 euros, double 70-90 (30-40 euro supplement for extra bed), breakfast included • Credit cards: MC, Visa, Bancomat • 2 rooms designed for use by the mobility challenged. Off-street parking. Small pets allowed (not in the restaurant) • Restaurant. Reading and TV room. Garden, terrace. 2 swimming pools, jacuzzi. Children's playground, horse-riding, compressed-air rifle shooting range, trekking course.

Bergi, a facility situated in the Madonie Park and more precisely in the Greco-Roman archeological site known as Vallone Saraceno, is a 7-hectare farm that grows vegetables, fruit and olives. It's the ideal place for those who want a peaceful vacation far from the chaos of city life. The very pleasant rooms are furnished rustic style in an unpretentious manner. The traditional breakfast includes a number of homemade items such as pastries, jams and honeys. The restaurant is also open to non-residents (average price of a meal 20 euros, wine excluded) and proposes traditional cuisine made with their own organic produce, which can also be bought directly from the farm. Half and full board in a double room cost 55 and 70 euros per person respectively. They often organize group cooking courses and guided excursions in the Madonie Park, which guests can also visit by renting a bicycle from the farm.

• 14 double rooms, with bathroom; several with air-conditioning, balcony • Prices: double room single use 46 euros, double 70 (35 euro supplement for extra bed), breakfast included • Credit cards: none • 2 rooms designed for use by the mobility challenged. Off-street parking. No pets allowed. Owners always present • Bar, restaurant. Garden, children's playground. Pool. Trekking course

CASTELBUONO

89 KM EAST OF PALERMO A 19 SS 113 AND 286

NANGALARRUNI

🍲 Restaurant
Via delle Confraternite 7
Tel. 0921 671428
Closed Wednesday
Open: lunch and dinner
Holidays: variable
Seating: 100 + 30 outdoors
Prices: 33-35 euros, wine excluded
All credit cards

A constant search for top quality local products has always been the mark of Peppe Carollo, owner of this very pleasant restaurant. Peppe, his friends also call him 'the president', is passionately fond of **mushrooms**, above all the types found in the woods around Castelbuono. Mushrooms that throughout the year remain the star turn on the menu: among the more delicious preparations, the classic, exquisite **soup**, also enhanced by certain types of legume.
You can start the meal with steamed basilischi mushrooms, dried tomatoes stuffed with basil and mint, local cured meats. Of the first courses try the **gramigna with cep mushrooms, artichokes and goat's milk ricotta**, tagliatelle with ragù and vegetables, rice with nettles. As for main course dishes, it's the triumph of the **Nebrodi black pig** – a Slow Food Presidia – prepared in many ways. Alternatively, **kid with potatoes and saffron** or shank of pork cooked in red wine and chestnut honey. Before moving on to the puddings, have a taste of Sicilian and other national cheeses from the board, take your pick and enjoy it together with delicious honey or pistachio creams. An appropriate end to the meal is the flan with almonds in a pistachio sauce or the two traditional Castelbuono specialties: **cosi chini** (a kind of small buccellati) and **testa di turco**, a yummy sweet fried 'lasagna'.
The wine cellar is the outcome of Peppe's other passion. He's very knowledgeable and will be able to offer you an interesting selection of Sicilian, national and foreign wines, with a few pleasant surprises and an excellent price:quality ratio.

CASTELLAMMARE DEL GOLFO

36 KM EAST OF TRAPANI

RISTORANTE DEL GOLFO

🍲 Restaurant
Via Segesta 153
Tel. 0924 30257
Closed Tuesday, never in summer
Open: lunch and dinner
Holidays: variable in winter
Seating: 30 + 25 outdoors
Prices: 35 euros, wine excluded
All credit cards except AE, Bancomat

The seaside village of Castellammare lies just a few kilometers from the Segesta archeological site and is a fascinating place, with a pretty historic center overlooking the harbor and the sea. Every day Liborio Giorlando uses his expert eye to select the very best of the day's catch that will later be served in his restaurant.
Depending on the season you can start with **pilchards allinguate in sweet-and-sour sauce**, pilchard a beccafico pie, a fried platter with moscardini, cicireddi or neonata, boiled octopus, small breaded cuttlefish, red prawns marinated with lemon, tuna or swordfish carpaccio. First course dishes are mainly made using fresh pasta: you can try **busiati con la neonata**, with swordfish and mint or with sea urchins, with dory fish roe, fennel and fava beans, with pistachio and prawns or cuttlefish ink. In winter months, in addition to seafood dishes there are a few peasant farmer-style recipes like legume soups and **fava bean macco**. You then continue with something from the day's catch cooked in one of the traditional ways: either grilled, in acquapazza, or cooked in the oven. Don't miss the opportunity to try swordfish alla pantesca or in roulades, local **prawns** and **scampi**; if booked ahead of time, also stuffed squid or cuttlefish, **tuna in sweet-and-sour sauce** or tomato sauce. To finish, try the **cassatella** (classic fried sweet raviolo with a lemon-flavored ricotta filling), cannoli, cassata or, in summer, homemade granite al limone and almond parfait.
Service is attentive and courteous. The wine list offers a good selection of regional bottles, and every year it expands to bring in interesting new labels.

CASTELLAMMARE DEL GOLFO
Scopello

36 KM EAST OF TRAPANI, 10 KM FROM CITY CENTER

TRANCHINA

🔑 1-Star Hotel
Via Diaz 7
Tel. 0924 541099
Fax 0924 541232
E-mail: pensionetranchina@interfree.it
Open all year

Located not far from the splendid Zingaro Nature Reserve, Scopello is a small seaside village that has been famous for centuries for its tuna fishing. This small hotel managed with professionalism and courtesy by Sicilian Salvatore Tranchina and his wife Marisin from Panama is the ideal place for those who want a quiet, intimate place for their seaside vacation. On the first floor there's the breakfast room (on request you can also have dinner, consisting mainly of fresh fish and vegetables from the garden; half board 55-83 euros per person) and a lounge with fireplace for moments of relaxation. A central staircase leads to the rooms, fitted with wooden and wrought-iron furniture, all of them recently fitted with air-conditioning. Some rooms have a balcony with a beautiful sea view. Marisin will be happy to recommend interesting sites to visit in the surrounding area: apart from Zingaro, Erice, Segesta and Selinunte.

• 6 single and 4 double rooms, with bathroom, air-conditioning, mini-bar; several with balcony • Prices: single 50-60 euros, double 72-92 (26 euro supplement for extra bed), breakfast included • Credit cards: all, Bancomat • Public parking outside. No pets allowed. Owners always present • Restaurant. Lounge

CASTELL'UMBERTO

114 KM WEST OF MESSINA

COLAMARCO

🔑 Holiday farm
Località Colamarco
Tel. 0941 438130-338 2375957
Fax 0941 438130
E-mail: info@agriturismocolamarco.it
Internet: www.agriturismocolamarco.it
Open all year

Surrounded by olive trees and citrus groves, Colamarco lies at an altitude of 300 meters. The buildings where the apartments are were formerly farmhouses that have been completely restructured. The apartments all have bathrooms, fully equipped kitchens, kitchenware and bedroom linen. One is a rather unusual studio inasmuch as it was previously an astronomical observatory and has a roof that opens to give a superb view of the stars. On request breakfast can include various products from the farm: milk, jams and homemade tarts. Dinner is cooked using their own produce and other produce sourced locally: it's reserved for residents only and costs 18 euros per person, including drinks. The owners organize excursions and guided tours of sites of artistic interest in the surrounding area. If you like exercise there's both a tennis and a boules court, mountain bikes for rent, and three kilometers away the municipal swimming pool.

• 6 apartments (2-4 persons), with bathroom, kitchen, TV • Prices: double room single use and double 50-66 euros, triple 75-99, four-bed 100-132; breakfast 6 euros per person • Credit cards: none • 1 room designed for use by the mobility challenged. Off-street parking. No pets allowed. Owners always reachable • Conference room, Lounge. Patio. Tennis court, boules court, table tennis table

CASTELVETRANO
Marinella di Selinunte

LA PINETA

Trattoria
Via Punta Cantone
Tel. 0924 46820
No closing day
Open: lunch and dinner
Holidays: variable
Seating: 100 + 150 outdoors
Prices: 32-35 euros, wine excluded
All credit cards, Bancomat

The name of this trattoria, which lies inside the River Belice protected area just a few yards from the center of Marinella di Selinunte, refers to the small pinewood behind it: magnificent setting that, above all on summer evenings, is sure to provide a memorable experience. The trattoria itself is a small wooden construction that also has tables outside directly on the beach, so you can eat with your feet in the sand. Angelo Rizzuto is front of house with his sons Giuseppe, Lorenzo and Salvatore, while his wife Maria Giuseppa runs the kitchen.

The choice offered by the menu depends on the day's catch. Among the possible antipasti, we recommend the skewer of prawns, mussel or **clam soup**, marinated anchovies, boiled octopus and seafood salad. First courses are also mainly based on seafood; really excellent **spaghetti with sea urchins**, with langoustine or mussels and clams, plus a Sicilian classic, **fettuccine with tomato and eggplants**. You can then continue with fresh local fish either baked in the oven or, better still, barbecued. Here they also serve the very tasty Castelvetrano black bread (Slow Food Presidium) and excellent Nocellara del Belice olive oil that brings out the best in any dish.

Lastly, cannoli filled with ricotta, fried **cassatella**, homemade ice cream and fresh fruit. The wine list offers a decent selection of Sicilian wines.

CASTROFILIPPO
Torre

OSTERIA DEL CACCIATORE

Traditional osteria
Contrada Torre
Tel. 0922 829824
Closed Wednesday
Open: lunch, dinner if you book
Holidays: variable
Seating: 100
Prices: 18-24 euros, wine excluded
No credit cards

Castrofilippo, a small inland Sicilian village, is worth making a detour to visit: to reach it take the main Caltanissetta-Agrigento road and you'll find it in the vicinity of Canicattì. The osteria is run by five sisters: Salvina prepares fresh pastas and shells for the cannoli; Giusi takes care of decorations and the antipasti; Graziella, the first courses, meat and pizza cooked in a wood-fired oven; Eleonora dies rabbit, tripe and wild boar; Maria Rita takes the orders. Mamma Antonia coordinates the five girls, prepares the ingredients and is specialized in cooking snails. The osteria has two large rooms that sometimes have only a few guests, but even on such occasions the quality of the food and their courtesy remain unchanged.

The menu varies with the season. The antipasti are nice: roast onion with bacon, **fuazza** (a very crispy rolled pizza) with spinach, zebinata (oven-cooked vegetables), eggs roasted with bacon, chicory and balsamic vinegar, mixed season's vegetables served with primosale cheese, cherry tomatoes and basil. Well worth trying among the first courses are the **homemade tagliatelle with wild boar ragù** or with ricotta and eggplant, ricotta scacciata and, in summer, cold **legume soups**. Among the main courses try the **stigliola** (kid's intestines rolled with liver, boiled egg, onion and then barbecued), **rabbit chasseur**, marinated tongue of veal and **tripe stew**. You can finish off with almond pastries and cannoli filled with a ricotta that, when the time for good grazing comes around, is supplied by a small local cheese producer.

They make both the olive oil and Nero d'Avola house wine themselves: as an alternative they have just a few local bottled wines.

AMBASCIATA DEL MARE

Restaurant
Piazza Duomo 6
Tel. 095 341003
Closed Monday
Open: lunch and dinner
Holidays: 15 days in December
Seating: 50
Prices: 30-35 euros, wine excluded
All credit cards

Piazza del Duomo, with its sumptuous baroque cathedral, the dome of Sant'Agata abbey and the Elephant fountain – emblem of the city – all lie in the heart of Catania. Somewhere that's a must to visit because you'll also find this small restaurant that sees a steady stream of visitors, because of its central location, certainly, but also because of the quality of the food. As the name suggests, seafood is the number one ingredient. To help you choose you'll find Alessandro Valastro and Ciro Scamporrino front of house, while their third partner, Francesco Valastro, runs the kitchen.
The list of antipasti can include **pilchards a beccafico**, mussels au gratin, marinated anchovies and shrimp, fried spatola, merluzzetti in sweet-and-sour sauce, fried baccalà. If you'd like to try a bit of everything then order the generous house antipasti. Among the first courses are tasty **bucatini with tuna roe**, tagliolini with scampi, linguine with sea urchin pulp, pennette with mussels and peppers, **pasta** with cuttlefish ink or with **fresh tuna ragù**. The day's catch obviously determines what's available for your main course. Among the dishes, one that's outstanding in terms of taste is the **grouper** (or other type of fish) **alla marinara, ricciola all'acqua di mare** or **dentex cooked in the oven with potatoes**.
For pudding, locally made tartellette with almonds and cannoli with a ricotta filling. The choice of regional wines is fair.

METRÒ

Restaurant-wine shop
Via Crociferi 76
Tel. 095 322098
Closed Saturday for lunch and Sunday
Open: lunch and dinner
Holidays: Easter, May 1, Christmas
Seating: 90 + 60 outdoors
Prices: 27-30 euros, wine excluded
All credit card

Maurizio Morabito and Aldo Bacciulli run a pleasant place that's remained the same for over 30 years. Either seated in one of the cozy rooms or, in summer, in the pretty outside area in Via Crociferi, you can have a snack or a more substantial meal choosing from a menu that includes traditional local and regional dishes plus a few personal creations. The common denominator in whatever you choose will be the high quality of the seasonal ingredients.
Among the antipasti, well worth a try are the herring and orange salad, wild greens with roasted cacio cheese or spatola parmigiana. In the right period try the **lattume of fried tuna and the** masculini da magghia timbale (made with local anchovies) with potatoes and capers. To follow, orecchiette with broccoli and sausage, Leonfante **fava bean soup**, pasta alla Norma, **penne with pesto alla trapanese**; among the seafood firsts, linguine with skate broth, risotto with squid and saffron, ravioli with a sea bass filling, tagliatelle with tuna botargo. Among main course fish dishes there's **polpette di muccu, tuna with onions**, swordfish cooked with citrus fruit. In wintertime good choices will be lamb in fricassea, fillet steak soused with Nero d'Avola, **Nebrodi black pig pork chop**. There's an interesting and well-balanced selection of Sicilian cheeses.
You finish with delicious home-made desserts like **cream of Bronte pistachios** and the almond blancmange. They have a very wide selection of quality wines and liqueurs.

OSTERIA ANTICA MARINA

Trattoria
Via Pardo 29
Tel. 095 348197
Closed Wednesday
Open: lunch and dinner
Holidays: 3 days mid-Aug., 15 days end Dec.
Seating: 65 + 60 outdoors
Prices: 35 euros, wine excluded
All credit cards

The atmosphere is always the same – lively and down-to-earth. Two communicating rooms, with the fish and antipasti laid out in front of the open-plan kitchen area, and on the walls, old photos of the Marina quarter and the Piscaria, Catania's oldest market right outside the trattoria.

And the food hasn't changed either, based on tried and tested recipes much appreciated by the numerous clientele, starting from the tray of antipasti. On average fifteen different nibbles that alone are much more than normal antipasti: an appetizing repertoire that includes lightly fried local shrimp, telline in tomato sauce, **oven-baked pilchard roulades**, squid and potatoes in tomato sauce, octopus salad, small cod in sweet-and-sour sauce, **caponata**, olive giardiniera, stuffed artichokes and other vegetables in season with various condiments. Often the first course dishes include **linguine with sea urchins**, with tuna roe or with zucchini flowers and mussels, **spaghetti with cuttlefish ink** or with anchovies and toasted breadcrumbs, **pasta with fresh tuna** or with prawns and almonds. Depending on what's available in the market the main course will include fish from the day's catch either grilled or alla marinara. Don't miss trying the tasty **fried platter** of local fish: scallops, red mullet, goby, totanetti, magghia anchovies. The rich **fish soup** is also good and can well be a meal in itself.

To drink there are a few acceptable Sicilian wines and you can usually round off your meal with lemon or tangerine sherbets.

SAN PLACIDO INN

Bed and breakfast
Piazza San Placido 3
Tel. 095 315100-335 7182036
Fax 095 315100
E-mail: sanplacidoinn@hotmail.com
Internet: www.sanplacidoinn.com
Open all year

This beautiful B&B is located behind Piazza Duomo, in an attic on the fourth floor of an 18th-century building not far from the ancient Via Etnea, the city's main shopping and entertainment area. The airy, spacious rooms all have private bathrooms and are furnished in 'arte povera' style, with handmade ceramics and items once used by Sicilian peasant farmers; some rooms look directly over the sea. The shared kitchen with two ranges means that guests can prepare their own meals. There are two large terraces available for soaking up the sun or eating a traditional breakfast and enjoying a beautiful view. It's just a short drive by car to get to La Plaja, Catania's most popular beach.

• 2 double and 1 triple room, with bathroom, air-conditioning, mini-bar, TV • Prices: double room single use 35-50 euros, double 55-80, triple 80-100 (25 euro supplement for extra bed), breakfast included • Credit cards: Visa, Bancomat • Public parking in the immediate vicinity. No pets allowed. Owners always present • Breakfast room. Terrace, solarium

20 KM NORTHWEST OF RAGUSA

TRATTORIA CASALINGA

🍲 Trattoria
Via Biondi 19
Tel. 095 311319
Closed Sunday
Open: lunch, Friday and Saturday also for dinner
Holidays: in August
Seating: 70
Prices: 25-28 euros, wine excluded
All credit cards

MAJORE

🍲 Restaurant
Via dei Martiri Ungheresi 12
Tel. 0932 928019
Closed Monday
Open: lunch and dinner
Holidays: in July
Seating: 105
Prices: 18-21 euros, wine excluded
All credit cards

This typical family-run trattoria has been in business for some time now near Corso Sicilia and Fera 'o luni, the city's largest open-air market. The owner is Nino Mannino, a friendly outgoing type who knows almost all his customers personally and who often has a few unusual stories to tell. His wife continues to run the kitchen with great flair while their son Salvatore lends a hand in the dining room. There's no menu as such and so you'll be told what's available. As the name of the trattoria suggests, dishes will be based on traditional Catania home-cooked recipes.

The antipasti counter will offer the season's vegetables – either fried, grilled or in omelets – caponata, alivi cunzati and a few seafood dishes. For first courses there's a good **pasta co' maccu di fave**, or with the classic sauce alla Norma, fresh beans with pasta, which in summer is eaten cold, and which in Catania is called **triaca pasta**. You may also find **pasta with swordfish ragù**, rice with shellfish, pasta with a tasty sauce made with tomato, anchovies, pine nuts and wild fennel. Depending on the catch, for main course you'll find **swordfish roulades**, paddlefish cutlet, **tuna with onions**. **Masculini**, that is, anchovies, can be eaten cooked in the oven or filleted and dressed uncooked. Among the meat dishes, the **veal roulade** is especially tasty – they make it by taking a slice of meat filled with cheese, breadcrumbs, capers and marjoram, dipped in whisked egg, then breaded and fried. You end with fresh fruit or the occasional pudding. There's a small selection of regional wines.

This restaurant, which has been run by members of the La Terra Majore family since way back in 1896, is in the medieval center behind the city's main square. On the upper floor, the restaurant has a large room that they open on days when it's particularly busy, whereas the ground-floor room is still the original, more fascinating small room with a few tables next to the kitchen. The food here is strongly linked to this area's traditions, in particular pork by-products and pork-based recipes. So here, as the Majore family motto states, it's 'all praise to the pig'.

You start with a taste of **jlatina** (pork in aspic), salami, speck, olive giardiniera and olive bunate, that is, olives that taste good thanks to the condiment in which they've been preserved. Among first course dishes you'll find **ravioli with a ricotta filling served with pork sauce**, the tasty risotto alla majorese with pork ragù and caciocavallo cheese or alternatively, cavateddi with tomato sauce, fried eggplant and salted ricotta. A dish that's a symbol and based on a very old recipe is the appetizing **stuffed pork chop** (cuosti chini). Other main course dishes are sausages either barbecued or in tomato sauce and an excellent **falsomagro** with pork mixed with cheese, salami, boiled egg and onion. Sometimes you'll even find **pork alla ciaramuntana** (pan-cooked) and fried pork chops. Instead, if you'd like to try the **cunigghiu à portuisa** you have to book a few days ahead: it's a sweet-and-sour pork dish with potatoes, olives and peppers.

There's a good selection of wines, whereas for dessert you'll probably only find almond parfait.

CORLEONE
Ficuzza

EGADI ISLANDS
Favignana

45 KM SOUTH OF PALERMO

20 MINUTES BY HYDROFOIL FROM TRAPANI

ANTICA STAZIONE FERROVIARIA DI FICUZZA

Trattoria/Holiday farm
Via Vecchia Stazione
Tel. 091 8460000-338 5741023
E-mail info@anticastazione.it
Internet: www.anticastazione.it
Always open
Open: lunch and dinner
Holidays: none
Seating: 80 +40 outdoors
Prices: 22-30 euros, wine excluded
All credit cards

LA BETTOLA

Trattoria
Via Nicotera 47
Tel. 0923 921988
Closed Thursday, never in summer
Open: lunch and dinner
Holidays: December 1-15
Seating: 30 + 50 outdoors
Prices: 33 euros, wine excluded
All credit cards, Bancomat

The young people of the Camelot cooperative have saved the old train station of the Palermo-San Carlo line from a long period of dereliction, converting it into a comfortable relaxation area and a gastronomic landmark for the entire district. The bountiful breakfast includes homemade jams and puddings, cured meats and a cheese board. The relaxation room has satellite TV, stereo and parlor games.

The cuisine uses top quality raw materials, mostly from round about. The menus are seasonal: to start you can try the timbale of local ham with spiced ricotta cheese, fresh goats' cheese of Godrano, ammuttunati cardoons (filled with cheese and anchovies) baked or fried, homemade (like most of the pasta) **tagliatelle with boar ragù**, **macco di fave**, pasta filled with Corleone eggplant, vastedda del Belice and ricotta. Of the main courses we highly recommend the black pork fillet of the Nebrodi al Nero d'Avola and the baked **stuffed rabbit**. To finish, wild berry mousse and ice-creams, all home-made.

The cellar offers the best of Sicilian wines. A set menu is available at 22 euros.

• 12 double rooms, en-suite; some with TV • Prices: double single use 35-65, double 50-110 euros (supplement for additional bed 28-60 euros), breakfast included • 1 room specifically designed for the mobility impaired. Internal uncovered parking area. Pets welcome. 24 hour porter service • Wine bar, restaurant. Relaxation room. Garden, park. Horse-riding

The largest of the three Egadi Islands – Favignana – is very popular with tourists and so it's not easy to find restaurants or trattorias offering an acceptable price-quality ratio. One exception to this is certainly this family-run trattoria that has an almost Spartan look about it but where you'll find very simple, traditional seafood cuisine. Bastiano will be there to welcome you and make you feel at home; his wife, Maria Teresa, runs the kitchen while their children Peppe and Maria take turns in working in the kitchen or serving customers.

When the time comes for the 'mattanza' you'll be able to taste **tuna**, the number one local ingredient, either roast, in sweet-and-sour sauce, in tomato sauce, tuna-meatballs or as an excellent condiment for busiati, the typical fresh homemade pasta. As for the antipasti, you can choose between the insalata corallina containing langoustine, lobster, red prawns and cherry tomatoes, octopus salad, mixed fried platter, mussel soup. Among the first courses we can recommend the **Trapani-style couscous** in fish or langoustine soup. Apart from tuna, **busiate** can be served **with cuttlefish ink sauce**, with botargo, with swordfish and eggplants, with shrimp, or with clams and cherry tomatoes. The best of the day's catch (white bream, sea bass, sea urchins) either baked or cooked all'acquapazza is your best bet for a main course. You finish with fried **cassatele** and fresh fruit.

They have a good selection of Sicilian wines, particularly those from around Trapani.

EGADI ISLANDS
Marettimo

IL TIMONE

⌒ Trattoria
Via Garibaldi 18
Tel. 0923 923142
No closing day
Open: lunch and dinner
Holidays: November-April
Seating: 15 + 60 outdoors
Prices: 32 euros, wine excluded
All credit cards except AE

The island of Marettimo is the furthest of the Egadi Islands from Trapani but also the most enchanting. Here you'll find one of the best trattorias, run with passion by the Citrolo family: Maria operates the kitchen while her husband Nino and children Pasquale and Rosa are front of house. Service is polite and prompt, but if you want to be sure to taste the more characteristic dishes we recommend you book ahead.

You start with a nice selection of cold and warm antipasti, among which mussels and clams both in soup and au gratin, fish carpaccio, seafood salad and eggplants stuffed with tuna. The first course dishes are this trattoria's real specialty: every day they prepare **fresh pasta**, like **busiate**, that go well with seafood sauces (**with sea urchins**, or dentex) or varieties like ravioli or cappelletti filled with fish or shellfish. One of the most characteristic first courses is **spaghetti broken up in langoustine soup**, a great, well-balanced dish but only available if booked in advance. The choice for main course will depend on what Nino finds daily in the market where he personally selects the fish. White bream, dentex, squid, prawns or scampi are prepared roasted, cooked in a salt crust, baked or barbecued.

For dessert, try the cassata siciliana, which also comes in a lighter version, or a mulberry or **orange semifreddo**. The cellar contains a good selection of regional labels.

EGADI ISLANDS
Marettimo

IL VELIERO

⌒ Trattoria
Via Umberto 22
Tel. 0923 923274
No closing day
Open: lunch and dinner
Holidays: none
Seating: 50 + 80 outdoors
Prices: 26-30 euros, wine excluded
All credit cards, Bancomat

Marettimo, a splendid mountain in the midst of the sea, will enchant you with its colors, crystal clear waters and aromas. On the only main road you'll find the Trattoria Il Veliero, a 'safe haven' for good food any day of the year. Zio Peppe, who runs the trattoria with his family, will make you feel at home. An ex-fisherman, he selects only the very best fish for the recipes he and his wife Paolina prepare.

Your meal will begin with a series of land and sea antipasti: olives, dried tomatoes, Primosale cheese, eggplant caponata, octopus salad. The first courses are classical dishes on the island: **couscous with fish**, pasta with pilchards, **spaghetti with palamita** or tuna **ragù**, with cuttlefish ink, with palamita and eggplants, alla carrettiera. Well worth trying (if you book first) is the spaghetti in langoustine soup, a divine dish but it'll inevitably raise the final bill. Plus grilled mackerel, **cuttlefish stew**, **palamita** or moray eel in **sweet-and-sour sauce**, fried cuttlefish, whitebait fritters or **mixed seafood platter**. To finish, fresh fruit, lemon sorbet and quaresimali accompanied by a small glass of Marsala.

Service is fast and with no frills. On offer a choice of a few regional wines.

⚑ At the La Cambusa grocery store, you'll find a wide selection of Sicilian cured meats and cheeses, including some Slow Food Presidia, and a good selection of island wines.

ENNA

ANTICA HOSTARIA

⌒ Trattoria
Via Castagna 9
Tel. 0935 22521
Closed Monday for dinner, Tuesday
Open: lunch and dinner
Holidays: 15 days in summer
Seating: 50 + 20 outdoors
Prices: 25-27 euros, wine excluded
Credit cards: MC, Visa, Bancomat

When you walk down Via Roma in the old center of Enna you pass the cathedral, the archeological museum and the church of Santa Chiara and other places worth visiting. Almost at the end of the street there's a turn-off that takes you into a quiet courtyard where chef Michele Bonaccorso runs his trattoria, together with his wife, Rita. The place has two rooms with a homely feel, while in summer you can also eat outside. The cuisine is traditional local and regional fare.
Antipasti include stuffed artichokes, eggplant caponata, potato or fresh tuma omelets, cured meats and Sicilian cheeses, among which **piacentinu** that's also laid on a lemon-tree leaf and cooked on the **hotplate**. Alternating in the choice of first courses are fusilli with ricotta and dried tomatoes, **orecchiette with Sicilian pesto**, **pasta all'ennese**, ditalini with **fava bean macco**, legume soup, tagliatelle with mussels, clams and dried tomatoes, pasta with pilchards. Seafood main course dishes, which are usually prepared at weekends, include octopus cooked in red wine, marinated anchovies, swordfish alla ghiotta and other fish the owner buys in the market in Licata or Aci Trezza. Especially in winter, there's a wider choice of meat dishes: roast pork with almonds, **stigghiole**, tripe in tomato sauce, meatballs in lemon, **roast lamb** with potatoes, eggplant parmigiana, peperonata.
To finish, home-made cakes and semifreddo. Quite a good wine list of mainly regional wines.

ERICE
Pizzolungo

6 KM NORTHEAST OF TRAPANI

L'APPRODO

🔑 3-Star Hotel
Via Enea 3
Tel. 0923 571555
Fax 0923 571541
E-mail: info@hotelapprodotrapani.it
Internet: www.hotelapprodotrapani.it
Open all year

Pizzolungo is a small seaside town a few kilometers from Trapani and Erice. This is were you'll find the Approdo hotel, a simple modern building overlooking the beach, part of which is reserved for the hotel's guests. The spacious, airy rooms all have en suite bathrooms and are furnished in essential, functional manner. The restaurant offers Mediterranean cuisine in the spacious dining room or, when the weather permits, on the large terraces. The cost of half board varies according to the period of the year from 61 to 65 euros per person, based on double room occupancy, or from 70 to 75 euros per person for those in a single. The hotel also has a terrace with solarium, private parking and an elegant gazebo that can be used for meetings and conferences.

• 2 single, 10 double and 1 triple room, with bathroom, air-conditioning, minibar, TV, safe; several rooms with veranda • Prices: single 53-60 euros, double 85-95, triple 116-122 (18 euro supplement for extra bed), breakfast included • Credit cards: all, Bancomat • Off-street parking Small pets allowed. Reception open 24 hours a day • Bar, restaurant. Gazebo, terrace-solarium. Private beach

MONTE SAN GIULIANO

Restaurant
Vicolo San Rocco 7
Tel. 0923 869595
Closed Monday
Open: lunch and dinner
Holidays: 15 days in January 15 in November
Seating: 70 + 100 outdoors
Prices: 32-35 euros, wine excluded
All credit cards, Bancomat

PIZZOLUNGO

Holiday farm
Contrada San Cusumano
Tel. 0923 563710
Fax 0923 569780
E-mail: fradr@tin.it
Internet: www.pizzolungo.it

Atop Mount San Giuliano, the western-most point of Sicily, you'll find Erice, one of the island's most beautiful medieval villages. Visited by tourists and scientists alike, from the panoramic viewing point you can admire the Egadi Islands, the salt beds of Trapani and, to the north on clearer days, you can even see the island of Ustica. It's in this enchanted setting that you'll find Matteo Giurlanda and Andrea Coppola's restaurant. Matteo runs the kitchen, while Andrea coordinates service in the three dining rooms and outdoors.

Those starting with antipasti can usually choose between **sardines a beccafico**, oven-baked eggplant and ricotta roulades, tuna mosciame, smoked fish rolls, swordfish carpaccio. The more classic first courses are certainly the **couscous in fish stock**, **busiati with pesto alla trapanese**, treccine with grouper sauce; a creative touch arrives in the form of spaghetti with fish roe, cherry tomatoes and fried zucchini, and ricotta-filled ravioli with cuttlefish ink. The best of the day's catch cooked on the barbecue is the highlight among the mains, although the **swordfish roulades** alla siciliana and **grouper alla matalotta** are also good. Meat dishes are much less common.

To end your meal, in summer semifreddi and ice-cream, in winter cassata di ricotta and cannoli. The wine list has a good selection of top Sicilian labels.

This agriturismo is just a short distance from the sea, at the foot of Mount Erice (800 m). The property includes 80 hectares of land cultivated organically: the farm's produce, among which wine and extra virgin olive oil, can be bought at the facility. The two and four-bed apartments are all equipped with telephones. The farmhouse dates back to the 19th century and faces onto a splendid Mediterranean garden. In summer you can bathe in an ancient stone pool that's fed by a spring. Bicycles can be rented and four kilometers away there's a tennis court and the same distance away you'll find scuba diving courses and underwater excursions.

• 6 apartments (2-4 persons), with bathroom, kitchen • Prices: double room single use 64-70 euros, double 80-90, triple 120-135, four-bed 160-180; breakfast 5 euros per person • Credit cards: none • Facility accessible for the mobility challenged. Off-street parking. Small pets allowed. Owners always reachable • Garden

Maria Grammatico, Via Vittorio Emanuele, 14, turns traditional Erice confectionery into an art form.

FICARRA

FATTORIA DI GRENNE

📟⚬Holiday farm
Località Grenne
Tel. 0941 582757–582098
Fax 0941 583135
E-mail: giuseppepiccolo2@tiscali.it
Internet: www.grenne.com
Open all year

This farmhouse, which started out in the 16th century as the hunting lodge of the Piccolo barons, stands on a hill offering a splendid view out to the Aeolian islands. Following a renovation project that included the stone entrance hall and the creation of guest rooms next to the old building, for about twelve years now it has functioned as a vacation farm. Around the estate managed by Giuseppe Piccolo and his wife Francesca there are fruit trees and vineyards; olives, vegetables and citrus fruit are grown organically; sauces, cheeses preserved in oil and fruit jams are all produced on the farm. In fact there's never a shortage of jams for breakfast, along with coffee, milk, bread and cookies. We also recommend you try Francesca's wholesome typical cuisine (a meal costs 25 euros per person, wine excluded, half board ranges from 50-60 euros and full board, from 60-70 euros per person). You have to book if you want to eat at the restaurant. There are a number of possible excursions in the surrounding area, for instance, a trip to the Nebrodi Park and Etna. But don't forget to visit the little 16th-century church in the woods on the estate.

• 5 double rooms, with bathroom, TV • Prices: double room single use 35-45 euros, double 70-80, breakfast included • Credit cards: major ones, Bancomat • Off-street parking. Small pets allowed. Owners always reachable • Restaurant. TV room, games room. Garden. Pool, boules court, archery

GALATI MAMERTINO

LA BETTOLA

🍲Trattoria
Via Cavour 159
Tel. 0941 434952
Closed Monday
Open: lunch and dinner
Holidays: variable
Seating: 60
Prices: 20-22 euros, wine excluded
All credit cards except AE

From whichever direction you arrive, you'll already have been struck by the intense greenery of the hazelnut groves, oak and pine woods, the abundance of ferns, wild roses, daphne and broom that bedeck the gorges and valleys, right up to the highest ridges. To all this add a large protected area in which they are reintroducing the roe deer, which was quite common in these parts up to the end of the nineteenth century, and the fascinating spectacle of the waters of the San Basilio torrent that with a drop of almost 30 meters amongst craggy rocks creates the Catafurco waterfall. In this fairytale scenario, not far from the center of Galati you'll find this cozy trattoria. In a neat, clean dining room Santina will give you a detailed description of the recipes that her parents lovingly prepare.

You'll start with oven-baked ricotta and Nebrodi Provola cheeses, cured meats, the much sought-after **dressed olives** and then, depending on the season, **omelets with wild herbs**. They have fresh pasta in the classical shapes: **maccarruni**, excellent **with ragù**, lightly fried with cheese or in roulades accompanied by eggplant. Also good are the gnocchetti with mushrooms and pine nuts and, in winter, the various **legume soups**. Meat is the main ingredient for main courses and it comes from local farms where animals are raised using an almost free-range approach: the chicken is very good and vies with the **roast kid** for first place. To finish, fresh fruit or hazelnut cookies.

Santina is a real wine enthusiast so although there's only a small list it's well thought out.

GANGI

VILLA RAINÒ

Restaurant/Holiday farm
Contrada Rainò
Tel. and fax 0921 644680
E-mail villaraino@tnet.it
Internet: www.villaraino.it
Always open
Open: lunch and dinner
Holidays: 1 week in July
Seating: 70 +70 outdoors
Prices: 20-24 euros, wine excluded
All credit cards

Villa Rainò stands a short distance from the center of Gangi, in a valley dominated by Mount Marone, at the extreme west end of the province of Palermo. This farmhouse in the countryside, a short distance before entering the village, was once home to the Li Destri barons. Today, home to the hospitable Aldo and Nino Conte, it offers 15 rooms en-suite, a swimming pool immersed in greenery and a seasonal menu serving local products.
The antipasti include **caponata of eggplant**, fried lamb's liver and kidney, ricotta and primosale madoniti, sautéed wild green vegetables. They continue with the traditional **macco di fave**, **ditali with wild herbs** (plentiful in the surrounding countryside), and maccheroni with wild rabbit ragù. The choice of main courses is vast and appetizing: highly recommended is the **baked boar** with mushrooms, the char-boiled lamb, and the traditional **stuffed lamb**. The truly sumptuous banquet ends with fried sfinci and unforgettable ricotta cakes.
Small and well-selected Sicilian cellar, caring and friendly service.

• 15 double rooms, en-suite • Prices: double single use 42 euros, double 70 euros (supplement for additional bed 15 euros), breakfast included • Establishment in part accessible to the mobility impaired, 1 room specifically designed for the mobility impaired. Internal open parking area. Pets welcome. Owners always available • Bar, restaurant. Reading room, TV room. Garden. Swimming pool

GIARRE

SAN MATTEO

Holiday farm
Strada San Matteo Baglio 83, 3
Tel. 095 7790559 – 360 564945
Fax 095 7790559
E-mail: s.matteo@tiscali.it
Internet: www.sanmatteofarm.it
Open all year

Carlo Limone, Piedmontese by birth but Catanese by adoption, has a farm on that part of the east coast facing the bay of Taormina where he grows citrus and other fruit and then sells his certified organically cultivated produce around Italy. The vacation farm is a restructured old farmhouse used in the past to take a break by groups of workers involved in the grape harvest and winemaking process. The farmhouse is divided into three independent units, which are decorated with implements used on Sicilian farms in the past century and that give onto a wide patio covered by a pergola, which acts as a natural air-conditioning system. For breakfast you'll be able to taste a delicious assortment of jams, honeys, jellies and other tasty preserves produced on the farm. There's a kitchen available for those guests who wish to prepare their own meals.

• 1 triple room and 2 apartments (2 persons), with bathroom, mini-bar, TV; 1 with kitchen • Prices: double room single use 50 euros, double 70-100, breakfast included •: All major credit cards • 1 room designed for use by the mobility challenged. Off-street parking. Small pets allowed. Owners always reachable. • Patio. Solarium

Joppolo Giancaxio

DA CARMELO

Trattoria
Via Roma 16
Tel. 0922 631376
Closed Wednesday
Open: only for dinner
Holidays: variable
Seating: 48 + 70 outdoors
Prices: 15-20 euros
No credit cards

After having worked abroad for some time, Carmelo Argento came back to this village inland from Agrigento about 15 years ago and opened his down-to-earth trattoria. One small room, simply decorated, with paper tablecloths and when the weather permits, tables in the road along the side of the piazza. Carmelo himself, together with his wife, runs the kitchen – on Saturday and public holidays some other family members lend a hand serving at the tables.
The Italian-style antipasti (rather uncharacteristic compared with the rest) include nibbles of cheese, salami, prosciutto, olives and grilled vegetables. Among the fresh pastas you'll find tagliatelle and **cavati** served **with meat ragù**, with tomato and eggplant sauce or all'arrabbiata. Alternatively there's spaghetti with garlic, chili pepper and olive oil, and various soups: chickpea, fava bean, bean, cardoon, and a nice **zarche** (wild greens) **soup with legumes**. Main courses are all very filling: **stewed kid**, rabbit in sweet-and-sour sauce, stuffed meat roulades, **pan-fried local snails**. They also barbecue pork and veal chops, **mutton**, sausages. There are several interesting recipes based on giblets: mixed tripe both cooked in tomato sauce and plain, crackling roulades, **pig's trotters** either **boiled** or cooked in tomato sauce, barbecued **stigghiole** (veal entrails), zireno (another part of the intestines) either roast or boiled.
Fresh fruit to round off a substantial, low-cost meal. There are a few bottled wines in addition to the house wine.

Lentini

A MAIDDA

Trattoria-pizzeria
Via Alfieri 2
Tel. 095 941537
Closed Wednesday
Open: dinner only
Holidays: in August
Seating: 80
Prices: 19-22 euros, wine excluded
All credit cards

This trattoria is situated near Piazza Duomo and was recently extended, but has kept its simple rustic air in the interiors and furnishings. The Maidda (local name for the kneading troughs where bread was made and kept) is run by Salvo Bordonaro and his wife Mariella, who offer some really good dishes prepared using only local produce.
For antipasti you will find sinape, anciti, wild fennel and other seasonal herbs tossed in the pan or used to make very good omelets, borrage rissoles, **caponata**, fried thistles, olives and baked onions, lemon and orange salads. The pizzas and a few typical focaccias, such as the so-called facci vecchia, are made in the wood-fired oven. Among the first courses the **pasta with broccoli** or with baby fava beans, penne alla Norma or with pistachio and zucchini, linguine with asparagus, spaghetti with Sicilian pesto, **lentil soup**, **bean soup with bacon**, chickpeas in vegetable broth. Very tasty main courses: roast sausage with wild sinàpa, **rabbit alla stimpirata**, tongue in aromas, **mutton**, roulades of sweet peppers in sweet and sour sauce. In season various types of **snails:** vavaluci, vaccareddi, 'ntuppateddi, crastuna are served. Occasionally you will find tench and eel caught in the nearby Biviere, which are then roasted or stewed. Dishes are served with a few regional wines at very fair prices.
To close, ricotta cannoli, lemon and almond blancmange, **citrus fruit tart** or ricotta tart.

Navarria at Via Conte Alaimo 12 sells traditional cakes and biscuits.

LETOJANNI

43 KM SOUTHWEST OF MESSINA

DA NINO

🗝 1-Star Hotel
Via Luigi Rizzo 29
Tel. 0942 36147
Fax 0942 651060
E-mail: danino.letojanni@tiscali.it
Open from March to November

Letojanni is a small seaside resort a few kilometers from the more famous, and therefore in summer more chaotic, Taormina and Giardini Naxos. This small hotel managed by the Ardizzone family is directly on the seafront. The hotel was created in a two-floor building once the home of fishermen that's annexed to the celebrated restaurant of the same name. The rooms are very clean and simply furnished in modern style, most of them offer a sea view and two have a terrace. Use of the private beach, including deckchairs and beach umbrellas, is included in the room price.

• 2 single and 10 double rooms, with bathroom, air-conditioning, TV; several with a terrace • Prices: single 40 euros, double 80, breakfast included • Credit cards: all, Bancomat • Public parking very nearby. Small pets allowed. Owners always reachable. • Restaurant. Private beach

🍷 The restaurant (50 euros, wine excluded) has a seafood menu and prepares dishes using really top-quality ingredients.

LETOJANNI
Mazzeo

44 KM SOUTH OF MESSINA A 18 OR SS 114

IL FICODINDIA ▮

🍲 Restaurant
Via Appiano 9
Tel. 0942 36301
Closed Monday, never in August
Open: lunch and dinner
Holidays: January-March
Seating: 80 + 100 outdoors
Prices: 35 euros, wine excluded
All credit cards

From the Taormina motorway junction, travel a few miles until you reach Mazzeo, a village on the Letojanni seafront. Walk through the lovely garden with its citrus trees and beautiful prickly pear tree to be warmly welcomed into the restaurant by the owner Rocco, who has ruled over the kitchen for more than thirty years, and his assistant chef Santino, who prepare strictly regional dishes with a few innovative and original touches.
The house antipasti offer a rich array of dishes, including the ring of zucchini and swordfish, octopus with Bronte pistachio, marinated anchovies and shrimps, swordfish cooked with tomatoes and cheese, caponata of tuna or stockfish, squid alla luciana, **sardines a beccafico**. Among the first courses we recommend the spaghetti with sea urchin, **ditali with fava beans and mussels** (in season), **linguine with Nassa shrimps**, gnocchi with pistachio and prawns, **pasta with tuna and wild fennel,** fusilli with swordfish and eggplant. Among the main courses, the **fish roulades Messina-style** and the **ghiotta di pesce stocco** are very good. Other suggestions: pauro with almonds, prawns in lemon leaves, marinated grouper. For puddings, flaky pastries with cream and strawberries, ricotta and strawberry semifreddo, **Bronte pistachio ice cream** and water ices made using citrus fruits from the garden.
A wide selection of wines, with special attention paid to Sicilian labels and a few interesting other Italian labels.

117 KM SOUTHEAST OF MESSINA

31 KM SOUTHWEST OF TRAPANI

PORTELLA GAZZANA

🍲 Restaurant-pizzeria
Contrada Portella Gazzana
Tel. 0941 485648
Closed Thursday, never in summer
Open: lunch and dinner
Holidays: September 25-October 25
Seating: 70
Prices: 22-25 euros, wine excluded
All credit cards

CENTRALE

🛏 1-Star Hotel
Via Salinisti 19
Tel. and fax 0923 951777
E-mail: info@hotelcentralemarsala.it
Internet: www.hotelcentralemarsala.it
Open all year

If you are visiting the Nebrodi you cannot fail to visit Portella Gazzana with its extraordinarily beautiful landscape: the Rocche del Crasto, formations of calcareous rock which rise up sheer and unattainable where eagles safely nest; the Mangalaviti Wood with its ancient groves of turkey oaks; the dense woods of beech, maple, ash, holly, wild apple and yew trees; the Lauro cave with its splendid stalactites and stalagmites. Against this wonderful backdrop the Drago family welcomes its guests to a restaurant where you will find the fire burning through until after May, which makes it even more pleasant to stop and relax there. Antonio prepares the menu following the seasons, with very inviting starters: omelet with wild chicory or beet, rissoles with wild fennel, fried bread, sausage and eggs, fried ricotta. Among the first courses we recommend the **spaghetti with wild fennel, maccheroni incaciati, mushroom soup, pasta with black pork ragù** from the Nebrodi. The main dishes all involve meat from local farms: **mutton**, lamb and potatoes, **boiled mutton, broadside of kid**. If you can't decide there is an excellent **mixed grill**. Very good pizzas are served from their authentic wood-fired oven with classic mozzarella or with flaky provola from the Nebrodi. To close, excellent hazelnut biscuits.
The wine list is simple but reasonable.

🍷 At the Roxy Bar, run by Francesco Lazzara, excellent granita of black mulberries, or hazelnut, almond and pistachio ice cream with freshly baked croissants.

This small hotel with its bright, comfortable rooms in the old fishermen's district has been created in an enchanting courtyard. The rooms are on the ground floor and on the two floors above, and have internal balconies. There's also a small terrace with a view over the roofs of the nearby houses. The hotel is on one of the roads that cross Via XI Maggio, practically right in the historic center, which can be explored by bicycles that the municipality provides tourists free of charge. For breakfast you'll be given vouchers that can be used in any one of three bars: if you don't want a croissant and cappuccino you can have a Sicilian granita and brioche or the even more typical pani cunzatu and a glass of Marsala. The hotel also has special arrangements with local restaurants. Among the many possible excursions in the surrounding area, don't miss out on a visit to the Phoenician island of Mozia in the middle of the Stagnone lagoon.

• 1 single and 6 double rooms, with bathroom, air-conditioning, mini-bar, safe, TV • Prices: double room single use 40-45 euros, double, 60-70 (25 euro supplement for extra bed), breakfast included • Credit cards: all, Bancomat • 1 room designed for use by the mobility challenged. Private parking in the immediate vicinity. No pets allowed; Owners always present • Terrace, chill-out area

GARIBALDI

Trattoria
Piazza dell'Addolorata 35
Tel. 0923 953006
Closed Saturday for lunch and Sunday for dinner
Open: lunch and dinner
Holidays: never
Seating: 110 + 140 outdoors
Prices: 23-27 euros, wine excluded
All major credit cards, Bancomat

IL GALLO E L'INNAMORATA

Trattoria
Via Stefano Bilardello 18
Tel. 329 2918503
Closed Tuesday
Open: lunch and dinner
Holidays: July-September
Seating: 32
Prices: 28-35 euros, wine excluded
All credit cards, Bancomat

Situated in the historic heart of the town, this traditional trattoria is ably and carefully run by Uccio and Salvatore, the former front of house and the latter in the kitchen. In summer, with the generous compliance of the local council, the trattoria also uses the small square in front, which, with its sun umbrellas becomes a patio guarding one of the ancient gates to the town – Porta Garibaldi, hence the name of the trattoria.

A wide choice of antipasti: seafood salad, **purpiceddi** (small boiled and seasoned octopus), caponata, different sardine dishes, eggplant tart prepared by Donna Josè. Among the first courses, the ever-present **fish couscous**, spaghetti with tuna ragù and peas, **bucatini with sardines**, **spaghetti with tuna botargo** from nearby Favignana. The fish market is just a few yards from the trattoria, and Salvatore goes there every morning to choose the best the sea has to offer, so it is obvious that the main dishes are all based on fish: tuna, cuttlefish, squid, sarago are all prepared true to the most traditional recipes. The meal ends with ricotta puddings in winter and ice cream in summer from a nearby confectioner's. There you will always find the famous **tagliancozzi**, almond biscuits to be served with a good glass of Marsala or vin passito.

The wine list offers the main Sicilian labels, with special attention to local production.

Gianfranco Vivona, at Via Bilardello 21, offers a good choice of typical cakes and biscuits.

Together with his cooks, wine buff Davide he decides the day's menu, which always offers a few strictly traditional dishes from the area, prepared with the best produce found at the market. They pay scrupulous attention to selecting the ingredients, including the **cured meats** of black Nebrodi pork and **vastedda** from Belice, both Slow Food Presidia.

The antipasti include bruschetta with tuna roe and cherry tomatoes or onions and sardines, rissoles with broccoli, panelle and arancinette. There are normally three first courses to choose from: one meat, one fish and one vegetables. Among the meat first courses excellent **busiati with pork ragù** from the meat of the black Nebrodi pig, **pasta with qualeddu** (Sicilian name for brassica) **and sausage.** Among the fish first courses, pasta with sardines, botargo and cherry tomatoes and **fish couscous**. Also very good pasta stuffed with vegetables and delicious **soup of crastuna**, local dialect for large snails. If you choose meat for your main course, you can go for spatchcock with ragù, sausage with qualeddu, **roast black pork** and, in season, local **game.** Alternatively, the day's catch of fish prepared in various ways, and in late spring excellent **tuna.** Very good home-made desserts: 'Turks' heads', cappidduzzi, cannoli and 'torta della nonna' made to an ancient recipe of Davide's family.

Late in the evening, the trattoria is a favorite place for friends to get together to taste a glass of some of the best Sicilian wines.

MARSALA
Birgi

LA TORRE

⬭ Restaurant
Contrada San Teodoro 269
Tel. 0923 966110
No closing day
Open: lunch and dinner
Holidays: from October to April
Seating: 60
Prices: 30-35 euro, wine excluded
All credit cards, Bancomat

Beneath the ancient San Teodoro tower, used as an outlook in medieval times, and in front of the mythical Mothia, a Phoenician column of inestimable value, you will find this typical seaside trattoria run by Caterina Principato and her husband Antonino Sansico. They work together in the kitchen to prepare fish dishes which are simple but rich in flavor and aromas, while their daughter Giuseppa and co-owner Francesco Gianquinto are front of house.

You start with **sardine rissoles** or neonata, Sicilian rissoles, **fried cappuccetto** (cuttlefish), sea snails, sea urchins, mussel soup, seafood salad. To continue we recommend the **gnoccoli**, typical fresh pasta similar to open maccheroni, served with **tuna ragù**, lobster or swordfish and eggplants. Alternatively spaghetti with seafood, al nero di seppia, with sea urchins or clams and, the highlight of Trapani cooking, **fish couscous**. If you book you can also try the lobster soup. The choice of main course depends on the day's catch: sarago, sea bass, squid either grilled, baked or fried. At the right time of year, you should try the **fritto di Stagnone**, fried freshly caught mullet and cuttlefish, and the **pisci rè**, very delicate fried fish, which the Marsala people adore.

All home-made desserts: fried **cappidduzzo,** a sort of sweet ravioli stuffed with sheep's cheese ricotta aromatized with lemon rind and cinnamon; fruit ice creams and ices. A short wine list with some of the most famous Sicilian labels

MARSALA

VILLA ALBARIA

⬗ Bed and breakfast
Contrada Spagnola 27
Tel. 0923 968373-348 1509823
Fax 0923 711361
E-mail: info@villaalbaria.it
Internet: www.villaalbaria.it
Open all year round

Sabina Giacalone and Enrico Vaccaro refurbished their villa in the protected area of Marsala's Stagnone Island Nature Park, turning most of it into a B&B while keeping the rest as their summer residence. From the first floor of the villa, especially from the terrace, you enjoy the most astonishing view of the Stagnone lagoon in the early hours of the day and again when the sun sets behind the Egadi Islands. The room in the tower has the best view. Room furnishings are mostly rustic, but there's also some period furniture and decorative objects. Breakfast, served on the veranda during summer, is traditional: tarts and other cakes are made by the owner.

• 1 single, 7 double and 2 triple rooms, with adjacent bathroom, TV (on request), terrace • Prices: single 35 euros, double 70-75, triple 85-90, breakfast included • Credit cards: none • Facility partly accessible to the mobility challenged. Free public parking close at hand. Small pets allowed. Owners always reachable • Reading room, TV room. Garden, veranda. Organized beach about 1 km away

MASCALI
Nunziata

MENFI
Porto Palo

30 KM NORTH OF CATANIA, 4 KM FROM CITY CENTER

87 KM NORTHWEST OF AGRIGENTO SS 115

LE CLEMENTINE

VITTORIO

Bed and breakfast
Via Pedata Sant'Agata 8-10
Tel. 095 969047–338 2714390–329 1612712
E-mail: info@villaleclementine.it
Internet: www.villaleclementine.it
Closed from 10/11 to 15/12, from 10/01 to 31/01

Restaurant/Rooms for rent
Via Friuli Venezia Giulia 9
Tel. 0925 78484-78381
Fax 0925 78381
E-mail vittorio@davittorioristorante.com
Internet: www.davittorioristorante.com
Closed Sunday and Monday for dinner
Open: lunch and dinner
Holidays: mid-December/mid-January
Seating: 100 +100 outdoors
Prices: 30-35 euros, wine excluded
All credit cards

In the Nunziata countryside you'll find this beautiful, refurbished villa surrounded by green citrus groves: 12 hectares of clementines, hence the name chosen for the B&B. The view stretching from Etna to the Ionian sea is indeed splendid and can be enjoyed from the terrace accessible from the three comfortable rooms. In order to make your stay more pleasurable Maurizio Vergnano and Rossella Lattes propose excursions in the mountains, trekking, fishing trips, cooking courses, Sicilian pastry-making courses, but also painting and decoupage. The swimming pool has a jacuzzi and a section where you're forced to swim against the stream. This B&B makes a good base as there are many towns and natural sites within easy reach in the surrounding area. A nice breakfast consisting of milk, coffee, tea, organic jams, fresh fruit, cheese and cured meats.

• 2 double and 2 triple or four-bed rooms, with bathroom, terrace, air-conditioning, mini-bar, satellite TV, 2 with kitchenette; 1 apartment (5 persons) • Prices: double room single use 60 euros, double 75, triple 95, four-bed 110, breakfast included • Credit cards: none • Facility and rooms accessible to the mobility challenged. Off-street parking. No pets allowed. Owners always reachable • Breakfast room. Garden, terrace. Swimming pool

This establishment lies in the ancient fishing village of Menfi and is managed by Vittorio Brignoli and his wife Francesca and children. The restaurant has a summer panoramic veranda and the rooms (available all week) face onto the sea and a fine sandy beach.
The cuisine is essentially fish based and so the menu depends a lot on the catch of the day. Antipasti usually include octopus salad, paranza fish fry, **sarde a beccafico**, marinated anchovies, sautéed **vuccuni** (winkles), sauté of real clams, eggplant cakes. The first courses include **spaghetti with cuttlefish** or clams and mussels, bavette with swordfish ragù or sea urchins, busiati with tuna or lobster. The **catch** of the day (blacktails, bass, dentex, prawns, sole, squid) is cooked **on the grill**, but you can also find **turbot served with potatoes**, swordfish with tomato, lobster Catalan style. The few meat dishes include pasta with broad beans and meatballs. For dessert, fruit in season and (except in the hotter months) orange tart and ricotta cake.
A short Sicilian wine list is available.

• 10 double rooms and 2 triples, en-suite, TV • Prices: double single use 50, double 60-70, triple 85-90 euros, breakfast included • Internal uncovered parking. Pets welcome. Owners available from 7am to 2am • Bar, restaurant

At Menfi, the Interrante dairy (contrada Cinquanta) also produces Vastedda della Valle del Belice, a rare spun curd sheep's cheese protected by a Slow Food Presidium.

AL PADRINO

🍲 Trattoria
Via Santa Cecilia 54-56
Tel. 090 2921000
Closed Saturday for dinner, Sunday and festivities
Open: lunch and dinner
Holidays: August
Seating: 50
Prices: 20-22 euros
Credit cards: Visa, Bancomat

VILLA MORGANA

🗝 3-Star Hotel
Via Consolare Pompea 1965
Tel. and fax 090 325575
E-mail: info@villamorgana.it
Internet: www.villamorgana.it
Open all year

In the center of town, at one of the crossroads with the long Viale San Martino, this trattoria has been open for about thirty years, a favorite for lunch with many of the office workers in the area. It has a genuinely homely atmosphere, with about twelve tables in the simply furnished dining hall, and a glass cabinet displaying various dishes. You are welcomed by the dynamic, ironic owner, Pietro Denaro, and his sister Cettina and other cooks in the kitchen.
To start there are usually eggplant roulades with baked ricotta, cauliflower fritters, stuffed sweet peppers, potato croquettes, boiled vegetables. The menu is read out to you and continues with **pasta and chickpeas**, **macco of fava beans**, maccheroni with tomatoes, eggplant and salt ricotta, **pasta alla carrettiera**, with sardines or prawns and zucchini. Among the appetizing fish dishes from the Strait of Messina we find **pesce stucco a ghiotta**, **alalunga a cipollata**, roulades of sardines or swordfish, spatula chops cooked a ghiotta with peas, roast alalunga surra, fried cicireddi, stuffed squid. If you choose meat there are very good Messina chop kebabs and **boiled ammuddicatu** (roast tip of brisket in bread crumbs).
To close, pastries with cream and fresh fruit. A few different wines and a passable house wine.

Riccardo Morichetti and his wife Federica manage this quiet little hotel created in a refurbished villa dating from the 70s, surrounded by lush green grounds with palms, ficus, pines, agaves, almond and tangerine trees. The property has a view of one of Ganzirri's two lakes linked to the open sea, where you are able to follow the flight of herons, cormorants, cinerini and other migratory birds. A view that can also be admired from some of the guest rooms, which all differ from one another. On the first floor there's a spacious, elegant hall with couches, wooden ceilings, a fireplace and a marble staircase. The Italian-style breakfast offers coffee, milk, hot chocolate, honey, croissants and fresh doughnuts and cookies. Use of a private beach in one of the most beautiful parts of the Messina coast is included in the room price.

• 2 single and 13 double rooms, with bathroom, air-conditioning, TV • Prices: single 40-55 euros, double room single use 60, double 65-90 (15 euro supplement for extra bed), breakfast included • Credit cards: all except DC, Bancomat • 2 rooms designed for use by the mobility challenged. Off-street parking. Small pets allowed (5 euros per day). Reception open 24 hours a day. • Restaurant. Breakfast room. Conference room. Garden. Private beach 2 km away

🍷 There is a wide selection of wines at the Abbate wine store, Via Garibaldi 66. Typical biscuits, 'nzuddi and pignolata from Colascione at Via Panoramica dello Stretto 1368.

MILAZZO

41 KM WEST OF MESSINA

MEDITERRANIMA

Restaurant
Via dei Gigli 13
Tel. 090 9210861-335 5981790
Closed Monday
Open: dinner, Sunday only for lunch in winter
Holidays: in October
Seating: 60 + 90 outdoors
Prices: 25-30 euros, wine excluded
All credit cards

At the fMilazzo junction, go west until you reach the sea front, where you continue towards Barcellona Pozzo di Gotto for just over a kilometer. At the first traffic light turn into the parallel Via Feliciata and, after another kilometer, you will find this restaurant situated in a lovely early 20th century villa. On summer evenings it is nice to eat outside in the luxuriant garden under the stars. Booking is essential here. You will be welcomed by Rossella Nastasi and Santino Vaccarino who have developed their cultural association as a tool for rediscovering the local culinary tradition, which shines through in some fish dishes inspired by old fishermen's recipes, expertly prepared in the kitchen by Salvatore.
To start, very good antipasti of **sea anemone in batter, lattume of fried tuna** in bread crumbs, marinated anchovies, roast and fried totani rings, spatula roulades with caponata, **scauratello** (tuna fish with eggplants and mint). Among the first courses very good **maccheroni with tuna ragù**, ravioli with grouper sauce, trenette with tuna eggs. To continue **alalunga with onion,** stuffed totani, roast spatula, sliced tuna steaks, **anciove 'rrusti e mancia** and other tasty dishes which vary every day depending on the local catch.
As dessert, orange jelly and lemon cream tart. A fair choice of regional wines.

The Bagatto wine bar at Via Regis 12 a, offers a good choice of Sicilian and other wines.

MODICA

14 KM SOUTHEAST OF RAGUSA

LA RUSTICANA

Trattoria
Viale Medaglie d'oro 34
Tel. 0932 942950
Closed Sunday for dinner, in summertime also for lunch
Open: lunch and dinner
Holidays: none
Seating: 40
Prices: 16-18 euros, wine excluded
Credit cards: CartaSi, Visa, Bancomat

The Giannone family has been running this genuine homely trattoria near the railway station for about 30 years. The owner and his children are front of house while his wife prepares the dishes of the day, which are listed on the blackboard set up by the dresser in the spacious dining hall. The very good cuisine is mainly meat-based, and strictly follows local recipes and methods.
To start we might find **pork in aspic**, dried spicy sausage, a few Sicilian cheeses. Among the first courses there are **lolli with fava beans**, cavatelli alla Norma, **ricotta ravioli in pork sauce**, pasta with wild vegetables, various pulse soups, tortellini in broth. For main courses there are various appetizing meat dishes: **rabbit alla stimpirata**, lamb stew, **boiled beef**, meatballs, **pork sausage and meat al sugo**, tripe, veal steak Palermo style. There are some very good omelets (especially the one with ricotta and asparagus), a tasty **salad of fave cottola** (a very good local variety), for side dishes boiled chicory, grilled eggplant and other fresh seasonal vegetables. Among the occasional puddings, delicious lemon and **almond geli**. To drink, a small selection of Sicilian labels,, besides the passable house wine.

At Vico De Naro 9, Don Puglisi produces excellent traditional Modica cakes ('mpanatigghi, nucatoli, mustazzola) and chocolate made from Ecuador cocoa paste.

MODICA
Frigintini

LE MAGNOLIA

Restaurant-pizzeria
Via Gianforma 179
Tel. 0932 908136
Closed Monday for lunch and Tuesday
Open: lunch and dinner
Holidays: two weeks in January
Seating: 120 + 100 outdoors
Prices: 25-32 euros, wine excluded
Credit cards: CartaSi, Visa

Olive oil, still a thriving activity in Frigintini, used to be made in the building where this restaurant is housed. There are well-furnished dining rooms on the ground and first floors, and a large terrace with a view of the countryside is used for al fresco dining in the summer. The owner Emanuela Macauda works in the kitchen with Massimo; her husband Giuseppe Giunta serves front of house. The menu changes with the seasons and market availability, offering traditional dishes with a few original touches.
Typical are the tasty antipasti of fresh ricotta, Provola, Ragusano with chili, seasoned olives, sun-dried tomatoes, **caponata**, Modica focaccia and dried sausage. Others starters are seafood salad and sliced tuna in sesame seeds. First courses: traditional **lolli with fava beans**, **ricotta ravioli with pork sauce**, pasta with tomato, eggplant and salted ricotta, ricotta gnocchi with smoked swordfish and mint, caserecce with sardines, wild fennel and breadcrumbs and tagliolini with shellfish ragù. For main course, **rabbit alla stimpirata**, **pork chops with potatoes**, excellent **baked dentex** and swordfish steaks. Desserts include very good lemon gelo and ricotta soufflé with almonds.
An excellent choice of Sicilian wines and other Italian wines and spirits comes with very honest markups.

In **Modica** (10 km), at Via Marchesi Tedeschi 5, the Casa del Formaggio offers a good selection of local dairy produce: fresh and mature Caciocavallo, Canestrato, Provola, salted ricotta.

MODICA
Frigintini

MARIA FIDONE

Trattoria
Via Gianforma 6
Tel. 0932 901135
Closed Monday
Open: dinner, festivities also for lunch
Holidays: second half of July
Seating: 90 + 70 outdoors
Prices: 18-19 euros, wine excluded
No credit cards

Situated on the main road running through Frigintini, this country trattoria takes its name from the owner, who faithfully interprets the most authentic Modica recipes. It has been open from more than 20 years and is formed of a large simply but attractively furnished dining hall. Maria is in the kitchen with her daughter Grazia, while her son Emanuele, helped by other relatives, is there to courteously serve the guests. The menu is read out loud and offers a choice of set dishes, with a few variations according to the season.
You start with olives, dried tomatoes, hot chili, cheese, pork in aspic, ricotta, all served with fragrant bread rolls, called 'nciminiteddi, which are cooked in their own wood oven. To enrich the antipasti there are croquettes in sauce, **tomasine** with sausage and ricotta and **scacce** filled with tomato, parsley and vegetables from the nearby orchard. Among the first courses of homemade pasta there are the **ravioli with ricotta and marjoram** garnished with pork sauce or fresh tomato sauce, **cavateddi** with ragout or **with eggplants and salt ricotta**, soup of **lolli with broad beans**. In the winter you will find the vegetable soups and always, at Easter and Christmas, the tagliolini in broth with chicken meatballs. For main course they serve excellent **rabbit stimpirata**, stuffed chicken and in the winter, **stuffed pork chops**.
The meal finishes with excellent lemon and almond geli. Unfortunately the wine is limited to a very ordinary house wine.

In **Modica** (10 km), in Via Cornelia 32, the L'Assaggio wine-bar offers a good selection of wines.

14 KM SOUTH-EAST OF RAGUSA

14 KM SOUTHEAST OF RAGUSA

RELAIS MODICA

🔑 3-Star Hotel
Via Campailla 99
Tel. 0932 754451–339 3123957
Fax 0932 754451
E-mail: info@hotelrelaismodica.it
Internet: www.hotelrelaismodica.it
Open all year

TAVERNA NICASTRO 🐌 ▮

🍲 Trattoria
Via Sant'Antonio 28
Tel. 0932 945884
Closed Sunday and Monday
Open: only for dinner
Holidays: one week in August
Seating: 100 + 40 outdoors
Prices: 18-20 euros, wine excluded
Credit cards: CartaSi, Visa, Bancomat

Along the central Corso Umberto, a stairway on the corner with the Istituto Magistrale leads up to this charming little hotel in an early 1800s noble palazzo, managed by Antonio Modica and his wife Francesca Baccolini who hails from Florence. Located on different floors of the building, every room varies in size and shape, although all are furnished with antiques. From some of the rooms – and in particular from the roof garden – there's a beautiful view of the historic center of this charming town, famous for its culinary tradition and confectionery. For breakfast you'll have a choice of coffee, yoghurt, cereal, orange juice, rusks, fresh fruit, croissants from the pastry shop, carob jam, dry cookies and local fresh milk.

• 4 double, 4 triple and 2 four-bed rooms, with bathroom, air-conditioning, satellite TV, modem connection • Prices: double room single use70-85 euros, double 85-105, triple 110-120, four-4 bed 120-140, breakfast included • Credit cards: all except AE, Bancomat • Public parking nearby. No pets allowed. Reception open 7am-midnight • Breakfast room. Terrace

Concetta Nicastro is responsible for what comes out of the kitchen in this trattoria, which she opened in Modica Alta together with her husband Michele back in 1948. It is situated on a panoramic stairway, where a few tables are laid in summer, and is now run by their son Salvatore who, besides helping his mother in the kitchen, welcomes guests to the simply furnished country style dining rooms. Among the strong points on the menu, the abundant antipasti that include **croquettes in ragù**, pork in aspic, cheese, grilled vegetables, vegetables in oil, **platter of mixed meats** and tomasine of sausage and ricotta. Virtually everything is homemade, including the cured meats that Salvatore prepares in the ripening room using exclusively local meats. The pasta, handmade by mum Concetta, becomes ricotta filled ravioli, tagliatelle, **cavatieddi** served with **pork sauce** or fresh tomatoes. Among the other first courses tagliolini in broth, traditional **lolli with fava beans** and in the winter pulse soups. Hearty main courses: Nicastro rabbit, **pork in sauce,** roast pork sausage and chops, **boiled veal**. If you book you can try the **'mpanata of lamb, tripe stew** and the fried pork inners. To finish lemon, cinnamon or almond geli and the liqueur digestive made from laurel leaves, again entirely homemade.
A good assortment of wines with honest markups.

🍴 From Antica Dolceria Bonajuto, Corso Umberto 159, excellent 'mpanatigghi, nucatoli, cedrata, cubbaita, chocolate with vanilla, cinnamon and chili.

MONTALLEGRO

Caracciolo

MONTELETUS

🍲 Trattoria
Contrada Caracciolo
Tel. 0922 845177-334 1650814
Closed Monday, never in August
Open: lunch and dinner
Holidays: in November
Seating: 70
Prices: 17-23 euros, wine excluded
No credit cards

This trattoria is a gastronomic landmark in the area between Sciacca and Agrigento (just a few miles from the lovely beach of Eraclea Minoa and its famous archeological site), and takes its name from the Latin name for the village of Montallegro. The charming hostess Adriana is helped in the kitchen by her mother Maria and the young Japanese chef Kenji.

Two menus are available: one turf and one surf. The former offers the more imaginative meals: potato flaky pastries with veal stew, roulades of primosale cheese, raviolini with broccoli and sausage, mushroom and spinach risotto, pork chops stuffed with sheep's cheese. The fish menu is more traditional, beginning with the antipasti: octopus salad, raw marinated swordfish, **swordfish roulades**, grilled sardines marinated in mint, panelle in garlic, **paddlefish in sweet and sour sauce**, fish rissoles, **sardines beccafico**, stewed rissoles, croquettes with prawns, in squid ink or creamed, croquettes with sheep's cheese and anchovies, or with tuna and potatoes. Among the first courses, we recommend the **gnocchetti with squid ink**, a delicate prawn risotto perfumed with citrus fruits, tasty **ravioli stuffed with grouper** and fish ragù. The choice of main course depends on the day's fish catch, cooked in the most traditional manner. Plus, **swordfish** with peppers and Primosale and prawns with vegetable ragù. For desserts, hot chocolate cake with lemon ice-cream, dark chocolate with pistachio parfait and crème brûlée.

The wine list offers a reasonable selection of local Sicilian labels.

NASO

LA PERLA

🍲 Restaurant
Località Contrada Franci
Tel. 0941 954135
Closed Monday, never in summer
Open: lunch and dinner
Holidays: none
Seating: 60 + 120 outdoors
Prices: 30 euros, wine excluded
All credit cards

On the state highway down the Messina Tyrrhenian coast, you come to Capo d'Orlando, where you'll find the turn-off for Piano San Cono in the direction of the village of Naso. Climbing up through all the twists and turns, after eight kilometers you come to this cozy, well-furnished restaurant with its pleasant summer patio and orchard. It is owned by Franco Mentesana, an expert cook, and his wife Isabella, who serves in the dining hall. They prepare mainly seafood dishes, using only the best quality ingredients. To start, the interesting mixed seafood antipasti include classics such as **sardines beccafico**, marinated anchovies, **mussels au gratin**, squid, mussels and prawn salad, **fish rissoles** with onion and fennel, and special preparations like palamita and artichokes, spatula in turmeric and squid maccheroncini with fresh fava beans. Among the first courses, very good tagliolini with swordfish roe and tomatoes, agnolotti stuffed with fish in prawn sauce, lasagne with squid ink, **bavette with pistachio and prawn pesto**. The right cooking methods highlight the freshness of the day's fish: grilled mullet, fried cod, **stewed capon**, boiled mackerel, **stuffed squid**.

Delicious semifreddo of pistachio and strawberries, orange jelly, ricotta cream puffs with cinnamon and crunchy wafers. The wine list contains a few good Sicilian labels.

NICOLOSI

LA GIARA

Bed and breakfast
Viale della Regione 12 A
Tel. and fax 095 7919022
E-mail: info@giara.it
Internet: www.giara.it
Open all year

Nicolosi lies at an altitude of 700 meters inside Etna Park. In the center of the village on a tree-lined avenue you'll find this villa surrounded by greenery, a few steps away from the ice rink. Patrizia Calvagna and her companion, who's a hotel activity technician, run this B&B. The bright, comfortable rooms are furnished in modern style, and offer a view stretching from the sea to the volcano. The filling breakfast includes milk, coffee (also barley coffee), chocolate, tea, brioches, toast, juices, jams, assorted cereals and yogurt. Clearly the territory offers interesting excursions in unique natural surroundings, including the volcano itself. 12 kilometers away there's the ski lift station to go up to the Sapienza shelter, while only 100 meters away there are tennis courts and an ice rink that's open all year round.

• 1 single and 3 double rooms, with bathroom, air-conditioning, TV • Prices: single 35-50 euros, double 50-75 (10-15 euro supplement for extra bed), breakfast included • Credit cards: MC, Visa, Bancomat • Off-street parking. Small pets allowed. Owners always reachable • Reading room with library, TV room, Internet point. Garden, terrace

NOTO

L'ARCA

Bed and breakfast
Via Rocco Pirri 14
Tel. 0931 838656–894202
Fax 0931 838656
E-mail: arcarooms@notobarocca.com
Internet: www.notobarocca.com/arcarooms
Open all year

The B&B run by Salvatore Buongiorno and his wife Arcangela is located in the historic center of Noto, in a courtyard with a rustic feel to it. You take the stairs up to the hospitality facility, which was previously an apartment they owned. The rooms are simple and furnished with couches, tables and small wardrobes. Breakfast is served in the room and offers cappuccino, coffee, tea, warm croissants and fruit juices. On request there are deckchairs available to sunbathe on the terrace overlooking Piazza XVI Maggio, site of the nineteenth-century Municipal Theater and the church of San Domenico. The surrounding hills offer many interesting natural, artistic and archeological sites to visit. A nice trip we recommend is the one along the Ionian coast down to the most southerly point of Correnti Island.

• 1 single, 2 double and 2 triple rooms, with bathroom, air-conditioning, fridge, TV • Prices: single 36-42 euros, double 50-72, triple 65-87, breakfast included • Credit cards: none • Public parking close by. No pets allowed • Internet point. Terrace

MASSERIA DEGLI ULIVI

🗝️3 Star Hotel
Contrada Porcari
Tel. and fax 0931 813019
E-mail: info@masseriadegliulivi.com
Internet: www.masseriadegliulivi.com
Closed from 10 January to 10 February

TERRA DI PACE

🗝️Holiday farm
Contrada Zisola
Tel. 0931 838472-347 3816097
Fax 0931 838472
E-mail: terradipace@aliceposta.it
Internet: www.agrituristsicilia.com/terradipace.htm
Open all year

In a late 19th-century farmhouse surrounded by olive and carob trees, Toto, Arianna and Junio Ambrogio have created a hospitality facility comprising both renovated and entirely new premises, in the typical architectural style seen in the Ibla area. The reception and communal areas are separate from the hotel proper, which has comfortable rooms with wooden ceilings and Sicilian terracotta tiles, and are furnished with hand-crafted cabinets and wardrobes. In the high season, from the third week of July to the end of August, prices are higher than indicated below (a double room costs 140 euros, breakfast included). This makes an ideal base for excursions to the baroque town of Noto, the Castelluccio archeological site and remains of Ancient Noto. The buffet breakfast consists of coffee, milk, tea, orange juice, homemade jams, along with sandwiches, cookies and pastries they produce themselves. The restaurant offers regional dishes, prepared with seasonal products – meals range from 25-30 euros, wine excluded.

• 6 double, 8 triple and 2 four-bed rooms, with bathroom, TV • Prices: double room single use 80-110 euros, double 90-120, triple 120-180, four-bed 130-210, breakfast included • Credit cards: all, Bancomat • 2 rooms designed for use by the mobility challenged. Off-street parking. No pets allowed • Bar, restaurant. Breakfast room. Swimming pool, tennis court, 2 boules courts

This agriturismo, perched on a hill surrounded by olive, almond and citrus groves, has a splendid view. Vincenzo Moscuzza, Pina Tinè and their children offer guests a pleasant stay in small houses that have been restructured and equipped according to bio-architectural methods. The wooden furniture and Sicilian terracotta tiles create a pleasant atmosphere for those who wish to take a break from the routine of everyday life. On summer days you can have a refreshing swim in the pool and you can also eat outside or on the veranda of the apartment. Just ask your hosts and they'll provide the ingredients you need to prepare your own breakfast: jams, citrus fruit and olive oil are produced organically on the farm. The sea is only six kilometers away and there are many possible excursions to places in the vicinity, among which the fascinating Cava Grande del Cassibile and Vendicari nature reserves.

• 6 apartments (2-3 persons), with bathroom, air-conditioning, kitchen, veranda • Prices: double room single use 28-35 euros, double 56-70, triple 84-105; breakfast 4 euros per person • Credit cards: none • Facility accessible to the mobility challenged. Off-street parking. Small pets allowed. Owners always reachable • Lounge. Playground. Swimming pool

NOTO

TRATTORIA DEL CROCIFISSO DA BAGLIERI

Trattoria
Via Principe Umberto 46-48
Tel. 0931 571151
Closed Wednesday
Open: lunch and dinner
Holidays: 1 week after Easter, 2 end-September
Seating: 46
Prices: 25-30 euros, wine excluded
All major credit cards, Bancomat

During a visit to Noto, a town that is famous the world over for its wonderful baroque architecture, we recommend stopping at this trattoria situated in the high part of the town. Just a few tables divided between two simply furnished dining rooms, where Marco Baglieri will serve you with the help of a couple of waiters. The homely cuisine is entrusted to the expert Mamma Corradina.
The rustic antipasti include potato rissoles, onion omelet, fried fennel and sweet peppers, breadcrumbed eggplant, grilled vegetables, caciocavallo, olives, dried tomatoes. Tasty hot boiled octopus, eggplant au gratin, **orange salad**. Among the fresh homemade pasta try the very good **ricotta ravioli with pork sauce**, cavatelli alla Norma and arrabbiata. Among the first courses of seafood, you will find **spaghetti with sardines**, with sea urchin, squid ink, swordfish and mint. In winter they prepare **pulse soups** and minestrone. Various appetizing main courses of meat: **rabbit alla stimpirata**, liver and onions, **beef stew with potatoes**, tripe in sauce, roast sausage and pork chops. Depending on the season, some succulent fish dishes such as **tuna cipuddata**, swordfish steak in citrus sauce, fried squid, sardines, anchovies, cod.
Among the homemade puddings, gelo of almonds, lemon, mandarin and traditional **nfigghiulata** of ricotta. A reasonable selection of Sicilian wines.

At Corso Vittorio Emanuele 125, Caffè Sicilia offers cakes, ice cream, ices, nougat, jams and honey of excellent quality. The Sarta bakers shop, in via Manzoni 1, makes good foccaccia, pizza and stuffed 'mpanate.

NOVARA DI SICILIA

LA PINETA

Trattoria
Via Nazionale 159
Tel. 0941 650522
Closed Monday
Open: only for dinner
Holidays: none
Seating: 60
Prices: 18-20 euros, wine excluded
All major credit cards

Novara di Sicilia is on the border between the Peloritani and the Nebrodi mountains. In this valley a sort of Gaelic-Italian language is still spoken; on the south the valley is closed off by Mount Salvatesta (known as the Matterhorn of Sicily) and is open to the north towards the Tyrrhenian Sea. At carnival time, the traditional maiurchea involves rolling Maiorchino cheeses (Slow Food Presidia) along the town streets. This attractive family run trattoria is situated in the center and offers the best of local cooking. The friendly hosts Giuseppe Giamboi and his wife, offer seasonal dishes with all the warmth of a family lunch.
You start with various antipasti including **fried ricotta**, mountain vegetable crepes, roast eggplant and zucchini, fried vegetable rissoles, sweet and sour onions, pumpkin au gratin with capers and olives, homemade pickles and preserves in oil. When the time comes, you will also find **maiorchino cheese**. The first courses are typical: hand drawn **maccheroni with a dense, creamy pork sauce**, doppiette with eggplants, **rigatoni with broccoli and sausage**, tagliatelle with fresh mushrooms. Among the appetizing main courses you will find tripe with tomatoes, **stoccafisso with onions** Novara style, stuffed suckling pig, roulades and roast meats, **roast kid**. Special mention goes to the **pork stew in sauce**, an ancient recipe excellently prepared by Mrs. Giamboi.
You close with cannolicchi, ricotta ravioli and a good home-made prickly pear rosolio. A selection of a few Sicilian wines and a fairly good local house wine.

PACECO

BAGLIO COSTA DI MANDORLA

Holiday farm
Via Verderame 37
Tel. 0923 409100-338 1035806
E-mail: info@costadimandorla.it
Internet: www.costadimandorla.it
Holidays variable

The vacation farm run by the Di Vita family is in a renovated late nineteenth century building just a short distance from the center of Paceco. It comprises four independent apartments, all with a kitchen, bathroom, living room, courtyard and a veranda with a view. Facilities available for guests include a swimming pool with outdoor showers, a solarium, boules court and barbecue area. During your stay you will be able to taste and buy the farm's produce, such as extra-virgin olive oil and jams of various kinds. There are many places to visit: Erice, Segesta, Selinunte, the Egadi Islands, the Trapani salt mines, Stagnone and Zingaro nature reserves and San Vito Lo Capo beach.

• 6 apartments (2-7 persons), with bathroom, kitchen, veranda; several with air-conditioning • Prices: 1-2 person apartments 80-105 euros, 3-7 persons 114-301, breakfast included • Credit cards: MC, Visa, Bancomat • 1 apartment accessible to the mobility challenged. Off-street parking. Small pets allowed. Owners always reachable • Breakfast room, TV room. Garden, solarium, children's playground. Swimming pool, boules court

PALAZZOLO ACREIDE

DA ANDREA

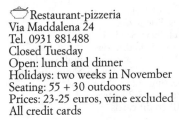

Restaurant-pizzeria
Via Maddalena 24
Tel. 0931 881488
Closed Tuesday
Open: lunch and dinner
Holidays: two weeks in November
Seating: 55 + 30 outdoors
Prices: 23-25 euros, wine excluded
All credit cards

Among the locations in the Noto Valley that have been declared human heritage sites by UNESCO, this village of beautiful churches and fine buildings is well worth a visit. The restaurant owned by Andrea Ali is in a side road off Corso Vittorio Emanuele. Andrea is the chef and he is helped in the kitchen by his brother Bruno and front of house by his wife Lucia.
They serve good local dishes that follow the seasons. Start with the local cured meats and cheeses, such as coppa, loin of pork, dried sausage, fresh Pecorino, Caciocavallo, baked ricotta, or capocollo with cabbage macerated in cooked must and, in season, sautéed **snails** and raw royal agaric mushrooms anointed with oil. First courses: **ricotta ravioli with pork** or stewed pumpkin, **cavateddi with asparagus and eggplant,** maccheroncini with fresh mushrooms and wild fennel, pasta with roast tomatoes, with diced veal, cherry tomatoes and mint, or with sausage, fennel, raisins and pine nuts, a mountain variation of the classic recipe with sardines. For main courses, Palazzolo **sausage**, roast or with sauce, pork stewed in Nero d'Avola wine, **roast lamb with potatoes,** fillet of veal with mushrooms, **sweet and sour rabbit** and pork chops with orange.
End with home-made ricotta and chocolate mousse or one of thee few other puddings. The wine list is dominated by Sicilian labels.

Try the home-made sausage from the Messina butcher's shop, Via Nazionale 28, and the bread and focaccia from the Vaccaro bakery, Via Annunziata 1.

PALAZZOLO ACREIDE   PALERMO

41 KM WEST OF SIRACUSA

TRATTORIA DEL GALLO

Osteria-trattoria
Via Roma 228
Tel. 0931 881334
Closed Wednesday
Open: dinner, on Sunday also for lunch
Holidays: August 16-September 10
Seating: 62
Prices: 18-20 euros
All credit cards

Just a short walk from the Chiesa Madre and the nearby Church of St. Paul, an admirable example of Baroque architecture, the osteria run by the Gallo family is open from the afternoon, if you want a snack with tasty **arancine al ragù**, freshly fried meatballs and hard boiled eggs. On alternate days the snack bar also offers slices of pizza with tomatoes, cheese and anchovies, and equally good **'mpanate** of broccoli, ricotta, potatoes, wild beet and other vegetables which are all prepared by Franca. Husband Salvatore and son Carlo are behind the counter and serve in the nearby dining room.
For antipasti, besides the rotisserie products, they normally serve dried sausage, marinated anchovies, olives, dried tomatoes, peppered pecorino, ricotta. The first courses always include cavateddi and **ricotta ravioli with pork sauce** or with tomatoes, tagliatelle with ragù, spaghetti with garlic, oil and chili. On Sunday there is also **baked pasta**, and, in the winter, pulse soup. Pork prevails in the main courses: roast sausage, **stuffed chops, pittinicchi al sugo.** Alternatively fried horsemeat steak, tripe in sauce, snails with tomato sauce and, occasionally, **roast kid** and rabbit chasseur. The meal ends with fresh fruit.
The wine is a painful note, just the house wine and a few odd bottles.

Excellent traditional cakes are made by the Corsino confectioners, Via Nazionale 2 and Caprice confectioners, Via Iudica 1.

AI CASCINARI

Trattoria
Via D'Ossuna 43-45
Tel. 091 6519804
Closed Mond., Tue.,Wed. for dinner
Open: lunch and dinner
Holidays: in August
Seating: 75
Prices: 28 euros, wine excluded
All major credit cards

Near to the historic Capo food market and the colorful antiques flea market, brothers Piero and Vito Riccobono run this trattoria, which is divided in five small dining rooms that are furnished simply and comfortably. Good quality cooking of classic Palermo dishes.
You start with boiled octopus salad with anchovies, olives and tomatoes, eggplant polpette in sauce, chickpea flour pancakes, potato croquettes plain or stuffed with ricotta, **sardines a beccafico**, and zucchini, cauliflower, mushrooms and fennel fried in batter. The menu changes every day and among the first courses you find **bucatini with sardines** (aromatized with wild fennel and raisins), fusilli with swordfish and tomatoes or broccoli and sausage, **spaghetti c'anciova and bread atturrata**, mezzemaniche with fresh beans and grated pecorino, pasta Lipari style with cherry tomatoes, anchovies, capers, eggplant and caciocavallo. Traditional main courses with tasty **baccalà sfincione**, succulent **bruciuluni** (falsomagro of veal), tripe and potatoes, **stuffed squid**, grilled tuna steaks, stuffed veal rolls al cartoccio, fried mixed fish.
The puddings come from a nearby confectioners: excellent cassata al forno. A reasonable selection of wines, mainly regional labels with average mark-ups.

All the tasty versions of Palermo bread (torcigliato, mafalda, filoni, pizziati) and traditional cookies (reginelle, quaresimali, algerini) from Fraterrigo bakers at Via Pannieri 26 and Tuttoilmondo at via Nebrodi 43.

ANTICA FOCACCERIA SAN FRANCESCO

🍲 Traditional osteria
Via A. Paternostro 58
Tel. 091 320264
No closing day
Open: lunch and dinner
Holidays: in winter
Seating: 200 + 100 outdoors
Prices: 3-20 euros, wine excluded
All credit cards

This historic osteria is built on three floors and is in the heart of old Palermo, in front of the lovely Church of San Francesco. It is run by Fabio and Vincenzo Conticello and is a real institution in the city. Here you find all the main specialties of traditional popular cuisine. Sitting at the cast iron tables made by the old Florio Foundry, placed around the smart Art Nouveau style counter, you can watch them preparing the **pani ca' meusa**, made with veal lungs and spleen to be tasted in the natural version with just a few drops of lemon added, or maritata, with slivers of Caciocavallo cheese. Alternatively, the fried chickpea flour **panelle, cazzilli** (potato croquettes), rice **arancine** stuffed with meat ragù, cardoons in batter, small pizzas, **sfincione**. If you prefer a complete meal, you can sit in the rooms upstairs and try, among others, the **baked timbale of anelletti**, **rigatoni with broccoli arriminati**, meat roulades stuffed with grated bread and aromas, to finish with a cannolo or slice of cassata. Good, mainly Sicilian, wine list. Professional and efficient service.

OTHER ADDRESSES FOR PANI CA' MEUSA
PANI CA' MEUSA
Porta Carbone – Via Cala 48
(In front of the tourist harbour)
FOCACCERIA BASILE
Piazza Nascé, 5
FOCACCERIA DI CARMELO BASILE
Via Ilardi, 22
FOCACCERIA TESTAGROSSA
Corso Calatafimi, 91

DAL MAESTRO DEL BRODO

🍲 Trattoria
Via Pannieri 7
Tel. 091 329523
Closed Monday
Open: lunch, Fri. and Sat. also for dinner
Holidays: two weeks mid-August
Seating: 60
Prices: 20-25 euros, wine excluded
All major credit cards

Damaged by time and neglect the Bocceria vecchia, the famous market that Palermo people have always called Vucciria, is still as fascinating as ever with its warm human atmosphere, colorful stalls and genuine characters like the seller of boiled octopus, the panellaro, u frittularu. Here in these poetic surroundings, which are unfortunately on their way out, Bartolo Arusa lived and grew up, working initially for others and then for himself, helped by his sons Sandro and Giuseppe. His spotless, friendly trattoria is situated at the entrance to the market on the side of the ancient Cassaro.

There are numerous buffet antipasti to choose from: sweet and sour pumpkin, **salad of mussu** (veal cartilage), eggplant roulades, caponata, fried squid and octopus. Very good first courses, including the **caserecce with swordfish and mint, bucatini with sardines,** tagliolini with zucchini and prawns. From the ancient recipes of "hearty soups" we have the steaming tortelli and the legendary **boiled meat with potatoes and saffron**, a rich single dish. Excellent main courses: breadcrumbed prawns, roast squid, very fresh grilled sargo, swordfish and tuna. The meal ends with fresh fruit and a few ice creams to choose from.

There is not a long wine list but there are some good quality labels. The price given above mainly refers to a fish meal; the price drops if meat dishes are chosen.

🍷 At bakers Fraterrigo, Via Pannieri 26, you will find flaky pastries, lemon taralli, small pizzas and enormous croissants with cream.

GARDENIA

2-Star Hotel
Via Mariano Stabile 136
Tel. 091 322761
Fax 091 333732
E-mail: gardeniahotel@gardeniahotel.com
Internet: www.gardeniahotel.com
Open all year

IL MEZZANINO DEL GATTOPARDO

Bed and breakfast
Via Alloro, 145
Tel. 091 6176120-333 4771703
Fax 091 6176120
E-mail: ilmezz.gattopardo@tiscali.it
Internet: www.bandbilmezzaninodelgattopardo.it
Open all year

The Gardenia Hotel is in the city center, between Piazza Ruggero Settimo and Piazza Verdi, on one of the roads that lead to the port. It was completely refurbished a few years ago and is equipped with very advanced technologies in compliance with EU regulations. You'll find the professional, efficient service usually associated with large hotels combined with that particularly cozy atmosphere typical of traditional Sicilian hospitality. All the rooms have en-suite bathrooms with shower and hair-drier; the majority also have a private terrace from which you can enjoy a view that stretches from Mount Pellegrino to the sea.

• 4 single, 10 double, 1 triple and 1 four-bed rooms, with bathroom, air-conditioning, TV, modem connection • Prices: single 65 euros, double 90, triple 130, four-bed 160; breakfast 5 euros per person • Credit cards: all, Bancomat • Garage (15 euros a day). Small pets allowed. Owners always reachable • Bar. TV room, reading room. Terrace

When you enter the historic center from Piazza Marina you come to Via Alloro, which was once an important residential street. Here, in front of the former Hotel Patria, you'll find architect Mimmo Targia's B&B on the second floor (the mezzanine floor) of a historic building that was inhabited by noble families back in the 15th century, and today has been carefully restored to recapture all of its original charm. The rooms are comfortable, pleasant and furnished with antique pieces. For breakfast, bread and cakes from the nearby bakery, organic jams and, on request, savory fare too. Guests can help themselves from the owner's fridge, pantry or wine cellar at any time of day. There are many fascinating things to see in the immediate vicinity if you stroll from the church of the Gancia to the regional art gallery in Palazzo Abatellis or the fourteenth-century Palazzo Steri and church of San Francesco d' Assisi (13th century). An itinerary that also offers stimulating chances to enjoy gastronomic delights and authentic specialties from the local cuisine.

• 2 double rooms, with bathroom, air-conditioning, mini-bar, safe, TV, kitchenette • Prices: double room single occupancy 80 euros, double 90-110, breakfast included • Credit cards: none • Public parking nearby. No pets allowed. Owners always reachable • Reading room with library, lounge. Hall organized for tasting typical products

PALERMO
Historic center

PALERMO
Old town

LA DIMORA DEL GENIO

☞—◑ Bed and breakfast
Via Garibaldi 58
Tel. 091 6166981-347 6587664
Fax 091 6166981-6164104
E-mail: paolamendola@ladimoradelgenio.it
Internet: www.ladimoradelgenio.it
Open all year

LETIZIA

☞—◑ 3-Star Hotel
Via dei Bottai, 30
Tel. and fax 091 589110
E-mail: booking@hotelletizia.com
Internet: www.hotelletizia.com
Open all year

This B&B run by Paola Mendola is in the city's monumental and commercial center, a few minutes from the railway station and located in a small, very well maintained historic building between the Piazza della Rivoluzione (where you will find Palermo's famous Fountain of the Genius) and Via Lincoln. The rooms, all of which have a private bathroom next door, are furnished with antiques and further enhanced by period frescos. Guests enjoy a generous breakfast consisting of Sicilian sweet specialties, jams and fruit juices that can either be eaten in one of the attractive communal rooms or, on request, in their own room. There are many palazzos, churches and monuments to visit in the surrounding area.

• 2 double and 1 triple rooms, with bathroom • Prices: double room single occupancy 70-80 euros, double 90-110, triple 120, breakfast included • Public parking nearby, private parking at a special rate (10 euros per day). No pets allowed. Owners always reachable • Breakfast room, lounge, TV room

The hotel is located between Corso Vittorio Emanuele, better known as Cassaro, and Piazza Marina. In the past this was the area the nobility chose for their palazzos around which the main public squares were then built. Communal areas are pleasant and cozy, furnished with antique pieces and Persian carpets. The rooms have been completely refurbished and now have parquet floors and are equipped with all modern comforts; some rooms also have a patio. The coffee bar itself faces onto a small patio planted with agaves and prickly pears. There's a generous, traditional Italian-style breakfast. You can rent cars and scooters. and on request management organizes private tours and excursions to Palermo and environs.

• 1 single, 11 double rooms and 1 suite, with bathroom (suite has a jacuzzi), air-conditioning, mini-bar, safe, TV • Prices: single 85-100 euros, double room single use 100-110, standard double 115, superior double 125, suite 118-150, breakfast included • Credit cards: all, Bancomat • Garage at a special rate (10 euros per day). Small pets allowed. Reception open 24 hours a day. • Bar. Breakfast room, Internet point

OSTERIA PARADISO

🍲 Trattoria
Via Serradifalco 23
No telephone
Closed Sunday
Open: lunch only
Holidays: second half of August
Seating: 35
Prices: 18-35 euros, wine excluded
No credit cards

A decidedly working-class atmosphere of yesteryear in this small local trattoria, which has been run by the Corona family since 1967. The simple traditional menu is read out to you and the fish can be chosen directly from a small counter, where you are certain to find the freshest and best quality available.

You start with a very tasty seafood salad, with boiled octopus or **fried cicirello** (type of small sardine). Among the first courses we should mention the spaghetti with clams or al nero di seppia, fresh **lasagnette** with **c'anciova** (small anchovies) and **toasted breadcrumbs atturrata**. There is then a wide choice of grilled sargo or swordfish, or **fish** cooked in **seawater**. If available, and to your liking, you should try the raw prawns seasoned with just a thread of oil and lemon juice. While fish is the main player here, there are also some good meat dishes: we recommend the boiled beef with anchovies and tomatoes and the **Palermo style roulades**. To close, fresh fruit, while if you want coffee it is best to go to the bar opposite. The choice of wines is rather limited.

As there is no phone in the trattoria, we advise arriving at opening time to be sure to get a seat; there are only six tables and it is quite normal to find yourself sitting at the same table as total strangers.

🍷 The Picone wine bar in Via Marconi 36, offers good wines from all over the world at reasonable prices.

PICCOLO NAPOLI

🍲 Trattoria
Piazzetta Mulino a Vento 4
Tel. 091 320431
Closed Sunday
Open: lunch, Oct.-June, Frid. and Sat. also for dinner
Holidays: 15-30 August
Seating: 52
Prices: 28-35 euros, wine excluded
All credit cards

The colorful stalls loaded with fruit and vegetables, the typical noise of the stallholders calling out their wares, are all still there thank heavens, in that kingdom of street food that is the historic market Borgo Vecchio: you will still find the fried food stands selling their panelle and rascature and peddlers selling sfincione and frittola which they press on you with their rough barking voices, all of it totally incomprehensible if you don't come from Palermo.

It was in the heart of this warm humanity in 1951 that the late lamented Orazio Corona gave life to what is now one of the most interesting trattorias in the city: with a combination of top quality ingredients (mainly fish), simple traditional cooking and a warm welcome that puts everyone at ease.

Gianni and Pippo, under the careful supervision of their mother Rosetta, will offer you a buffet antipasti to start, which includes fried calamari and prawns in the pot, **boiled octopus, eggplant caponata**. There are also a lot of first courses: we prefer the **bucatini with sardines**, spaghetti with sea urchins, **linguine with cuttlefish ink**. Seafood on the table for the main courses too: saraghi all'acquapazza, **roast cuttlefish**, grilled red mullet and **baked swordfish**, prepared using an ancient recipe which includes milk.

A small choice of desserts, including an excellent Sicilian cassata supplied by a famous confectioner. The wine list includes some very good Sicilian labels.

TRATTORIA DEGLI ARTISTI

Trattoria
Via Torquato Tasso 118
Tel. 339 4941920
Closed Sunday
Open: lunch and dinner
Holidays: two weeks in August
Seating: 38
Prices: 25 euros, wine excluded
No credit cards

This place is rather unusual for its position: it is unusual nowadays to find a plain traditional trattoria like this one in a residential area between the Libertà district and the smart Villa Sperlinga. When you pass through the entrance, you will find the small dining room with its basic furnishings which seats little more than thirty people, and facing you the open view of the clean and tidy kitchen. You don't have to be in a hurry here: the service is really slow, like the time it takes to eat lunch when the place is crowded. Giuseppe Di Blasi is in the kitchen (previously he worked in the local racecourse stables, but he has always loved cooking) and is helped by his wife, preparing the dishes with only top quality ingredients.

You can start with **boiled octopus**, seafood salad, **neonata**, marinated anchovies, raw prawns, fish carpaccio, impepata di cozze. Among the first courses, when in season, try the **pasta with tenerumi**, an excellent dish made using zucchini leaves. Alternatively try the **spaghetti** served with mussels and prawns, **with fish roe**, or with classic tomato sauce, enriched with fried eggplant and basil. The main courses are mainly meat: **falsomagro**, breadcrumbed roast, **roast lamb**. If you prefer to continue with fish, there is an excellent **tonno scottato**. Simple fresh side dish of tomato and green bean salad.

A few puddings, limited choice of local wines. Excellent quality-price ratio.

TRATTORIA PRIMAVERA

Trattoria
Piazza Bologni 4
Tel. 091 329408-329 2667775
Closed Monday
Open: lunch and dinner
Holidays: none
Seating: 50 + 35 outdoors
Prices: 20-25 euros, wine excluded
Credit cards: Visa

Located in one of the loveliest squares in the historic center of the city, surrounded by splendid baroque palazzos, this is the realm of Antonella and Ernesto Saviano. The cuisine is traditional Palermo with carefully selected ingredients. The passion of the restaurateurs, mother and son, was handed down to them by Antonella's parents who started up here in 1970.

The dishes change with the seasons. Among the antipasti, tasty **sardines a beccafico**, **sweet and sour spatula fish**, eggplant roulades, cold octopus salad. Traditional first courses include **bucatini with broccoli arriminati** (tossed in the pan) or with sardines, tagliatelle with swordfish and fresh mint, and tagliolini with zucchini, white prawns and tomatoes. The main courses are scrupulously prepared and unpretentious: **tuna a cipollata** (with onions), grilled veal brochettes, **swordfish roulades**. To finish, ricotta cassatele, Sicilian cassata, sorbets and ice-creams. The wine cellar gets better every year though it includes only Sicilian labels.

A special mention must be made of the efficient, reliable service, accompanied by a friendly smile. With just 18 euros, you can enjoy a complete and very satisfying set menu.

LA NICCHIA

Restaurant
Contrada Scauri Basso
Tel. 0923 916342
Closed Wednesday, never in summer
Open: only for dinner
Holidays: November 15-March 15
Seating: 50 + 50 outdoors
Prices: 32-35 euros, wine excluded
All credit cards, Bancomat

Gianni and Isabella once again confirm the name they've made for themselves over the years. Their restaurant continues to be one of the most interesting on the island thanks to their thoughtful, courteous, professional service and use of really high quality ingredients. If you make your reservation ahead of time you could be lucky enough to eat in the 'Pantelleria garden', a large circular construction surrounding a lemon tree to preserve it from the strong winds that sometimes hit the island.
You can start by choosing between the classic or the 'revisited' **caponata** made with eggplants, prawns, swordfish, tuna botargo and bitter cocoa. Among the firsts they have very good, ever-present **ravioli panteschi** (stuffed with ricotta and mint) with a fresh tomato sauce, cavatoni with tenerumi, mussels and botargo, tasty spaghetti with a condiment of capers, dried tomatoes, anchovies, chili pepper, breadcrumbs and a sprinkle of toasted almonds. Then on to the day's catch with either roast or fried fish: a special mention must go to the **king prawns allo zibibbo** and the **sea-urchins alla pantesca**, flavored with a Slow Food Presidia, the small Pantelleria capers with their strong aroma. To finish, there's nothing better than the **baci panteschi**, crisp layers of fried pasta filled with ricotta. Alternatively there are ice creams spiced with passito or cannoli. All of this, of course, accompanied by a nice glass of passito dessert wine.
The wine list is all Sicilian, with a special focus on the island's interesting new winemakers.

PANTELLERIA

6 HOURS BY FERRY FROM TRAPANI, 5 HOURS FROM MARSALA

LA VELA

Trattoria
Contrada Scauri Scalo
Tel. 0923 916566
No closing day
Open: lunch and dinner
Holidays: variable
Seating: 60 + 60 outdoors
Prices: 30 euros, wine excluded
No credit cards

A few meters from a slide used by fishermen to launch their boats near the port of Scauri, the island's second largest port, Elio and his wife run a trattoria that, as you might imagine, has made seafood cuisine a must. The menu has been tried and tested over the years and offers classic traditional dishes that, as always, are very capably prepared by Rina and Antonio.
You usually start with boiled octopus and the **mixed fried platter** or island vegetables (the zucchini are especially good). There's an interesting dish they call **ciakiciuka**, a kind of local revisited classic Sicilian caponata prepared with stewed vegetables. The first course is all based on seafood. Well worth a mention, the **couscous alla pantesca**, with vegetables and fish served whole on your plate, spaghetti with either sea urchins or scampi and cherry tomatoes. You then continue with whatever fish you ordered from the tray shown to you at the table, fish that's prepared in one of the more classic manners: fried, barbecued or all'acquapazza. For dessert, there's the ever-present **baci panteschi** (a kind of fried pasta in a flower shape, filled with ricotta) that will be served together with an excellent glass of passito di Pantelleria.
The cellar has mainly leading Sicilian wines but with a special focus on interesting new local labels.

At the Caper Producers Cooperative in Contrada Scauri Basso you'll find the famous Pantelleria capers, a Slow Food Presidium.

PANTELLERIA

ZINEDI

🍲 Holiday farm
Contrada Zinedi
Tel. 0923 914023
No closing day
Open: only for dinner
Holidays: from November to April
Seating: 100
Prices: 20 euros
No credit cards

This pleasant vacation farm run by the Valenza family is just below the airport on a ridge dominating the Punta Spadillo lighthouse. Every evening this restaurant marked by Matteo's thoughtful, courteous and fast service is open to non-residents who can enjoy a set menu priced at 20 euros.

You start with a generous buffet of antipasti that includes caper pâté, classic caponata and the revisited Pantelleria version, **ciakiciuka**, tasty local dried tomatoes and tumma, a fresh cheese they produce on the farm. After this you can choose from the exquisite **couscous pantesco** with vegetables and fish, the classic **ravioli filled with mint and ricotta** prepared by Matteo's aunt Franca, pasta with grouper and capers, with cuttlefish and peas, with limpets, with Pantelleria pesto. Main courses vary depending on the day's catch. Alongside the usual barbecued fish, special mention should be made of the **squid alla pantesca** (stuffed with bread, almonds, fresh tomato, capers, pine nuts and garlic), **oven-baked ricciola** and grouper. To end your meal, baci and mustazzoli go down well with the passito they produce themselves. The choice of wines is limited to a local house wine and a few bottles from small Sicilian growers.

The farm also has a small store where you can buy jams, zibibbo honey, extra-virgin olive oil and passito, and can offer hospitality for around thirty people in mini-apartments and double rooms.

PETRALIA SOPRANA

DA SALVATORE

🍲 Trattoria-pizzeria
Piazza San Michele 3
Tel. 0921 680169
Closed Tuesday, never in summer
Open: lunch and dinner
Holidays: variable
Seating: 40 + 30 outdoors
Prices: 18-22 euros, wine excluded
No credit cards

The SS120 trunk road seems to string together the four Sicilian parks of Alcantara, Etna, Nebrodi and Madonie and the two Petralia's are to be found right on the ridge: Petralia Soprana was founded by the Sicani and at 1147 m above sea level is the highest town in the Madonie area and the entire province. Some ugly modern buildings ruin the entrance to the village, but as you climb slowly up towards the center along the narrow winding roads, you will discover small and large squares obviously dating back to medieval times, churches and buildings in different styles, baroque balconies and open stone façades. A very attractive corner is the small Piazza San Michele, which is where in this attractive trattoria Salvatore offers you traditional Madonie dishes.

You start with very fresh ricotta before tasting the excellent provolone and cheeses in baskets. Among the antipasti the highlight is the **omelet with wild herbs**: the best in our opinion is with purretti (wild leeks). Salvatore personally harvests the excellent ingredients from the surrounding fields that his wife uses to prepare the tasty **pasta cchi virduri** or to enrich the various **soups**: with beans and chicory, broad beans, or with chickpeas. If you prefer pasta there is a very rich **pasta with mutton and sausage sauce** or with wild boar ragù. The meat all comes from local farms: excellent the **grilled** lamb, kid, veal or pork for main course.

You close with their homegrown fruit or some good traditional cookies. The house wine is reasonable but there are also a few good Sicilian labels to choose from.

MONACO DI MEZZO

Holiday farm
Contrada Monaco di Mezzo
Tel. 0934 673949
Fax 0934 676114
E-mail: info@monacodimezzo.com
Internet: www.monacodimezzo.com

PETRAELEJUM

Restaurant
Corso Pietro Agliata 113
Tel. 0921 641947
Closed Friday for dinner, never in summer
Open: lunch and dinner
Holidays: none
Seating: 46
Prices: 18-22 euros, wine excluded
All credit cards

For centuries Monaco di Mezzo has been the heart of the Feudo Monaco; this is where you'll find the recently refurbished church where mass used to be celebrated. Acquired by Baron Michele Pottino in 1855, today it's part of a working farm that as a sideline also offers vacations. The main farmhouse contains the rooms and apartments (the latter can be rented for a minimum of seven days), a restaurant and a communal area with lounge and TV room. There's also a tennis court, riding school and swimming pool. Guests can try many homemade products and buy them here too: wine, oil, cheeses, jams, cured meats and beef. Breakfast comprises both sweet and savory fare, and is also based on the farm's own produce. Half board 60-65 euros, full board 70-75 euros for person.

• 9 double rooms and 6 apartments (4-6 persons), with bathroom, air-conditioning, TV, modem connection; apartments with kitchenette • Prices: double room single occupancy 60-65 euros, double 80-90, breakfast 5 euros per person • Credit cards: all, Bancomat • 2 rooms designed for use by the mobility challenged. Off-street parking. Small pets allowed. Owners always present • Bar, restaurant. TV room, lounge. Swimming pool, tennis court, riding school

The Madonie mountains are the most ancient of Sicilian lands to emerge: the Carst grottos and the woods in which trees and plants such as beech, larch, basil and holly (which grows to an exceptional size here) are the two distinguishing features of the area. Petralia Sottana is on the left bank of the River Imera, on a rocky spur that overlooks a natural amphitheatre of woods and meadows. The Petraelejum is a small, efficient family-run restaurant and is situated on the main road of the village. There is a bar as you enter behind which you find two attractive dining rooms where you will be warmly welcomed by Vincenzo and his mother.
To start you will be offered ricotta and other cheeses supplied by the trusted local dairies. Vincenzo's father works in the kitchens preparing the excellent **wild vegetables in batter** (you must try the napruddi, wild thistles, which can also be baked) and the balls of wild fennel. Among the first courses, in borrage season, you must try the mountain crepes and the excellent **tagliatelle with ricotta and urranii**. Alternatively, they make very tasty **pasta with boar ragù**. The **stewed** lamb or kid is the best of the main courses, together with the grilled meats, all sourced from local farms.
The family has a passion for wine and there is a reasonable selection of good Sicilian labels. The house wine is also very pleasant.

POMIERI

🍲 Restaurant attached to the hotel
Contrada Pomieri
Tel. 0921 649998
No closing days
Open: lunch and dinner
Holidays: three weeks in November
Seating: 200
Prices: 18-22 euros, wine excluded
No credit cards

LA CASA SULLA COLLINA D'ORO

🛏️ Bed and breakfast
Via Mattarella
Tel. 0935 89680-333 4668829
Fax 0935 89680
E-mail: info@lacasasullacollinadoro.it
Internet: www.lacasasullacollinadoro.it
Open all year

This area is one of the most interesting in the Madonie mountains, a place of woods, green valleys, deep precipices and cool streams, where you suddenly come across enchanting little villages, rich in works of art and breathtaking views. The friendly inn that Ignazio Ganci and his family run is in a clearing just 2 kilometers from the ski station at Piano Battaglia, the only one in western Sicily, popular with sports fans and enthusiasts. The simple genuine cooking uses only carefully selected top quality ingredients and the recipes are the traditional mountain ones, varying according to the seasons.

You start with a hearty onion frittata, wild asparagus or mushrooms, **goat salami** and **pork in aspic**. These are followed by the bean soup, delicious **tagliatelle with boar ragù** or hare caught in the woods, pork cutlets with wild herbs, stigghiole of grilled lamb, u **bruciuluni** and, when in season, T-bone steak with Madonie cep mushrooms.

Desserts are traditional too: cannoli, cheesecake (**sfogghiu**) and almond semifreddo. The cellar boasts a few good Sicilian wines.

Located in a very nicely renovated late 19th-century house (also on the Relais de charme circuit), this B&B is only a few hundred meters from the historic center, with its wealth of examples of medieval and baroque architecture. The rooms are elegantly furnished and there are large communal areas, comprising two spacious lounges (one has a large window affording a magnificent view). But there's also a 1000 square-meter garden planted with indigenous flora and a terrace from which you can admire the ancient Canali quarter, with its cathedral and the Aragonese castle. The generous breakfast served in a relaxed family atmosphere consists of almond pastries, brioches, cookies and warm bread buns that can be filled with a variety of homemade jams. On request they can arrange guided tours (Italian or German tour guides are available) to the Casale Roman villa and to the archeological sites of Morgantina, Philosophiana and Rossomanno. There's also a shuttle-bus service to and from Catania airport or railway station.

• 5 double rooms, with bathroom, satellite TV • Prices: double room single occupancy 45 euros, double 70 (20 euro supplement for extra bed), breakfast included • Credit cards: none • Off-street parking. Small pets allowed. Owners always reachable • Breakfast, reading and conversation room, TV room. Garden, terrace, solarium

🍯 In contrada Tùdia, Tùdia makes and sells natural and biological preserves: marmalades and jams, bottled sauces, eggplant caponata and vegetables preserved in oil.

PIAZZA ARMERINA

LA RUOTA

Trattoria
Contrada Paratore
Tel. 0935 680542
No closing day
Open: only for lunch
Holidays: none
Seating: 32 + 50 outdoors
Prices: 20-25 euros, wine excluded
All credit cards

The trattoria is situated in a very old watermill in the valley where Platia (the ancient Piazza Armerina) used to lie, surrounded by the hills that saw the flourishing development of Sicilian civilization, about 500 meters from the archeological site of the Roman Villa in Casale, which is on the UNESCO world heritage list. The osteria is furnished in a very simple, friendly manner with a warm family atmosphere.

Fiorella's traditional homely cuisine gets the most out of the genuine local ingredients she uses, to offer guests a good choice of first courses of fresh homemade pasta, main courses using meat from animals bred in the Piazza Armerina area and fresh local vegetables. Among the first courses you must try the **maccheroncini with wild fennel** (when in season), or Norma style, or Sicilian style, or **alla carrettiera**; among the main courses excellent **rabbit alla stemperata**, veal or pork chops, **sausage, lamb chops**. Excellent typical side dishes: Sicilian **caponata** garnished with local extra virgin olive oil, grilled eggplant, baked peppers, **artichokes in tegame**. To close on a sweet note, choose from among the almond pastries, cannoli or fruit salad.

The wine list is not very long, but the wines that are available are very reasonably priced. In summer we recommend eating outside.

PIETRAPERZIA

BELVEDERE

Trattoria
Via Castello
Tel. 333 8307488-333 4274086
Closed Monday
Open: dinner, lunch if you book
Holidays: October 1-15
Seating: 45 + 120 outdoors
Prices: 15-20 euros, wine excluded
No credit cards

Take the Caltanissetta exit from the A19, and you enter the high road that leads to Gela: when you reach Ponte Capodarso, you will find signposts for Pietraperzia. In this old medieval village, near the castle, which provides a lovely view over the mountain landscape, Gabriele and Filippina have taken over a council-owned trattoria and furnished it in a very simple, tasteful style. Their two young sisters Giulia and Marta work in the dining room, although the whole family gives a hand when needed. The menu offers traditional local recipes and varies with the seasons. In winter they prepare excellent antipasti of **pork in aspic**, **small cheeses** personally made by Gabriele (he owns 300 goats), some cheeses and cured meats of local Slow Food Presidia. They are followed by **homemade maccheroni with aggrassato mutton sauce**, pasta pirzisa (Pietrina style) with broccoli, dried tomatoes, olives, capers and sausage, kid cooked in the canale (terracotta casserole), goats' ricotta cannoli. In summer you start with **caponata**, fresh fava beans with pecorino, roast ferla mushrooms. Continue with **fava bean macco** or the caserecce, garnished with fresh vegetables or cherry tomatoes, basil, garlic, capers and chopped almonds. **Grilled mutton**, sweet and sour meatballs, **fillet all'argintera** (tossed in the pan with garlic, oregano, vinegar and caciocavallo cheese).

Gabriele bakes his own bread and the oil is homemade. The wine list only has a few but good quality labels. During the summer you can eat outside in the cool shade of the citrus trees.

83 KM SOUTHWEST OF PALERMO, 15 KM FROM CITY CENTER

83 KM SOUTHEAST OF PALERMO

ANTICO FEUDO SAN GIORGIO

Holiday farm
Strada Statale 120, km 46
Tel. 0921 642613–333 4214946–347 3475890
Fax 0921 642613
E-mail: info@feudosangiorgio.it
Internet: www.feudosangiorgio.it
Open all year

ITRIA

Trattoria
Via Beato Gnoffi 8
Tel. 0921 688790
Closed Wednesday
Open: lunch and dinner
Holidays: 2 weeks after 25 September
Seating: 50 + 30 outdoors
Prices: 22-24 euros, wine excluded
No credit cards, Bancomat

This vacation farm is in the heart of the Madonie Park where the Fatta della Fratta family built a country house in the 19th century. After careful reclamation of the land and renovation of the buildings, 1994 saw the launch of the two activities seen today – organic agriculture and rural hospitality. The apartments – all spacious and with either one, two or three bedrooms, lounge and bathroom, while some also have a kitchenette – are tastefully furnished and offer all modern comforts. The single and double rooms all have en suite bathrooms. Meals in the restaurant cost 25 euros per person, including beverages, and are prepared using the farm's own produce, where available. In summer, lunch can be served on the panoramic terrace. Those who love walking will find a very wide choice of natural paths to explore in the Park.

• 5 double rooms and 9 apartments (4-7 persons), with bathroom; apartments with mini-bar • Prices: double room single use 40-45 euros, double 80-90, apartment 145-170, breakfast included • Credit cards: major ones, Bancomat • Facility accessible to the mobility challenged, 1 apartment designed for their use. Off-street parking. Small pets allowed • Restaurant. Reading room, TV room, games rooms. Garden with children's playground. Swimming pool, table tennis

Polizzi Generosa is situated in the heart of the Madonie, amidst luxuriant woods of oak, larch and hazelnut trees, one of the resources of the district. For lovers of artistic beauty, the village with its winding streets, offers numerous noble palazzos and churches, with the elegant lines of the cathedral, which contains a precious triptych from the Flemish school, standing out.
Itria is a simple village trattoria, lovingly and enthusiastically run by Giuseppina and Renato in a relaxing friendly atmosphere. In the kitchen the ingredients are all excellent local produce, enhancing, but never overwhelming, the genuine local flavors.
The menu changes with the seasons. You start with chickpea or lentil soup, tripe, grilled **stigghiole** (lamb giblets), omelet of wild asparagus or pore mushrooms (when in season). Very flavorsome first courses as well, **ditali with badda beans**, a Slow Food Presidia, strong tasty **bucatini with mutton ragù**. Among the main courses we recommend the roast pork shank, local grilled **wild boar chops** and roast madonita sausage. Good hearty puddings: hazelnut semifreddo, ricotta cannolo and, of course, the unforgettable **sfogghiu**, the local cheesecake.
A small but quality wine cellar, excellent family style service. Very reasonable prices.

Vinci confectioners, at Via Garibaldi 134, make traditional top quality cakes and a traditional sfogghiu.

PORTOPALO DI CAPO PASSERO

MAURÌ 1987

Restaurant-pizzeria
Via Tagliamento 22
Tel. 0931 842644
Closed Tuesday, never in summer
Open: lunch and dinner
Holidays: 3 weeks between Oct. and Nov.
Seating: 70 + 30 outdoors
Prices: 35 euros, wine excluded
All credit cards

On the southeast tip of Sicily, facing the village of Portopalo, the island of Capo Passero, together with the nearby Correnti island, acts as a breakwater between two seas: the Ionian to the northeast and the Strait of Sicily to the southwest.

In a side road off the main street, you find the restaurant run by Maurizio Morittu, with his brother Giovanni in the kitchen. It is also a pizzeria and is very busy during the summer when the tourists arrive. The strongpoint is the excellent locally caught fish.

For antipasti we would mention tuna botargo al salmoriglio, **polpette di novellame**, boiled polpetti di scoglio, salad of prawns marinated in orange, smoked swordfish and tuna. The choice of first courses includes fusilli with swordfish and Pachino cherry tomatoes, **risotto al nero di seppia** or with shrimps and seafood, spaghetti with botarga, **pasta with sardines,** linguine with scampi. From May to October you will find dishes making full use of local **tuna**: penne with tuna and pennyroyal, tuna slices grilled or stewed with onions, tuna ghiotta. Among the main courses grilled calamari, **swordfish alla matalotta** or fried with mint and vinegar. From the counter you can personally choose fish that has just been caught (dentex, sargo, mullet, aioli, shellfish) to be roasted, alla marinara, or all'acqua di mare.

For puddings, ricotta cannoli, homemade cakes and lemon sorbet. An extensive wine list with some interesting labels.

RAGALNA

IL PALMENTO DELL'ETNA

Bed and breakfast
Via Rocca 22
Tel. 095 620977-338 3445794
Fax 095 7122784
E-mail: info@ilpalmentodelletna.com
Internet: www.ilpalmentodelletna.com
Open all year

Ragalna lies on the south-western slopes of Etna at an altitude of approximately 850 meters and has a view over the countryside stretching from the Simeto valley to the bay of Augusta. The surrounding territory is popular for excursions as it contains a wealth of spontaneous vegetation, forests, large caves and desert-like areas extending up to the top of the crater. The B&B with rooms tastefully furnished in Sicilian arte povera style is in a renovated rural villa with a mill dating back to the second half of the nineteenth century. Grazia Di Stefano will welcome you to this house that was renovated thanks to the efforts of her daughter, Cettina. The buffet breakfast includes homemade jams and local produce, including cookies and cakes from the bakery, that you can enjoy on the terrace, in the garden or inside the mill.

• 2 triple and 1 four-bed rooms, with bathroom, TV • Prices: triple room single occupancy 40-60 euros, triple double occupancy 70-90, triple 90-100, four-bed 110-120, breakfast included • Credit cards: none • Off-street parking. Small pets allowed. Owners always reachable • Breakfast room, reading room. Terrace, garden

CUCINA E VINO

Recently opened osteria
Via Orfanotrofio 91
Tel. 0932 686447
Closed Wednesday
Open: lunch and dinner
Holidays: in February
Seating: 50 + 15 outdoors
Prices: 25-32 euros, wine excluded
All credit cards

In one of the many delightful corners of the historic center of Ibla, you will find this place on the ground floor of an early 19th century building that still retains the stone vaults of the original structure. The tables set in the three small, delightfully furnished rooms are joined in summer by several places in the inner courtyard. All management aspects are taken care of with great passion by Luigi Grasso and his son Luca, helped in the kitchen by the young and promising Giovanni. The menu includes dishes in keeping with the culinary traditions of Sicily with a few, lighter touches.

The excellent antipasti include omelets with asparagus or other vegetables, focaccine with tomatoes, olives and capers, vastedda del Belice with grilled vegetables and **eggplant alla parmigiana**. These are followed by **ravioli with ricotta and pork sauce**, cavateddi with ricotta and finocchietto or pumpkin and ricotta, **rigatoni with white meat sauce** and caserecce with vegetables and basil. There are delicious veal roulades with Marsala wine, potato pie and **shoulder of lamb with potatoes allo zafferano**. Other main courses include: crunchy pork with potatoes and wild herbs and pork fillet with a prune sauce. The **orange salad** with fennels and lettuce is also delicious, as well as the salad with cicorietta, fresh beans, raisins, pine nuts and flakes of Caciocavallo cheese.

Puddings include exquisite wafers with ricotta and home-made tarts. Small selection of Sicilian wines.

ORFEO

Restaurant
Via Sant'Anna 117
Tel. 0932 621035
Closed Sunday
Open: lunch and dinner
Holidays: two weeks in August
Seating: 45
Prices: 25-30 euros, wine excluded
All credit cards

Near Piazza San Giovanni and the cathedral, this place is furnished in a staid, basic manner; managed by the Criscione family since 1970, in the 1930s it was a typical osteria. The owner is front of house, while his wife looks after the kitchen. The menu embraces typical dishes from the Ragusa area and, more in general, Sicilian specialties, depending on seasonal supplies. Antipasti include caponata, omelets, stuffed artichokes, mushrooms and breaded eggplant, grilled Ragusa cheese. First courses include **penne with sanapo** (a local vegetable), **spaghetti mollicati**, gnocchi with red pumpkin and ricotta, **cavati with cappuliato and tomatoes**, sautéed orecchiette with broccoli, pasta with eggplant, swordfish, cherry tomatoes and almonds. In winter, dishes always include **macco di fave**, pea soup and lentil soup. There are many meat-based second courses: sausage cooked in Nero d'Avola wine, beef meat balls with potato puree, **veal stew** and **pork with a sauce topping**. Fish dishes include the interesting angler fish alla marinara and fillets of **baccalà alla ghiotta**.

Puddings include a delicious cassatella with ricotta, mousse of ricotta, almonds and honey. Several fair local wines are also served.

At Via Veneto 104, Di Pasquale has a good selection of pastry specialties. Casa del Formaggio Sant'Anna, at Corso Italia 330, has an interesting selection of local cheeses such as Provole, ricotta, fresh and mature Ragusano.

SAN GIORGIO E IL DRAGO

Trattoria
Piazza San Giorgio 28
Tel. 095 923972
Closed Tuesday
Open: lunch and dinner
Holidays: in January
Seating: 80 + 50 outdoors
Prices: 25-27 euros, wine excluded
All credit cards

VENEZIANO

Trattoria
Via Romano 8 A
Tel. 095 7991353
Closed Sunday for dinner and Monday
Open: lunch and dinner
Holidays: in July
Seating: 90
Prices: 25 euros, wine excluded
All credit cards

This mountain village has retained the urban layout of the original Medieval hamlet. Strolling in the lovely historic center, opposite the convent of San Giorgio, you will find this trattoria set in a XIX century cellar, with two very welcoming rooms that are often crowded on holidays (booking is advisable). You will be welcomed with a smile by Samantha and the kindness and helpfulness of Daniele Anzalone. Their mothers in the kitchen are the true soul of this place, preparing dishes in keeping with Etna traditions.

The house antipasti include provola, **baked ricotta**, cured meats, potato crocchettes, melted scamorza, omelets of vegetables, and cooked vegetables. First courses include home-made maccheroni with a spicy sauce, pansotti stuffed with eggplant with tomatoes and salted ricotta, **casarecce with sparacogne** (wild vegetables), ravioli al ragù. There are one or two more conventional dishes that the owner says are requested by the many tourists that come to dine here. There follow substantial meat second courses such as stewed rabbit, veal roulades, **sausage sauteed with cavuliceddi,** and **roast lamb**. In season, don't miss the dishes based on Etna cep **mushrooms**: such as the excellent braised meat with cep mushrooms and almonds.

Small selection of desserts. The wine list – entirely Sicilian – could be improved, including graphically.

Managed with great passion by a close-knit family group, this friendly trattoria has been open for more than 50 years. On entering the large dining room, you will be greeted by Salvatore and Massimo Munforte, who will describe the traditional dishes prepared by Maria (Salvatore's mother) and Rosa, the fourth generation of Veneziano family restaurateurs.

Starters include **baked ricotta**, followed by breaded ricotta and roast provola and pecorino. A taste of capocollo and salami is followed by a wealth of vegetables preserved in olive oil or vinegar. First courses include interesting pansotti stuffed with ricotta and spinach in a sauce of Bronte pistachio nuts and homemade **tagliolini** with **sparacogne** (typical wild herb of the area). There is an impressive menu based on Etna **cep mushrooms**, served in soups, sautéed, roast and breaded or as the basic ingredient of an aromatic sauce for rigatoni. There is a broad selection of main courses: roast pork with potatoes, **sauteed stoccafisso**, sausage and **mutton**.

Limited but interesting choice of puddings: flaky pastry with ricotta, Sicilian cassata, **cannolo with pistachio ice cream**. In August, it is possible to taste the aromatic tabacchiera peach (Slow Food Presidium). The wine list could be improved.

In **Bronte** (17 km), Pasticceria Conti Gallenti, Corso Umberto 275 sells biscuits and tiny cakes with almonds and pistachio nuts, excellent, home-made panettoni and colombe.

ROCCALUMERA
Allume

SAN CATALDO

CONTE D'ANTARES

Trattoria
Via Petricchia 1
Tel. 0942 746206
Closed Monday
Open: only for dinner, festivities also for lunch
Holidays: 1 week in June and 1 in September
Seating: 55 + 30 outdoors
Prices: 25-35 euros, wine excluded
All credit cards except AE, Bancomat

ANZALONE

Trattoria
Piazza Crispi 5
Tel. 0934 586624
Closed Sunday
Open: lunch and dinner
Holidays: August 15-30
Seating: 50
Prices: 18-20 euros, wine excluded
No credit cards

A few hundred meters from the Messina-Catania state road lies a village set in a tiny valley at the foot of the rocky ridge surmounted by the ruins of Fiumedinisi castle, an impressive-sounding name that conceals a delightful country trattoria serving exquisite local cuisine. On entering, you will find a delightful courtyard with roses, rosemary plants and wild prickly pears. The dining room with its slightly kitsch furnishing or the geraniums on the summer terrace see Graziela – an elegant lady who speaks several languages – describe the menu, make suggestions, serve and direct her children as she moves rapidly among the tables. The chef is her husband,'"mastro" Angelo: despite his vaguely demon-like appearance that makes him resemble more a stoker than a chef, he is actually very shy and kind; between pots, pans and the barbecue, he creatively yet simply prepares excellent ingredients to serve dishes that are a balanced combination of innovation and tradition.
Start with caponata, eggplant salad, parmigiana di zucchini, freshly baked **ricotta** and vegetable roulades, followed by **pappardelle with chestnuts**, ravioli with orange, **spaghetti with wild fennel**. The main courses, essentially meat, include pork roulades with bitter vegetables and ricotta, **lamb kebabs ammollicato** and **roast kid**. The puddings and **citrus fruit sorbets** change with the seasons and the mood of the moment. A limited but carefully selected list of Sicilian wines.

The trattoria that the Anzalone family has run for about twenty years is located in a small square overlooking the main street. This is a genuine family place, with son-in-law Claudio Rizzo front of house and Signora Ninetta in the kitchen preparing the typical dishes of the Sicilian hinterland.
The selection of antipasti includes sautéed mushrooms, eggplant caponata, cunsate olives, dried tomatoes, marinated anchovies, ricotta, sheep's cheeses and omelets with wild fennel, potatoes and onions or wild herbs such as mazzareddri. Typical first courses include **pasta** with meat sauce, **alla carrettiera**, with fresh tomato and eggplant, sparacelli and ricotta or sautéed broccoli. In cooler months, there is always **macco with beans**, chickpea and bean soups, a soup with local vegetables. Then come **beef stew with potatoes**, roast **mutton** and sausage, pork pancetta with sauce, delicious **stigghiole** (grilled veal offal), tripe alla parmigiana or in bianco, steamed or fried baccalà with olives, veal tail with sauce and **babbaluci**, wild snails usually sautéed. And only if you book: boiled **carcagnola** (pig's trotters).
Close with a tart of ricotta and pistachio nuts and, in summer, with citrus fruit sorbets. The cellar has a few good bottles of Sicilian wine.

At Piazza Giovanni XXIII 7, Pasticceria Gaetano Campisi offers an excellent torrone ice-cream with whole almonds. Also excellent small cakes prepared with pasta reale and pistachio nuts.

CASALE DEL PRINCIPE

Z'ALIA

Holiday farm
Contrada Dammusi
Tel. 091 8579910
Fax 091 8579168
E-mail: info@casaledelprincipe.it
Internet: www.casaledelprincipe.it
Open all year

Trattoria
Via Piana degli Albanesi 2
Tel. 091 8577065
Closed Tuesday
Open: lunch and dinner
Holidays: September 15-30
Seating: 50
Prices: 28 euros, wine excluded
All credit cards

Casale del Principe is just a few kilometers from Palermo in the heart of the Jato valley. A watchtower in the 16th-century, it was enlarged and transformed into a Jesuit convent in the 18th century and later became a farmhouse when the princes of Camporeale took over ownership. Today it has been renovated with full respect for the original structure and is now a beautiful vacation farm surrounded by poplars, ash and eucalyptus trees. The accommodation has been created around the two inner courtyards, in the former storerooms and the old chapel; most of the rooms have a private terrace with a beautiful view. In the restaurant and the baglio opposite, you can enjoy traditional dishes cooked using typical local organically grown products (22 euros, wine excluded). The farm also organizes recreational activities such as pottery and cooking courses, horse riding, archery and guided tours.

• 4 double rooms and 3 apartments, with bathroom, air-conditioning, minibar; several rooms with terrace • Prices: double room single use 45 euros, double and apartment 90, breakfast included • Credit cards: MC, Visa, Bancomat • 1 apartment designed for use by the mobility challenged. Off-street parking. No pets allowed. Owners always present • Bar, restaurant. TV room, lounge. Garden, children's playground. Horse riding, archery

Z'Alia is located in a small town not far from Palermo, on the road to Sciacca. The area is famed for its top quality wine cellars and confectionery, and we recommend a visit to the magnificent ruins of the ancient Jetas, a city founded by the mysterious Elimi people and then settled by the Greeks, Romans and Arabs. This place is managed by Maria and Gigi, helped by son Mario, and has a single, rustic-style room with wooden arches and beams and simple tables with straw chairs. The traditional cuisine focuses on home-made pasta and simple yet high quality ingredients.
Bear in mind that the menu is very seasonal. Try starting with **caponata**, green cunsate olives, timbale of baked eggplant, fresh sheep's ricotta, frittata with potatoes, Godrano Caciocavallo, vegetables and wild herbs or asparagus. First courses include **tagliatelle with sausage** and mountain fennel, **pappardelle with mutton sauce**, ravioli with ricotta and spinach, tagliolini with cep mushrooms (when in season). Main courses are all baked in the oven or cooked on lava stone: lamb chops, **Sicilian roulades**, sausage, **mutton**, pork chops. Puddings are a true anthology of tradition: cassatele with ricotta, cannoli, Sicilian cassata, tarts and iced fruit.
Aside from the robust house wine, about 20 good local labels are available. The family-style service is kind and friendly.

Salvatore Cerniglia, Via Palermo: high quality ice creams, confectionery and pastries, reflecting Albanian traditions in Sicily.

San Piero Patti
Sambuco

100 km northwest of Messina A 20 SP 122

Da luciana

Trattoria
Contrada Sambuco 1
Tel. 0941 660309
Closed Sunday for dinner and Monday
Open: lunch and dinner
Holidays: none
Seating: 80
Prices: 22-25 euros, wine excluded
All credit cards

Between the Peloritani and Nebrodi mountains, just a few kilometers from San Piero Patti, this country trattoria is managed by Luciana Bovaro with Giancarlo in an agreeable and friendly fashion. Luciana in the kitchen interprets the local cuisine with great skill and a few personal touches, using many products grown in the market-gardens around the trattoria.
The menu includes an impressive range of antipasti, starting with the delicate fresh ricotta accompanied by home-made jams; then come eggplant a funghetto, marinated zucchini, **peperoni ammollicati** , preserves in olive oil, peperoni, artichokes and eggplant, tasty hot dishes such as crispelle di tuma, fritters with wild herbs, **polpettine in lemon leaves**, bruschette with provola cheese, a basket with two types of cheese and caponata, pistachio nut pie, roast potatoes with a cream of mushrooms. First courses include risotto with yellow pumpkin and pistachio nuts, **tagliatelle with mushrooms** in season, eggplant roulade with baked ricotta, ravioli with hazelnuts. And if you are still hungry, main courses include traditional **mixed roast** meats as well as delicious **shank of pork**, lamb chops, **veal roulades** alla siciliana with mollica (breadcrumbs), artichokes and pecorino. The homemade puddings are fairly good: **cassatine with Bronte pistachio nuts**, chocolate cake, ricotta cannoli.
There are several regional labels and a reasonable house wine. The shop next door sells homemade liqueurs, infusions, jams, conserves and fresh fruit.

San Salvatore di Fitalia

103 km west of Messina

Casali di Margello

Holiday farm
Contrada Margello
Tel. 0941 486225
Fax 0941 486928
E-mail: info@casalidimargello.it
Internet: www.casalidimargello.it
Open all year

This vacation farm is surrounded by chestnut, hazel, citrus and olive trees, five kilometers from the village of San Salvatore in the Fitalia valley. Pippo Costanzo and Antonina Ciminata have restructured some farmhouses built in the early nineteenth century, refurbishing them in accordance with bio-architectural canons using traditional materials: terracotta tiles, wood, local stone and wrought iron. The attractive, comfortable rooms face onto the courtyard from where you reach the communal areas, which include the typical restaurant (a complete meal, including beverages, costs 23 euros). For breakfast you'll be offered milk, coffee, butter and jams, homemade tarts and cookies. In the hall they've preserved an old oil press with a grindstone and you can also visit their small ethnographic museum. The area offers many attractions and your hosts (who speak a bit of English and French) will be very happy to provide you with much useful information.

• 4 double and 4 four-bed rooms, with bathroom, mini-bar, TV • Prices: double room single occupancy 50-60 euros, double 70-90, four-bed 140-180, breakfast included • Credit cards: all, Bancomat • 1 room designed for use by the mobility challenged. Off-street parking. No pets allowed. Owners always reachable • Restaurant. TV room, reading or conference room. 2 swimming pools, boules court, five-a-side soccer field, table tennis, trekking course

ARRHAIS

Trattoria-pizzeria
Largo Marino, 6
Tel. 091 947127
Closed Wednesday
Open: lunch and dinner
Holidays: none
Seating: 60 + 150 outdoors
Prices: 35 euros, wine excluded
All credit cards

VILLA CEFALÀ

Holiday farm
Strada Statale 113, 48
Tel. 091 931545-328 0097781
Fax 091 941616
E-mail: info@tenutacefala.it
Internet: www.tenutacefala.it
Open all year

Porticello is a delightful seaside suburb of Santa Flavia, just a few kilometers from the Solunto archaeological site and little more than 15 km from Palermo. In summer, right opposite the small fishing port, we find the tables of this classic trattoria, managed by Giovanni and Calogero Tarantino, who opened in 1994. Inside, the place is set out on two floors, one of which serves as a pizzeria. Arrhais is the original Arab name of the cape where tuna were caught: and **tuna**, in season, is served here in various ways from the antipasti to the seconds. All the fish is procured at the nearby fish market, and is fresh and of excellent quality.

Start with sea urchins, snails in guazzetto, sweet and sour mussels and fasolari, excellent, **tuna sott'olio**, tasty croutons with botargo. First courses include **caserecce with fresh tuna and mint**, tagliatelle with spatula fillets and pumpkin flowers, **spaghetti con la neonata**, with sea urchins, sardines, or al nero di seppia. The main courses include a huge selection of fish, such as saraghi prepared with sea water, **stuffed squid**, grilled shrimps, stewed ricciole, **fritture di piccolo pesce azzurro**. Finish with Sicilian cassata, stuffed cannoli with ricotta and the always-available fruit sorbets.

The wine list is ample, inviting and balanced, with labels from Sicily and other regions.

This elegant country house was built for the counts Pilo di Capaci in 1778 in order to better manage a vast citrus grove. The original premises have been refurbished and transformed into rooms and apartments equipped with all major comforts. The rooms are in a building facing the olive grove; the apartments are scattered over four different buildings, each with its own view: the citrus grove, the sea and the inner courtyard of the villa. The stylishly cozy restaurant serves typical traditional dishes revisited with a touch of originality. During your meal you'll be able to taste Nero d'Avola wine, extra-virgin olive oil and the citrus honey produced on the farm and also available for purchase. There are many places to visit in the surrounding area: the bay of Solanto, the Solunto archeological site, Bagheria, Monreale and Palermo. You can also rent bicycles, cars and 11-meter rubber dinghies.

• 2 double, 1 four-bed rooms and 7 apartments (2-4 persons), with bathroom, air-conditioning, mini-bar, TV; kitchenette in the apartments • Prices: double room single occupancy and double 84-96 euros, four-bed 134-146, apartments 118-178 (20 euro supplement for extra bed), breakfast included • Off-street parking. Small pets allowed. Owners always reachable. • Restaurant. Multimedia room. Garden. Swimming pool

30 KM NORTH OF CATANIA

62 KM NORTHWEST OF AGRIGENTO ON SS 115 OR SS 624

CASE PERROTTA

AL MORO

🔑 Holiday farm
Via Andronico 2
Tel. and fax 095 968928
E-mail: caseperrotta@caseperrotta.it
Internet: www.caseperrotta.it
Open all year

🔑 Bed and breakfast
Via Liguori, 44
Tel. and fax 0925 86756
E-mail: almorosciacca@libero.it
Internet: www.almoro.com
Open all year

The vacation farm is on the slopes of Etna at an altitude of 700 meters, close to the one thousand year-old chestnut tree known as the 'Castagno dei cento cavalli'. The original structure dates from the late sixteenth century and was used as a convent by the Benedictine order but then over the centuries it has undergone several transformations. The last renovation in 1994 transformed Case Perrotta into what you see today: the ancient farmhouse and old mill now have ten comfortable rooms with en suite bathrooms. Breakfast offers a variety of tasty fare. Main meals (at 25 euros per person, wine excluded) can be eaten in the restaurant or also in the large gazebo or inner courtyard. Periodically they organize excursions and literary and culinary events. In addition you can purchase fruit, olive oil, jams and products preserved in olive oil produced on the farm.

• 1 single, 3 double and 6 triple rooms, with bathroom, mini-bar, safe, satellite TV • Prices: single 45 euros, double 75, triple 109 (32 euro supplement for extra bed), breakfast included • Credit cards: Visa, Bancomat • 1 room accessible to the mobility challenged. Off-street parking. Small pets allowed. Owners always reachable. • Restaurant. Grounds. Soccer field, boules court

The building dates back to the 16th century and has been carefully restored to respect local culture using bio-architectural techniques. The rooms are equipped to offer every comfort – for instance, telephone, mini-bar and satellite television – while providing a relaxing atmosphere. On the ground floor there's a reading area, Internet access points, leading to a spacious breakfast room and an inner garden. There's also a wine cellar created inside a traditional Muslim home where you can taste top Sicilian wines. The buffet breakfast consists of local traditional, biologically controlled produce. For main meals, guests of the B&B can go to the 'Hostaria del vicolo' with which special rates have been agreed.

• 8 double, 1 triple rooms and 1 suite, with bathroom, air-conditioning, mini-bar, satellite TV • Prices: double room single occupancy 45-55 euros, double 80-95, triple 105-120, suite 120-140, breakfast included • Facility partly accessible for the mobility challenged. Parking at special rates 50 meters away. Owners always reachable. • Bar, wine cellar. Breakfast room, reading room, TV room. Garden

SCIACCA
Scunchipani

SINAGRA

67 KM NORTHWEST OF AGRIGENTO

107 KM SOUTHWEST OF MESSINA SS 139

NNI MIA

FRATELLI BORRELLO

Bed and breakfast
Contrada Scunchipani
Tel. 0925 80111-338 6225540
Fax 0925 80128
E-mail: beb@nnimia.com
Internet: www.nnimia.com
Open all year

Trattoria
Contrada Forte
Tel. 0941 594436-594844
Closed Wednesday
Open: lunch and dinner
Holidays: 1 week in Italy
Seating: 150
Prices: 20-25 euros, wine excluded
All credit cards

This B&B is in a modern, two-floor villa surrounded by olive trees, citrus groves and palms. The rooms are pleasantly spacious and have been furnished with great attention to detail. There's an attractive veranda in the garden where breakfast is served – fresh fruit, pastries from the local bakery, almond milk and granite. On request the B&B (the name in dialect nni mia means 'at my place') offers various services: excursions on the family boat out of the tourist port of Sciacca; visits to wine stores in the area, with tasting of typical dishes; beauty treatments, sauna and swimming pool. Your very active hostess, Antonella Bondì, is a landscape architect and also organizes interesting trips to historic parks and private or public gardens. Her husband Roberto is a qualified physiotherapist and manages the Officina dell'Ozio fitness center (thalaxotherm, Turkish bath, relaxing and therapeutic massage).

• 5 double rooms, with bathroom, air-conditioning, mini-bar, satellite TV • Prices: double room single occupancy 55-65 euros, double 80-90 (22-28 euro supplement for extra bed), breakfast included • Credit cards: major ones, Bancomat • Off-street parking. Small pets allowed. Owners always reachable • Veranda, garden. Swimming pool, fitness center

The Borrello family trattoria, renowned for its succulent traditional cuisine, is located in the countryside near Sinagra, on the provincial road to Ucrìa. The food served is based on the produce of the attached farm, set up more than 40 years ago: livestock reared here includes cattle, sheep and the Nebrodi black pig (Slow Food Presidia), as well as mushrooms, olives and vegetables; sausages and cheese such as Nebrodi provola are also produced. These tasks are shared between brothers and sisters Pippo, Franco, Annamaria and Graziella (in the kitchen).
The pride of this trattoria is its huge range of antipasti with delicious **cured meats**, fresh and baked ricotta, pecorino and caprino cheese, provola flan in heated terracotta, various dishes based on **mushrooms**, sausage fried with eggs, cotica di maiale, fritters and omelets with seasonal vegetables and preserves in olive oil. Certain dishes change with the seasons but there is always an impressive menu. If you are still hungry, excellent first courses include **pasta 'ncaciata with broccoli**, tagliatelle with cep mushrooms, maccheroni with meat sauce and, in summer, pasta with artichokes and **maccheroncini with eggplant and zucchini**. Main courses always include **mutton**, sausage and roast pork ribs, grilled veal. Specialties such as **roast black pig** and **kid in padella** on the other hand must be booked in advance. Homemade puddings include mustazzola cooked in wine and hazelnut biscuits. Small selection of regional wines at fair prices.

SIRACUSA
Quartiere Santa Lucia

SIRACUSA
Ortigia
Old town

SIRACUSA SOUTH EXIT FROM SS 114 OR 115

GIUGGIULENA

🗝–0 Bed and breakfast
Via Pitagora da Reggio 35
Tel. and fax 0931 468142
E-mail: info@giuggiulena.it
Internet: www.giuggiulena.it
Open all year

GUTKOWSKI

🗝–0 3-Star Hotel
Lungomare Vittorini 26
Tel. 0931 465861
Fax 0931 480505
E-mail: info@guthotel.it
Internet: www.guthotel.it
Open all year

Giuggiulena, in Sicilian, means sesame seed, but it's also a type of sandstone, the characteristic stone of the cliff on which this B&B stands high above the sea. It's not too far from the Cappuccini latomia, a quarry that's just one of the places of historical and artistic interest to visit in the city. The rooms are comfortable and bright and have a lovely view. You can sunbathe on the terrace and go for a swim in the sea below. Sabrina Perasole, Neapolitan by birth though her grandmother was from Siracusa, gives guests a warm welcome (she'll come and pick you up with her own car, if necessary). A buffet breakfast is set out in a common room or on the terrace and includes freshly squeezed orange juice, local cheeses, organic jams, home-made cakes, sweet fare from local pastry shops and, during summer, granita with brioche.

• 6 double rooms, with bathroom, balcony, air-conditioning, mini-bar, satellite TV • Prices: double room single use 60-70 euros, double 85-95 (30-35 euro supplement for extra bed), breakfast included • Credit cards: all, Bancomat • 1 room designed for use by the mobility challenged. Parking in the immediate vicinity. Small pets allowed • Breakfast room, reading room, Internet point. Terrace, solarium

This hotel was opened in 1999 and is located in two adjacent buildings painted in pastel colors, the result of restructuring houses once inhabited by craftsmen and fishermen. It's close to the open-air market area in the old quarter of Ortigia. The rooms, some of which have a sea view, are comfortable, unpretentious but with original touches in the choice of furnishings. The young, courteous staff speak fluent English and French. Manager Paola Pretsch chose her Polish grandfather's name for the hotel as he was a man who was very fond of traveling and lived for many years in Siracusa. There's a nice breakfast offering an assortment of jams and honeys that are locally and organically produced, homemade cookies, orange juice, as well as coffee, milk, yoghurt, cheese and eggs.

• 3 single and 22 double rooms, with bathroom, air-conditioning, mini-bar, satellite TV • Prices: single 55-70 euros, double room single occupancy 65-80, double 80-100, breakfast included • Credit cards: all, Bancomat • 2 rooms designed for use by the mobility challenged. Parking in the immediate vicinity. Small pets allowed. Reception open 24 hours a day • Wine bar. Breakfast room, reading room with Internet point

LA FINANZIERA

Restaurant
Via Epicarmo 41
Tel. 0931 61888-463117
Closed Sunday, in summer Sunday for dinner
Open: lunch and dinner
Holidays: 15 days in July or August
Seating: 60
Prices: 30-35 euros, wine excluded
All credit cards

This restaurant, held in high regard for its excellent fish-based cuisine and located in a side-road off Corso Gelone, opposite the station of the Guardia di Finanza, has been run by Lucia Mela, since 1960. On entering, guests are welcomed into the cozily neat dining room, which is joined by another small room on the top floor. In the kitchen for an impressive 35 years, Pippo creates traditional dishes from classic Sicilian cuisine.

If you'd like to start with antipasti, the buffet next to the counter has the catch of the day, including tender **polpo bollito**, tasty stewed moscardini with tomato, crunchy scoppularicchi (squid) fried, anchovies (marinated or in olive oil), piscirovu (omelet) with cheese and parsley, fried or roast peppers, giardiniera of olives, boiled or grilled vegetables. First courses include some excellent **linguine coi ricci** and linguine with mussels and clams. Other excellent first courses are ravioli with scampi, risotto alla marinara, fettuccine alla siracusana dressed with anchovies, olives, capers and eggplant. Winter dishes usually include vegetable and **legume soups**. Main courses include: slices of grouper, rock fish or **ricciola alla matalotta** (the local term for marinara), stewed or pan fried mullet, masculinu (anchovies), saraghi, dentici, pauro or other grilled fish, fried prawns and squid. Very occasionally, there is **baccalà a ghiotta** and, in the short fishing season, **lampuga a cipollata**.

Puddings include seasonal fruit or a refreshing lemon sorbet. There is a fair selection of wines at reasonable prices.

LA GAZZA LADRA

Osteria
Via Cavour 8
Tel. 340 0602428
Closed Monday
Open: lunch and dinner
Holidays: July and August
Seating: 30
Prices: 15-20 euros, wine excluded
No credit cards

Marcello Foti and his wife from Treviso, Maria Grazia Troncon, have been running this friendly little place close to Piazza Duomo for ten years. The highly original tables in iron, wood and glass are set with straw-paper place mats. The walls are decorated with fine photos from various parts of the world; the kitchen is open to view, behind the glass counter. Here, you can enjoy a simple snack or a complete meal with home-made dishes based on seasonal, local produce.

Antipasti include **caponata of eggplant**, dried tomatoes, grilled or steamed vegetables, orange salad, local cheeses and cured meats, omelets with potatoes, onions or ricotta and mint. In winter, first courses include **pasta alla siracusana** with anchovies, toasted bread with thick tomato sauce, Norma with eggplant and salted ricotta, pasta with cream of pumpkin and vegetable sauces, tasty **soups** including onions, legumes, broad beans and borage. These are followed by roast pork sausage, **stew with potatoes**, **veal roulades**. The menu in spring tends more to fish: **pasta with sardines**, with nero di seppie, fresh tuna sauce, mucco and cod roe. Delicious **plain tuna**, fillets of spatola, squid in guazzetto, octopus salad, anchovies with baked citrus fruit.

Finish with almond blancmange or other home-made puddings. Small selection of regional wines also served by the glass.

Traditional confectionery at Artale, Via Landolina 32. Selection of Sicilian wines at Enoteca Solaria, Via Roma 86. Selection of wines and sweet-savory preserves at Antiche Siracuse, Piazza Archimede.

TAORMINA

TRAPANI
Old town

49 KM SOUTHWEST OF MESSINA

VILLA FIORITA

🗝3 Star Hotel
Via Pirandello 39
Tel. 0942 24122
Fax 0942 625967
E-mail: info@villafioritahotel.com
Internet: www.villafioritahotel.com
Open all year

AI LUMI

🗝Bed and breakfast
Corso Vittorio Emanuele, 71
Tel. and fax 0923 547720
E-mail: info@ailumi.it
Internet: www.ailumi.it
Open all year

Close to the historic center but protected by lush Mediterranean vegetation stands Villa Fiorita, the ideal place for those who want a peaceful, stylish vacation. Every room is different; all are pleasant and cozy, with prestigious furnishings; some have balconies or terraces, from which you can enjoy a splendid view of the Ionian sea. The swimming pool is surrounded by a large Mediterranean garden, filled with lemon and tangerine trees. The generous continental-style breakfast is served in the garden or in the dining room. In the garden you must take a look at the entrance to the only intact Roman tomb in Taormina. There's a heavy demand for the six parking spaces available so it's advisable to book them well in advance.

• 24 double rooms and 1 mini-suite (2-4 persons), with bathroom, air-conditioning, mini-bar, safe, TV • Prices: double room single occupancy 108 euros, double 120, mini-suite 155 (35 euro supplement for extra bed), breakfast included • Credit cards: all, Bancomat • Off-street parking, garage (12 euros a day). Small pets allowed. Reception open 24 hours a day • Bar. Breakfast room, reading room, lounge. Terrace, solarium. Swimming pool

This lovely B&B has been created in one of the many historic homes in an old, elegant street in the center of Trapani. It's run by a very friendly, helpful young couple, the Rizzos. Francesca, in particular, divides her time between the B&B and the Trapani Winemaking Cooperative of which she manages the sales office. The rooms are simple and furnished in an unpretentious manner. The Ai lumi restaurant nearby is managed by Francesca's husband and offers a 15% reduction on the check for the B&B's guests. This eatery is much appreciated for the quality of ingredients used in addition to the way dishes are prepared. Breakfast consists of homemade cakes and jams and is served at the restaurant for the guests staying in rooms; guests in the apartments receive everything they need to prepare their own breakfast.

• 1 single, 4 double rooms and 8 apartments (2-5 persons), with bathroom, television, mini-bar, air-conditioning; apartments with kitchenette • Prices: single and double room single occupancy 35-50 euros, double 70-100, breakfast included; apartments 80-165 euros • Credit cards: all, Bancomat • Parking in the immediate vicinity. No pets allowed. Owners always reachable

AL SOLITO POSTO

Trattoria
Via Orlandini 30 A
Tel. 0923 24545
Closed Sunday
Open: lunch and dinner
Holidays: 15 days in August
Seating: 50
Prices: 30 euros, wine excluded
All credit cards, Bancomat

Vito Basciano's trattoria keeps its promises and we find it worthy of all your attention this year too. The cuisine is essentially fish-based and the offering varies with the seasons and the catch. Start with a generous self-service buffet of antipasti, that always include **tuna roe in olive oil** and little seasonal omelets. The first courses reflect Sicilian traditions in general and those of Trapani in particular: a special mention to **spaghetti with sea urchins** or roe, lobster soup (if you book) and baked **sardine timbale**. The excellent, classic main courses are based on the catch of the day: grilled, all'acquapazza, a ghiotta or alla matalotta. May and June always focus on Favignana **tuna**, prepared in various ways: a cipollata and in sweet and sour sauce for antipasto, as a sauce for the exquisite busiati, marinated, grilled or ammuttunato (with cloves of garlic inside and cooked for a long time in a rich tomato sauce) as a main course. Puddings are only available if you book. Good, fast, polite and informal service. The wine list is limited to Sicilian labels, with special attention to the main local cellars.
Since the trattoria – especially at lunchtime – is very popular with staff from the local public offices, it is advisable to book.

🍯 Try the Sicilian cannoli, the traditional pastry, the cooked meats and takeaway dishes at Angelino, at Via Ammiraglio Staiti 87.

CANTINA SICILIANA 🐌🍷

Traditional osteria
Via Giudecca 32
Tel. 0923 28673
No closing day
Open: lunch and dinner
Holidays: variable
Seating: 45
Prices: 25-30 euros, wine excluded
All credit cards

The Giudecca Jewish quarter in the old time is home to this old osteria (it was opened in 1912 as a wine bar serving a few hot dishes), where Pino Maggiore has worked for about 40 years, initially as the cleaner, then as the chef and, since 1980, as the owner. A charismatic figure, he welcomes guests in the dining room with his trusted assistant Ibitsem, a young girl from Tunisia who speaks many languages; her sister Hajer works in the kitchen.
There's an impressive selection of antipasti: marinated fish, tuna roe, anchovy fritters, whitebait fritters, boiled octopus or octopus salad, eggplant caponata, **sarde allinguate**, smoked tuna and swordfish, tuna tartar with onions and capers. First courses include **frascatole** (traditional durum wheat pasta) in fish and prawn stock, bucatini with sardines, **busiati with pesto alla trapanese** and eggplant or with red prawns, almonds and cherry tomatoes, spaghetti with tuna roe and almonds or broken up in prawn soup, **cuscus with fish stock**, caserecce with swordfish, eggplant and mint. Main courses usually include roast prawns or squid, **stuffed cuttlefish**, swordfish roulades, **swordfish alla pantesca**. The few meat dishes include Marsala and Palermo cutlets. Puddings include **cassatelle** of ricotta (fried ravioloni filled with ricotta), Sicilian cassata, almond parfait and sgroppino, lemon ice cream blended with limoncello.
The excellent wine list has about 300 Sicilian and national labels, also on sale in the adjacent wine shop.

TRAPANI
Xitta

DUCA DI CASTELMONTE

Holiday farm
Via Motisi 3
Tel. 0923 526139
Fax 0923 883140
E-mail agriduca@libero.it
Internet: www.ducadicastelmonte.it
Always open May to September
in winter Thursday to Sunday
Open: dinner, Sunday also for lunch
Seating: 40 +40 outdoors
Prices: 27-30 euros
All major credit cards, Bancomat

The country residence built in the early 19th century by the Curatolo family has been converted into accommodation, and the structure which stored the must is now the dining area. A collection of farm tools of the time is preserved in one of the rooms which was once the oil mill. Conserves and jams are made with the farm produce, and fruit and vegetables of the area are often at the base of the cuisine. The meal starts with eggplant and field balm cakes, caponata, stuffed tomatoes, **melanzane ammuttunate**. This is followed by the **vegetable cuscus**, **pasta with sardines**, macco di fave, busiati with mixed meat ragù. The main courses include **larded rabbit**, shank of pork with pistachio, **bruciuluni** (traditional Sicilian meatloaf). The fresh sheep's cheese and hot ricotta are highly recommended. The homemade puddings are also very good: **fried cassatele**, ciaccole, fruit tarts and ricotta pies.
The cellar contains a fair number of regional labels, and the service is attentive and friendly.
The establishment closes in February and November.

• 7 apartments (1-7 persons), with bathrooms • Prices: single 38-45, double 76-90, triple 114-135, with 4 beds 152-180, with 5 beds 190-225, with 6 beds 228-270, with 7 beds 266-315 euros, breakfast included • Establishment accessible to the mobility impaired, as well as 1 apartment specifically designed for the mobility impaired. Internal covered parking area. Pets welcome. Owners always available • Restaurant. Children's play ground. Swimming pool, small football ground, volleyball court, bowling green

TRAPANI
Fontanasalsa

FONTANASALSA

Holiday farm
Via Cusenza 78
Tel. and fax 0923 591001
E-mail: bagliofontanasalsa@hotmail.com
Internet: www.fontanasalsa.it
Open all year

Managed by Maria Caterina Burgarella, this vacation farm is surrounded by approximately 60 hectares of olive groves and lies in the center of an immense plain set between the slopes of Mount Erice and the Stagnone lagoon. The rooms have all main comforts and are furnished in a reserved, elegant manner. All of them either face onto the orange grove or the courtyard with an oil press dating from the eighteenth century: they make an exceptionally high quality extra-virgin olive oil. Meals in the restaurant cost 25 euros per person, wine excluded. In summer guests can use the outdoor swimming pool. There are various itineraries for those who want to explore the area, either on foot or on horseback. In addition, Fontanasalsa is only a few kilometers from the center of Trapani, the Stagnone nature reserve and the island of Mozia.

• 10 double rooms, with bathroom, air-conditioning, mini-bar, TV • Prices: double room single occupancy 60-65 euros, double 90-100, breakfast included • Credit cards: all, Bancomat • 1 room accessible to the mobility challenged. Off-street parking. Small pets allowed. Owners always reachable • Restaurant. Wine-tasting room, lounge. Garden. Swimming pool

La bettolaccia

Trattoria
Via Generale Fardella 23
Tel. 0923 21695
Closed Sunday and Saturday for lunch
Open: lunch and dinner
Holidays: one month between October and November
Seating: 28
Prices: 28-35 euros, wine excluded
All credit cards, Bancomat

Podere San Giovanni

Holifay farm
Via Serro Mokarta 56
Tel. 0923 524148-348 7621146-348 0026500
Fax 0923 524148
E-mail: info@poderesangiovanni.com
Internet: www.poderesangiovanni.com
Open all year

Close to the port, a short stroll from the Cathedral and the chiesa del Purgatorio, this trattoria was founded about 70 years ago as a tavern serving rustic wine by the glass, accompanied by something hot to eat. Since it is close to the old prison, it later became a trattoria serving families visiting inmates. It has been managed for about seven years, with closer attention to service and menus, by Francesco Fileccia; his wife Giusy looks after the kitchen with one or two helpers. It is delightfully decorated with black and white photos of South American countries, which the owners are in love with.

Start with cold cuscus of fish and vegetables, marinated fish, tuna and **sardine polpette**, joined at times by other more imaginative dishes. First courses include **busiati**, fresh homemade pasta, **with pesto trapanese** and fried eggplant, **timbale of bucatini with sardines** and wild fennel, spaghetti swordfish roe, cherry tomatoes and capers, **cuscus alla trapanese**, served with soup and fried fish in keeping with local traditions. The main courses change on the basis of the catch that day but include spigola cooked in salt, grilled saraghi, cernia in a citrus fruit sauce, fillets of sampietro with red onions. In the tuna-fishing period, don't miss the classic **tuna** dishes: roast, sweet and sour or in a sauce (also as a topping for pasta), not forgetting **lattume fritto**.

All puddings are homemade: in summer – almond parfait, semifreddi and iced drinks; in winter – Sicilian cassata, fried and baked cassatelle. The wine cellar is extensive and focuses mainly on Sicilian labels.

An old 19th-century baglio among olive groves and vineyards, Podere San Giovanni has now been renovated by the Genovese family to offer all modern comforts while respecting the original structure of the building. The ten rooms, with Sicilian terracotta tile ceilings and wooden beams, all have air-conditioning and en suite bathrooms. In the spacious, comfortable dining room they serve typical dishes prepared using vegetables and olive oil produced by the farm (half board 60 euros per person, full board 78 euros). Two boules courts, a garden with a children's playground and a terrace with solarium are available for guests. Sports fans can use the nearby tennis courts and riding school at special rates.

• 1 single and 9 double or triple rooms, with bathroom, air-conditioning • Prices: single 38-44 euros, double 69-75, triple 90-110, breakfast included • Credit cards: all, Bancomat • Facility partly accessible to the mobility challenged. Off-street parking. No pets allowed. Reception open 4pm-10 pm • Restaurant. Reading room. Conference room. Garden, terrace, solarium. Boules courts

TRAPANI
Guarrato

USTICA

VULTAGGIO

MARIO

🍲 Holiday farm
Contrada Misiliscemi
Tel. 0923 864261-347 6696059
Fax 0923 865107
E-mail info@misiliscemi.it
Internet: www.misiliscemi.it
No closing day
Open: lunch and dinner
Holidays: 2 weeks in Nov., 2 in June
Seating: 48 +48 outdoors
Prices: 20-22 euros, wine excluded
All major credit cards, Bancomat

🍲 Trattoria
Piazza Umberto I 21
Tel. 091 8449505
Closed Monday, never in summer
Open: lunch and dinner
Holidays: in January
Seating: 30 + 50 outdoors
Prices: 25 euros, wine excluded
All major credit cards

On a small hill from which it enjoys an enchanting view over the Egadi Islands, the Vultaggio family will welcome you in all their simplicity and kindness. The rooms are modestly furnished, en-suite, and warmed by a heat pump. The buffet style breakfast is bountiful.

The meals start with caponata of eggplant or artichokes, fried panelle, **taroncioli** (balls of sheep tuma), alivi cunsate, tunnina salata, dried tomatoes, sweet and sour zucchinis. In winter you can taste the excellent **zabbina** of hot ricotta. Among the first courses we recommend the **country-style cuscus**, the **fresh pasta** dressed with Sicilian style **meat stew** and the cassatele of ricotta and hen broth. The main courses, all meat based, are mostly grilled and baked. Alternatively, **larded rabbit** and veal kebabs filled with tuma and fennel are served. The meal ends with blancmange, fried cassatelle, almond parfait and, in summer, fruit granita.

The cellar has numerous Sicilian labels, in addition to a good Nero d'Avola produced on the farm.

🗝🔑• 12 double rooms and 2 with 4 beds, en-suite • Prices: double single use 25-35, double 50-70, with 4 beds 100-140 euros, breakfast included • 2 rooms specifically designed for the mobility impaired. Internal uncovered parking area. Pets welcome. Owners always available • Restaurant. TV room. Garden, children's play ground. Bowling green, swimming pool

Even though last autumn Mario Russo had to step down for health reasons, nothing or little has changed at this trattoria, given that the staff is still the same and the food is truly a benchmark for those arriving on this volcanic island for a vacation. Comfortably seated inside, or better still, in the well-ventilated outside area where they serve you in summer, you'll be able to enjoy simple but very tasty seafood cuisine.

To start with they always have local shrimp served raw with just a trickle of olive oil and lemon, or **eggplant caponata**, **tuna in olive oil**, local tuma breaded and grilled. Among the first courses we can certainly recommend the **spaghetti with Ustica-style pesto** made with small, juicy local tomatoes, lots of fresh basil, capers, garlic and extra-virgin olive oil; alternatively, but by no means a second-best, the delicious pasta with sea urchins. Their **lentil soup** prepared in the traditional local manner is very popular – of course, made with the highly sought-after lentils, a Slow Food Presidium. There's also a nice **couscous** served with a succulent broth made from rock-fish and grouper. Among the main courses, we should mention the swordfish roulades and magnificent **grilled platters** of prawns, white bream and gilthead.

To close, plenty of local fruit. Wines available are Sicilian.

🍯 In the northern part of the island you'll find Nicola Longo in Contrada Tramontana, where he grows Albanella grapes that are used to make a wine of that name. His farm also produces Ustica lentils, beans, chickpeas, chili peppers and eggplants.

VALDERICE

9 KM EAST OF TRAPANI SP 187

BAGLIO SANTA CROCE

🔑🍲 3-Star Hotel
Strada Statale 187
Tel. 0923 891111
Fax 0923 891192
E-mail: hotel@bagliosantacroce.it
Internet: www.bagliosantacroce.it
Open all year round

Located on the slopes of Mount Erice, on a small hill not too far from the village, is this ancient farmhouse built in the seventeenth century that once belonged to the Battiata barony. The farmhouse was at once a stable, a home for a few peasant farmer families, a barn and a store for farm implements. After careful renovation carried out by the owner, Giuseppe Cusenza, in 1982 it became a small, elegant hotel. The rooms have original terracotta floors and wooden beams, and are furnished with wrought iron bedsteads and olive-wood chairs. The restaurant serves good quality dishes (the cost of a meal ranges from 20-25 euros per person, wine excluded), and there's a generous Italian-style breakfast. Among the many places worth visiting nearby are Erice, Mozia, Gibellina, Selinunte, Segesta, San Vito Lo Capo, the Egadi Islands and the Zingaro and Scopello nature reserves.

• 3 single, 16 double, 3 triple and 3 four-bed rooms, with bathroom, TV • Prices: single 60-75 euros, double 100-120, triple 140-168, four-bed 180-216, breakfast included • Credit cards: all, Bancomat • External parking reserved for guests. No pets allowed. Reception open 24 hours a day. • Bar, restaurant. TV room. Conference room. Garden. Swimming pool

VITTORIA
Scoglitti

38 KM WEST OF RAGUSA SS 115

FICHERA

🍲 Trattoria-pizzeria
Via Napoli 124
Tel. 0932 980000
No closing day
Open: lunch and dinner
Holidays: two weeks in October
Seating: 80
Prices: 30-32 euros, wine excluded
All credit cards

The Scoglitti beach near Ragusa is a favorite spot for sunbathing and swimming in summer. In this place of sea-faring traditions, the trattoria was opened by brothers Saro and Lucio Fichera near the fishing port in 1984, The trattoria is now run by Saro's four children: Elio and Salvatore look after the kitchen, Enzo and Giovanni are front of house. The trattoria is located on the ground floor of a small building, with a spacious dining area and plain furnishings. The menu focuses on the excellent, local sea food.
Start with the impressive mixed antipasti: specialties such as baby cod and **fried capputteddi** (moscardini), sliced boiled octopus, red prawns raw and fried, marinated anchovies and gamberetti, **sweet and sour rayfish**, breaded squid, **eggplant caponata**, and crunchy arancini. , First courses include excellent **ravioli of ricotta with cuttlefish ink**, pennette with red prawns, trofie (homemade pasta) with scampi and creamed zucchini, spaghetti with seafood en papilotte. Depending on the catch of the day, the menu may include sea bass and gilthead bream, tasty **stewed turbot** with flavorings and cherry tomatoes, 'turban' of sea bass baked with Fiore sicano cheese, tuna carpaccio, roast mullet and sole.
Finish the pastry cassata. There's also a broad selection of wines and spirits.

SARDEGNA

ALGHERO

SA MANDRA

⌂ Holiday farm
Strada Aeroporto Civile 21 A
Tel. 079 999150-333 2447521
Open Friday, Saturday and Sunday,
always in summer
Open: dinner, in summer lunch if
booked in advance
Holidays: February 1-15
Seating: 100 + 50 outside
Prices: 35 euros
All major credit cards, Bancomat

In the magnificent stretch of land between Alghero to Porto Ferro, there's a
farm that offers rural hospitality in a
number of well-furnished rooms and
serves meat cooked over an open fire. It
takes its name from the place sheep are
kept during milking and its cuisine from
the traditions of Barbagia, the part of
Sardinia where owners Mario Maroccu
and Rita Pirisi lived before moving to the
Nurra area with their children.
A member of the friendly staff will rattle
off a fixed menu for you, drawing attention to such treats as baskets loaded up
with carasau and guttiau bread. The antipasti include sausage and cheeses,
coppa, pancetta, **Monta Spada raw
ham**, **coratella alla barbaricina** (lamb
offal), thyme-flavored cream cheese,
homemade preserves in oil and sa vrue
(curds). Among the first courses are
ravioli with seven herbs, **maharrones
de pungiu** with veal sauce, **culurgiones** of cheese and potatoes, malloreddus and **tallarinas with porcini
mushrooms**. Tasty main course meat
dishes include mutton, either braised
with potatoes and wild fennel or boiled,
and you can't beat the **porcetto roasted
on the spit**.
Though you may be full by the time you
finish all that, you can round off the meal
with mixed fruit and traditional Sardinian
desserts. Don't miss the extraordinary
seadas here.
The house wine is served by the carafe,
but you can also order good labels from
other island producers. If you call ahead
of time, you can book a tour of the farm
and pleasant horse rides in the Nurra.
Booking is recommended.

ARZACHENA
Cudacciolu

DA TINA

🝰 Bed and breakfast
Località Cudacciolu
Tel. 0789 80808-328 7475809
Fax 0789 80808
E-mail: er.borali@tiscali.it
Open from May to September

Tina Borali operates this pleasant B&B a
few kilometers from the exclusive – and
extremely expensive – Costa Smeralda.
Rooms are modestly appointed with
modern furniture and offer views over
the grounds and the surrounding
Mediterranean shrub land. For breakfast, guests can enjoy pastries, cookies,
bread with butter and jams, coffee, milk,
tea, cured meats and cheeses. From
Arzachena, you can take the 'green
train' to Tempio Pausania. Be sure to
stop and visit Sant'Antonio di Gallura
and Lake Liscia before continuing on to
Calangianus and Luras in the woods of
Mount Limbara. There's good sightseeing in the area, once the site of the ancient Nuragic civilization, where you can
visit the Tomb of the Giants and other
impressive burial grounds. The geologi-
cal and archaeological museums in
Arzachena are also worth a visit.

• 3 double rooms with bathroom, 2
rooms with a common bathroom, 2
rooms with air-conditioning • Prices:
double room single use 30-50 euros,
double 60-80 (26 euro supplement for
extra bed), breakfast included • No
credit cards • 1 room handicap accessible. Off-street parking. Small pets allowed. Owners always present • Breakfast room. Garden

BARUMINI

SA LOLLA

Hotel-restaurant
Via Cavour 49
Tel. 070 9368419
Closed Monday
Open: lunch and dinner
Holidays: variable in winter
Seating: 200 + 20 outdoors
Prices: 24-30 euros, wine excluded
All major credit cards, Bancomat

Sa Lolla, situated in a renovated country house, is basically an all-purpose facility; the rooms of the small hotel are on the upper floor, and guests can use the adjacent sports facilities and attend various kinds of events held in the amphitheatre. On the ground floor, there's a large stone-walled dining room, and the garden is open for dining in summertime.

Visitors have a choice between a meat or a fish menu, both of which offer a number of well-prepared specialties based on seasonal ingredients. On the first, less expensive menu, there are vegetables in olive oil, sausages with olives and **snails in tomato sauce** (which are also used to flavor the **fregola**); then tagliolini with either porcini mushrooms or wild asparagus sauce, depending on the season, **culurgiones with potatoes and mint** or **malloreddus alla campidanese** (with tomato, diced pork and sausage). On Sundays, Sa Lolla offers **stewed mutton** with wild cardoon, as well as barbecued **suckling pig** or goat braised with arbutus honey. The seafood fare includes sardines in olive oil, crab, octopus alla diavola and shrimp alla catalana, followed by **spaghetti** al cartoccio, with **botargo** or **sea urchin** sauce and a piece of fish cooked with Vernaccia or a grill platter of crayfish, cuttlefish and prawns. The meal ends the same way for both menus – fresh fruit, fruit cocktail, gelato and the usual seadas with honey.

For those who don't want the house wine, which is included in the meal price, there's a small but comprehensive selection of regional labels.

BONARCADO

SA MOLA

Hotel-restaurant
Via Giardini
Tel. 0783 56588
Closed Monday
Open: lunch and dinner
Holidays: February
Seating: 80 + banqueting hall
Prices: 25-27 euros, wine excluded
All major credit cards, Bancomat

Old and new harmoniously coexist in Antonio Borrodde's facility. While the restaurant and hotel rooms are in a 19th-century country house, the residence, with 15 apartments, was added on only recently. As for the food, chef Sandro Sanna's dishes reflect the culinary traditions of this area, from olive oil to casizolu and meat from Sardinian Modicana cattle (a Slow Food Presidium).

You can start with **snails in tomato sauce** or boiled grouse, served in a tasty mushroom and caper sauce. But the dishes vary frequently, and with every season comes something new to try. Among the first courses, safe bets include **ravioli filled with oxmeat** or zucchini and ricotta mustia, **culurgiones with potatoes and mint**, typical malloreddus with sausage and also **fregola with donkeymeat stew**, which in summer you can get with zucchini flowers in scampi. Then you can move on to rabbit alla cacciatora, the excellent **tagliata of oxmeat**, **roast suckling pig** and braised donkey, sometimes with quite creative accompaniments such as duck's breast with string beans and arbutus honey. In autumn, mushrooms harvested in the area are used in pasta sauces or roasted to accompany meat dishes. Among the desserts, in addition to seada, there's citrus fruit semifreddo, tiramisu and flandilatte.

The wine list includes a number of regional labels.

In **Seneghe** (5 km) at the Cosseddu brothers' place (Via Iosto 3) you can buy excellent extra-virgin olive oil made from intensely fruity Sartos olives.

LA MARGHERITA

Restaurant-pizzeria
Via Parpaglia at the corner of Via Azuni
Tel. 0785 373723
Closed Wednesday, never in summer
Open: only for dinner
Holidays: 15 days in January
Seating: 80 + 60 outdoors
Prices: 30-32 euros, wine excluded
All major credit cards, Bancomat

SA PISCHEDDA

Hotel-restaurant
Via Roma 2
Tel. 0785 372000
Closed Tuesday, never from April through October
Open: lunch and dinner
Holidays: January
Seating: 100 + 120 outdoors
Prices: 28-30 euros, wine excluded
All major credit cards, Bancomat

The sea and the medieval village of Bosa attract so much tourism that the population doubles during the summer. It's here that Antonio Fiorelli's restaurant offers traditional Sardinian dishes, prepared simply and served in a comfortable environment. In the evenings, the excellent wood-oven pizzas draw a younger crowd.

Meat and seafood antipasti start off the meal, with local **cured meats**, selected by the owner, served alongside smoked salmon and swordfish or **mussel and clam soup**. The seafood is the star of the first course menu, and the selection is ample, including **risotto alla marinara**, which varies with the catch but is always rich, spaghetti with botargo or clams, handmade tagliatelle with cuttlefish ink, or with red mullet and zucchini, and excellent **ravioli di pesce** with shrimp and seasonal vegetables. Don't miss the agliata al sugo prepared with skate or dogfish – on the menu it's called **s'azzada** – and another of the local seafood specialties is the **lobster alla bosana**, just boiled and served with splash of olive oil, accompanied by boiled eggs and vegetables. There's also fish from the day's catch, which you can get grilled, baked or fried. For those who prefer meat and order ahead of time, there's superb **roast porcetto**, or tagliata and escalopes, cooked with olive oil and lemon or, when in season, with local wild mushrooms. For dessert, there are **seadas** and typical **pabassinos** stuffed with currants.

There's quite a good choice of wines, with many regional labels.

The old center of Bosa, on a hill at the foot of the Malaspina Castle, is well worth a visit. Right next to Ponte Vecchio is Sa Pischedda, a historic hotel that opened at the end of the 19th century and is now also a seafood restaurant. In warm months, you can sample its food on an airy veranda overlooking the River Temo and the lights of the town.

To start, **mullet botargo**, crab and lobster, as well as delicate mussel and clam soup, octopus salad and **agliata** cooked with dogfish or skate. There's a wide selection of first courses, including one of the classic dishes of Sardinian cuisine, **fregola with clams**. Or you could try **tagliatelle alla granseola** (crab), **anguleddas with botargo**, linguine with scampi, cuttlefish risotto, **Bosa-style fish soup** and a curious surf-and-turf combination, maltagliati with oysters and mushrooms. The day's catch – which could be frog-fish, caponi, or any number of other varieties – is enjoyable whether it's grilled, stewed or oven-baked in salt. An alternative to sea fare is fillet steak flavored with porcini mushrooms, tagliata of beef with arugula or grilled beef chops. Finally, there's a small selection of Pecorino cheeses and desserts, like pastry-wraps filled with ricotta and honey, nougat parfait with caramel al Grand Marnier and croccantini with hot chocolate that go well with a glass of Malvasia.

The wine cellar offers a great selection of the best Sardinian labels.

CABRAS

IL CAMINETTO

Restaurant
Via Battisti 8
Tel. 0783 391139
Closed Monday, never in August
Open: lunch and dinner
Holidays: 10 days in January, 15 in November
Seating: 130
Prices: 25-30 euros, wine excluded
All major credit cards, Bancomat

Il Caminetto is large and often busy with traditional cuisine that varies depending on the day's catch from the sea and the nearby pond. The **burrida cabrarese** is one of the typical antipasti here, along with **mussel and clam soups**, **fried orziadas** (sea anemones) and **sardines with seasonal vegetables** fried in batter. Among the first courses, spaghetti with mussels, clams or cuttlefish, linguine with sea urchins and **fregula e cocciua pintada**, a seafood soup. The main courses include **grilled fish platters**, cuttlefish and squid, either fried or stewed, lobsters, **merca** (preserved fish), **anguidda incasada** (eel) nd mullet roasted on cane embers. **Seada** is always on the dessert menu.
There are many modestly priced regional labels in the cellar.

• 6 single rooms, 15 doubles and 2 triples, with bathroom, air conditioning, balcony, fridge bar, satellite TV • Prices: single 48-70, double single use 61-83, double 76-120, triple 95-150 euros, breakfast included • 2 rooms handicap accessible. Free parking. Pets welcome. 24-hour doorman• Bar, restaurant. Breakfast room. Conference room. Internal garden.

Francesco Atzori produces a high quality, fruity extra-virgin olive oil (Provincial Road 4, km 2.5). The Antonio and Mario Casula bakery, Corso Umberto 1, sells Oristano's own style of mostaccioli, baked according to an ancient recipe.

CAGLIARI
Old town

CAGLIARI NOVECENTO

Hotel
Via Angioj 23
Tel. 070 650607
Fax 070 6401311
E-mail: cagliarinovecento@libero.it
Open all year round

After many years' experience in the building trade, Salvatore Carta recently purchased an 1870s building once used to host pilgrims. Completely restored, the common areas still boast some original frescoes, part of the original ceiling and sections of the old floor. Breakfast is served in the lounge and includes hot beverages, fruit juices and freshly made items from the local pastry shop. English breakfast is available on request. Located in the lower section of the Stampace area (a limited traffic zone), the hotel provides a comfortable base for guests that want to visit the impressive buildings of the town center and stroll along the promenade, Via Roma.

• 2 single and 4 double rooms, bathroom, air-conditioning, fridge, television • Prices: single 50 euros, double 72 (22 euro supplement for extra bed); breakfast included • Credit cards: all, Bancomat • External public parking. No pets allowed. Reception open 24 hours a day • Breakfast room, reading room

CRACKERS

Trattoria
Corso Vittorio Emanuele 195
Tel. 070 653912
Closed Wednesday
Open: lunch and dinner
Holidays: August 20-first week of September
Seating: 60
Prices: 35 euros, wine excluded
All major credit cards, Bancomat

Considering that the Stampace quarter of Cagliari is nowhere near Turin, it may seem strange that Cinus brothers' trattoria specializes in Piedmontese favorites such as agnolotti with gravy or risotto with Alba truffles (also used to their flavor fried eggs, fillet steak, and tagliata). The reason is that the brothers boast long years of restaurant experience in the Piedmontese capital.

The antipasti include oven-baked vegetables, swordfish carpaccio, frog-fish salad and, in the right season, royal agaric and porcini mushroom salad. The real specialties at Crackers, at least according to the visitors, are the **risottos**. With porcini mushrooms, Barolo, Champagne, truffles from Alba or Sardinia, artichokes, **wild asparagus**, or **cardoncelli**, there's a flavor for every palate. In addition to the agnolotti, you'll also find **ravioli campidanesi**, and some fish dishes too, ranging from **pasta with botargo** to spaghetti with shellfish or fish soup. If you want roast porcetto, you have to order it in advance; in winter, beef braised in Barolo and **costata di bue rosso** are always available. In summer, it's best to opt for the lighter fish dishes, either roasted or in the **mixed fry platter**. Among the desserts are panna cotta, trifle, crème caramel and strudel, plus some Sardinian specialties. The wine list includes selections from several regions; in addition to Sardinian labels, you can count on finding good Veneto and Trentino whites and Piedmontese and Tuscan reds. For the finishing touch to your meal, an amaro, a grappa or a Sardinian liqueur.

DOLMEN

Restaurant
Viale Sant'Avendrace 216
Tel. 070 281019
Closed Monday
Open: lunch and dinner
Holidays: August
Seating: 90
Prices: 30 euros, wine excluded
All major credit cards, Bancomat

This historic restaurant is in the suburbs, near the road that leads to the airport and old State Highway 131 (Viale Monastir), though it's not far from the center of town and the port. The area is full of restaurants and trattorias, but Dolmen stands out for its rustic furnishings, reminiscent of the Sardinian countryside, as well as for the freshness of its ingredients. Plus, there's not a boring dish on the menu.

This restaurant is 100% Cagliari and focuses on seafood; it was recently taken over by Lucio Mario Troilo, a member of the Cagliari school of cooking born in Calabria (the menu includes a pasta with Calabrian 'nduja salami). Troilo has decided to spice up the menu, so you'll find **oysters**, **orziadas** (sea anemones), with which they make truly exquisite pasta, **sea urchins**, rock-fish with potatoes and **dentex with Vernaccia**. Of course there's also a lot more: the traditional **mixed grill** that includes tender, tasty cuttlefish, a **fried fish platter**, crostini with 'nduja salami and barbecued or **oven-baked swordfish**.

Admittedly, some dishes, like oysters, will raise the cost of the bill, but for the most part this is quality cuisine at pretty low prices for the city. Additionally, the wine list focuses on areas that aren't frequently explored.

FLORA

⌂ Restaurant
Via Sassari 45
Tel. 070 664735-658219
Closed Sunday
Open: lunch and dinner
Holidays: 3 weeks in August, 1 week for New Year
Seating: 80 + 40 outdoors
Prices: 30-35 euros, wine excluded
All major credit cards, Bancomat

KAREL

⚷ Bed and breakfast
Via Sonnino 208
Tel. 070 3300029-328 8236847
Fax 070 3300030-178 6021297
E-mail: info@karel-bedeandbreakfast.it
Internet: www.karel-bedandbreakfast.it
Open all year round

Your host Beppe Deplano has spent many years running this place near the port of Cagliari with his daughter Laura, and he puts a lot of effort into his selection of local ingredients. He also happens to be an expert on Savoy silverware and a collector of early 20th-century toys, and his enthusiasm for these items is obvious from the cabinets filled with silverware, art nouveau vases and marble and bronze sculptures. Beppe transformed his old trattoria into a restaurant in the early 1990s without changing the spirit, cuisine or meticulous selection of ingredients.

The antipasti include fried meatballs, zucchini flowers, **mussel and clam soups**, raw porcini mushrooms (in season) and sometimes even **royal agaric mushrooms**. Among the first courses are **culurgiones ogliastrini made with potatoes and mint**, with sauce or fried in the traditional manner, artichoke or **onion ravioli**, chickpea or bean soups and minestrone. For the main course dishes, there are **cordula** (lamb's intestines) **with peas**, **mutton stewed in red wine**, sweetbreads and **tripe spiced with wild mint**. The seafood options include pasta with clams and zucchini, cartoccio of fish, an extremely light **mixed fried fish platter**, **rock-fish with potatoes**, crawfish or **lobster alla catalana**, which is even better in a sauce made from its own eggs. As for the homemade desserts, anything chocolate here is superb.

Beppe has a written menu, but he prefers to recite it, and if he likes you he'll tell you a joke or two. The wine list has a selection of the best Sardinian labels along with a few wines from other Italian regions.

Marina, near the port, is one of the historic areas of Cagliari, maybe originating from a Roman military camp. The renovation of several buildings dating back to the mid-19th century in the area around the church of Saint Eulalia (archaeological excavations and a museum) has given the place a new lease of life. The B&B's comfortable rooms are spread out over five buildings, one of which doesn't have a common area. Breakfast is therefore served in the room. All rooms are painted in soft pastel colors, fitted with different style furniture and are always friendly and comfortable. A traditional breakfast of tea, coffee, milk, bread, jams, honey, cookies, yoghurt, pastries and cakes is offered.

• 8 double and 5 triple rooms, bathroom (2 rooms with bathroom in common), air-conditioning, television • Prices: double room single use 45-70 euros, double 60-120, triple 90, breakfast included • All major credit cards, Bancomat • Paid parking nearby. Small pets allowed. Owners always contactable • Breakfast room

LA VECCHIA TRATTORIA

Trattoria
Via Azuni 55
Tel. 070 652515-348 8239169
Closed Sunday
Open: lunch and dinner
Holidays: variable
Seating: 60 + 40 outdoors
Prices: 30-35 euros, wine excluded
All major credit cards, Bancomat

SAN CRISPINO

Restaurant
Corso Vittorio Emanuele 190
Tel. 070 651853
Closed Monday
Open: lunch and dinner
Holidays: none
Seating: 80
Prices: 30-33 euros, wine excluded
All credit cards except AE, Bancomat

Via Azuni is in one of Cagliari's oldest districts (Stampace), at the foot of the historic castle. If you start out at Piazza Yenne you can walk the entire length of the street (perhaps stopping to visit the church of Sant'Anna or the crypt of Santa Restituta) and you'll eventually end up at La Vecchia Trattoria. The trattoria has been open for a few decades now but was taken over two years ago by Claudio Ara, who has made a number of changes to the layout. The kitchen's on the left as you enter, and on the right there's a small dining room attached to a second, larger one.
Claudio Ara has two cooks helping him in the kitchen, whence he dispatches a fine variety of regional dishes, sometimes inventively but always tastefully reinterpreted. There's seafood but also typical dishes from central Sardinia, like **carne di bue rosso** (meat from the Sardinian Modicana, a Slow Food Presidia). The menu changes often, especially with the seasons. The best among the wide selection of antipasti are the **sardines on zucchini**, **fresh Arzana sausage**, **Ogliastrino ham** served with thin slices of melon and **mussels on carasau bread**. Among the home-made pastas available for the first course, it's certainly worth trying the ravioli with eggplant and **ciccioneddas with fish sauce**. For a main course, aside from the dishes made using bue rossp, there are always various types of **fresh fish** cooked Mediterranean-style. Among the desserts, we recommend the **tiramisù**. There isn't a wine list, but your host has some rather impressive bottles from some of the region's excellent producers. The same goes for grappas and liqueurs.

The Mura brothers have been busy with renovations recently, and though there is slightly less seating as a result, the place is now noticeably more comfortable. But even with the facelift, San Crispino is still reserved and elegant with straightforward, traditional cuisine. Located in the heart of Cagliari, this restaurant offers a menu that satisfies both the regulars and the many tourists who pass through the Sardinian capital. Every day you can choose from thirty different antipasti, warm or cold, including tuna carpaccio, stewed or baked eggplant, **snails in tomato sauce**, mussel or clam soups and excellent **orziadas fritters**. The spaghetti with sea urchin sauce is particularly good in winter, and the **fregola with clams** and **culurgiones** and the large ravioli stuffed with mint and potato are great all year round. Among the fish for the main course there's often filleted sea bass, gilthead or dentici with vegetables and a magnificent **mixed fried fish platter** with orziadas. The meat dishes are exceptional, too; there's **cordula** (goat or lamb's intestines) roasted and served with peas, stewed or **roast goat**, barbecued or grilled horsemeat steaks.
To round off the meal, there are seadas or a selection of traditional cookies with a glass of blueberry liqueur or limoncello. There's also quite a good selection of regional wines.

CAGLIARI
Old town

CAGLIARI
Near the old town

SARDINIA DOMUS

🗝Bed and breakfast
Largo Carlo Felice 26
Tel. 070 659783-338 1613081
Fax 070 659783
E-mail: info@sardiniadomus.it
Internet: www.sardiniadomus.it
Open all year round

VILLA CAO

🗝Bed and breakfast
Via Bacaredda 126
Tel. 070 401269-338 6133691
E-mail: silvanacao@libero.it
Internet: www.villacao.it
Closed in August and from December 21 to January 3

This B&B is in a renovated old building with all its original architecture, including wooden beams and brick walls. The rooms are spacious and bright, with simple but comfortable furniture. Breakfast is served in a pleasant lounge and includes a variety of sweets. Close to both the port and the railway station, the B&B is a good home base if you want to sightsee in Cagliari without having to rely on a car or public transportation. Attractions include the cathedral and the Palazzo Viceregio in the historic Castello area, and the museum complex in Piazza Arsenale houses both the National Archaeological Museum and the botanical gardens.

• 5 double rooms and 1 with 4 beds, bathroom, air-conditioning, television, modem connection; 2 rooms with balcony • Prices: double room single use 55 euros, double 70, triple 100, quadruple 120, breakfast included • Credit cards: all, Bancomat • Paid parking out front and nearby. Small pets allowed (5 euros per day). Owners always reachable • Breakfast room

This B&B is a beautiful, tastefully furnished house with an elegant, friendly atmosphere, just a short walk away from the opera house. It's a family-run establishment and the owner, Silvana Cao, who inherited Cagliari's famous furniture production business, lives there. One of the entrances leads out onto a charming old town alleyway, and there's a tidy garden and a portico where guests can relax. Rooms are fitted with modern furniture; one room has a small mezzanine study area, and two particularly quiet rooms look out onto the courtyard. The filling breakfast includes coffee, tea, fruit juices or freshly squeezed orange juice, cookies, fresh bread, toast, butter, jam and honey.

• 1 single and 2 double rooms, bathroom (separate for the single room), air-conditioning, television; double rooms with mini-bar • Prices: single 44 euros, double 72 (23 euro supplement for extra bed), breakfast included • Credit cards: none • Off-street parking. Small pets allowed. Owners always present • Breakfast room, lounge, library, internet point. Garden

CAGLIARI
Giorgino

CALANGIANUS

9 KM EAST OF TEMPIO PAUSANIA, 35 KM FROM OLBIA ON SS 127

ZENIT

🍲 Restaurant
Viale Pula-Villaggio dei pescatori
Tel. 070 250009
Closed Monday
Open: lunch and dinner
Holidays: January
Seating: 60 + 60 outdoors
Prices: 25 euros, wine excluded
All major credit cards, Bancomat

IL TIRABUSCIÒ

🍲 Restaurant
Via Nino Bixio 5
Tel. 079 661849
Closed Sunday
Open: lunch and dinner
Holidays: between January and February
Seating: 30
Prices: 30-35 euros, wine excluded
All major credit cards, Bancomat

If you head west from the center of Cagliari, towards Pula and the Santa Gilla lagoon, you'll find a fishermen's village with at most 40 houses. Both the beach and the sea are in easy reach of this simply furnished, marine-themed restaurant.

As you can imagine, the menu recited here is all about the fish caught that day. And since it's so fresh, the fish doesn't require much in the way of preparation to taste really good. For example, there's a very nice **burrida** made with either dogfish or skate, simply marinated in a vinegar-based sauce. There are soups and broths made with several kinds of fish or featuring just one (we recommend the **eel soup**), **spaghetti** with shellfish sauce or, in winter, **with sea urchin sauce** and, lastly, **fregola with clams**. As a main course, you can enjoy one of many kinds of baked fish or the **mixed fish platter**, in which you'll often find fish that other restaurants don't usually serve, like moray eel. When it's time for dessert, you'll find Sardinian cakes and cookies, an original blancmange al limoncello and some standard offerings like crema catalana.

To accompany your meal there are house wines in addition to the local and regional wines on the list.

Known as the capital of cork production, Calangianus is tucked away in the ancient oak groves of Sardinia. The small, friendly restaurant Antonio Fele operates in his grandparents' old house is in the town center. Renovations uncovered several original granite decorations that now give the surroundings a note of reserved elegance.

The antipasti are rather unique and include carpaccio of zucchini with salty ricotta cheese, honey and botargo, fried artichoke hearts, mushrooms au gratin or quail drumsticks browned in Nebbiolo wine. After that, though, the meals prepared by chef Andrea Sassu stick to the traditions of Gallura and inland Sardinia. Depending on the season, the first courses include **sweet pulingioni** (typical Gallura-style ravioli), **chjusoni with hare sauce**, tagliatelle with wild boar sauce and linguine with mussels and peppers. Provided you order it in advance, you can also enjoy an excellent **Gallura-style soup**. Meat is central to the main course list; depending on what's available from local producers you can try **donkey meat with garlic and parsley**, fillet steak in Cannonau wine sauce or lamb chops with rosemary. The **porcetto**, like the soup, must be ordered in advance.

There are about 50 labels on the wine list, mostly reasonably priced regional wines.

CALASETTA
Sant'Antioco Island

28 KM SOUTH-WEST OF CARBONIA, 28 KM FROM IGLESIAS

DA PASQUALINO

🍲 Trattoria
Via Regina Margherita 85
Tel. 0781 88473
Closed Tuesday, never in summer
Open: lunch and dinner
Holidays: in winter at various times
Seating: 80 + 20 outdoors
Prices: 25-35 euros, wine excluded
All major credit cards, Bancomat

As soon as you reach Calasetta, take the road leading to the port and you'll find the new Pasqualino, which relocated from via Roma a few years ago. The new place admittedly lacks charm, but Annamaria's fish dishes are still excellent.

A good starting point would be any of the various preparations of tuna available: **musciame**, smoked or boiled **cuts** preserved in olive oil and **botargo**. Or you can have mussels alla marinara, mixed seafood or octopus salad or **clam soup**. First courses include, in addition to fish soup, **spaghetti** with tuna sauce, **alla calasettana** (with tuna, mullet botargo and musciame) or alla marinara. Two dishes here that you don't see very often in Sardinia are the **cascà** (couscous), which comes with a rich sauce of shrimp, squid, cuttlefish and other small fish, and the **pilau** (fregola spiced with saffron) with clams, mussels and prawns. **Mixed fried fish platters** and various types and sizes of grilled fish are typical main courses, but there are meat dishes too, like rabbit chasseur, **porcetto** (which must be ordered in advance), horsemeat steaks and pork chops. To round off the meal, there's homemade tiramisu, a few kinds of gelato, warm **seadas** with honey and Ricotta cheese pardula.

There's a house wine from the nearby Cantina Sociale, but there is also a small selection of island labels. Given the many visitors in summer, it's always best to make reservations.

🍞 In **Sant'Antioco** (10 km) at the Calabrò bakery in front of the town hall, you can buy traditional, naturally leavened bread.

CODRONGIANOS

18 KM SOUTHEAST OF SASSARI ON SS 131

FUNTANARENA

🔑 3-Star Hotel
Via S'Istradoneddu 8-10
Tel. 079 435048
Fax 079 216179
E-mail: info@funtanarena.it
Internet: www.funtanarena.it
Open from April to September

The term 'funtanarena' is a Sardinian word meaning 'spring from the sand'. This small hotel, run by a company called L'isola che c'è, is in a 19th-century manor house near the historic center of Codrongianos. Each room is furnished differently and named for either a natural oil or the dominant theme of its decorations; all rooms are quiet and have views of the olive grove and the orchard. The furnishings are antique and there's no TV, but there are books available from the well-stocked library. For breakfast there's a simple buffet of pastries, hot beverages and fruit juices, fresh bread and jam. The restaurant offers regional and national dishes at 20-30 euros a meal, excluding wine.

• 2 single and 7 double rooms, bathroom • Prices: double room single use 54-65 euros, double 81-96 (30-36 euro for extra bed), breakfast included • Credit cards: all, Bancomat • 2 rooms handicap accessible. Off-street parking. Small pets allowed. Reception open from 9 am to 9 pm • Bar, restaurant. Television room. Conference room. Garden

CUGLIERI

DESOGOS

Hotel-trattoria
Via Cugia 6
Tel. 0785 39660
Closed Friday
Open: lunch and dinner
Holidays: 15 days in November
Seating: 60
Prices: 25 euros, wine excluded
All major credit cards, Bancomat

Cuglieri is on the western slope of Montiferru, about 10 kilometers from some of the treasures of the Oristano coastline. The village has strong ties to the surrounding land, which yields many quality products, like sheep and cattle (including Sardinian Modicana breed, a Slow Food Presidium), local olive oils and casizolu. These ingredients are building blocks for the tasty dishes the Desogos sisters make in their trattoria, which is attached to a ten-room hotel they also own.

There's a fixed menu that varies with the seasons and with what's available in the market. Start with **panadinas** filled with meat or seasonal vegetables, legume salads spiced with wild fennel, local cured meats and **pane frissu cun petta imbinada** (meat marinated in wine). Then you can choose from among ravioli with chard and ricotta, **minestra cun casu friscu**, pappardelle with wild boar sauce and **malloreddus cun su ghisadu** (a traditional sauce made from mutton or lamb on the bone). Then on to the meat dishes, which include veal, sausages, **stewed** or **roast suckling pig**, **pitta cun ulìa** (red beef with olives) and game – wild boar or hare are hunted nearby – usually cooked in salmi. In summer there are also fish dishes, mainly to keep the tourists happy.

As an alternative to the house wine served by the carafe (included in the fixed price), the cellar stocks a few regional labels.

DOLIANOVA

CASA MASCIA

Bed and breakfast
Via Manzoni 7
Tel. 070 743481-347 6204208-349 8010617
E-mail: casamascia@tiscali.it
Open all year round

Dolianova is a relatively young town 20 kilometers from the sea, formed in 1905 from two villages called San Pantaleo and Sicci San Biagio. Right in the middle of old Sicci is the Lepori family's 19th-century house, elegantly appointed with period furniture, a courtyard, a garden and a summer gazebo. The family lives in one part of the house, and the remainder has been converted into guest rooms. One of the rooms has a mezzanine floor with a separate sleeping area. The common areas include a kitchen/living room where guests can enjoy a breakfast of tea, milk, coffee, Sardinian cookies, fresh pastries, bread, butter, jam, honey and seasonal fruit.

• 3 double rooms with bathroom • Prices: double room single use 30-35 euros, double 50-60 (15 euro supplement for extra bed), breakfast included • Credit cards: none • Off-street parking for 1 car and free public parking outside. Small pets allowed. Owners always present • Dining room. Garden

DORGALI
Ispinigoli

ELMAS

32 KM EAST OF NUORO ON SS 129 AND 125

8 KM NORTH OF CAGLIARI ON SS 130

ISPINIGOLI

Hotel-restaurant
Strada Statale 125 km 210
Tel. 0784 95268-94293
Never closed
Open: lunch and dinner
Holidays: beginning of November-end of February
Seating: 300 + 100 outdoors
Prices: 25-35 euros, wine excluded
All major credit cards except DC, Bancomat

PANI E CASU

Trattoria
Via Moguru
Tel. 070 216691
Closed Sunday
Open: lunch and dinner
Holidays: 2 weeks in August
Seating: 90
Prices: 23-25 euros
All major credit cards, Bancomat

Pietro Mula's restaurant offers such a wide variety of dishes that it's difficult to summarize them. The large dining rooms are also good for hosting banquets and special occasions, and there is a covered terrace that can seat up to 100 people in good weather. In addition to the restaurant, Ispinigoli has a hotel with a number of additional services, like a play area and an indoor disco. As this is not really a classic osteria, you may be surprised by the well-crafted traditional dishes.

There are three different menus, each of which includes a selection of antipasti, a first course, a main course and dessert – the vegetarian meal, more traditional fare and seafood. You also get three or four different kinds of bread with your meal. Among the antipasti, you'll usually find **marinated grouper**, raw swordfish with cherry tomatoes, diced wild boar with vegetables and local cured meats, **cervelletta** and **cordedda in salsa**. After that, there's **minestra chin frue** (goat's milk whey), carasau soup with broth, cottu bread, **anzelottos** with cheese and mint and **maccarones furriaos**, with a sauce made of cheeses, saffron and armidda (a typical local herb) or **fregola with clams**. Then you can opt for **roast porceddu** or **purpuzza de porcu** (morsels of suckling pig flambé), beef and horsemeat or, if you order it in advance, kid and lamb. Otherwise, go for fried, grilled or baked fish. And if this isn't enough, there's a wide selection of **cheeses** including various kinds of pecorino, caprino, mozzarella and Fiore sardo.

To finish, there's taedda with honey, seadas and casadinas. The wine list has about 350 labels. There's also a special children's menu.

This trattoria is just outside Elmas on the road to Assemini. If it wasn't for the sign outside, you'd probably miss it, because it looks like any other unassuming farmhouse in the countryside. It's furnished very simply with rustic wooden tables, checked tablecloths and old photos on the walls. The atmosphere is informal and a bit chaotic, especially on weekends, so if you want to guarantee yourself a nice traditional Sardinian dinner, you should probably make reservations. The menu is always the same; this kitchen shies away from elaborate preparations, focusing instead on quality products from this area. Antipasti include vegetables from their garden, either raw or preserved in olive oil, with fine regional and **local cured meats**, semi-seasoned pecorino cheese in a spicy cream, and **snails in tomato sauce**. After this come the classic **culurgiones**, pasta stuffed with durum wheat flour, traditional ravioli with either tomato or walnut sauce or just lightly fried in butter and **malloreddus alla campidanese**. For the main course, there's veal, horsemeat, **donkey-meat** or, when in season, **wild boar** either barbecued or stewed and served in generous portions. The **sweetbreads**, brains, udder and sausages are excellent too. To finish, there are traditional seadas and typical cookies.

There's a house wine to go with your meal (included in the fixed price), or you can take the advice of your host, Efisio Mameli, on which regional label goes best with the dishes you choose. Plus classic Sardinian liqueurs.

GAVOI

SANTA RUGHE

Restaurant
Via Carlo Felice 2
Tel. 0784 53774
Closed Wednesday, never in August
Open: lunch and dinner
Holidays: variable
Seating: 80 + 20 outdoors
Prices: 27-30 euros, wine excluded
All major credit cards, Bancomat

Gavoi is a large village once famous for producing horse harnesses, though today its most important product is cheese, especially Fiore sardo. The most memorable part of Gavoi for us, though, was Santa Rughe (named after the nearby church of Santa Croce), for the meal and the smiling welcome we got there, and for the way the place fits in so magnificently with its surroundings. The food here is quintessentially local, starting with the **Pecorino cheeses**, served seasoned as an opener, roasted halfway through the meal or smoked at the end. Just as recommendable are the cured meats – sausage, prosciutto, pancetta and **lardo di Gavoi** – served with porcini mushrooms, olives, eggplant and fava beans. Then you can get brain fritters, sweetbread, tripe and **purpuzza** (marinated pieces of pork). The first courses also highlight the location: **malloreddus** with sheep's milk ricotta, saffron and mint, **ravioli stuffed with cheese** and **lisandros** (similar to fettucine) with porcini mushrooms. Then there are trays piled high with meat – veal, donkey, horse – and the ever-present **roast porcetto**, and in winter, wild boar stew or **lamb stew**. Lastly, traditional desserts like **seadas** and sweet ricotta raviolini flavored with lemon or orange peel.
There's a good selection of local wines (some available by the glass), but there are also wines from the rest of Italy as well as a wide variety of grappas and typical liqueurs. If you want, you can get pizza here, too.

GIBA

LA ROSELLA

Hotel-restaurant
Via Principe di Piemonte 135
Tel. 0781 964029
Closed Wednesday, never in summer
Open: lunch and dinner
Holidays: from Christmas to New Year
Seating: 120
Prices: 30-32 euros, wine excluded
All major credit cards, Bancomat

Here at La Rosella fish is showing up on the menu more and more – the Gulf of Palmas and the Mediterranean are less than 10 kilometers away – and Lucia Pennisi handles it with the same flair as she does the meat and vegetables. Her daughter Stefania gives her a hand, taking care of the service and selecting the ingredients, notably the sheep and goat's milk cheeses from a cooperative in Villamassargia. There are also around 20 rooms for those wishing to prolong their stay.
There are elements of both sea and land throughout the meal, starting with the antipasti, which include wild cardoons and **alga and sea anemone frittata**, **goat ham** and tuna with onions, stuffed hot peppers and fregola with crab sauce. As a first course you might want to try the **pillus**, bran puff pastry dressed with goat or **lamb ragù** or black and white tagliolini (colored black with cuttlefish ink) allo scoglio. The stuffed pastas, such as **ravioli with wild asparagus** or artichokes, or the **gnocchetti with chard and ricotta** are good too. If you've never tried it, you've got to order the **plaited sheep's intestines** flavored with artichokes and peas and cooked slowly on an open fire. But every one of the dishes is mouthwatering, from the **grive (thrush) cooked with blueberries**, leg of lamb or suckling pig with chickpeas, to the eel cooked on a skewer to the shellfish soups, fregola with artichokes, cardoons and porcini mushrooms. We've already mentioned the cheeses, and for dessert you can count on the seadas, raviolini filled with sweet ricotta or quince jelly and cakes with lemon cream.
The wine list focuses on the best regional labels.

GAZEBO MEDIOEVALE

⌒ Restaurant
Via Musio 21
Tel. 0781 30871
Closed Sunday, never in August
Open: lunch and dinner
Holidays: between October and November
Seating: 90 + 40 outdoors
Prices: 28-30 euros, wine excluded
All major credit cards, Bancomat

DA RICCARDO

⌒ Trattoria
Via Vittorio Emanuele 13-15
Tel. 0785 35631
Closed Tuesday
Open: lunch and dinner
No holidays taken
Seating: 40
Prices: 25-30 euros, wine excluded
No credit cards

Capital of a new double province, Iglesias boasts a noteworthy old center in the shadow of the Salvaterra Castle, still partly surrounded by the original Pisan walls. The sea is not far away, and there's a lovely stretch of coast extending from Cape Altano to the Pan di Zucchero rock. This is where the restaurant gets most of its ingredients.

Once you're seated in one of the two elegant dining rooms, you can start with tuna **carpaccio**, swordfish, sea bass, grouper and gilthead. If they have it, you should try the delicate **luvaro carpaccio** (deep-sea dentex). Or you can opt for marinated or spiced anchovies and **guazzetto of mussels and clams**. If you order it in advance, you can try a rich **seafood couscous** and paella with shellfish and pork. But there are many alternatives, ranging from **orecchiette with mussels and chickpeas** to **fregola with clams**, trofiette with shellfish, **spaghetti** with various accoutrements, like clams and porcini mushrooms, **botargo and sea asparagus**, **granseola crab and vegetables**. As for main dishes, there are **mixed fried** and grilled platters, **tagliata of tuna** with tomatoes and onions and Mediterranean-style fillet of perch with seasonal vegetables. There are also a few dishes with meat from the local markets. For dessert, we suggest the black fig mousse or citrus fruit semifreddo.

The wine list has a good number of regional labels, mainly whites, to accompany the seafood.

Riccardo, Paola and Graziella's trattoria is in Magomadas, a village in the Planargia area just steps from the sea. And in fact, the sea provides most of the ingredients they use in their summer dishes, which change from day to day. For 24 euros you can get a fixed menu – mixed antipasti, two first courses, a main course, dessert and a liqueur. Possible options are **anguidda incasada (eel)**, octopus salad, carpaccio of swordfish and a tasty salad of stuffed cuttlefish dressed with balsamic vinegar. Then comes **spaghetti with botargo**, or with clams, fusilli with shrimp and zucchini and, moving on to the main course, a mixed grilled platter, **prawns cooked with blueberries**, **sea bass flavored with wild fennel** and **crayfish alla catalana**.

In the fall, mushrooms rule, with twenty different types of porcini, galletti and sanguinelli used to prepare flans, pasta sauces and soups. We recommend bavette with porcini mushrooms and swordfish or the **porcini mushroom soup**. Winter is legume season here, and you'll mostly find them with various types of shellfish; creamed chickpeas with clams and shrimp or beans with mussels are just two examples. Other dishes that come to mind are the **panadinas** filled with meat and vegetables, minestrone and barley soup, **petta imbinada** and the mixed grilled meat platter. Lastly, there are various typical desserts available, like grilled seadas or papassinos and almond-flavored treats. But if you're a cheese lover, go for a plate of seasoned pecorino and ricotta served with honey.

In the cellar there are a number of excellent regional wines, many of them on tap.

MURAVERA
Villaputzu

NUORO

68 KM NORTHEAST OF CAGLIARI

SU TALLERI

� Restaurant
Bivio Porto Corallo
Tel. 070 997574
Closed Sunday evenings
Open: lunch and dinner
Holidays: 2 weeks in October and 2 at Christmas
Seating: 120
Prices: 28-32 euros, wine excluded
All major credit cards, Bancomat

IL RIFUGIO

⌖container Trattoria-pizzeria
Via Antonio Mereu 28-36
Tel. 0784 232355
Closed Wednesday
Open: lunch and dinner
Never takes holidays
Seating: 80
Prices: 25-30 euros, wine excluded
All major credit cards except DC, Bancomat

Even though it can't boast a picturesque setting, this restaurant is near the coast in an area olive, almond and citrus trees. The offerings here are reliable and inexpensive, and at 30 euros, the fixed menu offers mixed antipasti, two first courses, grilled fish with a side plate, house wine, coffee and a glass of blueberry liqueur or homemade limoncello. You start with crostini with olive oil and cherry tomatoes followed by octopus salad, sauté of mussels and clams, mussels au gratin and carpionata of fish. Often you'll also find tappadas, which are **monacelle snails** in a hot red sauce or alongside fregola in the first course. **Fregola** is also served with **sea anemones** or clams with botargo, or you could try the seafood risotto with mussels, clams, scampi, crab, shrimp and tomato or the **spaghetti with botargo**, truffles or sea urchin sauce. In sauces the fish is often combined with vegetables, like the rockfish in the tagliolini with asparagus or zucchini. You'll also find various kinds of fish, prawns and cuttlefish in the mixed grill; or get the **mixed fish fry**, capone alla catalana or, if you don't mind spending a bit more, **lobster alla catalana** or lobster boiled and served with olive oil and lemon juice. Lastly, try some typical Sardinian sweets like seada, pardula and pistoccheddu.
To accompany your meal you can choose from among the locally produced wines or from the small selection of Sardinian labels.

🍴 In Località **Canne Frau** (10 km) the Bresca Dorada farm produces wine, honey and excellent orange and prickly pear flavored liqueurs.

Silverio Nanu's place is in the middle of town, not far from the cathedral and the three museums, which feature exhibitions on Grazia Deledda, archeology and Sardinian traditions. In this friendly, informal atmosphere you'll have a chance to taste local specialties made from that day's market offerings.
Among the antipasti you'll find cured mutton, ham, vegetables preserved in olive oil and smoked sausage. The first course specialties include **malloreddus alla nuorese** (with meat sauce), **maccarones with red sauce and rissoles** and, if you order it in advance, **su filindeu** (durum wheat bran pasta cooked in mutton broth), a dish that's so complicated that nowadays it's only made for special occasions. Then **tripe alla paesana**, horse fillet and steak, roast pork, **mutton in cappotto** with potatoes and beans or **in cassola alla nuorese**. Although the sea is some distance away, there's a surprising variety of seafood dishes, from marinated sardines to mussels au gratin, octopus alla diavola and seafood salad. Following this, there's spaghetti with botargo, **fregola** with shellfish or **eel broth** and lastly, a mixed grilled fish platter, roast mullet and gilthead alla Vernaccia. To round off your meal there's a small selection of fresh and seasoned pecorino cheeses and roasted cow's milk cheese, or you can go directly to the seadas with honey or other more unusual desserts such as mousses and semifreddi.
The wine list is respectable and includes some good regional labels. After your meal, have a glass of blueberry liqueur or filuferru. Il Rifugio also serves excellent pizzas but only for dinner.

NUXIS

OLBIA

LETIZIA

Restaurant-pizzeria
Via San Pietro 12
Tel. 0781 957021
Closed Tuesday
Open: lunch and dinner
Never takes holidays
Seating: 80 + 100 outdoors
Prices: 30-32 euros, wine excluded
All major credit cards, Bancomat

BARBAGIA

Restaurant-pizzeria
Via Galvani 94
Tel. 0789 51640
Closed Wednesday, never in summer
Open: lunch and dinner
Holidays: January
Seating: 100 + 60 outdoors
Prices: 30-35 euros, wine excluded
All major credit cards, Bancomat

It surprised us to discover just how many ingredients Letizia uses in her **perdingianu a scabecciu** (eggplant a scapece), gureu scettau (cardoons buried in tarragon) and faixeddas (fava beans) a cassola. The balance of tastes in each dish is exceptional, thanks also to the clever use of herbs that's one of the hallmarks of Elio Fanutza's restaurant. Aside from the main courses, the menu has a vegetarian focus and will expose you to local products and recipes, interpreted here in a charming, personal way. Among the antipasti, apart from the dishes already mentioned, you will find **fresh cheese with mastic tree oil**, crostini with mushrooms and a new dish this year, mousse di ovinfort (herbed Sardinian pecorino). Then it's time for crespelle with goat's milk cheese and nettles, **borage ravioli** with nettle and walnut pesto, lasagnette with porcini mushrooms and a typical local dish, **eggplant mazzamurru**. You'll only find meat in the main course dishes, but if you want, you can subsitute filling vegetable or mushroom dishes. Apart from **mutton in cappotto** boiled with onions, laurel and potatoes, and **suckling pig roasted in blueberry leaves**, among the new treats worth mentioning is the duck's breast with a blueberry-flavored chocolate sauce. The desserts are always good, from the unusual anicini mushroom ice-cream to sweet millefoglie di carasau with cinnamon cream and wild blackberries, wild fennel sorbet or saffron-flavored semifreddo with honey and almonds. To go with these, there are dessert wines that are homemade like the olive oil. The cellar is stocked with the top local wines, some available by the glass. To finish, arbutus-, sage- and laurel-flavored grappas.

Anyone who has planned a vacation to the beaches of Costa Smeralda will have to pass through Olbia. And just because you're near the sea doesn't mean you shouldn't try some meaty country cuisine. Though Barbagia is on one of the roads leading to the port, its food is drawn from the land.
Just ignore the standard dishes on this menu, like the bresaola and arugula and the prosciutto with melon; go for the real delicacies right from the antipasti. If there are two of you, ask for the **mixed Sardinian antipasti**, with local cured meats and cheeses, grilled vegetables, **pigs' trotters and pork in aspic**, fried sweetbread and brains. When you're ready for a first course, go for the **maccarones furriaos** or de busa (with wild boar sauce), potato **culungiones** and the **malloreddus**. The 'three tastes' option will give you a chance to try all three types of pasta, but don't forget the 'newly-weds dish', which is spaghetti with tomato sauce and meatballs. **Roast porcetto** or lamb, **lamb cordula**, wild boar in sweet and sour sauce, meat skewer, chops and sausages are the most popular main courses. The menu doesn't completely shun seafood, however. There's a wide selection that includes **mullet botargo**, clams alla marinara, spaghetti with crab or crawfish sauce, sea bass and gilthead cooked in salt, grilled eel and many more dishes.
A small selection of cheeses, not just local ones, seadas, gugligliones and a wine list of main regional labels complete the menu.

Da Gesuino

Hotel-restaurant
Via Garibaldi 3
Tel. 0789 22395
Closed Sunday, never in summer
Open: lunch and dinner
Holidays: December 24-26
Seating: 70
Prices: 32-35 euros
All major credit cards, Bancomat

Da Gesuino is the quintessential family-run establishment, both because it's been operated by the Dessena family for over fifty years and because two of the children – Sebastiana and Gesuino – have now taken the reins. And by the look of it they've learned a lot from their predecessors. Sebastiana runs the kitchen and cooks the day's fresh fish, while her brother takes care of the dining room, always ready to advise you on the dishes, which change daily depending on the catch.
To start with there's a mixed antipasti that always has between seven and ten dishes: seafood or **octopus salad** with tomatoes and olives, **mullet botargo**, salmon and onion quiche, mussels or razor-shells au gratin and shrimp cocktail are some of the possibilities. If you want to try the real house specialties, it's best to order them in advance, particularly the **fish soup**, for which the cook has to find the right varieties of fish, and the **fish ravioli** served with mussels, clams and fresh cherry tomatoes. Otherwise, go for the trofie with mussels and potatoes, **penne with pilchards** or tagliatelle with shrimp and fresh tomatoes. You'll be surprised at how good it all is. The seafood menu ends with excellent grilled fish and a tasty **mixed fried fish platter**. There are also some inland dishes, such as the local cured meats, **ravioli with a ricotta filling and tomato sauce** and roast Sardinian sausage. The cheese board has some of the region's most noteworthy varieties. Lastly, there are nice desserts like lemon mousse, bavarese all'amarena and the typical seadas.
The wine list has a wide selection of the best regional labels at reasonable prices. There's an attached hotel with 28 rooms for those who want to stay a little longer.

12 km southeast of Nuoro

CK

Restaurant/3-Star Hotel
Corso Martin Luther King 2-4
Tel. 0784 288024-0784 288733
Fax 0784 288733
E-mail: ci.kappa@tiscali.it
Internet: www.cikappa.com
Open: every day, for lunch and dinner
Holidays: none
Seating: 150 + 70 outdoors
Prices: 30 euros, wine excluded
All major credit cards, Bancomat

In the historic town center of Oliena, Cenceddu and Killeddu offer tasty Sardinian cuisine in their restaurant and comfortable hospitality in cozy rooms furnished country style. Half board (minimum of three days) costs 44 euros per person, full board 57. The meals open with local **cured meats** and a list of warm samplings of meat and vegetables, which vary with the season. The traditional first course Sardinian dishes follow: **macarrones de busa**, **culurgiones with potatoes and mint** and ravioli with tomato or ragù. The main courses include **prattu de cassa** (single dish of game, potato and onion, flavored with a mix of local aromatic herbs), **parasembene**, roast **suckling pig**, mutton and **goat al Cannonau** or stewed with the sauce and **lamb with wild fennel**. Alternatives to the meat are the cheese board with local cheeses, some seafood specials and, for dinner only, pizza cooked in a wood oven. Desserts include **sa pompia** (the fruit used to prepare it is a Slow Food Presidium) and **seada**. The cellar offers regional and national wines.

• 5 doubles and 2 triples, bathroom attached (2 with shared bathroom), air conditioning, TV • Prices: double single use 36, double 50, triple 65 euro; breakfast not included • Restaurant handicap accessible. Private uncovered parking. Pets welcome. Doorman service available from 7 am to 9 pm • Bar, restaurant. Veranda

Salumificio Puddu, in Orbuddai: excellent quality hams, cured meat, large sausages, fresh and seasoned sausages, pancetta, coppa and capocollo.

ANTICA TRATTORIA DEL TEATRO ☺

Trattoria
Via Parpaglia 11
Tel. 0783 71672
Closed Wednesday, never in July and August
Open: lunch and dinner
Holidays: three weeks in October
Seating: 30
Prices: 30-35 euros, wine excluded
All major credit cards, Bancomat

You'll find this small place in the center of town, in front of the Eleonora d'Arborea Theatre. The trattoria is constantly evolving, its most significant new development this year being two small menus dedicated entirely to **cheese**. You can either get a cheese board with only Sardinian cheeses (herbed, pecorino and raw goat's milk cheeses) or a sampling of international varieties (Spanish, Portuguese, French and English); these, and all 30 cheeses on the trolley, go nicely with a Le Baladin or other beers from tiny Belgian brewers.

Apart from cheese you can choose one of the three set menus that feature both seafood and meat– the one priced at 35 euros offers two antipasti, two first courses, a main course, a few cheeses and dessert of your choice. We recommend the **quail cooked with blueberries** and, as your first course, the classic **lorighittas with white-meat ragù and pecorino cheese**. **Skewers of mutton** and suckling pig medallions complete the list of meat dishes, while among the fish, a good dish to start with is **panada of eel** gratinée al casizolu. Other dishes that come to mind are **fregola with Marceddì clams**, escalope of mullet in brown bread crust, tagliata of tuna with vegetable caponata and artichoke raviolini, which comes with sea urchin eggs in winter. To finish up, there are seadas, dark chocolate cake and other desserts of the cook's own invention.

Wines include the top regional labels. The other two set menus – which are definitely a challenge to finish given the size of portions – cost 40 and 45 euros.

CRAF

Restaurant
Via De Castro 34
Tel. 0783 70669
Closed Sunday
Open: lunch and dinner
No holidays taken
Seating: 40
Prices: 25-30 euros
All credit cards

A mandatory stop for anyone visiting the old town center is this restaurant in a 17th-century building that was a tavern 20 years ago. Now Salvatore Pippia runs the place and offers up the typical cuisine of inland Oristano. Salvatore is a real character, somehow both gruff and hospitable, and the other resident personality is his wife Rita, who will advise you on what to order.

When in season, wild asparagus and mushrooms (porcini and antunna) figure into the antipasti arrangement along with a good selection of typical **cured meats**, preserves in olive oil and olives. Among the first courses, we recommend the cheese ravioli, artichoke risotto and tagliatelle with game sauces (wild boar and hare), and you have to try the **bread, mushroom and cheese soup**. Once it gets cold, warm up with legume soups with cotiche and wild herbs. There's an interesting selection of barbecued meats with many cuts and types to choose from, including **mutton**, **lamb ribs** and horse or **donkey fillet**. In summer, seafood and Oristano lagoon fish dishes lighten up the menu, including **burrida cabrarese** and incasadas eel. For side plates there are grilled vegetables and **roast antunna mushrooms**. There's a nice cheese board, too, with variously seasoned Pecorino cheeses and Casizolu del Montiferru. The usual desserts are produced by artisans in Bonarcado and go well with Vernaccia di Oristano, and there's an excellent seada with bitter arbutus honey. You'll find all the most appealing regional labels in the wine list, all at a good value.

DA GINO

⌒Trattoria
Via Tirso 13
Tel. 0783 71428
Closed Sunday
Open: lunch and dinner
Holidays: third week in January, August 15-September 10
Seating: 40
Prices: 30-32 euros, wine excluded
Credit cards: MC, Visa, Bancomat

IL GIGLIO

⌒Holiday farm
Santa Caterina-Case Sparse
Tel. 347 3483744-349 1447955
Fax 0783 329049
E-mail: info@agriturismoilgiglio.com
Internet: www.agriturismoilgiglio.com
Open: every day, lunch and dinner
Holidays: none
Seating: 90 + 30 outdoors
Prices: 23-33 euros, wine excluded
No credit cards

Da Gino's cuisine is no longer primarily focused on game as it once was. This trattoria near the sea has shifted its offerings toward seafood fare made from ingredients caught that day in the gulf and the lagoon.

To start with, have a look at the trolley full of uncooked seafood, and you'll certainly find something good to try. Then you can move on to the crispy fried **orziadas** (sea anemones) and the light **mussel and clam soups**. The **minestra di fregula e cocciua**, a dish that's popular on the coast, is also made with clams but is heartier and served as a first course. Alternatively, you might prefer the spaghetti with clams or orziadas or, at the end of winter, the **pennette with sea urchin sauce**. Then on to the **mixed fried platters** that, depending on availability, can include red mullet, squid and goby or grilled gilthead, sea bass and prawns. Aside from seafood there are also dishes made using vegetables or antunna and porcini mushrooms. Desserts include a classic **seada** with honey, coppa all'amaretto or a fresh fruit cocktail.

There's a house wine as well as a few bottled regional wines. Service is basic and fast.

The land surrounding Il Giglio grows vegetables, fruit and olive trees, and supports the poultry, cattle and pigs that are used in the restaurant's seasonal cuisine. The communal areas are welcoming, the breakfast abundant. Half-board costs 55-60 euros, and in August a minimum stay of a week is required with half-board obligatory. The antipasti include homemade cured meats (**mustela** and sausage), samples of vegetables, quiche and sometimes **testina di maiale in aspic**. After this comes the handmade pasta, including **ravioli of ricotta and chard with meat sauce**, **malloreddus**, **fregola** with dressings of meat or vegetables or different kinds of soups. The main courses include **roast suckling pig**, served cold with myrtle berries (for large groups, if you order in advance) or stewed with lemon, **stuffed spatchcock**, barbecued meats and stewed eel. Among the home-made desserts, we recommend the fried simbua, the sweet sanguinaccio, the gattò and Sardinian sweets.

The house wine is served by the carafe and included in the price, and some regional wines are also available.

🔑• 10 double rooms en suite, air-conditioning • Prices: double single use 50, double 70-80 euros, breakfast included • Handicap accessible premises, 5 suitably equipped rooms • Private uncovered parking. Pets welcome. Owners always available • Restaurant. Conference room. Garden

🏵 In the S'Antiga Bontade bakery, Via Campania 61, Valentina Abis prepares excellent traditional Oristano cakes and biscuits (amaretti, gueffus, capigliette, tiliccas, pabassinos, mostaccioli), classic impanatine and other savory specialties. People also speak highly of the zippole and other treats made at Carnival time.

PADRIA

ZIA GIOVANNA

☞ Trattoria
Via Fratelli Sulis 9
Tel. 079 807074
Closed Saturday
Open: lunch, dinner only with reservations
Holidays: December 20 through January 5
Seating: 50
Prices: 18-20 euros
No credit cards

This small trattoria in central Padria has a bit of a dated look; tables are lined up in two rows, the dining room walls are covered with matchboards and the floors are the same ones the place had when Zia Giovanna opened it in the 1960s. But with its well-managed kitchen, this place has different kind of beauty, as any of the regulars can attest. The dishes offered here are extremely simple, starting with the variously seasoned pecorino cheeses or cured meats (sausage, ham and pancetta) that open the meal. Alternatively you can have equally simple samplings of vegetables: in olive oil, with onions in sweet and sour sauce and wild cardoons. Two dishes you'll always find for your first course are **panadinas** filled with meat or vegetables **with red sauce** and **raviolone**, a roll of pasta filled with meat, vegetables, red sauce and cheese, served in slices. In winter the menu is longer and includes **minestrone** and chickpea or lentil soups. If the **cordula** (stewed plaited lamb's intestines) isn't available, you can always fall back on equally tasty dishes like **roast porcetto** and **lamb**, **pork in sweet and sour sauce** and veal roulades. But because chef Gianfranco knows there are people who eat here every day ensures variety in their diet with his Friday fried fish platter, mussels and sardines. There are **seadas** and sweet raviolini with a ricotta and candied fruit filling for dessert.
There's a fairly good house red to accompany all dishes. The trattoria is only open at lunchtime, so if you want to have dinner you have to reserve in advance.

PORTOSCUSO

SA MUSCIARA

☞ Restaurant
Via Nuoro 25
Tel. 0781 507099
Closed Sunday, never in summer
Open lunch and dinner
Holidays: various in winter
Seating: 90
Prices: 30-35 euros, wine excluded
All major credit cards, Bancomat

Portoscuso's economy relies heavily on its age-old fishing tradition, and its old tuna processing factories are still used for canning tuna and drying tuna roe. Even if this old fishing village wasn't on your list of places to visit, it's worth the trip just to try the food at Sa Musciara. Owner Alberto Gai is passionate about sailing – as all the regatta photos here indicate – and he's also a charming host. Alberto's father-in-law Giuseppe Marongiu prepares dishes focused on the sea's riches.
Unsurprisingly, the main ingredient in most cases is tuna, and Giuseppe is a true artist in its preparation. To start with, an extremely simple **tuna in olive oil** is one of the antipasti, then there's **spaghetti a Sa Musciara** (with botargo, tuna and red tomato sauce) and **tuna Portoscuso-style**, a kind of tuna stew cooked in red wine or **tuna tripe** cooked in a pot. But let's not forget the other seafood dishes, such as various kinds of smoked fish, mollusks and shellfish cooked in white wine or in guazzetto. In winter, there's **tagliolini with sea urchin sauce**, risotto alla pescatora, carpaccio of fish, mixed grilled platters and **octopus with potatoes**. If you're not fond of fish there are some solid alternatives, among which is an excellent fried eggs with onions.
There's a good selection of wines, including the region's top labels. Apart from limoncello and blueberry liqueur there's also a small selection of grappas.

SANT'ANTONIO DI GALLURA

25 KM NORTHEAST OF TEMPIO PAUSANIA, 26 KM FROM OLBIA

DA AGNESE

Restaurant-pizzeria
Via Brunelleschi 12
Tel. 079 669185-339 2649798
Closed Tuesday
Open: lunch and dinner
No holidays taken
Seating: 70 + 20 outdoors
Prices: 30-35 euros, wine excluded
All major credit cards, Bancomat

Rita Malu and Antonio Spano are intent on reviving the traditional recipes of an area with no shortage of quality ingredients. And the effort these two are making seems to be bearing fruit, judging by Da Agnese's constantly growing menu with its heavy emphasis on local vegetables and meat as well as traditional desserts and homemade pasta.
You start with mixed cured meats, vegetables (onions, tomatoes, eggplants) stuffed and grilled or preserved in olive oil, zucchini flan with tomatoes and mozzarella or various kinds of omelets (there's one with eggplant and mushrooms). If they have it, order the **mazzafrissa** (a dish made from fresh cheese and cream, which also comes in an excellent sweet version). When you reach the first course there's another specialty, **suppa cuata**, with mixed meat broths, grated pecorino cheese and dry bread. But there's no lack of alternatives, like the excellent **pulilgioni** (sweet ravioli filled with ricotta) and **chjusoni** (Gallura-style gnocchi) served in a tomato sauce with or without wild boar or beef, porcini mushrooms or just basil. When in season we recommend the tagliatelle with mushrooms. For the main course there's **rabbit** that, depending on when you go, will be cooked in sweet and sour sauce, alla cacciatore or with cream; there's also roast veal with porcini mushrooms or zucchini, meat brochettes and ribs. If you want to eat **roast porcetto**, kid or lamb, you have to order in advance. Apart from the aforementioned mazzafrissa, there's chocolate, lemon or apple cake and seadas.
The wine list contains some of the region's best wines and the markups are fairly reasonable.

SANTU LUSSURGIU

33 KM NORTH OF ORISTANO

ANTICA DIMORA DEL GRUCCIONE

Hotel
Via Michele Obinu 31
Tel. 0783 552035-550300
Fax 0783 552036
E-mail: info@anticadimora.com
Internet: www.anticadimora.com
Closed 2 weeks after Epiphany

The Antica Dimora del Gruccione is managed with flair by Gabriella Bellodi and gives guests the opportunity to stay in an atmospheric 18th-century mansion. The rooms are all unique and spacious, each one furnished with family antiques. Some rooms have a kitchenette and one has a working fireplace. The common areas include a lounge with a well-stocked library where guests will also find videos and a selection of classical music. Breakfast is varied and generous and includes cornflakes, muesli, homemade jams, honey, coffee, milk, tea, seasonal fruit, cakes, homemade yoghurt and savory items available on request. The restaurant is normally open only to guests staying at the hotel and only with reservations (half board 60 euros, full board 76 euros per person).

• 3 single and 5 double rooms, bathroom, air-conditioning, television, modem connection; some with kitchenette • Prices: single 38 euros, double 76, breakfast included • All major credit cards, Bancomat • Some rooms handicap accessible. Off-street parking for motorcycles and bicycles, car parking available nearby. Small pets allowed. Owners always contactable• Restaurant. Garden

SANTU LUSSURGIU

SAS BENAS

Hotel-restaurant
Piazza San Giovanni 1
Tel. 0783 550870-347 8979611
Fax 0783 552100
E-mail: nuova.armonia@tiscali.it
Open: every day, lunch and dinner
Holidays: Christmas
Seating: 50
Prices: 25-30 euros, wine excluded
All major credit cards, Bancomat

Four aristocratic buildings have been converted into this hotel of nine bedrooms attached to a cozy dining room. The rooms face onto the cobbled streets and are furnished with the work of local craftsmen. The food on offer makes use of local produce and recipes from the hinterland. To start there's a selection of local cured meats, **leg of mutton with myrtle berry sauce**, excellent **salads of red ox meat** (Slow Food Presidium), vegetables in oil and bruschette al casziolu. In winter you should order the **pennette alla lussurgese** (with sausage and a little tomato); in other seasons the linguine with porcini mushrooms or boar sauce, or you can order in advance for a traditional country dish, **chibuddadu boncardese**. The many main courses include straccetti of boar with porcini mushrooms, veal or suckling pig **roasts**, **tagliata di sardo modicana** and roulade en croute. The meal ends with a selection of cheeses, including the unforgettable Casizolu, or almond sweets, seadas with honey, parfait of myrtle berry or white strawberries.
You can get a house wine in a carafe or one of the good regional labels.

• 9 double rooms and 1 suite, with bathroom, TV • Prices: double single use 37, double 62, 80 euros suite. Premises handicap accessible, with 1 suitably equipped room. Private uncovered parking. Pets not welcome. Staff always available • Bar (only for guests), restaurant. Conference room.

SAN VITO

I GLICINI

Bed and breakfast
Via Nazionale 187
Tel. 070 9929042-328 0222762
E-mail: cp.iglicini@tiscali.it
Internet: www.bedandbreakfastiglicini.com
Closed from December 20 to January 20

The San Vito B&B is a two-level building with a courtyard in the middle of an oak forest. All rooms are furnished in the Sardinian style with a big bathroom and shower, and there's a handicap accessible room on the ground floor. A Mediterranean breakfast is served in the lounge. Guests who like the sea are in luck, as there's a beach only seven kilometers away. Your host, a fishing enthusiast, will be pleased to suggest the best spots for fishing and the best seafood restaurants. You can also visit the nearby Flumendosa Valley and the old mines of Mount Narba.

• 5 double rooms with bathroom, television • Prices: single 32 euros, double 56-60, breakfast included • Credit cards: none • 1 room handicap accessible. Free public parking nearby. No pets allowed. Owners always contactable• Breakfast room, television room. Garden

SARULE

SASSARI

DA CANNONE ⊗

🍲 Trattoria
Via Togliatti 2-4
Tel. 0784 76075
Never closes
Open: lunch and dinner
Never takes holidays
Seating: 150 + 20 outdoors
Prices: 20-25 euros, wine excluded
No credit cards accepted

It's not often that you are offered **pane frattau** as a first course. It's a poor man's dish, traditional inland fare made with slices of carasau or carta da musica (music paper) dipped in broth and sprinkled with squashed tomatoes, red sauce or lamb ragù, grated pecorino and topped with a poached egg. It is uncommon now, as many eateries have forgotten how to make the dishes yesteryear and stick to more banal, standardized food. Luckily, memories live on in villages well off the classic tourist routes, kept alive in places like Giovanna Boneddu's trattoria.

Certainly the menu is rather short but it does offer an exhaustive panorama of typical dishes from the Barbagia area. You'll get off to a great start with a selection of **cured meats** they make themselves – sausage, capocollo, pancetta and ham –, wild boar salami when it's there and then a taste of artichoke hearts, wild cardoons, eggplants and peppers in olive oil. Then in addition to pane frattau, there's **malloreddus** hollowed out with a special implement made of cane and **maccarones de busa**, made by winding pasta around a knitting needle, served with meat or fresh tomato sauces. Main courses include just a few meat dishes, such as **roast porcetto**, lamb and **kid**, stewed or roasted and **boiled mutton** with potatoes. The **cheese board** includes a good number of variously seasoned Pecorinos, while the homemade desserts include treats like amaretti, aranzada made with orange peel, honey and almonds, pistiddos filled with cooked must and gueffus.

Portions are generous and there's a house wine or a few regional bottles to go with your meal.

DA GESUINO

🍲 Trattoria-pizzeria
Via Torres 17 G
Tel. 079 273392
Closed Sunday
Open: lunch and dinner
Holidays: mid-August
Seating: 150
Prices: 25-30 euros, wine excluded
All major credit cards, Bancomat

The trattoria run by partners Gesuino Correddu and Antonio Sacca is in the center of Sassari, a short distance from the Sant'Anna National Museum. There are three simply furnished dining rooms where you'll find well-prepared seafood and meat dishes.

From the buffet of antipasti you'll probably want to try the grilled vegetables, mixed cured meats, various kinds of smoked fish and a tasty **ricotta mustia** served with salmon or artichokes accompanied by **botargo**. All the **pastas** – gnocchetti, tagliolini and straccetti – are handmade and come with seasonal sauces made with **wild asparagus**, porcini mushrooms, **sea urchins**, wild boar ragù or **scampi and fresh tomato** and zucchini and shrimp. Among the main courses are some tasty horsemeat cuts and **asinello (donkey) alla sassarese**, as well as roasted snails, **lamb cordula (intestines) with peas** and, every Wednesday, **oven-baked porcetto**. Otherwise there are a few fish dishes like capone with potatoes, red shellfish soup, fish soup and baked or barbecued portions of fish. To round off, try a homemade dessert like tiramisu, semifreddi, tarts, trifle and various biscuits and cakes.

The cheese board gives a good sample of Sardinian specialties, with a very nice selection of pecorino cheeses. There's also a good selection of reasonably priced Sardinian wines.

🫒 Nuovo Oleificio San Pasquale, Località **Caniga**: made from Bosa olives, four excellent extra-virgin olive oils, among which is a fruity and an organically grown variety.

SERDIANA

SA MUSKERA

Trattoria
Via Regina Margherita 8 A
Tel. 070 743687-349 3153297
Closed Tuesday
Open: lunch and dinner
Holidays: variable, in winter
Seating: 65 + 30 outside
Prices: 25-35 euros, wine excluded
Credit cards: none

In old Sardinian houses, sa muskera was the corner closed off by a mosquito net where fresh and cured meats were stored. Today it's the name of this little osteria in a restored early 19th-century house inland from Cagliari. The owner and chef Bruno Paba, assisted in the kitchen and dining room by his wife and sister in law, has sought to conserve the original features of the place, including the inside courtyard where it's possible to eat al fresco in summer. Here the dishes 'speak Sardinian dialect' and follow the seasons.

The generous antipasti start with a selection of local cured meats and cheeses (sheep's cheeses at various stages of maturity, goat's cheeses and casu marzu) followed by **cordula** with peas, tripe in tomato sauce with field mint, **favata**, sweetbreads and courgettes with sausage, plus, in winter, **head of pig** or wild boar with dried fava beans. Bruno really struts his stuff in the first courses with **fregola incasada** (with ham, sausage and Sardinian cheeses), risotto with chestnuts or 'alla sarda' with saffron, sausage and pork, **malloreddus alla campidanese** and **ravioli** of ricotta and wild chard or ravioli of **potatoes and field mint**. **Pork**, pickled with pepper according to tradition, may be **roasted** or fried or, in winter, boiled with potatoes or fava beans. If you phone ahead, you can also have roast lamb, kid and mutton. For dessert, classics such as gueffus and seadas, plus an array of specialties from the Barbagia and Sassari areas.

The wine list contains 50 labels, including the best of the area (Serdiana boasts three cellars) and the rest of Sardinia, while the oil selection is no less impressive.

SINNAI

CASA ANEDDA

Bed and breakfast
Via Oristano 38
Tel. 070 767268-333 6525644-339 7609801
Fax 070 767686
E-mail: casanedda@tiscali.it
Internet: web.tiscali.it/casanedda
Open all year round

This is a typical local house dating from the late 19th century; it has a lodge and a spacious, sunny courtyard planted with orange and lemon trees. It was once the residence of a small landowner, and you can still identify the areas once used to store food and tools. Elena Anedda manages the B&B, which opened just a few years ago. Rooms are quite spacious, fitted with some of the family's antique furniture, and one of them still boasts an original period fresco. Breakfast includes hot beverages, typical Sardinian cookies, freshly baked pastries, bread and jams. Savory items are available on request. The living room has a separate reading area and guests are welcome to use the fully equipped kitchen.

• 4 double rooms with bathroom, air-conditioning, television • Prices: double room single use 35 euros, double 50 (20 euro supplement for extra bed), breakfast included • Credit cards: none • 1 room designed for use by the mobility challenged. Off-street parking, some of which is covered. No pets allowed. Owners always contactable • Lounge with kitchen. Internal courtyard.

SINNAI
Torre delle Stelle

SORGONO

35 KM EAST OF CAGLIARI

71 KM SOUTHWEST OF NUORO ON SS 128

TORRE DELLE STELLE

DA NINO

Bed and breakfast
Via Lattea 29
Tel. 348 3401311
E-mail: info@sardabb.com
Internet: www.sardabb.com
Open all year round

Hotel-restaurant
Corso IV Novembre 26
Tel. 0784 60127
Closed every fortnight on Saturday and Sunday, never in summer
Open: lunch and dinner
Holidays: from Christmas to end of January
Seating: 100 + 60 outdoors
Prices: 20-35 euros, wine excluded
All major credit cards except DC, Bancomat

The strong point of this B&B managed by Salvatore Pala is without question its location, as it's only minutes away from one of the most famous beaches on the coast that stretches from Cagliari along the southeastern part of the island. The beach is easily reachable by foot or car. The B&B is in a modern two-level house, and the terraces and garden are accessible from each of the comfortable rooms. Breakfast is served in the lounge and consists of fresh pastries, bread, jams and honey, fruit, yogurt and hot beverages. Larger groups have the option of renting out the whole house, though breakfast is not included with this option.

• 4 double rooms with bathroom, air-conditioning, safe • Prices: double room single use 90-110 euros, double 100-120 (30 euro supplement for extra bed), breakfast included • Credit cards: none • Off-street parking. No pets allowed. Owners always contactable • Lounge with kitchen. Reading and television room. Garden, terrace

Sorgono is the main town in Mandrolisai, an area still heavily involved in sheep farming and agriculture. The town is on the western bluffs of the Gennargentu mountains, and that's where you'll find the Censoplano family's hotel-restaurant, particularly pleasant for those who like the mountains. The restaurant is just one unpretentious room, but in summer you can also eat out in the large courtyard. You can always count on finding traditional Sardinian inland food here; there are three fixed menus (priced at 20, 30 and 35 euros) that give you a chance to try a wide variety of specialties.

Usually you start with the homemade preserves in olive oil, cured meats and sausages, and with their nice **cordula** (plaited lamb's intestines) **with peas**. Follow that up with **ricotta ravioli**, culurgiones with botargo or meat sauce, pane frattau and **maccarrones de punzu**. Outstanding dishes to try in winter are the **vegetable minestrone** ampazzu and various legume and vegetable soups. The most popular second courses are the boiled mutton, **sa pezza imbinada**, roast porcetto and barbecued beef steak. In other seasons there's lamb, veal with asparagus, **goat cooked in the pan with olives, wild boar with porcini mushrooms**, ossobuco with beans. If you come at the right time there are a number of dishes made using **mushrooms**. To finish, there are nice cheeses supplied by a local sheep farmer.

The very nice red made by the local Cantina Sociale del Mandrolisai is the main wine available.

1033

SARDINIA

TERRALBA
Marceddì

TETI

27 KM SOUTHWEST OF ORISTANO

58 KM SOUTHWEST OF NUORO

DA LUCIO

L'OASI

Restaurant
Via Sardus Pater 34
Tel. 0783 867130-82633
Closed Thursday
Open: lunch and dinner; only lunch
between October 15 and June 15
Holidays: 1 week at the end of
October, Christmas and New Year
Seating: 60 + 25 outdoors
Prices: 32-35 euros, wine excluded
All major credit cards, Bancomat

Trattoria-pizzeria
Via Trento 10
Tel. 0784 68211
Closed Monday
Open: lunch and dinner
No holidays taken
Seating: 80
Prices: 18-27 euros, wine excluded
All credit cards accepted, Bancomat

Marceddì is a small seaside village about ten kilometers west of Terralba. There is an enchanting view of the fishermen's houses overlooking the lagoon, which is rich in eels, gilthead and mullet (much sought after in summer for the quality botargo made from its eggs), as well as sea bass and striped bass. In the restaurant launched by their grandfather in the 1950s, Cristiano, Stefano and Fabio depend on these ingredients. Depending on the day's catch, the antipasto may include **octopus and shrimp salad**, mussel and clam zuppette, mullet botargo presented on a bed of celery, **uncooked clams and mussels**, mussels au gratin and a local variation of **burrida**, made with spotted numb-fish instead of dogfish. For your first course we recommend the **minestra di fregola and cocciua niedda** (these are very special local clams) or if you order it in advance, the **fish soup**, which can be made with 10-15 different types of fish. A simpler but equally satisfying dish is the **spaghetti** in bianco **with clams** (also combined with botargo) or with a red sauce and shellfish. The main courses are also simply prepared to bring out all the flavor of the day's catch. So in addition to traditional grilled fish there are **mixed fried fish platters** or gilthead or sea bass cooked in Vernaccia or in verde. To finish, seadas with honey and **gueffus** (typical balls of marzipan).
To accompany your meal there are a few good regional labels or some other Italian bottles on the wine list.

The kitchen at L'Oasi gets most of its ingredients from the forests of oak, durmast, and holm-oak that surround the village of Teti. Here you'll find not only mushrooms like porcini, prataioli, gallinacci and cardaroli, but also wild boar and hare with rich accoutrements. Luigi Dearca in the dining room guarantees a good supply of quality ingredients, while his wife Annamaria runs the kitchen.
If you don't eat too much you'll spend around 18 euros, but if you've got a big appetite there's a fixed menu at 27 euros that offers 10-15 antipasti, two first and main courses, cheese, fruit, dessert, coffee, a digestive (blueberry and filoferru) and the house wine. Apart from local cured meats, the antipasti include **goatmeat rissoles**, wild boar or pork with olives, rabbit in sweet and sour sauce, small focaccia with mushrooms and homemade preserves in olive oil. After that come some nice **maccarones de busa** served with **game sauce** and **cheese and potato culurgiones** with fresh tomato sauce. When it's in season, you can have **porcini mushroom soup** and tagliatelle or cavatelli with sausage meat and mushroom sauce. Then the classic **suckling pig**, roasted or cooked with blueberries, **ribs of mutton**, quail with mushrooms and **hare stew**. If you've still got room for more after all that, try the variously seasoned pecorino cheeses and typical sweets, among which are the candelaos made with marzipan molded into fruit or animal shapes. From Friday to Sunday evenings they also offer pizzas cooked in a wood-fired oven.
Apart from the house wine, the cellar also holds a few regional wines.

VILLAMASSARGIA

A CASA DI NONNA

🔑 Bed and breakfast
Via Centrale 11
Tel. 0781 74403-328 0678022
Fax 0781 74403
E-mail: deborap83@tiscali.it
Internet: www.acasadinonna.it
Open all year round

Debora Porrà is the charming hostess of this three-floor B&B in a beautiful 19th-century home that's been refurbished from the inside out. Rooms are comfortably fitted with antique family furniture and all have bathrooms. Bed and bath linens are all hand-woven in this village's own patterns. Breakfast is served in the spacious first floor lounge and features local breads and pastries, cakes and homemade jams. On the ground floor is a comfortable reading room where guests can relax and watch TV. There are tables and chairs on the porch, which is an ideal place to kick back.

• 3 double rooms with bathroom • Prices: double room single use 30-35 euros, double 55-60, breakfast included • Credit cards: none • Whole facility and 1 room handicap accessible. Parking area reserved for guests outside. Small pets allowed. Owners always present • Breakfast room, reading and television room. Internal courtyard

VILLANOVA MONTELEONE

SU CANTARU

🔑 Bed and breakfast
Via Nazionale 331
Tel. 079 961032-348 7429762-340 6247545
Fax 079 961032
E-mail: giovanni.ch@tiscalinet.it
Closed from December to March

Villanova Monteleone is on the slopes of Santa Maria Hill, just a 15-minute drive from the rugged Poglina coastline. In the middle of this village you'll find Su Cantaru, a recently renovated B&B that still features beautiful stone arches and ancient millstone. Rooms are tastefully furnished with cast iron beds, and all the linens were embroidered by village women. Guests can relax in the courtyard, which opens onto a beautiful garden. The very filling, traditional breakfast features homemade cakes and jams.

• 1 single and 3 double rooms, bathroom, television; 1 room with mini-bar • Prices: single 35 euros, double room single use 40, double 60, breakfast included • Credit cards: none • Free public parking nearby. No pets allowed. Owners always contactable • Breakfast room, television room. Internal courtyard

VILLANOVAFORRU

SA MUREDDA

🔑 Bed and breakfast
Vico San Sebastiano
Tel. 070 9331142-338 3047160
Fax 070 9331142
E-mail: samuredda@samuredda.it
Internet: www.samuredda.it
Open all year round

Sa Muredda, in the heart of the Marmilla district, is built entirely of stone, traditional from its foundations to its furniture. It features terracotta tile flooring throughout, spacious rooms tastefully decorated in wood and cast-iron and a charming garden. The Nature Museum a few kilometers away is between two parks linked by a panoramic chairlift that takes you as far as the Giara di Siddi.

• 3 double and 1 triple room, bathroom
• Prices: double room single use 42 euros, double 65, triple 85, breakfast included • Credit cards: none • 1 room handicap accessible. Off-street parking. Small pets allowed. Owners always contactable • Breakfast room. Garden

VILLASALTO

PAOLO PERELLA

🍲 Restaurant
Corso Repubblica 8
Tel. 070 956298
Never closes
Open: lunch and dinner
Holidays: variable
Seating: 20
Prices: 32-35 euros
No credit cards

It's often the case that if a restaurateur mentions 'restructuring', what he wants to do is make the place bigger and squish the tables closer together to fit in more paying customers. But not here at Paolo Perella's, where the emphasis has always been on meeting the needs and comfort of the customers present rather than trying to fit more of them. The restaurant's dining room is now even cozier, with seating for no more than twenty. When you phone – you'll need reservations – you'll speak with Giusta, the owner's wife, who will ask you what you'd like to eat, and both meat and fish (purchased in Carloforte or Muravera) are worth ordering.

Food from the land includes **goat's milk mozzarella** and ricotta cheeses and raw milk cheese. Then you can continue on to **ravioli filled with goat's milk ricotta** and served with unusual sauces like wild pear or blackberry. After that comes **roast suckling pig** and **goat** prepared in many different ways, even with tripe, as well as large and small-sized **game**. The wild boar, for instance, is usually stewed, and the rabbit is excellent al cartoccio with herbs and Vernaccia. A lot of work goes into the desserts, which combine traditional ingredients with creative flair. In addition to **goat's milk icecream** with carob, fresh pistachio nuts and saffron, we recommend the almond cakes hot from the oven and the **dolci della sposa**.

House wine is included in the price, but as an alternative you can choose from a small selection of quality Sardinian wines. Afterwards, there are some excellent grappas produced by Paolo and aged in juniper kegs.

GLOSSARY
OF **ITALIAN**
REGIONAL
CULINARY
TERMS

Slow Food Editore

A

abbacchio a lamb that has been slaughtered when still suckling or when it has just begun to graze, recognizable by the pale pink color of the meat

abbacchio alla svinatora a type of chasseur with garlic, white wine and fresh tomatoes

abbuot alla fressor entrails of milk-fed lamb browned in oil (Latina province)

accio/accia dialect name for celery in Campania, Calabria and Sicily

acciugata Ligurian sauce based on salty anchovies dissolved in warm oil until a paste is obtained for dressing fish, eggs, boiled vegetables

acciughe ripiene A Genoan recipe where, before frying, fresh anchovies are stuffed with a mixture of bread soaked in milk, egg, Parmigiano, oregano and pulped anchovies themselves

accomodato stew with potatoes for white meats (you usually add tomato) and stockfish (also without tomato)

aceto balsamico made from cooked, naturally fermented grape must aged in small wooden casks for at least five years; production of the 'traditional' variety (Modena and Reggio Emilia) is rigidly disciplined

aciugheta, aciughete agre in Veneto, small anchovies (*alici*) marinated in vinegar, usually with onions

acquacotta originally a dish for the poor in Maremma, Tuscany, made using stale bread, water, oil, eggs and seasonal vegetables

acquapazza (all') a way of cooking fish using garlic, oil, tomatoes and water (once sea water); today other aromas and vegetables are added as well

agerti regional name for mackerel

agghiotta/a ghiotta/alla ghiotta in the South this means stewing fresh or preserved fish, flavored with tomatoes, olives, capers and sometimes raisins; in Umbria and Tuscany it is the sauce pigeon is cooked in

aggiada A Ligurian sauce consisting of crushed garlic and bread soaked in vinegar and flavored with oil, salt; used for flavoring liver and rabbit

agglassato o aggrassato describes lamb, kid or veal, stewed with wine and peeled tomatoes

aglione condiment for **pici** (see) based on cooked and mashed tomatoes and cloves of garlic lightly fried in oil

agnello abbottonato shoulder of lamb boned and stuffed with a mixture of bread, egg, almonds, Parmigiano, parsley (Abruzzo)

agnello cac' e ova or cacio and eggs; a typical Abruzzo preparation, a variant is also found in Basilicata: after cooking, the pieces of lamb, or kid, are sprayed with beaten egg and grated cheese

agnello sotto la coppa cut in pieces, in Molise lamb was traditionally cooked on the hearthstone, under an iron lid strewn with embers

agnellotti same as **agnolotti** (see)

agnoli/agnolini stuffed pasta from Mantua shaped like cappelletti

agnolotti dal plin small sized pasta filled with meat, very fine pastry, pinched to seal; typical of the Langhe area

agnolotti see **ravioli**

agresto a long-known sauce based on vinegar, tart grapes, sugar, broth, garlic, chopped hazelnuts and almonds; used to accompany meats

agro (all') a preparation in which lemon juice or vinegar are used as a condiment

alici all'ammiraglia marinated in white wine and vinegar and then seasoned with oil, parsley, garlic, oregano (Lazio)

alici scattiate anchovies sautéed in a frying pan with aromas and vinegar

alivi cunzati (olive condite) olives boiled in water and vinegar, are strained and dressed with garlic, mint, oregano; covered in extravirgin olive oil, they keep for many months (Sicily)

allulur (l') bundles of lamb tripe flavored and wrapped in rumen; after boiling, they are sliced and dressed with oil and lemon (Molise)

amatriciana (all') a pasta sauce based on browned pork cheek, onion, tomatoes, pepper or chili pepper, grated Pecorino; originally from the town of Amatrice, in the region of Lazio

ambariegl a dialect term for lake shrimp (Latina province, Lazio)

ammollicate (di verdure) vegetables lightly fried in the pan with stale bread cubes and grated cheese

ammugliatielli lamb giblets wrapped round a stick and aromatized with garlic, parsley, cheese and chili pepper

ammuttunatu said of a vegetable or slice of fish cooked in tomato sauce, inside which garlic cloves and mint leaves have been inserted

ancìti dialect name for wild chards

anellini alla pecorara ring-shaped strings of pasta dressed with a sauce of guanciale, beef, mushrooms, summer vegetables, Pecorino and ricotta

anguidda incasada/incasata eel boiled with flavors and lightly baked with grated Pecorino (Sardinia)

anguilla a becco d'asino brodetto (see) of eel cut up and cooked with onion, tomato concentrate, water, and served with broiled polenta (Comacchio, Emilia-Romagna)

anguleddas pasta of hard wheat bran, water, lard, yeast and salt (Sardinia)

annoglia sausage obtained from pigskin or from the poor parts of the pig

anolini small, round egg pasta ravioli usually served in broth (Emilia)

antunna Sardinian name for **cardoncelli** mushrooms (see)

anzelottos/anzollotos/angiolottus) Sardinian ravioli of hard wheat bran with vegetable filling

apfelschmarrn see **kaiserschmarrn**

aragosta alla bossana boiled lobster served with olive oil, boiled eggs and vegetables

aragosta alla catalana lobster cooked with cacao, tomatoes, garlic, onion, brandy

arancino rice balls dressed with meat and tomato or chicken giblet sauces, then breaded and fried; popular all over the Centre-South

aranzada a sweet from the Nuoro district of Sardinia based on candied orange peel, almonds and honey

arista loin of pork roasted with the bone, in the oven or on the spit; term of Tuscan origin

armidda Sardinian dialect term for wild thyme

arna Veneto name for duck

arrabbiata(all') spicy sauce for pasta based on tomatoes, onion, chili pepper; in some regions meats such as rabbit are also done in this way

arreganato seasoned with oregano

arrosticini/rosticini pieces of mutton threaded onto wooden spits and cooked over a charcoal fire (Abruzzo)

arrostita on the Adriatic coast, indicates grilled fish

arrosto della vena a particularly tender cut of beef used for roasting and braising

arrosto morto way of cooking meat which starts by browning and continues as though for stewing, namely by adding fluids (pot roast)

arrusti e mancia/'rrusti e mancia grilled meat or fish to be eaten as soon as cooked (literally 'roast and eat', Sicily)

arselle regional term for clams

arvolto pizza fried in olive oil and served with hot tomato sauce and garlic

asìno/asìn soft, cow's milk cheese from Friuli, may be ripened or fresh

asulette rye flour soup from the Val d'Aosta served with slices of bread and fontina cheese

B

babà a small soft dough sweet which, straight out of the oven, is soaked in a syrup of water, sugar and rum

babbaluci Sicilian dialect name for small snails

baccalà a ciauredda a soup from Basilicata based on baccalà, tomatoes and abundant fresh spring onions served with toasted bread

baccalà alla fiorentina baccalà stewed with potatoes and tomatoes, garnished with sliced garlic

baccalà alla perticaregna baccalà in casserole with sweet and chili peppers, to eat hot or cold

baccalà alla trentina stoccafisso cooked in a frying pan with potatoes and onions

baccalà in cassuola fried baccalà dressed with tomato sauce, capers, olives, pine nuts and raisins

baccalà mantecato stoccafisso boiled, cut into pieces and pounded together with garlic, adding a drizzle of oil as you go until a cream is formed; some salt and pepper is then added

baccalà sotto il pesto fried baccalà covered with garlic, chili pepper, oil and plenty of vinegar

baccalà a preserved fish from the Baltic that has been absorbed perfectly into Italian cuisine. Baccalà is cod preserved in salt, while in Veneto it is called stoccafisso, namely dried cod.

baci panteschi sheets of fried pastry filled with ricotta typical of Pantelleria

bacicci wild herb

bacio di dama cookie consisting of two half-moons of flour pastry, hazelnuts (or almonds), sugar and butter linked by a drop of chocolate (Piedmont)

baffo kind of pig's cheek lightly fried in the pan

bagna caoda sauce based on garlic, anchovies and olive oil, to be savored hot together with raw or boiled vegetables (Piedmont)

bagnèt (rosso o verde) Piedmontese sauce made with parsley and anchovies (green sauce) or tomatoes (red sauce), used traditionally for flavoring boiled meats

bagòss hard texture cheese obtained from partially skimmed milk, typical of Bagolino (Brescia)

baìcoli hard cookies made of dough leavened more than once, typical of Venice

barbagiuai fried ravioli, prepared with a pasta of flour and water, filled with pumpkin, rice, eggs, chards, Parmigiano and aromatic herbs (Liguria)

barbotta focaccia made of maize flour, milk, onion, oil, Parmigiano

barbozzo Umbrian name for pig's cheek obtained from preserving this part of the pig under salt and pepper

barcarola (alla) recipe with vinegar and onions used for cooking fresh (pike) or preserved (*baccalà*) fish, but also giblets (liver)

bargnolino liqueur obtained from the infusion of wild plums

barzigole sheep or lamb marrow marinated and flavored, then grilled

basotti egg tagliolini cooked in broth then baked au gratin

batsoà pig's trotters boiled in water and vinegar, then boned, breaded and fried (Piedmont)

bavette flat spaghetti

bazzòffia soup with artichokes, peas, chards or wild lettuce, egg and Pecorino (South Lazio)

bensone see **ciambella**

berlingozzi sweet crumbly doughnuts with an aroma of lemon peel and vanilla, originally linked to Carneval (Tuscany)

bertagnino this is the name in Veneto and in some areas of Lombardy for the salt cod known in the rest of Italy as baccalà

bettelmat a Piedmontese cow's milk soft pressed paste cheese

bianchetti young anchovies or sardines, boiled and dressed in oil and lemon or prepared in fry-ups or in fritters

biancomangiare sort of almond blancmange typical of eastern Sicily, although it is common elsewhere too

biancostato term used in Lombardy for the flank steak cut of beef

bibarasse in cassopipa in Veneto, clams stewed slowly in a lidded earthenware pan

bichi long pasta similar to maccheroni alla **chitarra** (see)

bigoli/bigoi pasta of soft wheat flour extruded through a special press to become big spaghetti; common all over the north-east, it is topped traditionally with sardines and duck ragù

biroldo sausage, to be eaten fresh or cooked, based on pig's blood, entrails, spices, sometimes pine nuts and sultanas (North Tuscany)

bisato sull'ara oven-baked eel, a specialty of Murano (Venice)

biscotto cegliese produced exclusively at Ceglie Messapica (Puglia), this is a cookie of ground almonds mixed with sugar, eggs and cooked wine

biscotto di Agerola savory biscuit of whole wheat flour and maize

bisi in Veneto, young peas, see **risi e bisi**

bistecca alla palermitana veal chop or cutlet, dipped in oil and coated with breadcrumbs mixed with grated caciocavallo, and grilled on the plate or on charcoal

bitto cheese produced with cow's milk and to a small extent goat's milk in the pastures of the Bitto valley (Lombardy)

bleons/blecs/biechi maltagliati of egg pasta with wheat meal and buckwheat flour (Friuli)

blu del Moncenisio marbled cheese of cow's, ewe's and goat's milk, with a striking similarity to Gorgonzola

bobici (minestra di) maize soup, beans and potatoes flavored with lardo; typical of the Carso area

boboli da vida in Veneto, small snails topped with oil and parsley

bocconata pancetta stuffed with salami paste

bocconotto filled short pastry sweetmeat, widespread in Calabria (filled with cream or jam) and in Molise (filled with dry fruit, cacao, cinnamon, cooked must)

bogóni name used in Veneto for snails

bollito ammuddicatu breast of veal breaded and roasted (Sicily)

bollito misto dish common to all regions where cattle are raised, it comprises various cuts of beef, sausage too in some places, boiled in flavored water and served with various sauces. On the coast of the Marche region the term is used for a medley of steamed fish and seafood

bomba di riso rice timbale filled with pigeon meat, giblets (or sausage), cep mushrooms (sometimes), truffle, eggs (Parma and Piacenza, Emilia)

bombette/bomboletti term from the Marche region for sea snails (mollusc), in Abruzzo *bummalitt'*

bondiola cured meat, a synonym in Lombardy of *coppa piacentina*; in Veneto of *bondola*, a sausage of which a number of variants are known

bonet traditional Piedmontese pudding prepared with milk, eggs, sugar, cacao, amaretti, rum and in some cases, coffee

bordatino soup from Leghorn based on maize flour, beans and vegetables

boreto (brodetto) fish soup flavored with vinegar, served with bread croutons or polenta (Veneto)

borlenghi very fine focaccia cooked in a tin-plated copper pan to taste filled with a pesto sauce of bacon, sausage, aromas (Modena, Emilia)

borragine borrage, annual plant of the Mediterranean countries, the edible leaves of which are used in numerous gastronomic preparations

bossolano leavened ring cake aromatized with vanilla and grated lemon peel, sometimes with jam (Lombardy, Veneto, Emilia)

bottaggio see **casoeula**

bottarga artisan preparation, shaped like square salami, of mullet or tuna roe salted, pressed and aged

boudin salami based on pig's blood (today owing to legal restrictions it is substituted partially or totally by beets), and spices

bovoeti in Veneto, small land snails

braciola/brasciola in southern Italy a roulade of meat or swordfish, filled in various ways; in the case of meat it is cooked with tomatoes and wine

braciole di cotica roulades of pork rind filled with bread crumbs, raisins, pine nuts, Pecorino

brandacujun dish based on stockfish and potatoes, flavored with chopped garlic, parsley and pine nuts (Liguria)

brasato (al Barbera, al Barolo, al Sangiovese...) chunk of beef which is marinated in wine and vegetables before being cooked at length with spices and aromatic herbs

brasiola de Piave exclusive sausage recipe created by a restaurant owner of Musile di Piave (Venice)

brasolara pork fillet cured with salt and spices, wrapped in the mixture used to make soppressa and sausage

brazadela in Veneto and Emilia, **ciambella (see)**

bresaola/brisaola a lean beaf product made in Valtellina and in the val d'Ossola with cuts of beef or horsemeat cured and aged

brezel/bretzel bread bun shaped like an eight first boiled and then cooked in the oven, according to Austrian tradition (Alto Adige)

briciolata sauce based on stale bread crumbled and fried in oil with garlic cloves, used to dress **pici (see)**

brigidini sweet round wafers tasting of short pastry and anise cooked on special plates with tongs; originally from Tuscany

brisa (**1**) a Trento dialect word, cep mushroom (*Boletus edulis*) (**2**) white pumpkin soup, sour milk and beans, typical of the northeast regions

broccoli arriminati a pasta dressing: the cauliflower is boiled and then stirred together with onions, anchovies, raisins, pine nuts, tomato concentrate, chili pepper (Sicily)

broccolo fiolaro variety of broccoli typical of the province of Vicenza (Veneto)

brodetto preparation of stewed fish (a fairly close relation of the soups of filleted fish) typical of the Adriatic riviera and with many local variants: frequently flavored with vinegar, unripe peppers, chili peppers, or peppers

brovada/brovade turnips fermented in marc cut into thin slices and eaten raw or cooked; typical of Friuli

bruciatini toasted bacon served with chicory

bruciuluni big roulade of meat consisting of a slice of veal stuffed with minced meat, beaten eggs, bread crumbs, cheese, spices and, if you wish, boiled eggs (Sicily)

bruscandoli/bruscansi wild spring shoots: of hops in the province of Padua, of butcher's broom in the province of Verona

bruschetta toasted bread rubbed with garlic while still hot, dressed with oil, salt and pepper (of Tuscan origin, very widespread, many garnishing variations)

bruscitt beef stew minced and chopped, browned in butter and lardo with fennel seeds and cooked with red wine (Lombardy)

bruss/brusso spreadable cream cheese, intense flavor, obtained from the fermentation of pieces of different cheeses (Piedmont, Lombardy, Liguria)

brustico pike (or tench) grilled with lake reeds, typical of Umbria

brutti e buoni cookies made with almonds and/or hazelnuts, sugar, egg white and vanilla

bucatini al soffritto pasta dressed with pig entrails and chili pepper preserve

bucatini name used in Lazio for a type of long dry pasta with a hole in the middle

buccellato sweet widespread in Liguria, Tuscany, Sicily but with very different characteristics: leavened and puffy (flour, butter, milk, eggs, dry fruit) in Liguria and Tuscany, compact and filled (dry figs, candied fruit, dry fruit, spices) in Sicily; it is almost always ring-shaped

buccuni Sicilian and Sardinian term for murex, mollusc similar to a sea snail; in Calabria it's called a stargazer

bue grasso a castrated ox, of Piedmontese breed, more than four years old

bue rosso a breed of red beef cattle present in Sardinia

buglione in Tuscany indicates a stew with aromatic flavors and aromas: the meats are reduced to pulp and the sauce is served on slices of toasted bread

buione see **buglione**

buonenrico a perennial plant (*Chenopodium bonus-henricus*), in English good King Henry, used for cooking

buridda fish soup typical of Liguria

buristo variant of **biroldo** (see)

burrata stretchy string cow's milk cheese from Puglia, filled with fresh cream

burrida typical Sardinian marinade used to dress fish (especially catshark and skate)

burtlèina fritter made with a fluid batter flavored with spring onions, or, more traditionally served with soups or leftover risotto (Piacenza, Emilia)

busecca tripe soup typical of Piedmont and Lombardy, where the term in the narrow sense indicates all the parts that make up the fore-stomach of cows

busiati/ busiate fresh pasta obtained by winding pieces of dough round a knitting needle

bussolan/bussolà/buzolà see **bossolano**

butòon de pajàas a stew made with pieces of chopped pork sausage which, on cooking, take on the appearance of a clown's buttons

C

cacciatora (alla) preparation for poultry or game: it's a stew which includes onion, lardo, tomato, or – in southern Italy – garlic, rosemary and vinegar

cacciucco a fish soup typical of Leghorn but popular all over Versilia based on different varieties of seafood and molluscs; made with tomatoes with the addition of vinegar, red wine and chili pepper during the cooking

cacigni wild vegetable eaten in Abruzzo

cacio all'argintera o all'argentiera thin slices of caciocavallo fried with garlic and vinegar and sprinkled with oregano and pepper (Sicily)

cacio e pepe by extension, indicates a pasta dressed with Pecorino and plenty of fresh grated pepper

cacio marcetto spreadable cheese made very spicy by fermentation (Abruzzo and Molise); similar to Piedmontese bruss

caciocavallo stretchy string cow's milk cheese typical of southern cheese-making tradition

cacioricotta in Puglia the name for firm, salty ricotta, in Abruzzo known as *cagliata*

caciotta a more or less spherical form of cheese obtained from cow's, ewe's goat's or mixed cheeses

caciuf polenta – solidified and fried – cooked mixing beans, bacon, sausage and Parmigiano (Ferrara, Emilia)

calamarata a typical Campania form of ring-shaped pasta which resembles squid

calariddhe/calariello lamb cooked in a pan with vegetables and field herbs (Puglia)

calcione raviolone of bread dough, sweet-savory filled with eggs, sugar, Pecorino and lemon peel (Marche)

caldarroste chestnuts roasted with the peel

calsù stuffed pasta with a curious short-trouser shape obtained by modeling tiny pinces on the edge of the pasta, typical of Brescia

calzagatti/calzagàtt/cassagài polenta cooked together with a stew of beans and served with Parmigiano (Emilia); once solid it may be fried

calzoncelli small filled wafers, once of cooked must, today with a filling of ground almonds, chocolate, chestnut flour, grated orange peel

calzone pizza folded into a half-moon traditionally stuffed with ricotta, scraps of pork fat and black pepper; there are many variants

campofiloni very thin egg noodles; they take the name of the place where they are typical (Marche)

canci/cancij meat-less ravioli served with cheese, melted butter and sesame seeds, Ladino specialty (Alto Adige)

candelaos Sardinian sweets made

with ground almonds and presented in fruit or animal shapes

canederli ripieni o gnocchi boemi small sweet balls of potatoes and eggs filled with a plum (or an apricot), sprinkled with sugar and cinnamon (Trentino)

canederli the Italian name, used in Trentino and Veneto, for Alto Adige **knödel** (see)

canestrato hard or semi-hard ewe's or cow's cheese; of cylindrical shape, it bears the imprint of the basket in which the curd is left to drain

cannelloni alla sorrentina cannelloni filled with ricotta, scamorza, raw ham, and covered with ragù

cannoli Sicilian cannoli are flaky cylinders fried (rarely cooked in the oven) and filled with ricotta cream enriched with candied fruit and pieces of chocolate; in Calabria they are flour wafers, sugar and wine, rolled up, fried and covered with honey

canochie/canoce term from the Veneto for squill (*pannocchie*, mantis shrimps)

cantucci/cantuccini Tuscan cookies with almonds, pine nuts and aniseeds, traditional at end of meal, dipped in Vinsanto

cao the first cream to appear from fresh milk

capèl de prete priest's hat, a beef cut corresponding to the upper part of the shoulder

capelli d'angelo long and thin dry pasta cooked in broth

capetroccole tiny octopus called 'nail heads' (Lazio)

capocollo cured meat widespread in central and southern Italy, made with the upper portion of the neck and with part of the pork's shoulder

capomazzo pajatina of lamb with potatoes

caponata cold dish based on eggplants first fried and then mixed in a bitter-sweet sauce made of tomato concentrate, olives, capers, celery, onion and vinegar (Sicily, with some variants also common in Campania)

caponet bundle of pumpkin flowers or savoy cabbage leaves filled with boiled or roasted meat, cooked salami, parsley, garlic, eggs, Parmigiano (Piedmont)

cappellacci filled egg pasta shaped like a big tortello; the better known variety from Ferrara are filled with pumpkin and Parmigiano

cappelletti stuffed egg pasta typical of Emilia, common all over Italy and produced industrially; traditional varieties are produced in Reggio Emilia and Romagna: the same shape but a bit different in the filling which in Romagna sees the use of ricotta and raveggiolo (see) as well as meat and Parmigiano (see); both served in broth

cappidduzzo sweet ravioli filled with sheep ricotta aromatized with lemon peel and cinnamon (Sicily)

cappon magro Ligurian dish composed of layers of fish and boiled vegetables mixed together with an egg sauce, parsley, bread, vinegar, garlic, capers, olives and anchovies

cappone alla Stefani sweet and sour capon cooked according to the recipe of the head chef of the court of the Gonzagas

cappone in canavera capon meat stewed in a pig's bladder connected to a piece of bamboo cane that acts as an airhole (Veneto)

cappone incapponato stuffed gurnard (Tuscany)

cappuccetto/capputteddi baby cuttlefish in Sicilian dialect

cappuccio variety of compact cabbage

with waxy, light green or reddish leaves; basic ingredient of **crauti** (see)

capra alla neretese stewed in chunks and with many herbs, then seasoned with fried peppers (Teramo province, Abruzzo)

capra murata meat timbale cooked in a pan with potatoes and tomatoes (Sicily)

caprese (1) salad of Campania origin, very widespread, based on tomatoes and mozzarella dressed with oil, garlic and oregano or basil **(2)** cake made of almonds, chocolate and ground cookies (Campania)

capù di romice roulade prepared with wild herbs and stuffed with meat

capuc made of bread, herbs and cheese rolled up in a cabbage or vine leaf (Trentino)

capuliato/cappuliato condiment for pasta based on more or less spicy dried tomatoes (Sicily)

capunsei bread gnocchi typical of the Manta area dressed with melted butter, sage and Parmigiano Reggiano

carabaccia traditional Florentine minestra based on onions, peas and fresh fava beans, served in the bowl on toasted bread and garnished with a poached egg and flakes of Pecorino

caramelle filled pasta, whose shape recalls one of the commonest confectionery products

carbonade beef cooked in red wine, once prepared with meat kept in salt (Val d'Aosta)

carbonara (alla) pasta condiment consisting of browned bacon (cheek) and eggs amalgamated with grated Pecorino; recent use in Roman cooking

carcagnola boiled pig's trotters, cut into pieces, flavored with lemon juice, oil, salt, pepper, parsley and

served cold; frequently served with **mussu** (see) (Sicily)

carcerato soup from the Pistoia area (Tuscany) made with stale bread, broth of the less noble parts of veal, pepper and grated Pecorino

carciofi alla giudia cimaroli artichokes, shuffled into a corolla shape, boiled briefly and then fried on both sides until crispy (Rome, recipe of Jewish tradition)

carciofi alla romana cimaroli artichokes, larded with garlic and parsley cooked in water and oil with fresh mint

carciofi alla villanella artichokes cooked in a pan with anchovies and garlic

cardoncelli mushrooms (*Pleurotus fuscus*) with white, chewy meat, very common in Puglia and Basilicata

cardone typical soup of the Christmas season based on chicken broth, cardoons, meatballs, beaten egg and cheese (South Italy)

cargiò big ravioli filled with ricotta (Marche)

carletti see **silene**

carmasciano Pecorino produced in Carmasciano (Campania)

carne all'albese/carne cruda raw beef typical of Piedmont, minced, hand chopped or cut into thin slices, dressed with oil, lemon, salt, pepper

carne fumada smoked meat

carne salada piece of meat (except pork) marinated for about a fortnight with salt and ground pepper, widespread in Trentino and in Veneto

carpa regina fresh-water fish that prefers deep, slow moving water

carpaccio raw meat and fish (sometimes also vegetables) cut into thin slices and served with oil, lemon, salt and pepper

carpegna area of the Marche region which gives its name to a much appreciated ham

carpione/carpionata marinade for eggs, breaded meat, fish, zucchini, based on vinegar, oil, garlic and sage

carrati flour and water gnocchi cooked with Pecorino, fried bacon and beaten eggs; maccheroni alla chitarra are also called 'carrati' in Abruzzo,

cartellate/'ncartellate popular Apulian and Calabrian sweets based on fried pastry and flavored in cooked must

cartoccio (al) cooking method which consists in wrapping up food in wax or aluminum paper

casadinas see **pardulas**

casatella fresh cow's milk cheese typical of Romagna

cascà Sardinian cuscus served with a vegetable gravy and minced meat, with spices

casera Valtellina cheese produced in the valley floor with Alpine Brown milk sold fresh or medium aged

caserecce short pasta shape, slightly twisted

casieddu goat's cheese produced exclusively in the province of Potenza, made with a very aromatic herb and packaged in fern leaves

casizolu kneaded-paste cheese typical of Montiferru (Sardinia)

casoeula Milanese winter dish made with cabbage, various cuts of pork, including spareribs, pork rind, trotters, salamini

casolèt whole milk mountain cheese of soft texture (Trentino)

casoncelli/casunziei pasta filled with cured meats, bread, eggs, cheese and not meat (Lombardy and Veneto)

cassata sponge cake filled with ricotta mixed with sugar, chocolate, candied fruit, vanilla and liqueur, and iced with almond paste; Sicilian specialty. Cassata is also the name used for an ice-cream prepared in a similar way, and an Abruzzo sweet

cassatelle/cassatele fried ravioli filled with ricotta cream, typical of the Trapanese area

cassoncini bundles of folded pasta, similar to **piadina** (see), filled with wild herbs, usually fried (Romagna, Marche)

cassuola a dialect term from southern Italy which means casserole and, by extension, certain dishes that are cooked in a casserole

castagnaccio originally a Tuscan preparation – also widespread in Liguria – based on chestnut flour, a little sugar, pine nuts and raisins cooked in the oven

castelmagno cow's milk cheese, semi-hard, tinged with blue, originating in Castelmagno, Piedmont

castrato/crastu lamb castrated at a young age, with a tender, tastey meat; prevalently eaten grilled

castraùre baby artichokes, grown in the gardens of the Venice lagoon

casu marzu creamy cheese with a spicy taste obtained by fermenting Pecorino, mainly Fiore Sardo

cauzuni ravioli with ricotta and mint eaten in Basilicata

cavallucci Siena (Tuscany) sweets made of soft dough with walnuts and orange peel

cavatelli/cavatieddi/cavatiddi short pasta common in southern Italy and the islands shaped like cylinders which are poked by the finger to form little oval shells

caviale del Trasimeno pike eggs

cavrèt in tecia in Veneto and Venezia Giulia, kid in a skillet

cavuliceddi Sicilian dialect name for purple rocket (*Diplotaxis erucoides*)

cazzariell' hot chili pepper in Abruzzo dialect

cazzilli potatoes boiled and mashed, kneaded with parsley and grated cheese; shaped in small cylinders and fried in piping hot oil (Sicily)

cecamariti sort of **pancotto** (see) traditional in Puglia based on **friselle** (see) crumbled and garnished with turnip tops and pea cream

cecatelli see **cavatelli**

ceciliani local pasta made using a knitting needle (Viterbo, Lazio)

cecina name given in Tuscany (Leghorn) to chickpea **farinata** (see)

cenci Carnival sweets of crumbly pastry cut into various shapes and then fried and sprinkled with sugar; many different interpretations, many regional names

cencioni tagliatelle prepared with fava bean flour

ceppe homemade bucatini obtained by wrapping the dough around a wooden stick (Abruzzo and Molise)

cevapcici sausages of mixed minced meats (veal, pork, mutton or lamb) grilled, widespread on the borders with Slovenia

chiacchiere see **cenci**

chianina a breed of cattle originating in the Chiana Valley (Tuscany) often used for the **fiorentina** (see) steak

chibuddadu onion soup (Sardinia)

chicche della nonna green gnocchetti of potatoes and spinach

chiodini mushrooms shaped like semispherical nails that lend themselves to be stewed with tomatoes or sautéed with garlic and parsley

chiscïöi buckwheat fritters, casera cheese and a drop of grappa

chitarre/chitarrine long square pasta made by passing strips of fresh pasta over a frame with metal strings, like those of a guitar; maccheroni alla chitarra is a typical Abruzzo dish

chjusoni gnocchetti in Gallura fashion (Sardinia)

ciabattoni (**1**) broad white beans (Lazio) (**2**) giant maccheroni (Marche)

ciabbotto/ciabotta stew of summer pulses (Abruzzo)

ciaccia leavened focaccia in the form of small bread with bacon mixed into the dough

ciakiciuka version of **caponata** (see) eaten in Pantelleria, prepared with stewed vegetables

cialledda see **frisella**

ciambella leavened sweet based on flour, eggs, butter, lemon peel, baked in the oven; in Emilia, where it's typical, you usually dip it in wine

ciambelletti al vino sweets made of flour, sugar, oil, aniseed, white wine (central Italy)

ciambotta preparation based on vegetables, including eggplants, tomatoes, peppers, widespread in the whole of the South and subject to variations

ciammelle sort of twisted grissini of leavened pasta, first boiled then oven-cooked (Ciociaria, Lazio). Elsewhere they are sweets shaped like knots covered in julep

cianfotta see **ciambotta**

ciaurella vegetable stew

ciauscolo/ciavuscolo pork cured meat, typical of Marche, soft texture, spreadable

cibreo chicken giblet sauce traditional in Tuscany; like **fricassea** (see), it's topped with an egg sauce and lemon juice

cicci maritati soup based on numerous types of cereal and legumes (lentils, beans, chickpeas, peas, fava beans, wheat, corn, grasspeas…)

ciccioli pork rind from the processing of pig fat presenting as nut-colored pieces of irregular shape

ciccioneddas Sardinian pastries filled with jam or cream

cicerchia small legume of age old tradition (grasspea) today grown above all in the Marche; used for soups

ciceri e tria Puglian soup made with chickpeas and wide handmade tagliatelle, flavored with chili pepper and oil in which part of the pasta is browned

cicheti in Veneto and Friuli Venezia Giulia, appetizer served with **ombra** (glass of wine)

cicinielli/cicenielli whitebait in Campania dialect

cicireddi/cicirello the dialect name for cicerello, a small silver fish largely scale-free, excellent fried or marinated

cicoria impazzita chicory dipped in batter and fried

cicorielle a'zise chicory cooked with tomatoes, in meat broth and flavored with grated Pecorino; an Puglian recipe

cif e ciaf/ciffe ciaffe meat stew cooked with onions, garlic, parsley, chili pepper (Abruzzo)

cima breast of veal similar to a pocket and stuffed in various ways (meat, eggs, Parmigiano) served in slices (Liguria)

cimbro cheese from Lessinia (Veneto)

cinghiale al cioccolato see **dolceforte**

cinghiale alla maremmana wild boar pieces marinated and stewed, with wine, tomatoes, wild fennel

cinta senese autochthonous pig breed raised in the province of Siena (Tuscany), distinguished by its black pelt and white collar

ciociara (alla) in Ciociarìa fashion (Lazio)

cioncia stew of some parts of veal head with chili pepper, black olives, spices, typical of the Pistoia area (Tuscany)

ciopa di pane dialect term indicating the type of bread roll eaten in the Trento area, smaller than the Venetian equivalent

cipollata (a) preparation of fish slices cooked lightly and covered with onions cooked in sweet and sour sauce (Sicily)

cipollata onion and tomato soup to which eggs and grated Pecorino are added at the end of the cooking process (central Italy)

ciriole big handmade spaghetti, made with water and flour

cisrà chickpea soup typical of the Monferrato area prepared with pork rind, carrots, celery, broth, aromatic herbs

ciùiga pork sausage from the Trento area (made from the less noble parts of the pig) and minced turnips, aged

ciuppin fish broth with vegetables and fresh tomatoes, served with slices of toasted bread (Liguria)

civet furred game (or rabbit) stew marinated in red wine and aromas, cooked with aromatic herbs and vegetables

cjalsòns half-moon ravioli typical of Carnia (Friuli) with sweet-savory taste; innumerabile filling and condiment variations but smoked ricotta is almost always present

coccio/cuoccio regional name for the capon (gurnard), a sea fish with white, firm flesh

cocciua Sardinian name for clams, of which there are several varieties: niedda, pintada...

cocule meatballs made with potatoes, Pecorino, bread crumbs, eggs and served in broth

coda alla vaccinara stew made with tomatoes, onion, carrot and plenty of celery in which pieces of oxtail are cooked; the sauce is also used as a condiment for pasta (Rome)

codeghin cotechino in northern dialect

cognà (or grape mostarda) sauce based on grape must, martine pears, hazelnuts and cloves; it accompanies boiled meat, cheeses and polenta (Piedmont)

colatura di alici fluid obtained by preserving anchovies in salt for 4-5 months; it is used to dress pasta and vegetables

collo d'oca ripieno goose neck, stuffed with beef, egg, Parmigiano, aromas, may be served cold, sliced, or hot with tomato sauce (Tuscany)

colombaccio migratory bird (*Columba palumbus*) which is hunted, popular for the sauce obtained from it (Tuscany)

comaut pumpkin soup, potatoes, onions, with the addition of butter and sage (Provencal Valleys, Piedmont)

composta di mele, di cipolle compote obtained by cooking the main ingredient with water, sugar and possibly orange or lemon peel, cloves and cinnamon

conciato romano ewe's, goat's, cow's or mixed milk cheese which is washed with water and with a sauce of oil, vinegar, piperna and ground chili pepper, and aged in terracotta jars

condiggiun/condiggion Ligurian salad based on vegetables, **mosciame** (see), anchovies, boiled eggs, oil and vinegar

coniglio alla stimpirata stewed rabbit cooked in wine, with peppers, capers and fresh mint

coniglio da fossa all'ischitana rabbit, raised in deep ditches dug into the ground, cooked in a skillet with white wine and cherry tomatoes

coniglio de casada rabbit reared on a farm

consiero in Veneto, meat ragù without tomatoes

conzier rustego in Veneto, sauce made with chicory and chicken liver

copete/cupete little pieces of nougat based on chopped almonds, sugar, egg white and cinnamon, cooked in the oven between two wafers

coppa sausage made from the pickled and aged cervical muscle of the pig; called 'summer coppa' (Piacenza, Parma, Mantua)

coppa di testa cured meat made with pig's head and cartilage, cooked and compacted with many aromas including pistacchio and orange peel; called 'winter coppa' (Emilia)

coppiette slice of boar meat or dry beef, aromatized and smoked (Tuscany)

coratella entrails, generally lamb or kid

coratella alla barbaricina coratella cut into tiny pieces and served with fava beans and baby carrots (Sardinia)

cordula braided entrails of kid or lamb to be grilled or stewed (Sardinia)

corzetti fresh egg pasta typical of Liguria; there are two types: that so-called from Val Polcevera (Genoa), shaped like an eight, and the hand-stamped type shaped like a medalion

cosi chini sort of small *buccellati* (see)

costoleccio this is what they call barbecued spareribs in some areas in Tuscany

cotechino cured meat that needs cooking made of pork, lardo, spices and pork rind; common in Piedmont, Val d'Aosta, Lombardy and in Emilia Romagna with slight variations

cotechino in camicia o in galera cotechino first boiled then wrapped in slices of cooked ham and veal

cotica 'bbiturata slivers of pork rind boiled and served in small discs with tomatoes and marjoram

cotiche ripiene see **braciola di cotica**

cotoletta alla bolognese slice of veal breaded and fried, covered with raw ham and soft grana, passed in the oven and if in season, sprinkled with truffle

cotoletta alla petroniana see **cotoletta alla bolognese**

coujette/cojëtte potato gnocchi from the Cuneo mountains (Piedmont)

cozze ripiene see **muscoli ripieni**

crafun krapfen (see) traditional Ladino savory (Alto Adige) usually filled with game

crapiata typical soup from Matera based on legumes, including beans and fava beans

crastuna Sicilian dialect name for big snails like *Helix aspersa*

crauti (sauerkraut) thinly sliced cabbage, salted and fermented (regions linked to Austrian and German culture)

crème brûlée sweet based on egg yolks, sugar, milk cream, lemon peel, baked au gratin

cremolato/a di frutta sort of creamy water-ice prepared with the same system as sorbet, using fruit juices (Lazio)

cren root with a spicy taste used for cooking, generally grated, used for preparing sauces

cresc' tajat dialect term for maltagliati, but with maize flour (North Marche)

crescentina thin focaccia cooked in special molds called tigelle, to be accompanied with cured meats or with chopped lardo, garlic and rosemary (Modena, Emilia)

crescia sfogliata sweet version of **crescia** (see), rolled, it contains sugar, raisins, aniseed (Marche)

crescia leavened pizza dough with holes on top to be garnished with salt, oil, onions and rosemary

crespella alla valdostana very thin omelet (crêpe) filled with ham and fontina, covered with fonduta; originated in the Val d'Aosta in the Sixties, but this dish does not belong to the region's traditional recipes

crespelle thin, light omelets prepared with eggs, flour, milk, butter and a pinch of salt, filled with a sweet or savory stuffing

crispelle fritters from Catania, prepared either in a savory version (with anchovies and ricotta or Tuma cheese) or sweet (with rice, milk and eggs)

croccante confectionery consisting of almonds or hazelnuts bound with caramel

crocchè/crocchette see **cazzilli**

crocette a dialect term from the Marche for pellican's foot (mollusc)

crostata chiusa short pastry cake filled with jam

crostini di milza in brodo o zuppa di milza meat broth enriched with small 'buns' filled with spleen mixed with eggs and marjoram

crostini neri toasted bread spread with a sauce of chicken livers (or veal spleen) flavored with anchovies, capers and frequently Vinsanto (Tuscany)

crostolo pasta medal of flour, eggs and milk of the texture of the **piadina** from Romagna (see), and used in similar fashion (North Marche)

crudaiola (alla) raw condiment for pasta or fish based on oil and aromas, sometimes with the addition of cherry tomatoes

crustoli fried sweets of which there are various regional variations

cròstuli/kròstuli see **cartellate**

cube rolle a kind of marinated tagliata

cuccìa (1) in Basilicata and Calabria it's a wheat soup cooked with oil **(2)** in Sicily it's a sweet of cooked wheat enriched with honey, or sugar, and ricotta

cuculli Ligurian potato fritters, pine nuts, marjoram, eggs and cheese (same name as another type of fritter made with chickpea flour)

cucunci/cucunceddi little oval berries, the fruit of the caper plant

culaccia/culatta culatello (see) with pork rind, obtained from the prime part of leg of pork

culatello sausage obtained from the prime part of boned pork leg, cured and aged for a long time (province of Parma)

culurgiones/culingiones/culurjones/cullurzones/gurigliones Sardinian ravioli of durum wheat pasta generally with a non-meat filling

cunicio in tecia in Veneto and Venezia Giulia, rabbit in a skillet

cunigghiu à portuisa variation of rabbit alla stimpirata where wine is replaced by Marsala

cuosti chini stuffed pork chop (Sicily)

cupa or head salami because it is prepared with meat from the pig's head

curzul/curzoli pasta of flour and water (Emilia-Romagna)

cuscus Arab dish in which the bran is combined with various condiments, savory or sweet, of meat, fish, or vegetables, typical of the province of Trapani

cutturiddi (a) way of cooking lamb common in Basilicata: the meat, in chunks, is cooked slowly in an earthenware pan together with onions, dices of potato, oil, bay leaves, chili pepper

cuzztil pasta of flour and water

D

delizie al limone on the Amalfi coast, sponge cake filled with lemon juice pastry cream and covered with a lemon sauce; at Sorrento, the pastry of the **raffioli** (see) covered with a mix of pastry cream, lemon peel and limoncello

diavolillo very hot red chili pepper, oval-shaped and small, widespread in Abruzzo and Calabria

ditali short dry pasta whose shape recalls the thimble (hence the name)

dolceforte (in) Tuscan preparation originating in the Renaissance in which the meat employed (tongue, hare, boar) is cooked with wine, vinegar, sugar, chocolate, candied fruit and raisins acquiring a distinct bitter-sweet flavor

durelli gizzard (stomach) of poultry

E

erbazzone typical savory pie from Reggio Emilia consisting of thin pastry containing a filling of chards, lardo, Parmigiano Reggiano, aromas

F

fagioli al fiasco traditional Tuscan side dish which involves cooking beans with water and aromas in a glass flask placed next to the embers of the fireplace

fagioli all'uccelletto Tuscan side dish of cannellini beans stewed with tomatoes, oil, garlic and sage

fagioli dall'occhio small white beans with a black ring, called 'eye'

fagioli del Purgatorio cannellini beans, so called in the Viterbo area (Lazio)

fagioli zolfini small, spherical, yellowish color and fine skin (Tuscany)

fagiolina del Trasimeno small beans cultivated in the Lake Trasimeno area

fagiolo badda flavorsome two-color legume, small and roundish (*badda* in Sicilian dialect means ball)

falsomagro/farsumagru see **bruciuluni**

faraona alla creta dish typical of the Piacenza and Cremon area: the guinea-fowl, aromatized and wrapped in wax paper, is cooked in the oven in a soft clay wrapping

faraona alla leccarda see **palomba alla leccarda**

faraona rodolada co'a peveràda guinea fowl roulade with **peveràda** sauce (see)

farecchiata polentina made with wild pea flour and flavored with anchovy sauce

farinata col cavolo nero maize flour polenta cooked with black leaf kale, flavored with garlic, oil and grated Parmigiano (Tuscany)

farinata Ligurian flat bread made of chickpea flour and olive oil to be eaten hot

farro cereal with characteristics similar to corn grown in Garfagnana and Central Italy; used mainly for soups

farrotto sort of risotto prepared with spelt together with mixed wild vegetables (Abruzzo)

fasoi in potacin, sofegai, embogonàdi in Veneto and Venezia Giulia, beans cooked very slowly, with or without tomatoes

fassone (carne di) particularly fine Piedmontese veal

fasui (uardi e fasui) dialect term in Friuli Venezia Giulia meaning beans, used in many regional dishes, among which the typical barley and bean soup

fasule e scarole bean and escarole soup

fava cottoia fine Modica variety of protein-rich fava beans

favata typical shepherd's dish consisting of fresh fava beans cooked with pork, tomatoes and aromas

fave 'ngrecciate fava beans boiled and served as a salad with garlic and mint (or marjoram) (Macerata, Marche)

fave e cicoria see **incapriata**

favetta con cicorie see **incapriata**

favò short pasta with fava beans, tomato and fontina cheese, served with bits of bread fried in butter (Val d'Aosta)

fegatelli nella rete bundles of liver stewed in pieces with herbs then wrapped in pig net (Prato, Tuscany)

fellata in Abruzzo and Molise indicates an antipasto consisting of cured meats and typical local cheeses

ferdinandi twice leavened bread sweet

ferratelle sweet wafers cooked in a special plier and filled with ricotta cream (Abruzzo)

ferrazzuoli type of long shaped pasta worked with a needle, similar to maccheroni

fettuccine egg pasta in flat ribbons about 1 cm wide, a bit thicker than the classic Emilian tagliatelle

fettunta Tuscan name for simple **bruschetta** (see)

fiadoni/fiadoncelli Abruzzese sweets filled with fresh and grated Pecorino, eggs and cinnamon (there's a version in Trentino filled with honey, almonds, rum, cloves and cinnamon)

ficazza tuna salami obtained by packing the minor cuts of tuna cured with salt and pepper into pig bladder (Sicily)

fico dottato variety of light-colored fig, used in Calabria for the preparation of sweets

fidighin mortadella typical of northeast Piedmont, made of pork liver, cheek and bacon

filacci (see **sfilacci**)

fileja Calabrese fresh pasta made of water and flour, long and twisted shape

filetto baciato raw salami, typical of the Acqui Terme area (Piedmont), made of pork fillet, cured with salt and aromas, wrapped in salami paste

filiferru o filoferru Sardinian eau de vie

filindeu durum wheat pasta made in very fine threads and used in sheep's soup, typical of festive occasions in Sardinia

finanziera a typical Piedmontese dish based on sweetbreads, brains, testicles, veal fillet, coxcombs, cep mushrooms, Parmigiano, Marsala, oil and vinegar

fini-fini egg tagliatelle 2 mm wide, typical of Ciociaria (Lazio) where normally pasta is wider and thicker

finocchiona typical cured meat from Florence and Siena aromatized with wild fennel seeds, garlic crushed in wine, black pepper and serpillo thyme

fiocco di culatello cured meat obtained from the high front part of the leg remaining after the culatello has been produced

fiocco di vitello cut of veal corresponding to the front part of the breast

fior di latte (**1**) milk pudding, sugar and egg cooked in the oven in a caramelized mold (Emilia) (**2**) fresh pasta filata cheese similar to cow's mozzarella, from which it differs for form and texture of the pasta

fiore sardo Pecorino cheese (industrially mixed milk is used) aged and produced all over Sardinia

fiorentina thick young beef steak on the bone with tenderloin and sirloin attached (weight between 500 grams and 1 kg); grilled or barbecued

fioretti short egg pasta

flan soft vegetable timbale

foiade cube shapes of puff pastry with sides of three or four centimeters, typical of Bergamo (Lombardy)

foiolo Milanese name for omasum, part of tripe

folpeti Venetian term for moscardini, molluscs like baby octopuses

fondue bourguignonne chunks of meat for cooking at table in a pan filled with boiling oil; they can be eaten accompanied by sauces

fonduta Piedmontese specialty also widespread in the Val d'Aosta consisting of fontina cream cheese, milk and egg yolk, served hot

formadi frant soft, friable cheese obtained from mixing dairy cheeses in flakes with milk or cream, salt and pepper

formaggio di fossa mainly Pecorino (goat or mixed) which, covered with leaves, is aged in tuff grottoes

formaggio grigio see **graukäse**

formai de mut literally mountain cheese; in local dialect, mut actually means mountain pasture

formai parat melted cheese

formajo imbriago in Veneto and Venezia Giulia, 'drunken' cheese aged in contact with marc

formajo verde in Veneto and Venezia Giulia, cheese with herbs

fracchiata polentina made with grasspea flour and spelt flavored with fava beans and browned pork cheek (Abruzzo)

fragaglia small fish left at the bottom of the net, generally served fried

franceschini small fish similar to **cicireddi** (see)

francesina see **lesso rifatto**

frascarelli/frascariegl' polentina of maize flour and potatoes dressed with oil and chili pepper, enriched with beans (or vegetables) and, traditionally, pork rind (Molise)

frascatelli water and flour pasta, rather thick

frascatole durum wheat flour to be prepared like **cuscus** (see)

fratto di fave minestra made by country people, traditional in Calabria and Basilicata, based on fava bean purée and pasta

frecacha beef and potato pie typical of the Val d'Aosta

fregnacce rough diamond shapes of fresh pasta to be topped with sauces or to be served folded and filled with ragù and grated Pecorino on side plates (Lazio, Abruzzo)

fregola/fregula durum wheat pasta in the form of irregular spherical shapes (similar to **cuscus**, see)

friarelli see **friggitelli**

friarielli Neapolitan name for turnip tops

fricandò stew of beef and pork with potatoes, vegetables, aromatic herbs, white and red wine and a bit of tomato

fricassea lamb or chicken stew mixed, when cooked, with egg and lemon

fricco' di pollo chicken cooked in wine, vinegar and aromas. You can also use lamb, duck, rabbit and veal stew

frichetti cheese, potato and onion pies

friciòle/fricieu/friciolin typical Piedmontese leavened savory fritters accompanied by cured meats

frico cheese (*montasio*) fried in oil, butter or lard (Friuli specialty), frequently served with potatoes

friggione side dish for meats based on onions and stewed tomatoes all steamed in vinegar (Emilia-Romagna)

friggitelli little green long-shaped peppers with a sweet taste; they can be fried – hence the name – or stuffed (Abruzzo, Puglia, Calabria)

friscalutu bread with mushrooms and Pecorino flakes (Sicily)

frisceu or **friscïöi** Ligurian terms for various types of fritters

friselle doughnut-shaped rusk to be bathed in water before serving, accompanied by dried tomatoes, salads and fresh vegetables; traditional in the south, particularly Puglia

frite di prat boiled herbs tossed in a frying pan

fritto misto all'ascolana fry-up that is a bit different from other Italian fry-ups in so far as it consists of stuffed olives, artichokes, zucchini (or zucchini flowers) lamb and cremini mushrooms

fritto misto rich dish made up of various ingredients and preparations (meats, giblets, vegetables, starches) breaded and fried in oil and/or butter. There are five regional versions: Piedmontese, Florentine, Bolognese, Romano, Neapolitan

frittole Calabrese dish prepared with entrails, muzzle, ears and pork rind cooked in their own fat in a copper pan

frittura di paranza mix of small fish captured with a net, floured and fried

frittura dolce sweet semolino breaded and fried

fuazza a very crispy, stuffed and rolled up pizza (Sicily)

funciddi biscuits made of almonds and hazelnuts (Sicily)

funghi trifolati mushrooms sautéed in a frying pan with oil, garlic and salt; you serve them covered with minced parsley

fusilli short, spiral-shaped pasta originating in southern Italy; today produced industrially, it is still made at home using a knitting needle

G

galàni north-east, **chiacchiere** (see) of Carnival; there is also a savory version

galantina cold dish, generally white meat made into a sausage with ham (and/or tongue), pistachios and Marsala, boiled and left to cool in its broth

galletti dialect name for *finferli*, mushrooms

ganassino/ganascino veal or pork cheek, stewed, braised or boiled

garganelli small pieces of hollow maccheroni made of egg pasta enriched with Parmigiano and nutmeg: obtained by wrapping pieces of pasta round a stick and passing them through a 'comb' (Romagna)

gargàti in Veneto, homemade egg maccheroni pasta

garmugia a soup made in Lucca of seventeenth century origin based on spring onions, asparagus, peas, fava beans, minced beef, bacon, meat broth

garofolato beef, stewed with wine, concentrate of tomatoes, loads of cloves (Lazio)

garùsoli Venetian dialect term for murex

gattafin big ravioli fried, filled with wild herbs, eggs, ricotta and Parmigiano (Liguria)

gattò (**1**) almond brittle from Sardinia prepared with almonds, sugar and lemon peel (**2**) potato timbale stuffed with salami, provola and mozzarella cheese (Campania, Sicily)

gedi Messinese name for chards

gelatina di maiale pork boiled and boned, the meat is put into a mold; cut into slices, it's covered with cold broth and kept cool; a Sicilian specialty

gelo sort of fruit blancmange, the most traditional is that made of watermelon (Sicily)

genovese (alla) traditional neopolitan meat and onion stew: the sauce is used to dress pasta, the meat is served as a main course

geretto Milanese dialect term which stands for a cut of veal

ghiotta (alla)/agghiotta/ghiotta di a stew preparation of fish flavored with tomatoes, olives, capers and sometimes raisins

giancheti see **bianchetti**

gianduia very soft and creamy hazelnut chocolate, typical of Turin

gianduiotto a dark chocolate from Turin made with cream of toasted hazelnuts from the Langhe, sugar and vanilla

giardiniera long preserved pickled vegetables

gibanica sweet from Slovenia in various layers (short pastry, ricotta, poppy seeds, walnuts)

ginestrata Tuscan soup based on broth, beaten egg, Marsala and cinnamon

girello adult beef cut

giuncata cream cheese made in a reed basket

gnaccheragatti pasta made of bran, chestnut flour and water (Marche)

gnocc de la cùa or gnocchi of the tail, Valcamonica dish (Lombardy)

gnocchi 'ncotti see **strozzapreti**

gnocchi a coda di soreca long pasta of water and flour, looking like the tail of a mouse

gnocchi alla romana discs of solidified semolina baked au gratin with butter and Parmigiano

gnocchi sbatùi flour gnocchi served with butter, cheese or smoked ricotta, typical dish from the Lessini mountains (Veneto)

gnocco fritto/gnoch frit leavened pasta cut into diamond shapes and fried; present throughout Emilia although its name changes

gnoccoli fresh pasta in the shape of open maccheroncini

gnucheit spoon polenta with butter and Toma cheese

gnudi spinach (or nettles) gnocchi, ricotta, Parmigiano and a bit of flour, passed in butter and aromatized with sage (Tuscany)

gnumarieddi/gnumaridde roulades of kid or lamb entrails usually grilled; very common all over southern Italy

gobeletti short pastry sweets filled with jam, typical of Genoa

gola soft aromatic salami made from pork's neck

gorgonzola a marbled cheese, namely veined by green mold

gota pork cheek, bacon

gòto in Verona dialect a glass of wine and, by extension, an aperitif; equivalent to the Venetian **ombra**

gramigna egg maccheroncini obtained by pressing pasta in a special press, to be served with sausage (Emilia-Romagna)

gran pistau wheat soup with leeks and pork rind (Liguria)

grano arso wheat burned with the stubble after reaping, from which a dark flour is obtained

gransipori in Veneto and Venezia Giulia, *granciporri* (big crabs)

gras pistà a preparation common in Emilia based on finely ground lardo with garlic, shallots, a bit of salt, parsley if you like, generally saved in jars

grattonato a traditional dish from Basilicata based on sheep's tripe and giblets minced and mixed with eggs and Pecorino all cooked in meat broth

graukäse cow's cheese of greyish color and grainy consistency obtained by acid fermentation (Alto Adige)

gremolada/gramolata Lombard condiment made of garlic, parsley and lemon peel used in the recipe for Milan style veal shank

gricia (alla) condiment used in Roman cuisine for dressing pasta based on oil, onion, pork cheek crumbled and lightly fried; it is a tomato-less *amatriciana*

grifi all'aretina stew (see) of veal muzzle

grive (1) pork meatballs, lung, liver and giblets, wrapped in pig omentum, floured and fried (Piedmont, where they're also called frisse) **(2)** in Sardinia, thrushes on the spit perfumed with myrtle

gröstl preparation consisting of sliced boiled beef, potatoes and onions tossed in the pan until browned (Alto Adige)

guancette part of calf muzzle

guanciale cured meat made from pork cheek

guazzetto a stew with tomatoes usually referred to fish, frogs, snails; in the Marche region, using unripe tomatoes, garlic, oil, parsley and wine, sometimes with a splash of vinegar

gubana a sweet from Friuli of leavened pastry laid out in sheets and filled with walnuts, pine nuts, raisins and other ingredients

gueffus round Sardinian sweets made of almond flour, sugar, lemon, orange flower water, liqueur

guglgliones sweets filled with honey pastry and almonds, covered with honey (Sardinia)

gulasch in the South Tyrol version, inspired by the Hungarian dish, a beef stew bathed in red wine and tomato concentrate, flavored with paprika and cumin

I

impepata seafood simply opened over the stove, served with cooking water and sprinkled with pepper

(today more frequently splashed with lemon)

incapriata preparation typical of Basilicata and Puglia consisting of a purée of dry fava beans and boiled wild chicory, all with an extravirgin olive oil condiment

infrascati pasta based on wheat and maize flour (Lazio)

insalata russa boiled vegetable salad, diced and served with mayonnaise

intoppo/'ntruppc ragù for pasta, usually strascinati, based on tomato, veal and pork, sausage (southern Italy)

involtini alla palermitana roulades filled with bread crumbs, raisins, pine nuts, cheese and aromatized with bay leaves and onion

inzimino a stew made using chards or spinach and eaten with cuttlefish, squid but also chickpeas and tripe (Liguria, Tuscany)

J

jambarei dialect term for fresh water shrimp (province of Latina)

jlatina see **gelatina di maiale**

jota minestra with beans eaten in Trieste, **brovada** (see) or sauerkraut, lardo or bacon or mixed vegetables, sometimes with the addition of meat

K

kaiserschmarrn sweet omelet enriched with apples and raisins, served hot with jam; there are many variations

kiffel/kipfel half-moon shaped bread from Friuli prepared with potatoes, flour, eggs and butter, fried and served as a side dish (sweet variations are served as a dessert)

knieküchel krapfen (see) filled with blueberry jam

knödel big gnocchi of stale bread, flour, milk and eggs typical of Alto Adige tradition; aromatized with cheese, spinach, mushrooms, speck, bacon, they are eaten in various ways: dry, in broth (mainly liver) and as a side dish

krapfen spelled in many different ways, it indicates a sweet fritter of round or half-moon shaped leavened bread, dusted with sugar or filled with cream; in Trentino and in Alto Adige, inspired by Austrian and German culture, it is filled with ricotta, raisins, pears

L

laciada (or cutizza) water and flour batter fried and sprinkled with sugar

laganari lasagne, or fresh pasta in rectangles eaten in southern Italy

lagane/làine/làane e ceci minestra common in southern Italy of chickpeas (but also beans), fresh pasta of rectangular shape (lasagne) and a light fry of garlic, oil and paprika

lampascioni bulbs of a herbaceous plant that grows wild (nowadays it is also cultivated, especially in Puglia); of bitterish taste, you eat them boiled, fried or pickled

lampredotto boiled tripe with vegetables and dressed with pepper and oil, eaten between two slices of bread and typical of Tuscany

lardiato larded

lasagne al forno alla bolognese Emilian preparation also common elsewhere: green pasta rectangles (made of spinach) sauced in layers with ragù, bechamel and Parmigiano, baked au gratin

lasagne mes-cie homemade pasta with chestnut flour (Lunigiana, Tuscany)

lasagne a bit thicker than tagliatelle, they are strips of egg pasta 10-15 cm long and 2-5 wide

lattaiolo sweet made of eggs, milk,

flour, cinnamon, lemon peel, baked in the oven and sprinkled with icing sugar (Marche)

latte alla portoghese see **fior di latte**

latte in piedi see **fior di latte**

latteria originally, in the north east, this term referred to cheese made in dairy farms; now it is the product of a dairy, without any specific standard

latteruolo o casadello milk cream, vanilla, sugar and egg cooked in the oven wrapped in pasta

lattuchedda filleted underbelly of veal

lattume tuna sperm, placed first in salt, then pickled; you eat it sliced, served with oil and parsley

leghe local name (Tuscany) for black leaf kale: farinata with leghe see **farinata col cavolo nero**

lesso rifatto beef previously boiled, diced and tossed in the frying pan with onions and tomatoes

limoncello liqueur obtained from the infusion of lemon peel in alcohol

lingua in giardino (or in green sauce) boiled veal tongue, cut into thin slices and served hot covered with a sauce of parsley, carrots, tomatoes, capers, garlic, oil, vinegar or a green sauce of parsley, garlic, oil and vinegar

lingua salmistrata ox tongue treated with salt and saltpetre, left to pickle, then boiled

linguine long dry pasta of lenticular section originating in Liguria, around 3 mm wide

lion mortadella in large intestine casing (Emilia)

liptauer creamy mixture based on ricotta, butter, onion, cumin, capers and paprika (Trieste)

lisandros pasta similar to fettuccine

litùmp mix of wild aromatic herbs picked before sunrise

loertis/lovertis see **luppolo**

lolli small fresh pasta of cylindrical

shape, often accompanied by fava beans

lombrichi, lombrichelli big handmade spaghetti made of water and flour, vaguely spindle shaped (Lazio)

lonza cut of meat, synonym of lombo (loin) in northern Italy

lonzino di fichi cylindrical sweet made of dried, ground figs mixed with cooked must, almonds, walnuts, aniseed, all wrapped in fig leaves (Marche)

lonzino pork cured meat (loin) salted, cured and aged

lorighittas a kind of spaghetti entirely hand made, twisted on itself and closed like a small ring (Sardinia)

lubjanska breaded steak filled with ham and cheese, typical of Friuli Venezia Giulia

luccio in consa pike, boiled and filleted, dressed with a sauce of oil, garlic and salty anchovies; served with polenta (Brescia province)

luccio in salsa pike, boiled and filleted, dressed in layers with a sauce of oil, capers, garlic, vinegar, parsley and salty anchovies; leave it to rest (Mantua, Verona)

luganega/lucanica trentina big sausage made of the noble parts of the pig aged for up to four months; when fresh, it is much used in cooking (Trentino)

lumache alla bobbiese shelled snails cooked with leeks, aromatic herbs and white wine (province of Piacenza, Emilia)

lumaconi big dry snail-shaped pasta

luppolo its sprouts are used in the cuisine of various Italian regions for soups, omelets, risottos; it has various regional names

luserna incovercià in Veneto, tub gurnard grilled and marinated in vinegar

luvertin see **luppolo**

M

macafame bread cake with milk, eggs, apples and dry fruit

macarrones de busa artisan pasta from Sardinia similar to bucatini handmade using the special implement or a knitting needle

maccagno Piedmontese cheese made from whole cow's milk treated raw, dense elastic texture with eyes

maccarones furriaos Sardinian gnocchetti made with durum wheet pasta and eggs and dressed with melted Pecorino cheese

maccaruni name used in southern Italy for certain forms of generally hollow long or short pasta

maccheroni del pettine see **garganelli**

macco rather thick broad bean purée, served alone or with pasta (Sicily)

madernassa variety of pear, suitable for cooking, widespread in the Cuneo area (Piedmont)

magatello a term from Lombardy for a cut of beef

magnana a dialect term from the Marche for **neonata di pesce** (see)

maiorchino rare ewe's or goat's cheese that ages up to 24 months (Sicily)

makaira square spaghetti made from barley (Abruzzo)

malfatti irregular shaped gnocchi made of spinach (or other leafed vegetable), flour, egg, grated cheese, boiled and served with melted butter (North Italy)

mallegato Tuscan sausage similar to **buristo** (see)

malloreddus cun su ghisadu pasta with traditional sauce obtained from cleaning the bones of lambs and sheep

malloreddus type of pasta with a shell shape (gnocchetti type) served with sausage and tomatoes (Sardinia)

maltagliati fresh pasta with an irregular diamond shape, mainly used for pulse-based soups

manate typical Basilicata pasta that undergoes complex manual processing: the result is a tangle of big spaghetti

mandilli de sea lasagne from Liguria with a very fine pastry sheet (silk handkerchiefs) served with a pesto condiment

mandorle atterrate almonds toasted with white wine and sugar

mandurlin del pont sweets based on almonds, sugar, flour and whipped egg whites (province of Ferrara, Emilia)

manfricoli see **ciriole**

manfrigole buckwheat pancakes filled with cheese and butter

manfrigoli hard pasta of flour and eggs rubbed gently between the hands until it reduces to tiny grains then cooked in broth (Romagna)

manzo all'olio specialty from Brescia in which priest's hats are cooked with oil, garlic and anchovies

maracucciata polenta of black wheat with pulses

maranin polenta Marano maize, a variety cultivated in the Verona area

marchigiana breed of cows native to the Marche

margiuola cured meat prepared with pork tongue

mariola cured meat obtained from grinding and tanning the less noble parts of the pig

marro lamb offal wrapped in the gut with pieces of Pecorino (sometimes also mortadella) cooked on the barbecue or in the oven (Puglia, Calabria)

martin sec ancient variety of rustic pears, widespread in Piedmont, cooked and served for dessert

marubini ravioli from the Cremona area cooked in a broth of mixed meats and then served dry

marzolina goat cheese from Ciociaria (Lazio)

masaro in Veneto, a drake

mascarpone kind of cheese of creamy texture obtained from milk cream; originally from lower Lombardy, in Emilia you serve it as a dessert garnished in various ways

mascherpa Lodi dialect term for ricotta

masculina da magghia anchovies caught when their heads are caught in the net (Sicily)

masenete in Veneto, female crabs in their fertile period

masorini in Veneto, wild ducks

matalotta (alla) preparation of sliced fish, cooked in a casserole with garlic, basil, parsley, green olives, capers and tomato concentrate (Sicily)

mattone sweet in layers alternating cookies bathed in coffee or liqueur and cream of butter or of eggs

mazza di tamburo popular name for *Lepiota bruna* mushroom

mazzafrissa milk cream, with the addition of flour, cooked in a skillet (Sardinia)

mazzamurru typical soup from Cagliari consisting of slices of wet stale bread, alternating with fresh tomato sauce and grated Pecorino

mazzareddri wild vegetables with a bitter taste

mazzarelle lamb entrails cut in strips and gathered up with herbs in bunches, wrapped in endive leaves and browned in the pan (procince of Teramo, Abruzzo)

mazzolina name used in the Marche for piper gurnard

'mbuttunatu stuffed or, more simply, larded; a dialect word from southern Italy

meascia Lombardy focaccia made of maize flour, raisins, walnuts and other dry fruit, buttermilk

medaglioni small, round cutlets cooked as appropriate to the various types of meat

meini, pan mein traditional Lombard sweet which used to be made with millet flour but is now made with wheat and maize flour

melanzane alla parmigiana see **parmigiana di melanzane**

melanzane con la cioccolata eggplants fried and stacked in layers, alternating milk cream and candied fruit, and chocolate cream

merca (1) at Oristano, mullet boiled and wrapped in the leaves of a plant typical of swamp land **(2)** at Nuoro, curdled goat's milk cut into slices and left to dry, slightly acid taste

merluzzo Piedmontese name for baccalà

mes-ciua minestra from La Spezia (Liguria) based on beans, chickpeas, wheat

mezzanelli/mezzanielli lardiati short dry pasta topped with tomato and pork cheek sauce

mezzano medium-ripe cheese

mezzelune half-moon shape filled pasta

mezzemaniche dry pasta of hollow cylindrical shape, like rigatoni

mezzina name given in Versilia (Tuscany) to pig bacon

micischia/misciska/muscisca spiced sheep or goat meat, cut into slices and dried, typical of Puglia

migliaccio sweet chocolate blood enriched with almonds, pine nuts, candied fruit, milk cream and flavors, cooked in a pastry envelope like puff pastry

milanese cutlet on the bone obtained from veal loin dipped in beaten egg and peppered, then in breadcrumbs and, finally, fried

millefoglie sweet consisting of several

very fine layers of puff pastry which are filled with custard or chantilly or eggnog

minchiareddhi maccheroni based on barley flour hollowed with a fine iron rod

minestra al/nel sacco a mixture served in broth made of eggs, Parmigiano, flour and nutmeg previously cooked in a cloth bag, then left to chill and cut into cubes (Emilia, Marche, Lazio)

minestra chin frue soup with curded goat's milk (Sardinia)

minestra cun casu friscu soup with fresh cheese (Sardinia)

minestra di cardone e polpette see **cardone**

minestra di pane Tuscan soup of beans soaked in their broth, tomatoes, various vegetables alternating with layers of bread; the basis for **ribollita** (see)

minestra maritata vegetable soup enriched, in a number of variations, with pork; popular all over southern Italy

minestra matta squares (or tagliolini) of pasta dressed with tomato sauce and lightly fried bacon with domesticated herbs (Emilia); elsewhere with various wild herbs

mischiglio/miskiglio fresh pasta from Basilicata, often cavatello-shaped, made with a mixture of vegetable flours and cereals and dressed in various ways

miserie de le femene spoon gnocchi based on flour and eggs

missoltini shad dried in the sun and wind and then grilled (Lombardy lakes)

misticanza mix of seasonal wild herbs to be eaten uncooked as a salad (Lazio)

mistrà high-grade liqueur obtained by soaking aniseed in alcohol

mocetta cured meat from Val d'Aosta

prepared traditionally with the meat of ibex, today with that of chamois, goat or cow

moleche/moeche Veneto term for male crabs in the moulting season; they have a soft shell and can be eaten whole, usually fried

mollica in Sicily often used to indicate breadcrumbs or the soft part of bread

mollicato see **ammollicato**

mondeghili meatballs made from leftovers of boiled meat (Milan area), eggs, cheese, sausage, bread drenched in milk, aromas, breaded and fried

mondiola medium aged cured pork meat ground to medium consistency and folded on itself (northwest Tuscany)

moniceddhi/municedde a dialect term from Puglia for snails the brown color of a friar's smock

montasio cow's milk cheese from Friuli cooked and semi-hard

monte veronese dop cow's milk cheese from Lessinia (Veneto)

montèbore cow's and ewe's milk cheese from Piedmont, smooth with eyes

moretta mixture of coffee, rum and other liqueurs prepared according to an old sea recipe, served as a digestive (Fano, Marche)

morlacco cow's cheese from the Grappa (Veneto) tableland

mortadella di fegato cooked pork sausage consisting of a mixture of liver, bits of meat and bacon. Aromatized with spices and red wine

mortadella oval or cylindrical cooked cured pork of typical pink color; the Bologna variety is best known but mortadella is produced throughout the center-north

mortadellina di Campotosto sausage of ground lean pork threaded with a strip of white lardo (Abruzzo)

mortandela pork sausage of round shape and heavily cured (Val di Non, Trentino)

morzeddu/morzello/morsello giblets boiled and then cooked in wine with a spicy tomato sauce (Calabrese specialty)

mosciame dried tuna fillet

moscioli variety of mussels specific to the Cònero area (Marche)

mose polenta timbale with herbs

mostaccioli/mostacciuoli/mustazzuola/mustazzoli hard pastry sweets traditional in various regions of Italy and with similar characteristics: flour, sugar, spices, sometimes honey, frequently cooked wine and almonds

mostarda spicy condiment from the Cremona area based on candied fruit in a syrup containing a variable quantity of white mustard

mosto cotto see **vino cotto**

mozzarella in carrozza sort of sandwich of stale bread and slices of mozzarella breaded and fried; originally from Campania, today it is sold in pizza houses and fried food outlets all over the center and south of Italy

'mpanata scacciata (see) tall and swollen

muas/mus polentina of yellow and white flour cooked in water and milk, served with butter (Trentino Alto Adige)

muccu see **neonata**

mugliatielli see **ammugliatielli**

mulinara (a) method for preparing fish, floured and cooked according to different recipes

murazzano Piedmontese cheese traditionally of ewe's milk (today with a percentage of cow's milk), soft texture

muscoli ripieni dialect term for mussels; in the La Spezia (Liguria) area they are stewed after filling the valves with a mixture of mortadella, part of the molluscs, bread soaked in milk, Parmigiano, aromatic herbs

muscolo (with red wine) cut of beef corresponding to heel, cooked in red wine

musetto/muset cured meat prepared with lean pork meat, parts of muzzle and rind, spices and white wine

muss/musso Venetian dialect names for donkey

mussillo the back of the baccalà

mussu boiled head and cartilage of veal, diced, flavored with lemon juice, oil, salt, pepper, parsley and served cold; frequently served with **carcagnola** (see)

mustazzola see **mostaccioli**

mustela sausage obtained from the processing of pork fillet or loin

nana term used in Tuscany for duck

N

napruddi name used in Madonia (Palermo) for wild thistles, usually cooked in the oven or fried in batter

'ncaciato sautéed in a frying pan with cheese

'nciminiteddi small buns covered with sesame seeds (Sicily)

'nduja spreadable and very spicy sausage (Calabria)

neccio the Tuscan term for chestnut and its flour and by extension (necci) thin focaccette of chestnut flour cooked on a special baking tray

neonata southern name for **bianchetti** (see)

nero (al) the dark fluid secreted by cephalopod molluscs such as cuttlefish or octopus used to dress pasta or fish

nervetti so-called in Lombardy and Piedmont, gristle from the knee and veal shank boiled, thinly sliced and served with oil, onion, parsley

'nfigghiulata focaccia (sweet or savory) filled with ricotta (Sicily)

nocciolini biscuits with chopped hazelnuts or almonds

nocetta regional name for a cut of beef also applied to other meats such as venison

nocino liqueur obtained by the infusion of husks and kernels of unripe walnuts in alcohol; called nocillo in southern Italy

O

oca in onto goose meat salted and preserved in terracotta jars with melted goose fat and bay leaves

'ntuppateddi Sicilian dialect word for green snails (*Helix aperta*)

ocio Tuscan term for goose

ola thick soup based on beans, vegetables and spareribs, cooked in the oven in an earthenware pot (typical of the Piedmontese mountains)

olive all'ascolana big tender olives, typical of Ascoli Piceno (Marche), filled with minced meat and aromas, breaded and fried

ombra North-east, glass of wine

orapi dialect name for wild spinach (central Italy)

orecchiette traditional pasta from Puglia, Basilicata and confining areas, small and round in shape, similar to a small ear

oriot/orión pig's ear and head boiled and cut into pieces, served with a spicy pepper sauce and vegetables (Piedmont)

orziadas sea anemones, in Sardinian dialect

orzotto/orzetto first course prepared with barley, vegetables and sundry other ingredients

ossobuco alla milanese veal shank cut in slices with bone and marrow, cooked in broth and white wine, flavored with lemon zest

ossocollo (salume) sausage from Friuli prepared wih the meat of pig's neck (unminced), lardo, salt and spices

ovinfort marbled ewe's cheese, typical of Sardinia

P

pabassinas/papassinos petit-fours with almonds and raisins, covered with icing, typical of Sardinia

paccheri large dimension pasta with a hole in the middle, originating in Campania

pajata/pagliata part of the small intestine that, in Roman cuisine is cooked with chyme, as the animals (lamb, kid or veal) are very young; it presents as a cutlet that is grilled or stewed; exclusively in Lazio

palacinke crêpes from Venezia Giulia filled with jam or hazelnut cream

palamita big sea fish similar to tuna

pallocco dialect term for sweet chicory (Lazio)

pallotte cac' e ova grated Pecorino meatballs, bread soaked in milk, eggs and aromas, fried in oil

pallotte del pastore ricotta and Pecorino cheese meatballs with tomato sauce (Abruzzo and Molise)

palomba alla leccarda dove cooked on the spit above a pot containing a sauce of wine, vinegar, oil, pulped olive, sage, garlic and other aromas; the fat and blood from the meat trickle into the pot and the result is spread over the cooking dove

pan dell'orso sweet consisting of a mixture of almonds, honey, sugar, eggs and butter, covered with chocolate (Abruzzo)

pan fritu/pan fritto slice of bread cooked on the hot plate of a stove and dressed with salt or sugar (Liguria)

panada di anguille timbale with pasta, dried tomatoes in oil, pieces of skinned eel and parsley (Sardinia)

panada/panade preparation of stale bread, cheese and aromas typical of Veneto and Friuli

panadinas pies consisting of sheets of durum wheat pasta filled with meat and vegetables (Sardinia)

pancetta de casada homemade bacon

pancotto born as a 'poor dish', prepared with stale bread together with seasonal vegetables, in Puglia in particular they use turnip tops, onions, wild chicory, cabbage

pane carasau also called music paper, bread prepared with flour, salt, yeast and warm water, it looks like a very thin, round wafer (Sardinia)

pane cottu see **pancotto**

pane cunzatu bread with tomatoes, anchovies, fresh cheese, extravergin olive oil, oregano, salt and pepper condiment

pane frissu bread fried with lardo and sausage

pane guttiau pane carasau (see) bread served with olive oil and salt, sometimes aromatized with garlic

pane saporito see **pane cunzatu**

panedda aglintesa cow's roasted string cheese (Sardinia)

panelle mixture of chickpea flour cut into thin slices and fried (Sicily)

panforte sweet typical of Siena, low and compact, of ancient origin, today also produced industrially; it is similar to **panpepato** (see) but enriched with almonds and walnuts and lined with communion wafers

pani ca' meusa sandwich filled with veal spleen fried in lard (Sicily)

paniccia/panizza polenta of chickpea flour, solidified and cut into cubes which are fried in oil; common in southern Piedmont and in Liguria

panicia soup based on vegetables, barley, beans and smoked pork (Ladino Valleys, Alto Adige)

panigacci fine discs of flour and water cooked on plates (of terracotta, grès or cast iron) and dressed in various ways; Lunigiana specialty (Tuscany)

paniscia typical risotto from Novara (Piedmont) prepared with borlotti beans, savoy cabbage, vegetables, pork rind, lardo and **salam d'la doja** (see)

panissa typical risotto (Vercelli, Piedmont) prepared with beans, lardo, salami and lean bacon

panna cotta spoon pudding from Piedmont consisting of liquid cream solidified with fish glue

pannerone whole milk cheese that owes its name to the Lodi (Lombardia) term *panéra* (milk cream)

pannicolo cut of beef

panocchie/pannocchie dialect term from the Marche for mantis shrimps

panpepato/pampepato sweet based on dry fruit, candied fruit, honey, chocolate and spices cooked in the oven (Emilia, Tuscany, Lazio)

panséta in Veneto, rolled up bacon

pansopà in Veneto, bread soup (soaked bread)

pansotti/pansoti traditional Ligurian filled pasta, stuffed with herbs and vegetables

panunto see **fettunta**

panzanella stale bread softened in water and vinegar and dressed with tomato, onion, cucumber, extravergin olive oil; typical of Tuscany

panzerotto rolled pasta with a sweet or savory filling, fried in lard or oil. It may also simply mean filled half-moon shaped filled pasta

papaccelle sweet peppers, flat and ribbed, traditionally preserved in vinegar

papàrele con fegadini in Veneto, fettuccine with chicken liver

pappa al pomodoro bread cooked with oil and garlic and aromatized with rosemary and basil, in summer with tomatoes

pappardelle the Tuscan name for ribbon-shaped lasagne has now taken on the meaning all over Italy of any wide strip egg pasta; typical Tuscan varieties are '*sulla lepre*', '*sul cinghiale*', 'sul coniglio'

pappicci tagliatelle of flour and water boiled with fresh tomatoes and served with lardo and onion

parasambene diaphragm of roast veal (Sardinia)

parasangue see **parasambene**

pardula Sardinian Easter treat consisting of a basket filled with fresh cheese and saffron, it may be served with honey

parmigiana di melanzane dish originating in southern Italy of which numerous variations exist; it is prepared with slices of fried eggplant set in layers and dressed with tomato sauce, mozzarella and grated Parmigiano, all lightly cooked in the oven

parrozzo sweet of recent origin (created by a confectioner in Pescara), made of flour, milk, eggs, sugar, ground almonds, orange peel, covered with chocolate

passatelli in brodo first course of Emilian origin prepared with a mixture of breadcrumbs, eggs, Parmigiano, appropriately grated nutmeg; the rough cylinders obtained are served in a broth

passavulanti cookies based on toasted almonds, sugar, egg white, cinnamon and vanilla (Sicily)

pasta 'ncasciata short pasta with a tomato sauce condiment, meatballs, eggplants, salami, breadcrumbs and other ingredients that vary with the region, finally lightly cooked in the oven (Calabria, Sicily)

pasta al sangue tagliatelle prepared with flour, eggs and ox blood (Trentino)

pasta alla buranella pasta with fish ragù

pasta alla carrettiera pasta served with a raw tomato sauce, garlic, basil, chili pepper, oil, salt

pasta alla cuncimata pasta served with pork ragù and wild fennel (Sicily)

pasta alla Norma pasta served with tomato sauce, fried eggplants and salty ricotta (Sicily)

pasta c'anciova the condiment, defined as the poor man's botargo, consists of anchovies (anciova) and toasted bread crumbs (Sicily)

pasta ca' nnocca literally 'pasta in spades', dressed with pilchards and stewed peas (Sicily)

pasta cresciuta leavened fried pasta

pasta e broccoli in brodo di arzilla traditional Roman soup based on skatefish broth (arzilla) in which broccoli and then pasta are cooked before frying lightly in the pan

pasta e fasoi Venetian pasta and beans, generally served with lardo or pork rind

pasta ro malutempu poor dish, once prepared with homegrown vegetables and wild herbs, when fishermen couldn't get out to sea, today it's prepared with broccoli, olives and anchovies (Sicily)

paste di meliga corn flour cookies; Piedmontese specialty

pasticciata alla pesarese beef stew cooked in red wine with lardo, garlic, cinnamon, cloves, tomato sauce

pasticcio ferrarese maccheroni pie dressed with bechamel, mushrooms and ragù of mixed meats, covered with sweet short pastry; old specialty of Ferrara (Emilia)

pasticciotto typical Lecce sweet made of short pastry and filled with custard

pastiera typical sweet from Naples tied to Easter and consisting of short pastry, ricotta, cooked wheat, candied fruit and orange flower water

pastiere focaccia from Modica filled with minced meat, Caciocavallo, eggs

pastìn o tastìn in Veneto, mixture of fresh salami, not in sausage form

pastisàda di cavallo – horse stew cooked with wine and tomato, specialty from Verona

pastizzà de musso in Veneto, donkey meat stew

pastorale mutton stew cooked with vegetables and aromas, traditional in Basilicata

patacche/pataccacce strips of tagliatelle-like rustic pasta obtained from a fairly thick sheet of pasta (Lazio)

patùgol sort of potato polenta flavored with browned onions, bacon, butter, grated Grana (Trentino)

pearà sauce from Verona based on toasted bread crumbs, marrow, pepper, beef broth; used to accompany mixed boiled meats

pecora alla callara o a cotturo mutton cooked in water, white wine, tomatoes, cultivated herbs (Teramo and L'Aquila, Abruzzo)

pecora fellata in other words sheep two or three years old

pecora in cappotto mutton boiled with potatoes and onions

Pecorino laticauda cheese obtained from the milk of laticauda sheep

peilà polenta based on potatoes and flour (barley or wheat) mixed with cheese and melted butter (Val d'Aosta)

pendolini small cherry tomatoes

pengiarelle/pincinelle gnocchetti shaped like fine spindles obtained from leavened pasta (Marche)

pennoni dry pasta in the shape of large penne

peoci Venetian term for molluscs which in Italian are called mussels

peperoni crusch/cruschi dried peppers, used in many Southern recipes

peposo alla fornacina diced veal cooked at length wine and grains of pepper, its origin is attributed to the inside of imprunetino terracotta ovens (Tuscany)

perbureira pasta and beans typical of the Monferrato area (Piedmont)

persegada a dense preserve of cotogne apples with a perfume of cloves and cinnamon (Veneto)

pesca tabacchiera small flat-shaped peach; the white pasta type is very sweet and soft

pescatora (alla) general condiment for pasta and rice based on seafood and shellfish

pesce finto consisting of potatoes, tunafish and pickles, shaped like a fish, served as antipasti

pesce stocco other name for stoccafisso

pesto di salame finely minced fresh salami used as a condiment for pasta or risottos

pesto ligure sauce used to dress first dishes, prepared with basil, pine nuts, garlic, grated Parmigiano and Sardinian Pecorino, olive oil, salt

pesto trapanese condiment for pasta based on garlic, basil, tomatoes, almonds, Pecorino; pesto all'usticese and pesto siciliano are similar

petta/pezza imbinada pork soaked in wine and aromas (Sardinia)

pettl' e fasul see **pettole e fagioli**

pettole e fagioli a first dish from

Campania based on fettuccine-like homemade pasta

pettole/pittule balls of leavened dough fried in oil, common in southern Italy, sweet, covered with sugar, or savory, filled with anchovies, pieces of baccalà and whatever

petuccia, pitina spicy cured meat from Friuli covered in maize flour and smoked on the fire, traditionally prepared with game, goat's meat or mutton, today refined with pork

peverada a Veneto sauce based on chicken liver and soppressa, it goes with game, guinea fowl and roast duckling

peveroni Veneto dialect term for peppers

pezzata milk-fed lamb stuffed with various aromas, olives, capers, anchovies, pickled peppers, grated cheese cooked with white wine (Abruzzo and Molise)

pezzenta sausage from Basilicata that employs pig's head and giblets, it is consumed as soon as grilled or boiled, or preserved in fat

pezzetti stew of horsemeat typical of the Lecce area, with a dense and spicy sauce

pezzogna dialect name for pagello (sea bream)

piacentino/u ewe's cheese aromatized with saffron (Enna, Sicily)

piada/piadina pasta ring based on flour, water, lardo and salt, cooked on a special plate called a testo (Romagna)

piave cow's milk cheese from the Belluno area (Veneto); aged or medium aged varieties

picagge fresh egg pasta cut into strips about 1 cm wide (Liguria)

piccata/piccatina Milanese preparation with veal escalopes cooked in Marsala or lemon

picchiapò (alla) sort of **lesso rifatto** (see); in Rome beef muscle is used and it is flavored and eaten sliced with onions, tomatoes and capers

pici/pinci big hand-made spaghetti of durum wheat flour (Siena, Tuscany)

pìcula ad cavàl minced horsemeat first sautéed and then stewed with tomatoes and peppers (Piacenza, Emilia)

pierrade mixed grilled meats and vegetables, accompanied with sauces

pignata copper or terracotta pot, rotund and narrow at the mouth; in the cuisine of southern Italy, beans, octopus and meats are cooked slowly in a pignata

pignattaccia mixed meats, vegetables and white wine cooked slowly in the oven in an earthenware pan (Viterbo, Lazio)

pilau kid sauce, mixed after cooking with egg yolks and lemon juice, for dressing boiled rice (pilaf); today it is varied by using durum wheat bran mixed with water and saffron

pillus sheet of bran dressed with lamb or goat ragù, Pecorino and baked au gratin

pinza stuffed focaccia, sweet or savory, common in several regions

pinzimonio condiment based on olive oil, salt and pepper, in which you dip raw vegetables

piopparelli/pioppini mushrooms (*Pholiota*) commonly used in central Italian cooking

pipeto prepared with savoy cabbage, garlic, egg, Grana Padano cheese, salt and pepper, can be used as a filling for boiled hen or, cooked as an omelet, as a side dish (province of Cremona, Lombardy)

pisarei e fasò gnocchetti of stale bread tossed in a bean sauce with sausage (or lardo and pork rind), tomatoes and homegrown aromas

(Piacenza, Emilia)

pisci rè Marsala fish fry

piscialandrea Ligurian pizza served with tomatoes, onion, anchovies, olives, capers and garlic

piscirovu omelet enriched with parsley and grated Pecorino (Sicily)

pistiddos sweets, typical of Sardinia, prepared for the festivity of Sant'Antonio, filled with cooked must

pistoccheddu typical Sardinian cookies covered with a special icing

pita traditional sweet from Friuli filled with apples, raisins and nuts

piticelle di rosamarina fritters prepared with a spicy sauce of whitebait

pitta cun ulìa red ox with olives (Sardinia)

pitta di patate sort of Apulian focaccia or pizza made with boiled potatoes amalgamated with onions, tomatoes and olives, cooked in the oven

pitta impigliata sweet from Calabria prepared with a dough based on flour, oil, honey, cloves, cinnamon, orange juice and filled with dry fruit

pitta Calabrian focaccia of which a number of variations exist, flat and irregular in shape or round with a hole in the middle; it is eaten with **morzeddu** (see) and with an infinite number of other garnishings

pittinicchi spare ribs

pizz'onta bread pasta fritter from Abruzzo

pizza di crema layered pie of short pastry and cream

pizza dolce/doce plain sweet made of sponge cake soaked in liqueur (alchermes, maraschino) and built up in layers with egg cream, covered with meringue and baked lightly in the oven (Abruzzo)

pizza e minestra rustic preparation which combines a corn focaccia cooked in the oven with potatoes and wild vegetables boiled and garnished (Molise)

pizza rianata pizza of wholemeal flour seasoned with oil, garlic, oregano and tomatoes

pizza teramana see **pizza dolce**

pizzaiola (alla) cooked in a frying pan with tomatoes, garlic, oregano

pizzicotti water and flour gnocchetti

pizzoccheri big dark tagliatelle prepared with buckwheat flour and wheat meal, typical of Valtellina (Lombardy)

podolica breed of cattle still present in the southern Apennines; Caciocavallo Podolico cheese is made from milk of these cows

poenta e s-cioss in Veneto, polenta and snails

polenta concia o grassa maize flour cooked in salted water with the addition of Fontina (or other soft cheeses) and melted butter

polenta di patate see **patùgol**

polenta di riso mixture of water and rice flour

polenta nera made with buckwheat

polenta taragna a recipe from the Valtellina (Lombardy) in which polenta is dressed with butter and cheese (scimud or bitto)

polenta uncia recipe from the Brianza area (Lombardy) in which every layer of polenta is garnished with Parmigiano Reggiano and butter aromatized with garlic or onion

pollo al mattone in other words chicken cooked in a frying pan, after being aromatized, with a non-porous terracotta tile as a lid

pollo alla diavola chicken grilled over a charcoal fire

polpettone an oval shaped mixture stewed or baked in the oven; ingredients vary from region to region, but the main ingredient is always minced meat

polpo alla luciana after being cooked in just a little sea water in a hermetically sealed pan, the octopus is flavored with oil, lemon, parsley and garlic

pompìa bitter orange peel, grapefruit or candied cedar

porcellitto aglio forno dialect expression for pork cooked in the oven (Latina province, Lazio)

porcetto/porchetto/porceddu milk-fed pork roasted or oven-cooked (Sardinia)

porchetta (in) preparation of meats (mainly poultry) for the spit or oven similar to way in which pork is treated, namely larded with garlic, salt, aromas and, sometimes, bacon and liver of the animal itself

porchetta whole young pig roasted in the oven, flavored with garlic and wild fennel; prepared mostly for feasts, common in central Italy sliced and cold

porchettato see **in porchetta**

porcospino sweet from Romagna with a heart of cookies (or sponge cake) soaked in coffee and covered with cream and toasted almonds

porzina boiled fat and lean pork meats, smoked and otherwise, typical of Trieste

potacchio (in) way of cooking meat or fish by stewing with white wine, aromatic herbs, garlic, chili pepper

poverazze dialect name in Romagna for clams

prattu de cassa Sardinian single dish consisting of game, potatoes, onions, aromatized with a mix of aromatic herbs

prebuggiun/preboggion mix of aromatic herbs, prevalently wild, the make-up of which varies from place to place and with the season (Liguria)

prebugiun single dish eaten by country people made with potatoes and black leaf kale, typical of Ne (Liguria)

primo sale Pecorino aged for 15 days

prosciutto bazzone typical of the Garfagnana area (Tuscany)

provatura bufalo milk spun curd cheese similar to mozzarella; mostly used for cooking (Lazio)

provola bufalo milk spun curd or mixed cow's cheese, a bit more consistent than mozzarella

provolone del monaco caciocavallo (see) obtained from raw cow's milk and aged from 4 to 18 months

prugnoli mushrooms (*Calocibe gambosa*)

puìna Venetian term for ricotta

pulingioni/pulilgioni typical Gallura ravioli with ricotta

puncerle bread fritters filled with jam or toasted poppy seeds (Alto Adige)

punta di vitello ripiena al forno cut of meat opened like a 'pocket', stuffed with Parmigiano, bread crumbs and egg, cooked in the oven covered with bacon and aromas

puntarelle obtained from a variety of chicory, cut in such a way that the ends are curled, thus producing a salad that is garnished with garlic, oil and anchovies (Rome)

puntine di maiale spareribs, barbecued or stewed

puparul' crusch see **peperoni crusch**

purpazza de porcu flamed suckling pig in tiny morsels (Sardinia)

purpetielli affogati in Neapolitan dialect drowned baby octopi, in other words stewed

purpiceddi boiled baby octopi

purpo all'insalata octopus salad in Neapolitan dialect

purpuzza marinated diced pork (Sardinia)

putana sweet from Vicenza of wheat

and maize flour, enriched with dry figs, raisins and liqueur

puttanesca (alla) condiment for pasta based on tomatoes, olives, capers, anchovies; a new entry for central Italian cooking

puzzone raw cow's milk cheese with washed rind and some eyes, typical of Moena (Trentino)

Q

qualeddu Sicilian name for brassica, a sort of cabbage

quaresimali Sicilian cookies based on almonds, aromatized with candied orange and spices; different from the Tuscan variety, in the form of letters of the alphabet and covered with caramel or cacao

quartirolo fresh lean cheese that derives its name from the fourth cut forage on which the cows feed

quinto quarto complex of giblets and beef cuts of little economic value

R

rabatòn gnocchetti originating from Alessandria (Piedmont) prepared with herbs, ricotta, bread crumbs, Parmigiano and eggs, boiled in broth and then cooked au gratin

radic de l'ors bear's chicory, harvested at high altitudes in spring under the snow (Trentino)

radici de camp tarassaco

radici e fasioi pasta and beans with red chicory from Chioggia

raguse dialect term from the Marche for murex (molluscs)

rancetto condiment based on pork's cheek, onion, garlic, marjoram and Pecorino or Parmigiano

rape 'nfucate Apulian spicy side dish based on turnip tops, oil, garlic and chili pepper

rascatieddi/rascatelli see **cavatelli**

rascatura leftovers from processing **panelle** (see)

raschera Piedmontese cow's milk cheese (which can be adjusted with ewe's or goat's milk), soft and elastic

raspatura/raspadura specialty from Lodi (Lombardy) consisting of very fine flakes of local Grana cheese

ratafià liqueur of French-Piedmontese origin obtained from an infusion of sugared fruit juice adjusted with alcohol

ratatouille mix of fresh vegetables (zucchini, peppers, carrots, onions...) diced and stewed

raveggiolo fresh cheese from Romagna generally of cow's milk or mixed cow's and ewe's

raviòi co'e ortiche ravioli filled and sauced with nettle tips

ravioles potato and cheese gnocchi, long-shaped, sauced with melted butter and grated cheese; typical of the Cuneo mountains (Piedmont)

ravioli dolci ravioli filled with ricotta, sugar and lemon (Sardinia)

ravioli panteschi ravioli filled with ricotta and mint, typical of the Island of Pantelleria

ravioli egg pasta filled with various ingredients depending on the season and the region; the name may change but it is popular all over Italy

raviolo aperto dish interpreted by the chef Gualtiero Marchesi consisting of strips of folded pasta containing a sauce

renaz aged cow's milk cheese from the Belluno area (Veneto)

rènga Veneto dialect term for herring

ribollita Tuscan bean soup, stale bread, black-leaf kale and cabbage that is 'reboiled', namely put on the gas again covered with fresh bunching onion and a drizzle of extravirgin olive oil; traditionally leftover soup was used

ricciarelli crumbly cookies of diamond-shaped almond pastry, a specialty of Siena (Tuscany)

ricotta affumicata di burlina whey of Burlina cow's milk, a breed native to the Veneto which is at risk of extinction, re-cooked, aged and smoked

ricotta alla fuscella ultra-fresh ricotta left to take shape and drip into cone trunk baskets, rich in whey and with a very delicate flavor

ricotta infornata ricotta of cow's, ewe's or goat's milk, pure or mixed, cooked in the oven for half an hour

ricotta marzotica produced in Puglia in spring, it has a slightly spicy flavor

ricotta mustia ricotta produced with the whey of ewe's milk, shaped like a flat bun (Sardinia)

ricotta scante/schiante produced in Puglia; strong and spicy, used as a garnish for pasta

ridric di mont/radicc di mont name in Friuli dialect for Cicerbita alpina, a high mountain plant with bitterish sprouts which in Friuli are traditionally preserved in oil

rigaglie giblets (heart, liver, stomach, combs and wattles) of chickens or poultry in general

rigatoni short durum wheat pasta, ribbed and hollow; traditional in Rome and now produced industrially

ripieni mixture of vegetables with non-meat filling (onion, pepper, zucchini, eggplant) cooked in the oven (Liguria)

risi e bisi Veneto soup of rice and very soft peas

risotto al salto patties prepared from leftover risotto with saffron, fried in the pan till it becomes crispy

risotto all'onda risotto still slightly underdone, with a creamy texture

risotto alla pilota rice boiled in a hermetically sealed container and dressed with salamelle from Mantua and Parmigiano Reggiano

risotto alla sbiraglia/sbirraglia risotto with chicken and vegetables

risotto col pessìn de fosso in Veneto, risotto with *pesciolini di fosso* (newborn fish raised when rice fields are flooded)

risotto con i rovinassi in Veneto, risotto with giblets (chicken giblets)

risotto di gò risotto with lagoon goby, Veneto specialty

risotto in cagnone a recipe from Lombardy in which rice is boiled and dressed with butter, garlic, sage and Parmigiano Reggiano; variations exist in Piedmont and Liguria

risotto in caroman risotto with mutton, Veneto specialty

robiola soft, compact cheese typical of Piedmont (ewe's or mixed milk) and Lombardy (cow's milk)

roccaverano Piedmontese Robiola traditionally of goat's milk (today mixed too), white and compact

rocciata sweet typical of Assisi made with walnuts, almonds, raisins, plums, dried figs, apples, cinnamon and other

rollata (of rabbit or chicken, of veal) big meat roulade served in slices

rosa di Parma beef fillet with ham and Parmigiano

rosada egg cream, milk, sugar, grappa and crushed candied almonds (Trentino)

ròsole young poppy plants (rosolaccio)

rosolio sweet liqueur with a low alcohol content, a bit aromatized; the classic recipe once used rose petals

rossetti tiny white-yellow sea fish with a red spot on the belly

rosticciana collection of grilled meats, mainly spare ribs

rosticciata see **gröstl**

rostin negàa floured veal chops browned in butter, bacon and aromas, cooked with white wine and broth (Lombardy)

rufioi big ravioli with savoy cabbage and cheese (Trentino)

rustisciada/rustida pork and onion stew originating in Brianza which goes well with polenta (north-east Piedmont, Lombardy)

S

s'azzada (agliata da sugo) sauce condiment with garlic and parsley (Sardinia)

s'ciopeti see **bruscandoli**

sa vrue curdled ewe's or goat's milk left for 48 hours in a cork recipient to form a fresh cheese (Sardinia)

saba/sapa must just pressed and cooked at length aromatized with cinnamon and cloves (Emilia)

sabbiosa version of *torta paradiso* eaten in Pavia

sacòcia breast of veal stuffed with meat, green onions, eggs and cheese, boiled and served cold in slices (in Piedmontese dialect it means pocket)

sagne 'ncannulate strips of pasta rolled up holding one end and turning the other

sagne pelose lasagne, called 'hairy' because made using unrefined flour

salam 'd torgia typical salami of the Lanzo valleys (Piedmont), made with the meat of cows that are no longer productive, pig lardo, garlic, red wine and spices

salam d'la doja Piedmontese pork salami, immersed in the fat of the same animal and preserved in a terracotta recipient

salama da sugo sausage eaten in Ferrara going back to the Renaissance made of various ground parts of the pig; it is consumed (after long cooking and steaming) with mashed potatoes

salame di cioccolato see **salame dolce**

salame dolce o salame del papa sweet made of butter, cacao, eggs, sugar, toasted hazelnuts and biscuits, shaped like a cylinder and served in slices

salame moro see **salame dolce**

salignòn fat ricotta, left to dry, with the addition of ground chili pepper or paprica powder (Piedmont)

salmì way of preparing wild furred or feathered animals and sea birds, left to marinate in wine with vegetables, then cooked with the wine of the marinade and broth

salsa brusca typical Piedmontese sauce based on boiled eggs, olive oil, vinegar and, sometimes, mustard

saltarelli tiny fresh water shrimp typical of the Lombard-Veneto area, excellent fried or as an omelet

saltimbocca alla romana rapidly browned veal cutlets garnished with ham and sage

salva creamy cheese (Lombardy) which owes its name to the fact that it used to be produced in May so as to make use of surplus milk

sanapo/sinapa wild vegetable typical of eastern Sicily

sanguinaccio pork's blood clotted and aromatized. In the North and in Tuscany it is eaten as antipasti or a middle course in the form of sausage, in the South it is used as a sweet, enriched with dry fruit, sugar, candied fruit, chocolate

saor marinade for vegetables, fish and meats, prepared with onions browned in oil, wine, vinegar or lemon; the Venetian saor – sweet and sour – requires the addition of sugar, pine nuts, raisins

saragolla ancient native variety of durum wheat from which an excellent flour for pasta is obtained (centre-south Italy)

saras del fen Piedmontese ricotta whose forms are wrapped in hay

sarde a beccafico sardines opened like a book, boned and filled with bread crumbs, pine nuts, raisins and other variable ingredients, cooked briefly in the oven (Sicily)

sarde allinguate opened like a book and boned, the sardines are then floured and fried (Sicily)

sardela Veneto name for anchovies and sardines

sardella spreadable paste based on baby sardines, red pepper, wild fennel and oil

sardenaira Ligurian pizza flavored with a tomato dip, onion, sardines, olives, capers and garlic

sardo modicana breed of cattle present in Sardinia

sartù di riso rice timbale of Neapolitan origin, of which there exist two versions, one meatless and one with ragù

sasaka smoked and spiced lardo, minced and served on black bread croutons

sauersuppe tripe soup with a slightly acid taste given by the vinegar (Alto Adige)

sauté way of cooking molluscs (usually clams or mussels) in a frying pan

savor sauce obtained by the long cooking of grape must with various types of fresh autumnal and dry fruit (Emilia); similar to Piedmontese **cognà** (see)

sbrisolona/sbrisolosa dry cake of maize flour, butter and almonds with a strong tendency to crumble: the former is typical of the Mantua area, the latter of Cremona and environs (Lombardy)

sbroscia lake fish soup, vegetables and bread (Bolsena, Lazio)

sburrita di baccalà *baccalà* soup flavored with oil, garlic, calamint, thyme, chili pepper and served with toasted bread (Isola d'Elba, Tuscany)

scabeccio see **scapece**

scaccia scacciata (see) low and flat

scacciata focaccia eaten in Catania with a variable filling (anchovies, ham, olives, onions, tomatoes, potatoes, sausage, cauliflowers, Pecorino)

scafata soup of baby vegetables, including fava beans, peas and artichokes, flavored with onion, tomatoes and marjoram (Lazio)

scagliuozzi fried polenta

scaloppa slice of meat, generally white, or fish, requiring little cooking in the pan, flavored with lemon or Marsala

scamone cut of beef between the leg and the loin

scamorza in carrozza see **mozzarella in carrozza**

scamorza spun-curd cheese of cow's milk originally from Southern Italy

scandela Lombard dialect term for barley

scapece (a) preparation for fish and vegetables, first fried and then marinated in vinegar, garlic, mint; in Abruzzo they use saffron

scapicollata see **capocollo**

scarpariello fresh pasta similar to *alla chitarra*

scarpazzone see **erbazzone**

scarpinocc local variation of *casoncelli bergamaschi*, pasta filled with chopped meat, vegetables and aromas

scauratello tuna fish cooked with eggplants and mint

schenal de' porzel pork loin

schiaccia briaca sweet leavened focaccia of the Isle of Elba (Tuscany) with dry fruit, Aleatico wine, alchermes liqueur

schiacciata alla fiorentina sweet focaccia aromatized with vanilla, orange and saffron

schiaffoni see **paccheri**

schile/schie gray shrimp from the Venetian lagoon

schiz fresh summer pasture cheese from the Belluno area (Veneto)

schlutzer/schultzkrafen half-moon shaped ravioli from the Tyrol filled with spinach and flavored with onions and Parmigiano, served with melted butter

schmarrn see **kaiserscmarrn**

sciancui fresh egg pasta cut into irregular rectangles, as though torn (Liguria)

sciàtt buckwheat fritters filled with cheese, typical of Valtellina (Lombardy)

scilatedde/scilatelle/scialatelli big fresh pasta spaghetti rolled on a special rod that makes it hollow inside

scimud/scimudin cheese made of skimmed cow's milk typical of Valtellina (Lombardy)

sciurilli pumpkin flowers fried in batter

sclopìt regional name for the herb **silene** (see)

scoglio (allo) generic condiment for pasta based on fish, mostly shellfish and molluscs

sconcigli name used in Campania for murex

scoppularicchi fry of squid and cuttlefish

scorzone black truffle, *Tuber aestivum*

scottadito lamb chops grilled or fried

scottiglia stew of mixed meats (veal, pork, rabbit, chicken, pigeon or kid) cooked with tomatoes, traditional in Arezzo and the Maremma (Tuscany)

scottona young cow giving tender, veined meat

scrippelle 'mbusse traditional soup from Abruzzo consisting of thin rolled crêpes dressed with Pecorino and covered with chicken broth

scroccadenti/stracadent hard petit-fours made of crunchy almonds, honey, flour, egg whites

scrucchijata/scrucchiata grape jam (Abruzzo)

scurdigliata/scurdijata peas, turnips and fried bread (Puglia)

seadas/sebadas/sevadas big sweet ravioli filled with fresh Pecorino, fried and covered with hot honey. Typical of Sardinia

seirass fresh cow's milk ricotta (Piedmont)

selvaggina di valle feathered game hunted in the lagoon canals of the Po Delta (Veneto, Romagna)

sepa rosta Veneto dialect term for roast cuttlefish

sepoline da burcelo baby cuttlefish fished with the line in mid-summer in the Venetial lagoon

seppioline di rezzella baby cuttlefish caught with a net

seupa valpellenentse soup based on meat broth, stale bread, savoy cabbage and Fontina, au gratin (Val d'Aosta)

seupetta cogneintze risotto with bread and Fontina cheese, a Cogne specialty (Val d'Aosta)

sfilacci horsemeat dried on the wood fire in special fireplaces and then reduced to strips

sfinci d'ova cookies based on eggs, honey, sugar, salt and cinnamon (Sicily)

sfinci sweet fritters

sfincione (a) preparation of fish cooked in the oven with potatoes, onions, fennel seeds, bread crumbs (Sicily)

sfincione soft focaccia garnished with anchovies, tomatoes, cheese and lots of onion (Sicily)

sfogghiu pie made in Madonia (Sicily) whose filling includes grated **tuma** (see), lemon peel, chocolate flakes and pumpkin preserve

sfoiade big tagliatelle made of buckwheat (Trentino)

sfregolota see **torta de frègoloti**

sfrucculata dried figs filled with walnuts and fennel seeds

sgabei dough of fried bread used to accompany savory foods

sgnapa Venetian dialect term for grappa

sguazzetto alla becera (or **bechera**) stewed tripe with tomatoes

silene *Silene vulgaris garcke*, herbaceous plant the sprouts of which are used for risotti, gnocchi, soups and omelets

simbua fritta fried bran

sisàm dried bleak stewed with onion and vinegar

skilà vegetable soup from Valsesia (Piedmont) enriched with cheese cubes and rye bread

slikrofi little tortellini of potatoes and herbs typical of Friuli Venezia Giulia but of Slovene origin

soça/sorça beef (kept in salt for four or five days) cooked with savoy cabbage, potatoes and leeks, covered with fontina cheese which melts in the oven (Val d'Aosta)

soffritto pork entrails cooked for a long time in tomato sauce (Campania)

sopa coada bread and pigeon pie, cooked slowly in the oven; Treviso specialty

soppressa/sopressa a sausage typical of the Tre Venezie consisting of lean and fat parts of grossly minced pig

soppressata raw cured meat common in southern Italy of which there are a number of variations, prepared with fat pork and lean pork

ground in various ways, aromatized and pressed

söra ancient cheese from mountain pastures resembling the sole of a shoe

sorbir d'agnoli hot broth with **agnoli** (see) flavored with red wine before serving (Mantua, Lombardy)

spaccatelle short pasta slightly curved and opened lengthwise

spaghetti alla calasettana spaghetti with tuna botarga, mullet and **mosciame** (see) (Sardinia)

spalla cotta, spalla cruda sausages from the province of Parma (Emilia) obtained from lean pork shoulder with the bone; both are aromatized in pickle, the former is then cooked in water and wine, the latter aged raw

sparacelli Sicilian dialect name for broccoli

sparacogne wild herb typical of the Catania area

spatatata soup with potatoes, eggs, mint, cherry tomatoes and stale bread (Lazio)

spätzle/spätzli gnocchetti of flour and spinach obtained with a special sieve, you eat them in broth or as a side dish (Alto Adige)

speck obtained from the leg or boned shoulder of pig, dressed, dried and smoked

spetz tsaorì see **puzzone**

spezzatino small pieces of meat obtained from cuts of the less noble parts of veal, beef, lamb, pork, which must be cooked for a long period

spicchitedda cooked wine biscuits; rolled, decorated with almonds (Sicily)

spiedo bresciano, speo veneto historic recipe for huntable birds roasted on the spit and spaced out with sage leaves

spigatelli in Abruzzo, turnip tops

used as a pasta condiment

spinaroli prugnoli mushrooms

spoia lorda square raviolini which are filled with **squaquerone** (see), Parmigiano, nutmeg (Romagna)

sponcion/spuncioto snack or appetizer (**cicheto**) in Veneto and Friuli Venezia Giulia

spongarda see **spongata**

spongata ancient sweet that, in a shell of short pastry, contains fruit mustard, honey, walnuts, pine nuts, raisins, candied fruit, cinnamon; originating in Emilia it has spread to neighboring regions: to Liguria (*spungata*) and Lombardy (*spongarda*)

sporcamusi in Lecce, sweets of puff pastry sprinkled with icing sugar and stuffed with hot custard as a result of which your face gets covered in sugar if you blow on it

spressa cheese of skimmed cow's milk, compact and elastic (Trentino)

spumini/spumette small meringues with or without almonds

spungata see **spongata**

spuntature extremities of pork ribs

spunzoile/sponzali typical of Puglia, they are spring onions, white and long, similar to small leeks

squaquarone soft, fresh, lean cheese usually spread on focaccia and piadina (Romagna)

stigghiole/stigliole veal, lamb or kid entrails, mixed with scallions and barbecued (Sicily)

stoccafisso all'anconetana lengthy cooking procedure of pieces of stoccafisso with white wine, pesto of anchovies, capers and aromatic herbs, alternating with diced potatoes; bamboo reeds should be placed on the bottom of the casserole to prevent the fish sticking

stoccafisso alla livornese lengthy cooking procedure with potatoes, black olives, chili pepper, a bit of tomato sauce

stoccafisso codfish, stockfish, preserved by dehydration, or dried in the air. Common in the cuisine of nearly every region in Italy where it may take on other names: *stocche*, *stocco*, *pesce stocco*

stocco dialect term for stockfish in several southern Italian regions but also in Liguria

straccetti (di vitella) very small slices obtained from a larger slice of veal, cooked floured and browned and aromatized in various ways

straccetti (stracci) artisan egg pasta cut like lasagne

stracchino (1) fresh cheese ready to be eaten just a few days after production (2) ice-cream sweet from Piacenza in layers, each different (chocolate, almonds, coffee, vanilla, eggnog)

stracciata fresh kneaded-paste cheese, soft, made with cow's milk

stracciavocc' in Abruzzo dialect, squill

strachitund round Stracchino cheese

stracotto stewed meat (beef, horse or donkey), cooked for a long time in wine

straeca in Veneto, horse belly steak

strangolapreti/strozzapreti in the center-south, homemade potato gnocchi or rustic pasta of water and flour; in Trentino, gnocchi prepared with chards, stale bread, eggs, milk, flour and served with butter and sage

strangozzi/stringozzi rustic fettuccine, prepared with flour and water, worked with a rod to obtain the hollow maccheroni shape

strappatelli pasta obtained from a mixture of water and flour torn and thrown into boiling water

strascinati another name for orecchiette; in Basilicata the pieces of pasta are '*trascinati*' (dragged) over a special ridged board

strazzate cookies from Basilicata based on flour, almonds, sugar, eggs and bitter cocao

stricchetti short egg pasta with a butterfly shape, pinched in the middle (Emilia-Romagna)

stridoli/strigoli wild herb with long, thin leaves used to prepare omelets and condiments (Romagna)

stringhette di manzo see **straccetti**

strolghino taper-shaped pork salami of finely minced meat, to be eaten fresh (Emilia)

strongole big homemade spaghetti

strucchi/struki Friuli sweets of short pastry filled with walnuts, pine nuts, sugar and liqueur, fried or boiled

strudel sweet made of puff pastry rolled up and filled with a mixture of apples, dry fruit, sugar, cinnamon; savory versions have been introduced with a meat or vegetable filling (north-eastern regions)

subrich di patate fry of potatoes, eggs and cheese (Piedmont)

sugo finto sauce without meat based on tomato concentrate, aromas, spices

suppa cuata soup prepared with slices of bread, fresh cheese, aromas and lamb broth, layered and baked au gratin (Sardinia)

supplì ball of rice filled with ragù and mozzarella, breaded and fried, widespread in central Italy; in Rome, for the stringy cheese of the filling, it is called '*supplì al telefono*'

surgitti maize flour gnocchi with sausage and lemon flavoring, fried in oil

suri sottovento cold dish consisting of boiled, boned fish covered with a sauce of peppers, tomatoes and vinegar

T

tabulè cuscus of raw vegetables

tacchino alla canzanese turkey boned and baked in the oven with water together with bones and gristle, cooled in its aspic (province fo Teramo)

tacconi allo sgagg pasta of fava bean flour dressed with lardo and garlic

taccozze pasta of durum wheat flour cut into rough diamond shapes (Molise)

taedda caciocavallo of cow's milk

taeddha/taeddra tegamata (the dish takes its name from the recipient in which it is cooked) of zucchini, potatoes and mussels (southern Italy)

tagliancozzi see **quaresimali**

tagliata chop about five millimeters thick grilled or fried and served sliced and dressed with its gravy

taglierini/tagliolini thin tagliatelle

taiadeline dialect name in Veneto for tagliatelline and tagliolini

tajadèla dialect term in Trentino for tagliatelle

tajarin fresh pasta made with white flour and many eggs, cut long and fine, typical of Cuneo (Piedmont)

tajulì pilusi tagliolini of flour and water which, in the cooking, take on a velvety texture ('hairy') (Marche)

tajut term from Friuli dialect – the Italian is '*taglio*' or '*taglietto*' (cut) – for a glass of wine and, by extension, an aperitif; equivalent to the Venetian **ombra**

taleggio one of the very few Italian washed rind cheeses (Lombardy)

talli sprouts

tani butcher's broom sprouts

tappadas in Cagliari, snails

tapulone stewed, minced donkey meat, garlic, oil and aromatic herbs; a Borgomanero specialty (Piedmont)

taralli/tarallucci savory cookies variously flavored, typical of the South bu now widespread in the rest of Italy too

taratufi name in dialect for sea truffles, molluscs similar to clams but bigger

taroncioli tuma (see) cheese balls fried

taròzz side dish of potatoes and stringbeans flavored with butter and cheese

tartrà savory pudding prepared with milk, onions and leeks, eggs, butter, Parmigiano and aromas (Piedmont)

tartufata (torta) whipped cream cake with cream and hazelnuts, covered with layers of chocolate

tastasàl mixture of minced pork, salted and peppered, the same used to make salami

tastìn see **pastìn**

tecia name in Trieste for a pan, used to cook various dishes

tegamaccio (1) stew prepared with different types of fish from Lake Trasimeno (eel and perch or pike and tench) **(2)** in Lazio it's a stew of lamb, potatoes, artichokes, mint

tenerina oven-baked cake from Ferrara (Emilia) made of flour, eggs, dark chocolate and butter

tenerumi zucchini leaves with which you make a very refreshing soup

testa di turco sort of sweet lasagna, in which the layers of puff pastry alternate with milk cream

testarelle di agnello suitably cleaned abbacchio (see) heads, cooked in the oven with bread crumbs and aromas (Lazio)

testaroli thin focacce of flour, water and salt cooked in a testo e generalmente dressed with pesto, a first typical of the Lunigiana area (between Liguria and Tuscany)

testina all'agro calf's head boiled and served cold with onions, oil, vinegar

testina part of the calf's head, one of the seven cuts of Piedmontese mixed boiled meats; it is also served tossed in the pan with vinegar and aromas

teteùn typical Val d'Aosta cured meat obtained from processing the cow's udder

tiana a dialect term from the southern regions for a terracotta pan and, by extension, for a number of dishes cooked in it

tiella alla barese single dish of potatoes, mussels, rice, fresh tomatoes in layers, all cooked in the oven

tigelle see **crescentine**

timballo pasta or rice timbale, with layers of meat or vegetables, contained or otherwise in puff pastry, or broken and cooked in the oven in a mold; in Abruzzo it is made with *scrippelle* (thin flour crêpes), water and eggs

tiramisù spoon pudding common all over Italy based on Savoy biscuits and cream of mascarpone, sprinkled with cacao

tirtlan big ravioli of rye flour and wheat filled with sauerkraut (cabbage or spinach) and fried (Val Pusteria, Alto Adige)

toc' in braide sauce based on very soft polenta, meat sauce and melted cheese (Trentino, Lombardy)

tocco/tuccu/toccu Ligurian sauce made with tomatoes and flavored with a bit of wine, used to dress pasta dishes

tòcio generic term, used in the Northeast regions, for sauce, generally of tomatoes; *in tòcio* and *al tòcio* means stewed

tofeja bean and pork soup, typical of the Canavese area (Piedmont)

toma compact, elastic cow's milk cheese variously aged

tomasina focaccia from Ragusa filled with ricotta, cheese, sausage, boiled eggs

tomaxelle veal roulades typical of the Ligurian tradition

tombea cheese produced with raw milk from Bruno breed cows in the mountain pastures of Cima Rest and Tombea (Lombardy)

tonco de pontesel gulasch from Trentino made with various types of meat, a bit less spicy

tonnarelli dialect term (Lazio) for square maccheroni, similar to Abruzzo *spaghetti alla chitarra*

tonnina air-dried tuna fillet, compacted for cutting into slices

tonno alla portoscusese sort of tunafish stew cooked in red wine (Sardinia)

tonno di coniglio boiled rabbit, boned and saved in oil with garlic and sage (Piedmont)

tordelli ravioli from Lucca (Tuscany) half-moon shape with a filling based on brains, veal, ricotta, herbs, eggs, Pecorino and spices

törggelen traditional celebration of the successfully ended grape harvest, typical of vacation homes in Alto Adige when new wine and chestnuts are offered

torresani very young tower pigeons that have never flown

torta al testo traditional in Umbria, flat focaccia cooked on a refractory stone or earthenware disc called a testo

torta co' i becchi sweet tart from Lucca (Tuscany) filled with chards, pine nuts, raisins, sugar, grated cheese; the becchi is the garnishing

torta co' i bischeri Tuscan sweet tart filled with rice cooked in milk, chocolate, raisins, pine nuts, candied fruit; garnishing all round

torta d'erbi savory pie made with a pasta envelope containing a filling of wild herbs (Lunigiana, Tuscany)

torta de fregolòti crumbly sweet baked in the oven with a dense mixture (with or without chopped almonds) which is allowed to drop off in lumps (fregolòti in Trentino dialect)

torta di grano saraceno buckwheat flour is mixed with renette apples, hazelnuts, sugar and eggs (Trentino and Alto Adige)

torta di melanzane al cioccolato see **melanzane con la cioccolata**

torta di papavero made without flour but with sugar, eggs, yeast, cinnamon and poppy seeds, widely used in South Tyrol cuisine

torta di riso sweet specialty from Carrara (Tuscany) based on rice cooked in milk, eggs, sugar, vanilla and lemon aroma; in Emilia it's enriched with almonds, candied cedar, bitter almond liqueur and it's called Addobbi cake

torta di tagliatelle sweet from Ferrara made with very fine tagliolini and a mixture of layered almonds contained in a pasta envelope

torta fritta see **gnocco fritto**

torta pasqualina savory pie from Liguria with chards or artichokes, ricotta cheese, eggs and aromatic herbs

tortèl de patate flat bread cooked in the oven and made with boiled potato flakes mixed with eggs, maize flour and grated Grana (Trentino)

tortelli alla lastra made with a lean pasta (similar to that of **piadina**, see) filled with chards, pancetta and sausage, cooked in the appropriate testi or, failing that, on stone or in the oven

tortelli amari egg pasta typical of Castel Goffredo (Lombardy) the filling of which includes bitter cress or costmary

tortelli con la coda typical tortello from Piacenza with a filling of chards, ricotta and Grana Padano;

the very fine pasta is braided to form the 'tail'

tortelli di zucca egg pasta from the Mantua area with filling based on pumpkin, apple mustard, amaretti, Parmigiano Reggiano, salt and nutmeg

tortelli mugellani ravioli filled with boiled potatoes, bacon, Parmigiano; exclusive to the Mugello area (Tuscany)

tortellini filled egg pasta typical of Bologna and Modena; similar to **cappelletti** (see), smaller and thinner, the filling may be meat but also ham and mortadella; you boil them in broth

tortelloni big meat-less tortelli

tortiera di alici preparation in alternate layers of anchovies and a mixture of bread crumbs, Pecorino and aromatic herbs, cooked in the oven

tortiglioni dry, screw-shaped pasta

tortino di aliciotti e indivia Jewish recipe (Rome) in which layers of anchovies alternate with layers of escarole, cooked in the oven

tosèla cow's milk cheese to be eaten fresh or tossed in a pan (Trentino)

tosella cheese from the Asiago highlands (Veneto)

toumin dal mel soft, fat and white cow's milk cheese from the town of Melle (Piedmont)

tozzetti dry biscuits common in central and southern Italy containing bits of almonds and hazelnuts and, in some areas, flavored with anise

tracchie/tracchiolelle Neapolitan dialect term for spareribs

trainera (alla) sauce for pasta or meats based on tomato, oil and basil

treccia d'oro sweet from Vicenza (Veneto) of durum wheat flour with milk, butter, eggs, raisins, honey, vanilla

trenette typical long, dry pasta from Liguria, usually dressed with pesto; they are called '*avvantaggiate*' when whole grain flour is added to the wheat flour

triaca pasta pasta with fresh beans, also eaten cold in summertime (Sicily)

triglie alla livornese Tuscan preparation in which red mullet are cooked briefly in a tomato sauce

tripoline long pasta like broad tagliatelle with wavy edges

trippa all'olivetana convent recipe based on tripe, eggplants, tomatoes, boiled eggs, fresh Tuma and aged Pecorino (Sicily)

trippa alla fiorentina beef tripe stew cooked in tomatoes and garden aromas, garnished with Parmigiano

trippa alla parmigiana parboiled tripe, cut into strips and stewed with tomatoes and garden vegetables, served with grated Parmigiano

trippa alla reggiana tripe stew with tomatoes and bacon, ham, Parmigiano Reggiano, herbs

trippa alla romana tripe stew cut into strips with Roman mint and grated Pecorino (Lazio)

trippino term used in Lombardy for cleaned and blanched pig stomach

troccoli rustic tagliatelle from Puglia cut with a grooved rolling pin (troccolo)

trofie little gnocchi of white flour and water, twisted and tapered down at the ends

tubettini short, dry cylindrical pasta, with a hole in the middle

tuma fresh Pecorino (Sicily)

turcinieddu/torcinelli giblets of lamb or kid, wrapped in their own entrails, cooked over the fire (Puglia)

turtla round raviolo stuffed and fried, Ladino cuisine (Alto Adige)

U

ueca barley soup, vegetables, black bread and Fontina cheese (Val d'Aosta)

umbricelli see **ciriole**

urranii Sicilian dialect name for borage

V

vaccareddi Sicilian dialect name for small snails

vartis see **luppolo**

vastedda (1) round homemade bread (2) rare fresh ewe's string cheese typical of the Belice Valley (Sicily)

vavaluci see **babbaluci**

vecia col caval pist stew of peppers, tomatoes, stringbeans, potatoes, to which you add horse meatballs breaded and fried (Parma, Emilia)

ventresca arrosto roasted bacon (central Italy)

ventresca tuna in oil obtained from the white belly of the fish, much sought after

ventriceddi/ventricelle Calabrian dialect term for fish offal, used in various local preparations

ventricina cured sausage contained in pig stomach and typical of Abruzzo-Molise; various types of mixture depending on the place

vermicelli dry pasta of durum wheat bran, long and round; equivalent to spaghetti

verze sofegae stewed savoy cabbage

vettaioli late crop of cucumbers which in Tuscany are preserved in oil or pickled

vezzena cow's milk cheese from Trentino suitable for aging, also excellent grated

vignarola delicate stew of fava beans, artichokes and fresh peas, usually served in spring as antipasti (Lazio)

vincisgrassi oven-baked lasagne typical of the Marche region (Macerata) sauced with tomato-free minced meat and giblet ragù, enriched with mozzarella and Parmigiano

vino cotto/vin cotto sweet syrup of grapes prepared with must that has just been pressed; in Puglia it is also made with figs

violino di capra cured meat from Valchiavenna (Lombardy) prepared with goat leg and shoulder whose shape recalls the musical instrument of which it bears the name

virtù rich minestrone made of legumes, a great variety of diced seasonal vegetables, pieces of pork, and broken up homemade pasta, everything flavored with aromatic herbs, including dill; typical of Teramo (Abruzzo)

visciole type of cherry from which you can also make wine

vitalba herb for omelets

vitello alla fornaia/fornara breast (punta) of roast veal aromatized with garlic, rosemary, sage, served with potatoes (Lazio)

vitello tonnato boiled (or oven cooked) veal rump, served cold in slices with a sauce based on eggs, tunafish, capers, oil and lemon (Piedmont)

vuccuni sea snails

W

weinsuppe creamy soup obtained by mixing on a low gas, meat consommé, white wine, egg yolks, cream and cinnamon (Alto Adige)

weisswurst white meat frankfurter

Z

zabaione typical Piedmontese cream made of egg yolks, sugar and Marsala or Moscato

zabbina preparation based on hot ricotta and whey (Sicily)

zaleti/zaeti diamond-shaped biscuits

from Veneto, made of corn flour, butter, eggs and sugar

zampa alla parmigiana popular Tuscan dish where the veal trotter once boiled and boned is cut into strips and passed in onion and tomato sauce, then covered with grated Parmigiano

zampone minced swine meat, rind, muzzle and gristle in a pig's trotter skin casing, to be cooked (Modena, Emilia)

zanchette name which indicates flat fish similar to sole, common on the Adriatic coast.

zarche name from the Agrigento area for wild chards

zavardella soup of seasonal vegetables and legumes (Lazio)

zazzicchie dried sausages (Lazio)

zebinata oven-cooked vegetables

zemin Ligurian soup of chickpeas, chards and dried mushrooms

zeppole sweet fritters shaped like a doughnut, common all over southern Italy and prepared with ingredients that differ with the place

zerri sea fish belonging to the Mènola species, flesh that is not particularly tasty, to be fried, marinated or eaten in soup

zibibbo autochthonous vine that gives the strong sweet wine of the same name

zireno part of the entrails of the cow, can be roasted or boiled

ziti long dry pasta, it is traditionally combined with a dressing **alla genovese** (see)

zonclada/zonglada a pie from Treviso of medieval origin: short pastry, ricotta, candied fruit, raisins, cinnamon

zotoli Friuli and Venetian name for baby cuttlefish

zucca secca dry pumpkin, usually fried after being softened in water

zucchine alla poverella cut in discs and fried in oil until brown

zucchine alla velletrana sliced, floured and cooked in the oven with rosemary and garlic (Lazio)

zuccotto semifreddo of Tuscan origin shaped like a skullcap consisting of sponge cake filled with ricotta, whipped cream, chocolate and candied fruit

zuppa al vino see **weinsuppe**

zuppa all'etrusca soup with beans and wild turnips

zuppa del carbonaio based on legumes, sausage and various types of herbs (Tuscany)

zuppa di fosso soup with eels, snails, frogs, river shrimps, ditch herbs (Tuscany)

zuppa di soffritto see **soffritto**

zuppa di urtuti soup with various types of legumes and vegetables, including wild chicory and black-eye beans

zuppa frantoiana thick bean soup, black leaf kale, pumpkin, potatoes and aromas served, traditionally, with first press oil (Tuscany)

zuppa inglese a spoon pudding typical of Emilia but nowadays very common elsewhere too. To make, sponge cake is dipped in a liqueur such as Alchermes, then layered with whipped cream and chocolate cream

zuppa lombarda soup composed of homemade toasted bread, rubbed with garlic on which you pour a bean broth flavored with vinegar and dressed with oil (Tuscany)

INDEX OF ADDRESSES

A

A mangiare
Reggio Emilia, 494

Abbazia di San Pietro in Valle
San Pietro in Valle (Ferentillo, Tr), 627

Abbazia di San Vincenzo al Furlo
Furlo (Acqualagna, Pu), 649

Abbazia Il Roseto
Novello (Cn), 100

Abbazia
Monteveglio (Bo), 483

Abbondanza, Trattoria dell'
Pistoia, 589

Abraxas
Lucrino (Pozzuoli, Na), 877

Accademia
Venezia, 334

Accornero
Ca' Cima (Vignale Monferrato, Al), 139

Acquabella
Milano, 173

Acquapazza
Cetara (Sa), 849

Acquapazza
Pescara, 773

Acquario, L'
Castiglione del Lago (Pg), 623

Acquasanta, Osteria dell'
Acquasanta (Mele, Ge), 430

Acquolina, L'
Paterna (Terranuova Bracciolini, Ar), 610

Adriano
Villa Adriana (Tivoli, Rm), 746

Affrichella
Isola d'Elba (Marciana Marina, Li), 544

Afro, Da
Spilimbergo (Pn), 389

Aglio, olio e pomodoro
Barano d'Ischia Petrelle (Isola di Ischia, Na), 854

Agnello d'oro
Bergamo, 149

Agnello d'oro
Genova, 416

Agnello
San Martino in Passiria-Sankt Martin in Passeier (Bz), 258

Agnese, Da
Sant'Antonio di Gallura (Ot), 1029

Agnoletti, Antica trattoria
Giavera del Montello (Tv), 289

Agorà
Civita (Cs), 921

Agriturismo del Cimone
Canevare (Fanano, Mo), 465

Agriverde
Caldari (Ortona, Ch), 771

Aiole
Poggio Rosa (Castiglione d'Orcia, Si), 534

Aiòn
Montacuto (Ancona), 650

Airone, L'
Castelfranco d'Oglio (Drizzona, Cr), 162

Aiuole
Bivio Aiole (Arcidosso, Gr), 519

Alba, Trattoria dell'
Vho (Piadena, Cr), 192

Albana
Mazzolla (Volterra, Pi), 613

Albergo del Muletto
Villanova d'Asti (At), 141

Albergo del Teatro
Spello (Pg), 641

Albergo dell'Oca
Pescocostanzo (Aq), 776

Albergo della Corte
Benevento, 839

Albergotto, L'
Madonna dei Monti (Grazzano Badoglio, At), 84

Albero nascosto, L'
Trieste, 398

Aldina
Modena, 481

Aldo di Castiglione, Da
Asti, 43

Aldo Moro
Montagnana (Pd), 301

Aldo, Da
Biecina (Villa Basilica, Lu), 612

Allegria
Montesorbo (Mercato Saraceno, Fc), 480

Alloggio dei vassalli, L'
Napoli, 864

Alma
Marina di Ravenna (Ravenna), 492

Alpi, Alle
Cussignacco (Udine), 398

Alpina, La locanda
San Bartolomeo (Chiusa di Pesio, Cn), 73

Alpino da Rosa
Virle (Rezzato, Bs), 196

Belvedere
Gremiasco (Al), 85
Belvedere
Pessinate (Cantalupo Ligure, Al), 61
Belvedere
Pietraperzia (En), 988
Belvedere, Trattoria
Agnona (Borgosesia, Vc), 51
Benas, Sas
Santu Lussurgiu (Or), 1030
Benito, Da
Orentano (Castelfranco di Sotto, Pi), 534
Bere, La locanda del
Borgo Fàiti (Latina), 720
Bergi
Bergi (Castelbuono, Pa), 950
Bersagliere, Al
Verona, 342
Bersagliere, Antica osteria al
Vicenza, 345
Bettola, La
Galati Mamertino (Me), 961
Bettola, La
Isole Egadi (Favignana, Tp), 957
Bettolaccia, La
Trapani, 1004
Betulla, La
San Bernardino (Trana, To), 131
Bianca Lancia dal Baròn
San Vito (Calamandrana, At), 55
Bianchi, Osteria al
Brescia, 152
Binari, Osteria ai
Mombarone (Asti), 43
Binterhof
Castelrotto-Kastelruth (Bz), 243
Bistek
Trescore Cremasco (Cr), 206
Bistrò
San Prospero (Mo), 502
Bitta, La
Venezia, 339
Bivio
Cavallotti (Cerretto Langhe, Cn), 70
Blanch
Mossa (Go), 374
Boatina, La
Boatina (Cormons, Go), 360
Boccondivino
Bra (Cn), 52

Boccone del prete, Il
Porano (Tr), 639
Bogliaco
Bogliaco (Gargnano, Bs), 165
Boivin
Levico Terme (Tn), 223
Bologna, A
Bologna, 447
Bolognese, Trattoria
Vignola (Mo), 512
Bomboniera, La
Civitavecchia (Rm), 706
Bon reveil, Le
Bard (Ao), 18
Bonanni, Osteria
Turbone (Montelupo Fiorentino, Fi), 575
Borg da Ocjs
Borgnano (Cormons, Go), 359
Börg, Osteria dë
Rimini, 495
Borghetti
Parona di Valpolicella (Verona), 343
Borghetto, Il
Deruta (Pg), 626
Borgia, Osteria dei
Borgiano (Serrapetrona, Mc), 688
Borgo antico, Locanda
Dimezzano-Lucolena (Greve in Chianti, Fi), 558
Borgo antico, Osteria del
Gioia del Colle (Ba), 807
Borgo Colmello
Farra d'Isonzo (Go), 365
Borgo di Sumbilla
Campeggio (Monghidoro, Bo), 482
Borgo Maranzanis
Maranzanis-Povolaro (Comeglians, Ud), 358
Borgo Poscolle
Borgo Poscolle (Cavazzo Carnico, Ud), 355
Borgo Spoltino
Mosciano Sant'Angelo (Te), 770
Borgo, Al
Molinara (Bn), 860
Borgo, Il
Castellinaldo (Cn), 67
Borgo, Il
Ormea (Cn), 103
Borgo, Ostaria al
Bassano del Grappa (Vi), 271
Borgo, Osteria del
Massa, 569

Ca' d'Andrean
Manarola (Sp), 429
Ca' dei loff
Cison di Valmarino (Tv), 281
Ca' del re
Verduno (Cn), 135
Ca' del Vescovo
Porto Maurizio (Imperia), 420
Ca' Derton
Asolo (Tv), 268
Ca' Guerriera
Sustinente (Mn), 204
Ca' Ospitale
Beligna (Aquileia, Ud), 349
Ca' Poggioli
Lugo (Baiso, Re), 446
Ca' Rossa
Pegognaga (Mn), 191
Ca' San Ponzio
Vergne (Barolo, Cn), 47
Cabina, La
San Pio delle Camere (Aq), 780
Cacciani (ex Giadrina)
Frascati (Rm), 710
Cacciatore, Il
Città di Castello (Pg), 625
Cacciatore, Osteria del
Torre (Castrofilippo, Ag), 953
Cacciatori, Ai
Cavasso Nuovo (Pn), 354
Cacciatori, Ai
Cerneglons (Remanzacco, Ud), 381
Cadorna, Trattoria
Roma, 740
Café du bourg
Arvier (Ao), 17
Caffè grande
Rivergaro (Pc), 497
Caffè la crepa
Isola Dovarese (Cr), 167
Caffè ristorante Impero
Sizzano (No), 122
Caffè Roma
Costigliole d'Asti (At), 77
Cagliari Novecento
Cagliari, 1012
Cairoli
Genova, 418
Caldora, Taverna de li
Pacentro (Aq), 772

Calesse, Il
Montorio (Quarrata, Pt), 593
Calice, Al
Mestre (Venezia), 335
Caminella, La
Bure (San Pietro in Cariano, Vr), 318
Caminetto, Il
Cabras (Or), 1012
Caminetto, Il
Suvereto (Li), 609
Camino, Il
Marradi (Fi), 568
Camino, Il
Pianné (Matelica, Mc), 670
Camogliese, La
Camogli (Ge), 412
Campagna
Campagna (Arona, No), 41
Campana d'oro, La
Palmanova (Ud), 375
Campaniel, Al
Venezia, 335
Campanini
Madonna dei Prati (Busseto, Pr), 454
Campi di Marcello, Ai
Panzano (Monfalcone, Go), 372
Cancelletto, Al
Camin (Padova), 306
Cannata, 'A
Isole Eolie (Santa Marina Salina, Me), 945
Cannone, Da
Sarule (Nu), 1031
Canonica, La
Pagno (Cn), 104
Canonica, La
Casteldimezzo (Pesaro), 677
Cant del gal
Val Canali (Tonadico, Tn), 232
Cantacucco
Missano (Zocca, Mo), 514
Cantaru, Su
Villanova Monteleone (Ss), 1035
Cantina Colonna
Marino (Rm), 722
Cantina de Mananan, A
Corniglia (Vernazza, Sp), 415
Cantina dei cacciatori
Villa Superiore (Monteu Roero, Cn), 96
Cantina del Marchese, La
Marina (Camerota, Sa), 841

Cascina Collavini
Traniera (Costigliole d'Asti, At), 78
Cascina dei peri
Colombiera (Castelnuovo Magra, Sp), 414
Cascina Gaggioli
Milano, 177
Cascina Intersenga
San Lorenzo (Vignale Monferrato, Al), 140
Cascina La Commenda
Santa Margherita (Peveragno, Cn), 106
Cascina Lané
Baldichieri d'Asti (At), 45
Cascina Monsignorotti
San Nicolao (Nizza Monferrato, At), 99
Cascina Papa Mora
Cellarengo (At), 70
Cascina Schiavenza
Serralunga d'Alba (Cn), 118
Cascina Valdispinso
Villa (Santa Vittoria d'Alba, Cn), 117
Cascinari, Ai
Palermo, 978
Case Mori
San Martino Monte l'Abbate (Rimini), 495
Case Perrotta
Sant'Alfio (Ct), 997
Case Rosse, Le
Villa Verucchio (Verucchio, Rn), 511
Case, Le
Macerata, 669
Casentino
Poppi (Ar), 591
Caserma Guelfa
San Benedetto del Tronto (Ap), 681
Casetta, Dâ
Borgio Verezzi (Sv), 411
Casolare, Il
Fondi di Baia (Bacoli, Na), 836
Cassinazza, La
Orsenigo (Co), 189
Cassiopea
Preazzano (Vico Equense, Na), 889
Castagno, Il
Vivo d'Orcia (Castiglione d'Orcia, Si), 535
Castelletto, Il
Monteverde (Roma), 734
Castelletto, Il
Carovigno (Br), 798
Castelliere Pod Tabrom, Al
Zolla (Monrupino, Ts), 373

Castello da Diego, Al
Novello (Cn), 101
Castello di Frino
Ghiffa (Vb), 84
Castello di Luzzano
Luzzano (Rovescala, Pv), 199
Castello di Septe
Castello di Sette (Mozzagrogna, Ch), 771
Castello
Castello (Serle, Bs), 202
Castello
Pergine Valsugana (Tn), 226
Castello
Prato Sesia (No), 108
Castello
San Leo (Pu), 683
Castello, L'osteria del
Castell'Alfero (At), 66
Castelluccio, Taverna
Castelluccio (Norcia, Pg), 633
Castoro, Il
Preci (Pg), 639
Catagna, La
Bacoli (Na), 837
Catine, Da
Aonedis (San Daniele del Friuli, Ud), 382
Cattivelli, Antica trattoria
Isola Serafini (Monticelli d'Ongina, Pc), 484
Cavalier d'Arpino, Il
Arpino (Fr), 699
Cavalier Gino, Dal
Roma, 731
Cavalieri, Osteria dei
Pisa, 586
Cavallina, La
Polverina (Camerino, Mc), 657
Cavallina, La
Brisighella (Ra), 452
Cavallino bianco
Bolzano-Bozen, 240
Cavallino
Canè (Vione, Bs), 210
Caveja, La
Pietravairano (Ce), 872
Cencio, Antica osteria da
Cento (Fe), 460
Centrale
Marsala (Tp), 965

Colline del gelso, Le
Rossano (Cs), 934
Collinetta, La
Martone (Rc), 927
Colonna
Frascati (Rm), 711
Colonna
San Lorenzo (Vignale Monferrato, Al), 140
Colonna, Taverna
Paliano (Fr), 726
Combes, Les
Cheverel (La Salle, Ao), 25
Commercianti, Trattoria dei
Borgomanero (No), 50
Con calma
Torino, 126
Conca alla vecchia posta, La
L'Aquila, 769
Conca verde
Trescore Balneario (Bg), 205
Condo, Locanda da
Col San Martino (Farra di Soligo, Tv), 285
Contadin, Al
Combai (Miane, Tv), 295
Conte d'Antares
Allume (Roccalumera, Me), 993
Conte di Biancamano
Torino, 127
Conte matto
Trequanda (Si), 611
Conte, Da
Marano (Mira, Ve), 296
Contea, La
Neive (Cn), 98
Conti
Roncadelle (Bs), 198
Contrada, La
Desenzano del Garda (Bs), 161
Conventino, Il
Monteciccardo (Pu), 672
Convento San Colombo
Barisciano (Aq), 752
Convento, Il
Cetara (Sa), 849
Copertelle, Le
Serra San Quirico (An), 689
Coquus fornacis
Serra de' Conti (An), 687
Cornacchie, Osteria de le
Petritoli (Ap), 678

Corona
Bagni di Lucca (Lu), 521
Corona
San Sebastiano Curone (Al), 115
Corsaglia
Corsaglia (Montaldo di Mondovì, Cn), 95
Corso
Ascoli Piceno, 653
Corte Altavilla
Conversano (Ba), 801
Corte Gondina
La Morra (Cn), 87
Corte Marzago
Le Bugne (Valeggio sul Mincio, Vr), 333
Corte Pellegrini
Campalto (San Martino Buon Albergo, Vr), 317
Corte Salandini
Ponti sul Mincio (Mn), 194
Corte Virgiliana
Pietole (Virgilio, Mn), 211
Corte, La
Calamandrana (At), 55
Corte, Locanda la
San Lorenzo (Acciano, Aq), 751
Cortevecchia
Polesella (Ro), 309
Costa Casale
Chiaromonte (Pz), 896
Costa d'Orsola
Orsola (Pontremoli, Ms), 589
Costa della figura
Fontecorniale (Montefelcino, Pu), 673
Costa diva
Praiano (Sa), 878
Costa Salici
Cavalese (Tn), 217
Costa, La
Perego (Lc), 192
Costa, La
Sannicandro Garganico (Fg), 823
Costabella
San Zeno di Montagna (Vr), 321
Costachiara, Osteria
Badiola (Terranuova Bracciolini, Ar), 609
Costadoro
Bardolino (Vr), 270
Costalunga
Fara Vicentino (Vi), 285
Costantinopoli
Celso (Pollica, Sa), 875

G

Gabbiano, Il
Corte de' Cortesi (Cr), 157

Gabossi
Angone (Darfo Boario Terme, Bs), 160

Gagliano, Da
Sarteano (Si), 602

Gaia, Dal
Garolda (Roncoferraro, Mn), 199

Gajeta
Gaeta (Lt), 713

Gal vestì, Osteria dal
Santo Stefano Belbo (Cn), 116

Gallina sversa, Osteria della
Piana del Salto (Calosso, At), 57

Gallo e della volpe, Osteria del
Ospedaletto d'Alpinolo (Av), 869

Gallo e l'innamorata, Il
Marsala (Tp), 966

Gallo felice, Il
Martina Franca (Ta), 813

Gallo, Antica trattoria del
Vigano Certosino (Gaggiano, Mi), 163

Gallo, Osteria del
Villa d'Agri (Marsicovetere, Pz), 900

Gallo, Trattoria del
Palazzolo Acreide (Sr), 978

Gambero rosso, Al
San Piero in Bagno
(Bagno di Romagna, Fc), 445

Gambrinus 1847
San Polo di Piave (Tv), 318

Gardenia
Palermo, 980

Garibaldi innamorato, Il
Piombino (Li), 585

Garibaldi
Cisterna d'Asti (At), 74

Garibaldi
Marsala (Tp), 966

Garnì Ladinia
Pescul (Selva di Cadore, Bl), 324

Garsun
Mantena-Welschmontal
(Marebbe-Ennenberg, Bz), 249

Garzette, Le
Lido-Malamocco (Venezia), 340

Gaspar, Da
Zomeais (Tarcento, Ud), 392

Gastronomo, Il
Ponteromito (Montemarano, Av), 861

Gattara
Gattara (Casteldelci, Pu), 657

Gatto & la volpe, Il
Formia (Lt), 709

Gatto e la volpe, Il
Oleggio (No), 101

Gavarini
Mocrone (Villafranca in Lunigiana, Ms), 612

Gazebo medioevale
Iglesias (Ci), 1022

Gazza ladra, La
Siracusa, 1000

Gemma, Osteria da
Roddino (Cn), 111

Gennaro, Da
Santa Marina Alta (Pesaro), 677

Genzianella, La
Selvapiana (Fabbrica Curone, Al), 81

Germinal
Taggia (Im), 439

Gesù Cristo, Trattoria
Taranto, 826

Gesuino, Da
Olbia (Ot), 1025

Gesuino, Da
Sassari, 1031

Gesuiti, La taverna dei
Latronico (Pz), 899

Ghiaccio Bosco
Ghiaccio Bosco (Capalbio, Gr), 527

Ghiara, Trattoria della
Reggio Emilia, 494

Ghinè cambrì
Castellaccio (Livorno), 562

Ghironda, La
Montecchio Emilia (Re), 483

Giacaranda
San Marco (Castellabate, Sa), 845

Giaccò, Da
Isola Santa (Careggine, Lu), 528

Giancu, U
San Massimo (Rapallo, Ge), 435

Gianni a la vècia Bulàgna
Bologna, 449

Gianni Franzi
Vernazza (Sp), 440

Gianni, Osteria da
La Spezia, 423

Kofler am Kofl
Falzes-Pfalzen (Bz), 245
Kogoj
Medea (Go), 372
Kohlern
Colle di Villa-Bauernkohlern
(Bolzano-Bozen), 241
Kus, Taverna
San Zeno di Montagna (Vr), 321

L

La Cittadella dei Sibillini
La Cittadella (Montemonaco, Ap), 674
La Clusaz, Locanda
La Clusaz (Gignod, Ao), 24
Labbruto
Monti del Duca (Martina Franca, Ta), 813
Laghi verdi
Gramignazzo (Sissa, Pr), 506
Lago Laux
Laux (Usseaux, To), 134
Lalibera
Alba (Cn), 39
Lama San Giorgio
Rutigliano (Ba), 821
Lamarta
Vico (Treviso Bresciano, Bs), 206
Language and Art
Ascoli Piceno, 654
Lanterna, La
Mallare (Sv), 429
Lanterna, La
Somma Vesuviana (Na), 884
Lanzi
Alfero (Verghereto, Fc), 510
Lari, La taberna dei
Latina, 720
Latteria San Marco
Milano, 179
Laurino
Cavalese (Tn), 217
Legno
Sella (Borgo Valsugana, Tn), 213
Leiter am Waal
Plars di Mezzo-Mitterplars
(Lagundo-Algund, Bz), 247
Leon d'oro
Robilante (Cn), 109
Leon d'oro
San Leone (Agrigento), 946

Less, Al
Milano, 174
Letizia
Nuxis (Ci), 1024
Letizia
Palermo, 981
Libertino, Il
Trento, 234
Lina, La
Bagnone (Ms), 522
Lino, Da
Solighetto (Pieve di Soligo, Tv), 309
Lissidini
Stadolina (Vione, Bs), 210
Livio
Tessano (Dipignano, Cs), 925
Locanda al sole
Castello di Godego (Tv), 278
Locanda alce nero
Monastero di Montebello
Isola del Piano (Pu), 667
Locanda Alfieri
Termoli (Cb), 785
Locanda Cuccuini, La
Aia (Cavriglia, Ar), 536
Locanda degli artisti
Borgo San Lorenzo (Fi), 525
Locanda dei fattori
San Mauro Pascoli (Fc), 501
Locanda dei musici
Castagnole Monferrato (At), 65
Locanda dei Trecento
Sapri (Sa), 883
Locanda dei vagabondi
Corneliano d'Alba (Cn), 76
Locanda del Bricco
Arcagna (Dolceacqua, Im), 416
Locanda del canovaccio
Campiglia Marittima (Li), 526
Locanda del capitano
Montone (Pg), 631
Locanda del Castello
Frontone (Pu), 665
Locanda del cigno nero
Comago (Sant'Olcese, Ge), 437
Locanda del fiume-'A machina, La
Pisciotta (Sa), 874
Locanda del Gallo
Santa Cristina (Gubbio, Pg), 629

Mariano, Ostaria da
Mestre (Venezia), 341
Marie-Thérèse
Montina (Torreano, Ud), 394
Mariella, Locanda
Fragnolo (Calestano, Pr), 455
Marina Piccola
Manarola (Sp), 430
Marina, Ristorante
San Salvo Marina (San Salvo, Ch), 782
Marinella, Tavernetta
San Michele di Serino (Av), 881
Mario Enoteca dello Schioppettino, Da
Prepotto (Ud), 379
Mario
Firenze, 553
Mario
Isola di Ustica (Ustica, Pa), 1005
Mario, Da
Montegrotto Terme (Pd), 302
Marisa, Dalla
Venezia, 337
Marlen
Caldaro sulla Strada del Vino-
Kaltern an der Weinstrasse (Bz), 242
Marrucola
San Miniato (Pi), 601
Marsupino
Briaglia (Cn), 53
Martella, Antica trattoria
Avellino, 834
Martin pescatore
Milano, 181
Martinelli
Valle di Gresta (Ronzo Chienis, Tn), 228
Mas dei Girardei
San Giacomo (Brentonico, Tn), 214
Masale, La
Pesciano (Todi, Pg), 642
Maso Cantanghel
Forte (Civezzano, Tn), 219
Maso El Giata
Carano (Tn), 216
Maso Lizzone
Dro (Tn), 220
Maso Mistrin
Pinzolo (Tn), 226
Maso Palù
Brentonico (Tn), 214

Masoun dou Caro, A
Marine (Perloz, Ao), 27
Masseria Abate
Noci (Ba), 817
Masseria Barbera
Minervino Murge (Ba), 814
Masseria Canestrello
Canestrello (Candela, Fg), 797
Masseria Cerasella
Pescocostanzo (Aq), 776
Masseria Colombo
Contrada Pandaro (Mottola, Ta), 816
Masseria D'Elia
San Giorgio Lucano (Mt), 910
Masseria degli ulivi
Noto (Sr), 975
Masseria di Parco di Castro
Speziale (Fasano, Br), 803
Masseria Gattamora
Uggiano La Chiesa (Le), 827
Masseria Lamacavallo
Ostuni (Br), 818
Masseria Panareo
Porto Badisco (Otranto, Le), 819
Masseria Rienzo
Rienzo (Ostuni, Br), 818
Masseria Tolla
Tolla (Ostuni, Br), 819
Masseria Torricella
Castellana-Grotte (Ba), 799
Masseria, La
Petriglione (Guglionesi, Cb), 766
Massimo
Trino (Vc), 133
Mastrogiurato, Taverna del
Lanciano (Ch), 767
Matetti, I
Alassio (Sv), 405
Matricianella
Roma, 734
Matteuzzi
Ponterotto
(San Casciano in Val di Pesa, Fi), 596
Maurì 1987
Porto Palo di Capo Passero (Sr), 990
Maurizio, Ristorante del mercato da
Cravanzana (Cn), 78
Max
Cirò Marina (Kr), 920

Mazzini, Trattoria
Neviano degli Arduini (Pr), 484
Mecenate, Il
Gattaiola (Lucca), 564
Medioevo
Monte Sant'Angelo (Fg), 815
Mediterraneo
Amantea (Cs), 914
Mediterraneo
Gaeta (Lt), 713
Mediterraneo, Il
Cappellieri (Cirò, Kr), 919
Mediterranima
Milazzo (Me), 970
Melograno
Valrovina (Bassano del Grappa, Vi), 271
Melograno, Osteria del
Fossa (Aq), 762
Meloncello
Bologna, 450
Mendoza, Hostaria de
Rende (Cs), 933
Mercuri, Da Quintilia
Montefalcone Appennino (Ap), 673
Meridiana Ca' Reiné, La
Altavilla (Alba, Cn), 39
Meridiana, La
Fumane (Vr), 288
Meridiana, La
Saint-Pierre (Ao), 30
Metrò
Catania, 954
Metrò, Al
San Salvo Marina (San Salvo, Ch), 781
Mezzaluna
Nucifero (Palermiti, Cz), 930
Mezzanino del Gattopardo, Il
Palermo, 980
Mezzo Canale da Ninetta
Mezzocanale (Forno di Zoldo, Bl), 287
Mezzo, Osteria di
Salò (Bs), 200
Mezzosoldo
Mortaso (Spiazzo, Tn), 231
Michiletta
Cesena, 461
Middio, Da
Ascoli Piceno, 654
Milanese, Trattoria
Milano, 184

Milic
Sgonico (Ts), 388
Minicuccio
Vallesaccarda (Av), 888
Miramonti
La Santona (Lama Mocogno, Mo), 477
Miranda
Tellaro (Lerici, Sp), 426
Mirandolina
Tuscania (Vt), 746
Mirka e Marcello, Da
Milies (Segusino, Tv), 324
Miseno
Miseno (Bacoli, Na), 836
Mitraglieri, Hosteria ai
Camponogara (Ve), 276
Moderno
Carrù (Cn), 63
Moderno, Il
San Martino al Cimino (Viterbo), 748
Moiè
Padola (Comelico Speriore, Bl), 282
Mola, Sa
Bonarcado (Or), 1010
Molinella, La
Molinella (Isolabona, Im), 421
Molini, Ai
Faedo (Tn), 221
Monacelle, Le
Rioni Sassi (Matera), 902
Monaco di Mezzo
Petralia Sottana (Pa), 986
Monastero di Rolle, Al
Rolle (Cison di Valmarino, Tv), 281
Monastero, Al
Cividale del Friuli (Ud), 357
Monte a Pescia da Palmira
Monte a Pescia (Pescia, Pt), 582
Monte Rosa
Sebrey (Varallo, Vc), 134
Monte San Giuliano
Erice (Tp), 960
Monte, Ristorante al
Volto (Rosolina, Ro), 315
Montebello, Locanda
San Giacomo (Rocca Grimalda, Al), 110
Montecodruzzo, Osteria di
Montecodruzzo (Roncofreddo, Fc), 499
Montelaetus
Caracciolo (Montallegro, Ag), 973

Montepaolo
Montepaolo (Conversano, Ba), 802
Monterone
Ponzano Romano (Rm), 727
Monti, Trattoria
Roma, 740
Mora, Dalla
Venezia, 338
Moro
Mestre (Venezia), 340
Moro, Al
Sciacca (Ag), 997
Moro, Il
Capriata d'Orba (Al), 61
Moro, Osteria dal
Lido (Giulianova, Te), 763
Mosto, Antica trattoria dei
Conscenti (Ne, Ge), 431
Mulin vecio
Gradisca d'Isonzo (Go), 368
Mulinars, Ai
Clauzetto (Pn), 357
Mulinella, La
Pontenaia (Todi, Pg), 643
Mulino della Ricavata
Mulino della Ricavata (Urbania, Pu), 691
Mulino delle Tolle
Sevegliano (Bagnaria Arsa, Ud), 351
Mulino in pietra
Mulino di Leguigno (Casina, Re), 456
Mulino, Il
Comasine (Pejo, Tn), 225
Mundial 82
Cerva (Cz), 918
Municipio, Locanda al
Venzone (Ud), 401
Muraglie, Le
Muraglie (Conflenti, Cz), 922
Muredda, Sa
Villanovaforru (Ca), 1036
Musciara, Sa
Portoscuso (Ci), 1028
Musignano
Stabbia (Cerreto Guidi, Fi), 537
Muskera, Sa
Serdiana (Ca), 1032
Mustilli
Sant'Agata de' Goti (Bn), 881

N

Nadae, Da
Canale (Villadose, Ro), 346
Nangalarruni
Castelbuono (Pa), 951
Napoleonica, Alla
Bassura (Stroppo, Cn), 123
Napolit'amo
Napoli, 865
Narducci
Speziale (Fasano, Br), 804
Nazioni, Alle
San Quirino (Pn), 385
Né arte né parte
Roma, 735
Neapolis
Napoli, 865
Negri
Gonzaga (Mn), 165
Nena
Anghiari (Ar), 519
Nerbone, Da
Firenze, 549
Nerina
Malgolo (Romeno, Tn), 227
Nicastro, Taverna
Modica (Rg), 972
Nicchia, La
Isola di Pantelleria (Pantelleria, Tp), 984
Nicchio, Il
Vinci (Fi), 613
Niederhof
Foiana-Vollan (Lana, Bz), 248
Nino, Da
Letojanni (Me), 964
Nino, Da
Sorgono (Nu), 1033
Nni mia
Scunchipani (Sciacca, Ag), 998
Noce, Osteria del
Isola d'Elba (Marciana Castello, Li), 546
Nonna Bianca
Trecasali (Pr), 510
Nonna Gelsa, Locanda di
Niccone (Umbertide, Pg), 647
Nonna Gilda, Hosteria di
Spinacceto (Greccio, Ri), 715
Nonna Maria
Termoli (Cb), 786

Peillo de Mamagran, Lo
La Salle (Ao), 26
Penzo, Osteria da
Chioggia (Ve), 280
Peppe, Da
Rotonda (Pz), 909
Perbacco
Scorzè (Ve), 323
Perbacco
Cannara (Pg), 623
Perbacco
Pisciotta (Sa), 874
Perbacco
San Carlo (Villa San Secondo, At), 141
Perella, Paolo
Villasalto (Ca), 1036
Pergola, Alla
Fagnano (Trevenzuolo, Vr), 331
Pergola, La
Magliano Sabina (Ri), 721
Pergola, La
Mestre (Venezia), 339
Pergola, La
Capaccio Scalo (Capaccio, Sa), 842
Pergola, La
Gesualdo (Av), 852
Pergola, La
Scalo (Bovino , Fg), 796
Pergolina, Antica trattoria la
Fenili Belasi (Capriano del Colle, Bs), 153
Perla, La
Naso (Me), 973
Pero selvatico, Il
Roccelletta (Borgia, Cz), 916
Perret
Bonne (Valgrisenche, Ao), 32
Persei, Osteria
Prossedi (Lt), 729
Pertzes, Les
Cogne (Ao), 20
Pesca, La
Broccostella (Fr), 701
Pescatora, Alla
Scilla (Rc), 937
Pescatore, La taverna del
Santa Maria (Castellabate, Sa), 846
Pescatore, Osteria del
Tropea (Vv), 941
Pescatore, Trattoria del
Milano, 184

Pescatori, I
Orbetello (Gr), 580
Pescatori, Osteria dei
San Pietro (Portalbera, Pv), 195
Pesce azzurro, Al
Fano (Pu), 662
Pesce fresco, Trattoria del
Marina di Caulonia (Caulonia, Rc), 918
Peschiera, Alla
Fontanaluccia (Frassinoro, Mo), 473
Pesta, Sa
Genova, 420
Peta, La
Gazzo (Costa di Serina, Bg), 158
Petraelejum
Petralia Sottana (Pa), 986
Petralta
Petralta (Monte Santa Maria Tiberina, Pg), 631
Pettirosso
Rovereto (Tn), 228
Pettirosso, Il
Santa Croce (Duino Aurisina, Ts), 363
Pezzolla
Accettura (Mt), 893
Piacentino
Bobbio (Pc), 447
Piana dei mulini, La
Colle d'Anchise (Cb), 760
Pianaccio, Il
Podere Pianaccio (Montale, Pt), 574
Pianella, La
Serra San Quirico (An), 688
Piano, Al
Sarsina (Fc), 504
Piave, Al
Corona (Mariano del Friuli, Go), 371
Piazza Duomo
Sant'Agata de' Goti (Bn), 882
Piazza Garibaldi
Caltanissetta, 948
Piazza Nova
Ferrara, 469
Piazza Nuova, Osteria di
Bagnacavallo (Ra), 445
Piazza, La
Poggiardo (Le), 820
Piazzetta del sole, La
Farnese (Vt), 707
Piazzetta dell'erba, La
Assisi (Pg), 618

Ponte, Al
Bornio (Lusia, Ro), 295
Ponte, Al
Ponte sull'Oglio
(Acquanegra sul Chiese, Mn), 144
Ponte, Al
Sommacampagna (Vr), 326
Ponte, Ristorante del
Scheggino (Pg), 640
Ponti romani, Locanda ai
Vervaz (Challand-Saint-Victor, Ao), 18
Ponticello, Al
Comacchio (Fe), 462
Porta del tempo
Stroncone (Tr), 642
Porta di Felino, La
Casale (Felino, Pr), 466
Porta Mosa
Cremona, 159
Porta romana
Viterbo, 749
Porta vecchia 2004, La
Monopoli (Ba), 815
Porta, La
Monticchiello (Pienza, Si), 582
Portella Gazzana
Longi (Me), 965
Portella, La
Rivisondoli (Aq), 778
Porticciolo, Il
Lazise (Vr), 292
Portichetti
Verona, 344
Portici
Santuario di Vicoforte (Vicoforte, Cn), 138
Portico, Al
Conetta (Cona, Ve), 283
Porto, Al
Clusane (Iseo, Bs), 167
Portosalvo, Taverna
Villammare (Vibonati, Sa), 888
Posta
Glorenza-Glurns (Bz), 246
Posta
Montespluga (Madesimo, So), 170
Posta, Alla
Clodig (Grimacco, Ud), 368
Posta, La
Cavour (To), 69

Posta, La
Avigliano Umbro (Tr), 620
Postiglione, Il
Montodine (Cr), 186
Pozzetto, Al
Mure (Molvena, Vi), 299
Pozzo vecchio, Osteria del
Cavallino (Le), 799
Pozzo, Il
Pieve Fosciana (Lu), 585
Prà rosso
Salse di Nirano (Fiorano Modenese, Mo), 471
Prà-Sec
Romagnano (Trento), 235
Prato Gaio
Versa (Montecalvo Versiggia, Pv), 185
Presidenta, La
Olivola (Al), 102
Prestige
Lecce, 810
Pretzhof
Tulve-Tulfer (Vipiteno-Sterzing, Bz), 263
Primavera, La
Volterra (Pi), 615
Primavera, Trattoria
Palermo, 983
Priscilla
Roma, 737
Progresso
San Benedetto del Tronto (Ap), 682
Pulliero, Belvedere da
Campocroce (Mirano, Ve), 298
Pungolo, Il
Massa Marittima (Gr), 571
Puritate, La
Gallipoli (Le), 806
Purtù, El
Barco (Orzinuovi, Bs), 190
Puzelle, Le
Puzelle (Santa Severina, Kr), 936

Q

Quartina, La
Mergozzo (Vb), 91
Quartino, Osteria del
Brescia, 152
Quattro fontane, Le
Casagiove (Ce), 843
Quintilio
Altare (Sv), 406

R

Raganelle, Le
Diano Castello (Im), 415
Ragnatela, La
Scaltenigo (Mirano, Ve), 299
Ramo verde
Carema (To), 62
Re di Puglia
Coltano (Pisa), 586
Real Castello
Verduno (Cn), 136
Reale, Osteria
Gete (Tramonti, Sa), 887
Rechsteiner
San Nicolò (Ponte di Piave, Tv), 310
Recina, Taberna
Roma, 739
Regina
Pinerolo (To), 106
Reider
Salonetto-Schlaneid (Meltina-Moelten, Bz), 250
Relasi Modica
Modica (Rg), 972
Remo, Da
Foligno (Pg), 627
Renata, Da
Bonelli (Porto Tolle, Ro), 311
Renato, Da
Guinadi (Pontremoli, Ms), 590
Residence Verde
Lacco Ameno-Fango (Isola d'Ischia, Na), 855
Residenza del lago
Candia Canavese (To), 59
Residenza Pietrabruna
Pamparato (Cn), 105
Residenza Sveva
Termoli (Cb), 786
Ressignon, Lou
Cogne (Ao), 20
Restel de fer
Riva del Garda (Tn), 227
Rete, La
Beltiglio (Ceppaloni, Bn), 848
Rianata 'a vasulata
Camerota (Sa), 842
Riccardo, Da
Carrè (Vi), 277
Riccardo, Da
Magomadas (Or), 1022

Riccio, Il
Castiglione del Genovesi (Sa), 847
Riccio, Il
Montepulciano (Si), 576
Richetta, Da
Visso (Mc), 693
Richiastro, 'L
Viterbo, 749
Ridosso, A
Bacoli (Na), 835
Riffaioli, I
Firenze, 552
Rifugio Carota
Pieve d'Alpago (Bl), 308
Rifugio del lupo, Il
Dente San Nicola (Scanno, Aq), 782
Rifugio delle aquile
Acquachiara (Teramo), 785
Rifugio Olmata
Terracina (Lt), 745
Rifugio, Il
Nuoro, 1023
Righini
Monteleone (Inverno e Monteleone, Pv), 166
Riglarhaus
Lateis (Sauris, Ud), 386
Ripa del sole
Riomaggiore (Sp), 436
Riserva di Martignanello, La
Campagnano di Roma (Rm), 701
Risorgimento
Treiso (Cn), 132
Risotteria Melotti
Isola della Scala (Vr), 290
Rispoli, Trattoria da
Pogerola (Amalfi, Sa), 831
Ristor
Ruvo di Puglia (Ba), 822
Ristorantino, Al
Udine, 399
Ritrovo degli amici, Al
Martina Franca (Ta), 811
Ritrovo del platano, Al
Ponte di Campia (Gallicano, Lu), 556
Ritrovo, Il
Montepertuso (Positano, Sa), 876
Rive, Le
Onigo (Pederobba, Tv), 307
Roberto, Da
Barbianello (Pv), 147

Rocca verde
Candia (Ancona), 651
Rocca, Alla
Rocca Grimalda (Al), 110
Rocca, La
San Leo (Pu), 684
Rocco
Sirolo (An), 690
Rockhof
San Valentino-Sankt Valentin
(Villandro-Villanders, Bz), 263
Roma
Cutigliano (Pt), 543
Roma, Trattoria
Castelletto Stura (Cn), 66
Romano
Fori Imperiali (Roma), 737
Romeo, Da
Botteghino (Parma), 487
Roncal, Il
Cividale del Friuli (Ud), 356
Roncolato
Carcera (Soave, Vr), 325
Rondinella, La
Cannero Riviera (Vb), 59
Rondinella, La
Scalea (Cs), 936
Rosa dei venti, La
Ortezzano (Ap), 675
Rosa dei vini, La
Parafada (Serralunga d'Alba, Cn), 120
Rosa rossa, La
Monticelli d'Oglio (Verolavecchia, Bs), 208
Rosa rossa, Osteria della
Cherasco (Cn), 72
Rosa, Da
Macerata, 668
Rose, Trattoria alle
Salò (Bs), 200
Rosella, La
Giba (Ci), 1021
Rosen bar
Gorizia, 367
Rosetta, La
Alatri (Fr), 696
Rosier, Le
Saint-Vincent (Ao), 31
Rosso di sera
San Feliciano (Magione, Pg), 629

Rosso, Trattoria del
Bologna, 451
Rovere Dalla Riva
Arzene (Pn), 351
Roverino, Da
Comunanza (Ap), 660
Rua de li travaj
Patù (Le), 820
Rubbiara, Osteria di
Rubbiara (Nonantola, Mo), 485
Ruggero
Firenze, 553
Ruinello, Al
Ruinello (Santa Maria della Versa, Pv), 202
Ruota, Alla
Mazzano (Negrar, Vr), 304
Ruota, La
Piazza Armerina (En), 988
Rusticana, La
Modica (Rg), 970
Ruz
Azzolini (Lavarone, Tn), 222

S

S. Marco
Venezia, 341
Sabbia d'oro
Belvedere Marittimo (Cs), 915
Sagraro, Da
Mossano (Vi), 303
Saint Patrick
Terracina (Lt), 745
Sale e pepe
Stregna (Ud), 390
Sale, Locanda del
San Michele Cavana
(Lesignano de' Bagni, Pr), 478
Saletta, Dai
Torino, 127
Sali e tabacchi
Maggiana (Mandello del Lario, Lc), 171
Salini, Fratelli
Groppallo (Farini, Pc), 466
Salita, La
Monforte d'Alba (Cn), 95
Salon
Piano d'Arta (Arta Terme, Ud), 350
Saltini
Pomponesco (Mn), 193

Salumè
Forlì 473
Salvatore, Da
Catanzaro, 917
Salvatore, Da
Petralia Soprana (Pa), 985
San Bernardo
Verzuolo (Cn), 136
San Carlo
Cortemilia (Cn), 76
San Cesario, Osteria di
San Cesareo (Rm), 741
San Cipriano, Osteria
San Cipriano (Lonato, Bs), 169
San Crispino
Cagliari, 1015
San Frediano
Lucca, 565
San Galdino, Antica trattoria di
Zelo Surrigone (Mi), 211
San Giorgio e il drago
Randazzo (Ct), 992
San Giorgio
Termoli (Cb), 787
San Giovanni
Piacenza, 488
San Lorenzo Tre
Todi (Pg), 644
San Lorenzo
Alba (Cn), 40
San Lorenzo
San Lorenzo (Fiuggi, Fr), 708
San Martin
Giovinazzo (Ba), 807
San Martino
Lugo (Ra), 479
San Martino
San Martino d'Alpago
(Chies d'Alpago, Bl), 279
San Martino, Locanda
Cavizzana (Tn), 218
San Matteo
Giarre (Ct), 962
San Michele a Porta Pia
Porta Pia (Roma), 738
San Pietro Barisano
Rioni Sassi (Matera), 904
San Pietro
Cetara (Sa), 850

San Placido Inn
Catania, 955
San Teodoro Nuovo
Marconia (Pisticci, Mt), 906
Sangiovesa, La
Santarcangelo di Romagna (Rn), 503
Sansevero Degas
Napoli, 866
Sant'Alfonso
Furore (Sa), 851
Sant'Anna Da Emilia
Borgo dei Pescatori Marina Grande
(Sorrento, Na), 885
Sant'Anna
Argegno (Co), 145
Sant'Antonio
Lovere (Bg), 170
Santa Caterina
Orta San Giulio (No), 104
Santa Chiara
Guardiagrele (Ch), 764
Santa Emilia de Vialar
Aurelio (Roma), 738
Santa Lucia
Appignano del Tronto (Ap), 652
Santa Lucia
Sulmona (Aq), 784
Santa Rosalia
Santa Rosalia (Savigliano, Cn), 118
Santa Venere
Santa Venere (Cotronei, Kr), 922
Santarosa
Germaneto (Catanzaro), 917
Sante Rughe
Gavoi (Nu), 1021
Santi, I
Capocastello (Mercogliano, Av), 860
Santlhof
Cortaccia sulla strada del vino-
Kurtatsch an der Weinstrasse (Bz), 244
Santo Pietro
San Pietro (Pienza, Si), 583
Santo Stefano
Lenno (Co), 168
Saracena, La
Segni (Rm), 742
Sardinia Domus
Cagliari, 1016
Sardoc
Slivia (Duino Aurisina, Ts), 364

PLACE INDEX

A

Abano Terme (Pd), 266
Abbazia di Rosara (Ascoli Piceno), 655
Abetone (Pt), 518
Accettura (Mt), 893
Acciano (Aq), 751
Acquachiara (Teramo), 785
Acqualagna (Pu), 649
Acquanegra sul Chiese (Mn), 144
Acquasanta (Mele, Ge), 430
Acquate (Lecco), 168
Acquaviva (Ap), 649
Acquedolci (Me), 944
Acqui Terme (Al), 38
Agazzano (Pc), 444
Agerola (Na), 830
Agliano Terme (At), 38
Agnona (Borgosesia, Vc), 51
Agrigento, 946
Aia (Cavriglia, Ar), 536
Aidone (En), 946
Aiello del Sabato (Av), 830
Alassio (Sv), 405
Alatri (Fr), 696
Alba (Cn), 39, 40
Alba Adriatica (Te), 751
Alberobello (Ba), 792, 793
Albignano (Truccazzano, Mi), 207
Albisano (Torri del Benaco, Vr), 330
Albissola Marina (Sv), 405
Alessandria, 41
Alfero (Verghereto, Fc), 510
Alghero (Ss), 1009
Allein (Ao),
Allume (Roccalumera, Me), 993
Alseno (Pc), 444
Altamura (Ba), 793
Altare (Sv), 406
Altavilla (Alba, Cn), 39
Altipiani di Arcinazzo
    (Arcinazzo Romano, Fr), 698
Altomonte (Cs), 913
Amalfi (Sa), 831
Amandola (Ap), 650
Amantea (Cs), 913, 914
Amaseno (Fr), 696
Amatrice (Ri), 697
Ambivere (Bg), 144
Ameglia (Sp), 406
Amelia (Tr), 617
Ameto-Amaten (Brunico-Bruneck, Bz), 241
Anagni (Fr), 697
Ancona, 650, 651
Andreis (Pn), 349
Andria (Ba), 794

Andriano-Andrian (Bz), 239
Anduins (Vito d'Asio, Pn), 402
Anghiari (Ar), 518, 519
Angone (Darfo Boario Terme, Bs), 160
Annunziata (La Morra, Cn), 88
Ansedonia (Orbetello, Gr), 579
Anterselva di Mezzo-Antholz Mittertal
    (Rasun Anterselva-Rasen Antholz, Bz), 253
Antey-Saint-André (Ao), 15
Antignano (Livorno), 563
Anversa degli Abruzzi (Aq), 752
Aonedis (San Daniele del Friuli, Ud), 382
Aosta, 16
Apostolello (Simeri Crichi, Cz), 938
Appiano sulla Strada del Vino-
    Eppan an der Weinstrasse (Bz), 239
Appignano (Mc), 652
Appignano del Tronto (Ap), 652
Apricale (Im), 407
Aprilia (Lt), 698
Aquileia (Ud), 349
Arba (Pn), 350
Arbizzano (Negrar, Vr), 305
Arcagna (Dolceacqua, Im), 416
Arcara (Cava de' Tirreni, Sa), 847
Arcidosso (Gr), 519
Arcinazzo Romano (Fr), 698
Arco Felice (Pozzuoli, Na), 877
Arcore (Mi), 145
Arcugnano (Vi), 266
Arena-Metato (San Giuliano Terme, Pi), 598
Arezzo, 520, 521
Argegno (Co), 145
Ariano Irpino (Av), 832
Ariano nel Polesine (Ro), 267
Arnad (Ao), 17
Arnesano (Le), 794
Arola (Vico Equense, Na), 889
Arona (No), 41
Arpaise (Bn), 832
Arpino (Fr), 699
Arquà Polesine (Ro), 267
Arquata (Bevagna, Pg), 621
Arquata Scrivia (Al), 42
Arta Terme (Ud), 350
Artogne (Bs), 146
Arvier (Ao), 17
Arzachena (Ss), 1009
Arzene (Pn), 351
Ascoli Piceno, 653-655
Asolo (Tv), 268
Assisi (Pg), 617-619
Asti, 42-44
Atella (Pz), 893
Atrani (Sa), 833

Atripalda (Av), 833
Aurelio (Roma), 738
Avellino, 834
Avigliana (To), 44
Avigliano (Pz), 894
Avigliano Umbro (Tr), 620
Avigna-Afing
   (San Genesio Atesino-Jenensien, Bz), 256
Avolasca (Al), 45
Azzolini (Lavarone, Tn), 222
Azzurria (Gerace, Rc), 926

B

Bacoli (Na), 835-837
Badia Pavese (Pv), 146
Badia Polesine (Ro), 269
Badiola (Terranuova Bracciolini, Ar), 609
Bagheria (Pa), 947
Bagnacavallo (Ra), 445
Bagnaria Arsa (Ud), 351
Bagni di Lucca (Lu), 521
Bagno a Ripoli (Fi), 522
Bagno di Gavorrano (Gavorrano, Gr), 557
Bagno di Romagna (Fc), 445
Bagnoli Irpino (Av), 838
Bagnone (Ms), 522
Bagnoregio (Vt), 699
Bagolino (Bs), 147
Baiso (Re), 446
Baldichieri d'Asti (At), 45
Baldissero Torinese (To), 46
Bano (Monte San Savino, Ar), 577
Baone (Pd), 269
Barano d'Ischia Fiaiano
   (Isola di Ischia, Na), 854
Barberino Val d'Elsa (Fi), 523
Barbianello (Pv), 147
Barbuzzera (Dovera, Cr), 161
Barco (Orzinuovi, Bs), 190
Bard (Ao), 18
Bardolino (Vr), 270
Bardonecchia (To), 46
Barga (Lu), 523
Bargni (Serrungarina, Pu), 690
Bari, 795, 796
Barile (Pz), 894
Barisciano (Aq), 752
Barolo (Cn), 47, 48
Barumini (Md), 1010
Basaldella (Vivaro, Pd), 402
Baselga di Piné (Tn), 213
Bassano del Grappa (Vi), 271
Bassura (Stroppo, Cn), 123, 124
Battaglia (Casaletto Spartano, Sa), 844
Battella (Travacò Siccomario, Pv), 205

Baveno (Vb), 48
Beligna (Aquileia, Ud), 349
Bellagio (Co), 148
Bellante (Te), 753
Belluno, 272
Belluno Veronese (Brentino Belluno, Vr), 274
Belmonte Mezzagno (Pa), 947
Beltiglio (Ceppaloni, Bn), 848
Belvedere (Montefalco, Pg), 630
Belvedere (Povoletto, Ud), 378
Belvedere Marittimo (Cs), 915
Benevento, 839, 840
Beo (Monterosso, Sp), 431
Berceto (Pr), 446
Bereguardo (Pv), 148
Bergamo, 149
Bergantino (Ro), 272
Bergi (Castelbuono, Pa), 950
Bergolo (Cn), 49
Bergotto (Berceto, Pr), 446
Bernalda (Mt), 895
Besate (Mi), 149
Bettolle (Sinalunga, Si), 607
Bevagna (Pg), 620-622
Beverino (Sp), 407, 408
Biagiano (Assisi, Pg), 617
Biana (Ponte dell'Olio, Pc), 489
Bianzone (So), 150
Bibbona (Li), 524
Biecina (Villa Basilica, Lu), 612
Biella, 49
Bigallo (Bagno a Ripoli, Fi), 522
Birgi (Marsala, Tp), 967
Bisaccia (Av), 841
Bivio Aiole (Arcidosso, Gr), 519
Bivongi (Rc), 915
Boatina (Cormons, Go), 360, 361
Bobbio (Pc), 447
Bocale Secondo (Reggio Calabria), 933
Bogliaco (Gargnano, Bs), 164, 165
Bojano (Cb), 753
Bologna, 447-451
Bolsena (Vt), 700
Bolzano-Bozen, 240, 241
Bolzone (Ripalta Cremasca, Cr), 197
Bonarcado (Or), 1010
Bonassola (Sp), 408
Bonelli (Porto Tolle, Ro), 311
Bonne (Valgrisenche, Ao), 32
Bordano (Ud), 352
Bordighera (Im), 409, 410
Borghetto d'Arroscia (Im), 411
Borgia (Cz), 916
Borgiano (Serrapetrona, Mc), 688
Borgio Verezzi (Sv), 411

Canale (Villadose, Ro), 346
Canale d'Agordo (Bl), 276
Candela (Fg), 797
Candia (Ancona), 651
Candia Canavese (To), 59
Canè (Vione, Bs), 210
Canestrello (Candela, Fg), 797
Canevare (Fanano, Mo), 465
Cangelasio (Salsomaggiore Terme, Pr), 500
Cannara (Pg), 623
Cannero Riviera (Vb), 59
Cannobio (Vb), 60
Cantagallo (Po), 527
Cantalupa (To), 60
Cantalupo Ligure (Al), 61
Canzano (Te), 756
Capaccio (Sa), 842
Capaccio Scalo (Capaccio, Sa), 842
Capalbio (Gr), 527
Capannori (Lu), 528
Capocastello (Mercogliano, Av), 860
Capodacqua (Assisi, Pg), 618
Capoliveri (Li), 547
Cappellieri (Cirò, Kr), 919
Capracotta (Is), 756
Capreno (Sori, Ge), 438
Capri Leone (Me), 949
Capriano del Colle (Bs), 153
Capriata d'Orba (Al), 61
Capriva del Friuli (Go), 353
Caracciolo (Montallegro, Ag), 973
Carano (Tn), 216
Carcera (Soave, Vr), 325
Carcoforo (Vc), 62
Careggine (Lu), 528
Carema (To), 62
Carlentini (Sr), 950
Carmignano (Po), 529
Carovigno (Br), 798
Carovilli (Is), 757
Carpenedolo (Bs), 154
Carpi (Villa Bartolomea, Vr), 345
Carpineti (Re), 456
Carpineto Romano (Rm), 702, 703
Carrara, 529, 530
Carrè (Vi), 277
Carrù (Cn), 63, 64
Casa Villara (Beverino, Sp), 407
Casabella (Ziano Piacentino, Pc), 513
Casagiove (Ce), 843
Casaglia (Perugia), 637
Casale (Felino, Pr), 466
Casaletto Spartano (Sa), 844
Casali Lini (Fagagna, Ud), 365
Casalvieri (Fr), 704

Casareggio (Fortunago, Pv), 163
Caselle in Pittari (Sa), 844
Caserta, 845
Caserta Vecchia (Caserta), 845
Casevecchie (Bacoli, Na), 835
Casier (Tv), 277
Casignano-Gschnon
    (Montagna-Montan, Bz), 251
Casina (Re), 456
Casperia (Ri), 704
Cassano delle Murge (Ba), 798
Castagneto Carducci (Li), 531
Castagnito (Cn), 64
Castagnole Monferrato (At), 65
Castel Boglione (At), 65
Castel d'Aiano (Bo), 457
Castel del Piano (Gr), 531
Castel Maggiore (Bo), 458
Castel Morrone (Ce), 846
Castel Rocchero (At), 67
Castel San Pietro (Camino, Al), 58
Castel San Pietro Terme (Bo), 459
Castelbianco (Sv), 413
Castelbuono (Pa), 950, 951
Casteldelci (Pu), 657
Casteldimezzo (Pesaro), 677
Castelfranco d'Oglio (Drizzona, Cr), 162
Castelfranco di Sotto (Pi), 534
Castelfranco Emilia (Mo), 457, 458
Castelfranco Veneto (Tv), 278
Castell'Alfero (At), 66
Castell'Umberto (Me), 950
Castellabate (Sa), 845, 846
Castellaccio (Livorno), 562
Castellalto (Te), 757
Castellammare del Golfo (Tp), 951, 952
Castellana-Grotte (Ba), 799
Castellaro Lagusello
    (Monzambano, Mn), 186, 187
Castelletto (Brenzone, Vr), 274
Castelletto Stura (Cn), 66
Castelli (Monfumo, Tv), 300
Castelli (Te), 758
Castellina in Chianti (Si), 532, 533
Castellinaldo (Cn), 67
Castello (Certaldo, Fi), 538
Castello (Serle, Bs), 202
Castello di Godego (Tv), 278
Castello di Sette (Mozzagrogna, Ch), 771
Castelluccio (Norcia, Pg), 633
Castelmezzano (Pz), 895
Castelnovo del Friuli (Pn), 354
Castelnovo ne' Monti (Re), 459
Castelnuovo (Teolo, Pd), 328
Castelnuovo Berardenga (Si), 533

Osterie & Locande d'Italia

If you want to help us improve the guide next time round, feel free to fill in the coupon below and send it to:

Slow Food Editore
Redazione di Osterie d'Italia
via della Mendicità Istruita, 45
12042 Bra (Cn) – ITALY

Of the addresses listed in **Osterie & Locande d'Italia**, I have eaten/stayed at

Name: _____

Address: _____

Overall judgment:

❏ Positive   ❏ Negative

Reasons why _____

_____

_____

_____

I wish to propose a new address for inclusion in the next edition

Name _____

Address _____

Tel. _____

Reasons why _____

_____

_____

_____

My name _____

Address _____

Tel/email _____